Combined with the resources you have trusted throughout the years to provide you with the best business resources available are:

- **In the News** — New current events articles are added throughout the year. Each article is summarized by our teams of expert professors and is fully supported by exercises, activities, and instructor materials.
- **Online Study Guide** — Four quizzes are linked to each text chapter and include "hints" for each question. Quizzes graded immediately upon submission to provide immediate feedback on each given answer, and enable students to e-mail results to the instructor.
- **Research Area** — Your own personal resource library includes tutorials, descriptive links to virtual libraries, and a wealth of search engines and resources.
- **Internet Resources** — Discipline-specific sites, including preview information that allows instructors to review site information before viewing the site, ensure the best available business resources found by our learning community.

For the professor

- **Teaching Resources** provide material contributed by professors throughout the world—including teaching tips, techniques, academic papers, and sample syllabi—and **Talk to the Team,** a moderated faculty chat room.
- **Online Faculty** support includes downloadable supplements, additional cases, articles, links, and suggested answers to Current Events Activities.
- **What's New** gives you one-click access to all newly posted PHLIP resources.

For the student

- **Talk to the Tutor** schedules virtual office hours that allow students to post questions from any supported discipline and receive responses from the dedicated PHLIP/CW faculty team.
- **Writing Resource Center** provides an online writing center that supplies links to online directories, thesauruses, writing tutors, style and grammar guides, and additional tools.
- **Career Center** enables students to access career information, view sample resumes, even apply for jobs online.
- **Study Tips** provides an area where students can develop better study skills.

Online Learning Solutions—
Complete course content is pre-loaded!

Prentice Hall provides rich course content available in **your choice** of platforms: WebCT, Blackboard, or eCollege. The premium content of our online courses includes material that is specifically written to enhance – but not duplicate – text content. You may opt to use our content in its entirety or edit the material to suit your course. Features of each platform may vary, but most include:

- **Multiple-Section Chat Rooms**
- **Bulletin Board Conferencing**
- **Online Glossary**
- **Audio and Video Downloads**
- **Lectures and Review Sections**
- **Online Quizzes and Tests**
- **Course Management with Page Tracking**
- **Calendar and Syllabus Capabilities**

FINANCIAL ACCOUNTING

CHARLES T. HORNGREN SERIES IN ACCOUNTING

AUDITING: AN INTEGRATED APPROACH, 8/E
Arens/Loebbecke

FINANCIAL STATEMENT ANALYSIS, 2/E
Foster

GOVERNMENTAL AND NONPROFIT ACCOUNTING: THEORY AND PRACTICE, 6/E
Freeman/Shoulders

FINANCIAL ACCOUNTING, 4/E
Harrison/Horngren

COST ACCOUNTING: A MANAGERIAL EMPHASIS, 10/E
Horngren/Foster/Datar

ACCOUNTING, 4/E
Horngren/Harrison/Bamber

CASES IN FINANCIAL REPORTING, 3/E
Hirst/McAnally

INTRODUCTION TO FINANCIAL ACCOUNTING, 7/E
Horngren/Sundem/Elliott

INTRODUCTION TO MANAGEMENT ACCOUNTING, 11/E
Horngren/Sundem/Stratton

BUDGETING, 6/E
Welsch/Hilton/Gordon

revenue

investment

FINANCIAL ACCOUNTING

Fourth Edition

Walter T. Harrison Jr.
Baylor University

Charles T. Horngren
Stanford University

Upper Saddle River, New Jersey 07458

Executive Editor:	Debbie Hoffman
Associate Editor:	Kasey Sheehan
Senior Editorial Assistant:	Jane Avery
Editor-in-Chief:	P.J. Boardman
Senior Development Editor:	Ron Librach
Director of Development:	Steve Deitmer
Executive Marketing Manager:	Beth Toland
Senior Production Editor:	Anne Graydon
Managing Editor:	Sondra Greenfield
Senior Manufacturing Supervisor:	Paul Smolenski
Associate Director, Manufacturing:	Vincent Scelta
Design Director:	Pat Smythe
Interior Design:	Christine Cantera
Infographic Illustrations:	Kenneth Batelman
Photo Researcher:	Teri Stratford
Image Permissions Supervisor:	Kay Dellosa
Cover Design:	Pisaza Design Studio, Ltd.
Cover Image:	Jeff Brice
Composition and Full-service:	Progressive Information Technologies

Photo Credits: 2 Mark Richards/Contact Press Images Inc.; 50 Michael Newman/PhotoEdit; 104 Andrea McGinty, Chairman, It's Just Lunch! Inc.; 168 Michael Rosenfeld/Tony Stone Images; 218 Allsport Photography (USA), Inc.; 258 Teva, Deckers Outdoor Corporation; 310 Zigy Kaluzny/Liaison Agency, Inc.; 358 Uniphoto Picture Agency; 406 Michael Newman/PhotoEdit; 458 Adam Opel AG, used with permission of GM Media Archives; 498 Michael Quackenbush/The Image Bank; 534 Francie Manning/Index Stock Imagery, Inc.; 590 Daniel Grogan/Uniphoto Picture Agency

The Annual Report material in Appendix A is provided courtesy of Gap Inc.

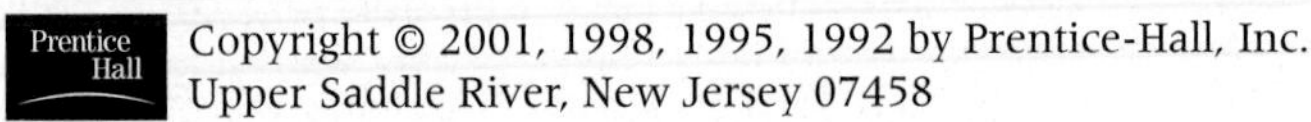

Library of Congress Cataloging-in-Publication Data

Harrison, Walter T.
Financial accounting / Walter T. Harrison, Jr., Charles T. Horngren. — 4th ed.
752 pp.
Includes indexes.

ISBN 0-13-012846-5
1. Accounting. I. Horngren, Charles T., II. Title
HF5635.H333 2000
657—dc21 00-029798

Prentice-Hall International (UK) Limited, London
Prentice-Hall of Australia Pty. Limited, Sydney
Prentice-Hall Canada, Inc., Toronto
Prentice-Hall Hispanoamericana, S.A., Mexico
Prentice-Hall of India Private Limited, New Delhi
Prentice-Hall of Japan, Inc., Tokyo
Pearson Education (Singapore), Pte. Ltd.
Editora Prentice-Hall do Brasil, Ltda., Rio de Janeiro

Printed in the United States of America
10 9 8 7 6 5 4 3 2

For our wives,

Nancy and Joan

The market leader in **Financial Accounting!**

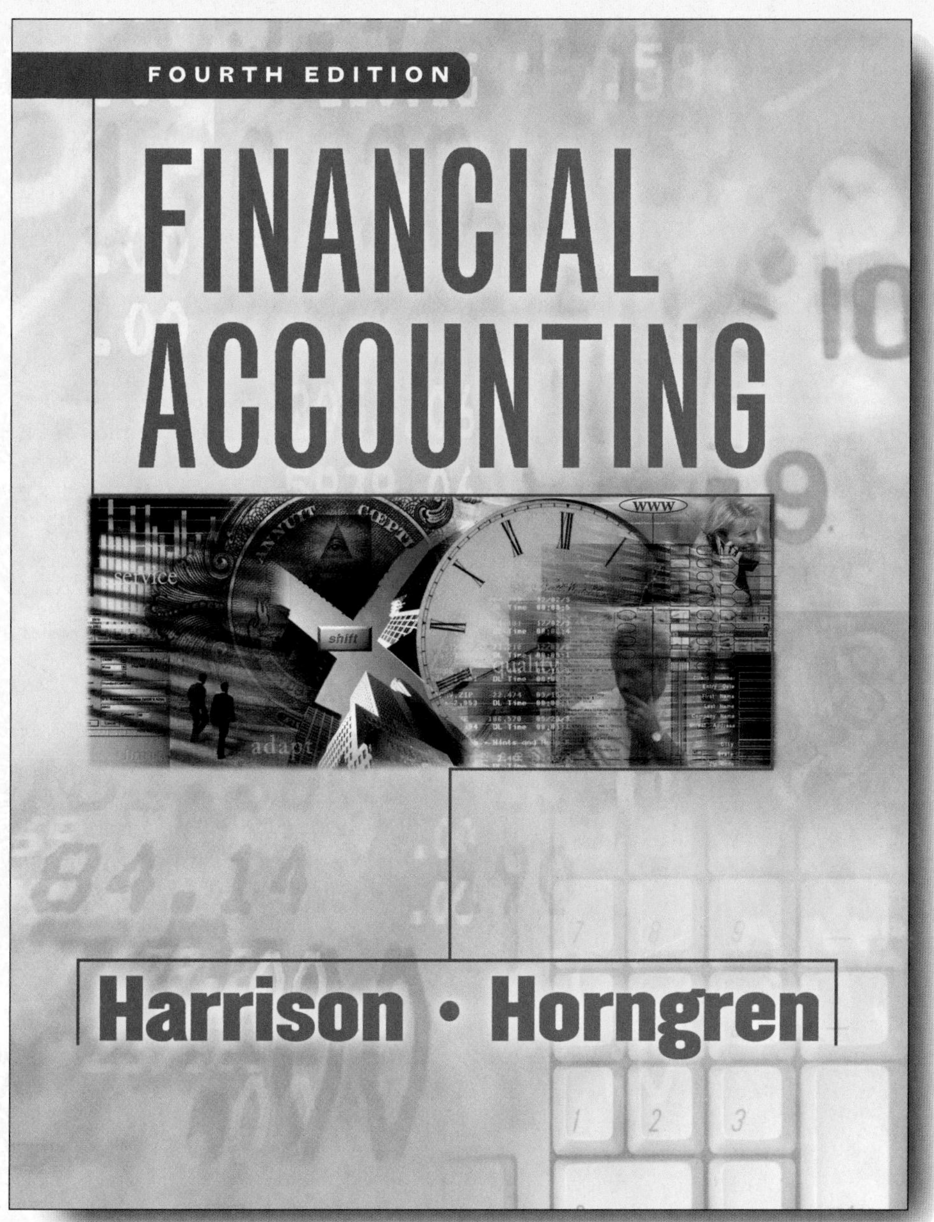

One *textbook delivers!*

The Fourth Edition of **Harrison and Horngren's *Financial Accounting*.**

You settle for nothing but the best quality stereo speakers for your music. You expect the highest return on your financial investments. You demand top performance from your students. And you also want a financial accounting textbook that delivers uncompromising performance.

Product Highlights

Can you name the financial accounting textbook that has more than tripled its market share?

featured Company & Video

Chapter 1

Financial Statements

- **New** information on cash flows

The Gap Inc. 

> *"I believe the strongest is Chapter 1. The chapter immediately gets the attention of the student with its opening discussion of The Gap. This serves to pique the student's curiosity about the usefulness of accounting information."*
>
> **Marsha H. Kertz,** San Jose State University

Chapter 2

Processing Information

- **New** section on "Effects of Transactions on the Financial Statements"
- Streamlined bookkeeping section

PepsiCo 

Chapter 3

Accrual Accounting

- **New section** on "Accrual Accounting and Cash Flows" based on *It's Just Lunch*
- **New** section on "Deferrals and Accruals"
- **New** diagram on the accounting cycle

It's Just Lunch UPDATED

Chapter 4

Internal Control and Cash

- Streamlined bank reconciliation material and added a new diagram on "The Paths that Two Checks Take" The diagram makes accounting for non-sufficient-funds checks easier to understand

Grant LeForge & Co. 

> *"I love the writing style and so do my students. Students are asked every quarter about the text. They really like it."*
>
> **Robert J. Shepherd,** University of California-Santa Cruz

Chapter 5

Short-term Investments and Receivables

- **New** chapter opener on Oracle Corporation's software shows how the New York Jets use it to teach their linemen how to block opponents
- Streamlined material on accounting for marketable securities, accounting for uncollectible receivables, and accounting for notes receivable

Oracle Corporation 

Chapter 6

Inventory

- Chapter is now based entirely on the perpetual inventory system. The periodic inventory system is now in a new chapter appendix
- Journal entries are moved back to Exhibit 6-13
- LIFO, FIFO, average-cost computations are now simplified
- **New** sections added on "Transition From Service Entities to Merchandisers," "What Goes Into Inventory Cost?," "The Cost-of-Goods-Sold Model Brings All the Inventory Data Together," "How Managers Decide the Amount of Inventory to Purchase," and "Complex Income Statement"

Teva Sandals 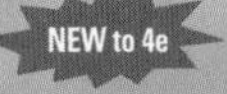

Chapter Enhancements

Field Tested/Market Tested

***Premium Performance** doesn't just happen.*
It results from careful attention to customer needs,

*evaluation of evolving media, and recognition of classroom challenges. Authors Tom Harrison and Charles Horngren deliver on each of these points in crafting each new edition of **Financial Accounting**. But don't listen to us. Listen to your students. Talk to them about their experience in using Harrison and Horngren. Listen to your colleagues. Also, listen to the market voice that recognizes the uncompromising performance this text delivers.*

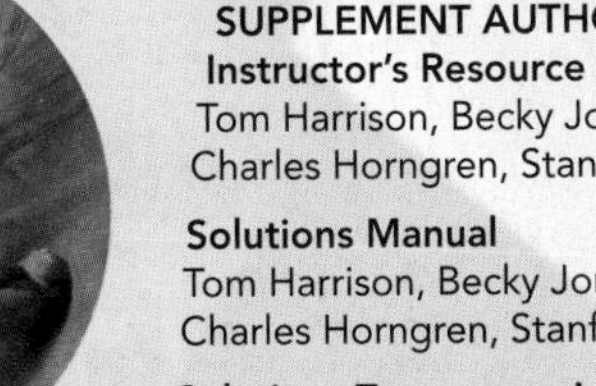

Fourth Edition Consultants:

TEXT REVIEWERS

Michael Bitter, Stetson University
Rada Brooks, University of California-Berkeley
Mark Camma, Atlantic Cape Community College
Lee Cannell, El Paso Community College
Jack M. Cathey, University of North Carolina-Charlotte
W. Michael Donovan, Southern Maine Technical College
Thomas G. Evans, University of Central Florida
Dennis Gutting, Orange County Community College
Paul P. Hoppe, Golden Gate University
Nancy L. Kelly, Middlesex Community Technical College
Marsha H. Kertz, San Jose State University
Gregory S. Kordecki, Clayton College and State University
Keith R. Leeseberg, Manatee Community College
June F. Li, University of Minnesota-Duluth
Angelo Luciano, Columbia College
Thomas W. Oliver, Clarion University
Kathy J. Perdue, DeVry Institute of Technology
Janet F. Phillips, Southern Connecticut State University
Patty Polk, University of Southern Mississippi
Sharon L. Robinson, Frostburg State University
Robert J. Shepherd, University of California-Santa Cruz
Alice B. Sineath, Forsyth Technical College
Victor Stanton, University of California-Berkeley
Kimberly Tarantino, California State University-Fullerton
Michael G. Vasilou, DeVry Institute, Chicago
Robert Walsh, Marist College
Martin E. Ward, DeVry Institute of Technology
Jeanne H. Yamamura, University of Nevada-Reno

SUPPLEMENT AUTHORS

Instructor's Resource Manual
Tom Harrison, Becky Jones, Betsy Willis, all of Baylor University
Charles Horngren, Stanford University

Solutions Manual
Tom Harrison, Becky Jones, Betsy Willis, all of Baylor University
Charles Horngren, Stanford University

Solutions Transparencies
Becky Jones, Betsy Willis, Tom Harrison, all of Baylor University
Charles Horngren, Stanford University

Test Item File
David S. Kerr, Texas A & M University

Study Guide
Steven Schaefer, Contra Costa College

Working Papers
Ellen Sweatt, Georgia Perimeter College

PowerPoint Slides
Joseph L. Morris, Southeastern Louisiana University

On Location! Videos
Beverly Amer, Northern Arizona University

Instructor's Resource CD-ROM
Various

PHAS General Ledger Software
Alfonso R. Oddo, Niagra University
Carroll Goeters
Jean Insinga, Middlesex Community and Technical College

PH Re-Enforcer Software
Carroll Goeters
Jean Insinga, Middlesex Community and Technical College

Spreadsheet Templates
Albert Fisher, Community College of Southern Nevada

Solutions to Spreadsheet Templates
Albert Fisher, Community College of Southern Nevada

Student CD-ROM Various

PHLIP/CW Karen Schoenebeck, Wichita State University

WebCT
Anthony Fortini, Maryann Pionegro

Gap Annual Report Gap/PH

SUPPLEMENT REVIEWERS

Thomas Hoar, Houston Community College
Robert Bauman, Allan Hancock College

At Prentice Hall,
nothing is left to chance.

THE answer *Harrison/Horngren, Financial Accounting*

Chapter 7

Plant Assets

- Simplified "Lump-Sum (Basket) Purchases of Assets"
- Moved "Capital Expenditures vs. Revenue Expenditures" up to where it belongs–near "Measuring the Cost of a Plant Asset"
- Shortened and simplified "Capitalizing the Cost of Interest"
- Streamlined "Changing the Useful Life of a Depreciable Asset"

Home Depot 

Chapter 8

Current and Long-term Liabilities

- Streamlined "Issuing Bonds Payable Between Interest Dates" to remove a journal entry
- Deleted sections on "Notes Payable Issued at a Discount," "Vacation Pay Liability," and "Off-Balance-Sheet Financing"

Home Depot UPDATED

Chapter 9

Stockholders' Equity

- Shortened and simplified "Accounting for Treasury Stock"
- Streamlined "Accounting for Stock Dividends" and "Retirement of Stock"
- Deleted the Stock Dividends Distributable account altogether (this reduces the number of journal entries to account for a stock dividend)
- Deleted "Accounting for Stock Conversions," "Donations Received by Corporations," "Closing Net Income to Retained Earnings," "Liquidation Value of Preferred Stock" (but kept "Redemption Value of Preferred Stock")

IHOP 

Chapter 10

Long-term Investments and International

- Shortened the sections on "Equity-Method Investments," "Accounting for Consolidated Subsidiaries," "Consolidation of Foreign Subsidiaries," and "Using the Cash-Flow Statement to Interpret Financial Statements"

General Motors UPDATED

Chapter 11

Using the Income Statement and the Statement of Stockholders' Equity

- Streamlined the section on "Accounting for Income Taxes by Corporations" by deleting some journal entries
- Deleted the section on "Using the Financial Statement Notes"

May Department Stores 

Chapter 12

The Statement of Cash Flows

- Focused more attention on the equation-approach to computing amounts for the statement of cash flows. The delivery is equation-approach first, followed by the T-account approach second

W. T. Grant

Chapter 13

Financial Statement Analysis

Bristol Myers-Squibb, Procter & Gamble

UPDATED

> *"I thought Chapter 11 was excellent–particularly the discussion on quality of earnings. I also thought Chapter 13 was very well done–very organized with good examples. I thought it was well written in a very conversationalist style. The Stop and Think's were excellent. It is too easy for the student to passively read the chapter without any real comprehension of how these rules can be applied."*
>
> **Marsha H. Kertz,** San Jose State University

Winning Features

You recall the moment...

...of turning on the ignition of your first new car and hearing it purr,

...of hearing the full-bodied baritone of your favorite performer echoing through surround sound speakers,

...when you solved the final clue in a difficult crossword puzzle

Ah! The satisfaction of accomplishment! Your students want to succeed. They want to see a meaningful connection between classroom concepts and **their** future business decisions. New features in the Fourth Edition of **Harrison/Horngren's *Financial Accounting*** spark their interest, **build their confidence,** and equip them for a **higher level of performance.**

Ah! The sweet satisfaction of accomplishment!

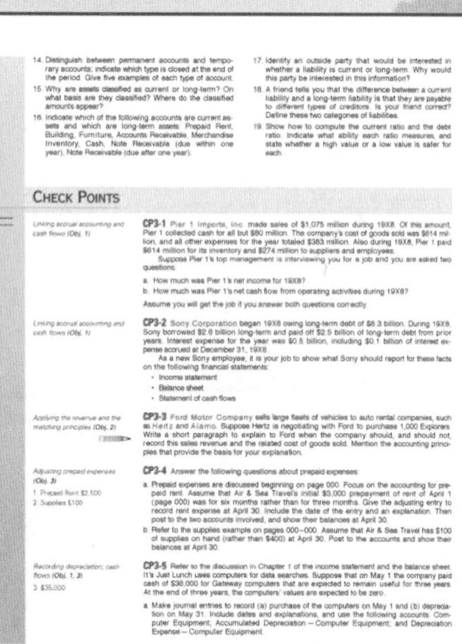

14. Distinguish between permanent accounts and temporary accounts; indicate which type is closed at the end of the period. Give five examples of each type of account.
15. Why are assets classified as current or long-term? On what basis are they classified? Where do the classified amounts appear?
16. Indicate which of the following accounts are current assets and which are long-term assets: Prepaid Rent, Building, Furniture, Accounts Receivable, Merchandise Inventory, Cash, Note Receivable (due within one year), Note Receivable (due after one year).
17. Identify an outside party that would be interested in whether a liability is current or long-term. Why would this party be interested in this information?
18. A friend tells you that the difference between a current liability and a long-term liability is that they are payable to different types of creditors. Is your friend correct? Define these two categories of liabilities.
19. Show how to compute the current ratio and the debt ratio. Indicate what ability each ratio measures, and state whether a high value or a low value is safer for each.

CHECK POINTS

Linking accrual accounting and cash flows (Obj. 1)

CP3-1 Pier 1 Imports, Inc. made sales of $1,075 million during 19X8. Of this amount, Pier 1 collected cash for all but $80 million. The company's cost of goods sold was $614 million, and all other expenses for the year totaled $383 million. Also during 19X8, Pier 1 paid $614 million for its inventory and $274 million to suppliers and employees.

Suppose Pier 1's top management is interviewing you for a job and you are asked two questions:

a. How much was Pier 1's net income for 19X8?
b. How much was Pier 1's net cash flow from operating activities during 19X8?

Assume you will get the job if you answer both questions correctly.

Linking accrual accounting and cash flows (Obj. 1)

CP3-2 Sony Corporation began 19X8 owing long-term debt of $8.3 billion. During 19X8, Sony borrowed $2.6 billion long-term and paid off $2.5 billion of long-term debt from prior years. Interest expense for the year was $0.5 billion, including $0.1 billion of interest expense accrued at December 31, 19X8.

As a new Sony employee, it is your job to show what Sony should report for these facts on the following financial statements:

- Income statement
- Balance sheet
- Statement of cash flows

Applying the revenue and the matching principles (Obj. 2)

CP3-3 Ford Motor Company sells large fleets of vehicles to auto rental companies, such as Hertz and Alamo. Suppose Hertz is negotiating with Ford to purchase 1,000 Explorers. Write a short paragraph to explain to Ford when the company should, and should not, record this sales revenue and the related cost of goods sold. Mention the accounting principles that provide the basis for your explanation.

Adjusting prepaid expenses (Obj. 3)

1. Prepaid Rent $2,500
2. Supplies $100

CP3-4 Answer the following questions about prepaid expenses:

a. Prepaid expenses are discussed beginning on page 000. Focus on the accounting for prepaid rent. Assume that Air & Sea Travel's initial $3,000 prepayment of rent of April 1 (page 000) was for six months rather than for three months. Give the adjusting entry to record rent expense at April 30. Include the date of the entry and an explanation. Then post to the two accounts involved, and show their balances at April 30.
b. Refer to the supplies example on pages 000–000. Assume that Air & Sea Travel has $100 of supplies on hand (rather than $400) at April 30. Post to the accounts and show their balances at April 30.

Recording depreciation; cash flows (Obj. 1, 3)

3. $35,000

CP3-5 Refer to the discussion in Chapter 1 of the income statement and the balance sheet. It's Just Lunch uses computers for data searches. Suppose that on May 1 the company paid cash of $36,000 for Gateway computers that are expected to remain useful for three years. At the end of three years, the computers' values are expected to be zero.

a. Make journal entries to record (a) purchase of the computers on May 1 and (b) depreciation on May 31. Include dates and explanations, and use the following accounts: Computer Equipment; Accumulated Depreciation—Computer Equipment; and Depreciation Expense—Computer Equipment.

42 Chapter 3

NEW ✔ Check Point Exercises

Check Points— Short exercises to open the assignment material for each chapter—are intended as warm-ups to help students build confidence in their problem-solving skills. **Check Points** use real companies whenever possible and are linked directly to the text so that students can review material before coming to class. The **Check Points** are ideal for faculty to use as daily quiz material.

"The best change in the pedagogy for the Fourth Edition is the Check Points. I like how they relate to the learning objectives [and] I plan to use them in class to emphasize certain points."

—**Mark Camma,** Atlantic Cape Community College

NEW Excel Application Problems

A unique feature

for the financial accounting market! **Decision Guidelines,** introduced in the Third Edition of Harrison/Horngren, appear in every chapter and show when, why, and how people use these accounting guidelines in order to make business decisions. Now, Harrison/Horngren innovate again with **new** optional **Excel spreadsheet applications** to accompany selected **Decision Guidelines.** Students can apply the **Decision Guidelines** material to a realistic situation and use the power of Excel to determine a solution.

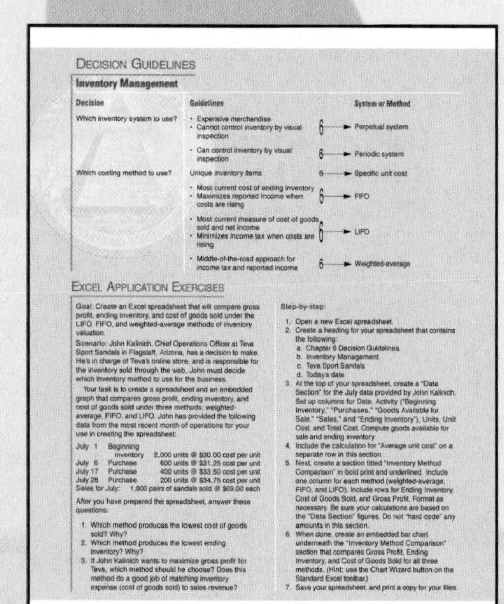

DECISION GUIDELINES

Inventory Management

Decision	Guidelines	System or Method
Which inventory system to use?	• Expensive merchandise • Cannot control inventory by visual inspection	Perpetual system
	• Can control inventory by visual inspection	Periodic system
Which costing method to use?	Unique inventory items	Specific unit cost
	• Most current cost of ending inventory • Maximizes reported income when costs are rising	FIFO
	• Most current measure of cost of goods sold and net income • Minimizes income tax when costs are rising	LIFO
	• Middle-of-the-road approach for income tax and reported income	Weighted-average

EXCEL APPLICATION EXERCISES

Goal: Create an Excel spreadsheet that will compare gross profit, ending inventory, and cost of goods sold under the LIFO, FIFO, and weighted-average methods of inventory valuation.

Scenario: John Kalinich, Chief Operations Officer at Teva Sport Sandals in Flagstaff, Arizona, has a decision to make. He's in charge of Teva's online store, and is responsible for the inventory sold through the web. John must decide which inventory method to use for the business.

Your task is to create a spreadsheet and an embedded graph that compares gross profit, ending inventory, and cost of goods sold under three methods: weighted-average, FIFO, and LIFO. John has provided the following data from the most recent month of operations for your use in creating the spreadsheet:

July 1	Beginning inventory	2,000 units @ $30.00 cost per unit
July 6	Purchase	600 units @ $31.25 cost per unit
July 17	Purchase	400 units @ $33.50 cost per unit
July 28	Purchase	200 units @ $34.75 cost per unit
Sales for July:		1,800 pairs of sandals sold @ $69.00 each

After you have prepared the spreadsheet, answer these questions:

1. Which method produces the lowest cost of goods sold? Why?
2. Which method produces the lowest ending inventory? Why?
3. If John Kalinich wants to maximize gross profit for Teva, which method should he choose? Does this method do a good job of matching inventory expense (cost of goods sold) to sales revenue?

Step-by-step:

1. Open a new Excel spreadsheet.
2. Create a heading for your spreadsheet that contains the following:
   a. Chapter 6 Decision Guidelines
   b. Inventory Management
   c. Teva Sport Sandals
   d. Today's date
3. At the top of your spreadsheet, create a "Data Section" for the July data provided by John Kalinich. Set up columns for Date, Activity ("Beginning Inventory," "Purchases," "Goods Available for Sale," "Sales," and "Ending Inventory"), Units, Unit Cost, and Total Cost. Compute goods available for sale and ending inventory.
4. Include the calculation for "Average unit cost" on a separate row in this section.
5. Next, create a section titled "Inventory Method Comparison" in bold print and underlined. Include one column for each method (weighted-average, FIFO, and LIFO). Include rows for Ending Inventory, Cost of Goods Sold, and Gross Profit. Format as necessary. Be sure your calculations are based on the "Data Section" figures. Do not "hard code" any amounts in this section.
6. When done, create an embedded bar chart underneath the "Inventory Method Comparison" section that compares Gross Profit, Ending Inventory, and Cost of Goods Sold for all three methods. (Hint: use the Chart Wizard button on the Standard Excel toolbar.)
7. Save your spreadsheet, and print a copy for your files.

MERCHANDISE INVENTORY, COST OF GOODS SOLD, AND GROSS PROFIT 21

Real-World Vignettes

6 Merchandise Inventory, Cost of Goods Sold, and Gross Margin

LEARNING OBJECTIVES

After studying this chapter, you should be able to

1. *Use the cost-of-goods-sold model*
2. *Apply the various inventory methods: specific unit cost, weighted-average, FIFO, and LIFO*
3. *Identify the income effects and the tax effects of the inventory methods*
4. *Measure the effects of inventory errors on cost of goods sold and net income*
5. *Use the gross profit percentage and the rate of inventory turnover to evaluate a business*
6. *Account for inventory transactions*
7. *Estimate inventory by the gross profit method*

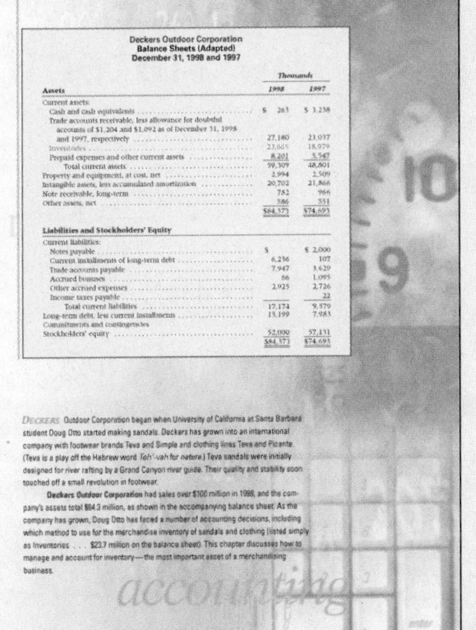

Deckers Outdoor Corporation
Balance Sheets (Adapted)
December 31, 1998 and 1997

	Thousands	
Assets	*1998*	*1997*
Current assets:		
Cash and cash equivalents	$ 263	$ 3,238
Trade accounts receivable, less allowance for doubtful accounts of $1,204 and $1,092 as of December 31, 1998 and 1997, respectively	27,180	23,037
Inventories	23,665	18,979
Prepaid expenses and other current assets	8,201	3,547
Total current assets	59,309	48,801
Property and equipment, at cost, net	2,994	2,509
Intangible assets, less accumulated amortization	20,702	21,866
Note receivable, long-term	782	966
Other assets, net	586	551
	$84,373	$74,693
Liabilities and Stockholders' Equity		
Current liabilities:		
Notes payable	$	$ 2,000
Current installments of long-term debt	6,236	107
Trade accounts payable	7,947	3,629
Accrued bonuses	66	1,095
Other accrued expenses	2,925	2,726
Income taxes payable		22
Total current liabilities	17,174	9,579
Long-term debt, less current installments	15,199	7,983
Commitments and contingencies		
Stockholders' equity	52,000	57,131
	$84,373	$74,693

DECKERS Outdoor Corporation began when University of California at Santa Barbara student Doug Otto started making sandals. Deckers has grown into an international company with footwear brands Teva and Simple and clothing lines Teva and Picante. (Teva is a play off the Hebrew word *Teh'-vah for nature*.) Teva sandals were initially designed for river rafting by a Grand Canyon river guide. Their quality and stability soon touched off a small revolution in footwear.

Deckers Outdoor Corporation had sales over $100 million in 1998, and the company's assets total $84.3 million, as shown in the accompanying balance sheet. As the company has grown, Doug Otto has faced a number of accounting decisions, including which method to use for the merchandise inventory of sandals and clothing (listed simply as Inventories . . . $23.7 million on the balance sheet). This chapter discusses how to manage and account for inventory—the most important asset of a merchandising business.

Real-World Vignettes

Each chapter begins with a real company story that introduces students to chapter-specific accounting issues. New companies include Teva Sandals, Oracle, and PepsiCo. These motivational stories are directly linked to our custom-crafted On Location! Videos.

"Harrison/Horngren is the clear winner here [as] the chapter opener ties to subsequent discussion."

—Gregory Kordecki,
Clayton College and State University

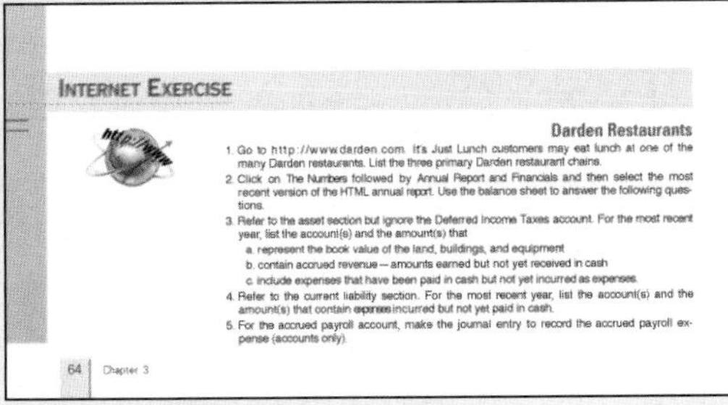

INTERNET EXERCISE

Darden Restaurants

1. Go to http://www.darden.com. It's Just Lunch customers may eat lunch at one of the many Darden restaurants. List the three primary Darden restaurant chains.
2. Click on The Numbers followed by Annual Report and Financials and then select the most recent version of the HTML annual report. Use the balance sheet to answer the following questions.
3. Refer to the asset section but ignore the Deferred Income Taxes account. For the most recent year, list the account(s) and the amount(s) that
   a. represent the book value of the land, buildings, and equipment
   b. contain accrued revenue—amounts earned but not yet received in cash
   c. include expenses that have been paid in cash but not yet incurred as expenses
4. Refer to the current liability section. For the most recent year, list the account(s) and the amount(s) that contain expenses incurred but not yet paid in cash.
5. For the accrued payroll account, make the journal entry to record the accrued payroll expense (accounts only).

64 Chapter 3

Internet Exercises

Exercises at the end of each chapter are directly linked to the chapter-opening story and video. Take a look at any chapter or check out online at **http://www.prenhall.com/harrison** to see samples.

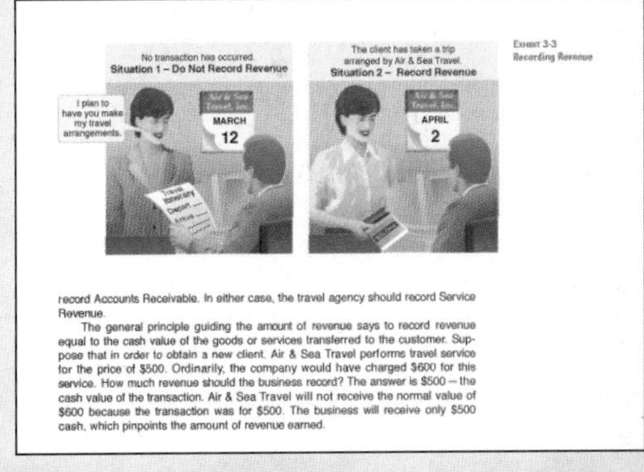

EXHIBIT 3-3
Recording Revenue

record Accounts Receivable. In either case, the travel agency should record Service Revenue.

The general principle guiding the amount of revenue says to record revenue equal to the cash value of the goods or services transferred to the customer. Suppose that in order to obtain a new client, Air & Sea Travel performs travel service for the price of $500. Ordinarily, the company would have charged $600 for this service. How much revenue should the business record? The answer is $500—the cash value of the transaction. Air & Sea Travel will not receive the normal value of $600 because the transaction was for $500. The business will receive only $500 cash, which pinpoints the amount of revenue earned.

Infographics

Help students understand concepts by providing visual displays of difficult material: one picture is worth a thousand words.

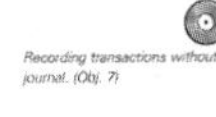

Recording transactions without a journal. (Obj. 7)

Net income captures much information: total revenues minus total expenses for the period. In essence, net income (or net loss) measures the ability of the business to generate revenues from its outputs (products or services) that exceed the costs of its inputs (merchandise, employee labor, supplies, utilities, and so on). A business that consistently earns net income, like It's Just Lunch, increases the value of the business for its owners, its employees, its customers, and society. The business is able to pay its debts. Net income captures these important aspects of a business.

An important step in financial statement preparation is the trial balance. ➸ The account balances in the trial balance include the effects of the transactions that occurred during the period—cash collections, purchases of assets, payments of bills, sales of assets, and so on. To measure its income, however, a business must do some additional accounting at the end of the period to update its records before preparing the financial statements. This process is called *adjusting the books*, and it consists of making special entries, called *adjusting entries*, that are needed to measure business income purchases of assets, payments of bills, sales of assets, and so on. To measure its income, however and generate accurate financial statements. This chapter also covers the process of closing the books at the end of the period.

➸ The trial balance, introduced in Chapter 2, page 74, lists the ledger accounts and their balances.

> The accounting profession has concepts and principles to guide the measurement of business income. To measure its income, however, a business must do some additional accounting at the end of the period to update its records before preparing the financial statements.
>
> This process is called *adjusting the books*, and it consists of making special additional accounting entries.

In this chapter, we apply these and other concepts and principles to measure the income and prepare the financial statements of Air & Sea Travel, Inc., for the month of April. The account balances in the trial balance include the effects of the transactions that occurred during the period. An important step in financial statement preparation is the trial balance.

444 Chapter 3

Concept Links Unique Concept Links point students to material covered in previous chapters. They take the student by the hand and lead him or her directly to the chapter and page on which the topic was introduced.

sources and uses of cash

Coverage of the Statement of Cash Flow

Grid for Statement of Cash Flows

Chapter	Cash Flow Coverage
1	The Gap's statement of cash flows is explained in detail. The relationships among all of the financial statements are illustrated.
2	Mid-Chapter Summary Problem requires preparation of the statement of cash flows.
3	New section on "Cash Flows and Accrual Accounting".
4	"Managing Cash" explains how companies speed the collection of cash. "Using a Budget to Manage Cash" introduces the cash budget. Internal controls are explained for cash.
5	Reporting short-term investments and receivables transactions on the statement of cash flows.
6	Reporting inventory transactions on the statement of cash flows.
7	Reporting plant asset transactions on the statement of cash flows.
8	Reporting financing activities on the statement of cash flows.
9	Reporting stockholders' equity transactions on the statement of cash flows.
10	Using the statement of cash flows to interpret a company's investing activities.
11	Analyzing both accounting income and cash flows to gain an overall picture of the company.
12	The statement of cash flows. Using the statement of cash flows in decision making.

"I like the discussion of cash flow effects in each chapter. I think it will help the students retain the concepts and utilize them more effectively. Again, the theory of continuing exposure should work here to help the students apply the concepts more quickly and more easily."

—Jeanne H. Yamamura
University of Nevada-Reno

technological support

> "**T**he market-leading text **delivers** the tools you need **today** to prepare tomorrow's business leaders. You pick the medium, and Harrison/Horngren's Financial Accounting, Fourth Edition provides the technology solution."

On Location! Videos

A set of custom-crafted videos (each 5-10 minutes in length) provided free upon adoption to faculty. Each video features real companies dealing with current accounting issues. Featured companies include: Teva Sandals, The Gap, Oracle, Home Depot, PepsiCo, IHOP, and more

Accounting Tutorial Video

These 15 newly created segments teach key financial accounting topics (a $100,000 video library!). Perfect for reviewing challenging topics or making up classes

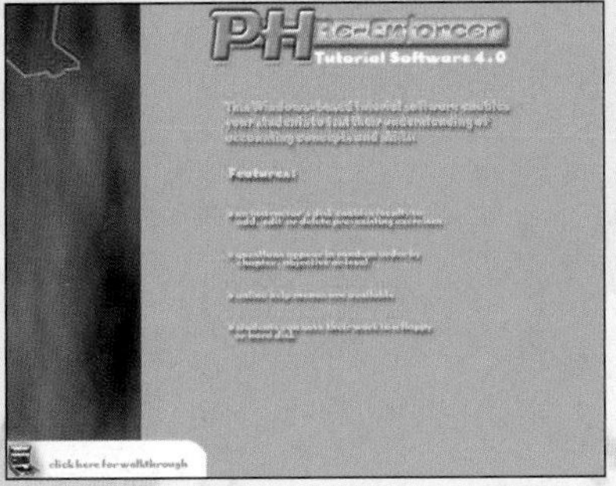

PH Re-Enforcer Software

This Windows-based tutorial software enables students to **test their understanding** through a variety of exercise types with immediate student feedback. The software can be networked and **downloaded from the Web site at no charge.** An Instructor's Disk enables faculty to add, edit, or delete pre-existing material

Accounting Made Easy

This Windows-based tutorial software provides another medium for students to **learn and test their understanding** of accounting concepts. It incorporates colorful animations, innovative feedback, personalities, and a variety of quiz materials linked to chapter topics. Available in two levels

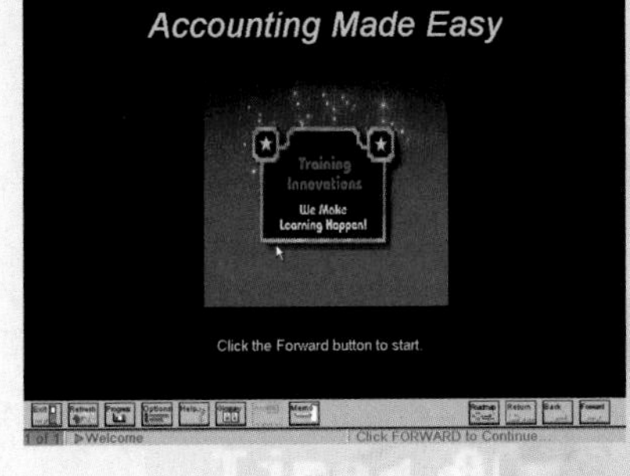

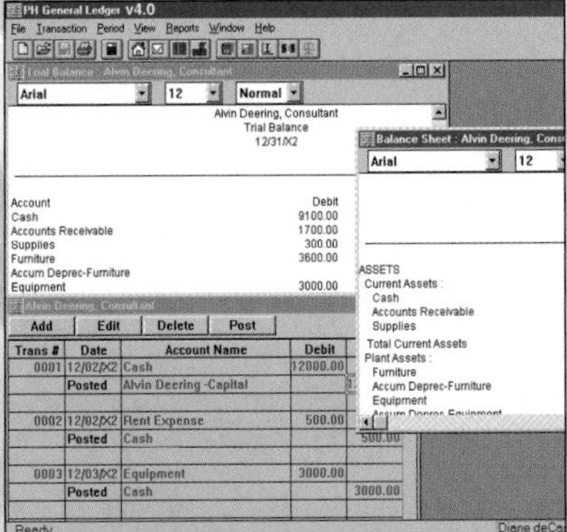

PHAS General Ledger

PHAS General Ledger software includes problem templates tied to selected text problems, and all users complete the entire accounting cycle: journalize, post, print reports, and close. A "Quick Tour" overviews the program and gives online "Help." The software may be **networked,** and adopters may **download the software** from the text Web site at **no additional charge**

Online Options

MyPHLIP/CW

Prentice Hall's Learning on the Internet Partnership/ Companion Web Site

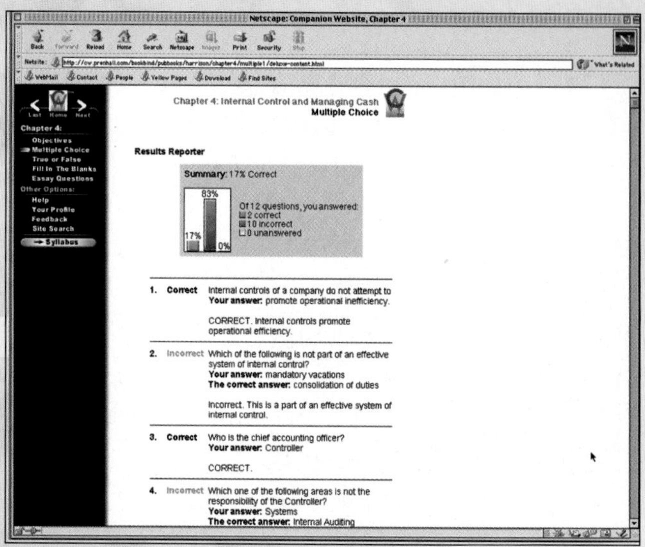

The most advanced text-specific site available on the Web. And it is available to adopters of Harrison/Horngren's *Financial Accounting*, Fourth Edition **free of charge!**	Harrison/ Horngren	Your Text
Current Events: (Articles available for each text chapter)		
■ Articles added every two weeks	Yes	?
■ Teaching tools for each article include: "Digging Deeper," "Group Activities," "Discussion Questions," "Thinking About the Future"	Yes	?
Internet Exercises:		
■ Available for each text chapter	Yes	?
■ Extra exercises (in addition to those in the text)	Yes	?
Study Guide:		
■ Four separate tests for each chapter (true/false, fill-in-the blank, multiple-choice, and essay)	Yes	?
■ "Hints" for each chapter	Yes	?
■ Immediate feedback on tests with total score, and explanations for each incorrect answer	Yes	?
■ Ability to e-mail results	Yes	?
Study Hall:		
■ Unique "Ask the Tutor" provides online tutor assistance from an accounting faculty member	Yes	?
■ Online chat room for students	Yes	?
■ Online research, study tips, and career resources	Yes	?
Syllabus Manager:		
■ Custom, online syllabi with calendar function	Yes	?
■ Can be linked to Web Sites	Yes	?
Faculty Resources:		
■ Password protected features	Yes	?
■ Downloads on online supplements		
■ Archive of materials created by faculty at other schools using this text	Yes	?
■ Chat room for faculty only	Yes	?
■ Teaching tools for current events and internet exercises	Yes	?

Test the power and features of the Harrison/Horngren text against the performance of your existing book!

http://www.prenhall.com/harrison

WebCT

webct

Customize your course for maximum results—even when your students aren't in the classroom with you.

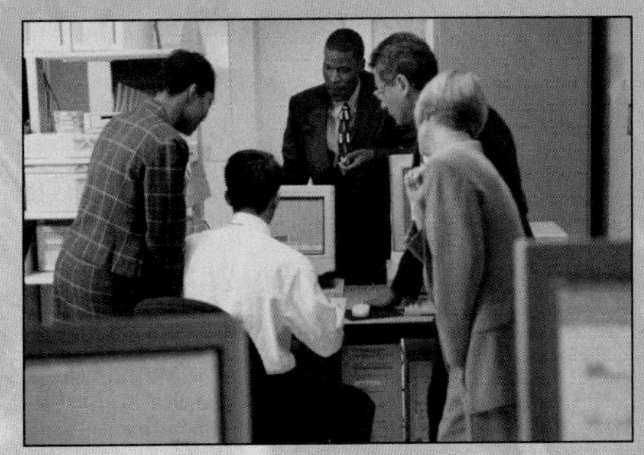

Features of **WebCT** include:

- Multiple Section Chat Rooms
- Bulletin Board Conferencing
- Audio and Video Downloads
- Lectures and Review Sections
- On-Line Quizzes and Tests
- Course Management with Page Tracking
- Calendar and Syllabus Capabilities
- Enables distance learning
- Pre-loaded content for Financial Accounting, 4/e
- "Point and Click" Systems for course customization

Special WebCT features available ONLY from Prentice Hall

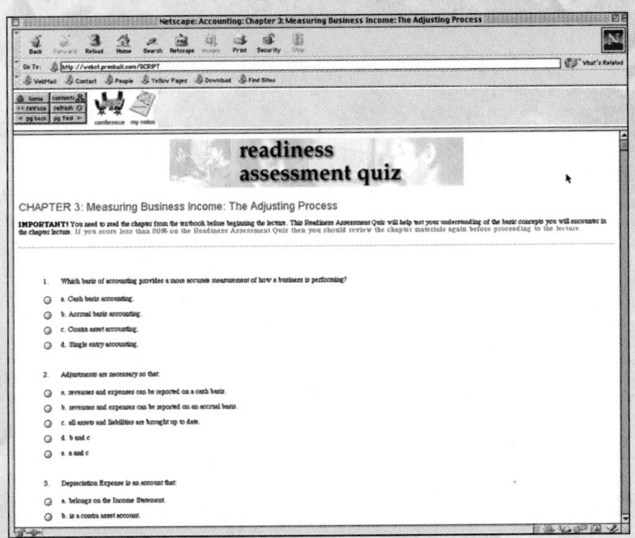

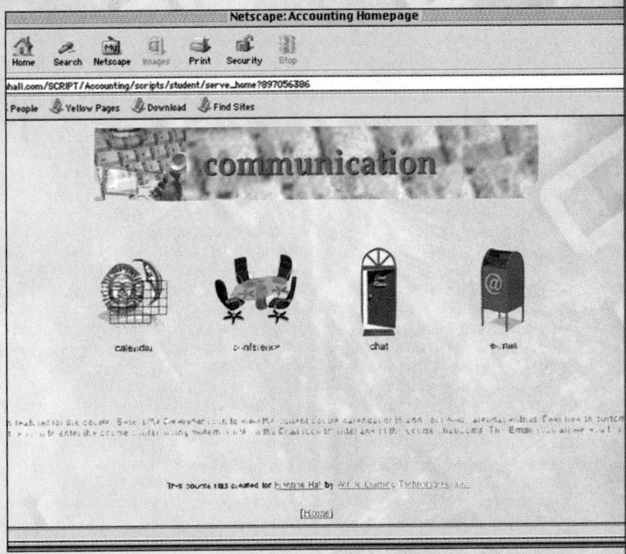

GOLD LEVEL SUPPORT **WebCT** and **Prentice Hall** have formed a unique alliance that provides all Prentice Hall online course customers with a special level Technical Support and a devoted WebCT 1-800# for adopters of Prentice Hall texts.

Because **you control the content** of the WebCT course, you can add to or delete from the online materials with a few simple key-strokes. Your **students perform better** because you can customize your class and course materials **on a daily basis.** Maximum responsiveness for premium performance!

http://www.prenhall.com/webct

Product Delivery

special thanks to Diane Colwyn

Focus Group Participants

Reviewers of the First, Second, and Third Editions

Salvador D. Aceves, Napa Valley College
Kim L. Anderson, Indiana University of Pennsylvania
Nina Brown, Tarrant County Junior College-Northwest
Kurt H. Buerger, Angelo State University
Glenn Bushnell, DeAnza College
Eric Carlson, Kean College of New Jersey
Wallace P. Carroll, J. Sargeant Reynolds Community College
Donna Chadwick, Sinclair Community College
Darrel W. Davis, University of Northern Iowa
S. T. Desai, Cedar Valley College
James M. Emig, Villanova University
Pat Evans, Auburn University
Kevin Feeney, Southern Connecticut State University
Carl J. Fisher, Foothill College
Jessica Frazier, Eastern Kentucky University
Marilyn Fuller, Paris Junior College
Roger Gee, San Diego Mesa College
Lucille Genduso, Nova University
James Genseal, Joliet Junior College
Barbara Gerrity, Berkeley School of Westchester
Gloria Grayless, Sam Houston State University
Ann Gregory, South Plains College
Timothy B. Griffin, University of Missouri-Kansas City & Johnson County Community College
Sue Gunckel, Albuquerque TVI Community College
Jim Haischer, Polk Community College
Debby Halik, Ivy Technical College
Jim Hansen, North Dakota State University
Saad Hassanein, Marymount University
Jimmie Henslee, El Centro College
Cynthia Holloway, Tarrant County Junior College-Northeast
Andrew Hrechek, Seton Hall University
Jean Insinga, Middlesex Technical and Community College
Tyronne James, Southern University of New Orleans
Fred R. Jex, Macomb Community College
Mary Thomas Keim, Indiana University of Pennsylvania
Nancy L. Kelly, Middlesex Technical and Community College
Randy Kidd, Penn Valley Community College
Raymond L. Larson, Appalachian State University
Cathy Larson, Middlesex Community College
Linda Lessing, SUNY College of Technology-Farmingdale
Lola Locke, Tarrant County Junior College
Cathy Lumbattis, Southern Illinois University
Paul Mihalek, University of Hartford
Graham Morris
Bruce Neumann, University of Colorado-Denver
Alfonso R. Oddo, Niagara University
Linda Overstreet, Hillsborough Community College
Robert Palmer, Troy State University
Patrick M. Premo, St. Bonaventure University
Karen Russom, North Harris College
Victoria Rymer, University of Maryland-College Park
Margaret Shelton, University of Houston, Downtown
Sherry Shively, Johnson County Community College
Kathleen Simione, Quinnipiac College
Dorothy Steinsapir, Middlesex Technical and Community College
Carolyn Streuly, Marquette University
Gracelyn Stuart, Palm Beach Community College
Diane L. Tanner, University of North Florida
Kathy Terrell, University of Central Oklahoma
Cynthia Thomas, Central Missouri State University
John Vaccaro, Bunker Hill Community College
Paul Waite, Niagara Community College
Martin Ward, DeVry Institute of Technology
Jim Weglin, North Seattle Community College
Bill Wempe, Wichita State University
Dale Westfall, Midland College
Joe Zernick, Ivy Technical College

English as a Second Language Reviewer

Zhu Zhu, Phoenix College

*"**Harrison/Horngren** is well written, well organized, and comprehensive in coverage. The problem material is good in terms of quantity and quality."*

—Keith R. Leeseberg
Manatee Community College

"I loved Chapters 11 and 13. They are much better than my current text. I like decision-making practice, so many of your exercises and problems would be very usable."

—Lee Cannell,
University of Texas-El Paso

Contents

Chapter 10
Long-Term Investments and International Operations 458

Chapter 11
Using the Income Statement and the Statement of Stockholders' Equity 498

Thematic Examples

Decision Guidelines

Internet Exercises—New

(Each chapter now concludes with an Internet-related exercise.)

ETHICS

(Ethical Issue exercises appear at the end of every chapter.)

CHAPTER	EXERCISE	PAGE
1	Introduction to ethical considerations in accounting and business	42
2	Ethics in recording business transactions	99
3	Ethical issues in accrual accounting	164
4	Ethics and internal/external controls	215
5	Ethics and uncollectible receivables	254
6	Ethical issues in inventory accounting	304
7	Ethical issues in accounting for plant assets and intangibles	356
8	Ethical issues in reporting contingent liabilities	404
9	Ethical considerations in accounting for the issuance of stock	455
	Ethical implications of treasury stock transactions	455
10	Ethics and the equity method of accounting for investments	496
11	Ethics and the income statement	532
12	Ethics and the statement of cash flows	587
13	Ethics and the current ratio	641

COMPUTERIZED ACCOUNTING SYSTEMS

CHAPTER	EXAMPLE	PAGE
1	The virtual office	48
2	Debits and credits in a computerized accounting system	64
	Using computers to record and journalize transactions immediately; computerized ledgers	70
	Computer preparation of trial balances	75
3	Use of computers to prepare monthly trial balances	113
	Computerized payroll modules for end-of-month adjustments	119
4	Automatic creation of permanent sales records in a computerized system and other computerized controls	173
	Electronic fund transfer	176
	Prevention of errors in account balances with computers	179
	Computers used to control cash receipts and disbursements	188,190
5	Using computers in the aging of accounts receivable	228
6	Use of computers in a perpetual inventory system	272
	Using computers to report inventory at LCM	277
7	Accounting for the the cost of buildings during construction with computers	314
	Using computerized systems to account for fixed assets and changes in accounting estimates	327
8	Accounting for current liabilities arising from many similar transactions; using computers to link the accounts payable	360
	Computerizing the payment of interest on notes payable	360
13	Using computers to calculate financial ratios and to compare companies' performance	604

Generally Accepted Accounting Principles (GAAP)

CHAPTER	EXAMPLE	PAGE
1	Introduction to generally accepted accounting principles: entity concept, reliability principle, cost principle, going-concern principle, stable-monetary unit concept	8
3	GAAP requirement that the accrual basis of accounting be used rather than the cash basis	107
	The time-period concept, revenue principle, and matching principle	107–110
4	GAAP rules regarding preparation of the statement of cash flows	193
6	Four inventory costing methods allowed by GAAP: specific unit cost, weighted-average cost, FIFO, and LIFO	264–266
	GAAP and practical considerations: a comparison of inventory methods	267–269
	GAAP's lower-of-cost-or-market rule	271
7	Accounting for plant assets and intangibles according to GAAP	312
	Matching an asset's expense against the revenue produced by that asset	322
	Rules regarding goodwill	335
	GAAP rules regarding the expensing of R&D costs	335
8	Accounting for contingent liabilities	365–366
	GAAP rules regarding use of the straight-line amortization	379
	Procedures for recording extraordinary gains and losses on the early retirement of debt	380
9	Recording small (0–20%) versus large (25%+) stock dividends	426–427
10	Bringing foreign subsidiaries' statements into conformity with American GAAP	478
	Comparision of GAAP in the United States with accounting principles in other countries	480
11	GAAP requirement that companies report the cumulative effect of a change in accounting principle	505
	Conformity to GAAP as explained in the statement of management responsibility	515
12	Accrual-basis accounting vs. cash-basis accounting	539–540
Appendix C	Summary of GAAP	677

FINANCIAL ACCOUNTING

1 The Financial Statements

Learning Objectives

After studying this chapter, you should be able to

1. Understand accounting vocabulary and use it in decision making
2. Analyze business activity with accounting concepts and principles
3. Use the accounting equation to describe an organization's financial position
4. Evaluate a company's operating performance, financial position, and cash flows
5. Explain the relationships among the financial statements

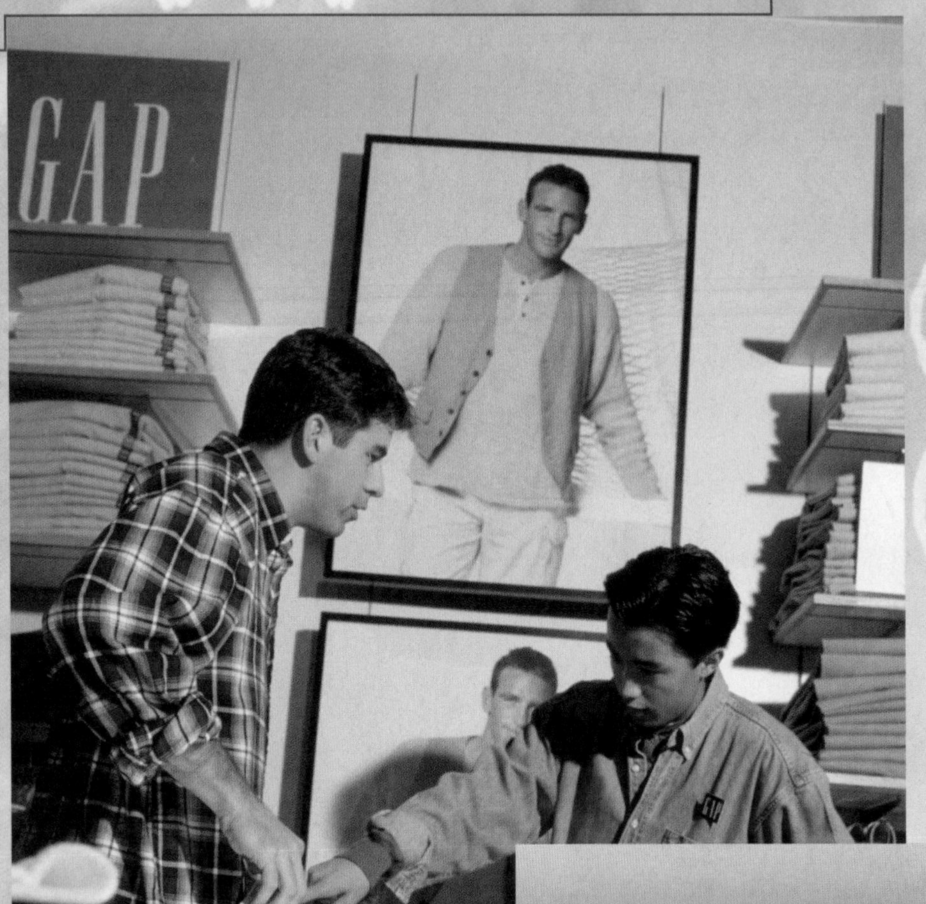

The Gap, Inc.
Anyone
Anywhere
Any time

The Gap, Inc.
Consolidated Statement of Earnings (adapted)

	($000)	Year Ended January 30, 1999	Percentage of Sales	Year Ended January 31, 1998	Percentage of Sales
1	Net sales revenue	$9,054,462	100.0%	$6,507,825	100.0%
2	Expenses				
3	Cost of goods sold	5,318,218	58.7	4,021,541	61.8
4	Advertising expense	419,000	4.6	175,000	2.7
5	Depreciation expense	326,036	3.6	269,706	4.1
6	Other operating expenses	1,658,329	18.3	1,190,311	18.3
7	Interest expense (revenue)	13,617	0.2	(2,975)	0.0
8	Earnings before income taxes	1,319,262	14.6	854,242	13.1
9	Income tax expense	494,723	5.5	320,341	4.9
10	Net earnings	$ 824,539	9.1%	$ 533,901	8.2%

From the streets of Philadelphia and Seattle, to the sidewalks of Boise and Tulsa, to the crowds of Tokyo and London, we want to be everywhere our customers are. One focus in 1998 was to bring our brands into our customers' homes. We expanded the convenience of shopping at our Gap Online Store at www.gap.com to bring the total brand — adults, kids, and babies — to online shoppers. Now customers anywhere in the United States can shop The Gap any time, day or night. It's perfect for people who just don't have time to get to our stores.

WHAT do advertising slogans such as "Anyone, Anywhere, Any time" have to do with accounting? A lot, because advertising leads to sales, and sales bring cash into **The Gap**. Also, advertising costs money, so businesses must budget their cash to pay for expensive ad campaigns. All these activities — advertising, buying merchandise, and selling products — are interesting to people outside The Gap because the information helps people make decisions about the company.

Accounting provides much of the information that people use to manage and evaluate businesses. In this course you will learn how to use accounting information just like investors on Wall Street and bankers on Main Street. In fact, the "Anyone, Anywhere, Any time" slogan of The Gap also applies to accounting: A person can make a wiser business decision if he or she knows how to use the information. In fact, the chances are good that accounting provided the right information for the decision. Let's begin our study of accounting by discussing some business decisions.

Managerial Decisions

In deciding how to operate the business, The Gap's managers must determine what merchandise they will sell and how to market it. Clearly, the company wants its revenues to exceed its expenses so that it will earn a profit. Accounting helps managers measure the revenues, expenses, and profit (or loss) of the business.

The income statement on page 14 reports that Gap, Inc., earned net sales revenue of over $9 billion during 1999 (line 1). Cost of goods sold, an expense (line 3), consumed over $5.3 billion. Additional expenses—advertising, depreciation, other operating expenses, and interest (lines 4–7 respectively)—totaled $2.4 billion, leaving The Gap with net earnings, the bottom line, of $825 million (line 10), after all expenses for the year ended January 30, 1999.

Gap managers must determine what types of assets to acquire for use in the business. For example, should they automate the warehouse and use robotic equipment to handle merchandise? If so, they will want to purchase equipment that moves goods rapidly and at the lowest cost. Accounting measures the cost of such equipment.

Finally, Gap managers must decide how the company will finance its operations. Which way of financing the business is better—selling stock (ownership shares) to the owners or borrowing from outsiders? There is no standard answer. Sometimes borrowing has the advantage. In other cases, it is better to issue stock. Accounting measures the cost of obtaining funds.

Investor Decisions

Suppose you have $50,000 to invest. You can deposit the money in a bank and earn interest. This investment is safe because deposits in U.S. banks are insured, but it will not grow very fast in a bank account. Or you could invest in land on the outskirts of town. There has been some talk that The Gap may open a store in the vicinity, and the land may increase in value. If so, your investment may double or triple in value, but it is also quite risky because The Gap may not locate near your land. Besides, others also know of The Gap's plan, and you may have to pay a high price for the land.

A third possible investment is buying stock in The Gap. This investment is more risky than depositing money in a bank account but less risky than buying land in hopes of selling it at a higher price. What information would you need before deciding to invest in Gap stock? You would prefer that The Gap have a track record of profitable operations—earning a profit (net earnings or net income) year after year. The company would need a steady stream of cash coming in and a manageable level of debt. How would you determine whether the company meets these criteria? The company's financial statements provide the information you need.

✔ CHECK POINT 1-1

ACCOUNTING—THE BASIS OF DECISION MAKING

Objective 1
Understand accounting vocabulary and use it in decision making

Accounting is the information system that measures business activities, processes that information into reports, and communicates the results to decision makers. For this reason, it is called "the language of business." The better you understand this language, the better you can manage your finances and the better your decisions will be. Personal planning, education expenses, loans, car payments, and income taxes all use the information system we call accounting.

Accounting: The Language of Business

Accounting: An Information System

A key product of an accounting information system is the set of **financial statements:** the documents that report financial information about a business en-

3. Businesses prepare reports to show the results of their operations.

EXHIBIT 1-1
The Flow of Information in an Accounting System

tity to decision makers. They tell us how well a business is performing in terms of profits and losses and where it stands in financial terms. In this chapter we focus on the financial statements of **The Gap.** As you complete this first chapter, you will be familiar with the financial statements that this well-known company uses to represent itself to the public. This book's major goal is to acquaint you with financial statements and to give you the expertise you need to use them for financial decision making.

Please don't mistake bookkeeping for accounting. Bookkeeping is the procedural element of accounting that processes the accounting data, just as arithmetic is a procedural element of mathematics. Exhibit 1-1 illustrates accounting's role in business. The process starts and ends with people making decisions.

CHECK POINT 1-2

Decision Makers Use Accounting Information

Decision makers need information. The more important the decision, the greater the need. All businesses and most individuals keep accounting records to aid in making decisions. The chapter-opening story reveals a key decision that Gap managers made in designing a slogan to expand the company. The result might be the company's income statement (page 14), which we also saw earlier. We will examine this and other financial statements in detail as we proceed through this chapter. First, however, let's look at some decision makers who use accounting information.

INDIVIDUALS. People use accounting information to manage their bank accounts, to evaluate job prospects, and to decide whether to rent an apartment or buy a house.

BUSINESSES. Managers of businesses use accounting information to set goals, to evaluate progress toward those goals, and to take corrective action if necessary. Decisions based on accounting information may include where to locate a Gap store, how many shirts to keep on hand, and how much cash to borrow.

INVESTORS AND CREDITORS. Investors and creditors provide the money a business needs to get started. When The Gap opened its first store, the company had no track record. To decide whether to help start a new venture, potential investors evaluate what income they can expect on their investment. This means analyzing the financial statements of the business. Before deciding to invest in The Gap, for example, you may examine the company's financial statements. Before making a loan to The Gap, banks evaluate the company's ability to meet scheduled payments.

GOVERNMENT REGULATORY AGENCIES. Most organizations face government regulation. For example, the Securities and Exchange Commission (SEC), a federal agency, requires businesses to report certain financial information to the investing public. The Gap and other companies publish annual reports. The company's income statement on page 14 was taken from The Gap's annual report for the year ended January 30, 1999.

TAXING AUTHORITIES. Local, state, and federal governments levy taxes on individuals and businesses. The Gap pays property tax on its assets and income tax on its profits. The Gap also collects sales tax from customers and forwards the money to the government. Individuals pay income tax on their earnings. All of these taxes are based on accounting data.

NONPROFIT ORGANIZATIONS. Nonprofit organizations—such as churches, hospitals, and government agencies, which operate for purposes other than profit—use accounting information as profit-oriented businesses do. Both for-profit organizations and nonprofit organizations deal with payrolls, rent payments, and the like—information from the accounting system.

OTHER USERS. Employees and labor unions demand wages that come from the employer's reported income. And newspapers report "improved profit pictures" of companies. Such news, which depends on accounting, reports information that affects our standard of living.

Financial Accounting and Management Accounting

The users of accounting information are diverse, but they may be categorized as *external users* or *internal users.* This distinction allows us to classify accounting into two fields—financial accounting and management accounting.

Financial accounting provides information to managers and to people outside the firm, such as investors on Wall Street and creditors who lend money to the company. Government agencies, such as the SEC, and the general public are also external users of a firm's accounting information. Financial accounting information must meet certain standards of relevance and reliability. This book deals primarily with financial accounting.

Management accounting generates confidential information for internal decision makers, such as top executives and department heads. Management accounting information is tailored to the needs of managers and thus does not have to meet external standards of reliability.

Ethical Considerations in Accounting and Business

Ethical considerations pervade all areas of accounting and business. The Y2K problem of the 1990s provided an ethical challenge for virtually all companies everywhere. A large-scale computer failure could have shut down operations and led to large losses. The business challenge was to alter computer programs to avoid the Y2K problem. The *ethical challenge* for accountants was to provide investors and creditors with enough information about how companies were dealing with the Y2K problem to enable them to make informed judgements about these companies.

By what criteria do accountants address questions that challenge their ethical conduct? *The American Institute of Certified Public Accountants (AICPA),* other professional accounting organizations, and most large companies have codes of ethics that require members and employees to honor high levels of ethical conduct. The AICPA is the country's largest organization of professional accountants, similar to the American Medical Association for physicians and the American Bar Association for attorneys.

STANDARDS OF PROFESSIONAL CONDUCT FOR ACCOUNTANTS. The Code of Professional Conduct was adopted by the members of the AICPA to provide guidance in performing their professional duties. Ethical standards in accounting are designed to produce *accurate information for decision making.* The preamble to the Code states: "[A] certified public accountant assumes an obligation of self-discipline above and beyond the requirements of laws and regulations . . . [and] an unswerving commitment to honorable behavior, even at the sacrifice of personal advantage." The result of ethical behavior by accountants is information that people can rely on for decision making. Without reliable information, people will not invest their money, and the failure to put resources to work will hurt our standard of living.

✔ CHECK POINT 1-3

The Boeing Company's Business Conduct Guidelines. Most organizations set standards of ethical conduct for their employees. For example, **The Boeing Company,** a leading manufacturer of aircraft, has a highly developed set of business conduct guidelines. In the introduction to those guidelines, the chairperson of the board and chief executive officer state: "We owe our success as much to our reputation for integrity as we do to the quality and dependability of our products and services. This reputation is fragile and can easily be lost."

Types of Business Organizations

A business takes one of three forms of organization, and in some cases, accounting procedures depend on which form the organization takes. Therefore, you should understand the differences among the three types of business organizations: proprietorships, partnerships, and corporations. Exhibit 1-2 compares the three types.

PROPRIETORSHIPS. A **proprietorship** has a single owner, called the proprietor, who is generally also the manager. The Gap may have started out as a proprietorship, with its founder as the owner. Proprietorships tend to be small retail stores or individual professional businesses, such as those of physicians, attorneys, and accountants. From the accounting viewpoint, each proprietorship is distinct from its proprietor. Thus, the accounting records of the proprietorship do not include the proprietor's personal financial records. From a legal perspective, however, the business *is* the proprietor and the proprietor is personally liable for the debts of the business.

PARTNERSHIPS. A **partnership** joins two or more persons together as co-owners. Each owner is a partner. Many retail establishments and some professional organizations of physicians, attorneys, and accountants are partnerships. Most partnerships are small or medium-sized, but some are gigantic, exceeding 2,000 partners. Accounting treats the partnership as a separate organization, distinct from the personal affairs of each partner. But the law views a partnership as the partners: Each partner is personally liable for all the debts of the partnership. For this reason, partnerships are viewed as quite risky.

EXHIBIT 1-2
Comparison of the Three Forms of Business Organization

	Proprietorship	*Partnership*	*Corporation*
Owner(s)	Proprietor—one owner	Partners—two or more owners	Stockholders—generally many owners
Life of entity	Limited by owner's choice or death	Limited by owners' choices or death	Indefinite
Personal liability of owner(s) for business debts	Proprietor is personally liable	Partners are personally liable	Stockholders are not personally liable
Accounting status	Accounting entity is separate from proprietor	Accounting entity is separate from partners	Accounting entity is separate from stockholders

CORPORATIONS. A **corporation** is a business owned by **stockholders,** or **shareholders**—people who own **stock,** or shares of ownership, in the business. The corporation is the dominant form of business organization in the United States. Proprietorships and partnerships are more numerous, but corporations transact much more business and are larger in terms of total assets, income, and number of employees. Most well-known companies, such as **The Gap, General Motors,** and **American Airlines,** are corporations. Their full names include *Corporation* or *Incorporated* (abbreviated *Corp.* and *Inc.*) to indicate that they are corporations—for example, The Gap, Inc., and General Motors Corporation. Some corporations bear the name "Company," such as Ford Motor Company. A proprietorship and a partnership can also bear the name "Company."

A corporation is a business entity formed under state law. From a legal perspective, a corporation is distinct from its owners. The corporation operates as an artificial person that exists apart from its owners. The corporation has many of the rights that a person has. For example, a corporation may buy, own, and sell property. Assets and debts in the business belong to the corporation. It may enter into contracts, sue, and be sued. Unlike proprietors and partners, stockholders have no personal obligations for corporation debts. The most that a stockholder can lose on an investment in corporate stock is the cost of the investment. But proprietors and partners are personally liable for the debts of their businesses.

The ownership interest of a corporation is divided into shares of stock. A person becomes a stockholder by purchasing the corporation's stock. The Gap, for example, has issued over 400 million shares of stock owned by thousands of shareholders. An investor with no personal relationship either to The Gap or to any other stockholder can become a co-owner by buying 1, 30, 100, 5,000, or any number of shares of its stock through the New York Stock Exchange.

The ultimate control of the corporation rests with the stockholders, who receive one vote for each share of stock they own. Stockholders elect the members of the **board of directors,** which sets policy for the corporation and appoints officers. The board elects a chairperson, who usually is the most powerful person in the corporation and often carries the title chief executive officer (CEO). The board also designates the president, who is the chief operating officer (COO) in charge of managing day-to-day operations. Most corporations also have vice presidents in charge of sales, manufacturing, accounting, finance, and other key areas.

ACCOUNTING PRINCIPLES AND CONCEPTS

Objective 2
Analyze business activity with accounting concepts and principles

Accountants follow professional guidelines. The rules that govern how accountants operate fall under the heading **GAAP,** which stands for **generally accepted accounting principles.**

In the United States, the *Financial Accounting Standards Board (FASB)* determines how accounting is practiced. The FASB works with the SEC and AICPA. Exhibit 1-3 diagrams the relationships among these organizations and the rules that govern them. The diagram starts at the top and moves to your right.

The primary objective of financial reporting is to provide information useful for making investment and lending decisions.

GAAP rests on a conceptual framework written by the FASB: To be useful, information must be relevant, reliable, and comparable. Accountants strive to meet those goals in the information they produce. This course will expose you to the generally accepted methods of accounting; we will discuss these as they become relevant in each chapter. We also summarize them in Appendix C. First, however, you need to understand several basic concepts that underlie accounting practice.

PUBLIC SECTOR

Law creates the Securities and Exchange Commission (SEC), a government agency, to regulate the stock and bond markets in the United States.

PRIVATE SECTOR

Accountants apply GAAP through the American Institute of Certified Public Accountants (AICPA) and other organizations.

Generally accepted accounting principles (GAAP) govern accounting information.

PRIVATE SECTOR

The Financial Accounting Standards Board (FASB) determines generally accepted accounting principles.

EXHIBIT 1-3
Key Accounting Organizations

The Entity Concept

The most basic concept in accounting is that of the **entity.** An accounting entity is an organization or section of an organization that stands apart as a separate economic unit. From an accounting perspective, sharp boundaries are drawn around each entity so as not to confuse its affairs with those of others.

Consider Julie DeFilippo, the owner of the catering firm An Extra Hand. DeFilippo's bank account shows a $2,000 balance at the end of the year, but only $1,200 came from the business. The other $800 was a gift from her grandparents. To follow the entity concept, DeFilippo will account for the $1,200 generated by the business—one economic unit—separately from the $800 she received from her family, which is a second economic unit. Only by accounting for the $1,200 and the $800 separately can DeFilippo evaluate her business clearly.

Now consider **Toyota,** which has several divisions. Toyota management evaluates each division as a separate accounting entity. If sales in the Lexus division are dropping drastically, Toyota should identify the reason. But if sales figures from all divisions of the company are combined into a single amount, then management cannot tell how many Lexuses the company is selling. To correct the problem, managers need sales data for each division—each separate entity—of the company.

In summary: The transactions of different entities should not be accounted for together. Each entity should be evaluated separately.

CHECK POINT 1-4

The Reliability (or Objectivity) Principle

To ensure that they are as accurate and as useful as possible, accounting records and statements are based on the most reliable data available. This guideline is the **reliability principle,** also called the **objectivity principle.** Reliable data (1) are verifiable and (2) can be confirmed by an independent observer. Ideally, accounting records are based on information that flows from activities documented by objective evidence. For example, an $18 purchase of a shirt by The Gap is supported by a paid invoice. This invoice is objective evidence of the company's cost of the shirt. Without the reliability principle, accounting records would be based on whims and opinions and subject to dispute.

Suppose you want to open a stereo shop and are trying to buy a small building. You believe the building is worth $155,000. Two real estate professionals appraise the building at $147,000. The owner of the building demands $160,000, and suppose you pay that price. The accounting value of the building is your cost of $160,000 because it is supported by the objective evidence of a completed transaction. The business should therefore record the building at its cost of $160,000.

The Cost Principle

The **cost principle** states that acquired assets and services should be recorded at their actual cost (also called *historical cost*). Even though the purchaser may believe the price paid is a bargain, the item is recorded at the price paid in the transaction and not at the "expected" cost. Suppose your stereo shop purchases stereo equipment from a supplier who is going out of business. Assume that you get a good deal on this purchase and pay only $2,000 for merchandise that would have cost you $3,000 elsewhere. The cost principle requires you to record this merchandise at its actual cost of $2,000, not the $3,000 that you believe it is worth.

The cost principle also holds that accounting records should maintain the historical cost of an asset for as long as the business holds the asset. Why? Because cost is a reliable measure. Suppose your store holds the stereo equipment for six months. During that time, stereo prices increase and the equipment can be sold for $3,500. Should its accounting value—the figure "on the books"—be the actual cost of $2,000 or the current market value of $3,500? According to the cost principle, the accounting value of the equipment remains at actual cost, $2,000.

The Going-Concern Concept

Another reason for measuring assets at historical cost is the **going-concern concept,** which holds that the entity will remain in operation for the foreseeable future. Most assets—that is, the firm's resources, such as supplies, land, buildings, and equipment—are acquired for use rather than for sale. Under the going-concern concept, accountants assume that the business will remain in operation long enough to use existing assets for their intended purpose. The market value of an asset—the price for which the asset can be sold—may change during the asset's life. Moreover, historical cost is a more reliable accounting measure for assets than market value is because cost is a historical fact.

Consider the alternative to the going-concern concept: going out of business. A store holding a going-out-of-business sale is trying to sell all its assets. In that case, the relevant measure of the assets is their current market value. But going out of business is the exception rather than the rule and for this reason accounting lists a going concern's assets at their historical cost.

The Stable-Monetary-Unit Concept

We think of a loaf of bread and a month's rent in terms of their dollar values. In the United States, accountants record transactions in dollars because the dollar is the medium of exchange. British accountants record transactions in pounds sterling, and Japanese accountants in yen.

Unlike the value of a liter or a mile, the value of a dollar or of a Mexican peso changes over time. A rise in the general price level is called *inflation.* During inflation, a dollar will purchase less milk, less toothpaste, and less of other goods. When prices are stable—when there is little inflation—a dollar's purchasing power is also stable.

Accountants assume that the dollar's purchasing power is relatively stable. The **stable-monetary-unit concept** is the basis for ignoring the effect of inflation in the accounting records. It allows accountants to add and subtract dollar amounts as though each dollar has the same purchasing power as any other dollar at any other time.

You are considering the purchase of land for future expansion. The seller is asking $50,000 for land that cost him $35,000. An appraisal shows a value of $47,000. You first offer $44,000, the seller makes a counteroffer of $48,000, and you agree on $46,000. What dollar value is reported for the land on your financial statements?

Answer: Report the land at $46,000, which is its historical cost.

THE ACCOUNTING EQUATION

Objective 3
Use the accounting equation to describe an organization's financial position

As we saw earlier, financial statements tell us how a business is performing and where it stands. They are the final product of the accounting process. But how do we arrive at the items and amounts that make up financial statements?

Assets and Liabilities

The financial statements are based on the most basic tool of accounting, the **accounting equation.** This equation presents the resources of the business and the claims to those resources.

- **Assets** are the economic resources of a business that are expected to be of benefit in the future. Cash, office supplies, merchandise, furniture, land, and buildings are examples of assets.

Claims to assets come from two sources:

- **Liabilities** are "outsider claims." They are economic obligations—debts—payable to outsiders, called *creditors*. For example, a creditor who has loaned money to a business has a claim—a legal right—to a part of the company's assets until the business repays the debt.
- **Owners' equity** (also called **capital**) represents the "insider claims" of a business. Equity means ownership, so these are the assets held by the owners of the business. An owner has a claim to the entity's assets because he or she has invested in the business. The amount that the founder of The Gap invested to start the business is an example.

The accounting equation shows the relationship among assets, liabilities, and owners' equity. Assets appear on the left-hand side of the equation. The legal and economic claims against the assets—the liabilities and owners' equity—appear on the right-hand side of the equation. As Exhibit 1-4 shows, the two sides must be equal:

Economic Resources	**= Claims to Economic Resources**
Assets	**= Liabilities + Owners' Equity**

Consider the assets and the liabilities of The Gap, Inc. What would be some of The Gap's assets? The first asset listed for all businesses is **cash,** the liquid (cash) asset that is the medium of exchange. Another important asset of The Gap is **merchandise inventory**—the shirts, slacks, and other goods—that Gap sells to customers. The Gap also has assets in the form of land, buildings, furniture, and equipment. These are the long-lived assets that Gap uses to sell its merchandise—store buildings, display racks, computers, and so on. Land, buildings, and equipment are called **plant assets,** or *property, plant, and equipment* (often abbreviated as *PPE*).

The Gap's liabilities include a number of payables, such as accounts payable and notes payable. The word *payable* always signifies a liability. An **account payable** is a liability for goods or services purchased on credit and supported only by the credit standing of the purchaser. A **note payable** is a written promise to pay on a certain date. **Long-term debt** is a liability that falls due beyond one year from the date of the financial statements.

EXHIBIT 1-4
The Accounting Equation

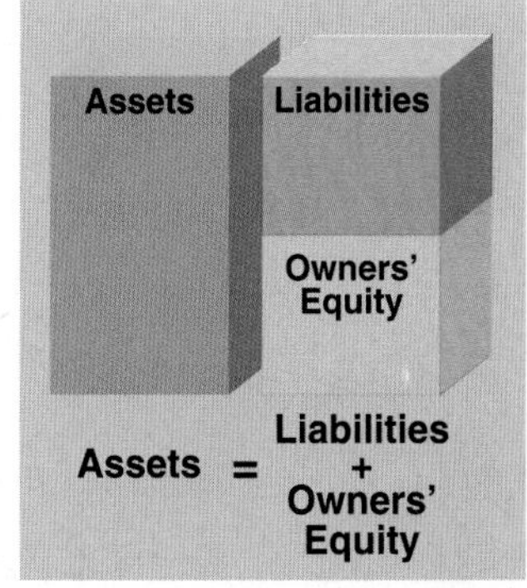

Owners' Equity

The owners' equity of The Gap, Inc., is the assets of the business minus its liabilities. This is true of any entity—from a private individual to the largest corporations such as **The Gap, IBM,** or **General Motors.** We often write the accounting equation to show that the owners' claim to business assets is a residual—something that is left over after a subtraction process:

Assets − Liabilities = Owners' Equity

The owners' equity of a corporation—called **stockholders' equity**—is divided into two main categories, paid-in capital and retained earnings. For a corporation, the accounting equation can be written as

CHECK POINT 1-5

Assets = Liabilities + Stockholders' Equity

Assets = Liabilities + Paid-in Capital + Retained Earnings

Paid-in, or **contributed, capital** is the amount invested in the corporation by its owners. The basic component of paid-in capital is **common stock,** which the corporation issues to stockholders as evidence of ownership.

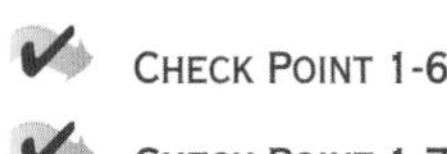

CHECK POINT 1-6

CHECK POINT 1-7

Retained earnings is the amount earned by income-producing activities and kept for use in the business. Two types of transactions that affect retained earnings are revenues and expenses.

- **Revenues** are increases in retained earnings from delivering goods or services to customers or clients. For example, a laundry's receipt of cash from a customer for cleaning a coat brings in revenue and increases the firm's retained earnings.
- **Expenses** are decreases in retained earnings that result from operations. For example, the wages that the laundry pays its employees constitute an expense and decrease retained earnings. Expenses are the cost of doing business and are the opposite of revenues. Expenses include office rent, salaries, and utility payments.

Businesses strive for profitability. When total revenues exceed total expenses, the result of operations is called **net income, net earnings,** or **net profit.** When expenses exceed revenues, the result is a **net loss.** Net income or net loss is the "bottom line" on an income statement. The Gap is profitable and refers to its bottom line as *net earnings* on page 14.

A successful business may pay dividends. **Dividends** are distributions to stockholders of assets (usually cash) generated by net income. Remember this: Dividends are not expenses. Exhibit 1-5 shows the relationships among

- retained earnings
- revenues − expenses = net income (or net loss)
- dividends

EXHIBIT 1-5
Components of Retained Earnings

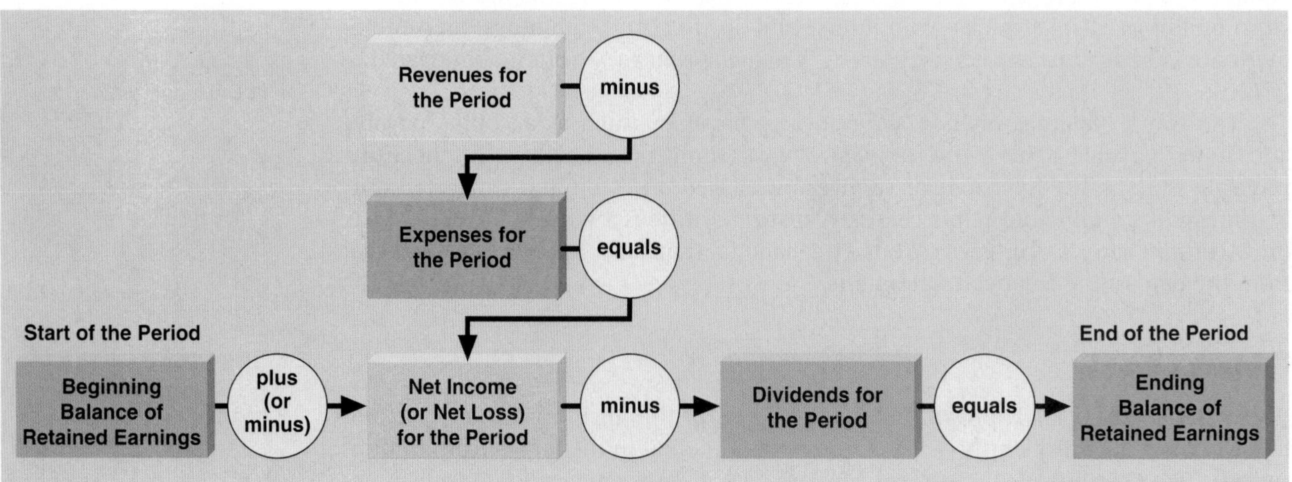

The owners' equity of proprietorships and of partnerships is different. These types of businesses make no distinction between paid-in capital and retained earnings. Instead, the equity of each owner is accounted for under the single heading of Capital—for example, Samuel Gap, Capital if the company were a proprietorship. The partnership of Pratt and Muesli has a separate record for the capital of each partner: Pratt, Capital, and Muesli, Capital.

1. If the assets of a business are $174,300 and the liabilities are $82,000, how much is the owners' equity?
2. If the owners' equity in a business is $22,000 and the liabilities are $36,000, how much are the assets?
3. A company reported monthly revenues of $77,600 and expenses of $81,300. What is the result of operations for the month?

Answers:

1. $92,300 ($174,300 − $82,000)
2. $58,000 ($22,000 + $36,000)
3. Net loss of $3,700 ($77,600 − $81,300); expenses minus revenues.

THE FINANCIAL STATEMENTS

Objective 4
Evaluate a company's operating performance, financial position, and cash flows

The end product of the accounting process is the set of financial statements that portrays the company in financial terms. Each financial statement relates to a specific date or covers a specific period of business activity, such as a year. What would managers and investors want to know about **The Gap** at the end of a period? Exhibit 1-6 summarizes the four basic questions that decision makers are likely to ask. The answer to each question is given by one of the financial statements: the income statement, the statement of retained earnings, the balance sheet, and the statement of cash flows.

EXHIBIT 1-6
Information Reported on the Financial Statements

Question	*Answer*	*Financial Statement*
1. How well did the company perform (or operate) during the period?	Revenues − Expenses Net income (or Net loss)	Income statement (also called the Statement of operations or the statement of earnings)
2. Why did the company's retained earnings change during the period?	Beginning retained earnings + Net income (or − Net loss) − Dividends Ending retained earnings	Statement of retained earnings (or Statement of stockholders' equity)
3. What is the company's financial position at the end of the period?	Assets = Liabilities + Owners' Equity	Balance sheet (also called the Statement of financial position)
4. How much cash did the company generate and spend during the period?	Operating cash flows ± Investing cash flows ± Financing cash flows Increase (or decrease) in cash during the period	Statement of cash flows

EXHIBIT 1-7
Income Statement (Statement of Earnings) (adapted)

THE GAP, INC.
Consolidated Statement of Earnings (adapted)

	($000)	*Year Ended January 30, 1999*	*Percentage of Sales*	*Year Ended January 31, 1998*	*Percentage of Sales*
1	Net sales revenue	$9,054,462	100.0%	$6,507,825	100.0%
2	Expenses				
3	Cost of goods sold	5,318,218	58.7	4,021,541	61.8
4	Advertising expense	419,000	4.6	175,000	2.7
5	Depreciation expense	326,036	3.6	269,706	4.1
6	Other operating expenses	1,658,329	18.3	1,190,311	18.3
7	Interest expense (revenue)	13,617	0.2	(2,975)	0.0
8	Earnings before income taxes	1,319,262	14.6	854,242	13.1
9	Income tax expense	494,723	5.5	320,341	4.9
10	Net earnings	$ 824,539	9.1%	$ 533,901	8.2%

To examine what the financial statements include and to learn how to read them, let's look at The Gap financial statements for the year ended January 30, 1999 (fiscal year 1999).

Let's begin with the income statement (statement of earnings) in Exhibit 1-7. Its final amount, net earnings (line 10), feeds into the statement of retained earnings (Exhibit 1-8, line 2), which also appears on the balance sheet (Exhibit 1-9, line 22). As you can see, there is a natural progression from the income statement, to the statement of retained earnings, to the balance sheet, and finally to the statement of cash flows (Exhibit 1-10). We discuss these financial statements in the pages that follow.

Income Statement (Statement of Earnings)

The **income statement, statement of operations,** or **statement of earnings,** reports the company's revenues, expenses, and net income or net loss for the period. At the top of Exhibit 1-7 (same as the income statement in the chapter opener) is the company's name, The Gap, Inc. The Gap, the parent company, owns other companies that are its subsidiaries. To give a full picture of all the resources that The Gap controls, the amounts reported on the statements include figures for both The Gap and its subsidiaries. Most companies' financial statements show the consolidation of a parent company and one or more subsidiaries. This is why they include the word *consolidated* in the title.

The date of the income statement is "For the years ended January 30, 1999 and January 31, 1998." The Gap's accounting year ends on the Saturday closest to January 31 of each year. If The Gap followed the calendar year, its accounting year would end on December 31, and its income statement would be dated "For the year ended December 31, 1999." The Gap uses a fiscal year that ends around January 31 because the company's big selling period winds down about a month after Christmas. **JC Penney, Wal-Mart Stores,** and most other retailers also use a fiscal year that ends on January 31. This is a general principle: Most companies adopt an accounting year that ends with the low point in their annual operations. For over 60% of large companies, the low point is December 31. A *fiscal year* is an accounting year that ends on a date other than December 31.

The Gap income statement reports operating results for two fiscal years, 1999 and 1998. The income statement includes more than one year's data to show the company's trends for sales and net income. To avoid cluttering the statement with zeros, The Gap reports its figures in thousands of dollars. During 1999, The Gap increased net sales from $6.5 billion to over $9 billion (see line 1). Net earnings increased from $534 million to $825 million (line 10). Continuation of this upward trend in net income would please the company's managers and investors.

The income statement reports two main categories:

- Revenues and gains
- Expenses and losses

In business we relate revenues and expenses to measure net income as follows:

Net Income = Total Revenues and Gains − Total Expenses and Losses

In accounting, the word "net" means the result after a subtraction has occurred. Net income is therefore the amount of income remaining after subtracting the expenses and losses from the revenues and gains.

REVENUES. Revenues and expenses do not always carry the terms *revenue* and *expense* in their titles. For example, *net sales* is really net sales revenue, but the term *revenue* is often omitted. During 1999, The Gap had net sales of $9,054,462,000 (line 1). The term *net* sales means that the company has subtracted from total sales the goods that Gap received from customers who returned merchandise.

EXPENSES. *Cost of goods sold* (also called *cost of sales,* line 3) represents the cost to The Gap of the goods it sold to customers. For example, suppose The Gap buys a shirt for $20 and sells it for $40. Sales revenue is $40, and cost of goods sold is $20. Cost of goods sold is the major expense of merchandising entities such as **The Gap, Wal-Mart** (the discount chain), and **Safeway** (the nationwide grocery company).

Additional major expenses are advertising, depreciation, and other operating expenses:

- *Advertising* (line 4) is the company's cost to promote its products in newspaper, television, and other advertising media.
- *Depreciation* (line 5) is the expense of using company-owned buildings, equipment, and furniture.
- *Other operating expenses* (line 6) is a broad category that includes salaries paid to employees, utilities expenses (for electricity, gas, and telephone), rent paid for leased property in shopping centers, and store supplies used for customer receipts. *Operating expenses* are those expenses directly related to The Gap's core operations, which consist of selling clothing.
- *Interest expense* is the cost of borrowed money. In 1999, The Gap incurred interest expense of $13.6 million. Note that in 1998, the company had no interest expense; rather, The Gap Company earned interest revenue of $2,975 million. The parentheses around $2,975 indicate that the interest amount for 1998 was revenue instead of expense. The parentheses around $2,975 reveal something to remember about the structure of financial statements:

Parentheses around dollar figures in a financial statement indicate a negative amount.

Find The Gap's interest revenue for 1998 in Exhibit 1-7. Note that interest revenue is listed among expenses. Because revenue and expense are opposites, we must subtract interest revenue from expenses. Why is interest revenue listed among expenses? Because interest revenue is a minor amount compared to the large amounts on the income statement. It is also convenient to list interest expense (revenue) on a single line of the statement rather than to show separate lines for a small amount of interest revenue and a small amount of interest expense.

Income before income taxes totaled $1.3 billion (line 8), and income tax expense (often labeled simply "Income taxes") absorbed $495 million of the company's profits (line 9). For fiscal year 1999, The Gap earned net income of $825 million after covering all expenses, including income tax.

✔ CHECK POINT 1-8

The Gap's income statement includes an interesting feature. Alongside the dollar amounts are percentages. The Gap shows the percentage of each sales dollar (sales = 100%) that is used up by the various expenses. See, for example, Cost of goods sold (line 3). During 1999, Cost of goods sold consumed 58.7 cents of every dollar of Gap's sales that year. This means that 41.3 cents ($1.00 − $0.587 = $0.413) of every sales dollar were left over to cover all other expenses and provide a profit. This information becomes more interesting when we compare 1999 to 1998.

The cost-of-goods-sold percentage dropped from 61.8% in 1998 to 58.7% in 1999 (line 3). Was this good news or bad news for Gap managers and stockholders? It was good news because it meant that The Gap's major expense, Cost of goods sold, had dropped. The result? Net earnings (line 10) increased from 8.2% in 1998 to 9.1% in 1999. Profits are growing and we can tell why: The Gap's cost of goods sold is decreasing.

CHECK POINT 1-9

Very few companies report percentages on their income statements the way The Gap does. As you can see, the percentages make the income statement more informative.

Comprehensive Income

The FASB also requires companies to report another income amount called comprehensive income. *Comprehensive income* includes net income from the income statement plus several additional items that we will cover in later chapters. However, because these additional items do not affect net income, they need not be reported on the income statement.

At this point, it remains to be seen how useful comprehensive income will be for decision making. Now let's move on to the statement of retained earnings in Exhibit 1-8.

Statement of Retained Earnings

The Gap's *retained earnings* represent exactly what the term implies: that portion of net income the company has retained, or kept for use in the business. As we saw in the income statement, the company earned net income of $824.5 million during 1999. This number from the income statement also appears on the **statement of retained earnings** (line 2 in Exhibit 1-8). Net income, therefore, is the link between these two financial statements. The net earnings for each year increase retained earnings.

After The Gap earns net income, the board of directors must decide whether to use some cash to pay a dividend to the stockholders. In both 1999 and 1998, The Gap paid dividends (line 3)—payments that decreased retained earnings (the parentheses indicate a subtraction). Gap, Inc., ended 1998 with retained earnings of $2,392,750,000. This ending balance carries over and becomes the beginning

CHECK POINT 1-10

EXHIBIT 1-8
Statement of Retained Earnings (adapted)

THE GAP, INC.
Consolidated Statement of Retained Earnings (adapted)

	($000)	*Year Ended January 30, 1999*	*Year Ended January 31, 1998*
	Retained earnings:		
1	Balance, beginning of year	$2,392,750	$1,938,352
2	Net earnings for the year	824,539	533,901
3	Less: Cash dividends declared and paid	(95,929)	(79,503)
4	Balance, end of year	$3,121,360	$2,392,750

balance of 1999. The Gap added more net income in 1999, paid dividends, and ended that year with a still larger balance of retained earnings (line 4).

Balance Sheet

The Gap balance sheet appears in Exhibit 1-9. Note that the balance sheet is dated January 30, 1999, the end of the company's fiscal year. The balance sheet gives a still picture (a snapshot) of the company's financial position at a moment in time—specifically the stroke of midnight on that day. This is in contrast to the dates of the other three statements: For the year ended January 30, 1999. The income statement, the statement of retained earnings, and the statement of cash flows (discussed in the next section) report on events that occurred throughout the year, from beginning to end.

A company's **balance sheet,** sometimes called its **statement of financial position,** reports three main categories of items: assets, liabilities, and owners' equity (which The Gap calls *shareholders' equity*).

EXHIBIT 1-9
Balance Sheet (adapted)

THE GAP, INC.
Consolidated Balance Sheet (adapted)

	($000)	*January 30, 1999*	*January 31, 1998*
	ASSETS		
	Current Assets:		
1	Cash	$ 565,253	$ 913,169
2	Merchandise inventory	1,056,444	733,174
3	Prepaid expenses	250,127	184,604
4	Total current assets	1,871,824	1,830,947
	Property and Equipment		
5	Leasehold improvements	1,040,959	846,791
6	Furniture and equipment	1,601,572	1,236,450
7	Land and buildings	405,796	220,718
8	Total property and equipment	3,048,327	2,303,959
9	Accumulated depreciation	(1,171,957)	(938,713)
10	Property and equipment, net	1,876,370	1,365,246
11	Intangible and other assets	215,725	141,309
12	Total assets	$3,963,919	$3,337,502
	LIABILITIES		
	Current Liabilities:		
13	Notes payable, short-term	$ 90,690	$ 84,794
14	Accounts payable	684,130	416,976
15	Accrued expenses payable	655,770	406,181
16	Income taxes payable	122,513	83,597
17	Total current liabilities	1,553,103	991,548
	Long-Term Liabilities		
18	Long-term debt	496,455	496,044
19	Other long-term liabilities	340,682	265,924
20	Total long-term liabilities	837,137	761,968
	SHAREHOLDERS' EQUITY		
21	Common stock	398,912	254,884
22	Retained earnings	3,121,360	2,392,750
23	Treasury stock	(1,902,400)	(1,010,251)
24	Other equity	(44,193)	(53,397)
25	Total shareholders' equity	1,573,679	1,583,986
26	Total liabilities and shareholders' equity	$3,963,919	$3,337,502

ASSETS. Assets are subdivided into two categories: current assets and long-term assets. **Current assets** are those assets that the company expects to convert to cash, sell, or consume during the next 12 months or within the business's normal operating cycle if longer than a year. The *operating cycle* is the time span during which (1) cash is used to acquire goods and services and (2) these goods and services are sold to customers, from whom the business collects cash.

Current assets for The Gap consist of Cash, Merchandise inventory, and Prepaid expenses (lines 1–3). The Gap has *no* Receivables, which are amounts to be collected from others. Most companies list Accounts receivable as the second asset under Cash. **Accounts receivable** are amounts collectible from customers to whom the company has sold merchandise on credit with the understanding that the customers will pay within a month or two. For The Gap, total current assets are almost $1.9 billion (line 4) at January 30, 1999. Let's examine each current asset.

The Gap had over $565 million in cash. Cash is the liquid asset that is the medium of exchange. The company does not sell to customers on credit and therefore reports no Accounts receivable. But The Gap does take credit cards. It deposits in the bank the credit-card slips, which are treated as cash, less a fee charged by the bank.

Merchandise inventory (line 2) is the company's largest current asset, totaling over $1 billion. *Inventory* is a common abbreviation for *Merchandise inventory,* and the two names are used interchangeably. Prepaid expenses represent prepayments for advertisements and for rent, insurance, and supplies that have not yet been used up. They are assets because The Gap will benefit from these expenditures in the future. *An asset must represent a future benefit.*

The main category of *long-term assets* is Property and Equipment (lines 5–8). We have already discussed furniture and equipment (line 6). Leasehold improvements (line 5) are another type of long-term asset. The Gap leases many of its stores and decorates them for its own purposes. The decorations—including counters, displays, and dressing rooms—make up leasehold improvements, and The Gap's cost of these assets totaled over $1 billion on January 30, 1999. Property and equipment cost a total of $3.048 billion (line 8). The property and equipment are partially used up, as indicated by the accumulated depreciation of $1.172 billion (line 9). (*Depreciation* is the accounting process of allocating an asset's cost to expense; we discuss depreciation in later chapters.) The net amount of property and equipment is $1.876 billion (cost of $3.048 billion − accumulated depreciation of $1.172 billion = net of $1.876 billion, line 10).

The Gap has Intangible and other assets of $215.7 million. Intangibles are assets with no physical form, such as trademarks and patents. *Other assets* are a catchall group of small dollar amounts that do not fall into any of the standard asset categories (such as Current Assets or Property and Equipment). Most companies, including The Gap, list Intangible and other assets as the final item on the balance sheet. At the end of fiscal year 1999, The Gap had total assets of $3,963,919,000 (line 12).

LIABILITIES. Liabilities are also divided into current and long-term categories. **Current liabilities** (lines 13–17) are debts payable within one year or within the entity's normal operating cycle if longer than a year. Chief among the current liabilities for Gap, Inc., are Notes payable, short-term; Accounts payable; Accrued expenses payable; and Income taxes payable. *Long-term liabilities* are payable after one year.

Notes payable, short-term (line 13) are promissory notes that The Gap has promised to pay back within one year or less. Accounts payable (line 14) represents amounts owed for goods and services that The Gap has purchased but not yet paid for. Accounts payable exceeded $684 million on January 30, 1999. The company's second largest current liability is Accrued expenses payable (line 15)—almost $656 million. Included among Accrued expenses payable are salaries payable to Gap employees, payroll taxes owed to the government, and interest owed on borrowed money. Income taxes payable (line 16) are amounts owed to the federal government for income taxes.

On January 30, 1999, Gap, Inc., owed total current liabilities of $1,553,103,000 (line 17) that will be paid within a few months. How will The Gap pay this huge amount? It will pay it with cash generated from selling inventory and collecting cash from customers. Recall that current assets totaled $1.9 billion. Would you feel safe if you had $1.9 billion of current assets to pay $1.6 billion of current liabilities within a year? Most managers of large businesses would feel safe because of the greater amount of current assets.

Gap, Inc., is in the enviable position of owing very little long-term debt (line 18). The company's long-term liabilities total $837 million. In sum, The Gap has total liabilities of around $2.4 billion (current liabilities of $1.6 billion + long-term liabilities of $0.8 billion). This sum is quite low relative to total assets of almost $4.0 billion.

OWNERS' EQUITY. The accounting equation states that

Assets − Liabilities = Owners' Equity

The assets (resources) and the liabilities (debts) of The Gap are fairly easy to understand. Owners' equity is harder to pin down. At a purely mathematical level, owners' equity is simple to calculate by the foregoing equation. But what does owners' equity really *mean*?

Gap, Inc., calls its owners' equity *shareholders' equity* (line 25), and this title is descriptive. Remember that a company's owners' equity represents the shareholders' ownership of the assets of the business. Owners' equity for The Gap consists of common stock, represented by millions of shares that the company has sold to stockholders for approximately $399 million as of January 30, 1999 (line 21).

The largest part of the owners' equity is Retained earnings of $3.1 billion (line 22). The large amount of Retained earnings explains why long-term liabilities are so low: Profitable operations, not long-term debt, have financed most of the company's operations. You should trace the $3.1 billion ending balance of retained earnings from the statement of retained earnings in Exhibit 1-8 (line 4) to the balance sheet (line 22). Retained earnings is the link between the statement of retained earnings and the balance sheet.

The Gap's shareholders' equity holds two other items. Treasury stock (line 23) is The Gap's own common stock that the company has issued to stockholders in the past, has repurchased, and is still holding in its treasury. The amount of treasury stock is reported in parentheses because it is a negative amount of owners' equity. Treasury stock is negative because the company has repurchased its own stock; for now, simply remember that treasury stock is a negative element of equity. The last category of shareholders' equity, Other equity, can be ignored because it is a collection of miscellaneous items.

At January 30, 1999, The Gap had Total shareholders' equity of $1,573,679,000 (line 25). We can now prove that The Gap's total assets equal the company's total liabilities and shareholders' equity, as we know it must (amounts in $000):

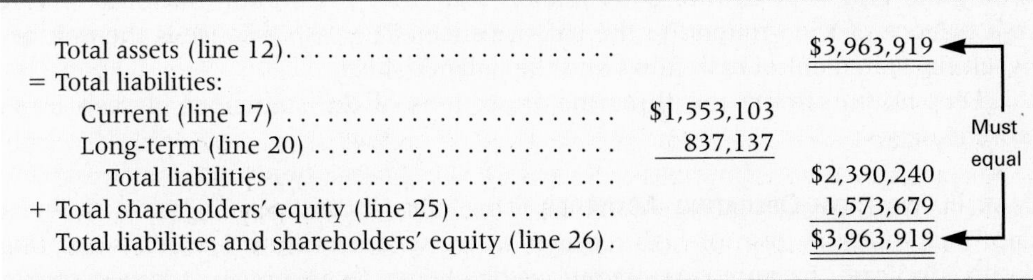

Total assets (line 12)		$3,963,919	← Must equal
= Total liabilities:			
Current (line 17)	$1,553,103		
Long-term (line 20)	837,137		
Total liabilities		$2,390,240	
+ Total shareholders' equity (line 25)		1,573,679	
Total liabilities and shareholders' equity (line 26)		$3,963,919	←

CHECK POINT 1-11

The statement of cash flows is the last required financial statement. We examine it next.

Operating, Investing, and Financing Activities

Organizations engage in three basic types of activities:

1. **Operating activities**
2. **Investing activities**
3. **Financing activities**

The **statement of cash flows** reports cash receipts and cash payments under these three categories. Think about the cash flows (cash receipts and cash payments) in each category:

- ***Companies operate by buying goods and services, which they turn around and sell to customers.*** Operating activities both increase cash (a cash receipt) and decrease cash (a cash payment). For example, **The Gap's** sales bring in cash receipts, and its purchases of merchandise require cash payments to pay for the goods. The Gap also pays cash for such expenses as salaries and the rent on store buildings. These are operating cash flows. Operating cash flows are the most important of the three types of activities because operations are the driving force of any organization.
- ***Companies invest in long-term assets that they use to run the business.*** The Gap pays cash to purchase land, buildings, furniture, and equipment. When these assets wear out, the company sells them for cash. Both purchases and sales of long-term assets are investing cash flows. Investing cash flows are the second most important because what a company invests in determines where its cash comes from.
- ***Companies finance themselves to get the funds needed to operate.*** Financing includes issuing stock and borrowing money. The Gap has issued stock to its shareholders and has borrowed money on long-term debt. These are cash receipts. The company pays dividends to its stockholders, purchases treasury stock, and pays off long-term debt. These cash payments are financing cash flows.

Overview of the Statement of Cash Flows

In Exhibit 1-10, The Gap's statement of cash flows is organized around its operating, investing, and financing activities. Each category includes both cash receipts and cash payments. Cash receipts are positive amounts with no signs. Cash payments are negative amounts enclosed by parentheses.

Fortunately, operating activities generated the lion's share of The Gap's cash (almost $1.4 billion in fiscal year 1999; see line 6). Investing activities include more cash payments than cash receipts, for a net cash outflow of $826 million (line 11). Financing activities resulted in a net cash outflow of $918 million (line 17). Overall, the company decreased its cash balance by $348 million during 1999 (line 19), ending the year with cash of $565 million (line 21). You should trace the ending cash balance of $565 million to the balance sheet. The cash balance is the link between the statement of cash flows and the balance sheet.

Let's now examine the three major sections of the statement of cash flows more closely.

CASH FLOWS FROM OPERATING ACTIVITIES. The bulk of the operating cash flows at Gap, Inc., took the form of cash received from customers (line 1). This is a strong positive indicator because core operations had better be a company's largest source

EXHIBIT 1-10
Statement of Cash Flows (adapted)

THE GAP, INC.
Consolidated Statement of Cash Flows (adapted)

	($000)	*Year Ended January 30, 1999*	*Year Ended January 31, 1998*
	CASH FLOWS FROM OPERATING ACTIVITIES		
1	Cash received from customers	$9,054,462	$6,507,825
2	Cash received from interest revenue	—	2,975
3	Cash paid to suppliers and employees	(7,190,877)	(5,337,599)
4	Cash paid for interest expense	(13,617)	—
5	Cash paid for income tax expense	(455,807)	(328,550)
6	Net cash provided by operating activities	1,394,161	844,651
	CASH FLOWS FROM INVESTING ACTIVITIES		
7	Sales of short-term investments	—	174,709
8	Purchase of long-term investments	—	(2,939)
9	Purchase of property and equipment	(797,592)	(465,843)
10	Acquisition of other assets	(28,815)	(19,779)
11	Net cash used for investing activities	(826,407)	(313,852)
	CASH FLOWS FROM FINANCING ACTIVITIES		
12	Borrowing on notes payable	1,357	44,462
13	Borrowing on long-term debt	—	495,890
14	Issuance of common stock	49,421	30,653
15	Purchase of treasury stock	(892,149)	(593,142)
16	Cash dividends paid	(76,888)	(79,503)
17	Net cash used for financing activities	(918,259)	(101,640)
18	Other	2,589	(1,634)
19	Net (decrease) increase in cash	(347,916)	427,525
20	Cash at beginning of year	913,169	485,644
21	Cash at end of year	$ 565,253	$ 913,169

of cash. The largest cash payments went to suppliers and to the company's employees (line 3). The net result of The Gap's operations during 1999 was net cash inflow of $1.394 billion—a healthy sum indeed.

CASH FLOWS FROM INVESTING ACTIVITIES. During 1999, Gap, Inc., spent almost $798 million to purchase property and equipment (line 9). The company sold no property and equipment during the year. If it had, it would have reported "Sales of property and equipment" at a positive amount representing the amount of cash received from the sale of the assets (during 1998, the company sold some short-term investments; see line 7). During 1999, net cash outflow from investing activities totaled $826 million (line 11). A net cash outflow from investing activities is generally healthy because it indicates that a company is buying new assets.

CASH FLOWS FROM FINANCING ACTIVITIES. Borrowing (line 12) was modest during 1999. The largest financing cash flow was an $892 million payment for the purchase of treasury stock (line 15). This means that The Gap bought back some of its own stock that it had issued earlier to its stockholders. The cash flow statement reports dividend payments of almost $77 million during 1999 (line 16). The overall effect of The Gap's financing activities during fiscal 1999 was a net cash outflow of $918 million (line 17).

NET INCREASE (DECREASE) IN CASH. The final result of the statement of cash flows is the net increase (or decrease) in cash during the year. As we have seen, The Gap's cash decreased by $348 million during 1999 (line 19). Lines 20 and 21 of the cash flow statement show both the beginning cash balance and the ending cash balance for the year. Gap began 1999 with $913 million and ended with $565 million. You should trace both of these amounts to the balance sheet in Exhibit 1-9 (line 1). They are needed to prepare a statement of cash flows. We give more attention to this statement in Chapter 12.

Preparation of the statement of cash flows begins with the final result—the increase (or decrease) in cash during the year. You can simply take the difference between beginning and ending cash from the balance sheet, and this is your final check figure for the statement of cash flows. Therefore, you start to prepare the statement of cash flows with knowledge of the final result. **The purpose of the statement of cash flows is to show *why* cash changed during the year.**

✔ CHECK POINT 1-12

Should The Gap be alarmed because cash decreased by $348 million during 1999? For three reasons, probably not:

1. The cash balance is still a healthy $565 million.
2. Net cash inflow from operating activities was very large and showed a large increase over the preceding year.
3. Net income on the income statement is growing both in dollar amount and as a percentage of net sales.

These are but a few of the evaluations you will be learning to make throughout this course. Now let's review the relationships among the financial statements.

RELATIONSHIPS AMONG THE FINANCIAL STATEMENTS

Objective 5
Explain the relationships among the financial statements

Exhibit 1-11 summarizes the relationships among the financial statements. Study the exhibit carefully because you will use these relationships throughout your business career. Specifically, note the following:

1. The income statement for the year ended December 31, 2000.
   a. Reports all revenues and all expenses during the period. Revenues and expenses are reported only on the income statement.
   b. Reports net income of the period if total revenues exceed total expenses. If total expenses exceed total revenues, a net loss is reported instead.
2. The statement of retained earnings for the year ended December 31, 2000.
   a. Opens with the retained earnings balance at the beginning of the period.
   b. Adds net income (or subtracts net loss, as the case may be). Net income (or net loss) comes directly from the income statement (see arrow ① in Exhibit 1-11).
   c. Subtracts dividends.
   d. Ends with the retained earnings balance at the end of the period.
3. The balance sheet at December 31, 2000, the end of the fiscal year.
   a. Reports all assets, all liabilities, and stockholders' equity of the business at the end of the period. No other financial statement reports assets and liabilities.
   b. Reports that total assets equal the sum of total liabilities plus total stockholders' equity. This balancing feature gives the balance sheet its name; it is based on the accounting equation.
   c. Reports the ending retained earnings, taken directly from the statement of retained earnings (see arrow ②).
4. The statement of cash flows for the year ended December 31, 2000.
   a. Reports cash flows from operating activities, investing activities, and financing activities during the year. Each category results in a net cash inflow or a net cash outflow for the period.
   b. Reports a net increase (or a net decrease) in cash during the year and ends with the cash balance on December 31, 2000. This is the amount of cash reported on the balance sheet (see arrow ③).

✔ CHECK POINT 1-13

Exhibit 1-11
Relationships Among the Financial Statements (all amounts assumed for the illustration)

Income Statement—Year Ended December 31, 2000
(Details given in Exhibit 1-8)

Revenues	$700,000
Expenses (detailed)	
Total Expenses	670,000
Net income	$ 30,000

Statement of Retained Earnings—Year Ended December 31, 2000

Beginning retained earnings	$180,000
Net income	30,000
Cash dividends	(10,000)
Ending retained earnings	$200,000

①

Balance Sheet—December 31, 2000

ASSETS	
Cash	$ 25,000
All other assets	275,000
Total assets	$300,000
LIABILITIES	
Total liabilities	$120,000
STOCKHOLDERS' EQUITY	
Common stock	40,000
Retained earnings	200,000
Other equity	(60,000)
Total liabilities and stockholders' equity	$300,000

② ③

Statement of Cash Flows—Year Ended December 31, 2000

Net cash flows provided by operating activities	$ 90,000
Net cash flows used for investing activities	(110,000)
Net cash flows provided by financing activities	40,000
Net increase in cash	20,000
Beginning cash	5,000
Ending cash	$ 25,000

1. Suppose you are considering investing in the stock of The Gap, Inc. Which financial statement would you examine to see whether the company is profitable? What would you look for?
2. Suppose you are a bank considering a loan of $50 million to The Gap. Which financial statement would you look at to see how much the company already owes other creditors? What would you look for?
3. Identify the links between (a) the income statement and the statement of retained earnings, (b) the statement of retained earnings and the balance sheet, and (c) the statement of cash flows and the balance sheet.

Answers:

1. Look for net income on the income statement.
2. Look for liabilities on the balance sheet.
3. (a) Net income (or net loss), (b) Ending retained earnings, (c) Ending cash.

The following Decision Guidelines feature summarizes the ways in which stockholders and creditors use financial statements. Decision Guidelines features appear throughout this book to summarize how people use accounting information to make key decisions.

DECISION GUIDELINES

How Stockholders and Creditors Use the Financial Statements

Group	Mainly Interested In	Reason	What They Look For
Stockholders	Net income	*Net income* means the company is profitable. Stockholders enhance their personal wealth through (a) an increase in the market price of the company's stock and (b) dividends received. Net income affects both stock prices and dividends.	Steadily rising level of net income over time means the company's profits look solid.
	Cash flows	*Cash flows* report how the company generates and uses its cash. Wise use of cash produces net income and more cash.	Operating activities should be the main source of cash.
Bankers and other creditors	Assets and liabilities	*Liabilities* indicate how much the company owes other creditors. *Assets* show what the company can pledge as collateral that a creditor can take if the company fails to pay its debts.	Assets far in excess of liabilities, or assets increasing faster than liabilities over time.
	Net income	Profitable companies can usually pay their debts.	Same as for stockholders.
	Cash flows	Same as for stockholders.	Same as for stockholders.

End-of-Chapter

SUMMARY PROBLEM FOR YOUR REVIEW

Air & Sea Travel, Inc., a travel agency, began operations on April 1, 20X1. During April, the business provided travel services for clients. It is now April 30, and investors wonder how well Air & Sea Travel performed during its first month. They also want to know the business's financial position at the end of April and its cash flows during the month.

They have assembled the following data, listed in alphabetical order. They have requested your help in preparing the Air & Sea Travel financial statements at the end of April 20X1.

Accounts payable	$ 100	Office supplies	$ 500
Accounts receivable	2,000	Payments of cash:	
Cash balance at beginning of April	-0-	Acquisition of land	40,000
Cash balance at end of April	33,300	Dividends	2,100
Cash receipts:		To suppliers and employees	3,100
Collections from customers	6,500	Rent expense	1,100
Issuance (sale) of stock to owners	50,000	Retained earnings at beginning of April	-0-
Sale of land	22,000	Retained earnings at end of April	?
Common stock	50,000	Salary expense	1,200
Dividends	2,100	Service revenue	8,500
Land	18,000	Utilities expense	400

Required

1. Prepare the income statement, the statement of retained earnings, and the statement of cash flows for the month ended April 30, 20X1, and the balance sheet at April 30, 20X1. Draw arrows linking the pertinent items in the statements.
2. Answer the investors' underlying questions.
   a. How well did Air & Sea Travel perform during its first month of operations?
   b. Where does Air & Sea Travel stand financially at the end of the first month?
3. If you were a banker, would you be willing to lend money to Air & Sea Travel, Inc.?

Answers

Requirement 1

Financial Statements of Air & Sea Travel, Inc.

AIR & SEA TRAVEL, INC.
Income Statement
Month Ended April 30, 20X1

Revenue:		
Service revenue		$8,500
Expenses:		
Salary expense	$1,200	
Rent expense	1,100	
Utilities expense	400	
Total expenses		2,700
Net income		$5,800

①

AIR & SEA TRAVEL, INC.
Statement of Retained Earnings
Month Ended April 30, 20X1

Retained earnings, April 1, 20X1	$ 0
Add: Net income for the month	5,800
	5,800
Less: Dividends	(2,100)
Retained earnings, April 30, 20X1	$3,700

AIR & SEA TRAVEL, INC.
Balance Sheet
April 30, 20X1

Assets		*Liabilities*	
Cash	$33,300	Accounts payable	$ 100
Accounts receivable	2,000		
Office supplies	500	***Stockholders' Equity***	
Land	18,000	Common stock	50,000
		Retained earnings	3,700
		Total stockholders' equity	53,700
		Total liabilities and	
Total assets	$53,800	stockholders' equity	$53,800

② ③

AIR & SEA TRAVEL, INC.
Statement of Cash Flows
Month Ended April 30, 20X1

Cash flows from operating activities:		
Collections from customers		$ 6,500
Payments to suppliers and employees		(3,100)
Net cash inflow from operating activities		3,400
Cash flows from investing activities:		
Acquisition of land	$(40,000)	
Sale of land	22,000	
Net cash outflow from investing activities		(18,000)
Cash flows from financing activities:		
Issuance (sale) of stock	$ 50,000	
Payment of dividends	(2,100)	
Net cash inflow from financing activities		47,900
Net increase in cash		$33,300
Cash balance, April 1, 20X1		0
Cash balance, April 30, 20X1		$33,300

Requirements 2 and 3

a. The company performed rather well in April. Net income was $5,800—very good in relation to service revenue of $8,500. The company was able to pay cash dividends of $2,100.

b. The business ended April with cash of $33,300. Total assets of $53,800 far exceed total liabilities of $100. Stockholders' equity of $53,700 provides a good cushion against which the business can borrow. The business's financial position at April 30, 20X1, is strong.

c. The company has plenty of cash, and assets far exceed liabilities. Operating activities generated positive cash flow in the first month of operations. Lenders like to see these features before making a loan. Thus, most bankers would be willing to lend to Air & Sea Travel at this time.

SUMMARY OF LEARNING OBJECTIVES

1. ***Understand accounting vocabulary and use it in decision making.*** *Accounting* is an information system for measuring, processing, and communicating financial information. As the "language of business," accounting helps a wide range of decision makers. Accountants are expected to perform their jobs in an ethical manner consistent with generally accepted accounting principles (GAAP).

   The three forms of business organization are the proprietorship, the partnership, and the corporation. In some cases, accounting procedures depend on a company's form of organization.

2. ***Analyze business activity with accounting concepts and principles.*** Accountants use the *entity concept* not only to keep the business's records separate from the personal records of the people who run it but to separate corporate divisions from one another. Other important concepts that guide accountants are the *reliability principle,* the *cost principle,* the *going-concern concept,* and the *stable-monetary-unit concept.*

3. ***Use the accounting equation to describe an organization's financial position.*** In its most common form, the accounting equation is

   Assets = Liabilities + Owners' Equity

   Assets are the economic resources of a business that are expected to be of benefit in the future. *Liabilities* are economic debts payable to people or organizations outside the firm. *Owners' equity* refers to the claims held by the owners of a proprietorship or partnership. In a corporation, owners' equity is usually called *stockholders' equity* and is subdivided into two categories: *paid-in capital* and *retained earnings.*

4. ***Evaluate a company's operating performance, financial position, and cash flow.*** The *financial statements* communicate financial information about a business entity to decision makers. The income statement reports the company's revenues, expenses, and net income or net loss for a period. The *statement of retained earnings* summarizes the changes in a corporation's retained earnings during the period. The *balance sheet* is a snapshot of a business on a particular day; it reports on three main categories of items—assets, liabilities, and owners' equity. The *statement of cash flows* reports cash receipts and cash payments over a period, classified according to the entity's major activities: operating, investing, and financing.

5. ***Explain the relationships among the financial statements.*** The bottom line of the income statement, net income, feeds into the statement of retained earnings. The final value of retained earnings then appears on the balance sheet. The final cash balance on the statement of cash flows also appears on the balance sheet.

ACCOUNTING VOCABULARY

Accounting, like many other subjects, has a special vocabulary. It is important that you understand the following terms. They are defined in the chapter and also in the glossary at the end of the book.

account payable (p. 11).
accounts receivable (p. 18).
accounting (p. 4).
accounting equation (p. 4).
asset (p. 11).
balance sheet (p. 17).
board of directors (p. 8).
capital (p. 11).
cash (p. 11).
common stock (p. 12).
contributed capital (p. 12).
corporation (p. 8).
cost principle (p. 10).
current assets (p. 18).
current liabilities (p. 18).
dividend (p. 12).
entity (p. 9).
expense (p. 12).
financial accounting (p. 6).
financial statements (p. 4).
financing activities (p. 20).
generally accepted accounting principles (GAAP) (p. 8).
going-concern concept (p. 10).
income statement (p. 14).
investing activities (p. 20).
liability (p. 11).
long-term debt (p. 11).
management accounting (p. 6).
merchandise inventory (p. 11).
net earnings (p. 12).
net income (p. 12).
net loss (p. 12).
net profit (p. 12).
note payable (p. 11).
objectivity principle (p. 9).
operating activities (p. 20).
owners' equity (p. 11).
paid-in capital (p. 12).
partnership (p. 7).
plant assets (p. 11).
proprietorship (p. 7).
reliability principle (p. 9).
retained earnings (p. 12).
revenue (p. 12).
shareholder (p. 8).
stable-monetary-unit concept (p. 10).
statement of cash flows (p. 20).
statement of earnings (p. 14).
statement of financial position (p. 17).
statement of operations (p. 14).
statement of retained earnings (p. 16).
stock (p. 8).
stockholder (p. 8).
stockholders' equity (p. 12).

QUESTIONS

1. Distinguish between accounting and bookkeeping.
2. Identify five users of accounting information and explain how they use it.
3. What organization formulates generally accepted accounting principles? Is this organization a government agency?
4. What are the owner(s) of a proprietorship, a partnership, and a corporation called?
5. Why do ethical standards exist in accounting?
6. Why is the entity concept so important to accounting?
7. Give four examples of accounting entities.
8. Briefly describe the reliability principle.
9. What role does the cost principle play in accounting?
10. If assets = liabilities + owners' equity, then how can liabilities be expressed?
11. Explain the difference between an account receivable and an account payable.
12. In what two ways can a business use its net income?
13. Give a more descriptive title for the balance sheet.
14. What feature of the balance sheet gives this financial statement its name?
15. Give another title for the income statement.
16. Which financial statement is like a snapshot of the entity at a specific time?
17. What information does the statement of retained earnings report?
18. What piece of information flows from the income statement to the statement of retained earnings? What information flows from the statement of retained earnings to the balance sheet?
19. List the cash-flow activities in the order they are likely to occur for a new business. Then rank the cash-flow activities in the order of their importance to investors.

CHECK POINTS

Making management and investor decisions (Obj. 1)

CP1-1 Suppose you manage a Gap store. As the store manager, what are three decisions you must make? How will accounting help you make these decisions? Answer in your own words.

Now suppose you are an investor who is considering the purchase of Gap stock as an investment. Study The Gap's income statement (statement of earnings) at the beginning of the chapter (page 14) and identify certain items that will help you decide whether to make this investment.

Distinguishing accounting from bookkeeping (Obj. 1)

CP1-2 Briefly discuss the difference between accounting and bookkeeping. How does bookkeeping fit into accounting?

Making ethical judgments (Obj. 1)

CP1-3 Accountants follow ethical guidelines in the conduct of their work. What are these standards of professional conduct designed to produce? Why is this goal important? Assume that there are no ethical guidelines for accountants and that companies can report to the public whatever they wish about their results of operations and their financial position. What would be a likely result?

Applying accounting concepts (Obj. 2)

CP1-4 Return to the discussion of Julie DeFilippo's catering business, An Extra Hand, on page 9. Suppose DeFilippo treats the full \$2,000 in her bank account as the product of An Extra Hand's operations. Answer these questions about DeFilippo's finances:

1. What can DeFilippo be misled into believing?
2. Which accounting concept applies to this situation?
3. How can the proper application of this accounting concept give DeFilippo a realistic view of her business? Explain in detail.

Using the accounting equation (Obj. 3)

CP1-5 Review the accounting equation on page 11.

1. Suppose you know the amounts of X-Ray Copy Center's assets and liabilities. Show how to determine the amount of owners' equity.
2. If you know assets and owners' equity, how can you measure liabilities? Give the equation.
3. Can you compute assets with the knowledge of owners' equity and liabilities? If so, show how. If not, explain why it is impossible.

Defining key accounting terms (Obj. 1)

CP1-6 Accounting definitions are precise, and you must understand each definition before you can use accounting information. Sharpen your understanding of key terms by answering the following questions:

1. How do *assets* and *owners' equity* differ? Which one (assets or owners' equity) must be at least as large as the other? Which one can be smaller than the other?
2. How are *liabilities* and *owners' equity* similar? Different?

Classifying assets, liabilities, and owners' equity (Obj. 1)

CP1-7 Classify the following items as an Asset (A), a Liability (L), or an Owners' Equity (E):

a. Accounts payable	**g.** Cash
b. Common stock	**h.** Long-term debt
c. Receivables	**i.** Merchandise inventory
d. Retained earnings	**j.** Notes payable
e. Land	**k.** Accrued expenses payable
f. Prepaid expenses	**l.** Equipment

Using the income statement (Obj. 4)

CP1-8 Use The Gap's income statement in Exhibit 1-7 (page 14) to answer the following questions about the company's operations during the year ended January 30, 1999:

1. Identify the two basic categories of items on The Gap's income statement.
2. What do we call the bottom line of the income statement?
3. The Gap's total assets are almost $4 billion, as reported on the company's balance sheet (page 17). How are total assets used to measure net earnings? Explain your answer.

Preparing an income statement (Obj. 4)

CP1-9 Return to The Gap's income statement in Exhibit 1-7 (page 14). Suppose the percentage of cost of goods sold to sales remained the same in 1999 as in 1998 (61.8% of net sales revenue). The Gap's income tax rate during 1999 was 37.5% (.375); this percentage is multiplied by earnings before income taxes to compute Income tax expense.

Prepare a revised income statement for The Gap for 1999. Round all amounts to the nearest $1 million. For example, treat net sales revenue of $9,054,462,000 as $9,054, and so on.

Preparing a statement of retained earnings (Obj. 4)

CP1-10 McCullough Water Systems began the year 2000 with retained earnings of $60,000. Revenues during the year were $600,000, and expenses totaled $530,000. McCullough declared and paid dividends of $30,000. What was the company's ending balance of retained earnings? To answer this question, prepare McCullough Water Systems' statement of retained earnings for the year ended December 31, 2000, complete with its appropriate heading.

Preparing a balance sheet (Obj. 4)

CP1-11 At December 31, 2000, McCullough Water Systems has cash of $13,000, receivables of $2,000, and inventory of $25,000. The company's land, buildings, and equipment total $110,000, and other assets amount to $10,000. McCullough owes accounts payable of $8,000 and short-term notes payable of $12,000 and also has a long-term debt of $80,000.

Common stock is $15,000. The general manager of McCullough knows the company has been profitable, but he is unsure about the amount of retained earnings.

Prepare McCullough Water Systems' balance sheet at December 31, 2000, complete with its appropriate heading.

Preparing a statement of cash flows (Obj. 4)

CP1-12 McCullough Water Systems ended the year 1999 with cash of $23,000. During 2000, McCullough made sales of $600,000 but collected only $580,000 from customers. Expenses for the year totaled $530,000, of which McCullough paid $520,000 to suppliers and employees.

McCullough paid $300,000 to expand its plant during 2000. McCullough had to borrow half of this amount by signing a long-term note payable. During the year, McCullough paid dividends of $10,000 and sold old water system equipment, receiving cash of $90,000.

Prepare McCullough Water Systems' statement of cash flows for the year ended December 31, 2000, complete with its appropriate heading. Follow the format of the summary problem on pages 24–26.

Identifying items with the appropriate financial statement (Obj. 5)

CP1-13 Identify each item with its appropriate financial statement, using the following abbreviations: Income statement (IS), Statement of retained earnings (SRE), Balance sheet (BS), and Statement of cash flows (SCF). Four items appear on two financial statements.

1. Dividends ________	**8.** Cash ________
2. Depreciation expense ________	**9.** Cash flows from financing activities ________
3. Inventory ________	**10.** Accounts payable ________
4. Sales revenue ________	**11.** Common stock ________
5. Retained earnings ________	**12.** Interest revenue ________
6. Operating cash flows ________	**13.** Long-term debt ________
7. Net income (or net loss) ________	**14.** Increase or decrease in cash ________

EXERCISES

Organizing a business
(Obj. 1)

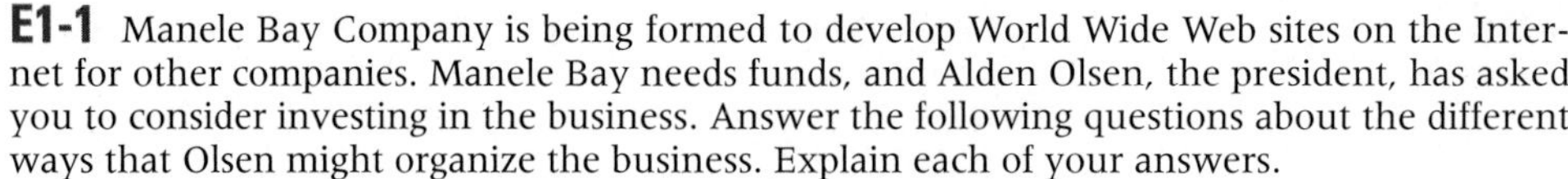

E1-1 Manele Bay Company is being formed to develop World Wide Web sites on the Internet for other companies. Manele Bay needs funds, and Alden Olsen, the president, has asked you to consider investing in the business. Answer the following questions about the different ways that Olsen might organize the business. Explain each of your answers.

a. What form of business organization will give Olsen the most freedom to manage the business as he wishes?

b. What form of organization will give creditors the maximum protection in the event that Manele Bay fails and cannot pay its liabilities?

c. What form of organization will enable the owners of Manele Bay to limit their risk of loss to the amount they have invested in the business?

d. Under what form of organization will Manele Bay be likely to have the longest life?

e. What form of organization will probably enable Manele Bay to raise the most money from owners' equity over the life of the business?

If you were Olsen and could organize the business as you wish, what form of organization would you choose for Manele Bay Company? Explain your reasoning.

Explaining the income statement and the balance sheet
(Obj. 1)

E1-2 Nick Barzoukas wants to open a Greek restaurant in Miami. In need of cash, he asks Florida Bank & Trust for a loan. The bank requires borrowers to submit financial statements to show likely results of operations for the first year and the expected financial position at the end of the first year. With little knowledge of accounting, Barzoukas doesn't know how to proceed. Explain to him the information provided by the statement of operations (the income statement) and the statement of financial position (the balance sheet). Indicate why a lender would require this information.

Applying acccounting concepts and principles
(Obj. 2)

E1-3

a. **Dell Computer** began in Michael Dell's dorm room at The University of Texas at Austin. Suppose Dell kept a single checkbook to account for both his personal affairs and Dell Computer transactions. Would he be able to determine the success or failure of the business? Which accounting concept or principle is applicable to Dell's situation?

b. Dell Computer owns real estate around Austin, Texas. Suppose the company purchased land for $3 million in 1995, and its value has risen. The business is offering the land for sale. One real estate appraiser says the land is worth $10 million; another appraises the land at $15 million. Should Dell record a gain on the value of the land, or should Dell wait to record the gain after it has actually sold the land? Which accounting concept or principle controls this situation?

c. Dell Computer has several divisions. Managers of each division are evaluated on their division's profit performance. Which concept or principle helps Dell Computer design an accounting system to identify the most profitable division managers?

d. Suppose Dell Computer decides to get out of the magnetic imaging business and offers its magnetic imaging division for sale. Which accounting concept or principle helps Dell account for its magnetic imaging division differently from its main operations?

e. Dell Computer must pay for the materials, labor, and overhead inputs to its computers. After assembly, a computer is much more valuable than the sum of the inputs. Which accounting concept or principle provides guidance on how to account for the materials, labor and overhead?

Accounting equation
(Obj. 3)

E1-4 Compute the missing amount in the accounting equation for each entity (amounts in billions):

	Assets	*Liabilities*	*Owners' Equity*
IBM	$?	$67	$19
Hershey Foods	3.3	?	0.9
SONY	49	35	?

Accounting equation
(Obj. 3, 4)

E1-5 **Pier 1 Imports** has current assets of $402 million; property, plant, and equipment of $216 million; and other assets totaling $35 million. Current liabilities are $122 million, long-term debt is $115 million, and other long-term liabilities add up to $24 million.

Required

1. Use these data to write Pier 1's accounting equation.

2. How much in resources does Pier 1 have to work with?

3. How much does Pier 1 owe?

4. How much of the company's assets do the Pier 1 stockholders actually own?

Accounting equation (Obj. 3)

E1-6 Assume **The Rawlings Sporting Goods Company's** balance sheet at August 31, 2000, and August 31, 1999, reports (in millions):

	Aug. 31, 2000	*Aug. 31, 1999*
Total assets	$132	$101
Total liabilities	88	61

Required

Three situations about Rawlings' issuance of stock and payment of dividends during the year ended August 31, 2000, are given. For each situation, compute the amount of Rawlings' net income or net loss during the year ended August 31, 2000.

1. Rawlings issued $1 million of stock and paid no dividends.

2. Rawlings issued no stock but paid dividends of $3 million.

3. Rawlings issued $10 million of stock and paid dividends of $2 million.

Accounting equation (Obj. 3, 4)

E1-7 Answer these questions about two actual companies.

1. The Gap began the year with total liabilities of $1.8 billion and total stockholders' equity of $1.6 billion. During the year, total assets increased by 16.6%. How much are total assets at the end of the year? Compare your results to The Gap balance sheet on page 17.

2. Johnson & Johnson, famous for Band-Aids and other health-care products, began the year with total assets of $12.2 billion and total liabilities of $6.7 billion. Net income for the year was $2.0 billion, and dividends and other decreases in stockholders' equity totaled $0.4 billion. How much is stockholders' equity at the end of the year?

Identifying financial statement information (Obj. 4)

E1-8 Managers at **PepsiCo** are planning an expansion of their bottling operations in Canada. They must decide where to locate the bottling plant, how much to spend on the building, and how to finance its construction. Of central importance is the level of net income they can expect to earn from operating the new plant. Identify the financial statement where these decision makers can find the following information about PepsiCo, Inc. (In some cases, more than one statement will report the needed data.)

a. Cash spent to acquire the building
b. Selling, general, and administrative expenses
c. Cash collections from customers
d. Ending cash balance
e. Liabilities that must be paid next year
f. Net income
g. Total assets
h. Long-term debt
i. Revenue
j. Common stock
k. Cash spent for income tax
l. Dividends
m. Income tax expense
n. Ending balance of retained earnings
o. Cost of goods sold

Business organization, balance sheet (Obj. 2, 5)

E1-9 Balances of the assets and liabilities of **The Home Depot** as of January 31, 1999, are adapted as follows. Also included are the revenue and expense figures of the business for the year ended on that date (amounts in millions):

Sales revenue	$30,219	Property and equipment	$8,532
Accounts receivable	469	Merchandise inventory	4,402
Accounts payable	1,586	Other liabilities	3,139
Common stock	2,864	Other expenses (summarized)	1,650
Cost of goods sold	21,614	Cash	62
Selling and store operating expense	5,341	Retained earnings, beginning	4,430
		Retained earnings, ending	?

Required

1. What type of business organization is The Home Depot? How can you tell?
2. Prepare the balance sheet of The Home Depot, Inc., at January 31, 1999.

Income statement (Obj. 2, 5)

E1-10 This exercise should be worked only in connection with Exercise 1-9. Refer to the data of **The Home Depot, Inc.,** in Exercise 1-9.

Required

1. Prepare the income statement of The Home Depot, Inc., for the year ended January 31, 1999.
2. What amount of dividends did Home Depot pay during the year ended January 31, 1999?

Statement of cash flows (Obj. 2, 4, 5)

E1-11 **Sprint Corporation,** the telecommunications company, began the year 20X1 with $113 million in cash. During 20X1, Sprint earned a net income of $395 million. Assume the company collected $12,629 million in cash from customers and paid $9,900 million to suppliers and employees during the year. Investing activities used cash of $3,141 million, and financing activities provided a net cash inflow of $422 million. Sprint ended 20X1 with total assets of $15,195 million and total liabilities of $10,553 million.

Required

Prepare Sprint Corporation's statement of cash flows for the year ended December 31, 20X1. Identify the data items given that do not appear on the statement of cash flows and note which financial statement reports these items.

Preparing an income statement and a statement of retained earnings (Obj. 5)

E1-12 Kink's Copy Service, Inc., ended the month of July 20X1, with these data:

Cash balance at beginning of July	$ 0	Payments of cash:	
Cash balance at end of July	6,100	Acquisition of copy equipment	$30,000
Cash receipts:		Dividends	1,200
Collections from customers	2,400	To suppliers	100
Issuance (sale) of stock to owners	35,000	Rent expense	700
Common stock	35,000	Retained earnings at beginning of July	0
Dividends	1,200	Retained earnings at end of July	?
Copy equipment	30,000	Service revenue	2,400
Office supplies	1,200	Utilities expense	200
		Accounts payable	2,000

Required

Prepare the income statement and the statement of retained earnings of Kink's Copy Service, Inc., for the month ended July 31, 20X1.

Preparing a balance sheet (Obj. 5)

E1-13 Refer to the data in the preceding exercise. Prepare the balance sheet of Kink's Copy Service, Inc., at July 31, 20X1.

Preparing a statement of cash flows (Obj. 5)

E1-14 Refer to the data in Exercise 1-12. Prepare the statement of cash flows of Kink's Copy Service, Inc., for the month ended July 31, 20X1. Draw arrows linking the pertinent items in the statements you prepared for Exercises 1-12 through 1-14.

Advising a business (Obj. 4, 5)

E1-15 This exercise should be used in conjunction with Exercises 1-12 through 1-14.

The owners of Kink's Copy Service, Inc., now seek your advice as to whether they should cease operations or continue the business. Write a report giving them your opinion of operating results, dividends, financial position, and cash flows during their first month of operations. Cite specifics from the financial statements to support your opinion. Conclude your report with advice on whether to stay in business or cease operations.

E1-16 Apply your understanding of the relationships among the financial statements to answer these questions.

Applying accounting concepts to explain business activity (Obj. 2, 5)

a. If you could pick a single source of cash for your business, what would it be? Why?

b. Give two reasons why a business can have a steady stream of net income over a five-year period and still experience a shortage of cash.

c. How can a business lose money several years in a row and still have plenty of cash?

d. How can a business earn large profits but have a small balance of retained earnings?

e. Suppose your business has $100,000 of current liabilities that must be paid within the next three months. Your current assets total only $70,000, and your sales and collections from customers are slow. Identify two ways to finance the extra $30,000 that you will need to pay your current liabilities when they come due.

PROBLEMS

(Group A)

P1-1A Take the role of an analyst for **PaineWebber** and suppose it is your job to write recommendations to the firm's investment committee. Helix Corporation has submitted these summary data to support its request for PaineWebber to purchase $100,000 of the company's stock.

Analyzing a loan request (Obj. 1, 5)

STATEMENT OF CASH FLOW DATA	*2002*	*2001*	*2000*
Net cash flow from operations	$190,000	$170,000	$170,000
Net cash flow from investing	(180,000)	(180,000)	(50,000)
Net cash flow from financing	30,000	20,000	(110,000)
Increase (decrease) in cash	$ 40,000	$ 10,000	$ 10,000
INCOME STATEMENT DATA			
Total revenues	$950,000	$820,000	$720,000
Total expenses	640,000	570,000	540,000
Net income	$310,000	$250,000	$180,000
STATEMENT OF RETAINED EARNINGS DATA			
Dividends	$160,000	$140,000	$120,000
BALANCE SHEET DATA			
Total assets	$990,000	$720,000	$590,000
Total liabilities	$440,000	$320,000	$300,000
Total stockholders' equity	550,000	400,000	290,000
Total liabilities and stockholders' equity	$990,000	$720,000	$590,000

Required

Analyze these financial statement data to decide whether the firm should purchase $100,000 of Helix's stock. Write a one-paragraph recommendation to the investment committee.

P1-2A Assume that **Ford Motor Company** experienced the following transactions during the year ended December 31, 20X1:

Applying accounting concepts and principles to the income statement (Obj. 2, 4, 5)

a. Ford sold automobiles and other manufactured products for $119.1 billion. Company management believes that the value of these products is approximately $130 billion. Other revenues totaled $46.6 billion.

b. It cost Ford $101.2 billion to manufacture the products it sold. If Ford had purchased the products instead of manufacturing them, Ford's cost would have been $122.6 billion.

c. Selling and administrative expenses were $6.0 billion. All other expenses, excluding income taxes, totaled $23.4 billion for the year. Income tax expense was 36% of income before tax.

d. Ford has several operating divisions: Ford, Mercury, Lincoln, and Financial Services. Each division is accounted for separately so that top management can see how well each division is performing. However, the company's financial statements combine the statements of all the divisions in order to show the operating results of the company as a whole.

e. Inflation affects the amounts that Ford must pay for steel and other components of the company's manufactured goods. If Ford's financial statements were to show the effects of inflation, assume the company's reported net income would drop by $0.7 billion.

f. If Ford were to go out of business, the sale of its assets would bring in over $250 billion in cash.

Required

1. Prepare Ford Motor Company's income statement for the year ended December 31, 20X1.
2. For a through f, identify the accounting concept or principle that provides guidance in accounting for the item described. State how you have applied the concept or principle in preparing Ford's income statement.

Using the accounting equation (Obj. 3)

P1-3A Compute the missing amounts for each company (adapted and in billions).

	Coca-Cola Co.	*Ford Corp.*	*Sara Lee Corp.*
BEGINNING:			
Assets	$17	$279	$13
Liabilities	10	228	9
ENDING:			
Assets	$19	$?	$11
Liabilities	11	204	9
OWNERS' EQUITY:			
Issuances of stock	$ 0	$ 1	$?
Dividends	3	9	1
INCOME STATEMENT:			
Revenues	$19	$119	$20
Expenses	?	97	21

Balance sheet (Obj. 2, 5)

P1-4A The manager of Nocona, Inc., prepared the balance sheet of the company while the accountant was ill. The balance sheet contains numerous errors. In particular, the manager knew that the balance sheet should balance, so he plugged in the stockholders' equity amount needed to achieve this balance. The stockholders' equity amount, however, is not correct. All other amounts are accurate.

NOCONA, INC.
Balance Sheet
Month Ended July 31, 20X1

Assets		*Liabilities*	
Cash	$15,000	Accounts receivable	$12,000
Office furniture	10,000	Service revenue	50,000
Note payable	16,000	Property tax expense	800
Rent expense	4,000	Accounts payable	9,000
Office supplies	1,000		
Land	44,000	***Stockholders' Equity***	
Advertising expense	2,500	Stockholders' equity	20,700
Total assets	$92,500	Total liabilities	$92,500

Required

1. Prepare the correct balance sheet and date it properly. Compute total assets, total liabilities, and stockholders' equity.
2. Identify the accounts listed above that should not be presented on the balance sheet. State why you excluded them from the correct balance sheet you prepared for Requirement 1. Which financial statement should these accounts appear on?

Balance sheet, entity concept (Obj. 2, 5)

P1-5A Kristina Peña is a realtor. She buys and sells properties on her own, and she also earns commission as a real estate agent for buyers and sellers. Peña organized her business as a corporation on November 24, 2000, by investing $50,000 to acquire the business's common stock. Consider these facts, which were accurate as of November 30, 2000:

a. Peña had $10,000 in her personal bank account and $12,000 in the business bank account.

b. Peña owed $1,800 on a personal charge account with the **Nordstrom** department store.

c. Peña acquired business furniture for $17,000 on November 25. Of this amount, her business owed $6,000 on open account at November 30.

d. Office supplies on hand at the real estate office totaled $1,000.

e. Peña's business owed $40,000 on a note payable for some undeveloped land that the business had acquired for a total price of $120,000.

f. Peña's business had spent $20,000 for a **Century 21** real estate franchise, which entitles her to represent herself as a Century 21 agent. Century 21 is a national affiliation of independent real estate agents. This franchise is a business asset.

g. Peña owed $100,000 on a personal mortgage on her personal residence, which she acquired in 1998 for a total price of $190,000.

Required

1. Prepare the balance sheet of the real estate business of Kristina Peña, Realtor, Inc., at November 30, 2000.
2. Identify the personal items given in the preceding facts that would not be reported on the balance sheet of the business.

Income statement, statement of retained earnings, balance sheet (Obj. 5)

P1-6A Given are the amounts of (a) the assets and liabilities of Liberty Corporation as of December 31 and (b) the revenues and expenses of the company for the year ended on that date. The items are listed in no particular order.

Land	$ 98,000	Accounts payable	$ 19,000
Note payable	85,000	Accounts receivable	12,000
Property tax expense	4,000	Advertising expense	13,000
Rent expense	23,000	Building	110,000
Cash	10,000	Salary expense	63,000
Common stock	100,000	Salary payable	1,000
Furniture	20,000	Service revenue	180,000
Interest expense	9,000	Supplies	3,000

The beginning amount of retained earnings was $50,000, and during the year dividends totaled $70,000.

Required

1. Prepare the income statement of Liberty Corporation for the year ended December 31 of the current year.
2. Prepare Liberty's statement of retained earnings for the year ended December 31.
3. Prepare Liberty's balance sheet at December 31. You will need to compute the amount of retained earnings.

Preparing a statement of cash flows (Obj. 4)

P1-7A The *data at the top of the next page* are adapted from the financial statements of **Nike, Inc.,** at the end of a recent year (in millions).

Required

Prepare Nike, Inc.'s statement of cash flows for the year ended May 31, 20X0.

Follow the format of the summary problem on pages 24–26. Not all the items given appear on the statement of cash flows.

Nike, Inc.

Revenues	$9,187	Sales of property, plant, and equipment	$ 24
Cash, beginning of year	262	Cost of goods sold	5,503
end of year	445	Other investing cash receipts	33
Purchases of property, plant, and equipment	510	Accounts receivable	1,754
Long-term debt	296	Borrowing on long-term debt	388
Collections from customers	8,779	Payment of dividends	101
Payments to employees and suppliers	8,456	Common stock	2,858
Retained earnings	2,974	Issuance of common stock	26

Analyzing a company's financial statements (Obj. 4, 5)

P1-8A Z-Mart, Inc., operates discount shoe stores. Condensed versions of the company's financial statements, with certain items omitted, follow for two recent years.

	20X1	***20X0***
STATEMENT OF INCOME	***(Thousands)***	
Revenues	$ k	$88,412
Cost of goods sold	74,564	a
Other expenses	15,839	13,564
Income before income taxes	4,346	9,262
Income taxes (36.95% in 20X1)	l	1,581
Net income	$ m	$ b
STATEMENT OF RETAINED EARNINGS		
Beginning balance	$ n	$ 9,987
Net income	o	c
Dividends	(559)	(455)
Ending balance	$ p	$ d
BALANCE SHEET		
Assets:		
Cash	$ q	$ e
Property, plant, and equipment	23,894	20,874
Other assets	r	16,900
Total assets	$ s	$37,819
Liabilities:		
Current liabilities	$ t	$ 9,973
Long-term debt and other liabilities	11,331	10,120
Total liabilities	22,785	f
Shareholders' Equity:		
Common stock	$ 229	$ 230
Retained earnings	u	g
Other shareholders' equity	133	283
Total shareholders' equity	v	17,726
Total liabilities and shareholders' equity	$ w	$ h
STATEMENT OF CASH FLOWS		
Net cash provided by operating activities	$ x	$ 2,906
Net cash used in investing activities	(3,332)	(3,792)
Net cash provided by financing activities	987	911
Increase (decrease) in cash	38	i
Cash at beginning of year	y	20
Cash at end of year	$ z	$ j

Required

1. Determine the missing amounts denoted by the letters.

2. Use Z-Mart's financial statements to answer these questions about the company. Explain each of your answers.

a. Did operations improve or deteriorate during 20X1?

b. What is the company doing with most of its income—retaining it for use in the business or using it for dividends?

c. How much in total resources does the company have to work with as it moves into the year 20X2? How much in total resources did the company have at the end of 20X0?

d. At the end of 20X0, how much did the company owe outsiders? At the end of 20X1, how much did the company owe?

e. What is the company's major source of cash? What is your opinion of the company's ability to generate cash? How is the company using most of its cash? Is the company growing or shrinking?

(Group B)

P1-1B As an analyst for **Merrill Lynch,** it is your job to write recommendations to the firm's loan committee. Alcoa Tire Company has submitted these summary data to support the company's request for a $300,000 loan.

Analyzing a loan request (Obj. 1, 5)

STATEMENT OF CASH FLOW DATA	*2002*	*2001*	*2000*
Net cash flow from operations	$ 70,000	$ 90,000	$110,000
Net cash flow from investing	(40,000)	(100,000)	60,000
Net cash flow from financing	(80,000)	(40,000)	(190,000)
Increase (decrease) in cash	$(50,000)	$(50,000)	$(20,000)
INCOME STATEMENT DATA			
Total revenues	$890,000	$830,000	$820,000
Total expenses	640,000	570,000	540,000
Net income	$250,000	$260,000	$280,000
STATEMENT OF RETAINED EARNINGS DATA			
Dividends	$290,000	$280,000	$270,000
BALANCE SHEET DATA			
Total assets	$730,000	$700,000	$660,000
Total liabilities	$390,000	$320,000	$260,000
Total stockholders' equity	340,000	380,000	400,000
Total liabilities and stockholders' equity	$730,000	$700,000	$660,000

Required

Analyze these financial statement data to determine whether the firm should lend $300,000 to Alcoa Tire Company. Write a one-paragraph recommendation to the loan committee.

P1-2B Assume that the **Chrysler Division of DaimlerChrysler Corporation,** the automaker, experienced the following transactions during the year ended December 31, 20X1:

Applying accounting concepts and principles to the income statement (Obj. 2, 4, 5)

a. Chrysler sold automobiles and other manufactured products for the discounted price of $69.4 billion. Under normal conditions Chrysler would have sold these products for $73 billion. Other revenues totaled $5.8 billion.

b. It cost Chrysler $59.0 billion to manufacture the products it sold. If Chrysler had purchased the products instead of manufacturing them, the cost would have been $61.6 billion.

c. Selling and administrative expenses were $3.9 billion. All other expenses, excluding income taxes, totaled $4.5 billion for the year. Income tax expense was 36% of income before tax.

d. Chrysler has several operating divisions: Plymouth, Dodge, Chrysler, Jeep, and Eagle. Each division is accounted for separately so that top management can see how well each division is performing. However, Chrysler's financial statements combine the statements of all the divisions in order to show the operating results of The Chrysler Division as a whole.

e. Inflation affects the amounts that Chrysler must pay for steel and other components of the company's manufactured goods. If Chrysler's financial statements were to show the effects of inflation, the company's reported net income would drop by $0.4 billion.

f. If Chrysler were to go out of business, the sale of its assets would bring in over $90 billion in cash.

Required

1. Prepare The Chrysler Division's income statement for the year ended December 31, 20X1.
2. For a through f, identify the accounting concept or principle that provides guidance in accounting for the item described. State how you have applied the concept or principle in preparing Chrysler's income statement.

Using the accounting equation (Obj. 3)

P1-3B Compute the missing amounts (?) for each company.

	Granite Co.	*Shale Corp.*	*Marble, Inc.*
BEGINNING:			
Assets	$150,000	$ 60,000	$ 80,000
Liabilities	70,000	30,000	60,000
ENDING:			
Assets	$180,000	$ 90,000	$?
Liabilities	70,000	55,000	80,000
OWNERS' EQUITY:			
Issuances of stock	$?	$ 0	$ 10,000
Dividends	70,000	40,000	30,000
INCOME STATEMENT:			
Revenues	$400,000	$240,000	$400,000
Expenses	320,000	?	300,000

Balance sheet (Obj. 2, 5)

P1-4B The manager of **Shipp Belting, Inc.,** which manufactures conveyor belts, prepared the company's balance sheet while the accountant was ill. The balance sheet contains numerous errors. In particular, the manager knew that the balance sheet should balance, so he plugged in the stockholders' equity amount needed to achieve this balance. The stockholders' equity amount, however, is not correct. All other amounts are accurate.

SHIPP BELTING, INC.
Balance Sheet
Month Ended October 31, 20X1

Assets		*Liabilities*	
Cash	$ 15,400	Notes receivable	$ 14,000
Office furniture	6,700	Interest expense	2,000
Accounts payable	3,000	Office supplies	800
Utilities expense	2,100	Accounts receivable	2,600
Advertising expense	300	Note payable	50,000
Land	80,500		
Salary expense	3,300	*Stockholders' Equity*	
		Stockholders' equity	41,900
Total assets	$111,300	Total liabilities	$111,300

Required

1. Prepare the correct balance sheet and date it properly. Compute total assets, total liabilities, and stockholders' equity.
2. Identify the accounts listed on the incorrect balance sheet that should not be presented on the balance sheet. State why you excluded them from the correct balance sheet you prepared for Requirement 1. On which financial statement should these accounts appear?

P1-5B Bob Hearn is a realtor. He buys and sells properties on his own, and he also earns commission as a real estate agent for buyers and sellers. He organized his business as a corporation on March 10, 2000, by investing $60,000 to acquire the business's common stock. Consider the following facts as of March 31, 2000:

Balance sheet, entity concept (Obj. 2, 5)

a. Hearn had $9,000 in his personal bank account and $16,000 in the business bank account.

b. Office supplies on hand at the real estate office totaled $1,000.

c. Hearn's business had spent $15,000 for a **Century 21** franchise, which entitles him to represent himself as an agent. Century 21 is a national affiliation of independent real estate agents. This franchise is a business asset.

d. Hearn's business owed $33,000 on a note payable for some undeveloped land that the business acquired for a total price of $100,000.

e. Hearn owed $65,000 on a personal mortgage on his personal residence, which he acquired in 1999 for a total price of $90,000.

f. Hearn owed $300 on a personal charge account with **Sears.**

g. Hearn had acquired business furniture for $12,000 on March 26. Of this amount, Hearn's business owed $6,000 on open account at March 31.

Required

1. Prepare the balance sheet of the real estate business of Bob Hearn, Realtor, Inc., at March 31, 2000.

2. Identify the personal items given in the preceding facts that would not be reported on the balance sheet of the business.

P1-6B Given are the amounts of (a) the assets and liabilities of Jaworsky Legal Associates as of December 31, and (b) the revenues and expenses of the company for the year ended on that date. The items are listed in no particular order.

Income statement, statement of retained earnings, balance sheet (Obj. 5)

Equipment	$31,000	Land	$ 8,000
Interest expense	4,000	Note payable	31,000
Interest payable	1,000	Property tax expense	2,000
Accounts payable	12,000	Rent expense	14,000
Accounts receivable	6,000	Salary expense	38,000
Building	26,000	Service revenue	115,000
Cash	4,000	Supplies	2,000
Common stock	10,000	Utilities expense	3,000

The beginning amount of retained earnings was $11,000, and during the year dividends totaled $42,000.

Required

1. Prepare the income statement of Jaworsky Legal Associates for the year ended December 31 of the current year.

2. Prepare the company's statement of retained earnings for the year ended December 31.

3. Prepare the company's balance sheet at December 31. You will need to compute the amount of retained earnings.

P1-7B The following data are adapted from the financial statements of **The Home Depot, Inc.,** at the end of a recent year (in millions):

Preparing a statement of cash flows (Obj. 4)

Purchases of property, plant, and equipment	$ 2,320	Other investing cash payments	$ 1
Long-term debt	1,566	Accounts receivable	469
Collections from customers	30,306	Borrowing on short-term debt	238
Payments to employees and suppliers	28,389	Payment of dividends	157
Revenues	30,219	Common stock	2,928
Cash, beginning of year	172	Issuance of common stock	168
end of year	62	Sales of property, plant, and equipment	45
Cost of goods sold	21,614	Retained earnings	5,876

Required

Prepare The Home Depot, Inc.'s statement of cash flows for the year ended January 31, 20X0. Follow the format of the summary problem on pages 24–26.

Analyzing a company's financial statements (Obj. 4, 5)

P1-8B McConnell Corporation manufactures recreational aircraft. Adapted versions of the company's financial statements are given for two recent years.

	20X1	20X0
STATEMENT OF OPERATIONS	*(In Thousands)*	
Revenues	$ k	$15,487
Cost of goods sold	11,026	a
Other expenses	1,230	1,169
Earnings before income taxes	920	1,496
Income taxes (35% in 20X1)	l	100
Net earnings	$ m	$ b
STATEMENT OF RETAINED EARNINGS		
Beginning balance	$ n	$ 2,702
Net earnings	o	c
Dividends	(65)	(55)
Ending balance	$ p	$ d
BALANCE SHEET		
Assets:		
Cash	$ q	$ e
Property, plant, and equipment	1,597	1,750
Other assets	r	10,190
Total assets	$ s	$13,026
Liabilities:		
Current liabilities	$ t	$ 5,403
Notes payable and long-term debt	2,569	3,138
Other liabilities	69	72
Total liabilities	$ 8,344	$ f
Shareholders' Equity:		
Common stock	$ 117	$ 118
Retained earnings	u	g
Other shareholders' equity	179	252
Total shareholders' equity	v	4,413
Total liabilities and shareholders' equity	$ w	$ h
STATEMENT OF CASH FLOWS		
Net cash provided by operating activities	$ x	$ 475
Net cash provided by investing activities	58	574
Net cash used by financing activities	(709)	(1,045)
Increase (decrease) in cash	335	i
Cash at beginning of year	y	1,082
Cash at end of year	$ z	$ j

Required

1. Determine the missing amounts denoted by the letters.

2. Use McConnell's financial statements to answer these questions about the company. Explain each of your answers.

a. Did operations improve or deteriorate during 20X1?

b. What is the company doing with most of its income—retaining it for use in the business or using it for dividends?

c. How much in total resources does the company have to work with as it moves into the year 20X2?

d. At the end of 20X0, how much did the company owe outsiders? At the end of 20X1, how much did the company owe? Is this trend good or bad in comparison to the trend in assets?

e. What is the company's major source of cash? Is cash increasing or decreasing? What is your opinion of the company's ability to generate cash?

EXTENDING YOUR KNOWLEDGE

DECISION CASES

Using financial statements to evaluate a loan request (Obj. 1, 2)

Case 1. Two businesses, Swinger Staple and Zalenski Medical Records, Inc., have sought business loans from you. To decide whether to make the loans, you have requested their balance sheets.

SWINGER STAPLE COMPANY
Balance Sheet
August 31, 2002

Assets		*Liabilities*	
Cash	$ 11,000	Accounts payable	$ 3,000
Accounts receivable . . .	4,000	Notes payable	388,000
Office supplies	1,000	Total liabilities	391,000
Office furniture	36,000		
Land	79,000	*Owners' Equity*	
Equipment	300,000	Owners' equity	40,000
		Total liabilities and	
Total assets	$431,000	owners' equity	$431,000

ZALENSKI MEDICAL RECORDS, INC.
Balance Sheet
August 31, 2002

Assets		*Liabilities*	
Cash	$ 9,000	Accounts payable	$ 12,000
Accounts receivable . . .	14,000	Note payable	18,000
Merchandise inventory	85,000	Total liabilities	30,000
Store supplies	500		
Furniture and fixtures .	9,000	*Stockholders' Equity*	
Building	82,000	Stockholders' equity . .	183,500
Land	14,000	Total liabilities and	
Total assets	$213,500	stockholders' equity .	$213,500

Required

1. Solely on the basis of these balance sheets, to which entity would you be more comfortable lending money? Explain fully, citing specific items and amounts from the respective balance sheets.
2. In addition to the balance sheet data, what other information would you require? Be specific.

Using accounting information (Obj. 1, 2, 3, 4, 5)

Case 2. A friend learns that you are taking an accounting course. Knowing that you do not plan a career in accounting, the friend asks you why you are "wasting your time." Explain to the friend how you and your friends will use accounting information in

a. Your personal life.
b. The business of your friend, who plans to be a farmer.
c. The business life of another friend, who plans a career in sales.

Ethical Issue

The board of directors of **Oriental Rug Company** is meeting to discuss the past year's results before releasing financial statements to the public. The discussion includes this exchange:

> **P.J. Boardman, company president:** "Well, this has not been a good year! Revenue is down and expenses are up—way up. If we don't do some fancy stepping, we'll report a loss for the third year in a row. I can temporarily transfer some land that I own into the company's name, and that will beef up our balance sheet. Ron, can you shave $500,000 from expenses? Then we can probably get the bank loan that we need."
> **Ron Librach, company chief accountant:** "P.J., you are asking too much. Generally accepted accounting principles are designed to keep this sort of thing from happening."

Required

1. What is the fundamental ethical issue in this situation?
2. Discuss how Boardman's proposals violate generally accepted accounting principles. Identify the specific concept or principle involved, and also refer to specifics from the AICPA Code of Professional Conduct.

Financial Statement Cases

Identifying items from a company's financial statements (Obj. 4)

Case 1. This and similar problems in succeeding chapters focus on the financial statements of **The Gap, Inc.** As you study each problem, you will gradually build the confidence that you can understand and use actual financial statements.

Required

Refer to The Gap financial statements in Appendix A at the end of the book.

1. Use The Gap income statement for the current year to answer these questions: Suppose you own stock in Gap, Inc. If you could pick one item on the company's income statement to increase year after year, what would it be? Why is this item so important? Did this item increase or decrease during fiscal year 1999? Is this good news or bad news for the company? What two items on the income statement are driving the change in this item from 1998 to 1999?
2. Use The Gap's statement of retained earnings in Exhibit 1-8 (page 16) to answer these questions: What is The Gap doing with most of its net earnings? How can you tell?
3. Use the balance sheet of The Gap in Exhibit 1-9 (page 17) to answer these questions: At the end of fiscal year 1999, how much in total resources did The Gap have to work with? How much did the company owe? How much of its assets did the company's stockholders actually own? Use these amounts to write the company's accounting equation at January 30, 1999. Round to the nearest $1 million.
4. Use The Gap's statement of cash flows in Exhibit 1-10 (page 21) (not the cash-flow statement in Appendix A at the back of the book) to answer these questions: It takes a lot of money to operate a company the size of The Gap. Where does The Gap get its cash? How does the company spend its cash? How much cash did it have at the beginning of the most recent year? How much cash did it have at the end of the year?

Identifying items from a company's financial statements (Obj. 4)

Case 2. Obtain the annual report of a company of your choosing. Annual reports are available in various forms, including the original document in hard copy and available on most companies' Web sites. Computerized databases such as Disclosure, Inc., and the SEC's EDGAR database, also provide companies' financial statements.

Required

Answer the following questions about the company. Concentrate on the current year in the annual report you select, except as directed for particular questions.

1. How much in cash (which may include cash equivalents) did the company have at the end of the current year? At the end of the preceding year? Did cash increase or decrease during the current year? By how much?
2. What were total assets at the end of the current year? At the end of the preceding year?
3. Write the company's accounting equation at the end of the current year by filling in the dollar amounts:

Assets = Liabilities + Owners' or Stockholders' Equity

4. Identify net sales revenue for the current year. The company may label this as Net sales, Sales, Net revenue, or as some other title. How much was the corresponding revenue amount for the preceding year?
5. How much net income or net loss did the company experience for the current year? For the preceding year? Evaluate the current year's operations in comparison with the preceding year.

Group Projects

Project 1. As instructed by your professor, obtain the annual report of a well-known company.

Required

1. Take the role of a loan committee of **Nation's Bank,** a large banking company headquartered in Charlotte, North Carolina. Assume the company has requested a loan from Nation's Bank. Analyze the company's financial statements and any other information you need to reach a decision regarding the largest amount of money you would be willing to lend. Go as deeply into the analysis and the related decision as you can. Specify the following:
   a. The length of the loan period—that is, over what period will you allow the company to pay you back?
   b. The interest rate you will charge on the loan. Will you charge the prevailing interest rate, a lower rate, or a higher rate? Why?
   c. Any restrictions you will impose on the borrower as a condition for making the loan.
   Note: The long-term debt note to the financial statements gives details of the company's existing liabilities.
2. Write your group decision in a report addressed to the bank's board of directors. Limit your report to two double-spaced word-processed pages.
3. If your professor directs, present your decision and your analysis to the class. Limit your presentation to 10 to 15 minutes.

Project 2. You are the owner of a company that is about to "go public"—that is, issue its stock to outside investors. You wish to make your company look as attractive as possible in order to raise $1 million of cash to expand the business. At the same time, you want to give potential investors a realistic picture of your company.

Required

1. Design a booklet to portray your company in a way that will enable outsiders to reach an informed decision as to whether to buy some of your stock. The booklet should include the following:
   a. Name and location of your company.
   b. Nature of the company's business (be as detailed as possible).
   c. How you plan to spend the money you raise.
   d. The company's comparative income statement, statement of retained earnings, balance sheet, and statement of cash flows for two years: the current year and the preceding year. Make the data as realistic as possible with the intent of receiving $1 million.
2. Word-process your booklet, not to exceed five pages.
3. If directed by your professor, make a copy for each member of your class. Distribute copies to the class and present your case with the intent of interesting your classmates in investing in the company. Limit your presentation to 10 to 15 minutes.

Internet Exercise

Harley-Davidson

Harley-Davidson is the only major domestic maker of motorcycles. It currently makes more than half the heavyweight bikes sold in the United States and one in four worldwide. The firm recently expanded production to reduce waiting lists to less than a year for its custom-made Road King and Fat Boy bikes. The Harley Web site allows you to explore model options and access the company's latest financial information.

1. Go to **http://www.harley-davidson.com.** Click on *The Company Index* scroll bar, select the *most recent annual report,* and click *go.* Click on *complete financial information* to display additional selections. Use the consolidated income statements (statements of operations) and balance sheets to answer the following questions.
2. For the three most recent years, identify the amounts reported for *Net sales* and *Net Income.* For each of these amounts comment on the direction of the trend, what the trend might indicate, and whether the trend is considered favorable or unfavorable. Is Harley-Davidson a profitable company?
3. For the two most recent years, identify or calculate the amounts reported for *Cash and Cash Equivalents, Total Assets, Total Liabilities,* and *Total Stockholders' Equity.* Does the accounting equation hold true? Are assets primarily financed by debt or stockholders' equity?
4. Record the number of *asset* accounts, *liability* accounts, and *stockholders' equity* accounts listed on the balance sheet. List the title of the account that reports the greatest dollar amount for each category.

APPENDIX TO CHAPTER 1

ACCOUNTING'S ROLE IN BUSINESS

ACCOUNTING'S RELATIONSHIP TO THE OTHER AREAS OF BUSINESS

Accounting professionals are more in demand than ever. Why do you suppose this is occurring? Let's step back for a moment and consider how organizations operate. Every organization has a primary mission. Hospitals provide health care. Law firms advise clients on legal matters. Auto dealers sell cars. All these organizations use *accounting* because it is impossible to physically observe all the aspects of a business. Accounting helps managers get a handle on the organization as a whole without drowning in the details. Let's see how businesspeople use accounting to make decisions.

How Owners and Managers Use Accounting

Suppose you own your own business, a consulting firm. How will you decide how much to spend on office rent, employee salaries, and computer software? You will be limited by the amount of cash you have in the bank, and you will know your cash balance because you've kept accounting records. After the business becomes a success, how will you decide how much to spend on a business expansion? Good contacts and intelligence are important, but they are not enough for sound decision making. You must "run the numbers" to determine how much you can expect to earn from the business. And those whom you ask to finance the business will be more impressed with a business plan than with a few vague ideas. Accounting will help you develop a business plan.

Good managers plan their activities in advance. They write their plans in terms of a *budget,* which is a formal plan often expressed in monetary terms. For example, a sales manager for **Xerox Corporation** will have an annual sales budget for which she is responsible. If she makes more sales than specified in the budget, she will receive a bonus. If you were this sales manager, would you like to be part of the budgeting process? Or do you want someone else to give you your marching orders each year? Budgeting is important, and you need to know how a budget is used to evaluate your own performance.

How Lenders and Investors Use Accounting

Accounting helps banks decide to whom they will lend money. Bankers cannot spend all their time observing borrowers' operations. But the bankers can study loan applicants' financial statements to get an idea of their ability to repay the loan. After making loans, bankers monitor borrowers' progress by examining their financial reports.

Accounting also provides important information that investors use to decide which stocks to buy and sell. An investor in Kansas may not have the time or the expertise to check every detail of a company in Florida before buying its stock. But the investor can examine the company's financial reports to decide whether the company appears to be profitable and well managed. It is amazing that investors buy the stock of a company that they have barely heard of. Why are investors willing to spend their money this way? Because accounting statements and other reports give a picture of the business that people trust. Accounting is usually divided into two areas: private accounting and public accounting.

PRIVATE ACCOUNTING

Private accountants work for a single business, such as a **Dillard's** department store, the **McDonald's** restaurant chain, or **Eastman Kodak Company.** Charitable organizations, educational institutions, and government agencies also employ private accountants. You'll find private accountants in Wall Street brokerage firms, agencies for the homeless, and rock-and-roll band organizations. Accountants' work varies according to the business or industry in which they operate.

Accountants in health-care organizations are playing a vital role in restructuring the nation's health-care system by guiding companies through government regulations. In the fast-paced world of entertainment and media, a private accountant might advise management on how to stay ahead of technological changes. While the specific missions of accountants vary, private accountants generally provide these services for their companies:

- *Budgeting* sets sales and profit goals and develops plans for achieving those goals. The most successful companies in the United States have been pioneers in the field of budgeting—**Procter & Gamble** and **General Electric,** for example.
- *Information systems design* identifies the organization's information needs, both internal and external. Systems designers develop and implement an information system to meet those needs.
- *Cost accounting* analyzes a business's costs to help managers control expenses.
- *Internal auditing* is performed by a business's own accountants. Many organizations—**Motorola, Bank of America,** and **3M** among them—have internal auditors who evaluate the firm's own accounting and management systems to improve operating efficiency.

A company's chief accounting officer usually has the title of controller, treasurer, or chief financial officer (CFO). This person carries the status of a vice president. Accountants who have met certain professional requirements in the area of management accounting are designated as *certified management accountants (CMAs).*

The CFO and other accounting professionals have become increasingly important as businesses compete in global markets. At **Federal Express,** some financial managers visited **Intel** to learn how to improve mailroom efficiency. At **Frito-Lay,** financial people set goals and stimulate the company's creativity. They might ask,

"How can our competitor produce a quality product at a lower price? How can we do even better?"

Clearly, this is a far cry from the old stereotype of the accountant sitting in a back room with record books and calculator in hand. Stephen Bollenbach, former CFO of **Walt Disney Company** recalls, "During the sixties the CFO served as a scorekeeper. Now the CFO's role includes critical functions like strategic planning—charting the company's long-term direction."

The changing nature of accountants' jobs means that people who choose accounting as a career need more than a sound financial and accounting background. They must be good communicators, analysts, and problem solvers, and they must be able to work in cross-functional teams composed of members from the company's different departments: operations, production, distribution, sales, and marketing.

Public Accounting

Public accountants serve the general public and collect professional fees for their work, much as doctors and lawyers do. Public accountants constitute a small fraction (about 10%) of all accountants. Accountants who have met certain professional requirements in accounting, auditing, and law are designated as *certified public accountants (CPAs).*

Like private accountants, public accountants provide many valuable services:

- *Consulting* describes the wide scope of advice CPAs provide to help managers run a business. CPAs look deep into a business's operations. With the insights they gain, they often make suggestions for improvements in the business's management structure and accounting systems.
- *Auditing* is an important service. In conducting an audit, CPAs from outside a business examine the business's financial statements. The CPAs report a professional opinion stating whether the firm's financial statements agree with generally accepted accounting principles. Stockholders and creditors, who have a financial stake in the company, need to know that the financial picture management shows them is complete and accurate.
- *Tax accounting* has two aims: complying with the tax laws and minimizing the company's tax bill. Because federal income tax rates run as high as 39.6% for individuals and 35% for corporations, reducing the company's tax bill is an important management consideration. Accountants plan business transactions to minimize taxes, and they advise clients on investments.

Most professional employees of accounting firms are CPAs. Accounting firms vary greatly in size. Some are small businesses and others large partnerships. Exhibit 1A-1 gives data on the ten largest U.S. accounting firms.

These firms are very large. **Andersen Worldwide** (the combination of **Arthur Andersen** and **Andersen Consulting**) generates annual revenues of almost $7 billion. The firm has almost 2,000 partners, more than 38,000 employees, and operates 98 offices around the world. The average Andersen partner brings in annual revenues exceeding $3.6 million and is paid over $500,000 per year. Partners in the other large accounting firms receive similar compensation. The accounting firms in Exhibit 1A-1 are the largest consulting, auditing, and tax firms in the world.

Accountants working as consultants have a major impact on their clients. The following actual examples describe how public accountants help their clients:

- A consultant specializing in health care simplified the way medical personnel interact with computers so that they can give more personal attention to patients.

EXHIBIT 1A-1
The 10 Largest U.S. Accounting Firms

Rank (1999)	*Firm Location*	*Net Revenue (in millions)*	*Partners*	*Number of Offices*	*Revenue per Partner (in millions)*
1	Andersen Worldwide New York	$6,828	1,897	98	$3.6
2	PricewaterhouseCoopers New York	$5,862	2,677	202	$2.2
3	Ernst & Young New York	$5,545	2,352	87	$2.4
4	Deloitte & Touche Wilton, Connecticut	$4,700	1,927	103	$2.4
5	KPMG New York	$3,800	1,611	136	$2.4
6	H&R Block Tax Services Kansas City, Missouri	$1,052	1,966	8,789	$0.5
7	Century Business Services* Cleveland, Ohio	$363	N/A	848	N/A
8	Grant Thornton Chicago	$336	281	48	$1.2
9	McGladrey & Pullen Bloomington, Minnesota	$296	374	63	$0.8
10	BDO Seidman Chicago	$250	312	42	$0.8

* Century Business Services, unlike the other firms, is not a partnership.

Source: Adapted from *Accounting Today* (March 15–April 4, 1999), Special Supplement.

- A CPA devised an ownership-succession plan for a small family-owned business. She brought together quarreling family members and anxious employees. With her help, the company reached an agreement for a smooth transition of ownership that was fair to both the family and the employees.

Public accountants spend most of their time at their clients' locations: across town, around the country, and around the world. Public accountants may even find themselves in some unlikely places. Consider the following examples:

- Josh Young's first consulting engagement for Arthur Andersen found him on the site of the Northridge earthquake outside of Los Angeles. One of his clients was a supermarket chain with 150 damaged stores. Young helped prepare insurance claims for his client and needed to visit the actual site at 4:00 A.M.—as the tremors continued—to determine how much damage had occurred.

- Mike Nugent, a supervising senior at **KPMG**, took on a consulting job, unaware that his business attire might include boots, overalls, and a hairnet. To conduct an audit for a chicken producer recently acquired by a Japanese company, Nugent drove to Heartland, Indiana, where he found himself surrounded by 2,000 screaming chickens!

- Jennifer Tufer is a **Deloitte & Touche** senior manager on assignment in Moscow. At the end of the day, she sifts through faxes that have arrived from various Deloitte & Touche offices around the world. A typical request comes from a U.S. manufacturer interested in setting up operations in

Russia. "The company wanted to know how they would be taxed," Ms. Tufer says.

Accounting Today

Today's accountants are as diverse as their job assignments. Accountants may be male or female, outgoing or conservative, but they are all analytical. They may have backgrounds in art history or computer programming. Their hobbies include rock climbing, scuba diving, and gourmet cooking. And they come from every ethnic and cultural background.

Accounting was once dominated by men, particularly in the "Big Five" firms—the five largest public accounting firms. Today, the Big Five, smaller CPA firms, and companies in general are hiring more women as professionals than ever before. Women are rising to top positions, such as CFO or partner. Deloitte & Touche, a Big Five firm has been cited as one of the best places to work in the United States.

Accountants are benefiting from today's flexible work arrangements. "I'm probably one of the first people who stayed in public accounting because of quality-of-life advantages," says Eileen Garvey, an audit partner at **Ernst & Young** in New York. Garvey was an early participant in flexible scheduling and worked a three-day-a-week schedule. The mother of two, Garvey was admitted to the partnership as a part-timer. Flexibility works for men, too. Carl Moellenkamp, a manager with Arthur Andersen in Chicago, took a summer's leave to pursue his other career as a chef.

Since the tools of the accounting trade are computers, phones, and fax machines, some accountants now work from home. **Janet Caswell,** a Michigan accountant with her own business, has a staff but no office. Her files, computer server, and other equipment are located in a rented storage space. Her telephone is a personal 800 number that can be programmed to follow her staff wherever they go. Her employees communicate and "meet" electronically. Caswell is one of a growing number of public accountants with this type of "virtual office."

What are the prospects for people entering the accounting field? Exhibit 1A-2 shows the accounting positions within public accounting firms and other organiza-

Exhibit 1A-2
Accounting Positions within Organizations

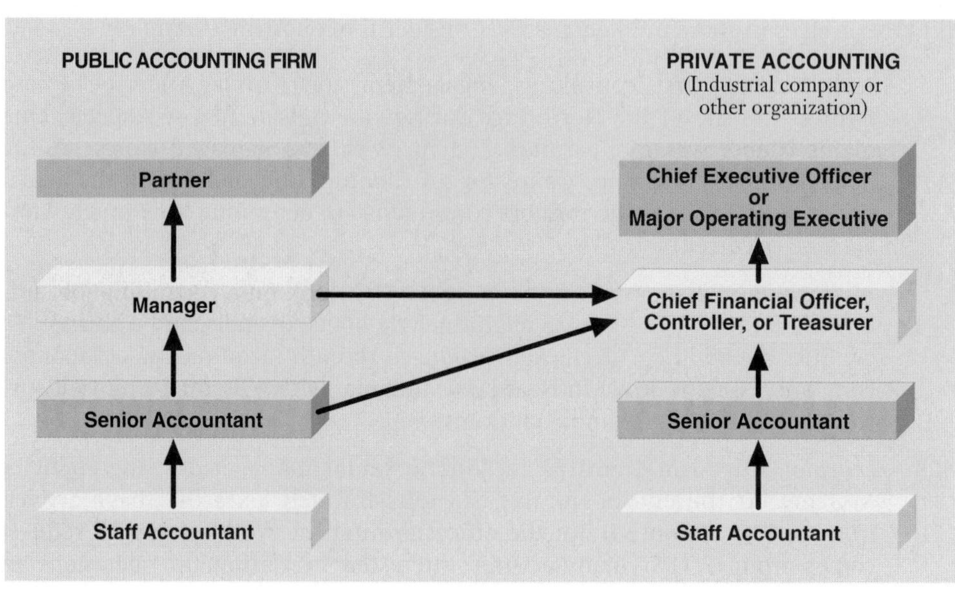

tions. Note the upward movement of accounting personnel, as indicated by the arrows. In particular, note how accountants may move from positions in public accounting to similar or higher positions in industry and government.

An accounting background can open doors in most lines of business. In short, accounting deals with all facets of an organization—purchasing, manufacturing, marketing, and distribution. This is why accounting provides such an excellent basis for gaining business experience.

2 Processing Accounting Information

Learning Objectives

After studying this chapter, you should be able to

1. Use key accounting terms
2. Analyze business transactions
3. Understand how double-entry accounting works
4. Record business transactions
5. Prepare and use a trial balance
6. Analyze transactions for quick decisions

PepsiCo, Inc.
Statement of Income (adapted)
Fiscal Years Ended December 26, 1998, December 27, 1997
(in millions)

	1998	1997
Net Sales	**$22,348**	$20,917
Expenses		
Cost of sales	**9,330**	8,525
Selling, general and administrative expenses	**9,924**	9,241
Amortization of intangible assets	**222**	199
Unusual impairment of assets	**288**	290
Operating Profit	**2,584**	2,662
Interest expense	**(395)**	(478)
Interest income	**74**	125
Income from Continuing Operations Before Income Taxes	**2,263**	2,309
Provision for Income Taxes (Income tax expense)	**270**	818
Income from Continuing Operations	**1,993**	1,491
Income from Discontinued Operations, net of tax	—	651
Net Income	**$ 1,993**	$ 2,142

PepsiCo, Inc. consists of three business units: Pepsi-Cola, Frito-Lay, and Tropicana. Frito-Lay is by far the most profitable segment. Frito-Lay uses only 35% of PepsiCo's total assets but produces 69% of the company's operating profit. Frito-Lay dominates the prepared snack-food industry worldwide.

How does Frito-Lay achieve this extraordinary success? The company's information system is one of the most sophisticated in the world. Frito-Lay route salespeople carry hand-held computers with amazing capabilities. Each day the route salesperson logs in the number of Frito-Lay snack food items left over from the day before. These data are downloaded to company headquarters in Dallas. Combined with yesterday's figures, Frito-Lay knows which products are selling and which products are not.

The great benefit of this information to Frito-Lay—and to PepsiCo, Inc.—is the elimination of waste. The company's accounting system enables managers to invest wisely in corn, potatoes, technology, and all the other factors that make the company successful. The bottom line of the income statement, net income, shows the result of wise decisions.

Chapter 1 gave you a good grounding in the financial statements, which are the focus of this course. Chapters 2 and 3 cover the accounting process that results in the financial statements.

Chapter 2 discusses the processing of accounting information. It begins with a basic approach that uses the accounting equation we studied in Chapter 1. The second half of the chapter extends the discussion to illustrate the way accounting systems work. Chapter 3 goes more deeply into how income is measured. It covers the end-of-period accounting process that results in the financial statements.

Throughout this chapter and the next, we illustrate service businesses such as a travel agency, a law practice, and a sports franchise like the Chicago Bulls. In later chapters, we move into merchandising businesses such as **Macy's** and **Wal-Mart**.

THE ACCOUNT

Objective 1
Use key accounting terms

Recall that in Chapter 1 we learned that the accounting equation is the most basic tool in accounting. It measures the assets of the business and the claims to those assets.

The basic summary device of accounting is the **account,** the detailed record of the changes that have occurred in a particular asset, liability, or stockholders' (or owners') equity during a period of time. Accounts are grouped in three broad categories, according to the accounting equation:

Assets = Liabilities + Stockholders' (or Owners') Equity

Assets

Assets are the economic resources that benefit the business and will continue to do so in the future. Most firms use the following asset accounts:

CASH. The Cash account shows the cash effects of a business's transactions. **Cash** means money and any medium of exchange that a bank accepts at face value, such as bank account balances, paper currency, coins, certificates of deposit, and checks. Most business failures result from a shortage of cash.

ACCOUNTS RECEIVABLE. A business may sell its goods or services in exchange for a promise for future cash receipt. Such sales are made on credit ("on account"). The Accounts Receivable account contains these amounts.

INVENTORY. **PepsiCo's** most important asset is its inventory—the drinks and snack foods that the company sells to customers. Other titles used for this account include *Merchandise* and *Merchandise Inventory.*

NOTES RECEIVABLE. A business may sell its goods or services in exchange for a note receivable called a *promissory note,* which is a written pledge that the customer will pay a fixed amount of money by a certain date.

PREPAID EXPENSES. A business often pays certain expenses in advance. A **prepaid expense** is an asset because the payment provides a future benefit for the business. Prepaid Rent, Prepaid Insurance, and Office Supplies are accounted for as prepaid expenses.

LAND. The Land account is a record of the cost of land a business owns and uses in its operations. Land held for sale is accounted for separately in an investment account.

BUILDINGS. The cost of a business's buildings—office, manufacturing plant, and the like—appears in the Buildings account.

Equipment, Furniture, and Fixtures. A business has a separate asset account for each type of equipment—Office Equipment, Manufacturing Equipment, Store Equipment, for example. The Furniture and Fixtures account shows the cost of these assets, which are similar to equipment.

Liabilities

Recall that a *liability* is a debt. Here are some of the most common types of liability accounts:

Notes Payable. The Notes Payable account is the opposite of the Notes Receivable account. Notes Payable includes the amounts that the business must pay because it signed promissory notes to borrow money or to purchase goods or services.

Accounts Payable. The Accounts Payable account is the opposite of the Accounts Receivable account. The promise to pay off debts arising from credit purchases of inventory and other goods appears in the Accounts Payable account. Such a purchase is said to be made "on account" or "on credit."

Accrued Liabilities. An **accrued liability** is a liability for an expense that has not yet been paid. Interest Payable and Salary Payable are accrued liability accounts for most companies. Income Taxes Payable is also an accrued liability.

LEARNING TIP: A receivable is always an asset.
A payable is always a liability.

Stockholders' (Owners') Equity

The owners' claims to the assets of a corporation are called *stockholders' equity, shareholders' equity,* or simply *owners' equity.* In a proprietorship, there is a single capital account. For a partnership, owner equity is often split into separate accounts for each owner's capital balance and each owner's withdrawals. A corporation uses Common Stock, Retained Earnings, and Dividends accounts.

Common Stock. The Common Stock account represents the owners' investment in the corporation. A person invests in a corporation by purchasing common stock. The corporation issues a stock certificate imprinted with the stockholder's name as proof of ownership.

Retained Earnings. A for-profit business must earn a profit to remain in operation. The Retained Earnings account shows the cumulative net income earned by the corporation over its lifetime, minus cumulative net losses and dividends.

Dividends. The owners of a corporation demand cash from the business. After profitable operations, the board of directors may (or may not) declare a cash dividend to be paid at a later date. Dividends are not required but are optional as decided by the board of directors. The corporation may keep a separate account titled *Dividends,* which indicates a decrease in Retained Earnings.

Revenues. The increase in stockholders' equity created by delivering goods or services to customers or clients is called *revenue.* The company uses as many revenue accounts as needed. PepsiCo uses a Sales Revenue account for amounts earned by selling merchandise to customers. A lawyer provides legal services for clients and thus uses a Service Revenue account. If a business loans money to an outsider, it will need an Interest Revenue account for the interest earned on the loan. If the business rents a building to a tenant, it will need a Rent Revenue account.

EXPENSES. The cost of operating a business is called *expense*. Expenses *decrease* stockholders' equity, which is the opposite effect of revenues. A business needs a separate account for each type of expense, such as Cost of Sales, Salary Expense, Rent Expense, Advertising Expense, and Utilities Expense. Businesses strive to minimize expenses and thereby maximize net income.

CHECK POINT 2-1

STOP & THINK

Name two things that (1) increase stockholders' equity; (2) decrease stockholders' equity.

Answer: (1) Sale of stock and net income (revenue greater than expenses). (2) Declaration and payment of dividends and net loss (expenses greater than revenue).

ACCOUNTING FOR BUSINESS TRANSACTIONS

Objective 2
Analyze business transactions

In accounting terms, a **transaction** is any event that both affects the financial position of the business entity and can be reliably recorded. Many events may affect a company, including (1) elections, (2) economic booms and recessions, (3) purchases and sales of merchandise inventory, (4) payment of rent, (5) collection of cash from customers, and so on. But accountants record only events with effects that can be measured reliably as transactions.

Which of the five events above would an accountant record? The answer is events 3, 4, and 5 because their dollar amounts can be measured reliably. The dollar effects of elections and economic trends cannot be measured reliably. Therefore, an accountant would not record a key election or a trend even though it might affect the business more than events 3, 4, and 5.

To illustrate accounting for business transactions, let's return to Gary and Monica Lyon. We met Gary and Monica in Chapter 1, when they opened a travel agency in April 20X1 and incorporated it as Air & Sea Travel, Inc. We will consider 11 events and analyze each in terms of its effect on the accounting equation of Air & Sea Travel.

TRANSACTION 1. The Lyons invest $50,000 of their money to begin the business, and Air & Sea Travel issues common stock to Gary and Monica Lyon. The effect of this transaction on the accounting equation of the business entity Air & Sea Travel, Inc., is a receipt of $50,000 cash and issuance of common stock as follows:

	Assets	=	*Liabilities* +	*Stockholders' Equity*	*Type of Stockholders' Equity Transaction*
	Cash			**Common Stock**	
(1)	+50,000			+50,000	Issued stock to owners

For every transaction, the net amount on the left side of the equation must equal the net amount on the right side. The first transaction increases both the assets (in this case, Cash) and the owners' equity of the business (Common Stock). The transaction involves no liabilities because it creates no obligation for Air & Sea Travel to pay an outside party. To the right of the transaction we write "Issued stock to owners" to record the reason for the $50,000 increase in stockholders' equity.

Effects of Transactions on the Financial Statements. Every transaction affects the financial statements, and we can prepare the statements after one, two, or any number of transactions. For example, Air & Sea Travel, Inc., could report the company's balance sheet after its first transaction, as shown at the top of page 55.

This balance sheet shows that Air & Sea Travel holds cash of $50,000 and that the company owes no liabilities. Thus, the stockholders own all of the assets of the

AIR & SEA TRAVEL, INC.
Balance Sheet
April 1, 20X1

Assets		*Liabilities*	
Cash	$50,000	None	
		Stockholders' Equity	
		Common stock............	$50,000
		Total stockholders' equity ..	50,000
		Total liabilities and	
Total assets	$50,000	stockholders' equity......	$50,000

business. But the balance sheet of a corporation does not reveal the names of the stockholders. Their equity in the assets of the business is denoted simply as *Common stock* on the balance sheet.

Air & Sea Travel's first transaction affected only cash and common stock—both *balance sheet* accounts. No revenue was affected, nor was any expense. Therefore, Air & Sea Travel would not report an income statement at this time.

As a practical matter, most entities report their financial statements at the end of the accounting period—not after each transaction. But with modern accounting systems they can produce statements whenever managers and owners need to know where the business stands. Now let's move on to Transaction 2.

TRANSACTION 2. Air & Sea Travel purchases land for a future office location, paying cash of $40,000. The effect of this transaction on the accounting equation is

	Assets		=	*Liabilities + Stockholders' Equity*	*Type of Stockholders' Equity Transaction*
	Cash	**+ Land**		**Common Stock**	
(1)	50,000			50,000	Issued stock to owners
(2)	−40,000	+40,000			
Bal.	10,000	40,000		50,000	
	50,000			50,000	

The cash purchase of land increases one asset (Land) and decreases another asset (Cash) by the same amount. After the transaction is completed, Air & Sea Travel has cash of $10,000, land of $40,000, no liabilities, and stockholders' equity of $50,000. Note that the sums of the balances (which we abbreviate Bal.) on both sides of the equation are equal. This equality must always exist.

CHECK POINT 2-2

TRANSACTION 3. The business buys stationery and other office supplies, agreeing to pay $500 to the office-supply store within 30 days. This transaction increases both the assets and the liabilities of the business. Its effect on the accounting equation is

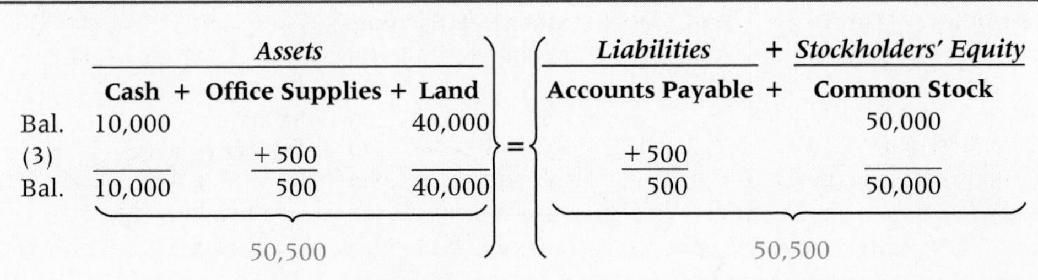

	Assets			=	*Liabilities*	*+ Stockholders' Equity*
	Cash	**+ Office Supplies**	**+ Land**		**Accounts Payable +**	**Common Stock**
Bal.	10,000		40,000			50,000
(3)		+500			+500	
Bal.	10,000	500	40,000		500	50,000
	50,500				50,500	

The asset affected is Office Supplies, and the liability is an Account Payable. Because Air & Sea Travel is obligated to pay $500 in the future but signs no formal promissory note, we record the liability as an account payable, not as a note payable.

TRANSACTION 4. Air & Sea Travel earns service revenue by providing travel-arrangement services for customers. Assume the business earns $5,500 and collects this amount in cash. The effect on the accounting equation is an increase in the asset Cash and an increase in Retained Earnings, as follows:

	Assets				*Liabilities* +	*Stockholders' Equity*		*Type of Stockholders' Equity Transaction*
	Cash	**+ Office Supplies**	**+ Land**		**Accounts Payable**	**+ Common Stock**	**+ Retained Earnings**	
Bal.	10,000	500	40,000	=	500	50,000		
(4)	+ 5,500						+ 5,500	Service revenue
Bal.	15,500	500	40,000		500	50,000	5,500	
	56,000				56,000			

TRANSACTION 5. Air & Sea Travel performs services for customers who do not pay immediately. In return for these services, Air & Sea receives the customers' promise to pay $3,000 within one month. This promise is an account receivable of Air & Sea Travel because the business expects to collect the cash in the future. (In accounting, we say that Air & Sea performed this service *on account.*) When the business performs a service for a client or a customer, the business earns revenue regardless of whether it receives cash immediately or expects to collect cash later. Air & Sea Travel records an increase in the asset Accounts Receivable and an increase in Retained Earnings as follows:

	Assets					*Liabilities* +	*Stockholders' Equity*		*Type of Stockholders' Equity Transaction*
	Cash	**+ Accounts Receivable**	**+ Office Supplies**	**+ Land**		**Accounts Payable**	**+ Common Stock**	**+ Retained Earnings**	
Bal.	15,500		500	40,000	=	500	50,000	5,500	
(5)		+ 3,000						+ 3,000	Service revenue
Bal.	15,500	3,000	500	40,000		500	50,000	8,500	
	59,000					59,000			

CHECK POINT 2-3

TRANSACTION 6. During the month, Air & Sea Travel pays $2,700 for the following cash expenses: office rent, $1,100; employee salary, $1,200 (for a part-time assistant); and total utilities, $400. The effect on the accounting equation is

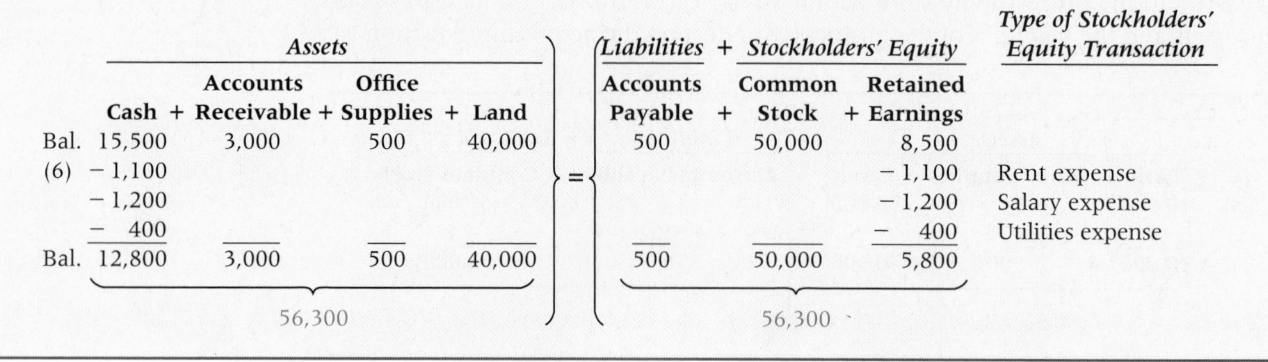

	Assets					*Liabilities* +	*Stockholders' Equity*		*Type of Stockholders' Equity Transaction*
	Cash	**+ Accounts Receivable**	**+ Office Supplies**	**+ Land**		**Accounts Payable**	**+ Common Stock**	**+ Retained Earnings**	
Bal.	15,500	3,000	500	40,000		500	50,000	8,500	
(6)	− 1,100				=			− 1,100	Rent expense
	− 1,200							− 1,200	Salary expense
	− 400							− 400	Utilities expense
Bal.	12,800	3,000	500	40,000		500	50,000	5,800	
	56,300					56,300			

TRANSACTION 7. Air & Sea Travel pays $400 to the store from which it purchased $500 worth of office supplies in Transaction 3. (In accounting, we say that Air & Sea Travel pays $400 *on account*.) The effect on the accounting equation is a decrease in the asset Cash and a decrease in the liability Accounts Payable as follows:

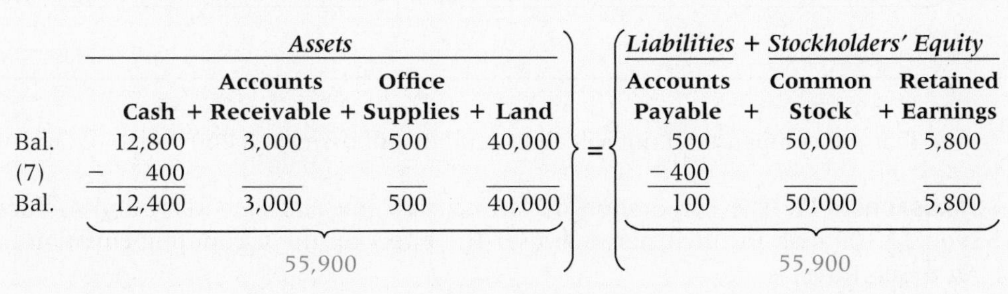

	Assets					*Liabilities + Stockholders' Equity*		
	Cash	**+ Accounts Receivable**	**+ Office Supplies**	**+ Land**		**Accounts Payable**	**+ Common Stock**	**+ Retained Earnings**
Bal.	12,800	3,000	500	40,000	=	500	50,000	5,800
(7)	− 400					−400		
Bal.	12,400	3,000	500	40,000		100	50,000	5,800
	55,900					55,900		

The payment of cash on account has no effect on the asset Office Supplies because the payment does not increase or decrease the supplies available to the business. The payment is not an expense; rather, the business is paying off a liability.

TRANSACTION 8. The Lyons remodel their home at a cost of $30,000, paying cash from personal funds. This event is *not* a transaction of Air & Sea Travel, Inc. It has no effect on Air & Sea's business affairs and therefore is not recorded by the business. It is a transaction of the *personal* entity the Lyon family, not the *business* entity Air & Sea Travel. We are focusing now solely on the business entity, and this event does not affect it. This transaction illustrates the application of the entity concept from Chapter 1.

TRANSACTION 9. In Transaction 5, Air & Sea Travel performed service for customers on account. The business now collects $1,000 from a customer. (We say that it *collects the cash on account*.) Air & Sea will record an increase in the asset Cash. It should not record an increase in service revenue because Air & Sea already recorded the revenue in Transaction 5, when it performed the service. The phrase "collect cash on account" means to record an increase in Cash and a decrease in the asset Accounts Receivable. The effect on the accounting equation is

	Assets					*Liabilities + Stockholders' Equity*		
	Cash	**+ Accounts Receivable**	**+ Office Supplies**	**+ Land**		**Accounts Payable**	**+ Common Stock**	**+ Retained Earnings**
Bal.	12,400	3,000	500	40,000	=	100	50,000	5,800
(9)	+ 1,000	−1,000						
Bal.	13,400	2,000	500	40,000		100	50,000	5,800
	55,900					55,900		

Total assets are unchanged from the preceding transaction's total. Why? Because Air & Sea Travel merely exchanged one asset for another.

TRANSACTION 10. Air & Sea Travel sells land for a price of $22,000, which is equal to the amount it paid for the land. Air & Sea receives $22,000 cash, and the effect on the accounting equation is

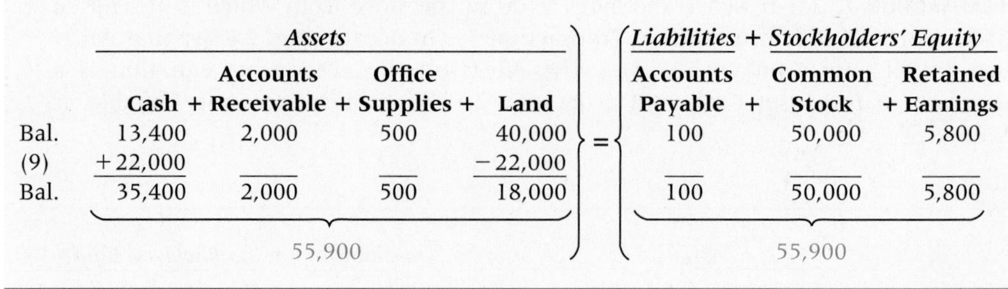

	Assets					Liabilities + Stockholders' Equity		
	Cash +	Accounts Receivable +	Office Supplies +	Land		Accounts Payable +	Common Stock	+ Retained Earnings
Bal.	13,400	2,000	500	40,000	=	100	50,000	5,800
(9)	+22,000			−22,000				
Bal.	35,400	2,000	500	18,000		100	50,000	5,800
	55,900					55,900		

Note that the company did not sell all its land; it still owns $18,000 worth of land.

Transaction 11. The corporation declares a dividend and pays Gary and Monica Lyon $2,100 cash for their personal use. The effect on the accounting equation of Air & Sea Travel is

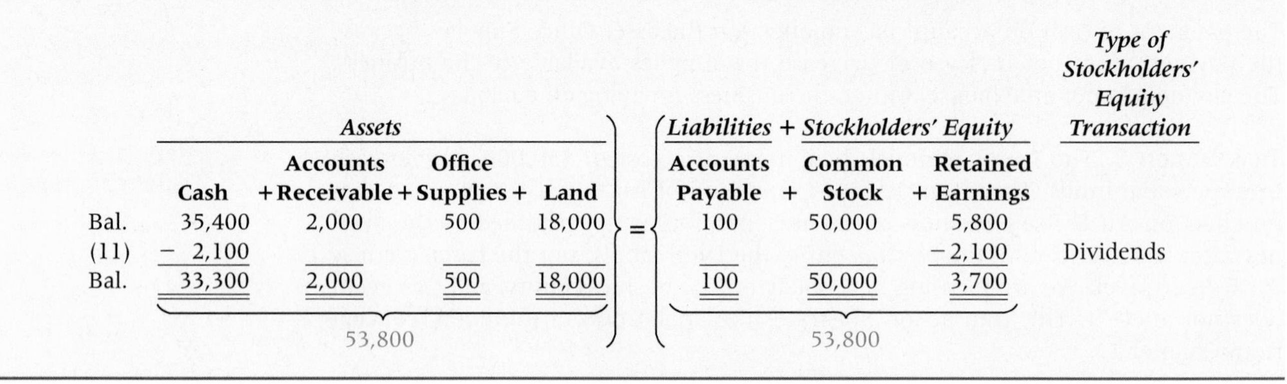

	Assets					Liabilities + Stockholders' Equity			*Type of Stockholders' Equity Transaction*
	Cash	+ Accounts Receivable	+ Office Supplies +	Land		Accounts Payable +	Common Stock	+ Retained Earnings	
Bal.	35,400	2,000	500	18,000	=	100	50,000	5,800	
(11)	− 2,100							−2,100	Dividends
Bal.	33,300	2,000	500	18,000		100	50,000	3,700	
	53,800					53,800			

The dividend decreases both the asset Cash and the retained earnings of the business. But dividends are not an expense.

Business Transactions and the Financial Statements

Exhibit 2-1 summarizes the 11 preceding transactions. Panel A summarizes the details of the transactions, and Panel B presents the financial analysis. As you study the exhibit, note that every transaction maintains the equality

ASSETS = LIABILITIES + STOCKHOLDERS' EQUITY

Exhibit 2-1 provides the data that Air & Sea Travel will use to create its financial statements:

- Data for the *statement of cash flows* are aligned under the Cash account. Cash receipts show up as increases in cash, and cash payments appear as decreases.
- *Income statement* data appear as revenues and expenses under Retained Earnings. The revenues increase retained earnings; the expenses decrease retained earnings.
- The *balance sheet* data are composed of the ending balances of the assets, liabilities, and stockholders' equities shown at the bottom of the exhibit. The accounting equation shows that total assets ($53,800) equal total liabilities plus stockholders' equity ($53,800).
- The *statement of retained earnings,* which shows net income (or net loss) and dividends, can be prepared from the income statement data.

Exhibit 2-1
Analysis of Air & Sea Travel, Inc., Transactions

PANEL A—Details of transactions

(1) Received $50,000 cash and issued stock to the owners who invested $50,000 cash in the business.
(2) Paid 40,000 cash for land.
(3) Bought $500 of office supplies on account.
(4) Received $5,500 cash from customers for service revenue earned.
(5) Performed services for customers on account, $3,000.
(6) Paid cash expenses: rent, $1,100; employee salary, $1,200; utilities, $400.
(7) Paid $400 on the account payable created in Transaction 3.
(8) Owners paid personal funds to remodel home. This is *not* a transaction of the business.
(9) Received $1,000 on the account receivable created in Transaction 5.
(10) Sold land for cash at its cost of $22,000.
(11) Declared and paid a dividend of $2,100 to the stockholders.

PANEL B—Analysis of transactions

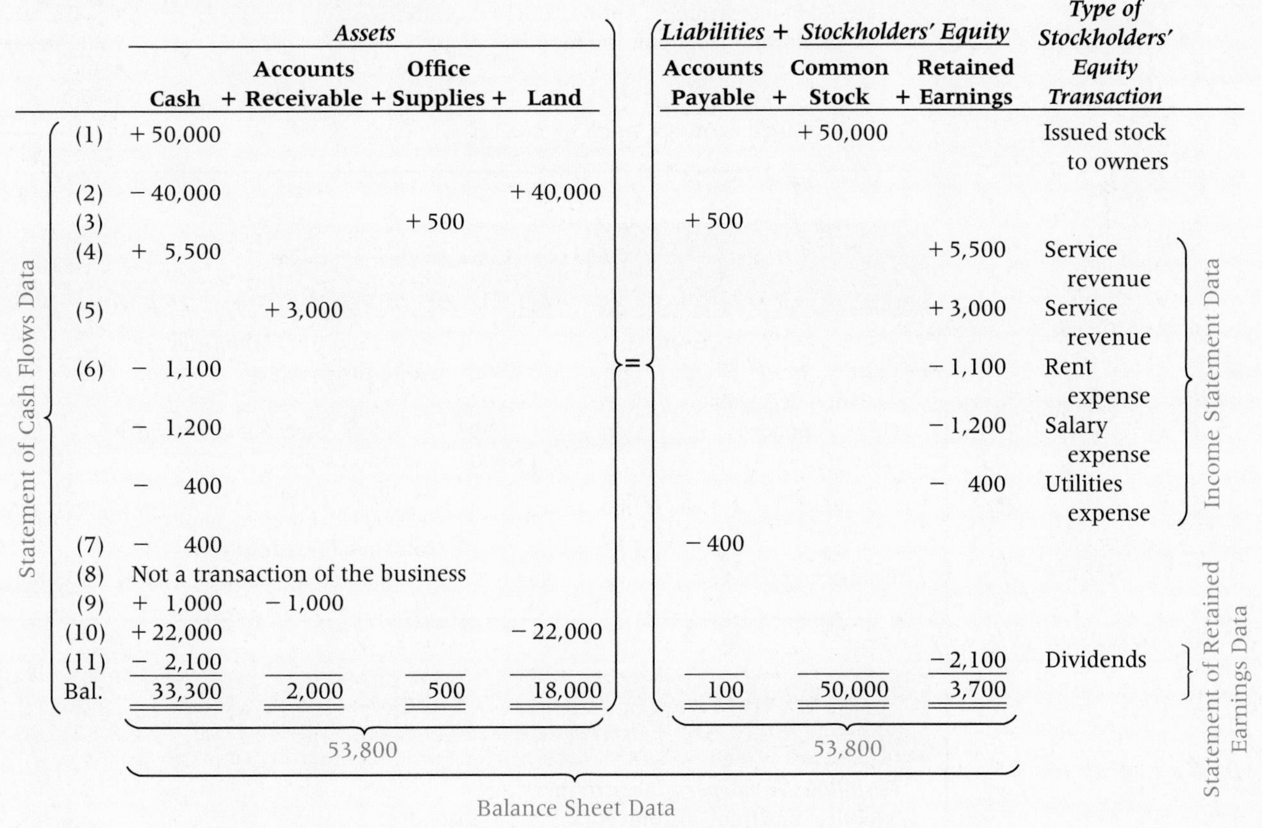

	Assets				*Liabilities* +	*Stockholders' Equity*		*Type of Stockholders' Equity Transaction*
	Cash +	Accounts Receivable +	Office Supplies +	Land	Accounts Payable +	Common Stock +	Retained Earnings	
(1)	+ 50,000					+ 50,000		Issued stock to owners
(2)	− 40,000			+ 40,000				
(3)			+ 500		+ 500			
(4)	+ 5,500						+ 5,500	Service revenue
(5)		+ 3,000					+ 3,000	Service revenue
(6)	− 1,100						− 1,100	Rent expense
	− 1,200						− 1,200	Salary expense
	− 400						− 400	Utilities expense
(7)	− 400				− 400			
(8)	Not a transaction of the business							
(9)	+ 1,000	− 1,000						
(10)	+ 22,000			− 22,000				
(11)	− 2,100						− 2,100	Dividends
Bal.	33,300	2,000	500	18,000	100	50,000	3,700	

Exhibit 2-2 shows Air & Sea Travel's financial statements at the end of April, the company's first month of operations. You will recognize the Air & Sea Travel statements from the solution to the summary problem at the end of Chapter 1. We repeat the financial statements here to reinforce your learning. Follow the flow of data to observe the following:

1. The income statement reports revenues, expenses, and either a net income or a net loss for the period. During April, Air & Sea earned net income of $5,800. Compare Air & Sea Travel's income statement to that of PepsiCo at the beginning of the chapter. Both income statements include only two categories of accounts: revenues and expenses.

(cont. on page 61)

Exhibit 2-2
Financial Statements of Air & Sea Travel, Inc.

AIR & SEA TRAVEL, INC.
Income Statement
Month Ended April 30, 20X1

Revenue:		
Service revenue ($5,500 + $3,000)		$8,500
Expenses:		
Salary expense	$1,200	
Rent expense	1,100	
Utilities expense	400	
Total expenses		2,700
Net income		$5,800 ①

AIR & SEA TRAVEL, INC.
Statement of Retained Earnings
Month Ended April 30, 20X1

Retained earnings, April 1, 20X1	$ 0
Add: Net income for the month	5,800 ①
	5,800
Less: Dividends	(2,100)
Retained earnings, April 30, 20X1	$3,700 ②

AIR & SEA TRAVEL, INC.
Balance Sheet
April 30, 20X1

Assets		***Liabilities***	
Cash ③	$33,300	Accounts payable	$ 100
Accounts receivable	2,000		
Office supplies	500	***Stockholders' Equity***	
Land	18,000	Common stock	50,000
		Retained earnings	3,700 ②
		Total stockholders' equity	53,700
		Total liabilities and	
Total assets	$53,800	stockholders' equity	$53,800

AIR & SEA TRAVEL, INC.
Statement of Cash Flows
Month Ended April 30, 20X1

Cash flows from operating activities:		
Collections from customers ($5,500 + $1,000)		$ 6,500
Payments to suppliers and employees ($2,700 + $400)		(3,100)
Net cash inflow from operating activities		3,400
Cash flows from investing activities:		
Acquisition of land	$ (40,000)	
Sale of land	22,000	
Net cash outflow from investing activities		(18,000)
Cash flows from financing activities:		
Issuance (sale) of stock	$ 50,000	
Payment of dividends	(2,100)	
Net cash inflow from financing activities		47,900
Net increase (decrease) in cash		$ 33,300
Cash balance, April 1, 20X1		0
Cash balance, April 30, 20X1 ③		$ 33,300

2. The statement of retained earnings starts with the beginning balance of retained earnings, which for a new business is zero. Add net income for the period (arrow ①), subtract dividends, and obtain the ending balance of retained earnings ($3,700).

3. The balance sheet lists the assets, liabilities, and stockholders' equity of the business at the end of the period. Included in stockholders' equity is retained earnings, which comes from the statement of retained earnings (arrow ②).

4. The statement of cash flows summarizes cash receipts and cash payments under three categories of activities: operating, investing, and financing. The result is an increase or a decrease in cash during the period. Add the beginning cash balance to the change in cash to compute the ending cash balance, which is reported on the balance sheet (arrow ③).

The transaction analysis that we've just examined can be used to prepare the financial statements. However, the kind of analysis in Exhibit 2-1 can become cumbersome for even the smallest of organizations. Consider **PepsiCo, Inc.,** with its hundreds of accounts and thousands of transactions. The spreadsheet to account for PepsiCo's transactions would be too large to use. For this reason, accountants use a different accounting system called *double-entry accounting* to create the financial statements. In the second half of this chapter we discuss double-entry accounting as it is used in business. But first, let's put into practice what you have learned thus far.

Mid-Chapter

Summary Problem for Your Review

Mike Cassell opens a research service near a college campus. He names the corporation Cassell Researchers, Inc. During the first month of operations, July 20X1, the business engages in the following transactions:

a. Mike Cassell invests $25,000 of personal funds, and the corporation issues its common stock to Cassell.
b. The company purchases on account office supplies costing $350.
c. Cassell Researchers pays cash of $20,000 to acquire a lot next to the campus. The company intends to use the land as a building site for a business office.
d. Cassell Researchers performs research for clients and receives cash of $1,900.
e. Cassell Researchers pays $100 on the account payable it created in Transaction b.
f. Mike Cassell pays $2,000 of personal funds for a vacation.
g. Cassell Researchers pays cash expenses for office rent ($400) and utilities ($100).
h. The business sells a small parcel of the land for its cost of $5,000.
i. The business declares and pays a cash dividend of $1,200.

Required

1. Analyze the preceding transactions in terms of their effects on the accounting equation of Cassell Researchers, Inc. Use Exhibit 2-1 as a guide.
2. Prepare the income statement, statement of retained earnings, balance sheet, and statement of cash flows of the business after recording the transactions. Draw arrows linking the statements.

Answers

Requirements 1 and 2

PANEL A—Details of Transactions

(a) Received $25,000 cash and issued common stock.
(b) Purchased $350 of office supplies on account.
(c) Paid $20,000 to acquire land as a building site.
(d) Earned service revenue and received cash of $1,900.
(e) Paid $100 on account.
(f) Paid for a personal vacation. This is not a transaction of the business.
(g) Paid cash expenses for rent ($400) and utilities ($100)
(h) Sold land for $5,000, its cost.
(i) Declared and paid cash dividends of $1,200.

PANEL B—Analysis of Transactions

	Assets				*Liabilities +*	*Stockholders' Equity*		*Type of Stockholders' Equity Transaction*
	Cash	**+ Office Supplies**	**+ Land**		**Accounts Payable**	**+ Common Stock**	**+ Retained Earnings**	
(a)	+25,000					+25,000		Issued stock to owner
(b)		+350			+350			
(c)	−20,000		+20,000					
(d)	+ 1,900						+ 1,900	Service revenue
(e)	− 100			=	− 100			
(f)	Not a transaction of the business							
(g)	− 400						− 400	Rent expense
	− 100						− 100	Utilities expense
(h)	+ 5,000		− 5,000					
(i)	− 1,200						− 1,200	Dividends
Bal.	10,100	350	15,000		250	25,000	200	
	25,450				25,450			

CASSELL RESEARCHERS, INC.
Income Statement
Month Ended July 31, 20X1

Revenue:		
Service revenue		$1,900
Expenses:		
Rent expense	$400	
Utilities expense	100	
Total expenses		500
Net income		$1,400

CASSELL RESEARCHERS, INC.
Statement of Retained Earnings
Month Ended July 31, 20X1

Retained earnings, July 1, 20X1	$ 0
Add: Net income for the month	1,400
	1,400
Less: Dividends	(1,200)
Retained earnings, July 31, 20X1	$ 200

CASSELL RESEARCHERS, INC.
Balance Sheet
July 31, 20X1

Assets		*Liabilities*	
Cash	$10,100	Accounts payable	$ 250
Office supplies	350		
Land	15,000	***Stockholders' Equity***	
		Common stock	25,000
		Retained earnings	200
		Total stockholders' equity	25,200
		Total liabilities and	
Total assets	$25,450	stockholders' equity	$25,450

CASSELL RESEARCHERS, INC.
Statement of Cash Flows
Month Ended July 31, 20X1

Cash flows from operating activities:		
Receipts:		
Collections from customers		$ 1,900
Payments:		
To suppliers ($100 + $400 + $100)		(600)
Net cash inflow from operating activities		1,300
Cash flows from investing activities:		
Acquisition of land	$(20,000)	
Sale of land	5,000	
Net cash outflow from investing activities		(15,000)
Cash flows from financing activities:		
Issuance (sale) of stock	$ 25,000	
Payment of dividends	(1,200)	
Net cash inflow from financing activities		23,800
Net increase in cash		$10,100
Cash balance, July 1, 20X1		0
Cash balance, July 31, 20X1		$10,100

DOUBLE-ENTRY ACCOUNTING

Objective 3
Understand how double-entry accounting works

Accounting is based on a **double-entry system,** which means that all business transactions have *dual effects: Each transaction affects at least two accounts.* For example, Air & Sea Travel's receipt of $50,000 from Gary and Monica Lyon and issuance of stock to them increased *both* the Cash *and* the Common Stock accounts of the business. It would be incomplete to record only the increase in the entity's cash without recording the increase in its stockholders' equity.

Consider a *cash purchase of supplies.* What are the dual effects of this transaction? The purchase (1) decreases cash and (2) increases supplies.

- A *purchase of supplies on credit* (1) increases supplies and (2) increases accounts payable.
- A *cash payment on account* (1) decreases cash and (2) decreases accounts payable. *All transactions have at least two effects on the entity.*

The T-Account

To record transactions, accountants often use *T-accounts.* The term gets its name from the capital letter *T.* The vertical line in the letter divides the account into its two sides: left and right. The account title rests on the horizontal line at the top of the T. For example, the Cash account of a business appears in the following T-account format:

CASH	
(Left side)	**(Right side)**
Debit	***Credit***

The left side of the account is called the *debit* side, and the right side is called the *credit* side. Often, beginners in the study of accounting are confused by the words *debit* and *credit*. To become comfortable using them, remember that

Debit = Left side

Credit = Right side

Even though *left side* and *right side* are more descriptive, the terms *debit* and *credit* are deeply entrenched in business.[1] *Every business transaction involves both a debit and a credit.*

Increases and Decreases in the Accounts

The type of account determines how we record increases and decreases in the account. For any given account, all increases are recorded on one side and all decreases on the other side.

- Increases in *assets* are recorded on the left (debit) side of the account. Decreases in assets are recorded on the right (credit) side.
- Conversely, increases in *liabilities* and *stockholders' equity* are recorded by *credits*. Decreases in liabilities and stockholders' equity are recorded by *debits*.

These are the *rules of debit and credit.*

In everyday conversation, we may praise someone by saying, "She deserves credit for her good work." As you study accounting, forget this general usage. Remember that in accounting

- *Debit means left side.*
- *Credit means right side.*

Whether an account is increased or decreased by a debit or credit depends on the type of account as shown in Exhibit 2-3.

EXHIBIT 2-3
Accounting Equation and the Rules of Debit and Credit

Accounting Equation:	Assets		=	Liabilities		+	Stockholders' Equity	
Rules of Debit and Credit:	Debit +	Credit −		Debit −	Credit +		Debit −	Credit +

In modern accounting systems, the computer interprets debits and credits as increases or decreases by account type. For example, a computer reads a debit to Cash as an increase to that account. But *debit* and *credit* are so deeply ingrained in accounting vocabulary that we use these terms even for computerized systems.

This pattern of recording debits and credits is based on the accounting equation:

ASSETS	=	LIABILITIES	+	STOCKHOLDERS' EQUITY
(DEBITS)		(CREDITS)		

[1]The words *debit* and *credit* have Latin origins (*debitum* and *creditum*). Pacioli, the Italian monk who wrote about accounting in the fifteenth century, used these terms.

Assets (debit-balance accounts) are on the opposite side of the equation from liabilities and stockholders' equity (credit-balance accounts). Therefore, increases and decreases in assets are recorded in the opposite manner from those in liabilities and stockholders' equity. And liabilities and stockholders' equity, which are on the same side of the equal sign, are treated in the same way. Exhibit 2-3 shows the relationship between the accounting equation and the rules of debit and credit.

To illustrate the ideas diagrammed in Exhibit 2-3, reconsider the first transaction in our earlier Air & Sea Travel illustration. Air & Sea received $50,000 cash and issued common stock to Gary and Monica Lyon. Which accounts of Air & Sea Travel are affected? By what amounts? On what side (debit or credit)? The answer is that both Assets and Common Stock increase by $50,000, as the following T-accounts show:

Assets		=	**Liabilities**	+	**Stockholders' Equity**	
CASH					COMMON STOCK	
Debit for Increase, 50,000						Credit for Increase, 50,000

Notice that Assets = Liabilities + Stockholders' Equity *and* that total debit amounts = total credit amounts.

The amount remaining in an account is called its *balance.* This first transaction gives Cash a $50,000 debit balance and Common Stock a $50,000 credit balance.

STOP & THINK

Can you prepare a balance sheet and an income statement for Air & Sea Travel at this point? What would the business's financial statements report?

Answer: You can prepare a balance sheet that would report Cash, an asset, of $50,000 and Common Stock, a stockholders' equity, of $50,000. You would not yet prepare an income statement because the business has experienced no revenues or expenses. For a review, return to the balance sheet that we prepared on page 55.

The second transaction in our Air & Sea Travel illustration is a $40,000 cash purchase of land. This transaction affects two assets: Cash and Land. It decreases (credits) Cash and increases (debits) Land, as shown in the T-accounts:

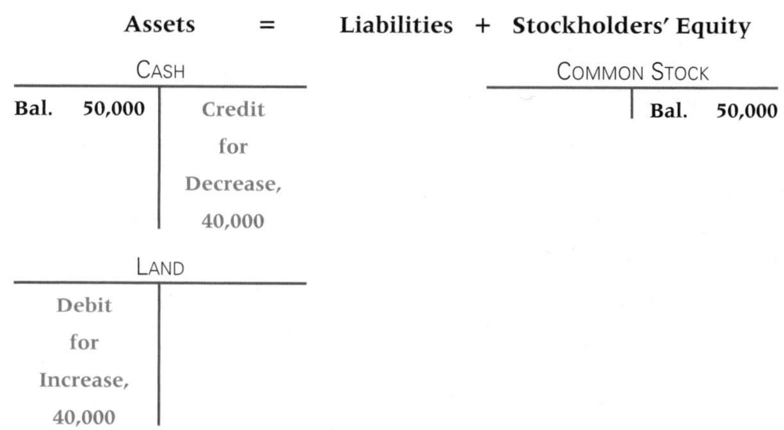

After this transaction, Cash has a $10,000 debit balance ($50,000 debit balance minus the $40,000 credit amount), Land has a debit balance of $40,000, and Common Stock has a $50,000 credit balance, as shown in Exhibit 2-4.

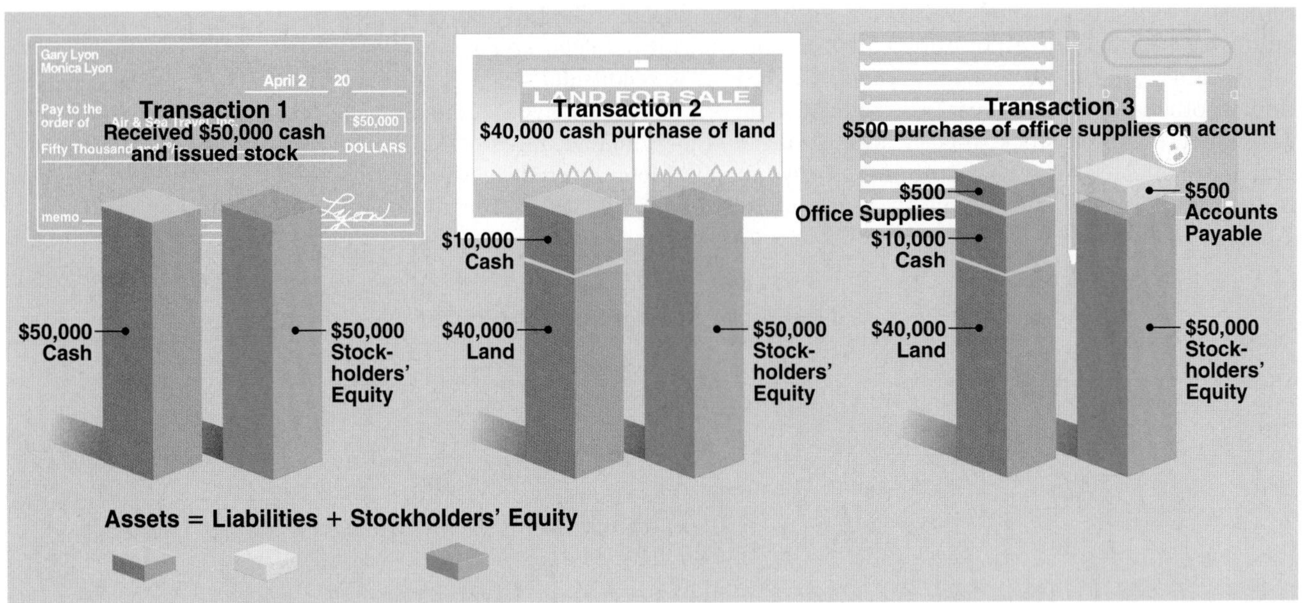

EXHIBIT 2-4
The Accounting Equation and the First Three Transactions of Air & Sea Travel, Inc.

Transaction 3 is a $500 purchase of office supplies on account. This transaction increases the asset Office Supplies and the liability Accounts Payable, as shown in the following T-accounts and in Exhibit 2-4:

Assets	=	**Liabilities**	+	**Stockholders' Equity**

CASH

Bal. **10,000**	

OFFICE SUPPLIES

Debit for Increase, 500	

LAND

Bal. **40,000**	

ACCOUNTS PAYABLE

	Credit for Increase, 500

COMMON STOCK

	Bal. **50,000**

Additional Stockholders' Equity Accounts: Revenues and Expenses

The stockholders' equity category includes the two types of income statement accounts, Revenues and Expenses:

- *Revenues* are increases in stockholders' equity that result from delivering goods or services to customers.
- *Expenses* are decreases in stockholders' equity due to the cost of operating the business.

Therefore, the accounting equation may be expanded as shown in Exhibit 2-5. Revenues and expenses appear in parentheses because their net effect—revenues minus expenses—equals net income, which increases stockholders' equity. If expenses are greater than revenues, there is a net loss, which decreases stockholders' equity.

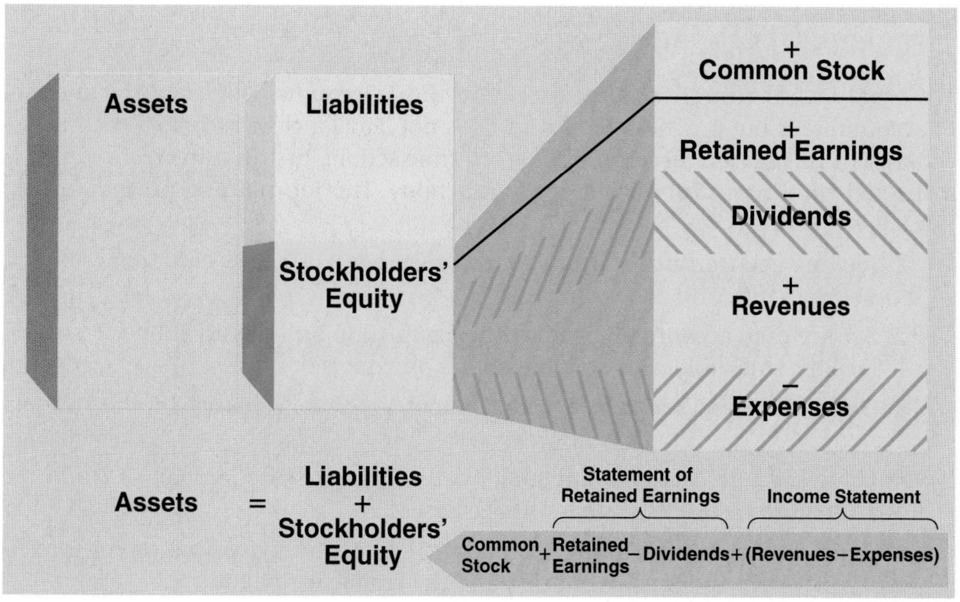

Exhibit 2-5
Expansion of the Accounting Equation

We can now express the rules of debit and credit in final form, as shown in Exhibit 2-6. **You should not proceed until you have learned the rules of debit and credit.** For example, you must remember that a debit increases an asset account and a credit records a decrease in an asset. Liabilities are the opposite. A credit increases a liability account and a debit decreases a liability. And so on for the other types of accounts.

Exhibit 2-6
Expanded Rules of Debit and Credit

Assets = Liabilities + Common Stock

Assets: Debit	Assets: Credit	Liabilities: Debit	Liabilities: Credit	Common Stock: Debit	Common Stock: Credit
Debit for Increase +	Credit for Decrease −	Debit for Decrease −	Credit for Increase +	Debit for Decrease −	Credit for Increase +

Account	Debit	Credit
Retained Earnings	Debit for Decrease −	Credit for Increase +
Dividends	Debit for Increase +	Credit for Decrease −
Revenues	Debit for Decrease −	Credit for Increase +
Expenses	Debit for Increase +	Credit for Decrease −

RECORDING TRANSACTIONS IN THE JOURNAL

Objective 4
Record business transactions

We could record all transactions directly in the T-accounts. However, this method of accounting is not practical because it does not leave a clear record of each transaction. For this reason, accountants record transactions first in a **journal,** which is a chronological record of an entity's transactions. The journalizing process follows five steps:

1. Identify the transaction from source documents, such as bank deposit slips, sales receipts, and check stubs.
2. Specify each account affected by the transaction and classify it by type (asset, liability, stockholders' equity, revenue, or expense).
3. Determine whether each account is increased or decreased by the transaction.
4. Using the rules of debit and credit, determine whether to debit or credit the account to record its increase or decrease.
5. Enter the transaction in the journal, including a brief explanation for the entry. The debit side is entered first and the credit side next.

Step 5, "Enter the transaction in the journal," means to record the transaction in the journal. This step is also called "making the journal entry" or "journalizing the transaction." Let's apply the five steps to journalize the first transaction of Air & Sea Travel, Inc.—receiving cash of $50,000 and issuing common stock.

STEP 1: The transaction is a cash receipt for the issuance of stock. The source documents are Air & Sea Travel's bank deposit slip and the stock certificate that the business issued to Gary and Monica Lyon.

STEP 2: Cash and Common Stock are the accounts affected by the transaction. Cash is an asset account and Common Stock a stockholders' equity account.

STEP 3: Both accounts, Cash and Common Stock, increase by $50,000.

STEP 4: Debit Cash to record an increase in this asset account. Credit Common Stock to record an increase in this stockholders' equity account.

STEP 5: The journal entry is

Date	*Accounts and Explanation*	*Debit*	*Credit*
Apr. 2[a]	Cash[b]	50,000[d]	
	Common Stock[c]		50,000[e]
	Issued common stock.[f]		

A complete journal entry includes

a. the date of the transaction
b. the title of the account debited (placed flush left)
c. the title of the account credited (indented slightly)

the dollar amounts of

d. the debit (left)
e. the credit (right)
f. a short explanation of the transaction (not indented).

Note that dollar signs are omitted in the money columns.

When analyzing a transaction, first pinpoint its effects (if any) on cash. Did cash increase or decrease? Next, find its effect on other accounts. Typically, it is easier to identify a transaction's cash effect than to identify its effects on other accounts.

In the introductory discussions that follow, we temporarily ignore the date of each transaction to focus on the accounts and their dollar amounts.

Copying Information (Posting) from the Journal to the Ledger

The journal is a chronological record of all company transactions listed by date of the transaction. But the journal does not indicate how much cash the business has to use. Another part of the accounting system, the ledger, gives the balance in each account. The **ledger** is a grouping of all the accounts with their balances. For example, the balance of the Cash account shows how much cash the business has. The balance of Accounts Receivable indicates the amount due from customers. The balance of Accounts Payable tells how much the business owes suppliers on open account, and so on.

In the phrase "keeping the books," *books* refers to the ledger. In most accounting systems, the ledger is computerized. Exhibit 2-7 shows how the asset, liability, and stockholders' equity accounts are grouped in the ledger.

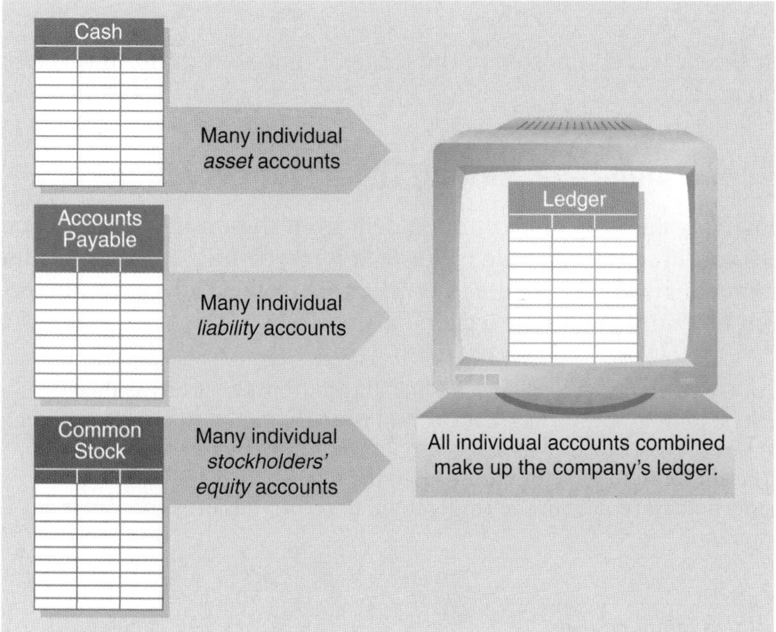

EXHIBIT 2-7
The Ledger (Asset, Liability, and Stockholders' Equity Accounts)

Entering transaction data in the journal does not place the data into the ledger. Data must be copied to the appropriate accounts in the ledger—a process called **posting.** Debits in the journal are posted as debits in the ledger, and credits in the journal as credits in the ledger. Exhibit 2-8 shows how the initial investment

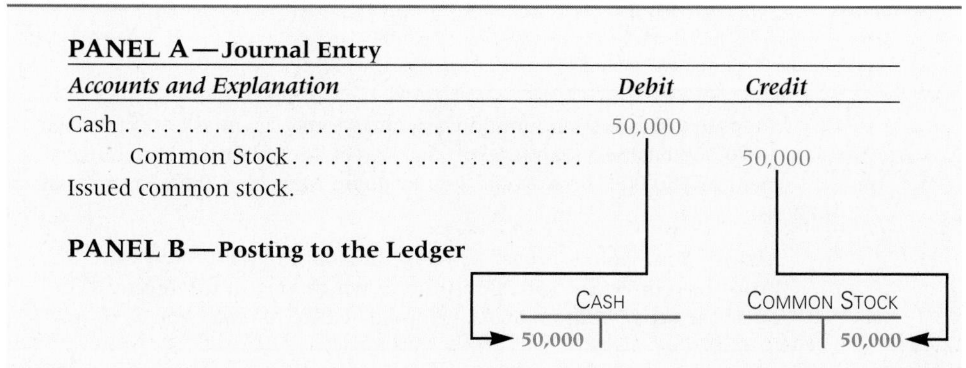

PANEL A—Journal Entry

Accounts and Explanation	*Debit*	*Credit*
Cash	50,000	
Common Stock		50,000
Issued common stock.		

PANEL B—Posting to the Ledger

CASH	
50,000	

COMMON STOCK	
	50,000

EXHIBIT 2-8
Journal Entry and Posting to the Ledger

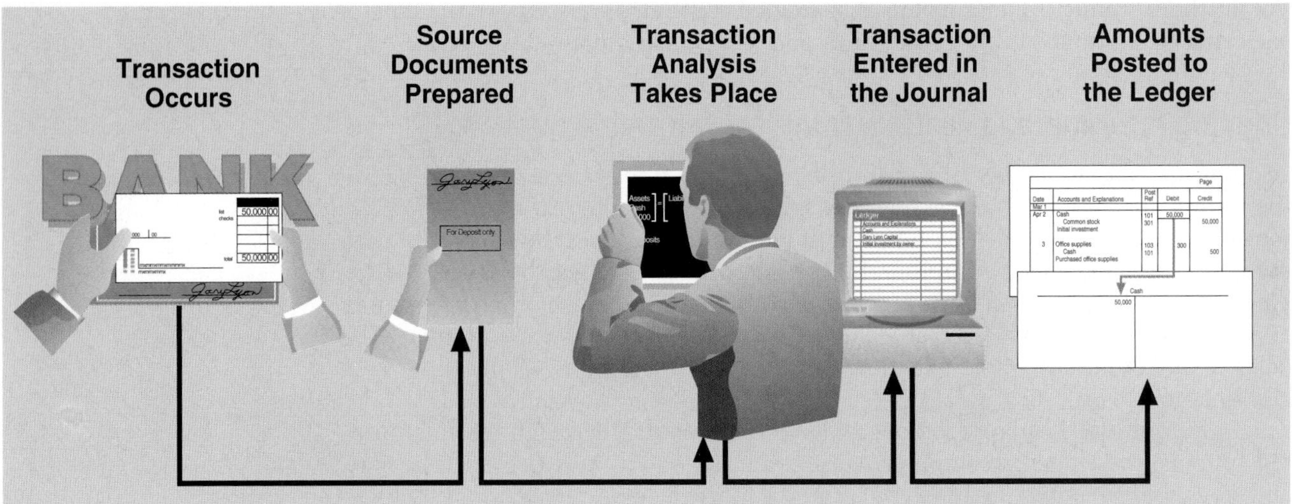

EXHIBIT 2-9
Flow of Accounting Data

transaction of Air & Sea Travel is posted to the ledger. Computers perform this task quickly and without error.

The Flow of Accounting Data: Putting Theory into Practice

Exhibit 2-9 summarizes the flow of accounting data from the business transaction to the ledger. Let's continue the example of Air & Sea Travel, Inc., and account for the same 11 transactions we illustrated earlier in terms of their effects on the accounting equation, the journal, and the ledger.

1. *Transaction analysis:* Air & Sea Travel, Inc., received $50,000 cash from the Lyons as their investment in the business and in turn issued common stock to them. Air & Sea Travel increased its asset cash; to record this increase, debit Cash. The corporation's issuance of stock to the owners increased the stockholders' equity of the corporation; to record this increase, credit Common Stock.

Journal entry:

	Debit	Credit
Cash	50,000	
Common Stock		50,000
Issued common stock.		

Accounting equation:	**Assets**	=	**Liabilities**	+	**Stockholders' Equity**
	50,000	=	***0***	+	***50,000***

Ledger accounts:

CASH	
(1) 50,000	

COMMON STOCK	
	(1) 50,000

Suppose you are a lender and Gary and Monica Lyon ask you to make a $10,000 business loan to Air & Sea Travel, Inc. After the initial investment of $50,000, how would you evaluate Air & Sea Travel as a credit risk?

Answer: You would probably view the loan request favorably. The Lyons have invested $50,000 of their own money in the business. Because the agency has no debts, it should be able to repay you.

2. *Transaction analysis:* The business paid $40,000 cash for land as a future office location. The purchase decreased cash; therefore, credit Cash. The purchase increased the entity's asset land; to record this increase, debit Land.

Journal entry:

Land	40,000	
Cash		40,000
Paid cash for land.		

Accounting equation:	**Assets**	=	**Liabilities**	+	**Stockholders' Equity**
	+40,000	=	*0*	+	*0*
	−40,000				

Ledger accounts:

CASH				LAND			
(1)	**50,000**	(2)	40,000	(2)	40,000		

3. *Transaction analysis:* The business purchased $500 office supplies on account payable. The credit purchase of office supplies increased this asset; to record this increase, debit Office Supplies. The purchase also increased the liability accounts payable; to record this, credit Accounts Payable.

Journal entry:

Office Supplies	500	
Accounts Payable		500
Purchased office supplies on account.		

Accounting equation:	**Assets**	=	**Liabilities**	+	**Stockholders' Equity**
	+500	=	*+500*	+	*0*

Ledger accounts:

OFFICE SUPPLIES				ACCOUNTS PAYABLE			
(3)	500					(3)	500

4. *Transaction analysis:* The business performed travel service for clients and received cash of $5,500. The transaction increased the business's cash, so debit Cash. Service revenue was increased. To record an increase in revenue, credit Service Revenue.

Journal entry:

Cash	5,500	
Service Revenue		5,500
Performed services for cash.		

Accounting equation:	**Assets**	=	**Liabilities**	+	**Stockholders' Equity**	+	**Revenues**
	+5,500	=	*0*	+		+	*5,500*

Ledger accounts:

CASH				SERVICE REVENUE			
(1)	**50,000**	**(2)**	**40,000**			(4)	5,500
(4)	5,500						

5. *Transaction analysis:* The business performed services for clients who did not pay immediately. Air & Sea Travel billed the clients for $3,000 on account. The transaction increased the asset accounts receivable; therefore, debit Accounts Receivable. Service revenue was also increased, so credit Service Revenue.

Journal entry:	Accounts Receivable	3,000	
	Service Revenue		3,000
	Performed services on account.		

Accounting equation:	Assets	=	Liabilities	+	Stockholders' Equity	+	Revenues
	+3,000	=	0	+		+	3,000

Ledger accounts:

ACCOUNTS RECEIVABLE			
(5)	3,000		

SERVICE REVENUE			
		(4)	**5,500**
		(5)	3,000

6. *Transaction analysis:* The business paid $2,700 for the following expenses: office rent, $1,100; employee salary, $1,200; and utilities, $400. The asset cash is decreased; therefore, credit Cash for the sum of the expense amounts. The following expenses are increased: Rent Expense, Salary Expense, and Utilities Expense. Debit each of these accounts.

Journal entry:	Rent Expense	1,100	
	Salary Expense	1,200	
	Utilities Expense	400	
	Cash		2,700
	Paid expenses.		

CHECK POINT 2-4

 CHECK POINT 2-5

 CHECK POINT 2-6

Accounting equation:	Assets	=	Liabilities	+	Stockholders' Equity	−	Expenses
	−2,700	=	0	+		−	2,700

Ledger accounts:

CASH			
(1)	**50,000**	**(2)**	**40,000**
(4)	**5,500**	(6)	2,700

RENT EXPENSE			
(6)	1,100		

SALARY EXPENSE			
(6)	1,200		

UTILITIES EXPENSE			
(6)	400		

7. *Transaction analysis:* The business paid $400 on the account payable created in Transaction 3. The payment decreased the asset cash; therefore, credit Cash. The payment also decreased the liability accounts payable; to record this decrease, debit Accounts Payable.

Journal entry:	Accounts Payable	400	
	Cash		400
	Paid cash on account.		

CHECK POINT 2-7

Accounting equation:	Assets	=	Liabilities	+	Stockholders' Equity
	−400	=	−400	+	0

Ledger accounts:

CASH			
(1)	**50,000**	**(2)**	**40,000**
(4)	**5,500**	**(6)**	**2,700**
		(7)	400

ACCOUNTS PAYABLE			
(7)	400	**(3)**	**500**

8. *Transaction:* The Lyons remodeled their personal residence. This is not a transaction of the travel agency, so the business makes no journal entry.

9. *Transaction analysis:* The business collected $1,000 cash on account from the clients in Transaction 5. The receipt of cash increased this asset; debit Cash. The asset accounts receivable decreased; therefore, credit Accounts Receivable.

Journal entry:

Cash	1,000	
Accounts Receivable		1,000
Collected cash on account.		

CHECK POINT 2-8

Accounting equation:	**Assets**	**=**	**Liabilities**	**+**	**Stockholders' Equity**
	+1,000	**=**	***0***	**+**	***0***
	−1,000				

Ledger accounts:

CASH				ACCOUNTS RECEIVABLE			
(1)	**50,000**	**(2)**	**40,000**	**(5)**	**3,000**	(9)	1,000
(4)	**5,500**	**(6)**	**2,700**				
(9)	1,000	**(7)**	**400**				

10. *Transaction analysis:* The business sold land for its cost of $22,000, receiving cash. The asset cash increased; debit Cash. The asset land decreased; credit Land.

Journal entry:

Cash	22,000	
Land.		22,000
Sold land.		

Accounting equation:	**Assets**	**=**	**Liabilities**	**+**	**Stockholders' Equity**
	+22,000	**=**	***0***	**+**	***0***
	−22,000				

Ledger accounts:

CASH				LAND			
(1)	**50,000**	**(2)**	**40,000**	**(2)**	**40,000**	(10)	22,000
(4)	**5,500**	**(6)**	**2,700**				
(9)	**1,000**	**(7)**	**400**				
(10)	22,000						

11. *Transaction analysis:* Air & Sea Travel, Inc., paid the Lyons cash dividends of $2,100. The dividends decreased the entity's cash; therefore, credit Cash. The transaction also decreased stockholders' equity and must be recorded by a debit to a stockholders' equity account. Decreases in a corporation's stockholders' equity that result from distributions to owners are debited to a separate stockholders' equity account entitled Dividends. Therefore, debit Dividends.

Journal entry:

Dividends	2,100	
Cash		2,100
Declared and paid dividends.		

Accounting equation:	**Assets**	**=**	**Liabilities**	**+**	**Stockholders' Equity**	**−**	**Dividends**
	−2,100	**=**	***0***	**+**		**−**	***2,100***

Ledger accounts:

CASH				DIVIDENDS			
(1)	**50,000**	**(2)**	**40,000**	(11)	2,100		
(4)	**5,500**	**(6)**	**2,700**				
(9)	**1,000**	**(7)**	**400**				
(10)	**22,000**	(11)	2,100				

Exhibit 2-10
Air & Sea Travel's Ledger Accounts after Posting

ASSETS = **LIABILITIES** + **STOCKHOLDERS' EQUITY**

ASSETS

Cash

	Debit		Credit
(1)	50,000	(2)	40,000
(4)	5,500	(6)	2,700
(9)	1,000	(7)	400
(10)	22,000	(11)	2,100
Bal.	33,300		

Accounts Receivable

	Debit		Credit
(5)	3,000	(9)	1,000
Bal.	2,000		

Office Supplies

	Debit		Credit
(3)	500		
Bal.	500		

Land

	Debit		Credit
(2)	40,000	(10)	22,000
Bal.	18,000		

LIABILITIES

Accounts Payable

	Debit		Credit
(7)	400	(3)	500
		Bal.	100

STOCKHOLDERS' EQUITY

Common Stock

	Debit		Credit
		(1)	50,000
		Bal.	50,000

Dividends

	Debit		Credit
(11)	2,100		
Bal.	2,100		

REVENUE

Service Revenue

	Debit		Credit
		(4)	5,500
		(5)	3,000
		Bal.	8,500

EXPENSES

Rent Expense

	Debit		Credit
(6)	1,100		
Bal.	1,100		

Salary Expense

	Debit		Credit
(6)	1,200		
Bal.	1,200		

Utilities Expense

	Debit		Credit
(6)	400		
Bal.	400		

Each journal entry posted to the ledger is keyed by date or by transaction number. In this way, any transaction can be traced from the journal to the ledger and, if need be, back to the journal. This linking allows you to locate efficiently any information you may need.

Accounts after Posting

Exhibit 2-10 shows how the ledger accounts look when the amounts of the preceding transactions have been posted. The exhibit groups the accounts under the accounting equation headings.

Each account has a balance, denoted as Bal. This amount is the difference between the account's total debits and its total credits. For example, the balance in the Cash account is the difference between the debits, \$78,500 (\$50,000 + \$5,500 + \$1,000 + \$22,000) and the credits, \$45,200 (\$40,000 + \$2,700 + \$400 + \$2,100). Thus, the cash balance is \$33,300. Because the balance amounts are not journal entries posted to the accounts, we set an account balance apart from the individual amounts by a horizontal rule that runs all the way across the account.

If the sum of an account's debits is greater than the sum of its credits, that account has a debit balance, as the Cash account does here. If the sum of its credits is greater, that account has a credit balance, as Accounts Payable does.

The Trial Balance

Objective 5
Prepare and use a trial balance

A **trial balance** is a list of all accounts with their balances—assets first, followed by liabilities and then stockholders' equity. It aids preparation of the financial statements by summarizing all the account balances. It also provides a check on accu-

EXHIBIT 2-11
Trial Balance

AIR & SEA TRAVEL, INC. Trial Balance April 30, 20X1		
	Balance	
Account Title	*Debit*	*Credit*
Cash	$33,300	
Accounts receivable	2,000	
Office supplies	500	
Land	18,000	
Accounts payable		$ 100
Common stock		50,000
Dividends	2,100	
Service revenue		8,500
Rent expense	1,100	
Salary expense	1,200	
Utilities expense	400	
Total	$58,600	$58,600

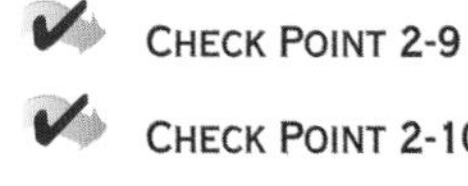
CHECK POINT 2-9
CHECK POINT 2-10

racy by showing whether total debits equal total credits. A trial balance may be taken at any time the postings are up-to-date, but the most common time is at the end of the period. Exhibit 2-11 is the trial balance of Air & Sea Travel, Inc., after its first 11 transactions have been journalized and posted.

Refer to the Air & Sea Travel trial balance in Exhibit 2-11. Suppose you are Monica Lyon, one of the owners. Your accountant is out of town, and the only accounting record available to you is the trial balance. You need a business loan, and your banker requests some information. Answer the following questions by developing the information from the trial balance:

1. How much are Air & Sea Travel's total assets?
2. Does the business already have any loans payable to other banks?
3. How much does the business owe in total?
4. How much equity do the owners have in the business—before considering revenues and expenses? Compute owners' equity by the accounting equation.
5. What was the business's net income or net loss for the month of April?

Answers:

1. $53,800 ($33,300 + $2,000 + $500 + $18,000)
2. No loans payable to other banks.
3. $100 for accounts payable.
4. $53,700 (Assets of $53,800 − Liabilities of $100)
5. Net income was $5,800 [Revenues of $8,500 − Expenses of $2,700 ($1,100 + $1,200 + $400)].

Correcting Accounting Errors

The term *trial balance* is appropriate. The list is prepared to *test* the accounts' balances by showing whether total debits equal total credits. If they are not equal, then accounting errors exist. Most computerized accounting systems prohibit the recording of unbalanced journal entries. Using computers, journal amounts are posted exactly as they have been journalized, and trial balances will always balance. Thus, computers minimize accounting errors. But they cannot *eliminate* errors, because human operators might input incorrect amounts.

You can detect the reasons(s) behind many out-of-balance conditions by computing the difference between total debits and total credits on the trial balance. Then perform one or more of the following actions:

1. Search the trial balance for a missing account. Trace each account and its balance from the ledger to the trial balance.
2. Search the journal for the amount of the difference between total debits and total credits. For example, suppose the total credits on the trial balance equal $58,600 and total debits are $58,400. A $200 transaction may have been recorded incorrectly in the journal or posted incorrectly to the ledger. Search the journal for a $200 transaction.
3. Divide the difference between total debits and total credits by 2. A debit treated as a credit, or vice versa, doubles the amount of error. Suppose Air & Sea Travel debited $300 to Cash instead of crediting the Cash account, or assume the accountant posted a $300 credit as a debit. Total debits contain the $300, and total credits omit the $300. The out-of-balance amount is $600, and dividing by 2 identifies the $300 amount of the transaction. Then search the journal for the $300 transaction and trace to the account affected.
4. Divide the out-of-balance amount by 9. If the result is evenly divisible by 9, the error may be a *slide* (example: writing $61 as $610) or a *transposition* (example: treating $61 as $16). Suppose Air & Sea Travel listed the $2,100 Dividends balance as $21,000 on the trial balance—a slide-type error. Total debits would differ from total credits by $18,900 ($21,000 − $2,100 = $18,900). Dividing $18,900 by 9 yields $2,100, the correct amount of the dividends. Trace this amount through the journal and then to the account affected.

CHECK POINT 2-11

Chart of Accounts

As you know, the ledger contains the business's accounts grouped under these headings:

1. **Balance sheet accounts: Assets, Liabilities, and Stockholders' Equity**
2. **Income statement accounts: Revenues and Expenses**

To keep track of accounts, organizations have a **chart of accounts,** which lists all accounts and account numbers. Account numbers usually have two or more digits. Assets are often numbered beginning with 1, liabilities with 2, stockholders' equity with 3, revenues with 4, and expenses with 5. The second, third, and higher digits in an account number indicate the position of the individual account within the category. For example, Cash may be account number 101, which is the first asset account. Accounts Payable may be number 201, the first liability account. All accounts are numbered by this system.

Organizations with many accounts use lengthy account numbers. For example, the chart of accounts of **Yankelovich-Clancy-Shulman,** a leading marketing research firm, uses five-digit account numbers. The chart of accounts for Air & Sea Travel, Inc., appears in Exhibit 2-12. Notice the gap between the account numbers 111 and 141. The Lyons realize that at some later date the business may need to add another category of receivables—for example, Notes Receivable, which may be numbered 121.

The appendix to this chapter gives two expanded charts of accounts that you will find helpful as you work through this course. The first chart lists the typical accounts that a large service corporation, such as Air & Sea Travel, would have after a period of growth. The second chart is for a merchandising corporation, one that sells a product rather than a service. Study the service corporation chart of accounts now and refer to the second chart of accounts later as needed.

EXHIBIT 2-12
Chart of Accounts—Air & Sea Travel, Inc.

BALANCE SHEET ACCOUNTS:

Assets	*Liabilities*	*Stockholders' Equity*
101 Cash	201 Accounts Payable	301 Common Stock
111 Accounts Receivable	231 Notes Payable	311 Dividends
141 Office Supplies		312 Retained Earnings
151 Office Furniture		
191 Land		

INCOME STATEMENT ACCOUNTS (PART OF STOCKHOLDERS' EQUITY):

Revenues	*Expenses*
401 Service Revenue	501 Rent Expense
	502 Salary Expense
	503 Utilities Expense

The Normal Balance of an Account

An account's *normal balance* is on the side of the account—debit or credit—where increases are recorded. That is, the normal balance is on the side that is positive. For example, because Cash and other assets usually have a debit balance (the debit side is positive and the credit side negative), the normal balance of assets is on the debit side. Assets are called *debit-balance accounts.* Conversely, because liabilities and stockholders' equity usually have a credit balance, their normal balances are on the credit side. They are called *credit-balance accounts.* Exhibit 2-13 illustrates the normal balances of all the assets, liabilities, and stockholders' equities, including revenues and expenses.

An account that normally has a debit balance may occasionally have a credit balance, which indicates a negative amount of the item. For example, Cash will have a temporary credit balance if the entity overdraws its bank account. Similarly, the liability Accounts Payable—normally a credit-balance account—will have a debit balance if the entity overpays its account. In other instances, the shift of a balance amount away from its normal balance indicates an accounting error. For example, a credit balance in Office Supplies, Office Furniture, or Buildings indicates an error because negative amounts of these assets do not exist.

As explained earlier, stockholders' equity usually contains several accounts. In total, these accounts show a normal credit balance for the stockholders' equity of the business. Each stockholders' equity account has a normal credit balance if it represents an *increase* in stockholders' equity (for example, the Common Stock account in Exhibit 2-13). However, if the individual stockholders' equity account represents a *decrease* in stockholders' equity, the account will have a normal debit balance (for example, the Dividends account in Exhibit 2-13).

 CHECK POINT 2-12

EXHIBIT 2-13
Normal Balances of the Accounts

Assets	Debit	
Liabilities		Credit
Stockholders' Equity—overall		Credit
Common stock		Credit
Retained earnings		Credit
Dividends	Debit	
Revenues		Credit
Expenses	Debit	

Four-Column Account Format

The ledger accounts illustrated thus far have been in a two-column T-account format, with the debit column on the left and the credit column on the right. The T-account clearly distinguishes debits from credits and is often used for illustrative purposes that do not require much detail.

Another standard format has four *amount* columns, as illustrated for the Cash account in Exhibit 2-14. The first pair of *amount* columns are for the debit and credit amounts posted from journal entries. The second pair of amount columns are for the account's balance. This four-column format keeps a running balance in the two rightmost columns of the account. For this reason, the four-column format is used more often than the two-column format. In Exhibit 2-14, Cash has a debit balance of $50,000 after Air & Sea's first transaction and a debit balance of $10,000 after its second transaction is posted. The "J.1" in the Journal Reference column indicates that the posted amount came from journal page 1.

Exhibit 2-14
Account in Four-Column Format

Account: **Cash** — Account No. 101

Date	Item	*Jrnl. Ref.*	*Debit*	*Credit*	*Balance*	
					Debit	*Credit*
20X1						
Apr. 2		J.1	50,000		50,000	
3		J.1		40,000	10,000	

This chapter has covered a lot of material on the processing of accounting information. The Decision Guidelines feature on page 79, "Analyzing and Recording Transactions," should help you focus on the essential elements covered in the chapter. The guidelines start with the most fundamental consideration in accounting: Has a transaction occurred? As you work through the guidelines, don't lose sight of your goal. The final guideline zeroes in on the financial statements, which are the focal points of the accounting process.

The statements are where the fun begins—the place people go for information to make decisions. As we proceed through this book, we will emphasize the use of the information for decision making. The more accounting you learn, the better equipped you will be to make decisions in your organization.

Quick Decision Making

Objective 6
Analyze transactions for quick decisions

Business people must often make quick decisions without the benefit of a complete accounting system. For example, the managers of **PepsiCo** may consider buying equipment. The equipment costs $100,000, and PepsiCo will borrow the money. To see how the borrowing and purchase of the equipment will affect Pepsi's financial position, the manager need not journalize the transactions and post to a ledger. For quick decision making he can analyze the effects of the transactions by going directly to T-accounts as follows (transaction amounts in color):

Transaction 1—Borrow $100,000 — T-accounts:

Cash		Note Payable	
100,000			100,000

Transaction 2—Purchase equipment — T-accounts:

Cash		Equipment		Note Payable	
100,000	100,000	100,000			**100,000**

This informal analysis shows immediately that PepsiCo's business will add $100,000 of equipment and a $100,000 note payable to its financial position. Assuming PepsiCo began with zero balances, the equipment and note payable transactions would result in the following balance sheet (date assumed for illustration only).

PEPSICO, INC.
Balance Sheet
September 12, 20X1

Assets		*Liabilities*	
Cash	$ 0	Note payable	$100,000
Equipment	100,000	Total liabilities	100,000
		Stockholders' Equity	0
Total assets	$100,000	Total liabilities and stockholders' equity	$100,000

✔ CHECK POINT 2-13

Companies do not actually keep their records in this shortcut fashion. But a decision maker who needs information immediately need not perform all the accounting steps to analyze the effect of transactions on the company's financial statements.

DECISION GUIDELINES

Analyzing and Recording Transactions

Decision	Guidelines
Has a transaction occurred?	If the event affects the entity's financial position and can be reliably recorded—*Yes* If either condition is absent—*No*
Where to record the transaction?	In the *journal*, the chronological record of transactions
What to record for each transaction?	Increases and/or decreases in all the accounts affected by the transaction
How to record an increase/decrease in the following accounts?	Rules of *debit* and *credit*:

	Increase	*Decrease*
Asset	Debit	Credit
Liability	Credit	Debit
Stockholders' equity	Credit	Debit
Revenue	Credit	Debit
Expense	Debit	Credit

Decision	Guidelines
Where to store all the information for each account?	In the *ledger*, the book of accounts and their balances
Where to list all the accounts and their balances?	In the *trial balance*
Where to report the Results of operations?	In the *income statement* (revenues − expenses = net income or net loss)
Financial position?	In the *balance sheet* (assets = liabilities + stockholders' equity)

END-OF-CHAPTER

End-of-Chapter

SUMMARY PROBLEM FOR YOUR REVIEW

The trial balance of Calderon Computer Service Center, Inc., on March 1, 20X2, lists the entity's assets, liabilities, and stockholders' equity on that date.

Account Title	*Balance*	
	Debit	*Credit*
Cash	$26,000	
Accounts receivable	4,500	
Accounts payable		$ 2,000
Common stock		10,000
Retained earnings		18,500
Total	$30,500	$30,500

During March, the business completed the following transactions:

a. Borrowed $45,000 from the bank. Calderon signed a note payable in the name of the business.
b. Paid cash of $40,000 to a real estate company to acquire land.
c. Performed service for a customer and received cash of $5,000.
d. Purchased supplies on credit, $300.
e. Performed customer service and earned revenue on account, $2,600.
f. Paid $1,200 on account.
g. Paid the following cash expenses: salaries, $3,000; rent, $1,500; and interest, $400.
h. Received $3,100 on account.
i. Received a $200 utility bill that will be paid next week.
j. Paid dividend of $1,800.

Required

1. Open the following accounts, with the balances indicated, in the ledger of Calderon Computer Service Center, Inc. Use the T-account format.
   - Assets—Cash, $26,000; Accounts Receivable, $4,500; Supplies, no balance; Land, no balance
   - Liabilities—Accounts Payable, $2,000; Note Payable, no balance
   - Stockholders' Equity—Common Stock, $10,000; Retained Earnings, $18,500; Dividends, no balance
   - Revenues—Service Revenue, no balance
   - Expenses—(none have balances) Salary Expense, Rent Expense, Interest Expense, Utilities Expense
2. Journalize the preceding transactions. Key journal entries by transaction letter.
3. Post to the ledger and show the balance in each account after all the transactions have been posted.
4. Prepare the trial balance of Calderon Computer Service Center, Inc., at March 31, 20X2.
5. To determine the net income or net loss of the entity during the month of March, prepare the income statement for the month ended March 31, 20X2. List expenses in order from the largest to the smallest.
6. Suppose the organizers of Calderon Computer Service Center ask you to invest $5,000 in the company's stock. Cite specifics from the income statement and the trial balance to support your decision.

Answers

Requirement 1

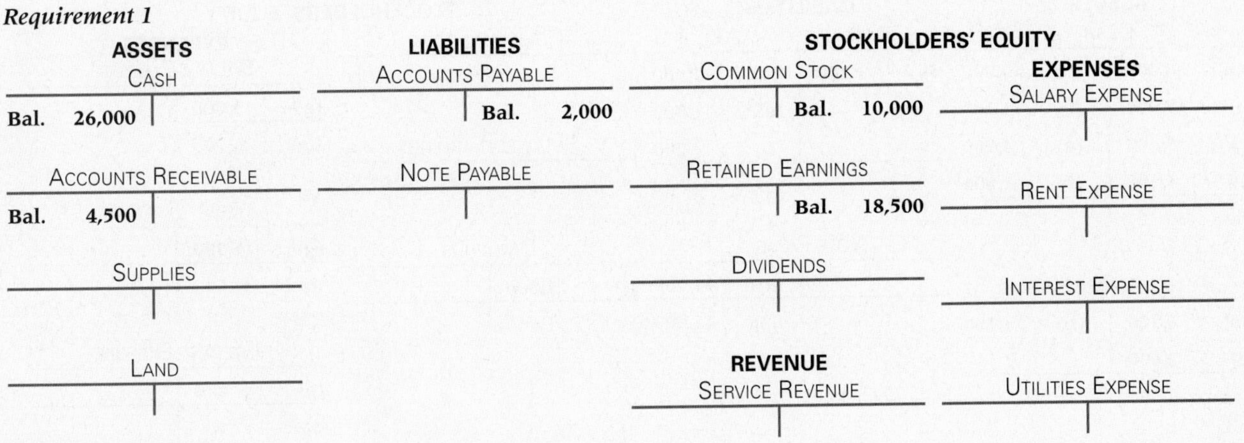

Requirement 2

Accounts and Explanation	*Debit*	*Credit*
a. Cash	45,000	
Note Payable		45,000
Borrowed cash on note payable.		
b. Land	40,000	
Cash		40,000
Purchased land for cash.		
c. Cash	5,000	
Service Revenue		5,000
Performed service and received cash.		
d. Supplies	300	
Accounts Payable		300
Purchased supplies on account.		
e. Accounts Receivable	2,600	
Service Revenue		2,600
Performed service on account.		
f. Accounts Payable	1,200	
Cash		1,200
Paid on account.		
g. Salary Expense	3,000	
Rent Expense	1,500	
Interest Expense	400	
Cash		4,900
Paid cash expenses.		
h. Cash	3,100	
Accounts Receivable		3,100
Received on account.		
i. Utilities Expense	200	
Accounts Payable		200
Received utility bill.		
j. Dividends	1,800	
Cash		1,800
Declared and paid dividends.		

Requirement 3

ASSETS

CASH

	Debit		Credit
Bal.	**26,000**	**(b)**	**40,000**
(a)	45,000	(f)	1,200
(c)	5,000	(g)	4,900
(h)	3,100	(j)	1,800
Bal.	31,200		

ACCOUNTS RECEIVABLE

	Debit		Credit
Bal.	**4,500**	**(h)**	**3,100**
(e)	2,600		
Bal.	4,000		

SUPPLIES

	Debit		Credit
(d)	300		
Bal.	300		

LAND

	Debit		Credit
(b)	40,000		
Bal.	40,000		

LIABILITIES

ACCOUNTS PAYABLE

	Debit		Credit
(f)	1,200	**Bal.**	**2,000**
		(d)	300
		(i)	200
		Bal.	1,300

NOTE PAYABLE

	Debit		Credit
		(a)	45,000
		Bal.	45,000

STOCKHOLDERS' EQUITY

COMMON STOCK

	Debit		Credit
		Bal.	10,000

RETAINED EARNINGS

	Debit		Credit
		Bal.	18,500

DIVIDENDS

	Debit		Credit
(j)	1,800		
Bal.	1,800		

REVENUE

SERVICE REVENUE

	Debit		Credit
		(c)	5,000
		(e)	2,600
		Bal.	7,600

EXPENSES

SALARY EXPENSE

	Debit		Credit
(g)	3,000		
Bal.	3,000		

RENT EXPENSE

	Debit		Credit
(g)	1,500		
Bal.	1,500		

INTEREST EXPENSE

	Debit		Credit
(g)	400		
Bal.	400		

UTILITIES EXPENSE

	Debit		Credit
(i)	200		
Bal.	200		

Requirement 4

CALDERON COMPUTER SERVICE CENTER, INC.
Trial Balance
March 31, 20X2

Account Title	*Balance* Debit	*Balance* Credit
Cash	$31,200	
Accounts receivable	4,000	
Supplies	300	
Land	40,000	
Accounts payable		$ 1,300
Note payable		45,000
Common stock		10,000
Retained earnings		18,500
Dividends	1,800	
Service revenue		7,600
Salary expense	3,000	
Rent expense	1,500	
Interest expense	400	
Utilities expense	200	
Total	$82,400	$82,400

Requirement 5

CALDERON COMPUTER SERVICE CENTER, INC. Income Statement Month Ended March 31, 20X2		
Revenue:		
Service revenue		$7,600
Expenses:		
Salary expense	$3,000	
Rent expense	1,500	
Interest expense	400	
Utilities expense	200	
Total expenses		5,100
Net income		$2,500

Requirement 6

A $5,000 investment in Calderon appears to be warranted because

a. The company earned net income of $2,500 on revenues of $7,600, so the business appears profitable.

b. Total assets of $75,500 ($31,200 + $4,000 + $300 + $40,000) far exceed total liabilities of $46,300 ($45,000 + $1,300), which suggests that Calderon can pay its debts and remain in business.

c. The stockholders have at least $10,000 of their own money invested in the business, as indicated by the balance of Common Stock. An investor can take comfort in the fact that the organizers are willing to risk their own money in the business.

d. Calderon is paying a dividend, so an investment in the stock may yield a quick return in the form of dividends.

SUMMARY OF LEARNING OBJECTIVES

1. ***Use key accounting terms.*** An *account* is the detailed record of the changes that have occurred in a particular asset, liability, or stockholders' equity during a period. *Assets* are the economic resources that benefit the business and will continue to do so in the future. *Liabilities* are debts payable to outsiders. *Stockholders' equity* (sometimes called *shareholders' equity* or simply *owners' equity*) are the owners' claims to the assets of a corporation. *Revenues* are increases in stockholders' equity created by delivering goods or services to customers. *Expenses* are the costs of doing business that decrease stockholders' equity.

2. ***Analyze business transactions.*** A *transaction* is any event that both affects the financial position of the business entity and can be reliably recorded. Analyzing business transactions involves determining each transaction's effects on the accounting equation: assets = liabilities + stockholders' equity. The summary of all the business's transactions over a period forms the basis for its financial statements.

3. ***Understand how double-entry accounting works.*** *Double-entry accounting* is an accounting system that uses debits and credits to record the dual effects of each business transaction. Every transaction involves both a debit and a credit, and the total amount debited must equal the total amount credited for each transaction. *Debits* are simply the left side of an account; *credits* are the right side of an account. Assets and expenses are increased by debits and decreased by credits. Liabilities, stockholders' equity, and revenues are increased by credits and decreased by debits.

4. ***Record business transactions.*** Accountants first record business transactions in a *journal,* a chronological record of the entity's transactions. Each journal entry includes a date, the titles of the accounts debited and credited, the dollar amounts debited and credited, and a short explanation of the transaction. This information is then *posted* (copied) to the *ledger,* a grouping of all the individual accounts and their balances. The balance of each account in the ledger may be taken after all posting is done.

5. ***Prepare and use a trial balance.*** A *trial balance* is a list of all accounts with their balances—assets first, followed by liabilities, stockholders' equity, revenues, and expenses. It provides an accuracy check by showing whether or not total debits equal total credits. If total debits do not equal total credits, an accounting error has occurred somewhere in journalizing or posting.

6. ***Analyze transactions for quick decisions.*** Decision makers must often make decisions without a complete accounting system. With some basic accounting knowledge, you can analyze certain situations by going directly to the ledger, thus compressing transaction analysis, journalizing, and posting into one step.

Accounting Vocabulary

account (p. 52).
accrued liability (p. 53).
cash (p. 52).
chart of accounts (p. 76).
credit (p. 64).
debit (p. 64).
double-entry system (p. 63).
journal (p. 68).
ledger (p. 69).
posting (p. 69).
prepaid expense (p. 52).
transaction (p. 54).
trial balance (p. 74).

Questions

1. Name the basic summary device of accounting. Name its two sides.

2. Is the following statement true or false? "Debit means decrease and credit means increase." Explain your answer.

3. What are the three basic types of accounts? Name two additional types of accounts. To which one of the three basic types are these two additional types of accounts most closely related?

4. What role do transactions play in accounting?

5. Briefly describe the flow of accounting information from the business transaction to the ledger.

6. Label each of the following transactions as increasing stockholders' equity (+), decreasing stockholders' equity (−), or having no effect on stockholders' equity (0). Write the appropriate symbol in the space provided.

___ a. Issuance of stock
___ b. Revenue transaction
___ c. Purchase of supplies on credit
___ d. Expense transaction
___ e. Cash payment on account
___ f. Dividends
___ g. Borrowing money on a note payable
___ h. Sale of service on account

7. Rearrange the following accounts in their logical sequence in the ledger:

Notes Payable	Cash
Accounts Receivable	Common Stock
Sales Revenue	Salary Expense

8. What is the meaning of the following statement? "Accounts Payable has a credit balance of $1,700."

9. Jack Brown Campus Cleaners launders the shirts of customer Bobby Baylor, who has a charge account at the cleaners. When Bobby picks up his clothes and is short of cash, he asks Jack Brown if he can pay later in the month. Bobby receives his monthly statement from the cleaners, writes a check on Dear Old Dad's bank account, and mails the check to Jack Brown. Identify the two business transactions described here. Which transaction increases Jack Brown's stockholders' equity? Which transaction increases cash?

10. Why do accountants prepare a trial balance?

11. To what does the normal balance of an account refer?

12. Indicate the normal balance of the five types of accounts.

Account Type	Normal Balance
Assets	________
Liabilities	________
Stockholders' equity	________
Revenues	________
Expenses	________

13. The accountant for Bower Construction Company mistakenly recorded a $500 purchase of supplies on account as a $5,000 purchase. He debited Supplies and credited Accounts Payable for $5,000. Does this error cause the trial balance to be out of balance? Explain your answer.

14. What is the effect on total assets of collecting cash on account from customers?

15. What is the advantage of analyzing transactions without the use of a journal? Describe how this "journalless" analysis works.

Check Points

Using key terms (Obj. 1)

CP2-1 There are three broad categories of accounts: assets, liabilities, and owners' equity.

1. Give a short (one- or two-word) synonym for an asset and a liability. Then list several individual assets and several specific liabilities.

2. Identify two categories of transactions that increase owners' equity. Name two categories of transactions that decrease owners' equity.

CP2-2 Ann Oliphant opened an architectural firm that immediately paid $15,000 for equipment. Was Oliphant's payment an expense of the business? If not, what did Oliphant acquire?

Explaining an asset versus an expense (Obj. 1)

CP2-3 Review transactions 4, 5, and 6 of Air & Sea Travel on page 56. Suppose Air & Sea Travel is applying for a business loan, and the bank requires the following financial information (after transaction 6 is completed):

Analyzing the effects of transactions (Obj. 2)

a. How much cash does the business have?

b. How much cash does the business hope to collect from clients?

c. How much in total assets does the business have?

d. How much does Air & Sea Travel owe?

e. Thus far, how much net income has the business earned?

Answer these questions.

CP2-4 Antonio Sevilla, M.D., opened a medical practice in Tucson, Arizona. The business completed the following transactions:

Analyzing transactions (Obj. 2)

June 1	Sevilla invested $64,000 cash to start his medical practice. The business issued stock to Sevilla.
1	Purchased medical supplies on account, $9,000.
2	Paid monthly office rent of $4,000.
3	Recorded $5,000 revenue for service rendered to patients. Received cash of $2,000 and sent bills to patients for the remainder.

After these transactions, how much cash and how much in accounts receivable does the business have to work with? Use T-accounts to show your answer.

CP2-5 Refer to Check Point 2-4. Which of the above transactions of Antonio Sevilla, M.D., increased the total assets of the business? Which transaction decreased total assets? For each transaction, identify the asset that was increased or decreased.

Analyzing transactions (Obj. 2)

CP2-6 After operating for several months, attorney Monica Peres completed the following transactions during the latter part of October:

Recording transactions (Obj. 3, 4)

Oct. 15	Borrowed $35,000 from the bank, signing a note payable.
22	Performed service for clients on account, $4,000.
30	Received cash on account from clients, $1,000.
31	Received a utility bill, $200, which will be paid during November.
31	Paid monthly salary to assistant, $3,000.
31	Paid interest expense of $300 on the bank loan.

Journalize the transactions of Monica Peres, Attorney. Include an explanation with each journal entry.

CP2-7 Architect Lisa Khoury purchased supplies on account for $2,000. Two weeks later, Khoury paid $1,500 on account.

Journalizing transactions; posting (Obj. 3, 4)

1. Journalize the two transactions on the books of Lisa Khoury, Architect. Include an explanation for each transaction.
2. Open a T-account for Accounts Payable and post to Accounts Payable. Compute the balance and denote it as Bal.
3. How much does Khoury's business owe after both transactions? In which account does this amount appear?

CP2-8 Grant Tobias performed legal service for a client who could not pay immediately. Tobias expected to collect the $3,000 the following month. A month later, Tobias received $2,000 cash from the client.

Journalizing transactions; posting (Obj. 3, 4)

1. Record the two transactions on the books of Grant Tobias, Attorney. Include an explanation for each transaction.

2. Open these T-accounts: Cash, Accounts Receivable, Service Revenue. Post to all three accounts. Compute each account's balance and denote as Bal.
3. Answer these questions based on your analysis:
   a. How much did Tobias earn? Which account shows this amount?
   b. How much in total assets did Tobias acquire as a result of the two transactions? Show the amount of each asset.

Preparing and using a trial balance (Obj. 5)

CP2-9 Assume that **Intel Corporation,** famous for the Pentium© family of processors, reported the following summarized data at December 31, 20X0. Accounts appear in no particular order; dollar amounts are in billions.

Revenues	$21	Other liabilities	$ 6
Other assets	20	Cash	4
Accounts payable	1	Expenses	16
Stockholders' equity	12		

Prepare the trial balance of Intel Corporation at December 31, 20X0. List the accounts in their proper order, as on page 75. How much was Intel's net income or net loss?

Using a trial balance (Obj. 5)

CP2-10 Refer to Air & Sea Travel's trial balance on page 75. Compute these amounts for the business:

1. Net income or net loss during April.
2. Total assets
3. Total liabilities

Using a trial balance (Obj. 5)

CP2-11 Refer to Air & Sea Travel's trial balance on page 75. The purpose of this check point is to help you learn how to correct three common errors in accounting:

Error 1 Mislabeling an item: Assume that Air & Sea Travel accidentally listed Accounts receivable as a credit balance rather than as a debit. Recompute the trial balance totals for debits and credits. Then take the difference between total debits and total credits. Finally, divide the difference by 2, and you get back to the original amount of Accounts receivable.

Error 2 Slide: Assume the trial balance lists Accounts receivable as $20,000 instead of $2,000. Recompute column totals, take the difference, and divide by 9. You get back to the original amount of Accounts receivable, $2,000.

Error 3 Transposition: Assume the trial balance lists Land as $81,000 instead of $18,000. Recompute column totals, take the difference, and divide by 9. The result is an integer (no decimals), which suggests that the error is either a transposition or a slide.

Using accounting terms (Obj. 1)

CP2-12 Accounting has its own vocabulary and basic relationships. Match the accounting terms at left with the corresponding definition or meaning at right.

___ 1. Receivable	A. Using up assets in the course of operating a business
___ 2. Owners' Equity	B. Always a liability
___ 3. Debit	C. Revenues − Expenses
___ 4. Expense	D. Grouping of accounts
___ 5. Net Income	E. Assets-Liabilities
___ 6. Ledger	F. Record of transactions
___ 7. Posting	G. Always an asset
___ 8. Normal balance	H. Left side of an account
___ 9. Payable	I. Side of an account where increases are recorded
___10. Journal	J. Copying data from the journal to the ledger

Analyzing transactions without a journal (Obj. 6)

CP2-13 Sports Depot, a health club, began by issuing common stock for cash of $80,000. The business immediately purchased equipment on account for $30,000.

1. Set up the following T-accounts of Sports Depot: Cash, Equipment, Accounts Payable, Common Stock.
2. Record the first two transactions of Sports Depot directly in the T-accounts without using a journal.
3. Compute the balance in each account and show that total debits equal total credits.

E2-1 Assume **Discount Tire Company** has opened a store in Tallahassee, Florida. Starting with cash and stockholders' equity (common stock) of $80,000, Scott Drake, the store manager, borrowed $420,000 by signing a note payable in the name of the store. Prior to opening the store, Drake purchased land for $70,000 and a building for $260,000. He also paid $100,000 for equipment and $40,000 for supplies to use in the business.

Reporting on business activities (Obj. 1)

Suppose the home office of Discount Tire Company requires a weekly report from store managers. Write Drake's memo to the home office to report on his borrowing and purchases. Include the store's balance sheet as the final part of your memo.

E2-2 For each of the following items, give an example of a business transaction that has the described effect on the accounting equation:

Business transactions and the accounting equation (Obj. 2)

a. Decrease an asset and decrease a liability.
b. Increase an asset and increase owners' equity.
c. Increase an asset and increase a liability.
d. Increase one asset and decrease another asset.
e. Decrease an asset and decrease owners' equity.

E2-3 The following events were experienced by either Haltom Oil Company, a corporation, or Casey Haltom, the major stockholder. State whether each event (1) increased, (2) decreased, or (3) had no effect on the total assets of the business. Identify any specific asset affected.

Transaction analysis (Obj. 2)

a. Haltom used personal funds to purchase a swimming pool for his home.
b. Sold land and received cash of $11,000 (the land was carried on the company's books at $11,000.)
c. Borrowed $50,000 from the bank.
d. Made cash purchase of land for a building site, $85,000.
e. Received $20,000 cash and issued stock to a stockholder.
f. Paid $60,000 cash on accounts payable (a payment to a supplier).
g. Purchased machinery and equipment for a manufacturing plant; signed a $100,000 promissory note in payment.
h. Performed service for a customer on account, $15,000.
i. The business paid Haltom a cash dividend of $4,000.
j. Received $90,000 cash from customers on accounts receivable.

E2-4 Refer to the data in Exercise 2-3. Use the data of Exercise 2-3 to prepare Haltom Oil Company's statement of cash flows for the year ended December 31, 20X1. Follow the format of the cash-flow statement given in Exercise 2-2. On the statement of cash flows that you prepare, key each line by the letter corresponding to the data item listed in Exercise 2-3. Cash receipts are positive amounts, and cash payments are negative amounts enclosed within parentheses. The beginning cash balance of Haltom Oil Company was $19,000.

Preparing a statement of cash flows (Obj. 2)

Data items a, g, and h do not appear on the statement of cash flows of Haltom Oil Company. Why not?

E2-5 Jacob Marr opens a medical practice to specialize in gynecology. During the first month of operation (February), his business, entitled Jacob Marr, Professional Corporation (P.C.), experienced the following events:

Transaction analysis; accounting equation (Obj. 2)

Feb.	6	Marr invested $25,000 in the business, which in turn issued its common stock to him.
	9	The business paid cash for land costing $15,000. Marr plans to build an office building on the land.
	12	The business purchased medical supplies for $2,000 on account.
	15	Jacob Marr, P.C., officially opened for business.
	15–28	During the rest of the month, Marr treated patients and earned service revenue of $8,000, receiving cash for half the revenue earned.
	15–28	The business paid cash expenses: employee salaries, $1,400; office rent, $1,000; utilities, $300.
	28	The business sold supplies to another physician for cost of $500.
	28	The business borrowed $10,000, signing a note payable to the bank.
	28	The business paid $1,500 on account.

Required

1. Analyze the effects of these events on the accounting equation of the medical practice of Jacob Marr, P.C. Use a format similar to that of Exhibit 2-1, Panel B, with headings for Cash, Accounts Receivable, Medical Supplies, Land, Accounts Payable, Note Payable, Common Stock, and Retained Earnings.
2. After completing the analysis, answer these questions about the business.
   a. How much are total assets?
   b. How much does the business expect to collect from patients?
   c. How much does the business owe in total?
   d. How much net income or net loss did the business experience during its first month of operations?

Journalizing transactions (Obj. 3, 4)

E2-6 Refer to Exercise 2-5. Record the transactions in the journal of Jacob Marr, Professional Corporation (P.C.). List the transactions by date and give an explanation for each transaction.

Analyzing transactions and determining net income (Obj. 2)

E2-7 The analysis of the transactions in which Consolidated Trucking, Inc., engaged during its first month of operations follows in their order of occurrence. The company earns service revenue. Consolidated Trucking paid no dividends during the period.

	Cash	+ *Accounts Receivable*	+ *Lease Equipment*	= *Note Payable*	+ *Common Stock*	+ *Retained Earnings*
(a)	+ 15,000				+ 15,000	
(b)			+ 100,000	+ 100,000		
(c)		+ 900				+ 900
(d)	− 750		+ 750			
(e)	+ 150	− 150				
(f)	− 1,000					− 1,000
(g)	+ 2,500					+ 2,500
(h)	− 10,000			− 10,000		

Required

1. Describe each transaction.
2. If these transactions fully describe the operations of Consolidated Trucking during the month, what was the amount of net income or net loss?

Journalizing transactions (Obj. 3, 4)

E2-8 Sylvania Learning System, Inc., engaged in the following transactions during June 20X3, its first month of operations:

June	1	Received $36,000 and issued common stock.
	2	Purchased $800 of office supplies on account.
	4	Paid $14,000 cash for land to use as a building site.
	6	Performed service for customers and received cash, $2,000.
	9	Paid $100 on accounts payable.
	17	Performed service for customers on account, $1,200.
	23	Received $1,200 cash from customers on account.
	30	Paid the following expenses: salary, $1,000; rent, $500.

Required

1. Record the preceding transactions in the journal of Sylvania Learning System, Inc. Key transactions by date and include an explanation for each entry, as illustrated in the chapter.
2. After these transactions, how much cash does Sylvania have to work with?

Posting to the ledger and preparing a trial balance (Obj. 4, 5)

E2-9 Refer to Exercise 2-8.

Required

1. After journalizing the transactions of Exercise 2-8, post the entries to the ledger, using T-account format. Key transactions by date. Date the ending balance of each account June 30.

2. Prepare the trial balance of Sylvania Learning System, Inc., at June 30, 20X3.
3. How much are total assets, total liabilities, and total stockholders' equity on June 30?

Journalizing transactions (Obj. 3, 4)

E2-10 The first seven transactions of Road & Track Company have been posted to the company's accounts as follows:

Cash

	Debit		Credit
(1)	16,000	(2)	7,000
(4)	100	(5)	6,000
(7)	7,000	(6)	300

Supplies

	Debit		Credit
(3)	600	(4)	100

Equipment

	Debit		Credit
(5)	6,000		

Land

	Debit		Credit
(2)	31,000		

Accounts Payable

	Debit		Credit
(6)	300	(3)	600

Note Payable

	Debit		Credit
		(2)	24,000
		(7)	7,000

Common Stock

	Debit		Credit
		(1)	16,000

Required

Prepare the journal entries that served as the sources for the seven transactions. Include an explanation for each entry.

Preparing a trial balance (Obj. 5)

E2-11 The accounts of California Instruments Company follow with their normal balances at May 31, 20X0. The accounts are listed in no particular order.

Account	*Balance*	*Account*	*Balance*
Common stock	$48,800	Building	$75,250
Accounts payable	4,300	Dividends	6,000
Sales revenue	22,000	Utilities expense	1,400
Land	29,000	Accounts receivable	15,500
Note payable	25,000	Delivery expense	300
Cash	21,000	Retained earnings	?
Salary expense	8,650		

Required

1. Prepare the company's trial balance at May 31, 20X0, listing accounts in proper sequence, as illustrated in the chapter. For example, Supplies comes before Building and Land. List the expense with the largest balance first, the expense with the next largest balance second, and so on.
2. Prepare the financial statement for the month ended May 31, 20X0, that will tell California Instruments' top managers the results of operations for the month.

Correcting errors in a trial balance (Obj. 5)

E2-12 The trial balance of Michigan Maple, Inc., at February 28, 20X1, does not balance:

Cash	$ 4,200	
Accounts receivable	13,000	
Inventory	1,400	
Supplies	600	
Land	46,000	
Accounts payable		$ 3,000
Common stock		47,900
Sales revenue		19,700
Salary expense	1,700	
Rent expense	800	
Utilities expense	300	
Total	$68,000	$70,600

Investigation of the accounting records reveals the following errors:

a. Recorded a $400 cash revenue transaction by debiting Accounts Receivable. The credit part of the entry was correct.

b. Posted a $1,000 credit to Accounts Payable as $100.

c. Did not record utilities expense or the related account payable in the amount of $200.

d. Understated Common Stock by $400.

e. Omitted Cost of Goods Sold, an expense of $3,900, from the trial balance.

Required

Prepare the correct trial balance at February 28, complete with a heading. Journal entries are not required.

Recording transactions without a journal (Obj. 6)

E2-13 Set up the following T-accounts: Cash, Accounts Receivable, Office Supplies, Office Furniture, Accounts Payable, Common Stock, Dividends, Service Revenue, Salary Expense, and Rent Expense.

Record the following transactions directly in the T-accounts without using a journal. Use the letters to identify the transactions.

a. Bob Hearn opened a law firm by investing $8,000 cash and office furniture valued at $5,400. Organized as a professional corporation, the business issued common stock to Hearn.

b. Paid monthly rent of $1,500.

c. Purchased office supplies on account, $800.

d. Paid employees' salaries, $1,800.

e. Paid $400 of the account payable created in transaction c.

f. Performed accounting service on account, $1,700.

g. Declared and paid dividends of $2,000.

Preparing a trial balance (Obj. 5)

E2-14 Refer to Exercise 2-13.

1. After recording the transactions in Exercise 2-13, prepare the trial balance of Bob Hearn, Esq., at July 31, 20X2.

2. How well did the business perform during its first month? Give the basis for your answer.

Serial Exercise

Exercise 2-15 begins an accounting cycle that is completed in Chapter 3.

Recording transactions and preparing a trial balance (Obj. 3, 4, 5)

E2-15 Donna Schulz, Certified Public Accountant, Professional Corporation (P.C.), completed these transactions during the first part of December:

Dec.	2	Received $7,000 cash from Schulz. Issued common stock to her.
	2	Paid monthly office rent, $500.
	3	Paid cash for a Dell computer, $3,000. The computer is expected to remain in service for five years.
	4	Purchased office furniture on account, $3,600. The furniture should last for five years.
	5	Purchased supplies on account, $300.
	9	Performed tax service for a client and received cash for the full amount of $800.
	12	Paid utility expenses, $200.
	18	Performed consulting service for a client on account, $1,700.

Required

1. Set up T-accounts for: Cash, Accounts Receivable, Supplies, Equipment, Furniture, Accounts Payable, Common Stock, Dividends, Service Revenue, Rent Expense, Utilities Expense, and Salary Expense.

2. Journalize the transactions. Explanations are not required.

3. Post to the T-accounts. Key all items by date and denote an account balance on December 18 as Bal.

(continued)

4. Prepare a trial balance at December 18. In the Serial Exercise of Chapter 3, we will add transactions for the remainder of December and will require a trial balance at December 31.

CHALLENGE EXERCISES

Computing financial statement amounts (Obj. 6)

E2-16 The owner of Quick Phone Service, Inc., is an engineer with little understanding of accounting. He needs to compute the following summary information from the accounting records:

a. Net income for the month of March.
b. Total cash paid during March.
c. Cash collections from customers during March.
d. Cash paid on a note payable during March.

The quickest way to compute these amounts is to analyze the following accounts:

	Balance		Additional Information for the Month of March
Account	*Feb. 28*	*Mar. 31*	
1. Retained Earnings	$ 6,200	$10,500	Dividends, $3,800
2. Cash	4,600	5,400	Cash receipts, $55,200
3. Accounts Receivable........	24,300	26,700	Sales on account, $60,500
4. Note Payable.............	13,900	21,400	New borrowing, $16,300

The net income for March can be computed as follows:

RETAINED EARNINGS

March dividends	**3,800**	**Feb. 28 Bal.**	**6,200**
		March net income x **= $8,100**	
		March 31	**Bal. 10,500**

Use a similar approach to compute the other three items. For total cash paid in March (item b), use only the Cash data (number 2). For cash collections (item c), use only Accounts Receivable (number 3), and so on.

Analyzing accounting errors (Obj. 3, 4, 5)

E2-17 Klutz Accountant has trouble keeping his debits and credits equal. During a recent month, he made the following errors:

a. In preparing the trial balance, Klutz omitted a $20,000 note payable.
b. Klutz recorded a $120 purchase of supplies on account by debiting Supplies and crediting Accounts Payable for $210.
c. In journalizing a cash sale, Klutz correctly debited Cash for $300 but accidentally credited Accounts Receivable.
d. Klutz posted a $200 utility expense as $20. The credit posting to Cash was correct.

Required

1. For each of these errors, state whether the total debits equal total credits on the trial balance.
2. Identify any accounts with misstated balances and indicate the amount and direction of the error (account balance too high or too low).

PROBLEMS

(Group A)

Analyzing a trial balance (Obj. 1)

P2-1A The owners of Baylor Magnetic Imaging, Inc., are selling the business. They offer the following trial balance to prospective buyers.

Your best friend is considering buying Baylor. She seeks your advice in interpreting this information. Specifically, she asks whether this trial balance is the same as a balance sheet and an income statement. She also wonders whether Baylor is a sound company. After all, the accounts are in balance.

BAYLOR MAGNETIC IMAGING, INC. **Trial Balance** December 31, 20XX		
Cash	$ 12,000	
Accounts receivable	47,000	
Prepaid expenses	4,000	
Equipment	181,000	
Accounts payable		$105,000
Note payable		92,000
Common stock		30,000
Retained earnings		50,000
Dividends	18,000	
Service revenue		84,000
Salary expense	63,000	
Rent expense	26,000	
Supplies expense	7,000	
Advertising expense	3,000	
	$361,000	$361,000

Required

Write a memo to answer your friend's questions. To aid her decision, state how she can use the information on the trial balance to compute Baylor's net income or net loss for the current period. State the amount of net income or net loss in your note.

Analyzing transactions with the accounting equation and preparing the financial statements (Obj. 2)

P2-2A Lisa Lane operates and is the major stockholder of an interior design studio called Lane Designers, Inc. The following amounts summarize the financial position of the business on April 30, 20X5:

	Assets				=	***Liabilities*** +	***Stockholders' Equity***	
	Cash +	*Accounts Receivable* +	*Supplies* +	*Land*	=	*Accounts Payable* +	*Common Stock* +	*Retained Earnings*
Bal.	1,720	2,240		24,100		5,400	10,000	12,660

During May 20X5, the business completed these transactions:

a. Lane received $12,000 as a gift and deposited the cash in the business bank account. The business issued common stock to Lane.

b. Paid $1,400 on accounts payable (a payment to a supplier).

c. Performed services for a client and received cash of $4,100.

d. Collected cash from a customer on account, $750.

e. Purchased supplies on account, $720.

f. Consulted on the interior design of a major office building and billed the client for services rendered, $5,000.

g. Received cash of $1,700 and issued common stock to Lane.

h. Recorded the following business expenses for the month (payments to supplier):

(1) Paid office rent—$1,200. (2) Paid advertising—$660.

i. Declared and paid a cash dividend of $2,400.

Required

1. Analyze the effects of the preceding transactions on the accounting equation of Lane Designers, Inc. Adapt the format of Exhibit 2-1, Panel B.

2. Prepare the income statement of Lane Designers, Inc., for the month ended May 31, 20X5. List expenses in decreasing order by amount.

3. Prepare the statement of retained earnings of Lane Designers, Inc., for the month ended May 31, 20X5.

4. Prepare the balance sheet of Lane Designers, Inc., at May 31.

5. Prepare the statement of cash flows of Lane Designers for the month ended May 31, 20X5.

P2-3A This problem should be used only in conjunction with Problem 2-2A. Refer to Problem 2-2A.

Recording transactions, posting (Obj. 3, 4)

Required

1. Journalize the transactions of Lane Designers, Inc. Explanations are not required.
2. Set up the following T-accounts: Cash, Accounts Receivable, Supplies, Land, Accounts Payable, Common Stock, Retained Earnings, Dividends, Service Revenue, Rent Expense, Advertising Expense. Insert in each account its balance as given (example: Cash $1,720). Post to the accounts.
3. Compute the balance in each account. For each asset account, each liability account, and for Common Stock, compare its balance to the ending balance you obtained in Problem 2-2A. Are the amounts the same or different? (In Chapter 3, we will complete the accounting process. There you will learn how the Retained Earnings, Dividends, Revenue, and Expense accounts work together in the processing of accounting information.)

P2-4A Angela Tekell practiced law with a large firm, a partnership, for 10 years after graduating from law school. Recently, she resigned her position to open her own law office, which she operates as a professional corporation. The name of the new entity is Angela Tekell, Attorney and Counselor, Professional Corporation (P.C.). Tekell experienced the following events during the organizing phase of her new business and its first month of operations. Some of the events were personal and did not affect the law practice. Others were business transactions and should be accounted for by the business.

Analyzing transactions with the accounting equation (Obj. 2, 3)

July	1	Tekell sold 1,000 shares of Eastman Kodak stock, which she had owned for several years, receiving $88,000 cash from her stockbroker.
	2	Tekell deposited in her personal bank account the $88,000 cash from sale of the Eastman Kodak stock.
	3	Tekell received $150,000 cash from her former partners in the law firm from which she resigned.
	5	Tekell deposited $60,000 cash in a new business bank account entitled Angela Tekell, Attorney and Counselor, P.C. The business issued common stock to Tekell.
	6	A representative of a large company telephoned Tekell and told her of the company's intention to transfer its legal business to the new entity of Angela Tekell, Attorney and Counselor, P.C.
	7	The business paid $550 cash for letterhead stationery for the law office.
	9	The business purchased office furniture. Tekell paid cash of $10,000 and agreed to pay the account payable for the remainder, $9,500, within three months.
	23	Tekell finished court hearings on behalf of a client and submitted her bill for legal services, $3,000. She expected to collect from this client within one month.
	29	The business paid $5,000 of its account payable on the furniture purchased on July 9.
	30	The business paid office rent, $1,900.
	31	The business declared and paid a cash dividend of $500.

Required

1. Classify each of the preceding events as one of the following:
   a. A business transaction to be recorded by the business of Angela Tekell, Attorney and Counselor, P.C.
   b. A business-related event but not a transaction to be recorded by the business of Angela Tekell, Attorney and Counselor, P.C.
   c. A personal transaction not to be recorded by the business of Angela Tekell, Attorney and Counselor, P.C.
2. Analyze the effects of the above events on the accounting equation of the business of Angela Tekell, Attorney and Counselor, P.C. Use a format similar to Exhibit 2-1, Panel B.
3. At the end of the first month of operations, Tekell has a number of questions about the financial standing of the business. Explain to her:
   a. How the business can have so much cash and so little in retained earnings.

b. How much in total resources the business has, how much it owes, and what Tekell's ownership interest is in the assets of the business.

4. Record the transactions of the business in its journal. Include an explanation for each entry.

Analyzing and recording transactions (Obj. 3, 4)

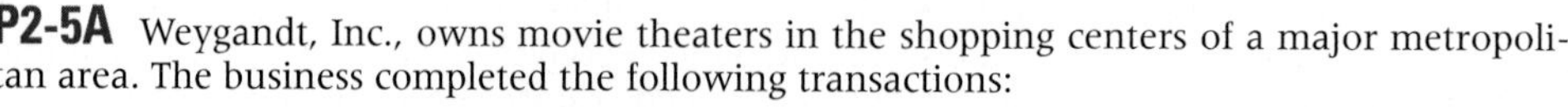

P2-5A Weygandt, Inc., owns movie theaters in the shopping centers of a major metropolitan area. The business completed the following transactions:

Feb. 1	Received cash of $30,000 and issued common stock to the investor.
2	Paid $20,000 cash and signed a $30,000 note payable to purchase land for a theater site.
5	Borrowed $70,000 from the bank to finance part of the construction of the new theater. Signed a note payable to the bank.
7	Received $15,000 cash from ticket sales and deposited that amount in the bank. (Label the revenue as Sales Revenue.)
10	Purchased theater supplies on account, $1,700.
15	Paid employees' salaries, $2,800, and rent on a theater building, $1,800.
15	Paid property tax expense, $1,200.
16	Paid $800 on account.
17	Declared and paid a cash dividend of $3,000.

Weygandt, Inc., uses the following accounts: Cash, Supplies, Land, Accounts Payable, Notes Payable, Common Stock, Dividends, Sales Revenue, Salary Expense, Rent Expense, and Property Tax Expense.

Required

1. Journalize each transaction. Explanations are not required.
2. After these transactions, how much cash does the business have? How much does it owe in total?

Journalizing transactions, posting, and preparing a trial balance (Obj. 3, 4, 5)

P2-6A Kermit Larson opened a law office on September 3 of the current year. During the first month of operations, the business completed the following transactions:

Sep. 3	Larson transferred $20,000 cash from his personal bank account to a business account entitled Kermit Larson, Attorney, Professional Corporation (P.C.). The corporation issued common stock to Larson.
4	Purchased supplies, $200, and furniture, $1,800, on account.
6	Performed legal services for a client and received $1,000 cash.
7	Paid $15,000 cash to acquire land for an office site.
10	Defended a client in court, billed the client, and received his promise to pay the $600 within one week.
14	Paid for the furniture purchased September 4 on account.
16	Paid the telephone bill, $120.
17	Received partial payment from client on account, $500.
24	Paid the water and electricity bills, $110.
28	Received $1,500 cash for helping a client sell real estate.
30	Paid secretary's salary, $1,200.
30	Declared and paid dividends of $2,400.

Required

Set up the following T-accounts: Cash, Accounts Receivable, Supplies, Furniture, Land, Accounts Payable, Common Stock, Dividends, Service Revenue, Salary Expense, and Utilities Expense.

1. Record each transaction in the journal, using the account titles given. Key each transaction by date. Explanations are not required.
2. Post the transactions to the T-accounts, using transaction dates as posting references. Label the ending balance of each account Bal., as shown in the chapter.
3. Prepare the trial balance of Kermit Larson, Attorney, P.C., at September 30 of the current year.

P2-7A Walter Steitz obtained a corporate charter from the state of New York and started a counseling service. During the first month of operations (June 20X3), the business completed the following selected transactions:

Recording transactions directly in T-accounts and preparing a trial balance (Obj. 5, 7)

a. Steitz began the business with an investment of $11,000 cash and a building valued at $60,000. The corporation issued common stock to Steitz.
b. Borrowed $30,000 from the bank; signed a note payable.
c. Purchased office supplies on account, $1,300.
d. Paid $18,000 for office furniture.
e. Paid employees' salaries, $2,200.
f. Performed counseling service on account for a client, $2,100.
g. Paid $800 of the account payable created in Transaction c.
h. Received a $600 bill for advertising expense that will be paid in the near future.
i. Performed counseling service for clients and received cash, $1,100.
j. Received cash on account, $1,200.
k. Paid the following cash expenses:
   (1) Rent on land, $700. (2) Utilities, $400.
l. Declared and paid dividends of $3,500.

Required

1. Set up the following T-accounts: Cash, Accounts Receivable, Office Supplies, Office Furniture, Building, Accounts Payable, Note Payable, Common Stock, Dividends, Service Revenue, Salary Expense, Advertising Expense, Rent Expense, Utilities Expense.
2. Record each transaction directly in the T-accounts without using a journal. Use the letters to identify the transactions.
3. Prepare the trial balance of Steitz Counseling Service, Inc., at June 30, 20X3.

(Group B)

P2-1B The owners of Bulova, Inc., are selling the business. They offer the following trial balance to prospective buyers:

Analyzing a trial balance (Obj. 1)

BULOVA, INC. Trial Balance December 31, 20XX		
Cash	$ 16,000	
Accounts receivable	11,000	
Prepaid expenses	4,000	
Land	231,000	
Accounts payable		$ 31,000
Note payable		120,000
Common stock		103,000
Retained earnings		40,000
Dividends	21,000	
Service revenue		46,000
Rent expense	14,000	
Advertising expense	3,000	
Wage expense	33,000	
Supplies expense	7,000	
	$340,000	$340,000

Your best friend is considering buying Bulova. He seeks your advice in interpreting this information. Specifically, he asks whether this trial balance is the same as a balance sheet and an income statement. He also wonders whether Bulova is a sound company. After all, the accounts are in balance.

Required

Write a short note to answer your friend's questions. To aid his decision, state how he can use the information on the trial balance to compute Bulova's net income or net loss for the current period. State the amount of net income or net loss in your note.

Analyzing transactions with the accounting equation and preparing the financial statements (Obj. 2)

P2-2B Lisa Sirbasku operates and is the major stockholder of an interior design studio called Sirbasku Interiors, Inc. The following amounts summarize the financial position of the business on August 31, 20X2:

	Assets				= Liabilities +	Stockholders' Equity	
	Cash +	Accounts Receivable +	Supplies +	Land =	Accounts Payable +	Common Stock +	Retained Earnings
Bal.	1,250	1,500		12,000	8,000	4,000	2,750

During September 20X2, the business completed these transactions:

a. Sirbasku inherited $20,000 and deposited the cash in the business bank account. The business issued common stock to Sirbasku.
b. Performed services for a client and received cash of $6,700.
c. Paid $5,000 on accounts payable (a payment to a supplier).
d. Purchased supplies on account, $1,000.
e. Collected cash from a customer on account, $500.
f. Received cash of $1,000 and issued common stock to Sirbasku.
g. Consulted on the interior design of a major office building and billed the client for services rendered, $2,400.
h. Recorded the following business expenses (payments to suppliers) for the month:
(1) Paid office rent—$900. (2) Paid advertising—$300.
i. Declared and paid a cash dividend of $1,800.

Required

1. Analyze the effects of the preceding transactions on the accounting equation of Sirbasku Interiors, Inc. Adapt the format of Exhibit 2-1, Panel B.
2. Prepare the income statement of Sirbasku Interiors, Inc., for the month ended September 30, 20X2. List expenses in decreasing order by amount.
3. Prepare the entity's statement of retained earnings for the month ended September 30, 20X2.
4. Prepare the balance sheet of Sirbasku Interiors, Inc., at September 30, 20X2.
5. Prepare the statement of cash flows of Sirbasku Interiors, Inc., for the month ended September 30, 20X2.

Recording transactions, posting (Obj. 3, 4)

P2-3B This problem should be used only in conjunction with Problem 2-2B. Refer to Problem 2-2B.

Required

1. Journalize the transactions of Sirbasku Interiors, Inc. Explanations are not required.
2. Set up the following T-accounts: Cash, Accounts Receivable, Supplies, Land, Accounts Payable, Common Stock, Retained Earnings, Dividends, Service Revenue, Rent Expense, and Advertising Expense. Insert in each account its balance as given (example: Cash $1,250). Post the transactions to the accounts.
3. Compute the balance in each account. For each asset account, each liability account, and for Common Stock, compare its balance to the ending balance you obtained in Problem 2-2B. Are the amounts the same or different? (In Chapter 3, we will complete the accounting process. There you will learn how the Retained Earnings, Dividends, Revenue, and Expense accounts work together in the processing of accounting information.)

Analyzing transactions with the accounting equation (Obj. 2, 3)

P2-4B Rod Tanner practiced law with a large firm, a partnership, for five years after graduating from law school. Recently, he resigned his position to open his own law office, which he operates as a professional corporation. The name of the new entity is Rod Tanner, Attorney, Professional Corporation (P.C.). Tanner experienced the following events during the organizing phase of his new business and its first month of operations. Some of the events were personal and did not affect his law practice. Others were business transactions and should be accounted for by the business.

Feb. 4	Tanner received $65,000 cash from his former partners in the law firm from which he resigned.
5	Tanner deposited $42,000 cash in a new business bank account entitled Rod Tanner, Attorney, P.C. The business issued common stock to Tanner.
6	The business paid $300 cash for letterhead stationery for the new law office.
7	The business purchased office furniture. The company paid cash of $10,000 and agreed to pay the account payable for the remainder, $7,000, within six months.
10	Tanner sold IBM stock, which he and his wife had owned for several years, receiving $75,000 cash from his stockbroker.
11	Tanner deposited the $75,000 cash from sale of the IBM stock in his personal bank account.
12	A representative of a large company telephoned Tanner and told him of the company's intention to transfer its legal business to Tanner.
18	Tanner finished court hearings on behalf of a client and submitted his bill for legal services, $4,000. Tanner expected to collect from this client within two weeks.
21	The business paid half its account payable for the furniture purchased on February 7.
25	The business paid office rent, $1,000.
28	The business declared and paid a cash dividend of $2,000.

Required

1. Classify each of the preceding events as one of the following:
   a. A business transaction to be recorded by the business of Rod Tanner, Attorney, P.C.
   b. A business-related event but not a transaction to be recorded by the business of Rod Tanner, Attorney, P.C.
   c. A personal transaction not to be recorded by the business of Rod Tanner, Attorney, P.C.

2. Analyze the effects of the preceding events on the accounting equation of the business of Rod Tanner, Attorney, P.C. Use a format similar to that in Exhibit 2-1, Panel B.

3. At the end of the first month of operations, Tanner has a number of questions about the financial standing of the business. Explain to him:
   a. How the business can have so much cash and so little in retained earnings.
   b. How much in total resources the business has, how much it owes, and what Tanner's ownership interest is in the assets of the business.

4. Record the transactions of the business in its journal. Include an explanation for each entry.

P2-5B Don Kieso practices medicine under the business title Don Kieso, M.D., Professional Corporation (P.C.). During May, Kieso's medical practice completed the following transactions:

Analyzing and recording transactions (Obj. 3, 4)

May 1	Kieso deposited $9,000 cash in the business bank account. The business issued common stock to him.
5	Paid monthly rent on medical equipment, $700.
9	Paid $5,000 cash and signed a $25,000 note payable to purchase land for an office site.
10	Purchased supplies on account, $1,200.
19	Paid $1,000 on account.
22	Borrowed $20,000 from the bank for business use. Kieso signed a note payable to the bank in the name of the business.
30	Revenues earned during the month included $6,000 cash and $5,000 on account.
30	Paid employees' salaries ($2,400), office rent ($1,500), and utilities ($400).
30	Declared and paid a cash dividend of $4,000.

Kieso's business uses the following accounts: Cash, Accounts Receivable, Supplies, Land, Accounts Payable, Notes Payable, Common Stock, Dividends, Service Revenue, Salary Expense, Rent Expense, and Utilities Expense.

Required

1. Journalize each transaction of Don Kieso, M.D., P.C. Explanations are not required.

2. After these transactions, how much cash does the business have? How much in total does it owe?

Journalizing transactions, posting, and preparing a trial balance (Obj. 3, 4, 5)

P2-6B Pat Libby opened a law office on January 2 of the current year. During the first month of operations, the business completed the following transactions:

Jan.	2	Libby deposited $28,000 cash in the business bank account Pat Libby, Attorney, Professional Corporation (P.C.). The corporation issued common stock to Libby.
	3	Purchased supplies, $500, and furniture, $2,600, on account.
	4	Performed legal service for a client and received cash, $1,500.
	7	Paid cash to acquire land for an office site, $22,000.
	11	Defended a client in court and billed the client $800.
	16	Paid for the furniture purchased January 3 on account.
	17	Paid the telephone bill, $110.
	18	Received partial payment from client on account, $400.
	22	Paid the water and electricity bills, $130.
	29	Received $1,800 cash for helping a client sell real estate.
	31	Paid secretary's salary, $1,300.
	31	Declared and paid dividends of $2,200.

Required

Set up the following T-accounts: Cash, Accounts Receivable, Supplies, Furniture, Land, Accounts Payable, Common Stock, Dividends, Service Revenue, Salary Expense, and Utilities Expense.

1. Record each transaction in the journal, using the account titles given. Key each transaction by date. Explanations are not required.

2. Post the transactions to the T-accounts, using transaction dates as posting references. Label the ending balance of each account Bal., as shown in the chapter.

3. Prepare the trial balance of Pat Libby, Attorney, P.C., at January 31 of the current year.

Recording transactions directly in T-accounts and preparing a trial balance (Obj. 5, 7)

P2-7B Joyce Plummer obtained a corporate charter from the state of Ohio and started CableVision, Inc. During the first month of operations (January 20X7), the business completed the following selected transactions:

a. Plummer began the business with an investment of $10,000 cash and a building valued at $50,000. The corporation issued common stock to Plummer.

b. Borrowed $20,000 from the bank; signed a note payable.

c. Paid $12,000 for transmitting equipment.

d. Purchased office supplies on account, $400.

e. Paid employees' salaries, $1,300.

f. Received $500 for cable TV service performed for customers.

g. Sold cable service to customers on account, $1,800.

h. Paid $100 of the account payable created in Transaction d.

i. Received a $600 bill for utility expense that will be paid in the near future.

j. Received cash on account, $1,100.

k. Paid the following cash expenses:
(1) Rent on land, $1,000. (2) Advertising, $800.

l. Declared and paid dividends of $2,600.

Required

1. Set up the following T-accounts: Cash, Accounts Receivable, Office Supplies, Transmitting Equipment, Building, Accounts Payable, Note Payable, Common Stock, Dividends, Service Revenue, Salary Expense, Rent Expense, Advertising Expense, and Utilities Expense.

2. Record the foregoing transactions directly in the T-accounts without using a journal. Use the letters to identify the transactions.
3. Prepare the trial balance of CableVision, Inc., at January 31, 20X7.

EXTENDING YOUR KNOWLEDGE

DECISION CASES

Recording transactions directly in T-accounts, preparing a trial balance, and measuring net income or loss (Obj. 5, 6)

Case 1. You have been requested by a friend named Carroll Fadal to give advice on the effects that certain business transactions will have on the entity he has started. Time is short, so you will not be able to do all the detailed procedures of journalizing and posting. Instead, you must analyze the transactions witout the use of a journal. Fadal will continue the business only if it can be expected to earn monthly net income of $5,000. The following transactions have occurred this month:

a. Fadal deposited $10,000 cash in a business bank account, and the corporation issued common stock to Fadal.
b. Borrowed $4,000 cash from the bank and signed a note payable due within one year.
c. Paid $300 cash for supplies.
d. Purchased advertising in the local newspaper for cash, $800.
e. Purchased office furniture on account, $4,400.
f. Paid the following cash expenses for one month: secretary's salary, $1,750; office rent, $600.
g. Earned revenue on account, $7,300.
h. Earned revenue and received $2,500 cash.
i. Collected cash from customers on account, $1,200.
j. Paid on account, $1,000.
k. Declared and paid dividends of $900.

Required

1. Set up the following T-accounts: Cash, Accounts Receivable, Supplies, Furniture, Accounts Payable, Notes Payable, Common Stock, Dividends, Service Revenue, Salary Expense, Advertising Expense, Rent Expense.
2. Record the transactions directly in the accounts without using a journal. Key each transaction by letter.
3. Prepare a trial balance at the current date. List expenses with the largest amount first, the next largest amount second, and so on. The business name will be Fadal Consulting, Inc.
4. Compute the amount of net income or net loss for this first month of operations. Would you recommend that Fadal continue in business? Why or why not?

Explaining debits and credits (Obj. 3)

Case 2. The following questions both deal with the accounting equation, but they are not related:

a. When you deposit money in your bank account, the bank credits your account. Is the bank misusing the word credit in this context? Why does the bank use the term *credit* to refer to your deposit, and not *debit*?
b. Your friend asks, "When revenues increase assets and expenses decrease assets, why are revenues credits, and expenses debits and not the other way around?" Explain to your friend why revenues are credits and expenses are debits.

ETHICAL ISSUE

Caritas, a charitable organization in Tucson, Arizona, has a standing agreement with Phoenix State Bank. The agreement allows Caritas to overdraw its cash balance at the bank when donations are running low. In the past, Caritas managed funds wisely and rarely used this privilege. Alex Mann has been named president of Caritas. To expand operations, he is acquiring office equipment and spending a lot for fund-raising. During Mann's presidency, Caritas has maintained a negative bank balance of about $3,000.

Required

What is the ethical issue in this situation? Do you approve or disapprove of Mann's management of Caritas's and Phoenix State Bank's funds? Why?

FINANCIAL STATEMENT CASES

Journalizing transactions (Obj. 3, 4)

Case 1. This problem helps to develop skill in recording transactions by using an actual company's account titles. Refer to **The Gap's** financial statements in Appendix A. Assume that Gap, Inc., completed the following selected transactions during the year ended January 30,1999:

a. Made sales on account, $9,054 million.

b. Incurred cost of goods sold (an expense) of $5,318 million. Credit the Merchandise Inventory account.

c. Paid operating expenses of $2,403 million.

d. Accrued interest expense, $14 million. Credit Interest Payable.

e. Paid income tax expense, $495 million.

Required

1. Set up T-accounts for: Cash (debit balance of $3,463 million); Accounts Receivable ($0 balance); Merchandise Inventory (debit balance of $6,374 million); Interest Payable ($0 balance); Net Sales Revenue ($0 balance); Cost of Goods Sold ($0 balance); Operating Expenses ($0 balance); Interest Expense ($0 balance); Income Tax Expense ($0 balance).
2. Journalize The Gap's transactions a–e. Explanations are not required.
3. Post to the T-accounts, and compute the balance for each account. Key postings by transaction letters a–e.
4. For each of the following accounts, compare the balance that you computed to The Gap's actual balance as shown on Gap's most recent income statement or balance sheet. All your amounts should agree to the actual figures, rounded to the nearest million dollars.

    a. Cash
    b. Merchandise Inventory
    c. Net Sales Revenue
    d. Cost of Goods Sold
    e. Operating Expenses
    f. Interest Expense
    g. Income Tax Expense (listed as Income Taxes on the income statement)

Journalizing transactions, preparing a trial balance (Obj. 4, 5)

Case 2. Obtain the annual report of a company of your choice. Assume that the company completed the following selected transactions during May of the current year:

May 3	Borrowed $350,000 by signing a short-term note payable (may be called short-term debt or other account title).
5	Paid rent for six months in advance, $4,600.
9	Earned revenue on account, $74,000.
12	Purchased equipment on account, $33,000.
17	Paid a telephone bill, $300 (this is Selling Expense).
19	Paid $90,000 of the money borrowed on May 3.
26	Collected half the cash on account from May 9.
30	Paid the account payable from May 12.

Required

1. Journalize these transactions, using the company's actual account titles taken from its annual report. Explanations are not required.
2. Set up a T-account for each account that you used in journalizing the transactions. (For clarity, insert no actual balances in the accounts.) Post the transaction amounts to the accounts, using the dates as posting references. Take the balance of each account.
3. Prepare a trial balance.

Group Projects

Project 1. Contact a local business and arrange with the owner to learn what accounts the business uses.

Required

1. Obtain a copy of the business's chart of accounts.
2. Prepare the company's financial statements for the most recent month, quarter, or year. You may use either made-up account balances or balances supplied by the owner.

If the business has a large number of accounts within a category, combine related accounts and report a single amount on the financial statements. For example, the company may have several cash accounts. Combine all cash amounts and report a single Cash amount on the balance sheet.

You will probably encounter numerous accounts that you have not yet learned. Deal with these as best you can. The charts of accounts given in the appendix to this chapter will be helpful.

Project 2. You are promoting a rock concert in your area. Your purpose is to earn a profit, so you will need to establish the formal structure of a business entity. Assume you organize as a corporation.

Required

1. Make a detailed list of ten factors you must consider as you establish the business.
2. Describe ten of the items your business must arrange in order to promote and stage the rock concert.
3. Identify the transactions that your business will undertake to organize, promote, and stage the concert. Journalize the transactions, and post to the relevant T-accounts. Set up the accounts you will need for your business's ledger. Refer to the chapter appendix if needed.
4. Prepare the income statement, statement of retained earnings, balance sheet, and statement of cash flows immediately after the rock concert—that is, before you have had time to pay all the business's bills and to collect all receivables.
5. Assume that you will continue to promote rock concerts if the venture is successful. If it is unsuccessful, you will terminate the business within three months after the concert. Discuss how you will evaluate the success of your venture and how you will decide whether to continue in business.

Internet Exercise

Disney Corporation

Disney has interests in ABC TV, ESPN, movie production, theme parks, publishing, a cruise line, Infoseek, and the NHL Mighty Ducks. Using the Disney Web site you can explore vacation options and get Disney's latest financial information.

1. Go to **http://www.disney.go.com/investors/**. Click on *Financial Publications* and then select the *most recent annual report.* At the bottom of the Annual Report cover page, click *next* to display options including the consolidated financial statements. Use the income statement, balance sheet, statement of stockholders' equity, and the statement of cash flows to answer the following questions.
2. For the three most recent years, list the amounts reported for *Revenues* and *Net Income.* For each of these amounts comment on the direction of the trend, what the trend might indicate, and whether the trend is considered favorable or unfavorable. *Net income* is reported on which two financial statements? Is net income the same amount on these two financial statements?
3. For the two most recent years, identify or calculate the amounts reported for *Cash and Cash Equivalents, Total Assets, Total Liabilities,* and *Total Stockholders' Equity.* Does the accounting equation hold true? Are assets primarily financed by debt or by shareholder contributions?
4. For the three most recent years, list the amounts reported for Cash provided (used) by Operations, Cash provided (used) by Investing Activities, and Cash provided (used) by Financing Activities. For each year, which activity is the primary source of cash? Parentheses indicate what about a dollar amount? On the statement of cash flows, identify the amounts reported for *Cash and Cash Equivalents, End of Year* for the two most recent years. On what other financial statement are Cash and Cash Equivalents reported? Do these two financial statements report the same amount for Cash and Cash Equivalents?

APPENDIX TO CHAPTER 2

TYPICAL CHARTS OF ACCOUNTS FOR DIFFERENT TYPES OF BUSINESSES

A SIMPLE SERVICE CORPORATION

Assets

Cash
Accounts Receivable
Allowance for Uncollectible Accounts
Notes Receivable, Short Term
Interest Receivable
Supplies
Prepaid Rent
Prepaid Insurance
Notes Receivable, Long-Term
Land
Furniture
Accumulated Depreciation—Furniture
Equipment
Accumulated Depreciation—Equipment
Building
Accumulated Depreciation—Building

Liabilities

Accounts Payable
Notes Payable, Short-Term
Salary Payable
Wages Payable
Payroll Taxes Payable
Employee Benefits Payable
Interest Payable
Unearned Service Revenue
Notes Payable, Long-Term

Stockholders' Equity

Common Stock
Retained Earnings
Dividends

Revenues and Gains

Service Revenue
Interest Revenue
Gain on Sale of Land (Furniture, Equipment, or Building)

Expenses and Losses

Salary Expense
Payroll Tax Expense
Employee Benefits Expense
Rent Expense
Insurance Expense
Supplies Expense
Uncollectible Account Expense
Depreciation Expense—Furniture
Depreciation Expense—Equipment
Depreciation Expense—Building
Property Tax Expense
Interest Expense
Miscellaneous Expense
Loss on Sale (or Exchange) of Land (Furniture, Equipment, or Building)

SERVICE PARTNERSHIP

Same as service corporation, except for owners' equity:

Owners' Equity

Partner 1, Capital
Partner 2, Capital
⋮
Partner *N*, Capital

Partner 1, Drawing
Partner 2, Drawing
⋮
Partner *N*, Drawing

A COMPLEX MERCHANDISING CORPORATION

Assets

Cash
Short-Term Investments
Accounts Receivable
Allowance for Uncollectible Accounts
Notes Receivable, Short-Term
Interest Receivable
Inventory
Supplies
Prepaid Rent
Prepaid Insurance
Notes Receivable, Long-Term
Investments in Subsidiaries
Investments in Stock (Available-for-Sale Securities)
Investments in Bonds (Held-to-Maturity Securities)
Other Receivables, Long-Term
Land
Land Improvements
Furniture & Fixtures
Accumulated Depreciation—Furniture & Fixtures
Equipment
Accumulated Depreciation—Equipment
Buildings
Accumulated Depreciation—Buildings
Organization Cost
Franchises
Patents
Leaseholds
Goodwill

Liabilities

Accounts Payable
Notes Payable, Short-Term
Current Portion of Bonds Payable
Salary Payable
Wages Payable
Payroll Taxes Payable
Employee Benefits Payable
Interest Payable
Income Tax Payable
Unearned Sales Revenue
Notes Payable, Long-Term
Bonds Payable
Lease Liability
Minority Interest

Stockholder's Equity

Preferred Stock
Paid-in Capital in Excess of Par—Preferred
Common Stock
Paid-in Capital in Excess of Par—Common
Paid-in Capital from Treasury Stock Transactions
Paid-in Capital from Retirement of Stock
Retained Earnings
Foreign Currency Translation Adjustment
Treasury Stock

Revenues and Gains

Sales Revenue
Interest Revenue
Dividend Revenue
Equity-Method Investment Revenue
Unrealized Holding Gain on Trading Investments
Gain on Sale of Investments
Gain on Sale of Land (Furniture & Fixtures, Equipment, or Buildings)
Discontinued Operations—Gain
Extraordinary Gains

Expenses and Losses

Cost of Goods Sold
Salary Expense
Wage Expense
Commission Expense
Payroll Tax Expense
Employee Benefits Expense
Rent Expense
Insurance Expense
Supplies Expense
Uncollectible Account Expense
Depreciation Expense—Land Improvements
Depreciation Expense—Furniture & Fixtures
Depreciation Expense—Equipment
Depreciation Expense—Buildings
Organization Expense
Amortization Expense—Franchises
Amortization Expense—Leaseholds
Amortization Expense—Goodwill
Income Tax Expense
Unrealized Holding Loss on Trading Investments
Loss on Sale of Investments
Loss on Sale (or Exchange) of Land (Furniture & Fixtures, Equipment, or Buildings)
Discontinued Operations—Loss
Extraordinary Losses

A MANUFACTURING CORPORATION

Same as merchandising corporation, except for Assets:

Assets

Inventories:
- Materials Inventory
- Work-in-Process Inventory
- Finished Goods Inventory

Factory Wages
Factory Overhead

3 Accrual Accounting and the Financial Statements

LEARNING OBJECTIVES

After studying this chapter, you should be able to

1. Link cash flows with accrual-basis accounting
2. Apply the revenue and matching principles
3. Adjust the accounts to update the financial statements
4. Prepare the financial statements
5. Understand what closing the books means
6. Use the current ratio and the debt ratio to evaluate a business

"None of my competitors had the low-tech, high level of personal service I was looking for."

—Andrea McGinty, President and Founder, It's Just Lunch

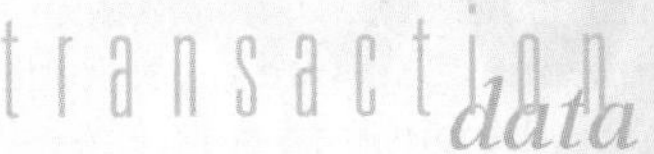

It's Just Lunch, Inc.
Income Statement (Adapted)
Year Ended December 31, 1998

Net Revenues		$20,175,920
Expenses		
Payroll	$ 7,696,355	
Advertising/Marketing	5,586,348	
Office	2,811,269	
Professional Fees	445,326	
Depreciation	424,526	
Travel	353,211	
Interest	272,502	
Insurance	235,991	
Miscellaneous	331,876	
Total Expenses	$18,157,404	
Net Income		$ 2,018,516

DISAPPOINTED by blind dates and personal ads, Andrea McGinty started her own dating firm and found a lucrative career.

In 1991, McGinty's fiancé walked out on her five weeks before the wedding. So it was back to the singles scene. One blind date threw a pizza against the wall when she got up to leave. There *had* to be a more civilized way to meet interesting people. Wouldn't it be nice if a dating service could arrange prescreened lunch dates for busy professionals like herself? "Lunch is over in an hour, and you don't have to kiss goodnight," McGinty reasoned.

McGinty followed her dream. Her company, **It's Just Lunch,** now has thousands of customers. McGinty charges $1,000 for arranging 12 dates. Lunch is extra, Dutch treat. "These are people who work long hours in fast-track careers. They need help with their social lives," says McGinty.

The business is a money-making machine, netting over $2 million in 1998 on revenues of $20 million.*

**Source:* Adapted from Suzanne Oliver, "Yuppie Yenta," *Forbes* (March 25, 1996), pp. 102–103.

What do we mean when we say that It's Just Lunch nets $2 million per year? As reported on its income statement, the business earns *net income,* or *profit,* of more than $2 million per year. What are the business's revenues? Service revenue fees of $1,000 per client to arrange 12 lunch dates. What are the business's expenses? Advertising, computer data searches, mailings to clients, and office expenses (such as employee salaries, rent, supplies, depreciation on office furniture, and computers and other office equipment). It's Just Lunch operates in much the same way as Air & Sea Travel, the travel agency we studied in Chapters 1 and 2.

Whether the business is It's Just Lunch, Air & Sea Travel, or The Gap, the profit motive increases the owners' drive to start and carry on the business. As you study this chapter, consider how important net income is to a business and how the pursuit of profit affects people's behavior.

How does a business know whether it is profitable or not? By preparing its financial statements. This chapter completes the accounting cycle, the process that begins with recording transactions (which we studied in Chapter 2) and ends with the financial statements that help measure profits and losses.

The Business Cycle

Businesses start with cash and work hard to collect more of it. They pay cash to buy goods and services, and then they sell those goods and services, receiving cash to complete the cycle. Exhibit 3-1 diagrams the business cycle. Start with circle 1 and proceed to the right.

The cycle for service entities such as **It's Just Lunch** or Air & Sea Travel is similar, except they do not hold inventory. The **accounting cycle** follows the business cycle to report on the following facts about the entity:

- Results of operations (income statement)
- Financial position (balance sheet)
- Cash flows (statement of cash flows)

Accrual-Basis Accounting Versus Cash-Basis Accounting

There are two basic ways to do accounting: the accrual basis and the cash basis. In **accrual-basis accounting,** an accountant recognizes the impact of a business

Exhibit 3-1
The Business Cycle

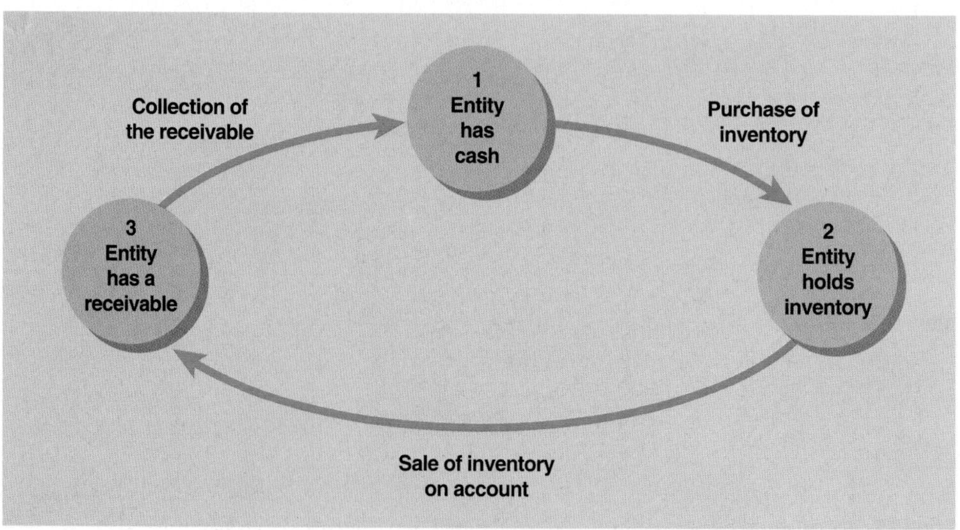

transaction as it occurs. When the business performs a service, makes a sale, or incurs an expense, the accountant records the transaction, whether or not cash has been received or paid. In **cash-basis accounting,** the accountant records a transaction only when cash is received or paid. Cash receipts are treated as revenues and cash payments are handled as expenses.

GAAP requires that businesses use the accrual basis. This means that the business records revenues as they are *earned* and expenses as they are *incurred*—not necessarily when cash changes hands.

Accrual Accounting and Cash Flows

Objective 1
Link cash flows with accrual-basis accounting

Accrual-basis accounting is more complex—and more complete—than cash-basis accounting. Accrual-basis accounting records both *cash* transactions, including

- Collecting from customers
- Receiving cash from interest earned
- Paying salaries, rent, income tax, and other expenses
- Borrowing money
- Paying off loans
- Issuing stock

It also records such *noncash* transactions as

- Purchases of inventory on account
- Sales on account
- Accrual of interest and other expenses incurred but not yet paid
- Depreciation expense
- Usage of prepaid insurance, supplies, and other prepaid expenses

The purpose of this chapter is to show how accrual-basis accounting completes the process that leads to the financial statements. Before launching into the end-of-period accounting procedures, however, let's illustrate how accrual-basis accounting and cash flows combine to give a complete picture of a company's operations, financial position, and cash flows. **It's Just Lunch** provides an interesting illustration.

Suppose that on August 1, 2000, It's Just Lunch receives from clients $1,000 in advance for the promise to provide a 12-date package. Assume that by December 31, 2000, It's Just Lunch has provided 9 (three-fourths) of the lunch dates. Under accrual-basis accounting, It's Just Lunch earned three-fourths of the $1,000, or $750, during the year 2000. At December 31, 2000, It's Just Lunch has a $250 liability to its clients because it still must provide them with 3 dates. During 2001, It's Just Lunch will arrange the remaining dates and earn the final $250 of revenue.

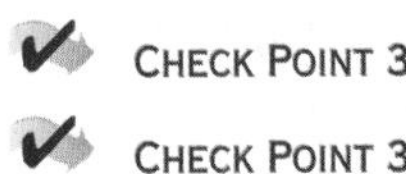

Exhibit 3-2 shows how accrual-basis accounting reports the full picture of the foregoing business activities of It's Just Lunch. Cash-basis accounting would show a different picture. If It's Just Lunch were to use the cash basis to account for this situation, the company would report only one thing: $1,000 of cash revenue in the year 2000, as shown on the statement of cash flows. Cash-basis accounting would not show the revenue when it was earned, as reported on the income statement. It would also ignore It's Just Lunch's $250 liability at December 31, 2000, as on the balance sheet. You can see how much more information the accrual basis provides.

Accrual accounting is based on a conceptual framework that includes a number of accounting concepts and principles. We turn now to the time-period concept, the revenue principle, and the matching principle.

The Time-Period Concept

The only way for a business to know for certain how successfully it has operated is to close its doors, sell all its assets, pay the liabilities, and return any leftover cash to

Exhibit 3-2
Accrual-Basis Accounting and Cash Flows for It's Just Lunch

	Year	
Results of operations	*2000*	*2001*
Income statement reports:		
Service revenue (when earned)	$ 750	$250
Financial position		
Balance sheet reports:		
Liabilities:		
Unearned service revenue (company still owes)	$ 250	$ 0
Cash flows		
Statement of cash flows reports:		
Cash flows from operating activities:		
Collections from customers		
(when cash was received)	$1,000	$ 0

the owners. This process, called *liquidation,* means going out of business. For going businesses it is not practical to measure income this way. Instead, businesses need periodic reports on their progress. Accountants slice time into small segments and prepare financial statements for specific periods. The **time-period concept** ensures that accounting information is reported at regular intervals.

The most basic accounting period is one year, and virtually all businesses prepare annual financial statements. For about 60% of large companies in a recent survey, the annual accounting period runs the calendar year from January 1 through December 31. It's Just Lunch also uses the calendar year as its annual reporting period. Retailers are a notable exception. For instance, **JC Penney Company** and most other retailers use a fiscal year ending on January 31 because the low point in their business activity falls during January, after Christmas sales. JC Penney does more than 30% of its yearly sales during November and December but only 5% in January.

However, managers and investors cannot wait until the end of the year to gauge a company's progress. Thus, companies prepare financial statements for interim periods of less than a year. Publicly owned companies must issue quarterly financial statements. Because managers want financial information even more often, monthly statements are common. A series of monthly statements can be combined for quarterly and semiannual periods. Although most of the discussions in this text are based on an annual accounting period, the procedures and statements can be applied to interim periods as well.

The Revenue Principle

Objective 2
Apply the revenue and matching principles

The **revenue principle** tells accountants two things:

1. *When* to record revenue by making a journal entry, and
2. The *amount* of revenue to record.

Revenue, defined in Chapter 1, page 12, is the increase in retained earnings from delivering goods and services to customers in the course of operating a business.

The general principle guiding *when* to record revenue says to record revenue when it has been earned—but not before. In most cases, revenue is earned when the business has delivered a completed good or service to the customer. The business has done everything required by the agreement and has transferred the good or service to the customer. Exhibit 3-3 shows two situations that provide guidance on when to record revenue. Situation 1 illustrates when *not* to record revenue: At this point, no transaction has occurred, so Air & Sea Travel makes no journal entry.

Situation 2 illustrates when revenue should be recorded: after a business transaction has occurred. If the client pays for Air & Sea Travel's service immediately, the business will record Cash. If the service is performed on account, Air & Sea will

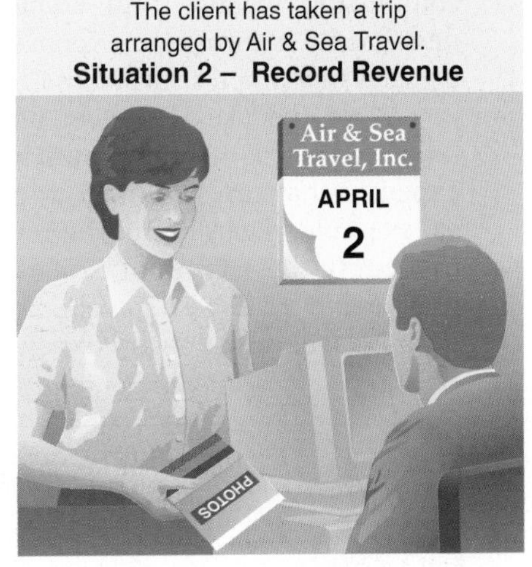

EXHIBIT 3-3
Recording Revenue

record Accounts Receivable. In either case, the travel agency should record Service Revenue.

The general principle guiding the *amount* of revenue says to record revenue equal to the cash value of the goods or services transferred to the customer. Suppose that in order to obtain a new client, Air & Sea Travel performs travel service for the price of $500. Ordinarily, the company would have charged $600 for this service. How much revenue should the business record? The answer is $500—the cash value of the transaction. Air & Sea Travel will not receive the normal value of $600 because the transaction was for $500. The business will receive only $500 cash, which pinpoints the amount of revenue earned.

The Matching Principle

The **matching principle** is the basis for recording expenses. Recall that expenses, such as rent, utilities, and advertising, are the costs of operating a business. *Expenses* are the costs of assets used up in the earning of revenue. The matching principle directs accountants to perform three activities:

> An expense, defined in Chapter 1, page 12, is a decrease in retained earnings that occurs in the course of operating a business.

1. Identify all expenses incurred during the accounting period,
2. Measure the expenses, and
3. Match expenses against revenues earned during the same period.

To match expenses against revenues means to subtract expenses from revenues in order to compute net income or net loss for the period. Exhibit 3-4 illustrates the matching principle.

There is a natural link between revenues and some types of expenses. For example, a business that pays sales commissions to its sales personnel will have

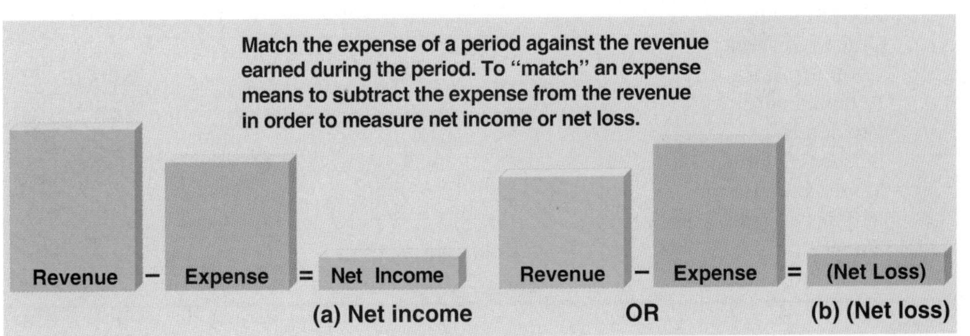

EXHIBIT 3-4
The Matching Principle

commission expense if the employees make sales. If they make no sales, the business has no commission expense. *Cost of goods sold* is another example. If there are no sales of women's suits, **Liz Claiborne, Inc.,** has no cost of goods sold.

✔ CHECK POINT 3-3

Some expenses, however, are not so easy to link with particular sales. Accountants follow the matching principle by first identifying a period's revenues and the expenses that can be linked to particular revenues. Monthly rent expense occurs, for example, regardless of the revenues. The matching principle directs accountants to identify these types of expenses with a particular time period, such as a month or a year. If Air & Sea Travel employs a secretary at a monthly salary of $1,900, the business will record salary expense of $1,900 at the end of each month.

1. A client pays Air & Sea $900 on March 15 for service to be performed April 1 to June 30. Has Air & Sea earned revenue on March 15?
2. Air & Sea Travel pays $4,500 on July 31 for office rent for the next three months. Has the company incurred an expense on July 31?

Answers:

1. No. Air & Sea has received the cash but will not perform the service until later. Air & Sea earns the revenue when it performs the service.
2. No. Air & Sea has paid cash, but the rent will not expire for three months. This prepaid rent is an asset because Air & Sea has the use of an office in the future.

Objective 3
Adjust the accounts to update the financial statements

UPDATING THE ACCOUNTS FOR THE FINANCIAL STATEMENTS: THE ADJUSTMENT PROCESS

At the end of the period, the business reports its financial statements. This accounting process begins with the trial balance that you saw in Chapter 2. Recall that the trial balance lists the accounts and their balances after the period's transactions have been recorded. Exhibit 3-5 is the trial balance of Air & Sea Travel, Inc., at April 30, 20X1.

See Chapter 2, pages 74–78, for a review of the trial balance.

EXHIBIT 3-5
Unadjusted Trial Balance

AIR & SEA TRAVEL, INC.
Unadjusted Trial Balance
April 30, 20X1

Cash	$24,800	
Accounts receivable	2,250	
Supplies	700	
Prepaid rent	3,000	
Furniture	16,500	
Accounts payable		$13,100
Unearned service revenue		450
Common stock		20,000
Retained earnings		11,250
Dividends	3,200	
Service revenue		7,000
Salary expense	950	
Utilities expense	400	
Total	$51,800	$51,800

This *unadjusted trial balance* includes some new accounts that we will explain here. It lists most, but not all, of the travel agency's revenue and expenses for the month of April. These trial balance amounts are incomplete because they omit certain revenue and expense transactions that affect more than one accounting period. This is why it is called an *unadjusted* trial balance. In most cases, however, we refer to it simply as the trial balance, without the label "unadjusted."

The accrual basis requires adjustments at the end of the period to produce correct balances for the financial statements. To see why, consider the Supplies account in Exhibit 3-5. Air & Sea Travel uses supplies in providing travel services for clients during the month. This use reduces the quantity of supplies on hand and thus constitutes an expense, just like salary expense or rent expense. Gary and Monica Lyon do not bother to record this expense daily, and it is not worth their while to record supplies expense more than once a month. It is time-consuming to make hourly, daily, or even weekly journal entries to record the expense for the use of supplies. So how does the business account for supplies expense?

By the end of the month, the Supplies balance is not current. The amount on the trial balance represents the cost of supplies available for use during the month minus any supplies that may have been sold. This balance fails to consider the supplies used (supplies expense) during the accounting period. It is necessary to count the supplies on hand at the end of the period, and this count determines the ending balance. This is the correct amount of supplies to report on the balance sheet. Adjusting the accounts brings the accounts up to date and produces accurate financial statements. Exhibit 3-6 illustrates the adjustment process for supplies and supplies expense.

To enter the adjustments into the accounting records, accountants make **adjusting entries** in the journal at the end of the period. Adjusting entries accomplish two purposes:

- They assign revenues to the period in which they are earned and expenses to the period in which they are incurred.
- They update the asset and liability accounts.

Adjusting entries are thus needed for two reasons:

1. To measure properly the period's income, and

2. To bring related asset and liability accounts to correct balances for the balance sheet.

For example, an adjusting entry is needed to transfer the amount of supplies used during the period from the asset account Supplies to the expense account Supplies Expense. The adjusting entry updates both the Supplies asset account and the Supplies Expense account. This adjustment achieves accurate measures of assets and expenses. Adjusting entries, which are the key to accurate accrual-basis accounting, are made before the financial statements are prepared.

EXHIBIT 3-6
The Adjustment of Supplies (and Supplies Expense) at the End of the Accounting Period

During April		April 30		
Supplies available for use during April	–	Supplies on hand at April 30	=	Supplies expense for April
TOTAL COST	–	**ASSET**	=	**EXPENSE**
$700	–	**$400**	=	**$300**

EXHIBIT 3-7
Summary of the Accounting Cycle

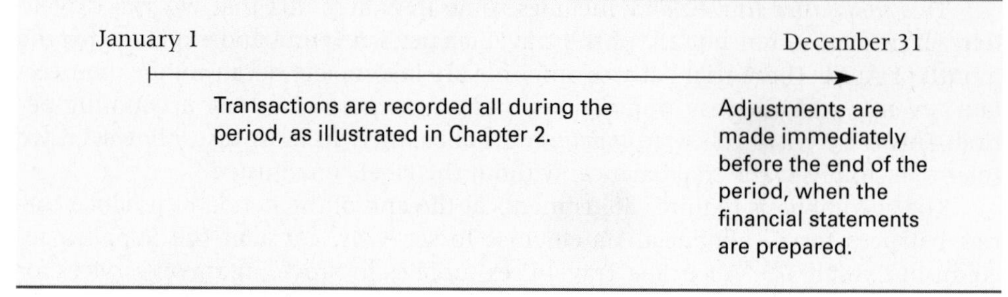

The end-of-period process of updating the accounts is called *adjusting the accounts, making the adjusting entries,* or *adjusting the books.* Exhibit 3-7 shows where the adjusting process fits into the accounting cycle.

Adjusting entries can be grouped into three basic categories: *deferrals, depreciation,* and *accruals.*

DEFERRALS. A **deferral** is an adjustment of an asset or a liability for which the business paid or received cash in advance. First, let's consider a deferral-type adjustment for the asset Supplies. **It's Just Lunch** purchases supplies for use in its operations. During the period, some supplies are used up and thus become expenses. At the end of the period, an adjustment is needed to remove from the Supplies account the cost of the supplies used up, which is Supplies Expense. Prepaid rent, prepaid insurance, and all other prepaid expenses require deferral-type adjustments.

There are also deferral-type adjustments for liabilities. Some companies collect cash in advance of earning the revenue. A prime example is It's Just Lunch, which collects cash up front and then arranges lunch dates for clients. When It's Just Lunch receives cash up front, the company has a liability to provide a service for the client. This liability is called Unearned Service Revenue. Then, over the course of the contract period, It's Just Lunch earns Service Revenue by providing the dates. This earning process requires an adjustment at the end of each accounting period. The adjustment removes from the liability account the amount of revenue earned during the period. Publishers such as **Time, Inc.,** and your local newspaper sell magazine and newspaper subscriptions and collect cash in advance. Their accounting parallels that of It's Just Lunch.

DEPRECIATION. **Depreciation** is the systematic allocation of the cost of a plant asset to expense over the asset's useful life. Therefore, depreciation is the most common long-term deferral. The business buys long-term plant assets, such as buildings, equipment, and furniture. As the company uses the assets, it records depreciation for their wear and tear and obsolescence. This end-of-period adjustment records Depreciation Expense and decreases the book value of the asset over its expected useful life. The process is identical to a deferral-type adjustment; the only difference is the type of asset involved.

ACCRUALS. An **accrual** is the opposite of a deferral. For an accrual the business records an expense or a revenue before paying or receiving cash. Salary Expense is an example of an accrual-type adjustment for an expense. As employees work for It's Just Lunch, the company's salary expense accrues with the passage of time. Suppose that at year end, It's Just Lunch owes employees salaries of $1,000 and will pay them on January 2 of the next year. At December 31, It's Just Lunch must record Salary Expense and Salary Payable for the $1,000. Other examples of expense accruals include interest expense, income tax expense, and indeed all expenses that the business has incurred but not yet paid.

There are also accrual-type adjustments for revenues. Suppose It's Just Lunch has earned interest revenue that it will collect in cash next year. At December 31, It's Just Lunch must accrue the interest revenue. The adjustment is made to the Interest Receivable account and the Interest Revenue account.

Let's see how the adjusting process actually works. We begin with prepaid expenses, which are assets, not expenses.

Prepaid Expenses

Prepaid expenses are expenses that are paid in advance and will be used up in the near future. Therefore, they are assets, not expenses, because they provide a future benefit for the owner. Let's start with prepaid rent.

PREPAID RENT. Landlords require tenants to pay rent in advance. This prepayment creates an asset for the renter because that tenant has purchased the future benefit of using the rented item. Suppose Air & Sea Travel prepays three months' rent on April 1, 20X1. If the lease specifies a monthly rental amount of $1,000, the entry to record the payment for three months debits Prepaid Rent as follows:

Apr. 1	Prepaid Rent ($1,000 × 3)	3,000	
	Cash		3,000
	Paid three months' rent in advance.		

The accounting equation shows that because one asset increases and another decreases, the amount of total assets is unchanged.

ASSETS	=	LIABILITIES	+	STOCKHOLDERS' EQUITY
3,000 −3,000	=	0	+	0

After posting, the Prepaid Rent account appears as follows:

PREPAID RENT	
Apr. 1 3,000	

Throughout April, the Prepaid Rent account maintains this beginning balance, as shown back in Exhibit 3-5 (p. 110).

At April 30, Prepaid Rent is adjusted to remove the expense from the asset account. The amount of rent expense is one month's worth of the prepayment ($3,000 × 1/3 = $1,000). The adjustment transfers one-third of the asset balance from Prepaid Rent to Rent Expense as follows:

*Apr. 30	Rent Expense ($3,000 × 1/3)	1,000	Adjusting entry a
	Prepaid Rent		1,000
	To record rent expense.		

The accounting equation shows that because of the expense, both assets and stockholders' equity decrease.

ASSETS	=	LIABILITIES	+	STOCKHOLDERS' EQUITY	−	EXPENSES
− 1,000	=	0			−	1,000

*See Exhibit 3-12, page 123, for a summary of adjustments a–g.

After posting, Prepaid Rent and Rent Expense appear as follows:

PREPAID RENT				→	RENT EXPENSE		
Apr. 1	3,000	Apr. 30	1,000	→	Apr. 30	1,000	
Bal.	2,000				Bal.	1,000	

Recording this expense illustrates the matching principle. The same analysis applies to a prepayment of three months' insurance premiums. The only difference is in the account titles, which would be Prepaid Insurance and Insurance Expense instead of Prepaid Rent and Rent Expense, respectively.

SUPPLIES. Supplies are another example of prepaid expenses. On April 2, Air & Sea Travel paid cash of $700 for office supplies:

Apr. 2	Supplies.	700	
	Cash		700
	Paid cash for supplies.		

ASSETS	=	LIABILITIES	+	STOCKHOLDERS' EQUITY
700 −700	=	0	+	0

Assume that the business purchased no additional supplies during April. The April 30 trial balance therefore lists Supplies with a $700 debit balance (Exhibit 3-5 [p. 110]).

During April, Air & Sea Travel used supplies in performing services for clients. The cost of the supplies used is the measure of *supplies expense* for the month. To measure the business's supplies expense during April, the owners count the supplies on hand at the end of the month. This is the amount of the asset still available to the business. Assume the count indicates that supplies costing $400 remain. Subtracting the entity's $400 supplies on hand at the end of April from the cost of supplies available during April ($700) measures supplies expense during the month ($300):

COST OF ASSET AVAILABLE DURING THE PERIOD	−	COST OF ASSET ON HAND AT THE END OF THE PERIOD	=	COST OF ASSET USED (EXPENSE) DURING THE PERIOD
$700	−	$400	=	$300

The April 30 adjusting entry to update the Supplies account and to record the supplies expense for the month debits the expense and credits the asset, as follows:

Apr. 30	Supplies Expense ($700 − $400).	300		Adjusting entry b
	Supplies		300	
	To record supplies expense.			

ASSETS	=	LIABILITIES	+	STOCKHOLDERS' EQUITY	−	EXPENSES
−300	=	0			−	300

After posting, the Supplies and Supplies Expense accounts appear as follows:

SUPPLIES				→	SUPPLIES EXPENSE		
Apr. 2	700	Apr. 30	300	→	Apr. 30	300	
Bal.	400				Bal.	300	

The Supplies account then enters the month of May with a $400 balance, and the adjustment process is repeated month after month.

CHECK POINT 3-4

At the beginning of the month, supplies were $5,000. During the month, $7,800 of supplies were purchased. At month's end, it was determined that $3,600 of supplies were still on hand. What are the adjusting entry and the ending balance in the Supplies account?

Answer:

Supplies Expense ($5,000 + $7,800 − $3,600)	9,200	
Supplies		9,200

Ending balance of supplies = $3,600 (the supplies still on hand)

Depreciation of Plant Assets

The logic behind accrual accounting is probably best illustrated by how businesses account for plant assets. **Plant assets** are long-lived tangible assets, such as land, buildings, furniture, machinery, and equipment used in the operations of the business. As one accountant has put it, "All assets but land are on a march to the junkyard." That is, all plant assets but land decline in usefulness as they age. This decline is an *expense* to the business. Accountants systematically spread the cost of each plant asset, except land, over the years of its useful life. This process of allocating cost to expense is called *depreciation.*

Consider Air & Sea Travel's operations. Suppose that on April 3 the business purchased furniture on account for $16,500:

Apr. 3	Furniture	16,500	
	Accounts Payable		16,500
	Purchased office furniture on account.		

ASSETS	=	LIABILITIES	+	STOCKHOLDERS' EQUITY
16,500	=	16,500	+	0

After posting, the Furniture account appears as follows:

FURNITURE		
Apr. 3	16,500	

Air & Sea Travel records an asset when the furniture is acquired. Then, a portion of the asset's cost is transferred from the asset account to Depreciation Expense during each period that the asset is used. This method matches the asset's expense to the revenue of the period—a practice that applies the matching principle. In many computerized systems, the adjusting entry for depreciation is programmed to occur automatically each month for the duration of the asset's life.

Gary and Monica Lyon believe their office furniture will remain useful for five years but will be virtually worthless at the end of its life. One way to compute the amount of depreciation for each year is to divide the cost of the asset ($16,500 in our example) by its expected useful life (five years). This procedure—called the *straight-line method*—gives annual depreciation of $3,300.

$16,500/5 years = $3,300 per year

Depreciation for the month of April is $275.

$3,300/12 months = $275 per month

Chapter 7 covers plant assets and depreciation in more detail.

THE ACCUMULATED DEPRECIATION ACCOUNT. Depreciation expense for April is recorded as follows:

Apr. 30	Depreciation Expense—Furniture	275	
	Accumulated Depreciation—Furniture. . . .		275
	To record depreciation on furniture.		

Adjusting entry c

Note that assets decrease by the amount of the expense:

ASSETS	=	LIABILITIES	+	STOCKHOLDERS' EQUITY	−	EXPENSES
− 275	=	0			−	275

Accumulated Depreciation is credited instead of Furniture because the original cost of the furniture remains in the original asset account as long as the business uses the asset. Accountants can always refer to that account if they need to know how much the asset cost.

The amount of depreciation is an *estimate.* Accountants use the **Accumulated Depreciation** account to show the cumulative sum of all depreciation expense from the date of acquiring the asset. Therefore, the balance in the Accumulated Depreciation account increases over the life of the asset.

Accumulated Depreciation is a *contra asset* account—an asset account with a normal credit balance. A **contra account** has two distinguishing characteristics:

1. It always has a companion account.

2. Its normal balance is opposite that of the companion account.

In this case, because Accumulated Depreciation is the contra (companion) account to the asset account Furniture, it appears directly after Furniture on the balance sheet.

A business carries an accumulated depreciation account for each depreciable asset. If a business has a building and a machine, for example, it will carry separate accounts for Accumulated Depreciation—Building and Accumulated Depreciation—Machinery.

After posting, the plant asset accounts of Air & Sea Travel, Inc., are as follows:

FURNITURE

Apr. 3	**16,500**		
Bal.	**16,500**		

ACCUMULATED DEPRECIATION—FURNITURE

		Apr. 30	**275**
		Bal.	**275**

DEPRECIATION EXPENSE—FURNITURE

Apr. 30	**275**		
Bal.	**275**		

BOOK VALUE. The net amount of a plant asset (cost minus accumulated depreciation) is called that asset's **book value,** *net book value,* or *carrying amount,* as shown here for Air & Sea's furniture:

Plant Assets:

Furniture	$16,500
Less Accumulated Depreciation	(275)
Book value	$16,225

CHECK POINT 3-5

Accumulated Depreciation is reported on the balance sheet with the Furniture account to determine the asset's book value. Exhibit 3-8 reports Air & Sea's plant assets at April 30.

PLANT ASSETS		
Furniture	$16,500	
Less Accumulated Depreciation	(275)	$16,225
Building	$48,000	
Less Accumulated Depreciation	(200)	47,800
Book value of plant assets		$64,025

EXHIBIT 3-8
Plant Assets on the Balance Sheet of Air & Sea Travel, Inc. (April 30)

STOP & THINK

1. What is the book value of Air & Sea Travel's furniture at the end of May?
2. Is book value what the furniture could be sold for?

Answers:

1. $16,500 − $275 − $275 = $15,950.
2. Not necessarily. Book value represents the part of the asset's cost that has not yet been depreciated. Book value is not necessarily related to the amount that an asset can be sold for.

Exhibit 3-9 shows how **Johnson & Johnson**—makers of Band-Aids, Tylenol, and other health-care products—reported Property, Plant, and Equipment in its annual report. Johnson & Johnson has real-estate holdings around the world; they are reported in line 1 of Exhibit 3-9. Line 2 includes the cost of buildings used in company operations. Machinery and equipment are given in line 3, and line 4 reports on assets that are under construction. Line 5 gives the sum of the accumulated depreciation on all Johnson & Johnson's plant assets. Line 6 shows the assets' book value of $4,115 million.

ACCRUED EXPENSES. Businesses often incur expenses before they pay cash. Consider an employee's salary. Because the employer's salary expense and salary payable grow as the employee works, the liability is said to accrue. Another example is interest expense on a note payable. Interest accrues as the clock ticks. The term **accrued expense** refers to a liability that arises from an expense that the business has incurred but has not yet paid.

It is time-consuming to make hourly, daily, or even weekly journal entries to record expenses. Consequently, the accountant waits until the end of the period. Then an adjusting entry brings each expense (and related liability) up-to-date just before the financial statements are prepared.

SALARY EXPENSE. Most companies pay their employees at set times. Suppose Air & Sea Travel pays its employee a monthly salary of $1,900, half on the 15th and half

1	Land and land improvements	$ 262
2	Buildings and building equipment	2,226
3	Machinery and equipment	3,143
4	Construction in progress	672
		6,303
5	Less Accumulated depreciation	(2,188)
6		$4,115

EXHIBIT 3-9
Johnson & Johnson's Reporting of Property, Plant, and Equipment (In millions)

on the last day of the month. The following calendar for April has the paydays circled:

			APRIL			
Sun.	*Mon.*	*Tue.*	*Wed.*	*Thur.*	*Fri.*	*Sat.*
					1	2
3	4	5	6	7	8	9
10	11	12	13	14	(15)	16
17	18	19	20	21	22	23
24	25	26	27	28	29	(30)

Assume that if either payday falls on the weekend, Air & Sea Travel pays the employee on the following Monday. During April, the agency paid its employee's first half-month salary of $950 and made the following entry:

Apr. 15	Salary Expense.	950	
	Cash		950
	To pay salary.		

ASSETS	=	LIABILITIES	+	STOCKHOLDERS' EQUITY	−	EXPENSES
−950	=	0			−	950

After posting, the Salary Expense account is

SALARY EXPENSE	
Apr. 15 950	

The trial balance at April 30 (Exhibit 3-5, page 110) includes Salary Expense, with its debit balance of $950. Because April 30, the second payday of the month, falls on a Saturday, the second half-month amount of $950 will be paid on Monday, May 2. At April 30, therefore, Air & Sea's accountant adjusts for additional *salary expense* and *salary payable* of $950 by recording an increase in each account as follows:

Apr. 30	Salary Expense	950		Adjusting entry d
	Salary Payable		950	
	To accrue salary expense.			

The accounting equation shows that liabilities increased and stockholders' equity decreased for the expense:

ASSETS	=	LIABILITIES	+	STOCKHOLDERS' EQUITY	−	EXPENSES
0	=	950			−	950

After posting, the Salary Payable and Salary Expense accounts appear as follows:

SALARY PAYABLE			
		Apr. 30	**950**
		Bal.	**950**

SALARY EXPENSE		
Apr. 15	**950**	
Apr. 30	**950**	
Bal.	**1,900**	

The accounts at April 30 now contain the complete salary information for the month. The expense account has a full month's salary, and the liability account shows the portion that the business still owes at April 30. All accrued expenses are recorded with similar entries—a debit to the expense account and a credit to the related liability account.

CHECK POINT 3-6

CHECK POINT 3-7

Many computerized systems contain a payroll module, or functional unit. The adjusting entry for accrued salaries is automatically journalized and posted at the end of each accounting period.

What is the adjusting entry at April 30 for the following situation? Weekly salaries for a five-day week total $3,500, payable on Friday; April 30 falls on a Tuesday.

Answer: $3,500 × 2/5 = $1,400. The adjusting entry is

Salary Expense	1,400	
Salary Payable.		1,400
To accrue salary expense.		

Accrued Revenues

Businesses often earn revenue before they receive the cash because collection occurs later. A revenue that has been earned but not yet received in cash is called an **accrued revenue.**

Assume that Guerrero Tours hires Air & Sea Travel on April 15 to perform services on a monthly basis. Suppose Guerrero will pay the travel agency $500 monthly, with the first payment on May 15. During April, Air & Sea will earn half a month's fee, $250, for work performed April 15 through April 30. On April 30, Air & Sea Travel makes the following adjusting entry:

Apr. 30	Accounts Receivable ($500 × 1/2)	250	Adjusting entry e
	Service Revenue		250
	To accrue service revenue.		

Both total assets and stockholders' equity increase because of the boost from revenue:

ASSETS	=	LIABILITIES	+	STOCKHOLDERS' EQUITY	+	REVENUES
250	=	0			+	250

Recall that Accounts Receivable has an unadjusted balance of $2,250, and the Service Revenue unadjusted balance is $7,000 (Exhibit 3-5, page 110). Posting this adjusting entry has the following effects on these two accounts:

ACCOUNTS RECEIVABLE

	Debit	Credit
	2,250	
Apr. 30	250	
Bal.	**2,500**	

SERVICE REVENUE

Debit		Credit
		7,000
	Apr. 30	250
	Bal.	**7,250**

All accrued revenues are accounted for similarly—by debiting a receivable and crediting a revenue.

CHECK POINT 3-8

Suppose Air & Sea Travel holds a note receivable from a client. At th end of April, $125 of interest revenue has been earned. Prepare the ad justing entry at April 30.

Answer:

Interest Receivable	125	
Interest Revenue		125
To accrue interest revenue.		

Unearned Revenues

Some businesses collect cash from customers before earning the revenue. Doin creates a liability called **unearned revenue,** which is an obligation arising from ceiving cash in advance of providing a product or a service. Only when the jo completed will the business earn the revenue. Suppose Baldwin Investm Bankers engages Air & Sea's services, agreeing to pay the travel agency $ monthly, beginning immediately. If Air & Sea Travel collects the first amount April 20, Air & Sea records this increase in assets and liabilities as follows:

Apr. 20	Cash	450	
	Unearned Service Revenue		450
	Received cash for revenue in advance.		

ASSETS	=	LIABILITIES	+	STOCKHOLDERS' EQUITY
450	=	450	+	0

After posting, the liability account appears as follows:

UNEARNED SERVICE REVENUE	
	Apr. 20 450

Unearned Service Revenue is a liability because it represents Air & Sea's o gation to perform service for the client. The April 30 unadjusted trial balance (hibit 3-5, page 110) lists this account with a $450 credit balance prior to adjusting entries. During the last 10 days of the month—April 21 through A 30—the travel agency will *earn* one-third (10 days divided by April's total of days) of the $450, or $150. Therefore, the accountant makes the following adj ment to decrease the liability, Unearned Service Revenue, and to record an incre in Service Revenue:

Apr. 30	Unearned Service Revenue ($450 × ⅓)	150	
	Service Revenue		150
	To record unearned service revenue that has been earned.		

Adjusting entry f

ASSETS	=	LIABILITIES	+	STOCKHOLDERS' EQUITY	+	REVENUES
0	=	−150			+	150

This adjusting entry shifts $150 of the total amount from the liability account the revenue account. After posting, the balance of Unearned Service Revenue is duced to $300, and the balance of Service Revenue is increased by $150:

UNEARNED SERVICE REVENUE			
Apr. 30	150	Apr. 20	450
		Bal.	300

SERVICE REVENUE			
			7,000
		Apr. 30	250
		Apr. 30	150
		Bal.	7,400

All types of revenues that are collected in advance are accounted for similarly.

CHECK POINT 3-9

An unearned revenue is a liability, not a revenue. An unearned revenue to one company can be a prepaid expense to the company that made the payment. For example, Baldwin Investment Bankers' prepayment to Air & Sea Travel is a prepaid expense of Baldwin.

Exhibit 3-10 diagrams the distinctive timing of prepaid- and accrual-type adjustments. Study prepaid expenses all the way across. Then study unearned revenues, and so on.

Summary of the Adjusting Process

Because one purpose of the adjusting process is to measure business income, each adjusting entry affects at least one income statement account—a revenue or an expense. The other purpose of the adjusting process is to update the balance sheet accounts. Therefore, the other side of each adjusting entry—a debit or a credit—affects an asset or a liability. No adjusting entry debits or credits Cash because cash transactions are recorded at other times. The end-of-period adjustment

EXHIBIT 3-10
Prepaid- and Accrual-Type Adjustments

PREPAIDS—THE CASH TRANSACTION OCCURS INITIALLY.

	Initially			*Later*		
Prepaid expenses	Pay cash and record an asset:			→ Record an expense and decrease the asset:		
	Prepaid Expense	XXX		Expense	XXX	
	Cash		XXX	Prepaid Expense ...		XXX
Unearned revenues	Receive cash and record unearned revenue:			→ Record a revenue and decrease unearned revenue:		
	Cash	XXX		Unearned Revenue	XXX	
	Unearned Revenue ...		XXX	Revenue ...		XXX

ACCRUALS—THE CASH TRANSACTION OCCURS LATER.

	Initially			*Later*		
Accrued expenses	Record (accrue) an expense and the related payable:			→ Pay cash and decrease the payable:		
	Expense	XXX		Payable	XXX	
	Payable ...		XXX	Cash		XXX
Accrued revenues	Record (accrue) a revenue and the related receivable:			→ Receive cash and decrease the receivable		
	Receivable ...	XXX		Cash	XXX	
	Revenue ...		XXX	Receivable .		XXX

The authors thank Darrel Davis and Alfonso Oddo for suggesting this exhibit.

EXHIBIT 3-11
Summary of Adjusting Entries

Category of Adjusting Entry	*Type of Account*	
	Debit	***Credit***
Prepaid expense	Expense	Asset
Depreciation	Expense	Contra asset
Accrued expense	Expense	Liability
Accrued revenue	Asset	Revenue
Unearned revenue	Liability	Revenue

Adapted from material provided by Beverly Terry.

process is reserved for the noncash transactions that are required by accrual-basis accounting. Exhibit 3-11 summarizes the adjusting entries.

Exhibit 3-12 on page 123 summarizes the adjustments of Air & Sea Travel, Inc., at April 30—the adjusting entries we've examined over the past few pages. Panel A repeats the data for each adjustment, Panel B gives the adjusting entries, and Panel C shows the accounts after the adjusting entries have been posted. The adjustments are keyed by letter.

➛ Recall from Chapter 2, page 69, that posting is the process of transferring amounts from the journal to the ledger.

Exhibit 3-12 includes an additional adjusting entry that we have not yet discussed: the accrual of income tax expense. Like individual taxpayers, corporations are subject to income tax. They typically accrue income tax expense and the related income tax payable as the final adjusting entry of the period. Air & Sea Travel, Inc., accrues income tax expense with adjusting entry g, as follows:

✔ CHECK POINT 3-10

Apr. 30	Income Tax Expense	540	Adjusting entry g
	Income Tax Payable		540
	To accrue income tax expense.		

THE ADJUSTED TRIAL BALANCE

This chapter began with the trial balance before any adjusting entries—the unadjusted trial balance (Exhibit 3-5, page 110). After the adjustments are journalized and posted, the accounts appear as shown in Exhibit 3-12, Panel C. A useful step in preparing the financial statements is to list the accounts, along with their adjusted balances, on an **adjusted trial balance.** This document has the advantage of listing all the accounts and their final balances in a single place. Exhibit 3-13 shows the adjusted trial balance of Air & Sea Travel.

Note how clearly this format presents the data. The information in the Account Title column and in the Trial Balance columns is drawn directly from the trial balance. The two Adjustments columns list the debit and credit adjustments directly across from the appropriate account title. Adjustment amounts are identified by the letter in parentheses that refers to the adjusting entry. For example, the debit labeled (e) on the work sheet refers to the debit adjusting entry of $250 to Accounts Receivable in Panel B of Exhibit 3-12. Likewise for adjusting credits: The corresponding credit—labeled (e)—refers to the $250 credit to Service Revenue.

The Adjusted Trial Balance columns give the final account balances. Each amount on the adjusted trial balance of Exhibit 3-13 is computed by taking the amounts from the unadjusted trial balance and adding or subtracting the adjustments. For example, Accounts Receivable starts with a balance of $2,250. Adding the $250 debit amount from adjusting entry (e) gives Accounts Receivable its ending balance of $2,500.

EXHIBIT 3-12

The Adjusting Process of Air & Sea Travel, Inc.

PANEL A—Information for Adjustments at April 30, 20X1

(a) Prepaid rent expired, $1,000.
(b) Supplies on hand, $400.
(c) Depreciation on furniture, $275.
(d) Accrued salary expense, $950.
(e) Accrued service revenue, $250.
(f) Amount of unearned service revenue that has been earned, $150.
(g) Accrued income tax expense, $540.

PANEL B—Adjusting Entries

	Account	Debit	Credit
(a)	Rent Expense	1,000	
	Prepaid Rent		1,000
	To record rent expense.		
(b)	Supplies Expense	300	
	Supplies		300
	To record supplies used.		
(c)	Depreciation Expense—Furniture	275	
	Accumulated Depreciation—Furniture		275
	To record depreciation on furniture.		
(d)	Salary Expense	950	
	Salary Payable		950
	To accrue salary expense.		
(e)	Accounts Receivable	250	
	Service Revenue		250
	To accrue service revenue.		
(f)	Unearned Service Revenue	150	
	Service Revenue		150
	To record unearned revenue that has been earned.		
(g)	Income Tax Expense	540	
	Income Tax Payable		540
	To accrue income tax expense.		

PANEL C—Ledger Accounts

ASSETS

CASH

Debit	Credit
Bal. 24,800	

PREPAID RENT

Debit	Credit
3,000	(a) 1,000
Bal. 2,000	

ACCOUNTS RECEIVABLE

Debit	Credit
2,250	
(e) 250	
Bal. 2,500	

FURNITURE

Debit	Credit
Bal. 16,500	

SUPPLIES

Debit	Credit
700	(b) 300
Bal. 400	

ACCUMULATED DEPRECIATION—FURNITURE

Debit	Credit
	(c) 275
	Bal. 275

LIABILITIES

ACCOUNTS PAYABLE

Debit	Credit
	Bal. 13,100

SALARY PAYABLE

Debit	Credit
	(d) 950
	Bal. 950

UNEARNED SERVICE REVENUE

Debit	Credit
(f) 150	450
	Bal. 300

INCOME TAX PAYABLE

Debit	Credit
	(g) 540
	Bal. 540

STOCKHOLDERS' EQUITY

COMMON STOCK

Debit	Credit
	Bal. 20,000

RETAINED EARNINGS

Debit	Credit
	Bal. 11,250

DIVIDENDS

Debit	Credit
Bal. 3,200	

REVENUE

SERVICE REVENUE

Debit	Credit
	7,000
	(e) 250
	(f) 150
	Bal. 7,400

EXPENSES

RENT EXPENSE

Debit	Credit
(a) 1,000	
Bal. 1,000	

SALARY EXPENSE

Debit	Credit
950	
(d) 950	
Bal. 1,900	

SUPPLIES EXPENSE

Debit	Credit
(b) 300	
Bal. 300	

DEPRECIATION EXPENSE—FURNITURE

Debit	Credit
(c) 275	
Bal. 275	

UTILITIES EXPENSE

Debit	Credit
Bal. 400	

INCOME TAX EXPENSE

Debit	Credit
(g) 540	
Bal. 540	

EXHIBIT 3-13
Adjusted Trial Balance

AIR & SEA TRAVEL, INC.
Preparation of Adjusted Trial Balance
April 30, 20X1

	Trial Balance		*Adjustments*		*Adjusted Trial Balance*	
Account Title	***Debit***	***Credit***	***Debit***	***Credit***	***Debit***	***Credit***
Cash	24,800				24,800	
Accounts receivable	2,250		(e) 250		2,500	
Supplies	700			(b) 300	400	
Prepaid rent	3,000			(a) 1,000	2,000	
Furniture	16,500				16,500	
Accumulated depr-furniture				(c) 275		275
Accounts payable		13,100				13,100
Salary payable				(d) 950		950
Unearned service revenue		450	(f) 150			300
Income tax payable				(g) 540		540
Common stock		20,000				20,000
Retained earnings		11,250				11,250
Dividends	3,200				3,200	
Service revenue		7,000		(e) 250 (f) 150		7,400
Rent expense			(a) 1,000		1,000	
Salary expense	950		(d) 950		1,900	
Supplies expense			(b) 300		300	
Depreciation expense			(c) 275		275	
Utilities expense	400				400	
Income tax expense			(g) 540		540	
	51,800	51,800	3,465	3,465	53,815	53,815

 CHECK POINT 3-11

PREPARING THE FINANCIAL STATEMENTS FROM THE ADJUSTED TRIAL BALANCE

Objective 4
Prepare the financial statements

The April financial statements of Air & Sea Travel can be prepared from the adjusted trial balance. Exhibit 3-14 shows how the accounts are distributed from the adjusted trial balance to the financial statements. The income statement (Exhibit 3-15) comes from the revenue and expense accounts. The statement of retained earnings (Exhibit 3-16) shows the reasons for the change in retained earnings during the period. The balance sheet (Exhibit 3-17) reports assets, liabilities, and stockholders' equity. Because the adjusting process does not affect cash, we can temporarily ignore the statement of cash flows.

Relationships Among the Financial Statements

➛ The relationships among the financial statements were introduced in Chapter 1, page 22.

The arrows in Exhibits 3-15, 3-16, and 3-17 illustrate the relationships among the income statement, the statement of retained earnings, and the balance sheet. Why is the income statement prepared first and the balance sheet last?

1. The income statement reports net income or net loss, calculated by subtracting expenses from revenues. Because revenues and expenses affect stockholders' equity, their net amount is then transferred to the statement of retained earnings.

(continued on page 126)

EXHIBIT 3-14
The Financial Statements of Air & Sea Travel, Inc., can be taken from the Adjusted Trial Balance

CHECK POINT 3-12

Account Title	Adjusted Trial Balance Debit	Adjusted Trial Balance Credit	
Cash	24,800		Balance Sheet (Exhibit 3-17)
Accounts receivable	2,500		
Supplies	400		
Prepaid rent	2,000		
Furniture	16,500		
Accumulated depr-furniture		275	
Accounts payable		13,100	
Salary payable		950	
Unearned service revenue		300	
Income tax payable		540	
Common stock		20,000	
Retained earnings		11,250	Statement of Retained Earnings (Exhibit 3-16)
Dividends	3,200		
Service revenue		7,400	Income Statement (Exhibit 3-15)
Rent expense	1,000		
Salary expense	1,900		
Supplies expense	300		
Depreciation expense	275		
Utilities expense	400		
Income tax expense	540		
	53,815	53,815	

EXHIBIT 3-15
Income Statement

AIR & SEA TRAVEL, INC.
Income Statement
Month Ended April 30, 20X1

Revenue:		
Service revenue		$7,400
Expenses:		
Salary expense	$1,900	
Rent expense	1,000	
Utilities expense	400	
Supplies expense	300	
Depreciation expense	275	3,875
Income before tax		3,525
Income tax expense		540
Net income		$2,985

EXHIBIT 3-16
Statement of Retained Earnings

CHECK POINT 3-12

AIR & SEA TRAVEL, INC.
Statement of Retained Earnings
Month Ended April 30, 20X1

Retained earnings, April 1, 20X1	$11,250
Add: Net income	2,985
	14,235
Less: Dividends	(3,200)
Retained earnings, April 30, 20X1	$11,035

Exhibit 3-17
Balance Sheet

AIR & SEA TRAVEL, INC.
Balance Sheet
April 30, 20X1

Assets			*Liabilities*	
Cash		$24,800	Accounts payable	$13,100
Accounts receivable		2,500	Salary payable	950
Supplies		400	Unearned service revenue	300
Prepaid rent		2,000	Income tax payable	540
Furniture	$16,500		Total liabilities	14,890
Less Accumulated depreciation	(275)	16,225		
			Stockholders' Equity	
			Common stock	20,000
			Retained earnings	11,035 ②
			Total stockholders' equity	31,035
Total assets		$45,925	Total liabilities and stockholders' equity	$45,925

2. Because Retained Earnings is a balance sheet account, the ending balance of retained earnings is transferred to the balance sheet. This amount is the final balancing element of the balance sheet. To solidify your understanding of this relationship, trace the $11,035 retained earnings figure from Exhibit 3-16 to Exhibit 3-17.

Mid-Chapter

Summary Problem for Your Review

The trial balance of State Service Company on page 127 pertains to December 31, 20X3, which is the end of its year-long accounting period. Data needed for the adjusting entries include the following:

a. Supplies on hand at year end, $2,000.
b. Depreciation on furniture and fixtures, $20,000.
c. Depreciation on building, $10,000.
d. Salaries owed but not yet paid, $5,000.
e. Accrued service revenue, $12,000.
f. Of the $45,000 balance of unearned service revenue, $32,000 was earned during the year.
g. Accrued income tax expense, $35,000.

Required

1. Open the ledger accounts with their unadjusted balances. Show dollar amounts in thousands, as shown for Accounts Receivable:

Accounts Receivable	
370	

2. Journalize State Service Company's adjusting entries at December 31, 20X3. Key entries by letter, as in Exhibit 3-12.
3. Post the adjusting entries.
4. Write the trial balance on a work sheet, enter the adjusting entries, and prepare an adjusted trial balance, as shown in Exhibit 3-13.
5. Prepare the income statement, the statement of retained earnings, and the balance sheet. (At this stage, it is not necessary to classify assets or liabilities as current or long-term.) Draw arrows linking these three financial statements.

STATE SERVICE COMPANY
Trial Balance
December 31, 20X3

Cash	$ 198,000	
Accounts receivable	370,000	
Supplies	6,000	
Furniture and fixtures	100,000	
Accumulated depreciation—furniture and fixtures		$ 40,000
Building	250,000	
Accumulated depreciation—building		130,000
Accounts payable		380,000
Salary payable		
Unearned service revenue		45,000
Income tax payable		
Common stock		100,000
Retained earnings		193,000
Dividends	65,000	
Service revenue		286,000
Salary expense	172,000	
Supplies expense		
Depreciation expense—furniture and fixtures		
Depreciation expense—building		
Income tax expense		
Miscellaneous expense	13,000	
Total	$1,174,000	$1,174,000

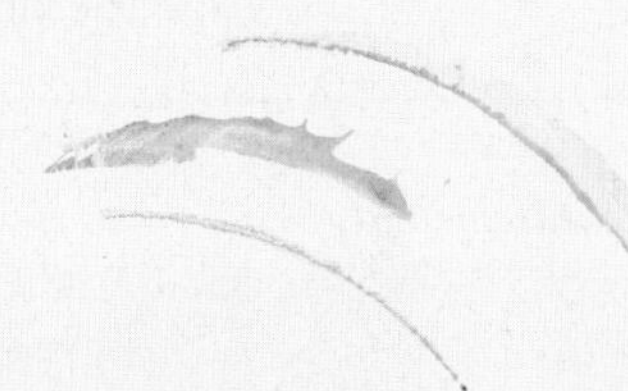

Answers

Requirements 1 and 3

ASSETS

CASH

Bal.	198		

ACCOUNTS RECEIVABLE

	370		
(e)	12		
Bal.	382		

SUPPLIES

	6	(a)	4
Bal.	2		

FURNITURE AND FIXTURES

Bal.	100		

ACCUMULATED DEPRECIATION—FURNITURE AND FIXTURES

			40
		(b)	20
		Bal.	60

BUILDING

Bal.	250		

ACCUMULATED DEPRECIATION—BUILDING

			130
		(c)	10
		Bal.	140

LIABILITIES

ACCOUNTS PAYABLE

		Bal.	380

SALARY PAYABLE

		(d)	5
		Bal.	5

UNEARNED SERVICE REVENUE

(f)	32		45
		Bal.	13

INCOME TAX PAYABLE

		(g)	35
		Bal.	35

STOCKHOLDERS' EQUITY

COMMON STOCK

		Bal.	100

RETAINED EARNINGS

		Bal.	193

DIVIDENDS

Bal.	65		

REVENUE

SERVICE REVENUE

			286
		(e)	12
		(f)	32
		Bal.	330

EXPENSES

SALARY EXPENSE

	172		
(d)	5		
Bal.	177		

SUPPLIES EXPENSE

(a)	4		
Bal.	4		

DEPRECIATION EXPENSE—FURNITURE AND FIXTURES

(b)	20		
Bal.	20		

DEPRECIATION EXPENSE—BUILDING

(c)	10		
Bal.	10		

INCOME TAX EXPENSE

(g)	35		
Bal.	35		

MISCELLANEOUS EXPENSE

Bal.	13		

Requirement 2

20X3				
(a)	Dec. 31	Supplies Expense ($6,000 − $2,000)	4,000	
		Supplies		4,000
		To record supplies used.		
(b)	31	Depreciation Expense—Furniture and Fixtures	20,000	
		Accumulated Depreciation—Furniture and Fixtures		20,000
		To record depreciation expense on furniture and fixtures.		
(c)	31	Depreciation Expense—Building	10,000	
		Accumulated Depreciation—Building		10,000
		To record depreciation expense on building.		
(d)	31	Salary Expense	5,000	
		Salary Payable		5,000
		To accrue salary expense.		
(e)	31	Accounts Receivable	12,000	
		Service Revenue		12,000
		To accrue service revenue.		
(f)	31	Unearned Service Revenue	32,000	
		Service Revenue		32,000
		To record unearned service revenue that has been earned.		
(g)	31	Income Tax Expense	35,000	
		Income Tax Payable		35,000
		To accrue income tax expense.		

Requirement 4

STATE SERVICE COMPANY
Preparation of Adjusted Trial Balance
December 31, 20X3

(Amounts in Thousands)

	Trial Balance		Adjustments		Adjusted Trial Balance	
	Debit	Credit	Debit	Credit	Debit	Credit
Cash	198				198	
Accounts receivable	370		(e) 12		382	
Supplies	6			(a) 4	2	
Furniture and fixtures	100				100	
Accumulated depreciation—furniture and fixtures		40		(b) 20		60
Building	250				250	
Accumulated depreciation—building		130		(c) 10		140
Accounts payable		380				380
Salary payable				(d) 5		5
Unearned service revenue		45	(f) 32			13
Income tax payable				(g) 35		35
Common stock		100				100
Retained earnings		193				193
Dividends	65				65	
Service revenue		286		(e) 12 (f) 32		330
Salary expense	172		(d) 5		177	
Supplies expense			(a) 4		4	
Depreciation expense—furniture and fixtures			(b) 20		20	
Depreciation expense—building			(c) 10		10	
Income tax expense			(g) 35		35	
Miscellaneous expense	13				13	
	1,174	1,174	118	118	1,256	1,256

Requirement 5

STATE SERVICE COMPANY
Income Statement
Year Ended December 31, 20X3

	(Amounts in Thousands)	
Revenue:		
Service revenue		$330
Expenses:		
Salary expense	$177	
Depreciation expense—furniture and fixtures	20	
Depreciation expense—building	10	
Supplies expense	4	
Miscellaneous expense	13	224
Income before tax		106
Income tax expense		35
Net income		$ 71

STATE SERVICE COMPANY
Statement of Retained Earnings
Year Ended December 31, 20X3

	(Amounts in Thousands)
Retained earnings, January 1,20X3	$193
Add: Net income	71
	264
Less: Dividends	(65)
Retained earnings, December 31, 20X3	$199

STATE SERVICE COMPANY
Balance Sheet
December 31, 20X3

(Amounts in Thousands)

Assets			*Liabilities*	
Cash		$198	Accounts payable	$380
Accounts receivable		382	Salary payable	5
Supplies		2	Unearned service revenue	13
Furniture and fixtures	$100		Income tax payable	35
Less Accumulated			Total liabilities	433
depreciation	(60)	40		
			Stockholders' Equity	
Building	$250			
Less Accumulated			Common stock	100
depreciation	(140)	110	Retained earnings	199
			Total stockholders' equity	299
			Total liabilities and	
Total assets		$732	stockholders' equity	$732

Ethical Issues in Accrual Accounting

Accrual accounting provides some ethical challenges that cash accounting can avoid. For example, suppose that in 2000, MajorCo prepays a $3 million advertising campaign to be conducted by Saatchi & Saatchi, a leading advertising agency. If the advertisements are scheduled to run during December, January, and February, MajorCo is buying an asset with a life of three months, and the company should record the expense over the three-month period. Suppose MajorCo pays for the advertisements on December 1 and the ads start running immediately. MajorCo should record one-third of the expense ($1 million) during the year ended December 31, 2000, and two-thirds ($2 million) during 2001.

Suppose 2000 is a great year for MajorCo and net income for the year is better than expected. MajorCo's top managers believe that 2001 will not be as profitable. In this case, the company has a strong incentive to expense the full $3 million during 2000 in order to report all the expense in the 2000 income statement. This unethical action will keep $2 million of advertising expense off the 2001 income statement and make 2001's operating results look better.

We are not suggesting that companies follow this course of action. Most companies follow standard procedures to keep all aspects of their business dealings ethical, including their accounting. Thus, MajorCo would expense $1 million in 2000 and $2 million in 2001, as required by generally accepted accounting principles. But violations of good accounting sometimes occur, and auditors—who must sign their names to their opinions of the financial statements they audit—are always on the lookout for these violations.

In cash-basis accounting, this particular ethical challenge could not arise. Under the cash basis, it would be appropriate for MajorCo to record the full $3 million as expense in December 2000 because the cash payment occurred during that month. But the cash basis is unacceptable because it distorts reported figures for assets, expenses, and net income. In this hypothetical example, MajorCo does in fact have a $2 million asset, prepaid advertising, at December 31, 2000. To expense the full $3 million in December denies the reality of the asset and overstates 2000's expenses. The main results? Assets and net income for 2000 are understated, and the company does not appear to be as successful as it really is.

Another ethical challenge in accrual accounting arises because it is easy to fail to record a liability at the end of the accounting period. Suppose it is now December 31, 2001, and—as expected—the year has not turned out very well for MajorCo. If top managers are unethical, the company can "manufacture" some net income by failing to record some of its expenses. For example, suppose the company owes $4 million in interest expense that it will pay in January 2002. At December 31, 2001, company accountants can "overlook" the $4 million interest expense accrual owed by the company at that later date.

How will this unethical action affect the financial statements? MajorCo's balance sheet will fail to report a $4 million liability for interest payable. Perhaps more important is the understatement of interest expense on the income statement. As a direct result, net income will be overstated, and operating results for 2001 will paint an overly rosy picture of the company's operations.

This ethical challenge cannot arise under the cash basis. With no cash payment to make in 2001, there is no expense to record for that year. Because the payment is made in January 2002, the cash basis dictates the accounting for the entire interest expense in the later year. But, as before, the cash basis is deficient because it fails to report the company's interest expense correctly for 2001. This approach overstates reported profits for 2001. The cash basis also fails to report the interest payable liability at December 31, 2001. This is why generally accepted accounting principles require the accrual basis, despite the ethical temptations it poses for accountants and managers.

Closing the Books

Objective 5
Understand what closing the books means

The term **closing the books** or **closing the accounts** refers to the end-of-period process of preparing the accounts for the next period's transactions. Closing the accounts consists of making **closing entries,** which set the balances of the revenue and expense accounts back to zero in order to measure the next period's net income. The idea is the same as setting the scoreboard back to zero after a football game.

Closing is a clerical procedure. Recall that the income statement reports only one period's income. For example, net income for **It's Just Lunch** or Air & Sea Travel for 2000 relates exclusively to 2000. At December 31, 2000, It's Just Lunch's accountants close the company's revenue and expense accounts for that year. Because these account balances relate to a particular accounting period, the revenue and expense accounts are called **temporary (nominal) accounts.** The Dividends account is also a temporary account because it measures dividends declared during a specific period. The closing process applies only to temporary accounts.

Let's contrast the nature of temporary accounts with that of the **permanent (real) accounts:** assets, liabilities, and stockholders' equity accounts. The permanent accounts are not closed at the end of the period because their balances are not used to measure income. Consider Cash, Accounts Receivable, Supplies, Buildings, Accounts Payable, Notes Payable, Common Stock, and Retained Earnings. Their balances at the end of one accounting period carry over to become the beginning balances of the next period.

Closing entries transfer the revenue, expense, and dividends balances from their respective accounts to the Retained Earnings account. There is no account for Net Income, which is merely the net result of all revenue and expense accounts.

Following are the steps in closing the accounts of a corporation such as Air & Sea Travel:

① Debit each revenue account for the amount of its credit balance. Credit Retained Earnings for the sum of the revenues. This entry transfers the sum of the revenues to the credit side of Retained Earnings.

② Credit each expense account for the amount of its debit balance. Debit Retained Earnings for the sum of the expenses. This entry transfers the sum of the expenses to the debit side of Retained Earnings.

③ Credit the Dividends account for the amount of its debit balance. Debit the Retained Earnings account. This entry transfers the dividends amount to the debit side of the Retained Earnings account. Remember that dividends are not expenses and do not affect net income or net loss.

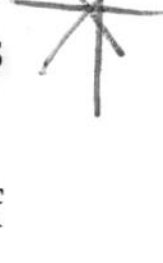

Suppose, for example, that Air & Sea Travel closes the books at the end of April. Exhibit 3-18 presents the complete closing process for the business. Panel A gives the closing journal entries, and Panel B shows the accounts after the closing entries have been posted. The closing process is completely automated in a computerized system. Accounts are identified as either temporary or permanent. The temporary accounts are closed automatically by selecting that option from the software menu. Posting also occurs automatically.

Detailed Classification of Assets and Liabilities

On the balance sheet, assets and liabilities are classified as either *current* or *long-term* to indicate their relative liquidity. **Liquidity** is a measure of how quickly an item can be converted to cash. Cash is the most liquid asset. Accounts receivable is relatively liquid because the business expects to collect the cash in the near future.

EXHIBIT 3-18
Journalizing and Posting the Closing Entries

✔ CHECK POINT 3-13

PANEL A—Journalizing **Page 5**

Closing Entries

	Date	Accounts	Debit	Credit
①	Apr. 30	Service Revenue	7,400	
		Retained Earnings		7,400
②	30	Retained Earnings	4,415	
		Rent Expense		1,000
		Salary Expense		1,900
		Supplies Expense		300
		Depreciation Expense		275
		Utilities Expense		400
		Income Tax Expense		540
③	30	Retained Earnings	3,200	
		Dividends		3,200

PANEL B—Posting

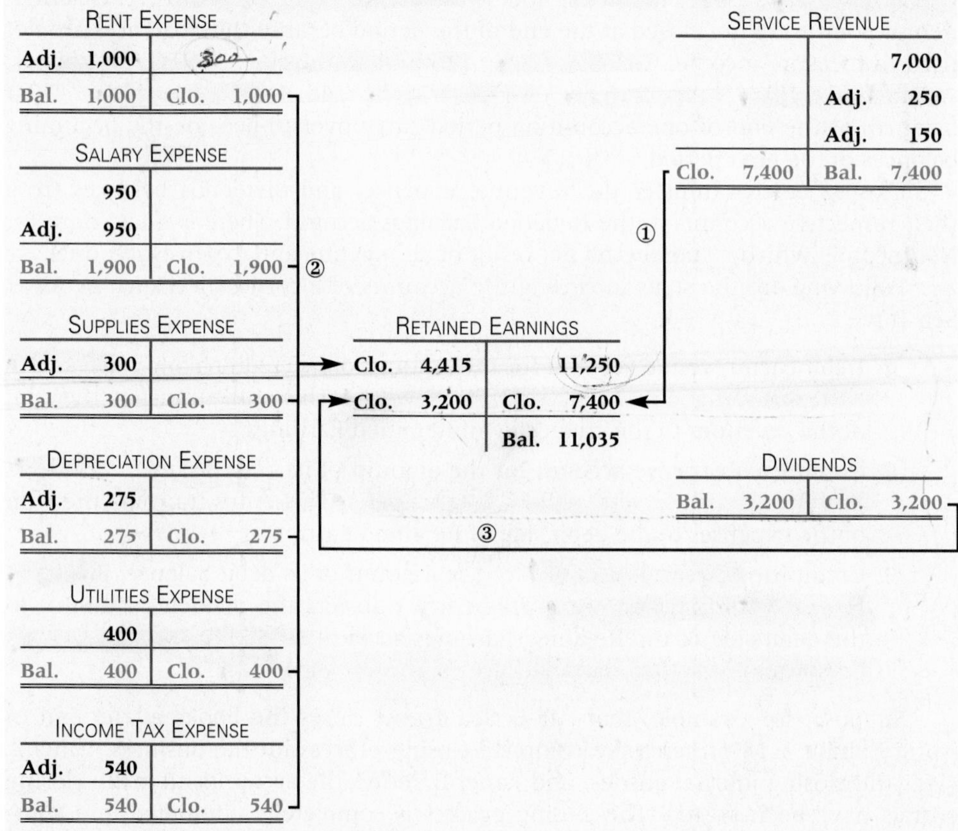

Adj. = Amount posted from an adjusting entry;
Clo. = Amount posted from a closing entry;
Bal. = Balance.

As arrow ② in Panel B shows, it is not necessary to make a separate closing entry for each expense. In one closing entry, we record one debit to Retained Earnings and a separate credit to each expense account.

Supplies are less liquid than accounts receivable, and furniture and buildings even less so.

Users of financial statements are interested in liquidity because serious problems, including bankruptcy, often arise from a shortage of cash. How quickly can the business convert an asset to cash and pay a debt? How soon must a liability be paid? These are questions of liquidity. Balance sheets list assets and liabilities in the order of their relative liquidity.

CURRENT ASSETS. As we saw in Chapter 1, **current assets** are assets that are expected to be converted to cash, sold, or consumed during the next 12 months or within the business's normal operating cycle if longer than a year. The **operating cycle** is the time span during which (1) cash is used to acquire goods and services and (2) these goods and services are sold to customers, from whom the business collects cash. For most businesses, the operating cycle is a few months. A few types of businesses have operating cycles longer than a year. Cash, Accounts Receivable, Notes Receivable due within a year or less, and Prepaid Expenses are current assets. Merchandising entities such as **Kmart, Sears,** and **Motorola** have an additional current asset, Inventory. This account shows the cost of goods that are held for sale to customers.

LONG-TERM ASSETS. Long-term assets are all of the assets that are not classified as current assets. They are not held for sale, but rather are used to operate the business. One category of long-term assets is plant assets, often labeled Property, Plant, and Equipment, as we saw earlier in the chapter. Land, Buildings, Furniture and Fixtures, and Equipment are plant assets. Of these, Air & Sea Travel has only Furniture. Other categories of long-term assets include Long-Term Investments, Intangible Assets, and Other Assets (a catchall category for assets that are not classified more precisely).

Those who use financial statements (such as bankers and other creditors) are interested in the due dates of an entity's liabilities. The sooner a liability must be paid, the more current it is. Liabilities that must be paid on the earliest future date create the greatest strain on cash. Therefore, the balance sheet lists liabilities in the order in which they are due. Balance sheets usually have at least two liability classifications, *current liabilities* and *long-term liabilities.*

CURRENT LIABILITIES. As we saw in Chapter 1, **current liabilities** are debts that are due to be paid within one year or within the entity's operating cycle if the cycle is longer than a year. Accounts Payable, Notes Payable due within one year, Salary Payable, Unearned Revenue, Interest Payable, and Income Tax Payable are current liabilities.

LONG-TERM LIABILITIES. All liabilities that are not current are classified as **long-term liabilities.** Many notes payable are long-term. Other notes payable are paid in installments, with the first installment due within one year, the second installment due the second year, and so on. In this case, the first installment would be a current liability and the remainder long-term liabilities.

Let's see how a real company reports these asset and liability categories on its balance sheet.

✔ CHECK POINT 3-14

Analyzing the Financial Statements of Hawaiian Airlines, Inc.

Exhibit 3-19 (Panels A through C) shows the actual classified balance sheet, the income statement, and the statement of cash flows of **Hawaiian Airlines, Inc.,** which provides service to and from the mainland and among the islands. A **classified balance sheet** shows the current assets separate from the long-term assets and the current liabilities separate from the long-term liabilities. Virtually all companies use a classified balance sheet to report their financial positions. You should be familiar with most of Hawaiian Airlines' account titles.

The classified balance sheet of Hawaiian Airlines is shown here in *report format,* with assets stacked at the top and liabilities and shareholders' equity beneath the assets. An alternative way to show the balance sheet, the *account format,* reports the assets on the left and the liabilities and stockholders' equity on the right. Exhibit 3-17, page 126, is an example of the account format of the balance sheet. Both formats are acceptable.

EXHIBIT 3-19
Financial Statements of Hawaiian Airlines, Inc.

HAWAIIAN AIRLINES, INC.
Classified Balance Sheet (Adapted)
December 31, 19X9 and 19X8

PANEL A

		(In thousands) 19X9	19X8
	ASSETS		
	Current Assets:		
1	Cash and cash equivalents	$ 5,389	$ 3,501
2	Accounts receivable	18,178	16,275
3	Inventories	7,648	6,234
4	Assets held for sale	1,344	1,594
5	Prepaid expenses	5,804	6,079
6	**Total current assets**	38,363	33,683
	Property and Equipment		
7	Flight equipment	40,659	34,702
8	Ground equipment, buildings, and leasehold improvements	5,775	3,976
9	Accumulated depreciation and amortization	(5,804)	(922)
10	Property and equipment, net	41,391	37,756
11	**Other Assets**	81,886	91,862
12	**Total Assets**	$161,640	$163,301
	LIABILITIES AND SHAREHOLDERS' EQUITY		
	Current Liabilities:		
13	Current portion of long-term debt	$ 6,027	$ 6,394
14	Current portion of capital lease obligations	2,662	2,907
15	Accounts payable	35,182	17,529
16	Air traffic liability	30,461	40,382
17	Other accrued liabilities	15,730	12,298
18	**Total current liabilities**	90,062	79,510
19	**Long-Term Debt**	5,523	14,152
20	**Capital Lease Obligations**	10,102	12,764
21	**Other Liabilities**	26,775	23,026
	SHAREHOLDERS' EQUITY		
22	Common stock	41,287	40,000
23	Other	(452)	—
24	Accumulated deficit	(11,657)	(6,151)
25	**Shareholders' equity**	29,178	33,849
26	**Total Liabilities and Shareholders' Equity**	$161,640	$163,301

(CONTINUED)

EXHIBIT 3-19 *(CONT.)*

HAWAIIAN AIRLINES, INC.
Statement of Operations (Adapted)
Year ended December 31, 19X9

PANEL B

		(In thousands) 19X9
	Operating Revenues:	
1	Passenger	$297,527
2	Charter	22,200
3	Cargo	18,169
4	Other	9,008
5	**Total**	346,904
	Operating Expenses:	
6	Flying operations	104,847
7	Maintenance	79,156
8	Passenger service	39,210
9	Aircraft and traffic servicing	54,616
10	Promotion and sales	43,162
11	General and administrative	18,377
12	Depreciation and amortization	7,437
13	Other	2,000
14	**Total**	348,805
15	**Operating Income (Loss)**	(1,901)
	Nonoperating Income (Expense):	
16	Interest expense	(4,341)
17	Interest income	762
18	Loss on disposition of equipment	(233)
19	Other, net	207
20	**Total**	(3,605)
21	**Net Income (Loss)**	$ (5,506)

PANEL C

		(In thousands) 19X9
	Cash Flows from Operating Activities:	
1	**Net cash provided by operating activities**	$18,788
	Cash Flows from Investing Activities:	
2	Additions to property and equipment	$ (9,165)
3	Net proceeds from disposition of equipment	4,225
4	**Net cash provided by (used in) investing activities**	**(4,940)**
	Cash Flows from Financing Activities:	
5	Issuance of long-term debt	$ 1,591
6	Repayment of long-term debt	(10,644)
7	Repayment of capital lease obligations	(2,907)
8	**Net cash provided by (used in) financing activities**	**(11,960)**
9	**Net increase (decrease) in cash and cash equivalents**	$ 1,888
10	Cash and cash equivalents—Beginning of year	3,501
11	**Cash and cash equivalents—End of year**	**$ 5,389**

On the balance sheet, Panel A of Exhibit 3-19, leasehold improvements are listed as assets, along with ground equipment and buildings (line 8). *Leasehold improvements* are modifications that Hawaiian Airlines has made to customize airplanes and other assets leased by the airline. The leasehold improvements are assets because they represent future benefits to Hawaiian even though the company does not own the leased assets. Hawaiian also reports *accumulated depreciation and amortization* (line 9). Amortization is similar to depreciation, except that amortization usually applies to intangible assets (those assets with no physical form)—in this case, the leasehold improvements.

Among the liabilities are *capital lease obligations*—lease payments the company must pay in the future to lease the airplanes (line 20). Observe the *accumulated deficit* in shareholders' equity (line 24). For its entire life, Hawaiian Airlines' net losses have exceeded the company's net incomes. The company therefore has an accumulated deficit, which is a negative amount of retained earnings.

The income statement—labeled the Statement of Operations in Panel B—shows why the company has an accumulated deficit. During 19X8, the company's net loss (as shown by the "bottom line," line 21) exceeded $5.5 million. In fact, Hawaiian has been losing money for several years and almost went bankrupt because it could not pay its debts. In 19X9, Hawaiian underwent a major reorganization. This explains why Exhibit 3-19 contains no comparative income statement for 19X8. The reorganized company is "new" insofar as its operations (revenues and expenses) are concerned.

Hawaiian Airlines reports its revenues by category, with passengers generating the bulk of company revenues (line 1). During 19X9, the company had total revenues of almost $347 million (line 5). In terms of expenses, flying operations—pilot and other salaries, fuel, and gate rentals at airports—consumed $105 million (line 6). Maintenance was the second largest expense, at $79 million (line 7). Hawaiian reports interest expense under the Nonoperating category along with interest income (same as interest revenue) and loss on disposition (sale) of equipment (lines 16–18). Not all companies report interest expense as a nonoperating item. Some companies consider interest expense—the cost of borrowing money—to be an operating expense.

During 19X9, Hawaiian had total operating expenses of $348.8 million (line 14) and total nonoperating expenses (net of interest income) of $3.6 million (line 20). The net loss for the year was $5.5 million (line 21).

The statement of cash flows, Panel C, indicates that operating activities were Hawaiian's main source of cash, bringing in $18.8 million (line 1). During 19X9, the airline invested in new property and equipment and sold some older equipment (lines 2–3). Regarding financing, the company paid off much more long-term debt and lease obligations than it borrowed during the year (lines 5–7).

Where else in Hawaiian Airlines' financial statements does the company report the effects of paying off more in long-term debt and lease obligations than it borrowed during the year?

Answer: The balance sheet (Panel A) also reports that long-term debt and capital lease obligations decreased during 1999 (see lines 19 and 20). You should be learning how to work back and forth among the financial statements in this manner—using the data on one statement to help explain the relationships in another statement.

Overall, Panel C shows that the company increased its cash by almost $1.9 million (line 9) and ended the year with cash of $5.4 million (line 11). In what two places does this information appear in Hawaiian Airlines' financial statements? Line 1 of the comparative balance sheet reports the beginning and ending balances of cash, and the statement of cash flows ends with this same information. Hawaiian is still experiencing financial difficulty, as shown by the accumulated deficit in retained earnings, the net loss on the income statement, and the small cash balance.

Let's now examine different formats for reporting the financial statements.

DIFFERENT FORMATS FOR THE FINANCIAL STATEMENTS

Companies can format their financial statements in different ways. Both the balance sheet and the income statement can be formatted in two basic ways.

Balance Sheet Formats

The **account format** lists the assets on the left and the liabilities and stockholders' equity on the right in the same way that a T-account appears, with assets (debits) on the left and liabilities and equity (credits) on the right.

The **report format** lists the assets at the top, followed by the liabilities and stockholders' equity below. The balance sheet of **Hawaiian Airlines** in Exhibit 3-19 illustrates the report format. Either format is acceptable. The report format is more popular, with approximately 60% of large companies using it.

Income Statement Formats

A **single-step income statement** lists all the revenues together under a heading such as Revenues or Revenues and Gains. The expenses appear in a separate category titled Expenses, Costs and Expenses, or perhaps Expenses and Losses. There is only one step, the subtraction of Expenses and Losses from the sum of Revenues and Gains, in arriving at net income.

A **multi-step income statement** contains a number of subtotals to highlight important relationships among revenues and expenses. For example, a merchandising company's multi-step income statement highlights gross profit (also called *gross margin*), income from operations, and other income and expense as follows (using assumed figures for illustrative purposes):

MULTI-STEP INCOME STATEMENT		
Net sales revenue		$150,000
Cost of goods sold		80,000
Gross profit		70,000
Operating expenses		
(listed individually)		40,000
Income from operations		30,000
Other income (expense):		
Interest revenue	$2,000	
Interest expense	(9,000)	
Gain on sale of equipment	3,000	(4,000)
Income before income tax		26,000
Income tax expense		10,000
Net income		$ 16,000

Most actual companies' income statements do not conform to either a pure single-step format or a pure multi-step format. Business operations are too complex for all companies to conform to rigid reporting formats. For example, Hawaiian Airlines' income statement in Exhibit 3-19 appears in a modified single-step format. Hawaiian lists all *operating* revenues together and all *operating* expenses together, as in the single-step format. But Hawaiian reports *nonoperating* income (expense) in a separate category—a practice that is more in keeping with the multi-step format. In practice, the multi-step format is more popular, with approximately 67% of large companies using it.

FINANCIAL STATEMENT ANALYSIS: USING ACCOUNTING RATIOS

Objective 6
Use the current ratio and the debt ratio to evaluate a business

As we've seen, the purpose of accounting is to provide information for decision making. A creditor considering lending money must predict whether the borrower can repay the loan. If the borrower already has a lot of debt, the probability of repayment is lower than if the borrower has a small amount of liabilities. To analyze a company's financial position, decision makers use ratios that are computed from various items in the financial statements.

Current Ratio

One of the most widely used financial ratios is the **current ratio,** which is the ratio of an entity's current assets to its current liabilities:

$$\textbf{Current ratio} = \frac{\textbf{Total current assets}}{\textbf{Total current liabilities}}$$

For Hawaiian Airlines (amounts in thousands for 19X9):

$$\frac{\$38{,}363}{\$90{,}062} = 0.426$$

The current ratio measures the company's ability to pay current liabilities with current assets. A company prefers to have a high current ratio, which means that the business has plenty of current assets to pay current liabilities. An increasing current ratio from period to period indicates improvement in financial position.

A rule of thumb: A strong current ratio is 2.00, which indicates that the company has $2.00 in current assets for every $1.00 in current liabilities. A company with a current ratio of 2.00 would probably have little trouble paying its current liabilities. Most successful businesses operate with current ratios between 1.50 and 2.00. A current ratio of 1.00 is considered quite low. **Hawaiian Airlines'** current ratio of 0.426 is very low and indicative of a weak current position.

Lenders and investors would view a company with a current ratio of 1.50 or 2.00 as substantially less risky. Such a company could probably borrow money on better terms and also attract more investors. The Decision Guidelines feature on page 139 provides some tips for using the current ratio.

Debt Ratio

A second aid to decision making is the **debt ratio,** which is the ratio of total liabilities to total assets:

$$\textbf{Debt ratio} = \frac{\textbf{Total liabilities}}{\textbf{Total assets}}$$

For Hawaiian Airlines (amounts in thousands for 19X9),

$$\frac{\$90{,}062 + \$5{,}523 + \$10{,}102 + \$26{,}775}{\$161{,}640} = \frac{\$132{,}462}{\$161{,}640} = 0.819$$

The debt ratio indicates the proportion of a company's assets that is financed with debt. This ratio measures a business's ability to pay both current and long-term debts—total liabilities.

A low debt ratio is safer than a high debt ratio. Why? Because a company with a small amount of liabilities has low required payments. Such a company is unlikely to get into financial difficulty. By contrast, a business with a high debt ratio, such as Hawaiian Airlines, may have trouble paying its liabilities, especially when sales are low and cash is scarce. When a company fails to pay its debts, its creditors can take it away from its owners. The largest retail bankruptcy in history, **Federated Department Stores** (parent company of **Bloomingdale's**), was due largely to high debt during a retail-industry recession. Federated was unable to weather the downturn and had to declare bankruptcy.

✔ CHECK POINT 3-15

In general, a *high* current ratio is preferable to a low current ratio. *Increases* in the current ratio indicate improving financial position. By contrast, a *low* debt ratio is preferable to a high debt ratio. Improvement is indicated by a *decrease* in the debt ratio. The Decision Guidelines suggest how to use the debt ratio.

Financial ratios are an important aid to decision making. Experienced managers, lenders, and investors evaluate a company by examining a large number of ratios over several years to spot trends and turning points. They also consider other factors, such as the company's cash position and its trend in net income. No single ratio gives the whole picture about a company.

Now, let's apply what we have learned. Please turn to the Decision Guidelines.

DECISION GUIDELINES

Using the Current Ratio

Decision	Guidelines
How to measure a company's ability to pay current liabilities with current assets?	$\text{Current ratio} = \dfrac{\text{Total current assets}}{\text{Total current liabilities}}$
Who uses the current ratio for decision making?	*Creditors,* who must predict whether a borrower can pay its current liabilities *Stockholders,* who know that a company that cannot pay its debts is not a good investment because it may go bankrupt *Managers,* who must have enough cash to pay the company's current liabilities
What is a good value of the current ratio?	Depends on the company's industry: A company with strong cash flow can operate successfully with a low current ratio of, say, 1.10–1.20 A company with weak cash flow needs a higher current ratio of, say, 1.50–1.60 Traditionally, a current ratio of 2.00 was considered ideal. Recently, acceptable values have decreased as companies have been able to operate more efficiently.

Using the Debt Ratio

Decision	Guidelines
How to measure a company's ability to pay total liabilities?	$\text{Debt ratio} = \dfrac{\text{Total liabilities}}{\text{Total assets}}$
Who uses the debt ratio for decision making?	*Creditors,* who must predict whether a borrower can pay its debts *Stockholders,* who know that a company that cannot pay its debts is not a good investment because it may go bankrupt *Managers,* who must have enough assets to pay the company's debts
What is a good value of the debt ratio?	Depends on the company's industry: A company with strong cash flow can operate successfully with a high debt ratio of, say, 0.70–0.80 A company with weak cash flow needs a lower debt ratio of, say, 0.60–0.70 Traditionally, a debt ratio of 0.50 was considered ideal. Recently, values have increased as companies have been able to operate more efficiently.

Decision Guidelines (cont.)

Using the Current Ratio

Decision	Guidelines
What happens when the current ratio is low?	The company must pay a higher interest rate when it borrows money.
Can the current ratio be too high?	Yes, because most of the current assets (cash, short-term investments, receivables, and prepaid expenses) are low-earning assets. Also, it costs money to keep inventory on hand. Therefore, managers strive for a current ratio that is high enough to pay the bills but not so high that it hurts profits.

Using the Debt Ratio

Decision	Guidelines
What happens when the debt ratio is high?	The company must pay a higher interest rate when it borrows money.
Can the debt ratio be too low?	Yes and no. *Yes,* because a company with no long-term debt gives up some profits it could earn from borrowing at a lower rate and investing the money at a higher rate. But, *no,* because a company with no long-term debt rarely gets into trouble due to the inability to pay its (low) debts.

Excel Application Problems

Goal: Create an Excel spreadsheet to calculate the current ratio and debt ratio for different companies, and use the results to answer questions about the companies. Requires Web research on The Gap and Lands' End.

Scenario: You are deciding whether to buy the stock of two well-known clothing retailers, The Gap and Lands' End. You know that the current ratio and the debt ratio measure whether a company has the assets to cover its liabilities.

Your task is to create a simple spreadsheet to compare the current ratio and the debt ratio for each company. When done, answer these questions:

1. Do both companies have an acceptable current ratio? How can you tell?
2. Do both companies have an acceptable debt ratio? How can you tell?
3. What is the trend (up or down) for the ratios of both companies? Is the trend for each company positive or negative? Why?
4. Which company has the "better" ending current ratio? The "better" ending debt ratio?

Step-by-step:

1. Locate the following current and prior year information for The Gap and Lands' End (found on the "Consolidated Balance Sheets"):
   - **a.** Current Assets
   - **b.** Total Assets
   - **c.** Current Liabilities
   - **d.** Long-Term Liabilities (This may have to be computed on the spreadsheet.)
   - **e.** Total Liabilities (This may have to be computed on the spreadsheet.)
   - **f.** Total Shareholders' Equity (Investment)
   - **g.** Total Liabilities and Shareholders' Equity (Investment)
2. Open a new Excel spreadsheet.
3. Create a bold-faced heading for your spreadsheet that contains the following:
   - **a.** Chapter 3 Decision Guidelines
   - **b.** The Current Ratio and Debt Ratio
   - **c.** The Gap and Lands' End Comparison
   - **d.** Today's date
4. Two rows down from your worksheet heading, create a column heading titled "The Gap (in 000's)." Make it bold and underline the heading.
5. One row down from The Gap's column heading, create a row with the following bold, underlined column titles:
   - **a.** Account
   - **b.** FYxx (xx = the most recent fiscal year, for example, 00)
   - **c.** FYyy (yy = the prior fiscal year, for example, 99)
6. Starting with the "Account" column heading, enter the data found in #1, above. You should have seven rows of data, with row descriptions (for example, "Current Assets"). Format the columns as necessary.
7. Skip a row at the end of your data, and then create a row titled "Current Ratio" and another row titled "Debt Ratio."
8. Enter the formula for each ratio in the "FYxx" and "FYyy" columns. You should have four formulas. Make both rows bold.
9. Repeat steps 4–8, substituting the Lands' End title and data as appropriate.
10. Save your work to disk, and print a copy for your files.

End-of-Chapter

Summary Problem for Your Review

Refer to the mid-chapter summary problem that begins on page 126.

Required

1. Make State Service Company's closing entries at December 31, 20X3. Explain what the closing entries accomplish and why they are necessary.

2. Post the closing entries to the Retained Earnings account and compare Retained Earnings' ending balance with the amount reported on the balance sheet on page 129. The two amounts should be the same.

3. Prepare State Service Company's classified balance sheet to identify the company's current assets and the company's current liabilities. (State has no long-term liabilities.) Then compute State Service Company's current ratio and debt ratio at December 31, 20X3.

4. The top management of State Service Company has asked you for a $500,000 loan to expand the business. State proposes to pay off the loan over a 10-year period. Recompute State's debt ratio assuming you make the loan. Use the company's financial statements plus the ratio values to decide whether to grant the loan at an interest rate of 8, 10, or 12%. State Service Company's cash flow is strong. Give the reasoning underlying your decision.

Answers

Requirement 1

20X1		*(In thousands)*	
Dec. 31	Service Revenue	330	
	Retained Earnings		330
31	Retained Earnings	259	
	Salary Expense		177
	Depreciation Expense—Furniture and Fixtures		20
	Depreciation Expense—Building		10
	Supplies Expense		4
	Income Tax Expense		35
	Miscellaneous Expense		13
31	Retained Earnings	65	
	Dividends		65

Explanation of Closing Entries:

The closing entries set the balance of each revenue account, each expense account, and the Dividends account back to zero for the start of the next accounting period. It is necessary to close these accounts because their balances relate only to a particular accounting period.

Requirement 2

Retained Earnings			
Clo.	**259**		**193**
Clo.	**65**	**Clo.**	**330**
		Bal.	**199**

The balance in the Retained Earnings account agrees with the amount reported on the balance sheet, as it should.

Requirement 3

$$\text{Current ratio} = \frac{\$582}{\$433} = 1.34 \qquad \text{Debt ratio} = \frac{\$433}{\$732} = 0.59$$

STATE SERVICE COMPANY
Balance Sheet
December 31, 20X3

(Amounts in Thousands)

Assets			*Liabilities*	
Current assets:			Current liabilities:	
Cash		$198	Accounts payable	$380
Accounts receivable		382	Salary payable	5
Supplies		2	Unearned service revenue	13
Total current assets		582	Income tax payable	35
Furniture and			Total current liabilities	433
fixtures	$100			
Less Accumulated			*Stockholders' Equity*	
depreciation	(60)	40	Common stock	$100
Building	$250		Retained earnings	199
Less Accumulated			Total stockholders' equity	299
depreciation	(140)	110	Total liabilities and	
Total assets		$732	stockholders' equity	$732

Requirement 4

$$\frac{\text{Debt ratio assuming}}{\text{the loan is made}} = \frac{\$433 + \$500}{\$732 + \$500} = \frac{\$933}{\$1{,}232} = 0.76$$

Decision: Make the loan at 10%.

Reasoning: Prior to the loan, the company's financial position and cash flow are strong. The current ratio is in a middle range, and the debt ratio is not too high. Net income (from the income statement) is high in relation to total revenue. Therefore, the company should be able to repay the loan.

The loan will increase the company's debt ratio from 59% to 76%, which is more risky than the company's financial position at present. On this basis, a mid-range interest rate appears reasonable—at least as the starting point for the negotiation between State Service Company and the bank.

SUMMARY OF LEARNING OBJECTIVES

1. ***Link cash flows with accrual-basis accounting.*** In *accrual-basis accounting,* an accountant recognizes the impact of a business event as it occurs, whether or not cash is received or paid. In *cash-basis accounting,* the accountant does not record a transaction unless cash changes hands. The cash basis omits important events, such as purchases and sales on account, and distorts the financial statements. For this reason, generally accepted accounting principles require the use of accrual-basis accounting.
2. ***Apply the revenue and matching principles.*** The *revenue principle* tells accountants (1) to record revenue when it has been earned, but not before, and (2) to record revenue equal to the cash value of the goods or services transferred to the customer. The *matching principle* directs accountants to identify all the expenses incurred during the accounting period, to measure those expenses, and to match the expenses against the revenues earned during that period in order to measure net income.
3. ***Adjust the accounts to update the financial statements.*** *Adjusting entries* assign revenues to the period in which they are earned and expenses to the period in which they are incurred. These entries, made at the end of the period, update the accounts for preparation of the financial statements. Adjusting entries fall into five categories: prepaid expenses, depreciation of plant assets, accrued expenses, accrued revenues, and unearned revenues.

Accountants prepare an adjusted trial balance by entering the adjusting entries next to the unadjusted trial balance and then computing each account's new balance.

4. ***Prepare the financial statements.*** Accountants use the adjusted trial balance to prepare three of the financial statements: the income statement, statement of retained earnings, and balance sheet. All financial statements should include the name of the entity, the title of the statement, the date or period covered by the statement, and the body of the statement. On the income statement, it is customary to list expenses in descending order, with Miscellaneous Expense appearing last and Income Tax Expense appearing after Income Before Tax.

   Income, shown on the *income statement,* increases retained earnings. This increase also appears on the *statement of retained earnings.* The ending balance of retained earnings appears on the *balance sheet.*

5. ***Understand what closing the books means.*** At the end of each accounting period accountants must close the *temporary accounts*—that is, the revenue, expense, and dividend accounts. The purpose is to set each account back to zero so that the next period's income can be measured accurately. The *permanent accounts*—assets, liabilities, and stockholders' equity—are not closed. The final check on the accuracy of the closing entries is the *postclosing trial balance.*

6. ***Use the current ratio and the debt ratio to evaluate a business.*** The *current ratio,* which measures a company's ability to pay current liabilities with current assets, is equal to total current assets divided by total current liabilities. The higher the current ratio, the stronger the company's financial position. The *debt ratio,* which measures a company's ability to pay its debts, equals total liabilities divided by total assets. In general, the lower the debt ratio, the stronger the company's financial position.

Accounting Vocabulary

account format (p. 137).
accounting cycle (p. 106).
accrual (p. 112).
accrual-basis accounting (p. 106).
accrued expense (p. 117).
accrued revenue (p. 119).
Accumulated Depreciation (p. 116).
adjusted trial balance (p. 122).
adjusting entry (p. 111).
book value (of a plant asset) (p. 116).
cash-basis accounting (p. 107).
classified balance sheet (p. 133).
closing the accounts (p. 131).
closing the books (p. 131).
closing entries (p. 131).
contra account (p. 116).
current asset (p. 133).
current liability (p. 133).
current ratio (p. 138).
debt ratio (p. 138).
deferral (p. 112).
depreciation (p. 112).
liquidity (p. 131).
long-term asset (p. 133).
long-term liability (p. 133).
matching principle (p. 109).
multi-step income statement (p. 137).
nominal accounts (p. 131).
operating cycle (p. 133).
permanent accounts (p. 131).
plant asset (p. 115).
prepaid expense (p. 113).
real accounts (p. 131).
report format (p. 137).
revenue principle (p. 108).
single-step income statement (p. 137).
temporary accounts (p. 131).
time-period concept (p. 108).
unearned revenue (p. 120).

Questions

1. Distinguish accrual-basis accounting from cash-basis accounting.
2. What two questions does the revenue principle help answer?
3. Briefly explain the matching principle.
4. Name five categories of adjusting entries and give an example of each.
5. Do all adjusting entries affect the net income or net loss of the period? Include the definition of an adjusting entry.
6. Manning Supply Company pays $1,800 for an insurance policy that covers three years. At the end of the first year, the balance of its Prepaid Insurance account contains two elements. What are the two elements, and what is the correct amount of each?
7. The title Prepaid Expense suggests that this type of account is an expense. If it is, explain why. If it is not, what type of account is it?
8. The manager of a Quickie-Pickie convenience store presents his entity's balance sheet to a banker when applying for a loan. The balance sheet reports that the entity's plant assets have a book value of $135,000 and accumulated depreciation of $65,000. What does *book value* of a plant asset mean? What was the cost of the plant assets?
9. Why is an unearned revenue a liability? Give an example.
10. Identify the types of accounts (assets, liabilities, and so on) debited and credited for each of the five types of adjusting entries.
11. Explain the relationships among the income statement, the statement of retained earnings, and the balance sheet.
12. Bellevue Company failed to record the following adjusting entries at December 31, the end of its fiscal year: (a) accrued expenses, $500; (b) accrued revenues, $850; and (c) depreciation, $1,000. Did these omissions cause net income for the year to be understated or overstated? By what overall amount?
13. Which types of accounts are closed? What purpose is served by closing the accounts?

14. Distinguish between permanent accounts and temporary accounts; indicate which type is closed at the end of the period. Give five examples of each type of account.

15. Why are assets classified as current or long-term? On what basis are they classified? Where do the classified amounts appear?

16. Indicate which of the following accounts are current assets and which are long-term assets: Prepaid Rent, Building, Furniture, Accounts Receivable, Merchandise Inventory, Cash, Note Receivable (due within one year), Note Receivable (due after one year).

17. Identify an outside party that would be interested in whether a liability is current or long-term. Why would this party be interested in this information?

18. A friend tells you that the difference between a current liability and a long-term liability is that they are payable to different types of creditors. Is your friend correct? Define these two categories of liabilities.

19. Show how to compute the current ratio and the debt ratio. Indicate what ability each ratio measures, and state whether a high value or a low value is safer for each.

CHECK POINTS

Linking accrual accounting and cash flows (Obj. 1)

CP3-1 **Pier 1 Imports, Inc.** made sales of $1,075 million during 19X8. Of this amount, Pier 1 collected cash for all but $80 million. The company's cost of goods sold was $614 million, and all other expenses for the year totaled $383 million. Also during 19X8, Pier 1 paid $614 million for its inventory and $274 million to suppliers and employees.

Suppose Pier 1's top management is interviewing you for a job and you are asked two questions:

a. How much was Pier 1's net income for 19X8?

b. How much was Pier 1's net cash flow from operating activities during 19X8?

Assume you will get the job if you answer both questions correctly.

Linking accrual accounting and cash flows (Obj. 1)

CP3-2 **Sony Corporation** began 19X8 owing long-term debt of $8.3 billion. During 19X8, Sony borrowed $2.6 billion long-term and paid off $2.5 billion of long-term debt from prior years. Interest expense for the year was $0.5 billion, including $0.1 billion of interest expense accrued at December 31, 19X8.

As a new Sony employee, it is your job to show what Sony should report for these facts on the following financial statements:

- Income statement
- Balance sheet
- Statement of cash flows

Applying the revenue and the matching principles (Obj. 2)

CP3-3 **Ford Motor Company** sells large fleets of vehicles to auto rental companies, such as **Hertz** and **Alamo.** Suppose Hertz is negotiating with Ford to purchase 1,000 Explorers. Write a short paragraph to explain to Ford when the company should, and should not, record this sales revenue and the related cost of goods sold. Mention the accounting principles that provide the basis for your explanation.

Adjusting prepaid expenses (Obj. 3)

CP3-4 Answer the following questions about prepaid expenses:

a. Prepaid expenses are discussed beginning on page 113. Focus on the accounting for prepaid rent. Assume that Air & Sea Travel's initial $3,000 prepayment of rent of April 1 (page 113) was for six months rather than for three months. Give the adjusting entry to record rent expense at April 30. Include the date of the entry and an explanation. Then post to the two accounts involved, and show their balances at April 30.

b. Refer to the supplies example on pages 114–115. Assume that Air & Sea Travel has $100 of supplies on hand (rather than $400) at April 30. Make the required journal entry. Then post to the accounts and show their balances at April 30.

Recording depreciation; cash flows (Obj. 1, 3)

CP3-5 Refer to the discussion in Chapter 1 of the income statement and the balance sheet. **It's Just Lunch** uses computers for data searches. Suppose that on May 1 the company paid cash of $36,000 for Gateway computers that are expected to remain useful for three years. At the end of three years, the computers' values are expected to be zero.

1. Make journal entries to record (a) purchase of the computers on May 1 and (b) depreciation on May 31. Include dates and explanations, and use the following accounts: Computer Equipment; Accumulated Depreciation—Computer Equipment; and Depreciation Expense—Computer Equipment.

2. Post to the accounts and show their balances at May 31.
3. What is the equipment's book value at May 31?
4. Which account(s) will It's Just Lunch report on the income statement for the month of May? Which account(s) will appear on the balance sheet of May 31? What will It's Just Lunch report on its statement of cash flows? Show the amount to report for each item on all three financial statements.

Applying the matching principle and the time-period concept (Obj. 2)

CP3-6 At December 31, 19X6, **Hawaiian Airlines** accrued salary expense by debiting Salary Expense and crediting Salary Payable for $2,500,000. Suppose Hawaiian Airlines paid $2,700,000 to its employees on January 3, 19X7, the company's next payday after the end of the 19X6 year. For this sequence of transactions,

1. How much Salary Expense would Hawaiian Airlines report on its 19X6 income statement? How much Salary Expense would the company report on its 19X7 income statement?
2. Show what Hawaiian Airlines would report on its statements of cash flows for 19X6 and 19X7.

Accruing and paying interest expense (Obj. 3)

CP3-7 Suppose Air & Sea Travel borrowed $10,000 on August 1 by signing a note payable to First Interstate Bank. The interest expense for each month is $80. The loan agreement requires Air & Sea Travel to pay August interest at the end of October, along with the interest that will accrue for September and October.

1. Make Air & Sea Travel's adjusting entry to record interest expense and interest payable at August 31, at September 30, and at October 31. Date each entry and include its explanation.
2. Post all three entries to the Interest Payable account. You need not take the balance of the account at the end of each month
3. Record the payment of interest at October 31.
4. On which financial statement and under what category will Air & Sea Travel report the interest payable? How much interest payable will Air & Sea Travel report at August 31, September 30, and October 31?

Accruing and receiving cash from interest revenue (Obj. 3)

CP3-8 Return to the situation in Check Point 3-7. Suppose you are accounting for the same transactions on the books of First Interstate Bank, which lent the money to Air & Sea Travel. Perform all three steps of Check Point 3-7 for First Interstate Bank using its own accounts: Interest Receivable and Interest Revenue.

Explaining unearned revenues (Obj. 3)

CP3-9 Write a paragraph to explain why unearned revenues are liabilities rather than revenues. In your explanation, use the following actual example: *Time* magazine collects cash from subscribers in advance and later mails the magazines to subscribers over a one-year period. Explain what happens to the unearned subscription revenue over the course of a year as *Time* mails the magazines to subscribers. Where (into what account) does the unearned subscription revenue go as *Time* mails magazines to subscribers? Give the adjusting entry that *Time* magazine would make to record the earning of $10,000 of Subscription Revenue. Include an explanation for the entry, as illustrated in the chapter.

Reporting prepaid expenses (Obj. 4)

CP3-10 Study the T-accounts in Exhibit 3-12, Panel C, on page 123. Focus on the Prepaid Rent account. Which amount in the Prepaid Rent account appeared on the *unadjusted* trial balance (Exhibit 3-13, page 124)? Which amount in the Prepaid Rent account will appear on the *adjusted* trial balance? Which amount will be reported on the balance sheet at April 30? Why will the balance sheet report this amount? Under what balance sheet category will Prepaid Rent appear?

Reporting on the financial statements (Obj. 4)

CP3-11 In the Adjustments columns of Exhibit 3-13, page 124, two adjustments affected Service Revenue.

1. Make journal entries for the two adjustments. Date the entries and include an explanation.
2. The journal entries you just made affected three accounts: Accounts Receivable, Unearned Service Revenue, and Service Revenue. Show how Air & Sea Travel will report all three accounts in its financial statements at April 30. For each account, identify its (a) financial statement, (b) category on the financial statement, and (c) balance.

Preparing the financial statements (Obj. 4)

CP3-12 The adjusted trial balance of **Rawlings Sporting Goods Company** at August 31, 19X8, lists these accounts, as adapted, with their amounts in thousands:

Retained earnings, August 31, 19X7	$ 14,037	Cost of goods sold	$119,151
Accounts receivable	40,352	Cash	862
Net revenues	170,604	Property and equipment, net	12,911
Total current liabilities	21,655	Common stock	26,555
All other expenses	47,793	Inventories	43,573
Other current assets	5,619	Long-term liabilities	66,625
Other assets	29,215		

Use these data to prepare Rawlings Sporting Goods Company's income statement for the year ended August 31, 19X8; statement of retained earnings for the year ended August 31, 19X8; and classified balance sheet at August 31, 19X8. Use the report format for the balance sheet. Draw arrows linking the three statements.

Making closing entries (Obj. 5)

CP3-13 Use the Rawlings Sporting Goods data in Check Point 3-12 to make the company's closing entries at August 31, 19X8. Then set up a T-account for Retained Earnings and post to that account. Compare Retained Earnings' ending balance to the amount reported on Rawlings' statement of retained earnings and balance sheet. What do you find?

Classifying assets and liabilities as current or long-term (Obj. 6)

CP3-14 **Lands' End** had sales of $1,119 million during the year ended January 31, 19X7, and total assets of $378 million at January 31, 19X7, the end of the company's fiscal year. The financial statements of Lands' End reported the following (amounts in millions):

Sales revenue	$1,119	Land and buildings	$ 72
Inventory	142	Accounts payable	77
Long-term debt	1	Operating expenses	424
Receivables	9	Accumulated depreciation	73
Interest expense	1	Accrued liabilities (such as Salary payable)	28
Equipment	99		
Prepaid expenses	17		

1. Identify the assets (including contra assets) and liabilities.
2. Classify each asset and each liability as current or long-term.

Using the current ratio and the debit ratio (Obj.6)

CP3-15 After closing its accounts at December 31, 19X6, **Sprint Corporation** had the following account balances (adapted) with amounts given in millions:

Property and equipment	$10,464	Long-term liabilities	$5,119
Cash	1,150	Other assets	2,136
Service revenue	-0-	Accounts receivable	2,464
Owners' equity	8,520	Total expenses	-0-
Other current assets	739	Accounts payable	1,027
Short-term notes payable	200	Other current liabilities	2,087

1. How much in current assets does Sprint have for each dollar of current liabilities that the company owes? Compute the current ratio to answer this question.
2. What percentage of Sprint's total assets are financed with debt? Compute the debt ratio to answer this question.
3. What percentage of Sprint's total assets do the stockholders of the company actually own free and clear of debt?

E3-1 During 1997, **Hershey Foods Corporation** made sales of $4,302 (assume all on account) and collected cash of $4,368 from customers. At December 31, 1997, Hershey reported Accounts Receivable of $361. All amounts are in millions.

Linking accrual accounting and cash flows (Obj. 1)

1. For these facts, show what Hershey reported on the following financial statements:
   - Income statement
   - Balance sheet
   - Statement of cash flows
2. Suppose Hershey had used the cash basis of accounting. What would Hershey have reported for these facts?

E3-2 **Williams-Sonoma, Inc.**, paid $585 to suppliers for inventory during fiscal year 1998. During that year, the company reported Cost of Goods Sold, its largest expense, of $557. The Williams-Sonoma balance sheet lists Accounts Payable of $58. All amounts are in millions.

Linking accrual accounting and cash flows (Obj. 1)

1. What does Williams-Sonoma report on the following financial statements:
   - Income statement?
   - Statement of financial position?
   - Statement of cash flows?
2. Which items would Williams-Sonoma report under the cash basis? Which items would the cash basis ignore?

E3-3 **Wal-Mart Stores, Inc.**, is the world's largest retailer, with almost 3,000 stores. Wal-Mart's balance sheet (adapted) follows.

Accrual basis of accounting (Obj. 1)

WAL-MART STORES, INC.
Balance Sheet (Adapted)
January 31, 19X9

	(In billions)
Current Assets:	
Cash	$ 1.9
Accounts receivable	1.1
Inventories	17.1
Prepaid expenses	1.1
Property, plant, and equipment, net	28.8
Total assets	$50.0
Current Liabilities:	
Accounts payable	$10.3
Other	6.5
Long-term liabilities	12.1
Shareholders' equity	21.1
Total liabilities & shareholders' equity	$50.0

Required

Identify every account listed in the Wal-Mart balance sheet that proves the company uses the accrual basis of accounting. For each account you identify, state how the cash basis of accounting would treat the item.

E3-4 Identify the accounting concept or principle that gives the most direction on how to account for each of the following situations:

Applying accounting concepts and principles (Obj. 2)

a. A construction company is building a highway system, and construction may take three years. When should the company record the revenue it earns?
b. A physician performs a surgical operation and bills the patient's insurance company. It may take three months to collect from the insurance company. Should the physician record revenue now or wait until cash is collected?

c. A utility bill is received on December 30 and will be paid next year. When should the company record utility expense?

d. Salary expense of $35,000 is accrued at the end of the period to measure income properly.

e. March has been a particularly slow month, and the business will have a net loss for the first quarter of the year. Management is considering not following its customary practice of reporting quarterly earnings to the public. Investors depend on quarterly earnings reports to decide whether to buy, hold, or sell the company's stock.

Applying accounting concepts (Obj. 2)

E3-5 Write a short paragraph to explain in your own words the concept of depreciation as it is used in accounting.

Journalizing adjusting entries and analyzing their effects on net income; accrual versus cash basis (Obj. 1, 3)

E3-6 An accountant made the following adjustments at December 31, the end of the accounting period:

a. Prepaid insurance, beginning, $600. Payments for insurance during the period, $2,000. Prepaid insurance, ending, $800.

b. Interest revenue accrued, $4,100.

c. Unearned service revenue, beginning, $800. Unearned service revenue, ending, $300.

d. Depreciation, $6,200.

e. Employees' salaries owed for two days of a five-day work week; weekly payroll, $9,000.

f. Income before income tax expense, $200,000. Income tax rate is 40%.

Required

1. Journalize the adjusting entries.
2. Suppose the adjustments were not made. Compute the overall overstatement or understatement of net income as a result of the omission of these adjustments.

Allocating supplies cost to the asset and the expense (Obj. 2, 3)

E3-7 Assume **PepsiCo, Inc.,** experienced four situations for its supplies. Compute the amounts indicated by question marks for each situation. For situations 1 and 2, journalize the needed entry. Consider each situation separately.

	Situation			
	1	*2*	*3*	*4*
Beginning supplies	$ 900	$500	$ 900	$ 200
Payments for supplies during the year (a payment to a supplier)	1,100	?	1,100	?
Total cost to account for	?	?	2,000	1,300
Ending supplies	500	800	?	400
Supplies expense	$?	$700	$1,400	$ 900

Linking accrual accounting and cash flows (Obj. 1,3)

E3-8 Return to the data in Exercise 3-7. For situation 2, show what PepsiCo would report on the following financial statements:

- Income statement
- Balance sheet
- Statement of cash flows

For each item, list the account and also give the dollar amount to report.

Journalizing adjusting entries (Obj. 3)

E3-9 Suppose **The Home Depot, Inc.** faced the following situations. Journalize the adjusting entry needed at December 31 for each situation. Consider each fact separately.

a. Equipment was purchased last year at a cost of $20,000. The equipment's useful life is four years. Record this year's depreciation.

b. On September 1, when we prepaid $1,200 for a one-year insurance policy, we debited Prepaid Insurance and credited Cash. This is a payment to a supplier.

c. The business will pay interest expense of $9,000 early in the next period. Of this amount, $3,700 is expense of the current year. Payment of interest is a separate category on the statement of cash flows.

d. Interest revenue of $900 has been earned but not yet received. The business holds a $20,000 note receivable that it will collect, along with the interest, next year.

e. On July 1, when we collected $6,000 rent in advance, we debited Cash and credited Unearned Rent Revenue. The tenant was paying for two years' rent.

f. Salary expense is $1,000 per day—Monday through Friday—and the business pays employees each Friday. This year, December 31 falls on a Thursday.

g. The unadjusted balance of the Supplies account is $3,100. The total cost of supplies on hand is $800.

Linking accrual accounting and cash flows (Obj. 1, 3)

E3-10 Use the data in Exercise 3-9 to answer these questions. Each letter links to the same lettered item in Exercise 3-9.

a. Refer to item a in Exercise 3-9. Show what Home Depot will report on its

1. Balance sheet (show all the data items needed to report the asset's book value)
2. Income statement

b. Refer to item b in Exercise 3-9. What will Home Depot report on its statement of cash flows?

c. Refer to item c in Exercise 3-9. Show what Home Depot will report on the following financial statements:

1. Income statement of the current year.
2. Balance sheet at end of the current year.
3. Statement of cash flows of the current year.
4. Income statement of the following year.
5. Balance sheet of the following year.
6. Statement of cash flows of the following year.

Recording adjustments in T-accounts (Obj. 3)

E3-11 The accounting records of Fort Lauderdale Art Supplies include the following unadjusted balances at May 31: Accounts Receivable, $1,600; Supplies, $900; Salary Payable, $0; Unearned Service Revenue, $900; Service Revenue, $4,700; Salary Expense, $1,200; Supplies Expense, $0. Fort Lauderdale Art Supplies' accountant develops the following data for the May 31 adjusting entries:

a. Supplies on hand, $400.

b. Salary owed to employee, $700.

c. Service revenue accrued, $350.

d. Unearned service revenue that has been earned, $550.

Open the foregoing T-accounts with their beginning balances. Then record the adjustments directly in the accounts, keying each adjustment amount by letter. Show each account's adjusted balance. Journal entries are not required.

Preparing the financial statements (Obj. 4)

E3-12 The adjusted trial balance of **The Coca-Cola Company** (adapted) follows.

THE COCA-COLA COMPANY
Adjusted Trial Balance (Adapted)
December 31, 19X8

(Millions)	*Adjusted Trial Balance*	
	Debit	***Credit***
Cash	1,800	
Accounts receivable	1,700	
Inventories	900	
Prepaid expenses	2,000	
Property, plant, equipment	5,700	
Accumulated depreciation		2,000
Other assets	9,000	
Accounts payable		3,400
Income tax payable		1,000
Other liabilities		6,300
Common stock		900
Retained earnings (beginning)		5,500
Dividends	1,500	
Sales revenue		18,800
Cost of goods sold	5,600	
Selling, administrative, and general expense	8,000	
Income tax expense	1,700	
	37,900	37,900

Required

Prepare Coca-Cola's income statement and statement of retained earnings for the year ended December 31, 19X8, and its balance sheet on that date. Draw the arrows linking the three statements.

Computing financial statement amounts (Obj. 3)

E3-13 The adjusted trial balances of Quartz Control Corporation at December 31, 20X2, and December 31, 20X1, include these amounts:

	20X2	*20X1*
Supplies	$ 2,100	$ 1,500
Salary payable	3,100	3,700
Unearned service revenue	14,200	16,300

Analysis of the accounts at December 31, 20X2, reveals these transactions for 20X2:

Purchases of supplies	$ 8,400
Cash disbursements for salaries	84,600
Cash receipts in advance for service revenue	180,200

Compute the amount of supplies expense, salary expense, and service revenue to report on the Quartz Control income statement for 20X2.

Closing the accounts (Obj. 5)

E3-14 Prepare the closing entries from the following accounts adapted from the records of **Sprint Corporation** at December 31, 19X8 (amounts in millions):

Unearned revenues	$ 229	Service revenue	$17,134
Cost of services sold (an expense)	8,787	Note payable	11,942
Accumulated depreciation	13,161	Depreciation expense	2,705
Selling, general, and administrative expense	5,273	Other revenue	450
Interest revenue	178	Dividends	457
Retained earnings, December 31, 19X7	3,693	Income tax expense	392
		Interest expense	190
		Income tax payable	440

How much net income did Sprint earn during 19X8? Prepare a T-account for Retained Earnings to show the December 31, 19X8, balance of Retained Earnings. What caused Retained Earnings to decrease during 19X8?

Identifying and recording adjusting and closing entries (Obj. 3, 5)

E3-15 The unadjusted trial balance and income statement amounts from the March adjusted trial balance of Impact Printing Company are given on page 151.

Required

Journalize the adjusting and closing entries of Impact Printing Company at March 31. There was only one adjustment to Service Revenue.

Preparing a classified balance sheet and using the ratios (Obj. 4, 6)

E3-16 Refer to Exercise 3-15.

Required

1. After solving Exercise 3-15, use the data in that exercise to prepare Impact Printing Company's classified balance sheet at March 31 of the current year. Use the report format.
2. Compute Impact Printing's current ratio and debt ratio at March 31. One year ago, the current ratio was 1.70 and the debt ratio was 0.20. Indicate whether Impact's ability to pay its debts has improved or deteriorated during the current year.

Impact Printing

E3-15

(Continued)

Account Title	*Unadjusted Trial Balance*		*From the Adjusted Trial Balance*	
Cash	9,100			
Supplies	2,400			
Prepaid rent	1,100			
Equipment	32,100			
Accumulated depreciation		6,200		
Accounts payable		4,600		
Salary payable				
Unearned service revenue		8,400		
Income tax payable				
Common stock		8,700		
Retained earnings		10,300		
Dividends	1,000			
Service revenue		11,700		19,100
Salary expense	3,000		3,800	
Rent expense	1,200		1,400	
Depreciation expense			300	
Supplies expense			400	
Income tax expense			1,600	
	49,900	49,900	7,500	19,100
Net income			11,600	
			19,100	19,100

SERIAL EXERCISE

Exercise 3-17 continues the Donna Schulz, Certified Public Accountant, P.C., situation begun in Exercise 2-15 of Chapter 2 (pp. 90–91).

Adjusting the accounts, preparing the financial statements, closing the accounts, and evaluating the business
(Obj. 3, 4, 5, 6)

E3-17 Refer to Exercise 2-15 of Chapter 2. Start from the trial balance and the posted T-accounts that Donna Schulz, Certified Public Accountant, Professional Corporation (P.C.), prepared for her accounting practice at December 18. A professional corporation is not subject to income tax. Later in December, the business completed these transactions:

Dec. 21	Received $900 in advance for tax work to be performed evenly over the next 30 days.
21	Hired a secretary to be paid $1,500 on the 20th day of each month.
26	Paid for the supplies purchased on December 5.
28	Collected $600 from the consulting client on December 18.
30	Declared and paid dividends of $1,600.

Required

1. Open these T-accounts: Accumulated Depreciation—Equipment, Accumulated Depreciation—Furniture, Salary Payable, Unearned Service Revenue, Retained Earnings, Depreciation Expense—Equipment, Depreciation Expense—Furniture, and Supplies Expense. Also, use the T-accounts opened for Exercise 2-15.

2. Journalize the transactions of December 21 through 30.

3. Post the December 21–30 transactions to the T-accounts, keying all items by date.

4. Prepare a trial balance at December 31. Also set up columns for the adjustments and for the adjusted trial balance, as illustrated in Exhibit 3-13, page 124.

5. At December 31, Schulz gathers the following information for the adjusting entries:

a. Accrued service revenue, $400.

b. Earned a portion of the service revenue collected in advance on December 21.

c. Supplies on hand, $100.

d. Depreciation expense—equipment, $50; furniture, $60.

e. Accrued expense for secretary's salary. Use a 30-day month to simplify the computation.

Make these adjustments directly in the adjustments columns and complete the adjusted trial balance at December 31.

6. Journalize and post the adjusting entries. Denote each adjusting amount as Adj. and an account balance as Bal.
7. Prepare the income statement and statement of retained earnings of Donna Schulz, Certified Public Accountant, P.C., for the month ended December 31 and the classified balance sheet at that date. Draw arrows to link the financial statements.
8. Journalize and post the closing entries at December 31. Denote each closing amount as Clo. and an account balance as Bal.
9. Compute the current ratio and the debt ratio of Schulz's accounting practice and evaluate these ratio values as indicative of a strong or weak financial position.

CHALLENGE EXERCISES

Computing revenue and cash amounts (Obj. 3)

E3-18 Chiang Finder Service aids Chinese students upon their arrival in the United States. Paid by the Chinese government, Ki Chiang collects some service revenue in advance. In other cases, he receives cash after performing relocation services. At the end of August—a particularly busy period—Chiang's books show the following:

	August 31	*July 31*
Accounts receivable	$1,200	$2,200
Unearned service revenue	1,200	300

a. During August, Chiang Finder Service received cash of $9,200 from the Chinese government. How much service revenue did the business earn during August? Show your computations.

b. Assume the service revenue of Chiang is $8,000 during August. How much cash did the business collect from the Chinese government during August? Show your computations.

Computing financial statement amounts (Obj. 3, 4)

E3-19 The unadjusted trial balance of Koele Hotel Company follows:

Cash	$ 4,200	Note payable, long-term	$ 6,000
Accounts receivable	7,200	Common stock	10,000
Rent receivable		Retained earnings	50,100
Supplies	1,100	Dividends	16,200
Prepaid insurance	2,200	Service revenue	4,100
Furniture	15,700	Rent revenue	101,000
Accumulated depreciation—furniture	1,300	Salary expense	32,700
Building	57,800	Depreciation expense—furniture	
Accumulated depreciation—building	14,900	Depreciation expense—building	
Land	51,200	Supplies expense	
Accounts payable	6,100	Insurance expense	
Salary payable		Interest expense	
Interest payable		Advertising expense	7,800
Property tax payable		Property tax expense	
Unearned service revenue	5,300	Utilities expense	2,700

Adjusting data at the end of the year include:

a. Unearned service revenue that has been earned, $1,900.

b. Accrued rent revenue, $1,200.

c. Accrued property tax expense, $900.

d. Accrued service revenue, $1,700.
e. Supplies used in operations, $600.
f. Accrued salary expense, $1,400.
g. Insurance expense, $1,800.
h. Depreciation expense—furniture, $800; building, $2,100.
i. Accrued interest expense, $500.

Mantu Koele, the principal stockholder, has received an offer to sell Koele Hotel Company. She needs to know the following information within one hour:

a. Net income for the year covered by these data.
b. Total assets.
c. Total liabilities.
d. Total stockholders' equity.
e. Proof that total assets = total liabilities + total stockholders' equity after all items are updated.

Required

Without opening any accounts, making any journal entries, or using a work sheet, provide Mantu Koele with the requested information. The business is not subject to income tax. Show all computations.

PROBLEMS

(Group A)

Linking accrual accounting and cash flows (Obj. 1)

P3-1A During 19X7, **Nike, Inc.,** earned revenues of $9.2 billion from the sale of shoes and clothing. Nike incurred a large number of expenses and ended the year with net income of $0.8 billion. Nike collected cash of $8.8 billion from customers and paid cash for all its 19X7 expenses plus an additional $0.1 billion for 19X6 expenses that were accrued at the end of 19X6. Answer these questions about Nike's operating results, financial position, and cash flows during 19X7:

1. How much were Nike's total expenses? Show your work.
2. Identify all the items that Nike will report on its income statement for 19X7. Show each amount.
3. How much cash did Nike pay for expenses and accrued liabilities during 19X7? These payments are labeled as "Payments to suppliers and employees."
4. Identify the appropriate financial statement and show how Nike will report its cash receipts and cash payments in its 19X7 annual report.
5. Nike began 19X7 with receivables of $1.4 billion. What was Nike's receivables balance at the end of 19X7? Identify the appropriate financial statement and show how Nike will report its ending receivable balance in the company's 19X7 annual report.
6. Nike began 19X7 owing accounts payable and accrued expenses payable totaling $0.9 billion. How much in accounts payable and accrued expenses payable did Nike owe at the end of 19X7? Identify the appropriate financial statement and show how Nike will report these two items in its 19X7 annual report. (For this requirement it is okay to combine accounts payable and accrued expenses payable into a single amount.)

Cash basis versus accrual basis (Obj. 1)

P3-2A Cadillac Jack's Restaurant had the following selected transactions during May:

May	1	Received $800 in advance for a banquet to be served later.
	5	Paid electricity expenses, $700.
	9	Received cash for the day's sales, $1,400.
	14	Purchased two video games, $3,000.
	23	Served a banquet, receiving a note receivable, $1,200.
	31	Accrued salary expense, $900.
	31	Prepaid building rent for June, July, and August, $3,000.

Required

1. Show how each transaction would be handled using the cash basis and the accrual basis. Under each column, give the amount of revenue or expense for May. Journal entries are not required. Use the following format for your answer, and show your computations:

Cadillac Jack's—Amount of Revenue (Expense) for May

Date	*Cash Basis*	*Accrual Basis*

2. Compute income (loss) before tax for May under the two accounting methods.
3. Which method better measures income and assets? Use the last transaction to explain.

Applying accounting principles (Obj. 1, 2)

P3-3A As the controller of Progressive Protection Company, you have hired a new employee, whom you must train. He objects to making an adjusting entry for accrued salaries at the end of the period. He reasons, "We will pay the salaries soon. Why not wait until payment to record the expense? In the end, the result will be the same." Write a reply to explain to the employee why the adjusting entry is needed for accrued salary expense.

Making accounting adjustments (Obj. 3)

P3-4A Journalize the adjusting entry needed on December 31, the end of the current accounting period, for each of the following independent cases affecting Fiber Optic Engineering, Inc. (FOE):

a. Each Friday, FOE pays its employees for the current week's work. The amount of the payroll is $4,500 for a five-day work week. The current accounting period ends on Monday.

b. FOE has received notes receivable from some clients for professional services. During the current year, FOE has earned accrued interest revenue of $2,640, which will be received next year.

c. The beginning balance of Engineering Supplies was $1,800. During the year, the entity purchased supplies costing $12,530, and at December 31 the inventory of supplies on hand is $2,970.

d. FOE is conducting tests of the strength of the steel to be used in a large building, and the client paid FOE $36,000 at the start of the project. FOE recorded this amount as Unearned Engineering Revenue. The tests will take several months to complete. FOE executives estimate that the company has earned three-fourths of the total fee during the current year.

e. Depreciation for the current year includes Office Furniture, $5,500; Engineering Equipment, $6,360; Building, $3,790. Make a compound entry.

f. Details of Prepaid Insurance are shown in the account:

Prepaid Insurance			
Jan. 1	**Bal.**	600	
Apr. 30		2,400	

FOE pays the annual insurance premium (the payment for insurance coverage is called a *premium*) on April 30 each year.

Analyzing and recording adjustments (Obj. 3)

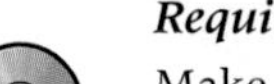

P3-5A Yellowhammer Auction Company's unadjusted and adjusted trial balances at December 31, 20X7, are given on page 155.

Required

Make the adjusting entries that account for the difference between the two trial balances. Yellowhammer Auction Company is not subject to income tax.

Preparing the financial statements and using the debt ratio (Obj. 4, 6)

P3-6A The adjusted trial balance of Unistar Communication, Inc., at December 31, 20X1 is on page 155.

Required

1. Prepare Unistar's 20X1 income statement, statement of retained earnings, and balance sheet. List expenses in decreasing order on the income statement and show total liabilities on the balance sheet. Draw arrows linking the three financial statements.
2. Unistar's lenders require that the company maintain a debt ratio no higher than 0.60. Compute Unistar's debt ratio at December 31, 20X1, to determine whether the company is in compliance with this debt restriction. If not, suggest an easy way that Unistar could have avoided this difficult situation by altering the amount of dividends.

P3-5A
(Continued)

YELLOWHAMMER AUCTION COMPANY
Adjusted Trial Balance
December 31, 20X7

Account Title	Trial Balance Debit	Trial Balance Credit	Adjusted Trial Balance Debit	Adjusted Trial Balance Credit
Cash	4,120		4,120	
Accounts receivable	11,260		12,090	
Supplies	1,090		780	
Prepaid insurance	2,600		910	
Office furniture	21,630		21,630	
Accumulated depreciation		8,220		10,500
Accounts payable		6,310		6,310
Salary payable				960
Interest payable				480
Note payable		12,000		12,000
Unearned commission revenue		1,840		1,160
Common stock		10,000		10,000
Retained earnings		3,510		3,510
Dividends	29,370		29,370	
Commission revenue		72,890		74,400
Depreciation expense			2,280	
Supplies expense			310	
Utilities expense	4,960		4,960	
Salary expense	26,660		27,620	
Rent expense	12,200		12,200	
Interest expense	880		1,360	
Insurance expense			1,690	
	114,770	114,770	119,320	119,320

P3-6A
(Continued)

UNISTAR COMMUNICATION, INC.
Adjusted Trial Balance
December 31, 20X1

	Debit	Credit
Cash	$ 2,340	
Accounts receivable	41,490	
Prepaid rent	1,350	
Equipment	75,690	
Accumulated depreciation		$ 22,240
Accounts payable		13,600
Unearned service revenue		4,520
Interest payable		2,130
Salary payable		930
Income tax payable		8,800
Note payable		36,200
Common stock		12,000
Retained earnings		20,380
Dividends	48,000	
Service revenue		178,370
Depreciation expense	11,300	
Salary expense	94,000	
Rent expense	12,000	
Interest expense	4,200	
Income tax expense	8,800	
Total	$299,170	$299,170

Preparing an adjusted trial balance and the financial statements; using the current ratio to evaluate the business (Obj. 3, 4, 6)

P3-7A Consider the unadjusted trial balance of IKON Advertising at October 31, 20X2, and the related month-end adjustment data.

IKON ADVERTISING
Trial Balance
October 31, 20X2

Cash	$ 5,300	
Accounts receivable	7,000	
Prepaid rent	4,000	
Supplies	600	
Furniture	36,000	
Accumulated depreciation		$ 3,000
Accounts payable		8,800
Salary payable		
Common stock		15,000
Retained earnings		21,000
Dividends	4,600	
Advertising revenue		14,400
Salary expense	4,400	
Rent expense		
Utilities expense	300	
Depreciation expense		
Supplies expense		
Total	$62,200	$62,200

Adjustment data:

a. Accrued advertising revenue at October 31, $2,000.

b. Prepaid rent expired during the month. The unadjusted prepaid balance of $4,000 relates to the period October 20X2 through January 20X3.

c. Supplies used during October, $200.

d. Depreciation on furniture for the month. The furniture's expected useful life is five years.

e. Accrued salary expense at October 31 for Tuesday through Friday. The five-day weekly payroll is $2,000.

Required

1. Using Exhibit 3-13, page 124, as an example, prepare the adjusted trial balance of IKON Advertising, at October 31, 20X2. Key each adjusting entry by letter.

2. Prepare the income statement, the statement of retained earnings, and the classified balance sheet. Draw arrows linking the three financial statements.

3. a. Compare the business's net income for October to the amount of dividends paid to the owners. Suppose this trend continues into 20X3. What will be the effect on the business's financial position, as shown by its accounting equation?

b. Will the trend make it easier or more difficult for IKON to borrow money if the business gets in a bind and needs cash? Why?

c. Does either the current ratio or the cash position suggest the need for immediate borrowing? Explain.

Preparing a classified balance sheet and using the ratios to evaluate the business (Obj. 4, 6)

P3-8A The accounts of Cookie Lapp Travel Agency, Inc., at December 31, 20X1, are listed in alphabetical order on page 157.

Required

1. All adjustments have been journalized and posted, but the closing entries have not yet been made. Prepare the company's classified balance sheet in report format at December 31, 20X1. Use captions for total assets, total liabilities, and total liabilities and stockholders' equity. The travel agency is not subject to income tax.

2. Compute Lapp's current ratio and debt ratio at December 31, 20X1. At December 31, 20X0, the current ratio was 1.52 and the debt ratio was 0.45. Did Lapp's overall ability to pay debts improve or deteriorate during 20X1?

Cookie Lapp Travel Agency

P3-8A

(Continued)

Accounts payable	$ 5,100	Insurance expense	$ 800
Accounts receivable	6,600	Note payable, long-term	9,800
Accumulated depreciation— furniture	11,600	Note receivable, long-term	4,000
Advertising expense	2,200	Other assets	3,600
Cash	6,500	Prepaid expenses	7,700
Commission revenue	93,500	Retained earnings, December 31, 20X0	5,300
Common stock	15,000	Salary expense	24,600
Current portion of note payable	2,200	Salary payable	3,900
Depreciation expense	1,300	Supplies expense	5,700
Dividends	47,400	Unearned commission revenue	5,400
Furniture	41,400		

Closing the books and evaluating retained earnings (Obj. 5)

P3-9A Refer back to Problem 3-8A.

1. Use the Cookie Lapp Travel Agency data in Problem 3-8A to journalize Lapp's closing entries at December 31, 20X1.
2. Set up a T-account for Retained Earnings and post to that account. What is the ending balance of Retained Earnings?
3. Did Retained Earnings increase or decrease during the year? What caused the increase or decrease?

Analyzing financial ratios (Obj. 6)

P3-10A This problem demonstrates the effects of transactions on the current ratio and the debt ratio of a well-known company. **Unocal Corporation** is a leading oil company, famous for its "76" gas stations. Unocal's condensed balance sheet at December 31, 19X8, is given.

	(In millions)
Total current assets	$1,576
Properties, net, and other assets	8,315
	$9,891
Total current liabilities	$1,316
Total long-term liabilities	5,645
Total stockholders' equity	2,930
	$9,891

Assume that during the first quarter of the following year, 19X9, Unocal completed the following transactions:

a. Paid half the current liabilities.
b. Borrowed $3 billion ($3,000 million) on long-term debt.
c. Earned revenue of $2.5 billion ($2,500 million) on account.
d. Paid selling expense of $1 billion ($1,000 million).
e. Accrued general expense of $800 million. Credit General Expense Payable, a current liability.
f. Purchased equipment, paying cash of $1.4 billion ($1,400 million) and signing a long-term note payable for $2.8 billion ($2,800 million).
g. Recorded depreciation expense of $600 million.

Required

1. Compute Unocal's current ratio and debt ratio at December 31, 19X8.
2. Compute Unocal's current ratio and debt ratio after each transaction. Consider each transaction separately.
3. Based on your analysis, you should be able to readily identify the effects of certain transactions on the current ratio and the debt ratio. Test your understanding by completing these statements with either "increase" or "decrease":

   a. Revenues usually ________________ the current ratio.
   b. Revenues usually ________________ the debt ratio.

c. Expenses usually ______________ the current ratio. (Note: Depreciation is an exception to this rule.)

d. Expenses usually ______________ the debt ratio.

e. If a company's current ratio is greater than 1.0, as it is for Unocal, paying off a current liability will always ______________ the current ratio.

f. Borrowing money on long-term debt will always ______________ the current ratio and ______________ the debt ratio.

(Group B)

Linking accrual accounting and cash flows (Obj. 1)

P3-1B **360° Communication Company** earned revenues of $1,347 million during 19X7 and ended the year with net income of $81 million. During 19X7, 360° collected $1,349 million from customers and paid cash for all but $306 million of its expenses. Answer these questions about 360° Communication's operating results, financial position, and cash flows during 19X7:

Required

1. How much were the company's total expenses? Show your work.
2. Identify all the items that 360° Communication Company will report on its 19X7 income statement. Show each amount.
3. How much cash did 360° pay for its 19X7 expenses?
4. Identify the appropriate financial statement, and show how 360° will report its cash receipts and cash payments in its 19X7 annual report. The cash payments are labeled as "Payments to suppliers and employees."
5. 360° Communication Company began 19X7 with receivables of $102 million. What was the company's receivables balance at the end of 19X7? Identify the appropriate financial statement, and show how 360° will report its ending receivables in the 19X7 annual report.
6. 360° began 19X7 owing accounts payable and accrued expenses payable totaling $279 million. How much in accounts payable and accrued expenses payable did the company owe at the end of the year? Identify the appropriate financial statement and show how 360° will report these two items in its 19X7 annual report. (For this requirement it is okay to combine accounts payable and accrued expenses payable into a single amount.)

Cash basis versus accrual basis (Obj. 1)

P3-2B Flowers Etching Service had the following selected transactions in October:

Oct.	1	Prepaid insurance for October through December, $900.
	4	Purchased equipment for cash, $800.
	5	Performed service and received cash, $700.
	8	Paid advertising expense, $300.
	11	Performed service on account, $1,800.
	19	Purchased equipment on account, $100.
	24	Collected for the October 11 service.
	26	Paid account payable from October 19.
	29	Paid salary expense, $900.
	31	Adjusted for October insurance expense (see Oct. 1).
	31	Earned revenue of $1,300 that was collected in advance back in September.

Required

1. Show how each transaction would be handled using the cash basis and the accrual basis. Under each column, give the amount of revenue or expense for October. Journal entries are not required. Use the following format for your answer, and show your computations:

Flowers Etching Service—
Amount of Revenue or Expense for October

Date	*Cash Basis*	*Accrual Basis*

2. Compute October income (loss) before tax under each accounting method.
3. Indicate which measure of net income or net loss is preferable. Use the transactions on October 11 and 24 to explain.

P3-3B Write a memo to explain for a new employee the difference between the cash basis of accounting and the accrual basis. Mention the roles of the revenue principle and the matching principle in accrual accounting.

Applying accounting principles (Obj. 1, 2)

P3-4B Journalize the adjusting entry needed on December 31, end of the current accounting period, for each of the following independent cases affecting Semitech Corporation.

Making accounting adjustments (Obj. 3)

a. Details of Prepaid Insurance are shown in the account:

PREPAID INSURANCE			
Jan. 1	**Bal.**	**600**	
Mar. 31		**3,000**	

Semitech prepays insurance each year on March 31.

b. Semitech pays its employees each Friday. The amount of the weekly payroll is $6,000 for a five-day work week, and the daily salary amounts are equal. The current accounting period ends on Monday.

c. Semitech has loaned money, receiving notes receivable. During the current year, the entity has earned accrued interest revenue of $509 that it will receive next year.

d. The beginning balance of Supplies was $2,680. During the year, the entity purchased supplies costing $6,180, and at December 31 the cost of supplies on hand is $2,150.

e. Semitech is servicing the air-conditioning system in a large building, and the owner of the building paid Semitech $12,900 as the annual service fee. Semitech recorded this amount as Unearned Service Revenue. Mari Potosi, the general manager, estimates that the company has earned one-fourth the total fee during the current year.

f. Depreciation for the current year includes Office Furniture, $700; Equipment, $2,730; and Trucks, $10,320. Make a compound entry.

P3-5B Interstate Rental Company's unadjusted and adjusted trial balances at September 30, 20X1, follow:

Analyzing and recording adjustments (Obj. 3)

INTERSTATE RENTAL COMPANY
Adjusted Trial Balance
September 30, 20X1

	Trial Balance		*Adjusted Trial Balance*	
Account Title	*Debit*	*Credit*	*Debit*	*Credit*
Cash	8,180		8,180	
Accounts receivable	6,360		6,840	
Interest receivable			300	
Note receivable	4,100		4,100	
Supplies	980		290	
Prepaid insurance	2,480		720	
Building	66,450		66,450	
Accumulated depreciation		16,010		17,110
Accounts payable		6,920		6,920
Wages payable				170
Unearned rental revenue		670		110
Common stock		18,000		18,000
Retained earnings		42,790		42,790
Dividends	3,600		3,600	
Rental revenue		9,940		10,980
Interest revenue				300
Wage expense	1,600		1,770	
Insurance expense			1,760	
Depreciation expense			1,100	
Property tax expense	370		370	
Supplies expense			690	
Utilities expense	210		210	
	94,330	94,330	96,380	96,380

Required

Make the adjusting entries that account for the differences between the two trial balances. Interstate Rental Company is not subject to income tax.

Preparing the financial statements and using the debt ratio (Obj. 4, 6)

P3-6B The adjusted trial balance of Anderson Consultants, Inc., at December 31, 20X6, follows:

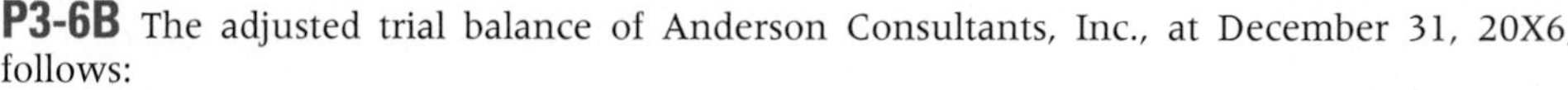

ANDERSON CONSULTANTS, INC. Adjusted Trial Balance December 31, 20X6		
Cash	$ 1,320	
Accounts receivable	8,920	
Supplies	2,300	
Prepaid rent	1,600	
Office equipment	30,180	
Accumulated depreciation		$ 4,350
Accounts payable		3,640
Interest payable		830
Unearned service revenue		620
Income tax payable		2,100
Note payable		11,620
Common stock		5,000
Retained earnings		1,090
Dividends	44,000	
Service revenue		127,910
Depreciation expense	1,680	
Salary expense	39,900	
Rent expense	10,300	
Interest expense	3,100	
Insurance expense	3,810	
Supplies expense	2,950	
Income tax expense	7,100	
Total	157,160	157,160

Required

1. Prepare Anderson's 20X6 income statement, statement of retained earnings, and balance sheet. List expenses (except for income tax) in decreasing order on the income statement and show total liabilities on the balance sheet. Draw arrows linking the three financial statements.
2. Anderson's lenders require that the company maintain a debt ratio no higher than 0.50. Compute Anderson's debt ratio at December 31, 20X6, to determine whether the company is in compliance with this debt restriction. If not, suggest an easy way that Anderson could have avoided this difficult situation by altering the amount of dividends.

Preparing an adjusted trial balance and the financial statements; using the current ratio to evaluate the business (Obj. 3, 4, 6)

P3-7B The unadjusted trial balance of Rebecca Kline, Attorney, Professional Corporation (P.C.), at July 31, 20X2, and the related month-end adjustment data follow at the top of page 161:

Adjustment data:

a. Accrued legal service revenue at July 31, $400.

b. Prepaid rent expired during the month. The unadjusted prepaid balance of $3,600 relates to the period July through October.

c. Supplies used during July, $600.

d. Depreciation on furniture for the month. The estimated useful life of the furniture is four years.

e. Accrued salary expense at July 31 for Monday through Wednesday. The five-day weekly payroll of $1,200 will be paid on Friday, August 2.

P3-7B *(Continued)*

REBECCA KLINE, ATTORNEY, P.C. Trial Balance July 31, 20X2		
Cash	$ 5,600	
Accounts receivable	11,600	
Prepaid rent	3,600	
Supplies	800	
Furniture	34,800	
Accumulated depreciation		$ 3,500
Accounts payable		10,450
Salary payable		
Common stock		25,000
Retained earnings		13,650
Dividends	4,000	
Legal service revenue		10,750
Salary expense	2,400	
Rent expense		
Utilities expense	550	
Depreciation expense		
Supplies expense		
Total	$63,350	$63,350

Required

1. Using Exhibit 3-13, page 124, as an example, prepare the adjusted trial balance of Rebecca Kline, Attorney, P.C., at July 31, 20X2. Key each adjusting entry by letter. A professional corporation is not subject to income tax.
2. Prepare the income statement, the statement of retained earnings, and the classified balance sheet. Draw arrows linking the three financial statements.
3. a. Compare the business's net income for July to the amount of dividends paid to the owners. Suppose this trend continues each month for the remainder of 19X2. What will be the effect on the business's financial position, as shown by its accounting equation?

   b. Will the trend make it easier or more difficult to borrow money if the business gets in a bind and needs cash? Why?

   c. Does either the current ratio or the cash position suggest the need for immediate borrowing? Explain.

P3-8B The accounts of Woodrow Engel, CPA, Professional Corporation (P.C.), at March 31, 20X3, are listed in alphabetical order.

Preparing a classified balance sheet and using the ratios to evaluate the business (Obj. 4, 6)

Accounts payable	$14,700	Furniture	$43,200
Accounts receivable	11,500	Insurance expense	600
Accumulated depreciation—building	47,300	Note payable, long-term	3,200
Accumulated depreciation—furniture	7,100	Note receivable, long-term	6,900
Advertising expense	900	Other assets	2,300
Building	55,900	Prepaid expenses	5,300
Cash	3,400	Retained earnings, March 31, 20X2	30,800
Common stock	9,100	Salary expense	17,800
Current portion of note payable	800	Salary payable	2,400
Depreciation expense	1,900	Service revenue	71,100
Dividends	31,200	Supplies	3,800
		Supplies expense	4,600
		Unearned service revenue	2,800

Required

1. All adjustments have been journalized and posted, but the closing entries have not yet been made. Prepare the company's classified balance sheet at March 31, 20X3. Use captions for total assets, total liabilities, and total liabilities and stockholders' equity. A professional corporation is not subject to income tax.

2. Compute Engel's current ratio and debt ratio at March 31, 20X3. At March 31, 20X2, the current ratio was 1.28 and the debt ratio was 0.29. Did Engel's ability to pay debts improve or deteriorate during 20X3? Evaluate Engel's overall debt position as strong or weak and give your reason.

Closing the books and evaluating retained earnings (Obj. 5)

P3-9B Refer back to Problem 3-8B.

1. Use the Woodrow Engel, CPA, P.C., data in Problem 3-8B to journalize Engel's closing entries at March 31, 20X3.

2. Set up a T-account for Retained Earnings and post to that account. What is the ending balance of Retained Earnings?

3. Did Retained Earnings increase or decrease during the year? What caused the increase or the decrease?

Analyzing financial ratios (Obj. 6)

P3-10B This problem demonstrates the effects of transactions on the current ratio and the debt ratio of a well-known company. **Texaco, Inc.,** is a leading oil company, famous for its Texaco gas stations. Texaco's condensed balance sheet at December 31, 19X8, is:

	(In millions)
Total current assets	$ 6,458
Properties, plant, equipment, and other assets	18,479
	$24,937
Total current liabilities	$ 5,206
Total long-term liabilities	10,212
Total stockholders' equity	9,519
	$24,937

Assume that during the first quarter of the following year, 19X9, Texaco completed the following transactions:

a. Paid half the current liabilities.

b. Borrowed $3 billion ($3,000 million) on long-term debt.

c. Earned revenue, $2.5 billion ($2,500 million) on account.

d. Paid selling expense of $1 billion ($1,000 million).

e. Accrued general expense of $800 million. Credit General Expense Payable, a current liability.

f. Purchased equipment, paying cash of $1.4 billion ($1,400 million) and signing a long-term note payable for $2.8 billion ($2,800 million).

g. Recorded depreciation expense of $600 million.

Required

1. Compute Texaco's current ratio and debt ratio at December 31, 19X8.

2. Compute Texaco's current ratio and debt ratio after each transaction. Consider each transaction separately.

3. Based on your analysis, you should be able to readily identify the effects of certain transactions on the current ratio and the debt ratio. Test your understanding by completing these statements with either "increase" or "decrease":

a. Revenues usually _______________ the current ratio.

b. Revenues usually _______________ the debt ratio.

c. Expenses usually _______________ the current ratio. (*Note:* Depreciation is an exception to this rule.)

d. Expenses usually _______________ the debt ratio.

(Continued)

e. If a company's current ratio is greater than 1.0, as it is for Texaco, paying off a current liability will always ______________ the current ratio.

f. Borrowing money on long-term debt will always ______________ the current ratio and ______________ the debt ratio.

Extending Your Knowledge

Decision Cases

Valuing a business on the basis of its net income (Obj. 3, 4)

Case 1. Chance Wayne has owned and operated Chance Wayne Advertising, Inc., since its beginning 10 years ago. From all appearances, the business has prospered. Recently, he mentioned that he has lost his zest for the business and would consider selling it for the right price.

Assume that you are interested in buying this business. You obtain its most recent monthly trial balance, which follows. Revenues and expenses vary little from month to month, and April is a typical month. Your investigation reveals that the trial balance does not include the effects of monthly revenues of $3,800 and expenses totaling $1,100. If you were to buy Chance Wayne Advertising, you would hire a manager so you could devote your time to other duties. Assume that this person would require a monthly salary of $4,000.

CHANCE WAYNE ADVERTISING, INC.
Trial Balance
April 30, 20XX

Cash	$ 9,700	
Accounts receivable	4,900	
Prepaid expenses	2,600	
Plant assets	221,300	
Accumulated depreciation		$189,600
Land	158,000	
Accounts payable		13,800
Salary payable		
Unearned advertising revenue		56,700
Common stock		50,000
Retained earnings		87,400
Dividends	9,000	
Advertising revenue		12,300
Rent expense		
Salary expense	3,400	
Utilities expense	900	
Depreciation expense		
Supplies expense		
Total	$409,800	$409,800

Required

1. Assume that the most you would pay for the business is 25 times the monthly net income *you could expect to earn* from it. Compute this possible price.
2. Wayne states that the least he will take for the business is its stockholders' equity on April 30. Compute this amount.
3. Under these conditions, how much should you offer Wayne? Give your reason.

Completing the accounting cycle to develop the information for a bank loan
(Obj. 3, 5)

Case 2. One year ago, Bob Cervenka founded Total Restoration Service, Inc. The business has prospered. Cervenka, who remembers that you took an accounting course while in college, comes to you for advice. He wishes to know how much net income the business earned during the past year. He also wants to know what the entity's total assets, liabilities, and stockholders' equity are. His accounting records consist of the T-accounts of his ledger, which were prepared by an accountant who moved to another city. The ledger at December 31 appears as follows:

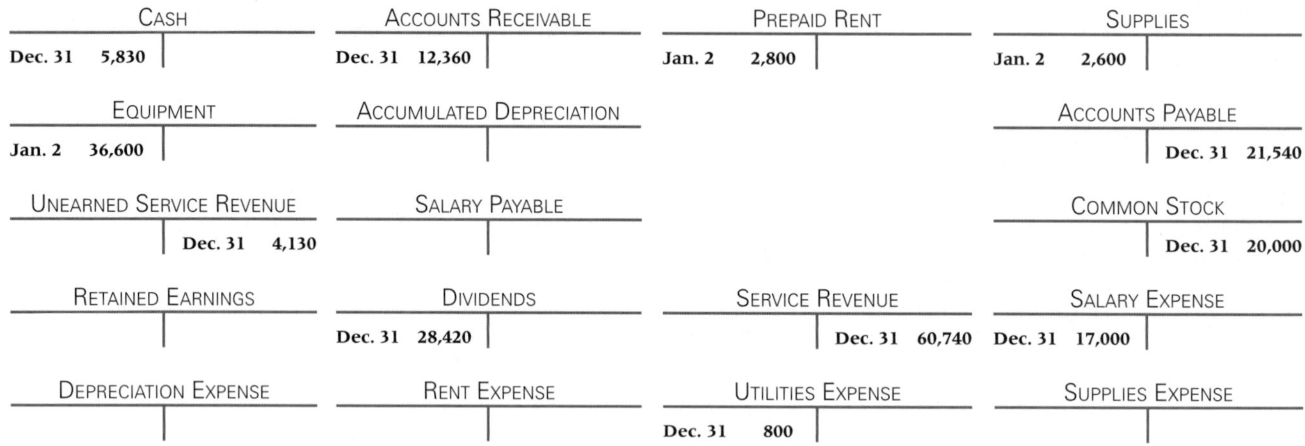

Cervenka indicates that at the year's end, customers owe him $1,600 accrued service revenue, which he expects to collect early next year. These revenues have not been recorded. During the year, he collected $4,130 service revenue in advance from customers, but he earned only $600 of that amount. Rent expense for the year was $2,400, and he used up $2,100 in supplies. Cervenka estimates that depreciation on his equipment was $5,900 for the year. At December 31, he owes his employee $1,200 accrued salary.

At the conclusion of your meeting, Cervenka expresses concern that dividends during the year might have exceeded net income. To get a loan to expand the business, Cervenka must show the bank that total stockholders' equity has grown from its original $20,000 balance. Has it? You and Cervenka agree that you will meet again in one week. You perform the analysis and prepare the financial statements to answer his questions.

ETHICAL ISSUES

Issue 1. CNA Associates, a management consulting firm, is in its third year of operations. The company was initially financed by owners' equity as the three partners each invested $30,000. The first year's slim profits were expected because new businesses often start slowly. During the second year, CNA landed a large contract with a paper mill, and referrals from that project brought in several other large jobs. To expand the business, CNA borrowed $100,000 from Synergy Bank of Kansas City. As a condition for making this loan, the bank required that CNA maintain a current ratio of at least 1.50 and a debt ratio of no more than 0.50.

Business during the third year has been good, but slightly below the target for the year. Expansion costs have brought the current ratio down to 1.47 and the debt ratio up to 0.51 at December 15. Jacques Pastille, the general manager, is considering the implication of reporting this current ratio to the bank. One course of action is to record in December of the third year some revenue on account that CNA will earn in January of their fourth year of operations. The contract for this job has been signed, and CNA will perform the management consulting service for the client during January.

Required

1. Journalize the revenue transaction, and indicate how recording this revenue in December would affect the current ratio and the debt ratio.

2. State whether it is ethical to record the revenue transaction in December. Identify the accounting principle relevant to this situation.
3. Propose for CNA Associates a course of action that is ethical.

Issue 2. The net income of Rollins, a department store, decreased sharply during 2000. Clay Rollins, owner of the store, anticipates the need for a bank loan in 2001. Late in 2000, he instructed the accountant to record a $40,000 sale of furniture to the Rollins family, even though the goods will not be shipped from the manufacturer until January 2000. Rollins also told the accountant *not* to make the following December 31, 2000, adjusting entries:

Salaries owed to employees	$1,800
Prepaid insurance that has expired	500

Required

1. Compute the overall effect of these transactions on the store's reported income for 2000. Is income overstated or understated?
2. Why did Rollins take these actions? Are they ethical? Give your reason, identifying the parties helped and the parties harmed by Rollins' action.
3. As a personal friend, what advice would you give the accountant?

Financial Statement Cases

Recording transactions and tracing account balances to the financial statements (Obj. 3, 6)

Case 1. The Gap, Inc.—like all other businesses—makes adjusting entries prior to year end in order to measure assets, liabilities, revenues, and expenses properly. Examine The Gap's balance sheet in Appendix A, and pay particular attention to Accumulated Depreciation and Amortization as well as Accrued Expenses and Other Current Liabilities.

Required

1. Open T-accounts for the first two accounts listed above. Insert The Gap's balances (in thousands) at January 31, 1998.
2. Journalize the following for the current year, ended January 30, 1999. Key entries by letter. Explanations are not required.

   Cash transaction (amounts in thousands):

   a. Paid the beginning balance of Accrued Expenses and Other Current Liabilities.

   Adjustments at January 30, 1999 (amounts in thousands):

   b. Accrued Expenses and Other Current Liabilities, $655,770. Debit Selling Expense.

   c. Recorded Depreciation Expense for the year, $233,244.
3. Post these entries and show that the balances in Accrued Expenses and Other Current Liabilities and in Accumulated Depreciation and Amortization agree with the corresponding amounts reported in the January 30, 1999 balance sheet.
4. Compute the current ratios and debt ratios for The Gap at January 30, 1999, and at January 31, 1998. Did the ratio values improve, deteriorate, or hold steady during the fiscal year ended January 30, 1999?

Adjusting the accounts of an actual company (Obj. 3)

Case 2. Obtain the annual report of a company of your choosing. Assume that the company accountants *failed* to make four adjustments at the end of the current year. For illustrative purposes, we shall assume that the amounts reported in the company's balance sheet for the related assets and liabilities are *incorrect*.
Adjustments omitted:

a. Depreciation of equipment, $800,000.
b. Salaries owed to employees but not yet paid, $230,000.
c. Prepaid rent used up during the year, $100,000.
d. Accrued sales (or service) revenue, $140,000.

Required

1. Compute the correct amounts for the following balance sheet items:
   a. Book value of plant assets
   b. Total liabilities
   c. Prepaid expenses
   d. Accounts receivable
2. Compute the amount of net income or net loss that the company would have reported if the accountants had recorded these transactions properly. Ignore income tax.

Group Project

Eric Caswell formed a lawn service company as a summer job. To start the business on May 1, he deposited $1,000 in a new bank account in the name of the corporation. The $1,000 consisted of a $600 loan from his father and $400 of his own money. The corporation issued 400 shares of common stock to Eric.

Eric rented lawn equipment, purchased supplies, and hired high-school students to mow and trim his customers' lawns. At the end of each month, Eric mailed bills to his customers. On August 31, Eric was ready to dissolve the business and return to Baylor University for the fall semester. Because he had been so busy, he had kept few records other than his checkbook and a list of amounts owed to him by customers.

At August 31, Eric's checkbook shows a balance of $840, and his customers still owe him $500. During the summer, he collected $4,400 from customers. His checkbook lists payments for supplies totaling $400, and he still has gasoline, weedeater cord, and other supplies that cost a total of $50. He paid his employees $1,900, and he still owes them $200 for the final week of the summer. Eric rented some equipment from Ludwig Tool Company. On May 1, he signed a six-month lease on mowers and paid $600 for the full lease period. Ludwig will refund the unused portion of the prepayment if the equipment is in good shape. In order to get the refund, Eric has kept the mowers in excellent condition. In fact, he had to pay $300 to repair a mower that ran over a hidden tree stump. To transport employees and equipment to jobs, Eric used a trailer that he bought for $300. He figures that the summer's work used up one-third of the trailer's service potential. The business checkbook lists an expenditure of $460 for dividends paid to Eric during the summer. Eric paid his father back during the summer.

Required

1. Prepare the income statement of Caswell Lawn Service, Inc., for the four months May through August. The business is not subject to income tax.
2. Prepare the classified balance sheet of Caswell Lawn Service, Inc., at August 31.
3. Prepare the statement of cash flows for Caswell Lawn Service, Inc., for the four months May through August.

Internet Exercise

Darden Restaurants

1. Go to **http://www.darden.com**. **It's Just Lunch** customers may eat lunch at one of the many **Darden** restaurants. List the three primary Darden restaurant chains.
2. Click on *The Numbers* followed by *Annual Report and Financials* and then select the most recent version of *the HTML annual report.* Use the balance sheet to answer the following questions.
3. Refer to the asset section but ignore the Deferred Income Taxes account. For the most recent year, list the account(s) and the amount(s) that
   a. represent the book value of the land, buildings, and equipment
   b. contain accrued revenue—amounts earned but not yet received in cash
   c. include expenses that have been paid in cash but not yet incurred as expenses
4. Refer to the current liability section. For the most recent year, list the account(s) and the amount(s) that contain *expenses* incurred but not yet paid in cash.

5. For the accrued payroll account, make the journal entry to record the accrued payroll expense (accounts only).
6. How many long-term liability accounts are listed? List the account titles.
7. Does Darden use cash-basis or accrual-basis accounting? How can you tell?
8. Which Darden balance sheet accounts are closed at the end of the year?
9. For the two most recent years, calculate Darden's *current ratio* and *debt ratio*. For each ratio state what the ratio indicates, the direction of the trend, and whether the trend is favorable or unfavorable.

4 Internal Control and Managing Cash

Learning Objectives

After studying this chapter, you should be able to

1. Describe an effective system of internal control
2. Use a bank reconciliation as a control device
3. Manage and account for cash
4. Apply internal controls to cash receipts
5. Apply internal controls to cash payments
6. Use a budget to manage cash
7. Weigh ethical judgments in business

"If all employees were always accurate and ethical, internal controls would not be necessary. Our ineffective internal control system gave one dishonest employee the opportunity to embezzle cash over several years' time. From now on, we're going to make it a lot harder to steal anything!"

Bill Bauer, Office Manager of Grant LeForge & Company

Grant LeForge & Company
Balance Sheet
June 30, 20X0

Assets	
Current assets:	
Cash	$ 1,710,934
Marketable securities	2,136,842
Receivables	859,763
Prepaid expenses	181,845
	4,889,384
Long-term investments	12,633,790
Property and equipment	5,436,211
Less accumulated depreciation	(1,707,946)
Other assets	663,582
	$21,915,021

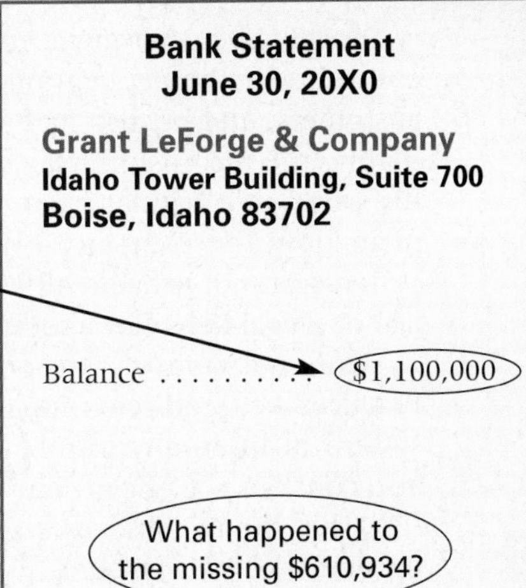
Bank Statement
June 30, 20X0

Grant LeForge & Company
Idaho Tower Building, Suite 700
Boise, Idaho 83702

Balance $1,100,000

What happened to the missing $610,934?

STEVE Lane was a cashier at the Boise, Idaho, office of the brokerage firm **Grant LeForge & Company.** His problems began when an auto accident forced him to miss work and Bill Bauer, manager of Grant LeForge, received complaints from customers who had not received credit for their deposits. Bauer uncovered an elaborate embezzlement scheme that Lane had begun five years earlier.

The court found that Lane had stolen a total of $610,934 in a "rob-Peter-to-pay-Paul scheme." He transferred customer deposits into his personal account and concealed the missing amounts with deposits from other customers. In this way, customer accounts always balanced as long as Lane was present to respond to customer inquiries. He simply explained that the account was temporarily out of balance. But while he was in the hospital, his replacement was unable to explain the irregularities in customers' accounts. When all the evidence came to light, it pointed in the direction of Lane, who was later tried and convicted of embezzlement. Bauer then understood why Lane had never taken a vacation.

What went wrong at the Grant LeForge office? There was a breakdown in the control over the accounting for cash. Steve Lane handled the cash received from customers, and he also had access to the company's accounting records. By manipulating the records, he was able to hide his theft for several years. No one checked his work on a regular basis. Several procedures that we discuss in this chapter explain how the company could have prevented this embezzlement. Such control systems cannot prevent all misconduct, but good controls can help to detect unethical or illegal behavior and limit its effects.

Internal controls are not optional for large companies. The Foreign Corrupt Practices Act requires companies under SEC jurisdiction to maintain an appropriate system of internal control, whether or not they have foreign operations. The act also contains specific prohibitions against bribery and other corrupt practices.

This chapter discusses *internal control*—the organizational plan and integrated framework that managers use to keep the business under control and protect company assets. The chapter applies these control techniques mainly to the management of cash (the most liquid asset) and provides a framework for making ethical judgments in business. Later chapters discuss how managers control other assets.

INTERNAL CONTROL

A key responsibility of managers is to control the operations of their business. Owners and the top managers set the entity's goals, managers lead the way, and employees carry out the plan. Good managers must decide where the organization is headed over the next several years. But if they don't control operations, the entity may not stay in business long enough for managers to put lofty plans into effect.

Internal control is the organizational plan and all the related measures that an entity adopts to

1. Safeguard assets,
2. Encourage adherence to company policies,
3. Promote operational efficiency, and
4. Ensure accurate and reliable accounting records.

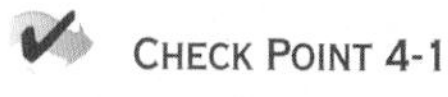

Exhibit 4-1 is an excerpt from the Responsibility for Consolidated Financial Statements of **Lands' End, Inc.** The company's top managers take responsibility for the financial statements and for the related system of internal control. The second paragraph refers to a system of internal control, the protection of assets, and the prevention of fraudulent financial reporting. Let's examine in more detail how companies create effective systems of internal control.

Establishing an Effective System of Internal Control

Objective 1
Describe an effective system of internal control

Whether the business is Grant LeForge, Lands' End, or a local department store, an effective system of internal controls has the following characteristics.

COMPETENT, RELIABLE, AND ETHICAL PERSONNEL. Employees should be *competent, reliable,* and *ethical.* Paying good salaries to attract top-quality employees, training them to do their jobs well, and supervising their work all help a company build a competent staff. A business adds flexibility to its staffing by rotating employees through various jobs. If one employee is sick or on vacation, a second employee is prepared to step in and do the job.

ASSIGNMENT OF RESPONSIBILITIES. A business with good internal controls overlooks no important duty. Each employee is assigned certain responsibilities. A model of

EXHIBIT 4-1
Management Statement About Internal Controls—Lands' End, Inc.

LANDS' END, INC.—Responsibility for Consolidated Financial Statements

The management of Lands' End, Inc., and its subsidiaries has the responsibility for preparing the accompanying financial statements and for their integrity and objectivity. The statements were prepared in accordance with generally accepted accounting principles applied on a consistent basis. The consolidated financial statements include amounts that are based on management's best estimates and judgments. Management also prepared the other information in the annual report and is responsible for its accuracy and consistency with the consolidated financial statements.

Management of the company has established and maintains a system of internal control that provides for appropriate division of responsibility, reasonable assurance as to the integrity and reliability of the consolidated financial statements, the protection of assets from unauthorized use or disposition, the prevention and detection of fraudulent financial reporting, and the maintenance of an active program of internal audits. Management believes that, as of January 29, 1999, the company's system of internal control is adequate to accomplish the objectives discussed herein.

David F. Dyer
Chief Executive Officer

Stephen A. Orum
Executive Vice President and Chief Financial Officer

Source: Lands' End, Inc., *Annual Report 1999,* p. 29. Courtesy of Lands' End.

such *assignment of responsibilities* appears in the corporate organizational chart in Exhibit 4-2. Notice that the corporation has a vice president of finance and accounting. Two other officers, the treasurer and the controller, report to that vice president. The treasurer is responsible for cash management. The **controller** is the chief accounting officer.

Within this organization, the controller may be responsible for approving invoices (bills) for payment, while the treasurer may actually sign the checks. Working under the controller, one accountant may be responsible for property taxes, another for income taxes. In sum, all duties are clearly defined and assigned to individuals who bear responsibility for carrying them out.

PROPER AUTHORIZATION. An organization generally has a written set of rules that outlines approved procedures. Any deviation from standard policy requires *proper authorization.* For example, managers or assistant managers of retail stores must approve customer checks for amounts above the store's usual limit. Likewise, deans or department chairs of colleges and universities must authorize juniors to enroll in courses restricted to seniors.

SEPARATION OF DUTIES. Smart management divides the responsibilities for transactions between two or more people or departments. *Separation of duties* limits the chances for fraud and promotes the accuracy of accounting records. The Lands' End responsibility statement (Exhibit 4-1) refers to a *division of responsibility.* This crucial component of the internal control system may be divided into four parts:

1. *Separation of operations from accounting.* The entire accounting function should be completely separate from operating departments, such as manufacturing and sales, so that reliable records may be kept. For example, product inspectors, not machine operators, should count units produced by a manufacturing process. Accountants, not salespeople, should keep inventory records. Observe the separation of accounting from production and marketing in Exhibit 4-2.

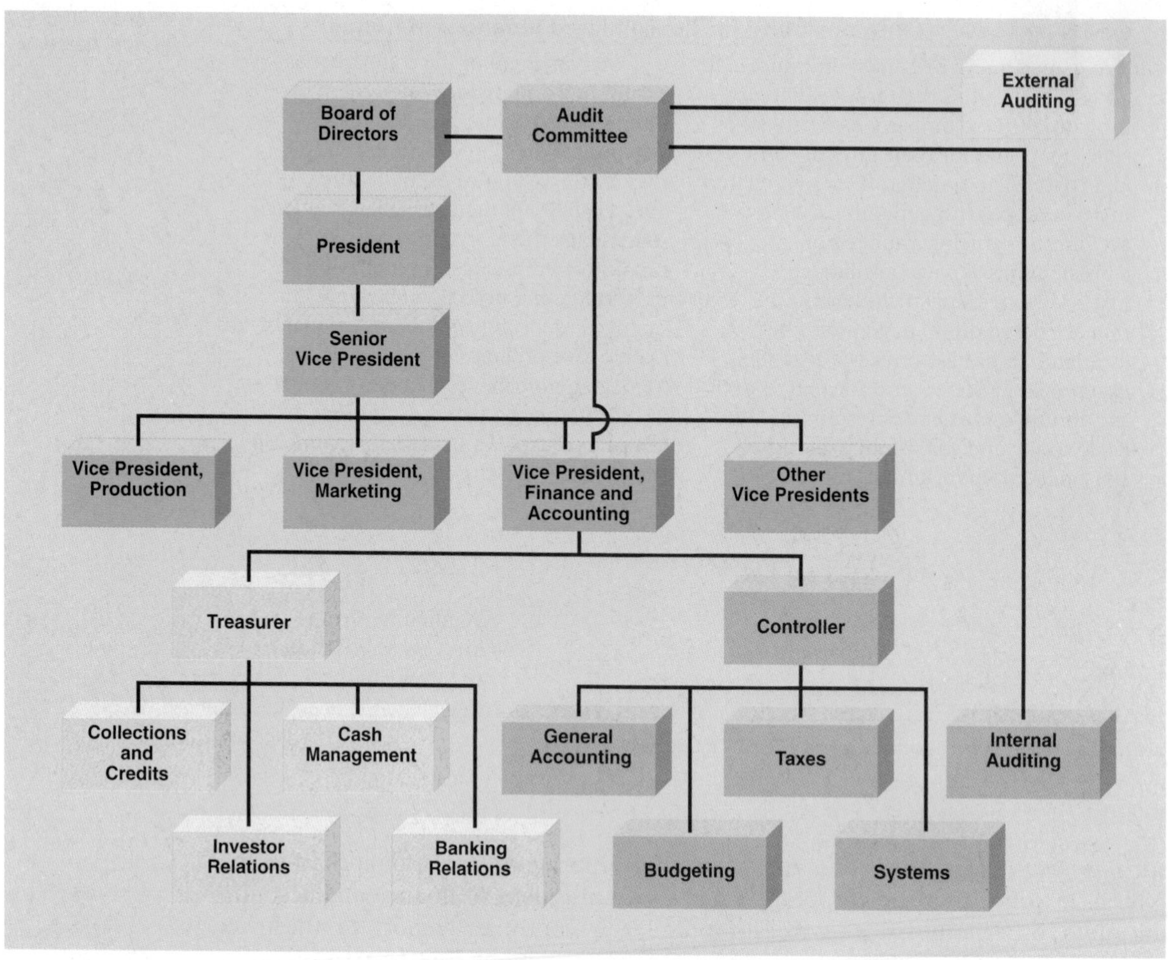

EXHIBIT 4-2
Organizational Chart of a Corporation

2. *Separation of the custody of assets from accounting.* Temptation and fraud are reduced if accountants are not allowed to handle cash and cashiers have no access to the accounting records. If one employee has both cash-handling and accounting duties, that person can steal cash and conceal the theft by making a bogus entry on the books. We see this component of internal control in Exhibit 4-2. The treasurer has custody of the cash while the controller accounts for the cash. Neither person has both responsibilities.

Steve Lane was able to apply one customer's cash deposit to another customer's account at Grant LeForge. Apparently, Lane, the cashier, controlled some data entered into the accounting system. This violation of the separation of duties cost Grant LeForge over $600,000.

Warehouse employees with no accounting duties should handle inventory. If they were allowed to account for the inventory, they could steal it and write it off as obsolete. A *write-off* is an entry that credits an asset account. This write-off could be recorded as a Loss on Inventory Obsolescence and a decrease in Inventory. A person with custody of assets should not have access to the computer programs. Similarly, the programmer should not have access to tempting assets such as cash.

3. *Separation of the authorization of transactions from the custody of related assets.* If possible, persons who authorize transactions should not handle the related asset. For example, the same person should not authorize the payment of a supplier's invoice and also sign the check to pay the bill. With both duties, the person can authorize payments to himself and then sign the checks. When these duties are separated, only legitimate bills are paid.

4. *Separation of duties within the accounting function.* Different people should perform the various phases of accounting to minimize both errors and opportunities for fraud. For example, different accountants should be responsible for recording cash receipts and cash disbursements. The employee who processes accounts payable and check requests should have nothing to do with the approval process.

✔ CHECK POINT 4-2

INTERNAL AND EXTERNAL AUDITS. To guarantee the accuracy of their accounting records, most companies undergo periodic audits. An **audit** is an examination of the company's financial statements and the accounting systems, internal controls, and records that produced them.

Because it is not economically feasible for auditors to examine all the transactions during a period, they must rely on the accounting system to produce accurate records. To gauge the reliability of the company's accounting system, auditors evaluate its system of internal controls. Auditors also spot the weaknesses in the system and recommend corrections. Auditors offer *objectivity* in their reports; managers immersed in operations have a tendency to overlook their own weaknesses.

Audits can be internal or external. Exhibit 4-2 shows *internal auditors* as employees of the business reporting directly to the audit committee. In some organizations, internal auditors report directly to a vice president. Throughout the year, they audit various segments of the organization to ensure that employees adhere to company policies. *External auditors* are entirely independent of the business. They are hired by a company such as **Lands' End, PepsiCo,** or **Xerox Corporation** to audit the entity as a whole. External auditors are concerned mainly with the financial statements and the factors affecting them. Both internal and external auditors are independent of the operations they examine.

An auditor may find that an employee, like Grant LeForge's Steve Lane, has both cash-handling and cash-accounting duties. In such cases, the auditor suggests improvements. Auditors' recommendations help the business run more efficiently.

DOCUMENTS AND RECORDS. Business *documents and records* vary considerably. They include source documents, such as invoices and purchase orders, and accounting journals and ledgers. Documents should be prenumbered. A gap in the numbered sequence calls attention to a missing document.

Prenumbering cash-sale receipts discourages theft by cashiers. The copies retained by the cashiers list the amount of the sale and can be checked against the actual amount of cash received. If the receipts are not prenumbered, the cashier can destroy the copy and pocket the cash received from the sale. However, if the receipts are prenumbered, the missing copy can easily be identified. In a computerized system, a permanent record of the sale is stored electronically when the transaction is completed.

In a bowling alley, a key document is the score sheet. The manager can check on cashiers by comparing the number of games scored with the amount of cash received. By multiplying the number of games by the price per game and comparing the result with each day's cash receipts, the manager can see whether the business is collecting all the revenue. If cash on hand is low, the cashier might be stealing.

ELECTRONIC AND COMPUTER CONTROLS. Businesses use electronic devices to control assets and operations. For example, retailers such as **Target Stores, Bradlees,** and **Dillard's** control inventories by attaching electronic sensors to their merchandise. The cashier removes the sensor when a sale is made. If a customer tries to leave the store with an item's sensor still attached, an alarm sounds. According to Checkpoint Systems, which manufactures electronic sensors, these devices reduce loss due to theft by as much as 50%.

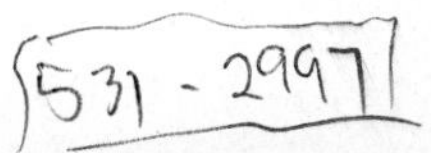

Accounting systems are relying less and less on documents and more and more on digital storage devices. Computers produce accurate records and enhance operational efficiency. But they do not automatically safeguard assets or encourage employees to behave in accordance with company policies. Computers have shifted the internal controls to the people who write the programs. All the controls that apply to accountants apply to computer programmers as well. They should not have access to the company's assets.

Within a single company, each department establishes controls over its assets and accounting records. Consider the retailer **Saks Fifth Avenue.** If the Saks system is well designed, each department maintains its own records. For example, the shoe department submits its sales totals for computer processing. The manager of the shoe department gets a printout showing a sales figure that should agree with the control total that she calculated *before* the documents went to the computer operators.

The accounts receivable department relies on computer operators to post correctly to thousands of customer accounts. Proper posting can be ensured by devising customer account numbers so that the last digit is a mathematical function of the previous digits (for example, 1359, where $1 + 3 + 5 = 9$). Any miskeying of a customer account number would trigger an error message to the keyboarder, and the computer would not accept the number.

OTHER CONTROLS. Businesses of all types keep cash and important business documents such as contracts and property titles in *fireproof vaults.* They use *burglar alarms* to protect buildings and other property.

Retailers receive most of their cash from customers on the spot. To safeguard cash, they use *point-of-sale terminals* that both serve as cash registers and record each transaction as it is entered into the machine. Several times each day, a supervisor removes the cash for deposit in the bank.

Employees who handle cash are in an especially tempting position. Many businesses purchase *fidelity bonds* on cashiers. The bond is an insurance policy that reimburses the company for losses due to employee theft. Before issuing a fidelity bond, the insurance company investigates the employee's past to ensure a record of ethical conduct. *Mandatory vacations* and *job rotation* require that employees be trained to do a variety of jobs. **General Electric, Eastman Kodak,** and other large companies move employees from job to job—often at six-month intervals. This practice enhances morale by giving employees a broad view of the business and helping them decide where they want to specialize. Knowing that someone else will be doing their job next month also keeps employees honest. If Grant LeForge had moved Steve Lane from job to job and required him to take a vacation, his embezzlement would probably have been detected much earlier. Or, he might not have been tempted to embezzle at all.

CHECK POINT 4-3

Ralph works the late movie at Galaxy Theater. Occasionally, he must both sell the tickets and take them as customers enter the theater. Standard procedure requires that Ralph tear the tickets, give one-half to the customer, and keep the other half. To control cash receipts, the theater manager compares each night's cash receipts with the number of ticket stubs on hand.

What is the internal control weakness in this situation? What might a dishonest employee do to steal cash? What additional steps should the manager take to strengthen the control over cash receipts?

Answer: The weakness is the lack of separation of duties. Ralph not only receives cash from customers but also controls the tickets. Good internal control would require that Ralph handle either cash or the tickets, but not both. If he were dishonest, he could fail to issue a ticket and then keep the customer's cash. To control such dishonest behavior, the manager could physically count the people watching a movie and compare that number with the number of ticket stubs collected. Otherwise, a dishonest employee could destroy some ticket stubs and keep the cash received from customers. To catch that dishonest behavior, the manager could account for all ticket stubs by serial number. Missing serial numbers would raise questions and lead to investigation.

The Limitations of Internal Control

Unfortunately, most internal control measures can be overcome. Systems designed to thwart an individual employee's fraud can be beaten by two or more employees working as a team—*colluding*—to defraud the firm. Consider our Galaxy Theater illustration in the Stop & Think feature. Ralph and a fellow employee could put together a scheme in which the ticket seller pockets the cash from ten customers and the ticket taker admits ten customers without tickets. To forestall this scheme, the manager could take additional control measures, such as matching the number of people in the theater against the number of ticket stubs retained. But that would take time away from other duties: The stricter the internal control system, the more expensive it becomes.

A system of internal control that is too complex can strangle the business with red tape. Efficiency and control are hurt rather than helped. Just how tight should an internal control be? Managers must make sensible judgments. Investments in internal control must be judged in light of the costs and benefits.

Using the Bank Account as a Control Device

Cash is the most liquid asset because it is the medium of exchange. Cash is easy to conceal, easy to move, and relatively easy to steal. As a result, most businesses use an elaborate system of internal controls to safeguard and manage their cash.

Keeping cash in a *bank account* is an important part of internal control because banks safeguard cash. Banks also provide depositors with detailed records of cash transactions. To take full advantage of these control features, the business should deposit all cash receipts in the bank account and make all cash payments through it (except petty cash disbursements, which we look at later in this chapter).

The documents used to control a bank account include the signature card, the deposit ticket, the check, the bank statement, and the bank reconciliation.

Signature Card. Banks require each person authorized to transact business through an account in that bank to sign a *signature card.* The bank compares the signatures on documents against signature cards to protect both the bank and the depositor against forgery.

Deposit Ticket. Banks supply standard forms such as *deposit tickets.* The customer fills in the dollar amount and the date of deposit. As proof of the transaction, the customer retains either (1) a duplicate copy of the deposit ticket or (2) a deposit receipt, depending on the bank's practice.

Check. To draw money from an account, the depositor writes a **check,** which is a document instructing the bank to pay the designated person or business a specified amount of money. There are three parties to a check: the *maker,* who signs the check; the *payee,* to whom the check is drawn; and the *bank* on which the check is

EXHIBIT 4-3
Check with Remittance Advice

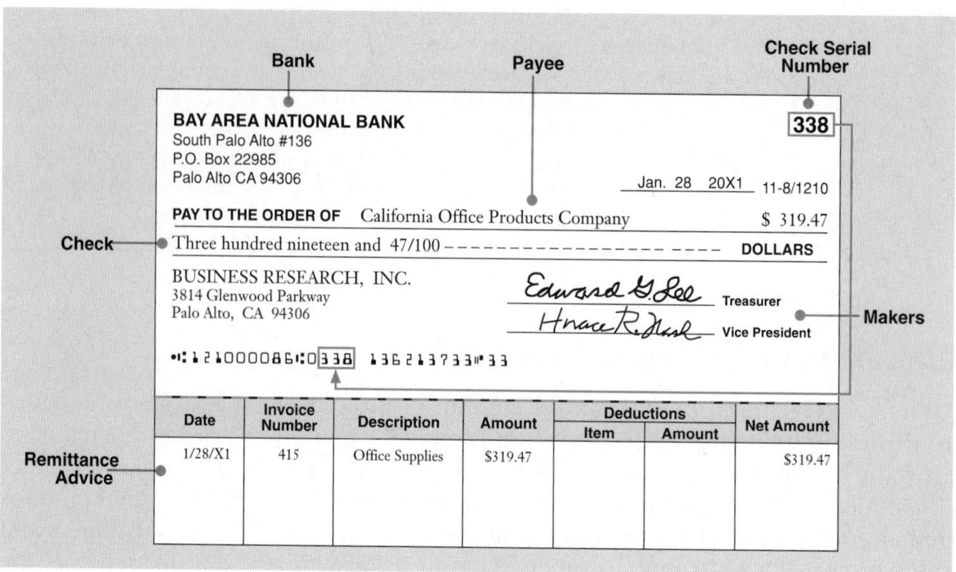

BAY AREA NATIONAL BANK
South Palo Alto #136
P.O. Box 22985
Palo Alto CA 94306

338

Jan. 28 20X1 11-8/1210

PAY TO THE ORDER OF California Office Products Company $ 319.47

Three hundred nineteen and 47/100 DOLLARS

BUSINESS RESEARCH, INC.
3814 Glenwood Parkway
Palo Alto, CA 94306

Treasurer
Vice President

Date	Invoice Number	Description	Amount	Deductions Item	Deductions Amount	Net Amount
1/28/X1	415	Office Supplies	$319.47			$319.47

drawn. Most checks are serially numbered and preprinted with the name and address of the maker and the bank.

Exhibit 4-3 shows a check drawn on the bank account of Business Research, Inc. The check has two parts, the check itself and the *remittance advice,* which is an optional attachment that tells the payee the reason for the payment. The maker (Business Research) retains a duplicate copy of the check for its recording in the check register (cash disbursements journal). Note that internal controls at Business Research require two signatures on checks.

BANK STATEMENT. Banks send monthly **bank statements** to their depositors. The statement shows the account's beginning and ending balance for the period and lists the month's transactions processed by the bank. Included with the statement are the maker's *canceled checks,* which the bank has paid on behalf of the depositor. The bank statement also lists any deposits and other changes in the account. Deposits appear in chronological order and checks in a logical order (usually by serial number), along with the date on which each check cleared the bank.

Exhibit 4-4 is the bank statement of Business Research, Inc., for the month ended January 31, 20X1. Many banks send some individual depositors their statements on the first of the month, some on the second, and so on. This spacing eliminates the clerical burden of supplying all the statements at one time. Most businesses—like Business Research—receive their bank statements at the end of each calendar month.

Electronic funds transfer (EFT) is a system that relies on electronic communications—not paper documents—to transfer cash. More and more businesses today rely on EFT for repetitive cash transactions. It is much cheaper for a company to pay employees by EFT (direct deposit) than by issuing hundreds of payroll checks. Also, many people make mortgage, rent, and insurance payments by prior arrangement with their banks and never write checks for those payments. The bank statement lists cash receipts by EFT among the deposits and cash payments by EFT among the checks and other bank charges.

The Bank Reconciliation

There are two records of a business's cash: (1) its Cash account in its own general ledger and (2) the bank statement, which records the actual amount of cash the

ACCOUNT STATEMENT

BAY AREA NATIONAL BANK

SOUTH PALO ALTO #136 P.O. BOX 22985 PALO ALTO, CA 94306

Business Research, Inc.
3814 Glenwood Parkway
Palo Alto, CA 94306

CHECKING ACCOUNT 136—213733

CHECKING ACCOUNT SUMMARY AS OF 01/31/X1

BEGINNING BALANCE	TOTAL DEPOSITS	TOTAL WITHDRAWALS	SERVICE CHARGES	ENDING BALANCE
6,556.12	4,352.64	4,963.00	14.25	5,931.51

CHECKING ACCOUNT TRANSACTIONS

DEPOSITS	DATE	AMOUNT
Deposit	01/04	1,000.00
Deposit	01/04	112.00
Deposit	01/08	194.60
EFT Collection of rent	01/17	904.03
Bank Collection	01/26	2,114.00
Interest	01/31	28.01

CHARGES	DATE	AMOUNT
Service Charge	01/31	14.25
Checks:		

CHECKS

Number	Date	Amount
332	01/12	3,000.00
656	01/06	100.00
333	01/12	150.00
334	01/10	100.00
335	01/06	100.00
336	01/31	1,100.00

BALANCES

Date	Balance	Date	Balance
12/31	6,556.12	01/17	5,264.75
01/04	7,616.12	01/20	4,903.75
01/06	7,416.12	01/26	7,017.75
01/08	7,610.72	01/31	5,931.51
01/12	4,360.72		

OTHER CHARGES	DATE	AMOUNT
NSF	01/04	52.00
EFT Insurance	01/20	361.00

MONTHLY SUMMARY

Withdrawals: 8 | Minimum Balance: 4,360.00 | Average Balance: 6,091.00

EXHIBIT 4-4
Bank Statement

business has in the bank. The balance in the firm's Cash account rarely equals the balance shown on the bank statement.

The books and the bank statement may show different amounts, but both may be correct. Except for errors by the bank or the business, any difference usually arises because of a time lag in recording certain transactions. When a firm writes a check, it immediately credits its Cash account. The bank, however, will not subtract the amount of the check from the business's balance until the bank receives the check and pays it. This step may take days, even weeks, if the payee waits to cash the check. Likewise, the business immediately debits Cash for all cash receipts, but it may take a day or so for the bank to add this amount to the firm's bank balance.

To ensure accuracy of the financial records, the firm's accountant must explain the reasons for the difference between the firm's records and the bank statement figures on a certain date. The result of this process is a document called the **bank reconciliation.** Properly done, the bank reconciliation ensures that all cash transactions have been accounted for and that the bank and book records of cash are correct. Knowledge of where cash comes from, how it is spent, and the balance of cash available is vital to success in business.

Here are some common items that cause differences between the bank balance and the book balance.

1. *Items recorded by the company but not yet recorded by the bank:*
   a. **Deposits in transit** (outstanding deposits). The company has recorded these deposits, but the bank has not.
   b. **Outstanding checks.** The company has issued these checks and recorded them on its books, but the bank has not yet paid them.
2. *Items recorded by the bank but not yet recorded by the company:*
   a. **Bank collections.** Banks collect money on behalf of depositors. Many businesses have their customers pay directly to the company bank account. This practice, called a *lock-box system,* places the business's cash in circulation faster than if the cash had to be collected and deposited by company personnel.
   b. *Electronic funds transfers.* The bank may receive or pay cash on behalf of the depositor. The bank statement will list the EFTs and may serve to notify the depositor to record these transactions.
   c. *Service charge.* This is the bank's fee for processing the depositor's transactions. The depositor learns the amount of the service charge from the bank statement.
   d. *Interest revenue on checking account.* Depositors earn interest if they keep a large enough balance of cash in their account. The bank notifies depositors of this interest on the bank statement.
   e. **NSF (nonsufficient funds) checks** received from customers. To understand how NSF checks *(hot checks)* are handled, consider the route a check takes. Exhibit 4-5 diagrams the check-clearing process.

EXHIBIT 4-5
The Paths That Two Checks Take

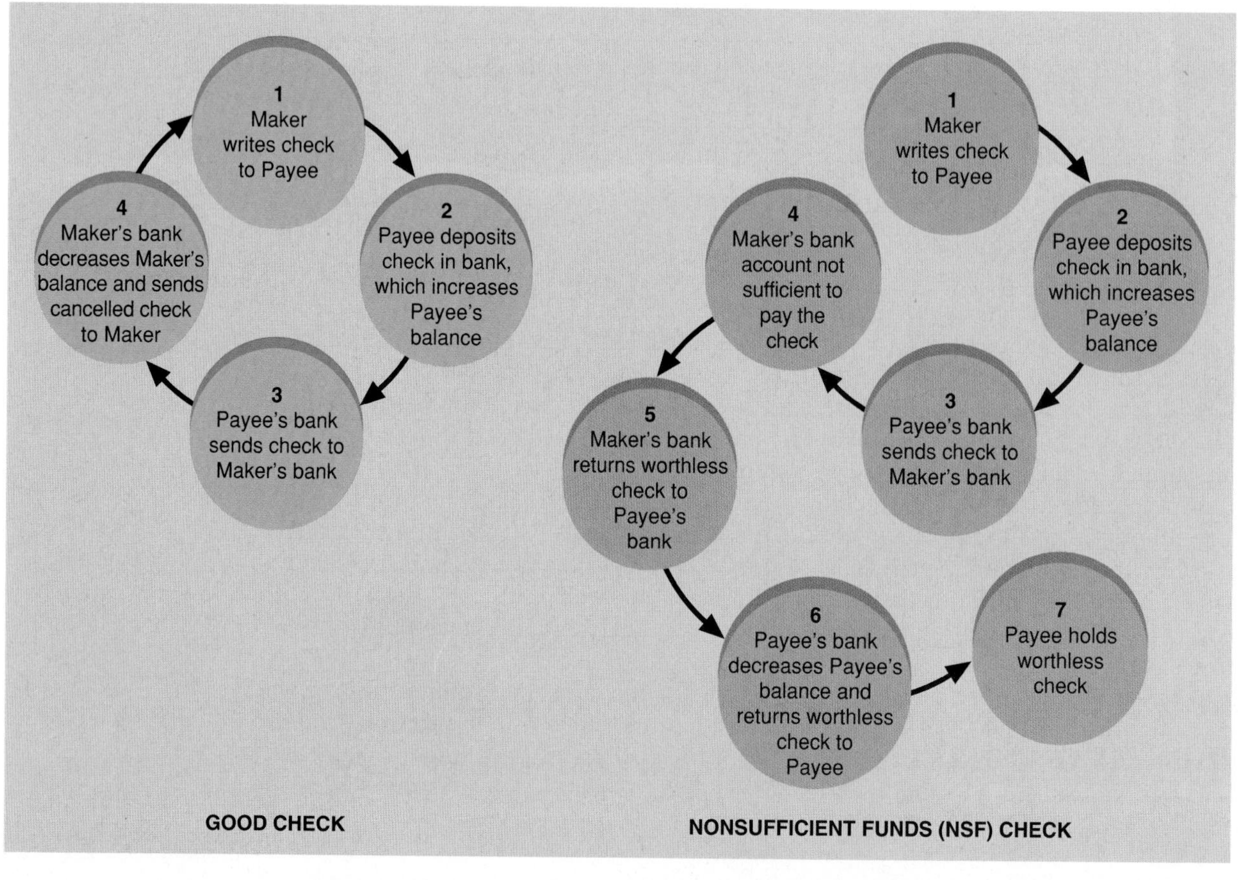

NSF checks are cash *receipts* that turn out to be worthless. If the maker's bank balance is insufficient to pay the check, the maker's bank refuses to pay the check and sends an NSF notice back to the payee's bank. The payee's bank then subtracts the amount from the payee's bank balance and notifies the payee of NSF action, as depicted in steps 5–7 of the exhibit. The payee may learn of NSF checks through the bank statement, which lists the NSF check as a charge (subtraction), as shown near the bottom of Exhibit 4-4 (p. 177).

f. *Checks collected, deposited, and returned to payee by the bank for reasons other than NSF.* Banks return checks to the payee if (1) the maker's account has closed, (2) the date is stale (some checks state "void after 30 days"), (3) the signature is not authorized, (4) the check has been altered, or (5) the check form is improper (for example, a counterfeit). Accounting for all returned checks is the same as for NSF checks.

g. *The cost of printed checks.* This charge against the company's bank account balance is handled as a service charge.

3. Errors by either the company or the bank. For example, a bank may improperly charge (decrease) the bank balance of Business Research, Inc., for a check drawn by another company, perhaps Business Research Associates. Or a company may miscompute its bank balance on its own books. Computational errors are becoming less frequent with the widespread use of computers. Nevertheless, all errors must be corrected, and the corrections will be a part of the bank reconciliation.

Objective 2
Use a bank reconciliation as a control device

BANK RECONCILIATION ILLUSTRATED. The bank statement in Exhibit 4-4 (p. 177) indicates that the January 31 bank balance of Business Research, Inc., is $5,931.51. However, as shown in Exhibit 4-6, the company's Cash account has a balance of $3,294.21. The following reconciling items explain why the two balances differ.

1. The January 30 deposit of $1,591.63 does not appear on the bank statement.
2. The bank erroneously charged to the Business Research, Inc., account a $100 check—number 656—written by Business Research Associates.

EXHIBIT 4-6
Cash Records of Business Research, Inc.

Ledger:

ACCOUNT Cash

Date	Item	Debit	Credit	Balance
20X1				
Jan. 1	Balance			6,556.12
2	Cash receipt	1,112.00		7,668.12
7	Cash receipt	194.60		7,862.72
31	Cash payments		6,160.14	1,702.58
31	Cash receipt	1,591.63		3,294.21

Cash Payments

Check No.	*Amount*	*Check No.*	*Amount*
332	$3,000.00	338	$ 319.47
333	510.00	339	83.00
334	100.00	340	203.14
335	100.00	341	458.53
336	1,100.00		
337	286.00	Total	$6,160.14

CHECK POINT 4-5

3. Five company checks issued late in January and recorded in the journal have not been paid by the bank:

Check No.	Date	Amount
337	Jan. 27	$286.00
338	28	319.47
339	28	83.00
340	29	203.14
341	30	458.53

4. The bank received $904.03 by EFT on behalf of Business Research, Inc. The bank statement serves as initial notification of this receipt of monthly rent revenue on unused office space.
5. The bank collected on behalf of the company a note receivable, $2,114 (including interest revenue of $214). Business Research has not recorded this cash receipt.
6. The bank statement shows interest revenue of $28.01, which the company has earned on its cash balance.
7. Check number 333 for $150 paid to Brown Company on account was recorded as a cash payment of $510, creating a $360 understatement of the Cash balance in the books.
8. The bank service charge for the month was $14.25.
9. The bank statement shows an NSF check for $52, which was received from customer L. Ross.
10. Business Research pays insurance expense monthly by EFT. The company has not yet recorded this $361 payment.

Exhibit 4-7 is the bank reconciliation based on the preceding data. Panel A lists the reconciling items, which are keyed by number to the reconciliation in Panel B. After the reconciliation, the adjusted bank balance equals the adjusted book balance. This equality is an accuracy check.

Each reconciling item is treated in the same way in every situation. Here is a summary of how to treat the various reconciling items:

Bank Balance—Always
- *Add* deposits in transit
- *Subtract* outstanding checks
- *Add* or *subtract* corrections of bank errors, as appropriate

Book Balance—Always
- *Add* bank collection items, interest revenues, and EFT receipts
- *Subtract* service charges, NSF checks, and EFT payments
- *Add* or *subtract* corrections of book errors, as appropriate

ACCOUNTING FOR TRANSACTIONS FROM THE RECONCILIATION. The bank reconciliation does not directly affect the journal or the ledger. The reconciliation is an accountant's tool, separate from the company's books.

The bank reconciliation acts as a control device by signaling the company to record the transactions listed as reconciling items in the Books section of the reconciliation. The company has not yet recorded these items. For example, the bank collected the note receivable on behalf of the company, but the company has not yet recorded this cash receipt. In fact, the company learned of the cash receipt only when it received the bank statement.

EXHIBIT 4-7
Bank Reconciliation

PANEL A—Reconciling Items

1. Deposit in transit, $1,591.63.
2. Bank error, add $100 to bank balance.
3. Outstanding checks: no. 337, $286; no. 338, $319.47; no. 339, $83; no. 340, $203.14; no. 341, $458.53.
4. EFT receipt of rent revenue, $904.03.
5. Bank collection, $2,114, including interest revenue of $214.
6. Interest earned on bank balance, $28.01.
7. Book error; add $360 to book balance.
8. Bank service charge, $14.25.
9. NSF check from L. Ross, $52.
10. EFT payment of insurance expense, $361.00

PANEL B—Bank Reconciliation

BUSINESS RESEARCH, INC.
Bank Reconciliation
January 31, 20X1

Bank			*Books*		
Balance, January 31		$5,931.51	Balance, January 31		$3,294.21
Add:			Add:		
1. Deposit of January 30 in transit		1,591.63	4. EFT receipt of rent revenue.............		904.03
2. Correction of bank error—Business Research Associates check erroneously charged against company account .		100.00	5. Bank collection of note receivable, including interest revenue of $214............		2,114.00
		7,623.14	6. Interest revenue earned on bank balance		28.01
			7. Correction of book error—overstated amount of check no. 333		360.00
					6,700.25
3. Less: Outstanding checks:			Less:		
No. 337	$286.00		8. Service charge.	$ 14.25	
No. 338	319.47		9. NSF check ...	52.00	
No. 339	83.00		10. EFT payment of insurance		
No. 340	203.14				
No. 341	458.53	(1,350.14)	expense	361.00	(427.25)
Adjusted bank balance		$6,273.00	Adjusted book balance		$6,273.00

Amounts agree.

CHECK POINT 4-6

On the basis of the reconciliation in Exhibit 4-7, Business Research, Inc., makes the following entries. They are dated January 31 to bring the Cash account to the correct balance on that date. Numbers in parentheses correspond to the reconciling items listed in Exhibit 4-7, Panel A.

Jan. 31 (4)	Cash	904.03	
	Rent Revenue		904.03
	Receipt of monthly rent.		

ASSETS	=	LIABILITIES	+	STOCKHOLDERS' EQUITY	+	REVENUES
904.03	=	0			+	904.03

Jan. 31 (5)	Cash	2,114.00	
	Notes Receivable		1,900.00
	Interest Revenue		214.00
	Note receivable collected by bank.		

ASSETS	=	LIABILITIES	+	STOCKHOLDERS' EQUITY	+	REVENUES
+2,114.00	=	0			+	214.00
−1,900.00						

Jan. 31 (6)	Cash	28.01	
	Interest Revenue		28.01
	Interest earned on bank balance.		

ASSETS	=	LIABILITIES	+	STOCKHOLDERS' EQUITY	+	REVENUES
28.01	=	0			+	28.01

Jan. 31 (7)	Cash	360.00	
	Accounts Payable—Brown Co.		360.00
	Correction of check no. 333.		

ASSETS	=	LIABILITIES	+	STOCKHOLDERS' EQUITY
360.00	=	360.00	+	0

Jan. 31 (8)	Miscellaneous Expense[1]	14.25	
	Cash		14.25
	Bank service charge.		

ASSETS	=	LIABILITIES	+	STOCKHOLDERS' EQUITY	−	EXPENSES
−14.25	=	0			−	14.25

Jan. 31 (9)	Accounts Receivable—L. Ross	52.00	
	Cash		52.00
	NSF check returned by bank.		

ASSETS	=	LIABILITIES	+	STOCKHOLDERS' EQUITY
+52.00	=	0	+	0
−52.00				

Jan. 31 (10)	Insurance Expense	361.00	
	Cash		361.00
	Payment of monthly insurance.		

ASSETS	=	LIABILITIES	+	STOCKHOLDERS' EQUITY	−	EXPENSES
−361.00	=	0			−	361.00

✔ CHECK POINT 4-7

These entries bring the business's books up to date.

The entry for the NSF check (entry 9) needs explanation. Upon learning that L. Ross's $52 check was not good, Business Research credits Cash to bring the Cash

[1]Note: Miscellaneous Expense is debited for the bank service charge because the service charge pertains to no particular expense category.

account up-to-date. Because Business Research still has a receivable from Ross, the company debits Accounts Receivable—L. Ross and pursues collection from him.

The bank statement balance is $4,500 and shows a service charge of $15, interest earned of $5, and an NSF check for $300. Deposits in transit total $1,200; outstanding checks are $575. The bookkeeper recorded as $152 a check of $125 in payment of an account payable.

1. What is the adjusted bank balance?
2. What was the book balance of cash before the reconciliation?
3. Prepare the journal entry(ies) highlighted by the bank reconciliation.

Answers:

1. $5,125 ($4,500 + $1,200 − $575).
2. $5,408 ($5,125 + $15 − $5 + $300 − $27). The adjusted book and bank balances are the same. The answer can be determined by working backward from the adjusted balance.
3.

Account	Debit	Credit
Miscellaneous Expense	15	
Cash		15
Cash	5	
Interest Revenue		5
Accounts Receivable	300	
Cash		300
Cash	27	
Accounts Payable		27

How Managers and Owners Use the Bank Reconciliation

As the following example illustrates, the bank reconciliation is a powerful control device in the hands of a business manager or owner.

Randy Vaughn is a CPA in Houston, Texas. He owns several apartment complexes that are managed by his aunt. His accounting practice keeps him busy, with little time to devote to his apartments. His aunt signs up tenants, collects the monthly rent checks, arranges custodial and maintenance work, hires and fires employees, writes the checks, and performs the bank reconciliation. In short, she does it all. This concentration of duties in one person is terrible from an internal control standpoint. Vaughn's aunt could be stealing from him, and as a CPA he is aware of this possibility.

Vaughn trusts his aunt because she is a member of the family. Nevertheless, he exercises some loose controls over her management of his apartments. Vaughn periodically drops by his properties to see whether the custodial/maintenance staff is keeping them in good condition. He asks tenants whether appliances are working and if their problems are being addressed promptly. These measures establish a degree of control over the buildings and grounds.

To control cash, Vaughn uses the bank statement and the bank reconciliation. He occasionally examines the bank reconciliation that his aunt has performed. Vaughn would know immediately if his aunt is writing checks to herself. By examining each check, Vaughn establishes control over cash disbursements.

Vaughn has a simple method for controlling cash receipts. He knows the occupancy level of his apartments. He also knows the monthly rent he charges. He multiplies the number of apartments—say 20—by the monthly rent (which averages $500 per unit) to arrive at expected monthly rent revenue of $10,000. By tracing the $10,000 revenue to the bank statement, Vaughn can tell if his rent money went into his bank account.

If his aunt is stealing cash and concealing it by manipulating the bank reconciliation, this too would come to light. To keep his aunt on her toes, Vaughn lets her know that he periodically audits her work.

CHECK POINT 4-8

CHECK POINT 4-9

Control activities such as these are critical in small businesses. Because there may be only a few employees, a separation of duties may not be feasible. But the manager or owner must oversee and control the operations of the business, or the assets will slip away, as they did for Grant LeForge & Company in our chapter-opening story.

MID-CHAPTER Mid-Chapter

SUMMARY PROBLEM FOR YOUR REVIEW

The Cash account of Bain Company at February 28, 20X3, is as follows:

CASH

Feb. 1	**Balance 3,995**	**Feb. 3**	**400**
6	**800**	**12**	**3,100**
15	**1,800**	**19**	**1,100**
23	**1,100**	**25**	**500**
28	**2,400**	**27**	**900**
Feb. 28	**Balance 4,095**		

Bain Company receives this bank statement on February 28, 20X3 (as always, negative amounts are in parentheses):

BANK STATEMENT FOR FEBRUARY 20X3

Beginning balance		$3,995
Deposits:		
Feb. 7	$ 800	
15	1,800	
24	1,100	3,700
Checks (total per day):		
Feb. 8	$ 400	
16	3,100	
23	1,100	(4,600)
Other items:		
Service charge		(10)
NFS check from M. E. Crown		(700)
Bank collection of note receivable for the company		1,000*
EFT—monthly rent expense		(330)
Interest on account balance		15
Ending balance		$3,070

* Includes interest of $119.

Additional data: Bain Company deposits all cash receipts in the bank and makes all cash payments by check.

Required

1. Prepare the bank reconciliation of Bain Company at February 28, 20X3.

2. Record the entries based on the bank reconciliation.

Answers

Requirement 1

BAIN COMPANY Bank Reconciliation February 28, 20X3		
Bank:		
Balance, February 28, 20X3		$3,070
Add: Deposit of February 28 in transit		2,400
		5,470
Less: Outstanding checks issued on Feb 25 ($500) and Feb. 27 ($900)		(1,400)
Adjusted bank balance, February 28, 20X3		$4,070
Books:		
Balance, February 28, 20X3		$4,095
Add: Bank collection of note receivable, including interest of $119		1,000
Interest earned on bank balance		15
		5,110
Less: Service charge	$ 10	
NSF check	700	
EFT—Rent expense	330	(1,040)
Adjusted book balance, February 28, 20X3		$4,070

Requirement 2

Date	Accounts	Debit	Credit
Feb. 28	Cash	1,000	
	Note Receivable ($1,000 − $119)		881
	Interest Revenue		119
	Note receivable collected by bank.		
28	Cash	15	
	Interest Revenue		15
	Interest earned on bank balance.		
28	Miscellaneous Expense	10	
	Cash		10
	Bank service charge.		
Feb. 28	Accounts Receivable—M. E. Crown	700	
	Cash		700
	NSF check returned by bank.		
28	Rent Expense	330	
	Cash		330
	Monthly rent expense.		

THE OPERATING CYCLE OF A BUSINESS

A company such as **Lands' End, Toys "Я" Us,** or **Macy's** buys inventory, sells the goods to customers, and uses the cash to purchase more inventory to repeat the cycle. Exhibit 4-8 diagrams the operating cycle for *cash sales* and for *sales on account.* For a cash sale, the cycle is from cash to inventory, which is purchased for resale, and back to cash. For a sale on account, the cycle is from cash to inventory to accounts receivable and back to cash. In all lines of business, managers strive to shorten the cycle in order to keep cash flowing as quickly as possible. The faster the sale of inventory and the collection of cash, the higher the company's profits.

EXHIBIT 4-8
Operating Cycle of a Business

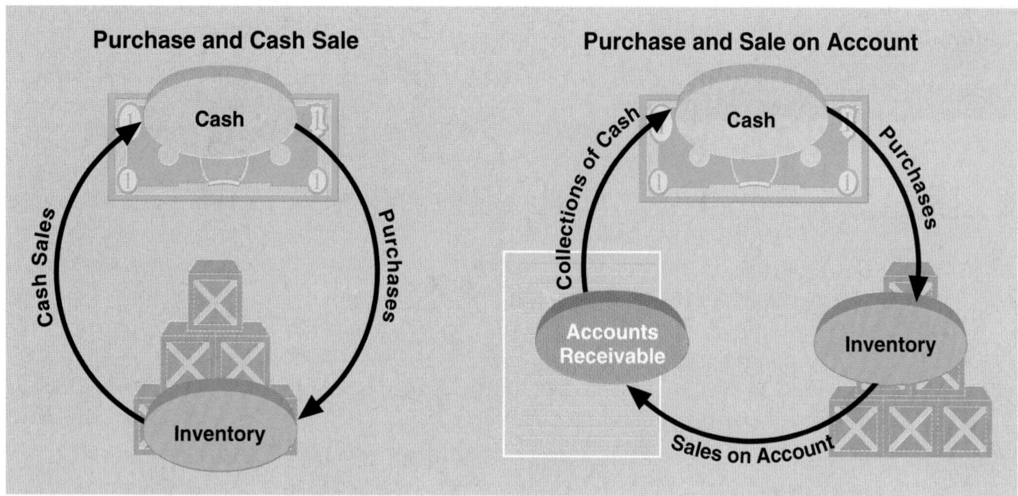

MANAGING CASH

Objective 3
Manage and account for cash

Managing cash requires a balancing act. **Lands' End, Toys "Я" Us,** and **Macy's** must have enough cash to pay their bills or they will go bankrupt. But cash is a relatively low-earning asset. Toys "Я" Us earns far more income by investing in inventory than by keeping most of its money in bank deposits. Therefore, companies strive to keep their cash circulating, as shown in Exhibit 4-8.

Companies use numerous techniques to manage their cash. In this section, we discuss some of these techniques.

Speeding the Collection of Cash from Sales

Manufacturers such as **Sony, Eastman Kodak,** and **Fisher-Price** (the toy maker) sell most of their goods on account to retail establishments. Consider a credit sale by Fisher-Price to Toys "Я" Us. Because Fisher-Price does not receive cash at the point of sale, it keeps a subsidiary accounts receivable ledger with a separate account for each customer. The sum of the amounts receivable from all Fisher-Price customers equals the balance in the company's Accounts Receivable account in the general ledger, as shown in Exhibit 4-9.

Like all companies, Fisher-Price uses the accounts receivable ledger to pursue collection from individual customers. For example, if **Kmart** fails to pay its account balance, Fisher-Price will follow up with additional billings.

EXHIBIT 4-9
Accounts Receivable Records for Fisher-Price

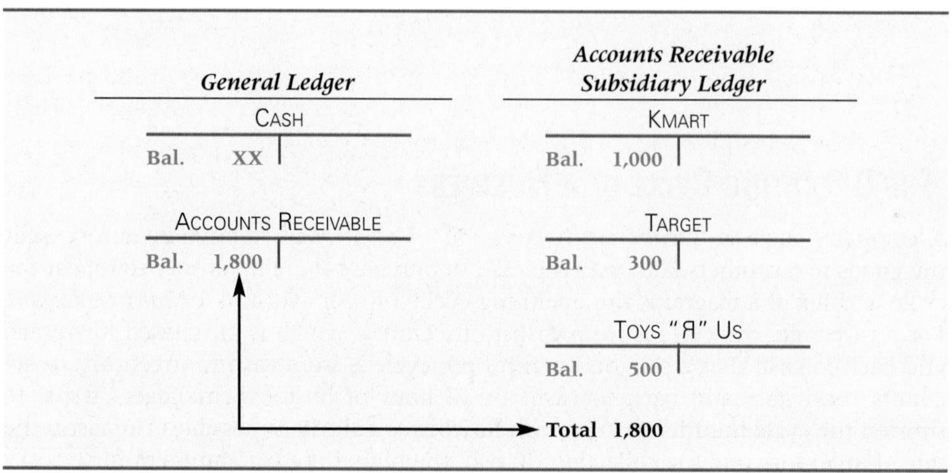

To speed the collection of cash, companies offer *sales discounts* that motivate customers to pay within a specified period, usually 10 days. Credit terms of "2/10 n/30" are common. This abbreviated discount formula means that the customer can take a 2% discount by paying within 10 days of the date of sale. Otherwise, the seller expects the buyer to pay the full amount within 30 days.

Suppose Fisher-Price makes a $50,000 sale to Toys "Я" Us on August 4. Assume credit terms of 2/10 n/30 and that Fisher-Price collects on August 14. Fisher-Price would record the sale and collection transactions with these journal entries:

Aug. 4	Accounts Receivable—Toys "Я" Us	50,000	
	Sales Revenue		50,000
	Sale on account.		

ASSETS	=	LIABILITIES	+	STOCKHOLDERS' EQUITY	+	REVENUES
50,000	=	0			+	50,000

Aug. 14	Cash ($50,000 × .98)	49,000	
	Sales Discounts ($50,000 × .02)	1,000	
	Accounts Receivable—Toys "Я" Us		50,000
	Collection on account.		

ASSETS	=	LIABILITIES	+	STOCKHOLDERS' EQUITY	−	CONTRA REVENUES
+49,000 −50,000	=	0			−	1,000

In this transaction, Fisher-Price received cash of $49,000 for a $50,000 sale. The customer took a $1,000 discount, which decreased Fisher-Price's net sales revenue to $49,000. The discount is recorded in a separate account, Sales Discounts, which is a contra account to Sales Revenue. As a contra account, Sales Discounts is subtracted from Sales Revenue to measure net sales revenue.

The 2% discount within 10 days works out to an annual interest rate of around 37%, which is high enough to motivate many customers to pay quickly. Why are companies such as Fisher-Price willing to offer this large discount? Because, as the saying goes, "A bird in the hand is worth two in the bush." By getting the cash immediately, the seller avoids a cash shortage and the resulting need to borrow, which is costly. The seller also avoids having to pursue collection later on. Chapter 5 discusses accounts receivable in more detail.

INTERNAL CONTROL OVER CASH RECEIPTS

Objective 4
Apply internal controls to cash receipts

Internal control over cash receipts ensures that all cash receipts are deposited in the bank and that the company's accounting record is correct. Many businesses receive cash over the counter and through the mail. Each source of cash receipts calls for its own security measures.

CASH RECEIPTS OVER THE COUNTER. The point-of-sale terminal (cash register) offers management control over the cash received in a store. Consider a **Macy's** store. First, the terminal should be positioned so that customers can see the amounts the cashier enters into the computer. Company policy should require issuance of a receipt to make sure that each sale is recorded by the cash register.

Second, the cash drawer opens only when the sales clerk enters an amount on the keypad, and the machine records each sale and cash transaction. At the end of the day, a manager proves the cash by comparing the total amount in the cash drawer against the machine's record of the days sales. This step helps prevent outright theft by the clerk. For security reasons, the clerk should not have access to the accounting record of the day's cash receipts.

At the end of the day, the cashier or some other employee with cash-handling duties deposits the cash in the bank. The accounting record of cash receipts goes electronically to the accounting department as the basis for an entry in the accounting records. Periodic onsite inspections by managers also discourage theft.

✔ CHECK POINT 4-10

CASH RECEIPTS BY MAIL. All incoming mail should be opened by a mailroom employee. This person should compare the amount of the check received with the attached remittance advice (the slip of paper that lists the amount of the check). If no advice was sent, the mailroom employee should prepare one and enter the amount of each receipt on a control tape. At the end of the day, this control tape is given to a responsible official, such as the controller, for verification. Cash receipts should be given to the cashier, who combines them with any cash received over the counter and prepares the bank deposit.

Requiring that a mailroom employee is the first person to handle postal cash receipts is another application of a good separation of duties. If the accountants opened postal cash receipts, they could easily hide thefts.

The mailroom employee forwards the remittance advices to the accounting department. These provide the data for entries in the cash books and postings to customers' accounts. As a final step, the controller compares the three records of the day's cash receipts:

(List continued on page 189)

EXHIBIT 4-10
Internal Controls over Cash Receipts

Element of Internal Control	*Internal Controls over Cash Receipts*
Competent, reliable, ethical personnel	Companies carefully screen employees for undesirable personality traits. They also spend large sums for training programs.
Assignment of responsibilities	Specific employees are designated as cashiers, supervisors of cashiers, or accountants for cash receipts.
Proper authorization	Only designated employees, such as department managers, can grant exceptions for customers, approve check receipts above a certain amount, and allow customers to purchase on credit.
Separation of duties	Cashiers and mailroom employees who handle cash do not have access to the accounting records. Accountants who record cash receipts have no opportunity to handle cash.
Internal and external audits	Internal auditors examine company transactions for agreement with management policies. External auditors examine the internal controls over cash receipts to determine whether the accounting system produces accurate amounts for revenues, receivables, and other items related to cash receipts.
Documents and records	Customers receive receipts as transaction records. Bank statements list cash receipts for reconciliation with company records (deposit tickets). Customers who pay by mail include a remittance advice showing the amount of cash they sent to the company.
Electronic and computer controls	Cash registers serve as transaction records. Each day's receipts are matched with customer remittance advices and with the day's deposit ticket from the bank.
Other controls	Cashiers are bonded. Cash is stored in vaults and banks. Employees are rotated among jobs and are required to take vacations.

- The control tape total from the mailroom;
- The bank deposit amount from the cashier;
- The debit to Cash from the accounting department.

Many companies use a *lock-box system* to separate cash duties and establish control over cash receipts. Customers send their checks directly to an address that is essentially a bank account. Internal control over the cash is enhanced because company personnel do not handle incoming cash. The lock-box system improves efficiency because the cash goes to work for the company immediately.

Exhibit 4-10 summarizes the controls over cash receipts.

INTERNAL CONTROL OVER CASH PAYMENTS

Objective 5
Apply internal controls to cash payments

Exercising control over cash payments is at least as important as controlling cash receipts.

Controls over Payment by Check

Payment by *check* is an important control over cash. First, the check provides a record of the payment. Second, to be valid, the check must be signed by an authorized official. Each payment by check, therefore, draws the attention of management. Before signing the check, the manager should study the evidence supporting the payment.

To illustrate the internal control over cash payments, suppose the business is buying inventory for sale to customers. Let's examine the process leading up to the cash payment.

CONTROLS OVER PURCHASING. The purchasing process—outlined in Exhibit 4-11—starts when the sales department identifies the need for merchandise and prepares a *purchase request* (or *requisition*). A separate purchasing department specializes in locating the best buys and mails a *purchase order* to the supplier, the outside company that sells the needed goods. When the supplier ships the goods to the requesting business, the supplier also mails the *invoice,* or bill, which is notification of the need to pay.

✔ CHECK POINT 4-11

As the goods arrive, the receiving department checks them for damage and lists the merchandise received on a document called the *receiving report.* The accounting department combines all the foregoing documents, checks them for accuracy and agreement, and forwards this *disbursement packet* to designated officers for approval and payment. The packet includes the invoice, receiving report, purchase order, and purchase request, as shown in Exhibit 4-12.

EXHIBIT 4-11
Purchasing Process

Business Document	*Prepared by*	*Sent to*
Purchase request (requisition)	Sales department	Purchasing department
Purchase order	Purchasing department	Outside company that sells the needed merchandise (supplier or vendor)
Invoice (bill)	Outside company that sells the needed merchandise (supplier or vendor)	Accounting department
Receiving report	Receiving department	Accounting department
Disbursement packet	Accounting department	Officer who signs the check

Exhibit 4-12
Disbursement Packet

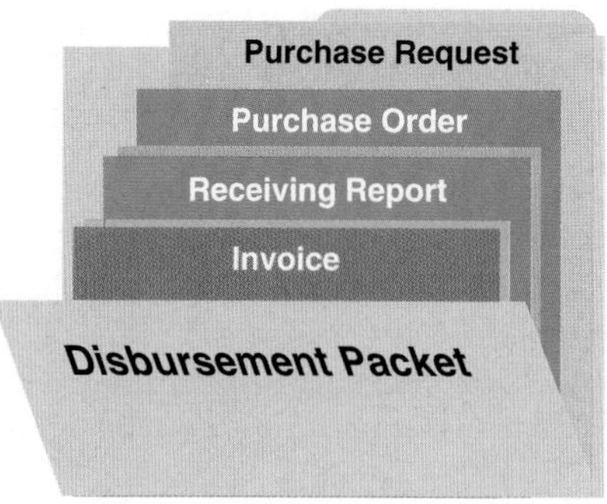

Controls over Approval of Payments. Before approving the disbursement, the controller and the treasurer should examine a sample of transactions to determine that the accounting department has applied the following controls:

1. The invoice is compared with a copy of the purchase order and purchase request to ensure that the business pays cash only for the goods that it ordered.
2. The invoice is compared with the receiving report to ensure that cash is paid only for the goods that were actually received.
3. The mathematical accuracy of the invoice is proved.

To avoid document alteration, some firms use indelible ink to stamp the amount on the check. After payment, the check signer can punch a hole through the disbursement packet. This hole denotes that the invoice has been paid and discourages dishonest employees from running the documents through the system for a duplicate payment.

Exhibit 4-13
Internal Controls over Cash Payments

Element of Internal Control	*Internal Controls over Cash Payments*
Competent, reliable, ethical personnel	Cash payments are entrusted to high-level employees, with larger amounts paid by the treasurer or assistant treasurer.
Assignment of responsibilities	Specific employees approve purchase documents for payment. Executives examine approvals, then sign checks.
Proper authorization	Large expenditures must be authorized by the top managers or the board of directors to ensure agreement with organizational goals.
Separation of duties	Computer operators and other employees who handle checks have no access to the accounting records. Accountants who record cash payments have no opportunity to handle cash.
Internal and external audits	Internal auditors examine company transactions for agreement with management policies. External auditors examine the internal controls over cash payments to determine whether the accounting system produces accurate amounts for expenses, assets, and other items related to cash payments.
Documents and records	Suppliers issue invoices that document the need to pay cash. Bank statements list cash payments (checks and EFT payments) for reconciliation with company records. Checks are prenumbered in sequence to account for payments.
Electronic, computer, and other controls	Blank checks are stored in a vault and controlled by a responsible official with no accounting duties. Machines stamp the amount on a check in indelible ink. Paid invoices are punched to avoid duplicate payment.

Information technology is streamlining cash payment procedures in many businesses. For example, the CPA firm of **Deloitte & Touche** is revamping the payment system of **Bank of America.** Exhibit 4-13 summarizes the internal controls over cash payments.

Controlling Petty Cash

It would be uneconomical and time-consuming for a business to write separate checks for an executive's taxi fare, floppy disks needed right away, or the delivery of a message across town. Therefore, companies keep a small amount of cash on hand to pay for such minor amounts. This fund is called **petty cash.**

The petty cash fund is opened with a particular amount of cash. A check for that amount is then issued to Petty Cash. Assume that on February 28, the business decides to establish a petty cash fund of $200. The custodian of the petty cash fund cashes the check and places the currency and coin in the fund, which may be a cash box, safe, or other device.

For each petty cash payment, the custodian prepares a *petty cash ticket* like the one illustrated in Exhibit 4-14. Control is established by recording on the petty cash ticket the date and purpose of the disbursement, the name of the person who received the cash, the account to be debited, and the amount of the payment.

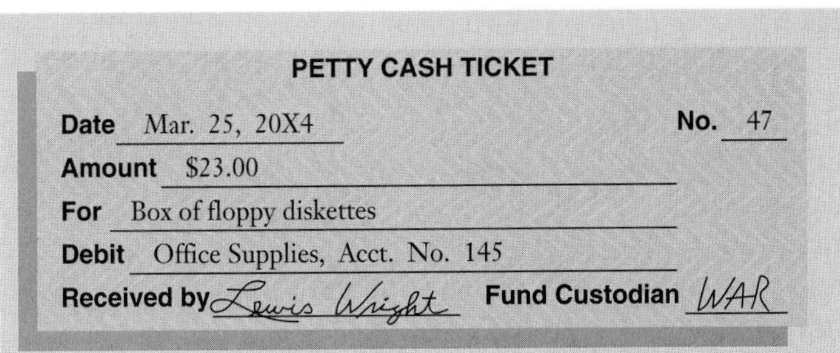
PETTY CASH TICKET

Date Mar. 25, 20X4 No. 47

Amount $23.00

For Box of floppy diskettes

Debit Office Supplies, Acct. No. 145

Received by Lewis Wright Fund Custodian WAR

EXHIBIT 4-14
Petty Cash Ticket

The sum of the cash in the petty cash fund plus the total of the ticket amounts should equal the opening balance at all times—in this case, $200. The Petty Cash account keeps its prescribed $200 balance at all times. Maintaining the Petty Cash account at this balance, supported by the fund (cash plus tickets), is characteristic of an **imprest system.** The control feature of an imprest system is that it clearly identifies the amount for which the custodian is responsible.

USING A BUDGET TO MANAGE CASH

Objective 6
Use a budget to manage cash

Managers control their organizations with the help of budgets. A **budget** is a quantitative expression of a plan that helps managers coordinate the entity's activities. Cash receives the most attention in the budgeting process because all transactions ultimately affect cash.

How, for example, does **MCI** decide when to invest millions in new telecommunications equipment? How will the company decide how much to spend? Will borrowing be needed, or can MCI finance the purchase with internally generated cash? Similarly, by what process do you decide how much to spend on your education? On an automobile? On a house? All these decisions depend to some degree on the information that a cash budget provides.

A cash budget helps a company manage its cash by planning the receipt and payment of cash during a future period. To prepare for the future, a company must determine how much cash it will need and then decide whether or not its operations will bring in the needed cash. To prepare for future cash needs, managers proceed in four steps:

1. Start with the entity's cash balance at the beginning of the period. The beginning balance tells how much cash is left over from the preceding period.
2. Add the budgeted cash receipts and subtract the budgeted cash payments. This is the most challenging part of the budgeting process because managers must predict the cash effects of all transactions of the budget period, including:
   a. Revenue and expense transactions (operating activities from the income statement)
   b. Asset acquisition and sale transactions (investing activities from the statement of cash flows)
   c. Liability and stockholders' equity transactions (financing activities from the statement of cash flows)

   Because foresight is imperfect, the actual figure will not always turn out as expected. However, it is important to develop *realistic* estimates of the cash receipts and payments during the budget period.
3. The beginning balance plus the expected receipts minus the expected payments equals the expected cash balance at the end of the period.
4. Compare the expected cash balance to the desired, or budgeted, cash balance at the end of the period. Managers know the minimum amount of cash they need (the budgeted balance) to keep the entity running. If there is excess cash, they can invest. If the expected cash balance falls below the budgeted balance, the company will need to obtain additional financing to reach the desired cash balance.

The budget period can span any length of time desired by managers. Large corporations use a daily cash budget because the amounts of money involved are so vast that a small mistake can cost millions of dollars in interest expense or lost interest revenue. Many organizations budget their cash at weekly or monthly intervals. The annual budget is simply the combination of all the daily, weekly, or monthly budgets for the year.

Exhibit 4-15 shows an example of a cash budget for **The Gap, Inc.,** for the year ended January 31, 20X2. Study it carefully because at some point in your career or personal affairs, you will use a cash budget.

Exhibit 4-15
Cash Budget

THE GAP, INC.
Cash Budget (Hypothetical)
For the Year Ended January 31, 20X2

		(In Millions)	
(1)	Cash balance, February 1, 20X1		$ 202.6
	Estimated cash receipts:		
(2)	Collections from customers		2,858.3
(3)	Interest and dividends on investments		6.2
(4)	Sale of store fixtures		4.9
			3,072.0
	Estimated cash payments:		
(5)	Purchases of inventory	$1,906.2	
(6)	Operating expenses	561.0	
(7)	Expansion of existing stores	206.4	
(8)	Opening of new stores	344.6	
(9)	Payment of long-term debt	148.7	
(10)	Payment of dividends	219.0	3,385.9
(11)	Cash available (needed) before new financing		(313.9)
(12)	Budgeted cash balance, January 31, 20X2		(200.0)
(13)	Cash available for additional investments, or (New financing needed)		$ (513.9)

Like the statement of cash flows, the cash budget has sections for cash receipts and cash payments. The budget, however, is prepared *before* the period's transactions, while the statement of cash flows reports on the effects of transactions *after* they have occurred. Also, the cash budget can take any form that helps managers make decisions. Because the cash budget is an internal document, used only by the managers of the business, it is not bound by generally accepted accounting principles.

The Gap's hypothetical cash budget in Exhibit 4-15 begins with $202.6 million of cash (line 1)—$2.6 million above the company's desired minimum balance of $200 million (line 12). The effects of the budgeted cash receipts and payments are expected to leave the company with a need for additional financing during the year. Observe that the budget for expanding existing stores will require $206.4 million (line 7), and the opening of new stores is expected to cost the company $344.6 million (line 8). Without these investing transactions, The Gap would not need additional cash. But long-term investments such as new stores and store expansions are needed to remain competitive.

Assume that managers of The Gap wish to maintain a cash balance of at least $200 million (line 12). Because the year's activity is expected to leave the company with a negative cash balance of $313.9 million (line 11), The Gap's managers need to arrange $513.9 million of financing (line 13). Line 11 of the cash budget identifies the amount of cash available or needed. Line 12 lists the minimum cash balance to maintain at all times. Add lines 11 and 12 to arrive at the amount of new financing needed.

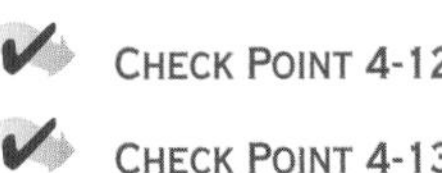

The cash budget provides information that should help managers arrange the financing in an orderly manner. With the cash, The Gap can expand its stores and search out exciting new products that keep customers coming back. Without the cash needed to make these kinds of investments, The Gap cannot compete with **The Limited, Macy's,** and other stores.

REPORTING CASH ON THE BALANCE SHEET

Cash is the first current asset listed on the balance sheet of most companies. Even small businesses have several bank accounts, but companies usually combine all cash amounts into a single total called "Cash and Cash Equivalents" on the balance sheet. Cash equivalents include liquid assets such as time deposits and certificates of deposit, which are interest-bearing accounts that can be withdrawn with no penalty after a short period of time. Although they are slightly less liquid than cash, they are sufficiently similar to be reported along with cash. For example, the balance sheet of **Intel Corporation,** maker of the Pentium® family of processors, recently reported the following:

INTEL CORP.
Consolidated Balance Sheet (Adapted)
December 31, 19X5 and December 31, 19X4

(In Millions)	*19X5*	*19X4*
Assets		
Current assets:		
Cash and cash equivalents	**$1,463**	**$1,180**
Short-term investments	995	1,230
Accounts receivable	3,116	1,978
Inventories	2,004	1,169
Other current assets	519	610
Total current assets	$8,097	$6,167

Intel's notes to the financial statements explain how the company accounts for cash equivalents and investments:

Notes to Consolidated Financial Statements

Investments. Highly liquid investments with original maturities of three months or less are classified as cash and cash equivalents. Investments with maturities greater than three months and less than one year are classified as short-term investments.

Ethics and Accounting

An article in the *Wall Street Journal* quoted a young entrepreneur in Russia as saying that he was getting ahead in business by breaking laws. He stated, "Older people have an ethics problem. By that I mean they *have* ethics." Conversely, Roger Smith, former chairman of **General Motors,** said, "Ethical practice is, quite simply, good business" because cheating never pays in the long run. Which perspective is valid? The latter, because first and foremost, practicing good ethics is the right thing to do. And second, unethical behavior always comes back to haunt you.

Corporate and Professional Codes of Ethics

Most large companies have a code of ethics designed to encourage ethical and responsible behavior by their employees. However, a set of general guidelines may not be specific enough to identify misbehavior, and a list of dos and don'ts can lead to the false view that anything is okay if it's not specifically forbidden. There is no easy answer. But most businesses are intolerant of unethical conduct by employees. As one executive has put it, "I cannot describe all unethical behavior, but I know it when I see it." Codes of conduct are insufficient by themselves. Senior management must set a high ethical tone at the top. This tone must be steadily reinforced by management words and actions.

Accountants have additional incentives to behave ethically. As professionals, they are expected to maintain higher standards than society in general. Why? Their ability to do business depends entirely on their reputations. Most independent accountants are members of the American Institute of Certified Public Accountants and must abide by the *AICPA Code of Professional Conduct.* Accountants who are members of the Institute of Management Accountants are bound by *the Standards of Ethical Conduct for Management Accountants.* These documents set standards of conduct for members. Unacceptable actions can result in expulsion from the organization—a penalty that makes it difficult for the person to remain in the accounting profession.

Refer to Chapter 1, page 6, for further discussion of these topics.

Ethical Issues in Accounting

Objective 7
Weigh ethical judgments in business

In many situations, the ethical choice is clear-cut. For example, stealing cash is illegal and unethical. In our chapter-opening story, the cashier's actions landed him in jail. In other cases, the choices are more difficult. In every instance, however, ethical judgments boil down to a personal decision: How should I behave in a given situation? Let's consider three ethical issues in accounting. The first two are easy to resolve. The third is more difficult.

SITUATION 1. Sonja Kleberg is preparing the income tax return of a client who has had a particularly good year—higher income than expected. On January 2, the client pays for newspaper advertising and asks Sonja to backdate the expense to the preceding year. The tax deduction would thus help the client more in the year just ended than in the current year. Backdating would increase expenses and decrease taxable income of the earlier year, and save the client a few dollars in tax payments. There is a difference of only two days between January 2 and December 31, and this client is important to Kleberg. What should she do? She should refuse the request because the transaction took place in January of the new year. What internal control device could prove that Kleberg behaved unethically if she backdated the transaction in the accounting records? An IRS audit and documents and records: The date of the cash payment could prove that the expense occurred in January rather than in December.

SITUATION 2. Jack Mellichamp's software company owes $40,000 to Bank of America. The loan agreement requires Mellichamp's company to maintain a current ratio (current assets divided by current liabilities) of 1.50 or higher. ➛ It is late in the year, and the bank will review Mellichamp's situation early next year. At present, the company's current ratio is 1.40. At this level, Mellichamp is in violation of his loan agreement. He can increase the current ratio to 1.53 by paying off some current liabilities right before year end. Is it ethical to do so? Yes, because the action is a real business transaction. But paying off the liabilities is only a delaying tactic. It will hold off the creditors for now, but time will tell whether the business can improve its underlying operations.

← For a review of the current ratio, see Chapter 3, page 138

SITUATION 3. Emilia Gomez, an accountant for the Democratic Party, discovers that her supervisor, Myles Packer, made several errors last year. Campaign contributions received from foreign citizens, which are illegal, were recorded as normal. It is not clear whether the errors were deliberate or accidental. Gomez is deciding what to do. She knows that Packer evaluates her job performance, and lately her work has been marginal. What should Gomez do? She is uncertain. To make her decision, Gomez could follow the framework outlined in the Decision Guidelines feature on page 196.

✓ CHECK POINT 4-14

Ethics and External Controls

There is another dimension to most ethical issues: *external controls,* which refer to the discipline on business conduct placed by outsiders who interact with the company. In situation 1, for example, Sonja Kleberg could give in to the client's request to backdate the advertising expense. But this action would be both dishonest and illegal. External controls arise from the business's interaction with the taxing authorities. An IRS audit of Kleberg's client could uncover her action.

In situation 2, the external controls arise from Jack Mellichamp's relationship with the bank that loaned money to his software company. As long as the loan agreement is in effect, the company must maintain a current ratio of 1.50 or higher. Paying off current liabilities to improve the current ratio would be a short-term solution to Mellichamp's problem. Over the long run, his business must generate more current assets through operations. His business will almost certainly need to borrow in the future and will probably face similar loan restrictions. Managers are wise to focus on long-term solutions to their problems if they hope to succeed in business.

The primary external control in situation 3 results from the laws of the United States and their enforcement through the U.S. legal system governing campaign financing. Campaign contributions are public information, and sooner or later the public will learn that the Democratic Party received illegal campaign contributions.

(continued on page 197)

Decision Guidelines

Ethical Judgments

Weighing tough ethical judgments requires a decision framework. Consider these six steps as general guidelines. Then apply them to Emilia Gomez's situation.

Question	Decision Guidelines
1. What are the facts?	1. *Determine the facts.*
2. What is the ethical issue, if any?	2. *Identify the ethical issues.* The root word of ethical is *ethics,* which Webster's dictionary defines as "the discipline dealing with what is good and bad and with moral duty and obligation." Gomez's ethical dilemma is to decide what she should do with the information she has uncovered.
3. What are the options?	3. *Specify the alternatives.* For Emilia Gomez, three alternatives are (a) report the errors to Packer, (b) report the errors to Packer's boss, and (c) do nothing.
4. Who is involved in the situation?	4. *Identify the people involved.* Individuals who could be affected include Gomez, Packer, the Democratic Party, and Gomez's co-workers who observe her behavior.
5. What are the possible consequences?	5. *Assess the possible outcomes.* (a) If Gomez reports the errors to Packer, he might penalize her, or he might reward her for careful work. Reporting the errors would preserve her integrity and probably would lead to returning the money to the donors. But the Democratic Party could suffer embarrassment if this situation were made public. (b) If Gomez reports to Packer's boss—going over Packer's head—her integrity would be preserved. Her relationship with Packer would surely be strained, and it might be difficult for them to work together in the future. Gomez might be rewarded for careful work. But if Packer's boss has colluded with Packer in recording the campaign contribution, Gomez could be penalized. If the error is corrected and outsiders notified, the Democratic Party would be embarrassed. Others observing this situation would be affected by the outcome. (c) If Gomez does nothing, she would avoid a confrontation with Packer or his boss. They might or might not discover the error. If they discover it, they might or might not correct it. All might criticize Gomez for not bringing the error to their attention. Fellow accountants might or might not learn of the situation.
6. What shall I do?	6. *Make the decision.* The best choice is difficult. Gomez must balance the likely effects on the various people against the dictates of her own conscience. Even though this framework does not provide an easy decision, it identifies the relevant factors. Gomez should report the errors. Ordinarily, Packer should be the first person contacted. If Packer fails to act in an honest way, then Gomez should inform Packer's boss. Senior management should always protect the messenger of accurate news, whether good or bad.

It would be in the party's best interest to admit its mistake and correct the errors as quickly as possible—by returning the illegal contributions to the donors. The situation will probably lead to tighter controls that will keep the organization from repeating the mistake. This is why organizations have codes of conduct and why, as Roger Smith put it, "Ethical practice is . . . good business."

STOP & THINK

Can you identify the external control in the chapter-opening story? How did it impose discipline on the cashier?

Answer: The external control was the monthly statement that Grant LeForge sends each client. When customers saw their account balances underreported on the monthly statements, they called in to ask why. Steve Lane must have spent half his time explaining the out-of-balance conditions of clients' accounts. Sooner or later he was bound to get caught. That's how external controls work.

End-of-Chapter

SUMMARY PROBLEM FOR YOUR REVIEW

Assume the following situation for PepsiCo, Inc.: PepsiCo ended 20X3 with total assets of $24 billion ($24,000 million), which included cash of $230 million. At December 31, 20X3, PepsiCo owed $17 billion, of which it expected to pay $6,600 million during 20X4. At the end of 20X3, Bob Detmer, the chief financial officer of PepsiCo, is preparing the budget for the next year.

During 20X4, Detmer expects PepsiCo to collect $26.4 billion from customers and an additional $90 million in interest earned from investments. PepsiCo expects to pay $12.5 billion for its inventories and $5.4 billion for operating expenses. To remain competitive, PepsiCo plans to spend $2.2 billion to upgrade production facilities and an additional $320 million to acquire other companies. PepsiCo also plans to sell older assets for approximately $300 million and to collect $220 million of this amount in cash. Because PepsiCo certainly expects to earn a profit during 20X4 (approximately $1.8 billion), the company is budgeting dividend payments of $550 million during the year. Finally, the company is scheduled to pay off $1.2 billion of long-term debt in addition to the current liabilities left over from 20X3.

Because of the increased level of activity planned for 20X4, Detmer budgets the need for a minimum cash balance of $330 million.

Required

1. How much must PepsiCo borrow during 20X4 to keep its cash balance from falling below $330 million? Prepare the 20X4 cash budget to answer this important question.
2. Consider the company's need to borrow $2,160 million. PepsiCo can avoid the need to borrow money in 20X4 by delaying one particular cash payment until 20X5 or later. Identify the item, and state why it would nevertheless be unwise to delay its payment.
3. To relate the cash budget to the statement of cash flows, suppose PepsiCo's transactions during 20X4 occurred as planned. Prepare PepsiCo's statement of cash flows for 19X4.

Answers

Requirement 1

PEPSICO, INC.
Cash Budget
For the Year Ended December 31, 20X4

		(In millions)
Cash balance, December 31, 20X3		$ 230
Estimated cash receipts:		
Collections from customers		26,400
Receipt of interest		90
Sale of assets		220
		26,940
Estimated cash disbursements:		
Purchases of inventory	$12,500	
Payment of operating expenses	5,400	
Upgrading of production facilities	2,200	
Acquisition of other companies	320	
Payment of dividends	550	
Payment of long-term debt and other liabilities ($1,200 + $6,600)	7,800	(28,770)
Cash available (needed) before new financing		(1,830)
Budgeted cash balance, December 31, 20X4		(330)
Cash available for additional investments, or (New financing needed)		$(2,160)

Requirement 2

PepsiCo can eliminate the need for borrowing $2,160 million by delaying the $2,200 million payment to *upgrade the company's production facilities.* The delay would be unwise because PepsiCo needs the upgrading to remain competitive.

Requirement 3

PEPSICO, INC.
Statement of Cash Flows
For the Year Ended December 31, 20X4

		(In millions)
Cash Flows from Operating Activities:		
Receipts:		
Collections from customers		$26,400
Receipt of interest		90
Payments:		26,490
Purchases of inventory	$(12,500)	
Payment of operating expenses	(5,400)	(17,900)
Net cash provided by operating activities		8,590
Cash Flows from Investing Activities:		
Upgrading of production facilities	$ (2,200)	
Acquisition of other companies	(320)	
Sales of assets	220	
Net cash used for investing activities		(2,300)
Cash Flows from Financing Activities:		
Borrowing	$ 2,160	
Payment of long-term debt and other liabilities	(7,800)	
Payment of dividends	(550)	
Net cash used for financing activities		(6,190)
Increase in cash		$ 100
Cash balance, beginning of year		230
Cash balance, end of year		$ 330

Summary of Learning Objectives

1. ***Describe an effective system of internal control.*** An effective internal control system includes these features: *competent, reliable, and ethical personnel; clear-cut assignment of responsibilities; proper authorization; separation of duties; internal and external audits; documents and records;* and *electronic and computer controls.* Many companies also make use of fireproof vaults, point-of-sale terminals, fidelity bonds, mandatory vacations, and job rotation. Effective computerized internal control systems must meet the same basic standards that good manual systems do.
2. ***Use a bank reconciliation as a control device.*** The *bank account* helps control and safeguard cash. Businesses use the *bank statement* and the *bank reconciliation* to account for cash and banking transactions and to bring the books up-to-date.
3. ***Manage and account for cash.*** Managers strive to keep cash flowing through their organization. To speed the collection of cash from sales, they offer sales discounts to people who pay within a specified period of time.
4. ***Apply internal controls to cash receipts.*** To control cash receipts over the counter, companies use point-of-sale terminals that customers can see and require that cashiers provide customers with receipts. As an additional control, the machine records each sale and cash transaction.

   To control cash receipts by mail, a mailroom employee should open the mail, compare the enclosed amount with the remittance advice, and prepare a control tape. This is an essential separation of duties—the accounting department should not open the mail. At the end of the day, the controller compares the three records of the day's cash receipts: the control tape total from the mailroom, the bank deposit amount from the cashier, and the debit to Cash from the accounting department.
5. ***Apply internal controls to cash payments.*** To control payments by check, checks should be issued and signed only when a *disbursement packet* including the purchase request, purchase order, invoice (bill), and receiving report (with all appropriate signatures) has been prepared. To control petty cash disbursements, the custodian of the fund should require a completed petty cash ticket for all payments.
6. ***Use a budget to manage cash.*** A budget is a quantitative expression of a plan that helps managers coordinate the entity's activities. To prepare for the future, a company must determine how much cash it will need and then decide whether its operations will bring in the needed cash. If not, then the company knows to arrange financing early. If operations will bring in an excess of cash, the company can be on the lookout for investment activities.
7. ***Weigh ethical judgments in business.*** To make ethical decisions, people should proceed in six steps: (1) Determine the facts. (2) Identify the ethical issues. (3) Specify the alternatives. (4) Identify the people involved. (5) Assess the possible outcomes. (6) Make the decision. Ethical business practice is simply good business.

Accounting Vocabulary

audit (p. 173).
bank collection (p. 178).
bank reconciliation (p. 177).
bank statement (p. 176).
budget (p. 191).
check (p. 175).
controller (p. 171).
deposit in transit (p. 178).
electronic funds transfer (EFT) (p. 176).
imprest system (p. 191).
internal control (p. 170).
nonsufficient funds (NSF) check (p. 178).
outstanding check (p. 178).
petty cash (p. 191).

Questions

1. What is the most basic goal of internal control? Why is it so important?
2. Are internal controls optional? If not, which federal law affects internal control procedures? What requirement does it place on management?
3. Identify the features of an effective system of internal control.
4. Separation of duties may be divided into four parts. What are they?
5. How can internal control systems be circumvented?
6. Are internal control systems designed to be foolproof and perfect? What is a fundamental constraint in planning and maintaining these systems?
7. Briefly state how each of the following serves as an internal control measure over cash: bank account, signature card, deposit ticket, and bank statement.
8. Each of the items in the following list must be accounted for in the bank reconciliation. Next to each item, enter the appropriate letter from these possible treatments: (a) bank side of reconciliation—add the item; (b) bank side of reconciliation—subtract the item;

(c) book side of reconciliation—add the item; (d) book side of reconciliation—subtract the item.

_______ Outstanding check
_______ NSF check
_______ Bank service charge
_______ Cost of printed checks
_______ Bank error that decreased bank balance
_______ Deposit in transit
_______ Bank collection
_______ Customer check returned because of unauthorized signature
_______ Book error that increased balance of Cash account

9. What purpose does a bank reconciliation serve?

10. How do accounts receivable records help a company manage its cash? How does offering discounts speed the collection of cash?

11. What role does a cash register play in an internal control system?

12. Describe the internal control procedures for cash received by mail.

13. What documents make up the disbursement packet? Describe three procedures that use the disbursement packet to ensure that each payment is appropriate.

14. Describe ways in which a budget helps a company manage its cash.

15. Suppose a company has six bank accounts, two petty cash funds, and three certificates of deposit that can be withdrawn on demand. How many cash amounts would this company likely report on its balance sheet?

16. "Our managers know that they are expected to meet budgeted profit figures. We don't want excuses. We want results." Discuss the ethical implications of this policy.

Check Points

Description of internal control (Obj. 1)

CP4-1 Internal controls are designed to safeguard assets, encourage employees to follow company policies, promote operational efficiency, and ensure accurate records. Which of these four goals of internal controls is most important? Stated differently, which goal must internal controls accomplish for the business to survive? Give your reason.

Characteristics of an effective system of internal control (Obj. 2)

CP4-2 Explain in your own words why separation of duties is often described as the cornerstone of internal controls for safeguarding assets. Describe what can happen if the same person has custody of an asset and also accounts for it.

Characteristics of an effective system of internal control (Obj. 2)

CP4-3 Review the characteristics of an effective system of internal controls that begin on page 170. Then identify two things that Grant LeForge & Company in the chapter-opening story could have done to make it harder for Steve Lane, the cashier, to steal from the company and hide the theft. Explain how each new measure taken by Grant LeForge would have accomplished its goal.

Bank reconciliation (Obj. 3)

CP4-4 Draw a simple diagram with three boxes and two arrows to show the relationships among (a) the bank statement, (b) the bank reconciliation, and (c) the accounting records. Use the arrows to show the flow of data.

Identifying reconciling items from bank documents (Obj. 3)

CP4-5 Compare Business Research, Inc.'s Cash account in Exhibit 4-6, page 179, with the bank statement that the company received in Exhibit 4-4, page 177.

1. Trace each cash receipt from the Cash account (Exhibit 4-6) to a deposit on the bank statement (Exhibit 4-4). Which deposit is in transit on January 31? Give its date and dollar amount.
2. Trace each of Business Research's checks from the cash payments record in Exhibit 4-6 to the bank statement in Exhibit 4-4. List all outstanding checks by check number and dollar amount.
3. On which side of the bank reconciliation do deposits in transit and outstanding checks appear—the bank side or the book side? Are they added or subtracted on the bank reconciliation?

Preparing a bank reconciliation (Obj. 3)

CP4-6 The Cash account of Cabletron, Inc., reported a balance of $1,585 at May 31. Included were outstanding checks totaling $900 and a May 31 deposit of $200 that did not appear on the bank statement. The bank statement, which came from Cornerstone Bank, listed a May 31 balance of $2,490. Included in the bank balance was a May 30 collection of $250 on account from a customer who pays the bank directly. The bank statement also shows a $20 service charge, $10 of interest revenue that Cabletron earned on its bank balance, and an NSF check for $35.

Prepare Cabletron's bank reconciliation at May 31.

CP4-7 After preparing Cabletron's bank reconciliation in Check Point 4-6, make the company's journal entries for transactions that arise from the bank reconciliation. Include an explanation with each entry.

Recording transactions from a bank reconciliation (Obj. 3)

CP4-8 Who in an organization should prepare the bank reconciliation? Should it be someone with cash-handling duties, someone with accounting duties, or someone with both duties? Does it matter? Give your reason.

Internal controls and the bank reconciliation (Obj. 2, 3)

CP4-9 Louise Goldsmith owns Goldsmith Financial Services. She fears that a trusted employee has been stealing from the company. This employee receives cash from customers and also prepares the monthly bank reconciliation. To check up on the employee, Goldsmith prepares her own bank reconciliation, as follows:

Using a bank reconciliation as a control device (Obj. 3)

GOLDSMITH FINANCIAL SERVICES
Bank Reconciliation
August 31, 20X7

Bank		*Books*	
Balance, August 31	$3,000	Balance, August 31	$2,100
Add:		Add:	
Deposits in transit.........	400	Bank collections	800
		Interest revenue	10
Less:		Less:	
Outstanding checks	(1,100)	Service charge............	(30)
Adjusted bank balance.......	$2,300	Adjusted book balance	$2,880

Does it appear that the employee has stolen from the company? If so, how much? Explain your answer. Which side of the bank reconciliation shows the company's true cash balance?

CP4-10 Max Emhart sells electrical appliances at Watson Electric Company in Joplin, Missouri. Company procedure requires Emhart to write a customer receipt for all sales. The receipt forms are prenumbered. Emhart is having personal financial problems and takes $500 that he received from a customer. To hide his theft, Emhart simply destroys the company copy of the sales receipt that he gave the customer. What will alert owner Murray Watson that something is wrong? What will his knowledge lead Watson to do?

Control over cash receipts (Obj. 4)

CP4-11 Answer the following questions about internal control over cash payments:

Internal control payments by check (Obj. 5)

1. Payment by check carries two basic controls over cash. What are they?
2. Suppose a purchasing agent receives the goods that he purchases and also approves payment for the goods. How could a dishonest purchasing agent cheat his company? How do companies avoid this internal control weakness?

CP4-12 Return to The Gap's hypothetical cash budget in Exhibit 4-15, page 192.

Preparing cash budgets with two different outcomes (Obj. 6)

1. Suppose The Gap were to postpone the opening of new stores until 20X3. How much new financing would The Gap need, or how much cash would the company have available for additional investments during the year ended January 31, 20X2?
2. Now suppose The Gap were to postpone both the expansion of existing stores and the opening of new stores until 20X3. How much new financing would The Gap need, or how much cash would the company have available for additional investments during the year ended January 31, 20X2?

CP4-13 Florida Progreso Growers is a major food cooperative. Suppose the company begins the year 2000 with cash of $6 million. Florida Progreso estimates cash receipts during 2000 will total $147 million. Planned payments for the year will require cash of $154 million. To meet daily cash needs, Florida Progreso must maintain a cash balance of at least $5 million.

Prepare Florida Progreso's cash budget for 2000. Identify two ways Florida Progreso can obtain the new financing.

Preparing a cash budget (Obj. 6)

CP4-14 Lane Gibbs, an accountant for Entergy Associates, discovers that his supervisor, Jules Duquet, made several errors last year. Overall, the errors overstated Entergy's net income by 20%. It is not clear whether the errors were deliberate or accidental. What should Gibbs do?

Making an ethical judgment (Obj. 7)

EXERCISES

Correcting an internal control weakness (Obj. 1)

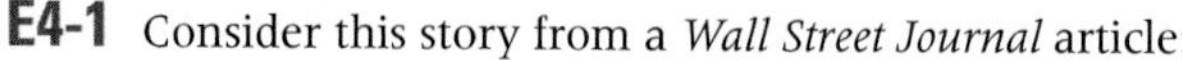

E4-1 Consider this story from a *Wall Street Journal* article:

> TOKYO—**Sumitomo Corp.**, the giant Japanese trading company, said unauthorized trades by its former head of copper trading over the past decade caused it huge losses that may total $1.8 billion.
>
> If Sumitomo's estimate pans out, the trading loss would be the largest in corporate history—dwarfing even the $1.3 billion lost by Nick Leeson of Barings PLC and the $1.1 billion lost by a trader at Japan's Daiwa Bank Ltd. And the fiasco adds a new name to the roll of all-time rogue traders: the flamboyant Yasuo Hamanaka, who until recently was the world's most powerful copper trader—and the one most feared by other traders.
>
> Sumitomo said it learned of the damage after Mr. Hamanaka called a superior and confessed to making unauthorized trades that led to the losses over a 10-year period. Mr. Hamanaka, according to a Sumitomo statement, admitted to concealing the losses by falsifying Sumitomo's books and records.

What internal control weakness at Sumitomo Corp. allowed this loss to grow so large? How could the company have avoided and/or limited the size of the loss?

Identifying internal control strengths and weaknesses (Obj. 1)

E4-2 The following situations describe two cash receipts situations and two equipment purchase situations. In each pair, one situation's internal controls are significantly better than the other's. Evaluate the internal controls in each situation as strong or weak, and give the reason for your answers.

Cash Receipts:

a. Cash received by mail goes straight to the accountant, who debits Cash and credits Accounts Receivable to record the collections from customers. The accountant then deposits the cash in the bank.

b. Cash received by mail goes to the mail room, where a mail clerk opens envelopes and totals the cash receipts for the day. The mail clerk forwards customer checks to the cashier for deposit in the bank and forwards the remittance slips to the accounting department for posting credits to customer accounts.

Equipment Purchases:

a. Centennial Homes policy calls for construction supervisors to request the equipment needed for construction jobs. The home office then purchases the equipment and has it shipped to the construction site.

b. Wayside Construction Company policy calls for project supervisors to purchase the equipment needed for construction jobs. The supervisors then submit the paid receipts to the home office for reimbursement. This policy enables supervisors to get the equipment they need quickly and keep construction jobs moving along.

Identifying internal controls (Obj. 1)

E4-3 Identify the missing internal control characteristic in the following situations:

a. When business is brisk, Stop-n-Shop and many other retail stores deposit cash in the bank several times during the day. The manager at another convenience store wants to reduce the time that employees spend delivering cash to the bank, so he starts a new policy. Cash will build up over Saturdays and Sundays, and the total two-day amount will be deposited on Sunday evening.

b. While reviewing the records of Pay Less Pharmacy, you find that the same employee orders merchandise and approves invoices for payment.

c. Business is slow at White Water Park on Tuesday, Wednesday, and Thursday nights. To reduce expenses, the owner decides not to use a ticket taker on those nights. The ticket seller (cashier) is told to keep the tickets as a record of the number sold.

d. The manager of a discount store wants to speed the flow of customers through checkout. To reduce the time that cashiers spend making change, she prices merchandise at round dollar amounts—such as $8.00 and $15.00—instead of the customary amounts—$7.95 and $14.95.

e. Grocery stores such as **Kroger** and **Winn Dixie** purchase large quantities of their merchandise from a few suppliers. At another grocery store, the manager decides to reduce paperwork. He eliminates the requirement that a receiving department employee prepare a receiving report, which lists the quantities of items received from the supplier.

E4-4 The following questions are unrelated except that they all pertain to internal control:

Explaining the role of internal control (Obj. 1)

1. Cash may be a relatively small item on the financial statements. Nevertheless, internal control over cash is very important. Why is this true?
2. Ling Ltd. requires that all documents supporting a check be canceled (stamped Paid) by the person who signs the check. Why do you think this practice is required? What might happen if it were not?
3. Many managers think that safeguarding assets is the most important objective of internal control systems, while auditors emphasize internal control's role in ensuring reliable accounting data. Explain why managers are more concerned about safeguarding assets and auditors are more concerned about the quality of the accounting records.
4. Separation of duties is an important consideration if a system of internal control is to be effective. Why is this so?

E4-5 The following items may appear on a bank reconciliation:

Classifying bank reconciliation items (Obj. 2)

1. Bank collection of a note receivable on our behalf.
2. Book error: We debited Cash for $200. The correct debit was $2,000.
3. Outstanding checks.
4. Bank error: The bank charged our account for a check written by another customer.
5. Service charge.
6. Deposits in transit.
7. NSF check.

Classify each item as (a) an addition to the bank balance, (b) a subtraction from the bank balance, (c) an addition to the book balance, or (d) a subtraction from the book balance.

E4-6 Jordan Ogden's checkbook lists the following:

Preparing a bank reconciliation (Obj. 2)

Date	*Check No.*	*Item*	*Check*	*Deposit*	*Balance*
10/1					$ 525
4	622	La Petite France Bakery	$ 19		506
9		Dividends		$ 116	622
13	623	General Tire Co.	43		579
14	624	Exxon Oil Co.	58		521
18	625	Cash	50		471
26	626	Fellowship Bible Church	25		446
28	627	Bent Tree Apartments	275		171
30		Paycheck		1,600	1,771

The October bank statement shows

Balance				$525
Add: Deposits				116
Deduct checks:	No.	Amount		
	622	$19		
	623	43		
	624	68*		
	625	50		(180)
Other charges:				
NSF check			$ 8	
Service charge			12	(20)
Balance				$441

* This is the correct amount for check number 624.

Required

Prepare Ogden's bank reconciliation at October 31, 20X0.

Preparing a bank reconciliation (Obj. 2)

E4-7 Evelyn Hupp operates four **7-11** stores. She has just received the monthly bank statement at May 31 from City National Bank, and the statement shows an ending balance of $1,840. Listed on the statement are an EFT rent collection of $300, a service charge of $12, two NSF checks totaling $74, and a $9 charge for printed checks. In reviewing her cash records, Hupp identifies outstanding checks totaling $467 and a May 31 deposit in transit of $1,788. During May, she recorded a $290 check for the salary of a part-time employee as $29. Hupp's Cash account shows a May 31 cash balance of $3,217. Prepare the bank reconciliation at May 31.

Making journal entries from a bank reconciliation (Obj. 2, 3)

E4-8 Using the data from Exercise 4-7, make the journal entries that Hupp should record on May 31. Include an explanation for each entry.

Applying internal controls to the bank reconciliation (Obj. 1, 2)

E4-9 A grand jury indicted the manager of Tried & True Bar for stealing cash from the company. Over a three-year period, the manager allegedly took almost $100,000 and attempted to cover the theft by manipulating the bank reconciliation.

Required

What is the most likely way that a person would manipulate a bank reconciliation to cover a theft? Be specific. What internal control arrangement could have prevented this theft?

Evaluating internal control over cash receipts (Obj. 4)

E4-10 **Kmart** stores use cash registers. The register display shows the amount of each sale, the cash received from the customer, and any change returned to the customer. The machine also produces a customer receipt but keeps no record of transactions. At the end of the day, the clerk counts the cash in the register and gives it to the cashier for deposit in the company bank account.

Required

Write a memo to convince the store manager that there is an internal control weakness over cash receipts. Identify the weakness that gives an employee the best opportunity to steal cash and state how to prevent such a theft.

Accounting for petty cash (Obj. 3, 5)

E4-11 Assume **Habitat for Humanity** in Baton Rouge, Louisiana, has created a $400 imprest petty cash fund. During the first month of use, the fund custodian authorized and signed petty cash tickets as follows:

Ticket No.	*Item*	*Account Debited*	*Amount*
1	Delivery of pledge cards to donors	Delivery Expense	$ 22.19
2	Mail package	Postage Expense	52.80
3	Newsletter	Supplies Expense	134.14
4	Key to closet	Miscellaneous Expense	2.85

Required

1. How much cash should the fund custodian request in order to replenish the petty cash fund?
2. Describe the items in the fund immediately before replenishment.
3. Describe the items in the fund immediately after replenishment.
4. Describe the internal control feature for this petty cash fund.

Preparing a cash budget (Obj. 6)

E4-12 Suppose **Sprint Corporation,** the long-distance telephone company, is preparing its cash budget for 20X1. The company ended 20X0 with $125.8 million, and top management foresees the need for a cash balance of at least $125 million to pay all bills as they come due.

Collections from customers are expected to total $11,504.2 million during 20X1, and payments for the cost of services and products should reach $6,166 million. Operating expense payments are budgeted at $2,543.6 million.

During 20X1, Sprint expects to invest $1,825.7 million in new equipment and $275 million in the company's cellular division and to sell older assets for $115.7 million. Debt payments scheduled for 20X1 will total $597.2 million. The company forecasts net income of $890.4 million for 20X1 and plans to pay dividends of $338 million.

Required

Prepare Sprint's cash budget for 20X1. Will the budgeted level of cash receipts leave Sprint with the desired ending cash balance of $125 million, or will the company need additional financing?

Evaluating the ethics of conduct by government legislators (Obj. 7)

E4-13 Approximately 300 current and former members of the U.S. House of Representatives—on a regular basis—wrote $250,000 of checks without having the cash in their accounts. Later investigations revealed that no public funds were involved. The House bank was a free-standing institution that recirculated House members' cash. In effect, the delinquent check writers were borrowing money from each other on an interest-free, no-service-charge basis. Nevertheless, the House closed its bank after the events became public.

Required

Suppose you are a new congressional representative from your state. Apply the decision guidelines for ethical judgments outlined on page 196 to decide whether you would write NSF checks on a regular basis through the House bank.

CHALLENGE EXERCISES

Internal control over cash disbursements, ethical considerations (Obj. 5, 7)

E4-14 Ann Oliver, the owner of Ann's Dress Shop, has delegated management of the business to Tom O'Grady, a friend. Oliver drops by the business to meet customers and check up on cash receipts, but O'Grady buys the merchandise and handles cash disbursements. Business has been brisk lately, and cash receipts have kept pace with the apparent level of sales. However, for a year or so, the amount of cash on hand has been too low. When asked about this, O'Grady explains that designers are charging more for dresses than in the past. During the past year, O'Grady has taken two expensive vacations, and Oliver wonders how O'Grady could afford these trips on his $35,000 annual salary and commissions.

Required

List at least three ways O'Grady could be defrauding Oliver's business of cash. In each instance also identify how Oliver can determine whether O'Grady's actions are ethical. Limit your answers to the dress shop's cash disbursements. The business pays all suppliers by check (no EFTs).

Preparing and using a cash budget (Obj. 6)

E4-15 Among its many products, **International Paper Company** makes paper for JC Penney shopping bags, the labels on Del Monte canned foods, and *Redbook* magazine. Marianne Parrs, the chief financial officer, is responsible for International Paper's cash budget for 20X2. The budget will help Parrs determine the amount of long-term borrowing needed to end the year with a cash balance of $300 million. Parrs' assistants have assembled budget data for 20X2, which the computer printed in alphabetical order. Not all the data items, reproduced below, are used in preparing the cash budget.

	(In millions)
Acquisition of other companies	$ 1,315
Actual cash balance, December 31, 20X1	270
Borrowing	?
Budgeted total assets before borrowing	23,977
Budgeted total current assets before borrowing	5,873
Budgeted total current liabilities before borrowing	4,863
Budgeted total liabilities before borrowing	16,180
Budgeted total stockholders' equity before borrowing	7,797
Collections from customers	19,467
Dividend payments	237
Issuance of stock	516
Net income	1,153
Other cash receipts	111
Payment of long-term and short-term debt	950
Payment of operating expenses	2,349
Purchases of inventory items	14,345
Purchase of property and equipment	1,518

Required

1. Prepare the cash budget to determine the amount of borrowing International Paper needs during 20X2.
2. Compute International Paper's expected current ratio and debt ratio at December 31, 20X2, both before and after borrowing on a short-term note payable. Based on these figures, and on the budgeted levels of assets and liabilities, would you lend the requested amount to International Paper? Give the reason for your decision.

PROBLEMS

(Group A)

Identifying the characteristics of an effective internal control system (Obj. 1)

P4-1A An employee of Ricoh Chiropractic Clinic, Inc., recently stole thousands of dollars of the company's cash. The company has decided to install a new system of internal controls.

Required

As a consultant for Ricoh, write a memo to the president explaining how a separation of duties helps to safeguard company assets.

Identifying internal control weaknesses (Obj. 1, 4, 5)

P4-2A Each of the following situations has an internal control weakness:

a. Discount stores such as **Wal-Mart** and **Kmart** receive a large portion of their sales revenue in cash, with the remainder in credit card sales. To reduce expenses, a store manager ceases purchasing fidelity bonds on the cashiers.

b. The office supply company from which Haught Air Conditioning Service purchases cash receipt forms recently notified Haught that the last-shipped receipts were not prenumbered. Jerry Haught, the owner, replied that he did not use the receipt numbers, so the omission is not important.

c. Digital Graphics is a software company that specializes in programs with accounting applications. The company's most popular program prepares all the accounting records and financial statements. In the company's early days, the owner and eight employees wrote the computer programs, lined up production of the diskettes, sold the products to ComputerLand and ComputerCraft, and performed the general management and accounting of the company. As Digital has grown, the number of employees has increased dramatically. Recently, the development of a new software program stopped while the programmers redesigned Digital's accounting system. Digital's own accountants could have performed this task.

d. Mona Belcher, a widow with no known sources of outside income, has been a trusted employee of Stone Products Company for 20 years. She performs all cash-handling and accounting duties, including opening the mail, preparing the bank deposit, accounting for all aspects of cash and accounts receivable, and preparing the bank reconciliation. Ms. Belcher has just purchased a new Lexus and a new home in an expensive suburb. Hortense Allison, the owner of the company, wonders how Ms. Belcher can afford these luxuries on her salary.

e. Ashley Webb employs three professional interior designers in her design studio. She is located in an area with a lot of new construction, and her business is booming. Ordinarily, Webb does all the purchasing of furniture, draperies, carpets, and other materials needed to complete jobs. During the summer, she takes a long vacation, and in her absence she allows each designer to purchase materials and labor. On her return, Webb reviews operations and notes that expenses are much higher and net income much lower than in the past.

Required

1. Identify the missing internal control characteristics in each situation.
2. Identify each firm's possible problem.
3. Propose a solution to the problem.
4. How will what you learned by solving this problem help you manage a business?

Using the bank reconciliation as a control device (Obj. 2)

P4-3A The cash receipts and the cash payments of Spies Hecker Paint Company for March 20X1 follow:

Cash Receipts (CR)		Cash Payments (CP)	
Date	*Cash Debit*	*Check No.*	*Cash Credit*
Mar. 4	$2,716	1413	$ 1,465
9	544	1414	1,004
11	1,655	1415	450
14	896	1416	8
17	367	1417	775
25	890	1418	88
31	2,038	1419	4,126
Total	$9,106	1420	970
		1421	200
		1422	2,267
		Total	$11,353

The Cash account of Spies Hecker shows the following information on March 31, 20X1:

Cash

Date	*Item*	*Jrnl. Ref.*	*Debit*	*Credit*	*Balance*
Mar. 1	Balance				10,188
31		CR. 10	9,106		19,294
31		CP. 16		11,353	7,941

On March 31, 20X1, Spies Hecker received this bank statement:

Bank Statement for March 20X1		
Beginning balance.		$10,188
Deposits and other Credits:		
Mar. 1.	$ 625 EFT	
5.	2,716	
10.	544	
11.	1,655	
15.	896	
18.	367	
25.	890	
31.	1,000 BC	8,693
Checks and other Debits:		
Mar. 8.	$ 441 NSF	
9.	1,465	
13.	1,004	
14.	450	
15.	8	
19.	340 EFT	
22.	775	
29.	88	
31.	4,216	
31.	25 SC	(8,812)
Ending balance		$10,069

Explanation: BC—bank collection, EFT—electronic funds transfer,
NSF—nonsufficient fund check, SC—service charge.

Additional data for the bank reconciliation:

a. The EFT deposit was a receipt of monthly rent. The EFT debit was payment of monthly insurance.

b. The NSF check was received late in February from Jay Andrews.

c. The $1,000 bank collection of a note receivable on March 31 included $122 interest revenue.

d. The correct amount of check number 1419, a payment on account, is $4,216. (The Spies Hecker accountant mistakenly recorded the check for $4,126.)

Required

1. Prepare the bank reconciliation of Spies Hecker Paint Company at March 31, 20X1.

2. Describe how a bank account and the bank reconciliation help the managers of Spies Hecker control the firm's cash.

Preparing a bank reconciliation and the related journal entries (Obj. 2)

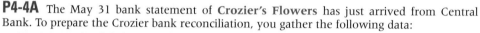

P4-4A The May 31 bank statement of **Crozier's Flowers** has just arrived from Central Bank. To prepare the Crozier bank reconciliation, you gather the following data:

a. The May 31 bank balance is $8,530.82.

b. Crozier's Cash account shows a balance of $7,521.55 on May 31.

c. The following Crozier checks are outstanding at May 31:

Check No.	*Amount*
616	$403.00
802	74.25
806	36.60
809	161.38
810	229.05
811	48.91

d. The bank statement includes two special deposits: $899.14, which is the amount of dividend revenue the bank collected from **General Electric Company** on behalf of Crozier; and $16.86, the interest revenue Crozier earned on its bank balance during May.

e. The bank statement lists a $6.25 subtraction for the bank service charge.

f. On May 31 the Crozier treasurer deposited $381.14, but this deposit does not appear on the bank statement.

g. The bank statement includes a $410.00 deduction for a check drawn by Marimont Freight Company. Crozier promptly notified the bank of its error.

h. The bank statement includes two charges for returned checks from customers. One is an NSF check in the amount of $67.50 received from Harley Doherty, recorded on the books by a debit to Cash, and deposited on May 19. The other is a $195.03 check received from Maria Shell and deposited on May 21. It was returned by Shell's bank with the imprint "Unauthorized Signature."

i. A few customers pay monthly flower bills by EFT. The May bank statement lists an EFT deposit for sales revenue of $200.

Required

1. Prepare the bank reconciliation for Crozier Flowers at May 31.

2. Record the entries necessary to bring the book balance of Cash into agreement with the adjusted book balance on the reconciliation. Include an explanation for each entry.

3. How will what you learned by solving this problem help you manage a business?

Identifying internal control weakness (Obj. 4)

P4-5A Mainframe Optical Products makes all sales on credit. Cash receipts arrive by mail, usually within 30 days of the sale. Liz Galeano opens envelopes and separates the checks from the accompanying remittance advices. Galeano forwards the checks to another employee, who makes the daily bank deposit but has no access to the accounting records. Galeano sends the remittance advices, which show the amount of cash received, to the accounting department for entry in the accounts. Galeano's only other duty is to grant sales allowances to customers. (A sales allowance decreases the amount that the customer must pay.) When she receives a customer check for less than the full amount of the invoice, she records the sales allowance and forwards the document to the accounting department.

Required

You are a new employee of Mainframe Optical. Write a memo to the company president identifying the internal control weakness in this situation. Explain how to correct the weakness.

P4-6A Louis Lipschitz, executive vice president and chief financial officer of **Toys "Я" Us, Inc.,** is responsible for the company's budgeting process. Suppose Lipschitz's staff is preparing the Toys "Я" Us cash budget for 20X1. Assume the starting point is the statement of cash flows of the current year, 20X0, reproduced in an adapted format as follows:

Preparing a cash budget and using cash-flow information (Obj. 6)

TOYS "Я" US, INC., AND SUBSIDIARIES
Consolidated Statement of Cash Flows (Adapted)

(In millions)	*20X0*
Cash Flows from Operating Activities	
Collections from customers	$8,089
Interest received	24
Purchases of inventory	(5,597)
Operating expenses	(1,858)
Net cash provided by operating activities	658
Cash Flows from Investing Activities	
Capital expenditures, net	(555)
Purchases of other assets	(58)
Net cash used in investing activities	(613)
Cash Flows from Financing Activities	
Short-term borrowings, net	119
Long-term borrowings	40
Long-term debt repayments	(1)
Issuance of stock	29
Share repurchases	(183)
Net cash provided by financing activities	4
Effect of foreign-currency exchange rate changes on cash and cash equivalents	(20)
Cash and Cash Equivalents	
(Decrease)/increase during year	29
Beginning of year	763
End of year	$ 792

Required

1. Prepare the Toys "Я" Us cash budget for 20X1. Date the budget simply "20X1" and denote the beginning and ending cash balances as "beginning" and "ending." Assume the company expects 20X1 to be the same as 20X0, but with the following changes:
   a. In 20X1, the company expects a 10% increase in collections from customers, an 11% increase in purchases of inventory, and a doubling of capital expenditures.
   b. The amount of borrowings and issuances of stock needed in 20X1 will be determined by the cash budget and thus does not appear on the cash budget. (But scheduled long-term debt repayments and share repurchases should be the same in 20X1 as they were in 20X0.)
   c. Lipschitz hopes to end the year with a cash balance of $500 million.

   You will find these explanations helpful:

   "Capital expenditures" are purchases of property and equipment.

   Toys "Я" Us does not pay cash dividends. Instead the company *repurchases* its stock from its stockholders. This is another way for a corporation to return cash to the stockholders.
2. Answer these questions about the company. Explain your reasoning for each answer.
   a. Does the company's cash budget for 20X1 suggest that Toys "Я" Us is growing, holding steady, or decreasing in size?
   b. Do the statement of cash flows for 20X0 and the cash budget for 20X1 suggest that operating activities are generating enough cash?

P4-7A TriState Bank in Durango, Colorado has a loan receivable from Yuma Construction Company. Yuma is six months late in making payments to the bank, and Leon Hess, a TriState vice president, is assisting Yuma to restructure its debt. With unlimited access to

Making an ethical judgment (Obj. 7)

Yuma's records, Hess learns that Yuma is depending on landing a construction contract from Maxey Glass Company, another TriState Bank client. Hess also serves as Maxey's loan officer at the bank. In this capacity, he is aware that Maxey is considering declaring bankruptcy. No one else outside Maxey Glass knows this. Hess has been a great help to Yuma Construction, and Yuma's owner is counting on Hess's expertise in loan workouts to advise the company through this difficult process. To help the bank collect on this large loan, Hess has a strong motivation to help Yuma to survive.

Required

Apply the ethical judgment framework outlined in the chapter to help Leon Hess plan his next action.

(Group B)

Identifying the characteristics of an effective internal control system (Obj. 1)

P4-1B Avalon Real Estate Development Company prospered during the economic expansion of the 1990s. Business was so good that the company bothered with few internal controls. A recent decline in the local real estate market has caused Avalon to experience a shortage of cash. Jean Martin-Ellis, the company owner, is looking for ways to save money.

Required

As a consultant for the company, write a memorandum to convince Ms. Martin-Ellis of the company's need for a system of internal control. Be specific in telling her how an internal control system could save the company money. Include the definition of internal control, and briefly discuss each characteristic of an effective internal control system, beginning with competent, reliable, and ethical personnel.

Identifying internal control weaknesses (Obj. 1, 4, 5)

P4-2B Each of the following situations reveals an internal control weakness.

a. Leah Kestner has been an employee of A&S Shoe Store for many years. Because the business is relatively small, Kestner performs all accounting duties, including opening the mail, preparing the bank deposit, and preparing the bank reconciliation.

b. Most large companies have internal audit staffs that continuously evaluate the business's internal control. Part of the auditor's job is to evaluate how efficiently the company is running. For example, is the company purchasing inventory from the least expensive wholesaler? After a particularly bad year, McGregor Cellular Company eliminates its internal audit department to reduce expenses.

c. Law firms, consulting firms, and other professional organizations use paraprofessional employees to perform routine tasks. For example, a legal paraprofessional might examine documents to assist a lawyer prepare a lawsuit. In the law firm of Dunham & Lee, Cecil Dunham, the senior partner, turns over a significant portion of his high-level legal work to his paraprofessional staff.

d. In evaluating the internal control over cash payments, an auditor learns that the purchasing agent is responsible for purchasing diamonds for use in the company's manufacturing process, approving the invoices for payment, and signing the checks. No supervisor reviews the purchasing agent's work.

e. Todd Wagoner owns a firm that performs engineering services. His staff consists of 12 professional engineers, and he manages the office. Often, his work requires him to travel to meet with clients. During the past six months, he has observed that when he returns from a business trip, the engineering jobs in the office have not progressed satisfactorily. He learns that when he is away, several of his senior employees take over office management and neglect their engineering duties. One employee could manage the office.

Required

1. Identify the missing internal control characteristic in each situation.
2. Identify each firm's possible problem.
3. Propose a solution to the problem.
4. How will what you learned by solving this problem help you manage a business?

Using the bank reconciliation as a control device (Obj. 2)

P4-3B The cash receipts and the cash payments of Radiofone Beepers for April 20X4 follow:

Cash Receipts (CR)		Cash Payments (CP)	
Date	*Cash Debit*	*Check No.*	*Cash Credit*
Apr. 2	$ 4,174	3113	$ 891
8	407	3114	147
10	559	3115	1,930
16	2,187	3116	664
22	1,854	3117	1,472
29	1,060	3118	1,000
30	337	3119	632
Total	$10,578	3120	1,675
		3121	100
		3122	2,413
		Total	$10,924

The Cash account of Radiofone shows the following information at April 30, 20X4:

Cash

Date	*Item*	*Jrnl. Ref.*	*Debit*	*Credit*	*Balance*
Apr. 1	Balance				1,911
30		CR. 6	10,578		12,489
30		CP. 11		10,924	1,565

Radiofone received the following bank statement on April 30, 20X4:

Bank Statement for April 20X4

Beginning balance		$ 1,911
Deposits and other Credits:		
Apr. 1	$ 326 EFT	
4	4,174	
9	407	
12	559	
17	2,187	
22	1,368 BC	
23	1,854	10,875
Checks and other Debits:		
Apr. 7	$ 891	
13	1,390	
14	903 US	
15	147	
18	664	
21	219 EFT	
26	1,472	
30	1,000	
30	20 SC	(6,706)
Ending balance		$ 6,080

Explanation: EFT—electronic funds transfer, BC—bank collection, US—unauthorized signature, SC—service charge.

Additional data for the bank reconciliation include the following:

a. The EFT deposit was a receipt of monthly rent. The EFT debit was a monthly insurance payment.

b. The unauthorized signature check was received from S. M. Holt.

c. The $1,368 bank collection of a note receivable on April 22 included $185 interest revenue.

d. The correct amount of check number 3115, a payment on account, is $1,390. (Radiofone's accountant mistakenly recorded the check for $1,930.)

Required

1. Prepare the Radiofone Beepers bank reconciliation at April 30, 20X4.
2. Describe how a bank account and the bank reconciliation help the managers of Radiofone Beepers control the business's cash.

Preparing a bank reconciliation and the related journal entries (Obj. 2)

P4-4B The August 31 bank statement of Computer Solutions, Inc. (CSI), has just arrived from **Texas First Bank.** To prepare the CSI bank reconciliation, you gather the following data:

a. CSI's Cash account shows a balance of $3,366.14 on August 31.

b. The August 31 bank balance is $4,484.22.

c. The bank statement shows that CSI earned $38.19 of interest on its bank balance during August. This amount was added to CSI's bank balance.

d. CSI pays rent ($750) and insurance ($290) each month by EFT.

e. The following CSI checks are outstanding at August 31:

Check No.	*Amount*
237	$ 46.10
288	141.00
291	578.05
293	11.87
294	609.51
295	8.88
296	101.63

f. The bank statement includes a deposit of $1,191.17, collected by the bank on behalf of CSI. Of the total, $1,011.81 is collection of a note receivable, and the remainder is interest revenue.

g. The bank statement lists a $10.50 subtraction for the bank service charge.

h. On August 31, the CSI treasurer deposited $316.15, but this deposit does not appear on the bank statement.

i. The bank statement includes a $300.00 deposit that CSI did not make. The bank had erroneously credited the CSI account for another bank customer's deposit.

j. The bank statement includes two charges for returned checks from customers. One is a $395.00 check received from Shoreline Express and deposited on August 20, returned by Shoreline's bank with the imprint "Unauthorized Signature." The other is an NSF check in the amount of $146.67 received from Lipsey, Inc. This check had been deposited on August 17.

Required

1. Prepare the bank reconciliation for Computer Solutions, Inc. (CSI).
2. Record the entries necessary to bring the book balance of Cash into agreement with the adjusted book balance on the reconciliation. Include an explanation for each entry.
3. How will what you learned by solving this problem help you manage a business?

Identifying internal control weakness (Obj. 4)

P4-5B TechLabs, Inc., makes all sales of its spreadsheet software on credit. Cash receipts arrive by mail, usually within 30 days of the sale. Matt Larosz opens envelopes and separates the checks from the accompanying remittance advices. Larosz forwards the checks to another employee, who makes the daily bank deposit but has no access to the accounting records. Larosz sends the remittance advices, which show the amount of cash received, to the accounting department for entry in the accounts. Larosz's only other duty is to grant sales allowances to customers. (A *sales allowance* decreases the amount that the customer must pay.) When Larosz receives a customer check for less than the full amount of the invoice, he records the sales allowance and forwards the document to the accounting department.

Required

You are a new employee of TechLabs, Inc. Write a memo to the company president identifying the internal control weakness in this situation. State how to correct the weakness.

Preparing a cash budget and using cash-flow information (Obj. 6)

P4-6B Louis Lipschitz, Executive Vice President and Chief Financial Officer of **Toys "Я" Us, Inc.,** is responsible for the company's budgeting process. Suppose Lipschitz's staff is preparing the Toys "Я" Us cash budget for 20X2. A key input to the budgeting process is last year's statement of cash flows, reproduced in an adapted format as follows:

TOYS "Я" US, INC., AND SUBSIDIARIES
Consolidated Statement of Cash Flows (Adapted)

(In millions)	*20X1*
Cash Flows from Operating Activities	
Collections from customers	$9,412
Interest received	17
Purchases of inventory	(6,750)
Operating expenses	(2,035)
Restructuring costs	(394)
Net cash provided by operating activities	250
Cash Flows from Investing Activities	
Capital expenditures	(468)
Purchases of other assets	(67)
Net cash used in investing activities	(535)
Cash Flows from Financing Activities	
Short-term borrowings	210
Long-term borrowings	82
Long-term debt repayments	(9)
Issuance of stock	16
Share repurchases	(200)
Net cash provided by financing activities	99
Effect of foreign-currency exchange rate changes on cash and cash equivalents	19
Cash and Cash Equivalents	
(Decrease)/increase during year	(167)
Beginning of year	370
End of year	$ 203

Required

1. Prepare the Toys "Я" Us cash budget for 20X2. Date the budget simply "20X2" and denote the beginning and ending cash balances as "beginning" and "ending." Assume the company expects 20X2 to be the same as 20X1, but with the following changes:
   a. In 20X2, the company expects a 15% increase in collections from customers and a 10% increase in purchases of inventory.
   b. The company expects to incur no restructuring costs in 20X2.
   c. The amount of any borrowings and the issuances of stock needed in 20X2 will be determined as a result of the cash budget and thus are not causal factors for the preparation of the budget. (But scheduled long-term debt repayments and share repurchases should be the same in 20X2 as they were in 20X1.)
   d. Lipschitz plans to end the year with a cash balance of $500 million.

You will find these explanations helpful:

"Capital expenditures" are purchases of property and equipment.

Toys "Я" Us does not pay cash dividends. Instead the company *repurchases* its stock from its stockholders. This is another way for a corporation to return cash to the stockholders.

2. Answer these questions about the company. Explain your reasoning for each answer.
   a. Does the company's cash budget for 20X2 suggest that Toys "Я" Us is growing, holding steady, or decreasing in size?
   b. Do the statement of cash flows for 20X1 and the cash budget for 20X2 suggest that operating activities are generating enough cash?

Making an ethical judgment (Obj. 7)

P4-7B Mel Boyd is executive vice president of Scott & White Investment Associates in Santa Fe, New Mexico. Active in community affairs, Boyd serves on the board of directors of UNIX Publishing Company. UNIX is expanding rapidly and is considering relocating its plant. At a recent meeting, UNIX board members decided to buy 200 acres of land on the edge of town. The owner of the property is Jerry Staas, a customer of Scott & White. Staas is completing a bitter divorce, and Boyd knows that Staas is eager to sell his property. In view of Staas's difficult situation, Boyd believes Staas would accept almost any offer for the land. Realtors have appraised the property at $3.6 million.

Required

Apply the ethical judgment framework outlined in the chapter Decision Guidelines to help Boyd decide what his role should be in UNIX's attempt to buy the land from Staas.

Decision Cases

Using the bank reconciliation to detect a theft (Obj. 2)

Case 1. Lionel Eyecare has poor internal control over its cash transactions. Recently Joseph Lionel, the owner, has suspected the cashier of stealing. Here are some details of the business's cash position at April 30.

a. The Cash account shows a balance of $20,102. This amount includes an April 30 deposit of $3,794 that does not appear on the April 30 bank statement.

b. The April 30 bank statement shows a balance of $16,624. The bank statement lists a $200 credit for a bank collection, an $8 debit for the service charge, and a $36 debit for an NSF check. The Lionel accountant has not recorded any of these items on the books.

c. At April 30, the following checks are outstanding:

Check No.	*Amount*
154	$116
256	150
278	353
291	190
292	206
293	145

d. The cashier handles all incoming cash and makes bank deposits. He also reconciles the monthly bank statement. Here is his April 30 reconciliation:

Balance per books, April 30		$20,102
Add: Outstanding checks		160
Bank collection		200
		20,462
Less: Deposits in transit	$3,794	
Service charge	8	
NSF check	36	3,838
Balance per bank, April 30		$16,624

Required

Lionel has requested that you determine whether the cashier has stolen cash from the business and, if so, how much. He also asks you to explain how the cashier has attempted to conceal the theft. To make this determination, you perform your own bank reconciliation using the format illustrated in the chapter. There are no bank or book errors. Lionel also asks you to evaluate the internal controls and to recommend any changes needed to improve them.

Correcting an internal control weakness (Obj. 1, 5)

Case 2. This case is based on an actual situation experienced by one of the authors. Bush Building Corporation, headquartered in Oklahoma City, built an office building in Edmond, a suburb north of Oklahoma City. The construction foreman, whose name was Slim, moved into Edmond in May to hire the 40 workers needed to complete the project. Slim hired the construction workers, had them fill out the necessary tax forms, and sent the employment documents to the home office, which opened a payroll file for each employee.

Work on the motel building began on June 1 and ended the following March. Each Thursday evening, Slim filled out a time card that listed the hours worked for each employee during the five-day work week ended at 5 P.M. on Thursday. Slim faxed the time sheets to the home office, which prepared the payroll checks on Friday morning. Slim drove to the home office after lunch on Friday, picked up the payroll checks, and returned to the construction site. At 5 P.M. on Friday, Slim distributed the payroll checks to the workers.

a. Describe in detail the internal control weakness in this situation. Specify what negative result could occur because of the internal control weakness.

b. Describe what you would do to correct the internal control weakness.

Ethical Issue

Lisa Stein owns apartment buildings in Iowa and Minnesota. Each property has a manager who collects rent, arranges for repairs, and runs advertisements in the local newspaper. The property managers transfer cash to Stein monthly and prepare their own bank reconciliations. The manager in Des Moines has been stealing large sums of money. To cover the theft, he understates the amount of the outstanding checks on the monthly bank reconciliation. As a result, each monthly bank reconciliation appears to balance. However, the balance sheet reports more cash than Stein actually has in the bank. In negotiating the sale of the Des Moines property, Stein is showing the balance sheet to prospective investors.

Required

1. Identify two parties other than Stein who can be harmed by this theft. In what ways can they be harmed?
2. Discuss the role accounting plays in this situation.

Financial Statement Cases

Internal controls and cash (Obj. 1, 3)

Case 1. Study The Gap's responsibility statement and the audit opinion of The Gap's financial statements given at the end of Appendix A. Answer the following questions about the company's internal controls and cash position.

Required

1. What is the name of The Gap's outside auditing firm? What office of this firm signed the audit report? How long after The Gap's year end did the auditors issue their opinion?
2. Who bears primary responsibility for the financial statements? How can you tell?
3. Does it appear that The Gap's internal controls are adequate? How can you tell?
4. What standard of auditing did the outside auditors use in examining The Gap's financial statements? By what accounting standards were the statements evaluated?

5. By how much did the company's cash position change during 1999? The statement of cash flows tells why this change occurred. Which type of activity—operating, investing, or financing—contributed the most to The Gap's cash flows during the year?

Audit opinion, management responsibility, internal controls, and cash (Obj. 1, 3)

Case 2. Obtain the annual report of a company of your choosing. Study the audit opinion and the management statement of responsibility (if present) in conjunction with the financial statements. Then answer these questions.

Required

1. What is the name of the company's outside auditing firm? What office of this firm signed the audit report? How long after the company's year end did the auditors issue their opinion?
2. Who bears primary responsibility for the financial statements? How can you tell?
3. Does it appear that the company's internal controls are adequate? Give your reason.
4. What standard of auditing did the outside auditors use in examining the company's financial statements? By what accounting standards were the statements evaluated?
5. By how much did the company's cash position (including cash equivalents) change during the current year? The statement of cash flows tells why this increase or decrease occurred. Which type of activity—operating, investing, or financing—contributed most to the change in the cash balance?
6. Where is the balance of petty cash reported? Name the financial statement and the account and identify the specific amount that includes petty cash.

Group Project

You are promoting a rock concert in your area. Assume you organize as a corporation, with each member of your group purchasing $10,000 of the corporation's stock. Therefore, each of you is risking some hard-earned money on this venture. Assume it is April 1 and that the concert will be performed on June 30. Your promotional activities begin immediately, and ticket sales start on May 1. You expect to sell all the firm's assets, pay all the liabilities, and distribute all remaining cash to the group members by July 31.

Required

Write an internal control manual that will help to safeguard the assets of the business. The manual should address the following aspects of internal control:

1. Assigning responsibilities among the group members.
2. Authorizing individuals, including group members and any outsiders that you need to hire, to perform specific jobs.
3. Separating duties among the group and any employees.
4. Describing all documents needed to account for and safeguard the business's assets.

Internet Exercise

Telemate.net Software Inc.

Corporate management now faces new internal control and ethical challenges with Internet access at the fingertips of many employees. Is it okay for an employee to log on to make a quick personal stock trade? What about sending personal e-mail, checking sports scores, playing games, visiting chat rooms, or shopping online? These are the new dilemmas facing corporate America.

1. Discuss several internal control issues that may concern management regarding personal use of the Internet by employees during working hours.
2. Do any special issues arise for company e-mail?
3. Many Web sites can trace and identify the company making visits. Do any special issues arise as to which Web sites are accessed by company employees?
4. Expanded Internet use has created a new industry to monitor Web site visits and the duration of employee time online. Go to **http://www.telemate.net/**. What services are provided by this company?

5. Telemate.Net Software Inc. had its initial public offering (IPO) of common stock on September 29, 1999. Must company financial statements before that date be made public? Would a company want to make those financial statements public? Explain.
6. Click on *Company* followed by *Company Fact Sheet.* In what year was the company founded? How much revenue did it earn during 1998? Comment on the size of this company.

5 Receivables and Short-Term Investments

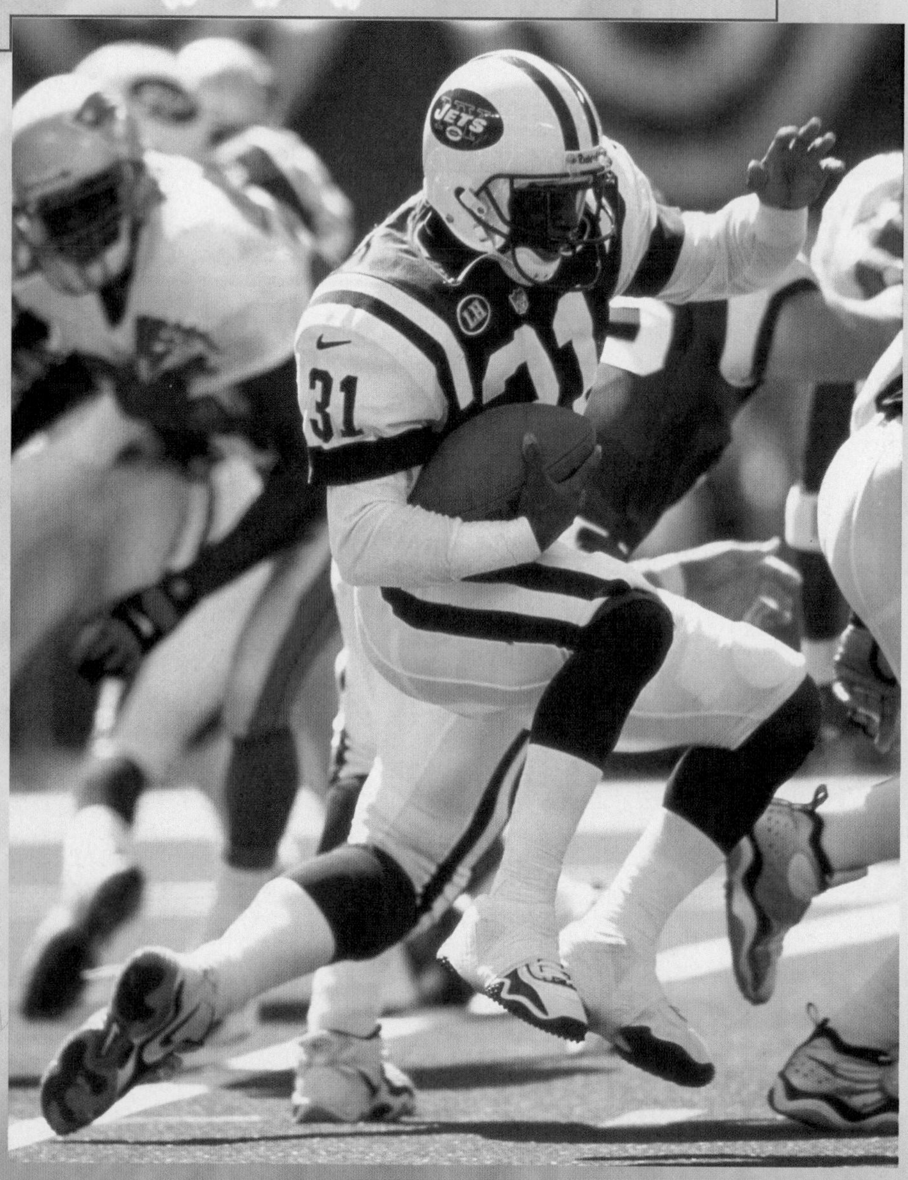

Learning Objectives

After studying this chapter, you should be able to

1. Understand short-term investments
2. Apply internal controls to receivables
3. Use the allowance method for uncollectible receivables
4. Account for notes receivable
5. Evaluate financial position with the acid-test ratio and days' sales in receivables
6. Report receivables and investment transactions on the statement of cash flows

Oracle Corporation
Condensed Balance Sheets (adapted)
May 31, 1998 and 1997

(Dollars in Thousands)	May 31, 1998	May 31, 1997
ASSETS		
CURRENT ASSETS		
Cash and cash equivalents	$1,273,681	$ 890,162
Short-term investments	645,518	323,028
Trade receivables, net of allowance for doubtful accounts of $195,609 in 1998 and $127,840 in 1997	1,857,480	1,540,470
Prepaid expenses and other current assets	546,371	517,436
Total current assets	4,323,050	3,271,096
Long-term investments	186,511	116,337
Property, net	934,350	868,948
Computer software development costs, net of accumulated amortization of $37,473 in 1998 and $36,303 in 1997	99,012	98,981
Other assets	276,088	268,953
Total assets	$5,819,011	$4,624,315
LIABILITIES AND STOCKHOLDERS' EQUITY		
CURRENT LIABILITIES		
Notes payable and current maturities of long-term debt	$ 2,924	$ 3,361
Accounts payable	239,698	185,444
Income taxes payable	181,354	203,646
Unearned revenues	877,087	602,862
Other current liabilities	1,183,102	926,826
Total current liabilities	2,484,165	1,922,139
Long-term debt	304,337	300,836
Other long-term liabilities	72,951	31,628
Stockholders' equity	2,957,558	2,369,712
Total liabilities and stockholders' equity	$5,819,011	$4,624,315

IN the New York Jets locker room, pregame reviews have taken on a whole new look. Gone are old-style playbooks with *X*-and-*O* diagrams of foes' alignments. In their place is an exciting world of multimedia. Desktop computers turn football formations into live animation. With help from **Oracle Corporation,** Carl Banks, director of player development, has turned passive training into an interactive success. Using Developer/2000 and multimedia software, Banks has a state-of-the-art teaching model to give the Jets a competitive edge. Banks states, "By the time [the players] hit the practice field, [they] lose the ability to visualize *X*'s and *O*'s as actual plays. Oracle has helped create [a] learning environment that increases [players'] retention by as much as 250%." Oracle is the world's second-largest software company. With annual revenues exceeding $8.0 billion, the company offers its products and services in more than 145 countries around the world.

Source: Adapted from Oracle Corporation Web site, June 17, 1999.

With exciting new products and services like Developer/2000, Oracle is growing rapidly. Revenues are increasing, and so are the company's receivables. As Oracle's balance sheet shows, Trade receivables (another name for Accounts receivable) are the company's largest asset. Receivables present a unique accounting challenge: How much of its receivables will the company be able to collect in cash? This chapter shows how to answer this and other questions about receivables. It also covers short-term investments, Oracle's second most liquid asset, which is listed immediately after cash on the balance sheet.

Some Basic Terminology

Before getting into the accounting for short-term investments and receivables, let's define some key terms.

- **Creditor.** The party to whom money is owed. The creditor has a receivable, which can also be called an *investment.*
- **Debtor.** The party who has a debt. The debtor has a payable.
- **Debt instrument.** A payable, usually some form of note or bond payable. The maker (issuer) of a debt instrument is the *debtor.* The holder of a debt instrument is the *creditor* (or investor) to whom the instrument is a receivable (or investment).
- **Equity securities.** Stock certificates that represent the investor's ownership of shares of stock in a corporation.
- **Maturity.** The date on which a debt instrument matures—that is, becomes payable.
- **Securities.** Notes payable or stock certificates that entitle the owner to the benefits of an investment.
- **Term.** The length of time until a debt instrument matures.

Short-Term Investments (Marketable Securities)

Objective 1
Understand short-term investments

Short-term investments, also called **marketable securities,** are investments that a company plans to hold for one year or less. These investments allow the company to "park" its cash temporarily and earn a modest return until the cash is needed. Short-term investments fall into three categories:

1. **Held-to-maturity investments,** which the investor expects to hold until the securities' maturity date. On held-to-maturity investments the investor earns interest revenue.
2. **Trading investments,** which the investor holds for the purpose of generating a gain by selling the securities within a few weeks or months.
3. **Available-for-sale investments,** which are all investments other than held-to-maturity investments and trading investments.[1]

All trading investments are short-term investments because companies intend to hold them for only a few months or less. Held-to-maturity investments and available-for-sale investments may be either short- or long-term investments, depending on the length of time that management intends to hold them. In the sections that follow, we explain how companies account for short-term investments.

[1]Available-for-sale investments are included here for completeness. Chapter 10 discusses the accounting for available-for-sale investments.

Held-to-Maturity Investments

A held-to-maturity investment earns interest revenue for the investor. Accounting for a held-to-maturity investment is the same as accounting for a note receivable, as discussed starting on page 223 of this chapter. This section focuses on trading investments.

Trading Investments

The investor intends to hold a trading investment for a very short time—a few months at most. The purpose of owning a trading investment is to sell it at a profit—for more than its cost.

Trading investments can be the stock of another company. Suppose **Oracle Corporation** purchases **Ford Motor Company** stock, intending to sell the Ford stock within a few months. This makes Oracle's investment a trading investment. If the market value of the Ford stock increases, Oracle will have a gain; if the price of the Ford stock drops, Oracle will have a loss. Along the way, Oracle may also receive dividend revenue from Ford Motor Company.

Suppose Oracle buys the Ford stock on May 18, paying $100,000 cash. Oracle records the purchase of the investment at cost:

May 18	Short-Term Investment	100,000	
	Cash		100,000
	Purchased investment.		

ASSETS	=	LIABILITIES	+	STOCKHOLDERS' EQUITY
+100,000 −100,000	=	0	+	0

Assume on May 27 Oracle receives a cash dividend of $4,000 from Ford. Oracle records the receipt of the dividend as follows:

May 27	Cash	4,000	
	Dividend Revenue		4,000
	Received cash dividend.		

ASSETS	=	LIABILITIES	+	STOCKHOLDERS' EQUITY	+	REVENUES
+4,000	=				+	4,000

PREPARING THE FINANCIAL STATEMENTS. Oracle's fiscal year ends on May 31, and Oracle prepares a balance sheet and an income statement. Assume the Ford stock has risen in value, and on May 31 the Ford investment has a current market value of $102,000. Market value is the amount the owner can receive when selling the investment. In this case Oracle has an *unrealized gain* on the investment:

- *gain* because the market value ($102,000) is greater than Oracle's cost of the investment ($100,000). A *gain* has the same effect as a revenue.
- *unrealized* gain because Oracle has not yet sold the investment

Trading investments are reported on the balance sheet at their current market value. Therefore, prior to preparing financial statements on May 31, Oracle adjusts the Ford investment to its current market value with this journal entry:

CHECK POINT 5-1

May 31	Short-Term Investment.	2,000	
	Unrealized Gain on Investment		2,000
	Adjusted investment to market value.		

ASSETS	=	LIABILITIES	+	STOCKHOLDERS' EQUITY	+	GAINS
+2,000	=	0	+	0	+	2,000

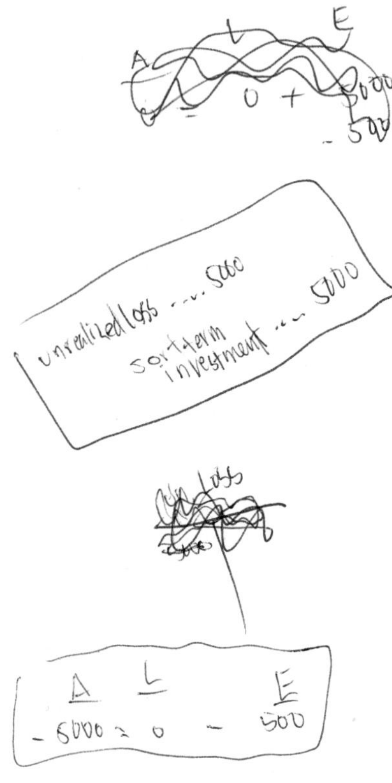

After the adjustment, Oracle's investment account appears as follows:

Short-Term Investment		
Cost	**100,000**	
Adjustment to market value	**2,000**	
Balance	**102,000**	

Now the Short-term Investment account is ready to be reported on the balance sheet—at current market value.

If Oracle's investment in Ford stock had decreased in value, say to $95,000, then Oracle would have had an unrealized loss. A *loss* has the same effect as an expense. In that case, Oracle would have made a different entry at May 31. For an unrealized loss,

- *debit* an Unrealized Loss account for $5,000 ($100,000 − $95,000) and
- *credit* the Short-term Investment account for $5,000 to reduce its carrying amount to current market value of $95,000.

In this case Oracle would report its short-term investment at current market value of $95,000.

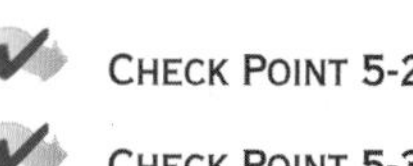

Reporting Short-Term Investments on the Balance Sheet and the Revenues, Gains, and Losses on the Income Statement

SHORT-TERM INVESTMENTS ON THE BALANCE SHEET. Short-term investments are current assets. They appear on the balance sheet immediately after cash because short-term investments are the next-most liquid type of asset after cash. (In business, *liquid* means close to cash.) Report trading investments at their current market value.

INTEREST REVENUE, DIVIDEND REVENUE, GAINS AND LOSSES ON THE INCOME STATEMENT. Investments earn interest revenue and dividend revenue. Investments also result in gains and losses, which, for trading investments are reported as Other revenue, gains, and (losses) on the income statement, as shown in Exhibit 5-1.

EXHIBIT 5-1
Reporting Short-Term Investments and the Related Revenues, Gains and Losses (amounts assumed)

Balance sheet	
Current assets:	
Cash	$ XXX
Short-term trading investments, at market value	102,000
Accounts receivable	XXX
Income statement	
Revenues	$ XXX
Expenses	XXX
Other revenue, gains, and (losses):	
Interest revenue	4,000
Dividend revenue	1,000
Unrealized gain on investment	2,000
⋮	⋮
Net income	$ XXX

CHECK POINT 5-2

CHECK POINT 5-3

Mid-Chapter

Summary Problem for Your Review

Humana, Inc., is one of the largest U.S. managed health-care companies. It provides a full array of health plans, including health maintenance organizations (HMOs) and other plans. The largest current asset on Humana's balance sheet is Marketable Securities (short-term investments). Their cost is $1,144 million, and their market value is $1,156 million.

If Humana holds the marketable securities in the hope of selling them at a profit within a few days or weeks, how will it classify the investment? At what amount will Humana report the investment on the balance sheet at December 31, 20X0? What will Humana report on its 20X0 income statement?

Answers

Trading investments, reported on the balance sheet as follows:

	(In millions)
Current assets:	
Cash	$ XX
Marketable securities (or short-term investments), at market value	1,156

Humana's income statement will report:

	(In millions)
Other revenue and gain:	
Unrealized gain on investments ($1,156 − $1,144 million)..................	$12

Accounts and Notes Receivable

Receivables are the third most liquid asset—after cash and cash equivalents and short-term investments. Receivables are usually good for a company because they are claims to someone else's cash. But a receivable can be bad news if the business cannot collect the receivable. In the remainder of the chapter, we discuss ways of controlling and managing receivables.

The Different Types of Receivables

Receivables are monetary claims against businesses and individuals. They are acquired mainly by selling goods and services and by lending money.

The two major types of receivables are accounts receivable and notes receivable. A business's *accounts receivable* are the amounts collectible from customers. Accounts receivable, which are *current assets,* are sometimes called *trade receivables,* as **Oracle Corporation** does on its balance sheet.

The Accounts Receivable account in the general ledger serves as a *control account* that summarizes the total amounts receivable from all customers. Companies also keep a *subsidiary ledger* of accounts receivable with a separate account for each customer, illustrated as follows:

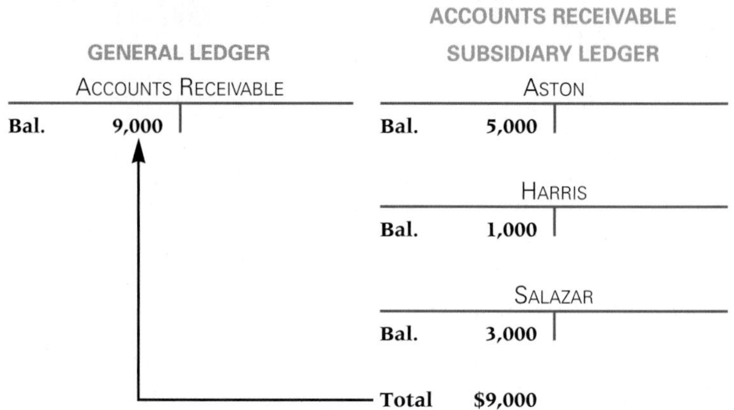

Notes receivable are more formal than accounts receivable. The debtor in a note receivable arrangement promises in writing to pay the creditor a definite sum at a specific future date—the *maturity* date. The note may require the debtor to pledge *security* for the loan. This means that the borrower promises that the lender may claim certain assets, called *collateral,* if the borrower fails to pay the amount due.

Notes receivable due within one year or less are current assets. Those notes due beyond one year are *long-term receivables* and are reported as Long-term Investments on the balance sheet. Oracle Corporation has some long-term investments on its balance sheet.

Some notes receivable are collected in periodic installments. The portion due within one year is a current asset and the remaining amount a long-term asset. **General Motors** may hold a $6,000 note receivable from you, but only the $1,500 you owe on it this year is a current asset to GM.

Other receivables is a miscellaneous category that includes loans to employees and subsidiary companies. Some companies report other receivables under the heading Other Assets on the balance sheet, as Oracle Corporation does. Usually, these are long-term receivables. Long-term notes receivable, and other receivables, are often reported on the balance sheet after current assets. Each type of receivable is a separate account in the general ledger.

The Decision Guidelines feature on page 225 identifies the main issues in controlling, managing, and accounting for receivables. These guidelines serve as a framework for the remainder of the chapter.

Establishing Internal Control over the Collection of Receivables

Objective 2
Apply internal controls to receivables

Businesses that sell on credit receive most of their cash receipts by mail. Internal control over collections of cash on account is an important part of the overall internal control system. Chapter 4 detailed control procedures over cash receipts, but a critical element of internal control deserves emphasis here—the separation of cash-handling and cash-accounting duties. Consider the following case:

> **Butler Supply Co.** is a small, family-owned business that takes pride in the loyalty of its workers. Most company employees have been with the Butlers for at least five years. The company makes 90% of its sales on account.
>
> The office staff consists of a bookkeeper and a supervisor. The bookkeeper maintains the general ledger and the accounts receivable subsidiary ledger. He also makes the daily bank deposit. The supervisor prepares monthly financial statements and any special reports the Butlers require. She also takes sales orders from customers and serves as office manager.

Can you identify the internal control weakness here? The bookkeeper has access to the general ledger, the accounts receivable subsidiary ledger, and the cash.

Decision Guidelines

Controlling, Managing, and Accounting for Receivables

It is easy to lose sight of the big picture—the main issues—in controlling, managing, and accounting for receivables. Most of the rest of this chapter relates to one or more of the following issues:

The main issues in *controlling* and *managing* the collection of receivables, along with a related plan of action, are

Issues	Plan of Action
1. Extending credit only to creditworthy customers, the ones most likely to pay us.	1. Run a credit check on prospective customers.
2. Separating cash-handling, credit, and accounting duties to keep employees from stealing the cash collected from customers.	2. Design the internal control system to separate duties.
3. Pursuing collection from customers to maximize cash flow.	3. Keep a close eye on collections from customers.

The main issues in *accounting* for receivables, and the related plans of action, are

Issues	Plan of Action
1. Measuring and reporting receivables on the balance sheet at their *net realizable value,* the amount we expect to collect. This is necessary to report assets accurately.	1. Report receivables at their net realizable value: **Balance sheet** Receivables .... $1,000 Less: Allowance for uncollectibles .. (80) Receivables, net .... $ 920
2. Measuring and reporting the expense associated with failure to collect receivables, which we call *uncollectible-account expense,* on the income statement. This helps to report net income at a reasonable amount.	2. Measure the expense of not collecting from customers: **Income statement** Sales (or service) revenue .... $8,000 Expenses: Uncollectible-account expense ... 190

The bookkeeper could take a customer check and write off the customer's account as uncollectible.[2]

How can this control weakness be corrected? The supervisor could open incoming mail and make the daily bank deposit. The bookkeeper should not be allowed to handle cash. Only the remittance advices would be forwarded to the bookkeeper to indicate which customer accounts to credit. By removing cash-handling duties from the bookkeeper and keeping the accounts receivable subsidiary ledger away from the supervisor, the company would separate duties and strengthen internal control. These actions would reduce an employee's opportunity to steal cash and then cover it up with a false credit to a customer account.

Using a bank lockbox would achieve the same separation of duties. Customers would send their payments directly to Butler Supply's bank, which would record and deposit the cash into the company's account. The bank would then forward the remittance advice to Butler Supply's bookkeeper to credit the appropriate customer accounts.

All Receivables Run the Risk of Not Being Collected

In Chapters 1–4, we have used many different companies to illustrate how to account for a business. Chapter 1 began with **The Gap,** a retail clothing establish-

[2]The bookkeeper would need to forge the endorsements of the checks and deposit them in a bank account that he controls.

ment. Chapter 2 featured **Frito-Lay** and **PepsiCo,** which are food concerns. Chapter 3 used **It's Just Lunch,** which provides a service for clients. Throughout, we have referred to Air & Sea Travel, another service provider. All these companies sell their products or services on credit and thus hold some receivables from customers.

By selling on account, and not getting cash at the point of sale, all companies run the risk of not collecting some of their receivables. In the final analysis, some customers simply do not pay the amounts they owe Frito-Lay and Oracle Corporation. The prospect that we may fail to collect from each customer provides the biggest challenge in accounting for receivables. We now turn to *uncollectible accounts,* also called *bad debts.*

Accounting for Uncollectible Accounts (Bad Debts): The Allowance Method

Selling on credit creates both a benefit and a cost:

- *The benefit:* Customers who are unwilling or unable to pay cash immediately may make a purchase on credit, and company revenues and profits rise as sales increase.
- *The cost:* The company will be unable to collect from some of its credit customers. Accountants label this cost **uncollectible-account expense, doubtful-account expense,** or **bad-debt expense.**

The extent of uncollectible-account expense varies from company to company. In certain businesses, a six-month-old receivable of $1 is worth only 67 cents, and a five-year-old receivable of $1 is worth only 4 cents. Uncollectible-account expense depends on the credit risk the business is willing to accept. At **Albany Ladder,** a $23 million construction equipment and supply firm headquartered in Albany, New York, 85% of company sales are on account. Albany's receivables grow in proportion to sales. Bad debts cost Albany Ladder about $100,000 a year, or about 1% to 1-1/2% of total sales. Albany undertakes careful credit screening and rigorous collection activity. It takes Albany Ladder an average of 70 days to collect its receivables.

For a firm that sells on credit, uncollectible-account expense is an operating expense along with salary expense and utilities expense. Uncollectible-account expense must be measured, recorded, and reported. To do so, accountants use the allowance method or, in certain limited cases, the direct write-off method (which we discuss on page 230).

The Allowance Method

Objective 3
Use the allowance method for uncollectible receivables

To present the most accurate financial statements possible, most firms use the **allowance method** to measure bad debts. This method records collection losses on the basis of estimates instead of waiting to see which customers the business will not collect from.

Rather than try to guess which accounts will go bad, managers estimate the total bad-debt expense for the period on the basis of the company's collection experience. The business records the estimated amount as Uncollectible-Account Expense and sets up **Allowance for Uncollectible Accounts** (or **Allowance for Doubtful Accounts**), a contra account related to Accounts Receivable. This allowance account shows the amount of the receivables that the business expects *not* to collect.

Subtracting the Allowance for Uncollectibles from Accounts Receivable yields the net amount that the company does expect to collect, as shown here (using assumed numbers):

Balance sheet (partial):	
Accounts receivable	$10,000
Less Allowance for uncollectible accounts	(900)
Accounts receivable, net	$ 9,100

Customers owe this company $10,000, of which it expects to collect $9,100. The company estimates that it will not collect $900 of its accounts receivable.

Another way to report these receivables follows the pattern used by Oracle Corporation, as follows:

Accounts receivable, net of allowance of $900	$9,100

 CHECK POINT 5-5

The income statement reports Uncollectible-account expense among the operating expenses, as follows (using assumed figures):

Income statement (partial):	
Expenses:	
Uncollectible-account expense	$2,000

Methods of Estimating Uncollectibles

The more accurate the estimate of uncollectible accounts, the more reliable the information in the financial statements. How are bad-debt estimates made? The most logical way to estimate uncollectibles is to examine the business's past records. There are two basic ways to estimate uncollectibles:

- *Percent-of-sales method*
- *Aging-of-accounts-receivable method*

PERCENT-OF-SALES. A **percent-of-sales method** computes uncollectible-account expense as a percentage of net credit sales. This method is also called the **income-statement approach** because it focuses on the amount of expense to be reported on the income statement. Uncollectible-account expense is recorded as an adjusting entry at the end of the period. Assume it is December 31, 20X3 and the accounts have these balances *before the year-end adjustments:*

ACCOUNTS RECEIVABLE		ALLOWANCE FOR UNCOLLECTIBLE ACCOUNTS	
120,000			**500**

Customers owe the business $120,000, and the Allowance for Uncollectible Accounts is too low. The $500 balance in the Allowance account is left over from the preceding period. Prior to any adjustments, the net receivable amount is $119,500 ($120,000 − $500), which is more than the business expects to collect from customers.

Based on prior experience, the credit department estimates that uncollectible-account expense is 1.5% of net credit sales, which were $500,000 for 20X3. The adjusting entry to record bad-debt expense for the year and to update the allowance is

(E) Expense

20X3		debit(+)	credit(−)
Dec. 31	Uncollectible-Account Expense ($500,000 × 0.015)	7,500	
	Allowance for Uncollectible Accounts		7,500
	Recorded expense for the year.		

The accounting equation shows that the transaction to record the expense decreases the business's assets by the amount of the expense:

ASSETS	=	LIABILITIES	+	STOCKHOLDERS' EQUITY	–	EXPENSES
–7,500	=	0			–	7,500

Now the accounts are ready for reporting in the 20X3 financial statements.

CHECK POINT 5-6

Accounts Receivable		Allowance for Uncollectible Accounts	
120,000			500
			7,500
			8,000

Customers still owe the business $120,000, but now the allowance for uncollectible accounts is realistic. The balance sheet will report accounts receivable at the net amount of $112,000 ($120,000 – $8,000). The income statement will report the period's uncollectible-account expense of $7,500, along with the other operating expenses for the period.

AGING OF ACCOUNTS RECEIVABLE. The second popular method for estimating uncollectible accounts is **aging-of-accounts-receivable.** This method is also called the **balance-sheet approach** because it focuses on accounts receivable. In the aging method, individual accounts receivable from specific customers are analyzed according to the length of time they have been receivable from the customer.

Computerized accounting packages prepare a report for aging accounts receivable. The computer accesses customer data and sorts accounts by customer number and by date of invoice. For example, Exhibit 5-2 shows that the credit department of Schmidt Builders Supply groups its accounts receivable into 30-day periods.

Schmidt's total balance of accounts receivable is $112,000. Of this amount, the aging schedule indicates that the company will *not* collect $3,769. But the allowance for uncollectible accounts is not yet up-to-date. Schmidt's accounts appear as follows *before the year-end adjustment:*

Accounts Receivable		Allowance for Uncollectible Accounts	
112,000			1,100

EXHIBIT 5-2
Aging the Accounts Receivable of Schmidt Builders Supply

	Age of Account				
Customer Name	*1–30 Days*	*31–60 Days*	*61–90 Days*	*Over 90 Days*	*Total Balance*
T-Bar-M Co.	$20,000				$ 20,000
Chicago Pneumatic Parts	10,000				10,000
Sarasota Pipe Corp.		$13,000	$10,000		23,000
Oneida, Inc.			3,000	$1,000	4,000
Other accounts*	39,000	12,000	2,000	2,000	55,000
Totals	$69,000	$25,000	$15,000	$3,000	$112,000
Estimated percent uncollectible	× 0.1%	× 1%	× 5%	× 90%	
Allowance for Uncollectible Accounts balance should be	$ 69 +	$ 250 +	$ 750 +	$2,700 =	$ 3,769

*Each of the "Other accounts" would appear individually.

The aging method is designed to bring the balance of the allowance account to the needed amount ($3,769), as determined by the aging schedule in Exhibit 5-2 (see the lower right corner for the final result).

To update the allowance, Schmidt makes this adjusting entry:

20X3			
Dec. 31	Uncollectible-Account Expense	2,669	
	Allowance for Uncollectible Accounts ($3,769 − $1,100)		2,669
	Recorded expense for the year.		

The recording of the expense decreases the business's assets by the amount of the expense. The accounting equation for the expense transaction is

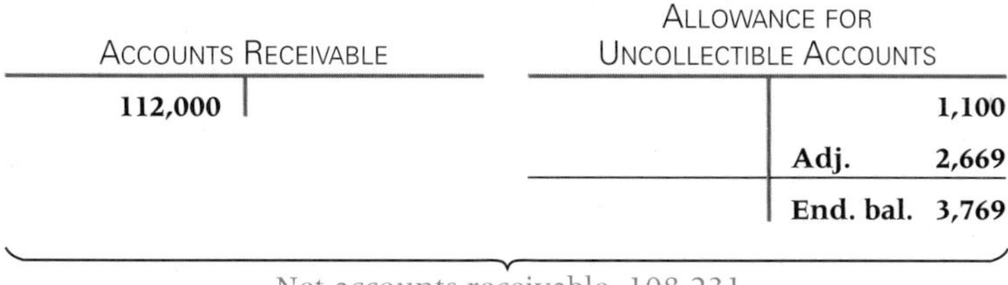

Now the balance sheet can report the amount that Schmidt expects to collect from customers, $108,231 ($112,000 − $3,769), as follows:

Accounts Receivable		Allowance for Uncollectible Accounts	
112,000			1,100
			Adj. 2,669
			End. bal. 3,769

Net accounts receivable, 108,231

As with the percent-of-sales method, the income statement reports the uncollectible-account expense.

Combining Percent-of-Sales and Aging Methods

In practice, companies use percent-of-sales and aging-of-accounts methods together.

- For *interim statements* (monthly or quarterly), companies use the percent-of-sales method because it is easier to apply. The percent-of-sales method focuses on the uncollectible-account *expense.* But that is not enough.
- At the end of the year, these companies use the aging method to ensure that Accounts Receivable is reported at *expected realizable value*—that is, the expected amount to be collected. The aging method focuses on the amount of the receivables—the *asset*—that is uncollectible.
- Using the two methods together provides good measures of both the expense and the asset. Exhibit 5-3 compares the two methods.

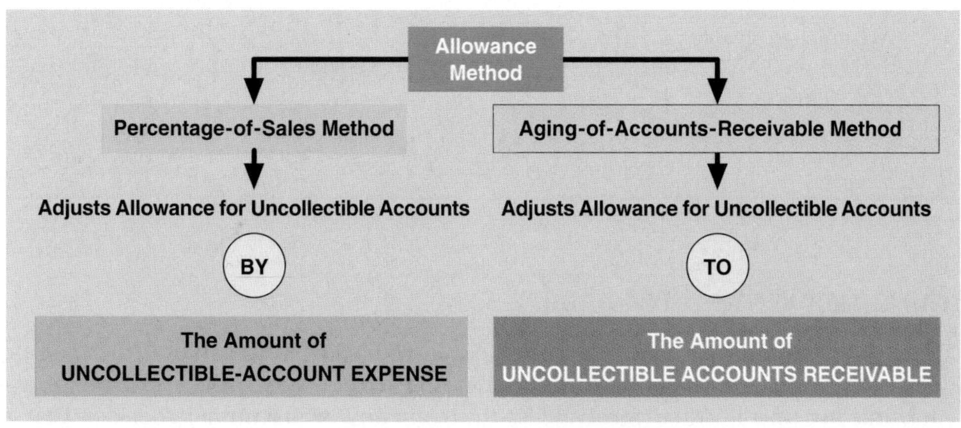

Exhibit 5-3
Comparing Percent-of-Sales and Aging Methods for Estimating Uncollectibles

WRITING OFF UNCOLLECTIBLE ACCOUNTS. Early in 20X4, Schmidt Builders Supply collects on most of its $112,000 accounts receivable as follows:

20X4			
Jan.–Mar.	Cash	92,000	
	Accounts Receivable		92,000
	Collected on account.		

Cash increases and Accounts Receivable decreases by the same amount. Total assets are unchanged:

ASSETS	=	LIABILITIES	+	STOCKHOLDERS' EQUITY
+92,000 −92,000	=	0	+	0

Suppose Schmidt's credit department determines that Schmidt cannot collect a total of $1,200 from customers Abbott and Smith. Schmidt's accountant then writes off Schmidt's receivables from the two delinquent customers with the following entry:

20X4			
Mar. 31	Allowance for Uncollectible Accounts	1,200	
	Accounts Receivable—Abbott		900
	Accounts Receivable—Smith		300
	Wrote off uncollectible accounts.		

CHECK POINT 5-7

CHECK POINT 5-8

CHECK POINT 5-9

CHECK POINT 5-10

The accounting equation shows that the write-off of uncollectible accounts has no effect on total assets or any other account:

ASSETS	=	LIABILITIES	+	STOCKHOLDERS' EQUITY
+1,200 −1,200	=	0	+	0

Because the write-off entry affects no expense account, it *does not affect net income.* The write-off has no effect on net receivables either, as shown for Schmidt Builders Supply in Exhibit 5-4.

EXHIBIT 5-4
Net Receivables Are the Same Before and After the Write-Off of Uncollectibles

	Before Write-Off		*After Write-Off*
Accounts receivable ($112,000 − $92,000)	$20,000	($20,000 − $1,200)	$18,800
Less Allowance for uncollectible accounts	(3,769)	($3,769 − $1,200)	(2,569)
Accounts receivable, net	$16,231	← same →	$16,231

The Direct Write-Off Method

There is an alternative way to account for uncollectible receivables. This method does *not* use an allowance account. Under the **direct write-off method** of accounting for uncollectible receivables, the company waits until it decides that a

CHECK POINT 5-11

ASSETS	=	LIABILITIES	+	STOCKHOLDERS' EQUITY	+	REVENUES
+ 1,045						
− 1,000	=	0			+	15
− 30						

Three aspects of these entries deserve mention:

1. Interest rates are always stated for an annual period unless they are specifically denoted otherwise. In this example, the annual interest rate is 9%. At December 31, 20X2, Continental Bank accrues interest revenue for the four months (4/12 of the year) the bank has held the note. The interest computation is

Principal	×	Interest rate	×	Time	=	Amount of Interest
$1,000	×	**.09**	×	**4/12**	=	**$30**

2. The December 31, 20X2, entry to accrue interest revenue includes a debit to Interest Receivable because the interest is in addition to the principal amount of the note. CHECK POINT 5-12
3. We often illustrate interest computations using a 360-day (12-month) year. This practice provides us with round numbers and enables us to focus on the concepts without the clutter of dollars and cents. In practice, computers eliminate the burden and use a 365-day year.

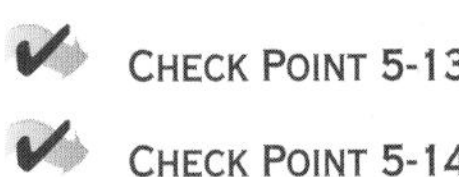
CHECK POINT 5-13
CHECK POINT 5-14

SELLING MERCHANDISE ON NOTES RECEIVABLE. Some companies sell their merchandise on notes receivable (versus selling on accounts receivable). This arrangement often occurs when the payment term extends beyond the customary accounts receivable period, which generally ranges from 30 to 60 days.

Suppose that on March 20, 20X0, **General Electric** sells household appliances for $15,000 to Dorman Builders. GE receives Dorman's 90-day promissory note at 10% annual interest. General Electric's entries to record the sale and collection from Dorman follow the pattern illustrated previously for Continental Bank and Lauren Holland, with one exception. At the outset, General Electric would credit Sales Revenue (instead of Cash) because GE is making a sale (and not lending money to Dorman).

A company may accept a note receivable from a trade customer whose account receivable is past due. The customer signs a note payable and gives it to the company. In this case, the company simply writes off the account receivable and debits a note receivable. We would say the company "received a note receivable from a customer on account."

Strategies for Speeding Up Cash Flow

All companies strive to speed up their cash receipts. Rapid cash flow improves profits because the business has cash to invest in new technology, research, and development. Instead of waiting 30, 60, or 90 days to collect receivables, companies find ways to collect cash immediately. Here are three common strategies:

- *Credit-card, or bankcard, sales.* The merchant sells merchandise and lets the customer pay with a credit card, such as **Discover** or **American Express,** or with a bankcard, such as **VISA** or **MasterCard.** To record a $100,000 sale on a VISA card, the seller may record this entry:

Cash	97,000	
Financing Expense	3,000	
Sales Revenue		100,000
Recorded bankcard sales.		

ASSETS	=	LIABILITIES	+	STOCKHOLDERS' EQUITY	+	REVENUES	−	EXPENSES
+97,000	=	0			+	$100,000	−	$3,000

The merchant deposits the VISA slip in its bank and immediately receives a discounted portion, say $97,000, of the $100,000 sale amount. VISA gets 3%, or $3,000 ($100,000 × .03 = $3,000). To the merchant, the financing expense is an operating expense similar to interest expense.

- *Selling receivables.* The company makes a normal sale on account, debiting Accounts Receivable and crediting Sales Revenue for the full $100,000. The company can then sell its accounts receivable to another business, called a *factor.* The factor earns its revenue by paying a discounted price for the receivable, say $95,000, and then hopefully collecting the full $100,000 from the customer. The benefit to the company is the immediate receipt of cash.

  To illustrate selling, or factoring, accounts receivable, let's return to Oracle Corporation's balance sheet at the beginning of the chapter (page 219). Observe that Trade receivables (same as Accounts Receivable) are Oracle's largest asset. Suppose Oracle wishes to speed up cash flow and sells $100,000 of trade receivables, and assume Oracle receives $95,000 cash. Oracle would record the sale of the receivables as follows:

Cash	95,000	
Financing Expense	5,000	
Trade (Accounts) Receivable		100,000
Sold accounts receivable.		

ASSETS	=	LIABILITIES	+	STOCKHOLDERS' EQUITY	−	EXPENSES
+95,000	=	0			−	5,000
−100,000						

  Again, financing expense is an operating expense that Oracle reports on its income statement.

- *Discounting notes receivable.* A company holding a note receivable may need cash immediately. The company can sell its note receivable at a discount. This arrangement, called *discounting a note receivable,* is similar to selling an account receivable, as in the foregoing entry. However, the credit is to Notes Receivable (instead of Accounts Receivable or Trade Receivables).

As you can see, all of these strategies enable the company to receive cash more quickly than by waiting to collect from customers.

USING ACCOUNTING INFORMATION FOR DECISION MAKING

Objective 5
Evaluate financial position with the acid-test ratio and days' sales in receivables

The balance sheet lists assets in the order of relative liquidity:

- Cash and cash equivalents
- Short-term investments
- Accounts (or trade) receivables

Oracle Corporation's balance sheet in the chapter-opening story shows the ordering of these accounts.

Acid-Test (or Quick) Ratio

In making decisions, owners and managers use some ratios based on the relative liquidity of assets. In Chapter 3, for example, we discussed the current ratio, which indicates the company's ability to pay current liabilities with current assets. A more stringent measure of the company's ability to pay current liabilities is the **acid-test** (or **quick**) **ratio:** ➛

The acid-test ratio is similar to the current ratio introduced in Chapter 3 (page 138), but it excludes inventory and prepaid expenses from the numerator.

For Oracle Corporation, 1998[3]
(Dollar amounts rounded to the nearest million)

$$\textbf{Acid-test ratio} = \frac{\textbf{Cash} + \textbf{Short-term investments} + \textbf{Net current receivables}}{\textbf{Total current liabilities}} = \frac{\$1{,}274 + \$646 + \$1{,}857}{\$2{,}484} = \textbf{1.52}$$

The higher the acid-test ratio, the better the business is able to pay its current liabilities. Oracle Corporation's acid-test ratio of 1.52 means that Oracle has $1.52 of quick assets to pay each $1 of current liabilities—a comfortable position.

Inventory, although included in the computation of the current ratio, is excluded from the acid-test ratio because it may not be easy to sell the goods. A company may have an acceptable current ratio and a poor acid-test ratio because of a large amount of inventory.

What is an acceptable acid-test ratio value? The answer depends on the industry. Automobile dealers can operate smoothly with an acid-test ratio of 0.20. They have almost no current receivables because they receive cash from customers, who borrow from banks and other lenders. In summary, car dealers need little in the way of liquid assets.

The acid-test ratio values for most department stores cluster about 0.80, while travel agencies average 1.10. In general, an acid-test ratio of 1.00 is considered safe. Oracle's ratio of 1.52 is quite high, as is that of competitor **Texas Instruments,** whose quick ratio is 1.29.

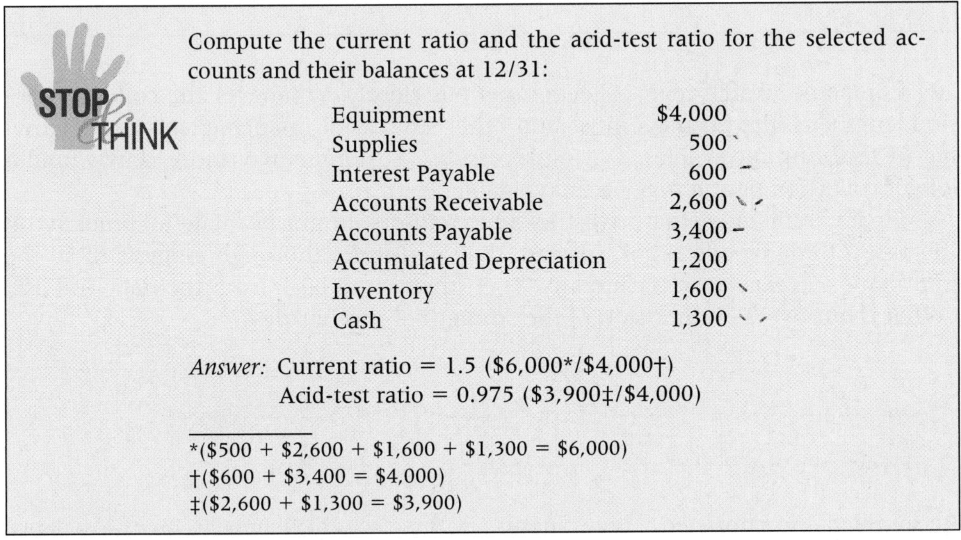

Compute the current ratio and the acid-test ratio for the selected accounts and their balances at 12/31:

Equipment	$4,000
Supplies	500
Interest Payable	600
Accounts Receivable	2,600
Accounts Payable	3,400
Accumulated Depreciation	1,200
Inventory	1,600
Cash	1,300

Answer: Current ratio = 1.5 ($6,000*/$4,000†)
Acid-test ratio = 0.975 ($3,900‡/$4,000)

*($500 + $2,600 + $1,600 + $1,300 = $6,000)
†($600 + $3,400 = $4,000)
‡($2,600 + $1,300 = $3,900)

Days' Sales in Receivables

After a business makes a credit sale, the *next* critical event in the business cycle is collection of the receivable. Several financial ratios center on receivables. **Days' sales in receivables,** also called the *average collection period,* indicates how many

[3]Taken from Oracle Corporation's 1998 balance sheet, page 219. Courtesy of Oracle Corporation.

days it takes to collect the average level of receivables. The shorter the collection period, the more quickly the organization can use cash for operations. The longer the collection period, the less cash is available to pay bills and expand. Days' sales in receivables can be computed in two steps, as follows:

For Oracle Corporation
(Dollar amounts rounded to the nearest million)

1. $\text{One day's sales} = \dfrac{\text{Net sales}}{\text{365 days}}$ $\qquad \dfrac{\$7{,}144^{4}}{365} = \$19.57 \text{ per day}$

2. $\text{Days' sales in average accounts receivable} = \dfrac{\text{Average net accounts receivable}}{\text{One day's sales}} = \dfrac{\left(\text{Beginning net receivables} + \text{Ending net receivables}\right) \div 2}{\text{One day's sales}}$

$$= \frac{(\$1{,}540 + \$1{,}857)/2}{\$19.57} = 87 \text{ days}$$

The length of the collection period depends on the credit terms of the company's sales. For example, sales on net 30 terms should be collected within approximately 30 days. When there is a discount, such as 2/10 net 30, the collection period may be shorter. Terms of net 45 or net 60 result in longer collection periods.

We discussed sales discounts in Chapter 4, page 187.

Oracle Corporation's collection period averaged 87 days during 1998. Which credit terms are more likely for Oracle's sales: net 80, or 3/30 net 80? Why?

Answer: Net 80. It takes Oracle 87 days to collect its receivables—a fact which suggests that the company does not offer discounts to customers who pay before 80 days.

Companies watch their collection periods closely. Whenever the collection period lengthens, the business must find other sources of financing, such as borrowing or factoring receivables. During recessions, customers pay more slowly, and a longer collection period may be unavoidable.

CHECK POINT 5-15

Finally, remember that investors and creditors do not evaluate a company on the basis of one or two ratios. Instead, they perform a thorough analysis of all the information available on a company. Then they stand back from the data and ask, "What is our overall impression of the strength of this business?"

Reporting Receivables and Short-Term Investment Transactions on the Statement of Cash Flows

Objective 6
Report receivables and investment transactions on the statement of cash flows

Receivables and short-term investments are assets, which appear on the balance sheet. We saw these in Oracle Corporation's balance sheet at the beginning of the chapter, and we've also seen how to report the related revenues, gains, and losses on the income statement. As we've discussed, because receivables and investment transactions affect cash, their effects must also be reported on the statement of cash flows.

Collections of receivables from customers are the most important source of cash for most companies. Collections from customers are cash receipts from *operating activities.*

[4]Taken from Oracle Corporation's 1998 income statement. Courtesy of Oracle Corporation.

EXAMPLE COMPANY **Statement of Cash Flows (Partial)** Year Ended December 31, 20XX	
Cash flows from operating activities:	
Collections from customers	$15,000
Receipts of interest	350
Receipts of dividends	150
Net cash inflow from operating activities	15,500
Cash flows from investing activities:	
Purchases of short-term investments	$ (1,400)
Sales of short-term investments	800
Loaned out money on notes receivable	(500)
Collected notes receivable	200
Net cash outflow from investing activities	(900)

EXHIBIT 5-6
Reporting the Effects of Receivables and Short-Term Investment Transactions on the Statement of Cash Flows

Exhibit 5-6 shows how the statement of cash flows can report receivables and short-term investment transactions. Each amount listed on the cash-flow statement is either a cash receipt, a positive amount, or a cash payment (a negative amount denoted by parentheses). First, let's consider the cash flows from *operating activities*. The largest amount is the cash receipt for collections from customers. Cash receipts of interest and dividends are also reported as cash flows from operating activities.

The second section of Exhibit 5-6 reports cash flows from *investing activities*. "Purchases of short-term investments . . . \$(1,400)" means that the company paid \$1,400 cash for investments during the year. "Sales of short-term investments . . . \$800" means that the company sold some short-term investments and received \$800 cash. Lending money is a cash payment for an investing activity because the company is investing in a note receivable. Collecting on a note receivable is a cash receipt for an investing activity.

 CHECK POINT 5-16

 CHECK POINT 5-17

1. During its first year of operations, Glade Corporation made credit sales of \$10,000. At the end of the year, Glade's accounts receivable total \$800. How much cash did Glade collect from customers during the year?
2. Glade's sales in its second year were \$15,000, and at year end, accounts receivable have grown to \$1,700. How much did Glade collect from customers during the second year? Ignore uncollectibles.

Answers:

1. \$9,200. Sales were \$10,000, but at year end, Glade had not collected the accounts receivable balance of \$800. Therefore, Glade must have collected \$9,200 (\$10,000 − \$800) from customers.
2. \$14,100. Early in the year, Glade collected last year's receivable balance of \$800. Sales during the second year were \$15,000, but Glade had not collected the ending receivables of \$1,700. Glade must have collected \$13,300 (\$15,000 − \$1,700) of the second year's sales. In all, Glade collected \$14,100 (\$800 + \$13,300) from customers during its second year.

(Continued)

Here is a shortcut computation—illustrated for the second year:

Cash collections = Sales for the period, $15,000 $\left\{ \begin{array}{l} \textbf{− an increase in accounts receivable, \$900} \\ \textbf{or} \\ \textbf{+ a decrease in accounts receivable} \end{array} \right.$

= $14,100

END-OF-CHAPTER

End-of-Chapter

Summary Problem for Your Review

CPC International, Inc., is the food-products company that produces Skippy peanut butter, Hellmann's mayonnaise, and Mazola corn oil. The company balance sheet at December 31, 20X7, reported:

	(In millions)
Notes and accounts receivable [total]	$549.9
Allowance for doubtful accounts	(12.5)

Required

1. How much of the December 31, 20X7, balance of notes and accounts receivable did CPC expect to collect? Stated differently, what was the expected realizable value of these receivables?

2. Journalize, without explanations, 20X8 entries for CPC International, assuming

a. Estimated Doubtful-Account Expense of $19.2 million, based on the percentage-of-sales method, all during the year.

b. Write-offs of uncollectible accounts receivable totaling $23.6 million.

c. December 31, 20X8, aging of receivables, which indicates that $15.3 million of the total receivables of $582.7 million is uncollectible at year end.

3. Show how CPC International's receivables and related allowance will appear on the December 31, 20X8, balance sheet.

4. Show what CPC International's income statement will report for the foregoing transactions.

Answers

Requirement 1

	(In millions)
Expected realizable value of receivables ($549.9 − $12.5)	$537.4

Requirement 2

a. Doubtful-Account Expense	19.2	
Allowance for Doubtful Accounts		19.2
b. Allowance for Doubtful Accounts	23.6	
Accounts Receivable.		23.6

ALLOWANCE FOR DOUBTFUL ACCOUNTS			
20X8 Write-offs	**23.6**	**Dec. 31, 20X7**	**12.5**
		20X8 Expense	**19.2**
		20X8 balance prior to December 31, 20X8	**8.1**

c. Doubtful-Account Expense ($15.3 − $8.1) 7.2
    Allowance for Doubtful Accounts 7.2

ALLOWANCE FOR DOUBTFUL ACCOUNTS	
	8.1
	7.2
	15.3

Requirement 3

	(In millions)
Notes and accounts receivable	$582.7
Allowance for doubtful accounts	(15.3)

Requirement 4

	(In millions)
Expenses: Doubtful-account expense for 20X8 ($19.2 + $7.2)	$26.4

SUMMARY OF LEARNING OBJECTIVES

1. ***Understand short-term investments.*** Short-term investments, also called *marketable securities,* are investments that a company plans to hold for one year or less. There are three types of short-term investments: held-to-maturity investments, trading investments, and available-for-sale investments. Trading investments are reported on the balance sheet at market value.

2. ***Apply internal controls to receivables.*** Businesses that sell on credit receive most of their cash receipts by mail. To ensure internal control, cash-handling duties must be separated from cash-accounting duties. A bank lockbox is often used to achieve this separation of duties.

3. ***Use the allowance method for uncollectible receivables.*** In the *percent-of-sales* method, uncollectible-account expense is estimated as a percentage of the company's net sales. Under the *aging-of-accounts-receivable* method, individual accounts are analyzed according to the length of time they have been receivable from the customer. This method adjusts Allowance for Uncollectible Accounts *to* the proper amount of uncollectible accounts receivable.

4. ***Account for notes receivable.*** *Notes receivable* are formal receivable arrangements in which the debtor signs a promissory note, agreeing to pay back both the principal borrowed plus a stated amount of interest on a certain date. To increase their cash flow, companies may discount, factor, or assign their receivables.

5. ***Evaluate financial position with the acid-test ratio and days' sales in receivables.*** The *acid-test ratio* measures a company's ability to pay current liabilities with the most liquid current assets. *Days' sales in receivables* indicates how long it takes a company to collect its average level of receivables.

6. ***Report receivables and investment transactions on the statement of cash flows.*** Because receivables and investment transactions affect cash, their effects are reported on the statement of cash flows. Collections from customers are cash receipts from *operating activities,* as are receipts of dividend and interest revenue. Purchases and sales of investments are *investing activities.*

Accounting Vocabulary

acid-test ratio (p. 235).
aging-of-accounts-receivable (p. 228).
Allowance for Doubtful Accounts (p. 226).
Allowance for Uncollectible Accounts (p. 226).
allowance method (p. 226).
available-for-sale investments (p. 220).
bad-debt expense (p. 226).
balance-sheet approach (p. 228).
creditor (p. 220).
days' sales in receivables (p. 235).
debt instrument (p. 220).
debtor (p. 220).
direct write-off method (p. 230).
doubtful-account expense (p. 226).
equity securities (p. 220).
held-to-maturity investments (p. 220).
income-statement approach (p. 227).
interest (p. 231).
marketable securities (p. 220).
maturity (p. 220).
percent-of-sales method (p. 227).
principal (p. 231).
quick ratio (p. 235).
receivable (p. 223).
securities (p. 220).
short-term investments (p. 220).
term (p. 220).
trading investments (p. 220).
uncollectible-account expense (p. 226).

Questions

1. Suppose you are the president of **Lands' End, Inc.** In general, would you be most inclined to make large investments in U.S. Treasury bills, the stock of **General Motors Corporation,** or new lines of merchandise in your main line of business? Explain your choice.

2. Describe the three categories of short-term investments. Indicate the amount to report on the balance sheet for trading investments.

3. MFS Communication, Inc., pays $100,000 to purchase Oracle stock as a short-term investment. MFS plans to hold the stock no longer than one month and hopes to sell the stock at a profit. Show how MFS will report the investment on its balance sheet, including the dollar amount, if at year end the market value of the Oracle stock is

a. $90,000 b. $107,000

Identify the category of assets in which the investment is reported and the accounts that come before and after the investment on the balance sheet.

4. Many businesses receive most of their cash on credit sales through the mail. Suppose you own a business in which you must hire employees to handle cash receipts and perform the related accounting duties. What internal control feature should you use to ensure that the cash received from customers is not taken by a dishonest employee?

5. Which of the two methods of accounting for uncollectible accounts—the allowance method or the direct write-off method—is preferable? Why?

6. Identify the accounts debited and credited to account for uncollectibles under (a) the allowance method and (b) the direct write-off method.

7. Identify and briefly describe the two ways to estimate bad-debt expense and uncollectible accounts under the allowance method.

8. Briefly describe how a company may combine both the percentage-of-sales method and the aging method to account for uncollectibles.

9. For each of the following notes receivable, compute the amount of interest revenue earned during 20X2:

	Principal	*Interest Rate*	*Interest Period*	*Maturity Date*
a. Note 1	$ 10,000	9%	60 days	11/30/20X2
b. Note 2	50,000	10%	3 months	9/30/20X2
c. Note 3	100,000	8%	18 months	12/31/20X3
d. Note 4	15,000	12%	90 days	1/15/20X3

10. Why does the payee of a note receivable usually need to make adjusting entries for interest at the end of the accounting period?

11. Show two ways to report Accounts Receivable of $100,000 and Allowance for Uncollectible Accounts of $2,800 on the balance sheet or in the related notes.

12. Why is the acid-test ratio a more stringent measure of the ability to pay current liabilities than the current ratio?

13. Which measure of days' sales in receivables is preferable, 30 or 40? Give your reason.

CHECK POINTS

CP5-1 Answer these questions about investments.

Classifying investments as current or long-term (Obj. 1)

1. Why is a trading investment always a current asset? Explain.
2. What is the amount to report for a trading investment on the balance sheet?

CP5-2 Assume **Intel Corporation** holds short-term trading investments. Suppose that on November 16, Intel paid $80,000 for a short-term trading investment in Coca-Cola stock. At December 31, the market value of the Coca-Cola stock is $81,000. For this situation, show everything that Intel would report on its December 31 balance sheet and on its income statement for the year ended December 31.

Accounting for a trading investment (Obj. 1)

CP5-3 Return to page 222 and the example of **Oracle Corporation's** short-term trading investment in **Ford Motor Company** stock.

Accounting for a trading investment (Obj. 1)

1. How much did Oracle pay for the short-term investment in Ford stock? Stated differently, what was Oracle's cost of the Ford stock?
2. Suppose the Ford stock had decreased in value to $97,000 at May 31. Make Oracle's journal entry to adjust the Short-Term Investment account to market value.
3. Show how Oracle would report the short-term investment on its balance sheet and the unrealized loss on its income statement.

CP5-4 Return to the Accounts Receivable T-accounts on page 224. Suppose Gary Bauer is the accountant responsible for these records. What duty will a good internal control system withhold from Bauer? Why?

Internal control over the collection of receivables (Obj. 2)

CP5-5 The allowance method of accounting for uncollectible receivables uses two accounts in addition to Accounts Receivable. Identify the two accounts and indicate which financial statement reports each account. Which of these is a contra account? Make up reasonable amounts to show how to report the contra account under its companion account on the balance sheet.

Applying the allowance method to account for uncollectibles (Obj. 3)

CP5-6 During its first year of operations, Zurich Film Production Company had net sales of $600,000, all on account. Industry experience suggests that Zurich's bad debts will amount to 1% of net credit sales. At December 31, 20X4, Zurich's accounts receivable total $90,000. The company uses the allowance method to account for uncollectibles.

Applying the allowance method (percent-of-sales) to account for uncollectibles (Obj. 3)

1. Make Zurich's journal entry for uncollectible-account expense using the percent-of-sales method.
2. Show how Zurich should report accounts receivable on its balance sheet at December 31, 20X4. Follow the reporting format illustrated at the top of page 227.

CP5-7 This exercise continues the situation of Check Point 5-6, in which Zurich Film Production Company ended the year 20X4 with accounts receivable of $90,000 and an allowance for uncollectible accounts of $6,000.

Applying the allowance method (percent-of-sales) to account for uncollectibles (Obj. 3)

During 20X5, Zurich Film Production Company completed the following transactions:

1. Net credit sales, $800,000
2. Collections on account, $780,000
3. Write-offs of uncollectibles, $5,000
4. Uncollectible-account expense, 1% of net credit sales

Journalize the 20X5 transactions for Zurich Film Production Company. Explanations are not required.

CP5-8 Use the solution to Check Point 5-7 to answer these questions about Zurich Film Production Company:

Applying the allowance method (percent-of-sales) to account for uncollectibles (Obj. 3)

1. Start with Accounts Receivable's beginning balance ($90,000) and then post to the Accounts Receivable T-account. How much do Zurich's customers owe the company at December 31, 20X5?
2. Start with the Allowance account's beginning credit balance ($6,000) and then post to the Allowance for Uncollectible Accounts T-account. How much of the receivables at December 31, 20X5, does Zurich expect *not* to collect?

(Continued)

3. At December 31, 20X5, how much cash does Zurich expect to collect on its accounts receivable?

4. Show what Zurich should report on its 20X5 balance sheet and income statement.

Applying the allowance method (aging-of-accounts-receivable) to account for uncollectibles (Obj. 3)

CP5-9 Guardian Medical Group started 20X0 with accounts receivable of $100,000 and an allowance for uncollectible accounts of $3,000. The 20X0 credit sales were $700,000, and cash collections on account totaled $720,000. During 20X0, Guardian wrote off uncollectible accounts receivable of $6,000. At December 31, 20X0, the aging of accounts receivable indicated that Guardian will *not* collect $2,000 of its accounts receivable.

Journalize Guardian's (a) credit sales, (b) cash collections on account, (c) write-offs of uncollectible receivables, and (d) uncollectible-account expense for the year. Explanations are not required. Prepare a T-account for Allowance for Uncollectible Accounts to show your computation of uncollectible-account expense for the year.

Applying the allowance method (aging-of-accounts-receivable) to account for uncollectibles (Obj. 3)

CP5-10 Perform the following operations for the receivables of Guardian Medical Group at December 31, 20X0.

1. Start with the beginning balances for these T-accounts:
   - Accounts Receivable, $100,000
   - Allowance for Uncollectible Accounts, $3,000

   Post the following 20X0 transactions to the T-accounts:
   a. Net credit sales of $700,000
   b. Collections on account, $720,000
   c. Write-offs of uncollectible accounts, $6,000
   d. Uncollectible-account expense (allowance method), $5,000
2. What are the ending balances of Accounts Receivable and Allowance for Uncollectible Accounts?
3. Show how Guardian will report accounts receivable on its balance sheet at December 31, 20X0. Follow the reporting format at the top of page 227.

Accounting for a note receivable (Obj. 4)

CP5-11 Metzger Bank lent $100,000 to Jean Nowlin on a 90-day, 8% note. Record the following for Metzger Bank:

a. Lending the money on May 19.

b. Collecting the principal and interest at maturity. Specify the date. For the computation of interest, use a 360-day year.

Explanations are not required.

CP5-12

Computing note receivable amounts (Obj. 4)

1. Compute the amount of interest during 20X1, 20X2, and 20X3 for the following note receivable: On April 30, 20X1, City National Bank of Cincinnati lent $1,000,000 to Marjorie Redwine on a two-year, 9% note.
2. Which party has a
   a. Note receivable? c. Interest revenue?
   b. Note payable? d. Interest expense?
3. How much in total would City National Bank collect if Redwine paid off the note early—say, on November 30, 20X1?

Accruing interest receivable and collecting a note receivable (Obj. 4)

CP5-13 Return to the promissory note in Exhibit 5-5, page 232. Assume the accounting year of Continental Bank ends on November 30, 20X2. Journalize Continental Bank's (a) lending money on the note receivable at August 31, 20X2, (b) accrual of interest at November 30, 20X2, and (c) collection of principal and interest at February 28, 20X3, the maturity date of the note.

Reporting receivables amounts (Obj. 6)

CP5-14 Using your answers to Check Point 5-13 for Continental Bank, show how the bank will report:

a. Note receivable and interest receivable on its classified balance sheet at November 30, 20X2.

b. Whatever needs to be reported on its income statement for the year ended November 30, 20X2.

c. Whatever needs to be reported for the note and related interest on its classified balance sheet at November 30, 20X3. You may ignore Cash.

d. Whatever needs to be reported on its income statement for the year ended November 30, 20X3.

CP5-15 **Cabletron Systems,** a cable TV company, reported the following items at February 28, 20X1 (amounts in millions, with 20X0 amounts also given as needed):

Using the acid-test ratio and days' sales in receivables to evaluate an actual company (Obj. 5)

Accounts payable	$ 69	Accounts receivable:	
Cash	215	February 28, 20X1	$ 235
Allowance for uncollectible		February 29, 20X0	160
accounts:		Cost of goods sold	575
February 28, 20X1	15	Short-term investments	165
February 29, 20X0	7	Other current assets	93
Inventories:		Other current liabilities	145
February 28, 20X1	198	Net sales revenue	1,406
February 29, 20X0	161	Long-term assets	416
Long-term liabilities	11		

Compute Cabletron's (a) acid-test ratio and (b) days' sales in average receivables for 20X1. Evaluate each ratio value as strong or weak. Assume Cabletron sells its goods on terms of net 45.

CP5-16 **Sprint Corporation,** the telecommunications company, included the following items in its financial statements (amounts in millions):

Reporting receivables and other accounts in the financial statements (Obj. 6)

Service revenue	$14,045	Unearned revenues	$ 200
Other assets	355	Allowance for	
Receivables, long-term	1,527	doubtful accounts	117
Cost of services sold		Cash	1,151
and other expenses	12,861	Accounts receivable	2,581
Notes payable	3,281	Accounts payable	1,027

1. Classify each item as (a) income statement or balance sheet and as (b) debit balance or credit balance.
2. How much net income did Sprint report for the year?
3. Show how Sprint reported receivables on its classified balance sheet. Follow the reporting format at the top of page 227.

CP5-17 In 20XX, Vulcan Steel Company, headquartered in Birmingham, Alabama, lent $100,000 to Taladega Mines to help Taladega extract iron ore from the ground. Later in 20XX, Vulcan collected from Taladega half of the note plus 8% interest for half the year. In addition, Vulcan received cash of $700,000 from customers on account.

Reporting cash flows from receivables transactions (Obj. 6)

Show how Vulcan Steel Company will report these cash flows on its statement of cash flows for the year ended December 31, 20XX. Include a complete heading for the statement and show cash payments in parentheses, as in Exhibit 5-6, page 237.

EXERCISES

E5-1 **Exxon,** the giant oil company, often has extra cash to invest. Suppose Exxon buys 1,000 shares of **Xerox Corporation** stock at $60 per share. Assume Exxon expects to hold the Xerox stock for one month and then sell it. The purchase occurs on December 20, 20X1. At December 31, the market price of a share of Xerox stock is $63 per share.

Accounting for a trading investment (Obj. 1)

Required

1. What type of investment is this to Exxon? Give the reason for your answer.
2. Record Exxon's purchase of the Xerox stock on December 20, and the adjustment to market value on December 31.
3. Show how Exxon would report this investment on its balance sheet at December 31, and any gain or loss on its income statement for the year ended December 31, 20X1.

Reporting a trading investment (Obj. 1, 6)

E5-2 On November 16, a company paid $48,000 for a trading investment in the stock of **Hewlett-Packard Company.** On December 12, the company received a $900 cash dividend from Hewlett-Packard. It is now December 31, and the market value of the Hewlett-Packard stock is $51,000. For this investment, show what the company should report in its income statement and balance sheet.

Accounting for a trading investment (Obj. 1)

E5-3 **Curtiss-Wright Corporation** developed the Wankel engine that thrust Mazda automobiles into prominence. Curtiss-Wright reports short-term investments on its balance sheet. Suppose Curtiss-Wright completed the following short-term investment transactions during 20X1:

20X1	
Nov. 6	Purchased 2,000 shares of Titan Corporation stock for $82,000. Curtiss-Wright plans to sell the stock at a profit in the near future.
27	Received a quarterly cash dividend of $0.85 per share on the Titan stock.
Dec. 31	Adjusted the investment in Titan stock. Current market value is $81,000, but Curtiss-Wright still plans to sell the stock at a profit early in 20X2.
20X2	
Jan. 11	Sold the Titan stock for $84,000.

Required

1. Prepare T-accounts for Cash; Short-Term Investment; Dividend Revenue; Unrealized Loss on Investment; and Gain on Sale of Investment, to show the effects of Curtiss-Wright's investment transactions. Start with a cash balance of $110,000; all the other accounts start at zero.
2. Show how Curtiss-Wright would report this investment on its balance sheets at December 31, 20X1 and 20X2, and the related revenues, gains, and losses on the 20X1 and 20X2 income statements.

Controlling cash receipts from customers (Obj. 2)

E5-4 As a recent college graduate, you land your first job in the customer collections department of Auto Accessories, Inc. Mingo Webb, one of the owners, has asked you to propose a system to ensure that cash received by mail from customers is handled properly. Draft a short memorandum identifying the essential element in your proposed plan and state why this element is important. Refer to Chapter 4 if necessary.

Reporting bad debts by the allowance method (Obj. 3)

E5-5 At December 31, 20X2, assume **Payless Shoes** has an accounts receivable balance of $137,000. Sales revenue for 20X2 is $950,000, including credit sales of $600,000. For each of the following independent situations, prepare the year-end adjusting entry to record doubtful-account expense. Show how the accounts receivable and the allowance for doubtful accounts are reported on the balance sheet. Use the reporting format of Oracle Corporation on page 219.

a. Allowance for Doubtful Accounts has a credit balance of $900 before the year-end adjustment. Payless Shoes estimates that doubtful-account expense for the year is 1/2 of 1% of credit sales.

b. Allowance for Doubtful Accounts has a debit balance of $600 before the year-end adjustment. Payless estimates that $3,400 of the accounts receivable will prove uncollectible.

Using the allowance method for bad debts (Obj. 3)

E5-6 On September 30, O'Malley Furniture Co. had a $28,000 balance in Accounts Receivable. During October, the company made sales of $137,000, which included $100,000 in credit sales. Other data include

- October collections on account were $91,000.
- Write-offs of uncollectible receivables totaled $1,070.
- Uncollectible-account expense is estimated as 2% of credit sales.
- September 30 credit balance in Allowance for Uncollectible Accounts is $1,600.

Required

1. Prepare journal entries to record sales, collections, write-offs of uncollectibles, and uncollectible-account expense by the allowance method (using the percent-of-sales approach) during October. Explanations are not required.
2. Show the ending balances in Accounts Receivable, Allowance for Uncollectible Accounts, and *Net* Accounts Receivable at October 31. How much does O'Malley expect to collect?
3. Show how O'Malley will report Accounts Receivable on its October 31 balance sheet. Use the Oracle Corporation format on page 219.

E5-7 Refer to Exercise 5-6.

Using the direct write-off method for bad debts (Obj. 3)

Required

1. Record uncollectible-account expense for October by the direct write-off method.
2. What amount of accounts receivable would O'Malley Furniture Co. report on its October 31 balance sheet under the direct write-off method? Does O'Malley expect to collect the full amount?

E5-8 At December 31, 20X1, the accounts receivable balance of First Missouri Corporation is $269,000. The allowance for doubtful accounts has a $5,910 credit balance. First Missouri prepares the following aging schedule for its accounts receivable:

Using the aging approach to estimate bad debts (Obj. 3)

Total Balance	Age of Accounts: 1–30 Days	31–60 Days	61–90 Days	Over 90 Days
$269,000	$107,000	$78,000	$69,000	$15,000
Estimated uncollectible	0.5%	1.2%	6.0%	50%

Required

1. Journalize the adjusting entry for doubtful accounts on the basis of the aging schedule. Show the T-account for the allowance.
2. Show how First Missouri will report Accounts Receivable on its December 31 balance sheet. Include the two accounts that come before receivables on the balance sheet, using assumed amounts.

E5-9 Record the following transactions in the journal of Canon Films, Inc. Round interest amounts to the nearest dollar.

Recording notes receivable and accruing interest revenue (Obj. 4)

Nov. 1	Loaned $100,000 cash to Sara Phillips on a one-year, 9% note.
Dec. 3	Sold goods to SMU, Inc., receiving a 90-day, 12% note for $3,750.
16	Received a $2,000, six-month, 12% note on account from McMaster Co.
31	Accrued interest revenue on all three notes receivable.

E5-10 Assume **Ricoh Copiers** completed these transactions:

Reporting the effects of note receivable transactions on the balance sheets, income statement, and statement of cash flow (Obj. 4)

20X3	
Apr. 1	Loaned $10,000 to Lee Franz on a one-year, 10% note.
Dec. 31	Accrued interest revenue on the Franz note.
20X4	
Apr. 1	Collected the maturity value of the note (principal plus interest) from Franz.

Show what Ricoh would report for these transactions on its 20X3 and 20X4 balance sheets, income statements, and statements of cash flows.

E5-11 **Aussie Wear, Inc.,** sells on account. When a customer account becomes three months old, Aussie Wear converts the account to a note receivable and immediately discounts the note to a bank. During 20X0, Aussie Wear completed these transactions:

Selling on notes receivable and discounting the note (Obj. 4)

Aug. 29	Sold goods on account to L. Moncrief, $4,000.
Dec. 1	Received a $4,000, 60-day, 10% note from Moncrief in satisfaction of his past-due account receivable.
1	Sold the Moncrief note by discounting it to a bank for $3,810.

Required

Record the transactions in Aussie Wear's journal.

Practical questions about receivables (Obj. 3, 4)

E5-12 Answer these questions about receivables and uncollectibles. For the true-false questions, explain why the statement is false:

1. Which receivables figure, the *total* amount that customers owe the company or the *net* amount the company expects to collect, is more interesting to investors as they consider buying the company's stock? Give your reason.
2. Show how to determine net accounts receivable. State exactly where this item is reported in the financial statements. Be very specific: statement, classification, position.
3. True or false? Credit sales increase receivables. Collections and write-offs decrease receivables.
4. True or false? The direct write-off method of accounting for uncollectibles overstates assets.
5. Stockton Bank lent $100,000 to California Company on a six-month, 6% note. Which party has interest receivable? Which party has interest payable? Interest expense? Interest revenue? How much interest will these organizations record one month after California signs the note?
6. When Stockton Bank accrues interest on the California Company note, show the directional effects on the bank's assets, liabilities, and equity (increase, decrease, or no effect). Also show the effects on California Company's assets, liabilities, and equity. For each company, indicate why its equity is affected.

Evaluating the acid-test ratio and days' sales in receivables (Obj. 5)

E5-13 **Salesman's Sample Company** reported the following amounts in its 20X6 financial statements. The 20X5 figures are given for comparison.

	20X6		*20X5*	
Current assets:				
Cash		$ 4,000		$ 9,000
Short-term investments		27,000		11,000
Accounts receivable	$80,000		$74,000	
Less Allowance for uncollectibles	(7,000)	73,000	(6,000)	68,000
Inventory		188,000		189,000
Prepaid insurance		2,000		2,000
Total current assets		294,000		279,000
Total current liabilities		101,000		107,000
Net sales		743,000		732,000

Required

1. Determine whether the acid-test ratio improved or deteriorated from 20X5 to 20X6. How does Salesman's Sample's acid-test ratio compare with the industry average of 0.90?
2. Compare the days' sales in receivables measure for 20X6 with the company's credit terms of net 30. What action, if any, should Salesman's Sample Company take?

Analyzing a company's financial statements (Obj. 5)

E5-14 **Wal-Mart Stores, Inc.,** is the largest retailer in the United States. Recently, Wal-Mart reported these figures in millions of dollars:

	1999	*1998*
Net sales	$137,634	$117,958
Receivables at end of year	1,118	976

The Wal-Mart financial statements include no uncollectible-account expense or allowance for uncollectibles.

Required

1. Compute Wal-Mart's average collection period on receivables during 1999.

2. Why are Wal-Mart's receivables so low? How can Wal-Mart have $1,118 million of receivables at January 31, 1999, and no significant allowance for uncollectibles?

E5-15 Nature Fresh, Inc., is a manufacturer of cosmetics, specializing in products for sensitive skin. During 20X0, Nature Fresh's net income reached $110 million on sales of $907 million, and Nature Fresh collected $887 million from customers.

Reporting receivables and investment transactions on the statement of cash flows (Obj. 6)

Sales and collections left the company with excess cash during the year, so the company invested $48 million in 90-day U.S. Treasury bills. Nature Fresh cashed in $46 million of the T-bills during the year. During 20X0, Nature Fresh earned interest revenue of $8.3 million. Of this amount, the company expects to collect the final $1.3 million early in 20X1 when the T-bills mature.

Required

Show what Nature Fresh, Inc., will report on its 20X0 cash-flow statement as a result of these transactions.

CHALLENGE EXERCISE

E5-16 Barry's Coffee Company, an importer of Colombian coffee, sells on credit and manages its own receivables. Average experience for the past three years has been as follows:

Determining whether to sell on bank cards (Obj. 2)

	Cash	*Credit*	*Total*
Sales	$200,000	$150,000	$350,000
Cost of goods sold	120,000	90,000	210,000
Uncollectible-account expense	—	4,000	4,000
Other expenses	34,000	27,000	61,000

Barry Christian, the owner, is considering whether to accept bank cards (VISA, MasterCard). He expects total sales to increase by 10%. If Barry's switches to bank cards, the business can save $2,000 on accounting and other expenses, but VISA and MasterCard charge 2% on bank-card sales. Christian figures that the increase in sales will be due to the increased volume of bank-card sales.

Required

Should Barry's Coffee Company start selling on bank cards? Show the computations of net income under the present plan and under the bank-card plan.

PROBLEMS

(Group A)

P5-1A During the fourth quarter of 20X0, the operations of Lybrand Canoe Company generated excess cash, which the company invested in securities, as follows:

Accounting for a trading investment (Obj. 1)

Nov. 2	Purchased 2,000 shares of common stock as a trading investment, paying $12.75 per share.
21	Received semiannual cash dividend of $0.45 per share on the trading investment.
Dec. 31	Adjusted the trading investment to its market value of $28,000.

Required

1. Prepare T-accounts for: Cash, balance of $400,000; Short-Term Investment; Dividend Revenue; Unrealized Gain on Investment.
2. Journalize the foregoing transactions and post to the T-accounts.
3. Show how to report the short-term investments on Lybrand's balance sheet at December 31.
4. Show how to report the dividend revenue and the unrealized gain on Lybrand's income statement.

Controlling cash receipts from customers (Obj. 2)

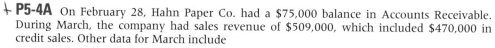

P5-2A Gunflint Outfitters distributes merchandise to sporting goods stores. All sales are on credit, so virtually all cash receipts arrive in the mail. Benjamin Nadir, the company president, has just returned from a trade association meeting with new ideas for the business. Among other things, Nadir plans to institute stronger internal controls over cash receipts from customers.

Required

Assume you are Benjamin Nadir, the company president. Write a memo to employees outlining a set of procedures to ensure that all cash receipts are deposited in the bank and that the total amounts of each day's cash receipts are posted as credits to customer accounts receivable.

Accounting for revenue, collections, and uncollectibles; %-of-sales method (Obj. 3)

P5-3A This problem takes you through the accounting for service revenue, accounts receivable, and uncollectible receivables for **America Online, Inc.,** the Internet service company. AOL sells its Internet services for cash and on account. By selling on credit, AOL cannot expect to collect 100% of its accounts receivable. At June 30, 1999, and June 30, 1998, respectively, AOL reported the following accounts receivable on its balance sheet (all amounts in millions of dollars):

	June 30,	
	1999	***1998***
Accounts receivable	$377	$226
Less Allowance for uncollectibles	(54)	(34)
Accounts receivable, net	$323	$192

During the year ended June 30, 1999, AOL earned service revenue of $4,777 million and collected cash of $4,455 million from customers. Assume uncollectible-account expense for the year was 4% of service revenue and that AOL wrote off uncollectible accounts receivable totaling $171 million. At year end AOL ended with the foregoing June 30, 1999, balances.

Required

1. Prepare T-accounts for Accounts Receivable and Allowance for Uncollectibles, and insert the June 30, 1998, balances as given.

2. Journalize the following transactions of AOL for the year ended June 30, 1999 (explanations are not required):

a. Service revenue on account, $4,777 million.

b. Collections on account, $4,455 million.

c. Uncollectible-account expense, 4% of service revenue (round to the nearest $1 million).

d. Write-offs of uncollectible accounts receivable, $171 million.

3. Post your entries to the Accounts Receivable and Allowance for Uncollectibles T-accounts that you created in Requirement 1.

4. Compute the ending balances for the two T-accounts and compare your balances to the actual June 30, 1999, amounts. They should be the same.

5. At June 30, 1999, how much did customers owe AOL? How much did AOL expect to collect from customers?

6. Show what AOL would report on its income statement for the year ended June 30, 1999, for the foregoing facts.

Accounting for uncollectibles by the direct write-off and allowance methods (Obj. 3)

P5-4A On February 28, Hahn Paper Co. had a $75,000 balance in Accounts Receivable. During March, the company had sales revenue of $509,000, which included $470,000 in credit sales. Other data for March include

- Collections on accounts receivable, $431,600
- Write-offs of uncollectible receivables, $6,500

Required

1. The unadjusted balance in Allowance for Uncollectible Accounts is $800 (debit). Uncollectible-Account Expense is estimated at 2% of credit sales. Record uncollectible-account expense and write-offs of customer accounts for March by the *allowance method.* Show all March activity in Accounts Receivable, Allowance for Uncollectible Accounts, and Uncollectible-Account Expense.

2. What amount of uncollectible-account expense will Hahn report on its March income statement? What amount of *net* accounts receivable will Hahn report on its March 31 balance sheet?
3. How will what you learned about uncollectible receivables help you manage a business?

P5-5A The June 30, 20X2, balance sheet of Burdette Silver Corporation reports the following:

Using the percent-of-sales and aging approaches for uncollectibles (Obj. 3)

Accounts Receivable.	$265,000
Allowance for Doubtful Accounts (credit balance)	(7,100)

At the end of each quarter, Burdette estimates doubtful-account expense to be 2% of credit sales. At the end of the year, the company ages its accounts receivable and adjusts the balance in Allowance for Doubtful Accounts to correspond to the aging schedule. During the second half of 20X2, Burdette completed the following selected transactions:

20X2

July 14	Made a compound entry to write off the following uncollectible accounts: Black & Lux, Inc., $766; TimeSaver Co., $2,413; and Twilley & Associates, $134.
Sept. 30	Recorded doubtful-account expense based on credit sales of $141,400.
Nov. 22	Wrote off the following accounts receivable as uncollectible: Monet Corp., $1,345; Blocker, Inc., $2,109; and M Street Plaza, $755.
Dec. 31	Adjusted the Allowance for Doubtful Accounts and recorded doubtful-account expense at year end, based on the following aging of accounts receivable:

	Age of Accounts			
Total Balance	*1–30 Days*	*31–60 Days*	*61–90 Days*	*Over 90 Days*
$296,600	$161,500	$86,000	$34,000	$15,100
Estimated uncollectible	0.2%	1.0%	4.0%	50.0%

Required

1. Record the transactions in the journal. Explanations are not required.
2. Open the Allowance for Doubtful Accounts and post entries affecting that account. Keep a running balance.
3. Most companies report two-year comparative financial statements. Show how Burdette will report its accounts receivable in a comparative balance sheet for 20X2 and 20X1. Use the reporting format at the top of page 227. At December 31, 20X1, the Burdette Accounts Receivable balance was $271,400 and the Allowance for Doubtful Accounts stood at $6,700.

P5-6A Assume that **Jones-Blair Co.,** a major paint manufacturer, completed the following selected transactions:

Uncollectibles, notes receivable, and accrued interest revenue (Obj. 3, 4)

20X4

Dec. 1	Sold goods to Kelly Moore Paint Co., receiving a $24,000, three-month, 10% note.
31	Made an adjusting entry to accrue interest on the Kelly Moore note.
31	Made an adjusting entry to record doubtful-account expense based on an aging of accounts receivable. The aging analysis indicates that $355,800 of accounts receivable will not be collected. Prior to this adjustment, the credit balance in Allowance for Doubtful Accounts is $339,100.

20X5

Feb. 18	Received a 90-day, 10%, $5,000 note from Altex Co. on account.
Mar. 1	Collected the maturity value of the Kelly Moore note.
8	Sold the Altex note to First State Bank, receiving cash of $4,619.
Nov. 11	Loaned $50,000 cash to Consolidated, Inc., receiving a 90-day, 9% note.
Dec. 31	Accrued the interest on the Consolidated, Inc., note.

Required

Record the transactions in the journal. Explanations are not required.

Using ratio data to evaluate a company's financial position (Obj. 5)

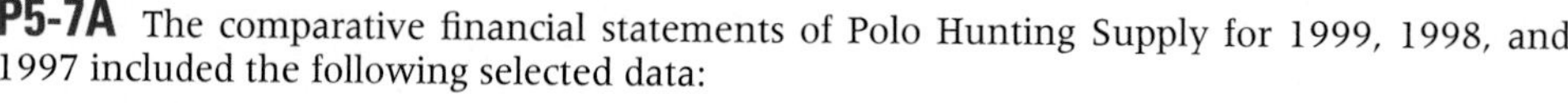

P5-7A The comparative financial statements of Polo Hunting Supply for 1999, 1998, and 1997 included the following selected data:

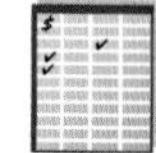

	1999	1998	1997
		(In millions)	
Balance sheet:			
Current assets:			
Cash	$ 27	$ 26	$ 22
Short-term investments	93	101	69
Receivables, net of allowance for doubtful accounts of $7, $6, and $4, respectively	176	154	127
Inventories	408	383	341
Prepaid expenses	32	31	25
Total current assets	736	695	584
Total current liabilities	440	446	388
Income statement:			
Net sales	$3,071	$2,505	$1,944
Cost of sales	1,380	1,360	963

Required

1. Compute these ratios for 1999 and 1998:
   a. Current ratio
   b. Acid-test ratio
   c. Days' sales in receivables
2. Write a memo explaining to top management which ratio values showed improvement from 1998 to 1999 and which ratio values deteriorated. State whether this trend is favorable or unfavorable for the company and give the reason for your evaluation.

(Group B)

Accounting for a trading investment (Obj. 1)

P5-1B During the fourth quarter of 20X1, Four Seasons, Inc., generated excess cash, which the company invested in securities, as follows:

Oct. 3	Purchased 5,000 shares of common stock as a trading investment, paying $9.25 per share.
14	Received cash dividend of $0.32 per share on the trading investment.
Dec. 31	Adjusted the trading investment to its market value of $45,500.

Required

1. Prepare T-accounts for: Cash, balance of $400,000; Short-Term Investment; Dividend Revenue; Unrealized (Loss) on Investment.
2. Journalize the foregoing transactions and post to the T-accounts.
3. Show how to report the short-term investment on the Four Seasons balance sheet at December 31.
4. Show how to report the dividend revenue and the unrealized (loss) on Four Seasons' income statement.

Controlling cash receipts from customers (Obj. 2)

P5-2B The Smile Center, a dental laboratory, prepares crowns, dentures, and other dental appliances. All work is performed on account, with monthly billing to participating dentists. Mark Sharp, accountant for The Smile Center, receives and opens the mail. Company procedure requires Sharp to separate customer checks from the remittance slips, which list the amounts that Sharp posts as credits to customer accounts receivable. Sharp deposits the checks in the bank. At the end of each day he computes the day's total amount posted to customer accounts and matches this total to the bank deposit slip. This procedure is intended to ensure that all receipts are deposited in the bank.

Required

As a consultant hired by The Smile Center, write a memo to management evaluating the company's internal controls over cash receipts from customers. If the system is effective, identify its strong features. If the system has flaws, propose a way to strengthen the controls.

Accounting for revenue, collections, and uncollectibles; %-of-sales method (Obj. 3)

P5-3B This problem takes you through the accounting for sales revenue, accounts receivable, and uncollectible receivables for **Pier 1 Imports, Inc.,** the specialty retailer. Pier 1 Imports, Inc. sells a variety of imported goods. By selling on credit, Pier 1 cannot expect to collect 100% of its accounts receivable. At February 28, 1998, and February 28, 1997, respectively (as adapted), Pier 1 Imports reported the following accounts receivable on its balance sheet (all amounts in thousands of dollars):

	February 28, 1998	February 28, 1997
Accounts receivable	$12,780	$4,395
Less Allowance for uncollectibles	(142)	(267)
Accounts receivable, net	$12,638	$4,128

During the year ended February 28, 1998, Pier 1 earned sales revenue of $1,075,405 thousand and collected cash of $1,056,141 thousand from customers. Assume uncollectible-account expense for the year was 1% of sales revenue and that Pier 1 wrote off uncollectible accounts receivable totaling $10,879 thousand. At year end Pier 1 ended with the foregoing February 28, 1998, balances.

Required

1. Prepare T-accounts for Accounts Receivable and Allowance for Uncollectibles and insert the February 28, 1997, balances as given.
2. Journalize the following transactions of Pier 1 Imports for the year ended February 28, 1998 (explanations are not required):
   a. Sales revenue on account, $1,075,405 thousand.
   b. Collections on account, $1,056,141 thousand.
   c. Uncollectible-account expense, 1% of sales revenue (round to the nearest $1 thousand).
   d. Write-offs of uncollectible accounts receivable, $10,879 thousand.
3. Post your entries to the Accounts Receivable and Allowance for Uncollectibles T-accounts that you created in Requirement 1.
4. Compute the ending balances for the two T-accounts and compare your balances to the actual February 28, 1998, amounts. They should be the same.
5. At February 28, 1998, how much did customers owe Pier 1 Imports? How much did Pier 1 expect to collect from customers?
6. Show what Pier 1 Imports would report on its income statement for the year ended February 28, 1998, for the foregoing facts.

Accounting for uncollectibles by the direct write-off and allowance methods (Obj. 3)

P5-4B On May 31, Marcus, Inc., had a $219,000 balance in Accounts Receivable. During June, the company had sales revenue of $789,000, which included $650,000 in credit sales. Other data for June include

- Collections on accounts receivable, $681,400
- Write-offs of uncollectible receivables, $8,900

Required

1. The unadjusted balance in Allowance for Uncollectible Accounts is $2,800 (credit). Uncollectible-Account Expense is estimated at 2% of credit sales. Record uncollectible-account expense and write-offs of customer accounts for June by the *allowance method.* Show all June activity in Accounts Receivable, Allowance for Uncollectible Accounts, and Uncollectible-Account Expense.
2. What amount of uncollectible-account expense will Marcus, Inc., report on its June income statement? What amount of *net* accounts receivable will Marcus, Inc., report on its June 30 balance sheet?
3. How will what you have learned about uncollectible receivables help you manage a business?

Using the percent-of-sales and aging approaches for uncollectibles
(Obj. 3)

P5-5B The June 30, 20X4, balance sheet of Swiss Tool Company reports the following:

Accounts Receivable	$143,000
Allowance for Doubtful Accounts (credit balance).	(3,200)

At the end of each quarter, Swiss Tool estimates doubtful-account expense to be 1 1/2% of credit sales. At the end of the year, the company ages its accounts receivable and adjusts the balance in Allowance for Doubtful Accounts to correspond to the aging schedule. During the second half of 20X4, the company completed the following selected transactions:

20X4	
July 31	Made a compound entry to write off the following uncollectible accounts: Zeff, Inc., $235; Khaki Co., $688; and L. Chino, $706.
Sept. 30	Recorded doubtful-account expense based on credit sales of $130,000.
Nov. 18	Wrote off as uncollectible the $767 account receivable from Bliss Co. and the $430 account receivable from Micro Data.
Dec. 31	Adjusted the Allowance for Doubtful Accounts and recorded doubtful-account expense at year end, based on the following aging of accounts receivable.

	Age of Accounts			
Total Balance	***1–30 Days***	***31–60 Days***	***61–90 Days***	***Over 90 Days***
$129,400	$74,600	$31,100	$14,000	$9,700
Estimated uncollectible	0.1%	0.8%	5.0%	30.0%

Required

1. Record the transactions in the journal. Explanations are not required.
2. Open the Allowance for Doubtful Accounts and post entries affecting that account. Keep a running balance.
3. Most companies report two-year comparative financial statements. Show how Swiss Tool will report its accounts receivable on a comparative balance sheet for 20X4 and 20X3. Use the reporting format at the top of page 227. At December 31, 20X3, Swiss Tool Company's Accounts Receivable balance was $112,000 and the Allowance for Doubtful Accounts stood at $2,700.

Uncollectibles, notes receivable, and accrued interest revenue
(Obj. 3, 4)

P5-6B Assume that **Del Monte Foods,** famous for its canned vegetables, completed the following selected transactions:

20X5	
Nov. 1	Sold goods to Kroger, Inc., receiving a $24,000, three-month, 6% note.
Dec. 31	Made an adjusting entry to accrue interest on the Kroger note.
31	Made an adjusting entry to record doubtful-account expense based on an aging of accounts receivable. The aging analysis indicates that $197,400 of accounts receivable will not be collected. Prior to this adjustment, the credit balance in Allowance for Doubtful Accounts is $193,900.
20X6	
Feb. 1	Collected the maturity value of the Kroger note.
23	Received a 90-day, 15%, $4,000 note from Bliss Co. on account.
Mar. 31	Sold the Bliss Co. note to Lakewood Bank, receiving cash of $3,810.
Nov. 16	Loaned $15,000 cash to McNeil, Inc., receiving a 90-day, 12% note.
Dec. 31	Accrued the interest on the McNeil, Inc., note.

Required

Record the transactions in the journal. Explanations are not required.

P5-7B The comparative financial statements of Valentini Clothiers, Inc., for 1999, 1998, and 1997 included the following selected data.

Using ratio data to evaluate a company's financial position (Obj. 5)

	1999	1998	1997
		(In millions)	
Balance sheet:			
Current assets:			
Cash	$ 76	$ 80	$ 60
Short-term investments	140	174	122
Receivables, net of allowance for doubtful accounts of $6, $6, and $5, respectively	257	265	218
Inventories	389	341	302
Prepaid expenses	21	27	46
Total current assets	883	887	748
Total current liabilities	503	528	413
Income statement:			
Net sales	$5,489	$4,995	$4,206
Cost of sales	2,734	2,636	2,418

Required

1. Compute these ratios for 1999 and 1998:
   a. Current ratio
   b. Acid-test ratio
   c. Days' sales in receivables
2. Write a memo explaining to top management which ratio values improved from 1998 to 1999 and which ratio values deteriorated. State whether this trend is favorable or unfavorable and give the reason for your evaluation.

Extending Your Knowledge

Decision Cases

Case 1. Manatech Health Foods sells to health food stores either for cash or on notes receivable. The business uses the direct write-off method to account for bad debts. Margaret Barzoukas, the owner, has prepared the company's financial statements. The most recent comparative income statements, for 20X2 and 20X1, follow:

Uncollectible accounts and evaluating a business (Obj. 3, 4)

	20X2	20X1
Total revenue	$220,000	$195,000
Total expenses	157,000	143,000
Net income	$ 63,000	$ 52,000

On the basis of the increase in net income, Barzoukas seeks to expand operations. She asks you to invest $50,000 in the business. From Barzoukas you learn that notes receivable from customers were $200,000 at the end of 20X0 and $400,000 at the end of 20X1. Also, total revenues for 20X2 and 20X1 include interest at 10% on the year's beginning notes receivable balance. Total expenses include doubtful-account expense of $2,000 each year, based on the direct write-off method. Barzoukas estimates that doubtful-account expense would be 5% of sales revenue if the allowance method were used.

Required

1. Prepare for Manatech Health Foods a comparative single-step income statement that identifies service revenue, interest revenue, doubtful-account expense, and other expenses, all computed in accordance with generally accepted accounting principles.
2. Consider whether sales revenue or interest revenue caused net income to increase during 20X2. Is Manatech's future as promising as Barzoukas' income statement makes it appear? Give the reason for your answer.

Estimating the collectibility of accounts receivable (Obj. 4)

Case 2. Assume that you work in the corporate loan department of Boston 1st Bank. Lane DuPont, owner of DuPont Mobile Homes, has come to you seeking a loan for $1 million to expand operations. DuPont proposes to use accounts receivable as collateral for the loan and has provided you with the following information from the company's most recent financial statements:

	20X4	*20X3*	*20X2*
	(In thousands)		
Sales	$1,475	$1,589	$1,502
Cost of goods sold	876	947	905
Gross profit	599	642	597
Other expenses	518	487	453
Net profit or (loss) before taxes	$ 81	$ 155	$ 144
Accounts receivable	$ 458	$ 387	$ 374
Allowance for doubtful accounts	23	31	29

Required

1. What analysis would you perform on the information DuPont has provided? Would you grant the loan on the basis of this information? Give your reason.
2. What additional information would you request from DuPont? Give your reason.
3. Assume that DuPont provided you with the information requested in Requirement 2. What would make you change the decision you made in Requirement 1?

ETHICAL ISSUE

E-Z Finance Company is in the consumer loan business. It borrows from banks and loans out the money at higher interest rates. E-Z's bank requires E-Z to submit quarterly financial statements in order to keep its line of credit. E-Z's main asset is Notes Receivable. Therefore, Uncollectible-Account Expense and Allowance for Uncollectible Accounts are important accounts.

Alicia Johnston, the company's owner, likes net income to increase in a smooth pattern, rather than increase in some periods and decrease in other periods. To report smoothly increasing net income, Johnston underestimates Uncollectible-Account Expense in some periods. In other periods, Johnston overestimates the expense. She reasons that the income overstatements roughly offset the income understatements over time.

Required

Is E-Z's practice of smoothing income ethical? Why or why not?

Financial Statement Cases

Case 1. **Eastman Kodak Company** reported these figures in a recent annual report:

Accounts receivable and cash flows (Obj. 6)

	Millions	
	19X7	*19X6*
From the income statement:		
Sales	$14,538	$15,968
From the balance sheet:		
Receivables	2,271	2,738
From the notes to the financial statements:		
Receivables are net of allowances of	112	90

Required

1. At year end 19X6 and at year end 19X7, how much did Eastman Kodak's customers owe the company? At each date how much did Eastman Kodak expect *not* to collect? How much did Eastman Kodak expect *to* collect?
2. Prepare T-accounts for Receivables and Allowances. In each account, write the description in words (no dollar amounts) of each item that appears in the account. Examples to start:

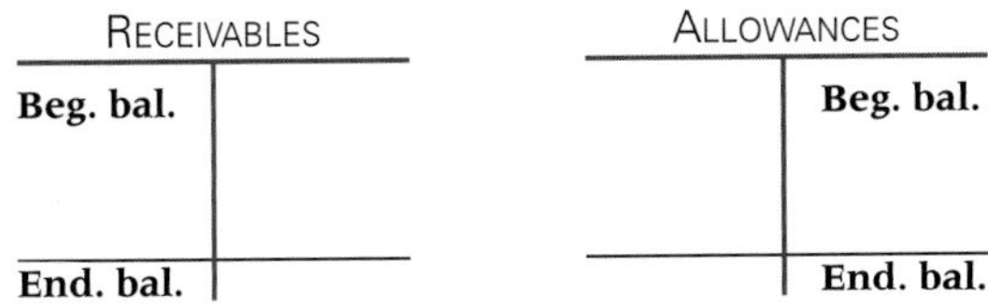

3. Assume that Eastman Kodak recorded uncollectible-account expense of $156 million during 19X7. How much were write-offs of uncollectible receivables during 19X7? Use the Allowances T-account you prepared for Requirement 2.
4. Compute the amount of cash that Eastman Kodak collected on account during 19X7. (Eastman Kodak could report this amount as "Collections from customers" on its statement of cash flows for 19X7.) Use the Receivables T-account you prepared for Requirement 2.

Case 2. Obtain the annual report of a company of your choosing.

Accounts receivable, uncollectibles, and notes receivable (Obj. 3, 4)

Required

1. How much did customers owe the company at the end of the current year? Of this amount, how much did the company expect to collect? How much did the company expect *not* to collect?
2. Assume that during the current year, the company recorded doubtful-account expense equal to 1% of net sales. Starting with the beginning balance, analyze the Allowance for Doubtful Accounts to determine the amount of the receivable write-offs during the current year.
3. If the company does not have notes receivable, you may skip this requirement. If notes receivable are present at the end of the current year, assume that their interest rate is 9%. Assume also that the company received no new notes receivable during the following year. Journalize these transactions, which took place during the following year:
   a. Received cash for 75% of the interest revenue earned during the year.
   b. Accrued the remaining portion of the interest revenue earned during the year.
   c. At year end, collected half the notes receivable.

Group Project

Rachel Joseph and Leah Jacobs worked for several years as sales representatives for **Xerox Corporation.** During this time, they became close friends as they acquired expertise with the company's full range of copier equipment. Now they see an opportunity to put their experience to work and fulfill lifelong desires to establish their own business. Navarro Community College, located in their city, is expanding, and there is no copy center within five miles of the campus. Business in the area is booming, office buildings and apartments are springing up, and the population of the Taft section of the city is growing.

Joseph and Jacobs want to open a copy center, similar to a Kinko's, near the Navarro campus. A small shopping center across the street from the college has a vacancy that would fit their needs. Joseph and Jacobs each have $35,000 to invest in the business, but they forecast the need for $200,000 to renovate the store and purchase some of the equipment they will need. Xerox Corporation will lease two large copiers to them at a total monthly rental of $6,000. With enough cash to see them through the first six months of operation, they are confident they can make the business succeed. The two women work very well together, and both have excellent credit ratings. Joseph and Jacobs must borrow $130,000 to start the business, advertise its opening, and keep it running for its first six months.

Required

Assume two roles: (1) Joseph and Jacobs, the partners who will own Navarro Copy Center; and (2) loan officers at Synergy Bank.

1. As a group, visit a copy center to familiarize yourselves with its operations. If possible, interview the manager or another employee. Then write a loan request that Joseph and Jacobs will submit to Synergy Bank with the intent of borrowing $130,000 to be paid back over three years. The loan will be a personal loan to the partnership of Joseph and Jacobs, not to Navarro Copy Center. The request should specify all the details of Joseph's and Jacobs' plan that will motivate the bank to grant the loan. Include a budget for each of the first six months of operation of the proposed copy center.
2. As a group, interview a loan officer in a bank. Write Synergy Bank's reply to the loan request. Specify all the details that the bank should require as conditions for making the loan.
3. If necessary, modify the loan request or the bank's reply in order to reach agreement between the two parties.

Internet Exercise

Microsoft

This chapter reported Oracle as the world's second largest software company. So which company is number one? **Microsoft.** Microsoft was added to the Dow Jones Industrial Average in November of 1999. Technology stocks such as Oracle, Microsoft, and Intel greatly influence our current economy.

1. Go to **http://www.microsoft.com/msft.** Click on the most recent *annual report* followed by *Start>*. Use the "Read Financial Review" scroll bar and select "Financial Highlights." Review the historical information presented for (1) revenue, (2) net income, (3) cash and short-term investments, and (4) total assets. Comment on the trends and what the trends of each might indicate.
2. Use the same scroll bar to select the financial statements and notes needed to answer the following questions.
3. For the most recent year, identify the amount reported as *investment income* on the income statement. What types of income are classified as investment income? Has this amount increased or decreased compared to the previous year? Does investment income increase net income? Is investment income included as part of operating income? Explain why or why not.
4. For the most recent year, identify the amount reported for *cash and short-term investments.* Why are these investments classified as short-term? Refer to the notes and list the five different types of short-term investments. (Note #2 in 1999.)

5. For the most recent year, identify the amount reported for *equity and other investments*. Refer to the notes and list the cost, net unrealized gain, and market value of these investments. (Note #3 in 1999.) Does the amount reported on the balance sheet for these investments reflect their cost or market value? Explain *net unrealized gain*.
6. For the two most recent years, calculate the *acid-test ratio*. Comment on the value of the ratio and what the ratio value indicates about the company's ability to pay its current liabilities. For the most recent year, calculate *days' sales in receivables*.

6 Merchandise Inventory, Cost of Goods Sold, and Gross Profit

Learning Objectives

After studying this chapter, you should be able to

1. Use the cost-of-goods-sold model
2. Apply the various inventory methods: specific unit cost, weighted-average, FIFO, and LIFO
3. Identify the income effects and the tax effects of the inventory methods
4. Measure the effects of inventory errors on cost of goods sold and net income
5. Use the gross profit percentage and the rate of inventory turnover to evaluate a business
6. Account for inventory transactions
7. Estimate inventory by the gross profit method

Deckers Outdoor Corporation
Balance Sheets (Adapted)
December 31, 1998 and 1997

	Thousands	
Assets	*1998*	*1997*
Current assets:		
Cash and cash equivalents	$ 263	$ 3,238
Trade accounts receivable, less allowance for doubtful accounts of $1,204 and $1,092 as of December 31, 1998 and 1997, respectively	27,180	23,037
Inventories	23,665	18,979
Prepaid expenses and other current assets	8,201	3,547
Total current assets	59,309	48,801
Property and equipment, at cost, net	2,994	2,509
Intangible assets, less accumulated amortization	20,702	21,866
Note receivable, long-term	782	966
Other assets, net	586	551
	$84,373	$74,693
Liabilities and Stockholders' Equity		
Current liabilities:		
Notes payable	$ —	$ 2,000
Current installments of long-term debt	6,236	107
Trade accounts payable	7,947	3,629
Accrued bonuses	66	1,095
Other accrued expenses	2,925	2,726
Income taxes payable		22
Total current liabilities	17,174	9,579
Long-term debt, less current installments	15,199	7,983
Commitments and contingencies		
Stockholders' equity	52,000	57,131
	$84,373	$74,693

DECKERS Outdoor Corporation began when University of California at Santa Barbara student Doug Otto started making sandals. Deckers has grown into an international company with footwear brands Teva and Simple and clothing lines Teva and Picante. (Teva is a play off the Hebrew word *Teh'-vah* for *nature.*) Teva sandals were initially designed for river rafting by a Grand Canyon river guide. Their quality and stability soon touched off a small revolution in footwear.

Deckers Outdoor Corporation had sales over $100 million in 1998, and the company's assets total $84.3 million, as shown in the accompanying balance sheet. As the company has grown, Doug Otto has faced a number of accounting decisions, including which method to use for the merchandise inventory of sandals and clothing (listed simply as Inventories . . . $23.7 million on the balance sheet). This chapter discusses how to manage and account for inventory—the most important asset of a merchandising business.

Inventory is the lifeblood of a merchandising company—its most important asset. The entity's major expense is **cost of goods sold** or **cost of sales,** the cost of the inventory that the business has sold to customers. For example, in 1998 Deckers reported cost of goods sold at $65.6 million, which far exceeded selling, general, and administrative expenses.

Accounting plays an important role in merchandising. The most obvious role is the recordkeeping required to stay abreast of quantities on hand in order to meet customer demand. Beyond that, there are several different methods of accounting for the cost of inventories. The choice of an inventory method can have a direct effect on income taxes, which in turn affect the company's cash flows. In short, accounting for inventory goes far beyond recordkeeping.

We begin this chapter by showing how the income statement and the balance sheet of a service company and a merchandiser are both similar and different. Then we move into the costs that go into inventory, followed by the basic concept of accounting for inventories.

Transition from Service Entities to Merchandisers

Chapters 1–5 have used both service entities and merchandisers to illustrate key accounting concepts. Chapter 6 steps into the world of merchandising with both feet. As you make this transition, the following summarized financial statements will show how the two types of companies are similar and different:

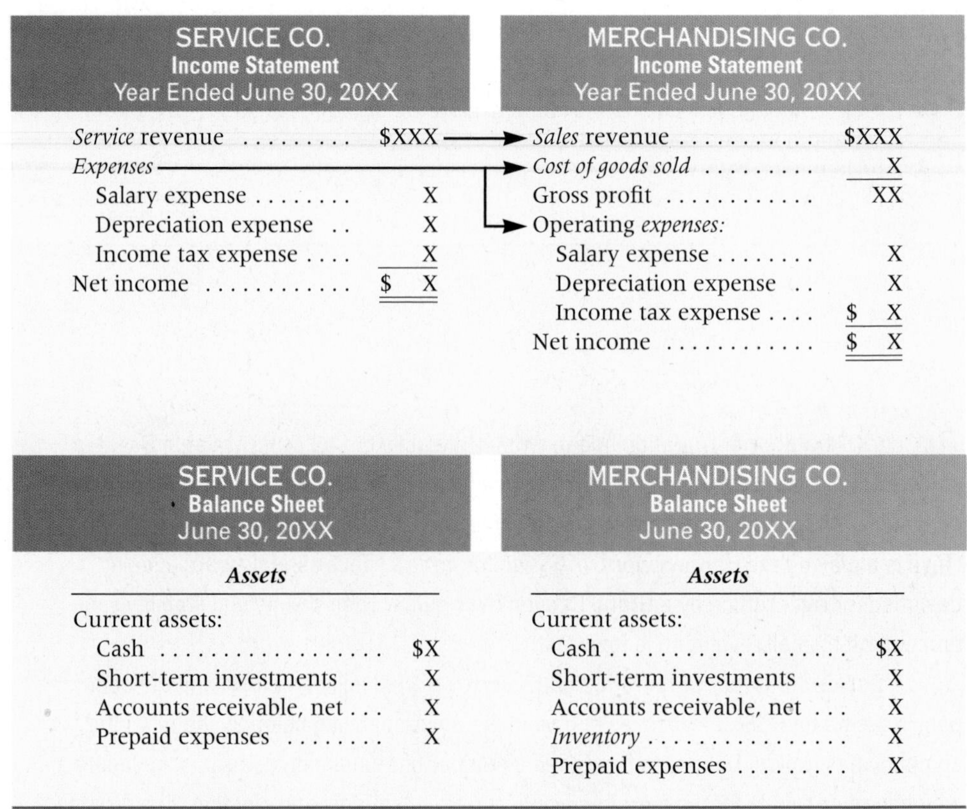

SERVICE CO.
Income Statement
Year Ended June 30, 20XX

Service revenue	$XXX
Expenses	
Salary expense	X
Depreciation expense	X
Income tax expense	X
Net income	$ X

MERCHANDISING CO.
Income Statement
Year Ended June 30, 20XX

Sales revenue	$XXX
Cost of goods sold	X
Gross profit	XX
Operating *expenses:*	
Salary expense	X
Depreciation expense	X
Income tax expense	$ X
Net income	$ X

SERVICE CO.
Balance Sheet
June 30, 20XX

Assets	
Current assets:	
Cash	$X
Short-term investments	X
Accounts receivable, net	X
Prepaid expenses	X

MERCHANDISING CO.
Balance Sheet
June 30, 20XX

Assets	
Current assets:	
Cash	$X
Short-term investments	X
Accounts receivable, net	X
Inventory	X
Prepaid expenses	X

What Goes into Inventory Cost?

The $23.7 million cost of inventory on **Deckers Outdoor Corporation's** balance sheet represents all the costs that Deckers incurred to bring the merchandise to the point of sale. Suppose Deckers employs a manufacturer in Hong Kong to make its Teva sandals. Deckers' cost of a pair of sandals would include

- Cost of the sandals—say $28 per pair.
- Customs duties paid to the U.S. Government in order to import the sandals. Suppose customs duties add $1 to the cost of each pair of sandals.
- Shipping cost from the manufacturer in Hong Kong to Deckers' location in California. This cost is called **freight-in.** Assume freight-in adds $0.70 to each pair of sandals.
- Insurance on the sandals while in transit—say, $0.30 per pair.

In total, Deckers' cost of a pair of sandals adds up to $30 ($28.00 + $1.00 + $0.70 + $0.30). The cost principle applies to all assets, as follows:

> **The cost of any asset is the sum of all the costs incurred to bring the asset to its intended use.**

For merchandise inventory, such as Teva sandals, the intended use is readiness for sale. After the goods are offered for sale, then other costs, such as advertising, display, and sales commissions, are expensed and thus are *not* included as the cost of inventory.

THE BASIC CONCEPT OF ACCOUNTING FOR INVENTORY

The basic concept of accounting for inventory is simple. Suppose **Deckers Outdoor Corporation** makes three pairs of sandals for $30 each, marks them up by $20, and sells two of the pairs for $50 each. Deckers' balance sheet reports the unit of inventory that the company still has, and the income statement reports the cost of goods sold for the two units sold, as follows:

Balance Sheet (partial)		*Income Statement (partial)*	
Current assets:		Sales revenue	
Cash	$XXX	(2 pairs @ $50)	$100
Short-term investments .	XXX	Cost of goods sold	
Accounts receivable	XXX	(2 pairs @ $30)	60
Inventory (1 pair @ $30).	30	Gross profit	$40
Prepaid expenses	XXX		

Gross profit, also called **gross margin,** is the excess of sales revenue over cost of goods sold. It is called *gross profit* because operating expenses have not yet been subtracted. Exhibit 6-1 on the next page shows actual inventory and cost of goods sold data from the financial statements of Deckers Outdoor Corporation.

Deckers' inventory balance of $23.7 million represents

Inventory (balance sheet) = **Number of units of inventory *on hand* at December 31, 1998** × **Cost per unit of inventory**

Deckers' cost of goods sold ($65.6 million) represents

Cost of goods sold (income statement) = **Number of units of inventory *sold* during 1998** × **Cost per unit of inventory**

EXHIBIT 6-1
Deckers Outdoor Corporation Inventory and Cost of Goods Sold (Cost of Sales)

DECKERS OUTDOOR CORPORATION
Balance Sheets (Adapted)
December 31, 1998 and 1997

	Thousands	
Assets	*1998*	*1997*
Current assets:		
Cash and cash equivalents	$ 263	$ 3,238
Trade accounts receivable, less allowance for doubtful accounts of $1,204 and $1,092 as of December 31, 1998 and 1997, respectively...	27,180	23,037
Inventories	23,665	18,979

DECKERS OUTDOOR CORPORATION
Statements of Operations (Adapted)
Years Ended December 31, 1998 and 1997

	Thousands	
	1998	*1997*
Net sales	$102,172	$106,713
Cost of sales (same as cost of goods sold)	65,592	62,453
Gross profit	36,580	44,260

What is the only difference between the computations of inventory (on the balance sheet) and cost of goods sold (on the income statement)? What element is common to both computations?

Answer: Inventory (on the balance sheet) represents *goods still on hand.* Cost of goods sold (on the income statement) represents *goods sold.* The common element to both computations is *cost per unit of inventory.*

NUMBER OF UNITS OF INVENTORY. The number of units of inventory on hand is determined from the accounting records and is backed up by a physical count of the goods at year end. Companies do not include in their inventory any goods that they hold on *consignment* for other entities because those goods belong to the other company. But they do include their own inventory that is out on consignment and being held for sale by another company.

COST PER UNIT OF INVENTORY. The cost per unit of inventory can pose an accounting challenge because companies purchase goods at different prices throughout the year. Which unit costs should be used to determine ending inventory for the balance sheet? Which unit costs should be used for cost of goods sold on the income statement?

The next section shows how the different accounting methods use inventory cost data to compute ending inventory for the balance sheet and cost of goods sold for the income statement. First, however, you need to understand the cost-of-goods-sold model.

Objective 1
Use the cost-of-goods-sold model

The Cost-of-Goods-Sold Model

The **cost-of-goods-sold model** brings together all the inventory data for the entire accounting period:

- Beginning inventory (balance left over from the preceding period)
- Purchases of inventory during the current period
- Ending inventory (balance on hand at the end of the current period)

We begin by illustrating the model for a situation in which the unit cost of inventory remains unchanged during the current period. Exhibit 6-2 presents the basic cost-of-goods-sold model, with all data assumed for the illustration.

EXHIBIT 6-2
Cost of Goods Sold (data assumed for the illustration)

Cost of goods sold:	
Beginning inventory (2 units @ $10 each)	$ 20
+ Purchases of inventory during the current period (10 units @ $10 each)	100
= Cost of goods available for sale (12 units @ $10 each)	120
− Ending inventory (3 units @ $10 each)	(30)
= Cost of goods sold (9 units @ $10 each)	$ 90

The logic behind the model is this: You start with some goods (beginning inventory). During the period, you buy some more goods (purchases). The sum of these two amounts is the cost of the goods available for sale during the period. At the end of the period, you have some goods left over (ending inventory). The excess of goods available over your ending inventory must be what you sold during the period. Because we account for inventory at cost, the excess is labeled cost of goods sold.

Exhibit 6-3 diagrams the cost-of-goods-sold model. Beginning inventory and Purchases go into goods available. Ending inventory and Cost of goods sold come out of goods available.

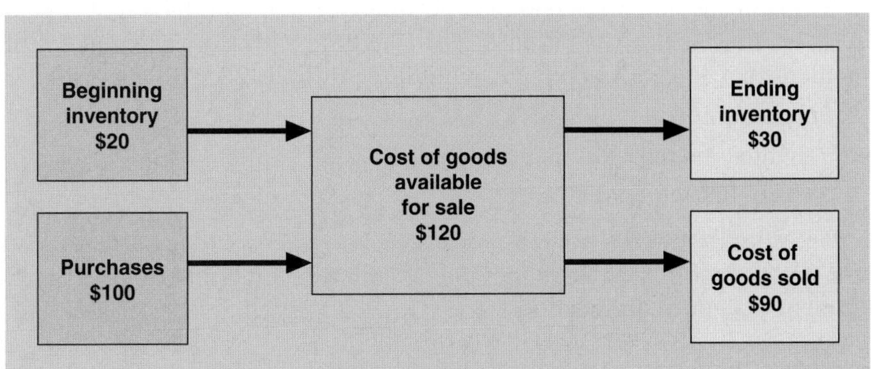

EXHIBIT 6-3
Diagram of the Cost-of-Goods-Sold Model

How Managers Decide the Amount of Inventory to Purchase

Suppose you are the buyer for a **Macy's** store. You are moving into the next period and planning your buying of Teva sandals. You have decided on several different lines of Tevas. What is your next inventory decision? You must decide how much inventory to purchase. If you buy too much inventory, you may be unable to sell it and may lose money. If you buy too little, you will be unable to satisfy your customers, who may take their business elsewhere.

How will you make the purchasing decision? The amount of inventory to purchase depends on three factors:

- Budgeted cost of goods sold
- Budgeted ending inventory
- Beginning inventory with which you started the period

A rearrangement of the cost-of-goods-sold formula helps you budget purchases as follows (all budgeted amounts are assumed for the next period):

1	Cost of goods sold (based on the budget for the next period)	$6,000
2	+ Ending inventory (based on the budget for the next period)	1,500
3	= Cost of goods available for sale, as budgeted	7,500
4	− Beginning inventory (actual amount left over from the prior period) ..	(1,200)
5	= Purchases (how much inventory managers need to buy)	$6,300

Most managers use this formula to determine how much to spend on inventory. The rationale for the formula is that goods available for sale (line 3) must come from a combination of beginning inventory (line 4), a past amount, and purchases (line 5), which the manager can still affect by future action. Focusing on the future, managers make their inventory purchases very cautiously. The power of the cost-of-goods-sold model lies in the key information it captures: beginning and ending inventory levels, purchases, and cost of goods sold. Now let's examine the different inventory costing methods.

INVENTORY COSTING METHODS

Objective 2
Apply the various inventory methods: specific unit cost, weighted-average, FIFO, and LIFO

Determining the unit cost of inventory is easy when the unit cost remains constant during the period, as we saw in Exhibit 6-2. But the unit cost often changes. For example, during times of inflation, prices rise. The sandals that cost Deckers $30 in January may cost $31 in June and $32 in October. Suppose Deckers sells 1,000 pairs of sandals in November. How many of them cost $30, how many cost $31, and how many cost $32? To compute cost of goods sold and the cost of inventory on hand, we must assign the business's actual cost to each item sold. The four costing methods that generally accepted accounting principles (GAAP) allow are:

1. Specific unit cost
2. Weighted-average cost
3. First-in, first-out (FIFO) cost
4. Last-in, first-out (LIFO) cost

A company can use any of these methods. Many companies use different methods for different categories of inventory.

SPECIFIC UNIT COST. Some businesses deal in inventory items that may be identified individually, such as automobiles, jewels, and real estate. These businesses usually cost their inventories at the specific unit cost of the particular unit. For instance, a Chevrolet dealer may have two vehicles in the showroom—a "stripped-down" model that cost $14,000 and a "loaded" model that cost $17,000. If the dealer sells the loaded model for $19,000, cost of goods sold is $17,000, the cost of the specific unit. The gross margin on this sale is $2,000 ($19,000 − $17,000). If the stripped-down auto is the only unit left in inventory at the end of the period, ending inventory is $14,000, the dealer's cost of the specific unit on hand.

The **specific-unit-cost method** is also called the *specific identification* method. This method is not practical for inventory items that have common characteristics, such as bushels of wheat, gallons of paint, or boxes of laundry detergent.

The weighted-average cost, FIFO (first-in, first-out) cost, and LIFO (last-in, first-out) cost methods are fundamentally different from the specific-unit-cost method. These methods do not assign to inventory the specific cost of a particular unit. Instead, they assume different flows of costs into and out of inventory.

WEIGHTED-AVERAGE COST. The **weighted-average cost method,** often called the *average-cost method,* is based on the weighted-average cost of inventory during the period. Weighted-average cost is determined as follows: Divide the cost of goods available for sale (beginning inventory plus purchases) by the number of units available for sale (beginning inventory plus purchases). Compute the ending inventory and cost of goods sold by multiplying the number of units by the weighted-average cost per unit.

Suppose **Deckers Outdoor Corporation** has 60 units of inventory, such as hiking socks, available for sale during the period. Ending inventory consists of 20 units, and cost of goods sold is based on 40 units. Panel A of Exhibit 6-4 gives the data for computing ending inventory and cost of goods sold for hiking socks. Note the question marks for the cost of ending inventory and for cost of goods sold. Panel B shows the weighted-average cost computations.

EXHIBIT 6-4
Inventory and Cost of Goods Sold under Weighted-Average, FIFO, and LIFO Cost

PANEL A—Illustrative Data

Beginning inventory (10 units @ $10 per unit)		$100
Purchases:		
No. 1 (25 units @ $14 per unit)	$350	
No. 2 (25 units @ $18 per unit)	450	
Total purchases		800
Cost of goods available for sale (60 units)		900
Ending inventory (20 units @ $? per unit)		?
Cost of goods sold (40 units @ $? per unit)		$?

PANEL B—Ending Inventory and Cost of Goods Sold

Weighted-Average Cost Method

Cost of goods available for sale—see Panel A (60 units @ average cost of $15* per unit)		$900
Ending inventory (20 units @ $15 per unit)		(300)
Cost of goods sold (40 units @ $15 per unit)		$600

FIFO Cost Method

Cost of goods available for sale (60 units—see Panel A)		$900
Ending inventory (cost of the *last* 20 units available):		
20 units @ $18 per unit (from purchase No. 2)		(360)
Cost of goods sold (cost of the *first* 40 units available):		
10 units @ $10 per unit (all of beginning inventory)	$100	
25 units @ $14 per unit (all of purchase No. 1)	350	
5 units @ $18 per unit (from purchase No. 2)	90	
Cost of goods sold		$540

LIFO Cost Method

Cost of goods available for sale (60 units—see Panel A)		$900
Ending inventory (cost of the *first* 20 units available):		
10 units @ $10 per unit (all of beginning inventory)	$100	
10 units @ $14 per unit (from purchase No. 1)	140	
Ending inventory		(240)
Cost of goods sold (cost of the *last* 40 units available):		
25 units @ $18 per unit (all of purchase No. 2)	$450	
15 units @ $14 per unit (from purchase No. 1)	210	
Cost of goods sold		$660

$$* \frac{\text{Cost of goods available for sale, \$900}}{\text{Number of units available for sale, 60}} = \text{Average cost per unit, \$15}$$

CHECK POINT 6-2

CHECK POINT 6-3

CHECK POINT 6-4

First-In, First-Out (FIFO) Cost. Under the **first-in, first-out (FIFO) method,** the first costs into inventory are the first costs out to cost of goods sold—hence, the name *first-in, first-out.* Ending inventory is therefore based on the costs of the latest purchases. In our example in Exhibit 6-4, the FIFO cost of ending inventory is $360. Cost of goods sold is $540. Panel A gives the data, and Panel B shows the FIFO computations.

Last-In, First-Out (LIFO) Cost. The **last-in, first-out (LIFO) method** is the opposite of FIFO. Under LIFO, the last costs into inventory are the first costs out to cost of goods sold. LIFO therefore leaves the oldest costs—those of beginning inventory *plus* the earliest purchases of the period—in ending inventory. In our example in Exhibit 6-4, the LIFO cost of ending inventory is $240. Cost of goods sold is $660.

Income Effects of FIFO, LIFO, and Weighted-Average Cost

In our example, the cost of inventory rose from $10 to $14 to $18 during the period. When inventory unit costs change this way, the different costing methods produce different cost-of-goods-sold and ending inventory figures, as Exhibit 6-4 shows. *When inventory unit costs are increasing,*

- FIFO ending inventory is *highest* because it is priced at the most recent costs, which are the highest.
- LIFO ending inventory is *lowest* because it is priced at the oldest costs, which are the lowest.

When inventory unit costs are decreasing,

- FIFO ending inventory is *lowest.*
- LIFO ending inventory is *highest.*

Exhibit 6-5 summarizes the income effects of the three inventory methods, using the data from Exhibit 6-4. Study the exhibit carefully, focusing on the differences in ending inventory, cost of goods sold, and gross profit.

Exhibit 6-5
Income Effects of the FIFO, LIFO, and Weighted-Average Inventory Methods

	FIFO		*LIFO*		*Weighted-Average*	
Sales revenue (assumed)		$1,000		$1,000		$1,000
Cost of goods sold:						
Goods available for sale (assumed)	$900		$900		$900	
Ending inventory	(360)		(240)		(300)	
Cost of goods sold		540		660		600
Gross profit		$ 460		$ 340		$ 400

Summary of Income Effects—When inventory unit costs are increasing

FIFO—Highest ending inventory
Lowest cost of goods sold
Highest gross profit

LIFO—Lowest ending inventory
Highest cost of goods sold
Lowest gross profit

Weighted-average—Results fall between the extremes of FIFO and LIFO

Summary of Income Effects—When inventory unit costs are decreasing

FIFO—Lowest ending inventory
Highest cost of goods sold
Lowest gross profit

LIFO—Highest ending inventory
Lowest cost of goods sold
Highest gross profit

Weighted-average—Results fall between the extremes of FIFO and LIFO

The Income Tax Advantage of LIFO

Objective 3
Identify the income effects and the tax effects of the inventory methods

Inventory methods dramatically affect income taxes, which have a direct impact on cash flow. When prices are rising, applying the LIFO method results in the *lowest taxable income* and thus the *lowest income taxes.* Let's use the gross profit data of Exhibit 6-5 to illustrate.

	FIFO	*LIFO*	*Weighted-Average*
Gross profit	$460	$340	$400
Operating expenses (assumed)	260	260	260
Income before income tax.	$200	$ 80	$140
Income tax expense (40%)	$ 80	$ 32	$ 56

CHECK POINT 6-5

Income tax expense is lowest under LIFO ($32) and highest under FIFO ($80). The most attractive feature of LIFO is reduced income tax payments, which is why over one-third of all companies use the LIFO method.

During periods of high inflation, many companies prefer LIFO for its tax advantage. Exhibit 6-6, based on an American Institute of Certified Public Accountants (AICPA) survey of 600 companies, indicates that FIFO remains the most popular inventory method.

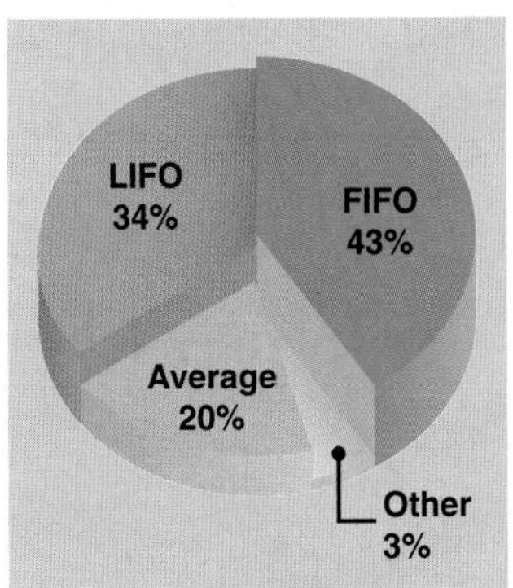

EXHIBIT 6-6
Use of the Various Inventory Methods

GAAP AND PRACTICAL CONSIDERATIONS: A COMPARISON OF INVENTORY METHODS

We may ask three questions to compare the weighted-average, FIFO, and LIFO inventory methods.

1. How well does each method match inventory expense—the cost of goods sold—to sales revenue on the income statement?

LIFO best matches the current value of cost of goods sold with current revenue by assigning to cost of sales the most recent inventory costs. Therefore, LIFO produces the cost-of-goods-sold figure that is closest to what it would cost the company to replace the goods sold. In contrast, FIFO matches the oldest inventory costs against the period's revenue—a poor matching of current expense with current revenue.

2. Which method reports the most up-to-date inventory amount on the balance sheet?

FIFO reports the most current inventory costs on the balance sheet. LIFO can result in misleading inventory costs on the balance sheet because it leaves the oldest prices in ending inventory.

3. What effects do the methods have on income taxes?

As shown earlier, LIFO results in the lowest tax payments when prices are *rising.* Taxes are highest under FIFO. When inventory prices are *decreasing,* tax payments are highest under LIFO and lowest under FIFO. The weighted-average cost method produces amounts between the extremes of LIFO and FIFO.

FIFO PRODUCES INVENTORY PROFITS. FIFO is sometimes criticized because it overstates income by so-called inventory profit during periods of inflation. Briefly, **inventory profit** is the difference between gross profit figured on the FIFO basis and gross profit figured on the LIFO basis. Exhibit 6-5 (p. 266) illustrates inventory profit. The $120 difference between FIFO and LIFO gross profits ($460 − $340) is called *FIFO inventory profit.* The company must replace the inventory it has sold in order to stay in business. The replacement cost of the merchandise is more closely approximated by the cost of goods sold under LIFO ($660) than by the FIFO amount ($540).

LIFO Allows Managers to Manage Reported Income—Up or Down. LIFO is criticized because it allows managers to manipulate net income. When inventory prices are rising rapidly and a company wants to show less income for the year (in order to pay less in taxes), managers can buy a large amount of inventory near the end of the year. Under LIFO, these high inventory costs immediately become expense—as cost of goods sold. As a result, the income statement reports a lower net income. Conversely, if the business is having a bad year, management may wish to increase reported income. To do so, managers can delay a large purchase of high-cost inventory until the next period. This high-cost inventory is not expensed as cost of goods sold in the current year. Thus, management avoids decreasing the current year's reported income. In the process, the company draws down inventory quantities, a practice known as *inventory liquidation.*

✔ Check Point 6-6

LIFO Liquidation. When the LIFO method is used and inventory quantities fall below the level of the previous period, the situation is called *LIFO liquidation.* To compute cost of goods sold, the company must dip into older layers of inventory cost. Under LIFO and during a period of rising inventory costs, that action shifts older, lower costs into cost of goods sold. The result is higher net income than the company would have reported if no LIFO liquidation had occurred. Managers try to avoid LIFO liquidation because it increases reported income and income taxes. **Owens-Corning,** the world's leading supplier of glass fiber materials, reported that LIFO liquidations added $2.7 million to its net income.

International Perspective. Many companies manufacture their inventory in foreign countries, and companies that value inventory by the LIFO method often must use another accounting method for their inventories in foreign countries. Why? LIFO is allowed in the United States, but other countries are not bound by U.S. accounting practices. Australia and the United Kingdom, for example, do not permit the use of LIFO. Virtually all countries permit FIFO and the weighted-average cost method. Exhibit 6-7 lists some countries that do and do not permit LIFO.

Exhibit 6-7
LIFO Use by Country

Country	*LIFO Permitted?*	*Country*	*LIFO Permitted?*
Australia	No	Netherlands	Yes
Brazil	Yes	Nigeria	No
Canada	Yes	Singapore	No
France	Yes	South Africa	Yes
Germany	Yes	Sweden	No
Hong Kong	No	Switzerland	No
Japan	Yes	United Kingdom	No
Mexico	Yes	United States	Yes

Higher Income or Lower Taxes? A company may want to report the highest income, and (as we've seen) FIFO meets this need when prices are rising. But the company also pays the highest income taxes under FIFO. When prices are falling, LIFO reports the highest income.

Which inventory method is better—LIFO or FIFO? There is no single answer to this question. Different companies have different motives for the inventory method they choose. **Polaroid Corporation** uses FIFO, **JC Penney Company** uses LIFO, and **Motorola, Inc.,** uses weighted-average cost. Still other companies use more than one method. **Black & Decker Corporation,** best known for its power tools and small appliances, uses both LIFO and FIFO. The following excerpt is from a Black & Decker annual report (amount in millions):

Inventories $390

Notes to Consolidated Financial Statements

Note 1: Summary of Accounting Policies

Inventories: The cost of United States inventories is based on the last-in, first-out (LIFO) method; all other inventories are based on the first-in, first-out (FIFO) method.

MID-CHAPTER Mid-Chapter

SUMMARY PROBLEM FOR YOUR REVIEW

Suppose a division of IBM Corporation that handles computer components has these inventory records for January 20X1:

Date	*Item*	*Quantity*	*Unit Cost*	*Sale Price*
Jan. 1	Beginning inventory	100 units	$ 8	
6	Purchase	60 units	9	
13	Sale	70 units		$20
21	Purchase	150 units	9	
24	Sale	210 units		22
27	Purchase	90 units	10	
30	Sale	30 units		25

Company accounting records reveal that operating expense for January was $1,900.

Required

1. Prepare the January income statement, showing amounts for FIFO, LIFO, and weighted-average cost. Label the bottom line "Operating income." (Round figures to whole-dollar amounts.) Show your computations, and use the model in Exhibit 6-2, page 263, to compute cost of goods sold.
2. Suppose you are the financial vice president of IBM. Which inventory method will you use if your motive is to
   a. Minimize income taxes?
   b. Report the highest operating income?
   c. Report operating income between the extremes of FIFO and LIFO?
   d. Report inventory on the balance sheet at the most current cost?
   e. Attain the best measure of net income for the income statement?

State the reason for each of your answers.

Answers

Requirement 1

IBM CORPORATION
Income Statement for Component
Month Ended January 31, 20X1

	FIFO		LIFO		Weighted-Average	
Sales revenue		$6,770		$6,770		$6,770
Cost of goods sold:						
Beginning inventory	$ 800		$ 800		$ 800	
Purchases	2,790		2,790		2,790	
Cost of goods available for sale	3,590		3,590		3,590	
Ending inventory	(900)		(720)		(808)	
Cost of goods sold		2,690		2,870		2,782
Gross margin		4,080		3,900		3,988
Operating expenses		1,900		1,900		1,900
Operating income		$2,180		$2,000		$2,088

Computations

Sales revenue:	(70 × \$20)	+ (210 × \$22) + (30 × \$25) = \$6,770
Beginning inventory:	100 × \$8	= \$800
Purchases:	(60 × \$9)	+ (150 × \$9) + (90 × \$10) = \$2,790
Ending inventory—FIFO:	90* × \$10	= \$900
LIFO:	90 × \$8	= \$720
Weighted-average:	90 × \$8.975**	= \$808 (rounded from \$807.75)

* Number of units in ending inventory = 100 + 60 − 70 + 150 − 210 + 90 − 30 = 90

** \$3,590/400 units† = \$8.975 per unit

† Number of units available = 100 + 60 + 150 + 90 = 400

Requirement 2

a. Use LIFO to minimize income taxes. Operating income under LIFO is lowest when inventory unit costs are increasing, as they are in this case (from \$8 to \$10). (If inventory costs were decreasing, income under FIFO would be lowest.)

b. Use FIFO to report the highest operating income. Income under FIFO is highest when inventory unit costs are increasing, as in this situation.

c. Use weighted-average cost to report an operating income amount between the FIFO and LIFO extremes. This is true in this situation and in others when inventory unit costs are increasing or decreasing.

d. Use FIFO to report inventory on the balance sheet at the most current cost. The oldest inventory costs are expensed as cost of goods sold, leaving in ending inventory the most recent (most current) costs of the period.

e. Use LIFO to attain the best measure of net income. LIFO produces the best matching of current expense with current revenue. The most recent (most current) inventory costs are expensed as cost of goods sold.

Accounting Principles and Their Relevance to Inventories

Several generally accepted accounting principles have special relevance to inventories. Among these are the consistency principle, the disclosure principle, the materiality concept, and accounting conservatism.

Consistency Principle

The **consistency principle** states that businesses should use the same accounting methods and procedures from period to period. Consistency makes it possible to compare a company's financial statements from one period to the next.

Suppose you are analyzing a company's net income pattern over a two-year period. The company switched from LIFO to FIFO during that time. Its net income increased dramatically, but only as a result of the change in inventory method. If you did not know of the change, you might believe that the company's income increased because of improved operations, which is not the case.

The consistency principle does not require that all companies within an industry use the same accounting method. Nor does it mean that a company may never change its accounting methods. However, a company making an accounting change must disclose the effect of the change on net income. **Sun Company, Inc.,** an oil company, disclosed the following in a note to its annual report:

> EXCERPT FROM NOTE 6 OF THE SUN COMPANY FINANCIAL STATEMENTS
>
> . . . Sun changed its method of accounting for the cost of crude oil and refined product inventories . . . from the FIFO method to the LIFO method. Sun believes that the use of the LIFO method better matches current costs with current revenues. . . . The change decreased the 19X1 net loss . . . by $3 million. . . .

Disclosure Principle

The **disclosure principle** holds that a company's financial statements should report enough information for outsiders to make knowledgeable decisions about the company. In short, the company should report *relevant, reliable,* and *comparable* information about its economic affairs. With respect to inventories, the disclosure principle means disclosing the accounting methods in use. Without knowledge of the inventory method, a banker could get an unrealistic impression of a company and make an unwise lending decision. For example, suppose the banker is comparing two companies—one using LIFO and the other, FIFO. The FIFO company reports higher net income, but only because it uses the FIFO inventory method. Without knowledge of the accounting methods the companies are using, the banker could loan money to the wrong business or could refuse a loan to a promising customer.

Materiality Concept

The **materiality concept** states that a company must perform strictly proper accounting only for items and transactions that are significant to the business's financial statements. Information is significant—or, in accounting terminology, *material*—when its inclusion and correct presentation in the financial statements would cause someone to change a decision because of that information. Immaterial—insignificant—items justify less-than-perfect accounting. The inclusion and proper presentation of *immaterial* items would not affect anyone's decision. The materiality concept frees accountants from having to compute and report every last item in strict accordance with GAAP. Thus, the materiality concept reduces the cost of accounting.

How does a business decide where to draw the line between the material and the immaterial? This decision rests to a great degree on how large the business is. The fast-food chain **Wendy's,** for example, has close to $500 million in assets. Management would likely treat as immaterial a $100 loss of inventory due to theft. Because a loss of this amount is immaterial to Wendy's total assets and net income, company accountants may not report the loss separately. Will this accounting treatment affect anyone's decision about Wendy's? Probably not, so it doesn't matter whether the loss is reported separately or simply embedded in cost of goods sold.

Accounting Conservatism

Conservatism in accounting means reporting items in the financial statements at amounts that lead to the gloomiest immediate financial results. Conservatism comes into play when there are alternative ways to account for an item. What advantage does conservatism give a business? Management often looks on the brighter side of operations and may overstate a company's income and asset values. Many accountants regard conservatism as a counterbalance to management's optimistic tendencies. The goal is for financial statements to present realistic figures.

Conservatism appears in accounting guidelines such as "anticipate no gains, but provide for all probable losses" and "if in doubt, record an asset at the lowest reasonable amount and a liability at the highest reasonable amount." Conservatism directs accountants to decrease the accounting value of an asset if it appears unrealistically high—even if no transaction occurs. Assume that a company paid $35,000 for inventory that has become obsolete and whose current value is only $12,000. Conservatism dictates that the inventory be *written down* to $12,000.

Lower-of-Cost-or-Market Rule

The **lower-of-cost-or-market rule** (abbreviated as **LCM**) shows accounting conservatism in action. LCM requires that inventory be reported in the financial statements at whichever is lower—its historical cost or its market value. Applied to inventories, *market value* generally means *current replacement cost* (that is, how much the business would have to pay now to purchase the amount of inventory that it has on hand). If the replacement cost of inventory falls below its historical cost, the business must write down the value of its goods because of the likelihood of incurring a loss on the inventory. GAAP requires this departure from historical cost accounting. The business reports ending inventory at its LCM value on the balance sheet. All this can be done automatically by a computerized accounting system. How is the write-down accomplished?

Suppose **Deckers Outdoor Corporation** paid $3,000 for inventory on September 26. By December 31, its value has fallen. The inventory can now be replaced for $2,200. Market value is below cost, and Deckers' December 31 balance sheet reports this inventory at its LCM value of $2,200. Usually, because the market value of inventory is higher than historical cost, inventory is valued at cost for most companies. Exhibit 6-8 presents the effects of LCM on the balance sheet and the income statement. The exhibit shows that the lower of (a) cost or (b) market

EXHIBIT 6-8
Lower-of-Cost-or-Market (LCM) Effects

Balance Sheet		
Current assets:		
Cash	$ XXX	
Short-term investments	XXX	
Accounts receivable	XXX	
Inventories, at market (which is lower than $3,000 cost)	2,200	
Prepaid expenses	XXX	
Total current assets	$X,XXX	
Income Statement		
Sales revenue		$20,000
Cost of goods sold:		
Beginning inventory (LCM = Cost)	$ 2,800	
Purchases	11,000	
Cost of goods available for sale	13,800	
Ending inventory—		
Cost = $3,000		
Replacement cost (market value) = $2,200		
LCM = Market	(2,200)	
Cost of goods sold		11,600
Gross profit		$ 8,400

CHECK POINT 6-7

value—the replacement cost—is the relevant amount for valuing inventory on the balance sheet.

Examine the income statement in Exhibit 6-8. What expense absorbs the impact of the $800 inventory write-down? Cost of goods sold is increased by $800 because ending inventory is $800 less at market ($2,200) than at cost ($3,000).

Companies disclose LCM in notes to their financial statements, as shown here for **CBS, Inc.,** the broadcasting conglomerate:

> NOTE 1: STATEMENT OF SIGNIFICANT ACCOUNTING POLICIES
> *Inventories.* Inventories are stated at the *lower of cost* (principally based on average cost) or *market value.* [Emphasis added.]

EFFECTS OF INVENTORY ERRORS

Objective 4
Measure the effects of inventory errors on cost of goods sold and net income

Businesses count their inventories at the end of the period. In the process of counting the items, applying unit costs, and computing amounts, errors may arise. The period 1 segment of Exhibit 6-9 below shows that an error in the ending inventory amount creates errors in the amounts for cost of goods sold and gross profit. Compare period 1, when ending inventory is overstated and cost of goods sold is understated, each by $5,000, with period 3, which is correct. *Period 1 should look exactly like period 3.*

Recall that one period's ending inventory is the next period's beginning inventory. Thus, the error in ending inventory carries over into the next period as shown for period 2. All the amounts in color in Exhibit 6-9 are incorrect. *Period 2 should also look exactly like period 3.*

Because ending inventory is *subtracted* in computing cost of goods sold in one period and the same amount is *added* as beginning inventory to compute next period's cost of goods sold, the error's effect cancels out at the end of the second period. The overstatement of cost of goods sold in period 2 counterbalances the understatement in cost of goods sold in period 1. Thus, the total gross profit amount for periods 1 and 2 is the correct $100,000 figure whether or not an error entered into the computation. These effects are summarized in Exhibit 6-10.

✔ CHECK POINT 6-8

✔ CHECK POINT 6-9

Inventory errors cannot be ignored, however, simply because they counterbalance. Suppose you are analyzing trends in Deckers' operations. Exhibit 6-9 shows a drop in gross profit from period 1 to period 2, followed by an increase in period 3.

EXHIBIT 6-9
Inventory Errors: An Example

	Period 1		*Period 2*		*Period 3*	
	Ending Inventory Overstated by $5,000		*Beginning Inventory Overstated by $5,000*		*Correct*	
Sales revenue		$100,000		$100,000		$100,000
Cost of goods sold:						
Beginning inventory	$10,000		$15,000		$10,000	
Purchases	50,000		50,000		50,000	
Cost of goods available for sale	60,000		65,000		60,000	
Ending inventory	(15,000)		(10,000)		(10,000)	
Cost of goods sold		45,000		55,000		50,000
Gross profit		$ 55,000		$ 45,000		$ 50,000
			$100,000			

Source: The authors thank Carl High for this example.

EXHIBIT 6-10
Effects of Inventory Errors

	Period 1		Period 2	
Inventory Error	*Cost of Goods Sold*	*Gross Profit and Net Income*	*Cost of Goods Sold*	*Gross Profit and Net Income*
Period 1 Ending inventory overstated	Understated	Overstated	Overstated	Understated
Period 1 Ending inventory understated	Overstated	Understated	Understated	Overstated

But that picture of operations is inaccurate because of the accounting error. The correct gross profit is $50,000 for each period. Providing accurate information for decision making requires that all inventory errors be corrected.

ETHICAL ISSUES IN INVENTORY ACCOUNTING

No area of accounting has a deeper ethical dimension than inventory. Managers of companies whose profits do not meet stockholder expectations are sometimes tempted to "cook the books" to increase reported income. The increase in reported income may lead investors and creditors into thinking the business is more successful than it really is.

What do managers hope to gain from fraudulent accounting? In some cases, they are trying to keep their jobs. In other cases, their bonuses are tied to reported income: the higher the company's net income, the higher the managers' bonuses. In still other cases, the business may need a loan. Financial statements that report high profits and large inventory values are more likely to impress lenders than low net income and inventory amounts.

There are two main schemes for cooking the books. The easiest is simply to overstate ending inventory. In the preceding section on the effects of inventory errors, we saw how an error in ending inventory affects net income. A company can intentionally overstate its ending inventory. Such an error understates cost of goods sold and overstates net income and retained earnings, as shown in the accounting equation that follows. The upward-pointing arrows indicate an overstatement—reporting more assets and equity than are actually present:

ASSETS	=	LIABILITIES	+	STOCKHOLDERS' EQUITY
↑	=	0	+	↑

Remember that an inventory error has an offsetting effect in the next period. This means that managers who misstate ending inventory can only hope to "buy some time" by hyping reported income in the short term. Next period's net income will be lower as a result of this period's error. As with all other deceptions, an inventory misstatement comes back to haunt the business.

The second way of using inventory to cook the books involves sales. Sales schemes are more complex than simple inventory overstatements. **Datapoint Corporation** and **MiniScribe,** both computer-related concerns, were charged with creating fictitious sales to boost their reported profits. Datapoint is alleged to have hired drivers to transport its inventory around San Antonio so that the goods could not be physically counted. Datapoint's logic seemed to be that excluding the goods from ending inventory would imply that the goods had been sold. The faulty reasoning broke down when the trucks returned the goods to Datapoint's warehouse. Datapoint had unrealistic amounts of sales returns. What would you think of a company with $10 million in sales and $3 million of goods returned by customers?

MiniScribe is alleged to have cooked its books by shipping boxes of bricks labeled as computer parts to its distributors right before year end. The bogus transactions increased the company's assets and stockholders' equity by $4 million—but only temporarily.

The scheme boomeranged in the next period, when MiniScribe had to record the sales returns. In virtually every area, accounting imposes a discipline that helps keep people honest in financial reporting.

CHECK POINT 6-10

ANALYZING FINANCIAL STATEMENTS

One key to successful management is to focus on the best way to sell the company's inventory. Owners, managers, and lenders use several ratios to evaluate operations.

Objective 5
Use the gross profit percentage and the rate of inventory turnover to evaluate a business

Gross Profit Percentage

A key decision-making tool for a merchandiser is based on gross profit, which we've seen equals sales revenue minus cost of goods sold. Merchandisers strive to increase their **gross profit percentage,** also called the **gross margin percentage,** which is computed as follows for **Deckers Outdoor Corporation.** Data are taken from Exhibit 6-1, page 262.

$$\textbf{Gross profit percentage} = \frac{\textbf{Gross profit}}{\textbf{Net sales revenue}} = \frac{\$36{,}580}{\$102{,}172} = .358 = 35.8\%$$

The gross profit (or gross margin) percentage is one of the most carefully watched measures of profitability. A 36% gross margin means that each dollar of sales generates 36 cents of gross profit. On average, the goods cost the seller 64 cents. For most firms, because the gross profit percentage changes little from year to year, a small downturn may signal an important drop in net income.

Deckers' gross profit percentage of 35.8% compares favorably with the industry average for sporting goods manufacturers, which is 36.3%. By contrast, the average gross profit percentage is 25.7% for shoes in general, 22.8% for grocery stores, and 14.1% for auto dealerships, according to Robert Morris Associates' *Annual Statement Studies.* Exhibit 6-11 compares Deckers' gross profit percentage to that of **Wal-Mart,** the leading discount chain.

Inventory Turnover

Owners and managers strive to sell inventory quickly because it generates no profit until it is sold. The faster the sales occur, the higher the company's income, and vice versa for slow-moving goods. Ideally, a business could operate with zero inventory. Most businesses, however, must keep goods on hand. **Inventory turnover,** the ratio of cost of goods sold to average inventory, indicates how rapidly inventory is sold. Its computation for Deckers Outdoor Corporation follows (data from Exhibit 6-1, page 262):

$$\textbf{Inventory turnover} = \frac{\textbf{Cost of goods sold}}{\textbf{Average inventory}} = \frac{\textbf{Cost of goods sold}}{\left(\textbf{Beginning inventory} + \textbf{Ending inventory}\right) \div 2}$$

$$= \frac{\$65{,}592}{(\$18{,}979 + \$23{,}665)/2} = \frac{\textbf{3.1 times per year}}{\textbf{(about every 119 days)}}$$

EXHIBIT 6-11
Gross Profit on $1.00 of Sales for Two Merchandisers

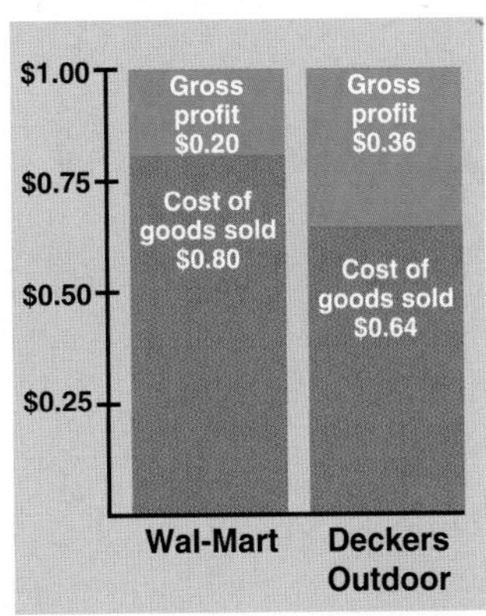

The inventory turnover statistic shows how many times the average level of inventory was sold (or turned over) during the year. Inventory turnover varies from industry to industry. Sporting goods manufacturers, in general, turn their goods over 3.2 times per year. Drugstores have higher turnover than auto dealerships. Exhibit 6-12 compares the inventory rate of Deckers Outdoor and Wal-Mart Stores, Inc., which turns its goods over very rapidly.

EXHIBIT 6-12
Rate of Inventory Turnover for Two Companies

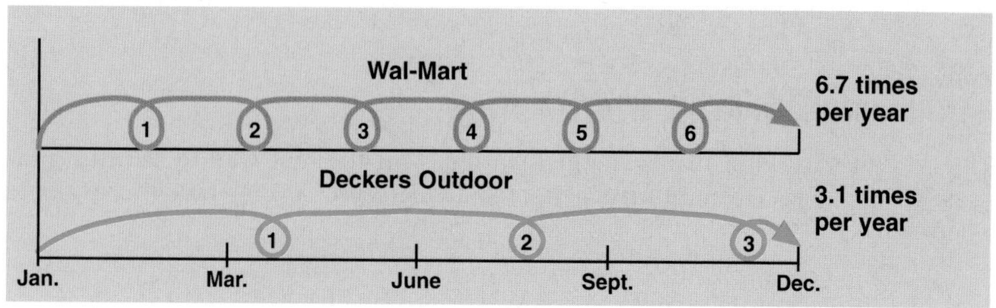

Exhibits 6-11 and 6-12 tell an interesting story. Wal-Mart sells a lot of inventory at a relatively low gross profit, and Wal-Mart turns its inventory over rapidly. Deckers Outdoor, a specialty company, prices inventory to earn a higher gross profit on each dollar of sales. As a result, Deckers cannot sell its merchandise as rapidly as Wal-Mart can. When analyzed together, gross profit percentage and rate of inventory turnover tell a lot about a company's merchandising strategy.

CHECK POINT 6-11

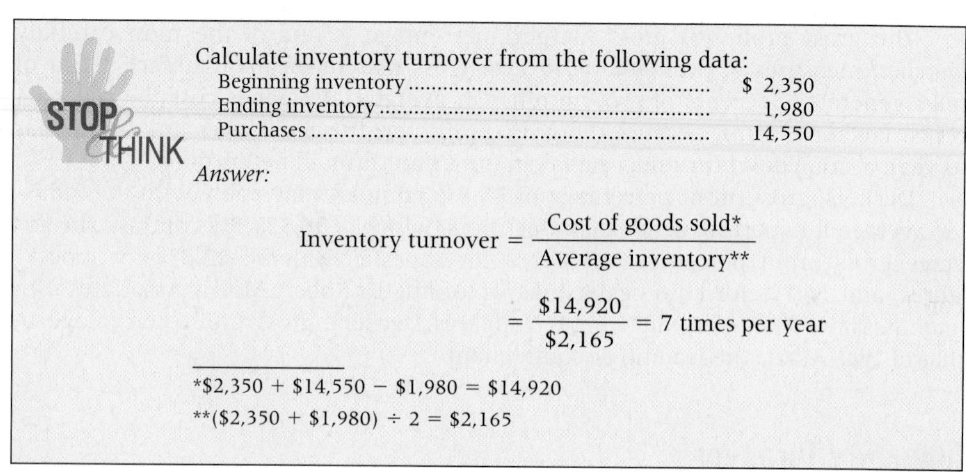

Calculate inventory turnover from the following data:

Beginning inventory	$ 2,350
Ending inventory	1,980
Purchases	14,550

Answer:

$$\text{Inventory turnover} = \frac{\text{Cost of goods sold*}}{\text{Average inventory**}}$$

$$= \frac{\$14,920}{\$2,165} = 7 \text{ times per year}$$

*$2,350 + $14,550 − $1,980 = $14,920

**($2,350 + $1,980) ÷ 2 = $2,165

INVENTORY ACCOUNTING SYSTEMS

Objective 6
Account for inventory transactions

There are two main types of inventory accounting systems: the periodic system and the perpetual system. The **periodic inventory system** is used by businesses that sell relatively inexpensive goods. Convenience stores without optical-scanning cash registers do not keep a daily running record of every loaf of bread and every six-pack of drinks they sell. Instead, these stores count their inventory periodically—at least once a year—to determine the quantities on hand. The inventory amounts are used to prepare the annual financial statements. Businesses such as restaurants and small department stores also use the periodic inventory system because the cost of accounting is low.

Perpetual Inventory System

Under the **perpetual inventory system,** the business maintains a running record of inventory on hand, usually by computer. This system achieves control over goods such as automobiles, jewelry, and furniture. The loss of one item would be significant, and this justifies the cost of a perpetual system. Because the cost of computers has come down, many small businesses are now using perpetual inventory systems for all types of goods.

Even under a perpetual system the business still counts the inventory on hand annually. The physical count establishes the correct amount of ending inventory and serves as a check on the perpetual records. The following chart compares the perpetual and periodic systems:

Perpetual Inventory System	Periodic Inventory System
• Keeps a running record of all goods bought and sold.	• Does not keep a running record of all goods bought and sold.
• Inventory counted once a year.	• Inventory counted at least once a year.
• Used for all types of goods.	• Used for inexpensive goods.

Perpetual inventory records provide information for the following decisions:

- When a department store calls Deckers Outdoor to see how soon it can get 100 pairs of Teva sandals, Deckers can answer by referring to the perpetual inventory record.
- The perpetual records alert the business to reorder when inventory becomes low. Sales may be lost if **Foot Locker** or **Macy's** cannot get the shoes they need from Deckers.
- At the end of each month, Deckers can prepare monthly financial statements. The perpetual inventory records show the company's ending inventory of Teva sandals, along with cost of goods sold for the month.

RECORDING TRANSACTIONS IN THE PERPETUAL SYSTEM. In the perpetual system, the business records purchases of inventory by debiting the Inventory account. When the business makes a sale, two entries are needed. The company records the sale in the usual manner—debits Cash or Accounts Receivable and credits Sales Revenue for the sale price of the goods. The company also debits Cost of Goods Sold (an expense account) and credits Inventory (the asset) for cost. The debit to Inventory (for purchases) and the credit to Inventory (for sales) keep an up-to-date record of the cost of inventory on hand.

Exhibit 6-13, page 278, shows the accounting for inventory in a perpetual system. Panel A gives the journal entries and the T-accounts, and Panel B presents the income statement and the balance sheet. All amounts are assumed. The chapter appendix illustrates the accounting for these transactions in a periodic inventory system.

In Exhibit 6-13, Panel A, the first entry to Inventory summarizes a lot of detail. The cost of the inventory, $560,000, is the *net* amount of the purchases, determined as follows (using assumed amounts):

Purchase price of the inventory from the seller	$600,000
+ Transportation cost to move the goods from the seller to the buyer **(freight-in)**	4,000
− **Purchase returns** for damaged or otherwise unsuitable goods returned to the seller...............	(25,000)
− **Purchase allowances** granted by the seller	(5,000)
− **Purchase discounts** for early payment	(14,000)
= Net purchases of inventory..........................	$560,000

EXHIBIT 6-13
Recording and Reporting Inventory—Perpetual System (amounts assumed)

Perpetual System

PANEL A—Recording Transactions and the T-accounts

1. Credit purchases of $560,000:

Inventory	560,000	
Accounts Payable		560,000

ASSETS	=	LIABILITIES	+	STOCKHOLDERS' EQUITY
560,000	=	560,000	+	0

2. Credit sales of $900,000 (cost $540,000):

Accounts Receivable.	900,000	
Sales Revenue.		900,000

ASSETS	=	LIABILITIES	+	STOCKHOLDERS' EQUITY	+	REVENUES
900,000	=	0			+	900,000

Cost of Goods Sold	540,000	
Inventory		540,000

ASSETS	=	LIABILITIES	+	STOCKHOLDERS' EQUITY	−	EXPENSES
−540,000	=	0			−	540,000

INVENTORY AND COST OF GOODS SOLD ACCOUNTS

Inventory (Dr.)	Inventory (Cr.)
100,000*	540,000
560,000	
120,000	

Cost of Goods Sold (Dr.)	Cost of Goods Sold (Cr.)
540,000	

PANEL B—Reporting in the Financial Statements

CHECK POINT 6-12

Income Statement (partial)

Sales revenue	$900,000
Cost of goods sold	540,000
Gross profit	$360,000

Ending Balance Sheet (partial)

Current assets:

Cash	$ XXX
Short-term investments	XXX
Accounts receivable	XXX
Inventory	120,000
Prepaid expenses.	XXX

*Beginning inventory was $100,000.

Freight-in is the transportation cost, paid by the buyer, to move goods from the seller to the buyer. Freight-in is accounted for as part of the cost of inventory.

A **purchase return** is a decrease in the cost of purchases because the buyer returned the goods to the seller. A **purchase allowance** is a decrease in the cost of purchases because the seller granted the buyer a subtraction (an allowance) from the amount owed. Purchase returns and allowances both decrease the buyer's cost of merchandise purchases and are often combined into a single account, Purchase Returns and Allowances. Throughout this book, we often refer to net purchases simply as Purchases, as in Exhibit 6-2 (p. 263).

A **purchase discount** is a decrease in the cost of purchases earned by making an early payment to the vendor. A common arrangement states payment terms of 2/10 n/30, which offers a 2% discount for payment within 10 days with the final amount due within 30 days.

In summary, **Net purchases = Purchases**
+ Freight-in
− Purchase returns & allowances
− Purchase discounts

Net sales are computed exactly as net purchases, except there is no freight-in to account for.

Net sales = Sales revenue
− Sales returns & allowances
− Sales discounts

Freight-out paid by the seller is not part of the cost of inventory. Instead, freight-out is the expense of delivering merchandise to customers. It is Delivery Expense.

The chapter appendix shows the accounting for these same transactions in a periodic accounting system.

Internal Control over Inventory

Internal control over inventory is important because inventory is such an important asset. Successful companies protect their inventory. Elements of good internal control over inventory include the following:

1. Physically count goods at least once each year regardless of which inventory accounting system is used.
2. Store inventory to protect it against theft, damage, and decay.
3. Allow access to inventory only to personnel who do *not* have access to the accounting records.
4. Keep perpetual inventory records for high-unit-cost merchandise.
5. Keep enough inventory on hand to prevent shortage situations, which lead to lost sales.
6. Do not stockpile too much inventory. This avoids the expense of tying up money in unneeded items.
7. Purchase inventory in economical quantities.

The annual physical count of inventory (item 1) is necessary because the only way to be certain of the amount of inventory on hand is to count it. When an error is detected, the records are brought into agreement with the physical count.

Keeping inventory handlers away from the accounting records (item 3) is an essential separation of duties, discussed in Chapter 4. An employee with access to both inventory and the accounting records can steal the goods and make an entry to conceal the theft. For example, the employee could increase the amount of an inventory write-down to make it appear that goods became obsolete when in fact they were stolen.

Computerized inventory systems allow companies to minimize both the amount of inventory on hand and the chances of running out of stock (items 5 and 6). In a competitive business environment, companies cannot afford to have cash tied up in too much inventory. Many manufacturing companies use *just-in-time (JIT) inventory systems,* which require suppliers to deliver materials just in time to be used in the production process. Just-in-time systems help minimize the amount of money a company has tied up in inventory.

ESTIMATING INVENTORY

Objective 7
Estimate inventory by the gross profit method

Often a business must *estimate* the value of its inventory. A fire may destroy inventory, and to file an insurance claim, the business must estimate the value of its loss. In this case, the business needs to estimate the value of ending inventory because it cannot count it. A widely used method for estimating ending inventory is the *gross profit method.*

Gross Profit (Gross Margin) Method

The **gross profit method,** also known as the *gross margin method,* is a way of estimating inventory on the basis of the familiar cost-of-goods-sold model.

	Beginning inventory
+	**Purchases**
=	**Cost of goods available for sale**
−	**Ending inventory**
=	**Cost of goods sold**

Rearranging *ending inventory* and *cost of goods sold* makes the model useful for estimating ending inventory and is illustrated in the following equations and in Exhibit 6-14:

	Beginning inventory
+	**Purchases**
=	**Cost of goods available for sale**
−	**Cost of goods sold**
=	**Ending inventory**

EXHIBIT 6-14
Estimating Ending Inventory

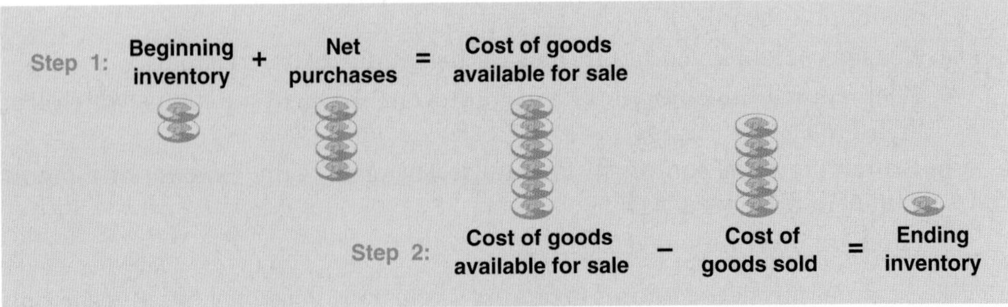

Suppose a fire destroys your business's inventory. To collect insurance, you must estimate the cost of the ending inventory. Beginning inventory and net purchases amounts can be taken directly from the accounting records. Sales Revenue less Sales Returns and Allowances and Sales Discounts indicates net sales up to the date of the fire. Using the entity's *normal gross profit rate* (that is, gross profit divided by net sales revenue), you can estimate cost of goods sold. The last step is to subtract cost of goods sold from goods available to estimate ending inventory. Exhibit 6-15 illustrates the gross profit method of estimating the cost of ending inventory.

EXHIBIT 6-15
Gross Profit Method of Estimating Inventory (amounts assumed)

Beginning inventory		$14,000
Purchases		66,000
Cost of goods available for sale		80,000
Cost of goods sold:		
Net sales revenue	$100,000	
Less estimated gross profit of 40%	(40,000)	
Estimated cost of goods sold		60,000
Estimated cost of *ending inventory*		$20,000

Accountants, managers, and auditors use this method to test the overall reasonableness of an ending inventory amount determined by a physical count. This method helps to detect large errors.

Beginning inventory is $70,000, net purchases total $292,000, and net sales are $480,000. With a normal gross profit rate of 40% of sales, how much is ending inventory?

Answer: $74,000 = [$70,000 + $292,000 − (0.60 × $480,000)]

REPORTING INVENTORY TRANSACTIONS ON THE STATEMENT OF CASH FLOWS

Let's return once again to the **Deckers Outdoor Corporation** example. In addition to the income statement and the balance sheet, Deckers publishes a statement of cash flows at the end of the year. Examine the Deckers income statement and balance sheet data on page 272. The income statement shows Deckers' revenues, cost of sales, and gross profit. The balance sheet reports the company's assets.

But how much cash did Deckers spend on inventory during the year? And how much cash did the company collect from customers? Did operations provide a net cash inflow, as they should for a successful company? Or were operating activities a drain on cash? Only the statement of cash flows answers these questions. Exhibit 6-16 shows that Deckers' operations generated negative cash flows. Let's examine the inventory-related cash flows.

Inventory-related transactions are *operating activities* because the purchase and the sale of merchandise set the pace for a company's operations. Collections from customers and payments for inventory are two large operating cash flows.

The cash-flow statement reports that Deckers collected $98 million from customers and paid $66 million for inventory during the year. These figures combine with Deckers' other operating activities to report that operations used a (negative) $10.1 million of cash during 1998. Overall, the company's operating cash flows look rather weak. We will reexamine the reporting of cash flows in Chapter 12.

Exhibit 6-16
Statement of Cash Flows for Deckers Outdoor Corporation

Check Point 6-13

DECKERS OUTDOOR CORPORATION
Statement of Cash Flows (partial, adapted)
Year Ended December 31, 1998

	Thousands
Cash flows from operating activities:	
Collections from customers	$ 98,029
Payments for inventory	(65,960)
Payments to other suppliers	(40,208)
Payments of interest	(1,171)
Other payments	(846)
Cash provided (used) by operating activities	$(10,156)

Detailed Income Statement

Exhibit 6-17 brings the chapter together by providing an example of a detailed income statement. You will find this example helpful for fitting all the pieces of the inventory puzzle together.

Exhibit 6-17
Detailed Income Statement

SILICON VALLEY SOFTWARE COMPANY
Income Statement
Year Ended December 31, 20XX

Sales revenue		$100,000	
Less: Sales discounts		(2,000)	
Sales returns & allowances		(3,000)	
Net sales revenue			$95,000*
Cost of goods sold:			
Beginning inventory		$ 10,000	
Purchases	$49,000		
Less: Purchase discounts	(1,000)		
Purchase returns & allowances	(4,000)		
Net purchases	4,000		
Freight-in	3,000	47,000	
Cost of goods available for sale		57,000	
Ending inventory		(12,000)	
Cost of goods sold			45,000**
Gross profit			50,000
Operating expenses:			
Selling:			
Sales commission expense		$ 5,000	
Freight-out (Delivery expense)		1,000	
Other expenses (detailed)		6,000	12,000
Administrative:			
Salary expense		$ 2,000	
Depreciation expense		2,000	
Other expenses (detailed)		4,000	8,000
Income before income tax			30,000
Income tax expense (40%)			12,000
Net income			$18,000

*Most companies report only the net sales revenue figure.
**Most companies report only the cost of goods sold total.

The Decision Guidelines feature summarizes the situations that call for a particular inventory accounting system and the motivation for using each costing method.

method produces the highest reported income? Which produces the lowest reported income?

5. Which inventory costing method produces the ending inventory valued at the most current cost? Which method produces the cost-of-goods-sold amount valued at the most current cost?

6. What is the most attractive feature of LIFO? Does LIFO have this advantage during periods of increasing prices or during periods of decreasing prices? Why has LIFO had this advantage recently?

7. What is inventory profit? Which method produces it?

8. Identify the chief criticism of LIFO.

9. How does the consistency principle affect accounting for inventory?

10. Briefly describe the influence that the concept of conservatism has on accounting for inventory.

11. Manley Company's inventory has a cost of $45,000 at the end of the year, and the current replacement cost of the inventory is $47,000. At which amount should the company report the inventory on its balance sheet? Now suppose the current replacement cost of the inventory is $42,000 instead of $47,000. At which amount should Manley report the inventory? What rule governs your answers to these questions?

12. Gabriel Company accidentally overstated its ending inventory by $40,000 at the end of period 1. Is gross profit of period 1 overstated or understated? Is gross profit of period 2 overstated, understated, or unaffected by the period 1 error? Is total gross profit for the two periods overstated, understated, or correct? Give the reason for your answers.

13. Identify an important method of estimating inventory amounts. What familiar model underlies this estimation method?

14. A fire destroyed the inventory of Olivera Company, but the accounting records were saved. The beginning inventory was $22,000, purchases for the period were $71,000, and sales were $140,000. Olivera's customary gross profit is 40% of sales. Use the gross profit method to estimate the cost of the inventory destroyed by the fire.

15. True or false? A company that sells inventory of low unit cost needs no internal controls over the goods. Any inventory loss would probably be small.

16. DuBois, Inc., made sales of $50,000 and collected $46,000 from customers. DuBois purchased inventory for $30,000, paying $20,000 cash and accruing the remainder. Cost of goods sold was $28,000. What will DuBois report on its income statement? On its statement of cash flows?

CHECK POINTS

Basic concept of accounting for inventory (Obj. 1)

CP6-1 Karas Enterprises purchased 1,000 units of inventory for $60 each and marked up the goods by $40 per unit. Karas then sold 800 units. For these transactions, show what Karas would report on its balance sheet at December 31, 20X0 and on its income statement for the year ended December 31, 20X0. Include a complete heading for each statement.

Applying the FIFO, LIFO, and weighted-average inventory methods (Obj. 1, 2)

CP6-2 Study Exhibit 6-4, page 265, and answer these questions.

1. In Panel A, are the company's inventory costs stable, increasing, or decreasing during the period? Cite specific figures to support your answer.
2. Which inventory method results in the *highest* amount for ending inventory (give this figure)? Explain why this method produces the highest amount for ending inventory. Does this method result in the highest, or the lowest, cost of goods sold? Explain why this occurs. Does this method result in the highest, or the lowest, gross profit? Explain your answer.
3. Which inventory method results in the *lowest* amount for ending inventory (give this figure)? Explain why this method produces the lowest amount for ending inventory. Does this method result in the highest or the lowest cost of goods sold? Explain why this occurs. Does this method result in the highest, or the lowest, gross profit? Explain your answer.

Applying the weighted-average, FIFO, and LIFO methods (Obj. 1, 2)

CP6-3 Return to Exhibit 6-4, page 265, and assume that the business sold 30 units of inventory during the period (instead of 40 units as in the exhibit). Compute ending inventory and cost of goods sold for each of the following costing methods:

a. Weighted-average **b.** FIFO **c.** LIFO

Follow the computational format illustrated in the exhibit.

Applying the weighted-average, FIFO, and LIFO methods (Obj. 2)

CP6-4 IKON Data Systems markets the ink used in laser printers. IKON started the year with 100 containers of ink (weighted-average cost of $9.14 each, FIFO cost of $9 each, LIFO cost of $8 each). During the year, IKON purchased 800 containers of ink at $13 and sold 700 units for $20 each. IKON paid operating expenses throughout the year, a total of $4,000. Assume IKON Data Systems is not subject to income tax.

Prepare IKON Data Systems' income statement for the current year ended December 31 under the weighted-average, FIFO, and LIFO inventory costing methods. Include a complete statement heading.

Income tax effects of the inventory costing methods (Obj. 3)

CP6-5 This check point should be used in conjunction with Check Point 6-4. IKON Data Systems in Check Point 6-4 is a corporation subject to a 40% income tax. Compute IKON's income tax expense under the weighted-average, FIFO, and LIFO inventory costing methods. Which method would you select in order to (a) maximize reported income and (b) minimize income tax expense? Format your answer as shown on page 266.

Income and tax effects of LIFO (Obj. 3)

CP6-6 **NIKE, Inc.,** uses the LIFO method to account for inventory. Suppose Nike is having an unusually good year, with net income far above expectations. Assume Nike's inventory costs are rising rapidly. What can Nike's managers do immediately before the end of the year to decrease reported profits and thereby save on income taxes? Explain how this action decreases reported income.

Applying the lower-of-cost-or-market rule to inventory (Obj. 4)

CP6-7 Return to the **Deckers Outdoor Corporation** data in Exhibit 6-1, page 262. At December 31, 1998, the controller of the company applied the lower-of-cost-or-market rule to Deckers' inventories. Suppose the controller determined that the current replacement cost (current market value) of the inventory was $22 million ($22,000 thousand, as in the statements). Show what Deckers would report for inventory and cost of goods sold.

Assessing the effect of an inventory error—one year only (Obj. 4)

CP6-8 Examine the Deckers Outdoor Corporation financial data in Exhibit 6-1, on page 262. Suppose Deckers' inventory at December 31, 1998, as reported, is overstated by $3 million ($3,000 thousand, as in the statements). What are Deckers' correct amounts for (a) inventory, (b) net sales, (c) cost of goods sold, and (d) gross profit?

Assessing the effect of an inventory error on two years' statements (Obj. 4)

CP6-9 Maggie Lang, staff accountant of Crestar Stores, learned that Crestar's $4 million cost of inventory at the end of last year was understated by $1.5 million. She notified the company president of the accounting error and the need to alert Crestar's lenders that last year's reported net income was incorrect. Michael LeVan, president of Crestar, explained to Lang that there is no need to report the error to lenders because the error will counterbalance this year. Even with no correction, LeVan reasons, gross profit for both years combined will be the same whether or not Crestar corrects its error.

1. Was last year's reported gross profit of $6.0 million overstated, understated, or correct? What was the correct amount of gross profit last year?
2. Is this year's gross profit of $6.8 million overstated, understated, or correct? What is the correct amount of gross profit for the current year?
3. Whose perspective is better, Lang's or LeVan's? Give your reason. Consider the trend of reported gross profit both without the correction and with the correction.

Ethical implications of inventory actions (Obj. 3, 4)

CP6-10 Determine whether each of the following actions in buying, selling, and accounting for inventories is ethical or unethical. Give your reason for each answer.

1. DTE Photo Film purchased lots of inventory shortly before year end to increase the LIFO cost of goods sold and decrease reported income for the year.
2. Edison Electrical Products delayed the purchase of inventory until after December 31, 20X3, in order to keep 20X2's cost of goods sold from growing too large. The delay in purchasing inventory helped net income of 20X3 to reach the level of profit demanded by the company's investors.
3. Dover Sales Company deliberately overstated ending inventory in order to report higher profits (net income).
4. Brazos River Corporation consciously overstated purchases to produce a high figure for cost of goods sold (low amount of net income). The real reason was to decrease the company's income tax payments to the government.
5. In applying the lower-of-cost-or-market rule to inventories, Fort Wayne Industries recorded an excessively low market value for ending inventory. This allowed the company to keep from paying income tax for the year.

Using ratio data to evaluate operations (Obj. 5)

CP6-11 Use the data in Exhibits 6-4 and 6-5, pages 265 and 266, to compute the company's gross profit percentage and rate of inventory turnover under

1. FIFO
2. LIFO

Which method makes the company look better on

3. Gross profit percentage? 4. Inventory turnover?

CP6-12 Magnum Auto Parts purchased inventory costing $100,000 and sold 70% of the goods for $120,000, with all transactions on account.

Accounting for inventory transactions (Obj. 6)

1. Journalize these two transactions under the perpetual inventory system.
2. For these transactions, show what Magnum will report for inventory, revenues, and expenses on its financial statements. Report gross profit on the appropriate statement.

CP6-13 Answer the following questions:

Estimating ending inventory by the gross profit method (Obj. 7)

1. Nextel Chemical Company began the year with inventory of $500,000. Inventory purchases for the year totaled $1,600,000. Nextel managers estimate that cost of goods sold for the year will be $1,800,000. How much is Nextel's estimated cost of ending inventory? Use the gross profit method.
2. Nextel Mining, a related company, began the year with inventory of $500,000 and purchased $1,600,000 of goods during the year (the same as in Question 1). Sales for the year are $3,000,000, and Nextel's gross profit percentage is 40% of sales. Compute Nextel's estimated cost of ending inventory by the gross profit method. Compare this answer to your answer in Question 1; they should be the same.

CP6-14

Accounting for inventory transactions and reporting on the statement of cash flows (Obj. 6)

1. Journalize the following transactions for **The Coca-Cola Company**:
   - Cash purchases of inventory, $7.0 billion
   - Sales on account, $18.0 billion
   - Cost of goods sold (perpetual inventory system), $6.9 billion
   - Collections on account, $17.8 billion
2. Which amounts are reported on the statement of cash flows? Are they operating cash flows, investing cash flows, or financing cash flows? Give your reason.

EXERCISES

E6-1 Supply the missing income statement amounts for each of the following companies:

Determining amounts for the income statement (Obj. 1)

Company	*Net Sales*	*Beginning Inventory*	*Purchases*	*Ending Inventory*	*Cost of Goods Sold*	*Gross Profit*
A	$94,700	$ (a)	$54,900	$22,600	$59,400	$ (b)
B	98,600	10,700	(c)	8,200	(d)	47,100
C	92,800	12,500	62,700	19,400	(e)	37,000
D	(f)	27,450	93,000	(g)	94,100	51,200

Prepare the income statement for company D, showing the computation of cost of goods sold. Company D's operating expenses for the year were $32,100, and its income tax rate is 40%.

Note: Exercise 6-12 builds on Exercise 6-1 with a profitability analysis of companies A–D.

E6-2 **Toys "Я" Us** is budgeting for the fiscal year ended January 31, 20X3. During the preceding year ended January 31, 20X2, sales totaled $9,400 million and cost of goods sold was $6,500 million. Inventory stood at $1,700 million at January 31, 20X1; and at January 31, 20X2, inventory stood at $1,900 million.

Budgeting inventory purchases (Obj. 1)

During the upcoming 20X3 year, suppose Toys "Я" Us expects sales and cost of goods sold to increase by 8%. The company budgets next year's ending inventory at $2,200 million.

Required

How much inventory should Toys "Я" Us purchase during the upcoming year in order to reach its budgeted figures?

Determining ending inventory and cost of goods sold by four methods (Obj. 2)

E6-3 Discount Computer Co. inventory records for computer chips indicate the following at October 31:

Oct. 1	Beginning inventory	5 units @	$160
8	Purchase	4 units @	160
15	Purchase	11 units @	170
26	Purchase	5 units @	176

The physical count of inventory at October 31 indicates that eight units are on hand, and there are no consignment goods.

Required

1. Compute ending inventory and cost of goods sold, using each of the following methods:
   a. Specific unit cost, assuming five $160 units and three $170 units are on hand
   b. Weighted-average cost
   c. First-in, first-out
   d. Last-in, first-out

2. Which method produces the highest cost of goods sold? Which method produces the lowest cost of goods sold? What causes the difference in cost of goods sold?

Computing the tax advantage of LIFO over FIFO (Obj. 3)

E6-4 Use the data in Exercise 6-3 to illustrate Discount Computer Co.'s income tax advantage of LIFO over FIFO. Sales revenue is $6,000, operating expenses are $1,100, and the income tax rate is 40%. How much in taxes would the company save by using the LIFO method?

Determining ending inventory and cost of goods sold (Obj. 1, 2)

E6-5 Holze Equipment Company specializes in printing equipment. Because each inventory item is expensive, Holze uses a perpetual inventory system. Company records indicate the following data for a line of collating machines:

Date	*Item*	*Quantity*	*Unit Cost*
May 1	Balance	5	$90
6	Sale	3	
8	Purchase	11	95
17	Sale	4	
30	Sale	3	

Required

1. Determine the amounts that Holze should report for ending inventory and cost of goods sold two ways:
   a. FIFO **b.** LIFO

2. Report inventory and cost of goods sold at FIFO in the financial statements. Include the names of all the current asset accounts on the balance sheet, and prepare the income statement through gross profit.

Measuring gross profit (Obj. 1, 2)

E6-6 Suppose a **Wal-Mart** store in Branson, Missouri, ended May 20X1 with 800,000 units of merchandise that cost an average of $6 each. Suppose the store then sold 600,000 units of merchandise for $4.4 million during June 20X1. Further, assume the store made two large purchases during June as follows:

June 6	100,000 units @ $6 =	$ 600,000
21	400,000 units @ $5 =	2,000,000

1. At June 30, the store manager needs to know the store's gross profit under both FIFO and LIFO. Supply this information.

2. What caused the FIFO and LIFO gross profit figures to differ? Does the difference go in the direction you would predict? Explain in detail.

Change from LIFO to FIFO (Obj. 3)

E6-7 Quaker Industries is considering a change from the LIFO inventory method to the FIFO method. Managers are concerned about the effect of this change on income tax expense and reported net income. If the change is made, it will become effective on March 1. Inventory on hand at February 28 is $63,000. During March, Quaker managers expect sales of $260,000, net purchases between $159,000 and $182,000, and operating expenses, excluding income tax, of $83,000. The income tax rate is 40%. Inventories at March 31 are budgeted as follows: FIFO, $85,000; LIFO, $78,000.

	A	B	C	D	E
1	QUAKER INDUSTRIES				
2	Estimated Income under FIFO and LIFO				
3	March 20XX				
4					
5		*FIFO*	*LIFO*	*FIFO*	*LIFO*
6					
7	Sales	$260,000	$260,000	$260,000	$260,000
8					
9	Cost of goods sold				
10	Beginning inventory	63,000	63,000	63,000	63,000
11	Purchases	159,000	159,000	182,000	182,000
12					
13	Cost of goods available				
14	Ending inventory	(85,000)	(78,000)	(85,000)	(78,000)
15					
16	Cost of goods sold				
17					
18	Gross profit				
19	Operating expenses	83,000	83,000	83,000	83,000
20					
21	Income from operations				
22	Income tax expense				
23					
24	Net income	$	$	$	$
25					

Required

Create a spreadsheet model to compute estimated net income for March under FIFO and LIFO. Format your answer as shown here.

Managing income taxes under the LIFO method (Obj. 3)

E6-8 Tomassini Corp. is nearing the end of its best year ever. With three weeks until year end, it appears that net income for the year will have increased by 70% over last year. Larry Tomassini, the principal stockholder and president, is pleased with the year's success but unhappy about the huge increase in income taxes that the business will have to pay.

He asks you, the financial vice president, to come up with a way to decrease the business's income tax burden. Inventory quantities are a little lower than normal because sales have been especially strong during the last few months. Tomassini Corp. uses the LIFO inventory method, and inventory costs have risen dramatically during the latter part of the year.

Required

Write a memorandum to Larry Tomassini to explain how the company can decrease its income taxes for the current year. Tomassini is a man of integrity, so your plan must be completely honest and ethical.

Identifying income, tax, and other effects of the inventory methods (Obj. 3)

E6-9 This exercise tests your understanding of the various inventory methods. In the space provided, write the name of the inventory method that best fits the description. Assume that the cost of inventory is rising.

FIFO	1.	Results in a cost of ending inventory that is close to the current cost of replacing the inventory.
specific Identification	2.	Used to account for automobiles, jewelry, and art objects.
FIFO	3.	Associated with inventory profits.
average	4.	Provides a middle-ground measure of ending inventory and cost of goods sold.
FIFO	5.	Maximizes reported income.
LIFO	6.	Enables a company to buy high-cost inventory at year end and thereby decrease reported income.
LIFO	7.	Enables a company to keep reported income from dropping lower by liquidating older layers of inventory.
LIFO	8.	Matches the most current cost of goods sold against sales revenue.
LIFO	9.	Results in an old measure of the cost of ending inventory.
LIFO	10.	Generally associated with saving income taxes.

Correcting an inventory error (Obj. 4)

E6-10 Pharmacia, Inc., uses a perpetual inventory system and reports inventory at the lower of FIFO cost or market. Prior to releasing its March 20X4 financial statements, Pharmacia's preliminary income statement is as follows:

INCOME STATEMENT (PARTIAL)	
Sales revenue	$92,000
Cost of goods sold	45,100
Gross profit	$46,900

During the year, Pharmacia purchased inventory at a cost of $30,000. The company has learned that beginning inventory was understated by $2,000. Ending inventory at March 31 is $9,400, and this amount is correct.

Show how Pharmacia should report the above data on its March income statement, and the company's inventory on its March 31 balance sheet.

Correcting an inventory error (Obj. 4)

E6-11 MERK Oil Company, a small independent producer, reported the following comparative income statement for the years ended September 30, 20X3 and 20X2:

MERK OIL COMPANY
Income Statement
Years Ended September 30, 20X3 and 20X2

	20X3		*20X2*	
Sales revenue		$137,300		$121,700
Cost of goods sold:				
Beginning inventory	$14,000		$12,800	
Purchases	72,000		66,000	
Cost of goods available	86,000		78,800	
Ending inventory	(16,600)		(14,000)	
Cost of goods sold		69,400		64,800
Gross profit		67,900		56,900
Operating expenses		30,300		26,100
Net income		$ 37,600		$ 30,800

During fiscal year 20X3, accountants discovered that ending 20X2 inventory was understated by $2,000. Prepare the corrected comparative income statement for the two-year period. What was the effect of the error on net income for the two years combined? Explain your answer.

E6-12 Refer to the data in Exercise 6-1 (p. 262). Which company is likely to be the most profitable, based on its gross profit percentage and rate of inventory turnover? Why should the company with the fastest inventory turnover have the lowest operating expenses?

Measuring profitability (Obj. 7)

Suppose you are a financial analyst, and a client has asked you to recommend an investment in one of these companies. Write a memo outlining which company you recommend and explain your reasoning.

E6-13 Schmeltekopf Corporation, which uses a perpetual inventory system, has these account balances at December 31, 20X4, prior to releasing the financial statements for the year:

Applying the lower-of-cost-or-market rule to inventories (Obj. 1)

INVENTORY		COST OF GOODS SOLD		SALES REVENUE	
Beg. bal. 12,400					
End. bal. 18,000		Bal. 110,000			Bal. 225,000

A year ago, when Schmeltekopf prepared its 20X3 financial statements, the replacement cost of ending inventory was $13,050. Schmeltekopf has determined that the replacement cost of the December 31, 20X4, ending inventory is $17,200.

Required

Prepare Schmeltekopf Corporation's 20X4 income statement through gross profit to show how the company would apply the lower-of-cost-or-market rule to its inventories.

E6-14 Accounting records for Goodrich, Inc., yield the following data for the year ended December 31, 20X1 (amounts in thousands):

Accounting for inventory transactions (Obj. 6)

Inventory, December 31, 20X0	$ 370
Purchases of inventory (on account)	2,900
Sales of inventory—80% on account; 20% for cash (cost $2,800)	4,390
Inventory at the lower of FIFO cost or market, December 31, 20X1	?

Required

1. Journalize Goodrich's inventory transactions for the year under the perpetual system. Show all amounts in thousands. Use Exhibit 6-13 as a model.
2. Report ending inventory, sales, cost of goods sold, and gross profit on the appropriate financial statement (amounts in thousands). Show the computation of cost of goods sold.

E6-15 Use the data in Exercise 6-3 (p. 263) to journalize the following transactions for Discount Computer Co., which uses the perpetual inventory system:

Recording inventory transactions (Obj. 6)

1. Total October purchases in one summary entry. All purchases were on credit.
2. Total October sales and cost of goods sold in two summary entries. The selling price was $300 per unit, and all sales were on credit. Discount Computer uses LIFO for inventory and cost of goods sold.
3. How much gross profit did Discount Computer earn? How much is the company's ending inventory?

E6-16 **The Home Depot** made sales of $30.2 billion in the year ended January 31, 1999. Collections from customers totaled $30.3 billion. The company began the year with $3.6 billion in inventories and ended with $4.3 billion. During the year purchases of inventory added up to $22.3 billion. Of the purchases, Home Depot paid $21.4 billion to suppliers.

Measuring gross profit and reporting cash flows (Obj. 1)

As an investor searching for a good investment, suppose you identify two critical pieces of information about Home Depot's operations during the year:

1. Compute Home Depot's gross profit.
2. What should Home Depot's statement of cash flows report for the foregoing data? Report the needed information.

E6-17 Georgia Technologies began January with inventory of $39,000. The business made net purchases of $37,600 and had net sales of $60,000 before a fire destroyed the company's inventory. For the past several years, Georgia's gross profit on sales has been 40%. Estimate the cost of the inventory destroyed by the fire. Identify another reason managers use the gross profit method to estimate inventory cost on a regular basis.

Estimating inventory by the gross profit method (Obj. 7)

CHALLENGE EXERCISES

Inventory policy decisions (Obj. 2, 3)

E6-18 For each of the following situations, identify the inventory method that you would use or, given the use of a particular method, state the strategy that you would follow to accomplish your goal:

a. Inventory costs have been stable for several years, and you expect costs to remain stable for the indefinite future. (Give the reason for your choice of method.)

b. Company management, like that of **IBM**, prefers a middle-of-the-road inventory policy that avoids extremes.

c. Your inventory turns over slowly. Inventory costs are increasing, and the company prefers to report high income.

d. Suppliers of your inventory are threatening a labor strike, and it may be difficult for your company to obtain inventory. This situation could increase your income taxes.

e. Inventory costs are decreasing, and your company's board of directors wants to minimize income taxes.

f. Inventory costs are increasing. Your company uses LIFO and is having an unexpectedly good year. It is near year end, and you need to keep net income from increasing too much.

LIFO liquidation (Obj. 2)

E6-19 Whirlpool Corporation, the world's leading manufacturer of major home appliances, reported these figures, as adapted, for 19X9 (in millions of dollars):

INCOME STATEMENT (ADAPTED)

Net revenues	$6,757
Cost of products sold	4,967
Operating expenses	1,397
Other expense (net)	93
Earnings before income taxes	300
Income taxes	100
Net earnings	$ 200

Note 4 of the financial statements disclosed:
Liquidation of prior years' LIFO inventory layers increased net earnings $8 million.

Required

1. Explain what the LIFO liquidation means and why it affects net earnings.

2. Would Whirlpool management be pleased or displeased at the increase in income due to the LIFO liquidation? Give your reason.

3. Prepare a revised income statement for Whirlpool Corporation if no LIFO liquidation had occurred. Assume the income tax rate was 33.3%.

Evaluating a company's profitability (Obj. 5)

E6-20 Hershey Foods Corporation reported these figures:

HERSHEY FOODS CORPORATION
Statement of Income
Years Ended December 31, 19X7 and 19X6

Millions	***19X7***	***19X6***
Sales	$4,302	$3,989
Cost of sales	2,489	2,302
Selling, marketing and administrative	1,183	1,124
Loss on disposal of businesses	—	35
Interest expense	76	48
Income tax expense	218	207
Net income	$ 336	$ 273

Required

Evaluate Hershey's operations during 19X7 in comparison to 19X6. Consider sales, gross profit, and net income. Track the gross profit percentage (to three decimal places) and the rate of inventory turnover (to one decimal place) in both years. Hershey's inventories at December 31, 19X7, 19X6, and 19X5, were $506, $475, and $516 million, respectively.

Required

1. Make summary journal entries to record the Lord & Taylor store's transactions for the year ended January 31, 20X0. The company uses a perpetual inventory system.
2. Determine the LIFO cost of the store's ending inventory at January 31, 20X0. Use a T-account.
3. Prepare the Lord & Taylor store's income statement for the year ended January 31, 20X0. Show totals for the gross profit, income before tax, and net income.

P6-9A Thornhill Oil Co. lost some chemical inventory in a fire. To file an insurance claim, Thornhill must estimate its inventory by the gross profit method. For the past two years, Thornhill's gross profit has averaged 20% of net sales. The company's inventory records reveal the following data:

Estimating inventory by the gross profit method; preparing the income statement (Obj. 7)

Inventory, March 1	$1,292,000
Transactions during March:	
Purchases	6,585,000
Purchase discounts	149,000
Purchase returns	8,000
Sales	8,657,000
Sales returns	17,000

Required

1. Estimate the cost of the lost inventory using the gross profit method.
2. Thornhill also asks you to prepare the company's March income statement through gross profit. Show the detailed computation of cost of goods sold in a separate schedule.

(Group B)

P6-1B Condensed versions of an **Exxon** convenience store's most recent income statement and balance sheet reported as follows. Because the business is organized as a proprietorship, it pays no corporate income tax.

Using the cost-of-goods-sold model to budget operations (Obj. 1)

EXXON CONVENIENCE STORE
Income Statement
Year Ended December 31, 20X4

Sales	$800,000
Cost of sales	660,000
Gross profit	140,000
Operating expenses	80,000
Net income	$ 60,000

EXXON CONVENIENCE STORE
Balance Sheet
December 31, 20X4

Assets		*Liabilities and Capital*	
Cash	$ 70,000	Accounts payable	$ 35,000
Inventories	35,000	Note payable	280,000
Land and buildings, net	360,000	Total liabilities	315,000
		Owner, capital	150,000
Total assets	$465,000	Total liabilities and capital	$465,000

The owner is budgeting for 20X5. He expects sales to increase by 10% and the gross profit *percentage* to remain unchanged. To meet customer demand for the increase in sales, ending inventory will need to be $50,000 at December 31, 20X5. The owner can lower operating expenses by doing some of the work himself. He hopes to earn a net income of $90,000 next year.

Required

1. A key variable the owner can control is the amount of inventory he purchases. Show how to determine the amount of purchases he should make in 20X5.
2. Prepare the store's budgeted income statement for 20X5 to reach the target net income of $90,000.

P6-2B Assume a **Reebok** outlet store began August 20X0 with 50 pairs of hiking boots that cost $40 each. The sale price of these boots was $70. During August, the store completed these inventory transactions:

Measuring cost of goods sold and ending inventory (Obj. 1, 2)

			Units	Unit Cost	Unit Sale Price
Aug.	3	Sale	16	$40	$70
	8	Purchase	80	41	72
	11	Sale	34	40	70
	19	Sale	9	41	72
	24	Sale	35	41	72
	30	Purchase	18	42	73
	31	Sale	8	41	72

Required

1. The preceding data are taken from the store's inventory records. Which cost method does the store use?
2. Determine the store's cost of goods sold for August. Also compute gross profit for August.
3. What is the cost of the store's August 31 inventory of hiking boots?

Computing inventory by three methods (Obj. 2, 3)

P6-3B Sequoia Carpet Co. began March with 73 yards of carpet that cost $23 per yard. During the month, Sequoia made the following purchases:

March	4	113 yards @ $27
	12	81 yards @ 29
	19	167 yards @ 32
	25	44 yards @ 35

At March 31 the ending inventory consists of 48 yards of carpet.

Required

1. Determine the ending inventory and cost-of-goods-sold amounts for March under (1) weighted-average cost, (2) FIFO cost, and (3) LIFO cost. Round weighted-average cost per unit to the nearest cent and round all other amounts to the nearest dollar.
2. How much income tax would Sequoia save during the month by using LIFO versus FIFO? The income tax rate is 40%.

Applying the different inventory costing methods (Obj. 2, 3)

P6-4B The records of Las Colinas Tennis Center include the following accounts at December 31 of the current year:

INVENTORY

Debit	Amount	Credit
Jan. 1 Balance (700 units @ $7.00)	4,900	
Jan. 6 Purchase 300 units @ $7.05	2,115	
Mar. 19 Purchase 1,100 units @ 7.35	8,085	
June 22 Purchase 8,400 units @ 7.50	63,000	
Oct. 4 Purchase 500 units @ 8.50	4,250	

SALES REVENUE

Debit	Credit	Amount
	Feb. 5 1,000 units @ $12.00	12,000
	Apr. 10 700 units @ 12.10	8,470
	July 31 1,800 units @ 13.25	23,850
	Sep. 4 3,500 units @ 13.50	47,250
	Nov. 27 3,100 units @ 14.00	43,400
	Dec. 31 Balance	134,970

Required

1. Prepare a partial income statement through gross profit under the weighted-average, FIFO, and LIFO methods. Use the cost-of-goods-sold model.
2. Which inventory method would you use to minimize income tax?

P6-5B MJ Design has recently been plagued with lackluster sales. The rate of inventory turnover has dropped, and some of the company's merchandise is gathering dust. At the same time, competition has forced MJ's suppliers to lower the prices that the company will pay when it replaces its inventory. It is now December 31, 20X2, and the current replacement cost of MJ Design's ending inventory is $1,000,000 below what MJ actually paid for the goods, which was $4,900,000. Before any adjustments at the end of the period, MJ's Cost of Goods Sold account has a balance of $29,600,000.

Applying the lower-of-cost-or-market rule to inventories (Obj. 4)

What action should MJ Design take in this situation? Give any journal entry required. At what amount should MJ report Inventory on the balance sheet? At what amount should the company report Cost of Goods Sold on the income statement? Discuss the accounting principle or concept that is most relevant to this situation.

P6-6B The Glen Oaks Boutique books show these data (in thousands):

Correcting inventory errors over a three-year period (Obj. 5)

	20X3		20X2		20X1	
Net sales revenue		$360		$285		$244
Cost of goods sold:						
Beginning inventory	$ 65		$ 55		$ 70	
Purchases	195		135		130	
Cost of goods available	260		190		200	
Less ending inventory	(70)		(65)		(55)	
Cost of goods sold		190		125		145
Gross profit		170		160		99
Operating expenses		113		109		76
Net income		$ 57		$ 51		$ 23

In early 20X4, internal auditors discovered that the ending inventory for 20X1 was overstated by $2 thousand and that the ending inventory for 20X3 was understated by $3 thousand. The ending inventory at December 31, 20X2, was correct.

Required

1. Show corrected income statements for the three years.
2. State whether each year's net income and owners' equity amounts are understated or overstated. Ignore income tax because Glen Oaks is a proprietorship. For each incorrect figure, indicate the amount of the understatement or overstatement.

P6-7B **Wal-Mart Stores, Inc.,** the world's largest retailer, reported these figures:

Using the gross profit percentage and the inventory turnover ratio to evaluate two retailers (Obj. 5)

WAL-MART STORES, INC.
Consolidated Statement of Income

(Amounts in millions)	*Fiscal Years Ended January 31* 19X6	19X5
Revenues:		
Net sales	$93,627	$82,494
Other income—net	1,122	918
	94,749	83,412
Costs and Expenses:		
Cost of sales	74,564	65,586
Operating, selling, and general and administrative expenses	14,951	12,858

WAL-MART STORES, INC.
Consolidated Balance Sheet

(Amounts in millions)	*January 31* 19X6	19X5
Assets		
Current Assets:		
Cash and cash equivalents	$ 83	$ 45
Receivables	853	900
Inventories	15,989	14,064
Prepaid expenses and other	406	329
Total Current Assets	$17,331	$15,338

For the same year ended January 31, 19X6, **The May Department Stores Company,** which owns over 300 upscale Lord & Taylor, Hecht's, Foley's, Robinson-May, Kaufmanns, Filene's Basement, and other stores, reported the following:

THE MAY DEPARTMENT STORES COMPANY
Consolidated Statement of Earnings

(Dollars in millions)	*Fiscal Year* 19X6	19X5
Net Retail Sales	$10,507	$9,759
Other revenues	445	348
Cost of sales	7,461	6,879
Selling, general and administrative expenses	2,081	1,916
Interest expense, net	250	233
Total cost of sales and expenses	9,792	9,028
Earnings from continuing operations before income taxes	1,160	1,079
Provision for income taxes	460	429
Net Earnings from Continuing Operations	$ 700	$ 650

THE MAY DEPARTMENT STORES COMPANY
Consolidated Balance Sheet

(Dollars in millions)	*Fiscal Year End* February 3, 19X6	January 28, 19X5
Assets		
Current Assets:		
Cash	$ 12	$ 8
Cash equivalents	147	40
Accounts receivable, net	2,403	2,432
Merchandise inventories	2,134	1,813
Other current assets	169	182
Net current assets of discontinued operation	232	243
Total Current Assets	$5,097	$4,718

Required

1. Compute both companies' gross profit percentage and inventory turnover ratio during 19X6.
2. What do these statistics reveal about Wal-Mart's and May's marketing strategies? Which company is clearly the discount merchandiser? Which company depends on higher markups to earn a profit?

P6-8B Toys "Я" Us purchases inventory in crates of merchandise, each unit of inventory is a crate of toys. Assume you are dealing with a single Toys "Я" Us store in San Antonio, Texas. The fiscal year of Toys "Я" Us ends each January 31.

Accounting for inventory in a perpetual system (Obj. 2, 6)

Assume the San Antonio Toys "Я" Us store began fiscal year 20X5 with an inventory of 20,000 units that cost a total of $1,200,000. During the year, the store purchased merchandise on account as follows:

April (30,000 units @ $65)	$ 1,950,000
August (50,000 units @ $65)	3,250,000
November (90,000 units @ $70)	6,300,000
Total purchases	$11,500,000

Cash payments on account during the year totaled $11,390,000.

During fiscal year 20X5, the store sold 180,000 units of merchandise for $16,400,000, of which $5,300,000 was for cash and the balance was on account. Toys "Я" Us uses the LIFO method for inventories.

Operating expenses for the year were $3,710,000. The store paid 80% in cash and accrued the rest. The store accrued income tax at the rate of 40%.

Required

1. Make summary journal entries to record the store's transactions for the year ended January 31, 20X5. Toys "Я" Us uses a perpetual inventory system.
2. Determine the LIFO cost of the store's ending inventory at January 31, 20X5. Use a T-account.
3. Prepare the store's income statement for the year ended January 31, 20X5. Show totals for the gross profit, income before tax, and net income.

P6-9B MacKay Rubber Company lost some of its inventory in a fire. To file an insurance claim, the company must estimate its inventory by the gross profit method. For the past two years, the gross profit has averaged 20% of net sales. The company's inventory records reveal the following data:

Estimating inventory by the gross profit method; preparing the income statement (Obj. 7)

Inventory, July 1	$ 367,000
Transactions during July:	
Purchases	5,789,000
Purchase discounts	26,000
Purchase returns	12,000
Sales	6,430,000
Sales returns	25,000

Required

1. Estimate the cost of the lost inventory, using the gross profit method.
2. The company also asks you to prepare its July income statement through gross profit. Show the detailed computation of cost of goods sold in a separate schedule.

EXTENDING YOUR KNOWLEDGE

DECISION CASES

Case 1. Bluebonnet Enterprises is nearing the end of its first year of operations. The company made inventory purchases of $745,000 during the year, as follows:

Assessing the impact of a year-end purchase of inventory (Obj. 2, 3)

January	1,000 units @	$100.00	=	$100,000
July	4,000	121.25		485,000
November	1,000	160.00		160,000
Totals	6,000			$745,000

Sales for the year will be 5,000 units for $1,200,000 of revenue. Expenses other than cost of goods sold and income taxes will be $300,000. The president of the company is undecided about whether to adopt the FIFO method or the LIFO method for inventories.

The company has storage capacity for 5,000 additional units of inventory. Inventory prices are expected to stay at $160 per unit for the next few months. The president is considering purchasing 1,000 additional units of inventory at $160 each before the end of the year. He wishes to know how the purchase would affect net income under both FIFO and LIFO. The income tax rate is 40%.

Required

1. To aid company decision making, prepare income statements under FIFO and under LIFO, both *without* and *with* the year-end purchase of 1,000 units of inventory at $160 per unit.
2. Compare net income under FIFO *without* and *with* the year-end purchase. Make the same comparison under LIFO. Under which method does the year-end purchase have the greater effect on net income?
3. Under which method can a year-end purchase be made in order to manage net income?

Assessing the impact of the inventory costing method on the financial statements (Obj. 2, 3, 4)

Case 2. The inventory costing method a company chooses can affect the financial statements and thus the decisions of the people who use those statements.

Required

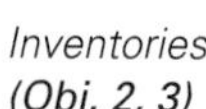

1. Conservatism is an accepted accounting concept. Would you want management to be conservative in accounting for inventory if you were (a) a shareholder or (b) a prospective shareholder? Give your reason.
2. Outback Cycle Company follows conservative accounting and writes the value of its inventory of bicycles down to market, which has declined below cost. The following year, an unexpected cycling craze results in a demand for bicycles that far exceeds supply, and the market price increases above the previous cost. What effect will conservatism have on the income of Outback over the two years?
3. A leading accounting researcher stated that one inventory costing method reports the most recent costs in the income statement, whereas another method reports the most recent costs in the balance sheet. In this person's opinion, the result is that one or the other of the statements is "inaccurate" when prices are rising. What did the researcher mean?

ETHICAL ISSUE

During 20X2, American Fabricators, Inc. (AFI) changed to the LIFO method of accounting for inventory. Suppose that during 20X3, AFI changes back to the FIFO method and the following year switches back to LIFO again.

Required

1. What would you think of a company's ethics if it changed accounting methods every year?
2. What accounting principle would changing methods every year violate?
3. Who can be harmed when a company changes its accounting methods too often? How?

FINANCIAL STATEMENT CASES

Inventories (Obj. 2, 3)

Case 1. The notes are an important part of a company's financial statements, giving valuable details that would clutter the tabular data presented in the statements. This case will help you learn to use a company's inventory notes. Refer to **The Gap's** statements and related notes in Appendix A at the end of the book and answer the following questions:

1. How much was the The Gap's merchandise inventory at January 30, 1999? At January 31, 1998?
2. How does The Gap value its inventories? Which cost method does the company use?
3. By rearranging the cost-of-goods-sold formula, you can determine purchases, which are not disclosed in The Gap's statements. How much were the company's inventory purchases during the year ended January 30, 1999? You can ignore ". . . and occupancy expenses" in the cost of goods sold title.

Case 2. Obtain the annual report of a company. Make sure that *Inventories* are included among its current assets. Answer these questions about the company.

Analyzing inventories (Obj. 2, 3)

1. How much were the company's total inventories at the end of the current year? At the end of the preceding year?
2. How does the company value its inventories? Which cost method or methods does the company use?
3. Depending on the nature of the company's business, would you expect the company to use a periodic inventory system or a perpetual system? Give your reason.
4. By rearranging the cost-of-goods-sold formula, you can solve for inventory purchases, which are not disclosed. Show how to compute the company's purchases during the current year. Examine the company's note titled Inventories, Merchandise Inventories, or a similar term. If the company discloses several categories of inventories, including a title similar to Finished Goods, use the beginning and ending balances of Finished Goods for the computation of purchases. If only one category of Inventories is disclosed, use these beginning and ending balances.

Group Project

Obtain the annual reports of ten companies, two from each of five different industries. Most companies' financial statements can be down loaded from their Web sites.

Comparing companies' inventory turnover ratios (Obj. 5)

1. Compute each company's gross profit percentage and rate of inventory turnover for the most recent two years. If annual reports are unavailable or do not provide enough data for multiple-year computations, you can gather financial statement data from *Moody's Industrial Manual.*
2. For the industries of the companies you are analyzing, obtain the industry averages for gross profit percentage and inventory turnover from Robert Morris Associates, *Annual Statement Studies;* Dun and Bradstreet, *Industry Norms and Key Business Ratios;* or Leo Troy, *Almanac of Business and Industrial Financial Ratios.*
3. How well does each of your companies compare to the other company in its industry? How well do your companies compare to the average for their industry? What insight about your companies can you glean from these ratios?
4. Write a memo to summarize your findings, stating whether your group would invest in each of the companies it has analyzed.

Internet Exercise

Nike Corporation

NIKE is the world's number-one shoe company and dominates the United States athletic shoe market with a 45% market share. The company designs and sells shoes for most sports and also has lines of dress and casual shoes, athletic apparel, and equipment. Nike products are sold in over 100 countries.

1. Go to **http://www.nikebiz.com/invest/financials.shtml**. Use the income statement, balance sheet, and note number 1 to answer the following questions and perform the following exercises.
2. For the most recent year, identify the amount reported for *Cost of Sales* and compute the total of all other expenses combined. Which is the larger amount? Comment on the significance of *Cost of Sales* for a manufacturing firm.
3. For the three most recent years, identify the amounts reported for *Revenues* and *Cost of Sales.* For each year, compute *Gross Profit* and *Gross Profit Percentage.* For each of these four amounts, comment on the direction of the trend, what the trend might indicate, and whether the trend should be considered favorable or unfavorable.
4. For the two most recent years, identify the amount reported for ending *Inventory.* For the most recent year, compute the *Inventory Turnover Ratio.* On average, how many days does Nike hold inventory before selling it?
5. Currently, which inventory costing method does Nike use? In 1998, which inventory costing method was used by Nike? As a result of this change in inventory costing method, would net income be expected to increase or decrease? Comment on whether this violates the consistency principle?

Appendix A to Chapter 6

Accounting for Inventory in the Periodic System

Periodic Inventory System

In the periodic inventory system, the business does not keep a continuous record of the inventory on hand. Instead, at the end of the period, the business makes a physical count of the inventory on hand and applies the unit costs to determine the cost of ending inventory. This inventory figure appears on the balance sheet and is used to compute cost of goods sold.

The periodic system is also called the *physical system* because it relies on the actual physical count of inventory. To use the periodic system effectively, the company's owner must be able to control inventory by visual inspection. For example, when a customer inquires about quantities on hand, the owner or manager should be able to eyeball the goods in the store.

Recording Transactions in the Periodic System. In the periodic system, the business records purchases of inventory in the Purchases account (an expense). Throughout the period, the Inventory account carries the beginning balance left over from the end of the preceding period. At the end of the period, the Inventory account must be updated for the financial statements. A journal entry removes the beginning balance, crediting Inventory and debiting Cost of Goods Sold. A second journal entry sets up the ending inventory balance, based on the physical count. The debit is to Inventory and the credit to Cost of Goods Sold. The final entry in this sequence transfers the amount of Purchases to Cost of Goods Sold. These end-of-period entries can be made during the closing process.

After the process is complete, Inventory has its correct balance of $120,000, and Cost of Goods Sold shows $540,000. Exhibit 6-A illustrates the accounting in the periodic system.

Exhibit 6-A
Recording and Reporting Inventories—Periodic System (Amounts assumed)

PERIODIC SYSTEM

PANEL A—Recording Transactions and the T-accounts

1. Credit purchases of $560,000:

Purchases	560,000	
Accounts Payable		560,000

ASSETS	=	LIABILITIES	+	STOCKHOLDERS' EQUITY	+	EXPENSES
0	=	560,000			+	560,000

2. Credit sales of $900,000:

Accounts Receivable	900,000	
Sales Revenue		900,000

ASSETS	=	LIABILITIES	+	STOCKHOLDERS' EQUITY	+	REVENUES
900,000	=	0			+	900,000

(Continued)

EXHIBIT 6-A (CONT.)

3. End-of-period entries to update Inventory and record Cost of Goods Sold:
   a. Transfer the cost of beginning inventory ($100,000) to Cost of Goods Sold.

Cost of Goods Sold	100,000	
Inventory (beginning balance)		100,000

   b. Record the cost of ending inventory ($120,000) based on a physical count.

Inventory (ending balance)	120,000	
Cost of Goods Sold		120,000

   c. Transfer the cost of purchases to Cost of Goods Sold.

Cost of Goods Sold	560,000	
Purchases		560,000

INVENTORY AND COST OF GOODS SOLD ACCOUNTS

Inventory		Cost of Goods Sold	
100,000*	**100,000**	**100,000**	**120,000**
120,000		**560,000**	
		540,000	

*Beginning Inventory was $100,000.

PANEL B—Reporting in the Financial Statements

Sales revenue		$900,000
Cost of goods sold:		
Beginning inventory	$100,000	
Purchases	560,000	
Cost of goods available	660,000	
Ending inventory	(120,000)	
Cost of goods sold		540,000
Gross profit		$360,000

Current assets:	
Cash	$ XXX
Short-term investments	XXX
Accounts receivable	XXX
Inventory	120,000
Prepaid expenses	XXX

CHECK POINTS

Recording inventory transactions in the periodic system

CP6-1A Magnum Auto Parts began the year with inventory of $20,000. During the year, Magnum purchased inventory costing $100,000 and sold goods for $140,000, with all transactions on account. Magnum ended the year with inventory of $40,000. Journalize all the necessary transactions under the periodic inventory system.

Computing cost of goods sold and preparing the income statement

CP6-2A Use the data in Check Point 6-1A to do the following:

1. Post to the Inventory and Cost of Goods Sold accounts.
2. Compute cost of goods sold by the cost-of-goods-sold model.
3. Prepare the income statement of Magnum Auto Parts through gross profit.

EXERCISES

Computing amounts for the GAAP inventory methods

E6-1A Abba Medical Supply's inventory records for industrial switches indicate the following at October 31:

Oct.	1	Beginning inventory	5 units @ $160
	8	Purchase	4 units @ 160
	15	Purchase	11 units @ 170
	26	Purchase	5 units @ 176

The physical count of inventory at October 31 indicates that eight units of inventory are on hand, and there are no consignment goods.

Required

Compute ending inventory and cost of goods sold, using each of the following methods:

1. Specific unit cost, assuming five $160 units and three $170 units are on hand
2. Weighted-average cost
3. First-in, first-out
4. Last-in, first-out

Journalizing inventory transactions in the periodic system; computing cost of goods sold

E6-2A Use the data in Exercise 6-1A to journalize the following for the periodic system:

1. Total October purchases in one summary entry. All purchases were on credit.
2. Total October sales in a summary entry. Assume that the selling price was $300 per unit and that all sales were on credit. Abba Medical Supply uses LIFO.
3. October 31 entries for inventory. Abba Medical Supply uses LIFO. Post to the Cost of Goods Sold T-account to show how this amount is determined. Label each item in the account.
4. Show the computation of cost of goods sold by the cost-of-goods-sold model.

PROBLEMS

Computing cost of goods sold and gross profit on sales

P6-1A An **American Tourister** outlet store began August 20X2 with 50 units of inventory that cost $40 each. The sale price of these units was $70. During August, the store completed these inventory transactions:

			Units	*Unit Cost*	*Unit Sale Price*
Aug.	3	Sale	16	$40	$70
	8	Purchase	80	41	72
	11	Sale	34	40	70
	19	Sale	9	41	72
	24	Sale	35	41	72
	30	Purchase	18	42	73
	31	Sale	6	41	72

Required

1. The preceding data are taken from the store's inventory records. Which cost method does the store use?
2. Determine the store's cost of goods sold for August under the periodic inventory system.
3. Compute gross profit for August.

P6-2A Accounting records for Big Gap, Inc., yield the following data for the year ended December 31, 20X5 (amounts in thousands):

Recording transactions in the periodic system; reporting inventory items in the financial statements

Inventory, December 31, 20X4	$ 370
Purchases of inventory (on account)	2,900
Sales of inventory—80% on account; 20% for cash	4,390
Inventory at the lower of FIFO cost or market, December 31, 20X5 . .	470

Required

1. Journalize Big Gap's inventory transactions for the year under the periodic system. Show all amounts in thousands. Use Exhibit 6-A as a model.
2. Report ending inventory, sales, cost of goods sold, and gross profit on the appropriate financial statement (amounts in thousands). Show the computation of cost of goods sold.

APPENDIX B TO CHAPTER 6

HOW ANALYSTS USE THE LIFO RESERVE—CONVERTING A LIFO COMPANY'S INCOME TO THE FIFO BASIS

Suppose you are a financial analyst, and it is your job to recommend stocks for your clients to purchase as investments. You have narrowed your choice to **Wal-Mart Stores, Inc.**, and **The Gap, Inc.** In your analysis, you observe that Wal-Mart uses the LIFO method for inventories and The Gap uses FIFO. The two companies' net incomes are not comparable because they use different inventory methods. To compare the two companies, you need to place them on the same footing.

The Internal Revenue Service allows companies to use LIFO for income-tax purposes only if they use LIFO for financial reporting. But companies may also report an alternative inventory amount in the financial statements. Doing so presents a rare opportunity to convert a company's net income from the LIFO basis to what the income would have been if the business had used FIFO. Fortunately, you can convert Wal-Mart's income from the LIFO basis, as reported in the company's financial statements, to the FIFO basis. Then you can compare Wal-Mart and The Gap.

Like many other companies that use LIFO, Wal-Mart reports the FIFO cost, a LIFO Reserve, and the LIFO cost of ending inventory. The **LIFO Reserve**[1] is the difference between the LIFO cost of an inventory and what the cost of that inventory would be under FIFO. Wal-Mart reported the following amounts:

WAL-MART USES LIFO:

	(In millions) 20X2	20X1
From the Wal-Mart balance sheet:		
Inventories (approximate FIFO cost)	$ 7,856	$6,207
Less LIFO reserve	(472)	(399)
LIFO cost	7,384	5,808
From the Wal-Mart income statement:		
Cost of goods sold	$34,786	
Net income	1,608	
Income tax rate	37%	

Converting Wal-Mart's 20X2 net income to the FIFO basis focuses on the LIFO Reserve because the reserve captures the difference between Wal-Mart's ending inventory costed at LIFO and at FIFO. Observe that during each year, the FIFO cost of ending inventory exceeded the LIFO cost. During 20X2, the LIFO Reserve increased by $73 million ($472 million − $399 million). *The LIFO Reserve can increase only when inventory costs are rising.* Recall that during a period of rising costs, LIFO produces the highest cost of goods sold and the lowest net income. Therefore, for 20X2, Wal-Mart's cost of goods sold would have been lower if the company had used the FIFO method for inventories. Wal-Mart's net income would have been higher, as the following computations show:

[1]The LIFO Reserve account is widely used in practice even though the term *reserve* is poor terminology.

IF WAL-MART HAD USED FIFO IN 20X2:	
	(In millions)
Cost of goods sold, as reported under LIFO	$34,786
− Increase in LIFO Reserve ($472 − $399)	(73)
= Cost of goods sold, if Wal-Mart had used FIFO	$34,713
Lower Cost of goods sold → Higher pretax income by	$ 73
Minus income taxes (37%)	(27)
Higher net income under FIFO	46
Actual net income under LIFO	1,608
Net income Wal-Mart would have reported for 20X2 if using FIFO	$1,654

Finally, you can compare Wal-Mart's net income with that of The Gap. All the ratios used for the analysis—current ratio, inventory turnover, and so on—can be compared between the two companies as though they both used the FIFO inventory method.

The LIFO Reserve provides another opportunity for managers and investors to answer a key question about a company:

How much income has the company saved over its lifetime by using the LIFO method to account for inventory?

Using Wal-Mart as an example, the computation at the end of 20X2 is (amounts in millions):

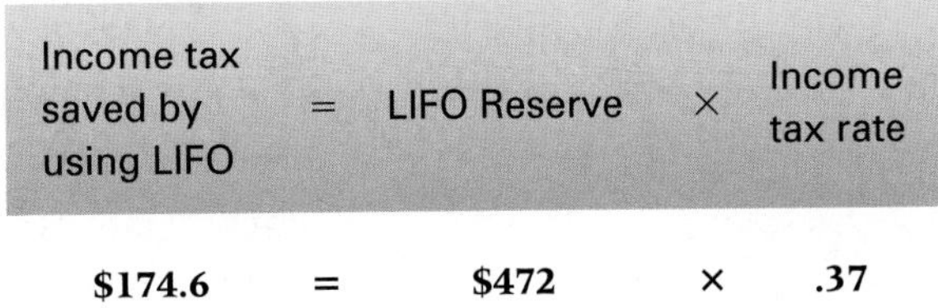

Income tax saved by using LIFO
=
LIFO Reserve
×
Income tax rate

$174.6 = **$472** × **.37**

Amazingly, by the end of 20X2, Wal-Mart has saved a total of $174.6 million by using the LIFO method to account for its merchandise inventory. Had Wal-Mart used the FIFO method, Wal-Mart would have almost $175 less cash to invest in the opening of new stores.

7 Plant Assets, Intangible Assets, and Related Expenses

Learning Objectives

After studying this chapter, you should be able to

1. Determine the cost of a plant asset
2. Account for depreciation
3. Select the best depreciation method for income tax purposes
4. Analyze the effect of a plant asset disposal
5. Account for natural resource assets and depletion
6. Account for intangible assets and amortization
7. Report plant asset transactions on the statement of cash flows

The Home Depot, Inc.
Balance Sheet (assets only, adapted)
Amounts in millions

		January 31, 1999	*February 1, 1998*
	Assets		
	Current Assets:		
1	Cash and Cash Equivalents	$ 62	$ 172
2	Short-Term Investments, including current maturities of long-term investments	—	2
3	Receivables, net	469	556
4	Merchandise Inventories	4,293	3,602
5	Other current assets	109	128
6	Total Current Assets	4,933	4,460
	Property and Equipment, at cost:		
7	Land	2,739	2,194
8	Buildings	3,757	3,041
9	Furniture, Fixtures and Equipment	1,761	1,370
10	Leasehold Improvements	419	383
11	Construction in Progress	540	336
12	Capital Leases	206	163
13		9,422	7,487
14	Less Accumulated Depreciation and Amortization	(1,262)	(978)
15	Net Property and Equipment	8,160	6,509
16	Long-Term Investments	15	15
17	Notes Receivable	26	27
18	Cost in Excess of the Fair Value of Net Assets Acquired, net of accumulated amortization of $24 at January 31, 1999 and $18 at February 1, 1998	268	140
19	Other	63	78
20	Total Assets	$13,465	$11,229

(Lines 7–15 bracketed: Plant Assets)

FOUNDED in 1978 in Atlanta, Georgia, **The Home Depot®** is the world's largest home improvement retailer and ranks among the 10 largest retailers in the United States. At January 31, 1999, the company was operating 761 stores from Canada to Chile. If the present growth rate continues, there will be over 1,600 Home Depot stores by the year 2002. For six consecutive years, The Home Depot has been named America's most admired specialty retailer by *Fortune* magazine.

Source: Adapted from *The Home Depot®* 1998 Annual Report, *Inside Cover*, p. 17.

HOW did The Home Depot grow so rapidly? By opening new stores at a fast pace, as its annual report describes. The Home Depot's balance sheet shows the effect of the company's growth. During the most recent year, total assets increased from $11.2 billion to $13.5 billion (line 20)—an increase of 20%. The bulk of the growth in assets shows up in Property and Equipment, collectively labeled *plant assets,* which we examine in this chapter.

In this chapter we also cover *intangible assets*—those assets without physical form, such as Cost in Excess of the Fair Value of Net Assets Acquired, better known as *goodwill.* This is the next-to-last asset reported on Home Depot's balance sheet (line 18). Finally, we discuss natural resource assets (such as oil, gas, timber, and gravel) and the expenses that relate to plant assets, natural resources, and intangible assets: depreciation, depletion, and amortization.

CHECK POINT 7-1

Chapter 7 concludes our coverage of asset topics, except for long-term investments, which we discuss in Chapter 10. By the time you complete this chapter, you should feel comfortable with your understanding of the various assets of a business and of the ways in which companies manage, control, and account for them.

TYPES OF ASSETS

Long-lived assets used in the operation of a business and not held for sale as investments can be divided into two categories: plant assets and intangible assets. **Plant assets,** or *fixed assets,* are long-lived assets that are tangible—for instance, land, buildings, and equipment. Their physical form provides their usefulness. The expense associated with plant assets is called *depreciation.* Of the plant assets, land is unique. Its cost is *not* depreciated—land is not expensed over time—because its usefulness does not decrease like that of other assets. Most companies report plant assets under the heading Property, plant, and equipment on the balance sheet.

We introduced the concept of depreciation in Chapter 3.

Intangible assets are useful not because of their physical characteristics, but because of the special rights they carry. Patents, copyrights, and trademarks are intangible assets. Accounting for intangibles is similar to accounting for plant assets that have physical form.

Accounting for intangibles has its own terminology. Different names apply to the individual plant assets and their corresponding expense accounts, as shown in Exhibit 7-1.

In the first half of the chapter we show how to identify the cost of a plant asset and how to expense its cost through depreciation. In the second half, we discuss the disposal of plant assets and how to account for natural resources and intangible assets. Unless stated otherwise, we describe accounting in accordance with generally accepted accounting principles for financial statement reporting, as distinguished from reporting to the IRS for income tax purposes.

EXHIBIT 7-1
Terminology Used for Plant Assets and Intangible Assets

Asset Account on the Balance Sheet	*Related Expense Account on the Income Statement*
Plant Assets	
Land	None
Buildings, Machinery and Equipment, Furniture and Fixtures, and Land Improvements	Depreciation
Natural Resources	Depletion
Intangibles	Amortization

Measuring the Cost of a Plant Asset

The *cost principle* ➡ directs a business to carry an asset on the balance sheet at the amount paid for the asset. The *cost of a plant asset* is the purchase price, applicable taxes, purchase commissions, and all other amounts paid to acquire the asset and to ready it for its intended use. In Chapter 6, we applied this principle to determine the cost of inventory. Because the types of costs differ for various categories of plant assets, we discuss the major groups individually.

Objective 1
Determine the cost of a plant asset

⬅ Refer to Chapter 1, page 10, for a discussion of the cost principle.

Land

The cost of land includes its purchase price (cash plus any note payable given), brokerage commission, survey fees, legal fees, and any back property taxes that the purchaser pays. Land cost also includes any expenditures for grading and clearing the land and for demolishing or removing any unwanted buildings.

The cost of land does *not* include the cost of fencing, paving, sprinkler systems, and lighting. These are separate plant assets—called *land improvements*—and are subject to depreciation.

Suppose **The Home Depot** signs a $300,000 note payable to purchase 20 acres of land for a new store site. Home Depot also pays $10,000 in back property tax, $8,000 in transfer taxes, $5,000 for removal of an old building, a $1,000 survey fee, and $260,000 to pave the parking lot—all in cash. What is the cost of this land?

Purchase price of land		$300,000
Add related costs:		
Back property tax	$10,000	
Transfer taxes	8,000	
Removal of building	5,000	
Survey fee	1,000	
Total related costs		24,000
Total cost of land		$324,000

✔ CHECK POINT 7-2

Note that the cost of paving the lot, $260,000, is *not* included, because the pavement is a land improvement. The Home Depot's entry to record purchase of the land is

Land	324,000	
Note Payable		300,000
Cash		24,000

ASSETS	=	LIABILITIES	+	STOCKHOLDERS' EQUITY
+324,000 −24,000	=	+300,000	+	0

Buildings

The cost of constructing a building includes architectural fees, building permits, contractors' charges, and payments for material, labor, and overhead. The time between the first expenditure for a new building and its completion can be many months, even years, and the number of separate expenditures numerous. If the company constructs its own assets, the cost of the building may also include the cost of interest on money borrowed to finance the construction. (We discuss this topic in the next section of this chapter.) Computers keep track of these details efficiently and assist in monitoring costs as they accumulate.

When an existing building (new or old) is purchased, its cost includes the purchase price, brokerage commission, sales and other taxes, and all expenditures for repairing and renovating the building for its intended purpose.

Machinery and Equipment

The cost of machinery and equipment includes its purchase price (less any discounts), transportation charges, insurance while in transit, sales and other taxes, purchase commission, installation costs, and any expenditures to test the asset before it is placed in service. After the asset is up and running, insurance, taxes, and maintenance costs are recorded as expenses.

Land and Leasehold Improvements

For a Home Depot store, the cost to pave a parking lot ($260,000) is not part of the cost of the land. Instead, the $260,000 would be recorded in a separate account entitled Land Improvements. This account includes costs for such other items as driveways, signs, fences, and sprinkler systems. Although these assets are located on the land, they are subject to decay, and their cost should therefore be depreciated. Also, the cost of a new building constructed on the land is a debit to the asset account Building.

The Home Depot leases some of its store buildings, warehouses, and vehicles. The company also customizes some of these assets to meet its special needs. For example, The Home Depot may paint its logo on a rental truck and install a special lift on the truck. These improvements are assets of The Home Depot even though the company does not own the truck. The cost of improvements to leased assets appears on the company's balance sheet as Leasehold Improvements (see line 10 of Home Depot's balance sheet on page 311). The cost of leasehold improvements should be depreciated over the term of the lease. Some companies refer to the depreciation on leasehold improvements as *amortization,* which is the same basic concept as depreciation.

Construction in Progress and Capital Leases

The Home Depot's balance sheet includes two additional categories of plant assets: Construction in Progress (line 11) and Capital Leases (line 12).

CONSTRUCTION IN PROGRESS. Construction in Progress is an asset, such as a warehouse, that the company is constructing for its own use. On the balance sheet date, the construction is incomplete. For The Home Depot, construction in progress is a plant asset because the company will use the asset in its operations.

CAPITAL LEASES. A capital lease is a lease arrangement similar to an installment purchase of the leased asset. Companies report assets rented through capital leases as assets even though they do not own the assets. Why? Because their lease payments secure the use of the asset over the term of the lease. For example, The Home Depot has capital leases on some of its store buildings. The Home Depot could report the cost of these assets either under Buildings or under Capital Leases. Either way, the asset shows up on the balance sheet as a plant asset. Chapter 8 discusses the long-term liability for a capital lease.

A capital lease is different from an operating lease, which is an ordinary rental agreement, such as an apartment lease or the rental of a Hertz automobile. The lessee (the renter) records an operating lease as Rent Expense.

Capitalizing the Cost of Interest

The Home Depot constructs some of its plant assets and finances part of the construction with borrowed money on which The Home Depot must pay interest. A company should generally include its interest cost as part of the cost of a self-constructed asset, such as a building or equipment that takes a long time to build. The practice of including interest as part of an asset's cost is called *capitalizing interest.* To **capitalize** a cost means to include it as part of an asset's cost. In accounting, we debit a capitalized cost to an asset (versus an expense) account.

Capitalizing interest cost is an exception to the normal practice of recording interest as an expense. Ordinarily, a company that borrows money records interest expense. But on assets that the business builds for its own use, the company should capitalize some of its interest cost. The logic goes like this: If The Home Depot buys a building from a construction company, the price of the building will include the builder's interest cost to finance the construction. To place self-constructed assets on the same footing, it makes sense to capitalize any interest incurred to finance the construction.

Lump-Sum (or Basket) Purchases of Assets

Businesses often purchase several assets as a group, or in a "basket," for a single lump-sum amount. For example, a company may pay one price for land and an office building. The company must identify the cost of each asset. The total cost is divided among the assets according to their relative sales (or market) values. This allocation technique is called the *relative-sales-value method.*

Suppose **Xerox Corporation** purchases land and a building in Kansas City for a midwestern sales office. The building sits on two acres of land, and the combined purchase price of land and building is $2,800,000. An appraisal indicates that the land's market (sales) value is $300,000 and that the building's market (sales) value is $2,700,000.

An accountant first figures the ratio of each asset's market value to the total market value. Total appraised value is $2,700,000 + $300,000 = $3,000,000. Thus, the land, valued at $300,000, is 10% of the total market value. The building's appraised value is 90% of the total. These percentages are then used to determine the cost of each asset, as follows:

Asset	*Market (Sales) Value*		*Total Market Value*		*Percentage of Total Market Value*		*Total Cost*		*Cost of Each Asset*
Land	$ 300,000	÷	$3,000,000	=	10%	×	$2,800,000	=	$ 280,000
Building	2,700,000	÷	3,000,000	=	90%	×	$2,800,000	=	2,520,000
Total	$3,000,000				100%				$2,800,000

If Xerox pays cash, the entry to record the purchase of the land and building is

	Debit	Credit
Land	280,000	
Building	2,520,000	
Cash		2,800,000

CHECK POINT 7-3

ASSETS	=	LIABILITIES	+	STOCKHOLDERS' EQUITY
+ 280,000	=			
+ 2,520,000	=	0	+	0
−2,800,000	=			

How would a business divide a $120,000 lump-sum purchase price for land, building, and equipment with estimated market values of $40,000, $95,000, and $15,000, respectively?

Answer:

	Estimated Market Value	Percentage of Total Market Value	×	Total Cost	=	Cost of Each Asset
Land	$ 40,000	26.7%*	×	$120,000	=	$ 32,040
Building	95,000	63.3%	×	120,000	=	75,960
Equipment	15,000	10.0%	×	120,000	=	12,000
	$150,000	100.0%				$120,000

*$40,000/$150,000 = 0.267, and so on.

Capital Expenditures versus Revenue Expenditures

When a company makes a plant asset expenditure, it must decide whether to debit an asset account or an expense account. In this context, *expenditure* refers to either a cash purchase or a credit purchase of goods or services related to the asset. Examples of these expenditures range from **General Motors'** purchase of robots for use in an assembly plant to your replacing the windshield wipers on a Chevrolet.

Expenditures that increase the asset's capacity or efficiency or extend its useful life are called **capital expenditures.** For example, the cost of a major overhaul that extends the useful life of a Home Depot delivery truck is a capital expenditure. Repair work that generates a capital expenditure is called a **major repair** or an **extraordinary repair.** The amount of the capital expenditure, said to be capitalized, is debited to an asset account. For an extraordinary repair on the truck, we would debit the asset account Equipment or Automobiles.

Other expenditures that do not extend the asset's capacity, but rather merely maintain it or restore it to working order, are called **revenue expenditures.** These costs are expenses and are matched against revenue. Examples include the costs of repainting a delivery truck, repairing a dented fender, and replacing tires. Revenue expenditures are debited to an expense account. For the **ordinary repairs,** or betterments, on the truck, we would debit Repair Expense.

The distinction between capital and revenue expenditures is often a matter of opinion. Does the cost extend the life of the asset (a capital expenditure), or does it only maintain the asset in good order (a revenue expenditure)? When doubt exists, companies tend to debit an expense, for two reasons. First, many expenditures are minor in amount, and most companies have a policy of expensing all expenditures below a specific minimum, such as $1,000. Second, the income tax motive favors

Exhibit 7-2
Capital Expenditure or Revenue Expenditure for a Delivery Truck

Debit an Asset Account for Capital Expenditures	Debit Repair and Maintenance Expense for Revenue Expenditures
Extraordinary repairs:	*Ordinary repairs:*
Major engine overhaul	Repair of transmission or other mechanism
Modification of body for new use of truck	Oil change, lubrication, and so on
Addition to storage capacity of truck	Replacement tires, windshield, and the like
	Paint job

debiting all borderline expenditures to expense in order to create an immediate tax deduction. Capital expenditures are not immediate tax deductions.

Exhibit 7-2 illustrates the distinction between capital expenditures and revenue expenditures (expense) for several delivery-truck expenditures. Note also the difference between extraordinary and ordinary repairs.

ACCOUNTING ERROR: EXPENSING A CAPITAL EXPENDITURE. Treating a capital expenditure as an expense, or vice versa, creates errors in the financial statements. Suppose **Intel Corporation** makes a capital expenditure and erroneously expenses this cost. A capital expenditure should have been debited to an asset account. This accounting error

- overstates Intel's expenses on the income statement.
- understates Intel's net income on the income statement.

On the Intel balance sheet,

- the equipment account (an asset) is understated.
- owners' (or stockholders') equity is understated.

Accounting Error: Company expenses a cost that should have been capitalized.

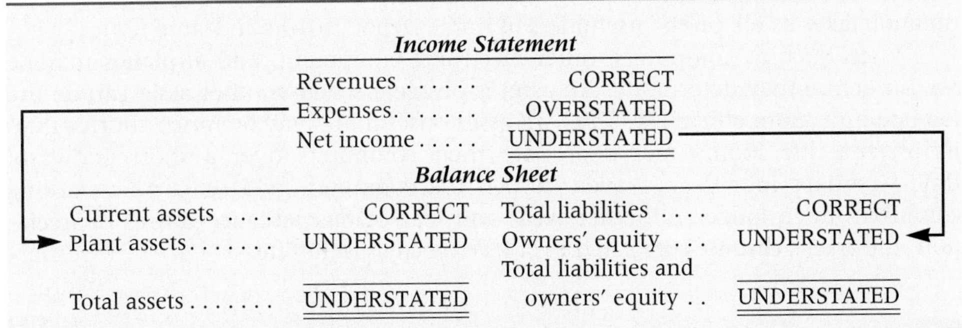

Income Statement

Revenues	CORRECT
Expenses.......	OVERSTATED
Net income.....	UNDERSTATED

Balance Sheet

Current assets	CORRECT	Total liabilities	CORRECT
Plant assets.......	UNDERSTATED	Owners' equity ...	UNDERSTATED
		Total liabilities and	
Total assets.......	UNDERSTATED	owners' equity ..	UNDERSTATED

CHECK POINT 7-4

ACCOUNTING ERROR: CAPITALIZING AN EXPENSE. Capitalizing the cost of an ordinary repair creates the opposite error. Expenses are then understated, and net income is overstated on the income statement. The balance sheet reports overstated amounts for both assets and owners' equity.

MEASURING THE DEPRECIATION OF PLANT ASSETS

The allocation of a plant asset's cost to expense over the period the asset is used is called *depreciation*. This allocation is designed to match the asset's expense against the revenue generated over the asset's life, as the matching principle directs. Exhibit 7-3 shows the depreciation process for the purchase of a Boeing 737 jet by **United Airlines.**

See Chapter 3 for a discussion of the matching principle.

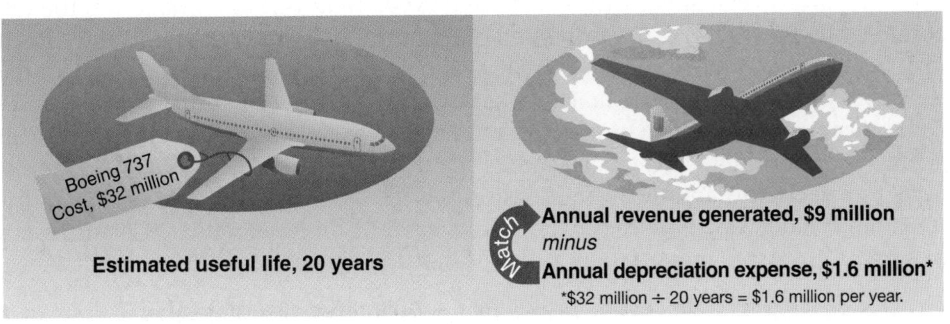

EXHIBIT 7-3
Depreciation and the Matching of Expense with Revenue

Suppose **The Home Depot** buys a computer for use in its accounting department. Home Depot believes it will get four years of service from the computer, which will then be worthless. Using the straight-line depreciation method (which we discuss later in this chapter), The Home Depot expenses one-quarter of the asset's cost in each of its four years of use.

Let's contrast what depreciation accounting is with what it is *not.*

1. *Depreciation is not a process of valuation.* Businesses do not record depreciation based on appraisals of their plant assets at the end of each period. Instead, businesses allocate the asset's cost to the periods of its useful life based on a specific depreciation method. (We discuss these methods on page 319.)
2. *Depreciation does not mean that the business sets aside cash to replace assets as they wear out.* Establishing a cash fund is a decision entirely separate from depreciation.

The Causes of Depreciation

Only land has an unlimited life. All other assets depreciate. For some plant assets, physical *wear and tear* is the primary cause of depreciation. For example, physical deterioration takes its toll on the usefulness of Home Depot's trucks and store fixtures.

Assets such as computers, other electronic equipment, and airplanes may be *obsolete* before they deteriorate. An asset is obsolete when another asset can do the job better or more efficiently. Thus, an asset's useful life may be much shorter than its physical life. Companies depreciate their computers over a short period of time—perhaps four years—even though the computers will remain in working condition much longer. Whether wear and tear or obsolescence causes depreciation, the asset's cost is depreciated over its expected useful life.

Measuring Depreciation

To measure depreciation for a plant asset, we must know its

1. Cost
2. Estimated useful life
3. Estimated residual value

We have already discussed cost, the purchase price of the asset, which is a known amount. The other two factors must be estimated.

Estimated useful life is the length of service the business expects to get from the asset—an estimate of how long the asset will be useful. Useful life may be expressed in years, units of output, miles, or another measure. For example, the useful life of a building is stated in years. The useful life of a bookbinding machine may be stated as the number of books the machine is expected to bind—that is, its expected units of output. A reasonable measure of a delivery truck's useful life is the total number of miles the truck is expected to travel. Companies base such estimates on past experience and information from industry magazines and government publications.

Estimated residual value—also called *scrap value* or *salvage value*—is the expected cash value of an asset at the end of its useful life. For example, Home Depot may believe that a machine's useful life will be seven years. After that time, Home Depot may expect to sell the machine as scrap metal. The amount the business believes it can get for the machine is the estimated residual value. In computations of depreciation, estimated residual value is *not* depreciated because Home Depot expects to receive this amount from disposing of the asset. The full cost of a plant asset is depreciated if the asset is expected to have no residual value. A plant asset's **depreciable cost** is measured as follows:

Depreciable cost = Asset's cost − Estimated residual value

Depreciation Methods

Four methods exist for computing depreciation:

Objective 2
Account for depreciation

- Straight-line
- Units-of-production
- Double-declining-balance
- Sum-of-years'-digits

(Double-declining-balance and Sum-of-years'-digits: Accelerated depreciation methods)

These four methods allocate different amounts of depreciation expense to each period. However, they all result in the same total amount of depreciation, the asset's depreciable cost over its life. Exhibit 7-4 presents the data we will use to illustrate depreciation computations by the three most widely used methods for a Home Depot truck. We omit the sum-of-years'-digits method because so few companies use it.

Straight-Line Method. In the **straight-line (SL) method,** an equal amount of depreciation expense is assigned to each year (or period) of asset use. Depreciable cost is divided by useful life in years to determine the annual depreciation expense. Applied to the Home Depot truck data from Exhibit 7-4, the equation for SL depreciation is

$$\textbf{Straight-line depreciation per year} = \frac{\textbf{Cost} - \textbf{Residual value}}{\textbf{Useful life, in years}}$$

$$= \frac{\$41{,}000 - \$1{,}000}{5}$$

$$= \$8{,}000$$

The entry to record this depreciation is

Depreciation Expense	8,000	
Accumulated Depreciation		8,000

ASSETS	=	LIABILITIES	+	STOCKHOLDERS' EQUITY	−	EXPENSES
−8,000	=	0			−	8,000

Assume that the truck was purchased on January 1, 20X1, and that Home Depot's fiscal year ends on December 31. A *straight-line depreciation schedule* is presented in Exhibit 7-5. The final column in Exhibit 7-5 shows the *asset's book value,* which is its cost less accumulated depreciation. Book value is also called *carrying amount* or *carrying value.* ➸

➸ We introduced the concept of book value/carrying value in Chapter 3.

As an asset is used, accumulated depreciation increases, and the book value decreases. (Compare the Accumulated Depreciation column and the Book Value column.) An asset's final book value is its *residual value* ($1,000 in Exhibit 7-5). At the end of its useful life, the asset is said to be *fully depreciated.*

Exhibit 7-4
Data for Depreciation Computations— A Home Depot Delivery Truck

Data Item	*Amount*
Cost of truck	$41,000
Less Estimated residual value	(1,000)
Depreciable cost	$40,000
Estimated useful life:	
Years	5 years
Units of production	100,000 units [miles]

Date	Asset Cost	Depreciation for the Year: Depreciation Rate		Depreciable Cost		Depreciation Expense	Accumulated Depreciation	Asset Book Value
1- 1-20X1	$41,000							$41,000
12-31-20X1		0.20*	×	$40,000	=	$8,000	$ 8,000	33,000
12-31-20X2		0.20	×	40,000	=	8,000	16,000	25,000
12-31-20X3		0.20	×	40,000	=	8,000	24,000	17,000
12-31-20X4		0.20	×	40,000	=	8,000	32,000	9,000
12-31-20X5		0.20	×	40,000	=	8,000	40,000	1,000

*$^1/_5$ years = 0.20 per year.

EXHIBIT 7-5
Straight-Line Depreciation Schedule for a Home Depot Truck

An asset with cost of $10,000, useful life of five years, and residual value of $2,000 was purchased on January 1. What was SL depreciation for the first year?

Answer: $1,600 = ($10,000 − $2,000)/5

UNITS-OF-PRODUCTION METHOD. In the **units-of-production (UOP) method,** a fixed amount of depreciation is assigned to each *unit of output,* or service, produced by the plant asset. Depreciable cost is divided by useful life, in units of production, to determine this amount. This per-unit depreciation expense is then multiplied by the number of units produced each period to compute depreciation for the period. The UOP depreciation equation for the Home Depot truck data in Exhibit 7-4 (page 319), in which the units are miles, is

$$\textbf{Units-of-production depreciation per unit of output} = \frac{\textbf{Cost} - \textbf{Residual value}}{\textbf{Useful life, in units of production}}$$

$$= \frac{\$41{,}000 - \$1{,}000}{100{,}000 \text{ miles}}$$

$$= \$0.40 \text{ per mile}$$

Assume that the truck is expected to be driven 20,000 miles during the first year, 30,000 during the second, 25,000 during the third, 15,000 during the fourth, and 10,000 during the fifth. The UOP depreciation schedule for this asset is shown in Exhibit 7-6.

The amount of UOP depreciation each period varies with the number of units the asset produces. In our example, the total number of units produced is 100,000, the measure of this asset's useful life. Therefore, UOP depreciation does not depend directly on time as do the other methods.

EXHIBIT 7-6
Units-of-Production Depreciation Schedule for a Home Depot Truck

Date	Asset Cost	Depreciation for the Year: Depreciation Per Unit		Number of Units		Depreciation Expense	Accumulated Depreciation	Asset Book Value
1- 1-20X1	$41,000							$41,000
12-31-20X1		$0.40*	×	20,000	=	$ 8,000	$ 8,000	33,000
12-31-20X2		0.40	×	30,000	=	12,000	20,000	21,000
12-31-20X3		0.40	×	25,000	=	10,000	30,000	11,000
12-31-20X4		0.40	×	15,000	=	6,000	36,000	5,000
12-31-20X5		0.40	×	10,000	=	4,000	40,000	1,000

*($41,000 − $1,000)/100,000 miles = $0.40 per mile.

The asset in the preceding Stop & Think produced 3,000 units in the first year, 4,000 in the second, 4,500 in the third, 2,500 in the fourth, and 2,000 units in the last year. Its estimated useful life is 16,000 units. What was UOP depreciation for each year?

Answers:

Depreciation per unit ($10,000 − $2,000)/16,000 units = $0.50 per unit

Yr. 1: $1,500 (3,000 × $0.50)
Yr. 2: $2,000 (4,000 × $0.50)
Yr. 3: $2,250 (4,500 × $0.50)
Yr. 4: $1,250 (2,500 × $0.50)
Yr. 5: $1,000 (2,000 × $0.50)

DOUBLE-DECLINING-BALANCE METHOD. An **accelerated depreciation method** writes off a relatively larger amount of the asset's cost nearer the start of its useful life than the straight-line method does. *Double-declining-balance* is one of the accelerated depreciation methods. **Double-declining-balance (DDB) depreciation** computes annual depreciation by multiplying the asset's book value by a constant percentage, which is two times the straight-line depreciation rate. DDB amounts are computed as follows:

- *First,* compute the straight-line depreciation rate per year. For example, a five-year truck has a straight-line depreciation rate of 1/5, or 20%. A ten-year asset has a straight-line rate of 1/10, or 10%, and so on.
- *Second,* multiply the straight-line rate by 2 to compute the DDB rate. The DDB rate for a ten-year asset is 20% per year (10% × 2 = 20%). For a five-year asset, such as the Home Depot truck in Exhibit 7-4 (page 319), the DDB rate is 40% (20% × 2 = 40%).
- *Third,* multiply the DDB rate by the period's beginning asset book value (cost less accumulated depreciation). Ignore the residual value of the asset in computing depreciation by the DDB method, except during the last year. The DDB rate for the truck in Exhibit 7-4 (page 319) is

$$\textbf{DDB depreciation rate per year} = \frac{1}{\textbf{Useful life, in years}} \times 2$$

$$= \frac{1}{5 \text{ years}} \times 2$$

$$= 20\% \times 2 = 40\%$$

 CHECK POINT 7-5

- *Fourth,* determine the final year's depreciation amount—that is, the amount needed to reduce the asset's book value to its residual value. In the DDB depreciation schedule in Exhibit 7-7, the fifth and final year's depreciation is

EXHIBIT 7-7
Double-Declining-Balance Depreciation Schedule for a Home Depot Truck

		Depreciation for the Year							
Date	*Asset Cost*	*DDB Rate*		*Asset Book Value*		*Depreciation Expense*	*Accumulated Depreciation*	*Asset Book Value*
1- 1-20X1	$41,000							$41,000
12-31-20X1		0.40	×	$41,000	=	$16,400	$16,400	24,600
12-31-20X2		0.40	×	24,600	=	9,840	26,240	14,760
12-31-20X3		0.40	×	14,760	=	5,904	32,144	8,856
12-31-20X4		0.40	×	8,856	=	3,542	35,686	5,314
12-31-20X5						4,314*	40,000	1,000

*Last-year depreciation is the amount needed to reduce asset book value to the residual value ($5,314 − $1,000 = $4,314).

$4,314—the $5,314 book value less the $1,000 residual value. The residual value should not be depreciated but should remain on the books until the asset's disposal.

Many companies change to the straight-line method during the next-to-last year of the asset's life. Under this plan, annual depreciation for 20X4 and 20X5 is $3,928. Look again at Exhibit 7-7. Depreciable cost at the end of 20X3 is $7,856 (book value of $8,856 less residual value of $1,000). Depreciable cost can be spread evenly over the last two years of the asset's life ($7,856 ÷ 2 remaining years = $3,928 per year).

The DDB method differs from the other methods in two ways:

1. The asset's residual value is ignored initially; in the first year, depreciation is computed on the asset's full cost.
2. Depreciation expense in the final year is whatever amount is needed to reduce the asset's book value to its residual value.

STOP & THINK

What is the DDB depreciation of the asset in the Stop & Think on page 320 for each year?

Answers:

Yr. 1: $4,000 ($10,000 × 40%)

Yr. 2: $2,400 ($6,000 × 40%)

Yr. 3: $1,440 ($3,600 × 40%)

Yr. 4: $160 ($10,000 − $4,000 − $2,400 − $1,440 − $2,000)*

*The asset is not depreciated below residual value.

Comparing the Depreciation Methods

Let's compare the three methods we've just discussed in terms of the yearly amount of depreciation:

CHECK POINT 7-6

	Amount of Depreciation Per Year		
			Accelerated Method
Year	*Straight-Line*	*Units-of-Production*	*Double-Declining-Balance*
1	$ 8,000	$ 8,000	$16,400
2	8,000	12,000	9,840
3	8,000	10,000	5,904
4	8,000	6,000	3,542
5	8,000	4,000	4,314
Total	$40,000	$40,000	$40,000

The yearly amount of depreciation varies by method, but the total $40,000 depreciable cost is the same under all methods.

Generally accepted accounting principles (GAAP) direct a business to match an asset's expense against the revenue that the asset produces. For a plant asset that generates revenue evenly over time, the straight-line method best meets the matching principle. During each period the asset is used, an equal amount of depreciation is recorded.

The units-of-production method best fits those assets that wear out because of physical use rather than obsolescence. Depreciation is recorded only when the asset is used, and the more units the asset generates in a given year, the greater the depreciation expense.

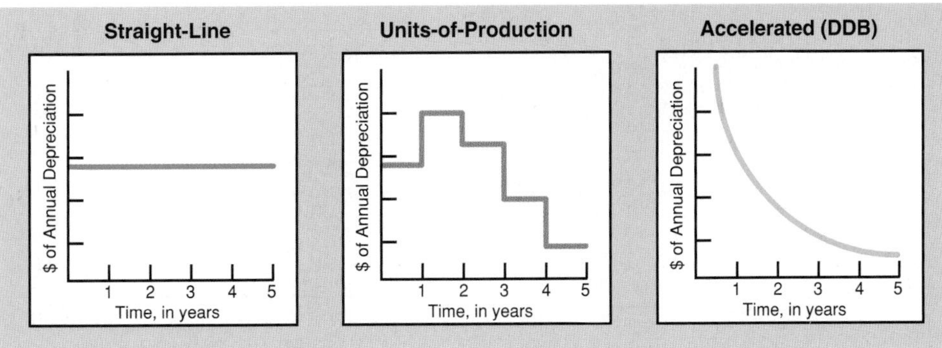

EXHIBIT 7-8
Depreciation Patterns Through Time

The accelerated method (DDB) applies best to those assets that generate greater revenue earlier in their useful lives. The greater expense recorded under the accelerated methods in the earlier periods is matched against the greater revenue of those periods.

Exhibit 7-8 graphs annual depreciation amounts for the straight-line, units-of-production, and accelerated depreciation (DDB) methods. The graph of straight-line depreciation is flat because annual depreciation is the same in all periods. Units-of-production depreciation follows no particular pattern because annual depreciation depends on the use of the asset. The greater the use, the greater the amount of depreciation. Accelerated depreciation is greatest in the asset's first year and less in the later years.

A recent survey of 600 companies conducted by the American Institute of CPA indicates that the straight-line method is most popular. Exhibit 7-9 shows the percentages of companies that use each of the depreciation methods.

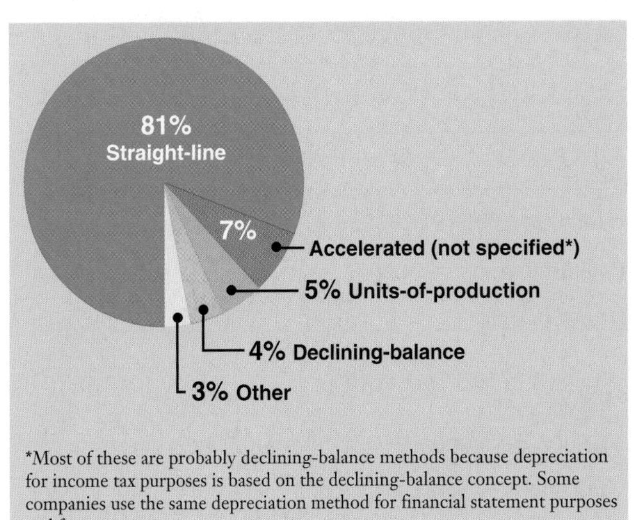

EXHIBIT 7-9
Use of the Depreciation Methods by 600 Companies

MID-CHAPTER

Mid-Chapter

SUMMARY PROBLEM FOR YOUR REVIEW

Hubbard Company purchased equipment on January 1, 20X3, for $44,000. The expected useful life of the equipment is 10 years or 100,000 units of production, and its residual value is $4,000. Under three depreciation methods, the annual depreciation expense and the balance of accumulated depreciation at the end of 20X3 and 20X4 are as follows:

	Method A		*Method B*		*Method C*	
Year	*Annual Depreciation Expense*	*Accumulated Depreciation*	*Annual Depreciation Expense*	*Accumulated Depreciation*	*Annual Depreciation Expense*	*Accumulated Depreciation*
20X3	$4,000	$4,000	$8,800	$ 8,800	$1,200	$1,200
20X4	4,000	8,000	7,040	15,840	5,600	6,800

Required

1. Identify the depreciation method used in each instance, and show the equation and computation for each. (Round off to the nearest dollar.)
2. Assume continued use of the same method through year 20X5. Determine the annual depreciation expense, accumulated depreciation, and book value of the equipment for 20X3 through 20X5 under each method, assuming 12,000 units of production in 20X5.

Answers

Requirement 1

Method A: Straight-Line

Depreciable cost = $40,000 ($44,000 − $4,000)

Each year: $40,000/10 years = $4,000

Method B: Double-Declining-Balance

$$\text{Rate} = \frac{1}{10 \text{ years}} \times 2 = 10\% \times 2 = 20\%$$

20X3: 0.20 × $44,000 = $8,800

20X4: 0.20 × ($44,000 − $8,800) = $7,040

Method C: Units-of-Production

$$\text{Depreciation per unit} = \frac{\$44{,}000 - \$4{,}000}{100{,}000 \text{ units}} = \$0.40$$

20X3: $0.40 × 3,000 units = $1,200

20X4: $0.40 × 14,000 units = $5,600

Requirement 2

	Method A: Straight-Line		
Year	*Annual Depreciation Expense*	*Accumulated Depreciation*	*Book Value*
Start			$44,000
20X3	$4,000	$ 4,000	40,000
20X4	4,000	8,000	36,000
20X5	4,000	12,000	32,000

	Method B: Double-Declining-Balance		
Year	*Annual Depreciation Expense*	*Accumulated Depreciation*	*Book Value*
Start			$44,000
20X3	$8,800	$ 8,800	35,200
20X4	7,040	15,840	28,160
20X5	5,632	21,472	22,528

	Method C: Units-of-Production		
Year	*Annual Depreciation Expense*	*Accumulated Depreciation*	*Book Value*
Start			$44,000
20X3	$1,200	$ 1,200	42,800
20X4	5,600	6,800	37,200
20X5	4,800	11,600	32,400

Computations for 20X5	
Straight-line	**$40,000/10 years = $4,000**
Double-declining-balance	**0.20 × $28,160 = $5,632**
Units-of-production	**$0.40 × 12,000 units = $4,800**

DEPRECIATION AND INCOME TAXES

Objective 3
Select the best depreciation method for income tax purposes

Most companies use the straight-line depreciation method for reporting to their stockholders and creditors on their financial statements. They also keep a separate set of depreciation records for computing their income taxes. For income tax purposes, most companies use an accelerated depreciation method.

Suppose you are a business manager. The IRS allows an accelerated depreciation method, which most managers prefer to straight-line depreciation. Why? Because it provides the most depreciation expense as quickly as possible, thus decreasing your immediate tax payments. You can then apply the cash you save to fit your business needs.

To understand the relationships between cash flow, depreciation, and income tax, recall our earlier depreciation example for a Home Depot truck:

- First-year depreciation is $8,000 under straight-line and $16,400 under double-declining-balance.
- DDB is permitted for income tax reporting.

EXHIBIT 7-10
The Cash-Flow Advantage of Accelerated Depreciation over Straight-Line Depreciation for Income Tax Purposes

	SL	*Accelerated*
① Cash revenues	$400,000	$400,000
② Cash operating expenses	300,000	300,000
③ Cash provided by operations before income tax	100,000	100,000
④ Depreciation expense (a noncash expense)	8,000	16,400
⑤ Income before income tax	92,000	83,600
⑥ Income tax expense (30%)	$ 27,600	$ 25,080
Cash-flow analysis:		
⑦ Cash provided by operations before income tax	$100,000	$100,000
⑧ Income tax expense	27,600	25,080
⑨ Cash provided by operations	$ 72,400	$ 74,920
⑩ Extra cash available for investment if DDB is used ($74,920 − $72,400)		$ 2,520

CHECK POINT 7-7

Assume that this store's lumber department has $400,000 in cash sales and $300,000 in cash operating expenses during the truck's first year and an income tax rate of 30%. The cash flow analysis appears in Exhibit 7-10.

Exhibit 7-10 highlights an important fact: The higher the depreciation expense, the lower the income before tax and thus the lower the tax payment. Therefore, accelerated depreciation helps conserve cash for use in the business. Exhibit 7-10 indicates that the business will have $2,520 (line 10) more cash at the end of the first year if it uses accelerated depreciation instead of SL.

MACRS DEPRECIATION FOR TAX PURPOSES. The Tax Reform Act of 1986 created a special depreciation method—used only for income tax purposes—called the **Modified Accelerated Cost Recovery System (MACRS).** Under this method, assets are grouped into one of eight classes identified by asset life, as shown in Exhibit 7-11. Depreciation for the first four classes is computed by the double-declining-balance method. Depreciation for 15-year assets and 20-year assets is computed by the 150%-declining-balance method. Under this method, the annual depreciation rate is computed by multiplying the straight-line rate by 1.50 (rather than by 2.00, as for DDB). For a 20-year asset, because the straight-line rate is 0.05 (1/20 = 0.05), the annual MACRS depreciation rate is 0.075 (0.05 × 1.50 = 0.075). Most real estate is depreciated by the straight-line method.

EXHIBIT 7-11
Details of the Modified Accelerated Cost Recovery System (MACRS) Depreciation Method

Class Identified by Asset Life (years)	*Representative Assets*	*Depreciation Method*
3	Race horses	DDB
5	Automobiles, light trucks	DDB
7	Equipment	DDB
10	Equipment	DDB
15	Sewage-treatment plants	150% DB
20	Certain real estate	150% DB
$27\frac{1}{2}$	Residential rental property	SL
39	Nonresidential rental property	SL

DEPRECIATION FOR PARTIAL YEARS

Companies purchase plant assets as needed. They do not wait until the beginning of a year or a month. Therefore, companies must develop policies to compute *depreciation for partial years.* Suppose the **County Line Bar-B-Q Restaurant** in Denver purchases a building on April 1 for $500,000. The building's estimated life is 20 years, and its estimated residual value is $80,000. The restaurant company's fiscal year ends on December 31. Let's consider how the company computes depreciation for the year ended December 31.

Many companies compute partial-year depreciation by first computing a full year's depreciation. Then they multiply that amount by the fraction of the year that they held the asset. Assuming the straight-line method, the year's depreciation for the restaurant building is $15,750, computed as follows:

$$\textbf{Full-year depreciation } \frac{\$500{,}000 - \$80{,}000}{20} = \$21{,}000$$

$$\textbf{Partial year depreciation } \$21{,}000 \times 9/12 = \$15{,}750$$

What if the company bought the asset on April 18? A widely used policy directs businesses to record no depreciation on assets purchased after the 15th of the month and to record a full month's depreciation on an asset bought on or before the 15th. Thus, the company would record no depreciation for April on an April 18 purchase. In that case, the year's depreciation would be $14,000 ($21,000 × 8/12).

How is partial-year depreciation computed under the other depreciation methods? Suppose County Line Bar-B-Q acquires the building on October 4 and uses the double-declining-balance method. For a 20-year asset, the DDB rate is 10% (1/20 = 5%; 5% × 2 = 10%). The annual depreciation computations for 20X1, 20X2, and 20X3 are shown in Exhibit 7-12.

EXHIBIT 7-12
Annual DDB Depreciation for Partial Years

		Depreciation for the Year									
Date	*Asset Cost*	*DDB Rate*		*Asset Book Value, Beginning*		*Fraction of the Year*		*Depreciation Expense*	*Accumulated Depreciation*	*Asset Book Value, Ending*
10- 4-20X1	$500,000									$500,000
12-31-20X1		1/20 × 2 = 0.10	×	$500,000	×	3/12	=	$12,500	$ 12,500	487,500
12-31-20X2		0.10	×	487,500	×	12/12	=	48,750	61,250	438,750
12-31-20X3		0.10	×	438,750	×	12/12	=	43,875	105,125	394,875

Most companies use computerized systems to account for fixed assets. Each asset has a unique identification number that links to the asset's cost, estimated life, residual value, and depreciation method. The system will automatically calculate the depreciation expense for each period. Both Accumulated Depreciation and book value are automatically updated.

CHECK POINT 7-8

CHANGING THE USEFUL LIFE OF A DEPRECIABLE ASSET

As we've discussed, a business must estimate the useful life of a plant asset to compute its depreciation. This prediction is the most difficult part of accounting for depreciation. After the asset is put into use, the business may refine its estimate on the basis of experience and new information. The **Walt Disney Company** made such a change, called a *change in accounting estimate.* Disney recalculated depreciation on the basis of revised useful lives of several of its theme park assets. The following note in Walt Disney's financial statements reports this change in accounting estimate:

Note 5

> . . . [T]he Company extended the estimated useful lives of certain theme park ride and attraction assets based upon historical data and engineering studies. The effect of this change was to decrease depreciation by approximately $8 million (an increase in net income of approximately $4.2 million . . .).

Assume that a Disney hot dog stand cost $40,000 and that the company originally believed the asset had an eight-year useful life with no residual value. Using the straight-line method, the company would record $5,000 depreciation each year ($40,000/8 years = $5,000). Suppose Disney used the asset for two years. Accumulated depreciation reached $10,000, leaving a remaining depreciable book value (cost *less* accumulated depreciation *less* residual value) of $30,000 ($40,000 − $10,000). From its experience, management believes the asset will remain useful for an additional 10 years. The company would spread the remaining depreciable book value over the asset's remaining life as follows:

Asset's remaining depreciable book value	÷	(New) Estimated useful life remaining	=	(New) Annual depreciation
$30,000	÷	**10 years**	=	**$3,000**

The yearly depreciation entry based on the new estimated useful life is

CHECK POINT 7-9

Depreciation Expense—Hot Dog Stand	3,000	
Accumulated Depreciation—Hot Dog Stand		3,000

ASSETS	=	LIABILITIES	+	STOCKHOLDERS' EQUITY	−	EXPENSES
−3,000	=	0			−	3,000

1. Suppose The Home Depot was having a bad year—net income is well below expectations and lower than last year's income. For depreciation purposes, Home Depot extended the estimated useful lives of its depreciable assets. How would this accounting change affect Home Depot's (a) depreciation expense, (b) net income, and (c) owners' equity?
2. Suppose that The Home Depot's accounting change turned a loss year into a profitable year. Without the accounting change, the company would have reported a net loss for the year. But the accounting change enabled The Home Depot to report net income. Under GAAP, Home Depot's annual report must disclose the accounting change and its effect on net income. Would investors evaluate The Home Depot as better or worse in response to these disclosures?

Answers:

1. An accounting change that lengthens the estimated useful lives of depreciable assets (a) decreases depreciation expense and (b, c) increases net income and owners' equity.
2. Investors' reactions are not always predictable. There is evidence, however, that companies cannot fool investors. In this case, investment advisers would *probably* subtract from Home Depot's reported net income the amount caused by the accounting change. Investors could then use the remaining net *loss* figure to evaluate Home Depot's lack of progress during the year. Investors would probably view The Home Depot as worse for having made this accounting change. For this reason, The Home Depot's managers would not engage in this type of activity.

Using Fully Depreciated Assets

A *fully depreciated asset* is an asset that has reached the end of its *estimated* useful life. No more depreciation is recorded for the asset. If the asset is no longer suitable for its purpose, it is disposed of, as discussed in the next section. However, the company may be in a cash bind and unable to replace the asset. Or the asset's useful life may have been underestimated at the outset. Foresight is not perfect. In any event, companies sometimes continue using fully depreciated assets. The asset account and its related accumulated depreciation account remain in the ledger even though no additional depreciation is recorded for the asset.

Remember: The total amount of depreciation recorded on an asset cannot exceed its depreciable cost. An asset *can* be used after it is fully depreciated.

DISPOSAL OF PLANT ASSETS

Objective 4
Analyze the effect of a plant asset disposal

Eventually, a plant asset ceases to serve a company's needs. The asset may have become worn out, obsolete, or for some other reason no longer useful to the business. Before accounting for the disposal of the asset, the business should bring depreciation up-to-date to measure the asset's final book value properly.

To account for disposal, credit the asset account and debit its related accumulated depreciation account. Suppose the final year's depreciation expense has just been recorded for a machine that cost $6,000 and is estimated to have zero residual value. The machine's accumulated depreciation thus totals $6,000. Assuming that this asset cannot be sold or exchanged, the entry to record its disposal is:

Accumulated Depreciation—Machinery	6,000	
Machinery		6,000
To dispose of fully depreciated machine.		

ASSETS	=	LIABILITIES	+	STOCKHOLDERS' EQUITY
+6,000 −6,000	=	0	+	0

If assets are junked before being fully depreciated, the company records a loss equal to the asset's book value. Suppose Wal-Mart store fixtures that cost $4,000 are disposed of in this manner. Accumulated depreciation is $3,000, and book value is therefore $1,000. Disposal of these store fixtures records a loss as follows:

Accumulated Depreciation—Store Fixtures	3,000	
Loss on Disposal of Store Fixtures	1,000	
Store Fixtures		4,000
To dispose of store fixtures.		

ASSETS	=	LIABILITIES	+	STOCKHOLDERS' EQUITY	−	LOSSES
+3,000 −4,000	=	0			−	1,000

Loss accounts such as Loss on Disposal of Store Fixtures decrease net income. Losses are reported as Other income (expenses) on the income statement.

Selling a Plant Asset

Suppose a Home Depot store sells fixtures on September 30, 20X4, for $5,000 cash. The fixtures cost $10,000 when purchased on January 1, 20X1, and have been depreciated on a straight-line basis. Managers estimated a 10-year useful life and no residual value. Prior to recording the sale of the fixtures, accountants must update depreciation. Suppose the business uses the calendar year as its accounting period. Partial-year depreciation must be recorded for the asset's expense from January 1, 20X4, to the sale date. The straight-line depreciation entry at September 30, 20X4, is

Sep. 30	Depreciation Expense ($10,000/10 years × 9/12)	750	
	Accumulated Depreciation—Fixtures		750
	To update depreciation.		

ASSETS	=	LIABILITIES	+	STOCKHOLDERS' EQUITY	−	EXPENSES
−750	=	0			−	750

After this entry is posted, the Fixtures account and the Accumulated Depreciation—Fixtures account appear as follows. The fixtures' book value is $6,250 ($10,000 − $3,750).

FIXTURES

Jan. 1, 20X1	10,000		

ACCUMULATED DEPRECIATION—FIXTURES

		Dec. 31, 20X1	1,000
		Dec. 31, 20X2	1,000
		Dec. 31, 20X3	1,000
		Sep. 30, 20X4	750
		Balance	3,750

Suppose the business sells the fixtures for $5,000 cash. The loss on the sale is $1,250, determined as follows:

Cash received from sale of the asset		$5,000
Book value of asset sold:		
Cost	$10,000	
Less accumulated depreciation up to date of sale .	(3,750)	6,250
Gain (loss) on sale of the asset.................		($1,250)

The entry to record sale of the fixtures for $5,000 cash is

Sep. 30	Cash	5,000	
	Accumulated Depreciation—Fixtures	3,750	
	Loss on Sale of Fixtures	1,250	
	Fixtures		10,000
	To sell fixtures.		

✔ CHECK POINT 7-10

ASSETS	=	LIABILITIES	+	STOCKHOLDERS' EQUITY	−	LOSSES
+5,000 +3,750 −10,000	=	0			−	1,250

When recording the sale of a plant asset, the business must remove the balances in the asset account (in this case, Fixtures) and its related accumulated depreciation account and also record a gain or a loss if the amount of cash received differs from the asset's book value.

If the sale price had been $7,000, the business would have had a gain of $750 (Cash, $7,000 − asset book value, $6,250). The entry to record this transaction would be

Sep. 30	Cash	7,000	
	Accumulated Depreciation—Fixtures	3,750	
	Fixtures		10,000
	Gain on Sale of Fixtures		750
	To sell fixtures.		

ASSETS	= LIABILITIES +	STOCKHOLDERS' EQUITY	+ GAINS
+7,000 +3,750 −10,000	= 0		+ 750

Gain on Sale of Fixtures is a credit-balance account, similar to a revenue. A gain is recorded when an asset is sold for a price greater than the asset's book value. A loss is a debit-balance account, similar to an expense. A loss is recorded when the sale price is less than book value. Gains increase net income. Gains and losses are reported on the income statement, as shown for **The Home Depot Inc.,** in the following Stop & Think.

STOP & THINK

Suppose The Home Depot's comparative income statement for two years included these items:

	(In billions) 20X2	20X1
Net sales	$30.2	$28.0
…		
Income from operations	2.7	3.2
Other income (expense):		
Gain on sale of store facilities	.8	
Income before income taxes	$ 3.5	$ 3.2

Which was a better year for Home Depot—20X2 or 20X1?

Answer: From a *sales* standpoint, 20X2 was better because sales were higher. But from an *income* standpoint, 20X1 was better. In 20X1, merchandising operations—the company's core business—generated $3.2 billion of income before taxes. In 20X2, merchandising produced only $2.7 billion of pre-tax income. Almost $1 billion of the company's income in 20X2 came from selling store facilities. A business cannot hope to continue on this path very long. This example illustrates why investors and creditors are interested in the sources of a company's profits, not just the final amount of net income.

Exchanging Plant Assets

Businesses often trade in their old plant assets for similar assets that are newer and more efficient. For example, a pizzeria may decide to trade in a five-year-old delivery car for a newer model. To record the exchange, the business must remove from the books the old asset and its related accumulated depreciation account.

In many cases, the business simply transfers the book value of the old asset plus any cash payment into the new asset account. For example, assume Mazzio Pizzeria's old delivery car cost $9,000 and has accumulated depreciation of $8,000. The car's book value is $1,000. If Mazzio's trades in the old automobile and pays cash of $10,000, the cost of the new delivery car is $11,000 (book value of the old asset, $1,000, plus cash given, $10,000). The pizzeria records the exchange transaction as follows:

Delivery Auto (new)	11,000	
Accumulated Depreciation (old)	8,000	
Delivery Auto (old)		9,000
Cash		10,000
Traded in old delivery car for new auto.		

ASSETS	=	LIABILITIES	+	STOCKHOLDERS' EQUITY
+11,000 +8,000 −9,000 −10,000	=	0	+	0

Under certain conditions, the business can have a loss on an exchange. Gains on the exchange of assets are not as common because accounting conservatism favors losses but not gains.

Accounting for Natural Resources and Depletion

Objective 5
Account for natural resource assets and depletion

Natural resources are plant assets of a special type, such as iron ore, petroleum (oil), natural gas, and timber. An investment in natural resources could be described as an investment in inventories in the ground (oil) or on top of the ground (timber). As plant assets (such as machines) are expensed through depreciation, so natural resource assets are expensed through depletion. **Depletion expense** is that portion of the cost of natural resources that is used up in a particular period. Depletion expense is computed in the same way as units-of-production depreciation.

An oil lease may cost $100,000 and contain an estimated 10,000 barrels of oil. The depletion rate would be $10 per barrel ($100,000/10,000 barrels). If 3,000 barrels are extracted during the year, depletion expense is $30,000 (3,000 barrels × $10 per barrel). The depletion entry for the year is

Depletion Expense (3,000 barrels × $10)	30,000	
Accumulated Depletion—Oil		30,000

ASSETS	=	LIABILITIES	+	STOCKHOLDERS' EQUITY	−	EXPENSES
−30,000	=	0			−	30,000

If 4,500 barrels are removed the next year, that period's depletion is $45,000 (4,500 barrels × $10 per barrel). Accumulated Depletion is a contra account similar to Accumulated Depreciation.

Natural resource assets can be reported on the balance sheet as follows:

Property, Plant, and Equipment:		
Land.		$120,000
Buildings	$800,000	
Equipment.	160,000	
	960,000	
Less: Accumulated depreciation	(410,000)	550,000
Oil	$340,000	
Less: Accumulated depletion.	(70,000)	270,000
Total property, plant, and equipment		$940,000

Pulp Products pays $500,000 for land that contains an estimated 500,000 board feet of timber. The land can be sold for $100,000 after the timber has been cut. If Pulp harvests 200,000 board feet in the year of purchase, how much depletion should be recorded?

Answer: ($500,000 − $100,000) ÷ 500,000 = $0.80 per board foot × 200,000 board feet = $160,000

ACCOUNTING FOR INTANGIBLE ASSETS AND AMORTIZATION

Objective 6
Account for intangible assets and amortization

As we saw earlier in the chapter, *intangible assets* are long-lived assets that are not physical in nature. Instead, these assets are special rights to future benefits from patents, copyrights, trademarks, franchises, leaseholds, and goodwill. Like equipment, an intangible asset is recorded at its acquisition cost and then systematically written off. Like depreciation, the intangible is written off through **amortization,** the systematic allocation of the intangible's cost to expense over its useful life.

Amortization is generally computed on a straight-line basis over a maximum period of 40 years. But obsolescence often cuts an intangible's useful life shorter than its legal life. Amortization expense for an intangible asset can be written off directly against the asset account rather than held in an accumulated amortization account. The residual value of most intangible assets is zero.

Assume that a business purchases a patent on a special manufacturing process. Legally, the patent may run for 20 years. The business realizes, however, that new technologies will limit the patented process's life to four years. If the patent cost $80,000, each year's amortization expense is $20,000 ($80,000/4). The balance sheet reports the patent at its acquisition cost less amortization expense to date. After one year, the patent has a $60,000 balance ($80,000 − $20,000), after two years a $40,000 balance, and so on.

Each type of intangible asset is unique.

- **Patents** are federal government grants giving the holder the exclusive right for 20 years to produce and sell an invention. The invention may be a product or a process—for example, **Sony** compact disk players and the **Dolby** noise-reduction process. Like any other asset, a patent may be purchased. Suppose a company pays $170,000 to acquire a patent on January 1, and the business believes the expected useful life of the patent is only five years. Amortization expense is $34,000 per year ($170,000/5 years). The company's acquisition and amortization entries for this patent are

Jan. 1	Patents	170,000	
	Cash		170,000
	To acquire a patent.		

ASSETS	=	LIABILITIES	+	STOCKHOLDERS' EQUITY
+170,000 −170,000	=	0	+	0

Dec. 31	Amortization Expense—Patents ($170,000/5)	34,000	
	Patents		34,000
	To amortize the cost of a patent.		

ASSETS	=	LIABILITIES	+	STOCKHOLDERS' EQUITY	−	EXPENSES
−34,000	=	0			−	34,000

- **Copyrights** are exclusive rights to reproduce and sell a book, musical composition, film, or other work of art. Copyrights also protect computer software programs, such as **Microsoft's** Windows® and **Excel's** spreadsheet. Issued by the federal government, copyrights extend 50 years beyond the author's (composer's, artist's, or programmer's) life. The cost of obtaining a copyright from the government is low, but a company may pay a large sum to purchase an existing copyright from the owner. For example, a publisher may pay the author of a popular novel $1 million or more for the book's copyright. Because the useful life of a copyright is usually no longer than two or three years, each period's amortization amount is a high proportion of the copyright's cost.
- **Trademarks** and **trade names** (or **brand names**) are distinctive identifications of products or services. The "eye" symbol that flashes across our television screens is the trademark that identifies the **CBS** television network. You are probably also familiar with **NBC's** peacock trademark. Seven-Up, Pepsi, Egg McMuffin, and Rice-a-Roni are everyday trade names. Advertising slogans that are legally protected include **United Airlines'** "Fly the friendly skies" and **Avis Rental Car's** "We try harder."

  The cost of a trademark or trade name is amortized over its useful life, not to exceed 40 years. The cost of advertising and promotions that use the trademark or trade name is not a part of the asset's cost, but rather a debit to the Advertising Expense account.

- **Franchises** and **licenses** are privileges granted by a private business or a government to sell a product or service in accordance with specified conditions. The **Dallas Cowboys** football organization is a franchise granted to its owner, Jerry Jones, by the National Football League. **McDonald's** restaurants and **Holiday Inns** are popular franchises. **Consolidated Edison Company (ConEd)** holds a New York City franchise right to provide electricity to residents. The acquisition costs of franchises and licenses are amortized over their useful lives rather than over legal lives, subject to the 40-year maximum.
- A **leasehold** is a prepayment of rent that a lessee (renter) makes to secure the use of an asset from a lessor (landlord). For example, Home Depot leases many of its store buildings from other entities. Often, leases require the lessee to make this prepayment in addition to monthly rental payments. The lessee records the monthly lease payments to the Rent Expense account. The prepayment, however, is prepaid rent recorded in an intangible asset account titled Leaseholds. This amount is amortized over the life of the lease by debiting Rent Expense and crediting Leaseholds.
- The term *goodwill* in accounting has a rather different meaning than in the everyday phrase "goodwill among men." In accounting, **goodwill** is defined as the excess of the cost of an acquired company over the sum of the market values of its net assets (assets minus liabilities). Recently, **Wal-Mart Stores, Inc.,** has been expanding into Mexico. Suppose Wal-Mart acquires Mexana Company at a cost of $10 million. The sum of the market values of Mexana's assets is $9 million, and its liabilities total $1 million. In this case, Wal-Mart paid $2 million for goodwill, computed as follows:

Purchase price paid for Mexana Company........		$10 million
Sum of the market values of Mexana		
Company's assets..........................	$9 million	
Less: Mexana Company's liabilities..............	(1 million)	
Market value of Mexana Company's net assets		8 million
Excess is called *goodwill*.......................		$ 2 million

Wal-Mart's entry to record the acquisition of Mexana Company, including its goodwill, would be

Assets (Cash, Receivables, Inventories, Plant Assets, all at market value)	9,000,000	
Goodwill	2,000,000	
Liabilities		1,000,000
Cash		10,000,000

✔ CHECK POINT 7-12

ASSETS	=	LIABILITIES	+	STOCKHOLDERS' EQUITY
+9,000,000 +2,000,000 −10,000,000	=	+1,000,000	+	0

Note that Wal-Mart has acquired both Mexana's assets *and* its liabilities.

Goodwill has special features, which include the following points:

1. Goodwill is recorded only when it is purchased in the acquisition of another company. Even though a favorable location, a superior product, or an outstanding reputation may create goodwill for a company, that entity never records goodwill for its own business. Instead, goodwill is recorded *only* by the acquiring company. A purchase transaction provides objective evidence of the value of the goodwill.
2. According to generally accepted accounting principles, goodwill is amortized over a period not to exceed 40 years. In reality, the goodwill of many entities increases in value. Nevertheless, the Accounting Principles Board specified in *Opinion No. 17* that the cost of all intangible assets must be amortized as expense. The Opinion prohibits a lump-sum write-off of the cost of goodwill upon acquisition.

RESEARCH AND DEVELOPMENT COSTS. Accounting for research and development (R&D) costs is one of the most difficult issues the accounting profession has faced. R&D is the lifeblood of companies such as **Procter & Gamble, General Electric, Intel,** and **Boeing.** At these and many other companies, R&D is vital to the development of new products and processes. Thus, it can be argued that the cost of R&D activities is one of these companies' most valuable (intangible) assets. But, in general, companies do not report R&D assets on their balance sheets.

GAAP requires companies to expense R&D costs as they incur them. Only in limited circumstances may the company capitalize the R&D cost as an asset. For example, assume that a company incurs R&D costs under a contract guaranteeing that the company will recover the costs from a customer. In this case, it is clear that the R&D cost is an asset, and the company records an intangible R&D asset when it incurs the cost. But this is the exception to the general rule.

In other situations, it is often unclear whether the R&D cost is an asset (with future benefit) or an expense (with no future benefit). The Financial Accounting Standards Board (FASB) could have let each company make the decision whether to capitalize or expense its R&D costs. Instead, the FASB decided to standardize accounting practice by requiring that R&D costs be expensed as incurred.

✔ CHECK POINT 7-13

INTERNATIONAL ACCOUNTING. Companies in The Netherlands (such as **Royal Dutch Shell** and **Phillips**), in Great Britain (such as **British Steel** and **British Airways**), and in other European nations do not have to record goodwill when they purchase another business. Instead, they may record the cost of goodwill as a decrease in owners' equity. Because these companies never have to amortize the cost of goodwill, their net income is higher than a U.S. company's would be. Not surprisingly, U.S. companies often cry "foul" when bidding against a European firm to acquire another business. Why? Americans claim the Europeans can pay higher prices because their income never takes a hit for amortization expense.

STOP & THINK

How could companies around the world be placed on the same accounting basis?

Answer: If all companies worldwide followed the same accounting rules, they would be reporting income and other amounts that are determined similarly. But this is not the case. Companies must follow the accounting rules of their own nations, and there are differences, as the goodwill situation illustrates. An international body, the International Accounting Standards Committee, has a set of accounting standards, but the organization has no enforcement power.

Ethical Issues in Accounting for Plant Assets and Intangibles

The main ethical issue in accounting for plant assets and intangibles is whether to capitalize or expense a particular cost. In this area, companies have split personalities. On the one hand, they all want to save on taxes. This desire motivates companies to expense all the costs they can in order to decrease taxable income. On the other hand, most companies also want their financial statements to look as good as they can, with high net income and high reported amounts for assets.

In most cases, a cost that is capitalized or expensed for tax purposes must be treated the same way for reporting to stockholders and creditors in the financial

Decision Guidelines

Plant Assets and Related Expenses

Decision	Guidelines
Capitalize or expense a cost?	General rule: Capitalize all costs that provide *future* benefit for the business. Expense all costs that provide *no future* benefit.
Capitalize or expense: • Cost associated with a new asset?	Capitalize all costs that bring the asset to its intended use.
• Cost associated with an existing asset?	Capitalize only those costs that add to the asset's usefulness or to its useful life. Expense all other costs as maintenance or repairs.
• Interest cost incurred to finance the asset's acquisition?	Capitalize interest cost only on assets constructed by the business for its own use. Expense all other interest cost.
Which depreciation method to use: • For financial reporting?	Use the method that best matches depreciation expense against the revenues produced by the asset.
• For income tax?	Use the method that produces the fastest tax deductions (MACRS). A company can use different depreciation methods for financial reporting and for income tax purposes. In the United States, this practice is considered perfectly legal and ethical.

statements. What, then, is the ethical path? Accountants should follow the general guidelines for capitalizing a cost: Capitalize all costs that provide a future benefit for the business and expense all other costs, as outlined in the Decision Guidelines feature.

Many companies have gotten into trouble by capitalizing costs they should have expensed. They made their financial statements look better than the facts warranted. But there are very few cases of companies getting into trouble by following the general guidelines, or even by erring on the side of expensing questionable costs. This is another example of accounting conservatism in action. It works.

We discussed accounting conservatism in Chapter 6.

REPORTING PLANT ASSET TRANSACTIONS ON THE STATEMENT OF CASH FLOWS

Objective 7
Report plant asset transactions on the statement of cash flows

Three main types of plant asset transactions appear on the statement of cash flows: acquisitions, sales, and depreciation (including amortization and depletion). Acquisitions and sales are *investing* activities. A company invests in plant assets by paying cash or by incurring a liability. The cash payments for plant and equipment are investing activities that appear on the statement of cash flows. The sale of plant assets results in a cash receipt, as illustrated in Exhibit 7-13, which excerpts data from the cash-flow statement of **The Home Depot, Inc.** The acquisitions, sales, and depreciation of plant assets are denoted in color (lines 5, 6, and 2).

Let's examine the investing activities first. During the fiscal year ended January 31, 1999, The Home Depot paid $2,059 million for plant assets (line 5). The cash-flow statement reports this cash payment as Capital Expenditures, a common description. During the year, the company sold property and equipment, receiving cash of $45 million (line 6). The Home Depot labels the cash received as Proceeds

EXHIBIT 7-13
Reporting Plant Asset Transactions on the Statement of Cash Flows

THE HOME DEPOT, INC.
Statement of Cash Flows (partial, adapted)
Fiscal Year Ended January 31, 1999

		(In millions)
	Cash Provided From Operations:	
1	Net earnings	$1,614
	Reconciliation of Net Earnings to Net Cash Provided by Operations:	
2	Depreciation and amortization	373
3	Other items (summarized)	(70)
4	Net Cash Provided by Operations	1,917
	Cash Flows From Investing Activities:	
5	Capital expenditures (Purchases of property and equipment)	(2,059)
6	Proceeds from sales of property and equipment	45
7	Other items (summarized)	(257)
8	Net Cash Used in Investing Activities	(2,271)
	Cash Flows From Financing Activities:	
9	Net Cash Provided by Financing Activities	248
10	Other items	(4)
11	Increase (decrease) in cash and cash equivalents	(110)
12	Cash and cash equivalents at beginning of year	172
13	Cash and cash equivalents at end of year	$ 62

CHECK POINT 7-14

from sales of property and equipment, also a common reporting practice. The $45 million is the amount of cash received from the sale of plant assets. It is neither the cost nor the book value of the assets sold. If the cash received from the sale differs from the asset's book value, the company reports a gain or a loss on the sale in the income statement.

The Home Depot's statement of cash flows reports Depreciation and amortization in the operating activities section (line 2). Observe that "Depreciation and amortization" is listed as a positive item under Reconciliation of Net Earnings to Net Cash Provided by Operations. You may be wondering why depreciation appears on the cash-flow statement. After all, depreciation does not affect cash.

In this particular statement format, the operating activities section of the cash-flow statement starts with net income (line 1) and reconciles to net cash provided by operating activities (line 4). Depreciation decreases net income in the same way that all other expenses do. It does not, however, have any effect on cash. Depreciation is therefore added back to net income in determining cash flow from operations. In effect, the add-back of depreciation to net income offsets the earlier subtraction of the expense. The sum of net income plus depreciation helps to reconcile net income (on the accrual basis) to cash flow from operations (a cash-basis amount). We revisit this topic in the full context of the statement of cash flows in Chapter 12.

Test your ability to use the cash-flow statement.

1. Make an entry in the journal to record The Home Depot's capital expenditures during the year.
2. Suppose the book value of the property and equipment that The Home Depot sold was $51 million (cost of $72 million minus accumulated depreciation of $21 million). Record the company's transaction to sell the property and equipment. Also write a sentence to explain why the sale transaction resulted in a loss for The Home Depot.
3. Where would The Home Depot report any gain or loss on the sale of the property and equipment—on which financial statement, under what heading?

Answers

	(In millions)	
1. Property and Equipment	2,059	
Cash		2,059
Made capital expenditures.		
2. Cash	45	
Accumulated Depreciation	21	
Loss on Sale of Property and Equipment	6	
Property and Equipment		72
Sold property and equipment.		

The company sold for $45 million assets that had book value of $51 million. The result of the sale was a loss of $6 million ($51 million − $45 million).

3. Report the loss on the *income statement* under the heading *Other income (expense).*

END-OF-CHAPTER

End-of-Chapter

Summary Problems for Your Review

Problem 1 The figures that follow appear in the *Answers to the Mid-Chapter Summary Problem,* Requirement 2, on page 324.

	Method A: Straight-Line			*Method B: Double-Declining-Balance*		
Year	*Annual Depreciation Expense*	*Accumulated Depreciation*	*Book Value*	*Annual Depreciation Expense*	*Accumulated Depreciation*	*Book Value*
Start			$44,000			$44,000
20X5	$4,000	$ 4,000	40,000	$8,800	$ 8,800	35,200
20X6	4,000	8,000	36,000	7,040	15,840	28,160
20X7	4,000	12,000	32,000	5,632	21,472	22,528

Required

Suppose the income tax authorities permitted a choice between these two depreciation methods. Which method would you select for income tax purposes? Why?

Problem 2 A corporation purchased the equipment described in the table on January 1, 20X5. Management has depreciated the equipment by using the double-declining-balance method. On July 1, 20X7, the company sold the equipment for $27,000 cash.

Required

Record depreciation for 20X7 and the sale of the equipment on July 1, 20X7.

Answers

Problem 1 For tax purposes, most companies select the accelerated method because it results in the most depreciation in the earliest years of the equipment's life. Accelerated depreciation minimizes taxable income and income tax payments in the early years of the asset's life, thereby maximizing the business's cash at the earliest possible time.

Problem 2 To record depreciation to date of sale, and then the sale of the equipment:

20X7			
July 1	Depreciation Expense—Equipment ($5,632 × 1/2 year)	2,816	
	Accumulated Depreciation—Equipment		2,816
	To update depreciation.		
July 1	Cash	27,000	
	Accumulated Depreciation—Equipment ($15,840 + $2,816)	18,656	
	Equipment		44,000
	Gain on Sale of Equipment		1,656
	To record sale of equipment.		

SUMMARY OF LEARNING OBJECTIVES

1. ***Determine the cost of a plant asset.*** Plant assets are long-lived tangible assets, such as land, buildings, and equipment, used in the operation of a business. The cost of a plant asset is the purchase price plus applicable taxes, purchase commissions, and all other amounts paid to acquire the asset and to prepare it for its intended use.
2. ***Account for depreciation.*** Businesses may account for depreciation (the allocation of a plant asset's cost to expense over its useful life) by four methods: the *straight-line method*, the *units-of-production method*, the *double-declining-balance method*, or the *sum-of-the-years'-digits method*. (In practice, the last method is not used much.) All these methods require accountants to estimate the asset's useful life and residual value.
3. ***Select the best depreciation method for income tax purposes.*** Most companies use an accelerated depreciation method for income tax purposes. Accelerated depreciation results in higher expenses, lower taxable income, and lower tax payments early in the asset's life.
4. ***Analyze the effect of a plant asset disposal.*** Before disposing of, selling, or trading in a plant asset, the company must update the asset's depreciation. Disposal is then recorded by removing the book balances from both the asset account and its related accumulated depreciation account. Sales often result in a gain or loss, which is reported on the income statement. When exchanging a plant asset, the company often carries forward the book value of the old asset plus any cash payment as the cost of the new asset and thus records no gain or loss on the exchange.
5. ***Account for natural resource assets and depletion.*** The cost of natural resources, a special category of long-lived assets, is expensed through *depletion*. Depletion is computed on a units-of-production basis. Accumulated Depletion is a contra account similar to Accumulated Depreciation.
6. ***Account for intangible assets and amortization.*** *Intangible assets* are assets that have no physical form. They give their owners a special right to current and expected future benefits. The major types of intangible assets are patents, copyrights, trademarks, franchises and licenses, leaseholds, and goodwill.

   The cost of intangibles is expensed through *amortization*, which is the same concept as depreciation. Amortization on intangibles is computed on a straight-line basis over a maximum of 40 years. However, the useful life of an intangible is often shorter than its legal life.
7. ***Report plant asset transactions on the statement of cash flows.*** Three main types of plant asset transactions appear on the statement of cash flows. Acquisitions and sales of plant assets appear in the investing activities section of the statement. Depreciation, depletion, and amortization appear in the statement's operating activities section as add-backs to net income.

ACCOUNTING VOCABULARY

accelerated depreciation method (p. 321).
amortization (p. 333).
brand name (p. 334).
capital expenditure (p. 316).
capitalize (p. 315).
copyright (p. 334).
depletion expense (p. 332).
depreciable cost (p. 318).
double-declining-balance (DDB) method (p. 321).
estimated residual value (p. 318).
estimated useful life (p. 318).
extraordinary repair (p. 316).
franchises and licenses (p. 334).
goodwill (p. 334).
intangible asset (p. 312).
leasehold (p. 334).
major repair (p. 316).
Modified Accelerated Cost Recovery System (MACRS) (p. 326).
ordinary repair (p. 316).
patent (p. 333).
plant asset (p. 312).
revenue expenditure (p. 316).
straight-line (SL) method (p. 319).
trademark, trade name (p. 334).
units-of-production (UOP) method (p. 320).

QUESTIONS

1. To what types of long-lived assets do the following expenses apply: depreciation, depletion, and amortization?
2. Describe how to measure the cost of a plant asset. Would an ordinary cost of repairing the asset after it is placed in service be included in the asset's cost?
3. When assets are purchased as a group for a single price and no individual asset cost is given, how is each asset's cost determined?
4. Distinguish a capital expenditure from a revenue expenditure. Explain the title "revenue expenditure," which is curious in that a revenue expenditure is a debit to an expense account.
5. Define depreciation. Present the common misconceptions about depreciation.
6. Explain the concept of accelerated depreciation. Which other depreciation method is used in the definition of

double-declining-balance depreciation? Which of the depreciation methods results in the most depreciation in the first year of the asset's life?

7. The level of business activity fluctuates widely for Harwood Delivery Service, reaching its peak around Christmas each year. At other times, business is slow. Which depreciation method is most appropriate for the company's fleet of Ford Aerostar minivans?

8. **Kinko's** uses the most advanced copy machines available to keep a competitive edge over other copy centers. To maintain this advantage, Kinko's replaces its machines before they are worn out. Describe the major factors affecting the useful life of a plant asset and indicate which factor seems most relevant to Kinko's copy machines.

9. Which type of depreciation method is best from an income tax standpoint? Why? How does depreciation affect income taxes? How does depreciation affect cash provided by operations?

10. What expense applies to natural resources? By which depreciation method is this expense computed?

11. How do intangible assets differ from most other assets? Why are they assets at all? What type of expense applies to intangible assets?

12. Why is the cost of patents and other intangible assets often expensed over a shorter period than the legal life of the asset?

13. Your company has just purchased another company for $400,000. The market value of the other company's net assets is $325,000. What is the $75,000 excess called? What type of asset is it? What is the maximum period over which its cost is amortized under generally accepted accounting principles?

14. **Microsoft** is recognized as a world leader in the development of software. The company's past success created vast amounts of business goodwill. Would you expect to see this goodwill reported on Microsoft's financial statements? Why or why not?

15. Describe the three types of plant asset transactions reported on a statement of cash flows. Indicate where and how each type of transaction appears on the statement.

CHECK POINTS

Cost and book value of a company's plant assets (Obj. 1)

CP7-1 Examine the balance sheet of **The Home Depot** at the beginning of this chapter. Answer these questions about the company:

1. When does The Home Depot's fiscal year end? Why does the company's fiscal year end on this date?
2. What is The Home Depot's largest category of assets?
3. What was The Home Depot's cost of property and equipment at January 31, 1999? What was the book value of property and equipment on this date?

Measuring the cost of a plant asset (Obj. 1)

CP7-2 Page 313 of this chapter lists the costs included for the acquisition of land. First is the purchase price of the land, which is obviously included in the cost of the land. The reasons for including the related costs are not so obvious. For example, property tax is ordinarily an expense, not part of the cost of an asset. State why the related costs listed on page 313 are included as part of the cost of the land. After the land is ready for use, will these related costs be capitalized or expensed?

Lump-sum purchase of assets (Obj. 1)

CP7-3 Return to the Stop & Think feature on page 316. Suppose at the time of your acquisition, the land has a current market value of $80,000, the building's market value is $60,000, and the equipment's market value is $20,000. Journalize the lump-sum purchase of the three assets for a total cost of $120,000. You sign a note payable for this amount.

Capitalizing versus expensing plant asset costs (Obj. 1)

CP7-4 Steitz Aviation repaired one of its Boeing 777 aircraft at a cost of $1 million, which Steitz paid in cash. The Steitz accountant erroneously capitalized this cost as part of the cost of the plane.

1. Journalize both the incorrect entry the accountant made to record this transaction and the correct entry that the accountant should have made.
2. Show the effects of the accounting error on Steitz Aviation's income statement and balance sheet, using the format illustrated on page 317.

Computing depreciation by three methods—first year only (Obj. 2)

CP7-5 At the beginning of 20X0, Steitz Aviation purchased a used Boeing 737 aircraft at a cost of $21,000,000. Steitz expects the plane to remain useful for five years (1 million miles) and to have a residual value of $6,000,000. Steitz expects the plane to be flown 150,000 miles the first year and 250,000 miles the last year.

1. Compute Steitz's first-year depreciation on the plane using the following methods:

   a. Straight-line **b.** Units-of-production **c.** Double-declining-balance

2. Show the airplane's book value at the end of the first year under each depreciation method.

Computing depreciation by three methods—final year only (Obj. 2)

CP7-6 Use the Steitz Aviation data in Check Point 7-5 to compute Steitz's fifth-year depreciation on the plane using the following methods:

a. Straight-line
b. Units-of-production
c. Double-declining-balance (you must compute depreciation for all five years)

Selecting the best depreciation method for income tax purposes (Obj. 3)

CP7-7 This exercise uses the Steitz Aviation data from Check Point 7-6. Assume Steitz Aviation is trying to decide which depreciation method to use for income tax purposes.

1. Which depreciation method offers the tax advantage for the first year? Describe the nature of the tax advantage.
2. How much income tax will Steitz save for the first year of the airplane's use as compared to using the straight-line depreciation method? Steitz's income tax rate is 40 percent. Ignore any earnings from investing the extra cash.

Partial-year depreciation (Obj. 2)

CP7-8 On March 31, 20X1, Steitz Aviation purchased a used Boeing 737 aircraft at a cost of $21,000,000. Steitz expects the plane to remain useful for five years (1,000,000 miles) and to have a residual value of $6,000,000. Steitz expects the plane to be flown 100,000 miles during the remainder of the first year ended December 31, 20X1. Compute Steitz's depreciation on the plane for the year ended December 31, 20X1, using the following methods:

a. Straight-line
b. Units-of-production
c. Double-declining-balance

Computing and recording depreciation after a change in useful life of the asset (Obj. 2)

CP7-9 Return to the example of the Disney World hot dog stand on page 328. Suppose that after using the hot dog stand for three years, the **Walt Disney Company** determines that the asset will remain useful for only three more years. Record Disney's depreciation on the hot dog stand for year 4 by the straight-line method.

Recording a gain or loss on disposal under two depreciation methods (Obj. 4)

CP7-10 Return to the Home Depot delivery-truck depreciation example in Exhibit 7-5 (page 320) and 7-7 (page 321). Suppose The Home Depot sold the truck on January 1, 20X3, for $20,000 cash, after using the truck for two full years.

1. Make a separate journal entry to record The Home Depot's sale of the truck under
   a. Straight-line depreciation (Exhibit 7-5, page 320).
   b. Double-declining-balance depreciation (Exhibit 7-7, page 321).
2. Why is there such a big difference between the gain or loss on disposal under the two depreciation methods?

Accounting for the depletion of a company's natural resources (Obj. 5)

CP7-11 **Texaco,** the giant oil company, holds reserves of oil and gas assets. At the end of 20X2, assume the cost of Texaco's mineral assets totaled approximately $22 billion, representing 2.4 billion barrels of oil in the ground.

1. Which depreciation method do Texaco and other oil companies use to compute their annual depletion expense for the minerals removed from the ground?
2. Suppose Texaco removed 0.6 billion barrels of oil during 20X3. Record Texaco's depletion expense for the year.
3. At December 31, 20X2, Texaco's Accumulated Depletion account stood at $15.0 billion. If Texaco did not add any new oil and gas reserves during 20X3, what would be the book value of the company's oil and gas reserves at December 31, 20X3? Cite a specific figure from your answer to illustrate why exploration activities are so important for companies such as Texaco.

Analyzing a company's goodwill (Obj. 6)

CP7-12 Examine the balance sheet of **The Home Depot** at the beginning of this chapter. Answer these questions about the company:

1. What account title does The Home Depot use for goodwill?
2. What was the book value of The Home Depot's goodwill at January 31, 1999? What was the amount of accumulated amortization on the goodwill? What was The Home Depot's cost of its goodwill on this date?
3. One year earlier, on January 31, 1998, The Home Depot had Goodwill at cost of $158 million, less Accumulated Amortization of $18 million, for a book value of $140 million. During the year ended January 31, 1999, The Home Depot sold no companies and thus sold none of its goodwill. Use your answer to requirement 2 to answer these questions:
   a. How much goodwill did The Home Depot purchase during the year ended January 31, 1999?
   b. How much amortization expense on its goodwill did the company record during the year?

CP7-13 This exercise summarizes the accounting for patents, which like copyrights, trademarks, and franchises, provide the owner with a special right or privilege. It also covers research and development costs.

Accounting for patents and research and development cost (Obj. 6)

Suppose **Oracle Software** paid $700,000 to research and develop a new software program. Oracle also paid $300,000 to acquire a patent on the new software. After readying the software for production, Oracle's sales revenue for the first year totaled $1,300,000. Cost of goods sold was $200,000, and operating (chiefly selling) expenses were $400,000. All these transactions occurred during 20X0. Oracle expects the patent to have a useful life of three years.

1. Prepare Oracle Software's income statement for the year ended December 31, 20X0, complete with a heading.
2. Considering the makeup of Oracle's expenses, what should the company's outlook for future profits be on the new software program?

CP7-14 During fiscal year 20X0, Kodan, Inc., a pharmaceutical company, purchased another company for $2 million. Kodan financed this purchase by paying cash of $1 million and borrowing the remainder. Also during fiscal 20X0, Kodan made capital expenditures of $4 million to expand its manufacturing plant. During the year, older equipment wore out, and Kodan sold the equipment, receiving cash of $0.3 million and suffering a loss of $0.2 million on the disposal. Overall, Kodan reported a net loss of $1.4 million during fiscal 20X0.

Reporting investing activities on the statement of cash flows (Obj. 7)

Show what Kodan, Inc., would report for cash flows from investing activities on its statement of cash flows for the year ended September 30, 20X0. Report a total amount for net cash provided (used) in investing activities.

EXERCISES

E7-1 Neon Enterprises purchased land, paying $90,000 cash as a down payment and signing a $150,000 note payable for the balance. In addition, Neon paid delinquent property tax of $2,000, title insurance costing $2,500, and a $5,400 charge for leveling the land and removing an unwanted building. The company paid $50,000 to remove earth for the foundation and then constructed an office building at a cost of $1,070,000. It also paid $72,000 for a fence around the boundary of the property, $10,400 for the company sign near the entrance to the property, and $6,000 for special lighting of the grounds. Determine the cost of the company's land, land improvements, and building.

Determining the cost of plant assets (Obj. 1)

E7-2 Persian Leasing Company bought three used machines in a $40,000 lump-sum purchase. An independent appraiser valued the machines as follows:

Allocating costs to assets acquired in a lump-sum purchase (Obj. 1)

Machine No.	*Appraised Value*
1	$12,000
2	20,000
3	16,000

Persian Leasing paid one-fourth in cash and signed a note payable for the remainder. Record the purchase in the journal, identifying each machine's individual cost in a separate Machine account. Round decimals to three places.

E7-3 Classify each of the following expenditures as a capital expenditure or a revenue expenditure (expense) related to machinery: (a) purchase price, (b) sales tax paid on the purchase price, (c) transportation and insurance while machinery is in transit from seller to buyer, (d) installation, (e) training of personnel for initial operation of the machinery, (f) special reinforcement to the machinery platform, (g) income tax paid on income earned from the sale of products manufactured by the machinery, (h) major overhaul to extend useful life by three years, (i) ordinary repairs to keep the machinery in good working order, (j) lubrication of the machinery before it is placed in service, (k) periodic lubrication after the machinery is placed in service.

Distinguishing capital expenditures from expenses (Obj. 1)

E7-4 During 20X4, Flowers by Design, Inc. (FBD), paid $100,000 for land and built a store in Nashville, Tennessee. Prior to construction, the city of Nashville charged FBD $1,000 for a building permit, which FBD paid. FBD also paid $10,000 for architect's fees. The construc-

Measuring, depreciating, and reporting plant assets (Obj. 1, 2)

tion cost of $530,000 was financed by a long-term note payable, with interest cost of $39,000 paid at December 31, 20X4. This interest cost was capitalized as part of the cost of the building. The building was completed June 30, 20X4. FBD depreciates the building by the straight-line method over 40 years, with estimated residual value of $100,000.

1. Journalize transactions for

   a. Purchase of the land

   b. All the costs chargeable to the building in a single entry

   c. Depreciation on the building

   Explanations are not required.

2. Report FBD's plant assets on the company's balance sheet at December 31, 20X4.

3. What will FBD's income statement for the year ended December 31, 20X4, report for the building?

Explaining the concept of depreciation (Obj. 2)

E7-5 Frank Becker has just slept through the class in which Professor Barshevski explained the concept of depreciation. Because the next test is scheduled for Wednesday, Becker telephones Emily Stein to get her notes from the lecture. Stein's notes are concise: "Depreciation—Sounds like Greek to me." Becker next tries Mark Haverhill, who says he thinks depreciation is what happens when an asset wears out. Clay Sherman is confident that depreciation is the process of building up a cash fund to replace an asset at the end of its useful life. Explain the concept of depreciation for Becker. Evaluate the explanations of Haverhill and Sherman. Be specific.

Determining depreciation amounts by three methods (Obj. 2, 3)

E7-6 Rambler Wholesale Grocers, Inc., bought a delivery van on January 2, 20X1, for $15,000. The van was expected to remain in service four years and to last 100,000 miles. At the end of its useful life, Rambler officials estimated that the van's residual value would be $3,000. The van traveled 34,000 miles the first year, 28,000 the second year, 18,000 the third year, and 20,000 in the fourth year. Prepare a schedule of *depreciation expense* per year for the van under the three depreciation methods. After two years under the double-declining-balance method, the company switches to the straight-line method. Show your computations.

Which method tracks the wear and tear on the van most closely? Which method would Rambler prefer to use for income tax purposes? Explain in detail why Rambler prefers this method.

Reporting plant assets, depreciation, and cash flow (Obj. 1, 2, 7)

E7-7 In January 20X2, American Eagle Restaurant purchased an old building, paying $20,000 cash and signing an $80,000 note payable. The restaurant paid $50,000 to remodel the building. Furniture and fixtures cost $30,000, and dishes and other supplies were obtained for $9,000.

American Eagle is depreciating the building over 20 years by the straight-line method, with estimated residual value of $40,000. The furniture and fixtures will be replaced at the end of five years; these assets are being depreciated by the double-declining-balance method, with zero residual value. The dishes and other supplies are treated as a current asset. At the end of the first year, the restaurant still has dishes and other supplies worth $2,000.

Show what the restaurant will report for its supplies, plant assets, and related cash flows at the end of the first year on its

- Income statement
- Balance sheet
- Statement of cash flows (investing cash flows only)

Show all computations.

Note: The purchase of dishes and other supplies is an operating cash flow because supplies are a current asset.

Units-of-production depreciation (Obj. 2)

E7-8 **Gold's Gym** purchased Nautilus exercise equipment at a cost of $100,000. In addition, Gold's paid $2,000 for a special platform on which to stabilize the equipment for use. Freight costs of $1,200 to ship the equipment were borne by **Nautilus.** Gold's will depreciate the equipment by the units-of-production method, based on an expected useful life of 50,000 hours of exercise. The estimated resale value of the equipment after 50,000 hours of use is $10,000. How many hours of usage can Gold's Gym expect for the machine if depreciation expense is $4,600 for the year 20X1?

Selecting the best depreciation method for income-tax purposes (Obj. 3)

E7-9 On June 30, 20X1, Elaine Penn Corp. paid $210,000 for equipment that is expected to have a seven-year life. In this industry, the residual value of equipment is approximately 10% of the asset's cost. Penn's cash revenues for the year are $100,000 and cash expenses total $60,000.

Select the appropriate MACRS depreciation method for income tax purposes. Then determine the extra amount of cash that Penn Corp. can invest by using MACRS depreciation, versus straight-line, for the year ended December 31, 20X1. The income tax rate is 40%.

Changing a plant asset's useful life (Obj. 2)

E7-10 Catholic Services, Inc., purchased a building for $900,000 and depreciated it on a straight-line basis over a 30-year period. The estimated residual value was $100,000. After using the building for 15 years, Catholic Services realized that the building will remain useful for a total of 40 years. Starting with the 16th year, Catholic Services began depreciating the building over a revised total life of 40 years and decreased the estimated residual value to $50,000. Record depreciation expense on the building for years 15 and 16.

Analyzing the effect of a sale of a plant asset; DDB depreciation (Obj. 4)

E7-11 On January 2, 20X0, a **Days Inn** purchased fixtures for $8,700 cash, expecting the fixtures to remain in service five years. Days Inn has depreciated the fixtures on a double-declining-balance basis, with $1,000 estimated residual value. On September 30, 20X1, Days Inn sold the fixtures for $3,000 cash. Record both the depreciation expense on the fixtures for 20X1 and the sale of the fixtures.

Measuring a plant asset's cost, using UOP depreciation, and trading in a used asset (Obj. 1, 2, 4)

E7-12 **Granite Shoals Corporation,** based in Branson, Missouri, is a large trucking company that operates throughout the midwestern United States. Granite Shoals uses the units-of-production (UOP) method to depreciate its trucks because its managers believe UOP depreciation best measures the wear and tear.

Granite Shoals trades in used trucks often to keep driver morale high and to maximize fuel efficiency. Consider these facts about one Mack truck in the company's fleet: When acquired in 20X2, the tractor-trailer rig cost $285,000 and was expected to remain in service for 10 years or 1,000,000 miles. Estimated residual value was $85,000. During 20X2, the truck was driven 75,000 miles; during 20X3, 120,000 miles; and during 20X4, 210,000 miles. After 40,000 miles in 20X5, the company traded in the Mack truck for a less expensive Freightliner rig. Granite Shoals paid cash of $50,000. Determine Granite Shoals' cost of the new truck. Journal entries are not required.

Recording natural resource assets and depletion (Obj. 5)

E7-13 Bryce Canyon Mines paid $298,500 for the right to extract ore from a 200,000-ton mineral deposit. In addition to the purchase price, Bryce Canyon also paid a $500 filing fee, a $1,000 license fee to the state of Utah, and $60,000 for a geological survey of the property. Because the company purchased the rights to the minerals only, it expected the asset to have zero residual value when fully depleted. During the first year of production, Bryce Canyon Mines removed 40,000 tons of ore. Make general journal entries to record (a) purchase of the mineral rights (debit Mineral Asset), (b) payment of fees and other costs, and (c) depletion for first-year production.

Recording intangibles, amortization, and a change in the asset's useful life (Obj. 6)

E7-14 ***Part 1.*** Hillcrest Dental Associates has recently purchased for $800,000 a patent for the design of a new X-ray machine. Although it gives legal protection for 20 years, the patent is expected to provide Hillcrest with a competitive advantage for only eight years. Assuming the straight-line method of amortization, make journal entries to record (a) the purchase of the patent and (b) amortization for year 1.

Part 2. After using the patent for four years, Hillcrest learns at a professional meeting that another company is designing a more efficient machine. On the basis of this new information, Hillcrest decides, starting with year 5, to amortize the remaining cost of the patent over two additional years, giving the patent a total useful life of six years. Record amortization for year 5.

Measuring goodwill (Obj. 6)

E7-15 Assume **Campbell Soup Company's** 20X1 statement of cash flows includes the following:

	20X1
	Millions
Cash Flows from Investing Activities:	
Businesses acquired	$(1,255)

Campbell's "Note 15. Intangible Assets," includes the following:

	20X1	*20X0*
	Millions	
Purchase price in excess of net assets of businesses acquired	$1,716	$542
Less: Accumulated amortization	(133)	(90)

Required

Answer these questions related to Campbell Soup Company's goodwill:

1. What title does Campbell Soup Company use to describe its goodwill? How well does Campbell's title agree with the text definition of goodwill?
2. How much did Campbell Soup Company pay to acquire other businesses during 20X1? How much of the purchase price was for goodwill? How much did Campbell pay for other assets? What other assets besides goodwill was Campbell Soup Company acquiring?

Measuring and recording goodwill (Obj. 6)

E7-16 **PepsiCo, Inc.,** dominates the snack-food industry with its Frito-Lay brand. Assume that PepsiCo, Inc., purchased O'Chip, Inc., for $7 million cash. The market value of O'Chip's assets is $14 million, and O'Chip has liabilities of $11 million.

Required

1. Compute the cost of the goodwill purchased by PepsiCo.
2. Record the purchase by PepsiCo.
3. Record amortization of goodwill for year 1, assuming the straight-line method and a useful life of 10 years.

Interpreting a cash-flow statement (Obj. 7)

E7-17 The following items are excerpted from the 19X8 annual report of **Sara Lee Corporation:**

SARA LEE CORPORATION

Consolidated Statement of Cash Flows (partial, adapted)

Year Ended June 30 (Millions of Dollars)	*19X8*
Operating Activities	
Net income	$523
Adjustments for noncash [expenses] included in net (loss)	
Depreciation	427
Amortization of intangibles	191
Investing Activities	
Purchases of property and equipment	474
Acquisitions of businesses	(393)
Sales of property	140
Dispositions of businesses	451

Required

Answer these questions:

1. Why are depreciation and amortization listed on the statement of cash flows?
2. Explain in detail each investing activity.

Challenge Exercises

Capitalizing versus expensing; measuring the effect of an error (Obj. 1)

E7-18 **Mirage Sportswear,** a catalog merchant in France, is similar to **L. L. Bean** and **Lands' End** in the United States. The company's assets consist mainly of inventory, a warehouse, and automated shipping equipment. Early in year 1, Mirage purchased equipment at a cost of 2 million francs (F 2 million). Management expects the equipment to remain in service five years. Because the equipment is so specialized, estimated residual value is negligible. Mirage uses the straight-line depreciation method. *Through an accounting error, Mirage accidentally expensed the entire cost of the equipment at the time of purchase.* Because the company is family owned and operated as a partnership, it pays no income tax.

Required

Prepare a schedule to show the overstatement or understatement in the following items at the end of each year over the five-year life of the equipment:

1. Total current assets
2. Equipment, net
3. Net income
4. Owners' equity

Reconstructing transactions from the financial statements (Obj. 2, 4)

E7-19 **Ford Motor Company's** comparative balance sheet reported these amounts (in millions of dollars):

	December 31, 19X9	19X8
Property:		
Land, plant, and equipment	$35,726.3	$34,825.1
Less accumulated depreciation	(19,422.0)	(18,486.8)
Net land, plant, and equipment	16,304.3	16,338.3
Unamortized special tools	6,218.0	5,869.5
Net property	$22,522.3	$22,207.8

Ford's income statement for 19X9 reported the following expenses (in millions):

Depreciation	$2,455.8
Amortization of special tools	1,822.1

Unamortized special tools refers to the remaining asset balance after amortization expense has been subtracted. Ford does not use an accumulated amortization account for special tools.

Required

1. There were no disposals of special tools during 19X9. Compute the cost of new acquisitions of special tools.
2. Assume that during 19X9 Ford sold land, plant, and equipment for $92 million and that this transaction produced a gain of $9 million. What was the book value of the assets sold?
3. Use the answer to Requirement 2 to compute the cost of land, plant, and equipment acquired during 19X9. For convenience, work with net land, plant, and equipment.

PROBLEMS

(Group A)

Identifying the elements of a plant asset's cost (Obj. 1, 2)

P7-1A McLennan Electric Cooperative incurred the following costs in acquiring land and a garage, making land improvements, and constructing and furnishing a district office building.

a. Purchase price of 3 1/2 acres of land, including a building that will be used as a garage for company vehicles (land market value is $700,000; building market value is $100,000)	$720,000
b. Delinquent real estate taxes on the land to be paid by McLennan Electric	3,700
c. Landscaping (additional dirt and earth moving)	3,550
d. Title insurance on the land acquisition	1,000
e. Fence around the boundary of the land	44,100
f. Building permit for the office building	200
g. Architect fee for the design of the office building	45,000
h. Company signs near front and rear approaches to the company property	53,550
i. Renovation of the garage	23,800
j. Concrete, wood, and other materials used in the construction of the office building	414,000
k. Masonry, carpentry, roofing, and other labor to construct the office building	734,000
l. Interest cost on construction loan for office building	3,400
m. Parking lots and concrete walks on the property	17,450
n. Lights for the parking lot, walkways, and company signs	8,900
o. Supervisory salary of construction supervisor (90% to office building; 6% to fencing, parking lot, and concrete walks; and 4% to garage renovation)	55,000

p. Office furniture for the office building	$123,500
q. Transportation of furniture from seller to the office building	1,300
r. Landscaping (trees and shrubs)	9,100

McLennan Electric depreciates buildings over 40 years, land improvements over 20 years, and furniture over 8 years, all on a straight-line basis with zero residual value.

Required

1. Set up columns for Land, Land Improvements, District Office Building, Garage, and Furniture. Show how to account for each of McLennan's costs by listing the cost under the correct account. Determine the total cost of each asset.

2. Assuming that all construction was complete and the assets were placed in service on March 19, record depreciation for the year ended December 31. Round figures to the nearest dollar.

3. How will what you learned in this problem help you manage a business?

Recording plant asset transactions; reporting on the balance sheet (Obj. 2)

P7-2A Terrell Alarm Protection Services has a hefty investment in security equipment, as reported in the company's balance sheet at December 31, 20X2:

Property, plant, and equipment, at cost:	
Land	$ 80,000
Buildings	110,000
Less Accumulated depreciation	(40,000)
Security equipment	620,000
Less Accumulated depreciation	(170,000)

In early July 20X3, Terrell purchased additional security equipment at a cost of $180,000. Terrell depreciates buildings by the straight-line method over 20 years with residual value of $30,000. Due to obsolescence, security equipment has a useful life of only 10 years and is being depreciated by the double-declining-balance method with zero residual value.

Required

1. Journalize Terrell's plant asset purchase and depreciation transactions for 20X3.

2. Report plant assets on the company's December 31, 20X3, balance sheet.

Recording plant asset transactions, exchanges, changes in useful life (Obj. 1, 2, 4)

P7-3A **Neilson & Associates** surveys American television-viewing trends. The company's balance sheet reports the following assets under Property and Equipment: Land, Buildings, Office Furniture, Communication Equipment, and Televideo Equipment. The company has a separate accumulated depreciation account for each of these assets except land. Assume that Neilson completed the following transactions:

Jan. 2	Traded in communication equipment with book value of $11,000 (cost of $96,000) for similar new equipment with a cash cost of $88,000. The seller gave Neilson a trade-in allowance of $15,000 on the old equipment, and Neilson paid the remainder in cash.
Aug. 31	Sold a building that had cost $475,000 and had accumulated depreciation of $353,500 through December 31 of the preceding year. Depreciation is computed on a straight-line basis. The building has a 30-year useful life and a residual value of $47,500. Neilson received $150,000 cash and a $450,000 note receivable.
Nov. 4	Purchased used communication and televideo equipment from the Gallup polling organization. Total cost was $80,000 paid in cash. An independent appraisal valued the communication equipment at $75,000 and the televideo equipment at $25,000.
Dec. 31	Recorded depreciation as follows: Equipment is depreciated by the double-declining-balance method over a five-year life with zero residual value. Record depreciation separately on the equipment purchased on January 2 and on November 4

Required

Record the transactions in the journal of Neilson & Associates.

P7-4A The board of directors of Overhead Door Company is having its regular quarterly meeting. Accounting policies are on the agenda, and depreciation is being discussed. A new board member, an attorney, has some strong opinions about two aspects of depreciation policy. Ben Morris, a physician, argues that depreciation must be coupled with a fund to replace company assets. Otherwise, there is no substance to depreciation, he argues. He also challenges the five-year estimated life over which Overhead Door is depreciating company computers. He notes that the computers will last much longer and should be depreciated over at least 10 years.

Explaining the concept of depreciation (Obj. 2)

Required

Write a paragraph or two to explain the concept of depreciation to Ben Morris and to answer his arguments.

P7-5A On January 2, 20X1, Marlin Credit Union purchased a computer at a cost of $63,000. Before placing the computer in service, the company spent $2,200 for special chips, $800 for a keyboard, and $4,000 for four-color monitors. Marlin management estimates that the computer will remain in service for six years and have a residual value of $16,000. The computer can be expected to process 18,000 documents in each of the first four years and 14,000 documents in each of the next two years. In trying to decide which depreciation method to use, Lisa Malasavas, the general manager, requests a depreciation schedule for each of the depreciation methods (straight-line, units-of-production, and double-declining-balance).

Computing depreciation by three methods and the cash-flow advantage of accelerated depreciation for tax purposes (Obj. 2, 3)

Required

1. Prepare a depreciation schedule for each of the depreciation methods, showing asset cost, depreciation expense, accumulated depreciation, and asset book value.
2. Marlin reports to creditors in the financial statements using the depreciation method that maximizes reported income in the early years of asset use. For income tax purposes, however, the company uses the depreciation method that minimizes income tax payments in those early years. Consider the first year that Marlin uses the computer. Identify the depreciation methods that meet the general manager's objectives, assuming the income tax authorities would permit the use of any of the methods.
3. Cash provided by operations before income tax is $150,000 for the computer's first year. The combined federal and state income tax rate is 30%. For the two depreciation methods identified in Requirement 2, compare the net income and cash provided by operations (cash flow). Show which method gives the net-income advantage and which method gives the cash-flow advantage.

P7-6A **Curtiss-Wright Corporation** is a medium-sized maker of high-tech parts used in commercial and military aircraft. The excerpts on page 350 come from Curtiss-Wright's 19X5 financial statements:

Analyzing plant asset transactions from a company's financial statements (Obj. 2, 4, 7)

Required

Answer these questions about Curtiss-Wright's plant assets.

1. How much was Curtiss-Wright's depreciation expense for 19X5? Why is the amount of depreciation expense so different from accumulated depreciation at December 31, 19X5?
2. At December 31, 19X5, what was Curtiss-Wright's cost of its plant assets? What was the amount of accumulated depreciation? What was the book value of the plant assets? Does book value measure how much Curtiss-Wright could sell the assets for? Why or why not?
3. How much were Curtiss-Wright's capital expenditures during 19X5? Prepare a T-account for Plant Assets at cost to determine whether Curtiss-Wright bought or sold more plant assets during the year.
4. How much cash did Curtiss-Wright receive for the sale of plant assets during 19X5? If the plant assets sold by the company had a book value of $1,642,000, did Curtiss-Wright experience a gain or a loss on the sale of plant assets? How much was the gain or loss?

P7-7A ***Part 1.*** **United Telecommunications, Inc.** (United Telecom) provides communication services in Florida, North Carolina, New Jersey, Texas, and other states. The company's balance sheet reports the asset Cost of Acquisitions in Excess of the Fair Market Value of the Net Assets of Subsidiaries. Assume that United Telecom purchased this asset as part of the acquisition of another company, which carried these figures:

Accounting for intangibles, natural resources, and the related expenses (Obj. 5, 6)

(continued near the bottom of page 350)

P7-6A
(continued here)
Curtis-Wright

CURTISS-WRIGHT CORPORATION
Balance Sheet

(In thousands)	*December 31, 19X5*	*19X4*
Assets		
Current assets:		
Cash and cash equivalents	$ 8,865	$ 4,245
Short-term investments	69,898	72,200
Receivables, net	36,277	32,467
Deferred tax assets (prepaid income tax expense)	7,149	8,204
Inventories	29,111	24,889
Other current assets	2,325	2,338
Total current assets	153,625	144,343
Property, plant and equipment, at cost:		
Land	4,504	4,655
Buildings and improvements	79,352	78,680
Machinery, equipment and other	114,195	119,653
	198,051	202,988
Less accumulated depreciation	(141,782)	(142,550)
Property, plant and equipment, net	56,269	60,438
Prepaid pension costs	31,128	28,092
Other assets	5,179	5,821
Total assets	$246,201	$238,694

CURTISS-WRIGHT CORPORATION
Statements of Cash Flows

(In thousands)	*For the Years Ended December 31, 19X5*	*19X4*
Cash flows from operating activities:		
Net earnings	$18,169	$19,303
Adjustments to reconcile net earnings to net cash provided by operating activities:		
Depreciation	9,512	10,883
Cash flows from investing activities:		
Proceeds from sales and disposals of plant assets	3,290	1,326
Additions to property, plant and equipment	(6,985)	(4,609)

P7-7A
(continued here)
United Telecommunications

Book value of assets	$640,000
Market value of assets	920,000
Liabilities	405,000

Required

1. What is another title for the asset Cost of Acquisitions in Excess of the Fair Market Value of the Net Assets of Subsidiaries?
2. Make the journal entry recording United Telecom's purchase of the other company for $800,000 cash.
3. Assuming United Telecom amortizes Cost of Acquisitions in Excess of the Fair Market Value of the Net Assets of Subsidiaries over five years, record the straight-line amortization for one year.

Part 2. **Continental Pipeline Company** operates a pipeline that provides natural gas to Atlanta; Washington, DC; Philadelphia; and New York City. The company's balance sheet includes the asset Oil Properties.

Suppose Continental paid $7 million cash for oil and gas reserves that contained an estimated 500,000 barrels of oil. Assume that the company paid $350,000 for additional geological tests of the property and $110,000 to prepare the surface for drilling. Prior to production, the company signed a $65,000 note payable to have a building constructed on the property. Because the building provides on-site headquarters for the drilling effort and will be abandoned when the oil is depleted, its cost is debited to the Oil Properties account and included in depletion charges. During the first year of production, Continental removed 82,000 barrels of oil, which it sold on credit for $18 per barrel. Operating expenses related to this project totaled $185,000 for the first year, all paid in cash. In addition, Continental accrued income tax at the rate of 40%.

Required

1. Record all of Continental's transactions for the year.
2. Prepare the company's income statement for this oil and gas project for the first year. Evaluate the profitability of the project.

Reporting plant asset transactions on the statement of cash flows (Obj. 7)

P7-8A At the end of 19X5, **Sprint Corporation,** the telecommunications company, had total assets of $15.2 billion and total liabilities of $10.5 billion. Included among the assets were property, plant, and equipment with a cost of $19.9 billion and accumulated depreciation of $10.2 billion.

Assume that Sprint completed the following selected transactions during 19X6: The company earned total revenues of $13.9 billion and incurred total expenses of $13.2 billion, which included depreciation of $1.5 billion. During the year, Sprint paid $2.1 billion for new property, plant, and equipment and sold old plant assets for $0.3 billion. The cost of the assets sold was $0.6 billion, and their accumulated depreciation was $0.4 billion.

Required

1. Explain how to determine whether Sprint had a gain or a loss on the sale of old plant assets. What was the amount of the gain or loss, if any?
2. Show how Sprint Corporation would report property, plant, and equipment on the balance sheet at December 31, 19X6.
3. Show how Sprint would report operating activities and investing activities on its statement of cash flows for 19X6. The company's cash-flow statement starts with net income.

(Group B)

Identifying the elements of a plant asset's cost (Obj. 1, 2)

P7-1B Tipton International, Inc., incurred the following costs in acquiring land, making land improvements, and constructing and furnishing its own sales building:

a. Purchase price of four acres of land, including an old building that will be used for a garage (land market value is $280,000; building market value is $40,000)	$250,000
b. Landscaping (additional dirt and earth moving)	8,100
c. Fence around the boundary of the land	17,650
d. Attorney fee for title search on the land	600
e. Delinquent real estate taxes on the land to be paid by Tipton	5,900
f. Company signs at front of the company property	1,800
g. Building permit for the sales building	350
h. Architect fee for the design of the sales building	19,800
i. Masonry, carpentry, roofing, and other labor to construct the sales building	709,000
j. Concrete, wood, and other materials used in the construction of the sales building	214,000
k. Renovation of the garage building	41,800
l. Interest cost on construction loan for sales building	9,000
m. Landscaping (trees and shrubs)	6,400
n. Parking lot and concrete walks on the property	52,300
o. Lights for the parking lot, walkways, and company signs	7,300
p. Supervisory salary of construction supervisor (85% to sales building; 9% to fencing, parking lot, and concrete walks; and 6% to garage building renovation)	40,000
q. Office furniture for the sales building	107,100
r. Transportation and installation of furniture	1,800

Tipton depreciates buildings over 40 years, land improvements over 20 years, and furniture over 8 years, all on a straight-line basis with zero residual value.

Required

1. Set up columns for Land, Land Improvements, Sales Building, Garage Building, and Furniture. Show how to account for each of Tipton's costs by listing the cost under the correct account. Determine the total cost of each asset.
2. Assuming that all construction was complete and the assets were placed in service on May 4, record depreciation for the year ended December 31. Round figures to the nearest dollar.
3. How will what you learned in this problem help you manage a business?

Recording plant asset transactions; reporting on the balance sheet (Obj. 2)

P7-2B Texas Oncology Associates reported the following on its balance sheet at December 31, 20X0:

Property, plant, and equipment, at cost:	
Land	$ 60,000
Buildings	200,000
Less Accumulated depreciation	(40,000)
Medical equipment	1,200,000
Less Accumulated depreciation	(260,000)

In early July 20X1, Texas Oncology expanded operations and purchased additional medical equipment at a cost of $500,000. The clinic depreciates buildings by the straight-line method over 20 years with residual value of $80,000. Due to obsolescence, the medical equipment has a useful life of only 10 years and is being depreciated by the double-declining-balance method with zero residual value.

Required

1. Journalize Texas Oncology Associates' plant asset purchase and depreciation transactions for 20X1.
2. Report plant assets on the clinic's December 31, 20X1, balance sheet.

Recording plant asset transactions, exchanges, changes in useful life (Obj. 1, 2, 4)

P7-3B Sykora Motor Freight provides local freight service in Kerrville, Texas. The company's balance sheet includes the following assets under Property, Plant, and Equipment: Land, Buildings, and Motor-Carrier Equipment. Sykora has a separate accumulated depreciation account for each of these assets except land. Assume that Sykora Motor Freight completed the following transactions:

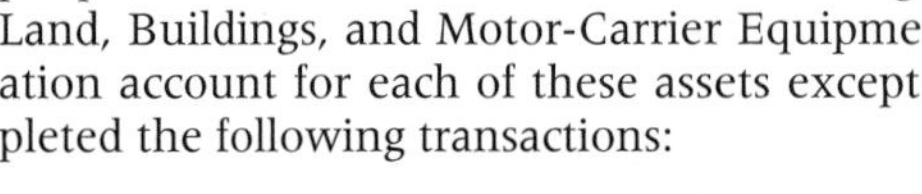

Jan. 2	Traded in motor-carrier equipment with book value of $47,000 (cost of $130,000) for similar new equipment with a cash cost of $176,000. Sykora received a trade-in allowance of $70,000 on the old equipment and paid the remainder in cash.
July 3	Sold a building that had cost $550,000 and had accumulated depreciation of $247,500 through December 31 of the preceding year. Depreciation is computed on a straight-line basis. The building has a 30-year useful life and a residual value of $55,000. Sykora received $100,000 cash and a $400,000 note receivable.
Oct. 29	Purchased land and a building for a single price of $300,000. An independent appraisal valued the land at $160,000 and the building at $200,000.
Dec. 31	Recorded depreciation as follows: Motor-carrier equipment has an expected useful life of five years and an estimated residual value of 5% of cost. Depreciation is computed on the double-declining-balance method. Depreciation on buildings is computed by the straight-line method. The new building carries a 40-year useful life and a residual value equal to 10% of its cost.

Required

Record the transactions in Sykora Motor Freight's journal.

P7-4B The board of directors of Greenlife Nursery is reviewing the 20X2 annual report. A new board member—a professor with little business experience—questions the company accountant about the depreciation amounts. The professor wonders why depreciation expense has decreased from $200,000 in 20X0 to $184,000 in 20X1 to $172,000 in 20X2. She states that she could understand the decreasing annual amounts if the company had been disposing of properties each year, but that has not occurred. Further, she notes that growth in the city is increasing the values of company properties. Why is the company recording depreciation when the property values are increasing?

Explaining the concept of depreciation (Obj. 2)

Required

Write a paragraph or two to explain the concept of depreciation to the professor and to answer her questions.

P7-5B On January 3, 20X0, SavOn Drugs paid $224,000 for a computer system. In addition to the basic purchase price, the company paid a setup fee of $6,200, $6,700 sales tax, and $3,100 for a special platform on which to place the computer. SavOn management estimates that the computer will remain in service five years and have a residual value of $20,000. The computer will process 50,000 documents the first year, with annual processing decreasing by 5,000 documents during each of the next four years (that is, 45,000 documents in 20X1; 40,000 documents in 20X2; and so on). In trying to decide which depreciation method to use, the company president has requested a depreciation schedule for each of three depreciation methods (straight-line, units-of-production, and double-declining-balance).

Computing depreciation by three methods and the cash-flow advantage of accelerated depreciation for tax purposes (Obj. 2, 3)

Required

1. For each of the generally accepted depreciation methods, prepare a depreciation schedule showing asset cost, depreciation expense, accumulated depreciation, and asset book value.
2. SavOn reports to stockholders and creditors in the financial statements using the depreciation method that maximizes reported income in the early years of asset use. For income tax purposes, however, the company uses the depreciation method that minimizes income tax payments in those early years. Consider the first year SavOn uses the computer. Identify the depreciation methods that meet SavOn's objectives, assuming the income tax authorities would permit the use of any of the methods.
3. Assume that cash provided by operations before income tax is $200,000 for the computer's first year. The combined federal and state income tax rate is 40%. For the two depreciation methods identified in Requirement 2, compare the net income and cash provided by operations (cash flow). Show which method gives the net-income advantage and which method gives the cash-flow advantage.

P7-6B **IBM** is the world's largest computer company. After a few lean years, IBM has rebounded strongly with some new products and improving profits. The excerpts shown on page 354 come from IBM's 19X5 financial statements:

Analyzing plant asset transactions from a company's financial statements (Obj. 2, 4, 7)

Required

Answer these questions about IBM's plant assets.

1. How much was IBM's depreciation expense for 19X5? Why is the amount of depreciation expense so different from accumulated depreciation at December 31, 19X5?
2. At December 31, 19X5, what was IBM's cost of its plant assets? What was the amount of accumulated depreciation? What percentage of the cost has been used up? Are IBM's plant assets at the end of 19X5 relatively new, of middle age, or relatively old? How can you tell?
3. How much were IBM's capital expenditures during 19X5? Prepare a T-account for Plant Assets at cost to determine whether IBM bought or sold more plant assets during the year.
4. How much cash did IBM receive for the sale of plant assets during 19X5? If the plant assets that IBM sold had a book value of $874 million, did IBM have a gain or a loss on the sale of plant assets? How much was the gain or loss?
5. IBM's balance sheet reports Software. What category of asset is software? How much of the cost of software did IBM amortize during 19X5? Is IBM's software relatively new or mostly used up? How can you tell?

P7-7B *Part 1.* **Collins Foods International, Inc.,** is the majority owner of Sizzler Restaurants. The company's balance sheet reports the asset Cost in Excess of Net Assets of Purchased Businesses. Assume that Collins purchased this asset as part of the acquisition of another company, which carried these figures:

Accounting for intangibles, natural resources, and the related expenses (Obj. 5, 6)

(continued near the bottom of page 354)

P7-6B
(continued here)
IBM

INTERNATIONAL BUSINESS MACHINES CORPORATION
Statement of Financial Position

(Dollars in millions) *At December 31:*	*19X5*	*19X4*
Assets		
Current assets:		
Cash	$ 1,746	$ 1,240
Cash equivalents	5,513	6,682
Marketable securities	442	2,632
Notes and accounts receivable—trade, net of allowances	16,450	14,018
Sales-type leases receivable	5,961	6,351
Other accounts receivable	991	1,164
Inventories	6,323	6,334
Prepaid expenses and other current assets	3,265	2,917
Total current assets	40,691	41,338
Plant, rental machines, and other property	43,981	44,820
Less: Accumulated depreciation	(27,402)	(28,156)
Plant, rental machines, and other property—net	16,579	16,664
Software, less accumulated amortization (19X5, $11,276; 19X4, $10,793)	2,419	2,963
Investments and sundry assets	20,603	20,126
Total assets	$80,292	$81,091

INTERNATIONAL BUSINESS MACHINES CORPORATION
Statement of Cash Flows

(Dollars in millions) *For the year ended December 31:*	*19X5*	*19X4*
Cash flow from operating activities:		
Net earnings	$4,178	$3,021
Adjustments to reconcile net earnings to cash provided from operating activities:		
Depreciation	3,955	4,197
Amortization of software	1,647	2,098
Cash flow from investing activities:		
Payments for plant, rental machines, and other property	(4,744)	(3,078)
Proceeds from disposition of plant, rental machines, and other property	1,561	900

P7-7B
(continued here)
Collins Foods

Book value of assets	$2.4 million
Market value of assets	3.1 million
Liabilities	2.2 million

Required

1. What is another title for the asset Cost in Excess of Net Assets of Purchased Businesses?
2. Make the journal entry to record Collins' purchase of the other company for $1.8 million cash.
3. Assuming Collins amortizes Cost in Excess of Net Assets of Purchased Businesses over five years, record the straight-line amortization for one year.

Part 2. **Georgia-Pacific Corporation** is one of the world's largest forest products companies. The company's balance sheet includes the assets Natural Gas, Oil, and Coal.

Suppose Georgia-Pacific paid $3.8 million cash for a lease giving the firm the right to work a mine that contained an estimated 100,000 tons of coal. Assume that the company paid $60,000 to remove unwanted buildings from the land and $45,000 to prepare the surface for mining. Further assume that Georgia-Pacific signed a $30,000 note payable to a landscaping company to return the land surface to its original condition after the lease ends. During the first year, Georgia-Pacific removed 35,000 tons of coal, which it sold on account for $67 per ton. Operating expenses for the first year totaled $240,000, all paid in cash. In addition, the company accrued income tax at the tax rate of 40%.

Required

1. Record all of Georgia-Pacific's transactions for the year.
2. Prepare the company's income statement for its coal operations for the first year. Evaluate the profitability of the coal operations.

Reporting plant asset transactions on the statement of cash flows (Obj. 7)

P7-8B At the end of 19X5, **The Coca-Cola Company** had total assets of $15.0 billion and total liabilities of $9.6 billion. Included among the assets were property, plant, and equipment with a cost of $6.7 billion and accumulated depreciation of $2.3 billion.

Assume that Coca-Cola completed the following selected transactions during 19X6: The company earned total revenues of $19.1 billion and incurred total expenses of $15.2 billion, which included depreciation of $0.5 billion. During the year, Coca-Cola paid $1.1 billion for new property, plant, and equipment and sold old plant assets for $0.5 billion. The cost of the assets sold was $0.6 billion, and their accumulated depreciation was $0.4 billion.

Required

1. Explain how to determine whether Coca-Cola had a gain or loss on the sale of old plant assets during the year. What was the amount of the gain or loss, if any?
2. Show how Coca-Cola would report property, plant, and equipment on the balance sheet at December 31, 19X6. What was the book value of property, plant, and equipment?
3. Show how Coca-Cola would report operating activities and investing activities on its statement of cash flows for 19X6. The company's cash-flow statement starts with net income.

EXTENDING YOUR KNOWLEDGE

DECISION CASES

Measuring profitability based on different inventory and depreciation methods (Obj. 2, 3)

Case 1. Suppose you are considering investing in two businesses, **360 Communications** and **Beepers Unlimited.** The two companies are virtually identical, and both began operations at the beginning of the current year. Assume that during the year, each company purchased inventory as follows:

Jan. 4	10,000 units at $4 =		$ 40,000
Apr. 6	5,000 units at 5 =		25,000
Aug. 9	7,000 units at 6 =		42,000
Nov. 27	10,000 units at 7 =		70,000
Totals	32,000		$177,000

During the first year, both companies sold 25,000 units of inventory.

In early January, both companies purchased equipment costing $150,000 that had a 10-year estimated useful life and a $20,000 residual value. 360 uses the inventory and depreciation methods that maximize reported income. By contrast, Beepers uses the inventory and depreciation methods that minimize income tax payments. Assume that both companies' trial balances at December 31 included the following:

Sales revenue	$370,000
Operating expenses	50,000

The income tax rate is 40%.

Required

1. Prepare both companies' income statements.

2. Write an investment newsletter to address the following questions for your clients: Which company appears to be more profitable? Which company has more cash to invest in promising projects? If prices continue rising in both companies' industries over the long term, which company would you prefer to invest in? Why?

Plant assets and intangible assets (Obj. 1, 6)

Case 2. The following questions are unrelated except that they all apply to fixed assets and intangible assets:

a. The manager of Columbia Valley Medical Clinic regularly buys plant assets and debits the cost to Repairs and Maintenance Expense. Why would he do that, since he knows this action violates GAAP?

b. The manager of Premier HealthCare regularly debits the cost of repairs and maintenance of plant assets to Plant and Equipment. Why would she do that, since she knows she is violating GAAP?

c. It has been suggested that, since many intangible assets have no value except to the company that owns them, they should be valued at $1.00 or zero on the balance sheet. Many accountants disagree with this view. Which view do you support? Why?

Ethical Issue

American Bank of St. Louis purchased land and a building for the lump sum of $4.3 million. To get the maximum tax deduction, the bank's managers allocated 80% of the purchase price to the building and only 20% to the land. A more realistic allocation would have been 60% to the building and 40% to the land.

Required

1. Explain the tax advantage of allocating too much to the building and too little to the land.
2. Was American Bank's allocation ethical? If so, state why. If not, why not? Identify who was harmed.

Financial Statement Cases

Plant assets and intangible assets (Obj. 2, 3, 6, 7)

Case 1. Refer to The Gap's, financial statements in Appendix A at the end of the book, and answer the following questions:

a. Which depreciation method does The Gap use for reporting to stockholders and creditors in the financial statements? What type of depreciation method does the company probably use for income tax purposes? Why is this method preferable for tax purposes?

b. Depreciation expense is embedded in the expense amounts listed on the income statement. The statement of cash flows gives the amount of depreciation and amortization expense. How much was The Gap's depreciation and amortization expense during the year ended January 30, 1999? How much was The Gap's accumulated depreciation and amortization at January 30, 1999? Explain why this amount exceeds depreciation and amortization expense for the current year.

c. Explain why The Gap adds depreciation and amortization expenses back to net income in the computation of net cash flows from operating activities.

d. Explain both of The Gap's investing activities on the statement of cash flows.

Plant assets and intangible assets (Obj. 2, 6, 7)

Case 2. Obtain the annual report of a company of your choosing. Answer these questions about the company. Concentrate on the current year in the annual report you select.

a. Which depreciation method or methods does the company use for reporting to stockholders and creditors in the financial statements? Does the company disclose the estimated useful lives of plant assets for depreciation purposes? If so, identify the useful lives.

b. Depreciation and amortization expenses are often combined because they are similar. Many income statements embed depreciation and amortization in other expense amounts. To learn the amounts of these expenses, it is often necessary to examine the statement of cash flows. Where does your company report depreciation and amortization? What were these expenses for the current year? (*Note:* The company you selected may have no amortization—only depreciation.)

c. How much did the company spend to acquire plant assets during the current year? Journalize the acquisitions in a single entry.

d. How much did the company receive on the sale of plant assets? Assume a particular cost and accumulated depreciation of the plant assets sold. Journalize the sale of the plant assets, assuming that the sale resulted in a $700,000 loss.

e. What categories of intangible assets does the company report? What is their reported amount?

Group Project

Visit a local business.

Required

1. List all its plant assets.
2. If possible, interview the manager. Gain as much information as you can about the business's plant assets. For example, try to determine the assets' costs, the depreciation method the company is using, and the estimated useful life of each asset category. If an interview is impossible, then develop your own estimates of the assets' costs, useful lives, and book values, assuming an appropriate depreciation method.
3. Determine whether the business has any intangible assets. If so, list them and gain as much information as possible about their nature, cost, and estimated useful lives.
4. Write a detailed report of your findings and be prepared to present your results to the class.

Internet Exercise

Wal-Mart

Wal-Mart is the world's largest retailer—bigger than **Sears, Kmart,** and **J.C. Penney** combined. It has over 3,500 Wal-Marts, Sam's Clubs, and Supercenters. Most of these stores are in the United States, Canada, and Mexico, but the company is expanding into South America, Asia, and Europe.

1. Go to **http://www.wal-mart.com** and use the *How May I Help You?* scroll bar, select the most recent *annual report,* and then click on *Go to Location.* Use the *financial statements* and the accompanying notes to answer the following questions.
2. At the two most recent year-ends, identify the amount reported for *Total Assets* and the four amounts used to calculate that total. Did total assets increase or decrease from the preceding year-end? What does this indicate? In general, is this trend favorable or unfavorable?
3. At the most recent year-end examine *Property, Plant and Equipment.* What is Wal-Mart's original cost of these assets? What is the book value? What amount of cost has already been expensed? Which category of PPE is never depreciated?
4. Refer to the financial statement you would expect to report depreciation expense. Which financial statement is this? For the most recent year, does this statement report the amount of depreciation expense? Find depreciation on another financial statement and give the name of that statement.
5. Which method of depreciation is used for financial statement purposes? for tax reporting purposes? Where did you find this information? Explain why a company uses different depreciation methods for tax reporting and for financial statement purposes. Is this ethical? Is it legal? Does this comply with the accounting principle of consistency?
6. What is Wal-Mart's range of useful lives for Buildings and improvements? Fixtures and equipment? Transportation equipment? Do these useful lives make sense? What is the range of useful lives for intangibles? Where did you find this information?
7. For the three most recent years, identify the amount of cash Wal-Mart paid to acquire Property, Plant and Equipment. Where do you find this information? Did these amounts increase or decrease? What does this indicate? Is this trend favorable or unfavorable?

8 Current and Long-Term Liabilities

Learning Objectives

After studying this chapter, you should be able to

1. Account for current liabilities
2. Identify and report contingent liabilities
3. Account for basic bonds-payable transactions
4. Measure interest expense by the effective-interest method
5. Explain the advantages and disadvantages of borrowing
6. Report liabilities on the balance sheet

revenue

investment

assets

The Home Depot, Inc.
Balance Sheet (adapted)

	Amounts in millions, except share data	*January 31, 1999*	*February 1, 1998*
	Assets		
	Current Assets:		
	Cash and Cash Equivalents	$ 62	$ 172
	Short-Term Investments, including current maturities of long-term investments	—	2
	Receivables, net	469	556
	Merchandise Inventories	4,293	3,602
	Other Current Assets	109	128
	Total Current Assets	4,933	4,460
	Property and Equipment, at cost:		
	Land	2,739	2,194
	Buildings	3,757	3,041
	Furniture, Fixtures and Equipment	1,761	1,370
	Leasehold Improvements	419	383
	Construction in Progress	540	336
	Capital Leases	206	163
		9,422	7,487
	Less Accumulated Depreciation and Amortization	(1,262)	(978)
	Net Property and Equipment	8,160	6,509
	Long-Term Investments	15	15
	Notes Receivable	26	27
	Cost in Excess of the Fair Value of Net Assets Acquired, net of accumulated amortization of $24 at January 31, 1999 and $18 at February 1, 1998	268	140
	Other	63	78
	Total Assets	$13,465	$11,229
1	Liabilities and Stockholders' Equity		
2	Current Liabilities:		
3	Accounts Payable	$ 1,586	$ 1,358
4	Accrued Salaries and Related Expenses	395	312
5	Sales Taxes Payable	176	143
6	Other Accrued Liabilities (or Accrued Expenses Payable)	586	530
7	Income Taxes Payable	100	105
8	Current Installments of Long-Term Debt	14	8
9	Total Current Liabilities	2,857	2,456
10	Long-Term Debt, excluding current installments	1,566	1,303
11	Other Long-Term Liabilities	208	178
12	Deferred Income Taxes	85	78
13	Minority Interest	9	116
14	**Stockholders' Equity**		
	Common Stock, par value $0.05. Authorized: 2,500,000,000 shares; issued and outstanding–1,475,452,000 shares at January 31, 1999 and 1,464,216,000 shares at February 1, 1998	74	73
	Paid-in Capital	2,854	2,626
	Retained Earnings	5,876	4,430
	Accumulated Other Comprehensive Income	(61)	(28)
		8,743	7,101
	Less: Shares Purchased for Compensation Plans	(3)	(3)
	Total Stockholders' Equity	8,740	7,098
15	Commitments and Contingencies		
16	**Total Liabilities and Stockholders' Equity**	$13,465	$11,229

(Margin labels: "Liabilities" bracketing lines 2–13; "Contingent Liabilities" beside line 15.)

See accompanying notes to consolidated financial statements.

AT JANUARY 31, 1999, **The Home Depot** owed a staggering $4,716,000,000. How can a company expect to pay back such a vast sum of money? By operating profitably to generate lots of cash and by keeping liabilities at a manageable level. The Home Depot does both very well.

Liabilities are debts. They are also a way that companies finance their purchases of assets. The Home Depot's balance sheet reports total assets of $13,465,000,000. (In Chapter 7 we examined the plant assets.) The Home Depot has financed its assets with a combination of debt (lines 1–13 of the balance sheet) and equity (line 14). When we consider Home Depot's total assets of $13.5 billion, liabilities of $4.7 billion don't seem so threatening.

This chapter discusses the various kinds of current and long-term liabilities of The Home Depot and other companies. It also covers contingent, or potential, liabilities that the business may have to pay (line 15 of the balance sheet). We begin with current liabilities (lines 1–9 of The Home Depot's balance sheet) and then move into long-term liabilities (lines 10–13).

CURRENT LIABILITIES OF KNOWN AMOUNT

Objective 1
Account for current liabilities

Recall that *current liabilities* are obligations due within one year or within the company's normal operating cycle if it is longer than one year. Obligations due beyond that period of time are classified as *long-term liabilities.*

Current liabilities and long-term liabilities were discussed in Chapter 3, page 133.

Current liabilities fall into one of two categories: liabilities of a known amount and those whose amount must be estimated. We look first at current liabilities of a known amount.

Accounts Payable

Amounts owed for products or services purchased on account are *accounts payable.* We have seen many accounts payable examples in preceding chapters. For example, **The Home Depot** purchases inventories on an account payable. The company reported Accounts Payable of $1,586 million at January 31, 1999 (see line 3 of the balance sheet on page 359).

One of a merchandiser's most common transactions is the credit purchase of inventory. A computer integrates the accounts payable and inventory systems. When merchandise dips below a certain level, the computer prepares a purchase order. The goods are received and the computer increases Inventory and Accounts Payable. For payments, the computer decreases Accounts Payable and Cash. The program also updates account balances for the financial statements.

Short-Term Notes Payable

Short-term notes payable, a common form of financing, are notes payable due within one year. Companies often issue short-term notes payable to borrow cash or to purchase inventory or plant assets. In addition to recording the note payable and its eventual payment, the business must also accrue interest expense and interest payable at the end of the period. The following entries are typical of this liability:

Recall from Chapter 3, page 117, that all adjusting entries for accrued expenses require a debit to an expense and a credit to a payable.

20X1			
Sep. 30	Inventory	8,000	
	Note Payable, Short-Term		8,000
	Purchase of inventory by issuing a one-year 10% note payable.		

This transaction increases both an asset and a liability.

ASSETS	=	LIABILITIES	+	STOCKHOLDERS' EQUITY
8,000	=	8,000		0

At year end, the company must accrue interest expense.

		Debit	Credit
Dec. 31	Interest Expense ($8,000 × 0.10 × 3/12)	200	
	Interest Payable		200
	Adjusting entry to accrue interest expense at year end.		

ASSETS	=	LIABILITIES	+	STOCKHOLDERS' EQUITY	−	EXPENSES
0	=	200			−	200

The balance sheet at December 31, 20X1, will report the Note Payable of $8,000 and the related Interest Payable of $200 as current liabilities. The 20X1 income statement will report interest expense of $200.

The following entry records the note's payment at maturity:

		Debit	Credit
20X2			
Sep. 30	Note Payable, Short-Term	8,000	
	Interest Payable	200	
	Interest Expense ($8,000 × 0.10 × 9/12)	600	
	Cash [$8,000 + ($8,000 × 0.10)]		8,800
	Payment of a note payable and interest at maturity.		

CHECK POINT 8-1

CHECK POINT 8-2

ASSETS	=	LIABILITIES	+	STOCKHOLDERS' EQUITY	−	EXPENSES
−8,800	=	−8,000 − 200			−	600

The cash payment entry must separate the total interest on the note between

- The interest expense accrued at the end of the previous period ($200)
- The current period's interest expense ($600).

Sales Tax Payable

Every state except Delaware, Montana, New Hampshire, and Oregon levies a sales tax on retail sales. Retailers charge their customers the sales tax in addition to the price of the item sold. Because the retailers owe the state the sales tax collected, the account Sales Tax Payable is a current liability. The Home Depot reported sales tax payable of $176 million at January 31, 1999. See line 5 of the company's balance sheet on page 359.

Suppose one Saturday's sales at a Home Depot Store totaled $200,000. The business collected an additional 5% in sales tax, which would equal $10,000 ($200,000 × 0.05). The store would record that day's sales as follows:

	Debit	Credit
Cash ($200,000 × 1.05)	210,000	
Sales Revenue		200,000
Sales Tax Payable ($200,000 × 0.05)		10,000
To record cash sales and the related sales tax.		

Observe that assets increased by $210,000, liabilities by $10,000 and revenues by $200,000.

ASSETS	=	LIABILITIES	+	STOCKHOLDERS' EQUITY	+	REVENUES
210,000	=	10,000			+	200,000

Sales Tax Payable is a very short-lived liability because companies pay the sales tax to the government at regular intervals.

Current Portion of Long-Term Debt

Some long-term debt must be paid in installments. The **current installment of long-term debt** (also called *current portion,* or *current maturity*) is the amount of the principal that is payable within one year. At the end of each year, a company reclassifies (from long-term debt to a current liability) the amount of its long-term debt that must be paid during the upcoming year.

The Home Depot's balance sheet (page 359) reports Current Installments of Long-Term Debt as the last current liability (line 8). It also reports Long-Term Debt, excluding current installments, immediately after total current liabilities (line 10). *Long-term debt* refers to the notes payable and bonds payable that we cover in the second half of this chapter.

Study The Home Depot's balance sheet and answer these questions about the company's current and long-term debt:

1. At January 31, 1999, how much in total did The Home Depot owe on current and long-term debt?
2. How much of the long-term debt did Home Depot expect to pay during the year ended January 31, 2000? How much was the company scheduled to pay during later years?

Answers:

1. Home Depot owed a total of $1,580 million ($14 million + $1,566 million).
2. Home Depot expected to pay the current installments of $14 million during the upcoming year and the remainder ($1,566 million) during later years.

The liabilities for the Current Installments of Long-Term Debt (line 8) and for the long-term portion (line 10) do *not* include any accrued interest payable. The two accounts, Current Installments of Long-Term Debt and Long-Term Debt, Excluding Current Installments, represent only the principal amounts owed. Interest Payable is a separate account for a different liability—the interest that must be paid. The Home Depot reports interest payable under the Current Liability caption Other Accrued Liabilities (line 6), which we discuss next.

Accrued Expenses (Accrued Liabilities)

An **accrued expense** is an expense that the business has incurred but has not yet paid. Therefore, it is also a liability, which explains why accrued expenses are also called **accrued liabilities.** Accrued expenses, such as The Home Depot's interest payable on its long-term debt, typically occur with the passage of time. By contrast, an account payable results from a particular transaction in which the company purchased a good or a service.

Like most other companies, Home Depot reports several categories of accrued expenses on its balance sheet:

- Accrued Salaries and Related Expenses (line 4)
- Other Accrued Liabilities (line 6)
- Income Taxes Payable (line 7)

Accrued Salaries and Related Expenses are the company's liabilities for salaries, wages, and related payroll expenses at the end of the period. This caption also includes payroll-related liabilities, such as taxes withheld from employee paychecks. Other Accrued Liabilities include the company's current liabilities for such items as interest payable. Income Taxes Payable is the amount of income tax The Home Depot still owes at year end.

Payroll Liabilities

Payroll, also called *employee compensation,* is a major expense of most businesses. For service organizations—such as CPA firms, real estate brokers, and travel agents—payroll is *the* major expense of conducting business. Because service organizations sell their personnel's services, employee compensation is their primary cost of doing business, just as cost of goods sold is the largest expense in a merchandising company.

Employee compensation takes different forms. Some employees collect a *salary,* which is pay stated at a yearly or monthly rate. Other employees work for *wages,* which are stated at hourly figures. Sales employees often receive a *commission,* which is a percentage of the sales the employee has made. Some companies reward excellent performance with a *bonus,* an amount over and above regular compensation. Accounting for all these forms of compensation follows the same pattern, which is illustrated in Exhibit 8-1 (using assumed figures).

Salary expense represents employees' *gross pay* (that is, pay before subtractions for taxes and other deductions). There are several payroll liabilities:

- Salary payable to employees is their *net* (take-home) *pay.*
- *Employee Income Tax Payable* is the employees' income tax that has been withheld from their paychecks.
- *FICA Tax Payable* is the employees' Social Security tax, which also is withheld from paychecks. (FICA stands for the Federal Insurance Contributions Act, which created the Social Security tax.) In addition, there is a liability for Medicare tax, which provides medical care for the elderly. The Medicare tax is similar to the FICA tax in that the company owes these liabilities to the U.S. government.
- In Exhibit 8-1, the employees have authorized the company to withhold union dues, which generates a payable to the union.

EXHIBIT 8-1
Accounting for Payroll Expenses and Liabilities

Salary Expense (or Wage Expense or Commission Expense)	10,000	
Employee Income Tax Payable		1,200
FICA Tax Payable		800
Employee Union Dues Payable		140
Salary Payable to Employees [take-home pay]		7,860
To record salary expense.		

ASSETS	=	LIABILITIES	+	STOCKHOLDERS' EQUITY	−	EXPENSES
		+ 1,200			−	10,000
0	=	+ 800				
		+ 140				
		+ 7,860				

In addition to salaries and wages, companies must pay some employer payroll taxes and expenses for employee fringe benefits. Accounting for these expenses is similar to the illustration in Exhibit 8-1.

Unearned Revenues

Unearned revenues are also called *deferred revenues, revenues collected in advance,* and *customer prepayments.* All these account titles indicate that the business has received cash from its customers before earning the revenue. The company has an obligation to provide goods or services to the customer. Let's consider an example.

The **Dun & Bradstreet (D&B) Corporation** provides credit evaluation services to businesses that subscribe to the D&B reports. When a company pays in advance to have D&B investigate the credit history of a potential customer, D&B collects cash and incurs a liability to provide future service. The liability account is called Unearned Subscription Revenue (or Unearned Subscription Income).

Assume that D&B charges a client $150 for a three-year subscription. D&B's entries would be as follows:

20X1			
Jan. 1	Cash	150	
	Unearned Subscription Revenue		150
	To receive cash for a three-year subscription.		

Dun & Bradstreet's assets and liabilities increase equally. There is no revenue yet.

ASSETS	=	LIABILITIES	+	STOCKHOLDERS' EQUITY
150	=	150	+	0

20X1, 20X2, 20X3			
Dec. 31	Unearned Subscription Revenue	50	
	Subscription Revenue ($150/3)		50
	To record revenue earned at the end of each year.		

The liability decreases as D&B earns the revenue.

YEAR	ASSETS	=	LIABILITIES	+	STOCKHOLDERS' EQUITY	+	REVENUES
20X1	0	=	−50			+	50
20X2	0	=	−50			+	50
20X3	0	=	−50			+	50

D&B's financial statements would report the following:

CHECK POINT 8-3

		December 31,	
Balance Sheet	***Year 1***	***Year 2***	***Year 3***
Current liabilities:			
Unearned subscription revenue	$50	$50	$-0-
Long-term liabilities:			
Unearned subscription revenue	$50	$-0-	$-0-
Income Statement	***Year 1***	***Year 2***	***Year 3***
Revenues:			
Subscription revenue	$50	$50	$50

CURRENT LIABILITIES THAT MUST BE ESTIMATED

A business may know that a liability exists and not know the exact amount. But the business must estimate the liability and report it on the balance sheet. Estimated liabilities vary among companies. Let's look at Estimated Warranty Payable, a liability account common among merchandisers.

Estimated Warranty Payable

Many merchandising companies guarantee their products under *warranty* agreements. The warranty period may extend for any length of time. Ninety-day warranties and one-year warranties are common for consumer products. The automobile companies—**BMW, General Motors,** and **Toyota,** for example—accrue liabilities for their vehicle warranties.

Whatever the warranty's lifetime, the matching principle demands that the company record the *warranty expense* in the same period that the business records sales revenue. ➜ After all, the warranty increases the amount of sales revenue, so the company must record warranty expense. At the time of the sale, however, the company does not know which products are defective. Because the exact amount of warranty expense cannot be known with certainty, the business must estimate its warranty expense and the related warranty liability.

← For a review of the matching principle, see Chapter 3, page 109.

Assume that **Black & Decker,** which manufactures products sold in **The Home Depot, Wal-Mart,** and other stores, made sales of $200,000,000 subject to product warranties. If, in past years, between 2% and 4% of products proved defective, Black & Decker could estimate that 3% of the products it sells this year will require repair or replacement. The company would estimate warranty expense of $6,000,000 ($200,000,000 × 0.03) for the period and make the following entry:

Warranty Expense	6,000,000	
Estimated Warranty Payable		6,000,000
To accrue warranty expense.		

ASSETS	=	LIABILITIES	+	STOCKHOLDERS' EQUITY	−	EXPENSES
0	=	6,000,000	+		−	6,000,000

Assume that defective merchandise totals $5,800,000. Black & Decker will replace it and record the following:

Estimated Warranty Payable	5,800,000	
Inventory		5,800,000
To replace defective products sold under warranty.		

If Black & Decker paid cash to satisfy the warranty, then the credit would be to the Cash account rather than to Inventory.

ASSETS	=	LIABILITIES	+	STOCKHOLDERS' EQUITY
−5,800,000	=	−5,800,000	+	0

Black & Decker's expense is $6,000,000 on the income statement. *When* the company repairs or replaces defective merchandise has no bearing on when the company records warranty expense. **Black & Decker records warranty expense at an estimated amount in the same period as the sale.** The company reports estimated warranty payable on the balance sheet under the current-liability caption Accrued Liabilities or Accrued Expenses Payable.

✔ CHECK POINT 8-4

✔ CHECK POINT 8-5

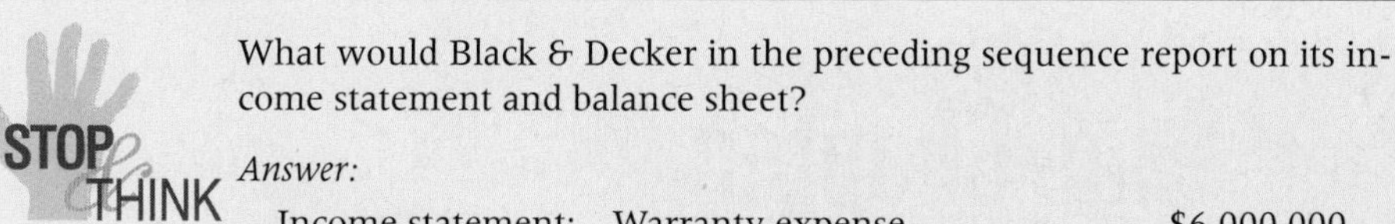

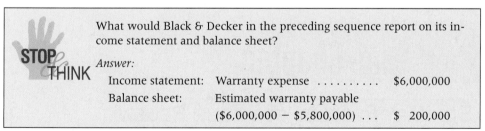

What would Black & Decker in the preceding sequence report on its income statement and balance sheet?

Answer:

Income statement:	Warranty expense	$6,000,000
Balance sheet:	Estimated warranty payable	
	($6,000,000 − $5,800,000) ...	$ 200,000

CONTINGENT LIABILITIES

Objective 2
Identify and report contingent liabilities

A *contingent liability* is not an actual liability. Instead, it is a potential liability that depends on a *future* event arising out of past events. The Financial Accounting Standards Board (FASB) provides these guidelines to account for contingent losses (or expenses) and their related liabilities:

1. Record an actual liability if it is *probable* that the loss (or expense) will occur and the *amount can be reasonably estimated.* Warranty expense is an example.
2. Report the contingency in a financial statement note if it is *reasonably possible* that a loss (or expense) will occur. Lawsuits in progress are a prime example.
3. There is no need to report a contingent loss that is *remote*—unlikely to occur. Instead, wait until an actual transaction clears up the situation. For example, suppose **Del Monte Foods** conducts business in Nicaragua, and the Nicaraguan government issues a mild threat to confiscate the assets of all foreign companies. Del Monte will report nothing about the contingency if the probability of a loss is considered remote.

The Home Depot reported its contingencies (type 2 above) in the following note (adapted):

> **Note 9, Commitments and Contingencies**
> 1. At January 31, 1999, the Company was contingently liable for approximately \$431 million under outstanding letters of credit issued primarily in connection with purchase commitments.
> 2. The Company is involved in litigation arising from the normal course of business. In management's opinion, this litigation is not expected to materially impact the Company's results of operation or financial condition.

Contingency 1 arises because The Home Depot has committed to purchase assets and has provided letters of credit, which are bank instruments. When the other company ships the assets to Home Depot, it can deposit the letters of credit into its bank account. If the other company never ships the goods, then Home Depot has no liability and will pay nothing.

Contingency 2 arises from lawsuits that claim wrongdoing by The Home Depot and seeks damages through the courts. If the court rules in favor of Home Depot, there is no liability. But if the ruling favors the plaintiff, then Home Depot has an actual liability.

It would be unethical to omit these disclosures from the financial statements. Investors need this information to properly evaluate The Home Depot's stock. Lenders may charge a higher interest rate because of a large contingent liability.

Contingent liabilities may be reported in a **short presentation,** after total liabilities on the balance sheet, but with no amounts given. In general, an explanatory note accompanies a short presentation. The Home Depot reported contingent liabilities this way (see line 15 of the balance sheet). Other companies report contingencies only in a note, as in the foregoing Note 9 for The Home Depot.

Mid-Chapter

Summary Problem for Your Review

Assume that **The Estée Lauder Companies, Inc.,** faced the following liability situations at June 30, 2001, the end of the company's fiscal year:

a. Long-term debt totals \$100 million and is payable in annual installments of \$10 million each. The interest rate on the debt is 7%, and interest is paid each December 31.

b. The company pays royalties on its purchased trademarks. Royalties for the trademarks are equal to a percentage of Estée Lauder's sales. Assume that sales in 2001 were \$400 million and were subject to a royalty rate of 3%. At June 30, 2001, Estée Lauder owes two-thirds of the year's royalty, to be paid in July.

c. Salary expense for the last payroll period of the year was $900,000. Of this amount, employees' withheld income tax totaled $88,000 and FICA taxes were $61,000. These payroll amounts will be paid early in July.

d. On fiscal year 2001 sales of $400 million, management estimates warranty expense of 2%. One year ago, at June 30, 2000, Estimated Warranty Liability stood at $3 million. Warranty payments were $9 million during the year ended June 30, 2001.

Show how Estée Lauder would report these liabilities on its balance sheet at June 30, 2001.

Answer

a. Current liabilities:	
Current installment of long-term debt	$10,000,000
Interest payable ($100,000,000 × .07 × 6/12)	3,500,000
Long-term debt ($100,000,000 − $10,000,000)	90,000,000
b. Current liabilities:	
Royalties payable ($400,000,000 × .03 × 2/3)	8,000,000
c. Current liabilities:	
Salary payable ($900,000 − $88,000 − $61,000)	751,000
Employee income tax payable	88,000
FICA tax payable	61,000
d. Current liabilities:	
Estimated warranty payable	2,000,000
[$3,000,000 + ($400,000,000 × .02) − $9,000,000]	

Financing Operations with Long-Term Debt

Large companies such as **The Home Depot** and **Daimler-Chrysler Corporation** cannot borrow billions from a single lender because no lender will risk that much money on a single company. How then do large corporations borrow huge amounts? They issue (sell) bonds to the public. **Bonds payable** are groups of notes payable issued to multiple lenders, called *bondholders*. The idea is that Chrysler can borrow large amounts by issuing bonds to thousands of individual investors, each buying a modest amount of Chrysler bonds. Chrysler receives the amount it needs, and each investor limits his or her risk by diversifying investments—not putting all the investor's "eggs in one basket."

In the pages that follow, we treat bonds payable and long-term notes payable together because their accounting is the same.

Bonds: An Introduction

To gain access to large amounts of cash, a company may issue bonds. Each bond is, in effect, a long-term note payable that pays interest. Bonds payable are debts of the issuing company.

Purchasers of bonds receive a bond certificate, which carries the issuing company's name. The certificate also states the *principal,* the amount that the company has borrowed from the bondholder. This figure, typically stated in units of $1,000, is also called the bond's *face value, maturity value,* or *par value.* The bond obligates the issuing company to pay the holder the principal amount at a specific future date called the *maturity date.* This date also appears on the bond certificate.

Bondholders loan their money to companies for a price: *interest on the principal.* The bond certificate states the interest rate that the issuer will pay the holder and the dates that the interest payments are due (generally twice a year). Some bond certificates name the bondholder (the investor). When the company pays back the

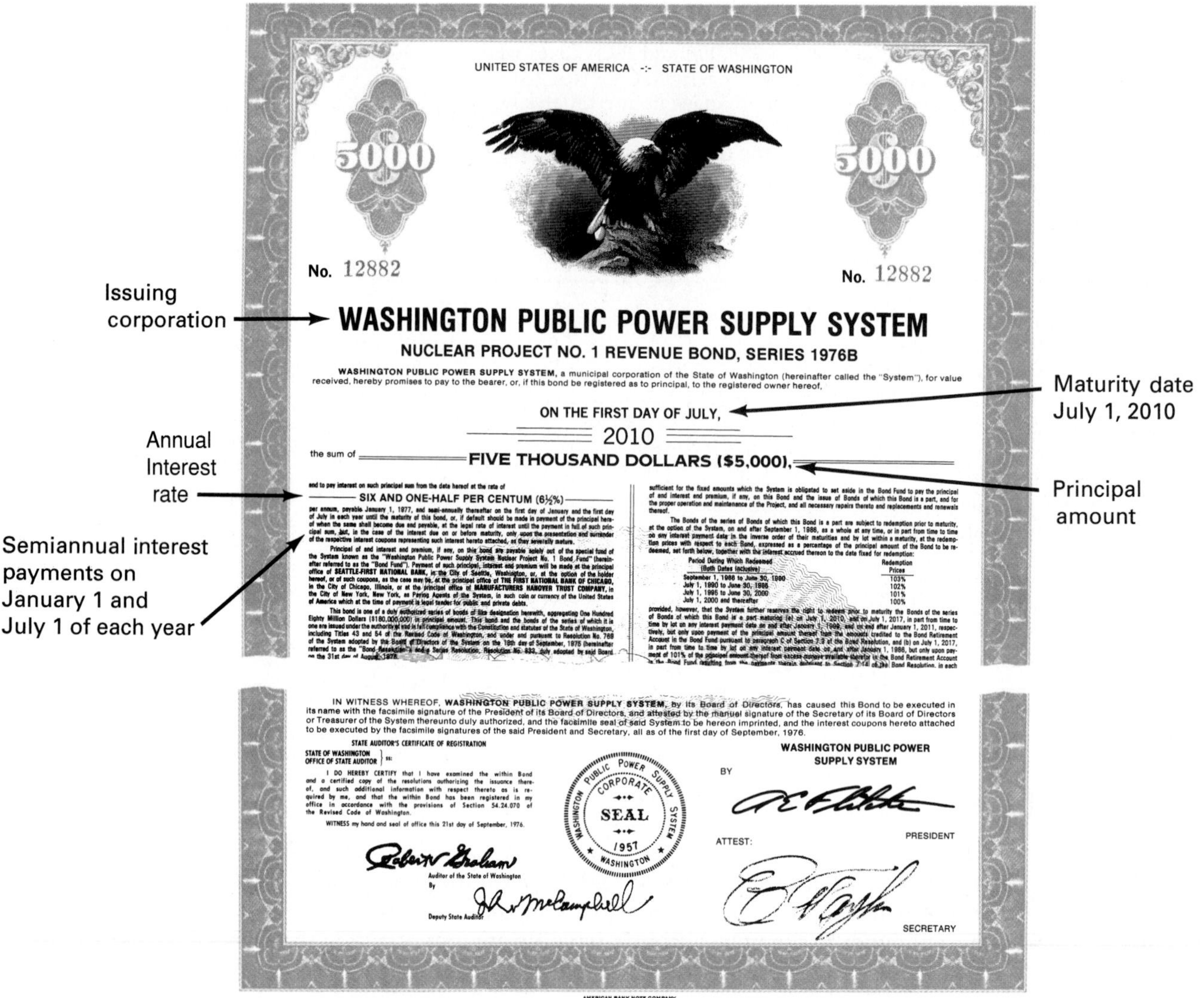

UNITED STATES OF AMERICA -:- STATE OF WASHINGTON

5000 5000

No. 12882 No. 12882

WASHINGTON PUBLIC POWER SUPPLY SYSTEM

NUCLEAR PROJECT NO. 1 REVENUE BOND, SERIES 1976B

WASHINGTON PUBLIC POWER SUPPLY SYSTEM, a municipal corporation of the State of Washington (hereinafter called the "System"), for value received, hereby promises to pay to the bearer, or, if this bond be registered as to principal, to the registered owner hereof,

ON THE FIRST DAY OF JULY,

2010

the sum of FIVE THOUSAND DOLLARS ($5,000),

SIX AND ONE-HALF PER CENTUM (6½%)

IN WITNESS WHEREOF, WASHINGTON PUBLIC POWER SUPPLY SYSTEM, by its Board of Directors, has caused this Bond to be executed in its name with the facsimile signature of the President of its Board of Directors, and attested by the manual signature of the Secretary of its Board of Directors or Treasurer of the System thereunto duly authorized, and the facsimile seal of said System to be hereon imprinted, and the interest coupons hereto attached to be executed by the facsimile signatures of the said President and Secretary, all as of the first day of September, 1976.

WASHINGTON PUBLIC POWER SUPPLY SYSTEM

BY PRESIDENT

ATTEST: SECRETARY

AMERICAN BANK NOTE COMPANY

Exhibit 8-2
Bond (Note) Certificate

principal, the holder returns the certificate, which the company retires (or cancels). Exhibit 8-2 shows an actual bond certificate.

The board of directors may authorize a bond issue. In some companies, the stockholders—as owners—may also have to vote their approval. Issuing bonds usually requires the services of a securities firm, such as **Merrill Lynch,** to act as the underwriter of the bond issue. The **underwriter** purchases the bonds from the issuing company and resells them to its clients, or it may sell the bonds in return for a commission from the issuer, agreeing to buy all unsold bonds.

Types of Bonds

All the bonds in a particular issue may mature at a specified time **(term bonds),** or they may mature in installments over a period of time **(serial bonds).** By issuing serial bonds, the company spreads its principal payments over time and avoids repaying the entire principal at one time. Serial bonds are like installment notes payable. The Home Depot's long-term debt is serial in nature because it comes due in installments.

Secured, or *mortgage, bonds* give the bondholder the right to take specified assets of the issuer if the company *defaults*—that is, fails to pay interest or principal. *Unsecured bonds,* called **debentures,** are backed only by the good faith of the borrower.

Debentures usually carry a higher rate of interest than secured bonds because debentures are riskier investments.

Bond Prices

Investors may buy and sell bonds through bond markets. The most famous bond market is the **New York Exchange,** which lists several thousand bonds. Bond prices are quoted at a percentage of their maturity value. For example, a \$1,000 bond quoted at 100 is bought or sold for \$1,000, which is 100% of its face value. The same bond quoted at $101\frac{1}{2}$ has a market price of \$1,015 (101.5% of face value = \$1,000 × 1.015). Prices are quoted to one-eighth of 1%. A \$1,000 bond quoted at $88\frac{3}{8}$ is priced at \$883.75 (\$1,000 × 0.88375).

Exhibit 8-3 contains actual price information for the bonds of **Ohio Edison Company,** taken from the *Wall Street Journal.* On this particular day, 12 of Ohio Edison's $9\frac{1}{2}$%, \$1,000 face-value bonds maturing in the year 2006 (indicated by 06) were traded. The bonds' highest price on this day was \$795 (\$1,000 × 0.795). The lowest price of the day was \$785 (\$1,000 × 0.785). The closing price (last sale price of the day) was \$795. This price was 2 points higher than the closing price of the preceding day. What was the bonds' closing price the preceding day? It was $77\frac{1}{2}$ ($79\frac{1}{2}$ − 2).

EXHIBIT 8-3
Bond Price Information for Ohio Edison Company (OhEd)

Bonds	*Volume*	*High*	*Low*	*Close*	*Net Change*
OhEd $9\frac{1}{2}$ 06	12	$79\frac{1}{2}$	$78\frac{1}{2}$	$79\frac{1}{2}$	+2

A bond issued at a price above its face (par) value is said to be issued at a **premium,** and a bond issued at a price below face (par) value has a **discount.** As a bond nears maturity, its market price moves toward par value. On the maturity date, a bond's market value exactly equals its par value because the company that issued the bond pays that amount to retire the bond.

CHECK POINT 8-7

Present Value

A dollar received today is worth more than a dollar to be received in the future. You may invest today's dollar immediately and earn income from it. But if you must wait to receive the dollar, you forgo the interest revenue. Money earns income over time, a fact called the *time value of money.* Let's examine how the time value of money affects the pricing of bonds.

Assume that a bond with a face value of \$1,000 reaches maturity three years from today and carries no interest. Would you pay \$1,000 to purchase the bond? No, because the payment of \$1,000 today to receive the same amount in the future provides you with no income on the investment. You would not be taking advantage of the time value of money. Just how much would you pay today to receive \$1,000 at the end of three years? The answer is some amount *less* than \$1,000. Let's suppose that you feel \$750 is a good price. By investing \$750 now to receive \$1,000 later, you earn \$250 interest revenue over the three years. The issuing company sees the transaction this way: It pays you \$250 interest for the use of your \$750 for three years.

The amount that a person would invest *at the present time* to receive a greater amount at a future date is called the **present value** of a future amount. In our example, \$750 is the present value of the \$1,000 amount to be received three years later.

Our \$750 bond price is a reasonable estimate. The exact present value of any future amount depends on

1. The amount of the future payment (or receipt)

2. The length of time from the investment to the date when the future amount is to be paid (or received)
3. The interest rate during the period

Present value is always less than the future amount. We discuss how present value is computed in Appendix B at the end of the book (page 671). We need to be aware of the present-value concept, however, in the discussion of bond prices that follows.

Bond Interest Rates

Bonds are sold at *market price,* which is the amount that investors are willing to pay at any given time. Market price is the bond's present value, which equals the present value of the principal payment plus the present value of the cash interest payments (which are made semiannually [that is, twice a year], annually, or quarterly over the term of the bond).

Two interest rates work to set the price of a bond.

- The **contract interest rate,** or **stated interest rate,** is the interest rate that determines the amount of cash interest the borrower pays—and the investor receives—each year. For example, Chrysler Corporation's 9% bonds have a contract interest rate of 9%. Thus, Chrysler pays $9,000 of interest annually on each $100,000 bond. Each semiannual interest payment is $4,500 ($100,000 × 0.09 × ½).
- The **market interest rate,** or **effective interest rate,** is the rate that investors demand for loaning their money. The market rate varies, sometimes daily. A company may issue bonds with a contract interest rate that differs from the prevailing market interest rate. Exhibit 8-4 shows how the contract (stated) interest rate and the market interest rate interact to determine the issuance price of a bond payable. Chrysler, for example, may issue its 9% bonds when the market rate has risen to 10%. Will the Chrysler bonds attract investors in this market? No, because investors can earn 10% on other bonds of similar risk. Therefore, investors will purchase Chrysler bonds only at a price less than par value. The difference between the lower price and face value is a *discount* (Exhibit 8-4). Conversely, if the market interest rate is 8%, Chrysler's 9% bonds will be so attractive that investors will pay more

EXHIBIT 8-4
How the Contract Interest Rate and the Market Interest Rate Interact to Determine the Price of a Bond Payable

				Issuance Price of Bonds Payable
Contract (stated) interest rate on a bond payable	equals	Market interest rate	implies	Par (face, or maturity) value
Example: 9%	=	*9%*	→	*Par: $1,000 bond issued for $1,000*
Contract (stated) interest rate on a bond payable	less than	Market interest rate	implies	Discount (price *below* par)
Example: 9%	<	*10%*	→	*Discount: $1,000 bond issued below $1,000*
Contract (stated) interest rate on a bond payable	greater than	Market interest rate	implies	Premium (price *above* par)
Example: 9%	>	*8%*	→	*Premium: $1,000 bond issued above $1,000*

 CHECK POINT 8-8

than face value for them. The difference between the higher price and face value is a *premium*.

ISSUING BONDS PAYABLE TO BORROW MONEY

Objective 3
Account for basic bonds payable transactions

Suppose **Chrysler Corporation,** a division of Daimler Chrysler Corporation, has $50 million in 9% bonds that mature in five years. Assume that Chrysler issues these bonds at par on January 1, 2000. The issuance entry is

2000			
Jan. 1	Cash	50,000,000	
	Bonds Payable		50,000,000
	To issue 9%, 5-year bonds at par.		

ASSETS	=	LIABILITIES	+	STOCKHOLDERS' EQUITY
50,000,000	=	50,000,000	+	0

Chrysler, the borrower, makes only a one-time entry to record the receipt of cash and the issuance of bonds. Afterward, investors buy and sell the bonds through the bond markets. The buy-and-sell transactions between investors do *not* involve the corporation that issued the bonds. Thus, Chrysler keeps no records of these transactions, except for the names and addresses of the bondholders. It needs this information to mail interest and principal payments.

Interest payments occur each January 1 and July 1. Chrysler's entry to record the first semiannual interest payment is:

2000			
July 1	Interest Expense		
	($50,000,000 × 0.09 × 6/12)	2,250,000	
	Cash		2,250,000
	To pay semiannual interest.		

ASSETS	=	LIABILITIES	+	STOCKHOLDERS' EQUITY	−	EXPENSES
−2,250,000	=	0	+		−	2,250,000

At year end, Chrysler must accrue interest expense and interest payable for six months (July through December), as follows:

2000			
Dec. 31	Interest Expense		
	($50,000,000 × 0.09 × 6/12)	2,250,000	
	Interest Payable		2,250,000
	To accrue interest.		

ASSETS	=	LIABILITIES	+	STOCKHOLDERS' EQUITY	−	EXPENSES
0	=	2,250,000	+		−	2,250,000

At maturity, Chrysler will record payment of the bonds as follows:

2005			
Jan. 1	Bonds Payable	50,000,000	
	Cash		50,000,000
	To pay bonds payable at maturity.		

CHECK POINT 8-9

ASSETS	=	LIABILITIES	+	STOCKHOLDERS' EQUITY
−50,000,000	=	−50,000,000		

Issuing Bonds and Notes Payable Between Interest Dates

The foregoing entries to record Chrysler's bond transactions are straightforward because the company issued the bonds on an interest payment date (January 1). However, corporations often issue bonds between interest dates.

Reconsider the Chrysler example. Assume that Chrysler issued its 9% bonds payable on February 28, 2000—two months after the bonds were dated (January 1, 2000). In this case, interest on the bonds has accrued for two months (January and February). On the next interest date (July 1), the bondholder will receive the full six months of interest. Therefore, at issuance on February 28, Chrysler Corporation will collect two months of interest from the bondholder and record issuance of the bonds as follows:

2000			
Feb. 28	Cash	50,750,000	
	Bonds Payable		50,000,000
	Interest Payable ($50,000,000 × 0.09 × 2/12)		750,000
	To issue 9%, 5-year bonds at par, two months after the original issue date.		

ASSETS	=	LIABILITIES	+	STOCKHOLDERS' EQUITY
50,750,000	=	50,000,000	+	0
		+ 750,000		

On June 30, Chrysler will make a semiannual interest payment. For the bondholder, receipt of six months of interest minus the two months of interest paid up front equals the four months of interest earned for March through June. Likewise, Chrysler Corporation has interest expense for the four months that the bonds have been outstanding.

Issuing Bonds Payable at a Discount

We know that market conditions may force the issuing corporation to accept a discount price for its bonds. Suppose Chrysler Corporation issues $100,000 of its 9%, five-year bonds when the market interest rate is 10%. The market price of the bonds drops below $100,000, and Chrysler receives $96,149[1] at issuance. The entry is

2000			
Jan. 1	Cash	96,149	
	Discount on Bonds Payable	3,851	
	Bonds Payable		100,000
	To issue 9%, 5-year bonds at a discount.		

ASSETS	=	LIABILITIES	+	STOCKHOLDERS' EQUITY
+96,149	=	− 3,851	+	0
		+ 100,000		

After posting, the bond accounts have the following balances:

Bonds Payable		Discount on Bonds Payable	
	100,000	**3,851**	

[1]Appendix B at the end of this book shows how to determine the price of this bond.

In this transaction, Chrysler Corporation borrowed $96,149. But Chrysler must pay back $100,000 at maturity. The $3,851 discount represents extra interest expense that Chrysler will recognize little-by-little over the life of the bond issue. Chrysler's interest expense will, therefore, be more than the cash interest that Chrysler will pay each six months. Chrysler's balance sheet immediately after issuance of the bonds would report the following:

Total current liabilities		$ XXX
Long-term liabilities:		
Bonds payable, 9%, due 2005	$100,000	
Less: Discount on bonds payable	(3,851)	96,149

Discount on Bonds Payable is a contra account to Bonds Payable, a decrease in the company's liabilities. Subtracting its balance from Bonds Payable yields the *carrying amount* of the bonds. Thus, Chrysler's liability is $96,149, which is the amount the company borrowed. If Chrysler were to pay off the bonds immediately (an unlikely occurrence), Chrysler's required outlay would be $96,149 because the market price of the bonds is $96,149.

Effective-Interest Method of Debt Amortization

Objective 4
Measure interest expense by the effective-interest method

Chrysler Corporation pays interest on its bonds semiannually, which is common practice for corporate bonds. Each semiannual interest *payment* remains the same amount over the life of the bonds:

$$\textbf{Semiannual interest payment} = \$100{,}000 \times .09 \times 6/12 = \$4{,}500$$

This payment amount is fixed by the bond contract.

But Chrysler's interest *expense* increases from period to period as the bonds march toward maturity. For bonds issued at a discount, the interest expense increases as the bonds' carrying amount increases.

Panel A of Exhibit 8-5 repeats the Chrysler bond data we've been using so far. Panel B provides an amortization table that determines the periodic interest expense. It also shows the bond carrying amount. Study the exhibit carefully because the amounts we will be using come directly from the amortization table. ➵ This exhibit is an example of the *effective-interest method of amortization.*

← Recall from Chapter 7, page 333, that *amortization* is the systematic reduction of a particular amount—in this case, the Discount on Bonds Payable.

Interest Expense on Bonds Issued at a Discount. In Exhibit 8-5, Chrysler Corporation borrows $96,149 cash but must pay $100,000 when the bonds mature. What happens to the $3,851 balance of the discount account over the life of the bond issue?

The $3,851 discount is really additional interest expense to the issuing company. That amount is a cost—beyond the stated interest rate—that Chrysler pays for using the investors' money. Exhibit 8-6 graphs the data from Exhibit 8-5: the interest expense (column B), the interest payment (column A), and the amortization of bond discount (column C).

Observe that the semiannual interest payment is fixed—by contract—at $4,500 (column A). But the amount of interest expense (column B) increases each period as the bond carrying amount is amortized upward toward maturity value.

The discount is interest expense that is not paid until the bonds are paid off at maturity. The discount is allocated to interest expense through amortization each period over the term of the bonds. Exhibit 8-7 illustrates the amortization of the bond discount from its beginning balance of $3,851 to its ending balance of $0. These amounts come from Exhibit 8-5, column D.

EXHIBIT 8-5 Debt Amortization for a Bond Discount

PANEL A—Bond Data

Issue date—January 1, 2000
Maturity (face, or par) value—$100,000
Contract interest rate—9%
Interest paid—$4\frac{1}{2}$% semiannually, $4,500 = $100,000 × 0.09 × $^6/_{12}$

Market interest rate at time of issue—10% annually, 5% semiannually
Issue price—$96,149
Maturity date—January 1, 2005

PANEL B—Amortization Table

	A	B	C	D	E
Semiannual Interest Date	*Interest* **Payment** *($4\frac{1}{2}$% of Maturity Value)*	*Interest* **Expense** *(5% of Preceding* **Bond** *Carrying Amount)*	*Discount Amortization (B − A)*	*Discount Account Balance (Preceding D − C)*	*Bond Carrying Amount ($100,000 − D)*
Jan. 1, 2000				$3,851	$ 96,149
July 1	$4,500	$4,807	$307	3,544	96,456
Jan. 1, 2001	4,500	4,823	323	3,221	96,779
July 1	4,500	4,839	339	2,882	97,118
Jan. 1, 2002	4,500	4,856	356	2,526	97,474
July 1	4,500	4,874	374	2,152	97,848
Jan. 1, 2003	4,500	4,892	392	1,760	98,240
July 1	4,500	4,912	412	1,348	98,652
Jan. 1, 2004	4,500	4,933	433	915	99,085
July 1	4,500	4,954	454	461	99,539
Jan. 1, 2005	4,500	4,961*	461	-0-	100,000

* Adjusted for effect of rounding.

Notes

- Column A The semiannual interest payments are constant—fixed by the bond contract.
- Column B The interest expense each period = the preceding bond carrying amount × the market interest rate. The amount of interest each period increases as the market interest rate, a constant, is applied to the increasing bond carrying amount (E).
- Column C The excess of each interest expense amount (B) over each interest payment amount (A) is the discount amortization for the period (C).
- Column D The discount balance (D) decreases by the amount of amortization for the period (C).
- Column E The bond carrying amount (E) increases from $96,149 at issuance to $100,000 at maturity.

EXHIBIT 8-6
Interest Expense on Bonds Payable Issued at a Discount

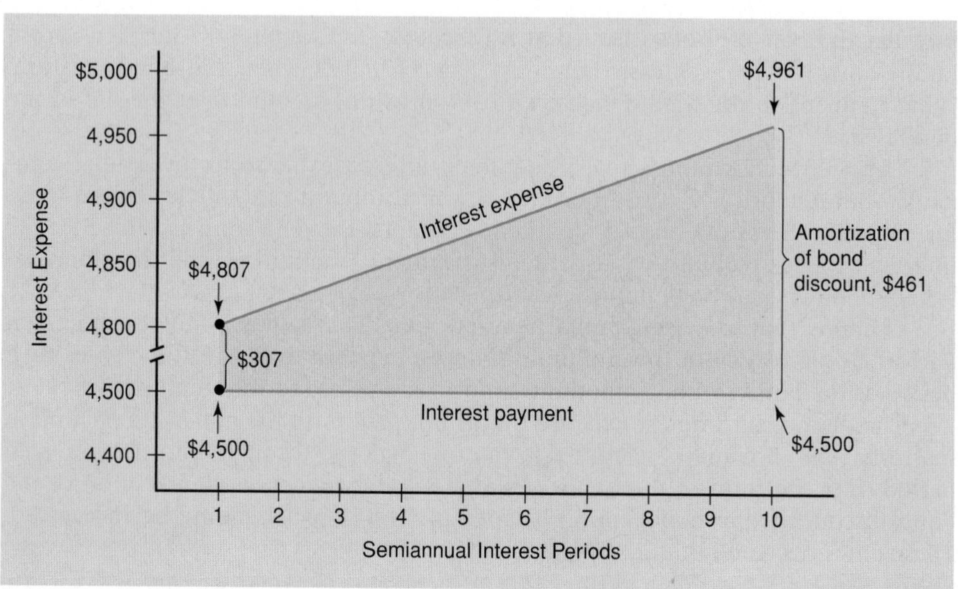

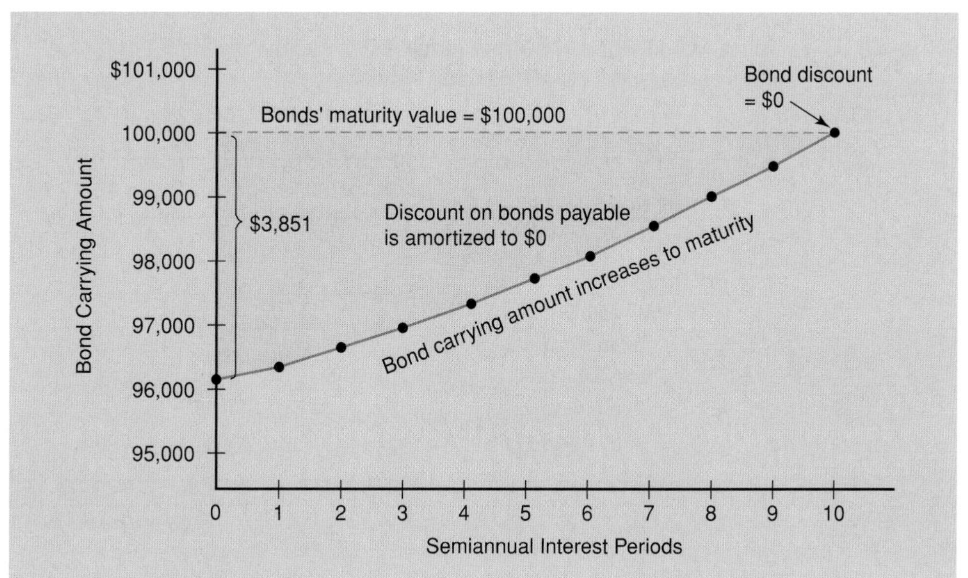

Exhibit 8-7
Amortizing Discount on Bonds Payable

Chrysler issues its bonds on January 1, 2000. On July 1, Chrysler makes the first $4,500 semiannual interest payment. On that date, Chrysler also amortizes (decreases) the bond discount because its balance must be reduced to zero over the term of the bonds. Chrysler's journal entry to record the interest payment and amortization of the bond discount follows (with all amounts taken from Exhibit 8-5):

2000			
July 1	Interest Expense	4,807	
	Discount on Bonds Payable		307
	Cash		4,500
	To pay semiannual interest and amortize bond discount.		

ASSETS	=	LIABILITIES	+	STOCKHOLDERS' EQUITY	−	EXPENSES
−4,500	=	+307			−	4,807

At December 31, 2000, Chrysler accrues interest and amortizes the bond discount for July through December with this entry (amounts from Exhibit 8-5):

✔ CHECK POINT 8-10

2000			
Dec. 31	Interest Expense	4,823	
	Discount on Bonds Payable		323
	Interest Payable		4,500
	To accrue semiannual interest and amortize bond discount.		

ASSETS	=	LIABILITIES	+	STOCKHOLDERS' EQUITY	−	EXPENSES
0	=	+ 323			−	4,823
		+4,500				

At December 31, 2000, Chrysler's bond accounts appear as follows:

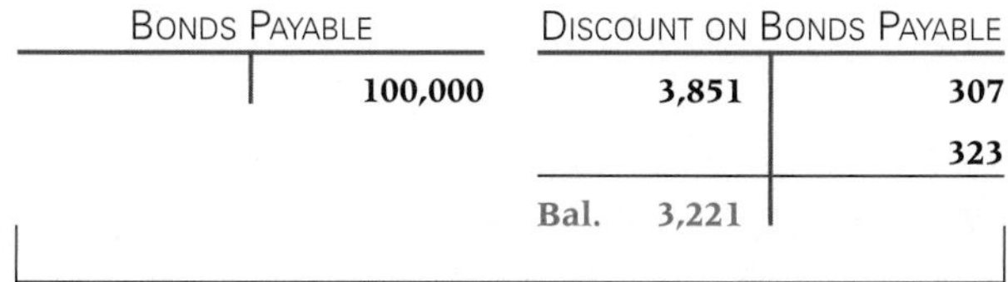

STOP & THINK

What would Chrysler Corporation's 2000 income statement and year-end balance sheet report for these bonds?

Answer:

Income Statement		
Interest expense ($4,807 + $4,823)		$ 9,630
Balance Sheet		
Current liabilities:		
Interest payable		$ 4,500
Long-term liabilities:		
Bonds payable	$100,000	
Less: Discount on bonds payable	(3,221)	96,779

CHECK POINT 8-11

At the bonds' maturity on January 1, 2005, the discount will have been amortized to zero, and the bonds' carrying amount will be $100,000. Chrysler will retire the bonds by making a $100,000 payment to the bondholders.

Issuing Bonds Payable at a Premium

Let's modify the Chrysler bond example to illustrate issuance of the bonds at a premium. Assume that Chrysler Corporation issues $100,000 of five-year, 9% bonds that pay interest semiannually. If the bonds are issued when the market interest rate is 8%, their issue price is $104,100.[2] The premium on these bonds is $4,100, and Exhibit 8-8 shows how to amortize the premium by the effective-interest method. In practice, bond premiums are rare because few companies issue their bonds to pay cash interest above the market interest rate.

Chrysler's entries to record issuance of the bonds on January 1, 2000, and to make the first interest payment and amortize the related premium on July 1, are as follows:

2000			
Jan. 1	Cash	104,100	
	Bonds Payable		100,000
	Premium on Bonds Payable		4,100
	To issue 9% bonds at a premium.		

ASSETS	=	LIABILITIES	+	STOCKHOLDERS' EQUITY
104,100	=	100,000	+	0
		+ 4,100		

2000			
July 1	Interest Expense	4,164	
	Premium on Bonds Payable	336	
	Cash		4,500
	To pay semiannual interest and amortize bond premium.		

ASSETS	=	LIABILITIES	+	STOCKHOLDERS' EQUITY	−	EXPENSES
− 4,500	=	− 336			−	4,164

[2]Again, Appendix B at the end of the book shows how to determine the price of this bond.

PANEL A—Bond Data

Issue date—January 1, 2000
Maturity (face, or par) value—$100,000
Contract interest rate—9%
Interest paid—$4\frac{1}{2}$% semiannually, $4,500 = $100,000 × 0.09 × $^6/_{12}$
Market interest rate at time of issue—8% annually, 4% semiannually
Issue price—$104,100
Maturity date—January 1, 2005

PANEL B—Amortization Table

	A	B	C	D	E
Semiannual Interest Date	*Interest* **Payment** *($4\frac{1}{2}$% of Maturity Value)*	*Interest* **Expense** *(4% of Preceding Bond Carrying Amount)*	*Premium Amortization (A − B)*	*Premium Account Balance (Preceding D − C)*	*Bond Carrying Amount ($100,000 + D)*
Jan. 1, 2000				$4,100	$104,100
July 1	$4,500	$4,164	$336	3,764	103,764
Jan. 1, 2001	4,500	4,151	349	3,415	103,415
July 1	4,500	4,137	363	3,052	103,052
Jan. 1, 2002	4,500	4,122	378	2,674	102,674
July 1	4,500	4,107	393	2,281	102,281
Jan. 1, 2003	4,500	4,091	409	1,872	101,872
July 1	4,500	4,075	425	1,447	101,447
Jan. 1, 2004	4,500	4,058	442	1,005	101,005
July 1	4,500	4,040	460	545	100,545
Jan. 1, 2005	4,500	3,955*	545	-0-	100,000

*Adjusted for effect of rounding.

Notes

- Column A The semiannual interest payments are constant—fixed by the bond contract.
- Column B The interest expense each period = the preceding bond carrying amount × the market interest rate. The amount of interest decreases each period as the bond carrying amount decreases.
- Column C The excess of each interest payment (A) over the period's interest expense (B) is the premium amortization for the period (C).
- Column D The premium balance (D) decreases by the amount of amortization for the period (C).
- Column E The bond carrying amount (E) decreases from $104,100 at issuance to $100,000 at maturity.

Immediately after issuing the bonds at a premium on January 1, 2000, Chrysler would report the bonds payable on the balance sheet as follows:

Total current liabilities.		$ XXX
Long-term liabilities:		
Bonds payable	$100,000	
Premium on bonds payable.	4,100	104,100

Note that the premium on bonds payable is *added* to the balance of bonds payable to determine the bonds' carrying amount.

INTEREST EXPENSE ON BONDS ISSUED AT A PREMIUM. In Exhibit 8-8 Chrysler Corporation borrows $104,100 cash but must pay only $100,000 at maturity. The $4,100 premium on the bonds is a reduction in Chrysler's interest expense over the term of the bonds. Exhibit 8-9 graphs Chrysler's interest expense (column B from Exhibit 8-8), interest payments (column A), and the premium amortization (column C).

Observe that the semiannual interest payment is fixed—by contract—at $4,500. The amount of interest expense each period decreases as the bond carrying amount is amortized downward toward maturity value.

EXHIBIT 8-9
Interest Expense on Bonds Payable Issued at a Premium

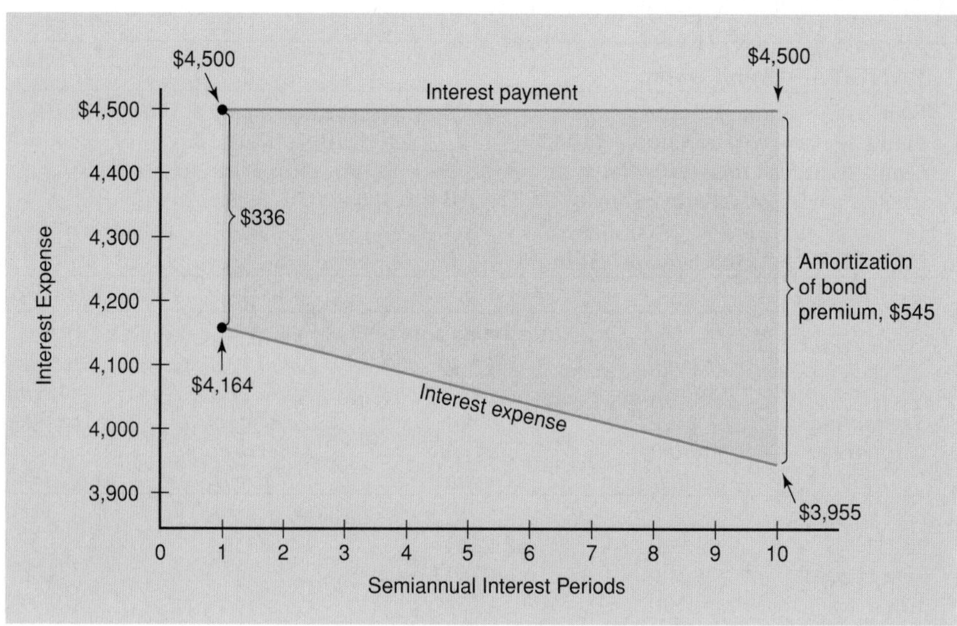

The premium is allocated as a subtraction of interest expense through amortization each period over the term of the bonds. Exhibit 8-10 diagrams the amortization of the bond premium from its beginning balance of $4,100 to its ending balance of $0. All amounts are taken from Exhibit 8-8.

Straight-Line Amortization of Bond Discount and Bond Premium

The tables in Exhibits 8-5 and 8-8 show the best way to amortize bond discounts and premiums (the effective-interest method). A less precise method is used for developing estimates and performing quick analyses that do not require a perfect measure of interest expense on a bond. Called the *straight-line amortization method,* it divides a bond discount (or premium) into equal periodic amounts over the bond's term. The amount of interest expense is thus the same for each interest period.

Let's apply the straight-line amortization method to the Chrysler Corporation bonds issued at a discount and illustrated in Exhibit 8-5 (p. 374). Suppose

EXHIBIT 8-10
Amortizing Premium on Bonds Payable

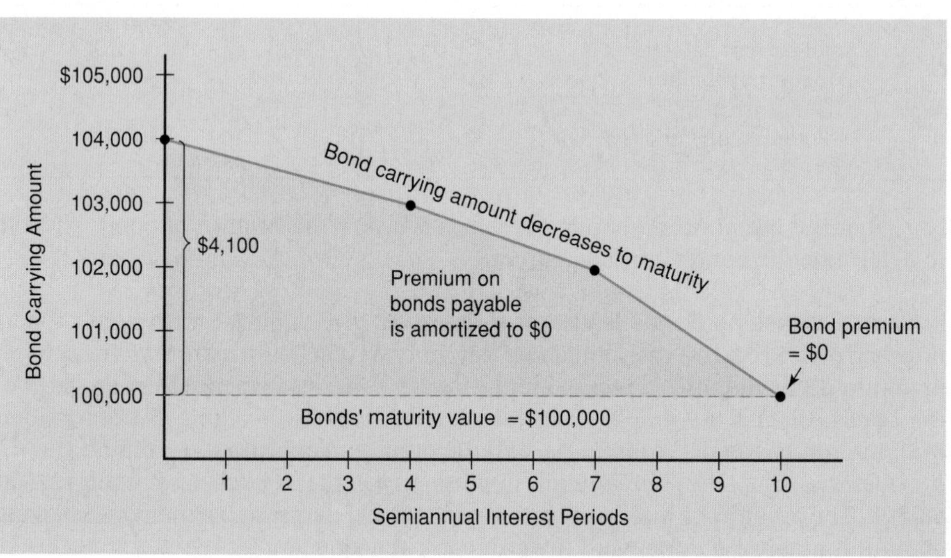

Chrysler's financial vice president is considering issuance of the 9% bonds at $96,149. To measure semiannual interest expense on the bonds, the executive can use the straight-line amortization method for the bond discount. Semiannual interest expense is estimated as follows:

Semiannual cash interest payment ($100,000 × 0.09 × 6/12)	$4,500
+ Semiannual amortization of discount ($3,851 ÷ 10)	385
= Estimated semiannual interest expense	$4,885

Chrysler's entry to record each semiannual interest payment and amortization of the discount under the straight-line amortization method would be

2000			
July 1	Interest Expense	4,885	
	Discount on Bonds Payable		385
	Cash		4,500
	To pay semiannual interest and amortize bond discount.		

CHECK POINT 8-12

CHECK POINT 8-13

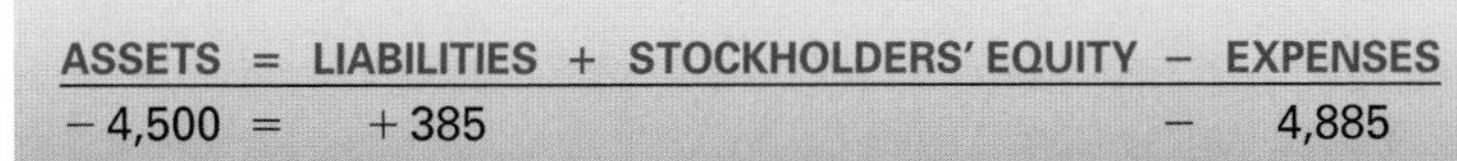

ASSETS = LIABILITIES + STOCKHOLDERS' EQUITY − EXPENSES
−4,500 = +385 − 4,885

Generally Accepted Accounting Principles (GAAP) permit the straight-line amortization method only when its amounts differ insignificantly from the amounts determined by the effective-interest method.

Early Retirement of Bonds Payable

Normally, companies wait until maturity to pay off, or *retire,* their bonds payable. But companies sometimes retire their bonds payable prior to maturity. The main reason for retiring bonds early is to relieve the pressure of making interest payments. Interest rates fluctuate. The company may be able to borrow at a lower interest rate and pay off old bonds bearing a higher interest rate.

Some bonds are **callable,** which means that the bonds' issuer may *call,* or pay off, those bonds at a specified price whenever the issuer so chooses. The call price is usually a few percentage points above the par value, perhaps 102 or 103. Callable bonds give the issuer the benefit of being able to pay off the bonds whenever it is most favorable to do so. The alternative to calling the bonds is to purchase them in the open market at their current market price.

Air Products and Chemicals, Inc., a producer of industrial gases and chemicals, has $70 million of debenture bond outstanding with unamortized discount of $350,000. Lower interest rates in the market may convince management to pay off these bonds now. Assume that the bonds are callable at 103. If the market price of the bonds is $99\frac{1}{4}$, will Air Products and Chemicals call the bonds or purchase them in the open market? Because the market price is lower than the call price, market price is the better choice. Retiring the bonds at $99\frac{1}{4}$ results in a gain of $175,000, computed as follows:

Par value of bonds being retired	$70,000,000
Less: Unamortized discount..........................	(350,000)
Carrying amount of the bonds	69,650,000
Market price ($70,000,000 × 0.9925)	69,475,000
Extraordinary gain on retirement	$ 175,000

The following entry records retirement of the bonds immediately after an interest date:

June 30	Bonds Payable	70,000,000	
	Discount on Bonds Payable		350,000
	Cash ($70,000,000 × 0.9925)		69,475,000
	Extraordinary Gain on Retirement of Bonds Payable		175,000
	To retire bonds payable before maturity.		

ASSETS	=	LIABILITIES	+ STOCKHOLDERS' EQUITY	+ GAINS
− 69,475,000	=	− 70,000,000		+ 175,000
		+ 350,000		

The entry removes the bonds payable and the related discount from the accounts and records an extraordinary gain on retirement. GAAP identifies gains and losses on early retirement of debts as *extraordinary,* and they are reported separately on the income statement.

If Air Products and Chemicals retired only half these bonds, the accountant would remove half the discount or premium. Likewise, if the price paid to retire the bonds exceeded their carrying amount, the retirement entry would record an extraordinary loss with a debit to Extraordinary Loss on Retirement of Bonds.

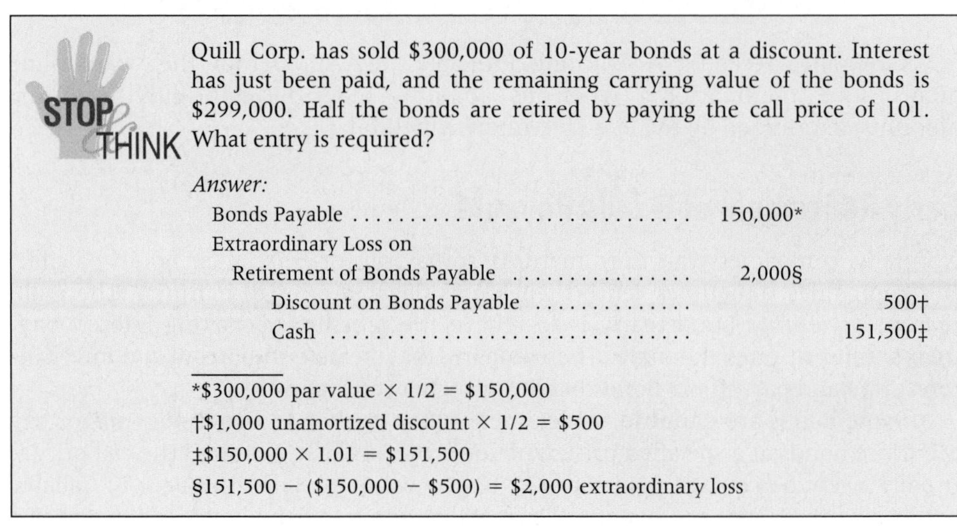

STOP & THINK

Quill Corp. has sold $300,000 of 10-year bonds at a discount. Interest has just been paid, and the remaining carrying value of the bonds is $299,000. Half the bonds are retired by paying the call price of 101. What entry is required?

Answer:

Bonds Payable	150,000*	
Extraordinary Loss on Retirement of Bonds Payable	2,000§	
Discount on Bonds Payable		500†
Cash		151,500‡

*$300,000 par value × 1/2 = $150,000

†$1,000 unamortized discount × 1/2 = $500

‡$150,000 × 1.01 = $151,500

§151,500 − ($150,000 − $500) = $2,000 extraordinary loss

Convertible Bonds and Notes

For a review of common stock, see Chapter 1, page 19.

Many corporate bonds and notes payable may be converted into the issuing company's common stock at the investor's option. These bonds and notes are called **convertible bonds** (or **notes**). For investors they combine the safety of assured receipt of interest and principal on the bonds with the opportunity for gains on the stock. The conversion feature is so attractive that investors usually accept a lower interest rate than they would on nonconvertible bonds. The lower cash interest payments benefit the issuer. Convertible bonds are recorded like any other debt at issuance. If the market price of the issuing company's stock gets high enough, the bondholders will convert the bonds into stock.

Prime Western, Inc., which operates hotels, had convertible notes outstanding carried on the books at $12.5 million. Assume that the maturity value of the notes was $13 million. If Prime Western's stock rises significantly, the noteholders will convert the notes into 400,000 shares of the company's $1 par common stock. Prime Western's entry to record this conversion is

May 14	Notes Payable	13,000,000	
	Discount on Notes Payable		500,000
	Common Stock (400,000 × $1 par)		400,000
	Paid-in Capital in Excess of Par-Common		12,100,000
	To record conversion of notes payable.		

ASSETS	=	LIABILITIES	+	STOCKHOLDERS' EQUITY
0	=	− 13,000,000	+	400,000
		+ 500,000		12,100,000

The carrying amount of the notes ($13,000,000 − $500,000) becomes stockholders' equity ($400,000 + $12,100,000). The notes payable account and its related discount or premium account are zeroed out. Common Stock is recorded at its *par value,* which is a dollar amount assigned to each share of stock. In this case, the credit to Common Stock is $400,000 (400,000 shares × $1 par value per share). Any extra carrying amount of the notes payable is credited to another stockholders' equity account, Paid in Capital in Excess of Par—Common. In effect, the carrying amount of the notes (or bonds) is transferred from a liability to stockholders' equity.

Advantages of Financing Operations with Bonds versus Stock

Businesses have different ways to acquire assets. The money to purchase the asset may be financed by the business's retained earnings, a stock issue, or bonds payable. Each financing strategy has its advantages:

Objective 5
Explain the advantages and disadvantages of borrowing

Advantages of Financing Operations by

1. Issuing Stock	*2. Issuing Notes or Bonds Payable*
• Creates no liabilities or interest expense. Less risky to the issuing corporation.	• Does not dilute stock ownership or control of the corporation. • Results in higher earnings per share because interest expense is tax-deductible.

Earnings per share (EPS) is the amount of a company's net income for each share of its stock. EPS is perhaps the single most important statistic used to evaluate companies because it is a standard measure of operating performance for comparing companies of different sizes and from different industries.

Suppose a corporation needs $500,000 for expansion. The company has net income of $300,000 and 100,000 shares of common stock outstanding. Management is considering two financing plans. Plan 1 is to issue $500,000 of 10% bonds payable, and plan 2 is to issue 50,000 shares of common stock for $500,000. Management believes the new cash can be invested in operations to earn income of $200,000 before interest and taxes.

Exhibit 8-11 shows the earnings-per-share advantage of borrowing. As you can see, our company's EPS amount is higher if the company borrows by issuing bonds. The business earns more on the investment ($90,000) than the interest it pays on the bonds ($50,000). Earning more income on borrowed money than the related interest expense increases the earnings for common stockholders and is called **trading on the equity.** It is widely used in business to increase earnings per share of common stock.

(continued on page 383)

Decision Guidelines

Financing with Debt or with Stock

Decision	Guidelines
How will you finance your business's operations?	Your financing plan depends on several factors, including the ability of the business's operations to generate cash flow, your willingness to give up some control of the business, the amount of financing risk you are willing to take, and the business's credit rating.
Do the business's operations generate enough cash to meet all its financing needs?	If yes, the business needs little outside financing. There is no need to borrow. If no, the business will need to issue additional stock or borrow the money it needs.
Are you willing to give up some of your control of the business?	If yes, then issue stock to other stockholders, who can vote their shares to elect the company's directors. If no, then borrow from bondholders, who have no vote in the management of the company.
How much financing risk are you willing to take?	If much, then borrow as much as you can. This will increase the business's debt ratio and the risk of being unable to pay its debts. If little, then borrow sparingly. This will hold the debt ratio down and reduce the risk of default on borrowing agreements.
How good is the business's credit rating?	The better the credit rating, the easier it is to borrow on favorable terms. A good credit rating also makes it easier to issue stock. Neither stockholders nor creditors will entrust their money to a company with a bad credit rating.

Excel Application Problem

Goal: Set up an Excel spreadsheet to compare earnings per share under two financing plans: borrowing and issuing stock.

Scenario: Clothes.com is thinking about building a new distribution warehouse to serve its growing web-based retail operations. In order to finance the warehouse, managers must recommend whether to borrow the funds for construction or issue stock. Construction costs are estimated at $5 million.

Plan 1 If borrowing is chosen, long-term bonds payable will be issued at 8% to raise the $5 million.

Plan 2 If stock is chosen, 80,000 shares will be issued to cover the $5 million cost.

Managers expect online sales to increase income before interest and income tax by $700,000 in the first year. Income tax expense is 40%. Net income before construction is $4 million, and shares outstanding before construction total 500,000.

Your task is to create a spreadsheet that compares earnings per share under the two plans. After completing the spreadsheet, answer these questions:

1. Which plan generates the higher earnings per share? Why?
2. Under what circumstances would Clothes.com consider using debt to finance its new warehouse?
3. Under what circumstances would Clothes.com consider the use of stock to finance its new warehouse?
4. Which option do you recommend for Clothes.com? Why? Does your recommendation change if the bond interest rate changes to 10%?

Step-by-step:

1. Open a new Excel spreadsheet.
2. Create a heading for your spreadsheet that contains the following:
   a. Chapter 8 Decision Guidelines
   b. Financing with Debt or Stock
   c. Clothes.com
   d. Today's date
3. Use Exhibit 8-11 in your textbook as a model for the layout of your spreadsheet. Label Plan 1 as "Issue $5 million of Bonds Payable" and Plan 2 as "Issue $5 million of Stock." Be sure to set up the spreadsheet so that you can change variables, such as the interest rate on the bonds, without re-typing any formulas in the body of the spreadsheet.
4. When finished, your spreadsheet should show earnings per share under both plans, and be capable of re-computing earnings per share simply by changing the interest rate on the bonds.
5. Save your work and print a copy of the worksheet (in landscape mode) for your files.

		Plan 1 Borrow $500,000 at 10%		Plan 2 Issue 50,000 Shares of Common Stock for $500,000
Net income before expansion		$300,000		$300,000
Expected project income before interest and income tax	$200,000		$200,000	
Less interest expense ($500,000 × 0.10)	(50,000)		-0-	
Expected project income before income tax	150,000		200,000	
Less income tax expense (40%)	(60,000)		(80,000)	
Expected project net income		90,000		120,000
Total company net income		$390,000		$420,000
Earnings per share after expansion:				
Plan 1 ($390,000/100,000 shares)		$3.90		
Plan 2 ($420,000/150,000 shares)				$2.80

EXHIBIT 8-11
Earnings-Per-Share Advantage of Borrowing

In this case borrowing results in higher earnings per share than issuing stock. Borrowing has its disadvantages, however. Interest expense may be high enough to eliminate net income and lead to a cash crisis or even bankruptcy. Also, borrowing creates liabilities that accrue during bad years as well as good years. In contrast, a company that issues stock can omit its dividends during a bad year. The Decision Guidelines feature provides some rules of thumb to help decide how to finance a company's operations.

CHECK POINT 8-14

LEASE LIABILITIES

A **lease** is a rental agreement in which the tenant **(lessee)** agrees to make rent payments to the property owner **(lessor)** in exchange for the use of the asset. Leasing allows the lessee to acquire the use of a needed asset without having to make the large initial cash down payment that purchase agreements require. Accountants distinguish between two types of leases: operating and capital.

Operating Leases

Operating leases are often short-term or cancelable. Many apartment leases and most car-rental agreements are for a year or less. These operating leases give the lessee the right to use the asset but provide the lessee with no continuing rights to the asset. The lessor retains the usual risks and rewards of owning the leased asset. To account for an operating lease, the lessee debits Rent Expense (or Lease Expense) and credits Cash for the amount of the lease payment. The lessee's books do not report the leased asset or any lease liability. Nevertheless, operating leases require the lessee to make rent payments. In a sense, therefore, an operating lease creates a liability.

Capital Leases

Most businesses use capital leasing to finance the acquisition of some assets. A **capital lease** is a long-term and noncancelable financing obligation that is a form of debt. How do you distinguish a capital lease from an operating lease? *FASB Statement No. 13* provides the guidelines. To be classified as a capital lease, a particular lease agreement must meet any *one* of the following criteria:

1. The lease transfers title of the leased asset to the lessee at the end of the lease term. Thus, the lessee becomes the legal owner of the leased asset.
2. The lease contains a *bargain purchase option.* The lessee can be expected to purchase the leased asset and become its legal owner.

3. The lease term is 75% or more of the estimated useful life of the leased asset. The lessee uses up most of the leased asset's service potential.
4. The present value of the lease payments is 90% or more of the market value of the leased asset. In effect, the lease payments operate as installment payments for the leased asset.

ACCOUNTING FOR A CAPITAL LEASE. Accounting for a capital lease is much like accounting for the purchase of an asset by the lessee. The lessee enters the asset into its own accounts and records a lease liability at the beginning of the lease term. Thus, the lessee capitalizes the asset in its own financial statements even though the lessee may never take legal title to the property.

Most companies lease some of their plant assets rather than buy them. The Home Depot leases store buildings under capital leases. At January 31, 1999, Home Depot reported its capital leases in Note 5 of its financial statements, excerpted as follows:

Note 5 Leases (partial)
The approximate future minimum lease payments under capital [. . .] leases at January 31, 1999 were as follows (in millions):

Fiscal Year	*Capital Leases*	
1999	$ 29	
2000	29	
2001	29	
2002	29	
2003	30	
Thereafter	396	
	542	
Less: Imputed interest	(362)	
Net present value of capital lease obligations	180	← This is Home Depot's total liability under the lease.
Less: Current installments	(2)	← Current liability
Long-term capital lease obligations, excluding current installments	$178	← Long-term liability

The note reveals that Home Depot must pay a total of $542 million on its capital leases. The present value of this liability is $180 million, of which $2 million is a current liability and $178 million is long-term debt. These amounts are included in the liability figures reported on The Home Depot's balance sheet. We now turn to the reporting of liabilities.

REPORTING LIABILITIES ON THE BALANCE SHEET

Objective 6
Report liabilities on the balance sheet

This chapter began with the liabilities reported on the balance sheet of **The Home Depot, Inc.** As a review of the material covered thus far, Exhibit 8-12 repeats the liabilities section of Home Depot's balance sheet.

You now have the tools to understand the two new categories of long-term liabilities listed on Home Depot's balance sheet. *Deferred income taxes* (line 12) are what the name implies: income tax liabilities that the company can defer and pay later. We cover accounting for income tax in more detail in Chapter 11. *Minority interest* (line 13) represents outside stockholders' interests, as opposed to The Home Depot's majority interest, in companies controlled by Home Depot. Minority interest isn't a liability that demands a payment. But neither is it Home Depot's owners' equity. Minority interest is usually included among the liabilities. We cover minority

THE HOME DEPOT, INC.
Balance Sheet (partial, adapted)

	Amounts in millions	
1	**Liabilities**	
2	Current Liabilities:	
3	Accounts Payable	$1,586
4	Accrued Salaries and Related Expenses	395
5	Sales Tax Payable	176
6	Other Accrued Liabilities (Accrued Expenses Payable)	586
7	Income Taxes Payable	100
8	Current Installments of Long-Term Debt (notes 2 and 5)	14 ←
9	Total Current Liabilities	2,857
10	Long-Term Debt, excluding current installments (notes 2 and 5)	1,566 ←
11	Other Long-Term Liabilities	208
12	Deferred Income Taxes	85
13	Minority Interest	9

Note 2 Long-Term Debt (adapted)
The Company's long-term debt at January 31, 1999, consisted of the following (amounts in millions):

	January 31, 1999
$3\frac{1}{4}$% Convertible Subordinated Notes, due October 1, 2001; convertible into shares of common stock of the Company	$1,103
Commercial Paper; weighted average interest rate of 4.8% at January 31, 1999	246
Capital Lease Obligations; payable in varying installments through January 31, 2019 (see note 5, page 384)	180
Other long-term debt	51
Total long-term debt	1,580
Less current installments	(14)
Long-term debt, excluding current installments	$1,566

EXHIBIT 8-12
Reporting Liabilities of The Home Depot, Inc.

interest in Chapter 10. Other long-term liabilities (line 11) may include long-term unearned revenue, also called *deferred credits.*

Exhibit 8-12 includes Note 2 from Home Depot's financial statements, which gives additional details about the company's liabilities. Note 2 shows the interest rates and the maturity dates of Home Depot's long-term debt. Investors need these data to evaluate the company. The note also reports the following:

- Capital lease obligations of $180 million included among the long-term debt
- Current installments of long-term debt ($14 million) as a current liability
- Long-term debt, excluding current maturities, of $1,566 million

Trace these amounts from Note 2 to the company's balance sheet. Working back and forth between the financial statements and the related notes is an important part of financial analysis.

CHECK POINT 8-15

Reporting the Fair Market Value of Long-Term Debt

FASB Statement Number 107 requires companies to report the fair market value of their financial instruments. Long-term debt, including notes and bonds payable, are financial instruments. At January 31, 1999, The Home Depot's Note 2 included this excerpt:

> The estimated fair [market] value of the $3\frac{1}{4}$% Notes, which are publicly traded, was approximately $2.9 billion based on the market price at January 31, 1999. The estimated fair value of commercial paper borrowings approximate their carrying value [of $246 million]. The estimated fair value of all other long-term borrowings was approximately $382 million compared to the carrying value of $231 million [$180 + $51].

Home Depot's $3\frac{1}{4}$% notes payable have a market value ($2.9 billion) that is almost three times as great as their carrying value ($1.1 billion in Note 2). This means that investors would pay $2.9 million for the notes.

What makes Home Depot's $3^{1}/_{4}\%$ notes payable so valuable? Is it their high interest rate? Explain.

Answer:

The notes payable are convertible into Home Depot stock. Apparently, Home Depot's stock is doing very well, and holders of the bonds can convert their bonds into the stock. As a result, the notes are very valuable. The high value of the notes does not result from their interest rate. As a matter of fact, $3^{1}/_{4}\%$ is quite low.

Pension and Postretirement Liabilities

Most companies have pension plans for their employees. A **pension** is employee compensation that will be received during retirement. Companies also provide postretirement benefits, such as medical insurance for their retired former employees. Because employees earn these benefits by their service, the company records pension and retirement-benefit expense while employees work for the company.

Pensions are one of the most complex areas of accounting. As employees earn their pensions and the company pays into the pension plan, the plan's assets grow. The obligation for future pension payments to employees also accumulates. At the end of each period, the company compares

- The fair market value of the assets in the pension plan—cash and investments—with
- The plan's accumulated benefit obligation. The *accumulated benefit obligation* is the present value of promised future pension payments to retirees.

If the plan assets exceed the accumulated benefit obligation, the plan is said to be *overfunded.* In this case, the asset and obligation amounts are to be reported only in the notes to the financial statements. However, if the accumulated benefit obligation, the pension liability, exceeds plan assets, the plan is *underfunded,* and the company must report the excess liability amount as a long-term pension liability on the balance sheet.

Suppose at December 31, 20X0, the pension plan of Mainstream Manufacturing, Inc., has

- Assets with a fair market value of $3 million and
- Accumulated pension benefit obligations of $4 million

Mainstream's balance sheet will report Long-Term Pension Liability of $1 million. This liability will be listed among the long-term liabilities. In this case, Mainstream will also report the $1 million as a negative component of other comprehensive income. *Comprehensive income* is the company's change in total stockholders' equity from all sources other than from the owners of the business. One such change in equity is the difference between the pension plan's accumulated benefit obligation and the market value of the pension plan assets.

Reporting Financing Activities on the Statement of Cash Flows

The Home Depot's balance sheet shows that the company finances most of its operations with equity. In fact, the company's debt ratio is only 35% (total liabilities of $4,725 million ÷ total assets of $13,465 million). Let's examine Home De-

Exhibit 8-13
Statement of Cash Flows (adapted) for The Home Depot, Inc.

	THE HOME DEPOT, INC. Statement of Cash Flows		
		Year Ended	
	(In millions)	*January 31 1999*	*February 1 1998*
	Cash Flow from Operating Activities:		
1	Net cash provided by operating activities	\$ 1,917	\$1,029
	Cash Flow from Investing Activities:		
2	Net cash used in investing activities	\$(2,271)	\$ (971)
	Cash Flow from Financing Activities:		
3	Borrowing by issuing commercial paper	\$ 246	\$ —
4	Proceeds from long-term borrowings	—	15
5	Payments of long-term debt	(8)	(40)
6	Proceeds from issuance of common stock	167	122
7	Payments of cash dividends	(168)	(139)
8	Other, net	7	10
9	Net cash provided by (used in) financing activities	\$ 244	\$ (32)
10	Increase (decrease) in cash	(110)	26
11	Cash at beginning of year	172	146
12	Cash at end of year	\$ 62	\$ 172

pot's financing activities as reported on its statement of cash flows. Exhibit 8-13 is an excerpt from the company's cash-flow statement.

During the year ended January 31, 1999, The Home Depot borrowed \$246 million by issuing commercial paper (line 3). The company paid \$8 million on its long-term debt (line 5). These were the only financing transactions that affected the company's liabilities during the year. Home Depot is able to finance most of its asset purchases with cash generated by operations (line 1). This is an indication of strong cash flows and a stable financial position.

End-of-Chapter

Summary Problem for Your Review

The Cessna Aircraft Company has outstanding an issue of 8% convertible bonds that mature in 2018. Suppose the bonds are dated October 1, 1998, and pay interest each April 1 and October 1.

Required

1. Complete the following effective-interest amortization table through October 1, 2000:

Bond Data

Maturity value—\$100,000

Contract interest rate—8%

Interest paid—4% semiannually, \$4,000 (\$100,000 × 0.08 × $^6/_{12}$)

Market interest rate at the time of issue—9% annually, $4^1/_2$% semiannually

Issue price—$90^3/_4$

Amortization Table

Semiannual Interest Date	A Interest Payment (4% of Maturity Amount)	B Interest Expense ($4\frac{1}{2}$% of Preceding Bond Carrying Amount)	C Discount Amortization (B − A)	D Discount Account Balance (Preceding D − C)	E Bond Carrying Amount ($100,000 − D)
10-1-98					
4-1-99					
10-1-99					
4-1-00					
10-1-00					

2. Using the amortization table, record the following transactions:

a. Issuance of the bonds on October 1, 1998.

b. Accrual of interest and amortization of discount on December 31, 1998.

c. Payment of interest and amortization of discount on April 1, 1999.

d. Conversion of one-third of the bonds payable into no-par stock on October 2, 2000. For no-par stock, transfer the bond carrying amount into the Common Stock account. There is no Additional Paid-in Capital.

e. Retirement of two-thirds of the bonds payable on October 2, 2000. Purchase price of the bonds was based on their call price of 102.

Answers

Requirement 1

Semiannual Interest Date	A Interest Payment (4% of Maturity Amount)	B Interest Expense ($4\frac{1}{2}$% of Preceding Bond Carrying Amount)	C Discount Amortization (B − A)	D Discount Account Balance (Preceding D − C)	E Bond Carrying Amount ($100,000 − D)
10-1-98				$9,250	$90,750
4-1-99	$4,000	$4,084	$84	9,166	90,834
10-1-99	4,000	4,088	88	9,078	90,922
4-1-00	4,000	4,091	91	8,987	91,013
10-1-00	4,000	4,096	96	8,891	91,109

Requirement 2

Date	Accounts	Debit	Credit
1998			
a. Oct. 1	Cash ($100,000 × 0.9075)	90,750	
	Discount on Bonds Payable	9,250	
	Bonds Payable		100,000
	To issue 8%, 20-year bonds at a discount.		
b. Dec. 31	Interest Expense ($4,084 × 3/6)	2,042	
	Discount on Bonds Payable ($84 × 3/6)		42
	Interest Payable ($4,000 × 3/6)		2,000
	To accrue interest and amortize bond discount for three months.		
1999			
c. Apr. 1	Interest Expense	2,042	
	Interest Payable	2,000	
	Discount on Bonds Payable ($84 × 3/6)		42
	Cash		4,000
	To pay semiannual interest, part of which was accrued, and amortize three months' discount on bonds payable.		

2000			
d. Oct. 2	Bonds Payable ($100,000 × 1/3)	33,333	
	Discount on Bonds Payable ($8,891 × 1/3)..................		2,964
	Common Stock ($91,109 × 1/3)......		30,369
	To record conversion of bonds payable.		
e. Oct. 2	Bonds Payable ($100,000 × 2/3)	66,667	
	Extraordinary Loss on Retirement of Bonds. .	7,260	
	Discount on Bonds Payable ($8,891 × 2/3)..................		5,927
	Cash ($100,000 × 2/3 × 1.02)		68,000
	To retire bonds payable before maturity.		

Summary of Learning Objectives

1. ***Account for current liabilities.*** *Current liabilities* are obligations due within one year or within the company's normal operating cycle if it is longer than one year. Obligations beyond that term are classified as *long-term liabilities.*
2. ***Identify and report contingent liabilities.*** *Contingent liabilities* are not actual liabilities but rather potential liabilities that depend on a future event arising out of a past transaction. Companies must report a liability if it is *probable* that the loss or expense will occur and the amount can be reasonably estimated. Contingencies should be reported in financial statement notes if it is *reasonably possible* that they will occur. There is no need to report contingent losses that are *remote possibilities.*
3. ***Account for basic bonds-payable transactions.*** Corporations may borrow by issuing long-term notes and/or bonds payable. A bond contract specifies the *maturity value* of the bonds, the *principal* (amount borrowed from the lender), a *contract interest rate,* and dates for the payment of interest and principal. Bonds issued above par are issued at a *premium,* and bonds issued below par are issued at a *discount. Market interest rates* fluctuate and may differ from the contract rate on a bond.
4. ***Measure interest expense by the effective-interest method.*** When a bond's contract interest rate differs from the market interest rate, the company's interest expense differs from period to period. For bonds issued at a discount, the amount of interest expense each period increases as the bond carrying amount increases. For bonds issued at a premium, the amount of interest expense each period decreases as the bond carrying amount decreases.

   To amortize a bond discount or premium over the life of the bond and calculate interest expense accurately, accountants use the *effective-interest method of amortization.* A less precise method is the *straight-line amortization method,* which divides a bond discount or premium into equal periodic amounts over the bond's term.
5. ***Explain the advantages and disadvantages of borrowing.*** A key advantage of borrowing versus issuing stock is that interest expense on debt is tax-deductible. Thus, selling bonds is less costly than issuing stock. Bonds also lead to a higher earnings per share than stock issues do. The key disadvantage of borrowing: The company must repay the loan and interest, in good times and in bad.
6. ***Report liabilities on the balance sheet.*** Many companies report additional categories of liabilities on the balance sheet. *Deferred income taxes* are income tax liabilities that the company has deferred and will pay later. *Deferred gains* and *deferred credits* are long-term unearned revenues.

Accounting Vocabulary

accrued expense (p. 362).
accrued liability (p. 362).
bonds payable (p. 367).
callable bonds (p. 379).
capital lease (p. 383).
contract interest rate (p. 370).
convertible bonds (*or* notes) (p. 380).
current installment of long-term debt (p. 362).
debentures (p. 368).
discount (on a bond) (p. 369).
earnings per share (EPS) (p. 381).
effective interest rate (p. 370).
lease (p. 383).
lessee (p. 383).
lessor (p. 383).
market interest rate (p. 370).
operating lease (p. 383).
payroll (p. 363).
pension (p. 386).
premium (on a bond) (p. 369).
present value (p. 369).
serial bonds (p. 368).
short presentation (p. 366).
short-term note payable (p. 360).
stated interest rate (p. 370).
term bonds (p. 368).
trading on the equity (p. 381).
underwriter (p. 368).

QUESTIONS

1. What distinguishes a current liability from a long-term liability? What distinguishes a contingent liability from an actual liability?
2. A company purchases a machine by signing a $60,000, 10%, one-year note payable on July 31. Interest is to be paid at maturity. What two current liabilities related to this purchase does the company report on its December 31 balance sheet? What is the amount of each current liability?
3. At the beginning of the school term, what type of account is the tuition that your college or university collects from students? What type of account is the tuition at the end of the school term?
4. Patton Company warrants its products against defects for three years from date of sale. During the current year, the company made sales of $300,000. Store management estimated that warranty costs on those sales would total $21,000 over the three-year warranty period. Ultimately, the company paid $22,000 cash on warranties. What was the company's warranty expense for the year? What accounting principle governs this answer?
5. Identify two contingent liabilities of a definite amount and two contingent liabilities of an indefinite amount.
6. Compute the price to the nearest dollar for the following bonds with a face value of $10,000:
   a. 100 **b.** 93 **c.** $88\frac{3}{4}$ **d.** $101\frac{3}{8}$ **e.** $122\frac{1}{2}$
7. In which of the following situations will bonds sell at par? At a premium? At a discount?
   a. 9% bonds sold when the market rate is 9%
   b. 9% bonds sold when the market rate is 8%
   c. 9% bonds sold when the market rate is 10%
8. Why are bonds sold for a price "plus accrued interest"? What happens to accrued interest when the bonds are sold by an individual?
9. A company retires 10-year bonds payable of $100,000 after five years. The business issued the bonds at 104 and called them at 103. Compute the amount of gain or loss on retirement. How is this gain or loss reported on the income statement?
10. Why are convertible bonds attractive to investors? Why are they popular with borrowers?
11. Contrast the effects on a company of issuing bonds versus issuing stock.
12. What characteristics distinguish a capital lease from an operating lease?
13. Distinguish an overfunded pension plan from an underfunded plan. Which situation requires the company to report a pension liability on the balance sheet? How is this liability computed?
14. What are the two main financing cash flows related to long-term debt?

CHECK POINTS

Accounting for a note payable (Obj. 1)

CP8-1 Return to the $8,000 purchase of inventory on a short-term note payable that begins on page 360. Assume that the purchase of inventory occurred on April 30, 20X1, instead of September 30, 20X1. Journalize the company's (a) purchase of inventory, (b) accrual of interest expense on December 31, 20X1, and (c) payment of the note plus interest on April 30, 20X2.

Reporting a short-term note payable and the related interest in the financial statements (Obj. 1)

CP8-2 This check point should be done in conjunction with Check Point 8-1.

1. Refer to the data in Check Point 8-1. Show what the company would report for the note payable on its balance sheet at December 31, 20X1, and on its income statement for the year ended on that date.
2. What one item will the financial statements for the year ended December 31, 20X2, report? Identify the financial statement, the item, and its amount.

Analyzing current liabilities (Obj. 1)

CP8-3 **Pier 1 Imports, Inc.,** reported the following current liabilities (adapted, all amounts in thousands):

	February 28,	
	19X8	19X7
Accrued payroll [. . .] liabilities	$27,194	$25,068
Gift certificates [. . .] outstanding	11,276	8,242

1. The purpose of this requirement is to show how Pier 1's ending balance of Accrued payroll . . . liabilities arose from the company's transactions during the year.

Create a T-account for Accrued Payroll . . . Liabilities. Insert the balance at February 28, 19X7 as the beginning balance. Assume that during the year ended February 28, 19X8, Pier 1 accrued payroll expense of $265,000 and paid $262,874 of this total. Post both of these amounts directly into the Accrued Payroll . . . Liabilities T-account and take its ending balance. Compare your result to Pier 1's actual ending balance. The two amounts should be equal.

2. Explain the nature of Pier 1's Gift Certificates . . . outstanding. What is another name for this account?

Accounting for warranty expense and estimated warranty payable (Obj. 1)

CP8-4 **DaimlerChrysler Corporation** warranties its automobiles for three years or 36,000 miles, whichever comes first. Suppose Chrysler's experience indicates that the company can expect warranty costs during the three-year period to add up to 5% of sales.

Assume that Four Corners Dodge in Durango, Colorado, made sales of $500,000 during 20X0, its first year of operations. Four Corners Dodge received cash for 30% of the sales and took notes receivable for the remainder. Payments to satisfy customer warranty claims totaled $22,000 during 20X0.

1. Record the sales, warranty expense, and warranty payments for Four Corners Dodge. Ignore any reimbursement Four Corners Dodge may receive from Chrysler Corporation.
2. Post to the Estimated Warranty Payable T-account. At the end of 20X0, how much in estimated warranty payable does Four Corners Dodge owe its customers? Why must the warranty payable amount be estimated?

Applying GAAP; reporting warranties in the financial statements (Obj. 1)

CP8-5 Refer to the data given in Check Point 8-4. What amount of warranty expense will Four Corners Dodge report during 20X0? Which accounting principle addresses this situation? Does the warranty expense for the year equal the year's cash payments for warranties? Explain how the accounting principle works for measuring warranty expense.

Interpreting a company's contingent liabilities (Obj. 2)

CP8-6 **Harley-Davidson, Inc.,** the motorcycle manufacturer, included the following note in its annual report:

> *NOTES TO CONSOLIDATED FINANCIAL STATEMENTS*
> *7(In Part): Commitments and Contingencies*
> The Company self-insures its product liability losses in the United States up to $3 million (catastrophic coverage is maintained for individual claims in excess of $3 million up to $25 million). Outside the United States, the Company is insured for product liability up to $25 million per individual claim and in the aggregate.

1. Why are these *contingent* (versus *real*) liabilities?
2. In the United States, how can the contingent liability become a real liability for Harley-Davidson? What are the limits to the company's product liabilities in the United States? Explain how these limits work.
3. How can a contingency outside the United States become a real liability for the company? How does Harley-Davidson's potential liability differ for claims outside the United States?

Pricing bonds (Obj. 3)

CP8-7 Compute the price of the following bonds:

a. $100,000 quoted at $97\frac{1}{2}$
b. $400,000 quoted at $102\frac{5}{8}$
c. $2,000,000 quoted at $89\frac{3}{4}$
d. $500,000 quoted at $110\frac{3}{8}$

Determining bond prices at par, discount, or premium (Obj. 3)

CP8-8 Determine whether the following bonds payable will be issued at par value, at a premium, or at a discount:

a. Sparta Corporation issued 8% bonds when the market interest rate was $6\frac{7}{8}$%.
b. Athens Company issued bonds payable that pay cash interest at the contract rate of 7%. At the date of issuance, the market interest rate was $8\frac{1}{4}$%.
c. The market interest rate is 9%. Corinth, Inc., issues bonds payable with a stated rate of $8\frac{1}{2}$%.
d. Macedonia Corp. issued $7\frac{1}{2}$% bonds payable when the market rate was $7\frac{1}{2}$%.

Journalizing basic bond payable transactions; bonds issued at par (Obj. 3)

CP8-9 Suppose **WPPSS** issued the 10-year bond in Exhibit 8-2, page 368, when the market interest rate was $6\frac{1}{2}$%. Assume that the fiscal year of WPPSS ends on June 30. Journalize the following transactions for WPPSS, including an explanation for each entry:

a. Issuance of the bond payable at par on July 1, 2000.
b. Payment of cash interest on January 1, 2001. (Round to the nearest dollar.)
c. Payment of the bonds payable at maturity. (Give the date.)

Issuing bonds payable and amortizing discount by the effective-interest method (Obj. 4)

CP8-10 AdTech, Inc., issued $500,000 of 7%, 10-year bonds payable at a price of 87 on March 31, 20X1. The market interest rate at the date of issuance was 9%, and the AdTech bonds pay interest semiannually.

1. Prepare an effective-interest amortization table for the bond discount through the first three interest payments. Use Exhibit 8-5, page 374, as a guide and round amounts to the nearest dollar.
2. Record AdTech's issuance of the bonds on March 31, 20X1, and, on September 30, 20X1, payment of the first semiannual interest amount and amortization of the bond discount. Explanations are not required.

Analyzing data on long-term debt (Obj. 4)

CP8-11 Use the amortization table that you prepared for AdTech, Inc. in Check Point 8-10 to answer these questions about the company's long-term debt:

1. How much cash did AdTech borrow on March 31, 20X1? How much cash will AdTech pay back at maturity on March 31, 20X11?
2. How much cash interest will AdTech pay each six months?
3. How much interest expense will AdTech report on September 30, 20X1? On March 31, 20X2? Why does the amount of interest expense increase each period? Explain in detail.

Determining bonds payable amounts; amortizing discount by the straight-line method (Obj. 3)

CP8-12 **Washington Public Power Supply System (WPPSS)** borrowed money by issuing the bond payable in Exhibit 8-2, page 368. Assume the issue price was $93\frac{1}{2}$ on July 1, 2000.

1. How much cash did WPPSS receive when it issued the bond payable?
2. How much must WPPSS pay back at maturity? When is the maturity date?
3. How much cash interest will WPPSS pay each six months? Carry the interest amount to the nearest cent.
4. How much interest expense will WPPSS report each six months? Assume the straight-line amortization method and carry the interest amount to the nearest cent.

Issuing bonds payable, accruing interest, and amortizing bond discount by the straight-line method (Obj. 3)

CP8-13 Return to the WPPSS bond in Exhibit 8-2, page 368. Assume that WPPSS issued the bond payable on July 1, 2000, at a price of 94. Also assume that WPPSS's accounting year ends on December 31. Journalize the following transactions for WPPSS, including an explanation for each entry:

a. Issuance of the bonds on July 1, 2000.

b. Accrual of interest expense and amortization of bond discount on December 31, 2000. (Use the straight-line amortization method, and round the interest amount to the nearest dollar.)

c. Payment of the first semiannual interest amount on January 1, 2001.

Earnings-per-share effects of financing with bonds versus stock (Obj. 5)

CP8-14 Greenhill Financial Services of Boise, Idaho, needs to raise $1 million to expand company operations into Montana. Greenhill's president is considering the issuance of either

- Plan A: $1,000,000 of 8% bonds payable to borrow the money
- Plan B: 100,000 shares of common stock at $10 per share

Before any new financing, Greenhill expects to earn net income of $350,000, and the company already has 200,000 shares of common stock outstanding. Greenhill believes the expansion will increase income before interest and income tax by $200,000. Greenhill's income tax rate is 40%.

Prepare an analysis similar to Exhibit 8-11, page 383, to determine which plan is likely to result in the higher earnings per share. Based solely on the earnings-per-share comparison, which financing plan would you recommend for Greenhill?

Reporting liabilities, including capital lease obligations (Obj. 6)

CP8-15 MNA Associates, Inc., includes the following selected accounts in its general ledger at December 31, 20X2:

Bonds payable	$350,000	Current obligation under capital lease	$ 8,000
Equipment under capital lease	114,000	Accounts payable	19,000
Interest payable (due March 1, 20X3)	7,000	Long-term capital lease liability	42,000
Current portion of bonds payable	50,000	Discount on bonds payable (all long-term)	6,000
Notes payable, long-term . . .	60,000		

Prepare the liabilities section of MNA's balance sheet at December 31, 20X2, to show how MNA would report these items. Report a total for current liabilities.

EXERCISES

Accounting for warranty expense and the related liability (Obj. 1)

E8-1 Assume the accounting records of **Jerry Stevens Firestone** included the following balances at the end of the period:

ESTIMATED WARRANTY PAYABLE		SALES REVENUE		WARRANTY EXPENSE	
	Beg. bal 8,100		**161,000**		

In the past, Stevens' warranty expense has been 6% of sales. During the current period, the business paid $10,430 to satisfy the warranty claims of customers.

Required

1. Record Stevens' warranty expense for the period and the company's cash payments during the period to satisfy warranty claims. Explanations are not required.
2. Show what Stevens will report on its income statement and balance sheet for this situation.

Recording and reporting current liabilities (Obj. 1)

E8-2 Assume **The Dallas Morning News** publishing company completed the following transactions during 20X1:

Nov. 1	Sold a six-month subscription, collecting cash of $120, plus sales tax of 5%.
Dec. 15	Remitted (paid) the sales tax to the state of Texas.
31	Made the necessary adjustment at year end.

Journalize these transactions (explanations not required). Then report any liability on the company's balance sheet.

Reporting payroll expense and liabilities (Obj. 1)

E8-3 A **Norwest Bank** has an annual salary expense of $900,000. In addition, the bank incurs payroll tax expense equal to 9% of the total payroll. At December 31, the end of the bank's accounting year, Norwest owes salaries of $4,000 and FICA and other payroll tax of $1,000. The bank will pay these amounts early next year.

Show what Norwest Bank will report for the foregoing on its income statement and year-end balance sheet.

Recording note payable transactions (Obj. 1)

E8-4 Record the following note-payable transactions of **Karr-Hunter Pontiac, Inc.,** in the company's journal. Explanations are not required.

20X2	
May 1	Purchased equipment costing $60,000 by issuing a one-year, 8% note payable.
Dec. 31	Accrued interest on the note payable.
20X3	
May 1	Paid the note payable at maturity.

Accounting for income tax (Obj. 1)

E8-5 Assume the following for **Campbell Soup Company.** At December 31, 20X0, Campbell Soup Company reported a current liability for income tax payable of $117 million. During 20X1, Campbell Soup earned income of $1,042 million before income tax. The company's income tax rate during 20X1 was 35%. Also during 20X1, Campbell Soup paid income taxes of $341 million.

How much income tax payable did Campbell Soup Company report on its balance sheet at December 31, 20X1? How much income tax expense did Campbell Soup report on its 20X1 income statement? Round amounts to nearest $1 million.

Analyzing liabilities (Obj. 1, 7)

E8-6 **Temple Industries** is a large holding company with major interests in paper, packaging, building products, and timber resources. Temple's 20X1 revenues totaled $2,794 million, and at December 31, 20X1, the company had $653 million in current assets. The December 31, 20X1, balance sheet reported the following (adapted):

At year end (In millions)	*20X1*	*20X0*
Liabilities and Shareholders' Equity		
Current Liabilities:		
Accounts payable	$ 138	$ 176
Accrued expenses	157	178
Employee compensation and benefits	37	25
Current portion of long-term debt	5	14
Total Current Liabilities	337	393
Long-Term Debt	1,489	1,316
Deferred Income Taxes	259	229
Postretirement Benefits Payable	132	126
Other Liabilities	21	17
Shareholders' Equity	2,021	1,783
Total Liabilities and Shareholders' Equity	$4,259	$3,864

Required

1. Describe each of Temple Industries' liabilities and state how the liability arose.
2. How much were Temple's total assets at December 31, 20X1? Was the company's debt ratio high, low, or in a middle range?

Reporting a contingent liability (Obj. 2)

E8-7 Hack Branch Distributing Company is a defendant in lawsuits brought against the distribution of its products. Damages of $2.3 million are claimed against the company, but the company denies the charges and is vigorously defending itself. In a recent press conference, the president of the company stated that he could not predict the outcome of the lawsuits. Nevertheless, he said management does not believe that any actual liabilities resulting from the lawsuits will significantly affect the company's financial position.

Required

1. Prepare a partial balance sheet to show how Hack Branch Distributing Company would report this contingent liability in a short presentation. Total actual liabilities are $7.1 million. Also, write the disclosure note to describe the contingency.
2. Suppose Hack Branch's attorneys believe it is probable that a judgment of $1.1 million will be rendered against the company. Report this situation in the Hack Branch Distributing Company financial statements. Journalize any entry required under GAAP. Explanations are not required.

Reporting current liabilities (Obj. 1)

E8-8 The top management of Polaris, Inc., examines the following company accounting records at December 29, immediately before the end of the year:

Total current assets	$ 450,000
Noncurrent assets	1,240,000
	$1,690,000
Total current liabilities	$ 230,000
Noncurrent liabilities	800,000
Owners' equity	660,000
	$1,690,000

Polaris's borrowing agreements with creditors require the company to keep a current ratio of 2.0 or better. How much in current liabilities should the company pay off within the next two days in order to comply with its borrowing agreements?

Reporting current and long-term liabilities (Obj. 1, 6)

E8-9 Assume that **Callaway Golf Corporation** completed these selected transactions during December 20X2:

a. **Sport Spectrum,** a chain of sporting goods stores, ordered $80,000 of golf equipment. With its order, Sport Spectrum sent a check for $80,000. Callaway will ship the goods on January 3, 20X3.

b. The December payroll of $104,000 is subject to employee withheld income tax of 9% and FICA tax of 8%. On December 31, Callaway pays employees their take-home pay and accrues all tax amounts.

c. Sales of $2,000,000 are subject to estimated warranty cost of 1.4%.

d. On December 1, Callaway signed a $100,000 note payable that requires annual payments of $20,000 plus 9% interest on the unpaid balance each December 1.

Required

Classify each liability as current or long-term and report the amount that would appear for these items on the Callaway Golf Corporation balance sheet at December 31, 20X2.

E8-10

Issuing bonds payable, paying and accruing interest, and amortizing discount by the straight-line method (Obj. 3)

1. On January 31, **Bayliner Boats** issues 10-year, 8% bonds payable with a face value of $1,000,000. The bonds were issued at 98 and pay interest on January 31 and July 31. Bayliner amortizes bond discount by the straight-line method. Record (a) issuance of the bonds on February 1, (b) the semiannual interest payment on July 31, and (c) the interest accrual on December 31.

2. If Bayliner issued the bonds payable on March 31, how much cash would the company receive upon issuance of the bonds?

E8-11 **Campbell Soup Company** has $200 million of 8.88% debenture bonds outstanding. The bonds mature in 2021. Assume the bonds were issued at 102 in 2001.

Measuring cash amounts for a bond; amortizing bond premium by the straight-line method (Obj. 3)

Required

1. How much cash did Campbell Soup receive when it issued these bonds?

2. How much cash in total will Campbell Soup pay the bondholders through the maturity date of the bonds?

3. Take the difference between your answers to Requirements 1 and 2. This difference represents Campbell Soup's total interest expense over the life of the bonds.

4. Compute Campbell Soup's annual interest expense by the straight-line amortization method. Multiply this amount by 20. Your 20-year total should be the same as your answer to Requirement 3.

E8-12 AMA Printing Company is authorized to issue $500,000 of 7%, 10-year bonds payable. On December 31, 20X1, when the market interest rate is 8%, the company issues $400,000 of the bonds and receives cash of $372,660. AMA amortizes bond discount by the effective-interest method. The semiannual interest dates are June 30 and December 31.

Issuing bonds payable; recording interest payments and the related discount amortization (Obj. 3, 4)

Required

1. Prepare an amortization table for the first four semiannual interest periods.

2. Record the second semiannual interest payment on December 31, 20X2, and the fourth payment on December 31, 20X3.

E8-13 On July 31, 2001, the market interest rate is 7%. Centurion Software, Inc., issues $300,000 of 8%, 20-year bonds payable at $110\frac{5}{8}$. The bonds pay interest on January 31 and July 31. Centurion amortizes bond premium by the effective-interest method.

Issuing bonds payable; recording interest accrual and payment and the related premium amortization (Obj. 3, 4)

Required

1. Prepare an amortization table for the first four semiannual interest periods.

2. Record issuance of the bonds on July 31, 2001, the accrual of interest at December 31, 2001, and the semiannual interest payment on January 31, 2002.

E8-14 **Richland Mall, Inc.**, issued $600,000 of $8\frac{3}{8}$% (0.08375), five-year bonds payable on January 1, 20X1, when the market interest rate was $9\frac{1}{2}$% (0.095). The mall pays interest annually at year end. The issue price of the bonds was $574,082.

Debt payment and discount amortization schedule (Obj. 4)

Required

Create a spreadsheet model to prepare a schedule to amortize the discount on these bonds. Use the effective-interest method of amortization. Round to the nearest dollar and format your answer as shown on page 396.

E8-15 The Viking Inn issued $400,000 of $8\frac{1}{2}$% notes payable on December 31, 20X0, at a price of $98\frac{1}{2}$. The notes' term to maturity is 10 years. After three years, the notes may be converted into the company's common stock. Each $1,000 face amount of notes is convert-

Recording conversion of notes payable (Obj. 3)

E8-14
(continued)
Richland Mall

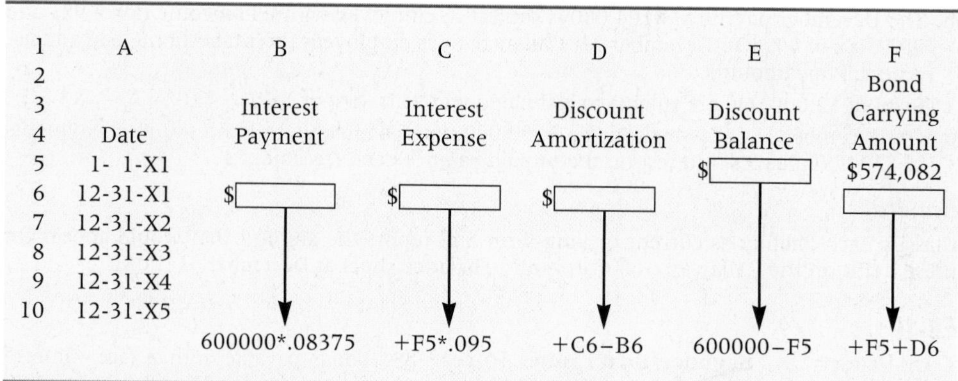

	A	B	C	D	E	F
1						
2						Bond
3		Interest	Interest	Discount	Discount	Carrying
4	Date	Payment	Expense	Amortization	Balance	Amount
5	1- 1-X1				$	$574,082
6	12-31-X1	$	$	$		
7	12-31-X2					
8	12-31-X3					
9	12-31-X4					
10	12-31-X5					
		600000*.08375	+F5*.095	+C6–B6	600000–F5	+F5+D6

E8-15
(continued)
Viking Inn

ible into 50 shares of $10 par stock. On December 31, 20X4, noteholders exercised their right to convert the notes into common stock.

Required

1. What would cause the noteholders to convert their notes into common stock?

2. Without making journal entries, compute the carrying amount of the notes payable at December 31, 20X4, immediately before the conversion. Viking Inn uses the straight-line method to amortize bond premium and discount.

3. All amortization has been recorded properly. Journalize the conversion transaction at December 31, 20X4.

Recording early retirement and conversion of bonds payable
(Obj. 3)

E8-16 IKON Office Solutions reported the following at September 30, immediately after the quarterly adjustments:

Long-term liabilities:		
Convertible bonds payable, 9%, 8 years to maturity	$300,000	
Discount on bonds payable	(6,000)	$294,000

Required

1. Record retirement of half the bonds on October 1 at the call price of 104.

2. Record conversion of the other half of the bonds into 4,000 shares of IKON's $10-par common stock on October 1. What would cause the bondholders to convert their bonds into stock?

Analyzing alternative plans for raising money
(Obj. 5)

E8-17 **Common Grounds Coffee Company** is considering two plans for raising $1,000,000 to expand operations. Plan A is to borrow at 9%, and plan B is to issue 100,000 shares of common stock. Before any new financing, Common Grounds has net income of $600,000 and 100,000 shares of common stock outstanding. Assume you own most of Common Grounds' existing stock. Management believes the company can use the new funds to earn additional income of $420,000 before interest and taxes. The income tax rate is 35%.

Required

1. Analyze Common Grounds' situation to determine which plan will result in higher earnings per share. Use Exhibit 8-11 (page 383) as a model.

2. Which plan results in the higher earnings per share? Which plan allows you to retain control of the company? Which plan creates more financial risk for the company? Which plan do you prefer? Why? Present your conclusion in a memo to Common Grounds' board of directors.

Reporting long-term debt and pension liability on the balance sheet
(Obj. 6)

E8-18 Consider the following situations.

a. A note to the financial statements of **Mapco, Inc.,** reported (in thousands):

Note 5: Long-Term Debt	
Total	$537,888
Less—Current portion	(22,085)
Discount	(1,391)
Long-term debt	$514,412

Assume that none of the debt discount is related to the current portion of long-term debt. Show how Mapco's classified balance sheet would report these liabilities.

b. Panafax Incorporated's pension plan has assets with a market value of $830,000. The plan's accumulated benefit obligation is $970,000. What amount of long-term pension liability, if any, will Panafax report on its balance sheet?

Challenge Exercise

Analyzing bond transactions (Obj. 3, 4)

E8-19 This (updated) advertisement appeared in the *Wall Street Journal*. (*Note:* A *subordinated debenture* is one whose rights are subordinated to the rights of other bondholders.)

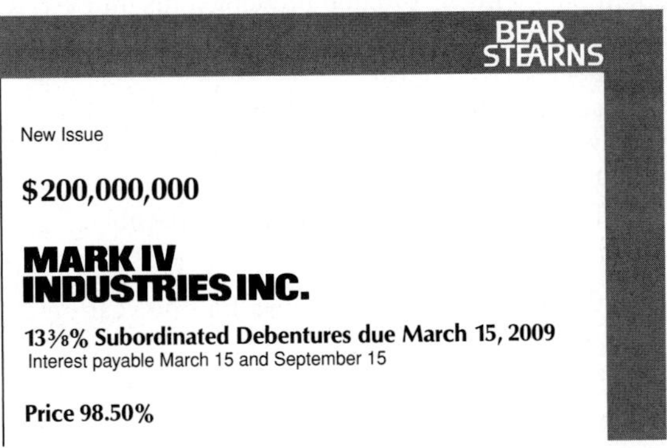

BEAR STEARNS
New Issue
$200,000,000
MARK IV INDUSTRIES INC.
13⅜% Subordinated Debentures due March 15, 2009
Interest payable March 15 and September 15
Price 98.50%

Required

Answer these questions.

1. Suppose investors purchased these securities at their offering price on March 15, 1999. Describe the transaction in detail, indicating who received cash, who paid cash, and how much.
2. Why is the contract interest rate on these bonds so high?
3. Compute the annual cash interest payment on the bonds.
4. Compute the annual interest expense under the straight-line amortization method.
5. Compute both the first-year (from March 15, 1999, to March 15, 2000) and the second-year interest expense (March 15, 2000, to March 15, 2001) under the effective-interest amortization method. The market rate of interest at the date of issuance was approximately 13.65%.
6. Suppose you purchased $500,000 of these bonds on March 15, 1999. How much cash did you pay? If you had purchased $500,000 of these bonds on March 31, 1999, how much cash would you have paid?

Problems

(Group A)

Measuring current liabilities (Obj. 1)

P8-1A Following are five pertinent facts about events during the current year at Discount Appliances, Inc.:

a. Sales of $430,000 were covered by Discount Appliances' product warranty. At January 1, estimated warranty payable was $12,400. During the year, Discount Appliances recorded warranty expense of $22,300 and paid warranty claims of $20,600.

b. Discount Appliances owes $100,000 on a long-term note payable. At December 31, 6% interest since July 31 and $20,000 of this principal are payable within one year.

c. December sales totaled $38,000, and Discount Appliances collected an additional state sales tax of 7%. This amount will be sent to the state of Ohio early in January.

d. On November 30, Discount Appliances received rent of $5,400 in advance for a lease on a building. This rent will be earned evenly over three months.

e. On September 30, Discount Appliances signed a six-month, 9% note payable to purchase equipment costing $12,000. The note requires payment of principal and interest at maturity.

Required

For each item, indicate the account and the related amount to be reported as a current liability on the Discount Appliances December 31 balance sheet.

Recording liability-related transactions (Obj. 1)

P8-2A The following transactions of Greenlawn Sprinkler Systems occurred during 20X4 and 20X5.

Required

Record the transactions in the company's journal. Explanations are not required.

20X4	
Jan. 9	Purchased a machine at a cost of $52,000, signing an 8%, six-month note payable for that amount.
Feb. 28	Borrowed $200,000 on a 9% note payable that calls for annual installment payments of $50,000 principal plus interest. Record the short-term note payable in a separate account from the long-term note payable.
July 9	Paid the six-month, 8% note at maturity.
Dec. 31	Accrued warranty expense, which is estimated at 3% of sales of $650,000.
31	Accrued interest on the outstanding note payable.
20X5	
Feb. 28	Paid the first installment and interest for one year on the outstanding note payable.

Identifying contingent liabilities (Obj. 2)

P8-3A **Sewell Motor Company** is the largest Cadillac dealer in the United States. The dealership sells new and used cars and operates a body shop and a service department. Grant Sewell, the general manager, is considering changing insurance companies because of a disagreement with Doug Barron, agent for the **Travelers Insurance Company.** Travelers is doubling Sewell's liability insurance cost for the next year. In discussing insurance coverage with you, a trusted business associate, Sewell brings up the subject of contingent liabilities.

Required

Write a memorandum to inform Sewell Motor Company of specific contingent liabilities arising from the business. In your discussion, define a contingent liability.

Recording bond transactions (at par) and reporting bonds payable on the balance sheet (Obj. 3)

P8-4A The board of directors of Bluebonnet Properties, Inc., authorizes the issue of $2 million of 8%, 20-year bonds payable. The semiannual interest dates are March 31 and September 30. The bonds are issued through an underwriter on March 31, 20X3, at par.

Required

1. Journalize the following transactions:
   a. Issuance of the bonds on March 31, 20X3.
   b. Payment of interest on September 30, 20X3.
   c. Accrual of interest on December 31, 20X3.
   d. Payment of interest on March 31, 20X4.
2. Report interest payable and bonds payable as they would appear on the Bluebonnet Properties, Inc., balance sheet at December 31, 20X3.

Issuing notes at a premium, amortizing by the straight-line method, and reporting notes payable on the balance sheet (Obj. 3, 6)

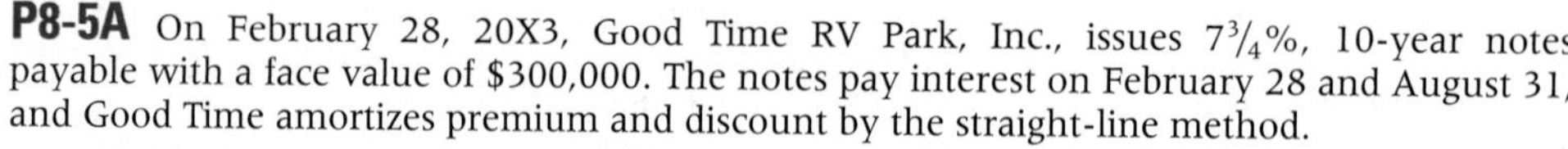

P8-5A On February 28, 20X3, Good Time RV Park, Inc., issues $7\frac{3}{4}$%, 10-year notes payable with a face value of $300,000. The notes pay interest on February 28 and August 31, and Good Time amortizes premium and discount by the straight-line method.

Required

1. If the market interest rate is $8\frac{1}{2}$% when Good Time issues its notes, will the notes be priced at par, at a premium, or at a discount? Explain.
2. If the market interest rate is 7% when Good Time issues its notes, will the notes be priced at par, at a premium, or at a discount? Explain.
3. Assume that the issue price of the notes is 102. Journalize the following note payable transactions:
   a. Issuance of the notes on February 28, 20X3.
   b. Payment of interest and amortization of premium on August 31, 20X3.
   c. Accrual of interest and amortization of premium on December 31, 20X3.
   d. Payment of interest and amortization of premium on February 28, 20X4.

4. Report interest payable and notes payable as they would appear on the Good Time balance sheet at December 31, 20X3.

P8-6A

Accounting for bonds payable at a discount and amortizing by the straight-line method
(Obj. 3)

1. Journalize the following transactions of Satellite Communications, Inc.:

2000	
Jan. 1	Issued $500,000 of 8%, 10-year bonds payable at 94.
July 1	Paid semiannual interest and amortized discount by the straight-line method on our 8% bonds payable.
Dec. 31	Accrued semiannual interest expense and amortized discount by the straight-line method on our 8% bonds payable.
2010	
Jan. 1	Paid the 8% bonds at maturity.

2. At December 31, 2000, after all year-end adjustments, determine the carrying amount of Satellite Communications' bonds payable, net.
3. For the year ended December 31, 2000, determine for Satellite Communications:
   a. Interest expense
   b. Cash interest paid

   What causes interest expense on the bonds to exceed cash interest paid during the year?

P8-7A Assume the notes to the **Homelite Products, Inc.,** financial statements reported the following data on September 30, Year 1 (the end of the fiscal year):

Analyzing a company's long-term debt and reporting the long-term debt on the balance sheet (effective-interest method)
(Obj. 3, 4, 6)

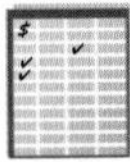

Note E—Long-Term Debt

5% bonds payable, due Year 14, net of discount of $31,645,000 (effective interest rate of 7.50%)	$119,855,000
Notes payable, interest rate of 8.67%, principal due in annual amounts of $26,000,000 in Years 5 through 10	156,000,000

Homelite amortizes discount by the effective-interest method.

Required

1. Answer the following questions about Homelite's long-term liabilities:
   a. What is the maturity value of the 5% bonds?
   b. What are Homelite's annual cash interest payments on the 5% bonds?
   c. What is the carrying amount of the 5% bonds at September 30, Year 1?
2. Prepare an amortization table through September 30, Year 4, for the 5% bonds. Round all amounts to the nearest thousand dollars and assume that Homelite pays interest annually on September 30. How much is Homelite's interest expense on the 5% bonds for the year ended September 30, Year 4?
3. Show how Homelite would report the 5% bonds payable and notes payable at September 30, Year 4.

P8-8A On December 31, 20X1, First Title Insurance Company issues 9%, 10-year convertible bonds with a maturity value of $300,000. The semiannual interest dates are June 30 and December 31. The market interest rate is 8%, and the issue price of the bonds is 106. First Title amortizes bond premium and discount by the effective-interest method.

Issuing convertible bonds at a premium, amortizing by the effective-interest method, retiring bonds early, converting bonds, and reporting the bonds payable on the balance sheet
(Obj. 3, 4, 6)

Required

1. Prepare an effective-interest-method amortization table for the first four semiannual interest periods.
2. Journalize the following transactions:
   a. Issuance of the bonds on December 31, 20X1. Credit Convertible Bonds Payable.
   b. Payment of interest and amortization of premium on June 30, 20X2.
   c. Payment of interest and amortization of premium on December 31, 20X2.
   d. Retirement of bonds with face value of $100,000 on July 1, 20X3. First Title pays the market price of 104.

e. Conversion by the bondholders on July 1, 20X3, of bonds with face value of $100,000 into 10,000 shares of First Titles' $1-par common stock.

3. Show how First Title would report the remaining bonds payable on its balance sheet at December 31, 20X3.

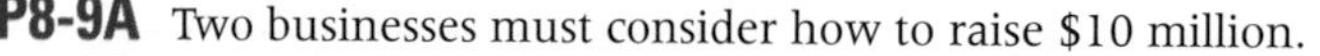

Financing operations with debt or with stock (Obj. 5)

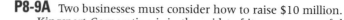

P8-9A Two businesses must consider how to raise $10 million.

Kingsport Corporation is in the midst of its most successful period since it began operations in 1952. For each of the past 10 years, net income and earnings per share have increased by 15%. The outlook for the future is equally bright, with new markets opening up and competitors unable to manufacture products of Kingsport's quality. Kingsport Corporation is planning a large-scale expansion.

Bristol Company has fallen on hard times. Net income has remained flat for five of the last six years, even falling by 10% from last year's level of profits, and cash flow also took a nose dive. Top management has experienced some turnover and has stabilized only recently. To become competitive again, Bristol Company needs $10 million for expansion.

Required

1. Propose a plan for each company to raise the needed cash. Which company should borrow? Which company should issue stock? Consider the advantages and the disadvantages of raising money by borrowing and by issuing stock and discuss them in your answer.
2. How will what you learned in this problem help you manage a business?

Reporting liabilities on the balance sheet (Obj. 6)

P8-10A The accounting records of Bellmead Food Stores, Inc., include the following items at December 31, 20X0:

Premium on bonds payable (all long-term)	$ 13,000	Interest expense	$ 47,000
Interest payable	6,200	Pension plan assets (market value)	402,000
Interest revenue	5,300	Bonds payable, current portion	60,000
Capital lease liability, long-term	73,000	Accumulated depreciation, building	88,000
Accumulated pension benefit obligation	436,000	Mortgage note payable, long term	467,000
Building acquired under capital lease	190,000	Bonds payable, long-term	180,000

Required

1. Show how these items would be reported on Bellmead's classified balance sheet, including headings and totals for current liabilities, long-term liabilities, and so on.
2. Answer the following questions about the financial position of Bellmead Food Stores at December 31, 20X0:
   a. What is the carrying amount of the bonds payable?
   b. During what year will Bellmead make its final payment on the bonds?
   c. Why is the interest payable amount so much less than the amount of interest expense?

(Group B)

Measuring current liabilities (Obj. 1)

P8-1B Following are five pertinent facts about events during the current year at Billboard Advertising, Inc.:

a. On August 31, Billboard signed a six-month, 7% note payable to purchase land costing $80,000. The note requires payment of principal and interest at maturity.

b. On October 31, Billboard received cash of $2,400 in advance for advertisements. This revenue will be earned evenly over six months.

c. December advertising revenue totaled $104,000, and, in addition, Billboard collected sales tax of 6%. This amount will be sent to the state of Alabama early in January.

d. Billboard owes $100,000 on a long-term note payable. At December 31, 6% interest for the year plus $20,000 of this principal are payable within one year.

e. Sales of $909,000 were covered by Billboard's service warranty. At January 1, estimated warranty payable was $11,300. During the year, Billboard recorded warranty expense of $31,100 and paid warranty claims of $28,100.

Required

For each item, indicate the account and the related amount to be reported as a current liability on Billboard Advertising's December 31 balance sheet.

P8-2B The following transactions of Canon Copy Center occurred during 20X2 and 20X3:

Recording liability-related transactions (Obj. 1)

20X2	
Feb. 3	Purchased a machine for $47,000, signing a six-month, 8% note payable.
Apr. 30	Borrowed $100,000 on a 9% note payable that calls for annual installment payments of $25,000 principal plus interest. Record the short-term note payable in a separate account from the long-term note payable.
Aug. 3	Paid the six-month, 8% note at maturity.
Dec. 31	Accrued warranty expense, which is estimated at 2% of sales of $145,000.
31	Accrued interest on the outstanding note payable.
20X3	
Apr. 30	Paid the first installment and interest for one year on the outstanding note payable.

Required

Record the transactions in the company's journal. Explanations are not required.

P8-3B Fox & Hound Stables provides riding lessons for girls ages 8 through 15. Most students are beginners, and none of the girls owns her own horse. K. K. Christy, the owner of Fox & Hound Stables, uses horses stabled at her farm and owned by the Gibneys. Most of the horses are for sale, but the economy has been bad for several years and horse sales have been slow. The Gibneys are happy that Christy uses their horses in exchange for rooming and boarding them. Because of a recent financial setback, Christy cannot afford liability insurance. She seeks your advice about her business's exposure to liabilities.

Identifying contingent liabilities (Obj. 2)

Required

Write a memorandum to inform Christy of specific contingent liabilities arising from the business. It will be necessary to define a contingent liability because she is a professional horse trainer, not a businessperson. Propose a way for Christy to limit her exposure to these liabilities.

P8-4B The board of directors of Digital Communications authorizes the issue of $3 million of 7%, 10-year bonds payable. The semiannual interest dates are May 31 and November 30. The bonds are issued through an underwriter on May 31, 20X0, at par.

Recording bond transactions (at par) and reporting bonds payable on the balance sheet (Obj. 3)

Required

1. Journalize the following transactions:
   a. Issuance of the bonds on May 31, 20X0.
   b. Payment of interest on November 30, 20X0.
   c. Accrual of interest on December 31, 20X0.
   d. Payment of interest on May 31, 20X1.
2. Report interest payable and bonds payable as they would appear on the Digital balance sheet at December 31, 20X0.

P8-5B On February 28, 20X4, Kindler Jewelry Corp. issues $8\frac{1}{2}$%, 20-year bonds payable with a face value of $500,000. The bonds pay interest on February 28 and August 31. Kindler amortizes premium and discount by the straight-line method.

Issuing bonds at a discount, amortizing by the straight-line method, and reporting bonds payable on the balance sheet (Obj. 3, 6)

Required

1. If the market interest rate is $8\frac{7}{8}$% when Kindler issues its bonds, will the bonds be priced at par, at a premium, or at a discount? Explain.
2. If the market interest rate is $7\frac{3}{8}$% when Kindler issues its bonds, will the bonds be priced at par, at a premium, or at a discount? Explain.
3. Assume that the issue price of the bonds is 97. Journalize the following bond transactions:

a. Issuance of the bonds on February 28, 20X4.
b. Payment of interest and amortization of discount on August 31, 20X4.
c. Accrual of interest and amortization of discount on December 31, 20X4.
d. Payment of interest and amortization of discount on February 28, 20X5.

4. Report interest payable and bonds payable as they would appear on the Kindler balance sheet at December 31, 20X4.

Accounting for bonds payable at a discount and amortizing by the straight-line method (Obj. 3)

P8-6B

1. Journalize the following transactions of Outré Cosmetics, Inc.:

2000	
Jan. 1	Issued $1,000,000 of 8%, 10-year bonds payable at 97.
July 1	Paid semiannual interest and amortized discount by the straight-line method on the 8% bonds payable.
Dec. 31	Accrued semiannual interest expense and amortized discount by the straight-line method on the 8% bonds payable.
2010	
Jan. 1	Paid the 8% bonds at maturity.

2. At December 31, 2000, after all year-end adjustments, determine the carrying amount of Outré's bonds payable, net.
3. For the year ended December 31, 2000, determine for Outré Cosmetics:
   a. Interest expense b. Cash interest paid
   What causes interest expense on the bonds to exceed cash interest paid during the year?

Analyzing a company's long-term debt and reporting long-term debt on the balance sheet (effective-interest method) (Obj. 3, 4, 6)

P8-7B The notes to Safelite Auto Glass's financial statements reported the following data on September 30, Year 1 (the end of the fiscal year):

Note 4. Indebtedness

Long-term debt at September 30, Year 1, included the following:	
5.00% bonds payable due Year 21 with an effective interest rate of 9.66%, net of discount of $81,223,000	$118,777,000
Other indebtedness with an interest rate of 8.30%, due $9,300,000 in Year 5 and $19,257,000 in Year 6	28,557,000

Safelite amortizes discount by the effective-interest method.

Required

1. Answer the following questions about Safelite's long-term liabilities:
   a. What is the maturity value of the 5.00% bonds?
   b. What are Safelite's annual cash interest payments on the 5.00% bonds?
   c. What is the carrying amount of the 5.00% bonds at September 30, Year 1?
2. Prepare an amortization table through September 30, Year 4, for the 5.00% bonds. Round all amounts to the nearest thousand dollars and assume that Safelite pays interest annually on September 30. How much is Safelite's interest expense on the 5.00% bonds for the year ended September 30, Year 4? Round interest to the nearest thousand dollars.
3. Show how Safelite would report the bonds payable and other indebtedness at September 30, Year 4.

Issuing convertible bonds at a discount, amortizing by the effective-interest method, retiring bonds early, converting bonds, and reporting the bonds payable on the balance sheet (Obj. 3, 4, 6)

P8-8B On December 31, 20X1, Hill Country Equipment Company issues 8%, 10-year convertible bonds with a maturity value of $500,000. The semiannual interest dates are June 30 and December 31. The market interest rate is 9%, and the issue price of the bonds is 94. Hill Country amortizes bond premium and discount by the effective-interest method.

Required

1. Prepare an effective-interest-method amortization table for the first four semiannual interest periods.
2. Journalize the following transactions:

a. Issuance of the bonds on December 31, 20X1. Credit Convertible Bonds Payable.
b. Payment of interest and amortization of discount on June 30, 20X2.
c. Payment of interest and amortization of discount on December 31, 20X2.
d. Retirement of bonds with face value of $200,000 July 1, 20X3. Hill Country purchases the bonds at 102 in the open market.
e. Conversion by the bondholders on July 1, 20X3, of bonds with face value of $200,000 into 50,000 shares of Hill Country's $1-par common stock.

3. Show how Hill Country would report the remaining bonds payable on its balance sheet at December 31, 20X3.

Financing operations with debt or with stock (Obj. 5)

P8-9B Marketing studies have shown that consumers prefer upscale restaurants, and recent trends in industry sales have supported the research. To capitalize on this trend, **Macaroni Grill, Inc.,** is embarking on a massive expansion. Assume plans call for opening 20 new restaurants during the next two years. Each restaurant is scheduled to be 30% larger than the company's existing locations, furnished more elaborately, and with upgraded menus. Management estimates that company operations will provide $3 million of the cash needed for expansion. Macaroni Grill must raise the remaining $1.5 million from outsiders. The board of directors is considering obtaining the $1.5 million either through borrowing or by issuing common stock.

Required

1. Write a memo to company management discussing the advantages and disadvantages of borrowing and of issuing common stock to raise the needed cash. Which method of raising the funds would you recommend?

2. How will what you learned in this problem help you manage a business?

Reporting liabilities on the balance sheet (Obj. 6)

P8-10B Assume the accounting records of **Watson Electric Co.** include the following items at December 31, 20X5:

Accumulated depreciation, equipment	$ 46,000	Capital lease liability, long-term	$ 81,000
Capital lease liability, current	18,000	Discount on bonds payable (all long-term)	7,000
Mortgage note payable, current	39,000	Interest revenue	5,000
Accumulated pension benefit obligation	419,000	Equipment acquired under capital lease	137,000
Bonds payable, long-term	675,000	Pension plan assets (market value)	382,000
Mortgage note payable, long-term	82,000	Interest payable	9,000
Bonds payable, current portion	75,000	Interest expense	57,000

Required

1. Show how these items would be reported on the Watson Electric Co. classified balance sheet, including headings and totals for current liabilities, long-term liabilities, and so on.

2. Answer the following questions about Watson's financial position at December 31, 20X5:
a. What is the carrying amount of the bonds payable?
b. During what year will Watson make the last payment on the bonds?
c. Why is the interest-payable amount so much less than the amount of interest expense?

EXTENDING YOUR KNOWLEDGE

DECISION CASES

Analyzing alternative ways of raising $5 million (Obj. 5)

Case 1. Business is going well for Dornoch Golf Corporation. The board of directors of this family-owned company believes that Dornoch could earn an additional $1.5 million income before interest and taxes by expanding into new markets. However, the $5 million that the business needs for growth cannot be raised within the family. The directors, who strongly wish to retain family control of the company, must consider issuing securities to outsiders. They are considering three financing plans.

Plan A is to borrow at 6%. Plan B is to issue 100,000 shares of common stock. Plan C is to issue 100,000 shares of nonvoting, \$3.75 preferred stock (\$3.75 is the annual dividend paid on each share of preferred stock).* Dornoch presently has net income of \$4 million and 1 million shares of common stock outstanding. The company's income tax rate is 40%.

Required

1. Prepare an analysis to determine which plan will result in the highest earnings per share of common stock.
2. Recommend one plan to the board of directors. Give your reasons.

Questions about long-term debt (Obj. 3 and Appendix B at end of the book)

Case 2. The following questions are not related:

a. Companies like to borrow for longer terms when interest rates are low and for shorter terms when interest rates are high. Why is this statement true?

b. If you were to win \$2 million from a Canadian lottery, you would receive the \$2 million at once, but if you won \$2 million in a U.S. lottery, you would receive 20 annual payments of \$100,000. Are the prizes equivalent? If not, why not?

c. Why do you think corporations prefer operating leases over capital leases? How do you think a wise shareholder would view an operating lease?

ETHICAL ISSUE 1

The Boeing Company, manufacturer of jet aircraft, was the defendant in numerous lawsuits claiming unfair trade practices. Boeing has strong incentives not to disclose these contingent liabilities. However, GAAP requires that companies report their contingent liabilities.

Required

1. Why would a company prefer not to disclose its contingent liabilities?
2. Describe how a bank could be harmed if a company seeking a loan did not disclose its contingent liabilities.
3. What is the ethical tightrope that companies must walk when they report their contingent liabilities?

ETHICAL ISSUE 2

SolarTech, manufacturer of solar energy panels, borrowed heavily to exploit the advantage of financing operations with debt. At first, SolarTech was able to earn operating income much higher than its interest expense and was therefore quite profitable. However, cheaper energy sources emerged, and SolarTech's debt burden pushed the company to the brink of bankruptcy. Operating income was less than interest expense.

Required

Is it unethical for managers to saddle a company with a high level of debt? Or is it just risky? Who could be hurt by a company's taking on too much debt? Discuss.

FINANCIAL STATEMENT CASES

Long-term debt (Obj. 3, 6)

Case 1. The Gap, Inc., income statement, balance sheet, and statement of cash flows in Appendix A at the end of the book provide details about the company's long-term debt. Use those data to answer the following questions:

1. How much cash did The Gap borrow during the year ended January 30, 1999? What account on the balance sheet shows the effect of the new borrowing? Record the borrowing transaction.
2. How much long-term debt did The Gap pay off during the year ended January 30, 1999?
3. How much long-term debt did The Gap issue during the year ended January 31, 1998? Compare this amount to the balances of long-term debt at January 31, 1998, and at January 30, 1999. What is the most likely explanation for the increases in the balances of long-term debt?
4. The Gap's borrowing agreements require that the company not exceed a certain debt ratio. Compute The Gap's debt ratio at January 30, 1999. Assume the maximum acceptable debt ratio is 60%. Compute the amount of liabilities that The Gap would need to pay off at January 30, 1999, in order to comply with this particular borrowing agreement.

---

*For a discussion of preferred stock, see Chapter 9.

Case 2. Obtain the annual report of a company of your choosing. Answer the following questions about the company. Concentrate on the current year in the annual report you select.

Long-term debt (Obj. 3, 6)

1. Examine the statement of cash flows. How much long-term debt did the company pay off during the current year? How much new long-term debt did the company incur during the year? Journalize these transactions, using the company's actual account balances.
2. Prepare a T-account for the Long-Term Debt account to show the beginning and ending balances and all activity in the account during the year. If there is a discrepancy, insert this amount in the appropriate place. (*Note:* Don't expect to be able to explain all details in real financial statements!)
3. Study the notes to the financial statements. Is any of the company's retained earnings balance restricted as a result of borrowings? If so, indicate the amount of the retained earnings balance that is restricted and the amount that is unrestricted. How will the restriction affect the company's dividend payments in the future?
4. Journalize in a single entry the company's interest expense for the current year. If the company discloses the amount of amortization of premium or discount on long-term debt, use the real figures. If not, assume the amortization of discount totaled $700,000 for the year.

GROUP PROJECTS

Project 1. Consider three different businesses:

1. A bank
2. A magazine publisher
3. A department store

For each business, list all of its liabilities—both current and long-term. Then compare the three lists to identify the liabilities that the three businesses have in common. Also identify the liabilities that are unique to each type of business.

Project 2. Alcenon Corporation leases the majority of the assets that it uses in operations. Alcenon prefers operating leases (versus capital leases) in order to keep the lease liability off its balance sheet and maintain a low debt ratio.

Alcenon is negotiating a 10-year lease on an asset with an expected useful life of 15 years. The lease requires Alcenon to make 10 annual lease payments of $20,000 each, with the first payment due at the beginning of the lease term. The leased asset has a market value of $135,180. The lease agreement specifies no transfer of title to the lessee and includes no bargain purchase option.

Write a report for Alcenon's management to explain what condition must be present for Alcenon to be able to account for this lease as an operating lease.

INTERNET EXERCISE

Boeing

The Boeing Company is the largest manufacturer of commercial jetliners and military aircraft, and the prime contractor for the International Space Station. It is the largest aerospace company in the world and the nation's leading exporter.

1. Go to **http://www.boeing.com** and click on *Investor/Financial*, then *Annual Report*, followed by the large *Next* arrow. At the bottom of the page click on the *Table of Contents* and use the financial statements and the accompanying notes to answer the following questions.
2. At the end of the two most recent years, identify or calculate total current liabilities, total long-term liabilities, and total liabilities. Which financial statement reports this information?
3. For the two most recent years, calculate Boeing's debt ratio (total liabilities / total assets). In regard to Boeing, state what this ratio indicates, the direction of the trend, what the trend might indicate, and whether the trend is favorable or unfavorable.
4. For the two most recent years, list the company's interest expense. Did interest expense increase or decrease? Which financial statement reports this information? What might cause interest expense to change? Does interest expense reflect the contract interest rates specified on bonds or effective interest rates?
5. During the most recent year, how much new borrowing did Boeing do? How much debt did Boeing repay? Was more debt borrowed or repaid? Calculate the amount of difference. This information is reported on which financial statement? for which category of cash-flow activity?
6. Refer to the Note reporting details on Debt. (Note #13 in 1998.) For the two most recent years, list the total amount of debt. Do these amounts agree with the amounts reported on the balance sheet?

9 Stockholders' Equity

Learning Objectives

After studying this chapter, you should be able to

1. Explain the advantages and disadvantages of a corporation
2. Measure the effect of issuing stock on a company's financial position
3. Describe how treasury stock transactions affect a company
4. Account for dividends and measure their impact on a company
5. Use different stock values in decision making
6. Evaluate a company's return on assets and return on stockholders' equity
7. Report stockholders' equity transactions on the statement of cash flows

IHOP Corp.
Consolidated Balance Sheets

	(In thousands, except per share amounts)	December 31, 1998	December 31, 1997
	Assets		
	Current assets		
	Cash and cash equivalents	$ 8,577	$ 5,964
	Receivables	28,461	30,490
	Reacquired franchises and equipment held for sale, net	2,284	2,321
	Inventories	1,222	1,378
	Prepaid expenses	274	629
	Total current assets	40,818	40,782
	Long-term receivables	217,156	171,967
	Property and equipment, net	161,689	142,751
	Reacquired franchises and equipment held for sale, net	12,943	13,151
	Excess of costs over net assets acquired, net	12,054	12,481
	Other assets	1,239	1,461
	Total assets	$445,899	$382,593
	Liabilities and Shareholders' Equity		
	Current liabilities		
	Current maturities of long-term debt	$ 5,386	$ 4,973
	Accounts payable	22,589	20,626
	Accrued employee compensation and benefits	6,017	4,595
	Other accrued expenses	5,309	4,602
	Deferred income taxes	2,560	3,468
	Capital lease obligations	1,388	1,062
	Total current liabilities	43,249	39,326
	Long-term debt	49,765	54,950
	Deferred income taxes	34,708	28,862
	Capital lease obligations and other	130,309	103,271
1	Shareholders' equity		
2	Preferred stock, $1 par value, 10,000,000 shares authorized; issued and outstanding: 1998 and 1997, no shares	—	—
3	Common stock, $.01 par value, 40,000,000 shares authorized; shares issued and outstanding: 1998, 9,881,580 shares (net of 4,620 treasury shares); 1997, 9,709,261 shares (net of 1,539 treasury shares)	99	97
4	Additional paid-in capital (net of treasury shares at cost: 1998, $154; 1997, $39)	60,100	54,629
5	Retained earnings	126,269	100,158
6	Contribution to ESOP	1,400	1,300
7	**Total shareholders' equity**	187,868	156,184
	Total liabilities and shareholders' equity	$445,899	$382,593

See the accompanying notes to the consolidated financial statements.

Based in Glendale, California, **IHOP Corp.** develops, franchises, and operates International House of Pancakes family restaurants. There are over 800 IHOPs in 37 states, Canada, and Japan—with large concentrations of IHOP restaurants in California, New York, New Jersey, Florida, and Texas.

IHOP serves up stacks of great pancakes, and you can buy IHOP stock as well. When IHOP Corp. went public, the company offered 6.2 million shares at $10 each. The shares got off to a strong start and have performed well. IHOP's stock lately has traded at about $25 per share.

6,7,8,9,10,15

What does it mean to "go public," as IHOP did? A corporation *goes public* when it sells its stock to the general public. A common reason for going public is to raise money for expansion. By offering its stock to the public, a company can raise more money than if the stockholders remain a small group. The IHOP Corp. balance sheet (lines 3 and 4) indicates that through the end of 1998, the company had received a little over $60 million (the sum of common stock and additional paid-in capital) from its stockholders.

Chapters 4–8 discussed accounting for the assets and the liabilities of a company. By this time, you should be familiar with all the assets and liabilities listed on IHOP's balance sheet. Let's focus now on the last part of the balance sheet—IHOP's stockholders' equity, which the company labels as *shareholders' equity*. In this chapter, we discuss the elements of stockholders' equity in detail. First, however, let's review what a corporation is and how it is organized.

CORPORATIONS: AN OVERVIEW

Objective 1
Explain the advantages and disadvantages of a corporation

The corporation is the dominant form of business organization in the United States. **IHOP** is an example. Proprietorships and partnerships are more numerous, but corporations transact more business and are larger in terms of total assets and sales revenue. Most well-known companies, such as **IHOP, CBS, The Gap,** and **IBM,** are corporations. Their full names may include *Corporation* or *Incorporated* (abbreviated *Corp.* and *Inc.*) to indicate that they are corporations—for example, CBS, Inc., and IHOP Corp.

Characteristics of a Corporation

Why is the corporate form of business so attractive? We now examine the key ways in which corporations differ from proprietorships and partnerships, as well as some of the advantages and disadvantages of corporations.

SEPARATE LEGAL ENTITY. A corporation is a business entity formed under state law. The state grants a **charter,** which is a document that gives a business the state's permission to form a corporation. Neither a proprietorship nor a partnership requires state approval to do business, because in the eyes of the law the business is the same as the owner(s).

From a legal perspective, a corporation is a distinct entity, an artificial person that exists apart from its owners, who are called **stockholders** or **shareholders.** The corporation has many of the rights that a person has. For example, a corporation may buy, own, and sell property. Assets and liabilities in the business belong to the corporation rather than to its owners. The corporation may enter into contracts, sue, and be sued.

The owners' equity of a corporation is divided into shares of **stock.** The corporate charter specifies how much stock the corporation can issue (sell).

CONTINUOUS LIFE AND TRANSFERABILITY OF OWNERSHIP. Most corporations have *continuous lives* regardless of changes in the ownership of their stock. The stockholders of IHOP or any corporation may transfer stock as they wish. They may sell or trade the stock to another person, give it away, bequeath it in a will, or dispose of it in any other way. The transfer of the stock does not affect the continuity of the corporation. In contrast, proprietorships and partnerships terminate when ownership changes.

NO MUTUAL AGENCY. *Mutual agency* is an arrangement whereby all owners act as agents of the business. A contract signed by one owner is binding for the whole company. Mutual agency operates in partnerships but *not* in corporations. A stockholder of IHOP Corp. cannot commit the corporation to a contract (unless he or she is also an officer in the business).

LIMITED LIABILITY OF STOCKHOLDERS. Stockholders have **limited liability** for corporation debts. That is, they have no personal obligation for corporation liabilities. The most that a stockholder can lose on an investment in a corporation's stock is the cost of the investment. In contrast, proprietors and partners are personally liable for all the debts of their businesses. This feature enables corporations to raise more capital from a wider group of investors than proprietorships and partnerships can.

SEPARATION OF OWNERSHIP AND MANAGEMENT. Stockholders own the corporation, but a *board of directors*—elected by the stockholders—appoints officers to manage the business. Thus, stockholders may invest $1,000 or $1 million in the corporation without having to manage the business or disrupt their personal affairs.

Management's goal is to maximize the firm's value for the stockholders' benefit. However, the separation between owners—stockholders—and management may create problems. Corporate officers may decide to run the business for their own benefit and not to the stockholders' advantage. Accounting provides information to help the stockholders evaluate their managers' performance.

CORPORATE TAXATION. Corporations are separate taxable entities. They pay a variety of taxes not borne by proprietorships or partnerships, including an annual franchise tax levied by the state. The franchise tax is paid to keep the corporate charter in force and enables the corporation to continue in business. Corporations also pay federal and state income taxes.

Corporate earnings are subject to **double taxation** of their income. First, corporations pay income taxes on their corporate income. Then, stockholders pay personal income tax on the cash dividends that they receive from corporations. Proprietorships and partnerships pay no business income tax. Instead, the tax falls solely on the owners.

GOVERNMENT REGULATION. Because stockholders have only limited liability for corporation debts, outsiders doing business with the corporation can look no further than the corporation for any claims that may arise against the business. To protect the creditors and the stockholders of a corporation, both federal and state governments monitor the affairs of corporations. This *government regulation* consists mainly of ensuring that corporations disclose the information that investors and creditors need to make informed decisions.

Exhibit 9-1 summarizes the advantages and disadvantages of the corporate form of business organization.

Organization of a Corporation

The process of creating a corporation begins when its organizers, called the **incorporators,** obtain a charter from the state. The charter includes the authorization

EXHIBIT 9-1
Advantages and Disadvantages of a Corporation

Advantages	*Disadvantages*
1. Can raise more capital than a proprietorship or partnership can	1. Separation of ownership and management
2. Continuous life	2. Corporate taxation
3. Ease of transferring ownership	3. Government regulation
4. No mutual agency of stockholders	
5. Limited liability of stockholders	

for the corporation to issue a certain number of shares of stock. The incorporators pay fees, sign the charter, and file required documents with the state. The corporation then comes into existence. The incorporators agree to a set of **bylaws,** which act as the constitution for governing the corporation.

The ultimate control of the corporation rests with the stockholders. The stockholders elect the members of the **board of directors,** which sets policy for the corporation and appoints the officers. The board elects a **chairperson,** who usually is the most powerful person in the corporation. The board also designates the **president,** who is the chief operating officer in charge of day-to-day operations. Most corporations also have vice presidents in charge of sales, manufacturing, accounting and finance, and other key areas. Exhibit 9-2 shows the authority structure in a corporation.

EXHIBIT 9-2
Authority Structure in a Corporation

CHECK POINT 9-1

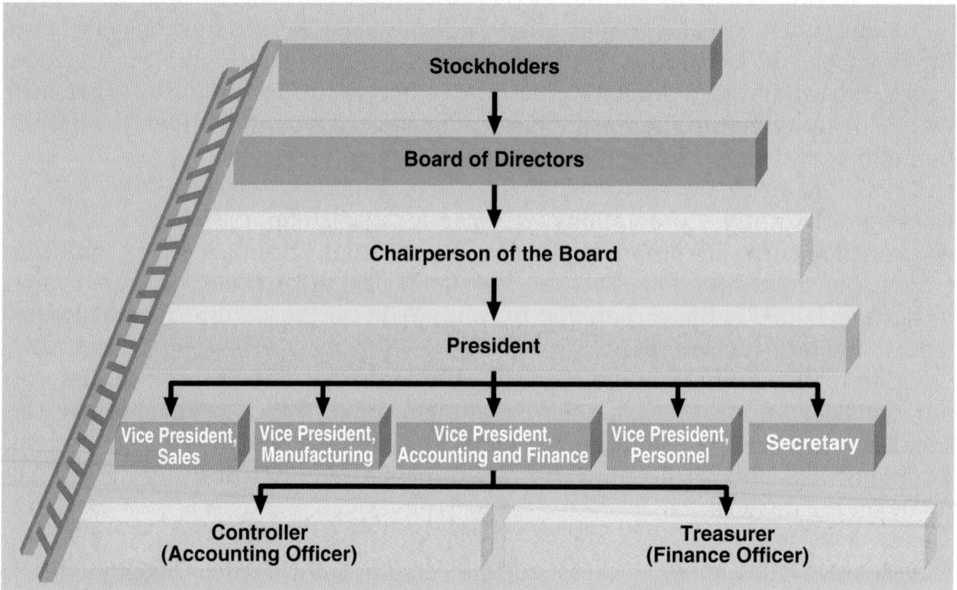

Stockholders' Rights

The ownership of stock entitles stockholders to four basic rights, unless specific rights are withheld by agreement with the stockholders:

1. *Vote.* The right to participate in management by voting on matters that come before the stockholders. This is the stockholder's sole right to a voice in the management of the corporation. A stockholder is entitled to one vote for each share of stock owned.
2. *Dividends.* The right to receive a proportionate part of any dividend. Each share of stock in a particular class receives an equal dividend.
3. *Liquidation.* The right to receive a proportionate share (based on number of shares held) of any assets remaining after the corporation pays its liabilities in liquidation. *Liquidation* means to go out of business, sell the entity's assets, pay its liabilities, and distribute any remaining cash to the owners.
4. *Preemption.* The right to maintain one's proportionate ownership in the corporation. Suppose you own 5% of a corporation's stock. If the corporation issues 100,000 new shares of stock, it must offer you the opportunity to buy 5% (5,000) of the new shares. This right, called the *preemptive right,* is usually withheld from the stockholders.

Stockholders' Equity: Paid-In Capital and Retained Earnings

As we saw in Chapter 1, **stockholders' equity** represents the stockholders' ownership interest in the assets of a corporation. Stockholders' equity is divided into two main parts:

1. **Paid-in capital,** also called **contributed capital,** is the amount of stockholders' equity that the stockholders have contributed to the corporation. Paid-in capital includes the stock accounts and any additional paid-in capital.
2. **Retained earnings** is the amount of stockholders' equity that the corporation has earned through profitable operations and has not given back to the stockholders—hence the term *retained* earnings.

Companies report each element of their stockholders' equity by source. They report paid-in capital separately from retained earnings because most states have laws prohibiting the declaration of cash dividends from paid-in capital. This means that cash dividends are declared from retained earnings, not from paid-in capital.

Capital Stock. A corporation issues *stock certificates* to its owners in exchange for their investments in the business. Because stock represents the corporation's capital, it is often called *capital stock.* The basic unit of capital stock is called a *share.* A corporation may issue a stock certificate for any number of shares it wishes—one share, 100 shares, or any other number—but the total number of *authorized* shares is limited by charter. Exhibit 9-3 depicts an actual stock certificate for 288 shares of **Central Jersey Bancorp** common stock. The certificate shows the company name, the stockholder name, the number of shares, and the par value of the stock (discussed later in this chapter).

Stock in the hands of a stockholder is said to be **outstanding.** The total number of shares of stock outstanding at any time represents 100% ownership of the corporation.

Exhibit 9-3
Stock Certificate

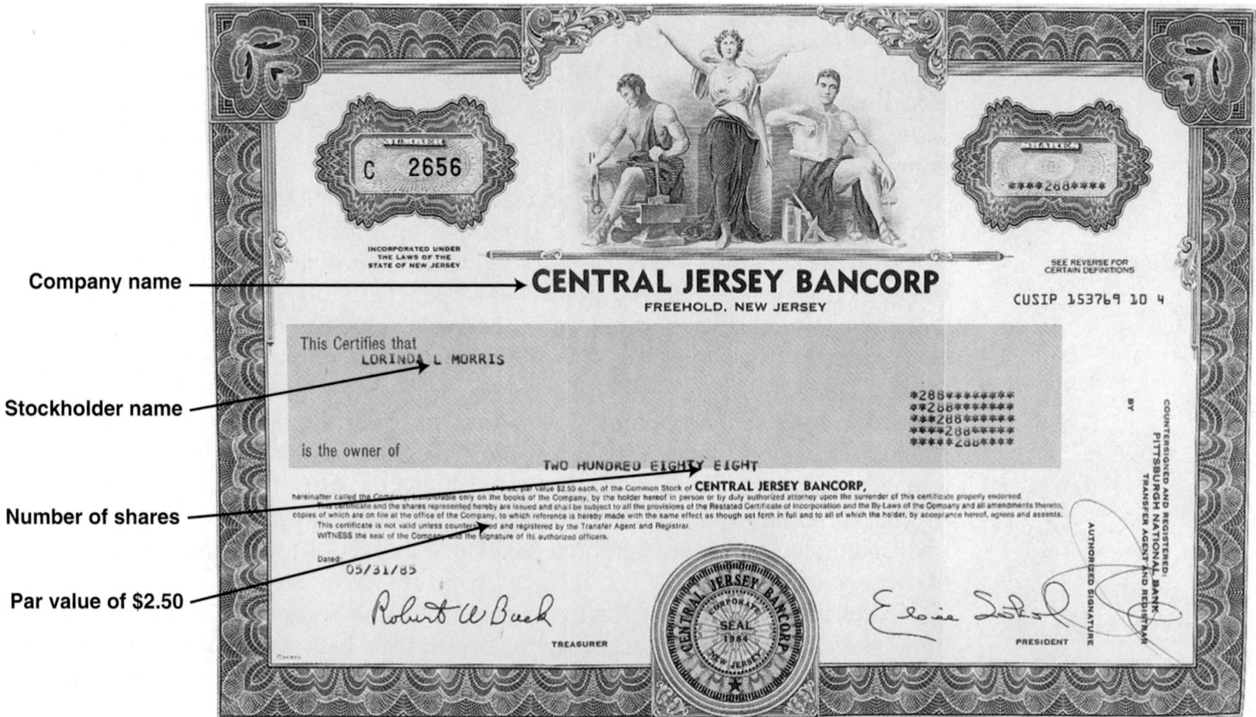

CLASSES OF STOCK

Corporations issue different types of stock to appeal to a variety of investors. The stock of a corporation may be either

- Common or preferred
- Par or no-par

Common and Preferred Stock

Every corporation issues **common stock,** the most basic form of capital stock. Unless designated otherwise, the word *stock* is understood to mean "common stock." Common stockholders have the four basic rights of stock ownership, unless a right is specifically withheld. For example, some companies issue Class A common stock, which usually carries the right to vote, and Class B common stock, which may be nonvoting. In describing a corporation, we would say the common stockholders are the owners of the business.

Investors who buy common stock take the ultimate risk with a corporation. If the corporation succeeds, it will pay dividends to its stockholders, but if net income and cash are too low, the stockholders may receive no dividends. The stock of successful corporations increases in value, and investors enjoy the benefit of selling the stock at a gain. But stock prices can decrease, leaving the investors holding worthless stock certificates. Because common stockholders take a risky investment position, they usually demand increases in stock prices or high dividends. If the corporation does not deliver, the stockholders sell the stock, and its market price falls. Short of bankruptcy, this is one of the worst things that can happen to a corporation because it means that the company cannot raise capital as needed.

Preferred stock gives its owners certain advantages over common stockholders. Preferred stockholders receive dividends before the common stockholders and receive assets before the common stockholders if the corporation liquidates. Some preferred stock is convertible into common stock. If the market price of the common goes high enough, the preferred stockholders turn in their preferred stock and receive common stock from the company.

Owners of preferred stock also have the four basic stockholder rights, unless a right is specifically denied. Often, the right to vote is withheld from preferred stockholders. Companies may issue different classes of preferred stock (Class A and Class B or Series A and Series B, for example). Each class is recorded in a separate account.

CHECK POINT 9-2

Investors who buy preferred stock take less risk than common stockholders do. Why? Because corporations pay a fixed amount of dividends on preferred stock. Investors usually buy preferred stock to earn those dividends. A large increase in the market value of preferred stock is less likely than a large increase in the market value of common stock because preferred-stock values do not fluctuate much.

Preferred stock operates as a hybrid between common stock and long-term debt. Like debt, preferred stock pays a fixed dividend amount to the investor. But like stock, the dividend becomes a liability only after the board of directors has declared the dividend. Also, companies must repay their debt but have no obligation to pay back true preferred stock. Preferred stock that must be redeemed (paid back) by the corporation is a liability masquerading as a stock. Experienced investors treat mandatorily redeemable preferred stock as part of total liabilities, not as part of owners' equity.

EXHIBIT 9-4
Preferred Stock

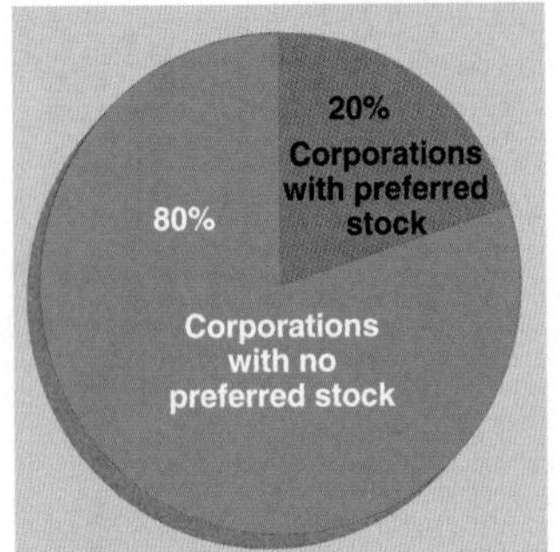

Preferred stock is rarer than you might think. A recent survey of 600 corporations revealed that only 120 of them (only 20%) had some preferred stock outstanding (Exhibit 9-4). All corporations have common stock. The balance sheet of **IHOP Corp.** (page 407) shows that IHOP is authorized to issue preferred stock. To date, however, IHOP has issued none of the preferred stock.

Preferred stock is unpopular mainly because dividend payments are not tax-deductible. **Dividends** are a distribution of assets created by earnings. Dividends are *not* an expense. If companies are going to commit to pay a fixed amount (of preferred dividends) each year, they want a tax deduction for the payment. Therefore, most companies would rather borrow money and get a tax deduction for the interest expense. Exhibit 9-5 summarizes the similarities and differences among common stock, preferred stock, and long-term debt.

EXHIBIT 9-5
Comparison of Common Stock, Preferred Stock, and Long-Term Debt

	Common Stock	*Preferred Stock*	*Long-Term Debt*
Investment risk	High	Medium	Low
Corporate obligation to repay principal	No	No	Yes
Dividends/interest	Dividends	Dividends not tax-deductible	Tax-deductible interest expense
Corporate obligation to pay dividends/interest	Only after declaration	Only after declaration	At fixed dates
Fluctuations in market value	High	Medium	Low

Par Value and No-Par Stock

Stock may be par value stock or no-par stock. **Par value** is an arbitrary amount assigned by a company to a share of its stock. Most companies set the par value of their common stock quite low to avoid legal difficulties from issuing their stock below par. Most states require companies to maintain a minimum amount of stockholders' equity for the protection of creditors, and this minimum is often called the corporation's legal capital. For corporations with par value stock, **legal capital** is the par value of the shares issued.

The common stock par value of **Coca-Cola Company** is $0.25 per share. **Hawaiian Airlines** common stock carries a par value of $0.01 per share, and **Pier 1 Imports** common stock par value is $1 per share. Par value of preferred stock is sometimes higher; $100 per share is typical, but some preferred stocks have par values of $25 and $10. As we shall see, par value is used to compute dividends on preferred stock.

No-par stock does not have par value. **Sara Lee Corporation** has 2,000 shares of preferred stock issued and outstanding with no par value. But some no-par stock has a **stated value,** which makes it similar to par-value stock. The stated value is an arbitrary amount similar to par value.

ISSUING STOCK

Objective 2
Measure the effect of issuing stock on a company's financial position

Large corporations such as **Coca-Cola, IHOP,** and **Microsoft** need huge quantities of money to operate. They cannot expect to finance all their operations through borrowing. They need capital that they raise by issuing stock. The charter that the incorporators receive from the state includes an **authorization of stock**—that is, a provision giving the state's permission for the business to issue (to sell) a certain number of shares of stock. Corporations may sell the stock directly to the stockholders or use the service of an *underwriter,* such as the brokerage firms **Merrill Lynch** and **Dean Witter.** An underwriter agrees to buy all the stock it cannot sell to its clients.

The corporation need not issue all the stock that the state authorizes. Management may hold some stock back and issue it later if the need for additional capital arises. The stock that the corporation issues to stockholders is called *issued stock.* Only by issuing stock—not by receiving authorization—does the corporation increase the asset and stockholders' equity amounts on its balance sheet.

The price that the stockholder pays to acquire stock from the corporation is called the *issue price.* Often, the issue price far exceeds the stock's par value because the par value was intentionally set quite low. For example, IHOP's common stock has a par value of $0.01 per share.

A combination of market factors—including the company's earnings record, financial position, and prospects for success—determines issue price. Investors will not pay more than market value for the stock. In the following sections, we show how companies account for the issuance of stock.

Issuing Common Stock

Companies often advertise the issuance of their stock to attract investors. The *Wall Street Journal* is the most popular medium for such advertisements, which are also called *tombstones.* Exhibit 9-6 is a reproduction of **IHOP's** tombstone, which appeared in the *Wall Street Journal.*

The lead underwriter of IHOP's public offering was **The First Boston Corporation.** Several other domestic brokerage firms and investment bankers sold IHOP stock to their clients. Altogether, IHOP hoped to raise approximately $62 million of capital. As it turned out, IHOP issued only 3.2 million shares at $10 per share and received cash of approximately $32 million.

ISSUING COMMON STOCK AT PAR. Suppose IHOP's common stock carried a par value of $10 per share. The entry for issuance of 3.2 million shares of stock at par would be

Jan. 8	Cash (3,200,000 × $10)	32,000,000	
	Common Stock		32,000,000
	To issue common stock at par.		

IHOP's assets and stockholders' equity increase by the same amount.

ASSETS	=	LIABILITIES	+	STOCKHOLDERS' EQUITY
32,000,000	=	0	+	32,000,000

The amount invested in the corporation, $32 million in this case, is paid-in capital of IHOP Corp.

ISSUING COMMON STOCK AT A PRICE ABOVE PAR. Many corporations set par value at a low amount, then issue common stock for a price above par value. The amount above par is called a *premium.* IHOP's common stock has a par value of $0.01 (1 cent) per share. The $9.99 difference between issue price ($10) and par value ($0.01) is additional paid-in capital. Both the par value of the stock and the additional amount are part of paid-in capital.

CHECK POINT 9-3

Because the entity is dealing with its own stockholders, a premium on the sale of stock is not gain, income, or profit to the corporation. This situation illustrates one of the fundamentals of accounting: *A company neither earns a profit nor incurs a loss when it sells its stock to, or buys its stock from, its own stockholders.*

With a par value of $0.01, IHOP's entry to record the issuance of the stock is

July 23	Cash (3,200,000 × $10)	32,000,000	
	Common Stock (3,200,000 × $0.01)		32,000
	Paid-in Capital in Excess of Par—Common (3,200,000 × $9.99)		31,968,000
	To issue common stock at a premium.		

(entry continued on page 416)

EXHIBIT 9-6
Announcement of Public Offering of IHOP Stock

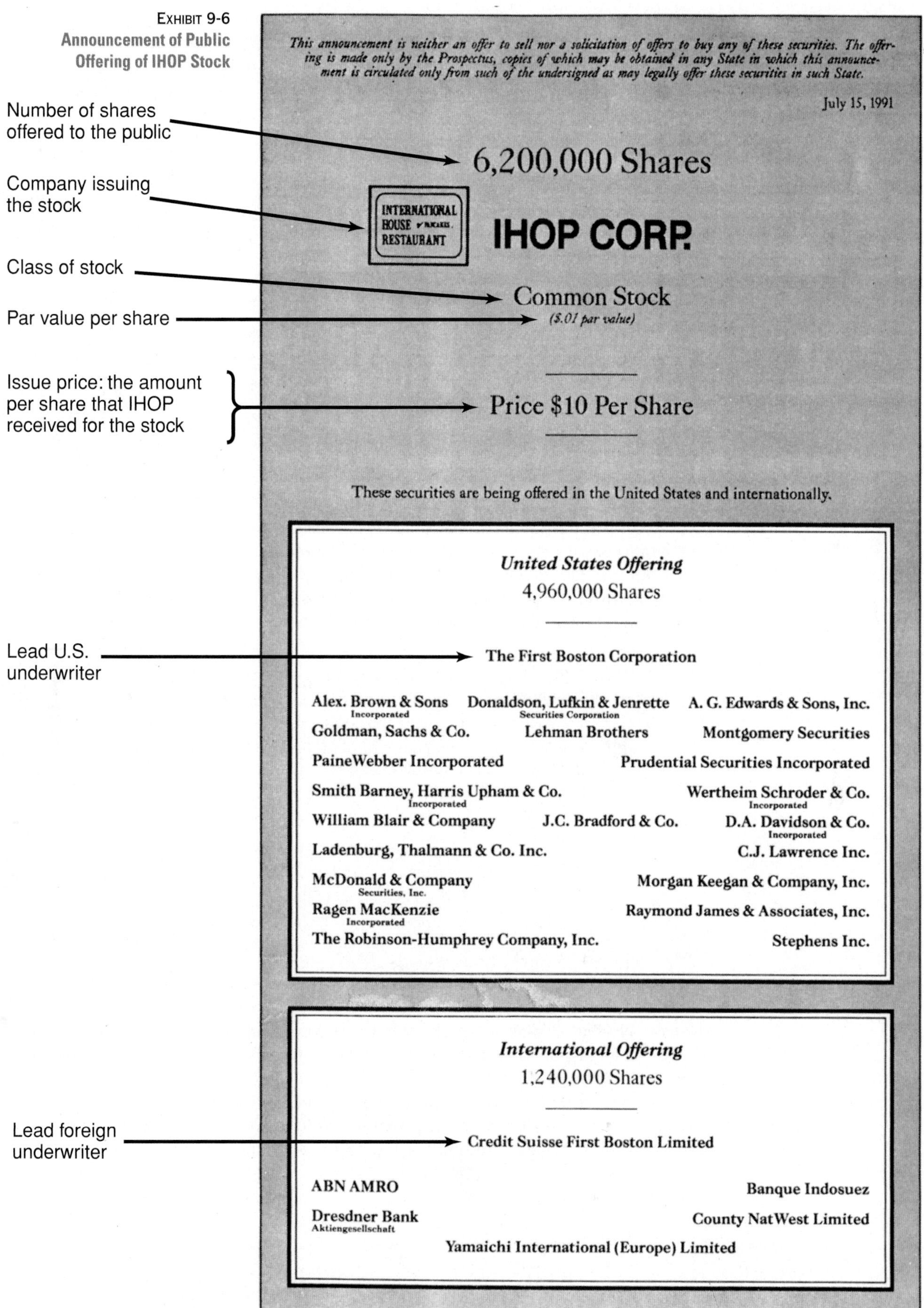

This announcement is neither an offer to sell nor a solicitation of offers to buy any of these securities. The offering is made only by the Prospectus, copies of which may be obtained in any State in which this announcement is circulated only from such of the undersigned as may legally offer these securities in such State.

July 15, 1991

6,200,000 Shares

INTERNATIONAL HOUSE of PANCAKES RESTAURANT

IHOP CORP.

Common Stock

($.01 par value)

Price $10 Per Share

These securities are being offered in the United States and internationally.

United States Offering

4,960,000 Shares

The First Boston Corporation

Alex. Brown & Sons Incorporated — Donaldson, Lufkin & Jenrette Securities Corporation — A. G. Edwards & Sons, Inc.

Goldman, Sachs & Co. — Lehman Brothers — Montgomery Securities

PaineWebber Incorporated — Prudential Securities Incorporated

Smith Barney, Harris Upham & Co. Incorporated — Wertheim Schroder & Co. Incorporated

William Blair & Company — J.C. Bradford & Co. — D.A. Davidson & Co. Incorporated

Ladenburg, Thalmann & Co. Inc. — C.J. Lawrence Inc.

McDonald & Company Securities, Inc. — Morgan Keegan & Company, Inc.

Ragen MacKenzie Incorporated — Raymond James & Associates, Inc.

The Robinson-Humphrey Company, Inc. — Stephens Inc.

International Offering

1,240,000 Shares

Credit Suisse First Boston Limited

ABN AMRO — Banque Indosuez

Dresdner Bank Aktiengesellschaft — County NatWest Limited

Yamaichi International (Europe) Limited

ASSETS	=	LIABILITIES	+	STOCKHOLDERS' EQUITY
32,000,000	=	0	+	+32,000
				+31,968,000

Another title for Paid-in Capital in Excess of Par—Common is Additional Paid-in Capital—Common. Since both par value and premium amounts increase the corporation's capital, they appear in the stockholders' equity section of the balance sheet.

At the end of the year, IHOP Corp. would report stockholders' equity on its balance sheet as follows, assuming that the corporate charter authorizes 40,000,000 shares of common stock and the balance of retained earnings is $26,000,000:

CHECK POINT 9-4

Stockholders' Equity	
Common stock, $0.01 par, 40 million shares authorized, 3.2 million shares issued	$ 32,000
Paid-in capital in excess of par	31,968,000
Total paid-in capital	32,000,000
Retained earnings	26,000,000
Total stockholders' equity	$58,000,000

All of the transactions recorded in this section include a receipt of cash by the corporation as it issues new stock to its stockholders. These transactions are different from the vast majority of stock transactions reported each day in the financial press. In those transactions, one stockholder sells his or her stock to another investor, and the corporation makes no journal entry.

Examine IHOP's balance sheet at December 31, 1998, given at the beginning of the chapter (page 407). Answer these questions:

1. What was IHOP's total paid-in capital at December 31, 1998?
2. What is the total amount of profits that IHOP has retained for use in the business through the end of 1998?
3. What is the fundamental difference between paid-in capital and retained earnings?

Answers:

1. Total paid-in capital: $60,199,000 ($99,000 + $60,100,000).
2. Retained earnings: $126,269,000.
3. Paid-in capital comes from stockholders' investments in the company. Retained earnings come from profits that the company has earned from customers.

ISSUING NO-PAR COMMON STOCK. When a company issues stock that has no par value, there can be no premium. A recent survey of 600 companies revealed that they had 67 issues of no-par stock.

When a company issues no-par stock, it debits the asset received and credits the stock account. Glenwood Corporation, which manufactures skateboards, issues 3,000 shares of no-par common stock for $20 per share. The stock issuance entry is

Aug. 14	Cash (3,000 × $20)	60,000	
	Common Stock		60,000
	To issue no-par common stock.		

ASSETS	=	LIABILITIES	+	STOCKHOLDERS' EQUITY
60,000	=	0	+	60,000

Regardless of the stock's price, Cash is debited and Common Stock is credited for the amount of cash received. There is no Paid-in Capital in Excess of Par for true no-par stock.

Glenwood Corporation's charter authorizes Glenwood to issue 10,000 shares of no-par stock, and the company has $46,000 in retained earnings. The corporation reports stockholders' equity on the balance sheet as follows:

Stockholders' Equity	
Common stock, no par, 10,000 shares authorized, 3,000 shares issued	$ 60,000
Retained earnings	46,000
Total stockholders' equity	$106,000

ISSUING NO-PAR COMMON STOCK WITH A STATED VALUE. Accounting for no-par stock with a stated value is identical to accounting for par value stock. The premium account for no-par common stock with a stated value is entitled Paid-in Capital in Excess of Stated Value—Common.

ISSUING COMMON STOCK FOR ASSETS OTHER THAN CASH. When a corporation issues stock in exchange for assets other than cash, it records the assets received at their current market value and credits the capital accounts accordingly. The assets' prior book value does not matter because the stockholder will demand stock equal to the market value of the asset given. Kahn Corporation issued 15,000 shares of its $1 par common stock for equipment worth $4,000 and a building worth $120,000. Kahn's entry is

CHECK POINT 9-5

Nov. 12	Equipment	4,000	
	Building	120,000	
	Common Stock (15,000 × $1)		15,000
	Paid-in Capital in Excess of Par—Common ($124,000 − $15,000)		109,000
	To issue common stock in exchange for equipment and a building.		

ASSETS	=	LIABILITIES	+	STOCKHOLDERS' EQUITY
+4,000 +120,000	=	0	+	+15,000 +109,000

How did this transaction affect Kahn Corporation's cash? Total assets? Paid-in capital? Retained earnings? Total stockholders' equity?

Answer:

	Cash	*Total Assets*	*Paid-in Capital*	*Retained Earnings*	*Total Stockholders' Equity*
Effect:	None	Increase $124,000	Increase $124,000	None	Increase $124,000

Issuing Preferred Stock

Accounting for preferred stock follows the pattern we illustrated for common stock. The charter of Brown-Forman Corporation, a distilling company, authorizes issuance of 1,177,948 shares of 4%, $10 par preferred stock. [The 4% refers to the annual cash dividend rate on the stock. Each Brown-Forman preferred stockholder receives an annual cash dividend of $0.40 ($10 par × .04). Note that the dividend is paid on the *par value*.] Assume that on July 31 the company issued all the shares at a price equal to the par value. The issuance entry is

July 31	Cash	11,779,480	
	Preferred Stock (1,177,948 × $10)		11,779,480
	To issue preferred stock at par.		

ASSETS	=	LIABILITIES	+	STOCKHOLDERS' EQUITY
11,779,480	=	0	+	11,779,480

If Brown-Forman had issued the preferred stock at a premium, the entry would have also credited an account titled Paid-in Capital in Excess of Par—Preferred. A corporation lists separate accounts for Paid-in Capital in Excess of Par on Preferred Stock and on Common Stock to differentiate the two classes of equity.

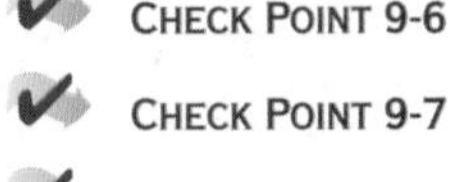

CHECK POINT 9-6

CHECK POINT 9-7

CHECK POINT 9-8

Accounting for no-par preferred stock follows the pattern we illustrated for no-par common stock. When reporting stockholders' equity on the balance sheet, a corporation lists preferred stock, common stock, and retained earnings—in that order.

ETHICAL CONSIDERATIONS IN ACCOUNTING FOR THE ISSUANCE OF STOCK

Issuance of stock for *cash* poses no serious ethical challenge. The company simply receives cash and issues the stock to the shareholders, giving them stock certificates as evidence of their purchase.

However, issuing stock for assets other than cash can pose an ethical challenge. The company issuing the stock often wishes to record a large amount for the noncash asset received (such as land or a building) and for the stock that it is issuing. Why? Because large asset and stockholders' equity amounts on the balance sheet make the business look more prosperous and more creditworthy. The motivation to look good can inject a subtle bias into the amount recorded for stock issued in return for assets other than cash.

As we discussed on page 417, a company is supposed to record an asset received at its current market value. But one person's perception of a particular asset's market value can differ from another person's perception. One person may appraise land at a market value of $400,000. Another may honestly believe the land is worth only $300,000. A company receiving land in exchange for its stock must decide whether to record the land received and the stock issued at $300,000, at $400,000, or at some amount in between.

The ethical course of action is to record the asset at its current fair market value, as determined by a good-faith estimate of market value from independent appraisers. It is rare for a public corporation to be found guilty of *understating* the asset values on its balance sheet, but companies have been embarrassed by *overstating* their asset values. Investors who rely on the financial statements may be able to prove that an overstatement of asset values caused them to pay too much for the company's stock. In this case, a court of law may render a judgment against the company. For this reason, companies often tend to value assets conservatively in order to avoid overstatement of book value.

Mid-Chapter

Summary Problems for Your Review

1. Test your understanding of the first half of this chapter by deciding whether each of the following statements is true or false.
   a. A stockholder may bind the corporation to a contract.
   b. The policy-making body in a corporation is called the board of directors.
   c. The owner of 100 shares of preferred stock has greater voting rights than the owner of 100 shares of common stock.
   d. Par value stock is worth more than no-par stock.
   e. Issuance of 1,000 shares of $5 par value stock at $12 increases contributed capital by $12,000.
   f. The issuance of no-par stock with a stated value is fundamentally different from issuing par value stock.
   g. A corporation issues its preferred stock in exchange for land and a building with a combined market value of $200,000. This transaction increases the corporation's owners' equity by $200,000 regardless of the assets' prior book values.
   h. Preferred stock is a riskier investment than common stock.
2. The brewery **Adolph Coors Company** has two classes of common stock. Only the Class A common stockholders are entitled to vote. The company's balance sheet included the following presentation:

Stockholders' Equity	
Capital stock	
Class A common stock, voting, $1 par value,	
authorized and issued 1,260,000 shares	$ 1,260,000
Class B common stock, nonvoting, no par value,	
authorized and issued 46,200,000 shares	11,000,000
	12,260,000
Additional paid-in capital	2,011,000
Retained earnings	872,403,000
	$886,674,000

Required

a. Record the issuance of the Class A common stock. Use the Coors account titles.
b. Record the issuance of the Class B common stock. Use the Coors account titles.
c. How much of Coors's stockholders' equity was contributed by the stockholders? How much was provided by profitable operations? Does this division of equity suggest that the company has been successful? Why or why not?
d. Write a sentence to describe what Coors's stockholders' equity means.

Answers

1. a. False **b.** True **c.** False **d.** False **e.** True **f.** False **g.** True **h.** False

2. a.

Cash	3,271,000	
Class A Common Stock		1,260,000
Additional Paid-in Capital		2,011,000
To record issuance of Class A common stock.		

b.

Cash	11,000,000	
Class B Common Stock		11,000,000
To record issuance of Class B common stock.		

c. Contributed by the stockholders: $14,271,000 ($12,260,000 + $2,011,000).
Provided by profitable operations: $872,403,000.
This division suggests that the company has been very successful because most of its stockholders' equity has come from profitable operations.

d. Coors's stockholders' equity of $886,674,000 means that the company's stockholders own $886,674,000 of the business's assets.

TREASURY STOCK

Objective 3
Describe how treasury stock transactions affect a company

A company's own stock that it has issued and later reacquired is called **treasury stock.**[1] In effect, the corporation holds the stock in its treasury. Corporations may purchase their own stock for several reasons:

1. The company has issued all its authorized stock and needs the stock for distributions to employees under stock purchase plans.
2. The purchase helps support the stock's market price by decreasing the supply of stock available to the public.
3. The business is trying to increase net assets by buying its shares low and hoping to sell them for a higher price later.
4. Management wants to avoid a takeover by an outside party.

The purchase of treasury stock decreases the company's assets and its stockholders' equity. The size of the company literally decreases, as shown on its balance sheet. Frames 1 and 2 of Exhibit 9-7, page 422, provide an illustration for **Eastman Kodak Company.** In frame 2, Eastman Kodak is smaller after having purchased $4 billion of treasury stock.

Purchase of Treasury Stock

We record the purchase of treasury stock by debiting Treasury Stock and crediting the asset given in exchange—usually Cash. Suppose that Jupiter Drilling Company had the following stockholders' equity before purchasing treasury stock:

Stockholders' Equity [Before Purchase of Treasury Stock]

Common stock, $1 par, 10,000 shares authorized, 8,000 shares issued	$ 8,000
Paid-in capital in excess of par—common	12,000
Retained earnings	14,600
Total stockholders' equity	$34,600

On November 22, Jupiter purchases 1,000 shares of its $1 par common as treasury stock, paying cash of $7.50 per share. Jupiter records the purchase of treasury stock as follows:

[1]In this text, we illustrate the *cost* method of accounting for treasury stock because it is used most widely. Other methods are presented in intermediate accounting courses.

Nov. 22	Treasury Stock, Common (1,000 × $7.50)	7,500	
	Cash		7,500
	Purchased 1,000 shares of treasury stock at $7.50 per share.		

The Treasury Stock account has a debit balance, which is the opposite of the other owners' equity accounts. Therefore, *Treasury Stock is a contra stockholders' equity account.* Treasury stock is recorded at cost, without reference to the stock's par value. The Treasury Stock account is often reported beneath Retained Earnings on the balance sheet. Treasury Stock's balance is subtracted from the sum of total paid-in capital and retained earnings, as follows:

***Stockholders' Equity* [After *Purchase of Treasury Stock*]**	
Common stock, $1 par, 10,000 shares authorized, 8,000 shares issued, 7,000 shares outstanding	$ 8,000
Paid-in capital in excess of par—common	12,000
Retained earnings	14,600
Subtotal	34,600
Less treasury stock, 1,000 shares at cost	(7,500)
Total stockholders' equity	$27,100

CHECK POINT 9-9

Total stockholders' equity decreases by the cost of the treasury stock. Also, shares of stock *outstanding* decrease. The number of *outstanding* shares, is computed as follows:

Number of shares of stock *issued*	8,000
Less Number of shares of treasury stock held	(1,000)
Number of shares of stock *outstanding*	7,000

Although the number of *outstanding shares* is not required to be reported on the balance sheet, this figure is important. Only outstanding shares have voting rights, receive cash dividends, and share in assets if the corporation liquidates.

Ethical Issue:

Treasury stock transactions have a serious ethical and legal dimension. A company such as **PENTAX** buying its own shares as treasury stock must be extremely careful that its disclosures of information are complete and accurate. Otherwise, a PENTAX stockholder who sold shares back to the company may claim that he or she was deceived into selling the stock at too low a price. What would happen if PENTAX purchased treasury stock at $17 per share and one day later announced a technological breakthrough that would generate millions of dollars in new business?

Answer:

PENTAX's stock price would likely increase in response to the new information. If it could be proved that PENTAX management withheld the information, a shareholder selling stock back to PENTAX may file a lawsuit to gain the difference per share. The stockholder would claim that with knowledge of the technological advance, he or she would have held the PENTAX stock until after the price increase.

Sale of Treasury Stock

A company may sell its treasury stock at a variety of prices.

SALE OF TREASURY STOCK AT COST. The company may sell its treasury stock at any price agreeable to the corporation and the purchaser. If the stock is sold for the same price that the corporation paid to reacquire it, the entry is a debit to Cash and a credit to Treasury Stock for the same amount.

SALE OF TREASURY STOCK ABOVE COST. If the sale price of treasury stock is greater than its reacquisition cost, the difference is credited to the account Paid-in Capital from Treasury Stock Transactions because the excess came from the company's stockholders. Suppose Jupiter Drilling Company resold its treasury shares for $9 per share (cost was $7.50 per share). The entry is:

Dec. 7	Cash (1,000 × $9)	9,000	
	Treasury Stock, Common		7,500
	Paid-in Capital from Treasury Stock Transactions		1,500
	To sell treasury stock at $9 per share.		

Paid-in Capital from Treasury Stock Transactions is reported with the other paid-in capital accounts on the balance sheet, beneath the Common Stock and Capital in Excess of Par accounts. Its balance can be combined as part of Additional Paid-in Capital, as shown for IHOP Corp. on page 407 (line 4).

CHECK POINT 9-10

SALE OF TREASURY STOCK BELOW COST. At times, the resale price of treasury stock is less than cost. The difference between these two amounts is debited to Paid-in Capital from Treasury Stock Transactions if this account has a credit balance, as in our example. If this account's balance is too small, then the company debits Retained Earnings for the remaining amount.

Treasury Stock Transactions: A Summary

Neither the purchase nor the sale of treasury stock creates a gain or a loss for the income statement, and thus treasury stock transactions have no effect on net income. Exhibit 9-7 illustrates a sequence of assumed treasury stock transactions for Eastman Kodak Company.

EXHIBIT 9-7
Effects of a Purchase and Resale of Treasury Stock (amounts in billions)

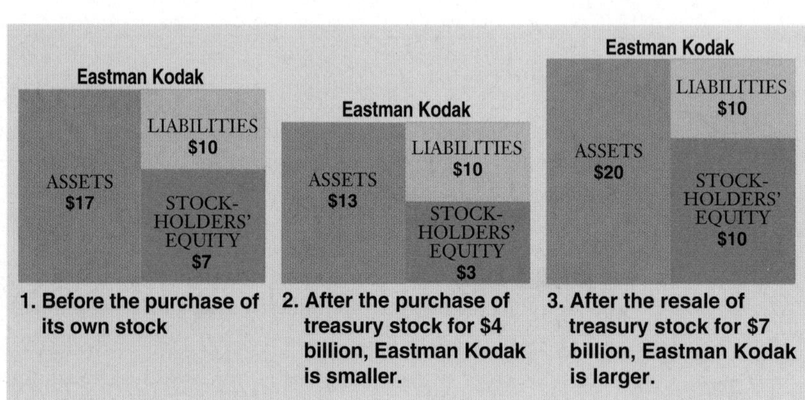

RETIREMENT OF STOCK

A corporation may purchase its own stock and *retire* it by canceling the stock certificates. Retirements of preferred stock occur more often than retirements of common stock, as companies seek to avoid having to pay dividends on the preferred stock. The retired stock cannot be reissued. Retiring stock, like purchasing treasury stock, decreases the corporation's outstanding stock. Retirement also decreases the number of shares issued. In retiring stock, the corporation removes the balances from all paid-in capital accounts related to the retired shares, such as Capital in Excess of Par.

Retained Earnings and Dividends

We have seen that the equity section of the corporation balance sheet is called *stockholders' equity* or *shareholders' equity.* The paid-in capital accounts and retained earnings make up the stockholders' equity section.

The Retained Earnings account carries the balance of the business's net income less its net losses and less any declared dividends accumulated over the corporation's lifetime. *Retained* means "held onto." Successful companies grow by reinvesting back into the business the assets they generate through profitable operations. **IHOP Corp.** is an example; the majority of its equity comes from retained earnings.

The Retained Earnings account is not a reservoir of cash waiting for the board of directors to pay dividends to the stockholders. In fact, the corporation may have a large balance in Retained Earnings but not have the cash to pay a dividend. Cash and Retained Earnings are two separate accounts with no particular relationship. A $500,000 balance in Retained Earnings simply means that $500,000 of owners' equity has been created by profits reinvested in the business. It says nothing about the company's Cash balance.

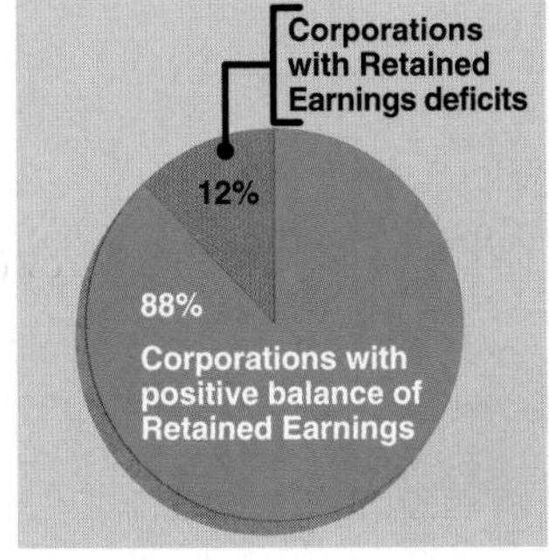

Exhibit 9-8
Retained Earnings of the *Accounting Trends & Techniques* 600 Companies

Retained Earnings Deficit. A credit balance in Retained Earnings is normal, indicating that the corporation's lifetime earnings exceed its lifetime losses and dividends. A debit balance in Retained Earnings arises when a corporation's lifetime losses and dividends exceed its lifetime earnings. The company has not been profitable. Called a **deficit,** this amount is subtracted from the sum of the other equity accounts to determine total stockholders' equity. In a recent survey, 72 of 600 companies (12%) had a retained earnings deficit (Exhibit 9-8).

Dividends and Dividend Dates

A dividend is a corporation's return to its stockholders of some of the benefits of earnings, most commonly in the form of cash payments to the stockholders. A corporation must declare a dividend before paying it. Only the board of directors has the authority to declare a dividend. The corporation has no obligation to pay a dividend until the board declares one, but once declared, the dividend becomes a legal liability of the corporation. Three relevant dates for dividends are as follows:

1. *Declaration date.* On the declaration date, the board of directors announces the intention to pay the dividend. The declaration creates a liability for the corporation. Declaration is recorded by debiting Retained Earnings and crediting Dividends Payable.
2. *Date of record.* As part of the declaration, the corporation announces the record date, which follows the declaration date by a few weeks. The corporation makes no journal entry on the date of record because no transaction occurs. Nevertheless, much work takes place behind the scenes to identify the stockholders who will receive the dividend.
3. *Payment date.* Payment of the dividend usually follows the record date by two to four weeks. Payment is recorded by debiting Dividends Payable and crediting Cash.

Dividends on Preferred and Common Stock

Objective 4
Account for dividends and measure their impact on a company

Declaration of a $50,000 cash dividend is recorded by debiting Retained Earnings and crediting Dividends Payable, as follows:[2]

[2]In Chapters 1–8, we debited the Dividends account, which is closed to Retained Earnings. Many businesses debit Retained Earnings directly, as shown here.

June 19	Retained Earnings	50,000	
	Dividends Payable		50,000
	To declare a cash dividend.		

ASSETS	=	LIABILITIES	+	STOCKHOLDERS' EQUITY
0	=	50,000	−	50,000

Payment of the dividend, which usually follows declaration by a few weeks, is recorded by debiting Dividends Payable and crediting Cash:

CHECK POINT 9-11

July 2	Dividends Payable	50,000	
	Cash		50,000
	To pay a cash dividend.		

ASSETS	=	LIABILITIES	+	STOCKHOLDERS' EQUITY
−50,000	=	−50,000	+	0

DIVIDENDS ON PREFERRED STOCK ARE PAID FIRST. When a company has issued both preferred and common stock, the preferred stockholders receive their dividends first. The common stockholders receive dividends only if the total declared dividend is large enough to pay the preferred stockholders first.

In addition to its common stock, Pine Industries, Inc., a furniture manufacturer, has 90,000 shares of preferred stock outstanding. Preferred dividends are paid at the annual rate of $1.75 per share. Assume that in 2001, Pine Industries declares an annual dividend of $1,500,000. The allocation to preferred and common stockholders is as follows:

Preferred dividend (90,000 shares × $1.75 per share)	$ 157,500
Common dividend (remainder: $1,500,000 − $157,500 . . .	1,342,500
Total dividend	$1,500,000

CHECK POINT 9-12

If Pine declares only a $200,000 dividend, preferred stockholders receive $157,500, and the common stockholders receive the remainder, $42,500 ($200,000 − $157,500).

DIFFERENCES BETWEEN PREFERRED STOCK AND COMMON STOCK. This example illustrates an important difference between preferred stock and common stock. To an investor, preferred stock is safer because it receives dividends first. For example, if Pine Industries earns only enough net income to pay the preferred stockholders' dividends, the owners of common stock receive no dividends. However, the earnings potential from an investment in common stock is much greater than the earnings potential of an investment in preferred stock. Preferred dividends are usually limited to the specified amount, but there is no upper limit on the amount of common dividends.

DIFFERENT WAYS TO EXPRESS THE DIVIDEND RATE ON PREFERRED STOCK. Dividends on preferred stock are stated either as a

- Percentage rate or
- Dollar amount

For example, preferred stock may be "6% preferred," which means that owners of the preferred stock receive an annual dividend of 6% of the stock's par value. If par value is $100 per share, preferred stockholders receive an annual cash dividend of $6 per share (6% of $100). The preferred stock may be "$3 preferred," which means that stockholders receive an annual dividend of $3 per share regardless of the preferred stock's par value. The dividend rate on no-par preferred stock is stated in a dollar amount per share.

STOP & THINK

Compute the amount of cash dividends that the following companies are paying on their preferred stock:

Company	Preferred Stock Outstanding
The LTV Corporation	$500,000 par value of 4.5% preferred stock
Chase Manhattan Corporation	$100,000,000 stated value of 9.76% preferred stock
The Washington Post Company	11,947 shares of $1 par value preferred stock that pays an annual dividend of $80 per share
The McGraw-Hill Companies	1,362 shares of $1.20 preference stock with par value of $10 per share

Answers:

LTV	$22,500 ($500,000 × 0.045)
Chase Manhattan	$9,760,000 ($100,000,000 × 0.0976)
Washington Post	$955,760 (11,947 shares × $80)
McGraw-Hill	$1,634 (1,362 shares × $1.20)

Dividends on Cumulative and Noncumulative Preferred Stock

The allocation of dividends may be complex if the preferred stock is *cumulative.* Corporations sometimes fail to pay a dividend to their preferred stockholders. This occurrence is called *passing the dividend,* and the passed dividends are said to be *in arrears.* The owners of **cumulative preferred stock** must receive all dividends in arrears plus the current year's dividend before the corporation can pay dividends to the common stockholders. *The law considers preferred stock cumulative unless it is specifically labeled as noncumulative.*

The preferred stock of Pine Industries is cumulative. Suppose the company passed the 2001 preferred dividend of $157,500. Before paying dividends to its common stockholders in 2002, the company must first pay preferred dividends of $157,500 for both 2001 and 2002, a total of $315,000.

Assume that Pine Industries passes its 2001 preferred dividend. In 2002, the company declares a $500,000 dividend. The entry to record the declaration is

Sep. 6	Retained Earnings	500,000	
	Dividends Payable, Preferred ($157,500 × 2)		315,000
	Dividends Payable, Common ($500,000 − $315,000)		185,000
	To declare a cash dividend.		

If the preferred stock is *noncumulative,* the corporation is not obligated to pay dividends in arrears. Suppose that Pine Industries preferred stock was noncumulative and the company passed the 20X4 preferred dividend of $157,500. The preferred stockholders would lose the 20X4 dividend forever. Having dividends in arrears on cumulative preferred stock is *not* a liability to the corporation. (A liability for dividends arises only when the board of directors declares the dividend.) Nevertheless, a corporation must report cumulative preferred dividends in arrears—usually in a note to the financial statements.

STOCK DIVIDENDS

A **stock dividend** is a proportional distribution by a corporation of its own stock to its stockholders. Stock dividends increase the stock account and decrease Retained Earnings. Because both these accounts are elements of stockholders' equity, total equity is unchanged by a stock dividend. There is merely a transfer from one stockholders' equity account to another, and no asset or liability is affected by a stock dividend. Stock dividends are fundamentally different from cash dividends because stock dividends do not transfer the corporation's assets to the stockholders.

The corporation distributes stock dividends to stockholders in proportion to the number of shares they already own. If you own 300 shares of **Xerox Corporation** common stock and Xerox distributes a 10% common stock dividend, you will receive 30 (300 × 0.10) additional shares. You would then own 330 shares of the stock. All other Xerox stockholders would receive additional shares equal to 10% of their prior holdings. You would all be in the same relative position after the dividend as you were before.

Reasons for Stock Dividends

In distributing a stock dividend, the corporation gives up no assets. Why, then, do companies issue stock dividends? A corporation may choose to distribute stock dividends for the following reasons:

1. *To continue dividends but conserve cash.* A company may want to keep cash in the business in order to expand, pay off debts, and so on. Yet the company may wish to continue dividends in some form. To do so, the corporation may distribute a stock dividend. Stockholders pay no tax on stock dividends.
2. *To reduce the market price of its stock.* Distribution of a stock dividend may cause the market price of a share of the company's stock to decrease because of the increased supply of the stock. Suppose the market price of a share of stock is $50. Doubling the number of shares of stock outstanding by issuing a stock dividend would drop the stock's market price by approximately half, to $25 per share. The objective is to make the stock less expensive and thus more attractive to a wider range of investors.

Recording Stock Dividends

The declaration of a stock dividend does *not* create a liability because the corporation is not obligated to pay assets. Instead, the corporation has declared its intention to distribute its stock. Assume that Louisiana Lumber Corporation has the following stockholders' equity prior to a stock dividend:

Stockholders' Equity	
Common stock, $10 par, 50,000 shares authorized, 20,000 shares issued	$200,000
Paid-in capital in excess of par—common	70,000
Retained earnings	85,000
Total stockholders' equity	$355,000

The entry to record a stock dividend depends on its size. Generally accepted accounting principles distinguish between a

- *Large* stock dividend (25% or more of issued stock)
- *Small* stock dividend (less than 20–25% of issued stock)

Stock Dividends between 20% and 25% are rare.

LARGE STOCK DIVIDENDS—25% OR MORE. A *large* stock dividend significantly increases the number of shares available in the market and usually decreases the stock price. A common practice is to transfer from Retained Earnings to Common Stock the par value of the dividend shares, as shown in Exhibit 9-9.

SMALL STOCK DIVIDENDS—LESS THAN 20–25%. A *small* stock dividend is less likely to affect the price of the company's stock significantly. For this reason, GAAP requires small stock dividends to be accounted for at their market value. Retained Earnings is decreased for the market value of the dividend shares, Common Stock is credited for the stock's par value, and Paid-in Capital in Excess of Par is credited for the remainder.

Assume Louisiana Lumber Corporation distributes a stock dividend when the market value of the company's common stock is $16 per share. Exhibit 9-9 illustrates the accounting if the dividend is large (a 50% dividend) or small (a 10% dividend):

EXHIBIT 9-9
Accounting for Stock Dividends

Large Stock Dividend—for example, 50% (Accounted for at **par value***)*			*Small Stock Dividend—for example, 10% (Accounted for at* **market value***)*		
Retained Earnings	100,000		Retained Earnings		
Common Stock			(20,000 × 0.10 × $16, market)	32,000	
(20,000 shares × 0.50 × $10, par)		100,000	Common Stock		
			(20,000 × 0.10 × $10, par)		20,000
			Paid-in Capital in Excess of Par.		12,000

Neither type of stock dividend affects assets, liabilities, or total stockholders' equity. A stock dividend merely rearranges the stockholders' equity accounts, leaving total equity unchanged.

A corporation issued 1,000 shares of its $15-par common as a stock dividend when the stock's market price was $25 per share. Assume that the 1,000 shares issued are (1) 10% of the outstanding shares and (2) 100% of the outstanding shares. Which stock dividend decreases total stockholders' equity?

Answer:
Neither a large stock dividend nor a small stock dividend affects total stockholders' equity.

 CHECK POINT 9-13

 CHECK POINT 9-14

STOCK SPLITS

A **stock split** is an increase in the number of authorized, issued, and outstanding shares of stock, coupled with a proportionate reduction in the stock's par value. For example, if the company splits its stock 2 for 1, the number of outstanding shares is doubled and each share's par value is halved. A stock split, like a large stock dividend, decreases the market price of the stock—with the intention of making the stock more attractive in the market. Most leading companies in the United States—**IBM, Ford Motor Company, Giant Food, Inc.,** and others—have split their stock. **Honeywell, Inc.,** which makes electronic controls, split its stock 2 for 1 twice in a three-year period.

The market price of a share of IBM common stock has been approximately $100. Assume that the company wishes to decrease the market price to approximately $25. IBM decides to split the common stock 4 for 1 to reduce the stock's market price from $100 to $25. A 4-for-1 stock split means that the company would have four times as many shares of stock outstanding after the split as it had before and that each share's par value would be quartered. Assume that IBM had 140 million shares of $5 par common stock issued and outstanding before the split:

IBM Stockholders' Equity (Adapted)

Before 4-for-1 Stock Split:	*(In millions)*	*After 4-for-1 Stock Split*	*(In millions)*
Common stock, $5 par, 187.5 million shares authorized, 140 million shares issued . . .	$ 700	Common stock, $1.25 par, 750 million shares authorized, 560 million shares issued . . .	$ 700
Capital in excess of par	6,800	Capital in excess of par	6,800
Retained earnings	11,630	Retained earnings	11,630
Other	3,293	Other	3,293
Total stockholders' equity	$22,423	Total stockholders' equity	$22,423

After the 4-for-1 stock split, IBM would have 750 million shares authorized and 560 million shares (140 million shares × 4) of $1.25 par ($5 ÷ 4) common stock. Indeed, the balance in the Common Stock account does not even change. Only the par value of the stock and the number of shares authorized, issued, and outstanding change. Compare the figures *in red* in the *preceding* stockholders' equity presentations for IBM. Because the stock split affects no account balances, no formal journal entry is necessary. Instead, the split is recorded in a memorandum entry such as the following:

Aug. 19	Called in the outstanding $5 par common stock and distributed four shares of $1.25 par common stock for each old share previously outstanding.

A company may engage in a reverse split to decrease the number of shares of stock outstanding. For example, IBM could split its stock 1 for 4. After the split, par value would be $20 ($5 × 4), shares authorized would be 35 million (140 million ÷ 4). Reverse splits are unusual.

Similarities and Differences between Stock Dividends and Stock Splits

Both stock dividends and stock splits increase the number of shares of stock owned per stockholder. Also, neither stock dividends nor stock splits change the investor's total cost of the stock owned or the company's total stockholders' equity.

Consider **Avon Products, Inc.,** whose beauty products are sold by independent sales representatives. Assume that you paid $3,000 to acquire 150 shares of Avon common stock. If Avon distributes a 100% stock dividend, your 150 shares increase to 300, but your total cost is still $3,000. Your new cost per share is $10 ($3,000 ÷ 300 shares). Likewise, if Avon distributes a 2-for-1 stock split, your shares increase in number to 300, and your total cost is unchanged. Neither type of stock action creates taxable income for the investor.

Both stock dividends and stock splits increase the corporation's number of shares of stock issued and outstanding. For example, a 100% stock dividend and a 2-for-1 stock split both double the number of outstanding shares and cut the stock's market price per share in half. They differ in that a stock *dividend* shifts an amount

Exhibit 9-10
Effects of Dividends and Stock Splits on Total Stockholders' Equity

Event	*Effect on Total Stockholders' Equity*
Declaration of cash dividend	Decrease
Payment of previously declared cash dividend	No effect
Distribution of stock dividend	No effect
Stock split	No effect

Source: Adapted from material provided by Beverly Terry.

from retained earnings to paid-in capital, leaving the par value per share unchanged. A stock *split* affects no account balances whatsoever. Instead, a stock split changes the par value of the stock. It also increases the number of shares of stock authorized, issued, and outstanding.

Exhibit 9-10 summarizes the effects of dividends and stock splits on total stockholders' equity.

Different Values of Stock

Objective 5
Use different stock values in decision making

The business community refers to several different *stock values* in addition to par value. These values include market value, redemption value, liquidation value, and book value.

Market Value

A stock's **market value,** or *market price,* is the price for which a person can buy or sell a share of the stock. The issuing corporation's net income, financial position, and future prospects and the general economic conditions determine market value. *In almost all cases, stockholders are more concerned about the market value of a stock than about any of the other values discussed next.* In the chapter opening story, **IHOP's** most recent stock price was quoted at 25, which means that the stock could be sold for, or bought for, $25 per share. The purchase of 100 shares of IHOP stock would cost $2,500 ($25.00 × 100), plus a commission. If you were selling 100 shares of IHOP stock, you would receive cash of $2,500, less a commission. The commission is the fee an investor pays to a stockbroker for buying or selling the stock. The price of a share of IHOP stock has fluctuated from $10 at issuance to a recent high of $26.50.

Redemption Value

Preferred stock that requires the company to redeem (pay to retire) the stock at a set price is called *redeemable preferred stock.* The company is *obligated* to redeem the preferred stock, so many view redeemable preferred stock not as stockholders' equity but instead as a liability. The price the corporation agrees to pay for the stock, which is set when the stock is issued, is called the *redemption value.*

The preferred stock of Pine Industries, Inc., has a redemption value of $25 per share. Beginning in 2001, Pine is "required to redeem annually 6,765 shares of the preferred stock ($169,125 annually)." Pine's annual redemption payment to the preferred stockholders will include this redemption value plus any dividends in arrears.

Book Value

The **book value** per share of common stock is the amount of owners' equity on the company's books for each share of its stock. If the company has only common stock outstanding, its book value is computed by dividing total stockholders' equity by the number of shares of common *outstanding*. For example, a company with stockholders' equity of \$180,000 and 5,000 shares of common stock outstanding has a book value of \$36 per share (\$180,000 ÷ 5,000 shares).

If the company has both preferred stock and common stock outstanding, the preferred stockholders have the first claim to owners' equity. Preferred stock often has a specified liquidation or redemption value. The preferred equity is its redemption value plus any cumulative preferred dividends in arrears. Book value per share of common is then computed as follows:

$$\text{Book value per share of common stock} = \frac{\text{Total stockholders' equity} - \text{Preferred equity}}{\text{Number of shares of common stock outstanding}}$$

Assume that the company balance sheet reports the following amounts:

Stockholders' Equity	
Preferred stock, 6%, \$100 par, 5,000 shares authorized, 400 shares issued, redemption value \$130 per share	\$ 40,000
Paid-in capital in excess of par—preferred	4,000
Common stock, \$10 par, 20,000 shares authorized, 5,500 shares issued	55,000
Paid-in capital in excess of par—common	72,000
Retained earnings	85,000
Treasury stock—common, 500 shares at cost	(15,000)
Total stockholders' equity	\$241,000

Suppose that four years' (including the current year) cumulative preferred dividends are in arrears and observe that preferred stock has a redemption value of \$130 per share. The book-value-per-share computations for this corporation are as follows:

Preferred equity	
Redemption value (400 shares × \$130)	\$ 52,000
Cumulative dividends (\$40,000 × 0.06 × 4 years)	9,600
Preferred equity	\$ 61,600*
Common equity	
Total stockholders' equity	\$241,000
Less preferred equity	(61,600)
Common equity	\$179,400
Book value per share [\$179,400 ÷ 5,000 shares outstanding (5,500 shares issued minus 500 treasury shares)]	\$ 35.88

* If the preferred stock had no redemption value, then preferred equity would be \$40,000 + \$4,000 + preferred dividends in arrears.

BOOK VALUE AND DECISION MAKING. How is book value per share used in decision making? Companies negotiating the purchase of a corporation may wish to know the book value of its stock. The book value of stockholders' equity may figure into the negotiated purchase price. Corporations—especially those whose stock is not publicly traded—may buy out a retiring executive, agreeing to pay the book value of the person's stock in the company.

Some investors compare the book value of a share of a company's stock with the stock's market value. The idea is that a stock selling below its book value is underpriced and thus a good buy. Let's compare two companies, **IHOP** and **Intel:**

Company	Recent Stock Price	Book Value Per Share (Common stockholders' equity)/(Number of shares of common stock outstanding)	
IHOP	$25	$187,868,000/9,881,580	= $19.01
Intel	$66	$23,377,000,000/3,315,000,000	= $ 7.05

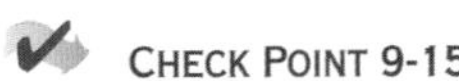

CHECK POINT 9-15

Neither company's stock is selling below its book value. But IHOP's book value per share is much closer to its market value than Intel's is. Does this mean IHOP's stock is the better investment? Not necessarily. Investment decisions should be based on more than one ratio. Let's turn now to two widely used measures of operating performance.

EVALUATING OPERATIONS: RATE OF RETURN ON TOTAL ASSETS AND RATE OF RETURN ON COMMON STOCKHOLDERS' EQUITY

Objective 6
Evaluate a company's return on assets and return on stockholders' equity

Investors and creditors are constantly evaluating managers' ability to earn profits. Investors search for companies whose stocks are likely to increase in value. Investment decisions often include a comparison of companies. But a comparison of **IHOP Corp.'s** net income with the net income of a new company in the restaurant industry simply is not meaningful. IHOP's profits may run into the millions of dollars, which far exceed a new company's net income. Does this automatically make IHOP a better investment? Not necessarily. To make relevant comparisons among companies of different size or scope of operations, investors use some standard profitability measures, including rate of return on total assets and rate of return on stockholders' equity.

Return on Assets

The **rate of return on total assets,** or simply **return on assets,** measures a company's success in using its assets to earn income for the two groups who finance the business:

- Creditors who have receivables from the corporation and thus earn interest.
- Stockholders who own the corporation's stock and expect it to earn net income.

The sum of interest expense and net income is the return to the two groups that have financed the corporation's activities, and this is the numerator of the return-on-assets ratio. The denominator is average total assets. Return on assets is computed as follows, using actual data from the 1998 annual report of IHOP Corp. (dollar amounts in thousands):

$$\text{Rate of return on total assets} = \frac{\text{Net income} + \text{Interest expense}}{\text{Average total assets}}$$

$$= \frac{\$26{,}111 + \$17{,}417}{(\$382{,}593 + \$445{,}899)/2} = \frac{\$43{,}528}{\$414{,}246} = 0.105$$

Net income and interest expense are taken from the income statement. Average total assets is computed from the beginning and ending balance sheets.

What is a good rate of return on total assets? There is no single answer because rates of return vary widely by industry. For example, high-technology companies earn much higher returns than do utility companies, groceries, and manufacturers of consumer goods such as toothpaste.

Return on Equity

Rate of return on common stockholders' equity, often called **return on equity,** shows the relationship between net income and average common stockholders' equity. The numerator is net income minus preferred dividends, information taken from the income statement. The denominator is *average common stockholders' equity*—total stockholders' equity minus preferred equity. IHOP Corp.'s rate of return on common stockholders' equity for 1998 is computed as follows (dollar amounts in thousands):

$$\textbf{Rate of return on common stockholders' equity} = \frac{\textbf{Net income} - \textbf{Preferred dividends}}{\textbf{Average common stockholders' equity}}$$

$$= \frac{\$26{,}111 - \$0}{(\$156{,}184 + \$187{,}868)/2} = \frac{\$26{,}111}{\$172{,}026} = 0.152$$

CHECK POINT 9-16

CHECK POINT 9-17

Because IHOP Corp. has no preferred stock, preferred dividends are zero. With no preferred stock outstanding, average *common* stockholders' equity is the same as average *total* equity—the average of the beginning and ending amounts.

IHOP's return on equity (15.2%) is higher than its return on assets (10.5%). This difference results from the interest-expense component of return on assets. Companies such as IHOP borrow at one rate (say, 7%) and invest the funds to earn a higher rate (say, 15%). Borrowing at a lower rate than the company's return on investments is called *using leverage*. Leverage increases net income as long as operating income exceeds the interest expense from borrowing.

Investors and creditors use return on common stockholders' equity in much the same way they use return on total assets—to compare companies. The higher the rate of return, the more successful the company. IHOP's 15.2% return on common stockholders' equity would be considered quite good in most industries. The Decision Guidelines feature offers suggestions for what to consider when investing in stock.

DECISION GUIDELINES

Investing in Stock

Investor Decision	Guidelines
Which category of stock to buy for:	
• A safe investment?	Preferred stock is safer than common, but for even more safety, invest in high-grade corporate bonds or government securities.
• Steady dividends?	Cumulative preferred stock. However, the company is not obligated to declare preferred dividends, and the dividends are unlikely to increase.
• Increasing dividends?	Common stock, as long as the company's net income is increasing and the company has adequate cash flow to pay a dividend after meeting all obligations and other cash demands.
• Increasing stock price?	Common stock, but again only if the company's net income and cash flow are increasing.
How to identify a good stock to buy?	There are many ways to pick stock investments. One strategy that works reasonably well is to invest in companies that consistently earn higher rates of return on assets and on equity than competing firms in the same industry. Also, select industries that are expected to grow.

EXCEL APPLICATION PROBLEM 

Goal: Create an Excel spreadsheet that compares the financial performance of several publicly traded stocks.

Scenario: Your task is to create an Excel spreadsheet that compares the historical performance of Abercrombie & Fitch, The Gap, and The Limited on three key financial measures. Embedded graphs of each financial dimension also must be created. All data used in your spreadsheet will come from Morningstar's website.

When you are finished, answer these questions:

1. Which of the three companies, if any, has earned a consistently higher return on equity than the others?
2. Which of the three companies, if any, has earned a consistently higher return on assets than the others?
3. Increasing cash flow from operations is a good sign for investing. Which of the companies, if any, has experienced increasing cash flows over the past five years?
4. Based on these very limited data, would you invest in any of these companies? Why or why not?

Step-by-step:

1. Locate www.morningstar.com on the Web.
2. Under the "Quotes & Reports" section, enter the ticker symbol for each company. Then, look under "Company Performance" and "Historical Overview." You should see a five-year summary of fiscal-year-end financial performance. Print out the Historical Overview for each company.
3. Open a new Excel spreadsheet.
4. Create a bold-faced heading for your spreadsheet that contains the following:
   - **a.** Chapter 9 Decision Guidelines
   - **b.** Investing in Stock
   - **c.** Stock Performance Analysis
   - **d.** Today's date
5. Under the heading, create a bold-faced, underlined section titled "Return on Equity %." Move down one row. Create one column each for the last five years (for example, "1999," "1998," and so on). Create one row each for The Gap, The Limited, and Abercrombie & Fitch.
6. Enter the return on equity data for the past five years, as found on the Morningstar Historical Overview for each company.
7. Repeat Steps 5 and 6 for "Return on Assets %" and "Operating Cash Flow (in millions)."
8. Using the Excel Chart Wizard, create separate graphs for Return on Equity %, Return on Assets %, and Operating Cash Flow. Resize and position each graph to the right of the data so that everything appears on one page when you print.
9. Save your work and print your spreadsheet in landscape mode (with graphs) for your files.

REPORTING STOCKHOLDERS' EQUITY TRANSACTIONS ON THE STATEMENT OF CASH FLOWS

Objective 7
Report stockholders' equity transactions on the statement of cash flows

Many of the transactions discussed in this chapter are reported on the statement of cash flows. Stockholders' equity transactions are *financing activities* because the company is dealing with its owners, the stockholders—the most basic group of people who finance the company. The financing transactions that affect stockholders' equity and cash (and thus appear on the statement of cash flows) fall into three main categories: issuances of stock, repurchases of stock, and dividends.

1. Issuances of Stock. *Issuances of stock* include basic transactions in which a company issues its stock for cash. Most companies, including **IHOP Corp.**, have employee stock ownership plans (ESOPs). In an ESOP, a company issues its stock to employees to increase their stake in the company because employees who own part of a company work hard to help it succeed. Most companies also have executive stock option plans that allow top managers to buy the company's stock at below-market prices. In both ESOPs and executive stock option plans, the transaction is essentially the same as a basic issuance of stock. The company receives cash and issues stock.

2. Repurchases of Stock. As we discussed earlier in the chapter, a company can repurchase its stock as treasury stock, or it can buy the stock and retire it. In both cases, the company pays cash to repurchase its own stock. A sale of treasury stock, like an issuance of stock, increases the company's cash.

3. Dividends. Most companies pay cash dividends to their stockholders. Dividend payments are a type of financing transaction because the company is paying its stockholders for the use of their money. In contrast, stock dividends are not reported on the statement of cash flows because the company pays no cash in a stock dividend.

The following report of cash flows from financing activities illustrates most of the cash flows that you will encounter. Cash receipts appear as positive amounts and cash payments as negative amounts, denoted by parentheses.

CHECK POINT 9-18

Cash Flows from Financing Activities	*(In millions)*
Proceeds from issuance of common stock	$ 16.9
Proceeds from issuance of stock to employees	41.4
Sale of treasury stock	37.0
Purchase of treasury stock	(24.0)
Repurchase and retirement of common stock	(1,034.0)
Payment of dividends	(351.5)
Net cash used by financing activities	$(1,314.2)

VARIATIONS IN REPORTING STOCKHOLDERS' EQUITY

Businesses often use terminology and formats in reporting stockholders' equity that differ from our general examples. We use a more detailed format in this book to help you learn the components of the stockholders' equity section. Companies assume that readers of their statements already understand the details they omit.

One of the most important skills you will learn in this course is the ability to understand the financial statements of real companies. Thus we present in Exhibit 9-11

EXHIBIT 9-11
Formats for Reporting Stockholders' Equity

General Teaching Format

Stockholders' equity	
Paid-in capital:	
Preferred stock, 8%, $10 par, 30,000 shares authorized and issued	$ 300,000
Paid-in capital in excess of par—preferred	10,000
Common stock, $1 par, 100,000 shares authorized, 60,000 shares issued	60,000
Paid-in capital in excess of par—common	2,140,000
Paid-in capital from treasury stock transactions, common	9,000
Paid-in capital from retirement of preferred stock	11,000
Total paid-in capital	2,530,000
Retained earnings	1,565,000
Subtotal	4,095,000
Less treasury stock, common (1,400 shares at cost)	(42,000)
Total stockholders' equity	$4,053,000

Real-World Format

Stockholders' equity	
Preferred stock, 8%, $10 par, 30,000 shares authorized and issued	$ 310,000
Common stock, $1 par, 100,000 shares authorized, 60,000 shares issued	60,000
Additional paid-in capital	2,160,000
Retained earnings	1,565,000
Less treasury stock, common (1,400 shares at cost)	(42,000)
	$4,053,000

a side-by-side comparison of our general teaching format and the format that you are more likely to encounter in real-world balance sheets. Note the following points in the real-world format:

1. The heading Paid-in Capital does not appear. It is commonly understood that Preferred Stock, Common Stock, and Additional Paid-in Capital are elements of paid-in capital.
2. Preferred stock is often reported in a single amount that combines its par value and premium.
3. For presentation in the financial statements, all additional paid-in capital—from capital in excess of par on common stock, treasury stock transactions, and stock retirement—appears as a single amount labeled "Additional Paid-in Capital." Because Additional Paid-in Capital belongs to the common stockholders, it follows Common Stock in the real-world format.
4. Total stockholders' equity ($4,053,000 in Exhibit 9-11) is not labeled.

End-of-Chapter

Summary Problem for Your Review

1. Use the following accounts and related balances to prepare the classified balance sheet of Whitehall, Inc., at September 30, 20X2. Use the account format of the balance sheet.

Common stock, $1 par, 50,000 shares authorized, 20,000 shares issued	$ 20,000	Long-term note payable ...	$ 80,000
		Inventory...............	85,000
Dividends payable	4,000	Property, plant, and equipment, net.........	226,000
Cash....................	9,000	Accounts receivable, net ...	23,000
Accounts payable.........	28,000	Preferred stock, $3.75, no-par, 10,000 shares authorized, 2,000 shares issued	24,000
Paid-in capital in excess of par—common.......	115,000	Accrued liabilities.........	3,000
Treasury stock, common, 1,000 shares at cost	6,000	Retained earnings	75,000

2. The balance sheet of Trendline Corp. reported the following at December 31, 20X1:

Stockholders' Equity	
Preferred stock, 4%, $10 par, 10,000 shares authorized and issued (redemption value, $110,000)	$100,000
Common stock, no-par, $5 stated value, 100,000 shares authorized	250,000
Paid-in capital in excess of par or stated value:	
Common stock..................................	239,500
Retained earnings	395,000
Less: Treasury stock, common (1,000 shares)	(8,000)
Total stockholders' equity	$976,500

Required

a. Is the preferred stock cumulative or noncumulative? How can you tell?
b. What is the total amount of the annual preferred dividend?
c. How many shares of common stock has the company issued?
d. Compute the book value per share of the preferred and the common stock. No preferred dividends are in arrears, and Trendline has not yet declared the 20X1 dividend.

Answers

1.

WHITEHALL, INC. Balance Sheet September 30, 20X2					
Assets		***Liabilities***			
Current:		Current:			
Cash	$ 9,000	Accounts payable			$ 28,000
Accounts receivable, net	23,000	Dividends payable			4,000
Inventory	85,000	Accrued liabilities			3,000
Total current assets	117,000	Total current liabilities			35,000
Property, plant and equipment, net	226,000	Long-term note payable			80,000
		Total liabilities			115,000
		Stockholders' Equity			
		Preferred stock, $3.75, no par, 10,000 shares authorized, 2,000 shares issued		$ 24,000	
		Common stock, $1 par, 50,000 shares authorized, 20,000 shares issued		20,000	
		Paid-in capital in excess of par—common		115,000	
		Retained earnings		75,000	
		Treasury stock, common, 1,000 shares at cost		(6,000)	
		Total stockholders' equity			228,000
Total assets	$343,000	Total liabilities and stockholders' equity			$343,000

2. a. The preferred stock is cumulative because it is not specifically labeled otherwise.
   b. Total annual preferred dividend: $4,000 ($100,000 × 0.04).
   c. Common stock issued: 50,000 shares ($250,000 ÷ $5 stated value).
   d. Book values per share of preferred and common stock:

Preferred:	
Redemption value	$110,000
Cumulative dividend for current year ($100,000 × 0.04)	4,000
Stockholders' equity allocated to preferred	$114,000
Book value per share ($114,000 ÷ 10,000 shares)	$ 11.40
Common:	
Total stockholders' equity	$976,500
Less stockholders' equity allocated to preferred	(114,000)
Stockholders' equity allocated to common	$862,500
Book value per share ($862,500 ÷ 49,000 shares)	$ 17.60

SUMMARY OF LEARNING OBJECTIVES

1. ***Explain the advantages and disadvantages of a corporation.*** The corporation is the dominant form of business in the United States. Corporations are separate legal entities that exist apart from their owners. The advantages

of corporations are their ability to raise capital, continuous life, transferability of ownership, lack of mutual agency, and limited liability of stockholders. The disadvantages of corporations are the separation of ownership from management, double taxation, and government regulation.

2. ***Measure the effect of issuing stock on a company's financial position.*** Corporations receive the authorization to sell (issue) a certain number of shares of stock. They may issue common or preferred stock, or par or no-par stock. Regardless of the type of stock, its issuance increases the company's assets and stockholders' equity.

3. ***Describe how treasury stock transactions affect a company.*** *Treasury stock* is a corporation's own stock that it has issued and later reacquired. The purchase of treasury stock decreases the company's assets and stockholders' equity. The sale of treasury stock increases the company's assets and stockholders' equity. Treasury stock is reported on the balance sheet as a contra element of stockholders' equity.

4. ***Account for dividends and measure their impact on a company.*** Companies may issue dividends in either cash or stock. Preferred stock has priority over common stock for dividends. The preferred dividend amount may be stated as a dollar value or as a percentage of the preferred stock's par value. In addition, the owners of *cumulative* preferred stock must receive all dividends in arrears before the corporation can pay dividends to the common stockholders.

   A *stock dividend* is a proportional distribution by a corporation of its own stock to its stockholders. Stock dividends increase the stock account and decrease Retained Earnings. Total stockholders' equity is unchanged. A *stock split* is an increase in the number of authorized, issued, and outstanding shares of stock, coupled with a proportionate reduction in the stock's par value. A stock split affects no account balances and therefore leaves total stockholders' equity unchanged.

5. ***Use different stock values in decision making.*** A stock's *market value* is the price for which a person could buy or sell a share of the stock. The price a company agrees to pay for a stock when buying it back is the stock's *redemption value*. *Liquidation value* is the amount the corporation agrees to pay the preferred stockholders per share if the corporation liquidates. A stock's *book value* is the amount of owners' equity on the company's books for each share of the stock outstanding.

6. ***Evaluate a company's return on assets and return on stockholders' equity.*** Return on assets and return on stockholders' equity are two measures of a corporation's profitability. *Return on assets* measures a company's success in using its assets to earn income for both the creditors and the stockholders. *Return on equity* shows the relationship between net income and average common equity to measure the company's ability to earn net income for the common stockholders. A healthy company's return on equity will exceed its return on assets.

7. ***Report stockholders' equity transactions on the statement of cash flows.*** Three main *financing* categories that affect stockholders' equity, and thus appear on the statement of cash flows, are (1) issuances of stock, (2) repurchases of stock, and (3) dividends.

ACCOUNTING VOCABULARY

authorization of stock (p. 413).
board of directors (p. 410).
book value (of a stock) (p. 429).
bylaws (p. 410).
chairperson (p. 410).
charter (p. 408).
common stock (p. 412).
contributed capital (p. 411).
cumulative preferred stock (p. 425).
deficit (p. 423).
dividends (p. 413).
double taxation (p. 409).
incorporators (p. 409).
legal capital (p. 413).
limited liability (p. 409).
market value (of a stock) (p. 429).
outstanding stock (p. 411).
paid-in capital (p. 411).
par value (p. 413).
preferred stock (p. 412).
president (p. 410).
rate of return on common stockholders' equity (p. 432).
rate of return on total assets (p. 431).
retained earnings (p. 411).
return on assets (p. 431).
return on equity (p. 432).
shareholder (p. 408).
stated value (p. 413).
stock (p. 408).
stock dividend (p. 426).
stockholder (p. 408).
stockholders' equity (p. 411).
stock split (p. 427).
treasury stock (p. 420).

QUESTIONS

1. Why is a corporation called a "creature of the state"? Briefly outline the steps in the organization of a corporation.

2. Identify the characteristics of a corporation and explain why corporations face a tax disadvantage.

3. Suppose H. J. Heinz Company issued 1,000 shares of its 3.65%, $100-par preferred stock for $120 per share. How much would this transaction increase the company's paid-in capital? How much would it increase Heinz's retained earnings? How much would it increase Heinz's annual cash dividend payments?

4. Rank the following accounts in the order they would appear on the balance sheet: Common Stock, Equipment, Preferred Stock, Retained Earnings, Dividends Payable. Also, give each account's balance sheet classification.

5. What effect does the purchase of treasury stock have on the (a) assets, (b) issued stock, and (c) outstanding stock of the corporation?
6. What is the normal balance of the Treasury Stock account? What type of account is Treasury Stock? Where is Treasury Stock reported on the balance sheet?
7. What effects do the purchase and retirement of common stock have on the (a) assets, (b) issued stock, and (c) outstanding stock of the corporation?
8. Briefly discuss the three important dates for a dividend.
9. As a preferred stockholder, would you rather own cumulative or noncumulative preferred? If all other factors are the same, would the corporation rather the preferred stock be cumulative or noncumulative? Give your reason.
10. Ametek, Inc., reported a cash balance of $73 million and a retained earnings balance of $162.5 million. Explain how Ametek can have so much more retained earnings than cash. In your answer, identify the nature of retained earnings and state how it relates to cash.
11. A friend of yours receives a stock dividend on an investment. He believes that stock dividends are the same as cash dividends. Explain why the two are not the same.
12. What is the difference between a small stock dividend and a large stock dividend? What is the main difference in accounting for small and large stock dividends?
13. Distinguish between the market value of stock and the book value of stock. Which is more important to investors?
14. Why should a healthy company's rate of return on stockholders' equity exceed its rate of return on total assets?

CHECK POINTS

Authority structure in a corporation (Obj. 1)

CP9-1 Consider the authority structure in a corporation, as diagrammed in Exhibit 9-2, page 410.

1. What group holds the ultimate power in a corporation?
2. Who is the most powerful person in the corporation?
3. Who is in charge of day-to-day operations?
4. Who manages the accounting?
5. Who has primary responsibility for the corporation's cash?

Characteristics of preferred and common stock (Obj. 1)

CP9-2 Answer the following questions about the characteristics of a corporation's stock:

1. Which stockholders are the real owners of a corporation?
2. Which right clearly distinguishes a stockholder from a creditor (who has lent money to the corporation)?
3. What privileges do preferred stockholders enjoy that common stockholders do not have?
4. Which class of stockholders would expect to reap greater benefits from a highly profitable corporation? Why?

Effect of a stock issuance on net income (Obj. 2)

CP9-3 Study **IHOP's** July 23 stock issuance entry given on page 414 and answer these questions about the nature of the IHOP transaction.

1. IHOP received $32,000,000 for the issuance of its stock. The par value of the IHOP Stock was only $32,000. Was the excess amount of $31,968,000 a profit to IHOP? If not, what was it?
2. Suppose the par value of the IHOP stock had been $1 per share, $5 per share, or $10 per share. Would a change in the par value of the company's stock affect IHOP's net income? Give the reasons for your answer.

Issuing stock and analyzing retained earnings (Obj. 2)

CP9-4 At December 31, 1998, **The Coca-Cola Company** reported the following on its comparative balance sheet, which included 1997 amounts for comparison (adapted, with all amounts except par value in millions):

	December 31,	
	1998	*1997*
Common stock $0.25 par value		
Authorized: 5,600 shares		
Issued: 3,460 shares in 1997	$ 865	
3,443 shares in 1998		$ 861
Paid-in capital in excess of par	2,195	1,527
Retained earnings	19,922	17,869

1. How much did Coca-Cola's total paid-in capital increase during 1998? What caused total paid-in capital to increase? How can you tell?
2. Journalize Coca-Cola's issuance of stock for cash during 1998.
3. Did Coca-Cola have a profit or a loss for 1998? How can you tell?

CP9-5 This Check Point shows the similarity and the difference between two ways to acquire plant assets.

Issuing stock to finance the purchase of assets (Obj. 2)

Case A—Issue stock and buy the assets in separate transactions:
Data Warehouse, Inc., issued 10,000 shares of its $5 par common stock for cash of $700,000. In a separate transaction, Data Warehouse then used the cash to purchase a warehouse building for $600,000 and equipment for $100,000. Journalize the two transactions.

Case B—Issue stock to acquire the assets:
Data Warehouse issued 10,000 shares of its $5 par common stock to acquire a warehouse building valued at $600,000 and equipment worth $100,000. Journalize this transaction.

Compare the balances in all accounts after making both sets of entries. Are the account balances similar or different?

CP9-6 Steitz Aviation Corp. has three classes of stock: Common, $1 par; Preferred Class A, $10 par; and Preferred Class B, no-par. Journalize Steitz's issuance of

Issuing stock (Obj. 2)

a. 1,000 shares of common stock for $40 per share
b. 1,000 shares of class A preferred stock for a total of $25,000
c. 1,000 shares of class B preferred stock for $18 per share

Explanations are not required.

CP9-7 The financial statements of Landa Computer, Inc., reported the following accounts (adapted, in millions except for par value):

Preparing the stockholders' equity section of a balance sheet (Obj. 2)

Net sales.	$1,031.5	Paid-in capital in excess of par . .	$ 26.2
Accounts payable.	62.4	Cost of goods sold	588.0
Retained earnings	166.2	Common stock $0.01 par;	
Other current liabilities	52.3	40.2 shares issued	0.4
Operating expenses	412.9	Long-term debt	7.6

Prepare the stockholders' equity section of the Landa Computer balance sheet. Net income has already been closed to Retained Earnings.

CP9-8 Use the Landa Computer data in Check Point 9-7 to compute Landa's

Using stockholders' equity data (Obj. 2)

a. net income **b.** total liabilities **c.** total assets (use the accounting equation).

CP9-9 The table on Jupiter Drilling's stockholders' equity section before the purchase of treasury stock appears on page 420. Suppose that Jupiter Drilling later purchases 500 shares of its common stock as treasury stock, paying cash of $5 per share.

Accounting for the purchase of treasury stock (Obj. 3)

1. Journalize the purchase of treasury stock.
2. Prepare the stockholders' equity section of Jupiter's balance sheet immediately after the purchase of treasury stock.
3. What effect does the purchase of treasury stock always have on total stockholders' equity? How did Jupiter's purchase of treasury stock affect the company's total stockholders' equity? Give the amount.

CP9-10 Return to the Jupiter Drilling Company situation in Check Point 9-9. After purchasing the 500 shares of treasury stock for $5 per share, Jupiter later sold 400 of the treasury shares for $8 per share.

Accounting for the sale of treasury stock (Obj. 3)

1. Journalize the sale of treasury stock.
2. Prepare the stockholders' equity section of Jupiter's balance sheet immediately after the sale of treasury stock.

3. What effect does the sale of treasury stock always have on total stockholders' equity? How did Jupiter's sale of treasury stock affect the company's total stockholders' equity? Give the amount.

Accounting for cash dividends (Obj. 4)

CP9-11 Augusta Company earned net income of $90,000 during the year ended December 31, 20X1. On December 15, Augusta declared the annual cash dividend on its 6% preferred stock (10,000 shares with total par value of $100,000) and a $0.50 per share cash dividend on its common stock (50,000 shares with total par value of $250,000). Augusta then paid the dividends on January 4, 20X2.

Journalize for Augusta Company:

a. Declaring the cash dividends on December 15, 20X1.

b. Paying the cash dividends on January 4, 20X2.

Did Retained Earnings increase or decrease during 20X1? By how much?

Dividing cash dividends between preferred and common stock (Obj. 4)

CP9-12 Refer to the allocation of dividends for Pine Industries on page 424. Answer these questions about Pine's cash dividends.

1. How much in dividends must Pine declare each year before the common stockholders receive cash dividends for the year?
2. Suppose Pine declares cash dividends of $100,000 for 20X1. How much of the dividends go to preferred? How much goes to common?
3. Is Pine's preferred stock cumulative or noncumulative? How can you tell?
4. Suppose Pine passed the preferred dividend in 20X0 and 20X1. In 20X2, Pine declares cash dividends of $500,000. How much of the dividends go to preferred? How much goes to common?

Recording a small stock dividend (Obj. 4)

CP9-13 Sprint Telex Company has 100,000 shares of $2.50 par common stock outstanding. Sprint distributes a 5% stock dividend when the market value of its stock is $13 per share.

1. Journalize Sprint's distribution of the stock dividend on March 19. An explanation is not required.
2. What was the overall effect of the stock dividend on Sprint Telex's total assets? On total stockholders' equity?

Recording a large stock dividend and reporting stockholders' equity (Obj. 4)

CP9-14 Pirelli Rubber Works has 20,000 shares of $1 par common stock outstanding. Pirelli issued this stock at a price of $10 per share. Pirelli then distributes a 50% stock dividend when the market value of its common stock is $62.50 per share.

1. Journalize Pirelli's distribution of the stock dividend on July 5. An explanation is not required.
2. Prepare the stockholders' equity section of Pirelli's balance sheet after issuance of the stock dividend. Retained Earnings had a balance of $60,000 before the dividend, and Pirelli's corporate charter authorizes the company to issue 100,000 shares of common stock.

Computing book value per share (Obj. 5)

CP9-15 Refer to the Real-World Format of Stockholders' Equity in Exhibit 9-11, page 434. That company has passed its preferred dividends for the current year and the two preceding years. Compute the book value of a share of the company's common stock.

Computing and explaining return on assets and return on equity (Obj. 6)

CP9-16 Give the formula for computing (a) rate of return on total assets and (b) rate of return on common stockholders' equity. Then answer these questions about the rate-of-return computations.

1. Why is interest expense added to net income to compute return on assets?
2. Why are preferred dividends subtracted from net income to compute return on common stockholders' equity?

Computing return on assets and return on equity for a leading company (Obj. 6)

CP9-17 **The Coca-Cola Company** has earned extraordinarily high rates of return on its assets and its stockholders' equity in recent years. Coca-Cola's 19X6 financial statements reported the following items, shown on the next page, with 19X5 figures given for comparison (adapted, in millions). Compute Coca-Cola's rate of return on total assets and rate of return on common stockholders' equity for 19X6. Evaluate the rates of return as strong or weak.

Measuring cash flows from financing activities (Obj. 7)

CP9-18 During 19X6, **Nike, Inc.,** earned net income of $553 million and paid cash dividends of $79 million. The company borrowed $53 million and paid off $30 million of debt. Nike raised $21 million by issuing common stock and paid $19 million to purchase treasury stock. Determine the amount of Nike's *net cash flow from financing activities* during 19X6.

CP9-17
Coca Cola (continued)

	19X6	19X5
Balance sheet		
Total current assets	$ 5,910	$ 5,450
Total long-term assets	10,251	9,591
Total assets	$16,161	$15,041
Total liabilities	$10,005	$ 9,649
Total stockholders' equity (all common)	6,156	5,392
Total liabilities and equity	$16,161	$15,041
Income statement		
Net sales	$18,546	
Cost of goods sold	6,738	
Gross margin	11,808	
Selling, administrative, and general expenses	7,893	
Interest expense	286	
All other expenses, net	137	
Net income	$ 3,492	

EXERCISES

Organizing a corporation (Obj. 1)

E9-1 Richard Barth and Michael Stephanopolous are opening a restaurant to be named Good Eats. They need outside capital, so they plan to organize the business as a corporation. Because your office is in the same building, they come to you for advice. Write a memorandum informing them of the steps in forming a corporation. Identify specific documents used in this process, and name the different parties involved in the ownership and management of a corporation.

Issuing stock and reporting stockholders' equity (Obj. 2)

E9-2 Studio Art Gallery, Inc., obtained a corporate charter that authorized the issuance of 100,000 shares of common stock and 5,000 shares of preferred stock. During its first year, the business completed the following stock issuance transactions:

Feb. 19	Issued 1,000 shares of $2.50 par common stock for cash of $6.50 per share.
Mar. 3	Sold 500 shares of $1.50 no-par preferred stock for $6,000 cash.
11	Received inventory valued at $11,000 and fixtures with market value of $8,500 for 3,300 shares of the $2.50 par common stock.

Required

1. Journalize the transactions. Explanations are not required.
2. Prepare the stockholders' equity section of Studio Art Gallery's balance sheet. The ending balance of retained earnings is a deficit of $20,000.

Issuing stock (Obj. 2)

E9-3 The balance sheet of **Gulf Resources & Chemical Corporation** (as adapted) reported the following stockholders' equity. Gulf Resources has two separate classes of preferred stock, labeled Series A and Series B. All dollar amounts, except for per-share amounts, are given in thousands.

GULF RESOURCES & CHEMICAL CORPORATION
Stockholders' Equity

Preferred stock, $1 par, authorized 4,000,000 shares (Note 7)	
Series A, 58,000 shares issued and outstanding	$ 58
Series B, 376,000 shares issued and outstanding	376
Common stock, $0.10 par, authorized 20,000,000 shares [issued and] outstanding 9,130,000 shares	913
Capital in excess of par	75,542

Required

1. Assume that all the preferred stock (Series A and Series B) was issued for $1 cash per share. At what price per share was the common stock issued?
2. Gulf Resources lists no treasury stock. How else can you tell that the company holds no treasury stock?

Stockholders' equity section of a balance sheet
(Obj. 2)

E9-4 The charter of Spenco Medical Corporation authorizes the issuance of 5,000 shares of class A preferred stock, 1,000 shares of class B preferred stock, and 10,000 shares of common stock. During a two-month period, Spenco completed these stock-issuance transactions:

June 23	Issued 1,000 shares of $1 par common stock for cash of $12.50 per share.
July 2	Sold 300 shares of $4.50, no-par class A preferred stock for $20,000 cash.
12	Received inventory valued at $25,000 and equipment with market value of $16,000 for 3,300 shares of the $1 par common stock.

Required

Prepare the stockholders' equity section of the Spenco balance sheet for the transactions given in this exercise. Retained earnings has a balance of $172,000. Journal entries are not required.

Measuring the paid-in capital of a corporation
(Obj. 2)

E9-5 Pavelka Corp. was recently organized. The company issued common stock to an attorney who gave legal services of $20,000 to help organize the corporation. Pavelka Corp. issued common stock to an inventor in exchange for his patent with a market value of $40,000. In addition, Pavelka received cash both for the issuance of 1,000 shares of its preferred stock at $110 per share and for the issuance of 26,000 shares of its common stock at $15 per share. During the first year of operations, Pavelka Corp. earned net income of $85,000 and declared a cash dividend of $26,000. Without making journal entries, determine the total paid-in capital created by these transactions.

Stockholders' equity section of a balance sheet
(Obj. 2, 3)

E9-6 Breedlove Construction, Inc., has the following selected account balances at June 30, 20X3. Prepare the stockholders' equity section of the company's balance sheet.

Common stock, no-par with $1 stated value, 500,000 shares authorized, 120,000 shares issued.	$120,000	Inventory.	$112,000
Accumulated depreciation—machinery and equipment	62,000	Machinery and equipment, net	109,000
Retained earnings	119,000	Preferred stock, 5%, $1 par, 20,000 shares authorized, 11,000 shares issued.	11,000
Accounts receivable, net	43,000	Paid-in capital in excess of stated value—common . . .	88,000
Notes payable, 8%	81,000	Treasury stock, common, 2,200 shares at cost	5,000

Recording treasury stock transactions and measuring their effects on stockholders' equity
(Obj. 3)

E9-7 Journalize the following transactions of Buzze Music Company:

Feb. 19	Issued 10,000 shares of no-par common stock at $15 per share.
Apr. 22	Purchased 900 shares of treasury stock at $14 per share.
June 11	Sold 200 shares of treasury stock at $16 per share.

What was the overall effect of these transactions on the company's stockholders' equity?

Recording stock issuance, treasury stock, and dividend transactions
(Obj. 2, 3, 4)

E9-8 At December 31, 1998, **Sprint Corporation** reported the stockholders' equity accounts, shown on page 443, (as adapted, with dollar amounts in millions, except par value per share). Assume that Sprint's 1999 transactions included the following:

a. Net income, $440 million.

b. Issuance of 6 million shares of common stock for $80 per share.

Common stock $2.50 par value per share, 615.2 million shares issued	$ 1,538
Capital in excess of par value	7,586
Retained earnings	3,651
Treasury stock, 8.5 million shares at cost	(426)
Other	99
Total stockholders' equity	$12,448

c. Purchase of 1 million shares of treasury stock for $7 million.

d. Declaration and payment of cash dividends of $300 million.

Journalize Sprint's transactions b, c, and d. Explanations are not required.

E9-9 Use the Sprint Corporation data in Exercise 9-8 to prepare the stockholders' equity section of the company's balance sheet at December 31, 1999.

Reporting stockholders' equity after a sequence of transactions (Obj. 2, 3, 4)

E9-10 Krisler Corporation reported the following shareholders' equity on its balance sheet:

Inferring transactions from a company's stockholders' equity (Obj. 2, 3, 4, 5)

Shareholders' Equity *(Dollars and shares in millions)*	***December 31*** ***19X9***	***19X8***
Preferred stock—$1 per share par value; authorized 20.0 shares; Series A Convertible Preferred Stock; issued and outstanding: 19X9 and 19X8—0.1 and 1.7 shares, respectively (aggregate liquidation preference $68 million and $863 million, respectively)	$ *	$ 2
Common stock—$1 per share par value; authorized 1,000.0 shares; issued: 19X9 and 19X8—408.2 and 364.1 shares, respectively	408	364
Additional paid-in capital	5,506	5,536
Retained earnings	6,280	5,006
Treasury stock, common—at cost: 19X9—29.9 shares; 19X8—9.0 shares	(1,235)	(214)
Total Shareholders' Equity	10,959	10,694
Total Liabilities and Shareholders' Equity	$53,756	$49,539

* Less than $1 million

Required

1. Identify two likely transactions that caused Krisler's preferred stock to decrease during 19X9.
2. Identify two likely transactions that caused Krisler's common stock to increase during 19X9.
3. How many shares of Krisler common stock were outstanding at December 31, 19X9?
4. Assume that during 19X9, Krisler sold no treasury stock. What average price per share did Krisler pay for the treasury stock the company purchased during the year? During 19X9, the market price of Krisler's common stock ranged from a low of $38.25 to a high of $58.13. Compare the average price Krisler paid for its treasury stock during 19X9 to the range of market prices during the year.
5. Krisler's net income during 19X9 was $2,025 million. How much were Krisler's dividends during the year?

E9-11 The following elements of stockholders' equity are adapted from the balance sheet of **Gulf Resources & Chemical Corporation.** All dollar amounts, except the dividends per share, are given in thousands.

Computing dividends on preferred and common stock (Obj. 4)

GULF RESOURCES & CHEMICAL CORPORATION Stockholders' Equity		
Preferred stock, cumulative, $1 par (Note 7)		
Series A, 58,000 shares issued	$	58
Series B, 376,000 shares issued		376
Common stock, $0.10 par, 9,130,000 shares issued		913

Note 7. Preferred Stock:	Designated Annual Cash Dividend per Share
Series A	$0.20
Series B	1.00

Assume that the Series A preferred has preference over the Series B preferred and that the company has paid all preferred dividends through 20X0.

Required

Compute the dividends to both series of preferred and to common for 20X1 and 20X2 if total dividends are $0 in 20X1 and $900,000 in 20X2. Round to the nearest dollar.

Recording dividends and reporting stockholders' equity (Obj. 4)

E9-12 Dade County Title Co., Inc., is authorized to issue 100,000 shares of $1 par common stock. The company issued 50,000 shares at $5 per share, and all 50,000 shares are outstanding. When the retained earnings balance was $150,000, Dade Title distributed a 50% stock dividend. Later, Dade declared and paid a $0.30 per share cash dividend.

Required

1. Journalize the distribution of the stock dividend.
2. Journalize the declaration and payment of the cash dividend.
3. Prepare the stockholders' equity section of the balance sheet after both dividends.
4. Which dividend decreased total stockholders' equity? By how much? Use the accounting equation to answer this question. Dade's total assets prior to the dividends stood at $900,000, paid-in capital was $250,000, and retained earnings were $150,000.

Recording a small stock dividend and reporting stockholders' equity (Obj. 4)

E9-13 The stockholders' equity for Pioneer Insurance Company on September 30, 20X0—end of the company's fiscal year—follows:

Stockholders' Equity	
Common stock, $10 par, 100,000 shares authorized, 50,000 shares issued	$500,000
Paid-in capital in excess of par—common	60,000
Retained earnings	300,000
Total stockholders' equity	$860,000

On October 6, the market price of Pioneer's common stock was $13 per share, and the company distributed a 10% stock dividend.

Required

1. Journalize the distribution of the stock dividend.
2. Prepare the stockholders' equity section of the balance sheet after the stock dividend.
3. Why is total stockholders' equity unchanged by the stock dividend?

Measuring the effects of stock issuance, dividends, and treasury stock transactions (Obj. 2, 3, 4)

E9-14 Identify the effects—both the direction and the dollar amount—of these assumed transactions on the total stockholders' equity of **Pier 1 Imports, Inc.** Each transaction is independent.

a. Purchase of 1,500 shares of treasury stock (par value $1) at $4.25 per share.
b. 10% stock dividend. Before the dividend, 69 million shares of $1 par common stock were outstanding; the market value was $7.625 at the time of the dividend.
c. Sale of 600 shares of $1 par treasury stock for $6.00 per share. Cost of the treasury stock was $4.25 per share.

d. A 3-for-1 stock split. Prior to the split, 69 million shares of $1 par common were outstanding.

e. A 50% stock dividend. Before the dividend, 69 million shares of $1 par common stock were outstanding; the market value was $13.75 at the time of the dividend.

E9-15 **The Gap, Inc.,** had the following stockholders' equity (adapted) at January 31 (dollars in millions):

Reporting stockholders' equity after a stock split (Obj. 4)

Common stock, $0.05 par, 500 million shares authorized, 440 million shares issued	$ 22
Additional paid-in capital	318
Retained earnings	2,393
Other	(1,149)
Total stockholders' equity	$1,584

Assume that on March 7, The Gap split its $0.05 par common stock 2 for 1. Make the memorandum entry to record the stock split and prepare the stockholders' equity section of the balance sheet immediately after the split. (Note: A stock split also increases the number of shares of stock authorized.)

E9-16 The balance sheet of Venture Business Systems reported the following, with all amounts, including shares, in thousands:

Measuring the book value per share of common stock (Obj. 5)

Redeemable preferred stock, 6%, redemption value $6,362; outstanding 100 shares	$ 4,860
Common stockholders' equity 11,120 shares issued and outstanding	181,360
Total stockholders' equity	$186,220

Required

1. Compute the book value per share for the common stock, assuming all preferred dividends are fully paid up (none in arrears).
2. Compute the book value per share of the common stock, assuming that three years' preferred dividends, including the current year, are in arrears.
3. Venture Business Systems' common stock recently traded at market value of $15.75. Does this mean that Venture's stock is a good buy at $15.75?

E9-17 **Ford Motor Company** reported these figures for 19X7 and 19X6 (in millions):

Evaluating profitability (Obj. 6)

	19X7	*19X6*
Income statement:		
Interest expense	$ 10,500	$ 10,399
Net income	6,920	4,446
Balance sheet:		
Total assets	279,097	262,867
Common stock	6,767	6,457
Retained earnings	25,234	20,334
Other equity	(1,267)	(29)
Total stockholders' equity	30,734	26,762

Compute Ford's rate of return on total assets and rate of return on common stockholders' equity for 19X7. Do these rates of return suggest strength or weakness? Give your reason.

E9-18 Assume **General Motors Corporation** included the following items on its statement of cash flows for 19X9 (amounts in millions):

Reporting investing and financing transactions on the statement of cash flows (Obj. 7)

Cash dividends paid to stockholders	$ 1,328
Decrease in long-term debt	9,636
Expenditures for real estate, plants, and equipment	6,351
Expenditures for special tools	3,726
Increase in long-term debt	12,130
Investment in [other] companies	616
Net increase in short-term loans payable	6,088
Proceeds from disposals of real estate, plants, and equipment	541
Proceeds from issuing common stock	505
Proceeds from the sale of various assets	183
Repurchases of common and preferred stocks	1,681

Required

1. Show how General Motors would report each of these items on its 19X9 statement of cash flows—as a cash flow from *investing activities* or as a cash flow from *financing activities*. Report cash payments in parentheses and list items in order of decreasing amounts.
2. Write a brief description of the three largest financing cash flows in your own words.

Challenge Exercises

Explaining the changes in stockholders' equity (Obj. 2, 3, 4)

E9-19 **Mobil Corporation,** the giant oil company, reported the following stockholders' equity data (adapted):

(In millions, except par value per share)	*December 31,* *19X7*	*19X6*
Preferred stock	$ 665	$ 686
Common stock, $1 par value	894	891
Additional paid-in capital	1,549	1,468
Retained earnings	20,661	19,108
Treasury stock, common	(3,158)	(2,643)

Mobil earned net income of $3,272 during 19X7. For each account except Retained Earnings, assume one transaction explains the change from the December 31, 19X6, balance to the December 31, 19X7, balance. Two transactions affected Retained Earnings. Give a full explanation, including the dollar amount, for the change in each account.

Accounting for changes in stockholders' equity (Obj. 2, 3, 4)

E9-20 Republic Group, Inc., began 20X0 with 8 million shares of $1 par common stock issued and outstanding. Beginning additional paid-in capital was $13 million, and retained earnings totaled $40 million. In March 20X0, Republic issued 2 million shares of common stock at a price of $2 per share. In May, the company distributed a 10% stock dividend at a time when Republic's common stock had a market value of $3 per share. Then in October, Republic's stock price dropped to $1 per share and the company purchased 2 million shares of treasury stock. For the year, Republic earned net income of $26 million and declared cash dividends of $5 million.

Complete the following tabulation to show what Republic should report for stockholders' equity at December 31, 20X0. Journal entries are not required.

(Amounts in millions)	*Common Stock*	*Additional Paid-In Capital*	*Retained Earnings*	*Treasury Stock*	*Total*
Balance, Dec. 31, 19X9	$8	$13	$40		$61
Issuance of stock					
Stock dividend				$	
Purchase of treasury stock					
Net income					
Cash dividends					
Balance, Dec. 31, 20X0	$	$	$	$	$

PROBLEMS

(Group A)

Explaining the features of a corporation's stock (Obj. 1)

P9-1A Answer the following questions about a corporation's stockholders' equity.

1. How is preferred stock similar to common stock? How is preferred stock similar to debt?
2. What makes convertible preferred stock more valuable than nonconvertible preferred stock? Name two economic benefits that an investor hopes to gain by purchasing convertible preferred stock.
3. MJ Designs purchased treasury stock for $50,000 and a year later sold it for $65,000. Explain to the manager of MJ Designs why the $15,000 excess is not profit to be reported on the company's income statement.
4. As an investor, would you prefer to receive cash dividends or stock dividends? Explain your reasoning.
5. Why do so many businesses organize as corporations if they have to pay an additional layer of income tax?

Recording corporate transactions and preparing the stockholders' equity section of the balance sheet (Obj. 2)

P9-2A The partnership of Livermore and McGregor needed additional capital to expand into new markets, so the business incorporated as LM, Inc. The charter from the state of Illinois authorizes LM, Inc., to issue 50,000 shares of 6%, $100 par preferred stock and 100,000 shares of no-par common stock with a stated value of $5 per share. In its first month, LM, Inc., completed the following transactions:

Dec.	2	Issued 300 shares of common stock to the promoter for assistance with issuance of the common stock. The promotional fee was $1,800. Debit the asset account Organization Cost.
	2	Issued 9,000 shares of common stock to Livermore and 12,000 shares to McGregor in return for cash equal to the stock's market value of $6 per share.
	10	Issued 400 shares of preferred stock to acquire a patent with a market value of $50,000.
	16	Issued 2,000 shares of common stock for cash of $12,000.

Required

1. Record the transactions in the journal.
2. Prepare the stockholders' equity section of the LM, Inc., balance sheet at December 31. The ending balance of Retained Earnings is $141,100.

Preparing the stockholders' equity section of the balance sheet (Obj. 2, 4)

P9-3A The following summary provides the information needed to prepare the stockholders' equity section of the Action Recycling, Inc., balance sheet:

> Action's charter authorizes the company to issue 5,000 shares of 5%, $100 par preferred stock and 500,000 shares of no-par common stock. Action issued 1,000 shares of the preferred stock at $105 per share. It issued 100,000 shares of the common stock for $519,000. The company's retained earnings balance at the beginning of 20X4 was $73,000. Net income for 20X4 was $80,000, and the company declared a 5% cash dividend on preferred stock for 20X4. Preferred dividends for 20X3 were in arrears.

Required

Prepare the stockholders' equity section of Action Recycling's balance sheet at December 31, 20X4. Show the computation of all amounts. Journal entries are not required.

Using stock dividends to fight off a takeover of the corporation (Obj. 4)

P9-4A Wooton, Inc., is positioned ideally in the clothing business. Located in White Plains, New York, Wooton is the only company with a distribution network for its imported goods. The company does a brisk business with specialty stores such as **Bloomingdale's**, **I. Magnin**, and **Bonwit Teller**. Wooton's recent success has made the company a prime target for a takeover. Against the wishes of Wooton's board of directors, an investment group from Philadelphia is attempting to buy 51% of Wooton's outstanding stock. Board members are convinced that the Philadelphia investors would sell off the most desirable pieces of the business and leave little of value.

At the most recent board meeting, several suggestions were advanced to fight off the hostile takeover bid. One suggestion is to increase the stock outstanding by distributing a 100% stock dividend.

Required

Suppose you are a significant stockholder of Wooton Corporation. Write a short memo explaining to the board whether distributing the stock dividend would make it more difficult or less difficult for the investor group to take over Wooton Corporation. Include in your memo a discussion of the effect the stock dividend would have on assets, liabilities, and total stockholders' equity—that is, the dividend's effect on the size of the corporation.

Measuring the effects of stock issuance, treasury stock, and dividend transactions on stockholders' equity (Obj. 2, 3, 4)

P9-5A The corporate charter of House of Carpets, granted by the state of Georgia, authorizes the company to issue 5,000,000 shares of $1 par common stock and 50,000 shares of $50 par preferred stock.

In its initial public offering during 20X1, House of Carpets issued 500,000 shares of its $1 par common stock for $5.00 per share. Over the next five years, House of Carpets' stock price increased in value and the company issued 400,000 more shares at prices ranging from $6 to $10.75. The average issue price of these shares was $8.50.

During 20X3, the price of House of Carpets' common stock dropped to $7, and the company purchased 60,000 shares of its common stock for the treasury. After the market price of the common stock increased in 20X4, House of Carpets sold 40,000 shares of the treasury stock for $8 per share.

During the five years 20X1–20X5, House of Carpets earned net income of $1,590,000 and declared and paid cash dividends of $640,000. Stock dividends of $220,000 were distributed to the stockholders in 20X4, with $35,000 transferred to common stock and $185,000 transferred to additional paid-in capital. At December 31, 20X5, the company has total assets of $13,100,000 and total liabilities of $6,350,000.

Required

Show the computation of House of Carpets' total stockholders' equity at December 31, 20X5. Present detailed computations of each element of stockholders' equity.

Analyzing the stockholders' equity and dividends of a corporation (Obj. 2, 4)

P9-6A **Bethlehem Steel Corporation** is one of the nation's largest steel companies. Bethlehem included the following stockholders' equity on its balance sheet:

Stockholders' Equity	*($ Millions)*
Preferred stock—	
Authorized 20,000,000 shares in each class; issued:	
$5.00 Cumulative Convertible Preferred Stock,	
at $50.00 stated value, 2,500,000 shares	$ 125
$2.50 Cumulative Convertible Preferred Stock,	
at $25.00 stated value, 4,000,000 shares	100
Common stock—$8 par value—	
Authorized 80,000,000 shares, issued 48,308,516 shares. .	621
Retained earnings	529
	$1,375

Observe that Bethlehem reports no Paid-in Capital in Excess of Par or Stated Value. Instead, the company reports those items in the stock accounts.

Required

1. Identify the different issues of stock Bethlehem has outstanding.
2. Which class of stock did Bethlehem issue at par or stated value, and which class did it issue above par or stated value?
3. Suppose Bethlehem passed its preferred dividends for one year. Would the company have to pay these dividends in arrears before paying dividends to the common stockholders? Why?
4. What amount of preferred dividends must Bethlehem declare and pay each year to avoid having preferred dividends in arrears?
5. Assume preferred dividends are in arrears for 19X8.
   a. Write Note 6 of the 19X8 financial statements to disclose the dividends in arrears.
   b. Journalize the declaration of an $82 million dividend for 19X9. No explanation is needed.

P9-7A Ski and Sea Corporation reported the following summarized balance sheet at December 31, 20X1:

Accounting for stock issuance, dividends, and treasury stock (Obj. 2, 3, 4)

Assets	
Current assets	$33,400
Property & equipment, net	51,800
Total assets	$85,200
Liabilities and Equity	
Liabilities	$37,800
Stockholders' equity	
$0.50 cumulative preferred stock, $5 par	2,000
Common stock, $1 par	6,000
Paid-in capital in excess of par, common	17,400
Retained earnings	22,000
Total liabilities and equity	$85,200

During 20X2, Ski and Sea Corporation completed these transactions that affected stockholders' equity:

Mar. 13	Issued 2,000 shares of common stock for $4 per share.
July 7	Declared the regular cash dividend on the preferred stock.
24	Paid the cash dividend.
Sept. 9	Distributed a 50% stock dividend on the common stock. Market price of the common stock was $7 per share.
Oct. 26	Reacquired 500 shares of common stock as treasury stock, paying $7 per share.
Nov. 20	Sold 200 shares of the treasury stock for $8 per share.

Required

1. Journalize Ski and Sea's transactions. Explanations are not required.

2. Report Ski and Sea's stockholders' equity at December 31, 20X2. Net income for 20X2 was $49,000.

P9-8A Assume that **IHOP Corp.** completed the following selected transactions during the current year:

Measuring the effects of dividend and treasury stock transactions on a company (Obj. 3, 4)

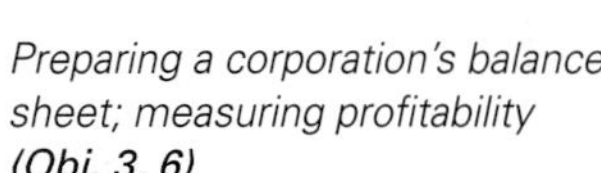

April 18	Declared a cash dividend on the 5%, $100 par preferred stock (1,000 shares outstanding).
May 23	Paid the cash dividends.
July 30	Distributed a 10% stock dividend on the 9.7 million shares of common stock outstanding. The market value of the common stock was $25 per share.
Oct. 26	Purchased 2,500 shares of the company's own common stock at $24 per share.
Nov. 8	Sold 1,000 shares of treasury common stock for $27 per share.

Required

Analyze each transaction in terms of its effect on the accounting equation of IHOP.

P9-9A The following accounts and related balances of Danka Office Solutions, Inc., are arranged in no particular order.

Preparing a corporation's balance sheet; measuring profitability (Obj. 3, 6)

Accounts payable	$ 31,000	Dividends payable	$ 3,000
Retained earnings	?	Total assets, November 30, 20X0	581,000
Common stock, $5-par; 100,000 shares authorized, 42,000 shares issued	210,000	Net income	36,200
Inventory	170,000	Common stockholders' equity November 30, 20X0	383,000
Property, plant, and equipment, net	278,000	Interest expense	12,800
Goodwill, net	6,000	Treasury stock, common 1,600 shares at cost	11,000
Preferred stock, 4%, $10 par, 25,000 shares authorized, 3,700 shares issued	37,000	Prepaid expenses	13,000
Cash	32,000	Patent, net	31,000
Additional paid-in-capital—common	140,000	Accrued liabilities	17,000
		Long-term note payable	104,000
		Accounts receivable, net	102,000

Required

1. Prepare the company's classified balance sheet in the account format at November 30, 20X1.
2. Compute rate of return on total assets and rate of return on common stockholders' equity for the year ended November 30, 20X1.
3. Do these rates of return suggest strength or weakness? Give your reason.

Analyzing the statement of cash flows (Obj. 7)

P9-10A The statement of cash flows of **Reebok International Ltd.** reported the following for the year ended December 31, 19X9:

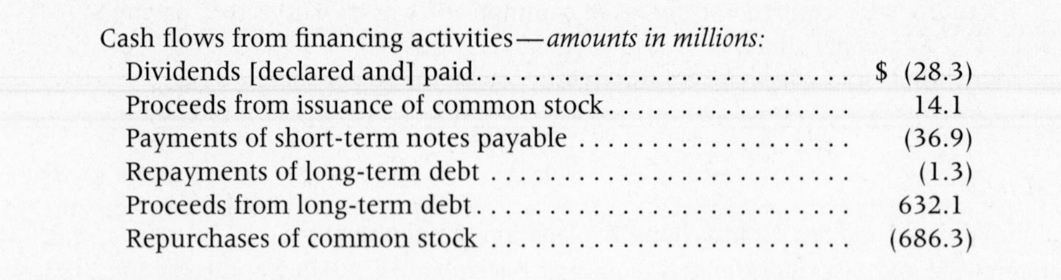

Cash flows from financing activities—*amounts in millions:*	
Dividends [declared and] paid	$ (28.3)
Proceeds from issuance of common stock	14.1
Payments of short-term notes payable	(36.9)
Repayments of long-term debt	(1.3)
Proceeds from long-term debt	632.1
Repurchases of common stock	(686.3)

Required

1. Make the journal entry that Reebok used to record each of these transactions.
2. From these transactions, would you expect Reebok's total liabilities, total stockholders' equity, and total assets to have grown or shrunk during 19X9? Reebok's net income for 19X9 was $135 million. State the reasoning behind your answer.

(Group B)

Explaining the features of a corporation's stock (Obj. 1)

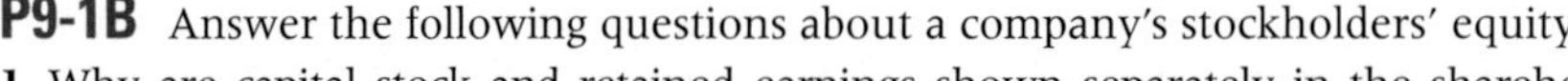

P9-1B Answer the following questions about a company's stockholders' equity.

1. Why are capital stock and retained earnings shown separately in the shareholders' equity section of the balance sheet?
2. Ann Martinelli, the major shareholder of Martinelli, Inc., proposes to give some land she owns to the company in exchange for common shares in Martinelli, Inc. What challenge does Martinelli, Inc., face in recording the transaction?
3. Preferred shares generally are preferred with respect to dividends and on liquidation. Why would investors buy common stock when preferred stock is available?
4. What does it mean if the redemption value of a company's preferred stock is greater than its book value?
5. Suppose you own 100 shares of stock in Stratagem Systems and someone offers to buy your shares for their book value. Under what circumstances would you accept the offer? Under what circumstances would you *not* accept the offer?

Recording corporate transactions and preparing the stockholders' equity section of the balance sheet (Obj. 2)

P9-2B The partners who own Depaul & Hancock wished to avoid the unlimited personal liability of the partnership form of business, so they incorporated as D&H Exploration, Inc. The charter from the state of Wyoming authorizes the corporation to issue 10,000 shares of 6%, $100 par preferred stock and 250,000 shares of no-par common stock with a stated value of $5 per share. In its first month, D&H Exploration completed the following transactions:

Dec. 3	Issued 500 shares of common stock to the promoter for assistance with issuance of the common stock. The promotional fee was $5,000. Debit the asset account Organization Cost.
3	Issued 5,100 shares of common stock to DePaul and 3,800 shares to Hancock in return for cash equal to the stock's market value of $10 per share.
12	Issued 1,000 shares of preferred stock to acquire a patent with a market value of $110,000.
22	Issued 1,500 shares of common stock for $10 cash per share.

Required

1. Record the transactions in the journal.
2. Prepare the stockholders' equity section of the D&H Exploration, Inc., balance sheet at December 31. The ending balance of Retained Earnings is $31,300.

Preparing the stockholders' equity section of the balance sheet (Obj. 2, 4)

P9-3B The following is stockholders' equity information for Water Works, Incorporated:

Water Works' charter authorizes the company to issue 10,000 shares of $2.50 preferred stock with par value of $100 and 120,000 shares of no-par common stock. The company issued 1,000 shares of the preferred stock at $104 per share. It issued 40,000 shares of the common stock for a total of $220,000. The company's retained earnings balance at the beginning of 20X3 was $63,000, and net income for the year was $90,000. During 20X3, Water Works declared the specified dividend on preferred and a $0.50 per share dividend on common. Preferred dividends for 20X2 were in arrears.

Required

Prepare the stockholders' equity section of Water Works, Incorporated's balance sheet at December 31, 20X3. Show the computation of all amounts. Journal entries are not required.

Purchasing treasury stock to fight off a takeover of the corporation (Obj. 3)

P9-4B Yuma Corporation is positioned ideally in its line of business. Located in Nogales, Arizona, Yuma is the only company between Texas and California with reliable sources for its imported gifts. The company does a brisk business with specialty stores such as Pier 1 Imports. Yuma's recent success has made the company a prime target for a takeover. An investment group from Mexico City is attempting to buy 51% of Yuma's outstanding stock against the wishes of Yuma's board of directors. Board members are convinced that the Mexico City investors would sell the most desirable pieces of the business and leave little of value.

At the most recent board meeting, several suggestions were advanced to fight off the hostile takeover bid. The suggestion with the most promise is to purchase a huge quantity of treasury stock. Yuma has the cash to carry out this plan.

Required

1. Suppose you are a significant stockholder of Yuma Corporation. Write a memorandum to explain to the board how the purchase of treasury stock would make it more difficult for the Mexico City group to take over Yuma. Include in your memo a discussion of the effect that purchasing treasury stock would have on stock outstanding and on the size of the corporation.
2. Suppose Yuma management is successful in fighting off the takeover bid and later sells the treasury stock at prices greater than the purchase price. Explain what effect these sales will have on assets, stockholders' equity, and net income.

Measuring the effects of stock issuance, treasury stock, and dividend transactions on stockholders' equity (Obj. 2, 3, 4)

P9-5B The corporate charter of Discount Auto Parts, Inc., granted by the state of Delaware, authorizes the company to issue 1,000,000 shares of $1 par common stock and 100,000 shares of $50 par preferred stock.

In its initial public offering during 20X2, Discount Auto Parts issued 200,000 shares of its $1 par common stock for $6.50 per share. Over the next five years, Discount's common stock price increased in value, and the company issued 200,000 more shares at prices ranging from $7 to $11. The average issue price of these shares was $9.25.

During 20X4, the price of Discount's common stock dropped to $8, and Discount purchased 30,000 shares of its common stock for the treasury. After the market price of the common stock increased in 20X5, Discount sold 20,000 shares of the treasury stock for $9 per share.

During the five years 20X2–20X6, Discount earned net income of $295,000 and declared and paid cash dividends of $119,000. Stock dividends of $110,000 were distributed to the stockholders in 20X3, with $14,000 transferred to common stock and $96,000 transferred to additional paid-in capital. At December 31, 20X6, total assets of the company are $6,290,000, and liabilities add up to $3,024,000.

Required

Show the computation of Discount Auto Parts' total stockholders' equity at December 31, 20X6. Present detailed computations of each element of stockholders' equity.

Analyzing the stockholders' equity and dividends of a corporation (Obj. 2, 4)

P9-6B **U and I Group,** which makes food products and livestock feeds, included the following stockholders' equity on its year-end balance sheet at February 28:

Stockholders' Equity	*(In thousands)*
Voting Preferred stock, 5.5% cumulative—par value $23 per share; authorized 100,000 shares in each class:	
Class A—issued 75,473 shares	$ 1,736
Class B—issued 92,172 shares	2,120
Common stock—par value $5 per share; authorized 5,000,000 shares; issued 2,870,950 shares	14,355
[Additional] Paid-in Capital	5,548
Retained earnings	8,336
	$32,095

Required

1. Identify the different issues of stock U and I has outstanding.
2. Give the summary entries to record issuance of all the U and I stock. Assume that all the stock was issued for cash and that the additional paid-in capital applies to the common stock. Explanations are not required.
3. Suppose U and I passed its preferred dividends for five years. Would the company have to pay those dividends in arrears before paying dividends to the common stockholders? Give your reason.
4. What amount of preferred dividends must U and I declare and pay each year to avoid having preferred dividends in arrears?
5. Assume that preferred dividends are in arrears for 20X1.
   a. Write Note 5 of the February 28, 20X1, financial statements to disclose the dividends in arrears.
   b. Record the declaration of a $600,000 dividend in the year ended February 28, 20X2. An explanation is not required.

Accounting for stock issuance, dividends, and treasury stock (Obj. 2, 3, 4)

P9-7B Bedford Corporation reported the following summarized balance sheet at December 31, 20X2:

Assets	
Current assets	$18,200
Property & equipment, net	34,700
Total assets	$52,900
Liabilities and Equity	
Liabilities	$ 6,200
Stockholders' equity:	
$5 cumulative preferred stock, $100 par	1,800
Common stock, $1 par	2,400
Paid-in capital in excess of par, common	23,500
Retained earnings	19,000
Total liabilities and equity	$52,900

During 20X3, Bedford Corporation completed these transactions that affected stockholders' equity:

Jan. 22	Issued 1,000 shares of common stock for $14 per share.
Aug. 4	Declared the regular cash dividend on the preferred stock.
24	Paid the cash dividend.
Oct. 9	Distributed a 50% stock dividend on the common stock. Market price of the common stock was $15 per share.
Nov. 19	Reacquired 800 shares of common stock as treasury stock, paying $12 per share.
Dec. 8	Sold 600 shares of the treasury stock for $15 per share.

Required

1. Journalize Bedford's transactions. Explanations are not required.
2. Report Bedford's stockholders' equity at December 31, 20X3. Net income for 20X3 was $66,000.

P9-8B Motorcycles, Inc., completed the following selected transactions during 20X0:

Measuring the effects of dividend, and treasury stock transactions on a company (Obj. 3, 4)

Feb. 6	Declared a cash dividend on the 10,000 shares of $1.70 no-par preferred stock.
Mar. 20	Paid the cash dividends.
Apr. 18	Distributed a 50% stock dividend on the 30,000 shares of common stock outstanding. The market value of the common stock was $15 per share.
June 18	Purchased 2,000 shares of the company's own common stock at $12 per share.
Dec. 22	Sold 700 shares of treasury common stock for $16 per share.

Required

Analyze each transaction in terms of its effect on the accounting equation of Motorcycles, Inc.

P9-9B The following accounts and related balances of Mayflower Movers, Inc., as of September 30, 20X2, are arranged in no particular order.

Preparing a corporation's balance sheet; measuring profitability (Obj. 3, 6)

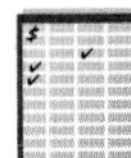

Interest expense	$ 6,100	Cash	$13,000
Property, plant, and equipment, net	247,000	Accounts receivable, net	24,000
Common stock, $1 par, 500,00 shares authorized, 115,000 shares issued	115,000	Paid-in capital in excess of par—common	19,000
Prepaid expenses	10,000	Accrued liabilities	26,000
Common stockholders' equity, September 30, 20X1	192,000	Long-term note payable	72,000
Net income	31,000	Inventory	59,000
Total assets, September 30, 20X1	304,000	Dividends payable	9,000
Treasury stock, common 18,000 shares at cost	22,000	Retained earnings	?
Goodwill, net	14,000	Accounts payable	31,000
		Trademark, net	9,000
		Preferred stock, $0.20, no-par, 10,000 shares authorized and issued	27,000

Required

1. Prepare the company's classified balance sheet in the account format at September 30, 20X2.
2. Compute rate of return on total assets and rate of return on common stockholders' equity for the year ended September 30, 20X2.
3. Do these rates of return suggest strength or weakness? Give your reason.

Analyzing the statement of cash flows (Obj. 7)

P9-10B The statement of cash flows of Ford Optical Company reported the following for the year ended December 31, 19X9:

Cash flows from financing activities—*amounts in millions:*	
Cash dividends [declared and] paid	$ (1,559)
Issuance of common stock	601
Proceeds from issuance of short-term debt	6,297
Proceeds from issuance of other debt	24,154
Principal payments on debt	(11,664)
Redemption of preferred stock	(1,875)

Required

1. Make the journal entry that Ford used to record each of these transactions.
2. From these transactions, would you expect Ford's total liabilities, total stockholders' equity, and total assets to have grown or shrunk during 19X9? Ford's net income for 19X9 was $4,139 million. State the reasoning behind your answer.

EXTENDING YOUR KNOWLEDGE

DECISION CASES

Evaluating alternative ways of raising capital (Obj. 2)

Case 1. Bob Libby and Kermit Larson have written a computer program for a video game that they believe will rival Nintendo and SegaGenesis. They need additional capital to market the product, and they plan to incorporate their partnership. They are considering alternative capital structures for the corporation. Their primary goal is to raise as much capital as possible without giving up control of the business. The partners plan to receive 110,000 shares of the corporation's common stock in return for the net assets of the partnership. After the partnership books are closed and the assets adjusted to current market value, Libby's capital balance will be $60,000, and Larson's balance will be $50,000.

The corporation's plans for a charter include an authorization to issue 5,000 shares of preferred stock and 500,000 shares of $1 par common stock. Libby and Larson are uncertain about the most desirable features for the preferred stock. Prior to incorporating, the partners are discussing their plans with two investment groups. The corporation can obtain capital from outside investors under either of the following plans:

- **Plan 1.** Group 1 will invest $160,000 to acquire 1,400 shares of 6%, $100 par nonvoting, noncumulative preferred stock.
- **Plan 2.** Group 2 will invest $105,000 to acquire 1,000 shares of $5, no-par preferred stock and $70,000 to acquire 70,000 shares of common stock. Each preferred share receives 50 votes on matters that come before the stockholders.

Required

Assume that the corporation is chartered.

1. Journalize the issuance of common stock to Libby and Larson. Debit each partner's capital account for its balance.
2. Journalize the issuance of stock to the outsiders under both plans.
3. Assume that net income for the first year is $85,000 and total dividends are $19,100. Prepare the stockholders' equity section of the corporation's balance sheet under both plans.
4. Recommend one of the plans to Libby and Larson. Give your reasons.

Analyzing cash dividends and stock dividends (Obj. 4)

Case 2. Willkommen, Inc., had the following stockholders' equity amounts on June 30 of the current year:

Common stock, no-par, 100,000 shares issued	$ 750,000
Retained earnings	830,000
Total stockholders' equity	$1,580,000

For years, Willkommen has paid an annual cash dividend of $0.88 per share. Last year, after paying the cash dividends, Willkommen distributed a 10% stock dividend. This year, the company declared and paid a cash dividend of $0.80 per share.

Suppose you own 10,000 shares of Willkommen common stock, acquired three years ago, prior to the 10% stock dividend. The market price of the stock was $22 per share before the stock dividend.

Required

1. How does the stock dividend affect your proportionate ownership in Willkommen, Inc.? Explain.
2. What amount of cash dividends did you receive last year? What amount of cash dividends will you receive after the above dividend action?
3. Immediately after the stock dividend was distributed, the market value of Willkommen stock decreased from $22 per share to $20 per share. Does this decrease represent a loss to you? Explain.
4. Suppose Willkommen announces at the time of the stock dividend that the company will continue to pay the annual $0.88 *cash* dividend per share, even after distributing the *stock* dividend. Would you expect the market price of the stock to decrease to $20 per share as in Requirement 3? Explain.

ETHICAL ISSUES

Ethical Issue 1. *Note: This case is based on a real situation.*
George Campbell paid $50,000 for a franchise that entitled him to market Success Associates software programs in the countries of the European Union. Campbell intended to sell individual franchises for the major language groups of western Europe—German, French, English, Spanish, and Italian. Naturally, investors considering buying a franchise from Campbell asked to see the financial statements of his business.

Believing the value of the franchise to be greater than $50,000, Campbell sought to capitalize his own franchise at $500,000. The law firm of McDonald & LaDue helped Campbell form a corporation chartered to issue 500,000 shares of common stock with par value of $1 per share. Attorneys suggested the following chain of transactions:

a. A third party borrows $500,000 and purchases the franchise from Campbell.
b. Campbell pays the corporation $500,000 to acquire all its stock.
c. The corporation buys the franchise from the third party, who repays the loan.

In the final analysis, the third party is debt-free and out of the picture. Campbell owns all the corporation's stock, and the corporation owns the franchise. The corporation balance sheet lists a franchise acquired at a cost of $500,000. This balance sheet is Campbell's most valuable marketing tool.

Required

1. What is unethical about this situation?
2. Who can be harmed? How can they be harmed? What role does accounting play here?

Ethical Issue 2. Muskogee Petroleum Company is an independent oil producer in Muskogee, Oklahoma. In February, company geologists discovered a pool of oil that tripled the company's proven reserves. Prior to disclosing the new oil to the public, Muskogee quietly bought most of its stock as treasury stock. After the discovery was announced, Muskogee's stock price increased from $6 to $27.

Required

1. Did Muskogee managers behave ethically? Explain your answer.
2. Identify the accounting principle relevant to this situation.
3. Who was helped and who was harmed by management's action?

FINANCIAL STATEMENT CASES

Analyzing stockholders' equity (Obj. 2, 3, 4)

Case 1. **The Gap, Inc.,** financial statements appear in Appendix A at the end of the book. Answer the following questions about the company's common stock.

1. What does The Gap call its stockholders' equity?
2. Show how The Gap computed the balance in the Common Stock account at January 30, 1999.
3. How many shares of common stock were authorized, issued, held in the treasury, and outstanding at January 30, 1999, and at January 31, 1998.
4. Journalize The Gap's transactions during the year ended January 30, 1999 to (a) issue common stock and (b) purchase treasury stock.
5. The Gap's balance of retained earnings increased during the year ended January 30, 1999. Identify both items that affected retained earnings and give their amounts.

Analyzing treasury stock and retained earnings (Obj. 3, 5)

Case 2. Obtain the annual report of a company of your choosing. Answer the following questions about the company. Concentrate on the current year in the annual report you select.

1. How many shares of common stock had the company issued through the end of the current year? How many shares were in the treasury? How many shares were outstanding on the date of the current balance sheet?
2. Compute average cost per share of treasury stock (common). Compare this figure to book value per share of common stock. Does it appear that the company was able to purchase treasury stock at book value? *Note:* This question can be answered only if the company reports the cost of treasury stock.
3. Prepare a T-account for Retained Earnings to show the beginning and ending balances and all activity in the account during the current year.

GROUP PROJECT

Competitive pressures are the norm in business. **Lexus** automobiles (made in Japan) have cut into the sales of **Mercedes-Benz** (a German company), **Jaguar Motors** (a British company), **General Motors' Cadillac Division,** and **Ford's Lincoln Division** (both U.S. companies). **Dell, Gateway,** and **Compaq** computers have siphoned business away from **Apple** and **IBM.** Foreign steelmakers have reduced the once-massive U.S. steel industry to a fraction of its former size.

Indeed, corporate downsizing has occurred on a massive scale. Each company or industry mentioned here has pared down plant and equipment, laid off employees, or restructured operations.

Required

1. Identify all the stakeholders of a corporation. A *stakeholder* is a person or a group who has an interest (that is, a stake) in the success of the organization.
2. Identify several measures by which a company may be considered deficient and in need of downsizing. How can downsizing help to solve this problem?
3. Debate the downsizing issue. One group of students takes the perspective of the company and its stockholders, and another group of students takes the perspective of other stakeholders of the company.

INTERNET EXERCISE

Motorola

Motorola is an electronics giant with operations in over 40 countries and about 50% of revenues generated outside the United States. Currently, **Motorola, Ericsson,** and **Nokia** vie for the number-one spot among mobile phone makers.

1. Go to **http://www.mot.com** and click on *Investor Information,* then *Financial Reports,* followed by the most recent *Summary Annual Report* in the html format. Use the *Condensed Consolidated Financial Statements* to answer the following questions.
2. How many types of stock have been authorized? issued? For the two most recent years identify total stockholders' equity. Of this total, identify the amount invested by shareholders. Did this amount increase or decrease? What caused this change?
3. Has the company reacquired any of its common stock? Explain how you can tell. What is reacquired stock called?

4. At the end of the two most recent years, identify the amount of stockholders' equity accumulated as the result of past profits. What is the name of this account? Did this amount increase or decrease? What may cause this change? Go to the consolidated statement of stockholders' equity to explain the change in these two amounts.
5. For the most recent year, what amount of cash was received from shareholders? Why was this cash received? Where did you find this information?
6. For the most recent year, what amount of cash was paid to shareholders? What are these payments called? Where did you find this information?

10 Long-Term Investments and International Operations

Learning Objectives

After studying this chapter, you should be able to

1. Account for available-for-sale investments
2. Use the equity method for investments
3. Understand consolidated financial statements
4. Account for long-term investments in bonds
5. Account for transactions stated in a foreign currency
6. Interpret a foreign-currency translation adjustment
7. Report investing transactions on the statement of cash flows

"GM Europe . . . designs, manufactures, and markets vehicles and components throughout that continent. Manufacturing facilities are located in 11 countries, and national sales companies operate in 25 countries."

—General Motors Annual Report, 1998

General Motors Corporation and Subsidiaries
Consolidated Balance Sheet (partial, adapted)

	Dollars in billions	December 31, 1998	1997
	Assets		
1	Total assets	$257.4	$231.8
	Liabilities		
2	Total liabilities	$242.4	$214.3
	Stockholders' equity		
3	Preference stocks	—*	—*
4	Common stocks, $1\frac{2}{3}$ par value	1.1	1.2
5	Capital surplus (principally additional paid-in capital)	12.6	15.4
6	Retained earnings	7.0	5.4
7	Subtotal	20.7	22.0
8	Accumulated foreign-currency translation adjustments	(1.1)	(0.9)
9	Net unrealized gains on investments	0.5	0.5
10	Other	(5.1)	(4.1)
11	Total stockholders' equity	15.0	17.5
12	Total liabilities and stockholders' equity	$257.4	$231.8

* Rounds to less than $0.5 billion

General Motors Corporation (GM) is the world's largest business entity, with annual revenues of $161 billion and assets totaling $257 billion, as shown on the company's 1998 balance sheet. The GM organization includes hundreds of individual corporations whose financial statements are combined and reported under the General Motors name. Among these are **GMAC, Hughes Electronics,** and **GM Locomotive.** GM's financial statements are called *consolidated* financial statements because they combine the reports of these and other GM companies.

Many of the companies that GM owns are located in foreign countries. A direct result of GM's foreign operations is *Accumulated foreign-currency translation adjustments,* which appear on the balance sheet in stockholders' equity (line 8).

General Motors also holds investments, and *Net unrealized gains on investments* appears on the balance sheet (line 9). On December 31, 1998, the current market value of GM's investments was $0.5 billion more than GM paid for the investments. In this chapter, we will examine all of these items.

Throughout this course, you have become increasingly familiar with the financial statements of companies such as **The Gap, Intel,** and **IHOP.** You have seen most of the items you will encounter in a set of financial statements. Only a few items remain. This chapter, which discusses long-term investments and international operations, continues your education in the financial statements and how to use them.

Accounting for Long-Term Investments

Investments come in all sizes and shapes—from the purchase of a few shares of stock to the acquisition of an entire company to an investment in bonds. In earlier chapters, we discussed stocks and bonds from the perspective of the company that issued the securities. In Chapter 5, we covered *short-term* investments. In this chapter, we examine *long-term* investments. First, however, let's review how investment transactions take place.

Stock Investments: A Review

Stock Prices

Investors buy more stock in transactions among themselves than from issuing companies. Each share of stock is issued only once, but it may be traded among investors many times thereafter. Individuals and businesses buy and sell stocks from each other in markets, such as the New York Stock Exchange and the American Stock Exchange. Brokers such as **Merrill Lynch** and **Edward Jones** handle stock transactions for a commission.

A broker may "quote a stock price," which means to *state the current market price per share.* The financial community quotes stock prices in dollars and one-eighth fractions. A stock selling at $32\frac{1}{8}$ costs \$32.125 per share. A stock listed at $55\frac{3}{4}$ sells at \$55.75.

Exhibit 10-1 presents information for the common stock of **The Boeing Company,** a large aircraft manufacturer, just as this information appeared in newspaper listings. During the previous 52 weeks, Boeing common stock reached a high price of \$114.50 and a low price of \$74.125 per share. The annual cash dividend is \$1.12 per share. During the previous day, 1,059,800 (10,598 × 100) shares of Boeing common stock were traded. The prices of these transactions ranged from a high of \$109.875 to a low of \$108.75 per share. The day's closing price of \$109.125 was \$0.50 lower than the closing price of the preceding day.

Exhibit 10-1
Stock Price Information for The Boeing Company

52 weeks								
High	*Low*	*Stock*	*Dividend*	*Sales 100s*	*High*	*Low*	*Close*	*Net Change*
$114\frac{1}{2}$	$74\frac{1}{8}$	Boeing	1.12	10598	$109\frac{7}{8}$	$108\frac{3}{4}$	$109\frac{1}{8}$	$-\frac{1}{2}$

Investors, Investees, and Types of Investments

To move further into our discussion of investments in stock, we need to define two key terms. The person or company that owns stock in a corporation is the *investor.* The corporation that issued the stock is the *investee.* If you own shares of Boeing common stock, you are an investor and Boeing is the investee.

Investments in stock are assets to the investor. The investments may be short-term or long-term. **Short-term investments**—sometimes called **marketable securities**—are current assets. To be listed on the balance sheet as short-term, investments must be *liquid* (readily convertible to cash). Also, the investor must intend either to convert the investments to cash within one year or to use them to pay a current liability. We saw how to account for short-term investments in Chapter 5.

Investments not meeting both requirements of short-term investments are classified as **long-term investments,** a category of noncurrent assets. Long-term investments include stocks and bonds that the investor expects to hold for longer than one year or that are not readily marketable. Exhibit 10-2 shows the positions of short-term and long-term investments on the balance sheet. For the remainder of this chapter, we focus on long-term investments.

EXHIBIT 10-2
Reporting Investments on the Balance Sheet

Current Assets		
Cash	$X	
Short-term investments	X	
Accounts receivable	X	
Inventories	X	
Prepaid expenses	X	
Total current assets		$X
Long-term investments [or simply Investments]		X
Property, plant, and equipment		X
Intangible assets		X
Other assets		X

We report assets in the order of their liquidity. Cash is the most liquid asset, followed by Short-Term Investments, Accounts Receivable, and so on. Long-Term Investments are less liquid than Current Assets but more liquid than Property, Plant, and Equipment. However, many companies report their long-term investments after property, plant, and equipment.

Stock Investments

We begin our discussion of stock investments with those situations in which the investor holds less than a 20% interest in the investee company. These investments in stock are classified as either

- trading investments, or
- available-for-sale investments.

Trading investments are expected to be sold in the very near future—days, weeks, or only a few months—with the intent of generating a profit on the sale. Trading investments are therefore classified as *current assets* (see Short-term investments in Exhibit 10-2).

Available-for-sale investments are all stock investments other than trading securities. They are classified as current assets if the business expects to sell the investments within the next year. All other available-for-sale investments are classified as long-term investments (Exhibit 10-2).

After classifying an investment as trading or as available-for-sale, the investor accounts for the two categories separately. We begin by illustrating the accounting for available-for-sale investments.

ACCOUNTING FOR AVAILABLE-FOR-SALE INVESTMENTS

Objective 1
Account for available-for-sale investments

The market value method is used to account for all available-for-sale investments in stock because the company expects to resell the stock at its market value. Under the **market value method,** *cost* is used only as the initial amount for recording the investments. These investments are reported on the balance sheet at their current *market* value.

Suppose that Dade, Inc., purchases 1,000 shares of **Hewlett-Packard Company** common stock at the market price of $35\frac{3}{4}$. Dade intends to hold this investment for longer than a year and therefore classifies it as an available-for-sale investment. Dade's entry to record the investment is:

20X1			
Feb. 23	Long-Term Investment (1,000 × $35.75)	35,750	
	Cash		35,750
	Purchased investment.		

ASSETS	=	LIABILITIES	+	STOCKHOLDERS' EQUITY
+35,750 −35,750	=	0	+	0

Assume that Dade receives a $0.22 per share cash dividend on the Hewlett-Packard stock. Dade's entry to record receipt of the dividend is

20X1			
July 14	Cash (1,000 × $0.22)	220	
	Dividend Revenue		220
	Received cash dividend.		

ASSETS	=	LIABILITIES	+	STOCKHOLDERS' EQUITY	+	REVENUES
220	=	0	+		+	220

For a review of stock dividends, see Chapter 9, page 424.

Receipt of a *stock* dividend is different from receipt of a cash dividend. For a stock dividend, the investor records no dividend revenue. Instead, the investor makes a memorandum entry in the accounting records to denote the new number of shares of stock held as an investment. Because the number of shares of stock held has increased, the investor's cost per share of the stock decreases. For example, suppose Dade, Inc., receives a 5% stock dividend from Hewlett-Packard Company. Dade would receive 50 shares (5% of 1,000 shares previously held) and make this memorandum entry in its accounting records:

MEMORANDUM—Receipt of stock dividend: Received 50 shares of Hewlett-Packard common stock in 5% stock dividend. New cost per share is $34.05 (cost of $35,750 ÷ 1,050 shares).

In all of Dade's future transactions that affect the Hewlett-Packard investment, Dade will use the new cost per share of $34.05.

Reporting Available-for-Sale Investments at Current Market Value

Because of the relevance of market values for decision making, available-for-sale investments in stock are reported on the balance sheet at their market value. This reporting requires an adjustment of the investments from their last carrying amount to current market value. Assume that the market value of Dade's investment in Hewlett-Packard's common stock is $36,400 on December 31, 20X1. In this case, Dade, Inc., the investor, makes the following adjustment:

20X1			
Dec. 31	Allowance to Adjust Investment to Market		
	($36,400 − $35,750)	650	
	Unrealized Gain on Investment		650
	Adjusted investment to market value.		

The increase in the investment's market value creates new stockholders' equity for the investor.

ASSETS	=	LIABILITIES	+	STOCKHOLDERS' EQUITY
650	=	0	+	650

Allowance to Adjust Investment to Market is a companion account that is used in conjunction with the Long-Term Investment account to bring the investment's carrying amount to current market value. In this case, the investment's cost ($35,750) plus the Allowance ($650) equals the investment carrying amount ($36,400).

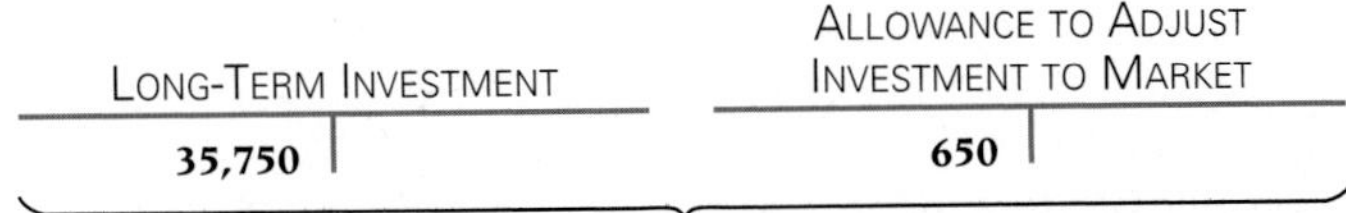

Investment carrying amount = Market value of $36,400

Here the Allowance has a debit balance because the market value of the investment increased. If the investment's market value declines, the Allowance is credited, and the investment carrying amount is its cost minus the Allowance.

The other side of the adjustment entry (bottom of page 462) is a credit to Unrealized Gain on Investment. If the market value of the investment declines, the company debits Unrealized Loss on Investment. An *unrealized* gain or loss results from a change in the investment's market value, not from the sale of the investment. For available-for-sale investments, the Unrealized Gain account or the Unrealized Loss account is reported in two places in the financial statements:

- *Other comprehensive income,* which can be reported on the *income statement* in a separate section below net income or in a separate statement of comprehensive income.
- *Accumulated other comprehensive income,* which is a separate section of stockholders' equity, below retained earnings, on the *balance sheet.*

The following display shows how Dade, Inc., reported its investment and the related unrealized gain in its financial statements at the end of 20X1 (all other figures are assumed for illustration in context):

Income statement:		
Revenues		$10,000
Expenses, including income tax		6,000
Net income		$ 4,000
Other comprehensive income:		
Unrealized gain on investments	$650	
Less Income tax (40%)	(260)	390
Comprehensive income		$ 4,390

Balance sheet:	
Assets:	
Total current assets	$ XXX
Long-term investments—at market value ($35,750 + $650)	36,400
Property, plant, and equipment, net	XXX
Stockholders' equity:	
Common stock	$ 1,000
Retained earnings	2,000
Accumulated other comprehensive income: Unrealized gain on investments	390
Total stockholders' equity	$ 3,390

CHECK POINT 10-1

The unrealized gain can be reported on the income statement as part of comprehensive income but not as part of net income. The unrealized gain is reported at its net-of-tax amount ($390) because it comes after net income, which also is an after-tax figure. The investments appear on the balance sheet at current market value. The balance sheet also reports the unrealized gain in a separate section of stockholders' equity, Accumulated other comprehensive income, which comes after Retained Earnings.

Selling an Available-for-Sale Investment

The sale of an available-for-sale investment can result in a *realized* gain or loss. Realized gains and losses measure the difference between the amount received from the sale of the investment and the cost of the investment.

Suppose Dade, Inc., sells its investment in Hewlett-Packard stock for $34,000 during 20X2. Dade would record the sale as follows:

20X2			
May 19	Cash	34,000	
	Loss on Sale of Investment	1,750	
	Long-Term Investment (cost)		35,750
	Sold investment.		

ASSETS	=	LIABILITIES	+	STOCKHOLDERS' EQUITY	−	LOSSES
34,000 −35,750	=	0	+		−	1,750

Dade would report the Loss on Sale of Investments as an "Other" item on the income statement. Then at December 31, 20X2, Dade must update the Allowance to Adjust Investment to Market and the Unrealized Gain on Investment accounts to their current balances. These adjustments are covered in intermediate accounting courses.

CHECK POINT 10-2

Suppose Xenon Corporation holds the following available-for-sale securities as long-term investments at December 31, 20X0:

Stock	*Cost*	*Current Market Value*
The Coca-Cola Company	$ 85,000	$71,000
Eastman Kodak Company	16,000	12,000
	$101,000	$83,000

Show how Xenon Corporation will report long-term investments on its December 31, 20X0, balance sheet.

Answer:

Assets

Long-term investments, at market value $83,000

ACCOUNTING FOR EQUITY-METHOD INVESTMENTS

Objective 2
Use the equity method for investments

An investor who holds less than 20% of the investee's voting stock usually plays no important role in the investee's operations. However, an investor with a larger stock holding—between 20 and 50% of the investee's voting stock—may *significantly influence* how the investee operates the business. Such an investor can likely affect the investee's decisions on dividend policy, product lines, sources of supply, and other important matters.

For this reason, investments in the range of 20 to 50% of another company's stock are common. For example, **General Motors** owns nearly 40% of **Isuzu Motors Overseas Distribution Corporation.** Because GM has a voice in shaping the policy and operations of Isuzu, some measure of Isuzu's success or failure should be included in GM's accounting for the investment. We use the **equity method** to account for investments in which the investor owns 20–50% of the investee's stock and thus can significantly influence the investee's decisions. These investee companies are often referred to as *affiliates;* thus Isuzu is an affiliate of General Motors.

Investments accounted for by the equity method are recorded initially at cost. Suppose **Phillips Petroleum Company** pays $400,000 for 30% of the common stock of White Rock Corporation. Phillips's entry to record the purchase of this investment follows:

Jan. 6	Long-Term Investment	400,000	
	Cash		400,000
	To purchase equity-method investment.		

ASSETS	=	LIABILITIES	+	STOCKHOLDERS' EQUITY
+400,000 −400,000	=	0	+	0

The Investor's Percentage of Investee Income

Under the equity method, Phillips, as the investor, applies its percentage of ownership—30%, in our example—in recording its share of the investee's net income and dividends. If White Rock reports net income of $250,000 for the year, Phillips records 30% of this amount as follows:

Dec. 31	Long-Term Investment ($250,000 × 0.30)	75,000	
	Equity-Method Investment Revenue		75,000
	To record investment revenue.		

ASSETS	=	LIABILITIES	+	STOCKHOLDERS' EQUITY	+	REVENUES
75,000	=	0	+		+	75,000

Because of the close relationship between the two companies, the investor increases the Investment account and records Investment Revenue when the investee reports income. As the investee's owners' equity increases, so does the Investment account on the investor's books.

Receiving Dividends under the Equity Method

Phillips records its proportionate part of cash dividends received from White Rock. When White Rock declares and pays a cash dividend of $100,000, Phillips receives 30% of this dividend and records this entry:

Dec. 31	Cash ($100,000 × 0.30)	30,000	
	Long-Term Investment		30,000
	To record receipt of cash dividend on equity-method investment.		

ASSETS	=	LIABILITIES	+	STOCKHOLDERS' EQUITY
30,000 −30,000	=	0	+	0

The Investment account is *decreased* for the receipt of a dividend on an equity-method investment. Why? Because the dividend decreases the investee's owners' equity and thus the investor's investment.

After the preceding entries are posted, Phillips's Investment account reflects its equity in the net assets of White Rock:

CHECK POINT 10-3

LONG-TERM INVESTMENT

Jan. 6	**Purchase**	**400,000**	**Dec. 31**	**Dividends**	**30,000**
Dec. 31	**Net income**	**75,000**			
Dec. 31	Balance	445,000			

Phillips would report the long-term investment on the balance sheet and the equity-method investment revenue on the income statement as follows:

Balance sheet (partial):		
Assets		
Total current assets	$	XXX
Long-term investments, at equity		445,000
Property, plant, and equipment, net		XXX
Income statement (partial):		
Income from operations	$	XXX
Other revenue:		
Equity-method investment revenue		75,000
Net income	$	XXX

Gain or loss on the sale of an equity-method investment is measured as the difference between the sale proceeds and the carrying amount of the investment. For example, sale of one-tenth of the White Rock common stock for $41,000 would be recorded as follows:

CHECK POINT 10-4

Feb. 13	Cash	41,000	
	Loss on Sale of Investment	3,500	
	Long-Term Investment ($445,000 × 1/10)		44,500
	Sold one-tenth of investment.		

ASSETS	=	LIABILITIES	+	STOCKHOLDERS' EQUITY	–	LOSSES
41,000 – 44,500	=	0	+		–	3,500

Summary of the Equity Method

The following T-account illustrates how to account for equity-method investments:

EQUITY-METHOD INVESTMENT

Original cost	**Share of losses**
Share of income	**Share of dividends**
Balance	

ACCOUNTING FOR CONSOLIDATED SUBSIDIARIES

Objective 3
Understand consolidated financial statements

Most large corporations own controlling interests in other companies. A **controlling** (or **majority**) **interest** is the ownership of more than 50% of the investee's voting stock. Such an investment enables the investor to elect a majority of the members of the investee's board of directors and thus control the investee. The investor is called the **parent company,** and the investee company is called the **subsidiary.** For example, because **Saturn Corporation** is a subsidiary of **General Motors,** the parent, the stockholders of GM control Saturn, as diagrammed in Exhibit 10-3.

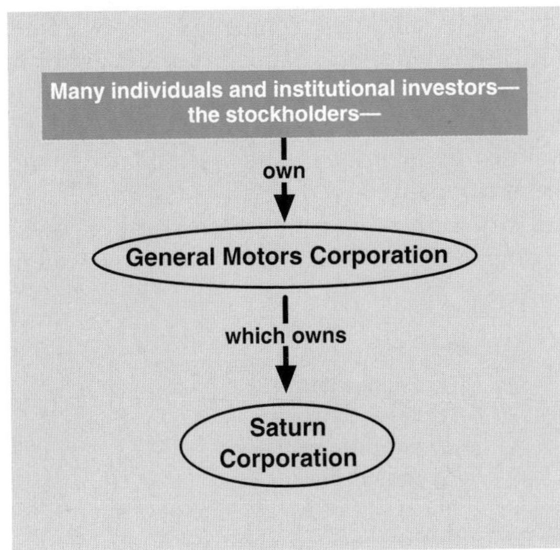

EXHIBIT 10-3
Ownership Structure of General Motors Corporation and Saturn Corporation

Exhibit 10-4 shows some of the more interesting subsidiaries of the "Big Two" U.S. automakers.

EXHIBIT 10-4
Selected Subsidiaries of the "Big Two" U.S. Automobile Manufacturers

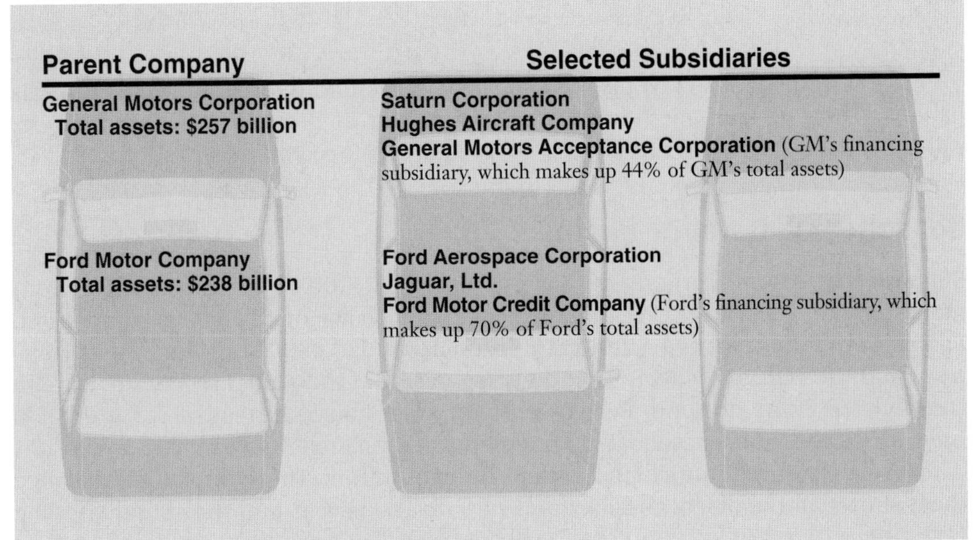

Parent Company	Selected Subsidiaries
General Motors Corporation **Total assets: $257 billion**	**Saturn Corporation** **Hughes Aircraft Company** **General Motors Acceptance Corporation** (GM's financing subsidiary, which makes up 44% of GM's total assets)
Ford Motor Company **Total assets: $238 billion**	**Ford Aerospace Corporation** **Jaguar, Ltd.** **Ford Motor Credit Company** (Ford's financing subsidiary, which makes up 70% of Ford's total assets)

Consolidation accounting is a method of combining the financial statements of two or more companies that are controlled by the same stockholders. This method reports a single set of financial statements for the consolidated entity, which carries the name of the parent company. Exhibit 10-5 illustrates the accounting method that should be used for stock investments according to the percentage of the investor's ownership in the investee company.

EXHIBIT 10-5
Accounting Methods for Stock Investment by Percentage of Ownership

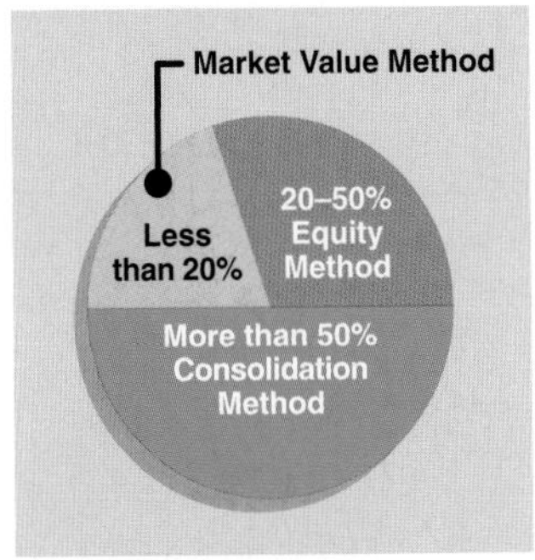

THE CONCEPT OF CONSOLIDATION ACCOUNTING. Almost all published financial reports include consolidated statements. To understand the statements you are likely to encounter, you need to know the basic concepts underlying consolidation accounting. **Consolidated statements** combine the balance sheets, income statements, and other financial statements of the parent company with those of majority-owned subsidiaries into an overall set of statements as if the parent and its subsidiaries were a single entity. The goal is to provide a better perspective on total operations than could be obtained by examining the separate reports of each individual company. The assets, liabilities, revenues, and expenses of each subsidiary are added to the parent's accounts. The consolidated financial statements present the combined account balances of the parent company and its subsidiary companies. For example, the balance in the Cash account of Saturn Corporation is added to the balance in the General Motors Cash account, and the sum of the two amounts is presented as a single amount in the consolidated balance sheet of General Motors Corporation. Each account balance of a subsidiary loses its identity in the consolidated statements, which bear the name of the parent company.

CHECK POINT 10-5

Exhibit 10-6 diagrams a corporate structure whose parent corporation owns controlling interests in five subsidiary companies and an equity-method investment in another investee company.

EXHIBIT 10-6
Parent Company with Consolidated Subsidiaries and an Equity-Method Investment

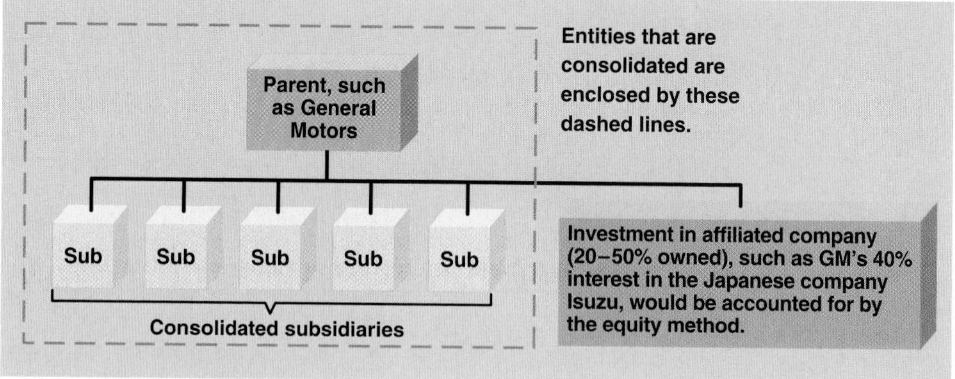

The sections that follow discuss the *purchase* method of accounting for consolidations. The purchase method is used most often in practice. Another method, called *pooling of interests* accounting, is covered in advanced accounting courses.

Consolidated Balance Sheet

Suppose that Parent Corporation has purchased all (100%) the outstanding common stock of Subsidiary Corporation at its book value of $150,000. In addition, Parent Corporation loaned Subsidiary Corporation $80,000. Both the parent company and the subsidiary keep their own separate and individual sets of books. The consolidated entity does not keep a separate set of books. Instead, a work sheet is used to prepare the consolidated statements. Companies may prepare a consolidated balance sheet immediately after the acquisition. The consolidated balance sheet shows all the assets and liabilities of both the parent and the subsidiary. The Investment in Subsidiary Corporation account on the parent's books represents all the assets and liabilities of Subsidiary. The consolidated statements cannot show both the investment amount *plus* the amounts for the subsidiary's assets and liabilities. Doing so would count the same resources twice. A key concept in consolidation accounting is to avoid double counting.

The Consolidation Work Sheet

Exhibit 10-7 shows the work sheet for consolidating the balance sheet. Consider elimination entry (a) for the parent-subsidiary ownership accounts. Entry (a) credits the parent's Investment account to eliminate its debit balance. It also eliminates the subsidiary's stockholders' equity accounts by debiting Common Stock and Retained Earnings for their full balances. Without this elimination, the consolidated

Assets	Parent Corporation	Subsidiary Corporation	Eliminations Debit	Eliminations Credit	Consolidated Amounts
Cash	12,000	18,000			30,000
Notes receivable from Subsidiary	80,000	—		(b) 80,000	—
Inventory	104,000	91,000			195,000
Investment in Subsidiary	150,000	—		(a) 150,000	—
Other assets	218,000	138,000			356,000
Total	564,000	247,000			581,000
Liabilities and Stockholders' Equity					
Accounts payable	43,000	17,000			60,000
Notes payable	190,000	80,000	(b) 80,000		190,000
Common stock	176,000	100,000	(a) 100,000		176,000
Retained earnings	155,000	50,000	(a) 50,000		155,000
Total	564,000	247,000	230,000	230,000	581,000

Exhibit 10-7
Work Sheet for Consolidated Balance Sheet—Parent Corporation Owns All of Subsidiary's Stock

financial statements would include both the parent company's investment in the subsidiary and the subsidiary company's equity. Because these accounts represent the same thing—Subsidiary's equity—they must be eliminated from the consolidated totals. If they weren't, the same item would be counted twice.

The resulting consolidated balance sheet (far right column) reports no Investment in Subsidiary account, and the consolidated totals for Common Stock and Retained Earnings are those of Parent Corporation only. Study the final column of the consolidation work sheet.

In this example, Parent Corporation loaned $80,000 to Subsidiary Corporation, and Subsidiary signed a note payable to Parent. Therefore, Parent's balance sheet includes an $80,000 note receivable and Subsidiary's balance sheet reports a note payable for the same amount. The parent's receivable and the subsidiary's payable represent the same resources—all entirely within the consolidated entity. Both therefore must be eliminated. Entry (b) accomplishes this. The $80,000 credit in the elimination column of the work sheet offsets Parent's Notes Receivable from Subsidiary. After this work sheet entry, the consolidated amount for Notes receivable is zero. The $80,000 debit in the elimination column offsets the Subsidiary's Notes Payable, and the resulting consolidated amount for notes payable is the amount owed to creditors outside the consolidated entity, which is appropriate. After the work sheet is complete, the consolidated amount for each account represents the total asset, liability, and equity amounts controlled by Parent Corporation.

Examine Exhibit 10-7. Why does the consolidated stockholders' equity ($176,000 + $155,000) exclude the equity of Subsidiary Corporation?

Answer:
Because the stockholders' equity of the consolidated entity is that of the parent only. Also, the subsidiary's equity and the parent company's investment balance represent the same resources. Therefore, including them both would amount to double counting.

Goodwill and Minority Interest

Goodwill and Minority Interest are two accounts that only a consolidated entity can have. *Goodwill,* which we studied in Chapter 7, arises when a parent company pays more to acquire a subsidiary company than the market value of the subsidiary's net assets. As we saw in Chapter 7, goodwill is the intangible asset that represents the parent company's excess payment to acquire the subsidiary.

Minority interest arises when a parent company purchases less than 100% of the stock of a subsidiary company. For example, suppose **Xerox Corporation** owns 80% of a subsidiary company. The remaining 20% of the subsidiary's stock is minority interest to Xerox Corporation. Minority Interest is reported among the liabilities on the balance sheet of the parent company.

CHECK POINT 10-6

Income of a Consolidated Entity

The income of a consolidated entity is the net income of the parent plus the parent's proportion of the subsidiaries' net income. Suppose Parent Company owns all the stock of Subsidiary S-1 and 60% of the stock of Subsidiary S-2. During the year just ended, Parent earned net income of $330,000, S-1 earned $150,000, and S-2 had a net loss of $100,000. Parent Company would report net income of $420,000, computed as follows:

	Net Income (Net Loss) of Each Company		*Parent's Ownership of Each Company*		*Parent's Consolidated Net Income (Net Loss)*
Parent Company	$ 330,000	×	100%	=	$330,000
Subsidiary S-1	150,000	×	100%	=	150,000
Subsidiary S-2	(100,000)	×	60%	=	(60,000)
Consolidated net income .					$420,000

LONG-TERM INVESTMENTS IN BONDS AND NOTES

Objective 4
Account for long-term investments in bonds

The major investors in bonds are financial institutions, such as pension plans, bank trust departments, mutual funds, and insurance companies. The relationship between the issuing corporation and the investor (bondholder) may be diagrammed as follows:

Issuing Corporation		*Investor (Bondholder)*
Bonds payable	⟷	Investment in bonds
Interest expense	⟷	Interest revenue

The dollar amount of a bond transaction is the same for issuer and investor, but the accounts debited and credited differ. For example, the issuing corporation's interest expense is the investor's interest revenue.

An investment in bonds is classified either as short-term (a current asset) or as long-term. Short-term investments in bonds are rare. Here, we focus on long-term investments in bonds and notes that the investor intends to hold until the bonds mature. These are called **held-to-maturity investments.**

We first encountered held-to-maturity investments in Chapter 5, page 220.

Accounting for Held-to-Maturity Investments—The Amortized Cost Method

Bond investments are recorded at cost. At maturity, the investor will receive the bonds' face value. For held-to-maturity investments, the discount or premium is amortized to account more precisely for interest revenue over the period the bonds will be held. The amortization of the discount or premium on a bond investment affects both Interest Revenue for the investor and the carrying amount of the bonds for the company that issued the bonds. Held-to-maturity investments in bonds are reported at their *amortized cost,* which determines the carrying amount.

Suppose an investor purchases $10,000 of 6% CBS bonds at a price of 95.2 on April 1, 20X2. The investor intends to hold the bonds as a long-term investment until their maturity. Interest dates are April 1 and October 1. Because these bonds mature on April 1, 20X6, they will be outstanding for 48 months. Assume amortization of the discount by the straight-line method. ➾ The following are the entries for this long-term investment:

➾ Straight-line amortization of premium or discount on a bond investment is calculated the same way as it is calculated for bonds payable (see Chapter 8, page 376).

20X2			
Apr. 1	Long-Term Investment in Bonds ($10,000 × 0.952) ...	9,520	
	Cash		9,520
	To purchase bond investment.		
Oct. 1	Cash ($10,000 × 0.06 × 6/12)	300	
	Interest Revenue		300
	To receive semiannual interest.		
Oct. 1	Long-Term Investment in Bonds		
	[($10,000 − $9,520)/48] × 6	60	
	Interest Revenue		60
	To amortize discount on bond investment for six months.		

At December 31, the year-end adjustments are

20X2			
Dec. 31	Interest Receivable ($10,000 × 0.06 × 3/12)	150	
	Interest Revenue		150
	To accrue interest revenue for three months.		
Dec. 31	Long-Term Investment in Bonds		
	[($10,000 − $9,520)/48] × 3	30	
	Interest Revenue		30
	To amortize discount on bond investment for three months.		

This amortization entry has two effects:

1. It increases the Long-Term Investment account on its march toward maturity value; and
2. It records the related interest revenue that the investor has earned as a result of the increase in the carrying amount of the investment.

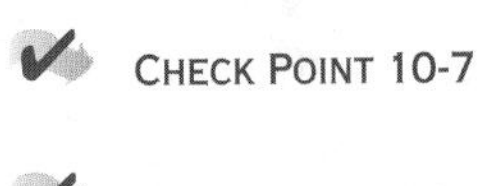

The financial statements at December 31, 20X2, report the following effects of this investment in bonds (assume that the market price is 102):

Balance sheet at December 31, 20X2:

Current assets:	
Interest receivable..	$ 150
Total current assets	X,XXX
Long-term investments in bonds ($9,520 + $60 + $30)—Note 6	9,610
Property, plant, and equipment	X,XXX

Income statement (multiple-step) for the year ended December 31, 20X2:

CHECK POINT 10-9

Other revenues:	
Interest revenue ($300 + $60 + $150 + $30)......................	$ 540

Note 6: Long-term investments:
Bond investments that will be held to maturity are reported at *amortized cost.* At December 31, 20X2, the market value of long-term investments in bonds was $10,200 ($10,000 × 1.02).

Summary of Accounting Methods

This chapter has illustrated how to account for various types of long-term investments. The Decision Guidelines feature shows which accounting method to use for each type of long-term investment.

DECISION GUIDELINES

Accounting Method to Use for Each Type of Long-Term Investment

Type of Long-Term Investment	Accounting Method
Investor owns less than 20% of investee stock (Available-for-sale investment classified as noncurrent asset)	Market value
Investor owns between 20% and 50% of investee/affiliate stock	Equity
Investor owns more than 50% of investee stock	Consolidation
Long-term investment in bonds (held-to-maturity investment)	Amortized cost

MID-CHAPTER

Mid-Chapter

SUMMARY PROBLEMS FOR YOUR REVIEW

1. Identify the appropriate accounting method for each of the following situations:

a. Investment in 25% of investee's stock

b. Available-for-sale investment in stock

c. Investment in more than 50% of investee's stock

2. At what amount should the following available-for-sale investment portfolio be reported on the December 31 balance sheet? All the investments are less than 5% of the investee's stock.

Stock	*Investment Cost*	*Current Market Value*
DuPont	$ 5,000	$ 5,500
Exxon	61,200	53,000
Procter & Gamble	3,680	6,230

Journalize any adjusting entry required by these data.

3. Investor paid $67,900 to acquire a 40% equity-method investment in the common stock of Investee. At the end of the first year, Investee's net income was $80,000, and Investee declared and paid cash dividends of $55,000. What is Investor's ending balance in its Equity-Method Investment account?

4. Parent Company paid $85,000 for all the common stock of Subsidiary Company, and Parent owes Subsidiary $20,000 on a note payable. Complete the consolidation work sheet at the top of page 474.

Assets	Parent Company	Subsidiary Company	Eliminations Debit	Eliminations Credit	Consolidated Amounts
Cash	7,000	4,000			
Note receivable from Parent	—	20,000			
Investment in Subsidiary	85,000	—			
Other assets	108,000	99,000			
Total	200,000	123,000			
Liabilities and Stockholders' Equity					
Accounts payable	15,000	8,000			
Notes payable	20,000	30,000			
Common stock	120,000	60,000			
Retained earnings	45,000	25,000			
Total	200,000	123,000			

Answers

1. **a.** Equity **b.** Market value **c.** Consolidation
2. Report the investments at market value: $64,730.

Stock	Investment Cost	Current Market Value
DuPont	$ 5,000	$ 5,500
Exxon	61,200	53,000
Procter & Gamble	3,680	6,230
Totals	$69,880	$64,730

Adjusting entry:

Unrealized Loss on Investments ($69,880 − $64,730)	5,150	
Allowance to Adjust Investment to Market		5,150
To adjust investments to current market value.		

3.

EQUITY-METHOD INVESTMENT

Cost	**67,900**	**Dividends**	**22,000****
Income	**32,000***		
Balance	**77,900**		

*$80,000 × .40 = $32,000
**$55,000 × .40 = $22,000

4. Consolidation work sheet:

Assets	Parent Company	Subsidiary Company	Eliminations Debit	Eliminations Credit	Consolidated Amounts
Cash	7,000	4,000			11,000
Note receivable from Parent	—	20,000		(a) 20,000	—
Investment in Subsidiary	85,000	—		(b) 85,000	—
Other assets	108,000	99,000			207,000
Total	200,000	123,000			218,000
Liabilities and Stockholders' Equity					
Accounts payable	15,000	8,000			23,000
Notes payable	20,000	30,000	(a) 20,000		30,000
Common stock	120,000	60,000	(b) 60,000		120,000
Retained earnings	45,000	25,000	(b) 25,000		45,000
Total	200,000	123,000	105,000	105,000	218,000

ACCOUNTING FOR INTERNATIONAL OPERATIONS

Did you know that **The Coca-Cola Company** earns most of its revenue outside the United States? It is common for U.S. companies to do a large part of their business abroad. Coca-Cola, **IBM,** and **Intel,** among many others, are very active in other countries. Exhibit 10-8 shows the percentages of international sales for these companies.

EXHIBIT 10-8
Extent of International Business

Company	*Percent of International Sales*
Coca-Cola	62%
IBM	57
Intel	56

Accounting for business activities across national boundaries makes up the field of *international accounting.* Electronic communication makes international accounting more important. This section starts with economic structures and their impact on international accounting and then shows several applications.

ECONOMIC STRUCTURES AND THEIR IMPACT ON INTERNATIONAL ACCOUNTING

The business environment varies widely across the globe. New York reflects the diversity of the market-driven economy of the United States. Japan's economy is similar to that of the United States, although Japanese business activity focuses more on imports and exports. International accounting deals with such differences in economic structures.

Foreign Currencies and Foreign-Currency Exchange Rates

Each country uses its own national currency. If **Boeing,** a U.S.-owned company, sells a 747 jet to **Air France,** will Boeing receive U.S. dollars or French francs? If the transaction takes place in dollars, Air France must exchange its francs for dollars to pay Boeing in U.S. currency. If the transaction takes place in francs, Boeing will receive francs, which it must exchange for dollars. In either case, a step has been added to the transaction: One of the companies must convert domestic currency into foreign currency.

The price of one nation's currency may be stated in terms of another country's monetary unit. This measure of one currency against another is called the **foreign-currency exchange rate.** In Exhibit 10-9, the dollar value of a French franc is $0.16. This means that one French franc can be bought for 16 cents. Other currencies, such as the pound and the yen (also listed in Exhibit 10-9), are similarly bought and sold.

EXHIBIT 10-9
Foreign-Currency Exchange Rates

Country	*Monetary Unit*	*Dollar Value*	*Country*	*Monetary Unit*	*Dollar Value*
Canada	Dollar	$0.66	Great Britain	Pound	$1.59
European Common Market	Euro	1.06	Italy	Lira	0.0005
			Japan	Yen	0.0086
France	Franc	0.16	Mexico	Peso	0.107
Germany	Mark	0.54			

Source: The *Wall Street Journal,* July 28, 1999, p. C21.

We use the exchange rate to convert the cost of an item given in one currency to its cost in a second currency. We call this conversion a *translation.* Suppose an item costs 200 French francs. To compute its cost in dollars, we multiply the amount in francs by the conversion rate: 200 French francs × $0.16 = $32.

Two main factors determine the supply and demand for a particular currency:

1. The ratio of a country's imports to its exports; and

2. The rate of return available in the country's capital markets.

THE IMPORT/EXPORT RATIO. Japanese exports usually surpass Japan's imports. Customers of Japanese companies must buy yen (the Japanese unit of currency) in the international currency market to pay for their purchases. This strong demand drives up the price—the foreign exchange rate—of the yen. In contrast, France imports more goods than it exports. French businesses must sell francs to buy the foreign currencies needed to acquire the foreign goods. As the supply of the French franc increases, its price decreases.

THE RATE OF RETURN. The rate of return available in a country's capital markets affects the amount of investment funds flowing into the country. When rates of return are high in a politically stable country such as the United States, international investors buy stocks, bonds, and real estate in that country. This activity increases the demand for the nation's currency and drives up its exchange rate.

Currencies are often described as "strong" or "weak." The exchange rate of a **strong currency** is rising relative to other nations' currencies. The exchange rate of a **weak currency** is falling relative to other currencies.

Suppose the *Wall Street Journal* listed the exchange rate for the British pound as $1.59 on October 14. On October 15, that rate has changed to $1.57. We would say that the dollar has risen against—is stronger than—the British pound. Because the pound has become less expensive, the dollar now buys more pounds. A stronger dollar would make travel to England more attractive to Americans.

Managing Cash in International Transactions

Objective 5
Account for transactions stated in a foreign currency

As international transactions become common, more companies are understanding the need to manage cash transactions conducted in foreign currencies. **D. E. Shipp Belting,** a small family-owned company in Waco, Texas, provides an example. Shipp makes conveyor belts that are used in a variety of industries. Farmers in the Rio Grande Valley along the Texas-Mexico border use Shipp conveyor belts to process vegetables. Because some of these customers are on the Mexican side of the border, Shipp conducts some of its business in pesos, the Mexican monetary unit. Conversely, the Swiss have developed some of the leading technologies for manufacturing high-grade conveyor belts. Shipp Belting therefore purchases inventory from Swiss companies. Some of these transactions are conducted in Swiss francs.

CASH RECEIPTS IN A FOREIGN CURRENCY. Consider Shipp Belting's sale of conveyor belts to **Artes de Mexico,** a vegetable grower in Matamoros, Mexico. The sale can be conducted either in dollars or in pesos. If Artes de Mexico agrees to pay in dollars, Shipp avoids the complication of dealing in a foreign currency, and the transaction is the same as selling to **M&M Mars** across town. But suppose that Artes de Mexico orders 1 million pesos (approximately $130,000) worth of conveyor belts from Shipp. Further suppose that Artes demands to pay in pesos and that Shipp agrees to receive pesos instead of dollars.

Because Shipp will need to convert the pesos to dollars, the transaction poses a challenge. What if the peso loses value—weakens, taking more pesos to obtain each dollar—before Shipp collects from Artes? In this case, Shipp will not earn as much as expected on the sale. The following example shows how to account for international transactions that result in the receipt of a foreign currency. It also shows how to measure the effects of such transactions on a company's cash position and profits.

Shipp Belting sells goods to Artes de Mexico for a price of 1 million pesos on July 28. On that date, a peso was worth $0.107, as quoted in exchange rate tables of the *Wall Street Journal.* One month later, on August 28, the peso has weakened against the dollar so that a peso is worth only $0.104. Shipp receives 1 million pesos from Artes on August 28, but the dollar value of Shipp's cash receipt is $3,000 less than expected. Shipp ends up earning less than hoped for on the transaction. The following journal entries show how Shipp would account for these transactions:

July 28	Accounts Receivable—Artes (1,000,000 pesos × $0.107)	107,000	
	Sales Revenue		107,000
	Sale on account.		

ASSETS	=	LIABILITIES	+	STOCKHOLDERS' EQUITY	+	REVENUES
107,000	=	0	+		+	107,000

Aug. 28	Cash (1,000,000 pesos × $0.104)	104,000	
	Foreign-Currency Transaction Loss	3,000	
	Accounts Receivable—Artes		107,000
	Collection on account.		

ASSETS	=	LIABILITIES	+	STOCKHOLDERS' EQUITY	−	LOSSES
104,000 − 107,000	=	0	+		−	3,000

✔ CHECK POINT 10-10

If Shipp had required Artes to pay at the time of the sale, Shipp would have received pesos worth $107,000. But by waiting the normal 30-day collection period to receive cash, Shipp exposed itself to *foreign-currency exchange risk,* the risk of loss in an international transaction. In this case, Shipp experienced a $3,000 foreign-currency transaction loss and received $3,000 less cash than expected, as shown in the collection entry.

If the peso had increased in value, Shipp would have experienced a foreign-currency transaction gain. When a company holds a receivable denominated in a foreign currency, it wants the foreign currency to remain strong so that it can be converted into more dollars. Unfortunately, this did not occur for Shipp Belting. One way of managing foreign-currency exchange risk is for the seller to simply quote a higher price for its goods in foreign markets. If the buyer accepts, the seller has protected itself against the risk of loss.

CASH DISBURSEMENTS IN A FOREIGN CURRENCY. Purchasing from a foreign company may also expose a company to foreign-currency exchange risk. To illustrate, assume Shipp Belting buys inventory from **Gesellschaft Ltd.,** a Swiss company. After lengthy negotiations, the two companies decide on a price of 20,000 Swiss francs. On September 15, when Shipp receives the goods, the Swiss franc is quoted in international currency markets at $0.799. When Shipp pays two weeks later, on September 29, the Swiss franc has weakened against the dollar—decreased in value to $0.781. Shipp would record the purchase and payment as follows:

Sept. 15	Inventory (20,000 Swiss francs × $0.799)	15,980	
	Accounts Payable—Gesellschaft Ltd.		15,980
	Purchase on account.		

ASSETS	=	LIABILITIES	+	STOCKHOLDERS' EQUITY
15,980	=	15,980	+	0

Sept. 29	Accounts Payable—Gesellschaft Ltd.	15,980	
	Cash (20,000 Swiss francs × $0.781)		15,620
	Foreign-Currency Transaction Gain		360
	Payment on account.		

ASSETS	=	LIABILITIES	+	STOCKHOLDERS' EQUITY	+	GAINS
−15,620	=	−15,980	+		+	360

CHECK POINT 10-11

The Swiss franc could have strengthened against the dollar, in which case Shipp would have had a foreign-currency transaction loss. A company with a payable denominated in a foreign currency hopes that the dollar gets stronger: When the payment date arrives, the company can use fewer dollars to purchase the foreign currency and thereby reduce its cost.

REPORTING FOREIGN-CURRENCY TRANSACTION GAINS AND LOSSES ON THE INCOME STATEMENT. The Foreign-Currency Transaction Gain account is the record of the gains on transactions settled in a currency other than the dollar. Likewise, the Foreign-Currency Transaction Loss account shows the amount of the losses on transactions conducted in foreign currencies. The company reports the *net amount* of these two accounts on the income statement as Other Revenues and Gains, or Other Expenses and Losses, as the case may be. For example, Shipp Belting would combine the $3,000 foreign-currency loss and the $360 gain and report the net loss of $2,640 on the income statement as follows:

Other Expenses and Losses:	
Foreign-currency transaction loss, net	$2,640

These gains and losses fall into the "Other" category because they arise from buying and selling foreign currencies, not from the main line of the company's business (in the case of D. E. Shipp Belting, selling conveyor belts). Companies seek to minimize their foreign-currency losses by a strategy called *hedging,* which we discuss next.

HEDGING—A STRATEGY TO AVOID FOREIGN-CURRENCY TRANSACTION LOSSES. One way for U.S. companies to avoid foreign-currency transaction losses is to insist that international transactions be settled in dollars. This requirement puts the burden of currency translation on the foreign party. This approach, however, may alienate customers and decrease sales. Another way for a company to protect itself from the effects of fluctuating foreign-currency exchange rates is by hedging.

Hedging means to protect oneself from losing money in one transaction by engaging in a counterbalancing transaction. A U.S. company selling goods to be collected in Mexican pesos expects to receive a fixed number of pesos in the future. If the peso is losing value, the U.S. company would expect the pesos to be worth fewer dollars than the amount of the receivable—an expected loss situation, as we saw for Shipp Belting.

The U.S. company may have accumulated payables stated in a foreign currency in the normal course of its business, such as the amount payable by Shipp to the Swiss company. Losses on the receipt of pesos may be approximately offset by gains on the payment of Swiss francs to Gesellschaft Ltd. Because most companies do not have equal amounts of receivables and payables in foreign currency, offsetting receivables and payables is an imprecise strategy. To obtain a more precise hedge, some companies buy *futures contracts,* which are contracts for foreign currencies to be received in the future. Futures contracts can effectively create a payable to exactly offset a receivable, and vice versa. Many companies that do business internationally use hedging techniques.

CONSOLIDATION OF FOREIGN SUBSIDIARIES

Objective 6
Interpret a foreign-currency translation adjustment

A U.S. company with a foreign subsidiary must consolidate the subsidiary's financial statements into its own statements for reporting to the public. The consolidation of a foreign subsidiary poses two special challenges:

1. Many countries outside the United States specify accounting treatments that differ from American accounting principles. For the purpose of reporting to the American public, accountants must first bring the subsidiary's statements into conformity with American generally accepted accounting principles (GAAP).
2. The second accounting challenge arises when the subsidiary statements are expressed in a foreign currency. One step in the consolidation process is to translate the subsidiary statements into dollars. Then the dollar-value statements of the subsidiary can be combined with the parent's statements in the usual manner, as illustrated in the first part of this chapter.

The process of translating a foreign subsidiary's financial statements into dollars usually creates a *foreign-currency translation adjustment.* This item appears in the financial statements of most multinational companies and is reported as part of other comprehensive income on the income statement and as part of stockholders' equity on the consolidated balance sheet. A translation adjustment arises due to changes in the foreign exchange rate over time. In general, *assets* and *liabilities* in the foreign subsidiaries' financial statements are translated into dollars at the exchange rate in effect on the date of the statements. However, *stockholders' equity* is translated into dollars at older, historical exchange rates. This difference in exchange rates creates an out-of-balance condition on the balance sheet. The translation adjustment amount brings the balance sheet back into balance. Let's use an example to see how the translation adjustment works.

U.S. Express Corporation owns Italian Imports, Inc., whose financial statements are expressed in lire (the Italian currency). U.S. Express must consolidate the Italian subsidiary's financial statements into its own statements. When U.S. Express acquired Italian Imports in 20X1, a lira was worth $0.00070. When Italian Imports earned its retained income during 20X1–20X6, the average exchange rate was $0.00067. On the balance sheet date in 20X6, a lira is worth only $0.00060. Exhibit 10-10 shows how to translate Italian Imports' balance sheet into dollars and shows how the translation adjustment arises.

EXHIBIT 10-10
Translation of a Foreign-Currency Balance Sheet into Dollars

Italian Imports, Inc., Amounts	*Lire*	*Exchange Rate*	*Dollars*
Assets	800,000,000	$0.00060	$480,000
Liabilities	500,000,000	0.00060	$300,000
Stockholders' equity:			
Common stock	100,000,000	0.00070	70,000
Retained earnings	200,000,000	0.00067	134,000
Accumulated other comprehensive income:			
Foreign-currency translation adjustment			(24,000)
	800,000,000		$480,000

The **foreign-currency translation adjustment** is the balancing amount that brings the dollar amount of the total liabilities and stockholders' equity of a foreign subsidiary into agreement with the dollar amount of its total assets (in Exhibit 10-10, total assets equal $480,000). Only after the translation adjustment of $24,000 do total liabilities and stockholders' equity equal total assets stated in dollars. In this case, the translation adjustment is negative, and total stockholders' equity becomes $180,000 ($70,000 + $134,000 − $24,000).

What in the economic environment caused the negative translation adjustment? A weakening of the lira since the acquisition of Italian Imports brought about the need for this adjustment. When U.S. Express acquired the foreign subsidiary in 20X1, a lira was worth $0.00070. When Italian Imports earned its retained income during 20X1 through 20X6, the average exchange rate was $0.00067. On the balance sheet date in 20X6, a lira is worth only $0.00060. Thus Italian Imports' net assets (assets minus liabilities) are translated into only $180,000 ($480,000 − $300,000).

To bring stockholders' equity to $180,000 requires a $24,000 negative amount. In a sense, a negative translation adjustment is like a loss. And it is reported as a contra item in the stockholders' equity section of the balance sheet, as shown in Exhibit 10-10. The interpretation of a negative translation adjustment is this: Measured in today's dollars, the book value of U.S. Express Corporation's investment in Italian Imports, Inc., is less than the amount U.S. Express invested to acquire the company.

The Italian Imports dollar figures in Exhibit 10-10 are the amounts that U.S. Express Corporation would include in its consolidated balance sheet. The consolidation procedures would follow those illustrated beginning on page 468.

International Accounting Standards

In this text, we focus on the principles of accounting that are generally accepted in the United States. Most of the methods of accounting are consistent throughout the world. Double-entry accounting, the accrual system, and the basic financial statements are used worldwide. Differences, however, do exist among countries, as shown in Exhibit 10-11.

Country	*Inventories*	*Goodwill*	*Research and Development Costs*
United States	Specific unit cost, FIFO, LIFO, weighted-average.	Amortized over period not to exceed 40 years.	Expensed as incurred.
Germany	Similar to U.S.	Amortized over 5 years.	Expensed as incurred.
Japan	Similar to U.S.	Amortized over 5 years.	May be capitalized and amortized over 5 years.
United Kingdom	LIFO is unacceptable for tax purposes and is not widely used.	Amortized over useful life or not amortized if life is indefinite.	Expense research costs. Some development costs may be capitalized.

EXHIBIT 10-11
Some International Accounting Differences

In discussing depreciation (Chapter 7), we emphasized that in the United States, the methods used for reporting to tax authorities differ from the methods used for reporting to shareholders. However, tax reporting and shareholder reporting are identical in many countries. For example, France has a "Plan Compatible" that specifies that a National Uniform Chart of Accounts be used for both tax returns and reporting to shareholders. German financial reporting is also determined primarily by tax laws. In Japan, certain principles are allowed for tax purposes only if they are also used for shareholder reporting.

For inventory, goodwill, and research and development costs, German accounting practices are more similar to those of the United States than to those of other countries. Despite the common heritage of the United States and the United Kingdom, U.S. and British accounting practices vary widely.

A company that sells its stock through a foreign stock exchange must follow the accounting principles of the foreign country. For example, because **British Petroleum Amoco (BPA)** stock is available through the New York Stock Exchange, BPA financial statements issued in the United States follow American GAAP.

The globalization of business enterprises and capital markets is creating much interest in establishing common, worldwide accounting standards. There are probably too many cultural, social, and political differences to expect complete worldwide standardization of financial reporting in the near future. However, the number of differences is decreasing.

✔ CHECK POINT 10-12

Several organizations are working to achieve worldwide harmony of accounting standards. Chief among these is the *International Accounting Standards Committee (IASC).* Headquartered in London, the IASC operates much as the Financial Accounting Standards Board in the United States. It has the support of the accounting professions in the United States, most of the British Commonwealth countries, Japan, France, Germany, the Netherlands, and Mexico. However, the IASC has no authority to require compliance with its standards. It must rely on cooperation by the various national accounting professions. Since its creation in 1973, the IASC has succeeded in narrowing some differences in international accounting standards.

USING THE STATEMENT OF CASH FLOWS TO INTERPRET A COMPANY'S INVESTING ACTIVITIES

Objective 7
Report investing transactions on the statement of cash flows

Investing activities include many types of transactions. In Chapter 7, we covered investing transactions in which companies purchase and sell long-term assets such as plant and equipment. As we have seen in this chapter, there is another type of investing activity that actually carries the name *investment.* The purchase and sale of investments in the stocks and bonds of other companies are also investing activities that are reported on the cash-flow statement.

Exhibit 10-12
Campbell Soup Company's Consolidated Statement of Cash Flows (partial, adapted)

	CAMPBELL SOUP CO. Consolidated Statement of Cash Flows		
	(In millions)	*19X5*	*19X4*
	Cash Flows from Operating Activities:		
1	Net cash provided by operating activities.	$ 1,185	$ 968
	Cash Flows from Investing Activities:		
2	Purchases of plant assets	(391)	(421)
3	Sales of plant assets	21	42
4	Businesses acquired.	(1,255)	(14)
5	Sales of businesses	12	27
6	Other	(45)	(41)
7	Net cash used in investing activities.	(1,658)	(407)
	Cash Flows from Financing Activities:		
8	Long-term borrowings.	312	115
9	Repayments of long-term borrowings.	(29)	(117)
10	Short-term borrowings	1,087	(50)
11	Repayments of short-term borrowings	(662)	(87)
12	Dividends paid.	(295)	(266)
13	Other	13	(129)
14	Net cash provided by (used in) financing activities	426	(534)

Investing activities are usually reported on the statement of cash flows as the second category, after operating activities and before financing activities. Exhibit 10-12 provides excerpts from **Campbell Soup Company's** statement of cash flows. During 19X5, Campbell Soup spent $1.255 billion to acquire other companies (line 4). Campbell Soup sold other companies for a total of $12 million (line 5).

How did Campbell Soup finance the acquisitions of other businesses? The cash-flow statement gives the answer. Campbell's operating activities provided cash of $1.185 billion during 19X5 (line 1). This amount alone covered most of the cost of acquiring the other companies—a sign of Campbell Soup's financial strength.

The financing-activities section of the cash-flow statement indicates that long-term borrowings provided cash of $312 million (line 8), with an additional $1.087 billion coming from short-term borrowing (line 10). Moreover, these amounts far exceeded Campbell Soup's repayments of borrowings (lines 9 and 11), which means that the company had the cash to expand.

End-of-Chapter

Summary Problem for Your Review

Translate the balance sheet of the Spanish subsidiary of Wrangler Corp., a U.S. company, into dollars. When Wrangler acquired this subsidiary, the exchange rate of the Spanish currency, the peseta, was $0.0060. The average exchange rate applicable to retained earnings is $0.0065. The peseta's current exchange rate is $0.0070.

Before performing the translation, predict whether the translation adjustment will be positive or negative. Does this situation generate a foreign-currency translation gain or a foreign-currency translation loss? Give your reasons.

	Pesetas
Assets	200,000,000
Liabilities	110,000,000
Stockholders' equity:	
Common stock	20,000,000
Retained earnings	70,000,000
	200,000,000

Answers

Translation of foreign-currency balance sheet:

This situation will generate a *positive* translation adjustment, which is like a gain. The gain occurs because the peseta's current exchange rate, which is used to translate net assets (assets minus liabilities), exceeds the historical exchange rates used for stockholders' equity.

The calculation follows.

	Pesetas	Exchange Rate	Dollars
Assets	200,000,000	$0.0070	$1,400,000
Liabilities	110,000,000	0.0070	$ 770,000
Stockholders' equity:			
Common stock	20,000,000	0.0060	120,000
Retained earnings	70,000,000	0.0065	455,000
Foreign-currency translation adjustment	—		55,000
	200,000,000		$1,400,000

Summary of Learning Objectives

1. ***Account for available-for-sale investments.*** *Available-for-sale securities* are all stock investments other than trading securities. They are classified as current assets if the business expects to sell them within a year or during the business's normal operating cycle if longer than a year. All other available-for-sale securities are classified as long-term investments. Available-for-sale investments are reported at current market value on the balance sheet.
2. ***Use the equity method for investments.*** The *equity method* is used when an investor owns 20–50% of the stock of an investee. The investor applies its percentage of ownership in recording its share of the investee's net income and dividends. Equity-method investment revenue is reported under Other revenues on the income statement.
3. ***Understand consolidated financial statements.*** Ownership of more than 50% of a company's voting stock creates a *parent-subsidiary* relationship, and the parent company must use the *consolidation method* to account for its subsidiaries. Because the parent has control over the subsidiary, the subsidiary's financial statements are included in the parent's consolidated financial statements.
4. ***Account for long-term investments in bonds.*** *Held-to-maturity investments* are bonds and notes that the investor intends to hold until maturity. The *amortized-cost method* is used to account for held-to-maturity investments. Investments in bonds are presented on the balance sheet after current assets; interest revenue from bond investments appears on the income statement under Other revenues.
5. ***Account for transactions stated in a foreign currency.*** When two or more currencies are involved in a transaction, each company may incur a gain or loss on foreign-currency exchanges. These gains and losses are reported on the income statement under the category Other gains and losses.
6. ***Interpret a foreign-currency translation adjustment.*** Consolidating a foreign subsidiary's financial statements into the parent company's statements requires adjusting the subsidiary statements to U.S. accounting principles, then translating the foreign-company statements into U.S. dollars. The translation process often creates a *translation adjustment,* which is needed to bring the dollar amount of the subsidiary's total liabilities and stockholders' equity into agreement with the dollar amount of total assets.
7. ***Report investing transactions on the statement of cash flows.*** Investing activities are the second major category of transactions reported on the statement of cash flows (after operating activities and before financing activities). The cash-flow statement provides vital information regarding a company's sources and uses of cash for investing activities.

ACCOUNTING VOCABULARY

available-for-sale investments (p. 461).
consolidated statements (p. 467).
controlling interest (p. 466).
equity method for investments (p. 465).
foreign-currency exchange rate (p. 475).
foreign-currency translation adjustment (p. 479).
hedging (p. 478).
held-to-maturity investments (p. 470).
long-term investment (p. 461).
majority interest (p. 466).
marketable security (p. 461).
market value method of accounting (for investments) (p. 461).
minority interest (p. 470).
parent company (p. 467).
short-term investment (p. 461).
strong currency (p. 475).
subsidiary company (p. 467).
trading investments (p. 461).
weak currency (p. 475).

QUESTIONS

1. How are stock prices quoted in the securities market? What is the investor's cost of 1,000 shares of Ford Motor Company stock at 55¾ with a brokerage commission of $1,350?
2. Show the positions of short-term investments and long-term investments on the balance sheet.
3. Outline the accounting methods for the different types of investments.
4. How does an investor record the receipt of a cash dividend on an available-for-sale investment? How does this investor record receipt of a stock dividend?
5. An investor paid $11,000 for 1,000 shares of stock—a trading investment—and later received a 10% stock dividend. At December 31, the investment's market value is $11,800. Compute the unrealized gain or loss on the investment.
6. When is an investment accounted for by the equity method? Explain how to apply the equity method. Mention how to record the purchase of the investment, the investor's proportion of the investee's net income, and receipt of a cash dividend from the investee. Describe how to measure gain or loss on the sale of this investment.
7. Why are intercompany items eliminated from consolidated financial statements? Name two intercompany items that are eliminated.
8. Name the account that expresses the excess of the cost of an investment over the market value of the subsidiary's owners' equity. What type of account is this, and where in the financial statements is it reported?
9. When a parent company buys more than 50% but less than 100% of a subsidiary's stock, a new category of ownership must appear on the balance sheet. What is this category called, and under what heading do most companies report it?
10. How would you measure the net income of a parent company with three subsidiaries? Assume that two subsidiaries are wholly (100%) owned and that the parent owns 60% of the third subsidiary.
11. McVey, Inc., acquired a foreign subsidiary when the foreign currency's exchange rate was $0.32. Over the years, the foreign currency has steadily risen against the dollar. Will McVey's balance sheet report a positive or a negative foreign-currency translation adjustment?
12. Describe the computation of a foreign-currency translation adjustment.

CHECK POINTS

Accounting for an available-for-sale investment; unrealized loss (Obj. 1)

CP10-1 TFC Financial, Inc., completed these long-term available-for-sale investment transactions during 20X1:

20X1	
Jan. 14	Purchased 300 shares of **Sysco** stock, paying $19¾ per share. TFC intends to hold the investment for the indefinite future.
Aug. 22	Received a cash dividend of $1.25 per share on the Sysco stock.
Dec. 31	Adjusted the Sysco investment to its current market value of $5,663.

1. Journalize TFC's investment transactions. Explanations are not required.
2. Show how to report the investment and any unrealized gain or loss on TFC's balance sheet at December 31, 20X1. Ignore income tax.

Accounting for the sale of an available-for-sale investment (Obj. 1)

CP10-2 Use the data given in Check Point 10-1. On August 4, 20X2, TFC Financial, Inc., sold its investment in Sysco stock for $21.50 per share.

1. Journalize the sale. No explanation is required.
2. How does the gain or loss that you recorded differ from the gain or loss that was recorded at December 31, 20X1?

Accounting for a 40% investment in another company (Obj. 2)

CP10-3 Suppose on January 6, 20X3, **General Motors** paid $100 million for its 40% investment in **Isuzu Motors.** Assume Isuzu earned net income of $12.5 million and paid cash dividends of $10 million during 20X3.

1. What method should General Motors use to account for the investment in Isuzu? Give your reason.
2. Journalize these three transactions on the books of General Motors. Show all amounts in millions of dollars and include an explanation for each entry.
3. Post to the Long-Term Investment T-account. What is its balance after all the transactions are posted?

Accounting for the sale of an equity-method investment (Obj. 2)

CP10-4 Use the data given in Check Point 10-3. Assume that in January 20X4, General Motors sold half its investment in Isuzu to **Toyota.** The sale price was $62 million. Compute General Motors' gain or loss on the sale.

Understanding consolidated financial statements (Obj. 3)

CP10-5 Answer these questions about consolidation accounting:

1. Define a parent company. Define a subsidiary company.
2. How do consolidated financial statements differ from the financial statements of a single company?
3. Which company's name appears on the consolidated financial statements? How much of the subsidiary's stock must the parent own before reporting consolidated statements?

Understanding goodwill and minority interest (Obj. 3)

CP10-6 Two accounts that arise from consolidation accounting are goodwill and minority interest.

1. What is goodwill, and how does it arise? Which company reports goodwill, the parent or the subsidiary? Where is goodwill reported?
2. What is minority interest, and which company reports it, the parent or the subsidiary? Where is minority interest reported?

Working with a bond investment (Obj. 4)

CP10-7 **Prudential Securities** owns vast amounts of corporate bonds. Suppose Prudential buys $1,000,000 of **Eastman Kodak** bonds at a price of 96. The Eastman Kodak bonds pay cash interest at the annual rate of 7% and mature at the end of five years.

1. How much did Prudential pay to purchase the bond investment? How much will Prudential collect when the bond investment matures?
2. How much cash interest will Prudential Securities receive each year from Eastman Kodak?
3. Will Prudential Securities' annual interest revenue on the bond investment be more or less than the amount of cash interest received each year? Give your reason.
4. Compute Prudential Securities' annual interest revenue on this bond investment. Use the straight-line method to amortize the discount on the investment.

Recording bond investment transactions (Obj. 4)

CP10-8 Return to Check Point 10-7, the Prudential Securities investment in Eastman Kodak bonds. Journalize on Prudential's books:

a. Purchase of the bond investment on January 2, 20X1. Prudential expects to hold the investment to maturity.
b. Receipt of annual cash interest on December 31, 20X1.
c. Amortization of discount on December 31, 20X1.
d. Collection of the investment's face value at the maturity date on January 2, 20X6. (Assume the receipt of 20X5 interest and amortization of discount for 20X5 have already been recorded, so you may ignore these entries.)

Recording interest revenue on a bond investment (Obj. 4)

CP10-9 Return to the bond investment situation on page 471. Assume the investor purchased the **CBS** bond investment on June 1, 20X2. Also assume that CBS pays cash interest on June 1 and December 1 each year. The bonds mature on June 1, 20X6.

1. Journalize the investor's accrual of cash interest and amortization of discount on the investment at December 31, 20X2. Use the straight-line amortization method.
2. What is the carrying amount of the bond investment at December 31, 20X2?

CP10-10 Suppose **Coca-Cola Company** sells soft-drink syrup to a Russian company on March 14. Coca-Cola agrees to accept 20,000,000 Russian rubles. On the date of sale, the ruble is quoted at $0.00017. Coca-Cola collects half the receivable on April 19, when the ruble is worth $0.00016. Then, on May 10, when the foreign-exchange rate of the ruble is $0.00019, Coca-Cola collects the final amount.

Journalize these three transactions for Coca-Cola.

Accounting for transactions stated in a foreign currency (Obj. 5)

CP10-11 Page 476 includes a sequence of Shipp Belting journal entries for transactions denominated in Mexican pesos. Suppose the foreign-exchange rate for a peso is $0.1370 on August 28. Record Ship Belting's collection of cash on August 28.

On page 477, Shipp Belting buys inventory for which Shipp must pay Swiss francs. Suppose a Swiss franc costs $0.8221 on September 29. Record Shipp Belting's payment of cash on September 29.

Accounting for transactions stated in a foreign currency (Obj. 5)

CP10-12 Exhibit 10-11, page 480, outlines some differences between accounting in the United States and accounting in other countries. American companies transact more business with British companies than with any other. Interestingly, however, there are several important differences between American and British accounting. In your own words, describe those differences for inventories, goodwill, and research and development.

International accounting differences (Obj. 6)

CP10-13 Companies divide their cash flows into three categories for reporting on the statement of cash flows.

1. List the three categories of cash flows in the order they appear on the statement of cash flows. Which category of cash flows is most closely related to this chapter?
2. Identify two types of transactions that companies report as cash flows from investing activities.

Reporting cash flows (Obj. 7)

EXERCISES

E10-1 Journalize the following long-term available-for-sale investment transactions of Fina Contractors:

Journalizing transactions for an available-for-sale investment (Obj. 1)

a. Purchased 400 shares (8%) of McDermott, Inc., common stock at $44 per share, with the intent of holding the stock for the indefinite future.

b. Received cash dividend of $1 per share on the McDermott investment.

c. At year end, adjusted the investment account to current market value of $45 per share.

d. Sold the McDermott stock for the market price of $50 per share.

E10-2 Late in the current year, IBEX, Inc., bought 3,000 shares of **Xerox** common stock at $37.375; 600 shares of **Coca-Cola** stock at $46.75; and 1,400 shares of **Panasonic** stock at $79—all as available-for-sale investments. At December 31, the *Wall Street Journal* reports Xerox stock at $39.125, Coca-Cola at $48.50, and Panasonic at $68.25.

Accounting for long-term investments (Obj. 1)

Required

1. Determine the cost and the market value of the long-term investment portfolio at December 31.
2. Record any adjusting entry needed at December 31.
3. What would IBEX report on its income statement and balance sheet for the information given? Make the necessary disclosures. Ignore income tax.

E10-3 **Sears, Roebuck and Co.** owns equity-method investments in several companies. Suppose Sears paid $800,000 to acquire a 25% investment in Thai Imports Company. Assume that Thai Imports Company reported net income of $640,000 for the first year and declared and paid cash dividends of $420,000. Record the following in Sears's journal: (a) purchase of the investment, (b) Sears's proportion of Thai Imports' net income, and (c) receipt of the cash dividends. What is the ending balance in Sears's investment account?

Accounting for transactions under the equity method (Obj. 2)

E10-4 Without making journal entries, record the transactions of Exercise 10-3 directly in the Sears account, Long-Term Investment in Thai Imports. Assume that after all the noted transactions took place, Sears sold its entire investment in Thai Imports for cash of $1,400,000. How much is Sears's gain or loss on the sale of the investment?

Measuring gain or loss on the sale of an equity-method investment (Obj. 2)

Applying the appropriate accounting method for a 40% investment (Obj. 2)

E10-5 Forbes Investments, Inc., paid $160,000 for a 40% investment in the common stock of Nye, Inc. For the first year, Nye reported net income of $84,000 and at year end declared and paid cash dividends of $46,000. On the balance sheet date, the market value of Forbes's investment in Nye stock was $184,000.

Required

1. Which method is appropriate for Forbes to use in accounting for its investment in Nye? Why?
2. Show everything that Forbes would report for the investment and any investment revenue in its year-end financial statements.

Preparing a consolidated balance sheet (Obj. 3)

E10-6 Mercedes, Inc., owns Benz Corp. The two companies' individual balance sheets are as follows:

Assets	*Mercedes*	*Benz*
Cash	$ 49,000	$ 14,000
Accounts receivable, net	82,000	53,000
Note receivable from Mercedes	—	12,000
Inventory	104,000	77,000
Investment in Benz	100,000	—
Plant assets, net	486,000	129,000
Other assets	22,000	8,000
Total	$843,000	$293,000
Liabilities and Stockholders' Equity		
Accounts payable	$ 44,000	$ 26,000
Notes payable	47,000	36,000
Other liabilities	82,000	131,000
Common stock	210,000	80,000
Retained earnings	460,000	20,000
Total	$843,000	$293,000

Required

1. Prepare the consolidated balance sheet of Mercedes, Inc. It is sufficient to complete the consolidation work sheet.
2. What is the amount of stockholders' equity of the consolidated entity?

Recording bond investment transactions (Obj. 4)

E10-7 On March 31, 20X3, **Audi, Inc.,** paid $95\frac{1}{2}$ for 7% bonds of **Mazda Corp.** as a long-term held-to-maturity investment. The maturity value of the bonds will be $20,000 on September 30, 20X7. The bonds pay interest on March 31 and September 30. At December 31, the bonds' market value is 93.

Required

1. What method should Audi, Inc., use to account for its investment in the Mazda bonds?
2. Using the straight-line method of amortizing the discount, journalize all of Audi's transactions on the bonds for 20X3.
3. Show how Audi would report the bond investment on its balance sheet at December 31, 20X3.

Managing and accounting for foreign-currency transactions (Obj. 5)

E10-8 Record the following foreign-currency transactions:

Nov. 17	Purchased inventory on account from a Japanese company. The price was 200,000 yen, and the exchange rate of the yen was $0.0090.
Dec. 16	Paid the Japanese supplier when the exchange rate was $0.0092.
19	Sold merchandise on account to a French company at a price of 60,000 French francs. The exchange rate was $0.16.
30	Collected from the French company when the exchange rate was $0.18.

On November 18, immediately after your purchase, and on December 20, immediately after your sale, which currencies did you want to strengthen? Which currencies did in fact strengthen? Explain your reasoning in detail.

E10-9 Translate into dollars the balance sheet of Pasta Systems Company's Italian subsidiary. When Pasta Systems acquired the foreign subsidiary, an Italian lira was worth $0.00050. The current exchange rate is $0.00085. During the period when retained earnings were earned, the average exchange rate was $0.00070.

Translating a foreign-currency balance sheet into dollars (Obj. 6)

	Lire
Assets	500,000,000
Liabilities	300,000,000
Stockholders' equity:	
Common stock	50,000,000
Retained earnings	150,000,000
	500,000,000

During the period covered by this situation, which currency was stronger, the dollar or the lira?

E10-10 During fiscal year 19X5, **The Home Depot, Inc.,** reported net income of $604 million and paid $162 million to acquire other businesses. Home Depot made capital expenditures of $1,103 million to open new stores and sold property, plant, and equipment for $50 million. The company purchased long-term investments in stocks and bonds at a cost of $94 million and sold other long-term investments for $454 million. During the year, the company also cashed in short-term investments for $96 million.

Preparing and using the statement of cash flows (Obj. 7)

Required

Prepare the investing activities section of The Home Depot's statement of cash flows. Based solely on The Home Depot's investing activities, does it appear that the company is growing or shrinking? How can you tell?

E10-11 Celera Corporation earns approximately 15% of its net income from financial services through its wholly-owned subsidiary, Celera Financial Corporation. As a result, Finance Receivables is the largest single long-term asset on Celera's balance sheet. At the end of a recent year, Celera's statement of cash flows reported the following for investing activities:

Using the statement of cash flows (Obj. 7)

CELERA CORPORATION AND CONSOLIDATED SUBSIDIARIES
Consolidated Statement of Cash Flows (Partial)

	(In millions)
Cash Flows from Investing Activities	
Purchases of short-term investments	$(4,700)
Finance receivables collected	9,616
Proceeds from sales of [intangible] assets	2,375
Proceeds from sales of property and equipment ($300) and investments ($161)	461
Expenditures for property and equipment	(1,761)
Net Cash (Used in) Provided by Investing Activities	$ 5,991

Required

For each item listed, make the journal entry that placed the item on Celera's statement of cash flows. Assume each asset that Celera sold had a book value equal to its sale price, so there were no gains or losses on the sale.

Challenge Exercise

Analyzing available-for-sale investments and the foreign-currency translation adjustment (Obj. 1, 6)

E10-12 Alpha Power Corporation, a world leader in the construction of power-generating plants, reported the following stockholders' equity on its balance sheet at December 31 (all amounts in thousands):

ALPHA POWER CORPORATION
Balance Sheet (Partial)

	(In Thousands) *19X9*
Shareholders' Equity:	
Common stock, without par value—	
Authorized 700,000 shares,	
issued 224,640 shares	$ 12,480
Retained earnings	2,329,691
Cumulative foreign-currency translation adjustments	131,711
Net unrealized investment gains	21,585

Required

1. How does the cumulative translation adjustment find its way onto Alpha Power's balance sheet? Is Alpha's cumulative translation adjustment at the end of 19X9 a gain or a loss? How can you tell?
2. Alpha's balance sheet also reports available-for-sale investments at $287,898,000 ($287,898 thousand). What was Alpha's cost of the investments? What was the market value of the investments on December 31, 19X9?
3. Suppose Alpha Power sold its available-for-sale investments in 20X0 for $259,000,000 ($259,000 thousand). Determine the gain or loss on sale of the investments.

Problems

(Group A)

Reporting investments on the balance sheet and the related revenue on the income statement (Obj. 1, 2)

P10-1A Valvon Corporation owns numerous investments in the stock of other companies. Assume that Valvon completed the following long-term investment transactions:

20X4	
May 1	Purchased 8,000 shares, which is 25% of the common stock of Zeus Company at total cost of $720,000.
Sep. 15	Received semiannual cash dividend of $1.40 per share on the Zeus investment.
Oct. 12	Purchased 1,000 shares of Mars Corporation common stock as an available-for-sale investment paying $22½ per share.
Dec. 14	Received semiannual cash dividend of $0.75 per share on the Mars investment.
Dec. 31	Received annual report from Zeus Company. Net income for the year was $350,000.

At year end the current market value of the Mars stock is $24,700. The market value of the Zeus stock is $725,000.

Required

1. For which investment is current market value used in the accounting? Why is market value used for one investment and not the other?
2. Show what Valvon would report on its year-end balance sheet and income statement for

these investment transactions. (It is helpful to use a T-account for the investment in Zeus stock.) Ignore income tax.

P10-2A The beginning balance sheet of Clarion Investment Company included the following:

Accounting for available-for-sale and equity-method investments (Obj. 1, 2)

Long-Term Investments in Affiliates (equity-method investments) . .	$657,000

Clarion completed the following investment transactions during the year:

Mar. 3	Purchased 5,000 shares of BCM Software common stock as a long-term available-for-sale investment, paying 9\frac{1}{4}$ per share.
May 14	Received cash dividend of $0.82 per share on the BCM investment.
Dec. 15	Received cash dividend of $29,000 from an affiliated company.
Dec. 31	Received annual reports from affiliated companies. Their total net income for the year was $620,000. Of this amount, Clarion's proportion is 30%.

The market values of Clarion's investments are BCM, $45,100; affiliated companies, $947,000.

Required

1. Record the transactions in the journal of Clarion Investment Company.
2. Post entries to the Long-Term Investments in Affiliates T-account and determine its balance at December 31.
3. Show how to report the Long-Term Available-for-Sale Investments and the Long-Term Investments in Affiliates on Clarion's balance sheet at December 31.

P10-3A This problem demonstrates the dramatic effect that consolidation accounting can have on a company's ratios. **General Motors Corporation (GM)** owns 100% of **General Motors Acceptance Corporation (GMAC),** its financing subsidiary. GM's main operations consist of manufacturing automotive products. GMAC mainly helps people finance the purchase of automobiles from GM and its dealers. The two companies' individual balance sheets are summarized as follows:

Analyzing consolidated financial statements (Obj. 3)

	General Motors (Parent)	*GMAC (Subsidiary)*
Total assets	$132.6	$94.6
Total liabilities.	$109.3	$86.3
Total stockholders' equity.	23.3	8.3
Total liabilities and equity.	$132.6	$94.6

Assume that GMAC's liabilities include $7.3 billion owed to General Motors, the parent company.

Required

1. Compute the debt ratio of General Motors Corporation considered alone.
2. Determine the consolidated total assets, total liabilities, and stockholders' equity of General Motors Corporation after consolidating the financial statements of GMAC into the totals of GM, the parent company.
3. Recompute the debt ratio of the consolidated entity. Why do companies prefer not to consolidate their financing subsidiaries into their own financial statements?

P10-4A Montalban, Inc., paid $179,000 to acquire all the common stock of InterShop Corp., and InterShop owes Montalban $55,000 on a note payable. Immediately after the purchase on May 31, 20X3, the two companies' balance sheets were as follows:

Consolidating a wholly-owned subsidiary (Obj. 3)

Assets	Montalban	InterShop
Cash	$ 18,000	$ 32,000
Accounts receivable, net	64,000	43,000
Note receivable from InterShop	55,000	—
Inventory	93,000	153,000
Investment in InterShop	179,000	—
Plant assets, net	305,000	138,000
Total	$714,000	$366,000
Liabilities and Stockholders' Equity		
Accounts payable	$ 76,000	$ 37,000
Notes payable	118,000	123,000
Other liabilities	44,000	27,000
Common stock	282,000	90,000
Retained earnings	194,000	89,000
Total	$714,000	$366,000

Required

1. Prepare Montalban's consolidated balance sheet. (It is sufficient to complete a consolidation work sheet.)
2. Why aren't total assets of the consolidated entity equal to the sum of total assets for both companies combined? Why isn't consolidated equity equal to the sum of the two companies' stockholders' equity combined?

Accounting for a bond investment purchased at a discount (Obj. 4)

P10-5A Financial institutions such as insurance companies and pension plans hold large quantities of bond investments. Suppose Hornblower & Weeks (H & W) purchases $500,000 of 6% bonds of **General Motors Corporation** for 92 on January 31, 20X0. These bonds pay interest on January 31 and July 31 each year. They mature on July 31, 20X8. At December 31, 20X0, the market price of the bonds is 93.

Required

1. Journalize H & W's purchase of the bonds as a long-term investment on January 31, 19X0 (to be held to maturity), receipt of cash interest and amortization of discount on July 31, 20X0, and accrual of interest revenue and amortization of discount at December 31, 20X0. The straight-line method is appropriate for amortizing discount.
2. Show all financial statement effects of this long-term bond investment on H & W's balance sheet and income statement at December 31, 20X0.

Recording foreign-currency transactions and reporting the transaction gain or loss (Obj. 5)

P10-6A Suppose **The Coca-Cola Company** completed the following transactions:

May 4	Sold soft-drink syrup on account to a Mexican company for $43,000. The exchange rate of the Mexican peso is $0.101, and the customer agrees to pay in dollars.
13	Purchased inventory on account from a Canadian company at a price of Canadian $100,000. The exchange rate of the Canadian dollar is $0.65, and payment will be in Canadian dollars.
20	Sold goods on account to an English firm for 70,000 British pounds. Payment will be in pounds, and the exchange rate of the pound is $1.50.
27	Collected from the Mexican company.
June 21	Paid the Canadian company. The exchange rate of the Canadian dollar is $0.62.
July 17	Collected from the English firm. The exchange rate of the British pound is $1.48.

Required

1. Record these transactions in Coca-Cola's journal and show how to report the transaction gain or loss on the income statement.
2. How will what you learned in this problem help you structure international transactions?

P10-7A Brocade, Inc., owns a subsidiary based in Denmark.

Measuring and explaining the foreign-currency translation adjustment (Obj. 6)

Required

1. Translate the foreign-currency balance sheet of the Danish subsidiary of Brocade, Inc., into dollars. When Brocade acquired this subsidiary, the Danish krone was worth $0.17. The current exchange rate is $0.14. During the period when the subsidiary earned its income, the average exchange rate was $0.16 per krone.

	Kroner
Assets	3,000,000
Liabilities	1,000,000
Stockholders' equity:	
Common stock	300,000
Retained earnings	1,700,000
	3,000,000

   Before you perform the foreign-currency translation calculation, indicate whether Brocade, Inc., has experienced a positive or a negative foreign-currency translation adjustment. State whether the adjustment is a gain or loss, and show where it is reported in the financial statements.
2. To which company does the translation adjustment "belong"? In which company's financial statements will the translation adjustment be reported?
3. How will what you learned in this problem help you understand published financial statements?

P10-8A Excerpts from **The Coca-Cola Company's** statement of cash flows, as adapted, appear as follows:

Using a cash-flow statement (Obj. 7)

THE COCA-COLA COMPANY AND SUBSIDIARIES
Consolidated Statements of Cash Flows

	Years Ended December 31,		
(In Millions)	*19X5*	*19X4*	*19X3*
Operating Activities			
Net cash provided by operating activities	**$ 3,115**	$ 3,183	$ 2,508
Investing Activities			
Collections of finance subsidiary receivables	**46**	50	44
Acquisitions and investments, principally bottling companies	**(338)**	(311)	(611)
Purchases of securities	**(190)**	(201)	(245)
Proceeds from disposals of investments	**580**	299	690
Purchases of property, plant, and equipment	**(937)**	(878)	(800)
Proceeds from disposals of property, plant, and equipment	**44**	109	312
Other investing activities	**(218)**	(105)	(275)
Net cash used in investing activities	**(1,013)**	(1,037)	(885)
Net cash provided by operations after reinvestment	**2,102**	2,146	1,623
Financing Activities			
Issuances of debt (borrowing)	**754**	491	445
Payments of debt	**(212)**	(154)	(567)
Issuances of stock	**86**	69	145
Purchases of stock for treasury	**(1,796)**	(1,192)	(680)
Dividends	**(1,110)**	(1,006)	(883)
Net cash used in financing activities	**(2,278)**	(1,792)	(1,540)
Effect of Exchange Rate Changes on Cash and Cash Equivalents	**(43)**	34	(41)
Cash and Cash Equivalents			
Net increase (decrease) during the year	**(219)**	388	42
Balance at beginning of year	**1,386**	998	956
Balance at end of year	**$ 1,167**	$ 1,386	$ 998

Required

As the chief executive officer of The Coca-Cola Company, your duty is to write the management letter to your stockholders explaining Coca-Cola's major investing activities during 19X5. Compare the company's level of investment with previous years and indicate how the company financed its investments during 19X5. Net income for 19X5 was $2,986 million.

(Group B)

Reporting investments on the balance sheet and the related revenue on the income statement (Obj. 1, 2)

P10-1B Chandra Corporation owns numerous investments in the stock of other companies. Assume that Chandra completed the following long-term investment transactions:

20X2	
Feb. 12	Purchased 20,000 shares, which is 35%, of the common stock of Polanyi, Inc., at total cost of $715,000.
Aug. 9	Received annual cash dividend of $1.26 per share on the Polanyi investment.
Oct. 16	Purchased 800 shares of Microdot Company common stock as an available-for-sale investment, paying $41½ per share.
Nov. 30	Received semiannual cash dividend of $0.60 per share on the Microdot investment.
Dec. 31	Received annual report from Polanyi, Inc. Net income for the year was $510,000.

At year end the current market value of the Microdot stock is $29,800. The market value of the Polanyi stock is $252,000.

Required

1. For which investment is current market value used in the accounting? Why is market value used for one investment and not the other?

2. Show what Chandra Corporation would report on its year-end balance sheet and income statement for these investment transactions. It is helpful to use a T-account for the investment in Polanyi stock. Ignore income tax.

Accounting for available-for-sale and equity-method investments (Obj. 1, 2)

P10-2B The beginning balance sheet of **E-Trade, Inc.,** included the following:

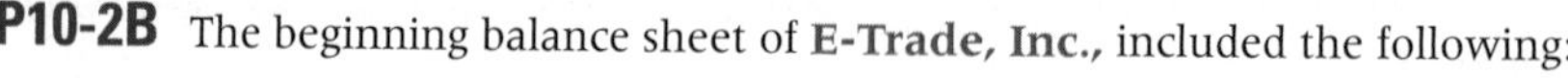

Long-Term Investments in Affiliates (equity-method investments) . .	$344,000

The company completed the following investment transactions during the year:

Mar. 2	Purchased 2,000 shares of ATI, Inc., common stock as a long-term available-for-sale investment, paying $12¼ per share.
Apr. 21	Received cash dividend of $0.75 per share on the ATI investment.
May 17	Received cash dividend of $47,000 from an affiliated company.
Dec. 31	Received annual reports from affiliated companies. Their total net income for the year was $550,000. Of this amount, E-Trade's proportion is 22%.

At year end the market values of E-Trade's investments are ATI, $26,800; affiliated company, $500,000.

Required

1. Record the transactions in the journal of E-Trade, Inc.

2. Post entries to the Long-Term Investments in Affiliates T-account and determine its balance at December 31.

3. Show how to report the Long-Term Available-for-Sale Investments and the Long-Term Investments in Affiliates accounts on E-Trade's balance sheet at December 31.

Analyzing consolidated financial statements (Obj. 3)

P10-3B This problem demonstrates the dramatic effect that consolidation accounting can have on a company's ratios. **Ford Motor Company** (Ford) owns 100% of **Ford Motor**

Credit Corporation (FMCC), its financing subsidiary. Ford's main operations consist of manufacturing automotive products. FMCC mainly helps people finance the purchase of automobiles from Ford and its dealers. The two companies' individual balance sheets are adapted and summarized as follows:

	Ford (Parent)	*FMCC (Subsidiary)*
Total assets	$89.6	$170.5
Total liabilities	$65.1	$156.9
Total stockholders' equity	24.5	13.6
Total liabilities and equity	$89.6	$170.5

Assume that FMCC's liabilities include $8.2 billion owed to Ford, the parent company.

Required

1. Compute the debt ratio of Ford Motor Company considered alone.
2. Determine the consolidated total assets, total liabilities, and stockholders' equity of Ford Motor Company after consolidating the financial statements of FMCC into the totals of Ford, the parent company.
3. Recompute the debt ratio of the consolidated entity. Why do companies prefer not to consolidate their financing subsidiaries into their own financial statements?

P10-4B Penske Logistics Corp. paid $266,000 to acquire all the common stock of LandStar, Inc., and LandStar owes Penske $81,000 on a note payable. Immediately after the purchase on June 30, 20X3, the two companies' balance sheets were as follows:

Consolidating a wholly-owned subsidiary (Obj. 3)

Assets	*Penske*	*LandStar*
Cash	$ 24,000	$ 20,000
Accounts receivable, net	91,000	42,000
Note receivable from LandStar	81,000	—
Inventory	145,000	214,000
Investment in LandStar	266,000	—
Plant assets, net	478,000	219,000
Total	$1,085,000	$495,000
Liabilities and Stockholders' Equity		
Accounts payable	$ 57,000	$ 49,000
Notes payable	177,000	149,000
Other liabilities	129,000	31,000
Common stock	274,000	118,000
Retained earnings	448,000	148,000
Total	$1,085,000	$495,000

Required

1. Prepare the consolidated balance sheet for Penske Logistics Corp. (It is sufficient to complete a consolidation work sheet.)
2. Why aren't total assets of the consolidated entity equal to the sum of total assets for both companies combined? Why isn't consolidated equity equal to the sum of the two companies' stockholders' equity amounts?

P10-5B Financial institutions such as insurance companies and pension plans hold large quantities of bond investments. Suppose Allstate Financial Service Company purchases $600,000 of 6% bonds of Eaton, Inc., for 103 on March 1, 20X1. These bonds pay interest on March 1 and September 1 each year. They mature on March 1, 20X8. At December 31, 20X1, the market price of the bonds is $103\frac{1}{2}$.

Accounting for a bond investment purchased at a premium (Obj. 4)

Required

1. Journalize Allstate's purchase of the bonds as a long-term investment on March 1, 20X1 (to be held to maturity), receipt of cash interest, and amortization of premium at December 31, 20X1. The straight-line method is appropriate for amortizing premium.
2. Show all financial statement effects of this long-term bond investment on Allstate Financial Services Company's balance sheet and income statement at December 31, 20X1.

Recording foreign-currency transactions and reporting the transaction gain or loss (Obj. 5)

P10-6B Suppose **Goodyear Tire & Rubber Company** completed the following transactions:

May	1	Sold inventory on account to **Fiat,** the Italian automaker, for \$82,000. The exchange rate of the Italian lira is \$0.0007, and Fiat agrees to pay in dollars.
	10	Purchased supplies on account from a Canadian company at a price of Canadian \$50,000. The exchange rate of the Canadian dollar is \$0.70, and payment will be in Canadian dollars.
	17	Sold inventory on account to an English firm for 100,000 British pounds. Payment will be in pounds, and the exchange rate of the pound is \$1.50.
	22	Collected from Fiat.
June	18	Paid the Canadian company. The exchange rate of the Canadian dollar is \$0.67.
	24	Collected from the English firm. The exchange rate of the British pound is \$1.47.

Required

1. Record these transactions in Goodyear's journal and show how to report the transaction gain or loss on the income statement.
2. How will what you learned in this problem help you structure international transactions?

Measuring and explaining the foreign-currency translation adjustment (Obj. 6)

P10-7B Assume **Sotheby, Inc.,** has a subsidiary company based in Japan.

Required

1. Translate into dollars the foreign-currency balance sheet of the Japanese subsidiary of Sotheby, Inc. When Sotheby acquired this subsidiary, the Japanese yen was worth \$0.0064. The current exchange rate is \$0.0086. During the period when the subsidiary earned its income, the average exchange rate was \$0.0080 per yen.

	Yen
Assets	300,000,000
Liabilities	80,000,000
Stockholders' equity:	
Common stock	20,000,000
Retained earnings	200,000,000
	300,000,000

   Before you perform the foreign-currency translation calculations, indicate whether Sotheby has experienced a positive or a negative translation adjustment. State whether the adjustment is a gain or a loss, and show where it is reported in the financial statements.
2. To which company does the foreign-currency translation adjustment "belong"? In which company's financial statements will the translation adjustment be reported?
3. How will what you learned in this problem help you understand published financial statements?

Using a cash-flow statement (Obj. 7)

P10-8B Excerpts from **Intel Corporation's** statement of cash flows, as adapted, appear as follows (shown at top of next page).

Required

As the chief executive officer of Intel Corporation, your duty is to write the management letter to your stockholders to explain Intel's investing activities during 19X5. Compare the company's level of investment with preceding years and indicate the major way the company financed its investments during 19X5. Net income for 19X5 was $3,566 million.

INTEL CORPORATION
Consolidataed Statement of Cash Flows (Partial)
Three Years Ended December 30, 19X5

(In Millions)	*19X5*	*19X4*	*19X3*
Cash and cash equivalents, beginning of year	**$ 1,180**	$ 1,659	$ 1,843
Net cash provided by operating activities	**4,026**	2,981	2,801
Cash flows provided by (used for) investing activities:			
Additions to property, plant, and equipment	**(3,550)**	(2,441)	(1,933)
Purchases of long-term, available-for-sale investments	**(129)**	(975)	(1,409)
Sales of long-term, available-for-sale investments	**992**	513	5
Net cash (used for) investing activities	**(2,687)**	(2,903)	(3,337)
Cash flows provided by (used for) financing activities:			
(Decrease) increase in short-term debt, net	**(179)**	(63)	197
Long-term borrowing	**—**	128	148
Retirement of long-term debt	**(4)**	(98)	—
Proceeds from sales of shares through employee stock plans and other	**277**	226	482
Repurchase and retirement of Common Stock	**(1,034)**	(658)	(391)
Payment of dividends to stockholders	**(116)**	(92)	(84)
Net cash (used for) provided by financing activities	**(1,056)**	(557)	352
Net increase (decrease) in cash and cash equivalents	**283**	(479)	(184)
Cash and cash equivalents, end of year	**$ 1,463**	$ 1,180	$ 1,659

Extending Your Knowledge

Decision Cases

Case 1. Diana Booker is the manager of Explorer Corp., whose year end is December 31. The company made two investments during the first week of January 20X2. Both investments are to be held for the indefinite future. Information about the investments follows:

Explaining the market value and equity methods of accounting for investments
(Obj. 1, 2)

a. One thousand shares of the common stock of Magellan Corporation were purchased as an available-for-sale investment for $95,000. During the year ended December 31, 20X2, Magellan paid Explorer a dividend of $3,000. Magellan earned a profit of $317,000 for that period, and at year end, the market value of Explorer's investment in Magellan stock was $87,000.

b. Explorer purchased 30% of the common stock of Cortes Co. for its book value of $150,000. During the year ended December 31, 20X2, Cortes earned $106,000 and paid a total dividend of $53,000. At year end, the market value of the Cortes investment is $261,000.

Booker has come to you to ask how to account for the investments. Explorer has never had such investments before. Explain the proper accounting to her by indicating which accounting method applies to each investment.

Required

Help Booker understand by writing a memo to

1. Describe the methods of accounting applicable to these investments.

2. Identify which method should be used to account for the investments in Magellan Corporation and Cortes Co. Also indicate the dollar amount to report for each investment on the year-end balance sheet.

Understanding the consolidation method for investments and international accounting (Obj. 3, 5)

Case 2. Jeff Bezos inherited some investments, and he has received the annual reports of the companies in which the funds are invested. The financial statements of the companies are puzzling to Bezos, and he asks you the following questions:

a. Notes to the statements indicate that "certain intercompany transactions, loans, and other accounts have been eliminated in preparing the consolidated financial statements." Why does a company eliminate transactions, loans, and accounts? Bezos states that he thought a transaction was a transaction and that a loan obligated a company to pay real money. He wonders if the company is juggling the books to defraud the IRS.

b. The balance sheet lists the asset Goodwill. What is goodwill? Does the presence of goodwill mean that the company's stock has increased in value?

c. The companies label their financial statements as *consolidated* balance sheet, *consolidated* income statement, and so on. What are consolidated financial statements?

d. The stockholders' equity section of the balance sheet reports Foreign-Currency Translation Adjustments. Bezos asks what is being translated and why this item is negative.

Required

Write a memo to respond to each of Bezos's questions.

ETHICAL ISSUE

Media One owns 18% of the voting stock of Web Talk, Inc. The remainder of the Web Talk stock is held by numerous investors with small holdings. Austin Cohen, president of Media One and a member of Web Talk's board of directors, heavily influences Web Talk's policies.

Under the market value method of accounting for investments, Media One's net income increases as it receives dividend revenue from Web Talk. Media One pays President Cohen a bonus computed as a percentage of Media One's net income. Therefore, Cohen can control his personal bonus to a certain extent by influencing Web Talk's dividends.

A recession occurs in 20X0, and Media One's income is low. Cohen uses his power to have Web Talk pay a large cash dividend. The action requires Web Talk to borrow in order to pay the dividend.

Required

1. In getting Web Talk to pay the large cash dividend, is Cohen acting within his authority as a member of the Web Talk board of directors? Are Cohen's actions ethical? Whom can his actions harm?

2. Discuss how using the equity method of accounting for investments would decrease Cohen's potential for manipulating his bonus.

FINANCIAL STATEMENT CASE

Investments in stocks (Obj. 1, 2, 3)

Obtain the annual report of a company of your choosing. Answer the following questions about the company. Concentrate on the current year in the annual report you select.

Required

1. Many companies refer to other companies in which they own equity-method investments as *affiliated companies.* This signifies the close relationship between the two entities even though the investor does not own a controlling interest.

Does the company have equity-method investments? Cite the evidence. If present, what were the balances in the investment account at the beginning and the end of the current year? If the company had no equity-method investments, skip the next question.

2. Scan the income statement. If equity-method investments are present, what amount of revenue (or income) did the company earn on the investments during the current year? Scan the statement of cash flows. What amount of dividends did the company receive during the current year from companies in which it held equity-method investments? *Note:* The amount of dividends received may not be disclosed. If not, you can still compute the amount of dividends received from the following T-account:

INVESTMENTS, AT EQUITY

Beg. bal. (from balance sheet)	**W**		
Equity-method revenue (from income statement)	**X**	**Dividends received** (unknown; must compute)	**Y**
End. bal. (from balance sheet)	**Z**		

3. The company probably owns some consolidated subsidiaries. You can tell whether the parent company owns 100% or less of the subsidiaries. Examine the income statement and the balance sheet to determine whether there are any minority interests. If so, what does that fact indicate?
4. The stockholders' equity section of most balance sheets lists Foreign-Currency Translation Adjustment or a similar account title. A positive amount signifies a gain, and a negative amount indicates a loss. The change in this account balance from the beginning of the year to the end of the year signals whether the U.S. dollar was strong or weak during the year in comparison to the foreign currencies. For the company you are analyzing, was the dollar strong or weak during the current year?

GROUP PROJECT

Pick a stock from the *Wall Street Journal* or other database or publication. Assume that your group purchases 1,000 shares of the stock as a long-term investment and that your 1,000 shares are less than 20% of the company's outstanding stock. Research the stock in *Value Line, Moody's Investor Record,* or other source to determine whether the company pays cash dividends and, if so, how much and at what intervals.

Required

1. Track the stock for a period assigned by your professor. Over the specified period, keep a daily record of the price of the stock to see how well your investment has performed. Each day, search the Corporate Dividend News in the *Wall Street Journal* to keep a record of any dividends you've received. End the period of your analysis with a month end, such as September 30 or December 31.
2. Journalize all transactions that you have experienced, including the stock purchase, dividends received (both cash dividends and stock dividends), and any year-end adjustment required by the accounting method that is appropriate for your situation. Assume you will prepare financial statements on the ending date of your study.
3. Show what you will report on your company's balance sheet, income statement, and statement of cash flows as a result of your investment transactions.

INTERNET EXERCISE

Ford

SEC regulations require all companies traded on a stock exchange to file periodic reports. Most of these reports are available on the Internet at the EDGAR (Electronic Data Gathering, Analysis, and Retrieval system) Web site.

1. Go to the EDGAR database Web site at **http://www.sec.gov** and click on the **EDGAR Database** button, then **Search the EDGAR Database,** followed by **Quick Forms Lookup.** Use the *"Select the form"* scroll bar to select form *10-K.* The 10-K contains business and financial information about a company that is filed annually. Scroll down the page to *"Enter a company",* type in FORD MOTOR CO. Then click on **Submit Choices.** Select the most recent *10-K* information, and choose the html format if available.
2. Within the 10-K report, scroll down and find *Item 6. Selected Financial Data* and review the *SUMMARY OF VEHICLE UNIT SALES* (page 33 of the 1998 10-K). For the most recent year, Ford sold how many cars and trucks in North America? Europe? Other international? Total worldwide?
3. Is Ford Motor Company an international company? What additional accounts would you expect to find on the financial statements of an international company? Where would you locate these accounts?
4. Scroll about halfway through the document until you find the CONSOLIDATED BALANCE SHEET (after page 60 in the 1998 10-K.) What does the term *consolidated* indicate in the title of this statement? For the most recent year, identify the amount reported for automotive "Marketable Securities" and "Equity in the net assets of affiliated companies." How is each account classified—current or long-term?
5. At the end of the most recent year, identify the amount reported for "Accumulated other comprehensive income." Is this amount a gain or a loss? How is this account classified? Describe what information (discussed in this chapter) may be included in this account.
6. Describe at least two possible Internet sources of corporate financial information.

11 Using the Income Statement and the Statement of Stockholders' Equity

Learning Objectives

After studying this chapter, you should be able to

1. Analyze a complex income statement
2. Account for a corporation's income tax
3. Analyze a statement of stockholders' equity
4. Understand managers' and auditors' responsibilities for the financial statements

"Our investors are interested in the level of income a company can expect to earn in the future. Therefore, we are most likely to base our recommendations on our review of a company's income from continuing operations rather than its net income."

—Murray Weintraub, Business Analyst, Sledd & Co. Investment Bankers

The May Department Stores Company
Consolidated Statement of Earnings (partial; adapted)

		Year Ended		
	(In millions, except per share)	January 30, 1999	January 31, 1998	February 1, 1997
1	Net retail sales	$13,072	$12,291	$11,492
2	Revenues	$13,413	$12,685	$12,000
3	Cost of sales	9,224	8,732	8,226
4	Selling, general, and administrative expenses	2,516	2,375	2,265
5	Interest expense, net	278	299	277
6	Total cost of sales and expenses	12,018	11,406	10,768
7	Earnings from continuing operations before income taxes	1,395	1,279	1,232
8	Provision for income taxes	546	500	483
9	**Net earnings from continuing operations**	**849**	**779**	**749**
10	Net earnings from discontinued operation	—	—	11
11	Net earnings before extraordinary loss	849	779	760
12	Extraordinary loss related to early extinguishment of debt, net of income taxes	—	(4)	(5)
13	Net earnings	$ 849	$ 775	$ 755
	Basic earnings per share:			
14	Continuing operations	$ 2.43	$ 2.18	$ 1.97
15	Discontinued operation	—	—	0.03
16	Net earnings before extraordinary loss	2.43	2.18	2.00
17	Extraordinary loss	—	(0.01)	(0.01)
18	Basic earnings per share	$ 2.43	$ 2.17	$ 1.99

The May Department Stores Company is one of the country's leading department store companies, operating 393 stores (including Lord & Taylor, Hecht's, Foley's, Robinsons-May, Filene's, and Kaufmann's). The company's total annual sales are $13.1 billion. May's operating results for the year ended January 30, 1999 are reported on the income statement (line 1).

Murray Weintraub, chief financial analyst for Sledd & Co. Investment Bankers, is evaluating May's net earnings. He and fellow analysts are trying to decide whether May's earnings are high enough to support the company's stock price at $30.25 per share. His decision will govern whether Sledd & Co. makes a "buy," "hold," or "sell" recommendation to its investment clients.

Investment analysts such as Weintraub use the financial statements and other data to predict the future net income and cash flows of companies, including May. Which income figure should investors use to evaluate a company's results? The answer depends on the decision you will make.

- If you want to measure how well the company has performed in light of all its activities, then you should look at net income (line 13).
- If you want to predict the level of income the company can expect to earn in the future, you should consider only those operations that repeat from year to year.

Murray Weintraub and his staff are probably more interested in income from continuing operations (line 9) than in net income. Most sophisticated investors and lenders concentrate their analysis on income from continuing operations because continuing operations can be expected to generate income in the future.

In this chapter, we discuss details of the corporate income statement and the statement of stockholders' equity. We also cover some other topics that will enhance your ability to analyze financial statements.

QUALITY OF EARNINGS

Objective 1
Analyze a complex income statement

A corporation's net income (net earnings) receives more attention than any other item in the financial statements. To stockholders, the larger the corporation's profit, the greater the likelihood of dividends. To creditors, the larger the profit, the better the ability to pay debts.

Suppose you are considering investing in the stock of two manufacturing companies. In reading their annual reports, you learn that the companies earned the same net income last year and that each company has increased its net income by 15% annually over the last five years.

The two companies, however, have generated income in different ways:

- Company A's income has resulted from the successful management of its central operations (manufacturing).
- Company B's manufacturing operations have been flat for two years. Its growth in net income has resulted from selling off segments of its business at a profit.

In which company would you invest?

Company A holds the promise of better earnings in the future. This corporation earns profits from *continuing operations.* We may expect the business to match its past earnings in the future. Company B shows no growth from operations. Its net income results from *one-time transactions*—the selling off of assets. Sooner or later, Company B will run out of assets to sell. When that occurs, the business will have no means of generating income. So your decision is to invest in the stock of Company A. Investors would say that Company A's earnings are of *higher quality* than Company B's earnings.

May Department Stores' earnings appear to be of high quality. The trends of sales (line 1), net income (line 13), and, most importantly, income from continuing operations (line 9) are up, up, up. To explore the makeup of net income, let's examine the various sources of income. Exhibit 11-1 provides a comprehensive example that we will use in the following discussions. It is the income statement of Allied Electronics Corporation, a small manufacturer of precision instruments.

Continuing Operations

In the income statement in Exhibit 11-1, the topmost section reports income from continuing operations (lines 1–10). This part of the business is expected to continue from period to period. We may use this information to predict that Allied Electronics will earn income of approximately $54,000 next year.

The continuing operations of Allied Electronics include three new items:

- During 20X2, the company restructured operations at a loss of $10,000 (line 6). Restructuring costs include severance pay to laid-off workers, mov-

Exhibit 11-1
Allied Electronics Corporation Income Statement

Section	Line	ALLIED ELECTRONICS CORPORATION Income Statement Year Ended December 31, 20X2		
Continuing operations	1	Sales revenue		$500,000
	2	Cost of goods sold		240,000
	3	Gross margin		260,000
	4	Operating expenses (detailed)		181,000
	5	Operating income		79,000
		Other gains (losses):		
	6	Loss on restructuring operations		(8,000)
	7	Gain on sale of machinery		19,000
	8	Income from continuing operations before income tax		90,000
	9	Income tax expense		36,000
	10	Income from continuing operations		54,000
Special items		Discontinued operations:		
	11	Operating income, $30,000, less income tax of $12,000	$18,000	
	12	Gain on disposal, $5,000, less income tax of $2,000	3,000	21,000
	13	Income before extraordinary item and cumulative effect of change in depreciation method		75,000
	14 15	Extraordinary flood loss, $20,000, less income tax savings of $8,000		(12,000)
	16	Cumulative effect of change in depreciation method, $10,000, less income tax of $4,000		6,000
	17	Net income		$ 69,000
Earnings per share		Earnings per share of common stock (20,000 shares outstanding):		
	18	Income from continuing operations		$2.70
	19	Income from discontinued operations		1.05
	20	Income before extraordinary item and cumulative effect of change in depreciation method		3.75
	21	Extraordinary loss		(0.60)
	22	Cumulative effect of change in depreciation method		0.30
	23	Net income		$3.45

✔ Check Point 11-1

✔ Check Point 11-2

✔ Check Point 11-3

ing expenses for employees transferred to other locations, and environmental cleanup expenses. The restructuring loss is part of continuing operations because Allied Electronics is remaining in the same line of business. But the restructuring loss is highlighted as an "Other" item on the income statement because its cause—restructuring—falls outside Allied Electronics' main business endeavor, which is selling electronics products.

- Allied also had a gain on the sale of machinery (line 7), which is outside the company's core business activity. This explains why the gain is reported separately from Allied's operating income (lines 1–5).
- Income tax expense (line 9) has been deducted in arriving at income from continuing operations. The tax that corporations pay on their income is a significant expense. The current maximum federal income tax rate for corporations is 35%. State income taxes run about 5% in many states. Thus, we use an income tax rate of 40% in our illustrations. The $36,000 income tax expense in Exhibit 11-1 equals the pretax income from continuing operations multiplied by the tax rate ($90,000 × 0.40 = $36,000).

How much was Allied Electronics' *total* income tax expense during 20X2? Consider lines, 9, 11, 12, 15, and 16 of the income statement in Exhibit 11-1.

Answer:

$46,000 = ($36,000 + $12,000 + $2,000 − $8,000 + $4,000)

Income tax is reported along with each separate category of income or loss:

Category of Income or Loss	*Income Tax Expense (Saving)*
Income from continuing operations	$36,000
Discontinued operations	
($12,000 + $2,000).	14,000
Extraordinary gains and losses	(8,000)
Cumulative effect of accounting change. .	4,000
Total income tax expense for 20X2.	$46,000

Note that $36,000 is the company's income tax expense from continuing operations; $46,000 is *total* income tax expense.

USING INCOME FROM CONTINUING OPERATIONS IN INVESTMENT ANALYSIS. How is income from continuing operations used in investment analysis? Suppose Murray Weintraub is estimating the value of Allied Electronics' common stock. Weintraub and his staff may believe that Allied Electronics can earn annual income of $54,000 each year for the indefinite future, based on Allied's 20X2 income from continuing operations.

To estimate the value of Allied's common stock, financial analysts determine the present value (present value means *today*) of Allied's stream of future income. Weintraub must use some interest rate to compute the present value. Assume that an appropriate interest rate (i) for the valuation of Allied Electronics is 12%. This rate is determined subjectively, based on the risk that Allied might not be able to earn annual income of $54,000 for the indefinite future. The rate is also called the **investment capitalization rate** because it is used to estimate the value of an investment in the capital stock of another company. The higher the risk, the higher the rate, and vice versa. The computation of the estimated value of a stock is

See Appendix B for a review of present value.

$$\textbf{Estimated value of Allied Electronics common stock} = \frac{\textbf{Estimated annual income in the future}}{\textbf{Investment capitalization rate}} = \frac{\$54{,}000}{.12} = \$450{,}000^*$$

Weintraub thus estimates that Allied Electronics Corporation is worth $450,000. He would then compare this estimate to the current market value of Allied Electronics' stock, which is $513,000. Allied Electronics' balance sheet reports that Allied has 108,000 shares of common stock outstanding, and the *Wall Street Journal* reports that Allied common stock is selling for $4.75 per share. The current market value of Allied Stock is thus

*This valuation model has many forms, which are covered in finance classes. Here we introduce the most basic form of a widely used valuation model to illustrate how accounting income can be used in actual practice.

Another way to estimate the value of a company's stock uses the price/earnings (P/E) ratio, which is roughly equal to the reciprocal of the investment capitalization rate. In the P/E formulation of company value, the analyst multiplies net income by the P/E ratio. The computation for Allied Electronics is net income ($54,000) multiplied by the P/E ratio (8.33), which equals the estimated value of $450,000.

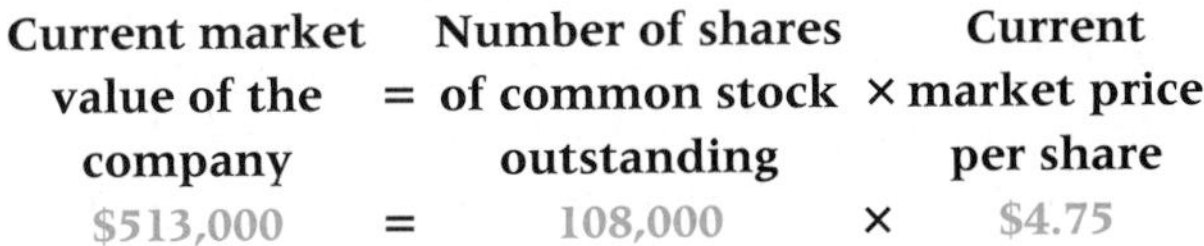

Current market value of the company
= Number of shares of common stock outstanding
× Current market price per share
$513,000 = 108,000 × $4.75

The investment decision rule may take this form:

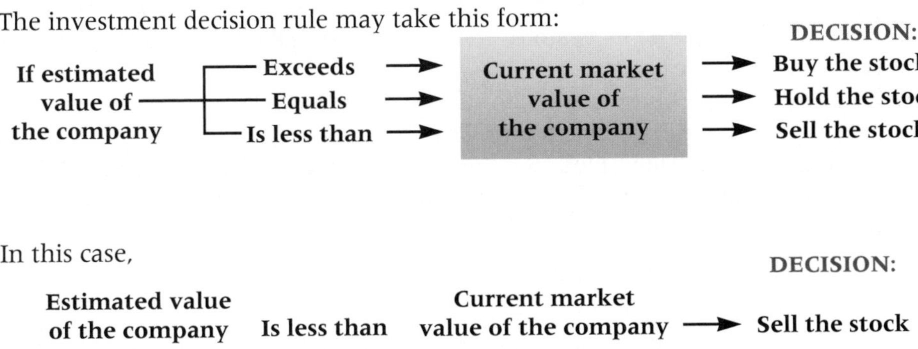

In this case,

Estimated value of the company		Current market value of the company		DECISION:
	Is less than		→	Sell the stock
$450,000		$513,000		

Sledd believes the stock price should fall below its current market value of $513,000 to somewhere in a range near $450,000. Based largely on its income from continuing operations, Sledd believes that Allied's stock would be more fairly valued at $450,000. Based on this analysis, Sledd & Co. Investment Bankers would recommend that investors holding Allied Electronics stock should sell it.

Investors often make their decisions based on the value of a single share of stock. They can estimate the value of one share of stock with a variation of the valuation computation that uses earnings per share (EPS) of common stock, as follows:

$$\text{Estimated value of one share of common stock} = \frac{\text{Estimated annual earnings per share}}{\text{Investment capitalization rate}}$$

CHECK POINT 11-4

The analysis based on one share of stock follows the pattern illustrated for the company as a whole.

Summary of the Investment Decision Process. Let's summarize the investment decision process. It begins with an income figure that experienced people believe Allied can earn year in and year out for the indefinite future. Most analysts use *income from continuing operations.* Some analysts also use *cash flows from operating activities* to estimate the value of an investment. Many analysts use both income from continuing operations and cash flows from operating activities. Chapter 12 covers cash-flow analysis in detail.

Suppose Murray Weintraub's investment team fears that Allied Electronics cannot earn $54,000 annually for the indefinite future. They may take a more conservative view—say, that Allied Electronics' income stream may be predictable for only 20 years into the future. In that case, analysts' estimate of the value of Allied's stock would be as follows:

Estimated value of Allied Electronics common stock		Estimated annual income in the future		Present value of annuity $n = 20$ periods; $i = 12\%$ (Appendix B, Table B-7)
	=		×	
	=	$ 54,000	×	7.469
	=	$403,326		

Based on this estimate, analysts would believe even more strongly that Allied's stock is overpriced at $513,000 ($4.75 per share).

Discontinued Operations

Most large corporations engage in several lines of business. For example, **Sears, Roebuck & Co.** has a real estate development company (**Homart**) and an insurance company (**Allstate**) in addition to its retail stores. We call each identifiable division of a company a **segment of the business.**

A company may sell a segment of its business. For example, **May Department Stores** sold **Payless**, its chain of shoe stores. The sale of a business segment is viewed as a one-time transaction. May's income statement for the year ended February 1, 1997, carries information on the segment that has been disposed of under the heading Discontinued Operations (line 10 on page 499).

Let's return to the Allied Electronics example in Exhibit 11-1 (page 501). The Discontinued Operations section of the income statement is divided into two components:

1. Operating income or (loss) on the segment that is disposed of, and

2. Gain (or loss) on the disposal.

Income and gain are taxed at the 40% rate and reported by Allied Electronics Corporation as follows:

Discontinued operations:		
Operating income, $30,000, less income tax, $12,000 . . .	$18,000	
Gain on disposal, $5,000, less income tax, $2,000	3,000	$21,000

It is necessary to separate discontinued operations into these two components because the company may operate the discontinued segment for part of the year. This is the operating income (or loss) component. Then, the disposal of the segment results in a gain (or loss). Trace this presentation to Exhibit 11-1, lines 11 and 12.

Discontinued operations relate to an identifiable segment of the business. In the normal course of business, companies dispose of old plant and equipment and buy new assets. Gains and losses on normal asset dispositions are *not* reported as discontinued operations because they don't relate to a segment of the business that is being discontinued. Gains and losses on normal asset dispositions can be reported along with operating revenues and expenses or highlighted in the "Other" section of the income statement (Exhibit 11-1, lines 6 and 7).

Financial analysts typically do not include income or loss on discontinued operations in predictions of future corporate income. The discontinued segments will not generate income for the company in the future.

Extraordinary Gains and Losses (Extraordinary Items)

Extraordinary gains and losses, also called **extraordinary items,** are both *unusual* for the company and *infrequent.* Losses from natural disasters (such as earthquakes, floods, and tornadoes) and the taking of company assets by a foreign government (expropriation) are extraordinary. Gains and losses on the early retirement of debt are also extraordinary items. May Department Store reports such an extraordinary loss (see page 499, line 12).

Extraordinary items are reported along with their income tax effect. During 20X2, Allied Electronics Corporation lost $20,000 of inventory in a flood (Exhibit 11-1, line 14). This flood loss, which reduced income, also reduced Allied's income tax. The tax effect decreases the net amount of the loss in the same way that the income tax reduces the amount of net income. Another way to report an extraordinary loss along with its tax effect is as follows:

Extraordinary flood loss.	$(20,000)
Less income tax saving.	8,000
Extraordinary flood loss, net of tax	(12,000)

Trace this item to the income statement in Exhibit 11-1 (lines 14 and 15). An extraordinary gain is reported in the same way, net of its income tax.

Gains and losses due to employee strikes, the settlement of lawsuits, discontinued operations, and the sale of plant assets are *not* extraordinary items. They are considered normal business occurrences. However, because they are outside the business's central operations, they are reported on the income statement as Other gains and losses. Examples include the gain on sale of machinery and the restructuring loss in the Other gains (losses) section of Exhibit 11-1 (page 501, lines 6 and 7).

Cumulative Effect of a Change in Accounting Principle

Companies sometimes change from one accounting method to another, such as from double-declining-balance (DDB) to straight-line depreciation, or from first-in, first-out (FIFO) to weighted-average cost for inventory. ➞ An accounting change makes it difficult to compare one period's financial statements with the statements of preceding periods. Without detailed information, investors and creditors can be misled into thinking that the current year is better or worse than the preceding year when in fact the only difference is a change in accounting method. To help investors separate the effects of regular business operations from those effects caused by a change in accounting method, companies report the effect of the accounting change in a special section of the income statement. This section usually appears after extraordinary items. Exhibit 11-1, line 16 gives an example for Allied Electronics.

← For a review of depreciation methods, see Chapter 7. For a review of inventory methods, see Chapter 6.

We need to know what cumulative effect an accounting change would have had on net income of prior years. GAAP (generally accepted accounting principles) requires companies that change accounting methods to disclose the difference between net income actually reported for past years and the net income that the company would have experienced if it had used the new method all along.

Allied Electronics Corporation changed from DDB to straight-line depreciation at the beginning of 20X2. How did this change in depreciation method affect the 20X2 financial statements? First, it decreased depreciation expense for 20X2 and thereby increased 20X2 income from continuing operations. Second, the change affected the cumulative amounts from previous years. If the company had been using straight-line depreciation in previous years, depreciation expense would have been less, and net income would have been $6,000 higher ($10,000 minus the additional income tax of $4,000). Exhibit 11-1 reports the cumulative effect of this accounting change on line 16.

Earnings per Share of Common Stock

The final segment of a corporation income statement presents the company's earnings per share. **Earnings per share (EPS)** is the amount of a company's net income per share of its *outstanding common stock.* EPS is a key measure of a business's success, computed as follows:

$$\textbf{Earnings per share} = \frac{\textbf{Net income} - \textbf{Preferred dividends}}{\textbf{Weighted-average number of shares of common stock outstanding}}$$

Just as the corporation lists its various sources of income separately—from continuing operations, discontinued operations, and so on—it also lists the EPS figure based on different income sources separately. Consider the EPS calculations for Allied Electronics Corporation. The final section (lines 18–23) of Exhibit 11-1 shows how the EPS figures are reported on the income statement:

	Earnings per share of common stock (20,000 shares outstanding):	
18	Income from continuing operations ($54,000/20,000).	$2.70
19	Income from discontinued operations ($21,000/20,000)	1.05
20	Income before extraordinary item and cumulative effect of change in depreciation method ($75,000/20,000)	3.75
21	Extraordinary loss ($12,000/20,000)	(0.60)
22	Cumulative effect of change in depreciation method ($6,000/20,000).	0.30
23	Net income ($69,000/20,000).	$3.45

WEIGHTED-AVERAGE SHARES OF COMMON STOCK OUTSTANDING. Computing EPS is straightforward if the number of common shares outstanding does not change during the period. For many corporations, however, shares outstanding vary from month to month. Consider a corporation that had 100,000 shares outstanding from January through November, then in December purchased 60,000 shares as treasury stock. This company's EPS would be misleadingly high if computed using the 40,000 shares outstanding at year end (100,000 − 60,000). To make EPS as meaningful as possible, corporations use the *weighted-average* number of shares of common stock outstanding during the period.

Let's assume that Diskette Demo Corporation had these shares of common stock outstanding for the following periods of a year:

- January through May—240,000 shares
- June through August—200,000 shares
- September through December—210,000 shares

We compute the weighted-average number of common shares outstanding by considering the outstanding shares per month as a fraction of the year:

Number of Common Shares Outstanding	×	*Fraction of Year*	*Period during the Year*	=	*Weighted-Average Number of Common Shares Outstanding*
240,000	×	5/12	January through May	=	100,000
200,000	×	3/12	June through August	=	50,000
210,000	×	4/12	September through December	=	70,000
			Weighted-average number of common shares outstanding during the year		220,000

The weighted-average number of common shares outstanding (220,000) would then be divided into net income to compute the corporation's EPS.

EFFECT OF PREFERRED DIVIDENDS ON EARNINGS PER SHARE. Holders of preferred stock have first claim on dividends but no claim to income beyond the stated preferred dividend. Therefore, preferred dividends affect EPS.

➛ Chapter 9, pages 417–418, provide detailed information on preferred stock.

Recall that EPS is earnings per share of *common* stock. ⟵ Therefore, preferred dividends must be subtracted from income subtotals in the computation of EPS. Preferred dividends are not subtracted from discontinued operations, extraordinary items, or the cumulative effect of accounting changes.

If Allied Electronics Corporation had 10,000 shares of preferred stock outstanding, each with a $1.00 dividend, the annual preferred dividend would be $10,000 (10,000 × $1.00). The $10,000 would be subtracted from each of the different income subtotals, resulting in the following EPS computations:

Earnings per share of common stock (20,000 shares outstanding):	
Income from continuing operations ($54,000 − $10,000)/20,000	$2.20
Income from discontinued operations ($21,000/20,000)	1.05
Income before extraordinary item and cumulative effect of change in depreciation method ($75,000 − $10,000)/20,000	3.25
Extraordinary loss ($12,000/20,000)	(0.60)
Cumulative effect of change in depreciation method ($6,000/20,000)	0.30
Net income ($69,000 − $10,000)/20,000	$2.95

CHECK POINT 11-5

CHECK POINT 11-6

EARNINGS PER SHARE DILUTION. Some corporations make their preferred stock attractive by offering convertible preferred stock. As we saw in Chapter 9, the holders of convertible preferred may exchange the preferred stock for common stock. When preferred is converted to common, the EPS is *diluted*—reduced—because more common shares are divided into net income. Corporations with complex capital structures present two sets of EPS figures:

- EPS based on actual outstanding common shares (*basic* EPS)
- EPS based on outstanding common shares plus the additional common shares that would arise from conversion of the preferred stock into common (*diluted* EPS)

Reporting Comprehensive Income

All companies report net income or net loss on their income statements. Companies with certain gains and losses are also required by FASB Statement 130 to report another income figure. **Comprehensive income** is the company's change in total stockholders' equity from all sources other than from the owners of the business. Comprehensive income includes net income plus some specific gains and losses. In Chapter 10, we saw two new components of comprehensive income:

- Unrealized gains (losses) on available-for-sale investments
- Foreign-currency translation adjustments

These items do not enter into the determination of net income but instead can be reported as Other comprehensive income, as shown in Exhibit 11-2. Assumed figures are used for all items.

EXHIBIT 11-2
Reporting Comprehensive Income

NATIONAL EXPRESS COMPANY
Income Statement
Year Ended December 31, 20X0

Revenues			$10,000
Expenses (including income tax)			6,000
Net income			4,000
Other comprehensive income:			
Unrealized gain on investment	$ 650		
Less income tax (40%)	260	$390	
Foreign-currency translation adjustment (loss)	$(900)		
Less income tax (40%)	360	(540)	
Other comprehensive income			(150)
Comprehensive income			$ 3,850

CHECK POINT 11-7

Earnings per share is *not* reported for Other comprehensive income.

Analyzing Both Accounting Income and Cash Flows to Gain an Overall Picture of a Company

For any one period, Allied Electronics' accounting income and net cash flow from operating activities may chart different paths. Accounting income arises from the accrual process as follows:

Total revenues and gains	−	Total expenses and losses	=	Net income (or Net loss)

As we have seen, revenues and gains are recorded when they occur, regardless of when the company receives or pays cash.

Net cash flow, on the other hand, is based solely on cash receipts and cash payments. During any particular period, a company may have lots of revenues and expenses and a hefty net income. But the company may have weak cash flow because it has not yet collected from all customers. The reverse may also be true: The company may have abundant cash flow but little accounting income.

The income statement and the statement of cash flows often paint different pictures of the company. Which financial statement provides better information? Neither; in fact, both statements are needed, along with the balance sheet and statement of stockholders' equity, for an overall view of the business.

Over long periods of time, a business's net income will equal its net cash flow because ultimately all revenues are realized in cash and all expenses are paid in cash. But until that happens, people will continue analyzing both accounting income and cash flows to make their investment, credit, and management decisions.

Accounting for Income Taxes by Corporations

Objective 2
Account for a corporation's income tax

Corporations pay income tax in the same way that individuals do. Corporate and personal tax rates differ, however. At this writing, the federal tax rate on most corporate income is 35%. Because most states also levy income taxes on corporations, most corporations have a combined federal and state income tax rate of approximately 40%.

To account for income tax, the corporation measures for each period

- *Income tax expense,* an expense on the income statement
- *Income tax payable,* a liability on the balance sheet

Accounting for income tax by a corporation follows the general principles that govern accounting for all other transactions. Suppose in 20X1 that **IHOP Corp.** reported income before tax (also called **pretax accounting income**) of $30 million. IHOP's combined income tax rate is 40%. Assume IHOP's income tax expense and income tax payable are the same. Then IHOP would record income tax for the year as follows (amounts in millions):

20X1			
Dec. 31	Income Tax Expense ($30 × 0.40)	12	
	Income Tax Payable		12
	Recorded income tax for the year.		

ASSETS	=	LIABILITIES	+	STOCKHOLDERS' EQUITY	−	EXPENSES
0	=	12	+		−	12

IHOP's 20X1 financial statements would report these figures (adapted, in millions):

Income statement		Balance sheet	
Income before income tax......	$ 30	Current liabilities:	
Income tax expense...........	(12)	Income tax payable...........	$12
Net income	$ 18		

Early in 20X2, IHOP would pay its income tax payable when the company files its 20X1 income tax return with the Internal Revenue Service.

In general, income tax expense and income tax payable can be computed as follows:*

Income tax *expense*	=	Income before income tax (from the *income statement*)	×	Income tax rate

Income tax *payable*	=	Taxable income (from the *income tax return* filed with the IRS)	×	Income tax rate

*The authors thank Jean Marie Hudson for suggesting this presentation.

The income statement and the income tax return are entirely separate documents:

- The *income statement* reports the results of operations that we have been working with throughout this course.
- The *income tax return* is filed with the Internal Revenue Service to determine how much tax the company must pay the government.

For most companies, income tax expense and income tax payable differ. Certain items of revenue and expense enter into the determination of income at different times for the purposes of measuring income for accounting purposes and for tax purposes. The most important difference between accounting income and **taxable income** occurs when a corporation uses straight-line depreciation for the financial statements and accelerated depreciation for the tax return. The tax depreciation method is called the *modified accelerated cost recovery system,* abbreviated as MACRS. ➛ For any one year, MACRS depreciation listed on the tax return usually differs from accounting depreciation on the income statement.

← We learned in Chapter 7 that the MACRS depreciation method is similar to the double-declining-balance method.

Continuing with the IHOP illustration, suppose for 20X2 that IHOP Corp. has

- Pretax accounting income of $40 million on the income statement
- Taxable income of $35 million on the company's income tax return

IHOP will record income tax for 20X2 as follows (dollar amounts in millions and an income tax rate of 40%):

20X2			
Dec. 31	Income Tax Expense ($40 × .40)	16	
	Income Tax Payable ($35 × .40)		14
	Deferred Tax Liability		2
	Recorded income tax for the year.		

ASSETS	=	LIABILITIES	+	STOCKHOLDERS' EQUITY	−	EXPENSES
0	=	14 + 2	+		−	16

Income tax expense is reported on the income statement, and income tax payable and deferred tax liability on the balance sheet, as follows for IHOP Corp. at the end of 20X2:

Income statement		**Balance sheet**	
Income before income tax......	$ 40	Current liabilities:	
Income tax expense...........	(16)	Income tax payable	$14
Net income	$ 24	Long-term liabilities:	
		Deferred tax liability	2**

**Assumes the beginning balance of Deferred tax liability was zero.

CHECK POINT 11-8

Early in 20X3, IHOP would pay its income tax payable of $14 million because this is a current liability. Deferred tax liability, however, is usually long-term, and the company may pay this liability over a longer period.

For a given year, Income Tax Payable can exceed Income Tax Expense. When that occurs, the company records a Deferred Tax Asset.

At January 30, 1999, **The May Department Stores Company** reported its liabilities as shown in Exhibit 11-3.

EXHIBIT 11-3
May's Consolidated Balance Sheet

THE MAY DEPARTMENT STORES COMPANY **Consolidated Balance Sheet (partial, adapted)**	
(In millions)	***January 30, 1999***
Liabilities	
Current Liabilities:	
Current maturities of long-term debt	$ 98
Accounts payable	1,017
Accrued expenses payable	755
Income taxes payable	189
Total Current Liabilities	2,059
Long-term debt	3,825
Deferred tax liability	482
Other liabilities	309

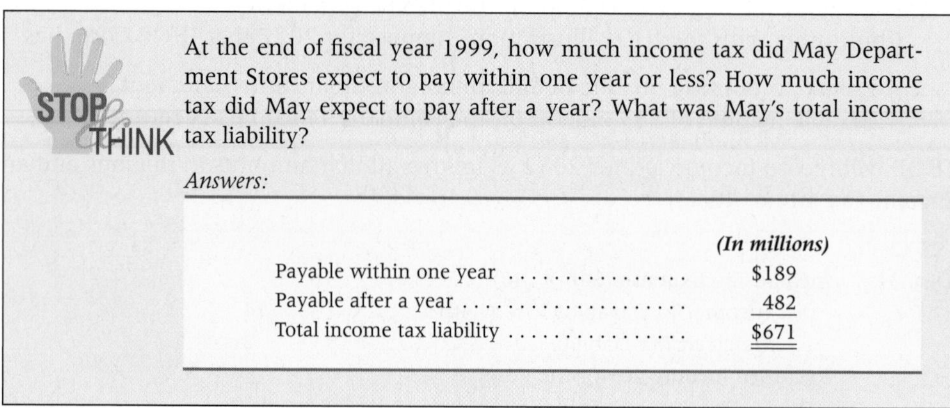

At the end of fiscal year 1999, how much income tax did May Department Stores expect to pay within one year or less? How much income tax did May expect to pay after a year? What was May's total income tax liability?

Answers:

	(In millions)
Payable within one year	$189
Payable after a year	482
Total income tax liability	$671

Prior-Period Adjustments

What happens when a company makes an error in recording revenues or expenses? If the error occurs in one period and is corrected in a later period, the balance of Retained Earnings will be wrong until the error is corrected.

Corrections to the beginning balance of Retained Earnings for errors of an earlier period are called **prior-period adjustments.** The correcting entry debits or credits Retained Earnings for the error amount and credits or debits the asset or liability account that was misstated. The prior-period adjustment appears on the corporation's statement of retained earnings to correct the Retained Earnings balance.

Assume that De Graff Corporation recorded income tax expense as $30,000. The correct amount was $40,000. This error resulted in understating 20X4 expenses by $10,000 and overstating net income by $10,000. A bill from the government in 20X5 for the additional $10,000 alerted De Graff's management to the mistake. The entry to record this prior-period adjustment in 20X5 is

20X5			
June 19	Retained Earnings	10,000	
	Income Tax Payable		10,000
	Prior-period adjustment to correct error in recording income tax expense of 20X4.		

Prior-period adjustments are not reported on the income statement. This prior-period adjustment would appear on the statement of retained earnings, as shown in Exhibit 11-4.

EXHIBIT 11-4
Reporting a Prior-Period Adjustment

DE GRAFF CORPORATION
Statement of Retained Earnings
Year Ended December 31, 20X5

Retained earnings balance, December 31, 20X4, as originally reported..................................	$390,000
Prior-period adjustment—debit to correct error in recording income tax expense of 20X4..................	(10,000)
Retained earnings balance, December 31, 20X4, as adjusted . .	380,000
Net income for 20X5................................	114,000
	494,000
Dividends for 20X5..................................	(41,000)
Retained earnings balance, December 31, 20X5............	$453,000

CHECK POINT 11-9

Restrictions on Retained Earnings

Dividends and purchases of treasury stock require payments by the corporation to its stockholders. ➼ In fact, treasury stock purchases are returns of paid-in capital to the stockholders. Because these outlays decrease the corporation's assets, fewer assets are available to pay liabilities. Therefore, a company's creditors seek to restrict a corporation's dividend payments and treasury stock purchases. For example, a bank may agree to loan $500,000 only if the borrowing corporation limits dividend payments and its purchases of treasury stock. Restrictions on dividends and stock purchases focus on the balance of retained earnings.

➼ For a review of treasury stock transactions and retirements of stock, see Chapter 9, pages 420–422.

Companies usually report their retained earnings restrictions in notes to the financial statements. **Alberto-Culver Company**—maker of Static Guard antistatic spray and Alberto VO5 hair products—had restrictions on retained earnings. These restrictions are indicated in Alberto-Culver's Note 3, as follows:

> ***Notes to Consolidated Financial Statements***
> *Note 3: Long-Term Debt*
> Various borrowing arrangements impose restrictions on such items as total debt, working capital [current assets minus current liabilities], dividend payments, treasury stock purchases, and interest expense. At September 30, 19X8, the company was in compliance with these arrangements, and $73 million of consolidated retained earnings was not restricted as to the payment of dividends and purchases of treasury stock.

Why would a borrower such as Alberto-Culver Company agree to restrict dividends as a condition for receiving a loan?

Answer:
To get a lower interest rate. Other things being equal, the greater the borrower's concessions, the more favorable the terms offered by the lender.

ANALYZING THE STATEMENT OF STOCKHOLDERS' EQUITY

Objective 3
Analyze a statement of stockholders' equity

Most companies report statements of stockholders' equity, which are more comprehensive than statements of retained earnings. The statement of stockholders' equity (often shortened to "statement of equity") is formatted in a manner similar to a statement of retained earnings but with columns for each element of stockholders' equity. The **statement of stockholders' equity** thus reports the changes in all categories of equity during the period.

Exhibit 11-5 is the statement of stockholders' equity for **Allied Electronics Corporation** for 20X2. Study its format. There is a column for each element of equity, with the far right column reporting total stockholders' equity. The top row (line 1) reports the beginning balance of each element, taken directly from last period's ending balance sheet. Each row of the statement reports the effect of a different category of transactions, starting with Issuance of stock (line 2). After explaining all the changes in stockholders' equity, the statement ends with the December 31, 20X2, balances (line 10), which appear on the ending balance sheet, given in Exhibit 11-6.

Explaining the Items Reported on a Statement of Stockholders' Equity

The statement of stockholders' equity provides information about a company's transactions, such as

1. Net income from the income statement
2. Details about the company's issuance of stock
3. Declaration of cash dividends
4. Distribution of stock dividends
5. Purchase and sale of treasury stock
6. Accumulated other comprehensive income:
  a. Unrealized gains and losses on available-for-sale investments
  b. Foreign-currency translation adjustment

EXHIBIT 11-5
Statement of Stockholders' Equity

ALLIED ELECTRONICS CORPORATION
Statement of Stockholders' Equity
Year Ended December 31, 20X2

					Accumulated Other Comprehensive Income		
	Common Stock, $1 Par	*Additional Paid-in Capital*	*Retained Earnings*	*Treasury Stock*	*Unrealized Gain (Loss) on Investments*	*Foreign-Currency Translation Adjustment*	*Total Stockholders' Equity*
1 Balance, December 31, 20X1...	$ 80,000	$160,000	$130,000	$(25,000)	$6,000	$(10,000)	$341,000
2 Issuance of stock	20,000	65,000					85,000
3 Net income			69,000				69,000
4 Cash dividends..............			(21,000)				(21,000)
5 Stock dividends—8%	8,000	26,000	(34,000)				-0-
6 Purchase of treasury stock.....				(9,000)			(9,000)
7 Sale of treasury stock.........		7,000		4,000			11,000
8 Unrealized gain on investments...........					1,000		1,000
9 Foreign-currency translation adjustment......						2,000	2,000
10 Balance, December 31, 20X2...	$108,000	$258,000	$144,000	$(30,000)	$7,000	$ (8,000)	$479,000

EXHIBIT 11-6
Stockholders' Equity Section of the Balance Sheet

ALLIED ELECTRONICS CORPORATION Balance Sheet (partial) December 31, 20X2 and 20X1		
	20X2	*20X1*
Total assets	$939,000	$886,000
Total liabilities	$460,000	$545,000
Stockholders' Equity		
Common stock, $1 par, shares issued—108,000 and 80,000, respectively	108,000	80,000
Additional paid-in capital	258,000	160,000
Retained earnings	144,000	130,000
Treasury stock	(30,000)	(25,000)
Accumulated other comprehensive income:		
Unrealized gain on investments	7,000	6,000
Foreign-currency translation adjustment	(8,000)	(10,000)
Total stockholders' equity	479,000	341,000
Total liabilities and stockholders' equity	$939,000	$886,000

Let's delve more deeply into the transactions that affected Allied Electronics' stockholders' equity during 20X2. Only after we understand what the business did can we decide whether we approve or disapprove. Let's use Exhibit 11-5 (page 512) to explain each category of transactions that changed Allied Electronics' stockholders' equity during 20X2.

ISSUANCE OF STOCK (LINE 2). During 20X2, Allied issued common stock for $85,000—the total increase in stockholders' equity for the issuance of stock, which is shown in the far right column of Exhibit 11-5. Of this total, $20,000 (par value) went into the Common Stock account, and $65,000 increased Additional Paid-in Capital. The issuance of stock increased Allied's total stockholders' equity by $85,000.

NET INCOME (LINE 3). During 20X2, Allied Electronics earned net income of $69,000, which increased Retained Earnings. The net income figure is the "bottom line" of Allied's income statement (Exhibit 11-1, page 501). Trace net income from the income statement, where it originates, to the Retained Earnings column of the statement of stockholders' equity (Exhibit 11-5). Then trace the beginning and ending amounts of Retained Earnings to the balance sheet in Exhibit 11-6. Moving back and forth among the financial statements is an important part of financial analysis.

DECLARATION OF CASH DIVIDENDS (LINE 4). The statement of stockholders' equity reports the amount of cash dividends the company declared during the year. Allied Electronics' cash dividends were $21,000, approximately one-third of net income. Exhibit 11-5 reports the decrease in retained earnings from the declaration of the cash dividends. Dividend *payments* may differ from dividends *declared.* ➵ The statement of cash flows (discussed in Chapter 12) reports the amount of cash dividends Allied *paid* during the year. The statement of stockholders' equity reports dividends *declared.*

← See Chapter 9, page 423–427, for a review of dividends.

DISTRIBUTION OF STOCK DIVIDENDS (LINE 5). During 20X2, Allied Electronics distributed to its stockholders stock dividends recorded at the market value of $34,000. This was a "small" stock dividend—8%, to be exact. Study the Common Stock column in Exhibit 11-5.

Prior to the stock dividend, Allied Electronics' Common Stock account had a balance of $100,000 (beginning balance of $80,000 + new issue of $20,000). The 8% stock dividend then added 8,000 shares of $1-par common stock, or $8,000, to the Common Stock account. But there was more to this stock dividend. Because the stock dividend was small—below 20–25% (recall from Chapter 9 the difference between "small" and "large" stock dividends)—Allied Electronics decreased (debited) Retained Earnings for the market value of the new shares issued in the stock dividend. This market value, $34,000, is reported under Retained Earnings in Exhibit 11-5. The difference between the market value of the dividend ($34,000) and the par value of the stock dividend ($8,000) was credited to Additional Paid-in Capital ($26,000).

PURCHASE AND SALE OF TREASURY STOCK (LINES 6 AND 7). The statement of stockholders' equity reports the purchases and sales of treasury stock. Recall from Chapter 9 that treasury stock is recorded at its cost. During 20X2, Allied Electronics paid $9,000 to buy treasury stock (line 6). This transaction decreased stockholders' equity by $9,000. Allied also sold some treasury stock during the year (line 7). The sale of treasury stock brought in $11,000 cash and increased total stockholders' equity by $11,000. The treasury stock that Allied sold had cost the company $4,000, and the extra $7,000 was added to Additional Paid-in Capital. At year end (line 10), Allied still owned treasury stock that cost the company $30,000 when it was purchased. The parentheses around the treasury stock figures in Exhibit 11-5 mean that treasury stock is a negative element of stockholders' equity.

ACCUMULATED OTHER COMPREHENSIVE INCOME (LINES 8 AND 9). Two categories of other comprehensive income are unrealized gains and losses on available-for-sale investments and the foreign-currency translation adjustment.

Unrealized Gains and Losses on Available-for-Sale Investments. In Chapter 10, we saw that available-for-sale investments are reported on the balance sheet at their *current market value.* The statement of stockholders' equity reports any unrealized gains and losses on these investments under the heading Accumulated Other Comprehensive Income (Exhibit 11-5). *Unrealized* means that the gain or loss did not result from the sale of the investments, but rather from a change in the investments' market value.

At December 31, 20X1, Allied Electronics held available-for-sale investments that were worth $6,000 more than Allied paid for them. This explains the $6,000 beginning balance (line 1) in Exhibit 11-5. Then, during 20X2, the market value of the investments increased by another $1,000 (line 8). At December 31, 20X2, Allied's portfolio of available-for-sale investments had a market value that exceeded Allied's cost by the accumulated amount of $7,000 (line 10). An unrealized loss on investments would appear on the statement of stockholders' equity as a negative amount.

Foreign-Currency Translation Adjustment. In Chapter 10, we discussed the foreign-currency translation adjustment that arises from consolidating the financial statements of a foreign subsidiary with a parent company. The foreign-currency translation adjustment, which can be either positive or negative, is like an unrealized gain or loss. At December 31, 20X1, Allied had a negative translation adjustment of $10,000 (see the beginning balance on line 1). During 20X2, the foreign currency strengthened against the dollar and decreased the negative amount of the translation adjustment by $2,000 (line 9). At December 31, 20X2, Allied's cumulative foreign-currency translation adjustment stood at $8,000—a negative amount that resembles an unrealized loss (line 10).

CHECK POINT 11-10

MANAGEMENT RESPONSIBILITY FOR THE FINANCIAL STATEMENTS

Objective 4
Understand managers' and auditors' responsibilities for the financial statements

The top managers of a corporation are responsible for the company's financial statements. Management issues a *statement of responsibility* along with the company's financial statements. Exhibit 11-7 is an excerpt from the statement of management's responsibility included in the annual report of **The May Department Stores Company.**

EXHIBIT 11-7
Statement of Management Responsibility (partial) for the Financial Statements—The May Department Stores Company

Management's Responsibility
Report of Management. Management is responsible for the preparation, integrity, and objectivity of the financial information included in this annual report. The financial statements have been prepared in conformity with generally accepted accounting principles applied on a consistent basis. The preparation of financial statements in conformity with generally accepted accounting principles requires management to make estimates and assumptions that affect the reported amounts. Although the financial statements reflect all available information and management's judgment and estimates . . . actual results could differ from those estimates. . . .

The members of the Audit Committee are Russell E. Palmer (chairman), Marsha J. Evans, Helen L. Kaplan, James M. Kilts, Edward H. Meyer, Michael R. Quinlan, William P. Stiritz, Robert D. Storey, and Murray L. Weidenbaum.

Management declares its responsibility for the financial statements. Management indicates that the financial statements conform to GAAP on a consistent basis. As we've seen throughout this book, GAAP is the standard for preparing the financial statements and is designed to produce relevant, reliable, and useful information for making investment and credit decisions. *Consistency* means that the company is not switching accounting methods back and forth to make itself look as good as possible. ➵

Management further states that preparation of the financial statements requires the company to make estimates and certain assumptions. As you have seen, accounting is not as exact as you might have imagined before taking this course.

➵ This is the consistency principle in action. See Chapter 6, page 270.

Auditor's Report on the Financial Statements

The Securities Exchange Act of 1934 requires most companies that issue their stock publicly to file audited financial statements with the Securities and Exchange Commission (SEC), a governmental agency. To comply with this requirement, companies engage outside auditors who are certified public accountants to examine their statements. The independent auditors decide whether the company's financial statements comply with GAAP and then issue an audit report. Exhibit 11-8 is the audit report on the financial statements of The May Department Stores Company for the year ended January 30, 1999.

EXHIBIT 11-8
Audit Report on the Financial Statements of The May Department Stores Company

Report of Independent Public Accountants

To the Board of Directors and Shareowners of
The May Department Stores Company:

We have audited the accompanying consolidated balance sheet of The May Department Stores Company (a Delaware corporation) and subsidiaries as of January 30, 1999, and January 31, 1998, and the related consolidated statements of earnings, shareowners' equity and cash flows for each of the three fiscal years in the period ended January 30, 1999.

(continued on page 516)

EXHIBIT 11-8 (CONT.)

These financial statements are the responsibility of the company's management. Our responsibility is to express an opinion on these financial statements based on our audits.

We conducted our audits in accordance with generally accepted auditing standards. Those standards require that we plan and perform the audit to obtain reasonable assurance about whether the financial statements are free of material misstatement. An audit includes examining, on a test basis, evidence supporting the amounts and disclosures in the financial statements. An audit also includes assessing the accounting principles used and significant estimates made by management, as well as evaluating the overall financial statement presentation. We believe that our audits provide a reasonable basis for our opinion.

In our opinion, the financial statements referred to above present fairly, in all material respects, the financial position of The May Department Stores Company and subsidiaries as of January 30, 1999, and January 31, 1998, and the results of their operations and their cash flows for each of the three fiscal years in the period ended January 30, 1999, in conformity with generally accepted accounting principles.

Arthur Andersen LLP
1010 Market Street
St. Louis, Missouri 63101-2089
February 10, 1999

The audit report is addressed to the board of directors and shareowners of the company. The auditing firm signs its name, in this case the St. Louis office of Arthur Andersen LLP (LLP is the abbreviation for limited liability partnership). The date of Andersen's audit report is February 10, 1999, shortly after the end of the company's fiscal year.

The audit report typically contains three paragraphs:

- The first paragraph identifies the audited financial statements.
- The second paragraph describes how the audit was performed, mentioning that generally accepted auditing standards are the benchmark for evaluating the audit's quality.
- The third paragraph states Andersen's opinion that May's financial statements conform to GAAP and that people can rely on them for decision making. May's audit report contains a *clean* opinion, more properly called an *unqualified* opinion. Audit reports usually fall into one of four categories:
  1. **Unqualified (clean).** The statements are reliable.
  2. **Qualified.** The statements are reliable, except for one or more items for which the opinion is said to be qualified.
  3. **Adverse.** The statements are unreliable.
  4. **Disclaimer.** The auditor was unable to reach a professional opinion.

The independent audit adds credibility to the financial statements. It is no accident that financial reporting and auditing are more advanced in the United States and Canada than anywhere else in the world and that these two countries' capital markets are the envy of the world. In addition, these two nations enjoy two of the highest living standards in the world.

The *Decision Guidelines* feature revisits the decision setting in which investors use accounting information for investment analysis. Study the guidelines to review the essence of this chapter.

Decision Guidelines

Using the Income Statement and the Related Notes in Investment Analysis

Decision	Factors to Consider		Decision Variable or Model
Which measure of profitability to use for investment analysis?	Are you interested in accounting income? →	Income including all revenues, expenses gains, and losses? →	Net income (bottom line)
	→	Income that can be expected to repeat from year to year? →	Income from continuing operations
	Are you interested in cash flows? →		Cash flows from operating activities (Chapter 12)

Note: A conservative strategy may use both income and cash flows and compare the two sets of results.

Decision	Factors to Consider	Decision Variable or Model
What is the estimated value of the stock?	If you believe the company can earn the income (or cash flow) indefinitely →	$\text{Estimated value} = \frac{\text{Annual income}}{\text{Investment capitalization rate}}$
	If you believe the company can earn the income (or cash flow) for a finite number of years →	$\text{Estimated value} = \text{Annual income} \times \text{Present value of annuity}$ (See Appendix B)
How does risk affect the value of the stock?	If the investment is high-risk →	Increase the investment capitalization rate
	If the investment is low-risk →	Decrease the investment capitalization rate

End-of-Chapter

Summary Problem for Your Review

The following information was taken from the ledger of **Kraft Corporation:**

Loss on sale of discontinued operations	$ 5,000	Paid-in capital in excess of par—preferred	$ 7,000
Prior-period adjustment—credit to Retained Earnings	5,000	Treasury stock, common (5,000 shares at cost)	25,000
Gain on sale of plant assets	21,000	Dividends	16,000
Cost of goods sold	380,000	Selling expenses	78,000
Income tax expense (saving):		Common stock, no par, 45,000 shares issued	180,000
Continuing operations	32,000	Sales revenue	620,000
Discontinued operations:		Interest expense	30,000
Operating income	10,000	Extraordinary gain	26,000
Loss on sale	(2,000)	Operating income, discontinued operations	25,000
Extraordinary gain	10,000	Loss due to lawsuit	11,000
Cumulative effect of change in inventory method	(4,000)	General expenses	62,000
Preferred stock, 8%, $100 par, 500 shares issued	50,000	Retained earnings, beginning as originally reported	103,000
		Cumulative effect of change in inventory method (debit)	(10,000)

Required

Prepare a single-step income statement (with all revenues grouped together) and a statement of retained earnings for Kraft Corporation for the current year ended December 31, 20XX. Include the earnings-per-share presentation and show computations. Assume no changes in the stock accounts during the year.

Answers

KRAFT CORPORATION **Income Statement** Year Ended December 31, 20XX		
Revenue and gains:		
Sales revenue		$620,000
Gain on sale of plant assets		21,000
Total revenues and gains		641,000
Expenses and losses:		
Cost of goods sold	$380,000	
Selling expenses	78,000	
General expenses	62,000	
Interest expense	30,000	
Loss due to lawsuit	11,000	
Income tax expense	32,000	
Total expenses and losses		593,000
Income from continuing operations		48,000
Discontinued operations:		
Operating income, $25,000, less income tax, $10,000	$ 15,000	
Loss on sale of discontinued operations, $5,000, less income tax saving, $2,000	(3,000)	12,000
Income before extraordinary item and cumulative effect of change in inventory method		60,000
Extraordinary gain, $26,000, less income tax, $10,000		16,000
Cumulative effect of change in inventory method, $10,000, less income tax saving, $4,000		(6,000)
Net income		$ 70,000
Earnings per share:*		
Income from continuing operations [($48,000 − $4,000)/40,000 shares]		$ 1.10
Income from discontinued operations ($12,000/40,000 shares)		0.30
Income before extraordinary item and cumulative effect of change in inventory method [($60,000 − $4,000)/40,000 shares]		1.40
Extraordinary gain ($16,000/40,000 shares)		0.40
Cumulative effect of change in inventory method ($6,000/40,000)		(0.15)
Net income [($70,000 − $4,000)/40,000 shares]		$ 1.65

*Computations:

$$\text{EPS} = \frac{\text{Income} - \text{Preferred dividends}}{\text{Common shares outstanding}}$$

Preferred dividends: $50,000 × 0.08 = $4,000

Common shares outstanding:

45,000 shares issued − 5,000 treasury shares = 40,000 shares outstanding

KRAFT CORPORATION **Statement of Retained Earnings** Year Ended December 31, 20XX	
Retained earnings balance, beginning, as originally reported	$103,000
Prior-period adjustment—credit	5,000
Retained earnings balance, beginning, as adjusted	108,000
Net income for current year	70,000
	178,000
Dividends for current year	(16,000)
Retained earnings balance, ending	$162,000

Summary of Learning Objectives

1. ***Analyze a complex income statement.*** A company's income statement reports on (1) continuing operations, (2) discontinued operations, (3) extraordinary gains and losses, and (4) the cumulative effect of accounting changes. It also reports income tax expense and *earnings per share (EPS)* for each of these categories.
2. ***Account for a corporation's income tax.*** Corporations pay income tax and must account for both income tax expense and income tax payable. *Income tax expense* is based on pretax accounting income. *Income tax payable* is based on taxable income. A difference between the expense and the payable creates another account, Deferred Tax Asset or Deferred Tax Liability.
3. ***Analyze a statement of stockholders' equity.*** A *statement of stockholders' equity* reports the changes in all categories of a company's equity during a period, including details about the company's (1) issuance of stock, (2) declaration of cash dividends, (3) distribution of stock dividends, (4) purchase and sale of treasury stock, (5) unrealized gains and losses on available-for-sale investments, and (6) the foreign-currency translation adjustment.
4. ***Understand managers' and auditors' responsibilities for the financial statements.*** The top managers of a company are responsible for the preparation and integrity of the company's financial statements. Independent CPAs audit the financial statements, then offer an objective opinion on whether the statements meet GAAP standards.

Accounting Vocabulary

adverse opinion (p. 516).
clean opinion (p. 516).
comprehensive income (p. 507).
disclaimer (p. 516).
earnings per share (EPS) (p. 505).
extraordinary gain or loss (p. 504).
extraordinary item (p. 504).
investment capitalization rate (p. 502).
pretax accounting income (p. 508).
prior-period adjustment (p. 510).
qualified opinion (p. 516).
segment of the business (p. 504).
statement of stockholders' equity (p. 512).
taxable income (p. 509).
unqualified (clean) opinion (p. 516).

Questions

1. Why is it important for a corporation to report income from continuing operations separately from discontinued operations and extraordinary items?
2. Explain how an investor can use income from continuing operations to estimate the value of a stock. Give the equation, using amounts of your own choosing.
3. Give two examples of extraordinary gains and losses and four examples of gains and losses that are *not* extraordinary.
4. Why is it important for companies to report the effects of their changes in accounting principles (accounting methods)? What appears on the income statement to alert investors that the company has made an accounting change?
5. What is the most widely used of all accounting statistics? Compute the price-to-earnings ratio for a company with EPS of $2 and market price of $12 per share of common stock.

6. What is the earnings per share of a company with net income of $5,500, issued common stock of 12,000 shares, and treasury common stock of 1,000 shares?
7. Identify three subtotals on the income statement that generate income tax expense. What is an income tax saving? How does it arise?
8. Explain the difference between the income tax expense and the income tax payable of a corporation. How is the amount of each item determined, and where does each item appear in the financial statements?
9. Why do creditors wish to restrict a corporation's payment of cash dividends and purchases of treasury stock?
10. What information does the statement of stockholders' equity report? Which other financial statement (besides the balance sheet and the notes) reports on the transactions that appear on the statement of stockholders' equity?
11. Who bears primary responsibility for the financial statements? What role do the independent auditors play? Of what value is the audit?

CHECK POINTS

Preparing a complex income statement (Obj. 1)

CP11-1 List the major parts of a complex corporate income statement for Harley-Davis Corporation for the year ended December 31, 20X1. Include all the major parts of the income statement, starting with net sales revenue and ending with net income (net loss). You may ignore dollar amounts and earnings per share.

Explaining the items on a complex income statement (Obj. 1)

CP11-2 Study the income statement of Allied Electronics Corporation in Exhibit 11-1 (page 501) and answer these questions about the company:

1. How much gross profit did Allied earn on the sale of its products—before deducting any operating expenses? How does Allied label gross profit on the income statement?
2. Why are the loss on restructuring and the gain on sale of machinery reported as "Other gains (losses)"?
3. What dollar amount of net income would most sophisticated investors predict for Allied Electronics to earn during 20X3 and beyond? Name this item, give its amount, and state your reason.
4. How do the discontinued operations differ from the extraordinary loss?

Preparing a complex income statement (Obj. 1)

CP11-3 XTE Corporation accounting records include the following items, listed in no particular order, at December 31, 20X1.

Extraordinary gain..........	$ 5,000	Other gains (losses).......	$ (2,000)
Cost of goods sold	71,000	Net sales revenue.........	182,000
Operating expenses	64,000	Loss on discontinued	
Accounts receivable.........	19,000	operations	(15,000)

Income tax of 40% applies to all items.

Prepare XTE's income statement for the year ended December 31, 20X1. Omit earnings per share.

Valuing a company's stock (Obj. 1)

CP11-4 **Hershey Foods Corporation** reported net sales of $4,302 million, net income of $336 million, and no discontinued operations, extraordinary items, or accounting changes for 19X7. At a capitalization rate of 6%, how much should the company be worth?

Earnings per share was $2.25. How much should one share of Hershey stock be worth? Compare your estimated stock price to Hershey's actual stock price as quoted in the *Wall Street Journal*, your newspaper, or over the Internet. Based on your estimated market value, should you buy, hold, or sell Hershey stock?

Reporting earnings per share (Obj. 1)

CP11-5 Return to the XTE Corporation data in CP11-3. XTE Corporation had 8,000 shares of common stock outstanding at December 31, 20X0. The company issued an additional 6,000 shares of common stock on August 31, 20X1. XTE declared and paid preferred dividends of $3,000 during 20X1.

Show how XTE Corporation reported earnings per share on its 20X1 income statement.

Interpreting earnings-per-share data (Obj. 1)

CP11-6 A corporation has preferred stock outstanding and issued additional common stock during the year.

1. Give the basic equation to compute earnings per share of common stock for net income.

2. List the income items for which the corporation must report earnings-per-share data.

3. What makes earnings per share so useful as a business statistic?

CP11-7 Use the XTE Corporation data in Check Point 11-3. In addition, XTE Corporation had unrealized losses of $1,000 on investments and a $2,000 foreign-currency translation adjustment (a gain) during 20X1. Both amounts are net of tax. Start with XTE Corporation's net income from CP11-3 and show how XTE could report other comprehensive income on its 20X1 income statement.

Reporting comprehensive income (Obj. 1)

Should XTE Corporation report earnings per share for other comprehensive income?

CP11-8 Pappadeaux Pizza had income before income tax of $100,000 and taxable income of $80,000 for 20X2, the company's first year of operations. The income tax rate is 40%.

Accounting for a corporation's income tax (Obj. 2)

1. Make the entry to record Pappadeaux's income taxes for 20X2.
2. Show what Pappadeaux Pizza will report on its 20X2 income statement starting with income before income tax. Also show what Pappadeaux will report for current and long-term liabilities on its December 31, 20X2, balance sheet.

CP11-9 Examine De Graff Corporation's statement of retained earnings on page 511. Suppose instead that De Graff had overpaid 20X4 income tax expense by $15,000. Show how De Graff would report this prior-period adjustment on the statement of retained earnings for 20X5.

Reporting a prior-period adjustment (Obj. 3)

CP11-10 Use the statement of stockholders' equity in Exhibit 11-5 (page 512) to answer the following questions about Allied Electronics Corporation:

Using the statement of stockholders' equity (Obj. 4)

1. At December 31, 20X2, Allied had total liabilities of $514,000. How much were the company's total assets?
2. How much cash did the issuance of common stock bring in during 20X2?
3. What was the cost of the treasury stock that Allied purchased during 20X2? What was Allied's cost of the treasury stock that Allied sold during the year? For how much did Allied sell the treasury stock during 20X2?
4. Was the stock dividend that Allied declared and distributed during 20X2 "large" or "small"? How can you tell? What was the par value of the stock that Allied distributed in the stock dividend? What was the market value of the stock distributed in the dividend?

EXERCISES

E11-1 **Texaco, Inc.,** the giant oil company, has reported a number of special items on its income statement. The following data, listed in no particular order, were adapted from Texaco's financial statements (amounts in millions):

Preparing and using a complex income statement (Obj. 1)

Preferred stock	$ 300	Retained earnings	$7,186
Total revenues	36,787	Income tax expense (saving):	
Foreign-currency translation adjustment	61	Continuing operations	258
Cumulative effect of accounting change—credit	147	Discontinued operations:	
Discontinued operations:		Net loss from operations	(2)
Net loss from operations	19	Net loss on disposal	(49)
Net loss on disposal	223	Cumulative effect of accounting change	26
Dividends paid	947	Unrealized net gain on investments	62
Total operating expenses	35,801	Short-term investments	35

Required

1. Show how the Texaco, Inc., income statement for 19X8 should appear. Omit earnings per share.
2. Although 19X8 was a bad year for Texaco, financial analysts believe that Texaco can easily earn its current level of income for the indefinite future. Therefore, they apply a 6% investment capitalization rate in estimating the value of Texaco stock. What is the analysts' esti-

mate of the market value of Texaco, Inc.? How can analysts use this figure to make an investment decision?

Preparing and using a complex income statement (Obj. 1)

E11-2 Visteon, Inc.'s accounting records contain the following information for 20X2 operations:

Extraordinary gain	$ 12,000
Sales revenue	130,000
Operating expenses (including income tax)	43,000
Cumulative effect of change in depreciation method (debit)	(15,000)
Cost of goods sold	45,000
Loss on discontinued operations	50,000
Income tax expense—extraordinary gain	4,800
Income tax saving—change in depreciation method	6,000
Income tax saving—loss on discontinued operations	20,000

Required

Prepare Visteon's income statement for 20X2. Omit earnings per share. Was 20X2 a good year or a bad year for Visteon? Explain your answer in terms of the outlook for 20X3.

Using an income statement (Obj. 1)

E11-3 **McDonnell Douglas,** manufacturer of the DC line of commercial aircraft and recently purchased by **The Boeing Company,** reported the following income statement, as adapted, for 19X7:

MCDONNELL DOUGLAS
Statement of Operations (partial)

Year Ended December 31 (In millions, except for share data)	*19X7*
Earnings from Continuing Operations	698
Discontinued operations, net of income taxes	57
Earnings Before Cumulative Effect of Accounting Change	755
Cumulative effect of initial application of new accounting standard for postretirement benefits	(1,536)
Net Earnings (Loss)	$ (781)
Earnings (Loss) Per Share:	
Continuing operations	$ 5.99
Discontinued operations	.49
Cumulative effect of accounting change	(13.18)
	$ (6.70)
Dividends Declared Per Share	$ .47

Required

1. Evaluate the results of operations for 19X7. Give the reasoning underlying your evaluation.
2. 19X7 was a loss year for McDonnell Douglas. Do you think the company's stock price dropped to near zero as a result of the net loss? Give your reason.
3. How could McDonnell Douglas afford to declare cash dividends during a loss year? How could the company afford to pay cash dividends during the year?

Using income data for investment analysis (Obj. 1)

E11-4 During 19X9, **PepsiCo, Inc.,** had sales of $28.5 billion, income from continuing operations of $1.8 billion, and net income of $1.7 billion. Earnings per share figures were $2.22 for continuing operations and $2.18 for net income. At December 31, 19X9, the market price of a share of PepsiCo's common stock closed at $38.25 on the New York Stock Exchange.

What investment capitalization rate did investors appear to be using to determine the value of one share of PepsiCo stock? The formula for the value of one share of stock uses earnings per share (EPS) in the calculation. Does this capitalization rate suggest high risk or low risk? What about PepsiCo's line of business is consistent with your evaluation of the company's risk?

E11-5 Downstream Corporation earned net income of $56,000 for the second quarter of 20X0. The ledger reveals the following figures:

Computing earnings per share (Obj. 1)

Preferred stock, $1.75 per year, no par, 1,600 shares issued and outstanding	$ 70,000
Common stock, $10 par, 52,000 shares issued	520,000
Treasury stock, common, 6,000 shares at cost	36,000

Required

Compute EPS for the quarter, assuming no changes in the stock accounts during the quarter.

E11-6 ETech Corp. had 40,000 shares of common stock and 10,000 shares of $10 par, 5% preferred stock outstanding on December 31, 20X0. On April 30, 20X1, the company issued 9,000 additional common shares and ended 20X1 with 49,000 shares of common stock outstanding. Income from continuing operations of 20X1 was $115,400, and loss on discontinued operations (net of income tax) was $8,280. The company had an extraordinary gain (net of tax) of $55,200.

Computing earnings per share (Obj. 1)

Required

Compute ETech's EPS amounts for 20X1, starting with income from continuing operations.

E11-7 For 20X0, its first year of operations, Capital Re Incorporated has pretax accounting income (on the income statement) of $420,000. Taxable income (on the tax return filed with the Internal Revenue Service) is $380,000. The income tax rate is 40%. Record Capital Re's income taxes for the year. What is the balance in the Deferred Tax Liability account at the end of the year? Show what Capital Re will report on its 20X0 income statement and balance sheet for this situation. Start the income statement with income before tax and recall that a company pays each year's income tax payable early in the next year.

Accounting for income tax by a corporation (Obj. 2)

E11-8 Upper 10, Inc., a soft-drink company, reported a prior-period adjustment in 19X9. An accounting error caused net income of prior years to be overstated by $3.8 million. Retained earnings at December 31, 19X8, as previously reported, stood at $395.3 million. Net income for 19X9 was $92.1 million, and dividends were $61.8 million.

Reporting a prior-period adjustment on the statement of retained earnings (Obj. 3)

Required

Prepare the company's statement of retained earnings for the year ended December 31, 19X9.

E11-9 The agreement under which Burgoyne Corp. issued its long-term debt requires the restriction of $250,000 of the company's retained earnings balance. Total retained earnings is $310,000, and total paid-in capital is $820,000.

Reporting a retained earnings restriction (Obj. 3)

Required

1. Show how to report stockholders' equity on Burgoyne's balance sheet, assuming Burgoyne discloses the retained earnings restriction in a note. Write the note.
2. Burgoyne's cash balance is $140,000. What is the maximum amount of dividends Burgoyne can declare?

E11-10 At December 31, 20X1, Taurus, Inc., reported stockholders' equity as follows:

Preparing a statement of stockholders' equity (Obj. 3)

Common stock, $5 par, 500,000 shares authorized, 300,000 shares issued	$1,500,000
Additional paid-in capital	3,100,000
Retained earnings	1,700,000
Treasury stock, 2,500 shares at cost	(78,000)
	$6,222,000

During 20X2, Taurus completed these transactions and events (listed in chronological order):

a. Declared and issued a 50% stock dividend. At the time, Taurus's stock was quoted at a market price of $31 per share.

b. Sold 1,000 shares of treasury stock for $36 per share (cost was $31).

c. Issued 500 shares of common stock to employees at the price of $28 per share.

d. Net income for the year, $340,000.

e. Declared cash dividends of $180,000, to be paid early in 20X3.

Required

Prepare Taurus, Inc.'s statement of stockholders' equity for 20X2, using the format of Exhibit 11-5 (page 512) as a model. Then use the statement you prepared to answer the following questions:

1. Did Taurus's retained earnings increase or decrease during 20X2? What caused retained earnings to change during the year?
2. How did the stock dividend affect total stockholders' equity? How did it affect total assets? Total liabilities?
3. How would creditors feel about Taurus's sale of treasury stock? Taurus's issuance of common stock? Why?

Analyzing a statement of stockholders' equity (Obj. 3)

E11-11 **The Coca-Cola Company** reported the following statement of stockholders' equity (adapted) for 19X8:

THE COCA-COLA COMPANY
Consolidated Statement of Share-Owners' Equity (adapted)

Year Ended December 31, 19X8	*Number of Common Shares Outstanding*	*Common Stock*	*Capital Surplus (Additional) Paid-In Capital)*	*Reinvested Earnings*	*Outstanding Restricted Stock*	*Accumulated Other Comprehensive Income* Foreign Currency Translation	*Unrealized Gain on Securities*	*Treasury Stock*
(In millions except per share data)								
Balance December 31, 19X7	1,276	$427	$1,173	$11,006	$(74)	$(272)	$48	$(7,073)
Stock issued to employees	4	1	85	—	—	—	—	—
Stock issued under restricted stock plans	—	—	7	—	6	—	—	—
Translation adjustments	—	—	—	—	—	(152)	—	—
Net change in unrealized gain on securities, net of deferred taxes	—	—	—	—	—	—	34	—
Purchases of stock for treasury	(29)	—	—	—	—	—	—	(1,796)
Treasury stock issued in connection with an acquisition	1	—	—	—	—	—	—	70
Net income	—	—	—	2,986	—	—	—	—
Dividends	—	—	—	(1,110)	—	—	—	—
Other	—	—	26	—	—	—	—	—
Balance December 31, 19X8	1,252	$428	$1,291	$12,882	$(68)	$(424)	$82	$(8,799)

Answer the following questions about The Coca-Cola Company:

Required

1. What were Coca-Cola's retained earnings balances at year end 19X7 and 19X8? Where else in the financial statements did Coca-Cola report these amounts? Was 19X8 a profitable year? How profitable?
2. Coca-Cola issued stock to employees who exercised their stock options and bought the company's stock. How much cash did Coca-Cola receive? Where else in the financial statements could you find this amount?
3. Did the market value of Coca-Cola's available-for-sale investments increase or decrease during 19X8? By how much?
4. How much did Coca-Cola pay to purchase treasury stock during the year? What was Coca-Cola's average cost per share of the treasury stock purchased this year?

E11-12 The annual report of **Sara Lee Corporation** included the following reports:

Identifying responsibility for the financial statements
(Obj. 4)

MANAGEMENT'S REPORT ON FINANCIAL INFORMATION (EXCERPTS)

Management of Sara Lee Corporation is responsible for the preparation and integrity of the financial information included in this annual report. The financial statements have been prepared in accordance with generally accepted accounting principles and, where required, reflect our best estimates and judgments. . . .

The corporation maintains high standards in selecting, training and developing personnel to help ensure that management's objectives of maintaining strong, effective internal controls and unbiased, uniform reporting standards are attained. We believe it is essential for the corporation to conduct its business affairs in accordance with the highest ethical practices as expressed in Sara Lee Corporation's Global Business Standards.

John H. Bryan
Chairman of the Board
and Chief Executive Officer

Judith A. Sprieser
Senior Vice President
and Chief Financial Officer

REPORT OF INDEPENDENT PUBLIC ACCOUNTANTS

To the Board of Directors and Stockholders, Sara Lee Corporation:
We have audited the accompanying consolidated balance sheets of SARA LEE CORPORATION (a Maryland corporation) AND SUBSIDIARIES as of June 27, 1998, June 28, 1997, and June 29, 1996, and the related consolidated statements of income, common stockholders' equity, and cash flows for each of the three years in the period ended June 27, 1998. These consolidated financial statements are the responsibility of the Corporation's management. Our responsibility is to express an opinion on these consolidated financial statements based on our audits.

We conducted our audits in accordance with generally accepted auditing standards. Those standards require that we plan and perform the audit to obtain reasonable assurance about whether the consolidated financial statements are free of material misstatement. An audit includes examining, on a test basis, evidence supporting the amounts and disclosures in the consolidated financial statements. An audit also includes assessing the accounting principles used and significant estimates made by management, as well as evaluating the overall consolidated financial statement presentation. We believe that our audits provide a reasonable basis for our opinion.

In our opinion, the consolidated financial statements referred to above present fairly, in all material respects, the financial position of Sara Lee Corporation and Subsidiaries as of June 27, 1998, June 28, 1997, and June 29, 1996, and the results of their operations and their cash flows for each of the three years in the period ended June 27, 1998, in conformity with generally accepted accounting principles.

Arthur Andersen, LLP
Chicago, Illinois
July 27, 1998

1. Who is responsible for Sara Lee Corporation's financial statements?
2. Which accounting firm, and which office of the accounting firm, audited Sara Lee's financial statements? What responsibility do the auditors take for Sara Lee's financial statements?
3. By what accounting standards did the auditors evaluate Sara Lee's financial statements? By what auditing standards did the auditors conduct their audit?

PROBLEMS

(Group A)

Preparing a complex income statement (Obj. 1)

P11-1A The following information was taken from the records of Delphi Systems, Inc., at September 30, 20X3. Delphi manufactures electronic control devices for elevators.

Prior-period adjustment—debit to Retained Earnings	$ 6,000	Treasury stock, common (1,000 shares at cost)	$ 11,000
Contributed capital from treasury stock transactions	7,000	Dividends	35,000
Interest expense	11,000	Interest revenue	4,000
Cost of goods sold	424,000	Extraordinary loss	30,000
Cumulative effect of change in depreciation method (debit)	(18,000)	Operating loss, discontinued segment	15,000
Loss on sales of plant assets	8,000	Loss on insurance settlement	12,000
Income tax expense (saving):		General expenses	113,000
Continuing operations	72,000	Preferred stock—5%, $40 par, 10,000 shares authorized, 5,000 shares issued	200,000
Discontinued segment:			
Operating loss	(6,000)	Paid-in capital in excess of par—common	20,000
Gain on sale	8,000		
Extraordinary loss	(12,000)	Retained earnings, beginning, as originally reported	88,000
Cumulative effect of change in depreciation method	(7,000)	Selling expenses	136,000
Gain on sale of discontinued segment	20,000	Common stock, $10 par, 25,000 shares authorized and issued	250,000
Sales revenue	833,000		

Required

1. Prepare Delphi Systems' single-step income statement, which lists all revenues together and all expenses together, for the fiscal year ended September 30, 20X3. Include earnings-per-share data.
2. Evaluate income for the year ended September 30, 20X3, in terms of the outlook for 20X4. Assume that 20X3 was a typical year, and Delphi's top managers hoped to earn income from continuing operations equal to 10% of sales.

Preparing a statement of retained earnings (Obj. 3)

P11-2A Use the data in Problem 11-1A to prepare Delphi Systems, Inc.'s statement of retained earnings for the year ended September 30, 20X3.

Using income data to make an investment decision (Obj. 1)

P11-3A Delphi Systems in Problem 11-1A holds significant promise for carving a niche in the electronic control device industry, and a group of Swiss investors is considering purchasing the company. Delphi's common stock is currently selling for $33.75 per share.

Business Today magazine recently carried a story that Delphi's income is bound to grow. It appears that the company can earn at least its current level of income for the indefinite future. Based on this information, the investors think that an appropriate investment capitalization rate for estimating the value of Delphi's common stock is 8%. Any capitalization rate below 8% would overvalue the stock. How much will this belief lead the investors to offer for Delphi Systems? Will the existing stockholders of Delphi be likely to accept this offer? Explain your answers.

Computing earnings per share and estimating the price of a stock (Obj. 1)

P11-4A The capital structure of Dexia Banking Corp. at December 31, 20X0, included 20,000 shares of $1.25 preferred stock and 44,000 shares of common stock. Common shares outstanding during 20X1 were 44,000 January through May, 50,000 June through August, and 60,500 September through December. Income from continuing operations during 20X1 was $81,100. The company discontinued a segment of the business at a gain of $6,630, and an extraordinary item generated a loss of $16,000. Dexia's board of directors restricts $80,000 of retained earnings for contingencies.

Required

1. Compute Dexia's earnings per share. Start with income from continuing operations. Income and loss amounts are net of income tax.
2. Analysts believe Dexia can earn its current level of income for the indefinite future. Estimate the market price of a share of Dexia common stock at investment capitalization rates of 8%, 10%, and 12%. The formula for estimating the value of one share of stock uses earnings per share. Which estimate presumes an investment in Dexia stock is the most risky? How can you tell?

Preparing a corrected income statement, including comprehensive income (Obj. 1)

P11-5A Ian Ewell, accountant for BCE Telecom, Inc., was injured in a motorcycle accident. Another employee prepared the accompanying income statement for the year ended December 31, 20X3.

The individual *amounts* listed on the income statement are correct. However, some *accounts* are reported incorrectly, and one does not belong on the income statement at all. Also, income tax (40%) has not been applied to all appropriate figures. BCE issued 52,000 shares of common stock in 20X1 and held 2,000 shares as treasury stock during 20X3.

BCE TELECOM, INC.
Income Statement
20X3

Revenue and gains:		
Sales		$362,000
Unrealized gain on available-for-sale investments		10,000
Paid-in capital in excess of par—common		80,000
Total revenues and gains		452,000
Expenses and losses:		
Cost of goods sold	$103,000	
Selling expenses	56,000	
General expenses	61,000	
Sales returns	11,000	
Dividends paid	7,000	
Sales discounts	6,000	
Income tax expense	50,000	
Total expenses and losses		294,000
Income from operations		158,000
Other gains and losses:		
Gain on sale of discontinued operations	$ 10,000	
Extraordinary gain	20,000	
Operating loss on discontinued segment	(13,000)	
Foreign-currency translation adjustment (loss)	(15,000)	
Total other gains, net		2,000
Net income		$160,000
Earnings per share		$ 3.20

Required

Prepare a corrected statement of income (single-step, which lists all revenues together and all expenses together), including comprehensive income, for 20X3; include earnings per share.

Accounting for a corporation's income tax (Obj. 2)

P11-6A The accounting (not the income tax) records of Rio Tonto, Inc., provide the following comparative income statement for 20X1 and 20X2, respectively:

	20X1	20X2
Total revenue	$930,000	$990,000
Expenses:		
Cost of goods sold	$430,000	$460,000
Operating expenses	270,000	280,000
Total expenses before tax	700,000	740,000
Pretax accounting income	$230,000	$250,000

Total revenue of 20X2 includes revenue of $15,000 for cash that was received late in 20X1. This revenue is included in 20X2 total revenue because it was earned in 20X2. However, revenue collected in advance is included in the taxable income of the year when the cash is received. In calculating taxable income on the tax return, this revenue belongs in 20X1. Also, the operating expenses of each year include depreciation of $50,000 computed under the straight-line method. In calculating taxable income on the tax return, Rio Tonto uses the modified accelerated cost recovery system (MACRS). MACRS depreciation was $80,000 for 20X1 and $20,000 for 20X2. The income tax rate is 35%.

Required

1. Compute Rio Tonto's taxable income for 20X1.
2. Journalize the corporation's income taxes for 20X1.
3. Prepare the corporation's income statement for 20X1.

Using a statement of stockholders' equity (Obj. 3)

P11-7A Transmeta, Inc., reported the following statement of stockholders' equity for the year ended October 31, 20X4:

TRANSMETA, INC.
Statement of Stockholders' Equity
Year Ended October 31, 20X4

(In millions)	Common Stock	Additional Paid-in Capital	Retained Earnings	Treasury Stock	Total
Balance, Nov. 1, 20X3	$427	$1,622	$904	$(117)	$2,836
Net income			336		336
Cash dividends			(194)		(194)
Issuance of stock (10,000,000 shares)	13	36			49
Stock dividend	22	61	(83)		—
Sale of treasury stock		9		19	28
Balance, Oct. 31, 20X4	$462	$1,728	$963	$ (98)	$3,055

Required

Answer these questions about Transmeta's stockholders' equity transactions:

1. The income tax rate is 40%. How much income before income tax did Transmeta, Inc., report on the income statement?
2. What is the par value of the company's common stock?
3. At what price per share did Transmeta issue its common stock during the year?
4. What was the cost of treasury stock sold during the year? What was the selling price of the treasury stock sold? What was the increase in total stockholders' equity?
5. Transmeta's statement lists the stock transactions in the order they occurred. What was the percentage of the stock dividend? Round to the nearest percentage.

P11-1B The following information was taken from the records of Networking Associates at November 30, 20X3. Networking Associates creates computer peripherals.

(Group B)

Preparing a complex income statement (Obj. 1)

Interest expense	$ 23,000	Dividends on common stock	$ 12,000
Gain on settlement of lawsuit	8,000	Sales revenue.	567,000
Paid-in capital from retirement of preferred stock	16,000	Retained earnings, beginning, as originally reported	63,000
Dividend revenue.	11,000	Selling expenses.	87,000
Treasury stock, common (2,000 shares at cost)	28,000	Common stock, no par, 22,000 shares authorized and issued.	350,000
General expenses	71,000	Extraordinary gain.	27,000
Loss on sale of discontinued segment	8,000	Loss on sale of plant assets. . .	10,000
Prior-period adjustment—debit to Retained Earnings.	4,000	Operating income, discontinued segment.	9,000
Income tax expense (saving):		Dividends on preferred stock .	?
Continuing operations . . .	28,000	Preferred stock, 6%, $25 par,. 20,000 shares authorized, 4,000 shares issued.	?
Discontinued segment:			100,000
Operating income	3,600	Cumulative effect of change in depreciation method (credit)	
Loss on sale	(3,200)		
Extraordinary gain	10,800		15,000
Cumulative effect of change in depreciation method.	6,000	Cost of goods sold	319,000

Required

1. Prepare Networking Associates' single-step income statement, which lists all revenues together and all expenses together, for the fiscal year ended November 30, 20X3. Include earnings-per-share data.
2. Evaluate income for the year ended November 30, 20X3, in terms of the outlook for 20X4. Assume that 20X3 was a typical year, and Networking Associates' top managers hoped to earn income from continuing operations equal to 10% of sales.

P11-2B Use the data in Problem 11-1B to prepare Networking Associates' statement of retained earnings for the year ended November 30, 20X3.

Preparing a statement of retained earnings (Obj. 3)

P11-3B Networking Associates in Problem 11-1B holds significant promise for carving a niche in the computer peripherals industry, and a group of Canadian investors is considering purchasing the company. Networking Associates' stock is currently selling for $32 per share.

Using income data to make an investment decision (Obj. 1)

Business Today magazine recently carried a story that Networking's income is bound to grow. It appears that the company can earn at least its current level of income for the indefinite future. Based on this information, the investors think that an appropriate investment capitalization rate for estimating the value of Networking Associates' common stock is 8%. Any capitalization rate below 8% would overvalue the stock. How much will this belief lead the investors to offer for Networking Associates? Will the existing stockholders of Networking be likely to accept this offer? Explain your answers.

P11-4B TNT Group's capital structure at December 31, 20X2, included 5,000 shares of $2.50 preferred stock and 130,000 shares of common stock. Common shares outstanding during 20X3 were 130,000 January through February; 119,000 during March; 121,000 April through October; and 128,000 during November and December. Income from continuing operations during 20X3 was $371,885. The company discontinued a segment of the business at a gain of $69,160, and an extraordinary item generated a loss of $49,510. The board of directors of TNT Group has restricted $280,000 of retained earnings for expansion of the company's office facilities.

Computing earnings per share and estimating the price of a stock (Obj. 1)

Required

1. Compute TNT's earnings per share. Start with income from continuing operations. Income and loss amounts are net of income tax.
2. Analysts believe TNT can earn its current level of income for the indefinite future. Estimate the market price of a share of TNT common stock at investment capitalization rates of 8%,

10%, and 12%. The formula for estimating the value of one share of stock uses earnings per share. Which estimate presumes an investment in TNT is the most risky? How can you tell?

Preparing a corrected income statement, including comprehensive income (Obj. 1)

P11-5B Clay Brown, accountant for Abbe National, Inc., was injured in a swimming accident. Another employee prepared the following income statement for the fiscal year ended June 30, 20X4:

ABBE NATIONAL, INC.
Income Statement
June 30, 20X4

Revenue and gains:		
Sales		$733,000
Foreign-currency translation adjustment—gain		11,000
Paid-in capital in excess of par—common		100,000
Total revenues and gains		844,000
Expenses and losses:		
Cost of goods sold	$383,000	
Selling expenses	103,000	
General expenses	74,000	
Sales returns	22,000	
Unrealized loss on available-for-sale investments	4,000	
Dividends paid	15,000	
Sales discounts	10,000	
Income tax expense	56,400	
Total expenses and losses		667,400
Income from operations		176,600
Other gains and losses:		
Extraordinary loss	$(30,000)	
Operating income on discontinued segment	25,000	
Loss on sale of discontinued operations	(40,000)	
Total other gains (losses)		(45,000)
Net income		$131,600
Earnings per share		$ 6.58

The individual *amounts* listed on the income statement are correct. However, some *accounts* are reported incorrectly, and one does not belong on the income statement at all. Also, income tax (40%) has not been applied to all appropriate figures. Abbe National, Inc., issued 24,000 shares of common stock in 20X1 and held 4,000 shares as treasury stock during the fiscal year 20X4.

Required

Prepare a corrected statement of income (single-step, which lists all revenues together and all expenses together), including comprehensive income, for fiscal year 20X4; include earnings per share.

Accounting for a corporation's income tax (Obj. 2)

P11-6B The accounting (not the income tax) records of Biltrite, Inc., provide the comparative income statement for 20X3 and 20X4, respectively:

	20X3	*20X4*
Total revenue	$680,000	$720,000
Expenses:		
Cost of goods sold	$290,000	$310,000
Operating expenses	180,000	190,000
Total expenses before tax	470,000	500,000
Pretax accounting income	$210,000	$220,000

Total revenue in 20X4 includes rent of $10,000 for cash that was received late in 20X3. This rent is included in 20X4 total revenue because the rent was earned in 20X4. However, rent revenue that is collected in advance is included in taxable income when the cash is received. In calculating taxable income on the tax return, this rent revenue belongs in 20X3.

In addition, operating expenses for each year include depreciation of $40,000 computed under the straight-line method. In calculating taxable income on the tax return, Biltrite uses the modified accelerated cost recovery system (MACRS). MACRS depreciation was $60,000 for 20X3 and $20,000 for 20X4. The income tax rate is 35%.

Required

1. Compute Biltrite's taxable income for 20X3.
2. Journalize the corporation's income taxes for 20X3.
3. Prepare the corporation's income statement for 20X3.

P11-7B BSR, Inc., reported the following statement of stockholders' equity for the year ended June 30, 20X4:

Using a statement of stockholders' equity (Obj. 3)

BSR, INC.
Statement of Stockholders' Equity
Year Ended June 30, 20X4

(In millions)	*Common Stock*	*Additional Paid-in Capital*	*Retained Earnings*	*Treasury Stock*	*Total*
Balance, July 1, 20X3	$173	$2,118	$1,702	$(18)	$3,975
Net income			520		520
Cash dividends.			(117)		(117)
Issuance of stock (5,000,000 shares)	7	46			53
Stock dividend.	18	272	(290)		—
Sale of treasury stock.		22		11	33
Balance, June 30, 20X4	$198	$2,458	$1,815	$ (7)	$4,464

Required

Answer these questions about BSR's stockholders' equity transactions.

1. The income tax rate is 35%. How much income before income tax did BSR report on the income statement?
2. What is the par value of the company's common stock?
3. At what price per share did BSR issue its common stock during the year?
4. What was the cost of treasury stock sold during the year? What was the selling price of the treasury stock sold? What was the increase in total stockholders' equity?
5. BSR's statement of stockholders' equity lists the stock transactions in the order in which they occurred. What was the percentage of the stock dividend? Round to the nearest percentage.

EXTENDING YOUR KNOWLEDGE

DECISION CASE

Clayton Homes, Inc., manufactures and sells houses across the southern part of the United States. Clayton's annual report includes Note 1—Summary of Significant Accounting Policies, as follows:

Using the financial statements in investment analysis (Obj. 1)

> **Income Recognition**
> [S]ales are recognized when cash payment is received or, in the case of credit sales, which represent the majority of . . . sales, when a down payment is received and the customer enters into an installment sales contract. Most of these installment sales contracts . . . are normally [collectible] over 36 to 180 months. . . .
> Premium [revenue] from . . . insurance policies [sold to customers] are recognized as income over the terms of the contracts. [E]xpenses are matched to recognize profits over the life of the contracts.

Magnuson Home Builders, Inc., a competitor of Clayton, includes the following note in its Summary of Significant Accounting Policies:

> **Accounting Policies for Revenues**
> Sales are recognized when cash payment is received or, in the case of credit sales, which represent the majority of . . . sales, when the customer enters into an installment sales contract. Customer down payments on credit sales are rare. Most of these installment sales contracts are normally [collectible] over 36 to 180 months. . . . Premium revenue from insurance policies sold to customers are recognized when the customer signs an insurance contract. Expenses are recognized over the life of the insurance contracts.

Suppose you have decided to invest in the stock of a home builder and you've narrowed your choices to Clayton and Magnuson. Which company's policies of accounting for revenues do you favor? Why? Will their accounting policies affect your investment decision? If so, how? Mention specific accounts in the financial statements that will differ between the two companies.

ETHICAL ISSUE

The income statement of **General Cinema Corporation** reported the following results of operations:

Earnings before income taxes, extraordinary gain, and cumulative effect of accounting change	$187,046
Income tax expense	72,947
Earnings before extraordinary gain and cumulative effect of accounting change	114,099
Extraordinary gain on elimination of debt, net.	419,557
Cumulative effect of change in accounting for postretirement healthcare benefits, net.	(39,196)
Net earnings	$494,460

Suppose General Cinema's management had reported the company's results of operations in this manner:

Earnings before income taxes and cumulative effect of accounting change	$886,307
Income tax expense	352,651
Earnings before cumulative effect of accounting change	533,656
Cumulative effect of change in accounting for postretirement healthcare benefits, net.	(39,196)
Net earnings	$494,460

Required

1. Does it really matter how a company reports its operating results? Why? Who could be helped by management's action? Who could be hurt?
2. Suppose General Cinema's management decides to report its operating results in the second manner. Evaluate the ethics of this decision.

FINANCIAL STATEMENT CASE

Using the financial statements for investment analysis (Obj. 1, 4)

The Gap's financial statements and related notes, which appear in Appendix A at the end of the book, contain a wealth of information that is useful for evaluating The Gap common stock as a potential investment.

Required

1. Track The Gap's net sales and net income for the three years presented on the income statement. Are the trends up or down? As an investor, which trend do you regard as most important?

2. Examine the Per-Share Data on The Gap's stock prices included in Management's Discussion and Analysis. Did The Gap's stock prices during the two years follow the path of the company's net income?
3. Estimate the year-end market price of a share of The Gap's stock by taking an average of the market high price and the market low price for the fourth quarter of fiscal year 1998. Assume it is reasonable to predict that The Gap can earn its current level of net income and earnings per share for the indefinite future. What investment capitalization rate does the market seem to be using in pricing a share of The Gap's stock (use Earnings per share—basic)? At its current level of income, does this rate suggest that analysts view The Gap as a high-risk investment or a low-risk investment?

GROUP PROJECT

Select a company and research its business. Search the business press for articles about this company. Obtain its annual report by requesting it directly from the company or from the company's Web site or from *Moody's Industrial Manual* (the exercise will be most meaningful if you obtain an actual copy and do not have to use *Moody's*).

Required

1. Based on your group's analysis, come to class prepared to instruct the class on six interesting facts about the company that can be found in its financial statements and the related notes. Your group can mention only the obvious, such as net sales or total revenue, net income, total assets, total liabilities, total stockholders' equity, and dividends, in conjunction with other terms. Once you use an obvious item, you may not use that item again.
2. The group should write a paper discussing the facts that it has uncovered. Limit the paper to two double-spaced, word-processed pages.

INTERNET EXERCISE

Sears, Roebuck and Co.

Hoover's Online: The Business Network offers free information on approximately 14,000 public and private companies. The Web site features capsules of company information, the latest financials, feature news stories, and a Company of the Day. Subscribers can view additional in-depth coverage.

1. Go to **http://www.hoovers.com**. Complete the line "Search Company for" by typing in *Sears, Roebuck,* then click on **Go.** Click on **Capsule.** This screen displays a wealth of information about Sears and links to even more information. Read the descriptive paragraph about Sears and note two items of interest.
2. Click on **Stock Chart**. Verify that Sears' ticker tape symbol "S" is displayed in *Enter Symbol(s):*. In the next scroll bar, select *5 years,* leave the next scroll bar at *No Events,* then click on **Draw Chart.** The top graph charts the daily market price of one share of stock and the lower graph charts the volume of shares traded. Describe the change in market price over the past five years. [For the fun of it, chart the information of the eBay (ebay) or Qualcomm (qcom) companies.] Go back to the page displaying the Company Capsule of information.
3. Click on **Financials.** Under the heading of *Free Financial Information,* click on **Annual Financials.** For the three most recent years, identify Total Revenue, Net Income, Net Profit Margin % (Net Income/Total Revenue), and Diluted EPS. For each amount, comment on the direction of the trend, what the trend might indicate, and whether the trend is considered favorable or unfavorable. Go back to the page displaying the Company Capsule of information.
4. Go to the Sears company Web site by clicking on the link **http://www.sears.com**. Get to the financial statements by clicking on **About Sears,** followed by **Information for our Shareholders, Financial Reports,** the most recent **Annual Report,** and finally **View the Table of Contents.** Use the *Consolidated Statements of Stockholders' Equity* to answer the following questions:
   a. For the most recent year, explain the changes within the Retained Earnings account and the Treasury Stock account.
   b. For the most recent year, identify the amount of Net Income and Accumulated Other Comprehensive Income. Compute Comprehensive Income for the most recent year.
   c. Describe at least two possible Internet sources of business and financial information for a company.

12 The Statement of Cash Flows

Learning Objectives

After studying this chapter, you should be able to

1. Identify the purposes of the statement of cash flows
2. Distinguish among operating, investing, and financing cash flows
3. Prepare a statement of cash flows by the direct method
4. Compute the cash effects of a wide variety of business transactions
5. Prepare a statement of cash flows by the indirect method

W. T. Grant Company
Statements of Cash Flows
Years Ended January 31,

		(In thousands) 19X8	19X7
	Cash flows from operating activities:		
1	Cash receipts from customers	$1,579,320	$1,317,218
2	Cash receipts from other revenues	10,057	8,924
3	Cash payments to suppliers and employees	(1,683,760)	(1,336,428)
4	Cash payments for interest	(21,127)	(16,452)
5	Cash payments for taxes	(8,459)	(8,143)
6	Other, net	9,704	7,964
7	Net cash inflow (outflow) from operating activities	(114,265)	(26,917)
	Cash flows from investing activities:		
8	Acquisition of property, plant, and equipment	$ (26,250)	$ (25,918)
9	Investments in securities	(2,040)	(5,951)
10	Other, net	2,149	(46)
11	Net cash inflow (outflow) from investing activities	(26,141)	(31,915)
	Cash flows from financing activities:		
12	New borrowing	$ 152,451	$ 100,000
13	Issuance of common stock	3,666	9,944
14	Retirement of debt	(1,760)	(13,823)
15	Payment of dividends	(21,141)	(21,139)
16	Purchase of treasury stock	(11,466)	—
17	Retirement of preferred stock	(252)	(308)
18	Net cash inflow (outflow) from financing activities	121,498	74,674
19	Increase (decrease) in cash	$ (18,908)	$ 15,842
20	Cash balance, beginning of year	49,851	34,009
21	Cash balance, end of year	$ 30,943	$ 49,851

THE classic case of **W. T. Grant Company** changed the information that companies report to the public. W. T. Grant was one of the leading retailers in the United States, a serious rival to **Kmart, Target,** and other discount chains. Coming as a shock to the business world, Grant's income statement reported rising profits as the company slid into bankruptcy. What went wrong? Despite its profitability, Grant's operations simply did not generate enough cash to pay the bills. If anyone had analyzed Grant's cash flows, the cash shortage would have been obvious. Line 7 of the reconstructed cash-flow statement above clearly shows that operating activities were draining cash at an alarming rate. The W. T. Grant ship was sinking fast.

Prior to Grant's bankruptcy, companies were not required to include a statement of cash flows in the annual report. After Grant's failure, investors, creditors, and the accounting profession realized that net income is *not* the only measure of success in business. After all, a company pays bills with cash, not with income. As we've seen throughout this text, the statement of cash flows is a basic financial statement on a par with the income statement and the balance sheet.

In preceding chapters, we included cash-flow analysis as it related to the topics covered: receivables, inventory, plant assets, long-term debt, and so on. But we have not yet discussed the statement of cash flows in its entirety. We do so in this chapter. Our goals are to round out your introduction to cash-flow analysis and to show how to prepare the statement of cash flows. We begin by explaining the statement format preferred by the Financial Accounting Standards Board (FASB). It is very clear and is thus called the *direct approach*. We end the chapter with the more common format of the statement of cash flows, the *indirect approach*. By the time you have worked through this chapter, you will feel more confident in your ability to analyze the cash flows of any company you might encounter.

THE STATEMENT OF CASH FLOWS: BASIC CONCEPTS

The balance sheet reports the company's cash balance at the end of the period. By examining balance sheets from two consecutive periods, you can tell whether cash increased or decreased during the period. However, the balance sheet does not indicate *why* the cash balance changed. The income statement reports revenues, expenses, and net income—clues about the sources and uses of cash—but the income statement does not tell *why* cash increased or decreased.

The **statement of cash flows** reports the entity's **cash flows**—cash receipts and cash payments—during the period. In other words, it shows where cash came from and how it was spent. It explains the *causes* of the change in the cash balance. The statement of cash flows covers a span of time and therefore is dated "Year Ended XXX" or "Month Ended XXX." Exhibit 12-1 illustrates the relative timing of the financial statements.

EXHIBIT 12-1
Timing of the Financial Statements

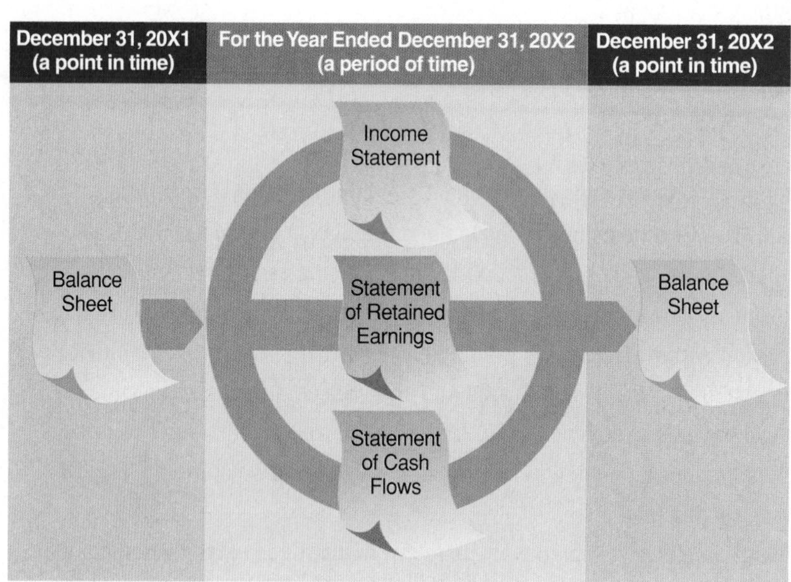

Overview of the Statement of Cash Flows

Objective 1
Identify the purposes of the statement of cash flows

The statement of cash flows is designed to serve the following purposes:

1. To *predict future cash flows*. In many cases, past cash receipts and payments are good predictors of future cash receipts and payments.
2. To *evaluate management decisions*. If managers make wise investment decisions, their business prospers. If they make unwise investments, the business suffers. The statement of cash flows reports the investments the company is

making in long-term assets and thus gives investors and creditors cash-flow information for evaluating managers' decisions.

3. To *determine the company's ability to pay dividends to stockholders and interest and principal to creditors.* Stockholders are interested in receiving dividends on their investments. Creditors want to receive their interest and principal amounts on time. The statement of cash flows helps investors and creditors predict whether the business can make these payments.
4. To *show the relationship of net income to the business's cash flows.* Usually, cash and net income move together. High levels of income tend to lead to increases in cash, and vice versa. However, a company's cash flow can suffer even when net income is high, and vice versa. The story of W. T. Grant illustrates this bitter lesson.

✔ CHECK POINT 12-1

Cash and Cash Equivalents

On a statement of cash flows, *Cash* means more than just cash on hand and cash in the bank. It includes **cash equivalents,** which are highly liquid, short-term investments that can be converted into cash with little delay. Examples of cash equivalents are money-market investments and investments in U.S. Government Treasury bills. Businesses invest their extra cash in these types of liquid assets rather than let the cash remain idle. Throughout this chapter, the term *cash* refers to cash and cash equivalents.

OPERATING, INVESTING, AND FINANCING ACTIVITIES

Objective 2
Distinguish among operating, investing, and financing cash flows

A business engages in three types of business activities:

- Operating activities
- Investing activities
- Financing activities

Operating activities are most important because operations represent the entity's day-to-day activities. Next come *investing activities* and then *financing activities.* Investing activities are generally more important than financing activities because *what* a company invests in is usually more important than *how* the company finances the acquisition.

The statement of cash flows in Exhibit 12-2 shows how cash receipts and payments are divided into operating activities, investing activities, and financing activities for **Anchor Corporation,** a small manufacturer of glass products. As Exhibit 12-2 illustrates, each set of activities includes both cash inflows (receipts) and cash outflows (payments). Outflows are shown in parentheses to indicate that payments must be subtracted. Each section of the statement reports a net cash inflow or a net cash outflow.

Operating activities create revenues and expenses, gains and losses. Therefore, operating activities affect the income statement, which reports the *accrual-basis* effects of operating activities. The statement of cash flows reports their impact on cash. The largest cash inflow from operations is the collection of cash from customers. Smaller inflows are receipts of interest on loans and dividends on stock investments. The operating cash outflows include payments to suppliers and employees and payments for interest and taxes. Exhibit 12-2 shows that Anchor's net cash inflow from operating activities is $68,000. A large positive operating cash flow is a good sign. *In the long run, operations must be the main source of a business's cash.* Otherwise, the company will die.

✔ CHECK POINT 12-2

Operating Activities Are Related to the Transactions That Make Up Net Income.*

*The authors thank Alfonso Oddo for suggesting this display.

EXHIBIT 12-2
Statement of Cash Flows (Direct Method for Operating Activities)

ANCHOR CORPORATION
Statement of Cash Flows
Year Ended December 31, 20X2

		(In thousands)
Cash flows from operating activities:		
Receipts:		
Collections from customers	$ 271	
Interest received on notes receivable	10	
Dividends received on investments in stock	9	
Total cash receipts		$ 290
Payments:		
To suppliers	$(133)	
To employees	(58)	
For interest	(16)	
For income tax	(15)	
Total cash payments		(222)
Net cash inflow from operating activities		68
Cash flows from investing activities:		
Acquisition of plant assets	$(306)	
Loan to another company	(11)	
Proceeds from sale of plant assets	62	
Net cash outflow from investing activities		(255)
Cash flows from financing activities:		
Proceeds from issuance of common stock	$ 101	
Proceeds from issuance of long-term debt	94	
Payment of long-term debt	(11)	
Payment of dividends	(17)	
Net cash inflow from financing activities		167
Net decrease in cash		**$ (20)**
Cash balance, December 31, 20X1		42
Cash balance, December 31, 20X2		$ 22

Cash flows from operating activities require analysis of each revenue and expense on the income statement, along with the related current asset or current liability from the balance sheet. The second half of the chapter illustrates this analysis.

Investing activities increase and decrease the business's long-term assets. The purchase of land, a building, or equipment is an investing activity, as is the purchase of an investment in the stock of another company. Sales of these assets are also investing activities. Making a loan is an investing activity because the loan creates a receivable for the lender, and then collecting the loan is also an investing activity. The acquisition of plant assets dominates Anchor Corporation's investing activities, which produce a net cash outflow of $255,000.

Investing Activities Require Analysis of the Long-Term Asset Accounts.

Investments in plant assets lay the foundation for future operations. A company that invests in plant and equipment appears stronger than one that is selling off large amounts of plant assets. Why? The latter company may run out of assets to sell. Its outlook is bleak.

Financing activities obtain from investors and creditors the cash needed to launch and sustain the business. Financing activities include issuing stock, borrowing money, buying or selling treasury stock, and paying dividends to stockholders. Payments to creditors include *principal* payments only. The payment of *interest* is an operating activity. Financing activities of Anchor Corporation brought in net cash of $167,000. One thing to watch among financing activities is whether the business is borrowing heavily. Excessive borrowing has been the downfall of many companies.

Financing Activities Require Analysis of the Long-Term Liability Accounts and the Owners' Equity Accounts.

NET INCREASE OR DECREASE IN CASH. Overall, Anchor's cash decreased by $20,000 during 20X2. The company began the year with cash of $42,000 and ended with $22,000, as shown in Exhibit 12-2.

Examine W. T. Grant's statement of cash flows on page 535 and reread the chapter-opening story. Which of the following statements explains W. T. Grant's cash outflow from operations? Give your reason.

a. W. T. Grant's cash drain resulted from investing too heavily in new properties.

b. Payments to suppliers and employees exceeded cash receipts from customers.

c. W. T. Grant did not borrow enough money to finance operations during the year.

d. Net income was too low.

Answer:

The answer is b. For both 19X8 and 19X7, cash payments to suppliers and employees exceeded cash receipts from customers.

Interest and Dividends

You may be puzzled by the listing of receipts of interest and dividends as operating activities. After all, these cash receipts result from investing activities. Equally puzzling is listing the payment of interest as part of operations. Interest expense results from borrowing money—a financing activity. After much debate, the FASB decided to include all these items as part of operations. Why? Mainly because they affect the computation of net income. Interest revenue and dividend revenue increase net income, and interest expense decreases income. Therefore, cash *receipts* of interest and dividends and cash payments of interest are reported as operating activities on the cash-flow statement.

In contrast, dividend *payments* are reported in the financing activities section of the cash-flow statement because they go to the entity's owners, who finance the business by holding its stock. This is apparent in Exhibit 12-3 (page 540), which summarizes the types of cash receipts and cash payments that are classified as operating, investing, and financing.

FORMAT OF THE STATEMENT OF CASH FLOWS

In *FASB Statement No. 95*, the FASB approved two formats for reporting cash flows from operating activities. The **direct method,** illustrated in Exhibit 12-2 (page 538), lists cash receipts from specific operating activities and cash payments for each major operating activity. *FASB Statement No. 95* expresses a clear preference for the direct method because it reports where cash came from and how it was spent on operating activities. The direct method is required for some insurance companies, and most governmental entities also use the direct method.

In keeping with generally accepted accounting principles (GAAP), companies' accounting systems are designed for accrual, rather than cash-basis, accounting. These systems make it easy for companies to compute cash flows from operating activities by a shortcut method. The **indirect method** starts with net income and

EXHIBIT 12-3 **Cash Receipts and Cash Payments on the Statement of Cash Flows**

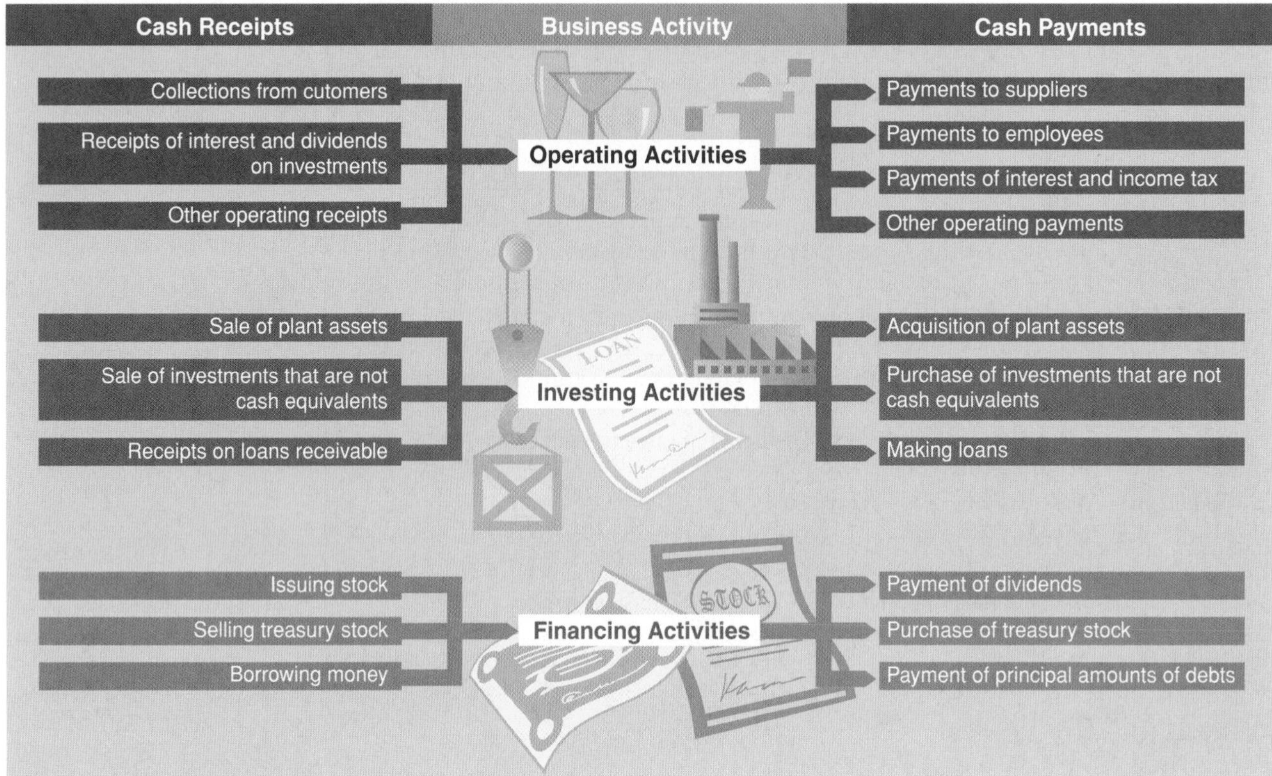

reconciles to cash flows from operating activities. Exhibit 12-4 gives an overview of the process of converting from accrual-basis income to the cash basis for the statement of cash flows.

The direct method is easier to understand, it provides more information for decision making, and the FASB prefers it. By learning it first, you will be learning how to determine the cash effects of business transactions. This is critical for analyzing financial statements because accrual-basis accounting often hides cash effects. Once you have a firm foundation in cash-flow analysis, it is easier to learn the indirect method. But if your instructor chooses to focus solely on the indirect method, you can study that method, which begins on page 556, with a minimum of references to earlier sections of this chapter.

The two basic ways of presenting the statement of cash flows arrive at the same subtotals for all three categories of activities and for the net change in cash. They differ only in the manner of reporting the cash flows from *operating activities.*

EXHIBIT 12-4
Converting from the Accrual Basis to the Cash Basis for the Statement of Cash Flows

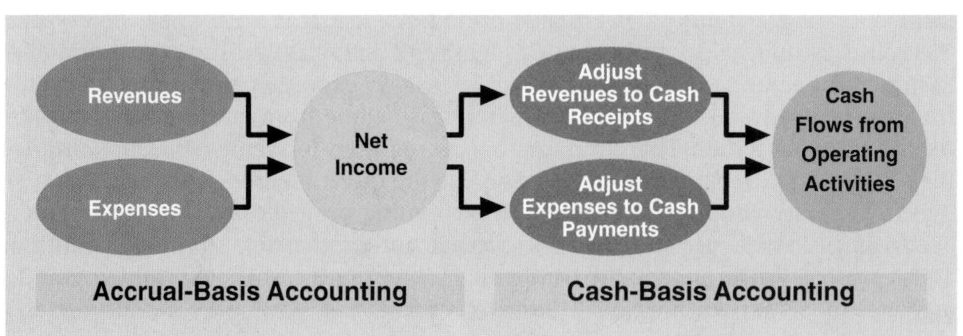

Preparing the Statement of Cash Flows: The Direct Method

Objective 3
Prepare a statement of cash flows by the direct method

Let's see how to prepare the statement of cash flows by the direct method illustrated in Exhibit 12-2. (This is the format of the statement of cash flows presented for **W. T. Grant Company** on page 535.)

Suppose **Anchor Corporation** has assembled the summary of 20X2 transactions in Exhibit 12-5. These summary transactions give the data for both the income statement and the statement of cash flows. Some transactions affect one statement, some the other. For example, although sales (item 1) are reported on the income statement, cash collections (item 2) appear on the cash-flow statement. Other transactions, such as the cash receipt of dividend revenue (item 5) affect both. *The statement of cash flows reports only those transactions with cash effects* (those with an asterisk in Exhibit 12-5).

To prepare the statement of cash flows, follow these steps:

1. Identify the activities that increased cash or decreased cash—those items with asterisks in Exhibit 12-5.

2. Classify each increase and each decrease in cash as an operating activity, an investing activity, or a financing activity.

3. Identify the cash effect of each transaction.

Cash Flows from Operating Activities

Operating cash flows are listed first because they are the largest and most important source of cash for most businesses. Exhibit 12-2 shows that Anchor is sound; its operating activities were the largest source of cash receipts, $290,000.

Cash Collections from Customers. Cash sales bring in cash immediately, and collections of accounts receivable take longer. On the other hand, credit sales increase

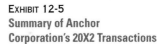

Exhibit 12-5
Summary of Anchor Corporation's 20X2 Transactions

Operating Activities:
1. Sales on credit, $284,000
*2. Collections from customers, $271,000
3. Interest revenue on notes receivable, $12,000
*4. Collection of interest receivable, $10,000
*5. Cash receipt of dividend revenue on investments in stock, $9,000
6. Cost of goods sold, $150,000
7. Purchases of inventory on credit, $147,000
*8. Payments to suppliers, $133,000
9. Salary and wage expense, $56,000
*10. Payments of salary and wages, $58,000
11. Depreciation expense, $18,000
12. Other operating expense, $17,000
*13. Interest expense and payments, $16,000
*14. Income tax expense and payments, $15,000

Investing Activities:
*15. Cash payments to acquire plant assets, $306,000
*16. Loan to another company, $11,000
*17. Proceeds from sale of plant assets, $62,000, including $8,000 gain

Financing Activities:
*18. Proceeds from issuance of common stock, $101,000
*19. Proceeds from issuance of long-term debt, $94,000
*20. Payment of long-term debt, $11,000
*21. Declaration and payment of cash dividends, $17,000

*Indicates a cash-flow transaction to be reported on the statement of cash flows.

Accounts Receivable but not Cash. All cash receipts are reported on the statement of cash flows as "Collections from customers . . . $271,000" in Exhibit 12-2.

CASH RECEIPTS OF INTEREST. Interest revenue is earned on notes receivable. The income statement reports interest revenue. As the clock ticks, interest accrues, but cash interest is received only on specific dates. Only the cash receipts of interest appear on the statement of cash flows—$10,000 in Exhibit 12-2.

CASH RECEIPTS OF DIVIDENDS. Dividends are earned on investments in stock. Dividend revenue is ordinarily recorded as an income-statement item when cash is received. This cash receipt is reported on the statement of cash flows—$9,000 in Exhibit 12-2. (Dividends *received* are part of operating activities, but dividends *paid* constitute a financing activity.)

PAYMENTS TO SUPPLIERS. Payments to suppliers include all cash disbursements for inventory and operating expenses except employee compensation, interest, and income taxes. *Suppliers* are those entities that provide the business with its inventory and essential services. For example, a clothing store's suppliers may include **Levi Strauss, Liz Claiborne,** and **Reebok.** Other suppliers provide advertising, utility, and various services that are operating expenses. In Exhibit 12-2, Anchor Corporation reports payments to suppliers of $133,000.

PAYMENTS TO EMPLOYEES. This category includes disbursements for salaries, wages, commissions, and other forms of employee compensation. Accrued amounts are excluded because they have not yet been paid. The statement of cash flows in Exhibit 12-2 reports only the cash payments ($58,000).

PAYMENTS FOR INTEREST EXPENSE AND INCOME TAX EXPENSE. These cash payments are reported separately from the other expenses. Interest payments show the cash cost of borrowing money. Income tax payments are also significant. In the Anchor Corporation example, interest and income tax expenses equal their cash payments amounts. Therefore, the same amount appears on the income statement and the statement of cash flows. In practice, this is rarely the case. Year-end accruals and other transactions usually cause the expense and cash payment amounts to differ. The cash-flow statement reports the cash payments for interest ($16,000) and income tax ($15,000).

CHECK POINT 12-4

DEPRECIATION, DEPLETION, AND AMORTIZATION EXPENSE. These expenses are *not* listed on the statement of cash flows in Exhibit 12-2 because they do not affect cash.

Cash Flows from Investing Activities

Many analysts regard investing as a critical activity because a company's investments determine its future course. Large purchases of plant assets signal expansion, which is usually a good sign. Low levels of investing activities over a lengthy period indicate that the business is not replenishing its capital assets.

CASH PAYMENTS TO ACQUIRE PLANT ASSETS AND INVESTMENTS AND LOANS TO OTHER COMPANIES. These cash payments are similar because they acquire a noncash asset. The first investing activity reported by Anchor Corporation in Exhibit 12-2 is the purchase of plant assets ($306,000). In the second transaction, Anchor makes an $11,000 loan and obtains a note receivable. These are investing activities because the company is investing in long-term assets. Another transaction that may fall in this category—one not shown in Exhibit 12-2—is a purchase of an investment in the stocks or bonds of another company.

PROCEEDS FROM THE SALE OF PLANT ASSETS AND INVESTMENTS AND THE COLLECTIONS OF LOANS. These cash receipts are the opposites of payments for plant assets and investments and making loans.

The sale of the plant assets needs explanation. The statement of cash flows in Exhibit 12-2 reports that Anchor Corporation received $62,000 cash from the sale of plant assets. The income statement shows an $8,000 gain on this transaction. What is the appropriate amount to show on the cash-flow statement? It is $62,000, the cash proceeds from the sale, not the $8,000 gain. Because a gain occurred, you may wonder why this cash receipt is not reported as part of operations. Operations consist of buying and selling *merchandise* or rendering *services* to earn revenue. Investing activities refer to the acquisition and disposition of long-term assets. Therefore, the FASB views the sale of plant assets and the sale of investments as cash inflows from investing activities.

Suppose **Scott Paper Company** sold timber land at a $35 million gain. The land cost Scott Paper $9 million when it was purchased in 1969. What amount will Scott Paper Company report as an investing activity for the sale of the land?

Answer:
Cash receipt of $44 million (cost of $9 million plus the gain of $35 million).

Investors and creditors are often critical of a company that sells large amounts of its plant assets. Such sales may signal an emergency. For example, budget cuts in the defense industry required the defense contractor **Grumman Corp.** to shed almost one-third of its facilities worldwide. Despite the downsizing, Grumman could no longer compete and was taken over by **Martin Marietta.**

In other situations, selling off fixed assets may be good news if, for example, the company is getting rid of an unprofitable division. Whether sales of plant assets are good news or bad news should be evaluated in light of a company's operating and financing characteristics.

Cash Flows from Financing Activities

Cash flows from financing activities include the following:

PROCEEDS FROM ISSUANCE OF STOCK AND DEBT. Readers of financial statements want to know how the entity obtains its financing. Issuing stock and borrowing money are two common ways to finance operations. In Exhibit 12-2, Anchor Corporation issued common stock and received cash of $101,000. Anchor also issued long-term debt to borrow $94,000.

PAYMENT OF DEBT AND PURCHASES OF THE COMPANY'S OWN STOCK. The payment of debt decreases cash, which is the opposite effect of borrowing. Anchor Corporation reports long-term debt payments of $11,000. Other transactions in this category are purchases of treasury stock and payments to retire the company's stock.

PAYMENT OF CASH DIVIDENDS. The payment of cash dividends decreases cash and is therefore a financing cash payment, as illustrated by Anchor's $17,000 payment in Exhibit 12-2. A *stock* dividend has no effect on Cash and is *not* reported on the cash-flow statement.

Now, let's put into practice what you have learned in the first half of the chapter.

MID-CHAPTER **Mid-Chapter**

SUMMARY PROBLEM FOR YOUR REVIEW

Drexel Corporation's accounting records include the following information for the year ended June 30, 20X3:

a. Salary expense, $104,000
b. Interest revenue, $8,000
c. Proceeds from issuance of common stock, $31,000
d. Declaration and payment of cash dividends, $22,000
e. Collection of interest receivable, $7,000
f. Payments of salaries, $110,000
g. Credit sales, $358,000
h. Loan to another company, $42,000
i. Proceeds from sale of plant assets, $18,000, including $1,000 loss
j. Collections from customers, $369,000
k. Cash receipt of dividend revenue on stock investments, $3,000
l. Payments to suppliers, $319,000
m. Cash sales, $92,000
n. Depreciation expense, $32,000
o. Proceeds from issuance of short-term debt, $38,000
p. Payments of long-term debt, $57,000
q. Interest expense and payments, $11,000
r. Loan collections, $51,000
s. Proceeds from sale of investments, $22,000, including $13,000 gain
t. Amortization expense, $5,000
u. Purchases of inventory on credit, $297,000
v. Income tax expense and payments, $16,000
w. Cash payments to acquire plant assets, $83,000
x. Cost of goods sold, $284,000
y. Cash balance: June 30, 20X2—$83,000
June 30, 20X3— ?

Required

Prepare Drexel Corporation's income statement and statement of cash flows for the year ended June 30, 20X3. Follow the cash-flow statement format of Exhibit 12-2 and the single-step format for the income statement (grouping all revenues together and all expenses together, as shown in Exhibit 12-6, page 546).

Answer

DREXEL CORPORATION
Income Statement
Year Ended June 30, 20X3

Item (Reference Letter)		*(In thousands)*	
	Revenue and gains:		
(g, m)	Sales revenue ($358 + $92)	$450	
(s)	Gain on sale of investments	13	
(b)	Interest revenue	8	
(k)	Dividend revenue	3	
	Total revenues and gains		$474
	Expenses and losses:		
(x)	Cost of goods sold	$284	
(a)	Salary expense	104	
(n)	Depreciation expense	32	
(v)	Income tax expense	16	
(q)	Interest expense	11	
(t)	Amortization expense	5	
(i)	Loss on sale of plant assets	1	
	Total expenses		453
	Net income		$ 21

Item (Reference Letter)	DREXEL CORPORATION Statement of Cash Flows Year Ended June 30, 20X3	(In thousands)	
	Cash flows from operating activities:		
	Receipts:		
(j, m)	Collections from customers ($369 + $92)	$ 461	
(e)	Interest received on notes receivable	7	
(k)	Dividends received on investments in stock	3	
	Total cash receipts		$ 471
	Payments:		
(l)	To suppliers	$(319)	
(f)	To employees	(110)	
(q)	For interest	(11)	
(v)	For income tax	(16)	
	Total cash payments		(456)
	Net cash inflow from operating activities		15
	Cash flows from investing activities:		
(w)	Acquisition of plant assets	$ (83)	
(h)	Loan to another company	(42)	
(s)	Proceeds from sale of investments	22	
(i)	Proceeds from sale of plant assets	18	
(r)	Collection of loans	51	
	Net cash outflow from investing activities		(34)
	Cash flows from financing activities:		
(o)	Proceeds from issuance of short-term debt	$ 38	
(c)	Proceeds from issuance of common stock	31	
(p)	Payments of long-term debt	(57)	
(d)	Dividends declared and paid	(22)	
	Net cash outflow from financing activities		(10)
	Net decrease in cash		$ (29)
(y)	Cash balance, June 30, 20X2		83
(y)	Cash balance, June 30, 20X3		$ 54

COMPUTING INDIVIDUAL AMOUNTS FOR THE STATEMENT OF CASH FLOWS

Objective 4
Compute the cash effects of a wide variety of business transactions

How do we compute the amounts for the statement of cash flows? Many accountants use the income statement and the *changes* in the related balance sheet accounts. For the *operating* cash-flow amounts, the adjustment process follows this basic approach:

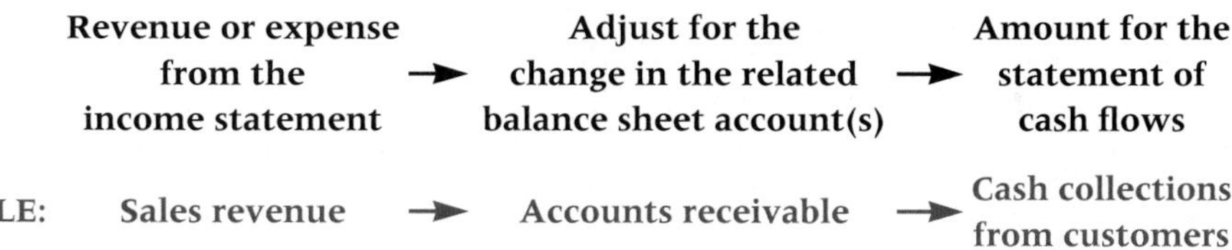

Learning this process is one of the most useful accounting skills you will acquire because it will enable you to identify the cash effects of a wide variety of transactions.

The following discussions use **Anchor Corporation's** income statement in Exhibit 12-6 and comparative balance sheet in Exhibit 12-7. The final result is the

Exhibit 12-6
Income Statement

ANCHOR CORPORATION
Income Statement
Year Ended December 31, 20X2

		(In thousands)
Revenues and gains:		
Sales revenue	$284	
Interest revenue	12	
Dividend revenue	9	
Gain on sale of plant assets	8	
Total revenues and gains		$313
Expenses:		
Cost of goods sold	$150	
Salary and wage expense	56	
Depreciation expense	18	
Other operating expense	17	
Interest expense	16	
Income tax expense	15	
Total expenses		272
Net income		$ 41

cash-flow statement in Exhibit 12-2. For continuity, trace the $22,000 and $42,000 cash amounts on the balance sheet in Exhibit 12-7 to the bottom part of the cash-flow statement in Exhibit 12-2, page 538.

Computing the Cash Amounts of Operating Activities

Computing Cash Collections from Customers. Collections can be computed by converting sales revenue (an accrual-basis amount) to the cash basis. Anchor Cor-

Exhibit 12-7
Comparative Balance Sheet

ANCHOR CORPORATION
Comparative Balance Sheet
December 31, 20X2 and 20X1

(In thousands)	20X2	20X1	Increase (Decrease)	
Assets				
Current:				
Cash	$ 22	$ 42	$(20)	
Accounts receivable	93	80	13	Changes in current assets—**Operating**
Interest receivable	3	1	2	
Inventory	135	138	(3)	
Prepaid expenses	8	7	1	
Long-term receivable from another company	11	—	11	Changes in noncurrent assets—**Investing**
Plant assets, net of depreciation	453	219	234	
Total	$725	$487	$238	
Liabilities				
Current:				
Accounts payable	$ 91	$ 57	$ 34	Changes in current liabilities—**Operating**
Salary and wage payable	4	6	(2)	
Accrued liabilities	1	3	(2)	
Long-term debt	160	77	83	Changes in long-term liabilities and paid-in capital accounts—**Financing**
Stockholders' Equity				
Common stock	359	258	101	
Retained earnings	110	86	24	Change due to net income—**Operating** and change due to dividends—**Financing**
Total	$725	$487	$238	

poration's income statement (Exhibit 12-6) reports sales of $284,000. Exhibit 12-7 shows that Accounts Receivable increased from $80,000 at the beginning of the year to $93,000 at year end, a $13,000 increase. Based on those amounts, Cash Collections equals $271,000, as shown in the following equation and the related T-account for Accounts Receivable. We must solve for cash collections (X).

Accounts Receivable

Beginning balance	+ Sales	− Collections	= Ending balance
$80,000	+ $284,000	− X	= $93,000
		− X	= $93,000 − $80,000 − $284,000
		X	= $271,000

ACCOUNTS RECEIVABLE

Beginning balance	80,000		
Sales	284,000	Collections	271,000
Ending balance	93,000		

Another explanation: Because Accounts Receivable increased by $13,000, Anchor Corporation must have received $13,000 less cash than sales revenue for the period. A decrease in Accounts Receivable would mean that the company received more cash than the amount of sales revenue. This computation is summarized as the first item in Exhibit 12-8.

All collections of receivables are computed in the same way. In our example, Anchor Corporation earned interest revenue of $12,000 (Exhibit 12-6). Interest Receivable's balance increased $2,000 (Exhibit 12-7). Cash receipts of interest must be $10,000 (Interest Revenue of $12,000 minus the $2,000 increase in Interest Receivable). Exhibit 12-8 shows how to make this computation.

COMPUTING PAYMENTS TO SUPPLIERS. This computation includes two parts:

- Payments for inventory
- Payments for expenses other than interest and income tax

EXHIBIT 12-8
Direct Method of Determining Cash Flows from Operating Activities

RECEIPTS / PAYMENTS	From Income Statement Account	Change in Related Balance Sheet Account	
RECEIPTS:			
From customers	Sales Revenue	+ Decrease in Accounts Receivable − Increase in Accounts Receivable	
Of interest	Interest Revenue	+ Decrease in Interest Receivable − Increase in Interest Receivable	
Of dividends	Dividend Revenue	+ Decrease in Dividends Receivable − Increase in Dividends Receivable	
PAYMENTS:			
To suppliers	Cost of Goods Sold	+ Increase in Inventory − Decrease in Inventory	+ Decrease in Accounts Payable − Increase in Accounts Payable
	Operating Expense	+ Increase in Prepaids − Decrease in Prepaids	+ Decrease in Accrued Liabilities − Increase in Accrued Liabilities
To employees	Salary (Wage) Expense	+ Decrease in Salary (Wage) Payable − Increase in Salary (Wage) Payable	
For interest	Interest Expense	+ Decrease in Interest Payable − Increase in Interest Payable	
For income tax	Income Tax Expense	+ Decrease in Income Tax Payable − Increase in Income Tax Payable	

We thank Barbara Gerrity for suggesting this exhibit.

Payments for inventory are computed by converting cost of goods sold to the cash basis. We accomplish this process by analyzing Cost of Goods Sold from the income statement and Accounts Payable from the balance sheet. Many companies also purchase inventory on short-term notes payable. In that case, we would analyze Short-Term Notes Payable in the same manner as Accounts Payable. The computation of Anchor Corporation's cash payments for inventory is given by the following equations (throughout, all amounts come from Exhibits 12-6 and 12-7):

Cost of Goods Sold

Beginning inventory	+ Purchases −	Ending inventory	=	Cost of goods sold
$138,000 +	X −	$135,000	=	$150,000
	X		=	$150,000 − $138,000 + $135,000
		X	=	$147,000

Now we can insert the figure (X) for purchases into Accounts Payable to determine the amount of cash payments for inventory (X), as follows:

Accounts Payable

Beginning balance	+ Purchases −	Payments for inventory	=	Ending balance
$57,000	+ $147,000	−X	=	$91,000
		−X	=	$91,000 − $57,000 + $147,000
		X	=	$113,000

The T-accounts show where the data come from.

Cost of Goods Sold			
Beg. inventory	138,000	End. inventory	135,000
Purchases	147,000		
Cost of goods sold	150,000		

Accounts Payable			
Payments for inventory	113,000	Beg. bal.	57,000
		Purchases	147,000
		End bal.	91,000

Beginning and ending inventory amounts are taken from the balance sheet, Cost of Goods Sold from the income statement. First, we must solve for purchases, $147,000. Then, we insert purchases into Accounts Payable and solve for *payments for inventory,* $113,000.

Another explanation: Payments for inventory appear in the Accounts Payable account. But we must first work through Cost of Goods Sold and the change in the Inventory account, as summarized in Exhibit 12-8 under Payments to Suppliers. Payments to suppliers ($133,000 in Exhibit 12-2) equal the sum of payments for inventory ($113,000) plus payments for operating expenses ($20,000), as explained next.

✔ CHECK POINT 12-7

COMPUTING PAYMENTS FOR OPERATING EXPENSES. Payments for operating expenses other than interest and income tax can be computed as plug figures by analyzing three accounts: Prepaid Expenses, Accrued Liabilities, and Other Operating Expenses, as follows for Anchor Corporation (again, all numbers are taken from Exhibits 12-6 and 12-7): For each account the purpose is to determine cash payments for operating expenses.

Prepaid Expenses

Beginning balance	+ Payments −	Expiration of prepaid expense	=	Ending balance
$7,000	+ X −	$7,000	=	$8,000
	X		=	$8,000 − $7,000 + $7,000
	X		=	$8,000

Accrued Liabilities

Beginning balance	+	Accrual of expense at year end	− Payments	=	Ending balance
$3,000	+	$1,000	−X	=	$1,000
			−X	=	$1,000 − $3,000 − $1,000
			X	=	$3,000

Other Operating Expenses (other than Salaries, Wages, Depreciation)

Accrual of expense at year end	+	Expiration of prepaid expense	+ Payments	=	Ending balance
$1,000	+	$7,000	+ X	=	$17,000
			X	=	$17,000 − $1,000 − $7,000
			X	=	$9,000

Total payments for operating expenses = $20,000

$8,000 + $3,000 + $9,000 = $20,000

The T-accounts give another picture of the same data.

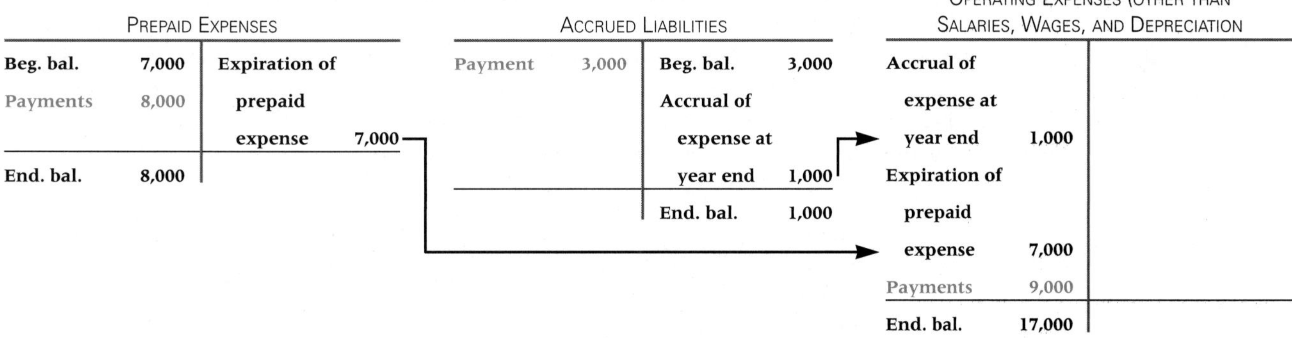

Another explanation: Increases in prepaid expenses require cash payments, and decreases indicate that payments were less than expenses. Decreases in accrued liabilities can occur only from cash payments; increases mean that cash was *not* paid. Exhibit 12-8 shows a streamlined version of this computation.

Computing Payments to Employees. The company may have separate accounts for salaries, wages, and other forms of compensation to employees. It is convenient to combine all payments to employees into one account. Anchor's calculation adjusts Salary and Wage Expense for the change in Salary and Wage Payable, as shown in the following equation, backed up by the Salary and Wage Payable T-account:

Salary and Wage Payable

Beginning balance	+	Salary and wage expense	− Payments =	Ending balance
$6,000	+	$56,000	− X	= $4,000
			− X	= $4,000 − $6,000 − $56,000
			X	= $58,000

CHECK POINT 12-8

SALARY AND WAGE PAYABLE

		Beginning balance	6,000
Payments to employees	58,000	Salary and wage expense	56,000
		Ending balance	4,000

Exhibit 12-8 (page 547) summarizes this computation under Payments to Employees.

COMPUTING PAYMENTS OF INTEREST AND INCOME TAXES. In our example, the expense and payment amounts are the same for interest and income tax. Therefore, no analysis is required to determine these payment amounts. If the expense and the payment differ, the payment can be computed by analyzing the related liability account (Interest Payable and Income Tax Payable, respectively), as illustrated for payments to employees; Exhibit 12-8 summarizes the procedure.

Computing the Cash Amounts of Investing Activities

Investing activities affect asset accounts, such as Plant Assets, Investments, and Notes Receivable. Most data for the computations of cash payments and receipts are taken directly from the income statement and the balance sheet.

COMPUTING ACQUISITIONS AND SALES OF PLANT ASSETS. Companies keep separate accounts for Land, Buildings, Equipment, and other plant assets. But for computing investing cash flows, it is helpful to combine these accounts into a single summary account. Also, we subtract accumulated depreciation from the assets' cost and get a net figure for plant assets. This approach allows us to work with a single plant asset account as opposed to a large number of plant asset and accumulated depreciation accounts.

To illustrate, observe that Anchor Corporation's

- Balance sheet reports beginning plant assets, net of depreciation, of $219,000 and an ending net amount of $453,000 (Exhibit 12-7).
- Income statement shows depreciation expense of $18,000 and an $8,000 gain on sale of plant assets (Exhibit 12-6).

Further, the acquisitions of plant assets total $306,000 (see Exhibit 12-2). How much, then, are the proceeds from the sale of plant assets? First, we must determine the book value of plant assets sold, as follows:

Plant Assets (net)

Beginning balance	+ Acquisitions	− Depreciation −	Book value of assets sold	= Ending balance
$219,000	+ $306,000	− $18,000	− X	= $453,000
			− X	= $453,000 − $219,000 − $306,000 + $18,000
			X	= $54,000

Now we can compute the sale proceeds:

$$\text{Sale proceeds} = \text{Book value of assets sold} + \text{Gain} - \text{Loss}$$
$$= \$54{,}000 + \$8{,}000 - \$0$$
$$= \$62{,}000$$

Trace the sale proceeds of $62,000 to the statement of cash flows in Exhibit 12-2. If the sale resulted in a loss of $3,000, the sale proceeds would be $51,000 ($54,000 − $3,000), and the statement would report $51,000 as a cash receipt from this investing activity.

The Plant Assets (net) T-account provides another look at the computation of the book value of the assets sold.

PLANT ASSETS (NET)

Beginning balance	**219,000**	**Depreciation**	**18,000**
Acquisitions	**306,000**	Book value of assets sold	54,000
Ending balance	**453,000**		

Proceeds from the sale of an asset need not equal the asset's book value. Remember:

Proceeds = Book value + Gain, or
Proceeds = Book value − Loss

The book-value information comes from the balance sheet; the gain or loss comes from the income statement.

COMPUTING ACQUISITIONS AND SALES OF INVESTMENTS, AND LOANS AND THEIR COLLECTIONS. The cash amounts of transactions involving investments can be computed in the manner illustrated for plant assets. Investments are easier to analyze, however, because there is no depreciation to account for, as shown in the following equation:

Investments (amounts assumed for illustration only):

$$\text{Beginning balance} + \text{Purchases} - \text{Book value of investments sold} = \text{Ending balance}$$
$$\$100{,}000 + \$50{,}000 - X = \$140{,}000$$
$$-X = \$140{,}000 - \$100{,}000 - \$50{,}000$$
$$X = \$10{,}000'$$

CHECK POINT 12-9

If you prefer to use T-accounts, this is the way it's done:

INVESTMENTS

Beginning balance*	**100**		
Purchases**	**50**	Book value of investments sold	10
Ending balance*	**140**		

*From balance sheet. **From statement of cash flows.

Loan transactions follow the pattern described on pages 546 and 547 for collections from customers, as follows:

Loans and Notes Receivable (amounts assumed for illustration only):

Beginning balance	+	New loans made	−	Collections	=	Ending balance
$90,000	+	$10,000		−X	=	$30,000
				−X	=	$30,000 − $90,000 − $10,000
				X	=	$70,000

LOANS AND NOTES RECEIVABLE

Beginning balance*	**90**		
New loans made**	**10**	Collections	70
Ending balance*	**30**		

*From balance sheet. **From statement of cash flows.

Exhibit 12-9 summarizes the computation of cash flows from investing activities. We must solve for the dollar amount of each item highlighted in color.

Computing the Cash Amounts of Financing Activities

Financing activities affect liability and stockholders' equity accounts, such as Notes Payable, Bonds Payable, Long-Term Debt, Common Stock, Paid-in Capital in Excess of Par, and Retained Earnings. The cash amounts of financing activities are computed by analyzing these accounts.

COMPUTING ISSUANCES AND PAYMENTS OF LONG-TERM DEBT. The beginning and ending balances of Long-Term Debt, Notes Payable, or Bonds Payable are taken from the balance sheet. If either the amount of new issuances or the amount of the payments is known, the other amount can be computed. For Anchor Corporation, new debt issuances total $94,000 (see Exhibit 12-2). The computation of debt payments follows from analysis of the Long-Term Debt account, using amounts from Anchor Corporation's balance sheet in Exhibit 12-7:

EXHIBIT 12-9 **Computation of Cash Flows from Investing Activities**

Receipts	
From sale of plant assets	Beginning plant assets (net) + Acquisition cost − Depreciation − Book value of assets sold = Ending plant assets (net)
	Cash received = Book value of assets sold + Gain on sale or − Loss on sale
From sale of investments	Beginning investments + Purchase cost of investments − Cost of investments sold = Ending investments
	Cash received = Cost of investments sold + Gain on sale or − Loss on sale
From collection of loans and notes receivable	Beginning loans or notes receivable + New loans made − Collections = Ending loans or notes receivable
Payments	
For acquisition of plant assets	Beginning plant assets (net) + Acquisition cost − Depreciation − Book value of assets sold = Ending plant assets (net)
For purchase of investments	Beginning investments + Purchase cost of investments − Cost of investments sold = Ending investments
For new loans made	Beginning loans or notes receivable + New loans made − Collections = Ending loans or notes receivable

Long-Term Debt

Beginning balance	+	Issuance of new debt	−	Payments of debt	=	Ending balance
$77,000	+	$94,000		−X	=	$160,000
				−X	=	$160,000 − $77,000 − $94,000
				X	=	$11,000

LONG-TERM DEBT

		Beginning balance	77,000
Payments	11,000	Issuance of new debt	94,000
		Ending balance	160,000

COMPUTING ISSUANCES AND RETIREMENTS OF STOCK, AND PURCHASES AND SALES OF TREASURY STOCK. The cash effects of these financing activities can be determined by analyzing the various stock accounts. For example, the amount of a new issuance of common stock is determined by combining the Common Stock and any related Capital in Excess of Par. It is convenient to work with a single summary account for stock as we do for plant assets. Using data from Exhibits 12-2 and 12-7, we have

Common Stock

Beginning balance	+	Issuance of new stock	−	Retirements of stock	=	Ending balance
$258,000	+	$101,000		−X	=	$359,000
				−X	=	$359,000 − $258,000 − $101,000
				X	=	0

CHECK POINT 12-10

COMMON STOCK

		Beginning balance	258,000
Retirements of stock	0	Issuance of new stock	101,000
		Ending balance	359,000

Cash flows affecting Treasury Stock can be analyzed by using the Treasury Stock account:

Treasury Stock (amounts assumed for illustration only)

Beginning balance	+	Purchase of treasury stock	−	Cost of treasury stock sold	=	Ending balance
$16,000	+	$3,000		−X	=	$5,000
				−X	=	$5,000 − $16,000 − $3,000
				X	=	$14,000

TREASURY STOCK

Beginning balance	16,000		
Purchases of treasury stock	3,000	Cost of treasury stock sold	14,000
Ending balance	5,000		

If either the purchase amount or the cost of treasury stock sold is known, the other amount can be computed. For a sale of treasury stock, the amount to report on the cash-flow statement is the sale proceeds. Suppose the company sold treasury stock that had originally cost $14,000, and the sale price was $2,000 less than cost. In this case, the statement of cash flows would report a cash receipt of $12,000 ($14,000 − $2,000).

COMPUTING DIVIDEND PAYMENTS. If dividend payments are not given elsewhere, they can be computed as follows. First, we must compute dividend declarations by analyzing the Retained Earnings account. Then we use the Dividends Payable account to solve for dividend payments. In this case, because Anchor Corporation has no Dividends Payable account, dividend payments must be the same as declarations. The following computations show how to determine the amount of Anchor Corporation's dividend payments:

Retained Earnings

Beginning balance	+	Net income	−	Dividend declarations	=	Ending balance
$86,000	+	$41,000		−X	=	$110,000
				−X	=	$110,000 − $86,000 − $41,000
				X	=	$17,000

Dividends Payable

Beginning balance	+	Dividend declarations	−	Dividend payments	=	Ending balance
$0	+	$17,000		−X	=	$0
				−X	=	$0 − $17,000 − $0
				X	=	$17,000

The T-accounts provide another view of this computation.

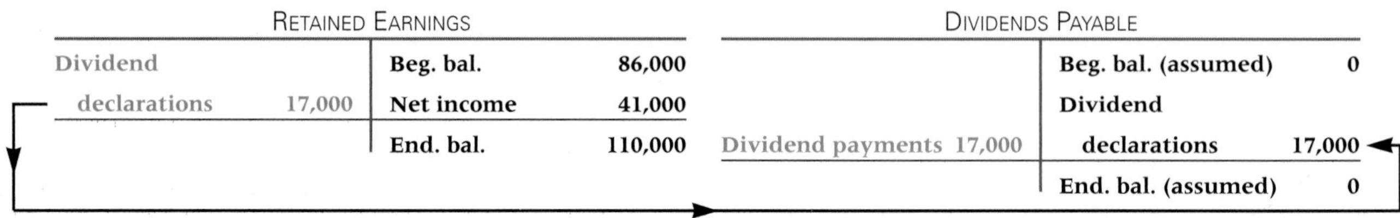

RETAINED EARNINGS
Dividend declarations 17,000
Beg. bal. 86,000
Net income 41,000
End. bal. 110,000
DIVIDENDS PAYABLE
Dividend payments 17,000
Beg. bal. (assumed) 0
Dividend declarations 17,000
End. bal. (assumed) 0

Exhibit 12-10 summarizes the computation of cash flows from financing activities. Amounts that must be computed are highlighted in color.

EXHIBIT 12-10
Computation of Cash Flows from Financing Activities

Receipts

From issuance of long-term debt	Beginning long-term debt + Cash received from issuance of long-term debt − Payment of debt = Ending long-term debt
From issuance of stock	Beginning stock + Cash received from issuance of new stock − Payments to retire stock = Ending stock
From sale of treasury stock	Beginning treasury stock + Purchase cost of treasury stock − Cost of treasury stock sold = Ending treasury stock
	Cash received = Cost of treasury stock sold + Extra amount of sale above cost or − amount of cost in excess of sale amount

(CONTINUED)

EXHIBIT 12-10 (CONT.)
Computation of Cash Flows from Financing Activities

Payments	
Of long-term debt	Beginning long-term debt + Cash received from issuance of long-term debt − Payment of debt = Ending long-term debt
To retire stock	Beginning stock + Cash received from issuance of new stock − Payments to retire stock = Ending stock
To purchase treasury stock	Beginning treasury stock + Purchase cost of treasury stock − Cost of treasury stock sold = Ending treasury stock
For dividends	Beginning retained earnings + Net income − Dividend declarations = Ending retained earnings
	Beginning dividends payable + Dividend declarations − Dividend payments = Ending dividends payable

NONCASH INVESTING AND FINANCING ACTIVITIES

Companies make investments that do not require cash. They also obtain financing other than cash. Our examples thus far have included none of these transactions. Now suppose that **Anchor Corporation** issued no-par common stock valued at $320,000 to acquire a warehouse. Anchor would journalize this transaction as follows:

Warehouse Building	320,000	
Common Stock		320,000

This transaction would not be reported on the cash-flow statement because Anchor paid no cash. But the investment in the warehouse and the issuance of stock are important. Noncash investing and financing activities like this transaction can be reported in a separate schedule that accompanies the statement of cash flows. Exhibit 12-11 illustrates how to report noncash investing and financing activities (all amounts are assumed). This information follows the cash-flow statement or can be disclosed in a note.

CHECK POINT 12-11

EXHIBIT 12-11
Noncash Investing and Financing Activities (in thousands; all amounts assumed for illustration only)

Noncash Investing and Financing Activities:	
Acquisition of building by issuing common stock	$320
Acquisition of land by issuing note payable	72
Payment of long-term debt by transferring investments to the creditor	104
Acquisition of equipment by issuing short-term note payable	37
Total noncash investing and financing activities	$533

RECONCILING NET INCOME TO NET CASH FLOW FROM OPERATING ACTIVITIES

The FASB requires companies that format operating activities by the direct method to report a reconciliation from net income to net cash flow from operating activities. The reconciliation shows how the company's net income is related to net cash flow from operating activities. Exhibit 12-12 shows the reconciliation for **Anchor Corporation.**

The end result—net cash inflow from operating activities of $68,000 (line 12)—is the same amount we derived earlier under the *direct* method (see Exhibit 12-2). The reconciliation is the *indirect* method of computing operating cash flows. We now turn to the indirect method.

EXHIBIT 12-12
Reconciliation of Net Income to Net Cash Inflow from Operating Activities

ANCHOR CORPORATION
Reconciliation of Net Income to Net Cash Inflow from Operating Activities

		(In thousands)	
1	Net income		$41
2	Add (subtract) items that affect net income and cash flow differently:		
3	Depreciation	$ 18	
4	Gain on sale of plant assets	(8)	
5	Increase in accounts receivable	(13)	
6	Increase in interest receivable	(2)	
7	Decrease in inventory	3	
8	Increase in prepaid expenses	(1)	
9	Increase in accounts payable	34	
10	Decrease in salary and wage payable	(2)	
11	Decrease in accrued liabilities	(2)	27
12	Net cash inflow from operating activities		$68

PREPARING THE STATEMENT OF CASH FLOWS: THE INDIRECT METHOD

Objective 5
Prepare a statement of cash flows by the indirect method

An alternative to the direct method for cash flows from *operating* activities is the *indirect method,* or the **reconciliation method,** as shown in Exhibit 12-12. This method starts with net income and shows the reconciliation from net income to operating cash flows. For example, the cash-flow statement of **The Washington Post Company** lists "Net income" first, followed by "Adjustments to reconcile net income to net cash provided by operating activities."

The indirect method shows the link between net income and operating cash flow better than the direct method. Perhaps that is why 590 companies (98.3%) of a 600-firm survey *(Accounting Trends and Techniques, 1998)* use the indirect method even though the FASB recommends the direct method.

These two methods (direct and indirect) affect only the operating activities section of the cash-flow statement. No difference exists in the reporting of investing activities or financing activities.

Exhibit 12-13 is **Anchor Corporation's** cash-flow statement prepared by the indirect method. Note that only the operating section of the statement differs from the direct method format in Exhibit 12-2. The new items are keyed to their explanations, as discussed in the following text. For ease of reference, we repeat Anchor Corporation's income statement and balance sheet here as Exhibits 12-14 and 12-15.

Logic Behind the Indirect Method

The operating section of the cash-flow statement begins with net income, taken from the income statement. Additions and subtractions, which follow, are labeled "Add (subtract) items that affect net income and cash flow differently." We discuss these items in the following sections.

DEPRECIATION, DEPLETION, AND AMORTIZATION EXPENSES.[A] These expenses are added back to net income when we go from net income to cash flow. Let's see why. Depreciation is recorded as follows:

Depreciation Expense	18,000	
Accumulated Depreciation		18,000

(continued on page 558)

EXHIBIT 12-13
Statement of Cash Flows—Indirect Method for Operating Activities

ANCHOR CORPORATION
Statement of Cash Flows
For the Year Ended December 31, 20X2

			(In thousands)
	Cash flows from operating activities:		
	Net income		$ 41
	Add (subtract) items that affect net income and cash flow differently:		
Ⓐ	Depreciation	$ 18	
Ⓑ	Gain on sale of plant assets	(8)	
Ⓒ	Increase in accounts receivable	(13)	
Ⓒ	Increase in interest receivable	(2)	
Ⓒ	Decrease in inventory	3	
Ⓒ	Increase in prepaid expenses	(1)	
Ⓒ	Increase in accounts payable	34	
Ⓒ	Decrease in salary and wage payable	(2)	
Ⓒ	Decrease in accrued liabilities	(2)	27
	Net cash inflow from operating activities		$ 68
From Exhibit 12-2	**Cash flows from investing activities:**		
From Exhibit 12-2	Acquisition of plant assets	$(306)	
From Exhibit 12-2	Loan to another comnpany	(11)	
From Exhibit 12-2	Proceeds from sale of plant assets	62	
From Exhibit 12-2	Net cash outflow from investing activities		$(255)
From Exhibit 12-2	**Cash flows from financing activities:**		
From Exhibit 12-2	Proceeds from issuance of common stock	$ 101	
From Exhibit 12-2	Proceeds from issuance of long-term debt	94	
From Exhibit 12-2	Payment of long-term debt	(11)	
From Exhibit 12-2	Payment of dividends	(17)	
From Exhibit 12-2	Net cash inflow from financing activities		167
From Exhibit 12-2	Net decrease in cash		$ (20)
From Exhibit 12-2	Cash balance, December 31, 20X1		42
	Cash balance, December 31, 20X2		$ 22

EXHIBIT 12-14
Income Statement (repeated from Exhibit 12-6)

ANCHOR CORPORATION
Income Statement
For the Year Ended December 31, 20X2

		(In thousands)
Revenues and gains:		
Sales revenue	$284	
Interest revenue	12	
Dividend revenue	9	
Gain on sale of plant assets	8	
Total revenues and gains		$313
Expenses:		
Cost of goods sold	$150	
Salary and wage expense	56	
Depreciation expense	18	
Other operating expense	17	
Interest expense	16	
Income tax expense	15	
Total expenses		272
Net income		$ 41

Exhibit 12-15
Comparative Balance Sheet (repeated from Exhibit 12-7)

ANCHOR CORPORATION
Comparative Balance Sheet
December 31, 20X2 and 20X1

(In thousands)	*20X2*	*20X1*	*Increase (Decrease)*
Assets			
Current:			
Cash	$ 22	$ 42	$(20)
Accounts receivable	93	80	13
Interest receivable	3	1	2
Inventory	135	138	(3)
Prepaid expenses	8	7	1
Long-term receivable from another company	11	—	11
Plant assets, net of depreciation	453	219	234
Total	$725	$487	$238
Liabilities			
Current:			
Accounts payable	$ 91	$ 57	$ 34
Salary and wage payable	4	6	(2)
Accrued liabilities	1	3	(2)
Long-term debt	160	77	83
Stockholders' Equity:			
Common stock	359	258	101
Retained earnings	110	86	24
Total	$725	$487	$238

This entry shows that depreciation expense has no effect on cash. However, depreciation expense, like all other expenses, is deducted from revenues in order to computate net income. Therefore, in going from net income to cash flows, we add depreciation back to net income. The addback cancels the earlier deduction.

The following example illustrates this practice: Suppose you had only two transactions during the period, a $1,000 cash sale and depreciation expense of $300. Net income is $700 ($1,000 – $300). Cash flow from operations is $1,000. To reconcile from net income ($700) to cash flow ($1,000), we must add back the depreciation amount of $300. Depletion and amortization are also added back. All expenses with no cash effects are added back to net income on the indirect form of the cash-flow statement. Some revenues do not bring in cash immediately. They too get special treatment. Revenues that do not provide cash are subtracted from net income. An example is a sale on account.

Gains and Losses on the Sale of Assets.[B] Sales of plant assets are *investing* activities. A gain or loss on the sale is an adjustment to income. Exhibit 12-13 (page 557) includes an adjustment for a gain. Recall that Anchor sold equipment for $62,000. Because the equipment's book value was $54,000, there was a gain of $8,000.

The $8,000 gain is reported on the income statement and is therefore included in net income. But the cash receipt from the sale is $62,000, and this amount includes the gain. To avoid counting the gain twice, we need to remove the gain from income and report the cash receipt of $62,000 as an investing activity. Starting with net income, we subtract the gain, which removes its effect from income. The sale of plant assets is then reported as a $62,000 cash receipt from an investing activity, as shown in Exhibits 12-2 and 12-13.

A loss on the sale of plant assets is also an adjustment to net income on the statement of cash flows. However, a loss is *added back* to income to compute cash flow from operations. The proceeds from selling the plant assets are then reported under investing activities.

Changes in the Current Asset and Current Liability Accounts.[C] Most current assets and current liabilities result from operating activities. Changes in the current accounts are reported as adjustments to net income on the cash-flow statement. The reasoning follows:

1. An *increase* in a current asset other than cash indicates a decrease in cash. Why? Because it takes cash to buy another asset. Suppose a company makes a sale on account. Accounts receivable are increased by the sale amount, but cash receipts are zero. Exhibit 12-15 (page 558) reports that Anchor Corporation's Accounts Receivable increased by $13,000 during 20X2. To compute the impact of revenue on Anchor's cash-flow amount, we must subtract the $13,000 increase in Accounts Receivable from net income in Exhibit 12-13. The reason is this: We have *not* collected this $13,000 in cash. The same logic applies to the other current assets. If they increase during the period, subtract the increase from net income to compute cash flow.

2. A *decrease* in a current asset other than cash indicates an increase in cash. Suppose Anchor's Accounts Receivable balance decreased by $4,000. Because cash receipts caused Accounts Receivable to decrease, add decreases in Accounts Receivable and the other current assets to net income.

3. A *decrease* in a current liability indicates a decrease in cash. The payment of a current liability causes both cash and the liability to decrease, so we subtract decreases in current liabilities from net income. In Exhibit 12-13, the $2,000 decrease in Accrued Liabilities is *subtracted* from net income to compute net cash inflow from operating activities.

4. An *increase* in a current liability indicates an increase in cash. Anchor's Accounts Payable increased during the year. This increase can occur only if cash is not spent to pay this liability. In that case, cash payments are less than the related expense and Anchor has more cash on hand. Thus, increases in current liabilities are *added* to net income.

CHECK POINT 12-12

CHECK POINT 12-13

CHECK POINT 12-14

As you can see, computing net cash inflow or net cash outflow from *operating* activities by the indirect method takes a path very different from that of the direct method. Nevertheless, both methods arrive at the same amount of net cash flow from operating activities ($68,000), as shown in Exhibits 12-2 and 12-13. Exhibit 12-16 summarizes the adjustments needed to convert net income to net cash flow from operating activities by the indirect method.

If you are studying *only* the indirect method for operating cash flows, please turn back to page 550 for coverage of investing and financing activities.

Exhibit 12-16
Indirect Method of Determining Cash Flows from Operating Activities

Net Income

Add (subtract) items that affect net income and cash flow differently:

- + Depreciation
- + Depletion
- + Amortization
- + Loss on disposal or exchange of long-term asset, or on early extinguishment of debt
- − Gain on disposal of long-term asset, or on early extinguishment of debt
- + Decrease in current asset other than cash
- − Increase in current asset other than cash
- + Increase in current liability*
- − Decrease in current liability*

Net cash inflow (or outflow) from operating activities

*Short-term notes payable for general borrowing, and current portion of long-term notes payable, are related to *financing* activities, not to operating activities.

We thank Barbara Gerrity and Jean Marie Hudson for suggesting this exhibit.

Nike's Statement of Cash Flows for Operating Activities—An Application of the Indirect Method

Nike, Inc., is a well-known maker of athletic shoes and clothing. As Exhibit 12-17 shows, Nike uses the indirect method to report cash flows from operating activities. We've discussed most of the items in Nike's statement of cash flows earlier, but three need clarification.

1. Deferred income taxes are added back to net income in the operating section. These taxes do not require current cash payments and are therefore similar to accrued liabilities.
2. Financing activities include proceeds from the exercise of options. This is the amount of cash received from issuance of stock to executives.
3. Changes in exchange rates show the cash effect of fluctuations in foreign currencies.

EVALUATION OF NIKE'S 19X7 CASH-FLOW RESULTS. Nike's cash flows for 19X7 look very strong. Cash increased from $18 million to almost $127 million. Virtually all the cash increase came from operations—a sign of strength. During 19X7, Nike invested in new plant and equipment ($11.9 million) and paid off more than $29 million ($10.7 million + $18.5 million) of debt. The company issued only $30 mil-

EXHIBIT 12-17
Nike, Inc., Statement of Cash Flows—Indirect Method

NIKE, INC.
Statement of Cash Flows
(Indirect Method for Operating Activities)
For the Year Ended May 31, 19X7

	(In thousands)
Cash provided (used) by operations:	
Net income	$ 35,879
Income charges (credits) not affecting cash:	
Depreciation	12,078
Deferred income taxes	8,486
Other	2,494
Changes in [current accounts]:	
Decrease in inventory	59,542
Decrease in accounts receivable	1,174
Decrease in other current assets	4,331
Increase in accounts payable, accrued liabilities, and income taxes payable	8,462
Cash provided by operations	132,446
Cash provided (used) by investing activities:	
Additions to property, plant, and equipment	(11,874)
Disposals of property, plant, and equipment	1,728
Additions to other assets	(930)
Cash used by investing activities	(11,076)
Cash provided (used) by financing activities:	
Additions to long-term debt	30,332
Reductions in long-term debt including current portion	(10,678)
Decrease in notes payable to banks	(18,489)
Proceeds from exercise of options	1,911
Dividends—common and preferred	(15,188)
Cash used by financing activities	(12,112)
Effect of exchange-rate changes on cash	(529)
Net increase (decrease) in cash	108,729
Cash and equivalents, beginning of year	18,138
Cash and equivalents, end of year	$126,867

lion of new debt. Nike's board of directors was so confident of the future that the board paid $15 million in dividends, almost half of net income.

Examine Anchor Corporation's statement of cash flows in Exhibit 12-13 (page 557). Answer each question, and classify it as *OPERATING, INVESTING,* or *FINANCING.*

a. Does Anchor Corporation appear to be growing or shrinking? How can you tell?

b. Where did Anchor's cash for expansion come from?

c. Suppose Accounts Receivable increased by $40,000 (instead of $13,000) during the current year. What would a $40,000 increase in Accounts Receivable signal about the company?

Answers:

a. This is an *INVESTING* question. Anchor appears to be growing. The company acquired more plant assets ($306,000) than it sold during the year.

b. This is a *FINANCING* question. The cash for expansion came from the issuance of common stock ($101,000) and from borrowing ($94,000).

c. This an *OPERATING* question. If accounts receivable had increased by $40,000, Anchor Corporation would have received $40,000 less cash during the year than the amount of sales revenue. A large increase in accounts receivable may signal either difficulty in collecting cash from customers or a sharp increase in sales. A manager, stockholder, or creditor of Anchor Corporation should compare current-year sales with sales revenue for the preceding year. If sales are up, higher accounts receivable are good news. If sales are down, higher receivables may signal a cash shortage.

USING CASH-FLOW INFORMATION IN INVESTMENT AND CREDIT ANALYSIS

The chapter-opening story of **W. T. Grant Company's** bankruptcy shows how crucial cash flows are to a company's survival. A cash shortage is usually the most pressing problem of a struggling organization. Abundant cash allows a company to expand, invest in research and development, and hire the best employees. How, then, do investors and creditors use cash-flow information to aid in decision making?

No single piece of information tells investors all they need to know about a company. Decision making is much more complex than plugging amounts into simple formulas. Investors analyze the financial statements, articles in the press, industry data, and economic predictions to decide whether to invest in a company's stock.

It has been said that cash-flow data help to spot losers better than they help to spot winners. This is often true. When a company's business is booming, profits are high and its financial position is improving. As the case of W. T. Grant Company vividly illustrates, a negative cash flow from operations warrants investigation. A cash downturn in a single year is not necessarily a danger signal. But negative cash flows for two consecutive years can be severe enough to kill a company. This is especially true if *operating* activities generate negative cash flows for two or more years. Without cash coming in from basic operations, a business simply cannot survive.

You may ask, "Can't the business raise money by issuing stock or by borrowing?" The answer is no: If operations cannot generate enough cash, then stockholders will not buy the company's stock. Nor will bankers lend money to it. A company that cannot generate cash from operations is doomed. The Decision Guidelines feature suggests how to use cash-flow information.

Decision Guidelines

Investors' and Creditors' Use of Cash-Flow and Related Information

Investors

Question	Factors to Consider*	Financial Statement Predictor/Decision Model*
1. How much in dividends can I expect to receive from an investment in stock?	Expected future net income	Income from continuing operations**
	Expected future cash balance	Net cash flows from (in order) • operating activities • investing activities • financing activities
	Future dividend policy	Current and past dividend policy
2. Is the stock price likely to increase or decrease?	Expected future net income	Income from continuing operations**
	Expected future cash flows from operating activities	Income from continuing operations** Net cash flow from operating activities
3. What is the future stock price likely to be?	Expected future income from • continuing operations, *and* • net cash flow from operating activities	$\text{Expected future price of a share of stock} = \frac{\text{Expected future earnings per share**}}{\text{Investment capitalization rate}}$ or $\text{Expected future price of a share of stock} = \frac{\text{Net cash flow from operations per share}}{\text{Investment capitalization rate}}$

Creditors

Question	Factors to Consider	Financial Statement Predictor
Can the company pay the interest and principal at the maturity of a loan?	Expected future net cash flow from operating activities	Income from continuing operations** —Net cash flow from • operating activities • investing activities

*There are many other factors to consider for making these decisions. These are some of the more common.
**See Chapter 11.

Measuring Cash Adequacy—Free Cash Flow

Throughout this chapter, we have focused on cash flows from operating, investing, and financing activities. Some investors, creditors, and managers make a further distinction. They seek to measure the amount of cash flow that a company can "free up" for opportunities that arise unexpectedly. The business world changes so quickly that new possibilities arise daily. The company with the most free cash flow is best able to respond to new opportunities. **Free cash flow** is the amount of cash available from operations after paying for planned investments in plant, equipment, and other long-term assets. Free cash flow can be computed as follows:

	Net cash flow		Cash outflow earmarked for
Free cash flow =	**from operating**	**–**	**investments in plant, equipment,**
	activities		**and other long-term assets**

PepsiCo, Inc., uses free cash flow to manage its operations. Suppose PepsiCo expects net cash inflow of $2.3 billion from operations. Assume PepsiCo plans to spend $1.9 billion to modernize its bottling plants. In this case, PepsiCo's free cash flow would be $0.4 billion ($2.3 billion – $1.9 billion). If a good investment opportunity comes along, PepsiCo should have $0.4 billion to invest in the other company. The managers of **Shell Oil Company, AT&T,** and **Briggs & Stratton** also use free cash flow analysis to manage their businesses.

A large amount of free cash flow is preferable because it means that a lot of cash is available for new investments. High-tech software companies such as **Intel, Microsoft,** and **America Online (AOL)** depend on technological breakthroughs for their competitive edge. These companies' investment opportunities may arise more quickly than those of older companies like **General Motors** and **Consolidated Edison,** the electric utility. For Intel, Microsoft, and AOL, free cash flow may be more important.

END-OF-CHAPTER End-of-Chapter

SUMMARY PROBLEM FOR YOUR REVIEW

Using the indirect method to report cash flows from operating activities, prepare the 20X3 statement of cash flows for Robins Corporation. In a separate schedule, report Robin's noncash investing and financing activities.

	December 31, 20X3	December 31, 20X2
Current Assets:		
Cash and cash equivalents	$19,000	$ 3,000
Accounts receivable	22,000	23,000
Inventories	34,000	31,000
Prepaid expenses	1,000	3,000
Current liabilities:		
Notes payable (for inventory purchases)	$11,000	$ 7,000
Accounts payable	24,000	19,000
Accrued liabilities	7,000	9,000
Income tax payable	10,000	10,000

Transaction Data for 20X3:

Purchase of equipment	$98,000	Depreciation expense	$ 7,000
Payment of cash dividends	18,000	Issuance of long-term note payable to borrow cash	7,000
Net income	26,000	Issuance of common stock for cash	19,000
Issuance of common stock to retire bonds payable	13,000	Sale of building	74,000
Purchase of long-term investment	8,000	Amortization expense	3,000
Issuance of long-term note payable to purchase patent	37,000	Purchase of treasury stock	5,000
		Loss on sale of building	2,000

Answer

ROBINS CORPORATION
Statement of Cash Flows
Year Ended December 31, 20X3

Cash flows from operating activities:		
Net income		$26,000
Add (subtract) items that affect net income and cash flow differently:		
Depreciation	$ 7,000	
Amortization	3,000	
Loss on sale of building	2,000	
Decrease in accounts receivable	1,000	
Increase in inventories	(3,000)	
Decrease in prepaid expenses	2,000	
Increase in notes payable, short-term	4,000	
Increase in accounts payable	5,000	
Decrease in accrued liabilities	(2,000)	19,000
Net cash inflow from operating activities		45,000
Cash flows from investing activities:		
Purchase of equipment	$(98,000)	
Sale of building	74,000	
Purchase of long-term investment	(8,000)	
Net cash outflow from investing activities		(32,000)
Cash flows from financing activities:		
Issuance of common stock	$ 19,000	
Payment of cash dividends	(18,000)	
Issuance of long-term note payable	7,000	
Purchase of treasury stock	(5,000)	
Net cash inflow from financing activities		3,000
Net increase in cash and cash equivalents		$16,000
Noncash investing and financing activities:		
Issuance of long-term note payable to purchase patent		$37,000
Issuance of common stock to retire bonds payable		13,000
Total noncash investing and financing activities		$50,000

SUMMARY OF LEARNING OBJECTIVES

1. ***Identify the purposes of the statement of cash flows.*** The *statement of cash flows* reports a business's cash receipts, cash payments, and net change in cash for the accounting period. It shows *why* cash increased or decreased during the period. A required financial statement, it gives a different view of the business from that given by accrual-basis statements. The cash-flow statement helps financial statement users predict the future cash flows of the entity and evaluate management decisions, determine the company's ability to pay dividends and interest, and ascertain the relationship of net income to cash flows. Cash includes cash and *cash equivalents.*

2. ***Distinguish among operating, investing, and financing cash flows.*** The cash-flow statement is divided into *operating activities, investing activities,* and *financing activities.* Operating activities create revenues and expenses. Investing activities increase and decrease long-term assets. Financing activities obtain the cash needed to launch and sustain the business. Each section of the statement includes cash receipts and cash payments and concludes with a net cash increase or decrease.

3. ***Prepare a statement of cash flows by the direct method.*** Two formats are used to report operating activities—the direct method and the indirect method. The *direct method* lists the major categories of operating cash receipts (collections from customers and receipts of interest and dividends) and cash payments (payments to suppliers, payments to employees, and payments for interest and income taxes).

4. ***Compute the cash effects of a wide variety of business transactions.*** The computation of the cash effects of business transactions requires analysis of the balance sheet, the income statement, and the related accounts.

5. ***Prepare a statement of cash flows by the indirect method.*** The *indirect method* starts with net income and reconciles to cash flow from operations. Although the FASB permits both the indirect and the direct methods, it prefers the direct method. However, the indirect method is more widely used.

Accounting Vocabulary

cash equivalents (p. 537).
cash flows (p. 536).
direct method (p. 539).
financing activities (p. 538).
free cash flow (p. 562).
indirect method (p. 539).
investing activities (p. 538).
operating activities (p. 537).
reconciliation method (p. 556).
statement of cash flows (p. 536).

Questions

1. What information does the statement of cash flows report that is not shown on the balance sheet, the income statement, or the statement of retained earnings?
2. Identify four purposes of the statement of cash flows.
3. Identify and briefly describe the three types of activities that are reported on the statement of cash flows.
4. How is the statement of cash flows dated, and why?
5. What is the check figure for the statement of cash flows? (In other words, which figure do you check to make sure you've done your work correctly?) Where is it obtained, and how is it used?
6. What is the most important source of cash for most successful companies?
7. How can cash decrease during a year when income is high? How can cash increase during a year when income is low? How can investors and creditors learn such facts about a company?
8. DeBerg, Inc., prepares its statement of cash flows by the *direct* method for operating activities. Identify the section of DeBerg's statement of cash flows where each of the following transactions will appear. If the transaction does not appear on the cash-flow statement, give the reason.
   a. Issuance of note payable
   b. Payment of salary expense
   c. Collection of sales revenue
   d. Amortization expense
   e. Payment of accounts payable
9. Why are depreciation, depletion, and amortization expenses *not* reported on a cash-flow statement that reports operating activities by the direct method? Why and how are these expenses reported on a statement prepared by the indirect method?
10. Mainline Distributing Company collected cash of $92,000 from customers and $6,000 interest on notes receivable. Cash payments included $24,000 to employees, $13,000 to suppliers, $6,000 as dividends to stockholders, and $5,000 as a loan to another company. How much was Mainline's net cash inflow from operating activities?
11. Summarize the major cash receipts and cash payments in the three categories of activities that appear on the cash-flow statement (direct method for operating cash flows).
12. Kirchner, Inc., recorded salary expense of $51,000 during a year when the balance of Salary Payable decreased from $10,000 to $2,000. How much cash did Kirchner pay to employees during the year? Where on the statement of cash flows should Kirchner report this item?
13. Marshall Corp.'s beginning plant asset balance, net of accumulated depreciation, was $193,000, and the ending amount was $176,000. Marshall recorded depreciation of $37,000 and sold plant assets with a book value of $9,000. How much cash did Marshall pay to purchase plant assets during the period? Where on the statement of cash flows should Marshall report this item?
14. How should issuance of a note payable to purchase land be reported in the financial statements? Identify three other transactions that fall into this same category.
15. An investment that cost $65,000 was sold for $80,000, resulting in a $15,000 gain. Show how to report this transaction on a statement of cash flows prepared by the indirect method.
16. Identify the cash effects of increases and decreases in current assets other than cash. What are the cash effects of increases and decreases in current liabilities?
17. Milano Corporation earned net income of $38,000 and had depreciation expense of $22,000. Also, noncash current assets decreased $13,000, and current liabilities decreased $9,000. What was Milano's net cash flow from operating activities?
18. What is free cash flow?

Check Points

Purposes of the statement of cash flows (Obj. 1)

CP12-1 How does the statement of cash flows help investors and creditors perform each of the following functions?

1. Predict future cash flows.
2. Evaluate management decisions.
3. Predict the company's ability to pay dividends and interest.

Using an actual statement of cash flows (Obj. 1)

CP12-2 Examine the statement of cash flows of **W. T. Grant Company** on page 535. What is the main danger signal about the company's cash flows?

Using an actual statement of cash flows (Obj. 1)

CP12-3 Return to the W. T. Grant Company cash-flow statement on page 535. Suppose Grant experiences two more years (19X9 and 20X0) exactly like 19X8. What will the company's cash balance be at the end of 20X0? What is likely to happen to the company?

Identifying operating cash flows (Obj. 2)

CP12-4 (Check Point 12-5 is an alternative exercise.) Mid-America Resources, Inc., accountants have assembled the following data for the year ended June 30, 20X0.

Payment of dividends.	$ 6,000	Cost of goods sold	$100,000
Proceeds from issuance		Payments to suppliers	80,000
of common stock	20,000	Purchase of equipment	40,000
Sales revenue	210,000	Payments to employees	70,000
Collections from customers . .	190,000	Payment of note payable	30,000
Payment of income tax	10,000	Proceeds from sale of land . . .	60,000
Purchase of treasury stock . . .	5,000	Depreciation expense.	15,000

Prepare the *operating* activities section of Mid-America's statement of cash flows for the year ended June 30, 20X0. Mid-America uses the direct method for operating cash flows.

Preparing a statement of cash flows—direct method (Obj. 3)

CP12-5 Use the data in Check Point 12-4 to prepare Mid-America's statement of cash flows for the year ended June 30, 20X0. Mid-America uses the *direct* method for operating activities. Use Exhibit 12-2, page 538, as a guide.

Preparing a statement of cash flows—direct method (Obj. 3)

CP12-6 Wellness Health Laboratories began 20X1 with cash of $104,000. During the year, Wellness earned service revenue of $600,000 and collected $590,000 from customers. Expenses for the year totaled $420,000, of which Wellness paid $410,000 in cash to suppliers and employees. Wellness also paid $140,000 to purchase equipment and a cash dividend of $50,000 to its stockholders during 20X1.

1. Compute net income for the year.
2. Determine the cash balance at the end of the year.
3. Prepare the company's statement of cash flows for the year. Format operating activities by the direct method.

Computing cash-flow amounts (Obj. 4)

CP12-7 Grace Chemical Company reported the following financial statements for 20X2:

GRACE CHEMICAL COMPANY
Income Statement
Year Ended December 31, 20X2

(In thousands)	
Sales revenue	$710
Cost of goods sold.	$340
Depreciation expense.	60
Salary expense	50
Other expenses.	150
Total expenses	600
Net income	$110

GRACE CHEMICAL COMPANY
Comparative Balance Sheet
December 31, 20X2 and 20X1

(In thousands)

Assets	**20X2**	**20X1**	**Liabilities**	**20X2**	**20X1**
Current:			Current:		
Cash	$ 19	$ 16	Accounts payable	$ 47	$ 42
Accounts receivable	54	48	Salary payable	23	21
Inventory	80	84	Accrued liabilities	8	11
Prepaid expenses	3	2	Long-term notes payable	66	68
Long-term investments	75	90			
Plant assets, net	225	185	**Stockholders' Equity**		
			Common stock	40	37
			Retained earnings	272	246
Total	$456	$425	Total	$456	$425

Compute the following operating cash flows:

a. Collections from customers
b. Payments for inventory

CP12-8 Use the Grace Chemical Company data in Check Point 12-7 to compute

Computing cash-flow amounts (Obj. 4)

a. Payments to employees
b. Payments of other expenses

CP12-9 Use the Grace Chemical Company data in Check Point 12-7 to compute the following:

Computing investing cash flows (Obj. 4)

a. Acquisitions of plant assets (all acquisitions were for cash). Grace sold no plant assets during the year.
b. Proceeds from the sale of long-term investments. Grace purchased no investments during the year.

CP12-10 Use the Grace Chemical Company data in Check Point 12-7 to compute the following:

Computing financing cash flows (Obj. 4)

a. New borrowing or payment of long-term notes payable. Grace had only one long-term note payable transaction during the year.
b. Issuance of common stock or retirement of common stock. Grace had only one common stock transaction during the year.
c. Payment of cash dividends (same as amount of dividends declared).

CP12-11 Return to the **Anchor Corporation** income statement (Exhibit 12-6) and comparative balance sheet (Exhibit 12-7), page 546. Assume that Anchor sold no plant assets during 20X2.

Noncash investing and financing transactions (Obj. 4)

1. Compute the cost of Anchor's plant asset acquisition during the year.
2. Anchor financed the plant asset by signing a long-term note payable for $83,000 and paying the remainder in cash. Journalize this transaction.
3. Show how to report Anchor's acquisition of the plant assets on the statement of cash flows.

CP12-12 Post Corporation is preparing its statement of cash flows for the year ended September 30, 20X4. Post reports cash flows from operating activities by the *indirect* method. The company's head bookkeeper has provided the following list of items for you to consider in preparing the company's statement of cash flows. Identify each item as an operating activity—addition to net income (O1), or subtraction from net income (O2); an investing activity (I); a financing activity (F); or an activity that is not used to prepare the cash-flow statement by the indirect method (N). Answer by placing the appropriate symbol in the blank space.

Identifying items for reporting cash flows from operations—indirect method (Obj. 5)

___	**a.** Loss on sale of land	___	**h.** Increase in accounts payable
___	**b.** Depreciation expense	___	**i.** Sales revenue
___	**c.** Increase in inventory	___	**j.** Payment of dividends
___	**d.** Decrease in prepaid expense	___	**k.** Decrease in accrued liabilities
___	**e.** Decrease in accounts receivable	___	**l.** Issuance of common stock
___	**f.** Purchase of equipment	___	**m.** Gain on sale of building
___	**g.** Collection of cash from customers	___	**n.** Retained earnings

Reporting cash flows from operating activities—indirect method (Obj. 5)

CP12-13 Grisham Publishing Company began 20X2 with accounts receivable, inventory, and prepaid expenses totaling $65,000. At the end of the year, the company had a total of $78,000 for these current assets. At the beginning of 20X2, Grisham owed current liabilities of $42,000, and at year end current liabilities totaled $40,000.

Net income for the year was $81,000, after including all revenues and gains and after subtracting all expenses and losses. Included in the computation of net income were a $4,000 gain on the sale of land and depreciation expense of $9,000.

Show how Grisham should report cash flows from operating activities for 20X2. Grisham uses the *indirect* method. Use Exhibit 12-13 (page 557) as a guide.

Preparing a statement of cash flows—indirect method (Obj. 5)

CP12-14 Grace Chemical Company reported its 20X2 financial statements as in Check Point 12-7, plus these additional data for 20X2:

a. Grace purchased no investments.
b. Grace sold no plant assets.
c. Grace had only one long-term note payable transaction.
d. Grace had only one common stock transaction.

Prepare Grace's statement of cash flows for the year ended December 31, 20X2. Grace uses the *indirect* method for operating activities. Use Exhibit 12-13 (page 557) as a guide.

Using an actual company's statement of cash flows (Obj. 5)

CP12-15 A friend is a stockholder in **Nike, Inc.,** and has received the company's statement of cash flows, which is reproduced in Exhibit 12-17 (page 560). Answer the following questions to help your friend understand this financial statement and its purpose:

1. What does the statement of cash flows reveal that you cannot learn from the income statement and the balance sheet? Use the W. T. Grant Company case to explain why cash flows are important.
2. Nike's statement indicates that the company uses the indirect method to report cash flows from operating activities. When you see a cash-flow statement, how can you tell that the company uses the indirect method?
3. Do Nike's cash flows for 19X7 look strong or weak? Give your reason. What are two things you should look for in evaluating a company's cash flows?

EXERCISES

Identifying the purposes of the statement of cash flows (Obj. 1)

E12-1 NEI Datacom has experienced an unbroken string of 10 years of growth in net income. Nevertheless, the business is facing bankruptcy! Creditors are calling all of NEI's outstanding loans for immediate payment, and the cash is simply not available. Attempts to explain where NEI went wrong make it clear that managers placed undue emphasis on net income and gave too little attention to cash flows.

Required

Write a brief memo, in your own words, to explain to the managers of NEI Datacom the purposes of the statement of cash flows.

Identifying activities for the statement of cash flows (Obj. 2)

E12-2 Identify each of the following transactions as an operating activity (O), an investing activity (I), a financing activity (F), a noncash investing and financing activity (NIF), or a transaction that is not reported on the statement of cash flows (N). Assume that the direct method is used to report cash flows from operating activities.

____ a. Collection of account receivable
____ b. Issuance of long-term note payable to borrow cash
____ c. Depreciation of equipment
____ d. Purchase of treasury stock
____ e. Issuance of common stock for cash
____ f. Payment of account payable
____ g. Issuance of preferred stock for cash
____ h. Payment of cash dividend
____ i. Sale of long-term investment
____ j. Amortization of bond discount
____ k. Acquisition of equipment by issuance of note payable
____ l. Payment of long-term debt
____ m. Acquisition of building by issuance of common stock
____ n. Accrual of salary expense
____ o. Purchase of long-term investment
____ p. Payment of wages to employees
____ q. Collection of cash interest
____ r. Cash sale of land
____ s. Distribution of stock dividend

Classifying transactions for the statement of cash flows (Obj. 2)

E12-3 Indicate where, if at all, each of the following transactions would be reported on a statement of cash flows prepared by the *direct* method and the accompanying schedule of noncash investing and financing activities.

a. Equipment	18,000	
Cash		18,000
b. Cash	7,200	
Long-Term Investment		7,200
c. Bonds Payable	45,000	
Cash		45,000
d. Building	164,000	
Note Payable, Long-Term		164,000
e. Cash	1,400	
Accounts Receivable		1,400
f. Dividends Payable	16,500	
Cash		16,500
g. Furniture and Fixtures	22,100	
Note Payable, Short-Term		22,100
h. Salary Expense	4,300	
Cash		4,300
i. Cash	81,000	
Common Stock		12,000
Paid-in Capital in Excess of Par—Common		69,000
j. Treasury Stock	13,000	
Cash		13,000
k. Retained Earnings	36,000	
Common Stock		36,000
l. Cash	2,000	
Interest Revenue		2,000
m. Land	87,700	
Cash		87,700
n. Accounts Payable	8,300	
Cash		8,300

Computing cash flows from operating activities—direct method (Obj. 3)

E12-4 Analysis of the accounting records of Auto Chef Corp. reveals the following:

Net income	$21,000	Payment of salaries and wages	$34,000
Payment of income tax	13,000	Depreciation	12,000
Collection of dividend revenue	7,000	Decrease in current liabilities	23,000
Payment of interest	16,000	Increase in current assets other than cash	17,000
Cash sales	9,000	Payment of dividends	7,000
Loss on sale of land	5,000	Collection of accounts receivable	93,000
Acquisition of land	37,000		
Payment of accounts payable	54,000		

Required

Compute cash flows from operating activities by the direct method. Use the format of the operating section of Exhibit 12-2 (page 538). Evaluate the operating cash flow of Auto Chef Corp. Give the reason for your evaluation.

Identifying items for the statement of cash flows—direct method (Obj. 3)

E12-5 Selected accounts of Crossroads Clinic, Inc., show the following:

DIVIDENDS RECEIVABLE

Beginning balance	**9,000**	**Cash receipts of dividends**	**38,000**
Dividend revenue	**40,000**		
Ending balance	**11,000**		

INVESTMENT IN LAND

Beginning balance	**90,000**	**Book value of investments sold**	**109,000**
Acquisitions	**127,000**		
Ending balance	**108,000**		

LONG-TERM DEBT

Payments	**69,000**	**Beginning balance**	**273,000**
		Issuance of debt for cash	**83,000**
		Ending balance	**287,000**

Required

For each account, identify the item or items that should appear on a statement of cash flows prepared by the direct method. State where to report the item.

Preparing the statement of cash flows—direct method (Obj. 3)

E12-6 The income statement and additional data of Crawford Properties, Inc., follow:

CRAWFORD PROPERTIES, INC.
Income Statement
Year Ended June 30, 20X1

Revenues:		
Sales revenue	$229,000	
Dividend revenue	8,000	$237,000
Expenses:		
Cost of goods sold	$103,000	
Salary expense	45,000	
Depreciation expense	29,000	
Advertising expense	11,000	
Interest expense	2,000	
Income tax expense	9,000	199,000
Net income		$ 38,000

Additional data:

a. Collections from customers are $15,000 more than sales.
b. Payments to suppliers are $9,000 less than the sum of cost of goods sold plus advertising expense.
c. Payments to employees are $1,000 more than salary expense.
d. Dividend revenue, interest expense, and income tax expense equal their cash amounts.
e. Acquisition of plant assets is $116,000. Of this amount, $101,000 is paid in cash, $15,000 by signing a note payable.
f. Proceeds from sale of land, $14,000.
g. Proceeds from issuance of common stock, $30,000.
h. Payment of long-term note payable, $15,000.
i. Payment of dividends, $11,000.
j. Change in cash balance, increase of $7,000.

Required

1. Prepare Crawford Properties' statement of cash flows and accompanying schedule of noncash investing and financing activities. Report operating activities by the *direct* method.
2. Evaluate Crawford's cash flows for the year. In your evaluation, mention all three categories of cash flows and give the reason for your evaluation.

E12-7 Compute the following items for the statement of cash flows:

Computing amounts for the statement of cash flows (Obj. 3, 4)

a. Beginning and ending Accounts Receivable are $22,000 and $18,000, respectively. Credit sales for the period total $81,000. How much are cash collections?

b. Cost of goods sold is $90,000. Beginning Inventory balance is $25,000, and ending Inventory balance is $21,000. Beginning and ending Accounts Payable are $11,000 and $8,000, respectively. How much are cash payments for inventory?

E12-8 Compute the following items for the statement of cash flows:

Computing investing and financing amounts for the statement of cash flows (Obj. 4)

a. Beginning and ending Retained Earnings are $45,000 and $73,000, respectively. Net income for the period is $62,000, and stock dividends are $8,000. How much are cash dividends?

b. Beginning and ending Plant Assets, net, are $103,000 and $107,000, respectively. Depreciation for the period is $16,000, and acquisitions of new plant assets are $27,000. Plant assets were sold at a $1,000 loss. What were the cash proceeds of the sale?

E12-9 The accounting records of Cottonwood Creek Golf Shop reveal the following:

Computing cash flows from operating activities—indirect method (Obj. 5)

Cash sales	$ 9,000	Payment of accounts payable	$48,000
Loss on sale of land	5,000	Net income	27,000
Acquisition of land	37,000	Payment of income tax	13,000
Collection of dividend revenue	7,000	Collection of accounts receivable	93,000
Payment of interest	16,000	Payment of salaries and wages	34,000
Increase in current assets other than cash	17,000	Depreciation	12,000
Payment of dividends	7,000	Decrease in current liabilities	23,000

Required

Compute cash flows from operating activities by the indirect method. Use the format of the operating section of Exhibit 12-13 (page 557). Then evaluate Cottonwood Creek's operating cash flows as strong or weak.

E12-10 Two transactions of Continental Credit Co. are recorded as follows:

Classifying transactions for the statement of cash flows (Obj. 3, 5)

a. Cash	17,000	
Accumulated Depreciation	83,000	
Equipment		93,000
Gain on Sale of Equipment		7,000
b. Land	210,000	
Cash		50,000
Note Payable		160,000

Required

1. Indicate where, how, and in what amount to report these transactions on the statement of cash flows and accompanying schedule of noncash investing and financing activities. Continental Credit reports cash flows from operating activities by the *direct* method.
2. Repeat Requirement 1, assuming that Continental Credit reports cash flows from operating activities by the *indirect* method.

E12-11 Use the income statement of Crawford Properties, Inc., in Exercise 12-6 (page 546), plus these additional data:

Preparing the statement of cash flows by the indirect method (Obj. 5)

a. Collections from customers are $15,000 more than sales.

b. Payments to suppliers are $9,000 less than the sum of cost of goods sold plus advertising expense.

c. Payments to employees are $1,000 more than salary expense.

d. Dividend revenue, interest expense, and income tax expense equal their cash amounts.

e. Acquisition of plant assets is $116,000. Of this amount, $101,000 is paid in cash, $15,000 by signing a note payable.
f. Proceeds from sale of land, $14,000.
g. Proceeds from issuance of common stock, $30,000.
h. Payment of long-term note payable, $15,000.
i. Payment of dividends, $11,000.
j. Change in cash balance, increase of $7,000.
k. From the balance sheet:

	June 30,	
	20X1	***20X0***
Current Assets:		
Cash	$27,000	$20,000
Accounts receivable	43,000	58,000
Inventory	83,000	77,000
Prepaid expenses	9,000	8,000
Current Liabilities:		
Notes payable (for inventory purchases)	$20,000	$20,000
Accounts payable	35,000	22,000
Accrued liabilities	23,000	21,000

Required

1. Prepare Crawford Properties, Inc.'s statement of cash flows for the year ended June 30, 20X1, using the indirect method.
2. Evaluate Crawford Properties' cash flows for the year. In your evaluation, mention all three categories of cash flows and give the reason for your evaluation.

Computing cash flows from operating activities—indirect method (Obj. 5)

E12-12 The accounting records of Ochoa, Inc., include these accounts:

CASH

Mar. 1	**5,000**		
Receipts	**447,000**	**Payments**	**448,000**
Mar. 31	**4,000**		

ACCOUNTS RECEIVABLE

Mar. 1	**18,000**		
Sales	**443,000**	**Collections**	**447,000**
Mar. 31	**14,000**		

INVENTORY

Mar. 1	**19,000**		
Purchases	**337,000**	**Cost of sales**	**335,000**
Mar. 31	**21,000**		

EQUIPMENT

Mar. 1	**93,000**		
Acquisition	**6,000**		
Mar. 31	**99,000**		

ACCUMULATED DEPRECIATION—EQUIPMENT

		Mar. 1	**52,000**
		Depreciation	**3,000**
		Mar. 31	**55,000**

ACCOUNTS PAYABLE

		Mar. 1	**14,000**
Payments	**332,000**	**Purchases**	**337,000**
		Mar. 31	**19,000**

ACCRUED LIABILITIES

		Mar. 1	**9,000**
Payments	**14,000**	**Expenses**	**11,000**
		Mar. 31	**6,000**

RETAINED EARNINGS

Quarterly		**Mar. 1**	**64,000**
dividend	**18,000**	**Net income**	**69,000**
		Mar. 31	**115,000**

Compute Ochoa's net cash inflow or outflow from operating activities during March. Use the indirect method. Does Ochoa have trouble collecting receivables or selling inventory? How can you tell?

E12-13 Consider three independent cases for the cash-flow data of Ken Nall & Associates:

Interpreting a cash-flow statement—indirect method (Obj. 5)

	Case A	*Case B*	*Case C*
Cash flows from operating activities:			
Net income	$ 30,000	$ 30,000	$ 30,000
Depreciation and amortization	11,000	11,000	11,000
Increase in current assets	(7,000)	(1,000)	(19,000)
Decrease in current liabilities	(8,000)	-0-	(6,000)
	$ 26,000	$ 40,000	$ 16,000
Cash flows from investing activities:			
Acquisition of plant assets	$ (91,000)	$(91,000)	$(91,000)
Sales of plant assets	4,000	8,000	97,000
	$ (87,000)	$(83,000)	$ 6,000
Cash flows from financing activities:			
New borrowing	$104,000	$ 50,000	$ 16,000
Payment of debt	(29,000)	(9,000)	(21,000)
	$ 75,000	$ 41,000	$ (5,000)
Net increase (decrease) in cash	$ 14,000	$ (2,000)	$ 17,000

For each case, identify from the cash-flow statement how Nall generated the cash to acquire new plant assets.

CHALLENGE EXERCISE

E12-14 **PepsiCo's** statement of cash flows for 19X8 is reproduced on page 574.

Analyzing an actual company's statement of cash flows (Obj. 5)

Required

1. Which format does PepsiCo use for reporting cash flows from operating activities?
2. What was PepsiCo's largest source of cash during 19X8? 19X7? 19X6?
3. The operating activities section of the statement lists (in millions):

Inventories	($11.8)
Income taxes	($16.9)

   Did these account balances increase or decrease during 19X8? How can you tell?
4. During 19X8, PepsiCo sold property, plant, and equipment. The gain or loss on this transaction is included in "Other noncash charges and credits, net" of $315.6 million. Assume that the book value of the plant assets that PepsiCo sold during 19X8 was $64.3 million. Journalize the sale of the property, plant, and equipment.

PROBLEMS

(Group A)

P12-1A Top managers of Henry's Interiors, Inc., are reviewing company performance for 20X4. The income statement reports a 15% increase in net income, the fifth consecutive year with an income increase above 10%. The income statement includes a nonrecurring loss without which net income would have increased by 16%. The balance sheet shows modest increases in assets, liabilities, and stockholders' equity. The assets posting the largest increases are plant and equipment because the company is halfway through a five-year ex-

Using cash-flow information to evaluate performance (Obj. 1)

E12-14 *(continued)* **Pepsi Co**

PEPSICO, INC., AND SUBSIDIARIES
Consolidated Statement of Cash Flows (partial, adapted)
Years Ended December 31, 19X8, 19X7 and 19X6

(In millions)	*19X8*	*19X7*	*19X6*
Cash Flows—Continuing Operations:			
Income from continuing operations	$ 1,301.7	$ 1,080.2	$ 1,090.6
Adjustments to reconcile income from continuing operations to net cash provided by continuing operations:			
Depreciation and amortization	1,214.9	1,034.5	884.0
Deferred income taxes	(52.0)	98.0	86.4
Other noncash charges and credits, net	315.6	227.2	2.1
Changes in current accounts:			
Accounts and notes receivable	(45.7)	(55.9)	(124.8)
Inventories	(11.8)	(54.8)	(20.9)
Prepaid expenses, taxes and other current assets	(27.4)	(75.6)	(41.9)
Accounts payable	(102.0)	57.8	25.4
Income taxes payable	(16.9)	(3.4)	136.3
Other current liabilities	135.2	122.3	72.8
Net Cash Provided by Continuing Operations	2,711.6	2,430.3	2,110.0
Cash Flows—Investing Activities:			
Acquisitions and investments in affiliates	(1,209.7)	(640.9)	(630.6)
Purchases of property, plant, and equipment	(1,549.6)	(1,457.8)	(1,180.1)
Proceeds from sales of property, plant, and equipment	89.0	69.6	45.3
Other, net	(83.2)	(246.7)	(171.9)
Net Cash Used for Investing Activities	(2,753.5)	(2,275.8)	(1,937.3)
Cash Flows—Financing Activities:			
Proceeds from issuances of long-term debt	1,092.7	2,799.6	777.3
Payments of short-term and long-term debt	(692.4)	(2,361.1)	(384.2)
Cash dividends paid	(395.5)	(343.2)	(293.9)
Purchases of treasury stock	(32.0)	(195.2)	(147.7)
Proceeds from exercises of stock options	82.8	15.8	9.3
Other, net	(30.9)	(47.0)	(37.9)
Net Cash Provided by (Used for) Financing Activities	24.7	(131.1)	(77.1)
Effect of Exchange Rate Changes on Cash and Cash Equivalents	0.4	(7.5)	(1.0)
Net Increase (Decrease) in Cash and Cash Equivalents	(16.8)	15.9	94.6
Cash and Cash Equivalents—Beginning of Year	186.7	170.8	76.2
Cash and Cash Equivalents—End of Year	$ 169.9	$ 186.7	$ 170.8

P12-1A *(continued)* **Henry's Interiors**

pansion program. No other assets and no liabilities are increasing dramatically. A summarized version of the cash-flow statement reports the following:

Net cash inflow from operating activities	$ 310,000
Net cash outflow from investing activities	(290,000)
Net cash inflow from financing activities	70,000
Increase in cash during 20X4	$ 90,000

Required

Write a memo giving top managers of Henry's Interiors your assessment of 20X4 operations and your outlook for the future. Focus on the information content of the cash-flow data.

Preparing an income statement, balance sheet, and statement of cash flows—direct method (Obj. 3)

P12-2A Dohn Corporation, a discounter of men's suits, was formed on January 1, 20X2, when Dohn issued its no-par common stock for $200,000. Early in January, Dohn made the following cash payments:

a. $50,000 for store fixtures
b. $120,000 for inventory (1,000 men's suits)
c. $12,000 for rent on a store building

In February, Dohn purchased 2,000 men's suits on account from a Chinese company. Cost of this inventory was $160,000. Before year end, Dohn paid $140,000 of this debt. Dohn uses the FIFO method to account for inventory.

During 20X2, Dohn sold 2,800 units of inventory for $200 each. Before year end, Dohn collected 90% of this amount.

The store employs three people. The combined annual payroll is $90,000, of which Dohn owes $3,000 at year end. At the end of the year, Dohn paid income tax of $64,000.

Late in 20X2, Dohn declared and paid cash dividends of $40,000.

For equipment, Dohn uses the straight-line depreciation method, over five years, with zero residual value.

Required

1. Prepare Dohn Corporation's income statement for the year ended December 31, 20X2. Use the single-step format, with all revenues listed together and all expenses together.
2. Prepare Dohn's balance sheet at December 31, 20X2.
3. Prepare Dohn's statement of cash flows for the year ended December 31, 20X2. Format cash flows from operating activities by the direct method.

Preparing the statement of cash flows—direct method (Obj. 2, 3)

P12-3A Patio Haus, Inc., accountants have developed the following data from the company's accounting records for the year ended July 31, 20X2:

a. Salary expense, $105,300
b. Cash payments to purchase plant assets, $181,000
c. Proceeds from issuance of short-term debt, $44,100
d. Payments of long-term debt, $18,800
e. Proceeds from sale of plant assets, $59,700, including $10,600 gain
f. Interest revenue, $12,100
g. Cash receipt of dividend revenue on stock investments, $2,700
h. Payments to suppliers, $673,300
i. Interest expense and payments, $37,800
j. Cost of goods sold, $481,100
k. Collection of interest revenue, $11,700
l. Acquisition of equipment by issuing short-term note payable, $35,500
m. Payments of salaries, $104,000
n. Credit sales, $608,100
o. Loan to another company, $35,000
p. Income tax expense and payments, $56,400
q. Depreciation expense, $27,700
r. Collections on accounts receivable, $681,100
s. Loan collections, $74,400
t. Proceeds from sale of investments, $34,700, including $3,800 loss
u. Payment of long-term debt by issuing preferred stock, $107,300
v. Amortization expense, $23,900
w. Cash sales, $146,000
x. Proceeds from issuance of common stock, $116,900
y. Payment of cash dividends, $50,500
z. Cash balance: July 31, 20X1—$53,800; July 31, 20X2—$?

Required

1. Prepare Patio Haus's statement of cash flows for the year ended July 31, 20X2. Follow the format of Exhibit 12-2, but do *not* show amounts in thousands. Include an accompanying schedule of noncash investing and financing activities.
2. Evaluate 20X2 in terms of cash flow. Give your reasons.

Preparing the statement of cash flows—direct method (Obj. 2, 3, 4)

P12-4A The 20X3 comparative balance sheet and income statement of Genie Marketing, Inc., follows on the next page.

Genie had no noncash investing and financing transactions during 20X3. During the year, there were no sales of land or equipment, no issuances of notes payable, no retirements of stock, and no treasury stock transactions.

Required

1. Prepare the 20X3 statement of cash flows, formatting operating activities by the direct method.
2. How will what you learned in this problem help you evaluate an investment?

P12-4A *(continued)*
Genie Marketing

GENIE MARKETING, INC.
Comparative Balance Sheet

	December 31, 20X3	20X2	Increase (Decrease)
Current assets:			
Cash and cash equivalents	$ 8,700	$ 15,600	$ (6,900)
Accounts receivable	46,500	43,100	3,400
Interest receivable	600	900	(300)
Inventories	94,300	89,900	4,400
Prepaid expenses	1,700	2,200	(500)
Plant assets:			
Land	35,100	10,000	25,100
Equipment, net	100,900	93,700	7,200
Total assets	$287,800	$255,400	$ 32,400
Current liabilities:			
Accounts payable	$ 16,400	$ 17,900	$ (1,500)
Interest payable	6,300	6,700	(400)
Salary payable	2,100	1,400	700
Other accrued liabilities	18,100	18,700	(600)
Income tax payable	6,300	3,800	2,500
Long-term liabilities:			
Notes payable	55,000	65,000	(10,000)
Stockholders' equity:			
Common stock, no-par	131,100	122,300	8,800
Retained earnings	52,500	19,600	32,900
Total liabilities and stockholders' equity	$287,800	$255,400	$ 32,400

GENIE MARKETING, INC.
Income Statement for 20X3

Revenues:		
Sales revenue		$438,000
Interest revenue		11,700
Total revenues		449,700
Expenses:		
Cost of goods sold	$205,200	
Salary expense	76,400	
Depreciation expense	15,300	
Other operating expense	49,700	
Interest expense	24,600	
Income tax expense	16,900	
Total expenses		388,100
Net income		$ 61,600

Preparing the statement of cash flows—indirect method (Obj. 2, 3, 5)

P12-5A Use the Genie Marketing, Inc., data from Problem 12-4A.

Required

1. Prepare the 20X3 statement of cash flows by the indirect method. If your instructor also assigned Problem 12-3A, prepare only the operating activities section of the statement.
2. How will what you learned in this problem help you evaluate an investment?

Preparing an income statement, balance sheet, and statement of cash flows—indirect method (Obj. 5)

P12-6A Use the Dohn Corporation data from Problem 12-2A.

Required

1. Prepare Dohn Corporation's income statement for the year ended December 31, 20X2. Use the single-step format, with all revenues listed together and all expenses together.
2. Prepare Dohn's balance sheet at December 31, 20X2.

3. Prepare Dohn's statement of cash flows for the year ended December 31, 20X2. Format cash flows from operating activities by the indirect method.

P12-7A Accountants for WWW.Smart, Inc. have assembled the following data for the year ended December 31, 20X4:

Preparing the statement of cash flows—indirect method (Obj. 2, 5)

	December 31, 20X4	*December 31, 20X3*
Current Accounts (All Result from Operations):		
Current assets:		
Cash and cash equivalents	$48,600	$34,800
Accounts receivable	70,100	73,700
Inventories	90,600	96,500
Prepaid expenses	3,200	2,100
Current liabilities:		
Notes payable (for inventory purchases)	$36,300	$36,800
Accounts payable	72,100	67,500
Income tax payable	5,900	6,800
Accrued liabilities	28,300	23,200

Transaction Data for 20X4:

Stock dividends	$ 12,600	Payment of cash dividends	$48,300
Collection of loan	10,300	Issuance of long-term debt to borrow cash	71,000
Depreciation expense	29,200	Net income	50,500
Acquisition of equipment	69,000	Issuance of preferred stock for cash	36,200
Payment of long-term debt by issuing common stock	89,400	Sale of long-term investment	12,200
Acquisition of long-term investment	44,800	Amortization expense	1,100
Acquisition of building by issuing long-term note payable	118,000	Payment of long-term debt	47,800
		Gain on sale of investment	3,500

Required

Prepare WWW.Smart's statement of cash flows using the *indirect* method to report operating activities. Include an accompanying schedule of noncash investing and financing activities.

P12-8A The comparative balance sheet of CNA Insurance, Inc., at December 31, 20X5, reported the following:

Preparing the statement of cash flows—indirect method (Obj. 2, 5)

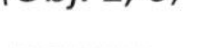

	December 31, 20X5	*December 31, 20X4*
Current Assets:		
Cash and cash equivalents	$ 8,400	$12,500
Accounts receivable	28,600	29,300
Inventories	51,600	53,000
Prepaid expenses	4,200	3,700
Current Liabilities:		
Notes payable (for inventory purchases)	$ 9,200	$ -0-
Accounts payable	21,900	28,000
Accrued liabilities	14,300	16,800
Income tax payable	11,000	14,300

CNA's transactions during 20X5 included the following:

Amortization expense	$ 5,000	Cash acquisition of building .	$124,000
Payment of cash dividends . . .	17,000	Net income.	31,600
Cash acquisition of equipment	55,000	Issuance of common stock for cash.	105,600
Issuance of long-term note payable to borrow cash	32,000	Stock dividend	13,000
Retirement of bonds payable by issuing common stock. . .	55,000	Sale of long-term investment	6,000
		Depreciation expense.	12,800

Required

1. Prepare the statement of cash flows of CNA Insurance, Inc., for the year ended December 31, 20X5. Use the *indirect* method to report cash flows from operating activities. Report noncash investing and financing activities in an accompanying schedule.
2. Evaluate CNA's cash flows for the year. Mention all three categories of cash flows and give the reason for your evaluation.

Preparing the statement of cash flows—direct and indirect methods (Obj. 3, 5)

P12-9A To prepare the statement of cash flows, accountants for Rolex Paper Company have summarized 20X8 activity in two accounts as follows:

CASH

Beginning balance	**87,100**	**Payments of operating expenses**	**46,100**
Issuance of common stock	**34,600**	**Payment of long-term debt**	**78,900**
Receipts of dividends	**1,900**	**Purchase of treasury stock**	**10,400**
Collection of loan	**18,500**	**Payment of income tax**	**8,000**
Sale of investments	**9,900**	**Payments on accounts payable**	**101,600**
Receipts of interest	**12,200**	**Payment of dividends**	**1,800**
Collections from customers	**308,100**	**Payments of salaries and wages**	**67,500**
Sale of treasury stock	**26,200**	**Payments of interest**	**21,800**
		Purchase of equipment	**79,900**
Ending balance	**82,500**		

COMMON STOCK

		Beginning balance	**103,500**
		Issuance for cash	**34,600**
		Issuance to acquire land	**62,100**
		Issuance to retire long-term debt	**21,100**
		Ending balance	**221,300**

Required

1. Prepare Rolex's statement of cash flows for the year ended December 31, 20X8, using the *direct* method to report operating activities. Also prepare the accompanying schedule of noncash investing and financing activities. Rolex's 20X8 income statement and selected balance sheet data follow.
2. Use these data to prepare a supplementary schedule showing cash flows from operating activities by the *indirect* method. All activity in the current accounts results from operations.

ROLEX PAPER COMPANY
Income Statement Year Ended December 31, 20X8

Revenues and gains:	
Sales revenue	$291,800
Interest revenue	12,200
Dividend revenue	1,900
Gain on sale of investments	700
Total revenues and gains	306,600

P12-9A *(continued)* **Rolex Income Statement**

Expenses:		
Cost of goods sold	$103,600	
Salary and wage expense	66,800	
Depreciation expense	20,900	
Other operating expense	44,700	
Interest expense	24,100	
Income tax expense	2,600	
Total expenses		262,700
Net income		$ 43,900

ROLEX PAPER COMPANY
Balance Sheet Data

	20X8 Increase (Decrease)
Current assets:	
Cash and cash equivalents	$?
Accounts receivable	(16,300)
Inventories	5,700
Prepaid expenses	(1,900)
Loan receivable	(18,500)
Investments	(9,200)
Equipment, net	59,000
Land	62,100
Current liabilities:	
Accounts payable	$ 7,700
Interest payable	2,300
Salary payable	(700)
Other accrued liabilities	(3,300)
Income tax payable	(5,400)
Long-term debt	(100,000)
Common stock	117,800
Retained earnings	42,100
Treasury stock	(15,800)

P12-10A Heart O'Kansas Optical Corporation's comparative balance sheet at September 30, 20X4, included the following balances:

Preparing the statement of cash flows—indirect and direct methods (Obj. 3, 4, 5)

HEART O'KANSAS OPTICAL
Balance Sheet September 30, 20X4 and 20X3

	20X4	20X3	Increase (Decrease)
Current assets:			
Cash	$ 11,700	$ 17,600	$ (5,900)
Accounts receivable	41,900	44,000	(2,100)
Interest receivable	4,100	2,800	1,300
Inventories	121,700	116,900	4,800
Prepaid expenses	8,600	9,300	(700)
Long-term investments	51,100	13,800	37,300
Equipment, net	131,900	92,100	39,800
Land	47,100	74,300	(27,200)
	$418,100	$370,800	$ 47,300

(continued)

P12-10A *(continued)* **Heart O'Kansas Optical, Balance Sheet**

Current liabilities:			
Notes payable, short-term	$ 22,000	$ -0-	$ 22,000
Accounts payable	61,800	70,300	(8,500)
Income tax payable	21,800	24,600	(2,800)
Accrued liabilities	17,900	29,100	(11,200)
Interest payable	4,500	3,200	1,300
Salary payable	1,500	1,100	400
Long-term note payable	123,000	121,400	1,600
Common stock	113,900	62,000	51,900
Retained earnings	51,700	59,100	(7,400)
	$418,100	$370,800	$ 47,300

Transaction data for the year ended September 30, 20X4:

a. Net income, $56,900
b. Depreciation expense on equipment, $8,500
c. Acquired long-term investments, $37,300
d. Sold land for $38,100, including $10,900 gain
e. Acquired equipment by issuing long-term note payable, $26,300
f. Paid long-term note payable, $24,700
g. Received cash of $51,900 for issuance of common stock
h. Paid cash dividends, $64,300
i. Acquired equipment by issuing short-term note payable, $22,000

Required

1. Prepare Heart O'Kansas Optical's statement of cash flows for the year ended September 30, 20X4, using the *indirect* method to report operating activities. Also prepare the accompanying schedule of noncash investing and financing activities. All current accounts except short-term notes payable result from operating transactions.
2. Prepare a supplementary schedule showing cash flows from operations by the *direct* method. The income statement reports the following: sales, $333,600; gain on sale of land, $10,900; interest revenue, $7,300; cost of goods sold, $161,500; salary expense, $63,400; other operating expenses, $29,600; income tax expense, $18,400; interest expense, $13,500; depreciation expense, $8,500.

(Group B)

Using cash-flow information to evaluate performance (Obj. 1)

P12-1B Top managers of Oasis Water, Inc., are reviewing company performance for 20X7. The income statement reports a 20% increase in net income over 20X6. However, most of the increase resulted from an extraordinary gain on insurance proceeds from storm damage to a building. The balance sheet shows a large increase in receivables. The cash-flow statement, in summarized form, reports the following:

Net cash outflow from operating activities	$(80,000)
Net cash inflow from investing activities	40,000
Net cash inflow from financing activities	50,000
Increase in cash during 19X7	$ 10,000

Required

Write a memo giving Oasis Water managers your assessment of 20X7 operations and your outlook for the future. Focus on the information content of the cash-flow data.

Preparing an income statement, balance sheet, and statement of cash flows—direct method (Obj. 3)

P12-2B Scott Corporation, a furniture store, was formed on January 1, 20X1, when Scott issued its no-par common stock for $300,000. Early in January, Scott made the following cash payments:

a. $150,000 for equipment
b. $120,000 for inventory (1,000 pieces of furniture)
c. $20,000 for 20X1 rent on a store building

In February, Scott purchased 2,000 units of furniture inventory on account from a Mexican company. Cost of this inventory was $260,000. Before year end, Scott paid $208,000 of this debt. Scott uses the FIFO method to account for inventory.

During 20X1, Scott sold 2,500 units of inventory for $200 each. Before year end, Scott collected 80% of this amount.

The store employs three people. The combined annual payroll is $95,000, of which Scott owes $4,000 at year end. At the end of the year, Scott paid income tax of $10,000.

Late in 20X1, Scott declared and paid cash dividends of $11,000.

For equipment, Scott uses the straight-line depreciation method, over five years, with zero residual value.

Required

1. Prepare Scott Corporation's income statement for the year ended December 31, 20X1. Use the single-step format, with all revenues listed together and all expenses together.
2. Prepare Scott's balance sheet at December 31, 20X1.
3. Prepare Scott's statement of cash flows for the year ended December 31, 20X1. Format cash flows from operating activities by the direct method.

Preparing the statement of cash flows—direct method (Obj. 2, 3)

P12-3B Accountants for Triad Associates, Inc., have developed the following data from the company's accounting records for the year ended April 30, 20X5:

a. Credit sales, $583,900
b. Loan to another company, $12,500
c. Cash payments to acquire plant assets, $59,400
d. Cost of goods sold, $382,600
e. Proceeds from issuance of common stock, $8,000
f. Payment of cash dividends, $48,400
g. Collection of interest, $4,400
h. Acquisition of equipment by issuing short-term note payable, $16,400
i. Payments of salaries, $93,600
j. Proceeds from sale of plant assets, $22,400, including $6,800 loss
k. Collections on accounts receivable, $448,600
l. Interest revenue, $3,800
m. Cash receipt of dividend revenue on stock investments, $4,100
n. Payments to suppliers, $368,500
o. Cash sales, $171,900
p. Depreciation expense, $59,900
q. Proceeds from issuance of short-term debt, $19,600
r. Payments of long-term debt, $50,000
s. Interest expense and payments, $13,300
t. Salary expense, $95,300
u. Loan collections, $12,800
v. Proceeds from sale of investments, $9,100, including $2,000 gain
w. Payment of short-term note payable by issuing long-term note payable, $63,000
x. Amortization expense, $2,900
y. Income tax expense and payments, $37,900
z. Cash balance: April 30, 20X4, $39,300
April 30, 20X5, $?

Required

1. Prepare Triad Associates' statement of cash flows for the year ended April 30, 20X5. Follow the format of Exhibit 12-2, but do *not* show amounts in thousands. Include an accompanying schedule of noncash investing and financing activities.
2. Evaluate 20X5 from a cash-flow standpoint. Give your reasons.

Preparing the statement of cash flows—direct method (Obj. 2, 3, 4)

P12-4B The 20X5 comparative balance sheet and income statement of Town East Press follow on page 582.

Town East had no noncash investing and financing transactions during 20X5. During the year, there were no sales of land or equipment, no issuances of notes payable, no retirements of stock, and no treasury stock transactions.

Required

1. Prepare the 20X5 statement of cash flows, formatting operating activities by the direct method.
2. How will what you learned in this problem help you evaluate an investment?

Preparing the statement of cash flows—indirect method (Obj. 2, 3, 5)

P12-5B Use the Town East Press data from Problem 12-4B.

Required

1. Prepare the 20X5 statement of cash flows by the indirect method. If your instructor also assigned Problem 12-3B, prepare only the operating activities section of the statement.
2. How will what you learned in this problem help you evaluate an investment?

P12-4B *(continued)*
Town East Press

TOWN EAST PRESS
Comparative Balance Sheet

	December 31, 20X5	December 31, 20X4	Increase (Decrease)
Current assets:			
Cash and cash equivalents	$ 10,500	$ 5,300	$ 5,200
Accounts receivable	25,300	26,900	(1,600)
Interest receivable	1,900	700	1,200
Inventories	83,600	87,200	(3,600)
Prepaid expenses	2,500	1,900	600
Plant assets:			
Land	89,000	60,000	29,000
Equipment, net	53,500	49,400	4,100
Total assets	$266,300	$231,400	$ 34,900
Current liabilities:			
Accounts payable	$ 31,400	$ 28,800	$ 2,600
Interest payable	4,400	4,900	(500)
Salary payable	3,100	6,600	(3,500)
Other accrued liabilities	13,700	16,000	(2,300)
Income tax payable	8,900	7,700	1,200
Long-term liabilities:			
Notes payable	75,000	100,000	(25,000)
Stockholders' equity:			
Common stock, no-par	88,300	64,700	23,600
Retained earnings	41,500	2,700	38,800
Total liabilities and stockholders' equity	$266,300	$231,400	$ 34,900

TOWN EAST PRESS
Income Statement for 20X5

Revenues:		
Sales revenue		$213,000
Interest revenue		8,600
Total revenues		221,600
Expenses:		
Cost of goods sold	$70,600	
Salary expense	27,800	
Depreciation expense	4,000	
Other operating expense	10,500	
Interest expense	11,600	
Income tax expense	29,100	
Total expenses		153,600
Net income		$ 68,000

Preparing an income statement, balance sheet, and statement of cash flows—indirect method (Obj. 5)

P12-6B Use the Scott Corporation data from Problem 12-2B.

Required

1. Prepare Scott Corporation's income statement for the year ended December 31, 20X1. Use the single-step format, with all revenues listed together and all expenses together.
2. Prepare Scott's balance sheet at December 31, 20X1.
3. Prepare Scott's statement of cash flows for the year ended December 31, 20X1. Format cash flows from operating activities by the indirect method.

Preparing the statement of cash flows—indirect method (Obj. 2, 5)

P12-7B Datex Corporation accountants have assembled the following data (at the top of page 583) for the year ended December 31, 20X7.

Required

Prepare Datex Corporation's statement of cash flows using the *indirect* method to report operating activities. Include an accompanying schedule of noncash investing and financing activities.

P12-7B *(continued)*
Datex Corporation

	December 31,	
	20X7	20X6
Current Accounts (All Result from Operations):		
Current assets:		
Cash and cash equivalents	$50,700	$22,700
Accounts receivable	69,700	64,200
Inventories	88,600	83,000
Prepaid expenses	5,300	4,100
Current liabilities:		
Notes payable (for inventory purchases)	$22,600	$18,300
Accounts payable	52,900	55,800
Income tax payable	18,600	16,700
Accrued liabilities	15,500	27,200

Transaction Data for 20X7:

Acquisition of land by issuing long-term note payable	$107,000	Purchase of treasury stock	$14,300
Stock dividends	31,800	Loss on sale of equipment	11,700
Collection of loan	8,700	Payment of cash dividends	18,300
Depreciation expense	21,800	Issuance of long-term note payable to borrow cash	34,400
Acquisition of building	125,300	Net income	57,100
Retirement of bonds payable by issuing common stock	65,000	Issuance of common stock for cash	41,200
Acquisition of long-term investment	31,600	Sale of equipment	58,000
		Amortization expense	5,300

Preparing the statement of cash flows—indirect method (Obj. 2, 5)

P12-8B The comparative balance sheet of Southern Bell Company at March 31, 20X3, reported the following:

	March 31,	
	20X3	20X2
Current Assets:		
Cash and cash equivalents	$19,900	$ 4,000
Accounts receivable	14,900	21,700
Inventories	63,200	60,600
Prepaid expenses	1,900	1,700
Current Liabilities:		
Notes payable (for inventory purchases)	$ 4,000	$ 4,000
Accounts payable	30,300	27,600
Accrued liabilities	10,700	11,100
Income tax payable	8,000	4,700

Southern Bell's transactions during the year ended March 31, 20X3, included the following:

Acquisition of land by issuing note payable	$76,000	Sale of long-term investment	$13,700
Amortization expense	2,000	Depreciation expense	15,300
Payment of cash dividend	30,000	Cash acquisition of building	47,000
Cash acquisition of equipment	78,700	Net income	70,000
Issuance of long-term note payable to borrow cash	50,000	Issuance of common stock for cash	11,000
		Stock dividend	18,000

Required

1. Prepare Southern Bell's statement of cash flows for the year ended March 31, 20X3, using the *indirect* method to report cash flows from operating activities. Report noncash investing and financing activities in an accompanying schedule.

2. Evaluate Southern Bell's cash flows for the year. Mention all three categories of cash flows and give the reason for your evaluation.

Preparing the statement of cash flows—direct and indirect methods (Obj. 3, 5)

P12-9B To prepare the statement of cash flows, accountants for Internet Guide, Inc., have summarized 20X3 activity in two accounts as follows:

CASH

Debit		Credit	
Beginning balance	53,600	Payments on accounts payable	399,100
Collection of loan	13,000	Payments of dividends	27,200
Sale of investment	8,200	Payments of salaries and wages	143,800
Receipts of interest	12,600	Payments of interest	26,900
Collections from customers	673,700	Purchase of equipment	31,400
Issuance of common stock	47,300	Payments of operating expenses	34,300
Receipts of dividends	4,500	Payment of long-term debt	41,300
		Purchase of treasury stock	26,400
		Payment of income tax	18,900
Ending balance	63,600		

COMMON STOCK

Debit		Credit	
		Beginning balance	84,400
		Issuance for cash	47,300
		Issuance to acquire land	80,100
		Issuance to retire long-term debt	19,000
		Ending balance	230,800

Required

1. Prepare the statement of cash flows of Internet Guide, Inc., for the year ended December 31, 20X3, using the *direct* method to report operating activities. Also prepare the accompanying schedule of noncash investing and financing activities.
2. Use the following data from Internet Guide's 20X3 income statement and balance sheet to prepare a supplementary schedule showing cash flows from operating activities by the *indirect* method. All activity in the current accounts results from operations.

INTERNET GUIDE, INC.
Income Statement
Year Ended December 31, 20X3

Revenues:		
Sales revenue		$701,300
Interest revenue		12,600
Dividend revenue		4,500
Total revenues		718,400
Expenses and losses:		
Cost of goods sold	$402,600	
Salary and wage expense	150,800	
Depreciation expense	19,300	
Other operating expense	44,100	
Interest expense	28,800	
Income tax expense	16,200	
Loss on sale of investments	1,100	
Total expenses		662,900
Net income		$ 55,500

INTERNET GUIDE, INC.
Balance Sheet Data
December 31, 20X3

	Increase (Decrease)
Current assets:	
Cash and cash equivalents	$?
Accounts receivable	27,600
Inventories	(11,800)
Prepaid expenses	600
Loan receivable	(13,000)
Long-term investments	(9,300)
Equipment, net	12,100
Land	80,100
Current liabilities:	
Accounts payable	$ (8,300)
Interest payable	1,900
Salary payable	7,000
Other accrued liabilities	10,400
Income tax payable	(2,700)
Long-term debt	(60,300)
Common stock, no-par	146,400
Retained earnings	28,300
Treasury stock	26,400

P12-10B The comparative balance sheet of Funny Bone Defensive Driving, Inc., at June 30, 20X1, included the following balances:

Preparing the statement of cash flows—indirect and direct methods
(Obj. 3, 4, 5)

FUNNY BONE DEFENSIVE DRIVING, INC.
Balance Sheet
June 30, 20X1 and 20X0

	20X1	*20X0*	*Increase (Decrease)*
Current assets:			
Cash	$ 24,500	$ 8,600	$ 15,900
Accounts receivable	45,900	48,300	(2,400)
Interest receivable	2,900	3,600	(700)
Inventories	68,600	60,200	8,400
Prepaid expenses	3,700	2,800	900
Long-term investment	10,100	5,200	4,900
Equipment, net	74,500	73,600	900
Land	42,400	96,000	(53,600)
	$272,600	$298,300	$(25,700)
Current liabilities:			
Notes payable, short-term (for general borrowing)	$ 13,400	$ 18,100	$ (4,700)
Accounts payable	42,400	40,300	2,100
Income tax payable	13,800	14,500	(700)
Accrued liabilities	8,200	9,700	(1,500)
Interest payable	3,700	2,900	800
Salary payable	900	2,600	(1,700)
Long-term note payable	47,400	94,100	(46,700)
Common stock	59,800	51,200	8,600
Retained earnings	83,000	64,900	18,100
	$272,600	$298,300	$(25,700)

Transaction data for the year ended June 30, 20X1:

a. Net income, $56,200
b. Depreciation expense on equipment, $13,400
c. Purchased long-term investment, $4,900
d. Sold land for $46,900, including $6,700 loss
e. Acquired equipment by issuing long-term note payable, $14,300
f. Paid long-term note payable, $61,000
g. Received cash for issuance of common stock, $3,900
h. Paid cash dividends, $38,100
i. Paid short-term note payable by issuing common stock, $4,700

Required

1. Prepare the statement of cash flows of Funny Bone Defensive Driving, Inc., for the year ended June 30, 20X1, using the *indirect* method to report operating activities. Also prepare the accompanying schedule of noncash investing and financing activities. All current accounts except short-term notes payable result from operating transactions.
2. Prepare a supplementary schedule showing cash flows from operations by the *direct* method. The income statement reports the following: sales, $245,300; interest revenue, $10,600; cost of goods sold, $82,800; salary expense, $38,800; other operating expenses, $42,000; depreciation expense, $5,400; income tax expense, $9,900; loss on sale of land, $6,700; interest expense, $6,100.

EXTENDING YOUR KNOWLEDGE

DECISION CASES

Preparing and using the statement of cash flows to evaluate operations (Obj. 4, 5)

Case 1. The 20X6 comparative income statement and the 20X6 comparative balance sheet of UPACK, Inc., have just been distributed at a meeting of the company's board of directors. The members of the board of directors raise a fundamental question: Why is the cash balance so low? This question is especially troublesome to the board members because 20X6 showed record profits. As the controller of the company, you must answer the question.

UPACK, INC.
Comparative Income Statement
Years Ended December 31, 20X6 and 20X5

(In thousands)	*20X6*	*20X5*
Revenues and gains:		
Sales revenue	$444	$310
Gain on sale of equipment (sale price, $33)	—	18
Totals	$444	$328
Expenses and losses:		
Cost of goods sold	$221	$162
Salary expense	48	28
Depreciation expense	46	22
Interest expense	13	20
Amortization expense on patent	11	11
Loss on sale of land (sale price, $61)	—	35
Total expenses and losses	339	278
Net income	$105	$ 50

UPACK, INC. **Comparative Balance Sheet** December 31, 20X6 and 20X5		
(In thousands)	***20X6***	***20X5***
Assets		
Cash	$ 25	$ 63
Accounts receivable, net	72	61
Inventories	194	181
Long-term investments	31	-0-
Property, plant, and equipment	369	259
Accumulated depreciation	(244)	(198)
Patents	177	188
Totals	$624	$554
Liabilities and Owners' Equity		
Notes payable, short-term (for general borrowing)	$ 32	$101
Accounts payable	63	56
Accrued liabilities	12	17
Notes payable, long-term	147	163
Common stock, no-par	149	61
Retained earnings	221	156
Totals	$624	$554

Required

1. Prepare a statement of cash flows for 20X6 in the format that best shows the relationship between net income and operating cash flow. The company sold no plant assets or long-term investments and issued no notes payable during 20X6. The changes in all current accounts except short-term notes payable arose from operations. There were *no* noncash investing and financing transactions during the year. Show all amounts in thousands.
2. Answer the board members' question: Why is the cash balance so low? In explaining the business's cash flows, identify two significant cash receipts that occurred during 20X5 but not in 20X6. Also point out the two largest cash disbursements during 20X6.
3. Considering net income and the company's cash flows during 20X6, was it a good year or a bad year? Give your reasons.

Using cash-flow data to evaluate an investment (Obj. 1, 2)

Case 2. Abba Medical, Inc., and Esquire Limousine Service are asking you to recommend their stock to your clients. Because Abba and Esquire earn about the same net income and have similar financial positions, your decision depends on their cash-flow statements, summarized as follows:

	Abba		***Esquire***	
Net cash inflows from operating activities		$ 70,000		$ 30,000
Cash inflows (outflows) from investing activities:				
Purchase of plant assets	$(100,000)		$(20,000)	
Sale of plant assets	10,000	(90,000)	40,000	20,000
Cash inflows (outflows) from financing activities:				
Issuance of common stock		30,000		—
Paying off long-term debt		—		(40,000)
Net increase in cash		$ 10,000		$ 10,000

Based on their cash flows, which company looks better? Give your reasons.

Ethical Issue

Terminix Pest Control is having a bad year. Net income is only $37,000. Also, two important clients are falling behind in their payments to Terminix, and Terminix's accounts receivable are ballooning. The company desperately needs a loan. The Terminix board of directors is considering ways to put the best face on the Terminix financial statements. The company's bank closely examines cash flow from operations. Joe Praco, Terminix's controller, suggests reclassifying as long-term the receivables from the slow-paying clients. He explains to the board that removing the $80,000 rise in accounts receivable will increase net cash inflow from operations. This approach will increase the company's cash balance and may help Terminix get the loan.

Required

1. Using only the amounts given, compute net cash inflow from operations both with and without the reclassification of the receivables. Which reporting makes Terminix look better?

2. Where else in Terminix's cash-flow statement will the reclassification of the receivable be reported? What cash-flow effect will this item report? What effect would the reclassification have on *overall* cash flow from all activities?

3. Under what condition would the reclassification of the receivables be ethical? Unethical?

Financial Statement Cases

Using the statement of cash flows (Obj. 1, 2, 3, 4, 5)

Case 1. Use **The Gap, Inc.,** statement of cash flows along with the company's other financial statements, all in Appendix A at the end of the book, to answer the following questions.

Required

1. By which method does The Gap report net cash flows from *operating* activities? How can you tell?

2. Suppose The Gap reported net cash flows from operating activities by the direct method. Compute these amounts for the year ended January 30, 1999:

a. Collections from customers

b. Payments for inventory

3. Evaluate the year ended January 30, 1999, in terms of net income, total assets, debt ratio, cash flows, and overall results. Be specific.

Computing cash-flow amounts and using cash-flow data for analysis (Obj. 1, 2, 3, 4, 5)

Case 2. Obtain the annual report of a company of your choosing. Answer the following questions about the company. Concentrate on the current year in the report.

Required

1. By which method does the company report net cash flows from *operating* activities? How can you tell?

2. Suppose the company reported net cash flows from operating activities by the direct method. Compute these amounts for the current year:

a. Collections from customers

b. Payments for inventory

3. Evaluate the current year in terms of net income (or net loss), total assets, debt ratio, cash flows, and overall results. Be specific.

Group Projects

Project 1. Each member of the group should obtain the annual report of a different company. Select companies in different industries. Evaluate each company's trend of cash flows for the most recent two years. In your evaluation of the companies' cash flows, you may use any other information that is publicly available—for example, the other financial statements (income statement, balance sheet, statement of stockholders' equity, and the related notes) and news stories from magazines and newspapers. Rank the companies' cash flows from best to worst and write a two-page report on your findings.

Project 2. Select a company and obtain its annual report, including all the financial statements. Focus on the statement of cash flows and, in particular, the cash flows from operating activities. Specify whether the company uses the direct method or the indirect method to report operating cash flows. As necessary, use the other financial statements (income statement, balance sheet, and statement of stockholders' equity) and the notes to prepare the company's cash flows from operating activities by the *other* method.

INTERNET EXERCISE

The Coca-Cola Company

The Coca-Cola Company has over 50% of the global soft-drink market with two-thirds of sales coming from outside the United States. Of the three top-selling soft drinks in the world, Coca-Cola Classic is #1, and Diet Coke is #3. (Pepsi is #2.) Among Coca-Cola's other brands are Minute Maid, Sprite, Barg's, Fruitopia, Powerade, Surge, and Dasani water.

1. Go to **http://www.thecoca-colacompany.com,** click on **Investors,** and then select the most recent **Annual Report.** Click on **Quick Index** and scroll down the index to find the consolidated financial statements. Use the *Consolidated Statements of Cash Flows* to answer the following questions.
2. Does Coca-Cola use the direct or indirect method of preparing the Statement of Cash Flows? How can you tell? How many activity sections are affected by the choice of method?
3. For the most recent year, list the amount of net cash inflow or outflow for each of the three major types of activities reported on the Statement of Cash Flows. Which type of activity is providing the most cash? Is this considered favorable or unfavorable?
4. For the most recent year, what amount is reported for *Net Income/(Loss)*and *Net Cash provided by Operating Activities?* Are these amounts the same? Explain why or why not.
5. For the most recent year, did Coca-Cola purchase *or* sell more property, plant, and equipment? Is this considered favorable or unfavorable? What was the net amount purchased/sold? Which activity section reports this information?
6. For the most recent year, did Coca-Cola issue or pay back more debt? What was the net amount issued/repaid? For the most recent year, did Coca-Cola issue or purchase more common stock? What was the net amount issued/purchased? For the most recent year, what amount of cash dividends did Coca-Cola pay out? Which activity section reports this information?

13 Financial Statement Analysis

Learning Objectives

After studying this chapter, you should be able to

1. Perform a horizontal analysis of comparative financial statements
2. Perform a vertical analysis of financial statements
3. Prepare and use common-size financial statements
4. Use the statement of cash flows in decision making
5. Compute the standard financial ratios used for decision making
6. Use ratios in decision making
7. Measure economic value added by a company's operations

"To compare the operating results of two companies like Bristol-Myers Squibb and Procter & Gamble, we need to use standard measures. Financial ratio analysis plays an important part in the recommendations we make to our clients regarding which companies' stock to buy."

—Angela Lane, Senior Analyst, Baer & Foster

Bristol-Myers Squibb Company
Consolidated Statement of Earnings (Adapted)

(In millions)	Year Ended December 31, 1998
Earnings	
1 **Net sales**	$18,284
2 **Expenses:**	
3 Cost of products sold	4,856
4 Marketing, selling and administrative	4,418
5 Advertising and product promotion	2,312
6 Research and development	1,577
7 Special charge	800
8 Provision for restructuring	201
9 Other	(148)
10	14,016
11 **Earnings before income taxes**	4,268
12 Provision for income taxes	1,127
13 **Net earnings**	$ 3,141

The Procter & Gamble Company
Consolidated Statement of Earnings (Adapted)

(In millions)	Year Ended June 30, 1998
1 Net sales	$37,154
2 Cost of products sold	21,064
3 Marketing, research, and administrative expenses	10,035
4 Operating income	6,055
5 Interest expense	548
6 Other income, net	201
7 Earnings before income taxes	5,708
8 Income taxes	1,928
9 Net earnings	$ 3,780

ANALYSTS at Baer & Foster, an investment banking firm, have identified health-care and consumer products as growth areas and will be recommending these companies' stocks to their clients. Angela Lane heads a team of analysts focusing on two companies: **Bristol-Myers Squibb** and **Procter & Gamble.** Bristol-Myers is best known for Clairol hair products, Ban deodorant, and Excedrin pain medicine. Procter & Gamble's key products include Crest toothpaste, Tide detergent, Pampers diapers, and Pringles chips.

Lane and her team wish to compare the performance of Bristol-Myers and Procter & Gamble. However, the two companies differ greatly in size and operate in slightly different industries. Procter & Gamble has sales of $37 billion, compared to $18 billion for Bristol-Myers Squibb. Procter & Gamble's total assets of $31 billion are almost double Bristol-Myers' assets of $16 billion. How can Lane's team compare two companies of such different size?

Investors and creditors face similar challenges every day. The way to compare companies of different size is to use *standard* measures. Throughout this book, we have discussed financial ratios, such as the current ratio, inventory turnover, and return on stockholders' equity. These ratios are standard measures that enable analysts to compare companies of different sizes. Managers use the ratios to monitor operations, and they use the financial statements to calculate most of these ratios. In this chapter, we discuss most of the basic ratios that managers use to run a company and that investors and lenders use to evaluate investments and loan prospects. These ratios are one reason accounting is called the "language of business."

Financial Statement Analysis

A major source of accounting information is the annual report. In addition to the financial statements (income statement, balance sheet, and statement of cash flows), annual reports contain the following:

1. Notes to the financial statements, including a summary of the accounting methods used
2. Management's discussion and analysis of the financial results
3. The auditor's report
4. Comparative financial data for a series of years

All of these items are covered in Chapter 11.

Management's discussion and analysis (MD&A) of financial results is especially important because top management is in the best position to know how well or how poorly the company is performing. The SEC requires the MD&A from public corporations. For example, the 1998 annual report of **Bristol-Myers Squibb Company** includes six pages entitled Financial Review, which begins as follows:

> In 1998, Bristol-Myers Squibb achieved record levels of sales, with all four of the company's business segments reporting sales increases. [. . .]. Worldwide sales grew to $18.3 billion, a 9% increase over 1997.

The graphs in Exhibit 13-1 show information that is important for stockholders. The graphs depict Bristol-Myers Squibb's three-year trend of net sales, market value of the company's stock, and cumulative return to the company's stockholders. How relevant are these facts for making decisions about a company such as Bristol-Myers Squibb or Procter & Gamble? They are very relevant because they help managers, investors, and creditors interpret the companies' financial statements.

Exhibit 13-1
Representative Financial Data of Bristol-Myers Squibb Company

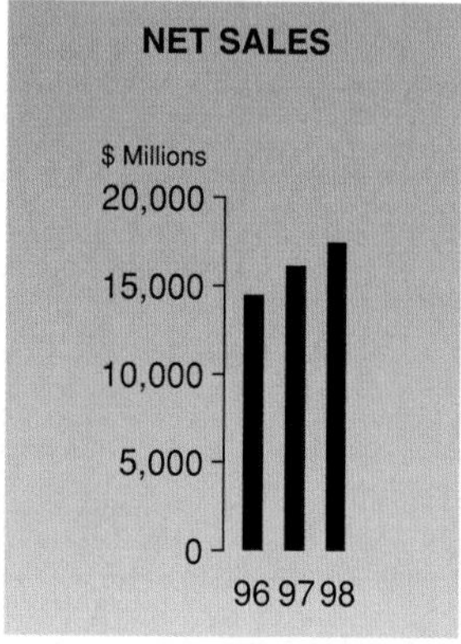

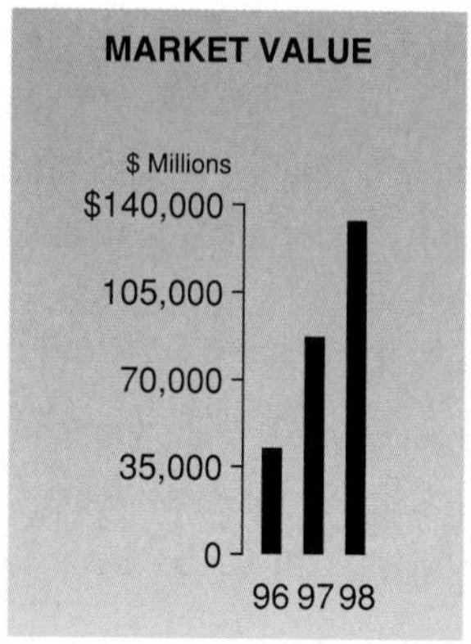

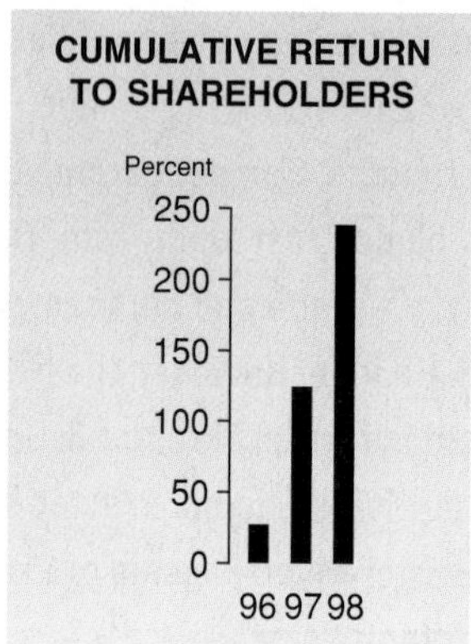

The Objectives of Financial Statement Analysis

Investors who purchase a company's stock hope to receive dividends and that the stock's value will increase. The middle graph shows that Bristol-Myers Squibb's stock price has increased dramatically. Investors bear the risk that they will not receive a good return on their investment. They use financial statement analysis to (1) predict their expected returns (see the last graph), and (2) assess the risks associated with those returns. Now let's examine some of the tools of financial analysis.

HORIZONTAL ANALYSIS

Objective 1
Perform a horizontal analysis of comparative financial statements

Many decisions hinge on whether the numbers—in sales, income, expenses, and so on—are increasing or decreasing over time. Has the sales figure risen from last year? By how much? We may find that sales have risen by $20,000. This fact may be interesting, but considered alone it is not very informative. The *percentage change* in sales over time enhances our understanding. It is more useful to know that sales have increased by 20% than to know that the increase in sales is $20,000.

The study of percentage changes in comparative statements is called **horizontal analysis.** Computing a percentage change in comparative statements requires two steps:

1. Computing the dollar amount of the change from the base (earlier) period to the later period
2. Dividing the dollar amount of change by the base-period amount

Horizontal analysis is illustrated for **Bristol-Myers Squibb** as follows (dollar amounts in millions):

			Increase (Decrease)	
	1998	*1997*	*Amount*	*Percent*
Sales	$18,284	$16,701	$1,583	9.5%

The percentage change in Bristol-Myers Squibb's sales during 1998 is 9.5%, computed as follows:

STEP 1. Compute the dollar amount of change in sales from 1997 to 1998:

1998		**1997**		**Increase**
$18,284	−	$16,701	=	$1,583

STEP 2. Divide the dollar amount of change by the base-period amount to compute the percentage change during the later period:

$$\textbf{Percentage change} = \frac{\textbf{Dollar amount of change}}{\textbf{Base-year amount}}$$

$$= \frac{\$1{,}583}{\$16{,}701} = 9.5\%$$

CHECK POINT 13-1

During 1998, Bristol-Myers Squibb's sales increased by 9.5%.

Detailed horizontal analyses are shown in the two right-hand columns of Exhibits 13-2 and 13-3, the financial statements of Bristol-Myers Squibb Company. The income statements (statements of earnings) reveal that net sales increased by 9.5% during 1998. Fortunately, cost of goods sold grew more slowly because gross profit grew by 9.7%—a good sign.

(Text continues on page 595)

EXHIBIT 13-2
Comparative Income Statement—Horizontal Analysis

BRISTOL-MYERS SQUIBB COMPANY
Statement of Earnings (Adapted)
Years Ended December 31, 1998 and 1997

(Dollar amounts in millions)	*1998*	*1997*	*Increase (Decrease) Amount*	*Percent*
Net sales	$18,284	$16,701	$1,583	9.5%
Cost of products sold	4,856	4,464	392	8.8
Gross profit	13,428	12,237	1,191	9.7
Operating expenses:				
Marketing, selling, and administrative	4,418	4,173	245	5.9
Advertising and product promotion	2,312	2,241	71	3.2
Research and development	1,577	1,385	192	13.9
Special charge	800	—	800	100.0*
Provision for restructuring	201	225	(24)	(10.7)
Other	(148)	(269)	(121)	(45.0)
Earnings before income taxes	4,268	4,482	(214)	(4.8)
Provision for income taxes	1,127	1,277	(150)	(11.7)
Net earnings	$ 3,141	$ 3,205	(64)	(2.0)

*An increase from zero to any positive number is treated as an increase of 100%.

EXHIBIT 13-3
Comparative Balance Sheet–Horizontal Analysis

BRISTOL-MYERS SQUIBB COMPANY
Balance Sheet (Adapted)
December 31, 1998 and 1997

(Dollar amounts in millions)	*1998*	*1997*	*Increase (Decrease) Amount*	*Percent*
Assets				
Current Assets:				
Cash and cash equivalents	$ 2,244	$ 1,456	$ 788	54.1%
Time deposits and marketable securities	285	338	(53)	(15.7)
Receivables, net	3,190	2,973	217	7.3
Inventories	1,873	1,799	74	4.1
Prepaid expenses	1,190	1,170	20	1.7
Total current assets	8,782	7,736	1,046	13.5
Property, plant, and equipment—net	4,429	4,156	273	6.6
Insurance recoverable	523	619	(96)	(15.5)
Goodwill	1,587	1,625	(38)	(2.3)
Other assets	951	841	110	13.1
	$16,272	$14,977	$1,295	8.6%
Liabilities				
Current Liabilities:				
Short-term borrowings	$ 482	$ 543	(61)	(11.2)%
Accounts payable	1,380	1,017	363	35.7
Accrued expenses payable	2,302	1,939	363	18.7
U.S. and foreign income taxes payable	750	865	(115)	(13.3)
Product liability*	877	668	209	31.3
Total current liabilities	5,791	5,032	759	15.1
Other liabilities	1,541	1,447	94	6.5
Long-term debt	1,364	1,279	85	6.6
Total liabilities	8,696	7,758	938	12.1

*Warranties, guarantees, and the like.

(CONTINUED)

EXHIBIT 13-3 (CONT.)
Comparative Balance Sheet–Horizontal Analysis

Stockholders' Equity				
Common stock	219	108	111	102.8
Capital in excess of par value of stock	1,075	544	531	97.6
Foreign-currency translation adjustments	(622)	(533)	(89)	(16.7)
Retained earnings	12,540	10,950	1,590	14.5
Less cost of treasury stock	(5,636)	(3,850)	(1,786)	(46.4)
Total stockholders' equity	7,576	7,219	357	4.9
	$16,272	$14,977	$1,295	8.6%

Other good news about 1998 operations: The two largest operating expenses—Marketing . . . and Advertising . . . —also grew more slowly than sales. Why then did net earnings decline during 1998? The special charge siphoned off $800 million before taxes. Bristol-Myers Squibb's notes reveal that the company expensed $800 million in 1998 for expected breast implant product liability the company may incur. This special charge casts a bit of a cloud over the company.

The comparative balance sheet in Exhibit 13-3 shows that 1998 was a year of expansion for Bristol-Myers Squibb. Total assets increased by $1,295 million, or 8.6%. The bulk of this growth occurred in current assets, which increased by 13.5%. Total liabilities increased by 12.1%, and total stockholders' equity grew by 4.9%.

Identify the item on Bristol-Myers Squibb's 1998 income statement that experienced the largest percentage increase from 1997. As Bristol-Myers Squibb moves into 1999 and beyond, will this item be very important to the company? Explain.

Answer:
The special charge increased by 100% from 1997 to 1998, from zero to $800 million. This item is very important because its amount is large and its future is uncertain.

Trend Percentages

Trend percentages are a form of horizontal analysis. Trends indicate the direction a business is taking. How have sales changed over a five-year period? What trend does gross profit show? These questions can be answered by trend percentages over a representative period, such as the most recent five or ten years. To evaluate the company, we examine more than just a two- or three-year period.

Trend percentages are computed by selecting a base year whose amounts are set equal to 100%. The amounts for each following year are expressed as a percentage of the base amount. To compute trend percentages, divide each item for following years by the corresponding amount during the base year:

$$\textbf{Trend \%} = \frac{\textbf{Any year \$}}{\textbf{Base year \$}}$$

Bristol-Myers Squibb Company showed sales, cost of goods sold, and gross profit for the past six years as follows:

(In millions)	*1998*	*1997*	*1996*	*1995*	*1994*	*1993*
Net sales	$18,284	$16,701	$15,065	$13,767	$11,984	$11,413
Cost of products sold	4,856	4,464	3,965	3,637	3,122	3,029
Gross profit	13,428	12,237	11,100	10,130	8,862	8,384

We want trend percentages for a five-year period starting with 1994. The base year is 1993. Trend percentages for net sales are computed by dividing each net sales amount by the 1993 amount of $11,413 million. To compute trend percentages for Cost of products sold, divide each Cost of products sold amount by $3,029 (the base-year amount). Compute trend percentages for Gross profit using gross profit of $8,384 as the base amount. The resulting trend percentages follow (1993, the base year = 100%):

CHECK POINT 13-2

	1998	*1997*	*1996*	*1995*	*1994*	*1993*
Net sales	160%	146%	132%	121%	105%	100%
Cost of products sold	160	147	131	120	103	100%
Gross profit	160	146	132	121	106	100%

Bristol-Myers Squibb's sales, cost of goods sold, and gross profit have trended upward at almost identical rates throughout the five-year period.

VERTICAL ANALYSIS

Objective 2
Perform a vertical analysis of financial statements

Horizontal analysis highlights changes in an item over time. However, no single financial analysis technique provides a complete picture of a business. Another method of analyzing a company is vertical analysis.

Vertical analysis of a financial statement reveals the relationship of each statement item to a specified base, which is the 100% figure. Every other item on the financial statement is then reported as a percentage of that base. For example, when an income statement is analyzed vertically, net sales is usually the base. Suppose under normal conditions a company's gross profit is 70% of net sales. A drop in gross profit to 60% of net sales may cause the company to suffer a loss. Management, investors, and creditors view a large decline in gross profit with alarm. Exhibit 13-4 shows the vertical analysis of **Bristol-Myers Squibb's** income statement as a percentage of net sales. In this case,

$$\textbf{Vertical analysis \%} = \frac{\textbf{Each income statement item}}{\textbf{Net sales}}$$

EXHIBIT 13-4
Comparative Income Statement—Vertical Analysis

BRISTOL-MYERS SQUIBB COMPANY
Statement of Earnings (Adapted)
Years Ended December 31, 1998 and 1997

	1998		*1997*	
(Dollar amounts in millions)	*Amount*	*Percent*	*Amount*	*Percent*
Net sales	$18,284	100.0%	$16,701	100.0%
Cost of products sold	4,856	26.6	4,464	26.7
Gross profit	13,428	73.4	12,237	73.3
Operating expenses:				
Marketing, selling, and administrative	4,418	24.2	4,173	25.0
Advertising and product promotion	2,312	12.6	2,241	13.4
Research and development	1,577	8.6	1,385	8.3
Special charge	800	4.4	—	—
Provision for restructuring	201	1.1	225	1.3
Other	(148)	(0.8)	(269)	(1.5)
Earnings before income taxes	4,268	23.3	4,482	26.8
Provision for income taxes	1,127	6.1	1,277	7.6
Net earnings	$ 3,141	17.2%	$ 3,205	19.2%

So, for example, the vertical analysis percentage for Cost of products sold for 1998 equals 26.6% ($4,856/$18,284 = 0.266). Exhibit 13-5 shows the vertical analysis of the balance sheet amounts as a percentage of total assets.

CHECK POINT 13-3

The vertical analysis of Bristol-Myers Squibb's income statement (Exhibit 13-4) shows no unusual relationships. The gross profit percentage increased a bit in 1998, but net income's percentage of sales declined because of the special charge.

The vertical analysis of Bristol-Myers Squibb's balance sheet (Exhibit 13-5) also yields few surprises. Both current assets' and current liabilities' percentages of total assets increased in 1998. The only bad news on the balance sheet is the increase in product liability.

Despite the ongoing litigation, the company's financial position remains strong. For example, the current ratio is 1.52 ($8,782 million/$5,791 million). The company has very little long-term debt, and retained earnings (profit from operations) is the largest single source of financing by far.

Recall from Chapter 3 (page 138) that the current ratio = total current assets divided by total current liabilities.

EXHIBIT 13-5
Comparative Balance Sheet—Vertical Analysis

BRISTOL-MYERS SQUIBB COMPANY
Balance Sheet (Adapted)
December 31, 1998 and 1997

	1998		1997	
(Dollar amounts in millions)	*Amount*	*Percent*	*Amount*	*Percent*
Assets				
Current Assets:				
Cash and cash equivalents	$ 2,244	13.8%	$ 1,456	9.7%
Time deposits and marketable securities	285	1.8	338	2.3
Receivables, net of allowances	3,190	19.6	2,973	19.9
Inventories	1,873	11.5	1,799	12.0
Prepaid expenses	1,190	7.3	1,170	7.8
Total current assets	8,782	54.0	7,736	51.7
Property, plant, and equipment—net	4,429	27.2	4,156	27.7
Insurance recoverable	523	3.2	619	4.1
Goodwill	1,587	9.8	1,625	10.9
Other assets	951	5.8	841	5.6
	$16,272	100.0%	$14,977	100.0%
Liabilities				
Current Liabilities:				
Short-term borrowings	$ 482	3.0%	$ 543	3.6%
Accounts payable	1,380	8.5	1,017	6.8
Accrued expenses payable	2,302	14.1	1,939	12.9
U.S. and foreign income taxes payable	750	4.6	865	5.8
Product liability	877	5.4	668	4.5
Total current liabilities	5,791	35.6	5,032	33.6
Other Liabilities	1,541	9.5	1,447	9.7
Long-Term Debt	1,364	8.3	1,279	8.5
Total liabilities	8,696	53.4	7,758	51.8
Stockholders' Equity				
Common stock	219	1.3	108	0.7
Capital in excess of par value of stock	1,075	6.6	544	3.6
Foreign-currency translation adjustments	(622)	(3.8)	(533)	(3.5)
Retained earnings	12,540	77.1	10,950	73.1
Less cost of treasury stock	(5,636)	(34.6)	(3,850)	(25.7)
Total stockholders' equity	7,576	46.6	7,219	48.2
	$16,272	100.0%	$14,977	100.0%

COMMON-SIZE STATEMENTS

Objective 3
Prepare and use common-size financial statements

The percentages in Exhibits 13-4 and 13-5 can be presented as a separate statement that reports only percentages (no dollar amounts). Such a statement is called a **common-size statement.**

On a common-size income statement, each item is expressed as a percentage of the net sales amount. Net sales is the *common size* to which we relate the other income-statement amounts. In the balance sheet, the common size is total assets *or* the sum of total liabilities and stockholders' equity. A common-size statement eases the comparison of different companies because their amounts are stated in percentages.

Common-size statements may identify the need for corrective action. Exhibit 13-6 is the common-size analysis of current assets taken from Exhibit 13-5. Exhibit 13-6 shows cash as a relatively high percentage of total assets at the end of each year. Receivables are a constant percentage of total assets. What could cause an increase in receivables? **Bristol-Myers Squibb** could grow lax in collecting accounts receivable, a policy that may lead to a cash shortage. If so, the company would need to pursue collection more vigorously. The company monitors its cash position and collection of receivables to avoid a cash shortage. Common-size statements provide information useful for this purpose.

STOP & THINK

Calculate the common-size percentages for the following income statement:

Net sales	$150,000
Cost of goods sold	60,000
Gross margin	90,000
Operating expense	40,000
Operating income	50,000
Income tax expense	15,000
Net income	$ 35,000

Answer:

Net sales	100%	(= $150,000 ÷ $150,000)
Cost of goods sold	40	(= $ 60,000 ÷ $150,000)
Gross margin	60	(= $ 90,000 ÷ $150,000)
Operating expense	27	(= $ 40,000 ÷ $150,000)
Operating income	33	(= $ 50,000 ÷ $150,000)
Income tax expense	10	(= $ 15,000 ÷ $150,000)
Net income	23%	(= $ 35,000 ÷ $150,000)

BENCHMARKING

Benchmarking is the practice of comparing a company to a standard set by other companies, with a view toward improvement.

Benchmarking Against the Industry Average

We study an individual company to gain insight into its past results and future performance. Still, that knowledge is limited to the one company. We may learn that gross profit has decreased and that net income has increased steadily for the last 10

Exhibit 13-6
Common-Size Analysis of Current Assets

BRISTOL-MYERS SQUIBB COMPANY
Common-Size Analysis of Current Assets
December 31, 1998 and 1997

	Percent of Total Assets	
	1998	*1997*
Current Assets:		
Cash and cash equivalents	13.8%	9.7%
Time deposits and marketable securities	1.8	2.3
Receivables, net	19.6	19.9
Inventories	11.5	12.0
Prepaid expenses	7.3	7.8
Total current assets	54.0	51.7
Long-Term Assets	46.0	48.3
Total Assets	100.0%	100.0%

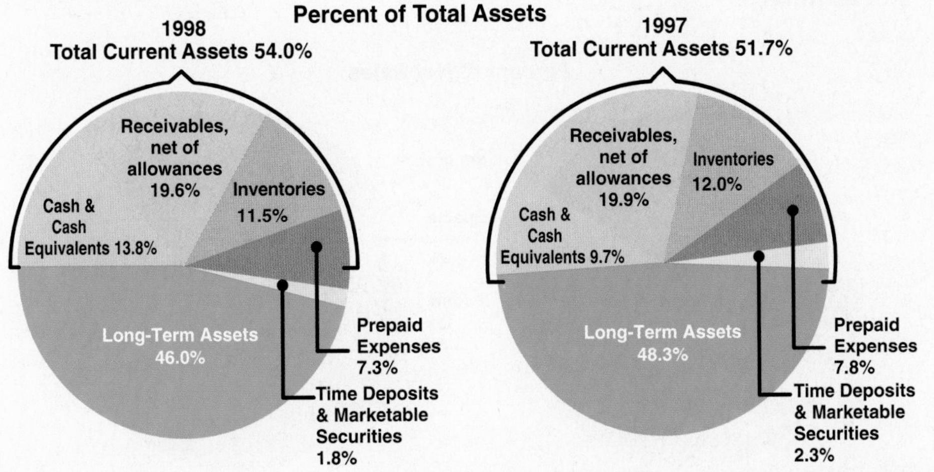

years. This information is helpful, but it does not consider how businesses in the same industry have fared over the same time period. Have other companies in the same line of business profited even more? Managers, investors, creditors, and other interested parties need to know how one company compares with other companies in the same line of business. For example, during the 1990s, **Apple Computer's** gross margin steadily declined in relation to its competitors', but it has rebounded recently.

Exhibit 13-7 gives the common-size income statement of **Bristol-Myers Squibb Company** compared with the average for the pharmaceuticals (health-care) industry. This analysis compares Bristol-Myers Squibb with all other companies in its line of business. The industry averages were adapted from Robert Morris Associates' *Annual Statement Studies.* Analysts at **Merrill Lynch, Edward Jones,** and other companies specialize in a particular industry and make such comparisons in deciding which companies' stocks to buy or sell. For example, financial-service companies such as Merrill Lynch have health-care industry specialists, airline-industry specialists, and so on. They compare a company with others in the same industry. Exhibit 13-7 shows that Bristol-Myers Squibb compares favorably with competing companies in its industry. Its gross profit percentage is much higher than the industry average. The company does a good job of controlling total expenses, and as a result, its percentage of net income is significantly higher than the industry average.

Exhibit 13-7
Common-Size Income Statement Compared with the Industry Average

BRISTOL-MYERS SQUIBB COMPANY
Common-Size Income Statement for Comparison with Industry Average
Year Ended December 31, 1998

	Bristol-Myers Squibb	*Industry Average*
Net sales	100.0%	100.0%
Cost of products sold	26.6	54.7
Gross profit	73.4	45.3
Operating expenses	50.1	36.5
Earnings from continuing operations before income tax	23.3	8.8
Income tax expense	6.1	2.3
Earnings from continuing operations	17.2	6.5
Special items (discontinued operations, extraordinary gains and losses, and effects of accounting changes)	—	1.4
Net earnings	17.2%	5.1%

Percent of Net Sales

Cost of goods sold 26.6%
Net income 17.2%
Income tax 6.1%
Operating expenses 50.1%

Bristol-Myers Squibb Company

Net income 5.1%
Special items 1.4%
Income tax 2.3%
Cost of goods sold 54.7%
Operating expenses 36.5%

Industry Average

Benchmarking Against a Key Competitor

Common-size statements are also used to compare the company to another specific company. Suppose you are a member of Angela Lane's team at Baer & Foster. You are considering an investment in the stock of a health-care company, and you are choosing between **Bristol-Myers Squibb** and **Procter & Gamble.** A direct comparison of their financial statements in dollar amounts is not meaningful because the amounts are so different (see the income statements on page 591). However, you can convert the two companies' income statements to common size and compare the percentages.

Exhibit 13-8 presents the common-size income statements of Bristol-Myers Squibb and Procter & Gamble. Procter & Gamble serves as an excellent benchmark because most of its products are market leaders. In this comparison, Bristol-Myers Squibb has higher percentages of gross profit, earnings from continuing operations, and net earnings.

CHECK POINT 13-4

USING THE STATEMENT OF CASH FLOWS IN DECISION MAKING

Objective 4
Use the statement of cash flows in decision making

The chapter has thus far focused on the income statement and balance sheet. We may also perform horizontal and vertical analysis on the statement of cash flows. In Chapter 12, we discussed how to prepare the statement. To continue our discussion of its role in decision making, let's use Exhibit 13-9, the statement of cash flows of DeMaris Corporation.

EXHIBIT 13-8
Common-Size Income Statement Compared with a Key Competitor

BRISTOL-MYERS SQUIBB COMPANY
Common-Size Income Statement for Comparison with Key Competitor
Year Ended December 31, 1998

	Bristol-Myers Squibb	*Procter & Gamble*
Net sales	100.0%	100.0%
Cost of products sold	26.6	56.7
Gross profit	73.4	43.3
Operating expenses	50.1	27.9
Earnings from continuing operations before income tax	23.3	15.4
Income tax expense	6.1	5.2
Earnings from continuing operations	17.2	10.2
Special items (discontinued operations, extraordinary gains and losses, and effects of accounting changes)	—	—
Net earnings	17.2%	10.2%

Percent of Net Sales

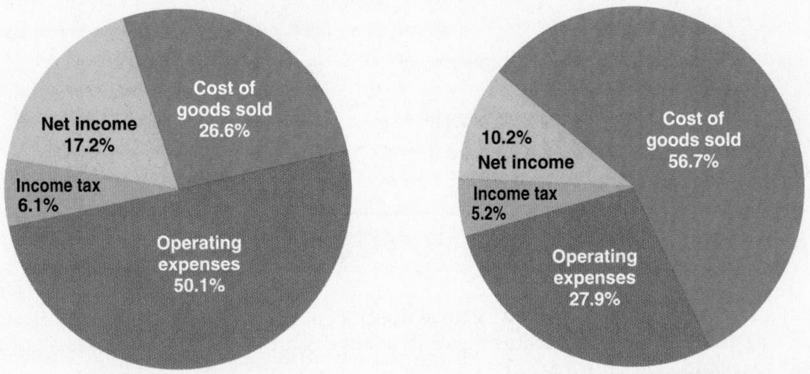

Bristol-Myers Squibb Company **Procter & Gamble**

EXHIBIT 13-9
Statement of Cash Flows

DEMARIS CORPORATION
Statement of Cash Flows
Year Ended December 31, 19X9

Operating activities:		
Income from operations		$ 35,000
Add (subtract) noncash items:		
Depreciation	$ 14,000	
Net increase in current assets other than cash	(15,000)	
Net increase in current liabilities	8,000	7,000
Net cash inflow from operating activities		42,000
Investing activities:		
Sale of property, plant, and equipment	$ 91,000	
Net cash inflow from investing activities		91,000
Financing activities:		
Issuance of bonds payable	$ 72,000	
Payment of long-term debt	(170,000)	
Purchase of treasury stock	(9,000)	
Payment of dividends	(33,000)	
Net cash outflow from financing activities		(140,000)
Increase (decrease) in cash		$ (7,000)

Some analysts examine cash flows to identify danger signals about a company's financial situation. For example, the statement in Exhibit 13-9 reveals what may be a weakness in DeMaris Corporation.

First, operations provided a net cash inflow of $42,000, which is much less than the $91,000 generated by the sale of fixed assets. An important question arises: Can the company remain in business by generating the majority of its cash by selling its property, plant, and equipment? No, because these assets are needed to manufacture the company's products in the future. Note also that borrowing by issuance of bonds payable brought in $72,000. No company can survive long by living on borrowed funds. DeMaris must eventually pay off the bonds. Indeed, the company paid $170,000 on older debt. Successful companies such as **General Mills, DuPont,** and **Intel** generate the greatest percentage of their cash from operations, not from selling their fixed assets or from borrowing. These conditions may be only temporary for DeMaris Corporation, but they are worth investigating.

Mid-Chapter

SUMMARY PROBLEM FOR YOUR REVIEW

Perform a horizontal analysis and a vertical analysis of the comparative income statement of **TRE Corporation,** which makes metal detectors. State whether 20X3 was a good year or a bad year, and give your reasons.

TRE CORPORATION
Comparative Income Statement
Months Ended December 31, 20X3 and 20X2

	20X3	*20X2*
Total revenues	$275,000	$225,000
Expenses:		
Cost of products sold	$194,000	$165,000
Engineering, selling, and administrative expenses	54,000	48,000
Interest expense	5,000	5,000
Income tax expense	9,000	3,000
Other expense (income)	1,000	(1,000)
Total expenses	263,000	220,000
Net earnings	$ 12,000	$ 5,000

Answer *(Horizontal analysis and vertical analysis on next page)*

The horizontal analysis shows that total revenues increased 22.2%. This percentage increase was greater than the 19.5% increase in total expenses, resulting in a 140% increase in net earnings.

The vertical analysis shows decreases in the percentages of net sales consumed by the cost of products sold (from 73.3% to 70.5%) and by the engineering, selling, and administrative expenses (from 21.3% to 19.6%). Because these two items are TRE's largest dollar expenses, their percentage decreases are quite important. The relative reduction in expenses raised December 20X3 net earnings to 4.4% of sales, compared with 2.2% the preceding December. The overall analysis indicates that December 20X3 was significantly better than December 20X2.

TRE CORPORATION
Horizontal Analysis of Comparative Income Statement
Months Ended December 31, 20X3 and 20X2

	20X3	*20X2*	*Increase (Decrease)* Amount	Percent
Total revenues	$275,000	$225,000	$50,000	22.2%
Expenses:				
Cost of products sold	$194,000	$165,000	$29,000	17.6
Engineering, selling, and administrative expenses	54,000	48,000	6,000	12.5
Interest expense	5,000	5,000	—	—
Income tax expense	9,000	3,000	6,000	200.0
Other expense (income)	1,000	(1,000)	2,000	—*
Total expenses	263,000	220,000	43,000	19.5
Net earnings	$ 12,000	$ 5,000	$ 7,000	140.0%

*Percentage changes are typically not computed for shifts from a negative amount to a positive amount, and vice versa.

TRE CORPORATION
Vertical Analysis of Comparative Income Statement
Months Ended December 31, 20X3 and 20X2

	20X3		*20X2*	
	Amount	*Percent*	*Amount*	*Percent*
Total revenues	$275,000	100.0%	$225,000	100.0%
Expenses:				
Cost of products sold	$194,000	70.5	$165,000	73.3
Engineering, selling, and administrative expenses	54,000	19.6	48,000	21.3
Interest expense	5,000	1.8	5,000	2.2
Income tax expense	9,000	3.3	3,000	1.4*
Other expense (income)	1,000	0.4	(1,000)	(0.4)
Total expenses	263,000	95.6	220,000	97.8
Net earnings	$ 12,000	4.4%	$ 5,000	2.2%

*Number rounded up.

USING RATIOS TO MAKE BUSINESS DECISIONS

Objective 5
Compute the standard financial ratios used for decision making

An important part of financial analysis is the calculation and interpretation of ratios. A ratio expresses the relationship of one number to another. For example, if the balance sheet shows current assets of $100,000 and current liabilities of $25,000, the ratio of current assets to current liabilities is $100,000 to $25,000. We can express this ratio as 4 to 1, or 4:1, or 4/1. Other ways to describe this ratio are (1) "current assets are 400% of current liabilities," (2) "the business has four dollars in current assets for every dollar of current liabilities," or, simply, (3) "the current ratio is 4.0." The last expression is most common.

We often reduce the ratio fraction by writing the ratio as one figure over the other—for example, 4/1—and then dividing the numerator by the denominator.

In this way, the ratio 4/1 may be expressed simply as 4. The 1 that represents the denominator of the fraction is understood, not written. Consider the ratio $175,000:$165,000. After dividing the first figure by the second, we come to 1.06:1, which we state as 1.06.

A manager, lender, or financial analyst may use any ratio that is relevant to a particular decision. Many companies include ratios in a special section of their annual financial reports. **Rubbermaid Incorporated**—the well-known manufacturer of plastic products—displays ratio data in the consolidated financial summary section of its annual report. Exhibit 13-10 shows an excerpt from that summary section. Investment services—**Moody's, Standard & Poor's, Robert Morris Associates,** and others—report these ratios for companies and industries.

EXHIBIT 13-10
Consolidated Financial Summary of Rubbermaid, Incorporated (dollar amounts in thousands except per-share amounts)

Years Ended December 31,	*19X8*	*19X7*	*19X6*	*19X5*
Operating Results				
Net earnings	$211,413	$164,095	$162,650	$143,520
Per common share	$1.32	$1.02	$1.02	$0.90
Percent of sales	10.8%	9.1%	9.8%	9.4%
Return on average shareholders' equity	20.0%	17.5%	19.7%	20.2%
Financial Position				
Current assets	$829,744	$699,650	$663,999	$602,697
Current liabilities	$259,314	$223,246	$245,500	$235,300
Working capital	$570,430	$476,404	$418,499	$367,397
Current ratio	3.20	3.13	2.70	2.56

The Decision Guidelines feature on pages 605–606 summarizes the widely used ratios that we will discuss in this chapter. The ratios may be classified as follows:

1. Ratios that measure the company's ability to pay current liabilities
2. Ratios that measure the company's ability to sell inventory and collect receivables
3. Ratios that measure the company's ability to pay long-term debt
4. Ratios that measure the company's profitability
5. Ratios used to analyze the company's stock as an investment

How much can a computer help in analyzing financial statements for investment purposes? Time yourself as you perform one of the financial-ratio problems in this chapter. Multiply your efforts by, say, 100 companies that you are comparing by means of this ratio. Now consider ranking these 100 companies on the basis of four or five additional ratios.

Online financial databases, such as **Lexis/Nexis** and the **Dow Jones News Retrieval Service,** offer quarterly financial figures for thousands of public corporations going back as far as 10 years. Assume that you want to compare companies' recent earnings histories. You might have the computer compare hundreds of companies on the basis of price/earnings ratio and rates of return on stockholders' equity and total assets. The computer could then give you the names of the 20 (or however many) companies that appear most favorable in terms of these ratios. Alternatively, you could have the computer download financial statement data to your spreadsheet and compute the ratios yourself.

Measuring a Company's Ability to Pay Current Liabilities

Working capital is defined as follows:

Working capital = Current assets − Current liabilities

(Text continues on page 606)

Decision Guidelines

Using Ratios in Financial Statement Analysis

Ratio	Computation	Information Provided
Measuring the company's ability to pay current liabilities:		
1. Current ratio	$\dfrac{\text{Current assets}}{\text{Current liabilities}}$	Measures ability to pay current liabilities with current assets.
2. Acid-test (quick) ratio	$\dfrac{\text{Cash} + \text{Short-term investments} + \text{Net current receivables}}{\text{Current liabilities}}$	Shows ability to pay all current liabilities if they come due immediately.
Measuring the company's ability to sell inventory and collect receivables:		
3. Inventory turnover	$\dfrac{\text{Cost of goods sold}}{\text{Average inventory}}$	Indicates saleability of inventory—the number of times a company sells its average inventory level during a year.
4. Accounts receivable turnover	$\dfrac{\text{Net credit sales}}{\text{Average net accounts receivable}}$	Measures ability to collect cash from credit customers.
5. Days' sales in receivables	$\dfrac{\text{Average net accounts receivable}}{\text{One day's sales}}$	Shows how many days' sales remain in Accounts Receivable—how many days it takes to collect the average level of receivables.
Measuring the company's ability to pay long-term debt:		
6. Debt ratio	$\dfrac{\text{Total liabilities}}{\text{Total assets}}$	Indicates percentage of assets financed with debt.
7. Times-interest-earned ratio	$\dfrac{\text{Income from operations}}{\text{Interest expense}}$	Measures the number of times operating income can cover interest expense.
Measuring the company's profitability:		
8. Rate of return on net sales	$\dfrac{\text{Net income}}{\text{Net sales}}$	Shows the percentage of each sales dollar earned as net income.
9. Rate of return on total assets	$\dfrac{\text{Net income} + \text{Interest expense}}{\text{Average total assets}}$	Measures how profitably a company uses its assets.
10. Rate of return on common stockholders' equity	$\dfrac{\text{Net income} - \text{Preferred dividends}}{\text{Average common stockholders' equity}}$	Gauges how much income is earned with the money invested by common shareholders.
11. Earnings per share of common stock	$\dfrac{\text{Net income} - \text{Preferred dividends}}{\text{Number of shares of common stock outstanding}}$	Gives the amount of net income per one share of the company's common stock.

(Continued)

Using Ratios in Financial Statement Analysis (cont.)

Ratio	Computation	Information Provided
Analyzing the company's stock as an investment:		
12. Price/earnings ratio	$\frac{\text{Market price per share of common stock}}{\text{Earnings per share}}$	Indicates the market price of $1 of earnings.
13. Dividend yield	$\frac{\text{Dividend per share of common (or preferred) stock}}{\text{Market price per share of common (or preferred) stock}}$	Shows the percentage of a stock's market value returned as dividends to stockholders each period.
14. Book value per share of common stock	$\frac{\text{Total stockholders' equity} - \text{Preferred equity}}{\text{Number of shares of common stock outstanding}}$	Indicates the recorded accounting amount for each share of common stock outstanding.

After covering these ratios in the section that follows, apply your new skills by working the Excel Application Problem on page 619.

Working capital is widely used to measure a business's ability to meet its short-term obligations with its current assets. In general, the larger the working capital, the better able is the business to pay its debts. Recall that capital, or owners' equity, is total assets minus total liabilities. Working capital is like a "current" version of total capital. The working-capital amount considered alone does not give a complete picture of the entity's working-capital position, however. Consider two companies with equal working capital:

	Company A	*Company B*
Current assets	$100,000	$200,000
Current liabilities	50,000	150,000
Working capital	$ 50,000	$ 50,000

Both companies have working capital of $50,000, but Company A's working capital is as large as its current liabilities. Company B's working capital is only one-third as large as its current liabilities. Which business has a better working-capital position? Company A, because its working capital is a higher percentage of current assets and current liabilities. To use working-capital data in decision making, it is helpful to develop ratios. Two decision-making tools based on working-capital data are the *current ratio* and the *acid-test ratio.*

We introduced the current ratio in Chapter 3 (page 138.)

Current Ratio. The most common ratio using current-asset and current-liability data is the **current ratio,** which is current assets divided by current liabilities. Recall the makeup of current assets and current liabilities. Inventory is converted to receivables through sales, the receivables are collected in cash, and the cash is used to buy inventory and pay current liabilities. A company's current assets and current liabilities represent the core of its day-to-day operations. The current ratio measures the company's ability to pay current assets with current liabilities.

Exhibit 13-11 gives the comparative income statement and balance sheet of Palisades Furniture, Inc. The current ratios of Palisades Furniture, Inc., at Decem-

EXHIBIT 13-11
Comparative Financial Statements

PALISADES FURNITURE, INC.
Comparative Income Statement
Years Ended December 31, 20X3 and 20X2

	20X3	*20X2*
Net sales	$858,000	$803,000
Cost of goods sold	513,000	509,000
Gross profit	345,000	294,000
Operating expenses:		
Selling expenses	126,000	114,000
General expenses	118,000	123,000
Total operating expenses	244,000	237,000
Income from operations	101,000	57,000
Interest revenue	4,000	—
Interest expense	24,000	14,000
Income before income taxes	81,000	43,000
Income tax expense	33,000	17,000
Net income	$ 48,000	$ 26,000

PALISADES FURNITURE, INC.
Comparative Balance Sheet
December 31, 20X3 and 20X2

	20X3	*20X2*
Assets		
Current Assets:		
Cash	$ 29,000	$ 32,000
Accounts receivable, net	114,000	85,000
Inventories	113,000	111,000
Prepaid expenses	6,000	8,000
Total current assets	262,000	236,000
Long-term investments	18,000	9,000
Property, plant, and equipment, net	507,000	399,000
Total assets	$787,000	$644,000
Liabilities		
Current liabilities:		
Notes payable	$ 42,000	$ 27,000
Accounts payable	73,000	68,000
Accrued liabilities	27,000	31,000
Total current liabilities	142,000	126,000
Long-term debt	289,000	198,000
Total liabilities	431,000	324,000
Stockholders' Equity		
Common stock, no par	186,000	186,000
Retained earnings	170,000	134,000
Total stockholders' equity	356,000	320,000
Total liabilities and stockholders' equity	$787,000	$644,000

ber 31, 20X3 and 20X2, follow, along with the average for the retail furniture industry:

Formula	*Palisades' Current Ratio* 20X3	*Palisades' Current Ratio* 20X2	*Industry Average*
Current ratio = $\frac{\text{Current assets}}{\text{Current liabilities}}$	$\frac{\$262{,}000}{\$142{,}000} = 1.85$	$\frac{\$236{,}000}{\$126{,}000} = 1.87$	1.70

CHECK POINT 13-5

The current ratio decreased slightly during 20X3. Lenders, stockholders, and managers closely monitor changes in a company's current ratio. In general, a higher current ratio indicates a stronger financial position. A higher current ratio suggests that the business has sufficient liquid assets to maintain normal business operations. Compare Palisades Furniture's current ratio of 1.85 with the industry average of 1.70 and with the current ratios of some well-known companies:

Company	*Current Ratio*
Chesebrough-Pond's Inc.	2.50
Wal-Mart Stores, Inc.	1.51
General Mills, Inc.	1.05

What is an acceptable current ratio? The answer depends on the nature of the industry. The norm for companies in most industries is between 1.60 and 1.90, as reported by Robert Morris Associates. Palisades Furniture's current ratio of 1.85 is within the range of those values. In most industries, a current ratio of 2.0 is considered good.

ACID-TEST RATIO. The **acid-test** (or **quick**) **ratio** tells us whether the entity could pay all its current liabilities if they came due immediately. That is, could the company pass this *acid test?* To do so, the company would have to convert its most liquid assets to cash.

→ We saw in Chapter 5 (page 235) that the higher the acid-test ratio, the better able is the business to pay its current liabilities.

To compute the acid-test ratio, we add cash, short-term investments, and net current receivables (accounts and notes receivable, net of allowances) and divide by current liabilities. Inventory and prepaid expenses are the two current assets *not* included in the acid-test computations because they are the least liquid of the current assets. A business may not be able to convert them to cash immediately to pay current liabilities. The acid-test ratio uses a narrower asset base to measure liquidity than the current ratio does.

Palisades Furniture's acid-test ratios for 20X3 and 20X2 follow:

Formula	*Palisades' Acid-Test Ratio* 20X3	*Palisades' Acid-Test Ratio* 20X2	*Industry Average*
Acid-test ratio = (Cash + short-term investments + net current receivables) / Current liabilities	(\$29,000 + \$0 + \$114,000) / \$142,000 = 1.01	(\$32,000 + \$0 + \$85,000) / \$126,000 = 0.93	0.40

The company's acid-test ratio improved considerably during 20X3 and is significantly better than the industry average. Compare Palisades' 1.01 acid-test ratio with the acid-test values of some well-known companies.

CHECK POINT 13-6

Company	*Acid-Test Ratio*
Chesebrough-Pond's Inc.	1.25
Wal-Mart Stores, Inc.	0.08
General Motors, Inc.	0.91

How can a leading company such as Wal-Mart function with so low an acid-test ratio? Wal-Mart has almost no receivables. Its inventory is priced low to turn over very quickly. The norm ranges from 0.20 for shoe retailers to 1.00 for manufacturers of paperboard containers and certain other equipment, as reported by Robert Morris Associates. An acid-test ratio of 0.90 to 1.00 is acceptable in most industries.

Palisades Furniture's current ratio is 1.85, which looks strong, while the company's acid-test ratio is 1.01, also strong. Suppose Palisades' acid-test ratio were dangerously low, say 0.48. What would be the most likely reason for the discrepancy between a high current ratio and a weak acid-test ratio?

Answer:
It would appear that the company is having difficulty selling its inventory. The level of inventory must be relatively high, and the inventory is propping up the current ratio. The rate of inventory turnover may be low. This prospect leads us into the next topic.

Measuring a Company's Ability to Sell Inventory and Collect Receivables

The ability to sell inventory and collect receivables is fundamental to business success. Recall the operating cycle of a merchandiser: cash to inventory to receivables and back to cash. ➛ In this section, we discuss three ratios that measure the company's ability to sell inventory and collect receivables.

➛ If you need to, refer to the discussion of the operating cycle in Chapter 3, page 133.

Inventory Turnover. Companies generally seek to achieve the quickest possible return on their investments, including their investments in inventory. The faster inventory sells, the sooner the business creates accounts receivable, and the sooner it collects cash.

Inventory turnover is a measure of the number of times a company sells its average level of inventory during a year. ➛ A high rate of turnover indicates relative ease in selling inventory; a low turnover indicates difficulty in selling. In general, companies prefer a high inventory turnover. A value of 6 means that the company's average level of inventory has been sold six times during the year. This is generally better than a turnover of 3 or 4. However, a high value can mean that the business is not keeping enough inventory on hand, and inadequate inventory can result in lost sales if the company cannot fill a customer's order. Therefore, a business strives for the most *profitable* rate of inventory turnover, not necessarily the *highest* rate.

➛ We introduced inventory turnover in Chapter 6, pages 275–276. Average inventory is computed as follows: (Beginning inventory + Ending inventory)/2.

To compute the inventory turnover ratio, we divide cost of goods sold by the average inventory for the period. We use the cost of goods sold—not sales—in the computation because both cost of goods sold and inventory are stated *at cost.* Sales are stated at the sales value of inventory and therefore are not comparable with inventory cost.

Palisades Furniture's inventory turnover for 20X3 is

Formula	*Palisades' Inventory Turnover*	*Industry Average*
$\text{Inventory turnover} = \dfrac{\text{Cost of goods sold}}{\text{Average inventory}}$	$\dfrac{\$513{,}000}{\$112{,}000} = 4.6$	3.0

Cost of goods sold appears in the income statement (Exhibit 13-11, page 607). Average inventory is figured by averaging the beginning inventory ($111,000) and ending inventory ($113,000). (See the balance sheet, Exhibit 13-11.) If inventory levels vary greatly from month to month, compute the average by adding the 12 monthly balances and dividing the sum by 12.

Inventory turnover varies widely with the nature of the business. For example, most manufacturers of farm machinery have an inventory turnover close to three times a year. In contrast, companies that remove natural gas from the ground hold their inventory for a very short period of time and have an average turnover of 30. Palisades Furniture's turnover of 4.6 times a year is high for its industry, which has an average turnover of 3.0. Palisades' high inventory turnover results from its policy of keeping little inventory on hand. The company takes customer orders and has its suppliers ship directly to some customers.

Inventory turnover rates can vary greatly within a company. At **Toys "Я" Us,** diapers and formula turn over more than 12 times a year, while seasonal toys turn over less than 3 times a year. The entire Toys "Я" Us inventory turns over an average of 3 times a year. The company's inventory is at its lowest point on January 31 and at its highest point around October 31.

To evaluate fully a company's inventory turnover, we must compare the ratio over time. A sharp decline in the rate of inventory turnover or a steady decline over a long period suggests the need for corrective action.

ACCOUNTS RECEIVABLE TURNOVER. Accounts receivable turnover measures a company's ability to collect cash from credit customers. In general, the higher the ratio, the more successfully the business collects cash and the better off its operations. However, a receivable turnover that is too high may indicate that credit is too tight, causing the loss of sales to good customers. To compute the accounts receivable turnover, we divide net credit sales by average net accounts receivable. The resulting ratio indicates how many times during the year the average level of receivables was turned into cash.

Palisades Furniture's accounts receivable turnover ratio for 20X3 is computed as follows:

Formula			*Palisades' Accounts Receivable Turnover*	*Industry Average*
Accounts receivable turnover	=	$\frac{\text{Net credit sales}}{\text{Average net accounts receivable}}$	$\frac{\$858{,}000}{\$99{,}500} = 8.6$	11.7

The net credit sales figure comes from the income statement. Palisades Furniture makes all sales on credit. If the company makes both cash and credit sales, this ratio is best computed by using only net credit sales. Average net accounts receivable is figured by adding the beginning accounts receivable balance ($85,000) and the ending balance ($114,000), then dividing by 2. If the accounts receivable balances exhibit a seasonal pattern, compute the average by using the 12 monthly balances.

Palisades' receivable turnover of 8.6 times per year is much lower than the industry average. The explanation is simple: Palisades is a hometown store that sells to local people who tend to pay their bills over a period of time. Many larger furniture stores sell their receivables to other companies called *factors,* a practice that keeps receivables low and receivable turnover high. But companies that factor (sell) their receivables receive less than face value of the receivables. Palisades Furniture follows a different strategy.

The sales of Comptronix, a manufacturer of computerized metering equipment, grew far faster than its receivables. Would this situation create an unusually high or an unusually low accounts receivable turnover?

Answer:
Receivable turnover would be unusually high. This high ratio would look strange in relation to the company's past measures of receivable turnover.

Days' Sales in Receivables. Businesses must convert accounts receivable to cash. All else equal, the lower the Accounts Receivable balance, the more successful the business has been in converting receivables into cash, and the better off the business is.

The **days'-sales-in-receivables** ratio tells us how many days' sales remain in Accounts Receivable. To compute the ratio, we follow a two-step process. *First,* divide net sales by 365 days to figure the average sales amount for one day. *Second,* divide this average day's sales amount into the average net accounts receivable.

Recall from Chapter 5 (pages 235–236) that days' sales in receivables indicates how many days it takes to collect the average level of receivables.

The data to compute this ratio for Palisades Furniture, Inc., for 20X3 are taken from the income statement and the balance sheet (Exhibit 13-11, page 607):

Formula	*Palisades' Days' Sales in Accounts Receivable*	*Industry Average*
Days' Sales in AVERAGE Accounts Receivable:		
1. One day's sales $= \frac{\text{Net sales}}{\text{365 days}}$	$\frac{\$858{,}000}{\text{365 days}} = \$2{,}351$	
2. Days' sales in average accounts receivable $= \frac{\text{Average net accounts receivable}}{\text{One day's sales}}$	$\frac{\$99{,}500}{\$2{,}351} = \text{42 days}$	12 days

Days' sales in average receivables can also be computed in a single step: \$99,500/(\$858,000/365 days) = 42 days.

Check Point 13-7

Palisades' ratio tells us that 42 average days' sales remain in accounts receivable and need to be collected. The company will increase its cash inflow if it can decrease this ratio. To detect any changes over time in the firm's ability to collect its receivables, let's compute the days'-sales-in-receivables ratio at the beginning and the end of 20X3:

Days' Sales in ENDING 20X2 Accounts Receivable:

$$\textbf{One day's sales} = \frac{\$803{,}000}{\text{365 days}} = \$2{,}200 \qquad \textbf{Days' sales in ENDING 20X2 accounts receivable} = \frac{\$85{,}000}{\$2{,}200} = \text{39 days at the beginning of 20X3}$$

Days' Sales in ENDING 20X3 Accounts Receivable:

$$\textbf{One day's sales} = \frac{\$858{,}000}{\text{365 days}} = \$2{,}351 \qquad \textbf{Days' sales in ENDING 20X3 accounts receivable} = \frac{\$114{,}000}{\$2{,}351} = \text{48 days at the end of 20X3}$$

This analysis shows a drop in Palisades Furniture's collection of receivables; days' sales in accounts receivable have increased from 39 at the beginning of the year to 48 at year end. The credit and collection department should strengthen its collection efforts. Otherwise, the company may experience a cash shortage in 20X4 and beyond.

The days' sales in receivables measure for Palisades is higher (worse) than the industry average because Palisades collects its own receivables. Many other furniture stores sell their receivables and carry fewer days' sales in receivables. Palisades Furniture remains competitive because of its personal relationship with its customers. Without their good paying habits, the company's cash flow would suffer.

Measuring a Company's Ability to Pay Long-Term Debt

The ratios discussed so far give us insight into current assets and current liabilities. They help us measure a business's ability to sell inventory, to collect receivables, and to pay current liabilities. Most businesses also have long-term debts. Bondholders and banks that loan money on long-term notes payable and bonds payable take special interest in the ability of a business to meet its long-term obligations. Two key indicators of a business's ability to pay long-term liabilities are the *debt ratio* and the *times-interest-earned ratio.*

DEBT RATIO. Suppose you are a loan officer at a bank and you are evaluating loan applications from two companies with equal sales revenue and total assets. Sales and total assets are the two most common measures of firm size. Both companies have asked to borrow $500,000 and have agreed to repay the loan over a 10-year period. The first firm already owes $600,000 to another bank. The second owes only $250,000. Other things equal, to which company are you more likely to lend money at a lower interest rate? Company 2, because the bank faces less risk by loaning to Company 2. That company owes less to creditors than Company 1 owes.

This relationship between total liabilities and total assets—called the **debt ratio**—tells us the proportion of the company's assets that it has financed with debt. If the debt ratio is 1, then debt has been used to finance all the assets. A debt ratio of 0.50 means that the company has used debt to finance half its assets and that the owners of the business have financed the other half. The higher the debt ratio, the higher the strain of paying interest each year and the principal amount at maturity. The lower the ratio, the lower the business's future obligations. Creditors view a high debt ratio with caution. If a business seeking financing already has large liabilities, then additional debt payments may be too much for the business to handle. To help protect themselves, creditors generally charge higher interest rates on new borrowing to companies with an already-high debt ratio.

We introduced the debt ratio in Chapter 3, page 138.

Calculation of the debt ratios for Palisades Furniture at the end of 20X3 and 20X2 is as follows:

Formula	Palisades' Debt Ratio 20X3	Palisades' Debt Ratio 20X2	Industry Average
$\text{Debt ratio} = \frac{\text{Total liabilities}}{\text{Total assets}}$	$\frac{\$431{,}000}{\$787{,}000} = 0.55$	$\frac{\$324{,}000}{\$644{,}000} = 0.50$	0.64

Palisades Furniture expanded operations by financing the purchase of property, plant, and equipment through borrowing, which is a common practice. This expansion explains the firm's increased debt ratio. Even after the increase in 20X3, the company's debt is not very high. Robert Morris Associates reports that the average debt ratio for most companies ranges around 0.57–0.67, with relatively little variation from company to company. Palisades' 0.55 debt ratio indicates a fairly low-risk debt position compared to the retail furniture industry average of 0.64.

TIMES-INTEREST-EARNED RATIO. The debt ratio measures the effect of debt on the company's *financial position* (balance sheet) but says nothing about its ability to pay interest expense. Analysts use a second ratio—the **times-interest-earned ratio**—to relate income to interest expense. To compute this ratio, we divide income from operations by interest expense. This ratio measures the number of times that operating income can *cover* interest expense. For this reason, the ratio is also called the *interest-coverage ratio.* A high times-interest-earned ratio indicates ease in paying interest expense; a low value suggests difficulty.

Calculation of Palisades' times-interest-earned ratios is as follows:

Formula			Palisades' Times-Interest-Earned Ratio 20X3		Palisades' Times-Interest-Earned Ratio 20X2		Industry Average
Times-interest-earned ratio	=	Income from operations / Interest expense	$101,000 / $24,000	= 4.21	$57,000 / $14,000	= 4.07	2.30

The company's times-interest-earned ratio increased in 20X3. This is a favorable sign, especially because the company's short-term notes payable and long-term debt rose substantially during the year. Palisades Furniture's new plant assets, we conclude, have earned more in operating income than they have cost the business in interest expense.

The company's times-interest-earned ratio of around 4.00 is significantly better than the 2.30 average for furniture retailers. The norm for U.S. business, as reported by Robert Morris Associates, falls in the range of 2.0 to 3.0 for most companies. On the basis of its debt ratio and its times-interest-earned ratio, Palisades Furniture appears to have little difficulty *servicing its debt*—that is, paying its liabilities.

CHECK POINT 13-8

Measuring a Company's Profitability

The fundamental goal of business is to earn a profit. Ratios that measure profitability play a large role in decision making. These ratios are reported in the business press, by investment services, and in companies' annual financial reports.

Suppose you are a personal financial planner who helps clients select stock investments. One client has $100,000 to invest in a chemical company. Over the next few years, you expect **Dow Chemical** to earn higher rates of return on its investments than analysts are forecasting for **Monsanto,** a competing company. Which company's stock will you recommend? Probably Dow's—for reasons that you will better understand after studying four rate-of-return measurements.

RATE OF RETURN ON NET SALES. In business, the term *return* is used broadly and loosely as an evaluation of profitability. Consider a ratio called the **rate of return on net sales,** or simply *return on sales.* (The word *net* is usually omitted for convenience, even though the net sales figure is used to compute the ratio.) This ratio shows the percentage of each sales dollar earned as net income. The rate-of-return-on-sales ratios for Palisades Furniture are calculated as follows:

Formula			Palisades' Rate of Return on Sales 20X3		Palisades' Rate of Return on Sales 20X2		Industry Average
Rate of return on sales	=	Net income / Net sales	$48,000 / $858,000	= 0.056	$26,000 / $803,000	= 0.032	0.008

Companies strive for a high rate of return. The higher the rate of return, the more net sales dollars are providing income to the business and the fewer net sales dollars are absorbed by expenses. The increase in Palisades Furniture's return on sales is significant and identifies the company as more successful than the average furniture store. Compare Palisades' rate of return on sales to the rates of some other companies:

Company	Rate of Return on Sales
General Motors	0.054
Kraft, Inc.	0.047
Wal-Mart Stores, Inc.	0.036

One strategy for increasing the rate of return on sales is to develop a product that commands a premium price, such as **Häagen-Dazs** ice cream, **Sony** products, and **Maytag** appliances. Another strategy is to control costs. If successful, either strategy converts a higher proportion of sales into net income and increases the rate of return on net sales.

A return measure can be computed on any revenue or sales amount. Return on net sales, as we have seen, is net income divided by net sales. *Return on total revenues* is net income divided by total revenues. A company can compute a return on other specific portions of revenue as its information needs dictate.

We first discussed the rate of return on total assets in Chapter 9, page 431.

RATE OF RETURN ON TOTAL ASSETS. The **rate of return on total assets,** or simply *return on assets,* measures a company's success in using its assets to earn a profit. Creditors have loaned money to the company, and the interest they receive is the return on their investment. Shareholders have invested in the company's stock, and net income is their return. The sum of interest expense and net income is thus the return to the two groups that have financed the company's operations, and this amount is the numerator of the return-on-assets ratio. Average total assets is the denominator. Computation of the return-on-assets ratio for Palisades Furniture is as follows:

Formula	Palisades' 20X3 Rate of Return on Total Assets	Industry Average
Rate of return on assets $= \dfrac{\text{Net income} + \text{Interest expense}}{\text{Average total assets}}$	$\dfrac{\$48{,}000 + \$24{,}000}{\$715{,}500} = 0.101$	0.042

Net income and interest expense are taken from the income statement (Exhibit 13-11, page 607). To compute average total assets, we take the average of beginning and ending total assets from the comparative balance sheet. Compare Palisades Furniture's rate of return on assets to the rates of some other companies:

Company	Rate of Return on Assets
The Gap, Inc.	0.170
Wal-Mart Stores, Inc.	0.129
General Mills, Inc.	0.124

We examined this ratio in detail in Chapter 9. For a review, see page 432.

RATE OF RETURN ON COMMON STOCKHOLDERS' EQUITY. A popular measure of profitability is **rate of return on common stockholders' equity,** which is often shortened to **return on stockholders' equity,** or simply *return on equity.* This ratio shows the relationship between net income and common stockholders' investment in the company—how much income is earned for every $1 invested by the common shareholders. To compute this ratio, we first subtract preferred dividends from net income. This calculation provides net income available to the common stockholders, which we need to compute the ratio. We then divide net income available to common stockholders by the average stockholders' equity during the year. Common stockholders' equity is total stockholders' equity minus preferred equity. The 20X3 rate of return on common stockholders' equity for Palisades Furniture is calculated as follows:

Formula	Palisades' 20X3 Rate of Return on Common Stockholders' Equity	Industry Average
$\text{Rate of return on common stockholders' equity} = \dfrac{\text{Net income} - \text{Preferred dividends}}{\text{Average common stockholders' equity}}$	$\dfrac{\$48{,}000 - \$0}{\$338{,}000} = 0.142$	0.121

We compute average equity by using the beginning and ending balances [($356,000 + $320,000)/2 = $338,000]. Common stockholders' equity is total equity minus preferred equity.

Observe that Palisades' return on equity (0.142) is higher than its return on assets (0.101). This difference results from borrowing at one rate—say, 0.08, or 8%—and investing the funds to earn a higher rate, such as the firm's 0.142, or 14.2%, return on stockholders' equity. This practice is called **trading on the equity,** or using **leverage.** ➛ It is directly related to the debt ratio. The higher the debt ratio, the higher the leverage. Companies that finance operations with debt are said to *leverage* their positions.

➛ For a review of trading on the equity, see Chapter 8, page 381.

For Palisades Furniture and for many other companies, leverage increases profitability. This is not always the case, however. Leverage can have a negative impact on profitability. If revenues drop, debt and interest expense still must be paid. Therefore, leverage is a double-edged sword, increasing profits during good times but compounding losses during bad times.

Compare Palisades Furniture's rate of return on common stockholders' equity with the rates of some leading companies:

Company	*Rate of Return on Common Equity*
Wal-Mart Stores, Inc.	0.25
Chesebrough-Pond's Inc.	0.20
General Motors	0.20

CHECK POINT 13-9

Palisades Furniture is not as profitable as these leading companies—perhaps because the larger companies must satisfy millions of stockholders worldwide. Palisades Furniture, on the other hand, is a much smaller company with stockholders who do not demand so high a return on their equity.

EARNINGS PER SHARE OF COMMON STOCK. *Earnings per share of common stock,* or simply **earnings per share (EPS),** is perhaps the most widely quoted of all financial statistics. EPS is the only ratio that must appear on the face of the income statement. EPS is the amount of net income per share of the company's outstanding *common* stock. Earnings per share is computed by dividing net income available to common stockholders by the number of common shares outstanding during the year. Preferred dividends are subtracted from net income because the preferred stockholders have a prior claim to their dividends. Palisades Furniture, Inc., has no preferred stock outstanding and thus has no preferred dividends. Computation of the firm's EPS for 20X3 and 20X2 follows (the company had 10,000 shares of common stock outstanding throughout 20X2 and 20X3):

Formula	Palisades' Earnings per Share 20X3	20X2
Earnings per share of common stock = $\dfrac{\text{Net income} - \text{Preferred dividends}}{\text{Number of shares of common stock outstanding}}$	$\dfrac{\$48{,}000 - \$0}{\$10{,}000} = \$4.80$	$\dfrac{\$26{,}000 - \$0}{10{,}000} = \$2.60$

Palisades Furniture's EPS increased 85%. Its stockholders should not expect such a significant boost in EPS every year. Most companies strive to increase EPS by 10–15% annually, and the more successful companies do so. But even the most dramatic upward trends include an occasional bad year.

Analyzing a Company's Stock as an Investment

Investors purchase stock to earn a return on their investment. This return consists of two parts: (1) gains (or losses) from selling the stock at a price that differs from the investors' purchase price, and (2) dividends, the periodic distributions to stockholders. The ratios we examine in this section help analysts evaluate stock in terms of market price or dividend payments.

PRICE/EARNINGS RATIO. The **price/earnings ratio** is the ratio of the market price of a share of common stock to the company's earnings per share. This ratio, abbreviated P/E, appears in the *Wall Street Journal* stock listings. P/E ratios play an important part in decisions to buy, hold, and sell stocks. They indicate the market price of $1 of earnings.

Calculations for the P/E ratios of Palisades Furniture, Inc., follow. The market price of its common stock was $50 at the end of 20X3 and $35 at the end of 20X2. These prices can be obtained from a financial publication, a stockbroker, or the company's Web site.

Formula	Palisades' Price/Earnings Ratio 20X3	20X2
P/E ratio = $\dfrac{\text{Market price per share of common stock}}{\text{Earnings per share}}$	$\dfrac{\$50.00}{\$4.80} = 10.4$	$\dfrac{\$35.00}{\$2.60} = 13.5$

Given Palisades Furniture's 20X3 P/E ratio of 10.4, we would say that the company's stock is selling at 10.4 times earnings. The decline from the 20X2 P/E ratio of 13.5 is not a cause for alarm because the market price of the stock is not under Palisades Furniture's control. Net income is more controllable, and it increased during 20X3. Like most other ratios, P/E ratios vary from industry to industry. P/E ratios range from 8 to 10 for electric utilities (**Pennsylvania Power and Light,** for example) to 40 or more for "glamour stocks" such as **Auto Zone,** an auto parts chain, and **Oracle Systems,** which develops computer software. The P/E ratios of many Internet stocks reach into the hundreds.

CHECK POINT 13-10

The higher a stock's P/E ratio the higher its *downside risk*—the risk that the stock's market price will fall. Many investors interpret a sharp increase in a stock's P/E ratio as a signal to sell the stock.

DIVIDEND YIELD. Dividend yield is the ratio of dividends per share of stock to the stock's market price per share. This ratio measures the percentage of a stock's market value that is returned annually as dividends, an important concern of stockholders. *Preferred* stockholders, who invest primarily to receive dividends, pay special attention to this ratio.

Palisades Furniture paid annual cash dividends of $1.20 per share of common stock in 20X3 and $1.00 in 20X2, and market prices of the company's common stock were $50 in 20X3 and $35 in 20X2. Calculation of the firm's dividend yields on common stock is as follows:

Formula		Dividend Yield on Palisades' Common Stock 20X3	Dividend Yield on Palisades' Common Stock 20X2
Dividend yield on common stock*	$= \dfrac{\text{Dividend per share of common stock}}{\text{Market price per share of common stock}}$	$\dfrac{\$1.20}{\$50.00} = 0.024$	$\dfrac{\$1.00}{\$35.00} = 0.029$

*Dividend yields may also be calculated for preferred stock.

An investor who buys Palisades Furniture common stock for $50 can expect to receive almost $2\frac{1}{2}\%$ of the investment annually in the form of cash dividends. Dividend yields vary widely, from 5% to 8% for older, established firms (such as **Procter & Gamble** and **General Motors**) down to the range of 0–3% for young, growth-oriented companies. Palisades Furniture's dividend yield places the company in the second group.

BOOK VALUE PER SHARE OF COMMON STOCK. Book value per share of common stock is simply common stockholders' equity divided by the number of shares of common stock outstanding. Common shareholders' equity equals total stockholders' equity less preferred equity. Palisades Furniture has no preferred stock outstanding. Calculations of its book-value-per-share-of-common-stock ratios follow. Recall that 10,000 shares of common stock were outstanding at the end of years 20X3 and 20X2.

Formula		Book Value per Share of Palisades' Common Stock 20X3	Book Value per Share of Palisades' Common Stock 20X2
Book value per share of common stock	$= \dfrac{\text{Total stockholders' equity} - \text{Preferred equity}}{\text{Number of shares of common stock outstanding}}$	$\dfrac{\$356{,}000 - \$0}{10{,}000} = \$35.60$	$\dfrac{\$320{,}000 - \$0}{10{,}000} = \$32.00$

Book value indicates the recorded accounting amount for each share of common stock outstanding. Many experts argue that book value is not useful for investment analysis. ➠ It bears no relationship to market value and provides little information beyond stockholders' equity reported on the balance sheet. But some investors base their investment decisions on book value. For example, some investors rank stocks on the basis of the ratio of market price to book value. To these investors, the lower the ratio, the more attractive the stock. These investors are called "value" investors, as contrasted with "growth" investors, who focus more on trends in a company's net income.

← Recall from Chapter 9, pages 429–430, that book value depends on historical costs, while market value depends on investors' outlook for dividends and an increase in the stock's value.

LIMITATIONS OF FINANCIAL ANALYSIS: THE COMPLEXITY OF BUSINESS DECISIONS

Objective 6
Use ratios in decision making

Business decisions are made in a world of uncertainty. As useful as ratios are, they have limitations. We may liken their use in decision making to a physician's use of

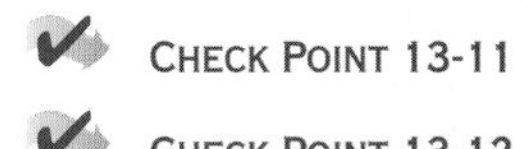

CHECK POINT 13-11

CHECK POINT 13-12

a thermometer. A reading of 101.6° Fahrenheit indicates that something is wrong with the patient, but the temperature alone does not indicate what the problem is or how to cure it.

In financial analysis, a sudden drop in a company's current ratio signals that *something* is wrong, but this change does not identify the problem or show how to correct it. The business manager must analyze the figures that go into the ratio to determine whether current assets have decreased, current liabilities have increased, or both. If current assets have dropped, is the problem a cash shortage? Are accounts receivable down? Are inventories too low? Only by analyzing the individual items that make up the ratio can the manager determine how to solve the problem. The manager must evaluate data on all ratios in the light of other information about the company and about its particular line of business, such as increased competition or a slowdown in the economy.

Legislation, international affairs, competition, scandals, and many other factors can turn profits into losses, and vice versa. To be most useful, ratios should be analyzed over a period of years to take into account a representative group of these factors. Any one year, or even any two years, may not be representative of the company's performance over the long term.

Economic Value Added—A New Measure of Performance

Objective 7
Measure economic value added by a company's operations

The top managers of **Coca-Cola, Quaker Oats,** and other leading companies use **economic value added (EVA®)** to evaluate a company's operating performance. EVA® combines the concepts of accounting income and corporate finance to measure whether the company's operations have increased stockholder wealth. EVA® can be computed as follows:

$$\textbf{EVA}^{\circledR} = \textbf{Net income} + \textbf{Interest expense} - \textbf{Capital charge}$$

where

$$\textbf{Capital charge} = \left(\begin{array}{c}\textbf{Notes}\\ \textbf{payable}\end{array} + \begin{array}{c}\textbf{Loans}\\ \textbf{payable}\end{array} + \begin{array}{c}\textbf{Long-term}\\ \textbf{debt}\end{array} + \begin{array}{c}\textbf{Stockholders'}\\ \textbf{equity}\end{array}\right) \times \begin{array}{c}\textbf{Cost of}\\ \textbf{capital}\end{array}$$

All amounts for the EVA® computation, except the cost of capital, are taken from the financial statements. The **cost of capital** is a weighted average of the returns demanded by the company's stockholders and lenders. The cost of capital varies with the company's level of risk. For example, stockholders would demand a higher return from a start-up computer software company than from Coca-Cola because the new company is untested and therefore more risky. Lenders would also charge the new company a higher interest rate because of this greater risk. Thus, the new company has a higher cost of capital than Coca-Cola. The cost of capital is a major topic in finance classes. In the following discussions we assume a value for the cost of capital (such as 10%, 12%, or 15%) to illustrate the computation of EVA® and its use in decision making.

The idea behind EVA® is that the returns to the company's stockholders (net income) and to its creditors (interest expense) should exceed the company's capital charge. The **capital charge** is the amount that stockholders and lenders *charge* a company for the use of their money. A positive EVA® amount indicates an increase in stockholder wealth, and the company's stock should remain attractive to investors. If the EVA® measure is negative, the stockholders will probably be unhappy with the company's progress and sell its stock, resulting in a decrease in the stock's price. Different companies tailor the EVA® computation to meet their own needs.

The Coca-Cola Company is a leading user of EVA®. Coca-Cola's EVA® for 1998 can be computed as follows, assuming a 12% cost of capital for the company (dollar amounts in millions):

$$\text{Coca-Cola's EVA}^{\circledR} = \text{Net income} + \text{Interest expense} - \left[\left(\text{Loans and notes payable} + \text{Long-term debt} + \text{Stockholders' equity}\right) \times \text{Cost of capital}\right]$$

$$= \$2{,}986 + \$272 - [(\$2{,}371 + \$1{,}141 + \$5{,}392) \times 0.12]$$

$$= \$3{,}258 - \$8{,}904 \times 0.12$$

$$= \$3{,}258 - \$1{,}068$$

$$= \$2{,}190$$

By this measure, Coca-Cola's operations during 1998 added $2.19 billion ($2,190 million) of value to its stockholders' wealth after meeting the company's capital charge. This performance is outstanding. Coca-Cola's positive EVA® measures explain why the company's stock price increased an average of 29% per year over the 10-year period from 1988 to 1998. A $100 investment in Coca-Cola stock in 1988 had grown to a value of $1,287 in 1998.

EFFICIENT MARKETS, MANAGEMENT ACTION, AND INVESTOR DECISIONS

An **efficient capital market** is one in which market prices fully reflect all information available to the public. Because stocks are priced in full recognition of all publicly accessible data, it can be argued that the stock market is efficient. Market efficiency has implications for management action and for investor decisions. It

(Please read all of the text material on this page and the next before doing this problem.)

EXCEL APPLICATION PROBLEM

This Excel Application Problem completes the Decision Guidelines, pages 605–606, which give the formulas for some of the ratios used in financial statement analysis.

Goal: Create an Excel spreadsheet that calculates financial ratios to compare The Gap and Lands' End. Then use the results to determine which company has the stronger financial performance.

Scenario: You've recently received a $1,000 bonus from your employer, The Gap. You've been thinking about investing the bonus in the stock of your employer, but your parents think the better investment would be Lands' End stock. Before making your purchase, you decide to create an Excel spreadsheet that compares both companies on several key financial ratios.

Your task is to create an Excel spreadsheet to compare the following ratios for The Gap and Lands' End:

1. Acid-test (quick) ratio
2. Inventory turnover
3. Times-interest-earned ratio
4. Return on net sales
5. Price/earnings ratio

When done with the spreadsheet, answer the following questions:

1. Which company is in a better position to pay all current liabilities if they come due immediately?
2. Which company moves its inventory faster?
3. Which company can cover its interest expense better?
4. Which company earned more profit, as a percentage, on each sales dollar?
5. Which company's earnings have a higher market price per dollar of earnings?

Step-by-step:

1. Locate the data required for each ratio in the annual reports of The Gap and Lands' End. These reports may be accessed via the Web.
2. Open a new Excel spreadsheet.
3. Create a bold-faced heading for your spreadsheet that contains the following:
   a. Chapter 13 Decision Guidelines
   b. Using Ratios in Financial Statement Analysis
   c. The Gap and Lands' End Comparison
   d. Today's date
4. In the first column, enter the names of all five ratios. Skip a row between each ratio name.
5. Create bold-faced, underlined column headings for The Gap and Lands' End.
6. Enter the data located in step 1, using the correct ratio formulas found in the Decision Guidelines. Format all cells as necessary.
7. Save your work, and print a copy for your files.

means that managers cannot fool the market with accounting gimmicks. If the information is available, the market as a whole can translate accounting data into a "fair" price for the company's stock.

Suppose you are the president of Anacomp Company. Reported earnings per share are $4, and the stock price is $40—so the P/E ratio is 10. You believe the corporation's stock is underpriced in comparison with other companies in the same industry. To correct this situation, you are considering changing your depreciation method from accelerated to straight-line. The accounting change will increase earnings per share to $5. Will the stock price then rise to $50? Probably not. The company's stock price will probably remain at $40 because the market can understand the accounting change. After all, the company merely changed its method of computing depreciation. There is no effect on the company's cash flows, and its economic position is unchanged. An efficient market interprets data in light of their true underlying meaning.

In an efficient market, the search for "underpriced" stock is fruitless unless the investor has relevant private information. Moreover, it is unlawful to invest on the basis of *inside* information. For outside investors, an appropriate strategy seeks to manage risk, diversify, and minimize transaction costs. The role of financial statement analysis consists mainly of identifying the risks of various stocks to manage the risk of the overall investment portfolio.

The Excel Application Problem provides an opportunity to apply your understanding of the ratios by writing an Excel spreadsheet.

End-of-Chapter

Summary Problem for Your Review

The following financial data are adapted from the annual report of **The Gap, Inc.**, which operates The Gap, Banana Republic, and Old Navy clothing stores:

THE GAP, INC.
Five-Year Selected Financial Data

*Operating Results**	*19X8*	*19X7*	*19X6*	*19X5*	*19X4*
Net sales	$2,960	$2,519	$1,934	$1,587	$1,252
Cost of goods sold and occupancy expenses excluding depreciation and amortization	1,856	1,496	1,188	1,007	814
Interest expense (net)	4	4	1	3	3
Income from operations	340	371	237	163	126
Income taxes	129	141	92	65	52
Net earnings	211	230	145	98	74
Cash dividends	44	41	30	23	18
Financial Position					
Merchandise inventory	366	314	247	243	193
Total assets	1,379	1,147	777	579	481
Working capital	355	236	579	129	434
Current ratio	2.06:1	1.71:1	1.39:1	1.69:1	1.70:1
Stockholders' equity	888	678	466	338	276
Average number of shares of common stock outstanding (in thousands)	144	142	142	141	145

*(Dollar amounts in thousands)

Required

Compute the following ratios for 19X5 through 19X8, and evaluate The Gap's operating results. Are operating results strong or weak? Did they improve or deteriorate during the four-year period?

1. Gross profit percentage
2. Net income as a percentage of sales
3. Earnings per share
4. Inventory turnover
5. Times-interest-earned ratio
6. Rate of return on stockholders' equity

Answers

Requirement	*19X8*	*19X7*	*19X6*	*19X5*
1. Gross profit percentage	$\frac{\$2,960 - \$1,856}{\$2,960}$ = 37.3%	$\frac{\$2,519 - \$1,496}{\$2,519}$ = 40.6%	$\frac{\$1,934 - \$1,188}{\$1,934}$ = 38.6%	$\frac{\$1,587 - \$1,007}{\$1,587}$ = 36.5%
2. Net income as a percentage of sales	$\frac{\$211}{\$2,960}$ = 7.1%	$\frac{\$230}{\$2,519}$ = 9.1%	$\frac{\$145}{\$1,934}$ = 7.5%	$\frac{\$98}{\$1,587}$ = 6.2%
3. Earnings per share	$\frac{\$211}{144}$ = \$1.47	$\frac{\$230}{142}$ = \$1.62	$\frac{\$145}{142}$ = \$1.02	$\frac{\$98}{141}$ = \$0.70
4. Inventory turnover	$\frac{\$1,856}{(\$366 + \$314)/2}$ = 5.5 times	$\frac{\$1,496}{(\$314 + \$247)/2}$ = 5.3 times	$\frac{\$1,188}{(\$247 + \$243)/2}$ = 4.8 times	$\frac{\$1,007}{(\$243 + \$193)/2}$ = 4.6 times
5. Times-interest-earned ratio	$\frac{\$340}{\$4}$ = 85 times	$\frac{\$371}{\$4}$ = 93 times	$\frac{\$237}{\$1}$ = 237 times	$\frac{\$163}{\$3}$ = 54 times
6. Rate of return on stockholders' equity	$\frac{\$211}{(\$888 + \$678)/2}$ = 26.9%	$\frac{\$230}{(\$678 + \$466)/2}$ = 40.2%	$\frac{\$145}{(\$466 + \$338)/2}$ = 36.1%	$\frac{\$98}{(\$338 + \$276)/2}$ = 31.9%

Evaluation: During this four-year period, The Gap's operating results were outstanding. Operating results improved, with all ratio values but return on stockholders' equity higher in 19X8 than in 19X5. Moreover, all the performance measures indicate high levels of income and return to investors.

Summary of Learning Objectives

1. ***Perform a horizontal analysis of comparative financial statements.*** *Horizontal analysis* is the study of percentage changes in financial statement items from one period to the next. To compute these percentage changes, (1) calculate the dollar amount of the change from the base (earlier) period to the later period, and (2) divide the dollar amount of change by the base-period amount. *Trend percentages* are a form of horizontal analysis.

2. ***Perform a vertical analysis of financial statements.*** *Vertical analysis* of a financial statement reveals the relationship of each statement item to a specified base, which is the 100% figure. In an income statement, net sales is usually the base. On a balance sheet, the base is the total assets figure.

3. ***Prepare and use common-size financial statements.*** A form of vertical analysis, *common-size statements* report only percentages, no dollar amounts. Common-size statements ease the comparison of different companies and may signal the need for corrective action. *Benchmarking* is the practice of comparing a company to a standard set by other companies, with a view toward improvement.

4. ***Use the statement of cash flows in decision making.*** Analysts use cash-flow analysis to identify danger signals about a company's financial situation. The most important information provided by the cash-flow statement is the net cash flow from operating activities.

5. ***Compute the standard financial ratios used for decision making.*** A ratio expresses the relationship of one item to

another. The most important financial ratios measure a company's ability to pay current liabilities (current ratio, acid-test ratio); ability to sell inventory and collect receivables (inventory turnover, accounts receivable turnover, days' sales in receivables); ability to pay long-term debt (debt ratio, times-interest-earned ratio); profitability (rate of return on net sales, rate of return on total assets, rate of return on common stockholders' equity, earnings per share of common stock); and its value as an investment (price/earnings ratio, dividend yield, book value per share of common stock).

6. ***Use ratios in decision making.*** Analysis of financial ratios over time is an important way to track a company's progress. A change in one of the ratios over time may reveal a problem. It is up to the company's managers to find the source of this problem and take actions to correct it.

7. ***Measure economic value added by a company's operations.*** *Economic value added (EVA)* measures whether a company's operations have increased its stockholders' wealth. EVA can be defined as the excess of net income and interest expense over the company's capital charge, which is the amount that the company's stockholders and lenders charge for the use of their money. A positive amount of EVA indicates an increase in stockholder wealth; a negative amount indicates a decrease.

Accounting Vocabulary

accounts receivable turnover (p. 610).
acid-test ratio (p. 608).
benchmarking (p. 598).
book value per share of common stock (p. 617).
capital charge (p. 618).
common-size statement (p. 598).
cost of capital (p. 618).
current ratio (p. 606).
days' sales in receivables (p. 611).
debt ratio (p. 612).
dividend yield (p. 616).
earnings per share (EPS) (p. 615).
economic value added (EVA) (p. 618).
efficient capital market (p. 619).
horizontal analysis (p. 593).
inventory turnover (p. 609).
leverage (p. 615).
price/earnings ratio (p. 616).
quick ratio (p. 608).
rate of return on common stockholders' equity (p. 614).
rate of return on net sales (p. 613).
rate of return on total assets (p. 614).
return on stockholders' equity (p. 614).
times-interest-earned ratio (p. 612).
trading on the equity (p. 615).
vertical analysis (p. 596).
working capital (p. 604).

Questions

1. Name the three broad categories of analytical tools that are based on accounting information.
2. Briefly describe horizontal analysis. How do decision makers use this analytical tool?
3. What is vertical analysis, and what is its purpose?
4. What is the purpose of common-size statements?
5. State how an investor might analyze the statement of cash flows. How might the investor analyze investing-activities data?
6. Identify two ratios used to measure the ability to pay current liabilities. Show how they are computed.
7. Why is the acid-test ratio given that name?
8. What does the inventory turnover ratio measure?
9. Suppose the days'-sales-in-receivables ratio of Gomez, Inc., increased from 36 at January 1 to 43 at December 31. Is this a good sign or a bad sign? What might Gomez management do in response to this change?
10. Company A's debt ratio has increased from 0.50 to 0.70. Identify a decision maker to whom this increase is important, and state how the increase affects this party's decisions about the company.
11. Which ratio measures the *effect of debt* on (a) financial position (the balance sheet) and (b) the company's ability to pay interest expense (the income statement)?
12. Company A is a chain of grocery stores, and Company B is a computer manufacturer. Which company is likely to have the higher (a) current ratio, (b) inventory turnover, and (c) rate of return on sales? Give your reasons.
13. Identify four ratios used to measure a company's profitability. Show how to compute these ratios and state what information each ratio provides.
14. The price/earnings ratio of **General Motors** was 6, and the price/earnings ratio of **American Express** was 45. Which company did the stock market favor? Explain.
15. **McDonald's Corporation** paid cash dividends of $0.20 per share when the market price of the company's stock was $40.875. What was the dividend yield on McDonald's stock? What does dividend yield measure?
16. Hold all other factors constant and indicate whether each of the following situations generally signals good or bad news about a company:
    a. Increase in current ratio
    b. Decrease in inventory turnover
    c. Increase in debt ratio
    d. Decrease in interest-coverage ratio
    e. Increase in return on sales
    f. Decrease in earnings per share
    g. Increase in price/earnings ratio
    h. Increase in book value per share
17. What is EVA, and how is it used in financial analysis?

CP13-1 **Nike, Inc.**, reported the following amounts on its 19X6 comparative income statement:

Horizontal analysis of revenues and gross profit (Obj. 1)

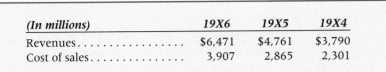

(In millions)	*19X6*	*19X5*	*19X4*
Revenues	$6,471	$4,761	$3,790
Cost of sales	3,907	2,865	2,301

Perform a horizontal analysis of revenues and gross profit—both in dollar amounts and in percentages—for 19X6 and 19X5.

CP13-2 Nike, Inc., reported the following revenues and net income amounts:

Trend analysis of revenues and net income (Obj. 1)

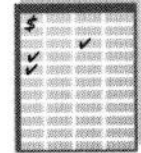

(In millions)	*19X6*	*19X5*	*19X4*	*19X3*	*19X2*	*19X1*
Revenues	$6,471	$4,761	$3,790	$3,930	$3,405	$3,004
Net income	553	400	299	365	329	287

1. Show Nike's trend percentages for revenues and net income. Start with 19X1 as the base year.
2. Which trend looks better—revenues or net income?

CP13-3 T-Shaft Sporting Goods reported the following amounts on its balance sheets at December 31, 20X2, 20X1, and 20X0:

Vertical analysis to correct a cash shortage (Obj. 2)

	20X2	*20X1*	*20X0*
Cash	$ 6,000	$ 6,000	$ 5,000
Receivables, net	46,000	32,000	19,000
Inventory	32,000	26,000	24,000
Prepaid expenses	2,000	2,000	1,000
Property, plant, and equipment, net	96,000	88,000	87,000
Total assets	$182,000	$154,000	$136,000

1. Sales and profits are high. Nevertheless, the company is experiencing a cash shortage. Perform a vertical analysis of T-Shaft's assets at the end of years 20X2, 20X1, and 20X0. Use the analysis to explain the reason for the cash shortage.
2. Suggest a way for T-Shaft to generate more cash.

CP13-4 **Nike, Inc.**, and **The Home Depot** are leaders in their respective industries. Compare the two companies by converting their income statements (adapted) to common size.

Common-size income statements of two leading companies (Obj. 3)

(In millions)	*Nike*	*Home Depot*
Net sales	$6,471	$19,536
Cost of goods sold	3,907	14,101
Selling and administrative expenses	1,589	3,846
Interest expense	39	16
Other expense	37	38
Income tax expense	346	597
Net income	$ 553	$ 938

Which company earns more net income? Which company's net income is a higher percentage of its net sales? Which company is more profitable? Explain your answer.

Evaluating the trend in a company's current ratio (Obj. 5, 6)

CP13-5 Examine the actual financial data of **Rubbermaid Incorporated** in Exhibit 13-10 (page 604). Show how to compute Rubbermaid's current ratio for each year 19X5 through 19X8. Is the company's ability to pay its current liabilities improving or deteriorating?

Evaluating a company's acid-test ratio (Obj. 5, 6)

CP13-6 Use the **Bristol-Myers Squibb** balance sheet data in Exhibit 13-3 (page 594).

1. Compute the company's acid-test ratio at December 31, 1998 and 1997.
2. Compare Bristol-Myers Squibb's ratio values to those of **Chesebrough-Pond's, General Motors,** and **Wal-Mart** on page 608. Is Bristol-Myers Squibb's acid-test ratio strong or weak? Explain.

Computing inventory turnover and days' sales in receivables (Obj. 5)

CP13-7 Use the Bristol-Myers Squibb 1998 income statement (page 594) and balance sheet (page 594) to compute the following:

a. The rate of inventory turnover for 1998.
b. Days' sales in average receivables during 1998. All sales are made on account. (Round dollar amounts to one decimal place.)

Measuring ability to pay long-term debt (Obj. 5, 6)

CP13-8 Use the actual financial statements of Bristol-Myers Squibb Company (pages 594 and 595).

1. Compute the company's debt ratio at December 31, 1998.
2. Compute the company's times-interest-earned ratio for 1998. For income from operations, use the sum of earnings before income taxes plus interest expense. Interest expense is not reported separately in the financial statements. Assume interest expense for 1998 was 7% of the sum of Short-term borrowings and Long-term debt at December 31, 1997. Round interest expense to the nearest million dollars.
3. Is Bristol-Myers Squibb's ability to pay its liabilities and interest expense strong or weak? Comment on the value of each ratio computed for requirements 1 and 2.

Measuring profitability (Obj. 5, 6)

CP13-9 Use the financial statements of Bristol-Myers Squibb Company (pages 594 and 595) to determine or, if necessary, to compute these profitability measures for 1998:

a. Rate of return on net sales.
b. Rate of return on total assets. Assume interest expense for 1998 was 7% of the sum of Short-term borrowings and Long-term debt at December 31, 1997. Round interest expense to the nearest million dollars.
c. Rate of return on common stockholders' equity. Are these rates of return strong or weak? Explain.

Computing EPS and the price/earnings ratio (Obj. 5)

CP13-10 The annual report of **The Home Depot** for the year ended January 31, 1997, included the following items:

Market price per share of common stock	$48
Preferred stock outstanding........................	$0
Net earnings (net income)........................	$937,739,000
Number of shares of common stock outstanding	487,752,000

1. Compute earnings per share (EPS) and the price/earnings ratio for The Home Depot's stock. Round to the nearest cent.
2. How much does the stock market say that $1 of The Home Depot's net income is worth?

Using ratio data to reconstruct an income statement (Obj. 5)

CP13-11 A skeleton of **Campbell Soup Company's** income statement (as adapted) appears as follows (amounts in millions):

Income Statement	
Net sales	$7,278
Cost of goods sold	(a)
Selling expenses	1,390
Administrative expenses	326
Interest expense	(b)
Other expenses	151
Income before taxes	1,042
Income tax expense	(c)
Net income	$ (d)

Use the following ratio data to complete Campbell Soup's income statement:

a. Inventory turnover was 5.53 (beginning inventory was $787; ending inventory was $755).

b. Rate of return on sales is 0.0959.

Using ratio data to reconstruct a balance sheet (Obj. 5)

CP13-12 A skeleton of Campbell Soup Company's balance sheet (as adapted) appears as follows (amounts in millions):

Balance Sheet			
Cash	$ 53	Total current liabilities	$2,164
Receivables	(a)	Long-term debt	(e)
Inventories	755	Other long-term liabilities	826
Prepaid expenses	(b)		
Total current assets	(c)	Common stock	185
Plant assets, net	(d)	Retained earnings	2,755
Other assets	2,150	Other stockholders' equity	(472)
Total assets	$6,315	Total liabilities and equity	$ (f)

Use the following ratio data to complete Campbell Soup's balance sheet:

a. Debt ratio is 0.6092.

b. Current ratio is 0.7306.

c. Acid-test ratio is 0.3161.

Measuring economic value added (Obj. 7)

CP13-13 Use the financial statements of Bristol-Myers Squibb (pages 594 and 595).

1. Compute economic value added (EVA®) by the company's operations during 1998. Use beginning-of-year amounts to compute the capital charge. Assume the company's cost of capital is 12% and that interest expense for 1998 was $128 million. Round all amounts to the nearest million dollars.
2. Should the company's stockholders be happy with the EVA® for 1998?

EXERCISES

Computing year-to-year changes in working capital (Obj. 1)

E13-1 What were the dollar amount of change and the percentage change in UTRECK Campgrounds' working capital during 2000 and 2001? Is this trend favorable or unfavorable?

	2001	*2000*	*1999*
Total current assets	$312,000	$290,000	$280,000
Total current liabilities	150,000	157,000	140,000

Horizontal analysis of an income statement (Obj. 1)

E13-2 Prepare a horizontal analysis of the following comparative income statement of **800-GO-RYDER, Inc.** Round percentage changes to the nearest one-tenth percent (three decimal places):

800-GO-RYDER, INC.
Comparative Income Statement
Years Ended December 31, 1999 and 1998

	1999	*1998*
Total revenue	$430,000	$373,000
Expenses:		
Cost of goods sold	$202,000	$188,000
Selling and general expenses	98,000	93,000
Interest expense	7,000	4,000
Income tax expense	42,000	37,000
Total expenses	349,000	322,000
Net income	$ 81,000	$ 51,000

Why did net income increase by a higher percentage than total revenues during 1999?

Computing trend percentages (Obj. 1)

E13-3 Compute trend percentages for **Kelly Realty's** net revenues and net income for the following five-year period, using year 1 as the base year. Round to the nearest full percent.

(In thousands)	*Year 5*	*Year 4*	*Year 3*	*Year 2*	*Year 1*
Net revenues	$1,470	$1,187	$1,106	$1,009	$1,043
Net income	147	114	83	71	85

Which grew faster during the period, net sales or net income?

Vertical analysis of a balance sheet (Obj. 2)

E13-4 The RV Center, Inc., has requested that you perform a vertical analysis of its balance sheet to determine the component percentages of its assets, liabilities, and stockholders' equity.

THE RV CENTER
Balance Sheet
December 31, 20X3

Assets	
Total current assets	$ 62,000
Property, plant, and equipment, net	227,000
Other assets	35,000
Total assets	$324,000
Liabilities	
Total current liabilities	$ 48,000
Long-term debt	128,000
Total liabilities	176,000
Stockholders' Equity	
Total stockholders' equity	148,000
Total liabilities and stockholders' equity	$324,000

Preparing a common-size income statement (Obj. 3)

E13-5 Prepare a comparative common-size income statement for 800-GO-RYDER, Inc., using the 1999 and 1998 data of Exercise 13-2 and rounding percentages to one-tenth percent (three decimal places). To an investor, how does 1999 compare with 1998? Explain your reasoning.

Analyzing the statement of cash flows (Obj. 4)

E13-6 Identify any weaknesses revealed by the statement of cash flows of Metro Roofing, Inc.

METRO ROOFING, INC. Statement of Cash Flows For the Current Year		
Operating activities:		
Income from operations		$ 32,000
Add (subtract) noncash items:		
Depreciation	$ 23,000	
Net increase in current assets other than cash	(45,000)	
Net decrease in current liabilities exclusive of short-term debt	(11,000)	(33,000)
Net cash outflow from operating activities		(1,000)
Investing activities:		
Sale of property, plant, and equipment		101,000
Financing activities:		
Issuance of bonds payable	$ 114,000	
Payment of short-term debt	(171,000)	
Payment of long-term debt	(79,000)	
Payment of dividends	(42,000)	
Net cash outflow from financing activities		(178,000)
Increase (decrease) in cash		$ (78,000)

E13-7 The financial statements of Slade Sign Company include the following items:

Computing five ratios (Obj. 5)

	Current Year	*Preceding Year*
Balance sheet:		
Cash	$ 17,000	$ 22,000
Short-term investments	11,000	26,000
Net receivables	64,000	73,000
Inventory	77,000	71,000
Prepaid expenses	16,000	8,000
Total current assets	185,000	200,000
Total current liabilities	151,000	91,000
Income statement:		
Net credit sales	$454,000	
Cost of goods sold	257,000	

Required

Compute the following ratios for the current year:

a. Current ratio

b. Acid-test ratio

c. Inventory turnover

d. Accounts receivable turnover

e. Days' sales in average receivables

E13-8 Canyon Oaks Spa has asked you to determine whether the company's ability to pay its current liabilities and long-term debts has improved or deteriorated during 20X2. To answer this question, compute the following ratios for 20X2 and 20X1:

Analyzing the ability to pay current liabilities (Obj. 5, 6)

a. Current ratio

b. Acid-test ratio

c. Debt ratio

d. Times-interest-earned ratio

Summarize the results of your analysis in a written report.

	20X2	20X1
Cash	$ 61,000	$ 47,000
Short-term investments	28,000	—
Net receivables	102,000	116,000
Inventory	226,000	263,000
Prepaid expenses	11,000	9,000
Total assets	543,000	489,000
Total current liabilities	205,000	241,000
Total liabilities	271,000	273,000
Income from operations	165,000	158,000
Interest expense	38,000	39,000

Analyzing profitability (Obj. 5, 6)

E13-9 Compute four ratios that measure ability to earn profits for Stone Mountain Carpets, Inc., whose comparative income statement follows:

STONE MOUNTAIN CARPETS, INC.
Comparative Income Statement
Years Ended December 31, 20X6 and 20X5

	20X6	20X5
Net sales	$174,000	$158,000
Cost of goods sold	93,000	86,000
Gross profit	81,000	72,000
Selling and general expenses	50,000	41,000
Income from operations	31,000	31,000
Interest expense	5,000	10,000
Income before income tax	26,000	21,000
Income tax expense	8,000	8,000
Net income	$ 18,000	$ 13,000

Additional data:

	20X6	20X5
Average total assets	$204,000	$191,000
Average common stockholders' equity	$ 96,000	$ 89,000
Preferred dividends	$ 3,000	$ 3,000
Shares of common stock outstanding	20,000	20,000

Did the company's operating performance improve or deteriorate during 20X6?

Evaluating a stock as an investment (Obj. 5, 6)

E13-10 Evaluate the common stock of Four-Day Tire Company as an investment. Specifically, use the three stock ratios to determine whether the common stock has increased or decreased in attractiveness during the past year.

	20X4	20X3
Net income	$ 58,000	$ 55,000
Dividends (half on preferred stock)	20,000	20,000
Common stockholders' equity at year end (80,000 shares)	580,000	500,000
Preferred stockholders' equity at year end	200,000	200,000
Market price per share of common stock at year end	$ 11.50	$ 7.75

Using economic value added to measure corporate performance (Obj. 7)

E13-11 Two companies with very different economic-value-added (EVA) profiles are **IHOP,** the restaurant chain, and **Texaco,** the giant oil company. Adapted versions of the two companies' 19X8 financial statements are presented here (in millions):

	IHOP	Texaco
Balance sheet data:		
Total assets	$252	$24,937
Interest-bearing debt	$ 35	$ 4,240
All other liabilities	109	11,177
Stockholders' equity	108	9,520
Total liabilities and equity	$252	$24,937
Income statement data:		
Total revenue	$164	$36,787
Interest expense	9	483
All other expenses	139	35,697
Net income	$ 16	$ 607

Required

1. Before performing any calculations, which company do you think represents the better investment? Give your reason.

2. Compute the EVA® for each company and then decide which company's stock you would rather hold as an investment. Assume each company's cost of capital is 10%.

CHALLENGE EXERCISES

E13-12 The following data (dollar amounts in millions) are from the financial statements of **McDonald's Corporation,** the restaurant chain.

Using ratio data to reconstruct a company's income statement (Obj. 2, 3, 5)

Average stockholders' equity	$3,605
Interest expense	$ 413
Preferred stock	-0-
Operating income as a percent of sales	24.04%
Rate of return on stockholders' equity	21.89%
Income tax rate	33.30%

Required

Complete the following condensed income statement. Report amounts to the nearest million dollars.

Sales	$?
Operating expense	?
Operating income	?
Interest expense	?
Pretax income	?
Income tax expense	?
Net income	$?

E13-13 The following data (dollar amounts in millions) are adapted from the financial statements of **Wal-Mart Stores, Inc.,** the largest retailer in the world:

Using ratio data to reconstruct a company's balance sheet (Obj. 2, 3, 5)

Total liabilities	$11,806
Preferred stock	$ -0-
Total current assets	$10,196
Accumulated depreciation	$ 1,448
Debt ratio	60.342%
Current ratio	1.51

Required

Complete the following condensed balance sheet. Report amounts to the nearest million dollars.

Current assets		$?
Property, plant and equipment	$?	
Less Accumulated depreciation	(?)	?
Total assets		$?
Current liabilities		$?
Long-term liabilities		?
Stockholders' equity		?
Total liabilities and stockholders' equity		$?

PROBLEMS

(Group A)

Trend percentages, return on common equity, and comparison with the industry (Obj. 1, 5, 6)

P13-1A Net revenues, net income, and common stockholders' equity for Bloom Irrigation, Inc., for a six-year period follow.

(In thousands)	*2003*	*2002*	*2001*	*2000*	*1999*	*1998*
Net revenues	$781	$714	$641	$662	$642	$634
Net income	51	45	32	48	41	40
Ending common stockholders' equity	366	354	330	296	272	252

Required

1. Compute trend percentages for each item for 1999 through 2003. Use 1998 as the base year. Round to the nearest percent.
2. Compute the rate of return on average common stockholders' equity for 1999 through 2003, rounding to three decimal places. In this industry, rates of 13% are average, rates above 16% are good, and rates above 20% are outstanding. Bloom has no preferred stock outstanding.
3. How does Bloom's return on common stockholders' equity compare with the industry?

Common-size statements, analysis of profitability, and comparison with the industry (Obj. 2, 3, 5, 6)

P13-2A Blaupunkt Stereo Shops has asked you to compare the company's profit performance and financial position with the average for the stereo industry. The proprietor has given you the company's income statement and balance sheet as well as the industry average data for retailers.

BLAUPUNKT STEREO SHOPS
Income Statement
Compared with Industry Average
Year Ended December 31, 20X6

	Blaupunkt	*Industry Average*
Net sales	$781,000	100.0%
Cost of goods sold	497,000	65.8
Gross profit	284,000	34.2
Operating expenses	163,000	19.7
Operating income	121,000	14.5
Other expenses	15,000	0.4
Net income	$106,000	14.1%

BLAUPUNKT STEREO SHOPS
Balance Sheet
Compared with Industry Average
December 31, 20X6

	Blaupunkt	Industry Average
Current assets	$350,000	70.9%
Fixed assets, net	74,000	23.6
Intangible assets, net	4,000	0.8
Other assets	22,000	4.7
Total	$450,000	100.0%
Current liabilities	$207,000	48.1%
Long-term liabilities	62,000	16.6
Stockholders' equity	181,000	35.3
Total	$450,000	100.0%

Required

1. Prepare a common-size income statement and balance sheet for Blaupunkt. The first column of each statement should present Blaupunkt's common-size statement, and the second column should show the industry averages.
2. For the profitability analysis, compute Blaupunkt's (a) ratio of gross profit to net sales, (b) ratio of operating income to net sales, and (c) ratio of net income to net sales. Compare these figures with the industry averages. Is Blaupunkt's profit performance better or worse than the industry average?
3. For the analysis of financial position, compute Blaupunkt's (a) ratio of current assets to total assets, and (b) ratio of stockholders' equity to total assets. Compare these ratios with the industry averages. Is Blaupunkt's financial position better or worse than the industry averages?

Using the statement of cash flows for decision making (Obj. 4)

P13-3A You have been asked to evaluate two companies as possible investments. The two companies, J & J Roofing, Inc., and Metal Components Corporation, are similar in size. Assume that all other available information has been analyzed, and the decision regarding which company's stock to purchase depends on their cash-flow data (below and page 632).

Required

Discuss the relative strengths and weaknesses of each company. Conclude your discussion by recommending one company's stock as an investment.

J & J ROOFING, INC.
Statement of Cash Flows
Years Ended September 30, 20X5 and 20X4

	20X5		20X4	
Operating activities:				
Income from operations		$ 17,000		$ 44,000
Add (subtract) noncash items:				
Total		(14,000)		(4,000)
Net cash inflow from operating activities		3,000		40,000
Investing activities:				
Purchase of property, plant, and equipment	$ (13,000)		$ (3,000)	
Sale of property, plant, and equipment	86,000		79,000	
Net cash inflow from investing activities		73,000		76,000
Financing activities:				
Issuance of short-term notes payable	$ 43,000		$ 19,000	
Payment of short-term notes payable	(101,000)		(108,000)	
Net cash outflow from financing activities		(58,000)		(89,000)
Increase in cash		$ 18,000		$ 27,000
Cash balance at beginning of year		31,000		4,000
Cash balance at end of year		$ 49,000		$ 31,000

METAL COMPONENTS CORPORATION
Statement of Cash Flows
Years Ended September 30, 20X5 and 20X4

	20X5		*20X4*	
Operating activities:				
Income from operations		$ 89,000		$ 71,000
Add (subtract) noncash items:				
Total		19,000		—
Net cash inflow from operating activities		108,000		71,000
Investing activities:				
Purchase of property, plant, and equipment	$(121,000)		$(91,000)	
Net cash outflow from investing activities		(121,000)		$(91,000)
Financing activities:				
Issuance of long-term notes payable	$ 46,000		$ 43,000	
Payment of short-term notes payable	(15,000)		(40,000)	
Payment of cash dividends	(12,000)		(9,000)	
Net cash inflow (outflow) from financing activities		19,000		(6,000)
Increase (decrease) in cash		$ 6,000		$(26,000)
Cash balance at beginning of year		54,000		80,000
Cash balance at end of year		$ 60,000		$ 54,000

Effects of business transactions on selected ratios (Obj. 5, 6)

P13-4A Financial statement data of Culligan Video, Inc., include the following items:

Cash	$ 22,000
Short-term investments	19,000
Accounts receivable, net	83,000
Inventories	141,000
Prepaid expenses	8,000
Total assets	657,000
Short-term notes payable	49,000
Accounts payable	103,000
Accrued liabilities	38,000
Long-term notes payable	160,000
Other long-term liabilities	31,000
Net income	71,000
Number of common shares outstanding	40,000

Required

1. Compute Culligan's current ratio, debt ratio, and earnings per share. Use the following format for your answer:

Requirement 1

Current Ratio	*Debt Ratio*	*Earnings per Share*

2. Compute the three ratios after evaluating the effect of each transaction that follows. Consider each transaction *separately.*
   a. Purchased merchandise of $26,000 on account, debiting Inventory.
   b. Borrowed $85,000 on a long-term note payable.
   c. Issued 5,000 shares of common stock, receiving cash of $120,000.
   d. Received cash on account, $19,000.
   e. Paid short-term notes payable, $32,000. Format your answer as follows:

Requirement 2

Transaction (letter)	*Current Ratio*	*Debt Ratio*	*Earnings per Share*

P13-5A Comparative financial statement data of Pro Sound Entertainment Co. follow.

Using ratios to evaluate a stock investment (Obj. 5, 6)

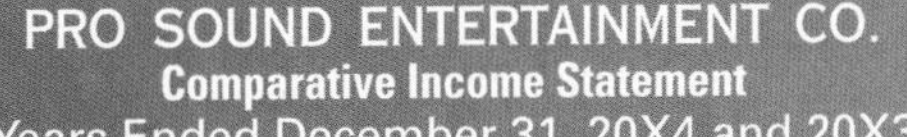

PRO SOUND ENTERTAINMENT CO.
Comparative Income Statement
Years Ended December 31, 20X4 and 20X3

	20X4	*20X3*
Net sales	$462,000	$427,000
Cost of goods sold	229,000	218,000
Gross profit	233,000	209,000
Operating expenses	136,000	134,000
Income from operations	97,000	75,000
Interest expense	11,000	12,000
Income before income tax	86,000	63,000
Income tax expense	30,000	27,000
Net income	$ 56,000	$ 36,000

PRO SOUND ENTERTAINMENT CO.
Comparative Balance Sheet
December 31, 20X4 and 20X3
(selected 20X2 amounts given for computation of ratios)

	20X4	*20X3*	*20X2*
Current assets:			
Cash	$ 96,000	$ 97,000	
Current receivables, net	112,000	116,000	$103,000
Inventories	172,000	162,000	207,000
Prepaid expenses	16,000	7,000	
Total current assets	396,000	382,000	
Property, plant, and equipment, net	189,000	178,000	
Total assets	$585,000	$560,000	598,000
Total current liabilities	$206,000	$223,000	
Long-term liabilities	119,000	117,000	
Total liabilities	325,000	340,000	
Preferred stockholders' equity, 6%, $100 par	100,000	100,000	
Common stockholders' equity, no par	160,000	120,000	90,000
Total liabilities and stockholders' equity	$585,000	$560,000	

Other information:

1. Market price of Pro Sound common stock: $53 at December 31, 20X4, and $32.50 at December 31, 20X3.
2. Common shares outstanding: 10,000 during 20X4 and 9,000 during 20X3.
3. All sales on credit.

Required

1. Compute the following ratios for 20X4 and 20X3:
   a. Current ratio
   b. Inventory turnover
   c. Times-interest-earned ratio
   d. Return on common stockholders' equity
   e. Earnings per share of common stock
   f. Price earnings ratio
2. Decide (a) whether Pro Sound's financial position improved or deteriorated during 20X4 and (b) whether the investment attractiveness of its common stock appears to have increased or decreased.
3. How will what you learned in this problem help you evaluate an investment?

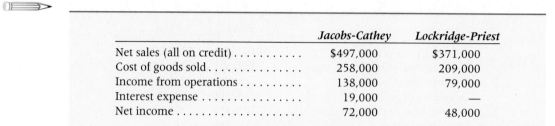

Using ratios to decide between two stock investments; measuring economic value added (Obj. 5, 6, 7)

P13-6A Assume that you are purchasing an investment and have decided to invest in a company in the air-conditioning and heating business. You have narrowed the choice to Jacobs-Cathey, Inc., and Lockridge-Priest Corp. and have assembled the following data:

Selected income statement data for current year:

	Jacobs-Cathey	*Lockridge-Priest*
Net sales (all on credit)	$497,000	$371,000
Cost of goods sold	258,000	209,000
Income from operations	138,000	79,000
Interest expense	19,000	—
Net income	72,000	48,000

Selected balance sheet and market price data at end of current year:

	Jacobs-Cathey	*Lockridge-Priest*
Current assets:		
Cash	$ 19,000	$ 22,000
Short-term investments	18,000	20,000
Current receivables, net	46,000	42,000
Inventories	100,000	87,000
Prepaid expenses	3,000	2,000
Total current assets	186,000	173,000
Total assets	328,000	265,000
Total current liabilities	98,000	108,000
Total liabilities	$131,000*	$108,000*
Preferred stock: 5%, $100 par	20,000	
Common stock, $1 par		
(10,000 shares)		10,000
$2.50 par (5,000 shares)	12,500	
Total stockholders' equity	197,000	157,000
Market price per share of common stock	$ 112	$ 51

*Includes notes payable: Jacobs-Cathey, $86,000
Lockridge-Priest, $1,000

Selected balance sheet data at beginning of current year:

	Jacobs-Cathey	*Lockridge-Priest*
Current receivables, net	$ 48,000	$ 40,000
Inventories	88,000	93,000
Total assets	270,000	259,000
Preferred stock, 5%, $100 par	20,000	—
Common stock, $1 par		
(10,000 shares)		10,000
$2.50 par (5,000 shares)	12,500	
Total stockholders' equity	126,000	118,000

Your investment strategy is to purchase the stocks of companies that have low price/earnings ratios but appear to be in good shape financially. Assume that you have analyzed all other factors and that your decision depends on the results of the ratio analysis to be performed.

Required

1. Compute the following ratios for both companies for the current year, and decide which company's stock better fits your investment strategy.
   1. Acid-test ratio
   2. Inventory turnover
   3. Days' sales in average receivables
   4. Debt ratio
   5. Times-interest-earned ratio
   6. Return on common stockholders' equity
   7. Earnings per share of common stock
   8. Price/earnings ratio
2. Compute each company's economic-value-added (EVA®) measure and determine whether their EVA®s confirm or alter your investment decision. Each company's cost of capital is 12%. Round all amounts to the nearest $1,000.

(Group B)

P13-1B Net sales, net income, and total assets for SW. Net, Inc., for a six-year period follow:

Trend percentages, return on sales, and comparison with the industry (Obj. 1, 5, 6)

(In thousands)	*20X6*	*20X5*	*20X4*	*20X3*	*20X2*	*20X1*
Net sales	$357	$313	$266	$281	$245	$241
Net income	29	21	11	18	14	13
Total assets	286	254	209	197	181	166

Required

1. Compute trend percentages for each item for 20X2 through 20X6. Use 20X1 as the base year and round to the nearest percent.
2. Compute the rate of return on net sales for 20X2 through 20X6, rounding to three decimal places. In this industry, rates above 5% are considered good, and rates above 7% are outstanding.
3. How does SW. Net's return on net sales compare with that of the industry?

P13-2B Top managers of Travelers Gym Supply have asked your help in comparing the company's profit performance and financial position with the average for the sporting goods industry. The accountant has given you the company's income statement and balance sheet and also the following data for the industry:

Common-size statements, analysis of profitability, and comparison with the industry (Obj. 2, 3, 5, 6)

TRAVELERS GYM SUPPLY
Income Statement
Compared with Industry Average
Year Ended December 31, 20X3

	Travelers	*Industry Average*
Net sales	$957,000	100.0%
Cost of goods sold	653,000	65.9
Gross profit	304,000	34.1
Operating expenses	257,000	28.1
Operating income	47,000	6.0
Other expenses	11,000	0.4
Net income	$ 36,000	5.6%

TRAVELERS GYM SUPPLY
Balance Sheet
Compared with Industry Average
December 31, 20X3

	Travelers	*Industry Average*
Current assets	$448,000	74.4%
Fixed assets, net	127,000	20.0
Intangible assets, net	42,000	0.6
Other assets	13,000	5.0
Total	$630,000	100.0%
Current liabilities	$246,000	35.6%
Long-term liabilities	136,000	19.0
Stockholders' equity	248,000	45.4
Total	$630,000	100.0%

Required

1. Prepare a common-size income statement and balance sheet for Travelers. The first column of each statement should present Travelers' common-size statement, and the second column should show the industry averages.
2. For the profitability analysis, compute Travelers' (a) ratio of gross profit to net sales, (b) ratio of operating income (loss) to net sales, and (c) ratio of net income (loss) to net sales. Com-

pare these figures with the industry averages. Is Travelers' profit performance better or worse than the average for the industry?

3. For the analysis of financial position, compute Travelers' (a) ratio of current assets to total assets and (b) ratio of stockholders' equity to total assets. Compare these ratios with the industry averages. Is Travelers' financial position better or worse than average for the industry?

Using the statement of cash flows for decision making (Obj. 4)

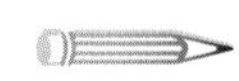

P13-3B You are evaluating two companies as possible investments. The two companies, similar in size, are commuter airlines that fly passengers from Phoenix to smaller cities in Arizona. All other available information has been analyzed and your decision of which company's stock to purchase depends on their cash flows, which are reported as follows:

EAGLE AIR CORP.
Statement of Cash Flows
Years Ended November 30, 20X5 and 20X4

	20X5		20X4	
Operating activities:				
Income (loss) from operations		$ (67,000)		$154,000
Add (subtract) noncash items:				
Total		84,000		(23,000)
Net cash inflow from operating activities		17,000		131,000
Investing activities:				
Purchase of property, plant, and equipment	$ (50,000)		$(91,000)	
Sale of long-term investments	52,000		4,000	
Net cash inflow (outflow) from investing activities		2,000		$(87,000)
Financing activities:				
Issuance of short-term notes payable	$ 122,000		$ 143,000	
Payment of short-term notes payable	(179,000)		(134,000)	
Payment of cash dividends	(45,000)		(64,000)	
Net cash outflow from financing activities		(102,000)		(55,000)
Increase (decrease) in cash		$ (83,000)		$(11,000)
Cash balance at beginning of year		92,000		103,000
Cash balance at end of year		$ 9,000		$ 92,000

KROFLITE, INC.
Statement of Cash Flows
Years Ended November 30, 20X5 and 20X4

	20X5		20X4	
Operating activities:				
Income from operations		$ 184,000		$ 131,000
Add (subtract) noncash items:				
Total		64,000		62,000
Net cash inflow from operating activities		248,000		193,000
Investing activities:				
Purchase of property, plant, and equipment	$(303,000)		$(453,000)	
Sale of property, plant, and equipment	46,000		72,000	
Net cash outflow from investing activities		(257,000)		$(381,000)
Financing activities:				
Issuance of long-term notes payable	$ 174,000		$ 118,000	
Payment of short-term notes payable	(66,000)		(18,000)	
Net cash inflow from financing activities		108,000		100,000
Increase (decrease) in cash		$ 99,000		$(88,000)
Cash balance at beginning of year		116,000		204,000
Cash balance at end of year		$ 215,000		$ 116,000

Required

Discuss the relative strengths and weaknesses of Eagle Air and Kroflite. Conclude your discussion by recommending one of the company's stocks as an investment.

P13-4B Financial statement data on Home & Garden, Inc., include the following items:

Effects of business transactions on selected ratios (Obj. 5, 6)

Cash	$ 47,000	Accounts payable	$ 96,000
Short-term investments	21,000	Accrued liabilities	50,000
Accounts receivable, net	102,000	Long-term notes payable	146,000
Inventories	274,000	Other long-term liabilities	78,000
Prepaid expenses	15,000	Net income	119,000
Total assets	933,000	Number of common shares outstanding	22,000
Short-term notes payable	72,000		

Required

1. Compute Home & Garden's current ratio, debt ratio, and earnings per share. Use the following format for your answer:

Requirement 1

Current Ratio *Debt Ratio* *Earnings per Share*

2. Compute the three ratios after evaluating the effect of each transaction that follows. Consider each transaction *separately.*
   a. Borrowed $76,000 on a long-term note payable.
   b. Issued 14,000 shares of common stock, receiving cash of $168,000.
   c. Received cash on account, $6,000.
   d. Paid short-term notes payable, $51,000.
   e. Purchased merchandise of $48,000 on account, debiting Inventory.

Format your answer as follows:

Requirement 2

Transaction letter *Current Ratio* *Debt Ratio* *Earnings per Share*

P13-5B Comparative financial statement data of Mastercraft Jewelry Company follow:

Using ratios to evaluate a stock investment (Obj. 5, 6)

MASTERCRAFT JEWELRY COMPANY
Comparative Income Statement
Years Ended December 31, 20X6 and 20X5

	20X6	*20X5*
Net sales	$667,000	$599,000
Cost of goods sold	378,000	283,000
Gross profit	289,000	316,000
Operating expenses	129,000	147,000
Income from operations	160,000	169,000
Interest expense	57,000	41,000
Income before income tax	103,000	128,000
Income tax expense	34,000	53,000
Net income	$ 69,000	$ 75,000

MASTERCRAFT JEWELRY COMPANY
Comparative Balance Sheet
December 31, 20X6 and 20X5
(Selected 20X4 amounts given for computation of ratios)

	20X6	*20X5*	*20X4*
Current assets:			
Cash	$ 37,000	$ 40,000	
Current receivables, net	208,000	151,000	$138,000
Inventories	352,000	286,000	184,000
Prepaid expenses	5,000	20,000	
Total current assets	602,000	497,000	
Property, plant, and equipment, net	287,000	276,000	
Total assets	$889,000	$773,000	707,000
Total current liabilities	$286,000	$267,000	
Long-term liabilities	245,000	235,000	
Total liabilities	531,000	502,000	
Preferred stockholders' equity, 4%, $20 par	50,000	50,000	
Common stockholders' equity, no par	308,000	221,000	148,000
Total liabilities and stockholders' equity	$889,000	$773,000	

Other information:

1. Market price of Mastercraft's common stock: $36.75 at December 31, 20X6, and $50.50 at December 31, 20X5.

2. Common shares outstanding: 15,000 during 20X6 and 14,000 during 20X5.

3. All sales on credit.

Required

1. Compute the following ratios for 20X6 and 20X5:

a. Current ratio
b. Inventory turnover
c. Times-interest-earned ratio
d. Return on assets
e. Return on common stockholders' equity
f. Earnings per share of common stock
g. Price/earnings ratio

2. Decide whether (a) Mastercraft's financial position improved or deteriorated during 20X6 and (b) the investment attractiveness of its common stock appears to have increased or decreased.

3. How will what you learned in this problem help you evaluate an investment?

Using ratios to decide between two stock investments; measuring economic value added (Obj. 5, 6, 7)

P13-6B Assume that you are considering purchasing stock in a company in the music industry. You have narrowed the choice to Keyboards of Texas and Lone Star Music and have assembled the following data:

Selected income statement data for current year:

	Keyboards	*Lone Star Music*
Net sales (all on credit)	$519,000	$603,000
Cost of goods sold	387,000	454,000
Income from operations	72,000	93,000
Interest expense	8,000	—
Net income	38,000	56,000

Selected balance sheet and market price data at end of current year:

	Keyboards	*Lone Star Music*
Current assets:		
Cash	$ 39,000	$ 25,000
Short-term investments	13,000	6,000
Current receivables, net	164,000	189,000
Inventories	183,000	211,000
Prepaid expenses	15,000	19,000
Total current assets	414,000	450,000
Total assets	938,000	974,000
Total current liabilities	338,000	366,000
Total liabilities	691,000*	667,000*
Preferred stock, 4%, $100 par	25,000	
Common stock, $1 par (150,000 shares)		150,000
$5 par (20,000 shares)	100,000	
Total stockholders' equity	247,000	307,000
Market price per share of common stock	$ 47.50	$ 9

*Includes notes and bonds payable: Keyboards, $303,000
Lone Star, $4,000

Selected balance sheet data at beginning of current year:

	Keyboards	*Lone Star Music*
Current receivables, net	$193,000	$142,000
Inventories	197,000	209,000
Total assets	909,000	842,000
Preferred stock, 4%, $100 par	25,000	
Common stock, $1 par (150,000 shares)		150,000
$5 par (20,000 shares)	100,000	
Total stockholders' equity	215,000	263,000

Your investment strategy is to purchase the stocks of companies that have low price/earnings ratios but appear to be in good shape financially. Assume that you have analyzed all other factors and that your decision depends on the results of the ratio analysis to be performed.

Required

1. Compute the following ratios for both companies for the current year and decide which company's stock better fits your investment strategy.

1. Acid-test ratio
2. Inventory turnover
3. Days' sales in average receivables
4. Debt ratio
5. Times-interest-earned ratio
6. Return on common stockholders' equity
7. Earnings per share of common stock
8. Price/earnings ratio

2. Compute each company's economic-value-added (EVA®) measure and determine whether their EVA®s confirm or alter your investment decision. Each company's cost of capital is 10%. Round all amounts to the nearest $1,000.

EXTENDING YOUR KNOWLEDGE

DECISION CASES

Understanding the components of accounting ratios (Obj. 5, 6)

Case 1. Consider the following business situations:

1. Bill Janus is the controller of Saturn Limited, a dance club whose year end is December 31. Janus prepares checks for suppliers in December and posts them to the appropriate accounts in that month. However, he holds on to the checks and mails them to the suppliers in January. What financial ratio(s) are most affected by the action? What is Janus's purpose in undertaking this activity?
2. Sara Fulton has asked you about the stock of a particular company. She finds it attractive because it has a high dividend yield relative to another stock she is also considering. Explain to her the meaning of the ratio and the danger of making a decision based on dividend yield alone.
3. Augusta National Corporation's owners are concerned because the number of days' sales in receivables has increased over the previous two years. Explain why the ratio might have increased.

Identifying action to cut losses and establish profitability (Obj. 2, 5, 6)

Case 2. Suppose you manage Whitewater Supply, Inc., a Wyoming sporting goods store that lost money during the past year. To turn the business around, you must analyze the company and industry data for the current year to learn what is wrong. The company's data follow.

WHITEWATER SUPPLY
Balance Sheet Data

	Whitewater Supply	*Industry Average*
Cash and short-term investments	3.0%	6.8%
Trade receivables, net	15.2	11.0
Inventory	64.2	60.5
Prepaid expenses	1.0	0.0
Total current assets	83.4	78.3
Fixed assets, net	12.6	15.2
Other assets	4.0	6.5
Total assets	100.0%	100.0%
Notes payable, short-term, 12%	17.1%	14.0%
Accounts payable	21.1	25.1
Accrued liabilities	7.8	7.9
Total current liabilities	46.0	47.0
Long-term debt, 11%	19.7	16.4
Total liabilities	65.7	63.4
Common stockholders' equity	34.3	36.6
Total liabilities and stockholders' equity	100.0%	100.0%

WHITEWATER SUPPLY
Income Statement Data

	Whitewater Supply	*Industry Average*
Net sales	100.0%	100.0%
Cost of sales	(68.2)	(64.8)
Gross profit	31.8	35.2
Operating expense	(37.1)	(32.3)
Operating income (loss)	(5.3)	2.9
Interest expense	(5.8)	(1.3)
Other revenue	1.1	0.3
Income (loss) before income tax	(10.0)	1.9
Income tax (expense) saving	4.4	(0.8)
Net income (loss)	(5.6)%	1.1%

Required

On the basis of your analysis of these figures, suggest four courses of action Whitewater Supply might take to reduce its losses and establish profitable operations. Give your reasons for each suggestion.

ETHICAL ISSUE

The Excelsior Hotel chain's long-term debt agreements make certain demands on the business. For example, Excelsior may not purchase treasury stock in excess of the balance of retained earnings. Also, long-term debt may not exceed stockholders' equity, and the current ratio may not fall below 1.50. If Excelsior fails to meet any of these requirements, the company's lenders have the authority to take over management of the hotel chain.

Changes in consumer demand have made it hard for Excelsior to attract travelers. Current liabilities have mounted faster than current assets, causing the current ratio to fall to 1.47. Before releasing financial statements, Excelsior management is scrambling to improve the current ratio. The controller points out that an investment can be classified as either long-term or short-term, depending on management's intention. By deciding to convert an investment to cash within one year, Excelsior can classify the investment as short-term—a current asset. On the controller's recommendation, Excelsior's board of directors votes to reclassify long-term investments as short-term.

Required

1. What effect will reclassifying the investments have on the current ratio? Is Excelsior's financial position stronger as a result of reclassifying the investments?
2. Shortly after the financial statements are released, sales improve; so, too, does the current ratio. As a result, Excelsior management decides not to sell the investments it had reclassified as short-term. Accordingly, the company reclassifies the investments as long-term. Has management behaved unethically? Give the reasoning underlying your answer.

FINANCIAL STATEMENT CASES

Measuring profitability and analyzing stock as an investment (Obj. 5, 6)

Case 1. Use the financial statements and the data labeled Ten-Year Selected Financial Data that appear before **The Gap's** financial statements (Appendix A at the end of the book) to answer the following questions.

Required

1. From the Ten-Year Summary, chart these ratios over the three most recent fiscal years: 1998, 1997, and 1996:
   a. Current ratio
   b. Net income per share—basic
   c. Rate of return on average assets
   d. Rate of return on average stockholders' equity
2. Compute these ratios for each of the three most recent fiscal years:
   a. Days' sales in average receivables.
   b. Inventory turnover. You will have to reconstruct ending inventory at January 31, 1997, and January 31, 1996, from the changes in the Inventory account given on the statement of cash flows.
3. Evaluate the company's progress (or lack of progress) in profitability and in its ability to pay current liabilities and to turn over inventory during this three-year period.

Measuring profitability and analyzing stock as an investment (Obj. 5, 6)

Case 2. Obtain the annual report of a company of your choosing.

Required

1. Use the financial statements and the multiyear summary data to chart the company's progress during the three most recent years, including the current year. Compute the following ratios that measure profitability and are used to analyze stock as an investment:

Profitability Measures

a. Rate of return on net sales
b. Rate of return on common stockholders' equity
c. Rate of return on total assets

Stock Analysis Measure

d. Price/earnings ratio (If given, use the average of the "high" and "low" stock prices for each year.)

2. Is the trend in the profitability measures consistent with the trend in the stock analysis measure? Evaluate the company's overall outlook for the future.

GROUP PROJECTS

Project 1. Select an industry you are interested in, and use the leading company in that industry as the benchmark. Then select two other companies in the same industry. For each category of ratios in the Decision Guidelines feature on pages 605–606, compute at least two ratios for all three companies. Write a two-page report that compares the two companies with the benchmark company.

Project 2. Select a company and obtain its financial statements. Convert the income statement and the balance sheet to common size and compare the company you selected to the industry average. Robert Morris Associates' *Annual Statement Studies,* Dun & Bradstreet's *Industry Norms & Key Business Ratios,* and Prentice Hall's *Almanac of Business and Industrial Financial Ratios,* by Leo Troy, publish common-size statements for most industries.

INTERNET EXERCISE

Merck

The Fortune 500 is a listing of the largest 500 domestic corporations determined by *Fortune* magazine. The *Fortune* magazine Web site offers the latest business news and information about the Fortune 500 companies and other Top Performer lists.

1. Go to **http://www.pathfinder.com/fortune** and click on **Fortune 500.** Identify the top three companies on the Fortune 500 list and their most recent annual revenues.

2. At the top of the page, click on **Top Performers** followed by **Highest Returns on Revenues.** In the text, this ratio is referred to as "Return on Sales." What is the formula for this ratio? What does this ratio measure? Identify the top three companies on this Top Performers list and their most recent Return on Revenues (Sales).

3. At the top of the page, click on **Industry List** and select the *pharmaceuticals* industry. The text refers to the ratio "profits as % of stockholders' equity" by what title? What is the formula for this ratio? What does this ratio measure? Identify "profits as % of stockholders' equity" for **Bristol-Myers Squibb, Johnson & Johnson, Merck,** and **Pfizer**—all pharmaceutical companies.

4. Click on **Merck** and go to Merck's Company Snapshot of information. Review the information provided and determine whether the company appears financially strong or weak. Defend your judgment with at least two supportive observations.

5. Describe at least two possible Internet sources of business and financial information for a company.

Appendix A

Annual Report of Gap, Inc.

Anyone Anywhere Anytime

Gap Inc.

1998 Annual Report

Financial Highlights

	Fifty-two Weeks Ended January 30, 1999	Fifty-two Weeks Ended January 31, 1998	Fifty-two Weeks Ended February 1, 1997
OPERATING RESULTS ($000)			
Net sales	$9,054,462	$6,507,825	$5,284,381
Percentage change year-to-year	39%	23%	20%
Earnings before income taxes	$1,319,262	$ 854,242	$ 748,527
Percentage change year-to-year	54%	14%	28%
Net earnings	$ 824,539	$ 533,901	$ 452,859
Percentage change year-to-year	54%	18%	28%
PER SHARE DATA			
Net earnings–diluted	$1.37	$.87	$.71
Cash dividends paid	.13	.13	.13
STATISTICS			
Net earnings as a percentage of net sales	9.1%	8.2%	8.6%
Return on average assets	22.6%	17.9%	18.2%
Return on average shareholders' equity	52.2%	33.0%	27.5%
Current ratio	1.21:1	1.85:1	1.72:1
Number of stores open at year-end	2,428	2,130	1,854
Comparable store sales growth	17%	6%	5%

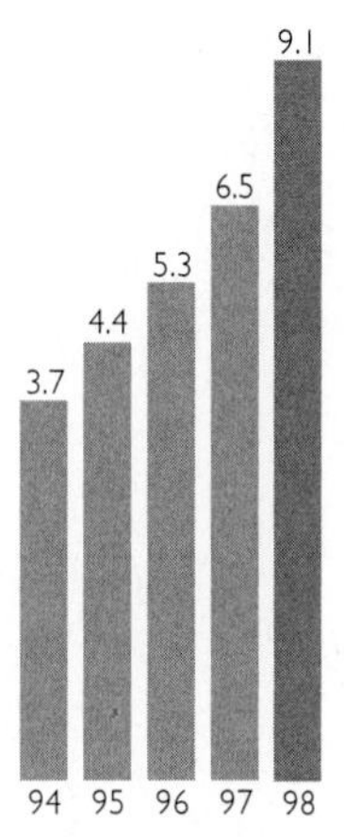

Net Sales
(in billions of dollars)

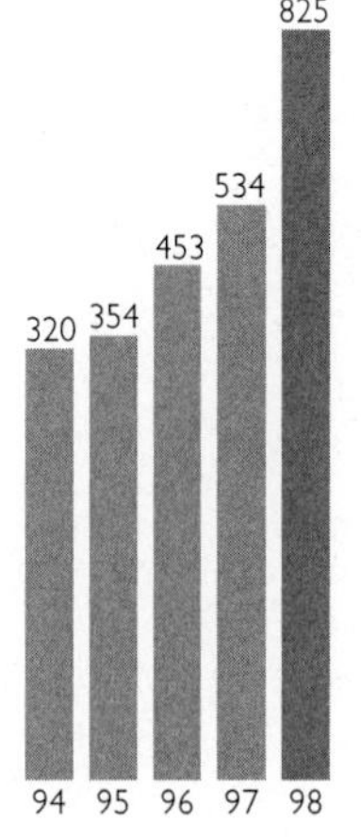

Net Earnings
(in millions of dollars)

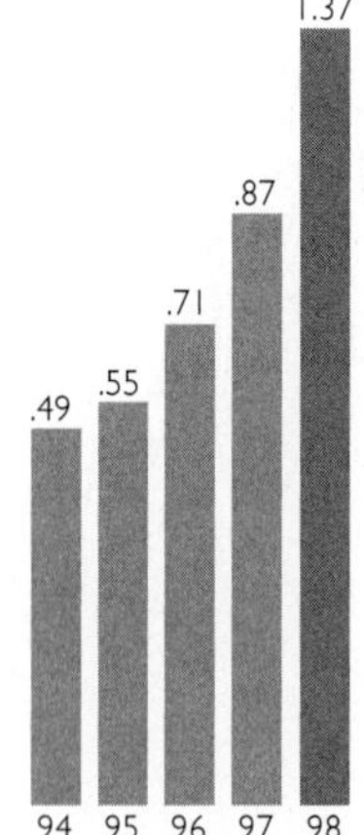

Earnings Per Share–Diluted
(in dollars)

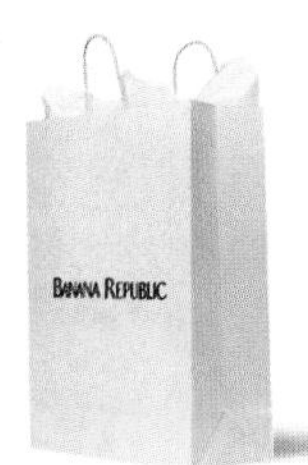

Store Growth

	Stores Opened Fiscal 1998 [a]	Total Stores at End Fiscal 1998	Planned Store Openings Fiscal 1999 [b]
GAP			150-200
Gap	75	944	
GapKids/babyGap	42	507	
International			80-100
United Kingdom	19	101	
Canada	9	117	
France	6	30	
Japan	15	31	
Germany	1	11	
BANANA REPUBLIC	32	279	40
International	1	10	
OLD NAVY	118	398	130
TOTAL	318	2,428	400

(a) Does not include store closings.
(b) Represents approximate numbers.

Financial Contents

Key Financial Statistics

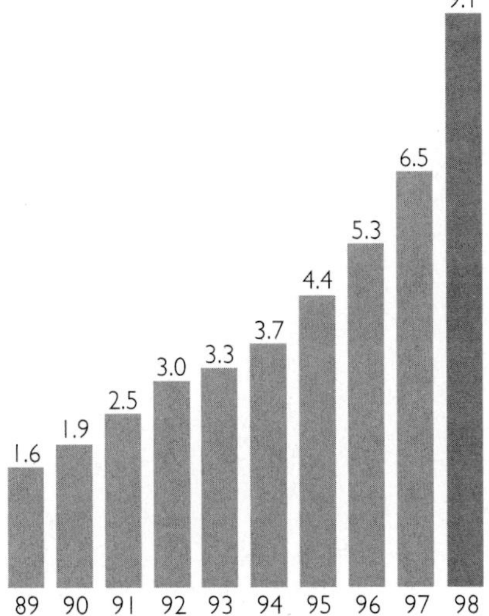

Net Sales
(in billions of dollars)
10-year CAGR=22%

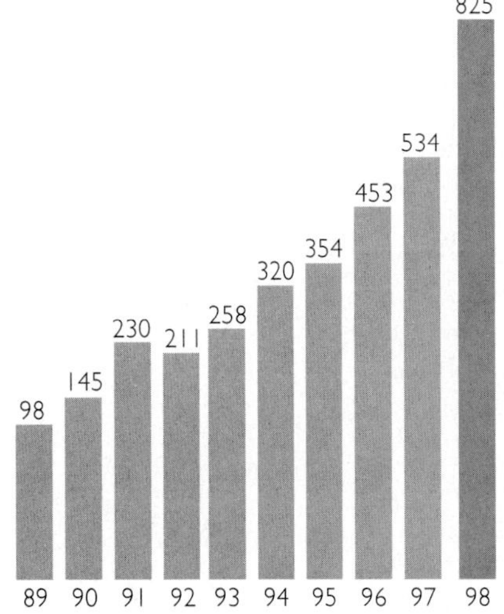

Net Earnings
(in millions of dollars)
10-year CAGR=27%

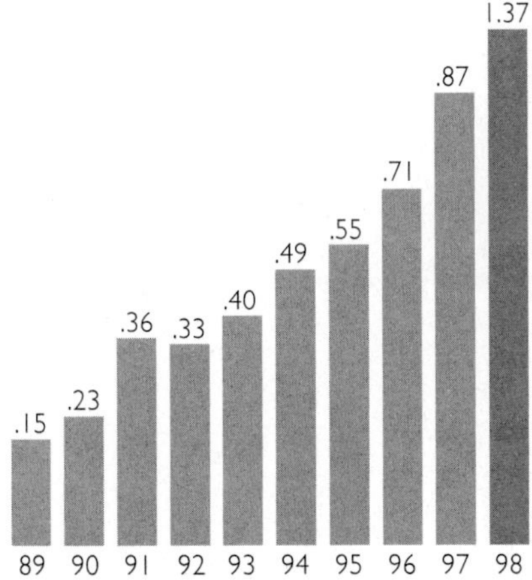

Earnings Per Share–Diluted
(in dollars)
10-year CAGR=29%

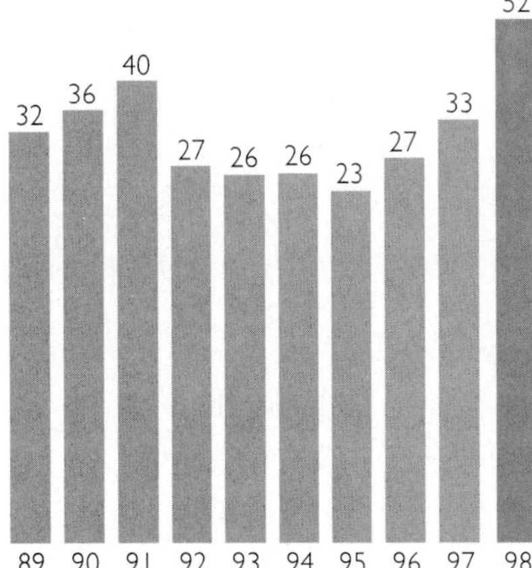

Return on Average Shareholders' Equity
(percent)

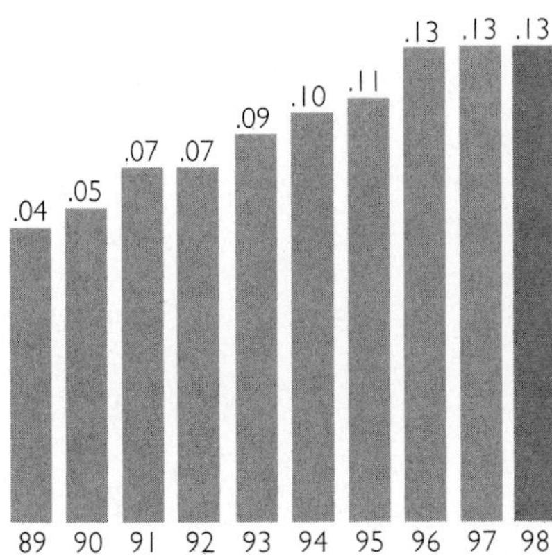

Dividends Paid Per Share
(in dollars)

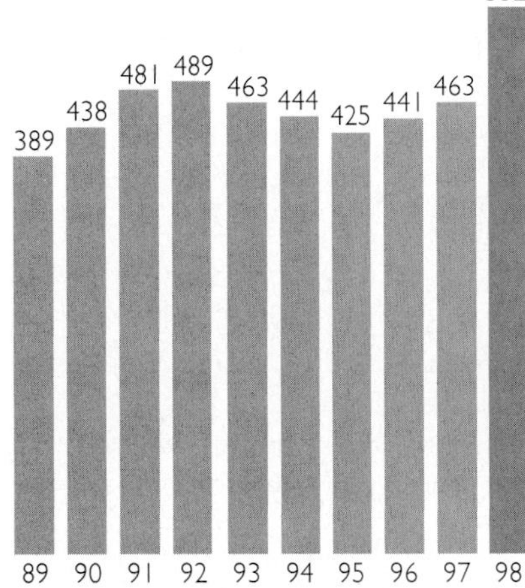

Sales Per Average Gross Square Foot†
(in dollars)

†52-week basis.

Ten-Year Selected Financial Data

	Compound Annual Growth Rate				
	3-year	5-year	10-year	1998 52 weeks	1997 52 weeks
OPERATING RESULTS ($000)					
Net sales	27%	22%	22%	$9,054,462	$6,507,825
Cost of goods sold and occupancy expenses, excluding depreciation and amortization	—	—	—	5,013,473	3,775,957
Percentage of net sales	—	—	—	55.4%	58.0%
Depreciation and amortization[(a)]	—	—	—	$ 304,745	$ 245,584
Operating expenses	—	—	—	2,403,365	1,635,017
Net interest expense (income)	—	—	—	13,617	(2,975)
Earnings before income taxes	31	25	26	1,319,262	854,242
Percentage of net sales	—	—	—	14.6%	13.1%
Income taxes	—	—	—	$ 494,723	$ 320,341
Net earnings	33	26	27	824,539	533,901
Percentage of net sales	—	—	—	9.1%	8.2%
Cash dividends paid	—	—	—	$ 76,888	$ 79,503
Capital expenditures	—	—	—	842,655	483,114
PER SHARE DATA					
Net earnings–basic	36%	28%	28%	$1.43	$.90
Net earnings–diluted	36	28	29	1.37	.87
Cash dividends paid[(b)]	—	—	—	.13	.13
Shareholders' equity (book value)	—	—	—	2.75	2.69
FINANCIAL POSITION ($000)					
Property and equipment, net	25%	20%	26%	$1,876,370	$1,365,246
Merchandise inventory	30	26	19	1,056,444	733,174
Total assets	19	18	23	3,963,919	3,337,502
Working capital	—	—	—	318,721	839,399
Current ratio	—	—	—	1.21:1	1.85:1
Total long-term debt, less current installments	—	—	—	$ 496,455	$ 496,044
Ratio of long-term debt to shareholders' equity	—	—	—	.32:1	.31:1
Shareholders' equity	—	—	—	$1,573,679	$1,583,986
Return on average assets	—	—	—	22.6%	17.9%
Return on average shareholders' equity	—	—	—	52.2%	33.0%
STATISTICS					
Number of stores opened	12%	24%	12%	318	298
Number of stores expanded	—	—	—	135	98
Number of stores closed	—	—	—	20	22
Number of stores open at year-end[(c)]	13	12	10	2,428	2,130
Net increase in number of stores	—	—	—	14%	15%
Comparable store sales growth (52-week basis)	—	—	—	17%	6%
Sales per square foot (52-week basis)[(d)]	—	—	—	$532	$463
Square footage of gross store space at year-end	19	20	17	18,757,400	15,312,700
Percentage increase in square feet	—	—	—	22%	21%
Number of employees at year-end	23	20	19	111,000	81,000
Weighted-average number of shares–basic	—	—	—	576,041,373	594,269,963
Weighted-average number of shares–diluted	—	—	—	602,916,255	615,301,137
Number of shares outstanding at year-end, net of treasury stock	—	—	—	571,973,354	589,699,542

(a) Excludes amortization of restricted stock, discounted stock options and discount on long-term debt.

(b) Excludes a dividend of $.0333 per share declared in January 1999 but paid in the first quarter of fiscal 1999.

(c) Includes the conversion of GapKids departments to their own separate stores. Converted stores are not classified as new stores.

(d) Based on weighted-average gross square footage.

Fiscal Year							
1996 52 weeks	1995 53 weeks	1994 52 weeks	1993 52 weeks	1992 52 weeks	1991 52 weeks	1990 52 weeks	1989 53 weeks
$5,284,381	$4,395,253	$3,722,940	$3,295,679	$2,960,409	$2,518,893	$1,933,780	$1,586,596
3,093,709	2,645,736	2,202,133	1,996,929	1,856,102	1,496,156	1,187,644	1,006,647
58.5%	60.2%	59.2%	60.6%	62.7%	59.4%	61.4%	63.4%
$ 191,457	$ 175,719	$ 148,863	$ 124,860	$ 99,451	$ 72,765	$ 53,599	$ 39,589
1,270,138	1,004,396	853,524	748,193	661,252	575,686	454,180	364,101
(19,450)	(15,797)	(10,902)	809	3,763	3,523	1,435	2,760
748,527	585,199	529,322	424,888	339,841	370,763	236,922	162,714
14.2%	13.3%	14.2%	12.9%	11.5%	14.7%	12.3%	10.3%
$ 295,668	$ 231,160	$ 209,082	$ 166,464	$ 129,140	$ 140,890	$ 92,400	$ 65,086
452,859	354,039	320,240	258,424	210,701	229,873	144,522	97,628
8.6%	8.1%	8.6%	7.8%	7.1%	9.1%	7.5%	6.2%
$ 83,854	$ 66,993	$ 64,775	$ 53,041	$ 44,106	$ 41,126	$ 29,625	$ 22,857
375,838	309,599	236,616	215,856	213,659	244,323	199,617	94,266
$ .72	$ .57	$ .51	$ .41	$ .34	$ .38	$ .24	$.16
.71	.55	.49	.40	.33	.36	.23	.15
.13	.11	.10	.09	.07	.07	.05	.04
2.68	2.53	2.11	1.72	1.37	1.06	.73	.53
$1,135,720	$ 957,752	$ 828,777	$ 740,422	$ 650,368	$ 547,740	$ 383,548	$ 238,103
578,765	482,575	370,638	331,155	365,692	313,899	247,462	243,482
2,626,927	2,343,068	2,004,244	1,763,117	1,379,248	1,147,414	776,900	579,483
554,359	728,301	555,827	494,194	355,649	235,537	101,518	129,139
1.72:1	2.32:1	2.11:1	2.07:1	2.06:1	1.71:1	1.39:1	1.69:1
—	—	—	$ 75,000	$ 75,000	$ 80,000	$ 17,500	$ 20,000
N/A	N/A	N/A	.07:1	.08:1	.12:1	.04:1	.06:1
$1,654,470	$1,640,473	$1,375,232	$1,126,475	$ 887,839	$ 677,788	$ 465,733	$ 337,972
18.2%	16.3%	17.0%	16.4%	16.7%	23.9%	21.3%	18.4%
27.5%	23.5%	25.6%	25.7%	26.9%	40.2%	36.0%	31.8%
203	225	172	108	117	139	152	98
42	55	82	130	94	79	56	7
30	53	34	45	26	15	20	38
1,854	1,680	1,508	1,370	1,307	1,216	1,092	960
10%	11%	10%	5%	7%	11%	14%	7%
5%	0%	1%	1%	5%	13%	14%	15%
$441	$425	$444	$463	$489	$481	$438	$389
12,645,000	11,100,200	9,165,900	7,546,300	6,509,200	5,638,400	4,762,300	4,056,600
14%	21%	21%	16%	15%	18%	17%	5%
66,000	60,000	55,000	44,000	39,000	32,000	26,000	23,000
625,719,947	626,577,596	632,466,639	626,858,004	618,944,994	610,511,282	602,947,623	599,771,631
640,900,830	641,628,773	647,429,741	643,406,853	640,602,521	635,531,438	629,967,009	630,929,312
617,663,996	647,432,964	651,441,371	653,619,276	648,833,571	641,355,003	635,688,135	632,481,318

Management's Discussion and Analysis
of Results of Operations and Financial Condition

The information below and elsewhere in this Annual Report contains certain forward-looking statements which reflect the current view of Gap Inc. (the "Company") with respect to future events and financial performance. Wherever used, the words "expect," "plan," "anticipate," "believe" and similar expressions identify forward-looking statements.

Any such forward-looking statements are subject to risks and uncertainties and the Company's future results of operations could differ materially from historical results or current expectations. Some of these risks include, without limitation, ongoing competitive pressures in the apparel industry, risks associated with challenging international retail environments, changes in the level of consumer spending or preferences in apparel, trade restrictions and political or financial instability in countries where the Company's goods are manufactured, disruption to operations from Year 2000 issues and/or other factors that may be described in the Company's Annual Report on Form 10-K and/or other filings with the Securities and Exchange Commission. Future economic and industry trends that could potentially impact revenues and profitability are difficult to predict.

The Company does not undertake to publicly update or revise its forward-looking statements even if experience or future changes make it clear that any projected results expressed or implied therein will not be realized.

Results of Operations

NET SALES

	Fifty-two Weeks Ended Jan. 30, 1999	Fifty-two Weeks Ended Jan. 31, 1998	Fifty-two Weeks Ended Feb. 1, 1997
Net sales ($000)	$9,054,462	$6,507,825	$5,284,381
Total net sales growth percentage	39	23	20
Comparable store sales growth percentage	17	6	5
Net sales per average gross square foot	$532	$463	$441
Square footage of gross store space at year-end (000)	18,757	15,313	12,645
Number of:			
New stores	318	298	203
Expanded stores	135	98	42
Closed stores	20	22	30

The total net sales growth for all years presented was attributable primarily to the increase in retail selling space, both through the opening of new stores (net of stores closed) and the expansion of existing stores. An increase in comparable store sales also contributed to net sales growth for all years presented.

The increase in net sales per average square foot for 1998 and 1997 was primarily attributable to increases in comparable store sales.

COST OF GOODS SOLD AND OCCUPANCY EXPENSES

Cost of goods sold and occupancy expenses as a percentage of net sales decreased 3.1 and .4 percentage points in 1998 from 1997 and in 1997 from 1996, respectively.

The decrease in 1998 from 1997 was attributable to a decrease in occupancy expenses as a percentage of net sales combined with an increase in merchandise margin. The decrease in occupancy expenses as a percentage of net sales was primarily due to leverage achieved through comparable store sales growth. The margin improvement was due to higher margins achieved on marked-down goods, as well as to an increase in the percentage of merchandise sold at regular price.

The decrease in 1997 from 1996 was primarily attributable to a decrease in occupancy expenses as a percentage of net sales, partially offset by a decrease in merchandise margin. The decrease in occupancy expenses as a percentage of net sales was primarily attributable to leverage achieved through comparable store sales growth.

As a general business practice, the Company reviews its inventory levels in order to identify slow-moving merchandise and broken assortments (items no longer in stock in a sufficient range of sizes) and uses markdowns to clear merchandise. Such markdowns may have an adverse impact on earnings, depending upon the extent of the markdown and the amount of inventory affected.

OPERATING EXPENSES

Operating expenses as a percentage of net sales increased 1.4 percentage points in 1998 from 1997 and 1.1 percentage points in 1997 from 1996.

In 1998, the increase was driven by significantly higher advertising/marketing costs as part of the Company's continued brand development efforts, partially offset by a decrease as a percentage of net sales in the write-off of leasehold improvements and fixtures associated with the remodeling, relocation and closing of certain stores planned for the next fiscal year, as well as to leverage from comparable store sales growth.

In 1997, the increase was primarily attributable to both increases in advertising/marketing costs and the write-off of leasehold improvements and fixtures.

NET INTEREST EXPENSE/INCOME

The change in 1998 to net interest expense from net interest income in 1997 was primarily due to the interest expense incurred for the full fiscal year related to the $500 million of debt securities issued during the third quarter of 1997. The Company's greater short-term borrowings in the last half of 1998 compared to 1997 also contributed to the increase in interest expense. The decrease in net interest income in 1997 from 1996 was due to the interest expense related to the long-term debt and to a decrease in gross average investments.

INCOME TAXES

The effective tax rate was 37.5 percent in 1998 and 1997 and 39.5 percent in 1996. The decrease in the effective tax rate in 1997 was a result of the impact of tax planning initiatives to support changing business needs.

Liquidity and Capital Resources

The following sets forth certain measures of the Company's liquidity:

	Fiscal Year		
	1998	1997	1996
Cash provided by operating activities ($000)	$1,394,161	$844,651	$834,953
Working capital ($000)	318,721	839,399	554,359
Current ratio	1.21:1	1.85:1	1.72:1

For the fiscal year ended January 30, 1999, the increase in cash provided by operating activities was due to an increase in net earnings and the timing of payments for certain payables, partially offset by investments in merchandise inventory. The decline in working capital and the current ratio was attributable to an increase in payables driven by business growth combined with a decrease in cash resulting from greater capital expenditures and share repurchases. For the fiscal year ended January 31, 1998, the increase in cash provided by operating activities was attributable to an increase in net earnings, offset by investments in merchandise inventory and the timing of payments for income taxes and certain payables.

The Company funds inventory expenditures during normal and peak periods through a combination of cash flows from operations and short-term financing arrangements. The Company's business follows a seasonal pattern, peaking over a total of about 10 to 13 weeks during the Back-to-School and Holiday periods. During 1998 and 1997, these periods accounted for 37 and 35 percent, respectively, of the Company's annual sales.

The Company has committed credit facilities totaling $950 million, consisting of an $800 million, 364-day revolving credit facility, and a $150 million, 5-year revolving credit facility through June 28, 2003. These credit facilities provide for the issuance of up to $450 million in letters of credit. The Company has additional uncommitted credit facilities of $400 million for the issuance of letters of credit. At January 30, 1999, the Company had outstanding letters of credit totaling approximately $677 million. The credit facilities also provide backup for the Company's $500 million commercial paper program. During the last half of fiscal 1998, the Company issued a total of $500 million of commercial paper to cover short-term borrowing needs. The Company had no commercial paper outstanding at January 30, 1999.

To provide financial flexibility, the Company filed a shelf registration statement in January 1999 with the Securities and Exchange Commission for $500 million of debt securities. The net proceeds from any issuance are expected to be used for general corporate purposes, including expansion of stores, distribution centers and headquarters facilities, brand investment, development of additional distribution channels and repurchases of the Company's common stock pursuant to its ongoing repurchase program. No assurances can be given that the Company will issue these debt securities.

In fiscal 1997, the Company issued $500 million of 6.9 percent ten-year debt securities. The proceeds were used for general corporate purposes similar to those described above.

In addition, during the first quarter of fiscal 1999, the Company's Japanese subsidiary issued $50 million of ten-year debt securities. The net proceeds are intended to be used for general corporate purposes. The cash flows relating to the bonds were swapped for the equivalent amounts in Japanese yen to minimize currency exposure.

Capital expenditures, net of construction allowances and dispositions, totaled approximately $797 million in 1998. These expenditures resulted in a net increase in store space of approximately 3.4 million square feet or 22 percent due to the addition of 318 new stores, the expansion of 135 stores and the remodeling of certain stores. Capital expenditures for 1997 and 1996 were $450 million and $359 million, respectively, resulting in a net increase in store space of 2.7 million square feet in 1997 and 1.5 million square feet in 1996.

The increases in capital expenditures in 1998 from 1997 and in 1997 from 1996 were primarily attributable to the number of stores opened, expanded and remodeled, as well as the expansion of headquarters facilities. The addition and expansion of distribution centers also contributed to the 1998 increase.

For 1999, the Company expects capital expenditures to exceed $1 billion, net of construction allowances. This represents the addition of 400 to 470 new stores, the expansion of approximately 100 to 110 stores and the remodeling of certain stores, as well as amounts for headquarters facilities, distribution centers and equipment. The Company expects to fund such capital expenditures with cash flow from operations and other sources of financing. Square footage growth is expected to be in excess of 20 percent before store closings. New stores are generally expected to be leased.

In 1997, the Company completed construction of a headquarters facility in San Bruno, California for approximately $60 million. The Company acquired land in 1998 in San Bruno and San Francisco on which to construct additional headquarters facilities. Construction commenced during the third quarter on the San Francisco property.

Also during 1997, the Company commenced construction on a distribution center for an estimated cost at completion of $60 million. The majority of the expenditures for this facility were incurred in 1998. The facility is expected to begin operations in early 1999.

On October 28, 1998, the Company's Board of Directors authorized a three-for-two split of its common stock effective November 30, 1998, in the form of a stock dividend for shareholders of record at the close of business on November 11, 1998. All share and per share amounts in the accompanying consolidated financial statements for all periods have been restated to reflect the stock split.

In October 1998, the Board of Directors approved a program under which the Company may purchase up to 45 million shares of its common stock. This program follows an earlier 67.5 million share repurchase program, under which the Company acquired 23.8 million shares for approximately $910 million during 1998. To date under the earlier program 66.1 million shares have been repurchased for approximately $1.7 billion.

During 1998, the Company entered into various put option contracts in connection with the share repurchase program to hedge against stock price fluctuations. The Company also continued to enter into foreign exchange forward contracts to reduce exposure to foreign currency exchange risk involved in its commitments to purchase merchandise for foreign operations. Additional information on these contracts and agreements is presented in the Notes to Consolidated Financial Statements (Note E). Quantitative and qualitative disclosures about market risk for financial instruments are presented on page 41.

Year 2000 Issue

The Year 2000 issue is primarily the result of computer programs using a two-digit format, as opposed to four digits, to indicate the year. Such computer systems will be unable to interpret dates beyond the year 1999, which could cause a system failure or other computer errors, leading to a disruption in the operation of such systems. In 1996, the Company established a project team to coordinate existing Year 2000 activities and address remaining Year 2000 issues. The team has focused its efforts on three areas: (1) information systems software and hardware; (2) facilities and distribution equipment and (3) third-party relationships.

The Program. The Company has adopted a five-phase Year 2000 program consisting of: Phase I—identification and ranking of the components of the Company's systems, equipment and suppliers that may be vulnerable to Year 2000 problems; Phase II—assessment of items identified in Phase I; Phase III—remediation or replacement of non-compliant systems and components and determination of solutions for non-compliant suppliers; Phase IV—testing of systems and components following remediation and Phase V—developing contingency plans to address the most reasonably likely worst case Year 2000 scenarios. The Company has completed Phases I and II and continues to make progress according to plan on Phases III, IV and V.

Information Systems Software and Hardware. The Company has completed Phase II and has made substantial progress on Phase III. Phase IV testing is being conducted concurrently with Phase III activities. Management believes that the Company is on track to complete remediation, testing and implementation of its individual information systems by mid-1999. Phase V contingency planning has begun and is expected to be complete by the end of the third quarter of 1999.

Facilities and Distribution Equipment. The Company has completed Phase II and is actively working on Phase III. Phase IV testing and Phase V contingency planning are scheduled to begin in the first quarter of 1999.

Third-Party Relationships. The Company has completed Phase II and is actively working on Phase III. Phase IV certification and Phase V contingency planning are expected to begin in the first quarter of 1999.

Risks / Contingency Plans. Based on the assessment efforts to date, the Company does not believe that the Year 2000 issue will have a material adverse effect on its financial condition or results of operations. The Company operates a large number of geographically dispersed stores and has a large supplier base and believes that these factors will mitigate any adverse impact. The Company's beliefs and expectations, however, are based on certain assumptions and expectations that ultimately may prove to be inaccurate.

The Company has identified that a significant disruption in the product supply chain represents the most reasonably likely worst case Year 2000 scenario. Potential sources of risk include (a) the inability of principal suppliers or logistics providers to be Year 2000-ready, which could result in delays in product deliveries from such suppliers or logistics providers and (b) disruption of the distribution channel, including ports, transportation vendors and the Company's own distribution centers as a result of a general failure of systems and necessary infrastructure such as electricity supply. The Company is preparing plans to flow inventory around an assumed period of disruption to the supply chain, which could include accelerating selected critical products to reduce the impact of significant failure.

The Company does not expect the costs associated with its Year 2000 efforts to be substantial. Approximately $30 million has been budgeted to address the Year 2000 issue, of which $16.5 million has been expensed through January 30, 1999. The Company's aggregate estimate does not include time and costs that may be incurred by the Company as a result of the failure of any third parties, including suppliers, to become Year 2000-ready or costs to implement any contingency plans.

Per Share Data

	Market Prices				Cash Dividends	
Fiscal	1998		1997		1998	1997
	High	Low	High	Low		
1st Quarter	$34 5/16	$26 5/16	$16 1/16	$12 11/16	$.0333	$.0333
2nd Quarter	44 15/16	33 11/16	19 7/8	13 5/8	.0333	.0333
3rd Quarter	45 5/16	30 1/4	23 13/16	18 11/16	.0333	.0333
4th Quarter	65	39 1/8	27 1/2	21 15/16	.0333[(a)]	.0333
Year					$.1332	$.1332

(a) Excludes a dividend of $.0333 per share declared in January 1999 but paid in the first quarter of fiscal 1999.

The principal markets on which the Company's stock is traded are the New York Stock Exchange and the Pacific Exchange. The number of holders of record of the Company's stock as of March 12, 1999 was 7,967.

Management's Report on Financial Information

Management is responsible for the integrity and consistency of all financial information presented in the Annual Report. The financial statements have been prepared in accordance with generally accepted accounting principles and necessarily include certain amounts based on Management's best estimates and judgments.

In fulfilling its responsibility for the reliability of financial information, Management has established and maintains accounting systems and procedures appropriately supported by internal accounting controls. Such controls include the selection and training of qualified personnel, an organizational structure providing for division of responsibility, communication of requirement for compliance with approved accounting control and business practices and a program of internal audit. The extent of the Company's system of internal accounting control recognizes that the cost should not exceed the benefits derived and that the evaluation of those factors requires estimates and judgments by Management. Although no system can ensure that all errors or irregularities have been eliminated, Management believes that the internal accounting controls in use provide reasonable assurance, at reasonable cost, that assets are safeguarded against loss from unauthorized use or disposition, that transactions are executed in accordance with Management's authorization and that the financial records are reliable for preparing financial statements and maintaining accountability for assets. The financial statements of the Company have been audited by Deloitte & Touche LLP, independent auditors whose report appears below.

The Audit and Finance Committee (the "Committee") of the Board of Directors is comprised solely of directors who are not officers or employees of the Company. The Committee is responsible for recommending to the Board of Directors the selection of independent auditors. It meets periodically with Management, the independent auditors and the internal auditors to assure that they are carrying out their responsibilities. The Committee also reviews and monitors the financial, accounting and auditing procedures of the Company in addition to reviewing the Company's financial reports. Deloitte & Touche LLP and the internal auditors have full and free access to the Committee, with and without Management's presence.

Independent Auditors' Report
To the Shareholders and Board of Directors of The Gap, Inc.:

We have audited the accompanying consolidated balance sheets of The Gap, Inc. and subsidiaries as of January 30, 1999 and January 31, 1998, and the related consolidated statements of earnings, shareholders' equity and cash flows for each of the three fiscal years in the period ended January 30, 1999. These financial statements are the responsibility of the Company's management. Our responsibility is to express an opinion on these financial statements based on our audits.

We conducted our audits in accordance with generally accepted auditing standards. Those standards require that we plan and perform the audit to obtain reasonable assurance about whether the consolidated financial statements are free of material misstatement. An audit includes examining, on a test basis, evidence supporting the amounts and disclosures in the financial statements. An audit also includes assessing the accounting principles used and significant estimates made by management, as well as evaluating the overall financial statement presentation. We believe that our audits provide a reasonable basis for our opinion.

In our opinion, such consolidated financial statements present fairly, in all material respects, the financial position of the Company and its subsidiaries as of January 30, 1999 and January 31, 1998, and the results of their operations and their cash flows for each of the three fiscal years in the period ended January 30, 1999 in conformity with generally accepted accounting principles.

Deloitte & Touche LLP

San Francisco, California
February 25, 1999

Consolidated Statements of Earnings

($000 except per share amounts)	Fifty-two Weeks Ended January 30, 1999	Percentage to Sales	Fifty-two Weeks Ended January 31, 1998	Percentage to Sales	Fifty-two Weeks Ended February 1, 1997	Percentage to Sales
Net sales	$9,054,462	100.0%	$6,507,825	100.0%	$5,284,381	100.0%
Costs and expenses						
Cost of goods sold and occupancy expenses	5,318,218	58.7	4,021,541	61.8	3,285,166	62.2
Operating expenses	2,403,365	26.5	1,635,017	25.1	1,270,138	24.0
Net interest expense (income)	13,617	0.2	(2,975)	0.0	(19,450)	(0.4)
Earnings before income taxes	1,319,262	14.6	854,242	13.1	748,527	14.2
Income taxes	494,723	5.5	320,341	4.9	295,668	5.6
Net earnings	$ 824,539	9.1%	$ 533,901	8.2%	$ 452,859	8.6%
Weighted-average number of shares–basic	576,041,373		594,269,963		625,719,947	
Weighted-average number of shares–diluted	602,916,255		615,301,137		640,900,830	
Earnings per share–basic	$1.43		$.90		$.72	
Earnings per share–diluted	1.37		.87		.71	

See Notes to Consolidated Financial Statements.

Consolidated Balance Sheets

($000 except par value)	January 30, 1999	January 31, 1998
ASSETS		
Current Assets		
Cash and equivalents	$ 565,253	$ 913,169
Merchandise inventory	1,056,444	733,174
Other current assets	250,127	184,604
Total current assets	1,871,824	1,830,947
Property and Equipment		
Leasehold improvements	1,040,959	846,791
Furniture and equipment	1,601,572	1,236,450
Land and buildings	160,776	154,136
Construction-in-progress	245,020	66,582
	3,048,327	2,303,959
Accumulated depreciation and amortization	(1,171,957)	(938,713)
Property and equipment, net	1,876,370	1,365,246
Lease rights and other assets	215,725	141,309
Total assets	$ 3,963,919	$ 3,337,502
LIABILITIES AND SHAREHOLDERS' EQUITY		
Current Liabilities		
Notes payable	$ 90,690	$ 84,794
Accounts payable	684,130	416,976
Accrued expenses and other current liabilities	655,770	406,181
Income taxes payable	122,513	83,597
Total current liabilities	1,553,103	991,548
Long-Term Liabilities		
Long-term debt	496,455	496,044
Deferred lease credits and other liabilities	340,682	265,924
Total long-term liabilities	837,137	761,968
Shareholders' Equity		
Common stock $.05 par value		
Authorized 1,500,000,000 shares; issued 664,997,475 and 659,884,262 shares; outstanding 571,973,354 and 589,699,542 shares	33,250	32,994
Additional paid-in capital	365,662	221,890
Retained earnings	3,121,360	2,392,750
Accumulated other comprehensive earnings	(12,518)	(15,230)
Deferred compensation	(31,675)	(38,167)
Treasury stock, at cost	(1,902,400)	(1,010,251)
Total shareholders' equity	1,573,679	1,583,986
Total liabilities and shareholders' equity	$ 3,963,919	$ 3,337,502

See Notes to Consolidated Financial Statements.

Consolidated Statements of Cash Flows

($000)	Fifty-two Weeks Ended January 30, 1999	Fifty-two Weeks Ended January 31, 1998	Fifty-two Weeks Ended February 1, 1997
CASH FLOWS FROM OPERATING ACTIVITIES			
Net earnings	$824,539	$533,901	$452,859
Adjustments to reconcile net earnings to net cash provided by operating activities:			
Depreciation and amortization[(a)]	326,447	269,706	214,905
Tax benefit from exercise of stock options and vesting of restricted stock	79,808	23,682	47,348
Deferred income taxes	(34,766)	(13,706)	(28,897)
Change in operating assets and liabilities:			
Merchandise inventory	(322,287)	(156,091)	(93,800)
Prepaid expenses and other	(77,292)	(44,736)	(16,355)
Accounts payable	265,296	63,532	88,532
Accrued expenses	231,178	107,365	87,974
Income taxes payable	38,805	(8,214)	25,706
Deferred lease credits and other long-term liabilities	62,433	69,212	56,681
Net cash provided by operating activities	1,394,161	844,651	834,953
CASH FLOWS FROM INVESTING ACTIVITIES			
Net maturity (purchase) of short-term investments	—	174,709	(11,774)
Net purchase of long-term investments	—	(2,939)	(40,120)
Net purchase of property and equipment	(797,592)	(465,843)	(371,833)
Acquisition of lease rights and other assets	(28,815)	(19,779)	(12,206)
Net cash used for investing activities	(826,407)	(313,852)	(435,933)
CASH FLOWS FROM FINANCING ACTIVITIES			
Net increase in notes payable	1,357	44,462	18,445
Net issuance of long-term debt	—	495,890	—
Issuance of common stock	49,421	30,653	37,053
Net purchase of treasury stock	(892,149)	(593,142)	(466,741)
Cash dividends paid	(76,888)	(79,503)	(83,854)
Net cash used for financing activities	(918,259)	(101,640)	(495,097)
Effect of exchange rate fluctuations on cash	2,589	(1,634)	2,155
Net (decrease) increase in cash and equivalents	(347,916)	427,525	(93,922)
Cash and equivalents at beginning of year	913,169	485,644	579,566
Cash and equivalents at end of year	$565,253	$913,169	$485,644

See Notes to Consolidated Financial Statements.

(a) Includes amortization of restricted stock, discounted stock options and discount on long-term debt.

Consolidated Statements of Shareholders' Equity

($000 except share and per share amounts)	Common Stock Shares	Common Stock Amount	Additional Paid-in Capital
Balance at February 3, 1996	710,935,439	$35,547	$315,445
Issuance of common stock pursuant to stock option plans	3,580,141	179	19,634
Net issuance of common stock pursuant to management incentive restricted stock plans	678,623	34	32,788
Tax benefit from exercise of stock options by employees and from vesting of restricted stock			47,348
Foreign currency translation adjustments			
Amortization of restricted stock			
Purchase of treasury stock			
Reissuance of treasury stock			6,969
Net earnings			
Cash dividends ($.13 per share)			
Balance at February 1, 1997	715,194,203	$35,760	$422,184
Issuance of common stock pursuant to stock option plans[a]	4,272,851	213	47,892
Net cancellations of common stock pursuant to management incentive restricted stock plans	(1,420,292)	(71)	(10,428)
Tax benefit from exercise of stock options by employees and from vesting of restricted stock			23,682
Foreign currency translation adjustments			
Amortization of restricted stock and discounted stock options			
Purchase of treasury stock			
Reissuance of treasury stock			7,344
Retirement of treasury stock	(58,162,500)	(2,908)	(268,784)
Net earnings			
Cash dividends ($.13 per share)			
Balance at January 31, 1998	659,884,262	$32,994	$221,890
Issuance of common stock pursuant to stock option plans[b]	5,050,130	253	46,836
Net issuance of common stock pursuant to management incentive restricted stock plans	63,083	3	4,362
Tax benefit from exercise of stock options by employees and from vesting of restricted stock			79,808
Adjustments for foreign currency translation ($1,893) and fluctuations in fair market value of financial instruments ($819)			
Amortization of restricted stock and discounted stock options			
Purchase of treasury stock			
Reissuance of treasury stock			12,766
Net earnings			
Cash dividends ($.17 per share [c])			
Balance at January 30, 1999	664,997,475	$33,250	$365,662

See Notes to Consolidated Financial Statements.

(a) Includes payout of cash for fractional shares resulting from the three-for-two split of common stock effective December 22, 1997.

(b) Includes payout of cash for fractional shares resulting from the three-for-two split of common stock effective November 30, 1998.

(c) Includes a dividend of $.0333 per share declared in January 1999 but paid in the first quarter of fiscal 1999.

Retained Earnings	Accumulated Other Comprehensive Earnings	Deferred Compensation	Treasury Stock Shares	Treasury Stock Amount	Total	Comprehensive Earnings
$1,569,347	$ (9,071)	$(48,735)	(63,502,475)	$ (222,060)	$1,640,473	
		(9,648)			10,165	
		(12,903)			19,919	
					47,348	
	3,884				3,884	$ 3,884
		23,448			23,448	
			(34,926,975)	(468,246)	(468,246)	
			899,243	1,505	8,474	
452,859					452,859	452,859
(83,854)					(83,854)	
$1,938,352	$ (5,187)	$(47,838)	(97,530,207)	$ (688,801)	$1,654,470	$456,743
		(18,166)			29,939	
		3,869			(6,630)	
					23,682	
	(10,043)				(10,043)	(10,043)
		23,968			23,968	
			(31,785,451)	(598,149)	(598,149)	
			968,438	5,007	12,351	
			58,162,500	271,692	0	
533,901					533,901	533,901
(79,503)					(79,503)	
$2,392,750	$(15,230)	$(38,167)	(70,184,720)	$(1,010,251)	$1,583,986	$523,858
		(10,351)			36,738	
		(3,873)			492	
					79,808	
	2,712				2,712	2,712
		20,716			20,716	
			(23,809,650)	(910,387)	(910,387)	
			970,249	18,238	31,004	
824,539					824,539	824,539
(95,929)					(95,929)	
$3,121,360	$(12,518)	$(31,675)	(93,024,121)	$(1,902,400)	$1,573,679	$827,251

Notes to Consolidated Financial Statements

For the Fifty-two Weeks ended January 30, 1999 (fiscal 1998), the Fifty-two Weeks ended January 31, 1998 (fiscal 1997), and the Fifty-two Weeks ended February 1, 1997 (fiscal 1996).

NOTE A: SUMMARY OF SIGNIFICANT ACCOUNTING POLICIES

Gap Inc. (the "Company") is a global specialty retailer which operates stores selling casual apparel, personal care and other accessories for men, women and children under a variety of brand names including Gap, Banana Republic and Old Navy. Its principal markets consist of the United States, Canada, Europe and Asia with the United States being the most significant.

On October 28, 1998, the Company's Board of Directors authorized a three-for-two split of its common stock effective November 30, 1998, in the form of a stock dividend for shareholders of record at the close of business on November 11, 1998. All share and per share amounts in the accompanying consolidated financial statements for all periods have been restated to reflect the stock split.

The consolidated financial statements include the accounts of the Company and its subsidiaries. Intercompany accounts and transactions have been eliminated.

The preparation of financial statements in conformity with generally accepted accounting principles requires Management to make estimates and assumptions that affect the reported amounts of assets and liabilities and disclosure of contingent assets and liabilities at the date of the financial statements and the reported amounts of revenue and expenses during the reporting period. Actual results could differ from those estimates.

Cash and equivalents represent cash and short-term, highly liquid investments with original maturities of three months or less.

Merchandise inventory is stated at the lower of FIFO (first-in, first-out) cost or market.

Property and equipment are stated at cost. Depreciation and amortization are computed using the straight-line method over the estimated useful lives of the related assets.

Lease rights are recorded at cost and are amortized over the estimated useful lives of the respective leases, not to exceed 20 years.

Costs associated with the opening or remodeling of stores, such as pre-opening rent and payroll, are expensed as incurred. The net book value of fixtures and leasehold improvements for stores scheduled to be closed or expanded within the next fiscal year is charged against current earnings.

Costs associated with the production of advertising, such as writing copy, printing and other costs, are expensed as incurred. Costs associated with communicating advertising that has been produced, such as television and magazine, are expensed when the advertising first takes place. Direct response costs of catalogs are capitalized and amortized over the expected lives of the related catalogs, not to exceed six months. Advertising costs were $419 million, $175 million and $96 million in fiscal 1998, 1997 and 1996, respectively.

Deferred income taxes arise from temporary differences between the tax basis of assets and liabilities and their reported amounts in the consolidated financial statements.

Translation adjustments result from translating foreign subsidiaries' financial statements into U.S. dollars. Balance sheet accounts are translated at exchange rates in effect at the balance sheet date. Income statement accounts are translated at average exchange rates during the year. Resulting translation adjustments are included in shareholders' equity.

The Company accounts for stock-based awards using the intrinsic value-based method under Accounting Principles Board (APB) Opinion No. 25, *Accounting for Stock Issued to Employees,* and has provided pro forma disclosures of net earnings and earnings per share in accordance with the provisions of Statement of Financial Accounting Standards (SFAS) No. 123, *Accounting for Stock-Based Compensation.* Restricted stock and discounted stock options represent deferred compensation and are shown as a reduction of shareholders' equity.

In fiscal 1998, the Company adopted SFAS No. 130, *Reporting Comprehensive Income*, which requires that an enterprise report, by major components and as a single total, the change in its net assets during the period from non-owner sources. The components of comprehensive earnings are shown in the Consolidated Statements of Shareholders' Equity.

The Company also adopted SFAS No. 131, *Disclosures About Segments of an Enterprise and Related Information*, which establishes annual and interim reporting standards for an enterprise's operating segments and related disclosures about its products, services, geographic areas and major customers. The Company has one reportable segment given the similarities of economic characteristics between the operations represented by the Company's three brands. Revenues of international retail operations represent 10.1 percent, 9.7 percent and 9.1 percent of Gap Inc.'s revenues for fiscal

1998, 1997 and 1996, respectively. Long-term assets of international operations, including retail and sourcing, represent 14.3 percent and 13.4 percent of Gap Inc.'s long-term assets for fiscal 1998 and 1997, respectively.

The Company adopted SFAS No. 133, *Accounting for Derivative Instruments and Hedging Activities*, on November 1, 1998. In accordance with the transition provisions of SFAS No. 133, the Company recorded the fair value of derivatives designated as fair-value and cash-flow hedges on the balance sheet. The Company also recorded a corresponding offset within the balance sheet to reflect the fair value of the hedged firm commitments. The net impact of the cumulative-effect adjustment for fair-value hedges was not material. The Company also recorded an immaterial cumulative-effect adjustment in comprehensive earnings to recognize at fair value all derivatives designated as cash-flow hedges.

Certain reclassifications have been made to the 1996 and 1997 financial statements to conform with the 1998 financial statements.

NOTE B: DEBT AND OTHER CREDIT ARRANGEMENTS

The Company has committed credit facilities totaling $950 million, consisting of an $800 million, 364-day revolving credit facility, and a $150 million, 5-year revolving credit facility through June 28, 2003. These credit facilities provide for the issuance of up to $450 million in letters of credit. The Company has additional uncommitted credit facilities of $400 million for the issuance of letters of credit. At January 30, 1999, the Company had outstanding letters of credit totaling $677,305,000.

Borrowings under the Company's credit agreements are subject to the Company not exceeding a certain debt ratio. The Company was in compliance with this debt covenant at January 30, 1999.

During fiscal 1997, the Company issued long-term debt which consists of $500 million of 6.9 percent unsecured notes, due September 15, 2007. Interest on the notes is payable semi-annually. The fair value of the notes at January 30, 1999 was approximately $552 million, based on the current rates at which the Company could borrow funds with similar terms and remaining maturities. The balance of the debt is net of unamortized discount.

Gross interest payments were $47,415,000, $8,399,000 and $2,800,000 in fiscal 1998, 1997 and 1996, respectively.

NOTE C: INCOME TAXES

Income taxes consisted of the following:

($000)	Fifty-two Weeks Ended Jan. 30, 1999	Fifty-two Weeks Ended Jan. 31, 1998	Fifty-two Weeks Ended Feb. 1, 1997
Currently Payable			
Federal	$438,110	$279,068	$266,063
State	55,716	33,384	36,167
Foreign	35,663	21,595	22,335
Total currently payable	529,489	334,047	324,565
Deferred			
Federal	(29,163)	(14,832)	(23,980)
State and foreign	(5,603)	1,126	(4,917)
Total deferred	(34,766)	(13,706)	(28,897)
Total provision	$494,723	$320,341	$295,668

The foreign component of pretax earnings before eliminations and corporate allocations in fiscal 1998, 1997 and 1996 was $190,864,000, $84,487,000 and $82,220,000, respectively. No provision was made for U.S. income taxes on the undistributed earnings of the foreign subsidiaries as it is the Company's intention to utilize those earnings in the foreign operations for an indefinite period of time or repatriate such earnings only when tax effective to do so. Undistributed earnings of foreign subsidiaries were $371,886,000 at January 30, 1999.

The difference between the effective income tax rate and the United States federal income tax rate is summarized as follows:

	Fifty-two Weeks Ended Jan. 30, 1999	Fifty-two Weeks Ended Jan. 31, 1998	Fifty-two Weeks Ended Feb. 1, 1997
Federal tax rate	35.0%	35.0%	35.0%
State income taxes, less federal benefit	2.5	3.2	4.4
Other	0.0	(0.7)	0.1
Effective tax rate	37.5%	37.5%	39.5%

Deferred tax assets (liabilities) consisted of the following:

($000)	Jan. 30, 1999	Jan. 31, 1998
Compensation and benefits accruals	$ 43,509	$ 31,367
Scheduled rent	54,687	44,451
Inventory capitalization	40,976	28,776
Nondeductible accruals	10,257	20,003
Other	22,031	17,854
Gross deferred tax assets	171,460	142,451
Depreciation	(4,058)	(9,553)
Other	(6,083)	(6,345)
Gross deferred tax liabilities	(10,141)	(15,898)
Net deferred tax assets	$161,319	$126,553

Net deferred tax assets at January 30, 1999 and January 31, 1998 are included in Other Current Assets ($101,048,000 and $66,120,000, respectively), and Lease Rights and Other Assets ($60,271,000 and $60,433,000, respectively) in the Consolidated Balance Sheets. Income tax payments were $410,919,000, $320,744,000 and $249,968,000 in fiscal 1998, 1997 and 1996, respectively.

NOTE D: LEASES

The Company leases most of its store premises and headquarters facilities and some of its distribution centers. These leases expire at various dates through 2017.

The aggregate minimum non-cancelable annual lease payments under leases in effect on January 30, 1999 are as follows:

Fiscal Year	($000)
1999	$ 511,335
2000	496,589
2001	472,029
2002	440,932
2003	385,126
Thereafter	1,322,334
Total minimum lease commitment	$3,628,345

Many leases entered into by the Company include options that may extend the lease term beyond the initial commitment period, subject to terms agreed to at lease inception. Some leases also include early termination options which can be exercised under specific conditions. If conditions did not warrant invoking early termination of any leases, and all renewal options were exercised for current lease agreements, the total lease commitment for the Company would be approximately $5.7 billion.

For leases that contain predetermined fixed escalations of the minimum rentals, the Company recognizes the related rental expense on a straight-line basis and records the difference between the recognized rental expense and amounts payable under the leases as deferred lease credits. At January 30, 1999 and January 31, 1998, this liability amounted to $154,897,000 and $129,981,000, respectively.

Cash or rent abatements received upon entering into certain store leases are recognized on a straight-line basis as a reduction to rent expense over the lease term. The unamortized portion is included in deferred lease credits.

Some of the leases relating to stores in operation at January 30, 1999 contain renewal options for periods ranging up to 30 years. Many leases also provide for payment of operating expenses, real estate taxes and for additional rent based on a percentage of sales. No lease directly imposes any restrictions relating to leasing in other locations (other than radius clauses).

Rental expense for all operating leases was as follows:

($000)	Fifty-two Weeks Ended Jan. 30, 1999	Fifty-two Weeks Ended Jan. 31, 1998	Fifty-two Weeks Ended Feb. 1, 1997
Minimum rentals	$460,715	$391,472	$337,487
Contingent rentals	75,601	38,657	30,644
Total	$536,316	$430,129	$368,131

NOTE E: FINANCIAL INSTRUMENTS

Foreign Exchange Forward Contracts

The Company operates in foreign countries which exposes it to market risk associated with foreign currency exchange rate fluctuations. The Company's risk management policy is to hedge substantially all merchandise purchases for foreign operations through the use of foreign exchange forward contracts to minimize this risk. At January 30, 1999, the Company had contracts maturing at various dates through 1999 to sell the equivalent of $309,775,000 in foreign currencies (83,200,000 British pounds, 171,100,000 Canadian dollars, 41,582,379,856 Italian lire, 3,254,000,000 Japanese yen and 1,334,870,281 Spanish pesetas) at the contracted rates.

Changes in the fair value of forward contracts designated as fair-value hedges, along with the offsetting changes in fair value of the related firm commitments to purchase foreign merchandise, are recorded in cost of sales in the current period. Changes in the fair value of forward contracts designated as cash-flow hedges are recorded as a component of comprehensive earnings, and are recognized in earnings when the hedged merchandise inventory is paid for. The related balance included in comprehensive earnings at January 30, 1999 will be recognized in earnings over the next 12 months. The critical terms of the forward contracts and the respective firm commitments and forecasted foreign purchase transactions are essentially the same. As a result, there were no amounts reflected in fiscal 1998 earnings resulting from hedge ineffectiveness.

NOTE F: EMPLOYEE BENEFIT AND INCENTIVE STOCK COMPENSATION PLANS

Retirement Plans

The Company has a qualified defined contribution retirement plan, called GapShare, which is available to employees who meet certain age and service requirements. This plan permits employees to make contributions up to the maximum limits allowable under the Internal Revenue Code. Under the plan, the Company matches all or a portion of the employee's contributions under a predetermined formula. The Company's contributions vest immediately. Company contributions to the retirement plan in 1998, 1997 and 1996 were $14,284,000, $12,907,000 and $11,427,000, respectively.

A nonqualified Executive Deferred Compensation Plan was established on January 1, 1999 which allows eligible employees to defer compensation up to a maximum amount. This plan superseded an earlier nonqualified Executive Deferred Compensation Plan, established on January 1, 1994, and a nonqualified Executive Capital Accumulation Plan, established on April 1, 1994. The Company does not match employees' contributions under the current plan.

A Deferred Compensation Plan was established on August 26, 1997 for nonemployee members of the Board of Directors. Under this plan, Board members may elect to defer receipt on a pre-tax basis of eligible compensation received for serving as nonemployee directors of the Company. In exchange for compensation deferred, Board members are granted discounted stock options to purchase shares of the Company's common stock. All options are fully exercisable upon the date granted and expire seven years after grant or one year after retirement from the Board, if earlier. The Company may issue up to 450,000 shares under the plan.

Incentive Stock Compensation Plans

The 1996 Stock Option and Award Plan (the "Plan") was established on March 26, 1996. The Board authorized 62,227,561 shares for issuance under the Plan, which includes shares available under the Management Incentive Restricted Stock Plan ("MIRSP") and an earlier stock option plan established in 1981, both of which were superseded by the Plan. The Plan empowers the Compensation and Stock Option Committee of the Board of Directors (the "Committee") to award compensation primarily in the form of nonqualified stock options or restricted stock to key employees. Stock options generally expire ten years from the grant date or one year after the date of retirement, if earlier. Stock options generally vest over a three-year period, with shares becoming exercisable in full on the third anniversary of the grant date. Nonqualified stock options are generally issued at fair market value but may be issued at prices less than the fair market value at the date of grant or at other prices as determined by the Committee. Total compensation cost for those stock options issued at less than fair market value and for the restricted shares issued was $20,845,000, $17,170,000 and $22,248,000 in 1998, 1997 and 1996, respectively.

In 1998, the Company established a stock option plan for non-officers, called Stock Up On Success, under which eligible employees may receive nonqualified stock options. The Board of Directors authorized 4,000,000 shares for issuance under Stock Up On Success. Stock options under the plan must be issued at not less than fair market value. On February 25, 1999, options to purchase 983,400 shares were granted to approximately 19,000 employees under the plan. These stock options have a vesting period of $1\frac{1}{2}$ years and expire ten years after the grant date.

Employee Stock Purchase Plan

The Company has an Employee Stock Purchase Plan under which all eligible employees may purchase common stock of the Company at 85 percent of the lower of the closing price of the Company's common stock on the grant date or the purchase date on the New York Stock Exchange Composite Transactions Index. Employees pay for their stock purchases through payroll deductions at a rate equal to any whole percentage from 1 percent to 15 percent. There were 960,410 shares issued under the plan during fiscal 1998, 968,438 during 1997 and 899,243 during 1996. All shares were acquired from reissued treasury stock. At January 30, 1999, there were 5,304,458 shares reserved for future subscriptions.

NOTE G: SHAREHOLDERS' EQUITY AND STOCK OPTIONS

Common and Preferred Stock

The Company is authorized to issue 60,000,000 shares of Class B common stock which is convertible into shares of common stock on a share-for-share basis; transfer of the shares is restricted. In addition, the holders of the Class B common stock have six votes per share on most matters and are entitled to a lower cash dividend. No Class B shares have been issued.

The Board of Directors is authorized to issue 30,000,000 shares of one or more series of preferred stock and to establish at the time of issuance the issue price, dividend rate, redemption price, liquidation value, conversion features and such other terms and conditions of each series (including voting rights) as the Board of Directors deems appropriate, without further action on the part of the shareholders. No preferred shares have been issued.

In October 1998, the Board of Directors approved a program under which the Company may purchase up to 45 million shares of its common stock. This program follows an earlier 67.5 million share repurchase program, under which the Company acquired 23.8 million shares for approximately

$910 million during 1998. To date under the earlier program 66.1 million shares have been repurchased for approximately $1.7 billion.

Stock Options

Under the Company's stock option plans, nonqualified options to purchase common stock are granted to officers, directors and employees at exercise prices equal to the fair market value of the stock at the date of grant or at other prices as determined by the Compensation and Stock Option Committee of the Board of Directors.

Stock option activity for all employee benefit plans was as follows:

	Shares	Weighted-Average Exercise Price
Balance at February 3, 1996	35,190,954	$ 7.61
Granted	14,046,165	13.73
Exercised	(3,580,141)	5.53
Canceled	(1,797,912)	9.90
Balance at February 1, 1997	43,859,066	$ 9.64
Granted	17,088,797	14.41
Exercised	(4,273,551)	7.10
Canceled	(3,838,943)	10.67
Balance at January 31, 1998	52,835,369	$11.31
Granted	18,963,355	32.18
Exercised	(5,068,828)	7.43
Canceled	(1,891,206)	17.91
Balance at January 30, 1999	64,838,690	$17.53

Outstanding options at January 30, 1999 have expiration dates ranging from March 26, 1999 to January 26, 2009.

At January 30, 1999, the Company reserved 88,981,648 shares of its common stock, including 69,260 treasury shares, for the exercise of stock options. There were 24,142,958 and 37,289,148 shares available for granting of options at January 30, 1999 and January 31, 1998, respectively. Options for 7,275,359, 6,449,771 and 6,559,833 shares were exercisable as of January 30, 1999, January 31, 1998 and February 1, 1997, respectively, and had a weighted-average exercise price of $8.26, $7.77 and $6.01 for those respective periods.

The Company accounts for its stock option and award plans in accordance with APB Opinion No. 25, under which no compensation cost has been recognized for stock option awards granted at fair market value. Had compensation cost for the Company's stock-based compensation plans been determined based on the fair value at the grant dates for awards under those plans in accordance with the provisions of SFAS No. 123, *Accounting for Stock-Based Compensation*, the Company's net earnings and earnings per share would have been reduced to the pro forma amounts indicated below. The effects of applying SFAS No. 123 in this pro forma disclosure are not indicative of future amounts. SFAS No. 123 does not apply to awards prior to fiscal year 1995. Additional awards in future years are anticipated.

	Fifty-two Weeks Ended Jan. 30, 1999	Fifty-two Weeks Ended Jan. 31, 1998	Fifty-two Weeks Ended Feb. 1, 1997
Net earnings ($000)			
As reported	$824,539	$533,901	$452,859
Pro forma	772,062	507,966	437,232
Earnings per share			
As reported–basic	$1.43	$.90	$.72
Pro forma–basic	1.34	.85	.70
As reported–diluted	1.37	.87	.71
Pro forma–diluted	1.28	.83	.68

The weighted-average fair value of the stock options granted during fiscal 1998, 1997 and 1996 was $11.25, $5.84 and $4.98, respectively. The fair value of each option granted is estimated on the date of the grant using the Black-Scholes option-pricing model with the following weighted-average assumptions for grants in 1998: dividend yield of .4 percent; expected price volatility of 32 percent; risk-free interest rates ranging from 5.3 percent to 5.7 percent and expected lives between 3.9 and 6.1 years. The fair value of stock options granted in 1997 was based on the following weighted-average assumptions: dividend yield of .7 percent; expected price volatility of 31 percent; risk-free interest rates ranging from 5.9 percent to 7.0 percent and expected lives between 3.9 and 5.8 years. The fair value of stock options granted prior to 1997 was based on the following weighted-average assumptions: dividend yield of 1.0 percent; expected price volatility of 30 percent; risk-free interest rates ranging from 5.5 percent to 6.5 percent and expected lives between 3.6 and 5.8 years.

The following table summarizes information about stock options outstanding at January 30, 1999:

	Options Outstanding			Options Exercisable	
Range of Exercise Prices	Number Outstanding at Jan. 30, 1999	Weighted-Average Remaining Contractual Life (in years)	Weighted-Average Exercise Price	Number Exercisable at Jan. 30, 1999	Weighted-Average Exercise Price
$ 5.45 to $ 8.69	19,519,642	4.71	$ 7.91	4,648,267	$ 6.89
8.94 to 13.91	14,180,163	7.30	12.88	2,395,097	9.86
13.92 to 22.73	12,926,859	7.71	16.06	164,610	15.13
22.75 to 62.22	18,212,026	9.15	32.49	67,385	29.48
$ 5.45 to $62.22	64,838,690	7.12	$17.53	7,275,359	$ 8.26

NOTE H: EARNINGS PER SHARE

Under SFAS No. 128, the Company provides dual presentation of EPS on a basic and diluted basis. The Company's granting of certain stock options and restricted stock resulted in potential dilution of basic EPS. The following summarizes the effects of the assumed issuance of dilutive securities on weighted-average shares for basic EPS.

	Fifty-two Weeks Ended Jan. 30, 1999	Fifty-two Weeks Ended Jan. 31, 1998	Fifty-two Weeks Ended Feb. 1, 1997
Weighted-average number of shares–basic	576,041,373	594,269,963	625,719,947
Incremental shares from assumed issuance of:			
Stock options	23,560,445	15,056,550	8,395,829
Restricted stock	3,314,437	5,974,624	6,785,054
Weighted-average number of shares–diluted	602,916,255	615,301,137	640,900,830

The number of incremental shares from the assumed issuance of stock options and restricted stock is calculated applying the treasury stock method.

Excluded from the above computation of weighted-average shares for diluted EPS were options to purchase 18,175 shares of common stock during fiscal 1998, 660,095 during 1997 and 7,627,467 during 1996. Issuance of these securities would have resulted in an antidilutive effect on EPS.

NOTE I: RELATED PARTY TRANSACTIONS

The Company has an agreement with Fisher Development, Inc. (FDI), wholly owned by the brother of the Company's chairman, setting forth the terms under which FDI may act as general contractor in connection with the Company's construction activities. FDI acted as general contractor for 302, 266 and 177 new stores' leasehold improvements and fixtures during fiscal 1998, 1997 and 1996, respectively. In the same respective years, FDI supervised construction of 135, 97 and 38 expansions, as well as remodels of existing stores and headquarters facilities. Total cost of construction was $342,030,000, $233,777,000 and $111,871,000, including profit and overhead costs of $28,877,000, $16,845,000 and $10,751,000, for fiscal 1998, 1997 and 1996, respectively. At January 30, 1999 and January 31, 1998, amounts due to FDI were $15,302,000 and $10,318,000, respectively. The terms and conditions of the agreement with FDI are reviewed annually by the Audit and Finance Committee of the Board of Directors.

NOTE J: QUARTERLY FINANCIAL INFORMATION (UNAUDITED)

Fiscal 1998

($000 except per share amounts)	Thirteen Weeks Ended May 2, 1998	Thirteen Weeks Ended Aug. 1, 1998	Thirteen Weeks Ended Oct. 31, 1998	Thirteen Weeks Ended Jan. 30, 1999	Fifty-two Weeks Ended Jan. 30, 1999
Net sales	$1,719,712	$1,904,970	$2,399,948	$3,029,832	$9,054,462
Gross profit	688,708	769,805	1,023,943	1,253,788	3,736,244
Net earnings	136,066	136,874	237,749	313,850	824,539
Earnings per share–basic	.23	.23	.42	.55	1.43
Earnings per share–diluted	.22	.22	.40	.53	1.37

Fiscal 1997

($000 except per share amounts)	Thirteen Weeks Ended May 3, 1997	Thirteen Weeks Ended Aug. 2, 1997	Thirteen Weeks Ended Nov. 1, 1997	Thirteen Weeks Ended Jan. 31, 1998	Fifty-two Weeks Ended Jan. 31, 1998
Net sales	$1,231,186	$1,345,221	$1,765,939	$2,165,479	$6,507,825
Gross profit	442,060	462,135	721,266	860,823	2,486,284
Net earnings	84,304	69,458	164,523	215,616	533,901
Earnings per share–basic	.14	.12	.28	.37	.90
Earnings per share–diluted	.14	.11	.27	.36	.87

Quantitative and Qualitative Disclosures About Market Risk

The table below provides information about the Company's market sensitive financial instruments as of January 30, 1999 and January 31, 1998.

The Company purchases foreign exchange forward contracts to hedge substantially all merchandise purchases made by foreign operations. These contracts are entered into with large reputable financial institutions, thereby minimizing the risk of credit loss. Further discussion of these contracts appears in the Notes to the Consolidated Financial Statements (Note E).

During fiscal 1997, the Company issued $500 million of unsecured notes, due September 15, 2007, with a fixed interest rate of 6.9 percent. By entering into the fixed-rate notes, the Company avoided interest rate risk from variable rate fluctuations.

A portion of the Company's fixed-rate short-term borrowings used to finance foreign operations is denominated in foreign currencies. By borrowing and repaying the loans in local currencies, the Company avoided the risk associated with exchange rate fluctuations.

	January 30, 1999			January 31, 1998		
($000)	Average Contract Rate[a]	Notional Amount of Forward Contracts in U.S. Dollars	Fair Value[b]	Average Contract Rate[a]	Notional Amount of Forward Contracts in U.S. Dollars	Fair Value[b]
Foreign exchange forward contracts(c)						
British pounds	.61	$137,222	$136,581	.60	$ 33,394	$ 33,269
Canadian dollars	1.51	112,967	112,228	1.40	32,984	31,757
Italian lire	1,700.06	24,459	25,052	1,743.25	35,924	35,383
Japanese yen	126.24	25,776	28,197	120.52	12,803	12,266
Spanish pesetas	142.75	9,351	9,189	151.98	8,125	8,112
Total foreign exchange forward contracts		$309,775	$311,247		$123,230	$120,787

	January 30, 1999		January 31, 1998	
($000)	Carrying Amount in U.S. Dollars	Fair Value[d]	Carrying Amount in U.S. Dollars	Fair Value[d]
Notes payable	$496,455	$551,818	$496,044	$526,128

(a) Currency per U.S. dollar.
(b) Calculated using forward spot rates at the dates presented.
(c) All contracts mature within one year.
(d) Based on the rates at which the Company could borrow funds with similar terms and remaining maturities at the dates presented.

Appendix B
Time Value of Money: Future Value and Present Value

The following discussion of future value lays the foundation for our explanation of present value in Chapter 8 but is not essential. For the valuation of long-term liabilities, some instructors may wish to begin on page 671.

The term *time value of money* refers to the fact that money earns interest over time. *Interest* is the cost of using money. To borrowers, interest is the expense of renting money. To lenders, interest is the revenue earned from lending. We must always recognize the interest we receive or pay. Otherwise, we overlook an important part of the transaction. Suppose you invest $4,545 in corporate bonds that pay 10% interest each year. After one year, the value of your investment has grown to $5,000. The difference between your original investment ($4,545) and the future value of the investment ($5,000) is the amount of interest revenue you will earn during the year ($455). If you ignored the interest, you would fail to account for the interest revenue you have earned. Interest becomes more important as the time period lengthens because the amount of interest depends on the span of time the money is invested.

Let's consider a second example, this time from the borrower's perspective. Suppose you purchase a machine for your business. The cash price of the machine is $8,000, but you cannot pay cash now. To finance the purchase, you sign an $8,000 note payable. The note requires you to pay the $8,000 plus 10% interest one year from the date of purchase. Is your cost of the machine $8,000, or is it $8,800 [$8,000 plus interest of $800 ($8,000 × 0.10)]? The cost is $8,000. The additional $800 is interest expense and not part of the cost of the machine.

FUTURE VALUE

The main application of future value is the accumulated balance of an investment at a future date. In our first example above, the investment earned 10% per year. After one year, $4,545 grew to $5,000, as shown in Exhibit B-1. If the money were invested for five years, you would have to perform five such calculations. You would also have to consider the compound interest that your investment is earning. *Compound interest* is not only the interest you earn on your principal amount,

EXHIBIT B-1
Future Value: An Example

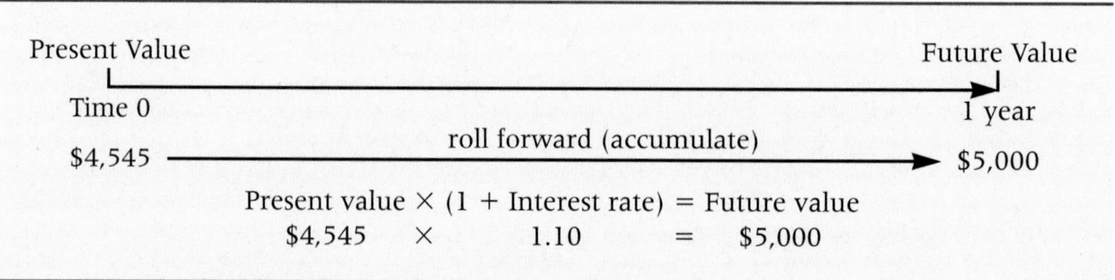

but also the interest you receive on the interest you have already earned. Most business applications include compound interest. The following table shows the interest revenue earned on the original $4,545 investment each year for five years at 10%:

End of Year	*Interest*	*Future Value*
0	—	$4,545
1	$4,545 × 0.10 = $455	5,000
2	5,000 × 0.10 = 500	5,500
3	5,500 × 0.10 = 550	6,050
4	6,050 × 0.10 = 605	6,655
5	6,655 × 0.10 = 666	7,321

Earning 10%, a $4,545 investment grows to $5,000 at the end of one year, to $5,500 at the end of two years, and $7,321 at the end of five years. Throughout this appendix we round off to the nearest dollar.

Future-Value Tables

The process of computing a future value is called *accumulating* because the future value is *more* than the present value. Mathematical tables ease the computational burden. Exhibit B-2, Future Value of $1, gives the future value for a single sum (a present value), $1, invested to earn a particular interest rate for a specific number of periods. Future value depends on three factors: (1) the amount of the investment, (2) the length of time between investment and future accumulation, and (3) the interest rate. Future-value and present-value tables are based on $1 because unity (the value 1) is so easy to work with.

In business applications, interest rates are always stated for the annual period of one year unless specified otherwise. In fact, an interest rate can be stated for any period, such as 3% per quarter or 5% for a six-month period. The length of the

EXHIBIT B-2
Future Value of $1

Future Value of $1

Periods	*4%*	*5%*	*6%*	*7%*	*8%*	*9%*	*10%*	*12%*	*14%*	*16%*
1	1.040	1.050	1.060	1.070	1.080	1.090	1.100	1.120	1.140	1.160
2	1.082	1.103	1.124	1.145	1.166	1.188	1.210	1.254	1.300	1.346
3	1.125	1.158	1.191	1.225	1.260	1.295	1.331	1.405	1.482	1.561
4	1.170	1.216	1.262	1.311	1.360	1.412	1.464	1.574	1.689	1.811
5	1.217	1.276	1.338	1.403	1.469	1.539	1.611	1.762	1.925	2.100
6	1.265	1.340	1.419	1.501	1.587	1.677	1.772	1.974	2.195	2.436
7	1.316	1.407	1.504	1.606	1.714	1.828	1.949	2.211	2.502	2.826
8	1.369	1.477	1.594	1.718	1.851	1.993	2.144	2.476	2.853	3.278
9	1.423	1.551	1.689	1.838	1.999	2.172	2.358	2.773	3.252	3.803
10	1.480	1.629	1.791	1.967	2.159	2.367	2.594	3.106	3.707	4.411
11	1.539	1.710	1.898	2.105	2.332	2.580	2.853	3.479	4.226	5.117
12	1.601	1.796	2.012	2.252	2.518	2.813	3.138	3.896	4.818	5.936
13	1.665	1.886	2.133	2.410	2.720	3.066	3.452	4.363	5.492	6.886
14	1.732	1.980	2.261	2.579	2.937	3.342	3.798	4.887	6.261	7.988
15	1.801	2.079	2.397	2.759	3.172	3.642	4.177	5.474	7.138	9.266
16	1.873	2.183	2.540	2.952	3.426	3.970	4.595	6.130	8.137	10.748
17	1.948	2.292	2.693	3.159	3.700	4.328	5.054	6.866	9.276	12.468
18	2.026	2.407	2.854	3.380	3.996	4.717	5.560	7.690	10.575	14.463
19	2.107	2.527	3.026	3.617	4.316	5.142	6.116	8.613	12.056	16.777
20	2.191	2.653	3.207	3.870	4.661	5.604	6.728	9.646	13.743	19.461

period is arbitrary. For example, an investment may promise a return (income) of 3% per quarter for six months (two quarters). In that case, you would be working with 3% interest for two periods. It would be incorrect to use 6% for one period because the interest is 3% compounded quarterly, and that amount differs from 6% compounded semiannually. *Take care in studying future-value and present-value problems to align the interest rate with the appropriate number of periods.*

Let's see how a future-value table like the one in Exhibit B-2 is used. The future value of $1.00 invested at 8% for one year is $1.08 ($1.00 × 1.080, which appears at the junction of the 8% column and row 1 in the Periods column). The figure 1.080 includes both the principal (1.000) and the compound interest for one period (0.080).

Suppose you deposit $5,000 in a savings account that pays annual interest of 8%. The account balance at the end of one year will be $5,400. To compute the future value of $5,000 at 8% for one year, multiply $5,000 by 1.080 to get $5,400. Now suppose you invest in a 10-year, 8% certificate of deposit (CD). What will be the future value of the CD at maturity? To compute the future value of $5,000 at 8% for 10 periods, multiply $5,000 by 2.159 (from Exhibit B-2) to get $10,795. This future value of $10,795 indicates that $5,000, earning 8% interest compounded annually, grows to $10,795 at the end of 10 years. Using Exhibit B-2, you can find any present amount's future value at a particular future date. Future value is especially helpful for computing the amount of cash you will have on hand for some purpose in the future.

Future Value of an Annuity

In the preceding example, we made an investment of a single amount. Other investments, called *annuities,* include multiple investments of an equal periodic amount at fixed intervals over the duration of the investment. Consider a family investing for a child's education. The Dietrichs can invest $4,000 annually to accumulate a college fund for 15-year-old Helen. The investment can earn 7% annually until Helen turns 18—a three-year investment. How much will be available for Helen on the date of the last investment? Exhibit B-3 shows the accumulation—a total future value of $12,860.

EXHIBIT B-3
Future Value of an Annuity

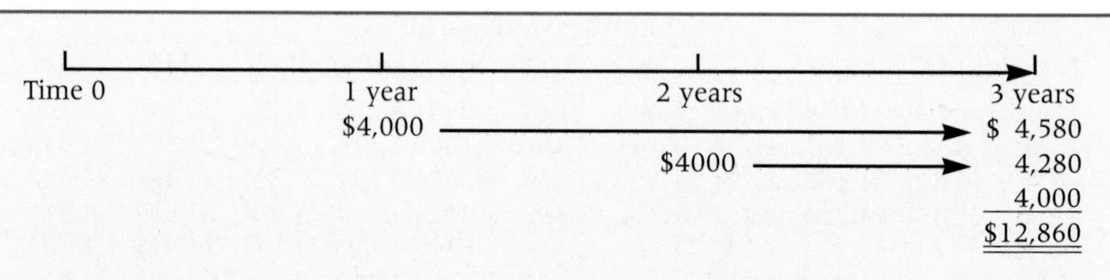

The first $4,000 invested by the Dietrichs grow to $4,580 over the investment period. The second amount grows to $4,280, and the third amount stays at $4,000 because it has no time to earn interest. The sum of the three future values ($4,580 + $4,280 + $4,000) is the future value of the annuity ($12,860), which can also be computed as follows:

End of Year	*Annual Investment*	*Interest*		*Increase for the Year*	*Future Value of Annuity*
0	—	—		—	0
1	$4,000	—		$4,000	$ 4,000
2	4,000	+ ($4,000 × 0.07 = $280)	=	4,280	8,280
3	4,000	+ ($8,280 × 0.07 = $580)	=	4,580	12,860

Future Value of Annuity of $1										
Periods	*4%*	*5%*	*6%*	*7%*	*8%*	*9%*	*10%*	*12%*	*14%*	*16%*
1	1.000	1.000	1.000	1.000	1.000	1.000	1.000	1.000	1.000	1.000
2	2.040	2.050	2.060	2.070	2.080	2.090	2.100	2.120	2.140	2.160
3	3.122	3.153	3.184	3.215	3.246	3.278	3.310	3.374	3.440	3.506
4	4.246	4.310	4.375	4.440	4.506	4.573	4.641	4.779	4.921	5.066
5	5.416	5.526	5.637	5.751	5.867	5.985	6.105	6.353	6.610	6.877
6	6.633	6.802	6.975	7.153	7.336	7.523	7.716	8.115	8.536	8.977
7	7.898	8.142	8.394	8.654	8.923	9.200	9.487	10.089	10.730	11.414
8	9.214	9.549	9.897	10.260	10.637	11.028	11.436	12.300	13.233	14.240
9	10.583	11.027	11.491	11.978	12.488	13.021	13.579	14.776	16.085	17.519
10	12.006	12.578	13.181	13.816	14.487	15.193	15.937	17.549	19.337	21.321
11	13.486	14.207	14.972	15.784	16.645	17.560	18.531	20.655	23.045	25.733
12	15.026	15.917	16.870	17.888	18.977	20.141	21.384	24.133	27.271	30.850
13	16.627	17.713	18.882	20.141	21.495	22.953	24.523	28.029	32.089	36.786
14	18.292	19.599	21.015	22.550	24.215	26.019	27.975	32.393	37.581	43.672
15	20.024	21.579	23.276	25.129	27.152	29.361	31.772	37.280	43.842	51.660
16	21.825	23.657	25.673	27.888	30.324	33.003	35.950	42.753	50.980	60.925
17	23.698	25.840	28.213	30.840	33.750	36.974	40.545	48.884	59.118	71.673
18	25.645	28.132	30.906	33.999	37.450	41.301	45.599	55.750	68.394	84.141
19	27.671	30.539	33.760	37.379	41.446	46.018	51.159	63.440	78.969	98.603
20	29.778	33.066	36.786	40.995	45.762	51.160	57.275	72.052	91.025	115.380

EXHIBIT B-4
Future Value of Annuity of $1

These computations are laborious. As with the Future Value of $1 (a lump sum), mathematical tables ease the strain of calculating annuities. Exhibit B-4, Future Value of Annuity of $1, gives the future value of a series of investments, each of equal amount, at regular intervals.

What is the future value of an annuity of three investments of $1 each that earn 7%? The answer, 3.215, can be found at the junction of the 7% column and row 3 in Exhibit B-4. This amount can be used to compute the future value of the investment for Helen's education, as follows:

Amount of each periodic investment	×	Future value of annuity of $1 (Exhibit B-4)	=	Future value of investment
$4,000	×	**3.215**	=	**$12,860**

This one-step calculation is much easier than computing the future value of each annual investment and then summing the individual future values. In this way, you can compute the future value of any investment consisting of equal periodic amounts at regular intervals. Businesses make periodic investments to accumulate funds for equipment replacement and other uses—an application of the future value of an annuity.

PRESENT VALUE

Often a person knows a future amount and needs to know the related present value. Recall Exhibit B-1, in which present value and future value are on opposite ends of the same time line. Suppose an investment promises to pay you $5,000 at the *end* of one year. How much would you pay *now* to acquire this investment? You would be willing to pay the present value of the $5,000 future amount.

Like future value, present value depends on three factors: (1) the *amount of payment (or receipt)*, (2) the length of *time* between investment and future receipt (or payment), and (3) the *interest rate*. The process of computing a present value is called *discounting* because the present value is *less* than the future value.

In our investment example, the future receipt is \$5,000. The investment period is one year. Assume that you demand an annual interest rate of 10% on your investment. With all three factors specified, you can compute the present value of \$5,000 at 10% for one year:

$$\textbf{Present value} = \frac{\textbf{Future value}}{\textbf{1 + Interest rate}} = \frac{\$5{,}000}{1.10} = \$4{,}545$$

By turning the data around into a future-value problem, we can verify the present-value computation:

Amount invested (present value)	\$4,545
Expected earnings (\$4,545 × 0.10).	455
Amount to be received one year from now (future value).	\$5,000

This example illustrates that present value and future value are based on the same equation:

$$\textbf{Future value} = \textbf{Present value} \times (1 + \textbf{Interest rate})$$

$$\textbf{Present value} = \frac{\textbf{Future value}}{\textbf{1 + Interest rate}}$$

If the \$5,000 is to be received two years from now, you will pay only \$4,132 for the investment, as shown in Exhibit B-5. By turning the data around, we verify that \$4,132 accumulates to \$5,000 at 10% for two years:

*

Amount invested (present value)	\$4,132
Expected earnings for first year (\$4,132 × 0.10)	413
Value of investment after one year	4,545
Expected earnings for second year (\$4,545 × 0.10)	455
Amount to be received two years from now (future value).	\$5,000

You would pay \$4,132—the present value of \$5,000—to receive the \$5,000 future amount at the end of two years at 10% per year. The \$868 difference between the amount invested (\$4,132) and the amount to be received (\$5,000) is the return on the investment, the sum of the two interest receipts: \$413 + \$455 = \$868.

EXHIBIT B-5
Present Value: An Example

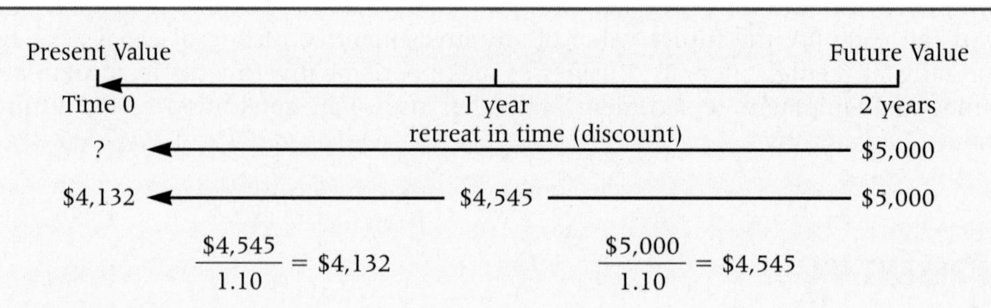

Present-Value Tables

We have shown the simple formula for computing present value. However, figuring present value "by hand" for investments spanning many years is time-consuming and presents too many opportunities for arithmetic errors. Present-value tables ease our work. Let's reexamine our examples of present value by using Exhibit B-6: Present Value of \$1.

Exhibit B-6
Present Value of $1

Present Value of $1

Periods	*4%*	*5%*	*6%*	*7%*	*8%*	*10%*	*12%*	*14%*	*16%*
1	0.962	0.952	0.943	0.935	0.926	0.909	0.893	0.877	0.862
2	0.925	0.907	0.890	0.873	0.857	0.826	0.797	0.769	0.743
3	0.889	0.864	0.840	0.816	0.794	0.751	0.712	0.675	0.641
4	0.855	0.823	0.792	0.763	0.735	0.683	0.636	0.592	0.552
5	0.822	0.784	0.747	0.713	0.681	0.621	0.567	0.519	0.476
6	0.790	0.746	0.705	0.666	0.630	0.564	0.507	0.456	0.410
7	0.760	0.711	0.665	0.623	0.583	0.513	0.452	0.400	0.354
8	0.731	0.677	0.627	0.582	0.540	0.467	0.404	0.351	0.305
9	0.703	0.645	0.592	0.544	0.500	0.424	0.361	0.308	0.263
10	0.676	0.614	0.558	0.508	0.463	0.386	0.322	0.270	0.227
11	0.650	0.585	0.527	0.475	0.429	0.350	0.287	0.237	0.195
12	0.625	0.557	0.497	0.444	0.397	0.319	0.257	0.208	0.168
13	0.601	0.530	0.469	0.415	0.368	0.290	0.229	0.182	0.145
14	0.577	0.505	0.442	0.388	0.340	0.263	0.205	0.160	0.125
15	0.555	0.481	0.417	0.362	0.315	0.239	0.183	0.140	0.108
16	0.534	0.458	0.394	0.339	0.292	0.218	0.163	0.123	0.093
17	0.513	0.436	0.371	0.317	0.270	0.198	0.146	0.108	0.080
18	0.494	0.416	0.350	0.296	0.250	0.180	0.130	0.095	0.069
19	0.475	0.396	0.331	0.277	0.232	0.164	0.116	0.083	0.060
20	0.456	0.377	0.312	0.258	0.215	0.149	0.104	0.073	0.051

For the 10% investment for one year, we find the junction of the 10% column and row 1 in Exhibit B-6. The figure 0.909 is computed as follows: $^{1}/_{1.10} = 0.909$. This work has been done for us, and only the present values are given in the table. To figure the present value for $5,000, we multiply 0.909 by $5,000. The result is $4,545, which matches the result we obtained by hand.

For the two-year investment, we read down the 10% column and across row 2. We multiply 0.826 (computed as $^{0.909}/_{1.10} = 0.826$) by $5,000 and get $4,130, which confirms our earlier computation of $4,132 (the difference is due to rounding in the present-value table). Using the table, we can compute the present value of any single future amount.

Present Value of an Annuity

Return to the investment example beginning at the asterisk on page 672. That investment provided the investor with only a single future receipt ($5,000 at the end of two years). *Annuity investments* provide multiple receipts of an equal amount at fixed intervals over the investment's duration.

Consider an investment that promises *annual* cash receipts of $10,000 to be received at the end of each of three years. Assume that you demand a 12% return on your investment. What is the investment's present value? That is, what would you pay today to acquire the investment? The investment spans three periods, and you would pay the sum of three present values. The computation is as follows:

Year	*Annual Cash Receipt*	*Present Value of $1 at 12% (Exhibit B-6)*	*Present Value of Annual Cash Receipt*
1	$10,000	0.893	$ 8,930
2	10,000	0.797	7,970
3	10,000	0.712	7,120
Total present value of investment			$24,020

The present value of this annuity is $24,020. By paying this amount today, you will receive $10,000 at the end of each of the three years while earning 12% on your investment.

This example illustrates repetitive computations of the three future amounts, a time-consuming process. One way to ease the computational burden is to add the three present values of $1 (0.893 + 0.797 + 0.712) and multiply their sum (2.402) by the annual cash receipt ($10,000) to obtain the present value of the annuity ($10,000 × 2.402 = $24,020).

An easier approach is to use a present value of an annuity table. Exhibit B-7 shows the present value of $1 to be received periodically for a given number of periods. The present value of a three-period annuity at 12% is 2.402 (the junction of row 3 and the 12% column). Thus, $10,000 received annually at the end of each of three years, discounted at 12%, is $24,020 ($10,000 × 2.402), which is the present value.

Present Value of Bonds Payable

The present value of a bond—its market price—is the present value of the future principal amount at maturity plus the present value of the future contract interest payments. The principal is a *single amount* to be paid at maturity. The interest is an *annuity* because it occurs periodically.

Let's compute the present value of the 9% five-year bonds of Chrysler Corporation (discussed on page 371). The face value of the bonds is $100,000, and they pay $4\frac{1}{2}$% contract (cash) interest semiannually (that is, twice a year).[1] At issuance, the market interest rate is expressed as 10% annually, but it is computed at 5% semiannually. Therefore, the effective interest rate for each of the 10 semiannual periods is 5%. We thus use 5% in computing the present value (PV)

[1]For a definition of contract interest rate, see page 370.

EXHIBIT B-7
Present Value of Annuity of $1

Present Value Annuity of $1

Periods	*4%*	*5%*	*6%*	*7%*	*8%*	*10%*	*12%*	*14%*	*16%*
1	0.962	0.952	0.943	0.935	0.926	0.909	0.893	0.877	0.862
2	1.886	1.859	1.833	1.808	1.783	1.736	1.690	1.647	1.605
3	2.775	2.723	2.673	2.624	2.577	2.487	2.402	2.322	2.246
4	3.630	3.546	3.465	3.387	3.312	3.170	3.037	2.914	2.798
5	4.452	4.329	4.212	4.100	3.993	3.791	3.605	3.433	3.274
6	5.242	5.076	4.917	4.767	4.623	4.355	4.111	3.889	3.685
7	6.002	5.786	5.582	5.389	5.206	4.868	4.564	4.288	4.039
8	6.733	6.463	6.210	5.971	5.747	5.335	4.968	4.639	4.344
9	7.435	7.108	6.802	6.515	6.247	5.759	5.328	4.946	4.607
10	8.111	7.722	7.360	7.024	6.710	6.145	5.650	5.216	4.833
11	8.760	8.306	7.887	7.499	7.139	6.495	5.938	5.453	5.029
12	9.385	8.863	8.384	7.943	7.536	6.814	6.194	5.660	5.197
13	9.986	9.394	8.853	8.358	7.904	7.103	6.424	5.842	5.342
14	10.563	9.899	9.295	8.745	8.244	7.367	6.628	6.002	5.468
15	11.118	10.380	9.712	9.108	8.559	7.606	6.811	6.142	5.575
16	11.652	10.838	10.106	9.447	8.851	7.824	6.974	6.265	5.669
17	12.166	11.274	10.477	9.763	9.122	8.022	7.120	6.373	5.749
18	12.659	11.690	10.828	10.059	9.372	8.201	7.250	6.467	5.818
19	13.134	12.085	11.158	10.336	9.604	8.365	7.366	6.550	5.877
20	13.590	12.462	11.470	10.594	9.818	8.514	7.469	6.623	5.929

of the maturity and of the interest. The market price of these bonds is $96,149, as follows:

	Effective annual interest rate ÷ 2	*Number of semiannual interest payments*	
PV of principal:			
$100,000 × PV of single amount at 5%		for 10 periods	
$100,000 × 0.614 (Exhibit B-6)			$61,400
PV of contract (cash) interest:			
$100,000 × 0.045 × PV of annuity at 5%		for 10 periods	
$4,500 × 7.722 (Exhibit B-7)			34,749
PV (market price) of bonds			$96,149

The market price of the Chrysler bonds shows a discount because the contract interest rate on the bonds (9%) is less than the market interest rate (10%). We discuss these bonds in more detail on pages 372–375.

Let's consider a premium price for the 9% Chrysler bonds. Assume that the market interest rate is 8% (rather than 10%) at issuance. The effective interest rate is thus 4% for each of the 10 semiannual periods:

	Effective annual interest rate ÷ 2	*Number of semiannual interest payments*	
PV of principal:			
$100,000 × PV of single amount at 4%		for 10 periods	
$100,000 × 0.676 (Exhibit B-6)			$67,600
PV of contract (cash) interest:			
$100,000 × 0.045 × PV of annuity at 4%		for 10 periods	
$4,500 × 8.111 (Exhibit B-7)			36,500
PV (market price) of bonds			$104,100

We discuss accounting for these bonds on pages 376–378. It may be helpful for you to reread this section ("Present Value of Bonds Payable") after you've studied those pages.

CAPITAL LEASES

How does a lessee compute the cost of an asset acquired through a capital lease? (See page 383 for a definition of capital leases.) Consider that the lessee gets the use of the asset but does *not* pay for the leased asset in full at the beginning of the lease. A capital lease is therefore similar to an installment purchase of the leased asset. The lessee must record the leased asset at the present value of the lease liability. The time value of money must be weighed.

The cost of the asset to the lessee is the sum of any payment made at the beginning of the lease period plus the present value of the future lease payments. The lease payments are equal amounts occurring at regular intervals—that is, they are annuity payments.

Consider a 20-year building lease that requires 20 annual payments of $10,000 each, with the first payment due immediately. The interest rate in the lease is 10%, and the present value of the 19 future payments is $83,650 ($10,000 × PV of annuity at 10% for 19 periods, or 8.365 from Exhibit B-7). The lessee's cost of the building is $93,650 (the sum of the initial payment, $10,000, plus the present value of the future payments, $83,650). The lessee would base its accounting for the leased asset (and the related depreciation) and for the lease liability (and the related interest expense) on the cost of the building that we have just computed.

Appendix Problems

PB-1 For each situation, compute the required amount.

a. Kellogg Corporation is budgeting for the acquisition of land over the next several years. Kellogg can invest $100,000 today at 9%. How much cash will Kellogg have for land acquisitions at the end of five years? At the end of six years?

b. Davidson, Inc. is planning to invest $50,000 each year for five years. The company's investment adviser believes that Davidson can earn 6% interest without taking on too much risk. What will be the value of Davidson's investment on the date of the last deposit if Davidson can earn 6%? If Davidson can earn 8%?

PB-2 For each situation, compute the required amount.

a. Intel, Inc. operations are generating excess cash that will be invested in a special fund. During 20X2, Intel invests $5,643,341 in the fund for a planned advertising campaign for a new product to be released six years later, in 20X8. If Intel's investments can earn 10% each year, how much cash will the company have for the advertising campaign in 20X8?

b. Intel, Inc. will need $10 million to advertise a new type of chip in 20X8. How much must Intel invest in 20X2 to have the cash available for the advertising campaign? Intel's investments can earn 10% annually.

c. Explain the relationship between your answers to *a* and *b*.

PB-3 Determine the present value of the following notes and bonds:

1. A $60,000, five-year note payable with contract interest rate of 9%, paid annually. The market interest rate at issuance is 10%.

2. Ten-year bonds payable with maturity value of $500,000 and contract interest rate of 12%, paid semiannually. The market rate of interest is 10% at issuance.

3. Same bonds payable as in number 2, but the market interest rate is 14%.

4. Same bonds payable as in number 2, but the market interest rate is 12%.

PB-4 On December 31, 20X1, when the market interest rate is 8%, Libby, Libby, & Short, a partnership, issues $400,000 of 10-year, 7.25% bonds payable. The bonds pay interest semiannually.

Required

1. Determine the present value of the bonds at issuance.

2. Assume that the bonds are issued at the price computed in Requirement 1. Prepare an effective-interest-method amortization table for the first two semiannual interest periods.

3. Using the amortization table prepared in Requirement 2, journalize issuance of the bonds and the first two interest payments and amortization of any premium or discount.

PB-5 St. Mere Eglise Children's Home needs a fleet of vans to transport the children to singing engagements throughout Normandy. Renault offers the vehicles for a single payment of 630,000 French francs due at the end of four years. Peugeot prices a similar fleet of vans for four annual payments of 150,000 francs at the end of each year. The children's home could borrow the funds at 6%, so this is the appropriate interest rate. Which company should get the business, Renault or Peugeot? Base your decision on present value, and give your reason.

PB-6 American Family Association acquired equipment under a capital lease that requires six annual lease payments of $40,000. The first payment is due when the lease begins, on January 1, 20X6. Future payments are due on January 1 of each year of the lease term. The interest rate in the lease is 16%.

Required

1. Compute the association's cost of the equipment.

Appendix C
Summary of Generally Accepted Accounting Principles (GAAP)

Every technical area has professional associations and regulatory bodies that govern the practice of the profession. Accounting is no exception. In the United States, generally accepted accounting principles (GAAP) are influenced most by the Financial Accounting Standards Board (FASB). The FASB has seven full-time members and a large staff. Its financial support comes from professional associations such as the American Institute of Certified Public Accountants (AICPA).

The FASB is an independent organization with no government or professional affiliation. The FASB's pronouncements, called *Statements of Financial Accounting Standards,* specify how to account for certain business transactions. Each new *Standard* becomes part of GAAP, the "accounting law of the land." In the same way that our laws draw authority from their acceptance by the people, GAAP depends on general acceptance by the business community. Throughout this book, we refer to GAAP as the proper way to do financial accounting.

The U.S. Congress has given the Securities and Exchange Commission (SEC), a government organization that regulates the trading of investments, ultimate responsibility for establishing accounting rules for companies that are owned by the general investing public. However, the SEC has delegated much of its rule-making power to the FASB. Exhibit C-1 outlines the flow of authority for developing GAAP.

The Objective of Financial Reporting

The basic objective of financial reporting is to provide information that is useful in making investment and lending decisions. The FASB believes that accounting information can be useful in decision making only if it is *relevant, reliable, comparable,* and *consistent.*

Relevant information is useful in making predictions and for evaluating past performance—that is, the information has feedback value. For example, PepsiCo's disclosure of the profitability of each of its lines of business is relevant for investor evaluations of the company. To be relevant, information must be timely. *Reliable* information is free from significant error—that is, it has validity. Also, it is free from the bias of a particular viewpoint—that is, it is verifiable and neutral. *Comparable*

Exhibit C-1
Flow of Authority for Developing GAAP

Concepts, Principles and Financial Statements	*Quick Summary*	*Text Reference*
Concepts		
Entity concept	Accounting draws a boundary around each organization to be accounted for.	Chapter 1, page 9
Going-concern concept	Accountants assume the business will continue operating for the foreseeable future.	Chapter 1, page 10
Stable-monetary-unit concept	Accounting information is expressed primarily in monetary terms that ignore the effects of inflation.	Chapter 1, page 10
Time-period concept	Ensures that accounting information is reported at regular intervals.	Chapter 3, page 108
Conservatism concept	Accountants report items in the financial statements in a way that avoids overstating assets, owners' equity, and revenues and avoids understating liabilities and expenses.	Chapter 6, page 271
Materiality concept	Accountants perform strictly proper accounting only for items that are significant to the company's financial statements.	Chapter 6, page 271
Principles		
Reliability (objectivity) principle	Accounting records and statements are based on the most reliable data available.	Chapter 1, page 9
Cost principle	Assets and services, revenues and expenses are recorded at their actual historical cost.	Chapter 1, page 10
Revenue principle	Tells accountants when to record revenue (only after it has been earned) and the amount of revenue to record (the cash value of what has been received).	Chapter 3, page 108
Matching principle	Directs accountants to (1) identify all expenses incurred during the period, (2) measure the expenses, and (3) match the expenses against the revenues earned during the period. The goal is to measure net income.	Chapter 3, page 109
Consistency principle	Businesses should use the same accounting methods from period to period.	Chapter 6, page 270
Disclosure principle	A company's financial statements should report enough information for outsiders to make informed decisions about the company.	Chapter 6, page 271
Financial Statements and Notes		
Balance sheet	Assets = Liabilities + Owners' Equity at a point in time.	Chapter 1
Income statement	Revenues and gains − Expenses and losses = Net income or net loss for the period.	Chapters 1 and 11
Statement of cash flows	Cash receipts − Cash disbursements = Increase or decrease in cash during the period, grouped under operating, investing, and financing activities.	Chapters 1 and 12
Statement of retained earnings	Beginning retained earnings + Net income (or − Net loss) − Dividends = Ending retained earnings.	Chapters 1 and 11
Statement of stockholders' equity	Shows the reason for the change in each stockholders' equity account, including retained earnings.	Chapter 11
Financial statement notes	Provide information that cannot be reported conveniently on the face of the financial statements. The notes are an integral part of the statements.	Chapter 11

EXHIBIT C-2
Summary of Important Accounting Concepts, Principles, and Financial Statements

and *consistent* information can be compared from period to period to help investors and creditors track the entity's progress through time. These characteristics combine to shape the concepts and principles that make up GAAP. Exhibit C-2 summarizes the concepts and principles that accounting has developed to provide useful information for decision making.

Appendix D
Check Figures

Chapter 1

Check Points

CP1-1 NCF
CP1-2 NCF
CP1-3 NCF
CP1-4 NCF
CP1-5 NCF
CP1-6 NCF
CP1-7 NCF
CP1-8 NCF
CP1-9 Net earnings $651 mil.
CP1-10 End. RE $100,000
CP1-11 Total assets $160,000
CP1-12 Cash bal. 12/31/00 $13,000
CP1-13 NCF

Exercises

E1-1 NCF
E1-2 NCF
E1-3 NCF
E1-4 IBM $86 bil.
E1-5 2. $653 mil.
E1-6 1. Net inc. $3 mil.
E1-7 1. $3,964 bil.
E1-8 NCF
E1-9 RE $5,876 mil.
E1-10 Net inc. $1,614 mil.; Div. $168 mil.
E1-11 End. cash bal. $123 mil.
E1-12 RE, 7/31/X1 $400
E1-13 Total assets $37,400
E1-14 Cash bal., 7/31/X1 $6,200
E1-15 NCF
E1-16 NCF

Problems

P1-1A NCF
P1-2A 1. Net inc. $22.5 bil.
P1-3A Coca-Cola Expenses $15 bil.
P1-4A 1. Total assets $82,000
P1-5A 1. Total assets $170,000
P1-6A 1. Net inc. $68,000; 3. Total assets $253,000
P1-7A Cash, ending $445 mil.
P1-8A 20X0 d. $17,213 thou.; 20X1 s. $42,541 thou.
P1-1B NCF
P1-2B 1. Net inc. $5.0 bil.
P1-3B Granite Issuance of stock $20,000
P1-4B 1. Total assets $120,000
P1-5B 1. Total assets $144,000
P1-6B 1. Net inc. $54,000; 3. Total assets $77,000
P1-7B Cash, ending $62 mil.
P1-8B 20X0 d. $4,043 thou.; 20X1 s. $13,216 thou.

Decision Cases

DC 1 NCF
DC 2 NCF

Financial Statement Cases

FS 1 3. Assets owned by stockholders $1,574 mil.

Chapter 2

Check Points

CP2-1 NCF
CP2-2 NCF
CP2-3 e. $5,800
CP2-4 Cash $62,000
CP2-5 NCF
CP2-6 NCF
CP2-7 2. Credit bal. $500
CP2-8 2. Accts. Rec. $1,000
CP2-9 Totals $40 bil.
CP2-10 2. Total assets $53,800
CP2-11 NCF
CP2-12 NCF
CP2-13 Total debits $110,000

Exercises

E2-1 Total assets $500,000
E2-2 NCF
E2-3 NCF
E2-4 Cash bal., ending $41,000
E2-5 2. a. $40,800; d. $5,300
E2-6 NCF
E2-7 2. $2,400
E2-8 2. $23,600
E2-9 2. Total SE $37,700
E2-10 NCF
E2-11 2. Net inc. $11,650
E2-12 Totals $72,100
E2-13 Cash bal. $2,300 debit
E2-14 2. Net loss $1,600
E2-15 4. T/B totals $13,400
E2-16 b. $54,400; c. $58,100; d. $8,800;
E2-17 NCF

Problems

P2-1A NCF
P2-2A 2. Net inc. $7,240; 4. Total assets $45,920
P2-3A 3. Cash bal. $14,610
P2-4A 2. Total debit bals. $65,100; 3. b. $65,100
P2-5A 2. Cash $85,400
P2-6A 3. T/B totals $23,300
P2-7A 3. T/B totals $105,300
P2-1B NCF
P2-2B 2. Net inc. $7,900; 4. Total assets $37,850
P2-3B 3. Cash bal. $21,450
P2-4B 2. Total debit bals. $46,500; 3. b. $46,500
P2-5B 2. Cash $20,000
P2-6B 3. T/B totals $32,600
P2-7B 3. T/B totals $83,200

Decision Cases

DC 1 3. T/B totals $27,200; 4. Net inc. $6,650
DC 2 NCF

Financial Statement Cases

FS 1 3. Cash bal. $565 mil.; Inventory bal. $1,056 mil.

Chapter 3

Check Points

CP3-1 Net inc. $78 mil.; Net cash inflow $107 mil.
CP3-2 NCF
CP3-3 NCF
CP3-4 a. Prepaid Rent $2,500 debit bal.
CP3-5 3. $35,000
CP3-6 1. 19X6 $2,500,000; 19X7 $200,000
CP3-7 2. Interest Payable $240 credit bal.
CP3-8 2. Interest Receivable $240 debit bal.
CP3-9 NCF
CP3-10 NCF
CP3-11 NCF

CP3-12 Net inc. $3,660 thou.; Total assets $132,532 thou.

CP3-13 RE $17,697 credit bal.

CP3-14 NCF

CP3-15 1. 1.31; 2. 0.50

Exercises

E3-1 NCF

E3-2 NCF

E3-3 NCF

E3-4 NCF

E3-5 NCF

E3-6 2. Net inc. overstated by $87,000

E3-7 1. Supplies Expense $1,500

E3-8 NCF

E3-9 NCF

E3-10 NCF

E3-11 Service Revenue $5,600 credit bal.

E3-12 Net inc. $3,500 mil.; Total assets $19,100 mil.

E3-13 Supplies expense $7,800 Salary expense $84,000

E3-14 Net inc. $415 mil.

E3-15 NCF

E3-16 Total assets $37,600; Current ratio 1.50

E3-17 7. Net inc. $1,690; Total assets $11,790

E3-18 a. $7,300 b. $9,900

E3-19 a. $58,600; b. $120,800; c. $18,300

Problems

P3-1A 3. $8.5 bil.; 5. $1.8 bil.; 6. $0.8 bil.

P3-2A 2. Cash loss $4,500; Accrual income $1,000

P3-3A NCF

P3-4A c. Debit Engineering Supplies Exp. $11,360 f. Debit Insurance Exp. $2,200

P3-5A Accounts Receivable 830
Commission Revenue 830

P3-6A 1. Net inc. $48,070; Total assets $98,630

P3-7A 2. Net inc. $8,300; Total assets $50,100

P3-8A 1. Total assets $58,200; 2. Current ratio 20X1 1.25

P3-9A 2. RE $16,800 credit bal.

P3-10A 2. a. Current ratio 1.40
Debt ratio 0.68

P3-1B 3. $960 mil.; 5. $100 mil.; 6. $585 mil.

P3-2B 2. Cash loss $500; Accrual income $2,300

P3-3B NCF

P3-4B a. Debit Insurance Exp. $2,850; d. Debit Supplies Exp. $6,710

P3-5B Accounts Receivable 480
Rental Revenue 480

P3-6B 1. Net inc. $59,070; Total assets $39,970

P3-7B 2. Net inc. $5,255; Total assets $51,075

P3-8B 1. Total assets $77,900; 2. Current ratio 20X3 1.16

P3-9B 2. RE $44,900 credit bal.

P3-10B 2. a. Current ratio 1.48;
Debt ratio 0.57

Decision Cases

DC 1 1. $167,500; 2. $139,100

DC 2 1. Net inc. $33,540; 2. Total assets $51,390

Financial Statement Cases

FS 1 2. Accrued Exp. and Other Current Liab. 406,181
Cash 406,181

Chapter 4

Check Points

CP4-1 NCF

CP4-2 NCF

CP4-3 NCF

CP4-4 NCF

CP4-5 NCF

CP4-6 Adj. bal. $1,790

CP4-7 NCF

CP4-8 NCF

CP4-9 Employee stole $580

CP4-10 NCF

CP4-11 NCF

CP4-12 1. New financing needed $169.3 mil.

CP4-13 New financing needed $6 mil.

CP4-14 NCF

Exercises

E4-1 NCF

E4-2 NCF

E4-3 NCF

E4-4 NCF

E4-5 NCF

E4-6 Adj. bal. $1,741

E4-7 Adj. bal. $3,161

E4-8 NCF

E4-9 NCF

E4-10 NCF

E4-11 1. $211.98

E4-12 1. New financing needed $124.8 mil.

E4-13 NCF

E4-14 NCF

E4-15 1. New financing needed $650 mil. 2. Current ratio after borrowing 1.18

Problems

P4-1A NCF

P4-2A NCF

P4-3A Adj. bal. $8,670

P4-4A Adj. bal. $8,368.77

P4-5A NCF

P4-6A New financing needed $229 mil.

P4-7A NCF

P4-1B NCF

P4-2B NCF

P4-3B Adj. bal. $2,657

P4-4B Adj. bal $3,003.33

P4-5B NCF

P4-6B Cash available to invest $359 mil.

P4-7B NCF

Decision Cases

DC 1 Cashier stole $1,000

DC 2 NCF

Financial Statement Cases

FS 1 NCF

Chapter 5

Check Points

CP5-1 NCF

CP5-2 NCF

CP5-3 NCF

CP5-4 NCF

CP5-5 NCF

CP5-6 A/R, net $84,000

CP5-7 NCF

CP5-8 3. $96,000

CP5-9 d. Uncollect. Accts. Exp. $5,000

CP5-10 3. A/R, net $72,000

CP5-11 NCF

CP5-12 3. $1,052,500

CP5-13 NCF

CP5-14 NCF

CP5-15 a. 2.80; b. 48 days

CP5-16 2. $1,184; 3. A/R, net $2,464

CP5-17 NCF

Exercises

E5-1 NCF

E5-2 NCF

E5-3 NCF

E5-4 NCF

E5-5 a. A/R, net $133,100; b. A/R, net $133,600

E5-6	3. A/R, net $33,400
E5-7	2. A/R, bal. $35,930
E5-8	2. A/R, net $255,889
E5-9	12/31 Interest Revenue $1,545
E5-10	NCF
E5-11	NCF
E5-12	NCF
E5-13	20X6 ratios: Acid-test 1.03; Days' sales in rec. 35 days
E5-14	1. 3 days
E5-15	NCF
E5-16	Net inc. w/o bank cards $75,000; w/cards $91,300

Problems

P5-1A	Short-term investment $28,000
P5-2A	NCF
P5-3A	3. Bals.: A/R $377 mil. debit; allowance $54 mil. credit
P5-4A	2. Uncollect. Acct. Exp. $9,400; A/R, net $104,800
P5-5A	3. 20X2 A/R, net $286,507
P5-6A	12/31/X4 Doubtful Acct. Exp. $16,700; 12/31/X5 Interest Revenue $625
P5-7A	1999 ratios: a. 1.67; b. 0.67; c. 20 days
P5-1B	Short-term investment $45,500
P5-2B	NCF
P5-3B	3. Bals.: A/R $12,780 thou. debit; allowance $142 thou. credit
P5-4B	2. Uncollect. Acct. Exp. $13,000; A/R, net $171,800
P5-5B	3. 20X4 A/R, net $125,467
P5-6B	12/31/X5 Doubtful Acct. Exp. $3,500; 12/31/X6 Interest Revenue $225
P5-7B	1999 ratios: a. 1.76; b. 1.02; c. 17 days

Decision Cases

DC 1	Net inc.: 20X1 $45,250; 20X2 $56,000
DC 2	NCF

Financial Statement Cases

FS 1	1. Customers owed Eastman Kodak $2,383 mil.; 3. $134 mil. 4. $14,849 mil.

Chapter 6

Check Points

CP6-1	Inventory $12,000; Gross profit $32,000
CP6-2	NCF
CP6-3	COGS: a. $450; b. $380; c. $520
CP6-4	Net inc.: Wtd.-avg. $1,201; FIFO $1,300; LIFO $900
CP6-5	Inc. tax exp.: Wtd.-avg. $480; FIFO $520; LIFO $360
CP6-6	NCF
CP6-7	COGS $67,257
CP6-8	c. $68,592; d. $33,580
CP6-9	1. $7.5 mil. 2. $5.3 mil.
CP6-10	NCF
CP6-11	GP%: FIFO 46%; LIFO 34%; Turnover: FIFO 2.3 times; LIFO 3.9 times
CP6-12	2. Gross profit $50,000
CP6-13	2. $300,000
CP6-14	NCF

Exercises

E6-1	a. $27,100; c. $49,000; Co. D net inc. $11,460
E6-2	Purchase $7,320
E6-3	1. COGS: Wtd. avg. $2,849; FIFO $2,800; LIFO $2,910
E6-4	LIFO saves $44
E6-5	1. COGS: a. $925; b. $950
E6-6	1. FIFO $0.8 mil.; LIFO $1.2 mil.
E6-7	Net inc. in sequence: $24,000; $19,800; $10,200; $6,000
E6-8	NCF
E6-9	NCF
E6-10	Gross profit $44,900; Inventory $9,400
E6-11	Net inc.: 20X3 $35,600; 20X2 $32,800
E6-12	A: GP% 37.3%; Turnover 2.4 times
E6-13	Gross profit $114,200
E6-14	2. Inventory $470 thou.; Gross profit $1,590 thou.
E6-15	3. Gross profit $2,190
E6-16	1. Gross profit $8.6 mil.
E6-17	$40,600
E6-18	NCF
E6-19	3. Net earnings-no liquidation $358 mil.
E6-20	19X7 GP% 42.1%; Turnover 5.1 times

Problems

P6-1A	1. Purchases budgeted $786,000 2. COGS $756,000
P6-2A	2. Gross profit $1,326
P6-3A	1. COGS: Wtd.-avg. $56,294; FIFO $55,300; LIFO $57,374
P6-4A	1. Gross profit: Wtd.-avg. $2,465; FIFO $2,587; LIFO $2,344
P6-5A	NCF
P6-6A	1. Net inc.: 20X3 $11,000; 20X2 $15,000; 20X1 $21,000
P6-7A	1. GP%; GM 11.9%; Ford 8.4%; Turnover: GM 11.7 times; Ford 14.8 times
P6-8A	2. $900,000; 3. Net inc. $654,000
P6-9A	1. $808,000
P6-1B	1. Purchases, budgeted $741,000 2. COGS $726,000
P6-2B	2. Gross profit $3,112
P6-3B	1. COGS: Wtd.-avg. $12,561; FIFO $12,295; LIFO $12,859
P6-4B	1. Gross profit: Wtd.-avg. $59,361; FIFO $59,870; LIFO $58,930
P6-5B	NCF
P6-6B	1. Net inc.: 20X3 $60,000; 20X2 $53,000; 20X1 $21,000
P6-7B	1. GP%: Wal-Mart 20.4%; May 29.0% Turnover: Wal-Mart 5 times; May 3.8 times
P6-8B	2. $600,000; 3. Net inc. $354,000
P6-9B	1. $994,000

Decision Cases

DC 1	1. Net inc. w/o year-end purchase: FIFO $189,000; LIFO $153,000 Net inc. w/year-end purchase: FIFO $189,000; LIFO $129,750
DC 2	NCF

Financial Statement Cases

FS 1	3. Purchases $5,641,488 thou.

Chapter 7

Check Points

CP7-1	3. Book value $8,160
CP7-2	NCF
CP7-3	Building cost $45,000
CP7-4	Net inc. Overstated
CP7-5	Book value: SL $18 mil.; UOP $18.75 mil.; DDB $12.6 mil.
CP7-6	Depr: UOP Year 5 $3,750,000; DDB Year 3 $1,560,000
CP7-7	2. Save $2,160,000
CP7-8	a. $2,250,000; b. $1,500,000; c. $6,300,000
CP7-9	Depr. Exp. $8,333
CP7-10	1. a. Loss $5,000; b. Gain $5,240
CP7-11	3. Book value $1.5 bil.
CP7-12	3. a. Goodwill $134 mil.; b. Amortiz. $6 mil.
CP7-13	1. Net loss $100,000
CP7-14	Net cash used for investing $4.7 mil.

Exercises

E7-1	Land $249,900; Land improve. $88,400

E7-2	Machine 1 $10,000; Machine 2 $16,680
E7-3	NCF
E7-4	2. Building, net $573,000
E7-5	NCF
E7-6	Depr. 20X4; SL $3,000; UOP $2,400; DDB $375
E7-7	B/S: Building, net $144,500; Furn. & fixt., net $18,000
E7-8	2,500 hours
E7-9	DDB saves $6,600
E7-10	Depr. year 16 $18,000
E7-11	Loss on Sale of Fixtures $654
E7-12	Cost of new truck $246,000
E7-13	c. Depletion $72,000
E7-14	Amortization: 1. b. $100,000; 2. $200,000
E7-15	Payments for : Goodwill $1,174 mil.; Other assets $81 mil.
E7-16	1. Cost of goodwill $4 mil.
E7-17	NCF
E7-18	Effects Year 2: 1. None; 2. F1.2 mil. under; 3. F0.4 over; 4. F1.2 under
E7-19	1. Acquisitions $2,170.6 mil.; 3. Acquisitions $2,504.8 mil.

Problems

P7-1A	1. Land $638,250; Land improve. $136,400; Office bldg. $1,246,100; Garage $116,000
P7-2A	2. A/Depr.: Bldg. $44,000; Security Equip. $278,000
P7-3A	12/31 Depr. Exp. on old equip. $33,600; on new equip. $4,000 and $1,333
P7-4A	NCF
P7-5A	3. Cash flow advantage of DDB $4,300
P7-6A	3. Cap. expend. $6,985,000 4. Gain on sale $1,648,000
P7-7A	Part 1. 3. Amortization $57,000 Part 2. 2. Net loss $64,260
P7-8A	1. Gain on sale $0.1 bil.; 2. PPE, net $10.1 bil.
P7-1B	1. Land $233,350; Land improve. $89,050; Sales bldg. $986,150;Garage $75,450
P7-2B	2. A/Depr.: Bldg. $46,000; Medical Equip. $498,000
P7-3B	12/31 Depr. Exp. on motor carrier equip. $61,200; on buildings $625
P7-4B	NCF
P7-5B	3. Cash-flow advantage of DDB $20,800
P7-6B	3. Cap. expend. $4,744 mil.; 4. Gain on sale $687 mil.
P7-7B	Part 1. 3. Amortization $180,000 Part 2. 2. Net inc. $436,650
P7-8B	1. Gain on sale $0.3 bil. 2. PPE, net $4.8 bil.

Decision Cases

DC 1	Net inc.: 360 $107,000; Beepers $84,600
DC 2	NCF

Financial Statement Cases

FS 1	b. Depr. & amort. exp. $326,447 thou.; Accum. depr. & amort. $1,171,957 thou.

Chapter 8

Check Points

CP8-1	4/30/X2 Debit: Note Pay. $8,000 Interest Pay. 533 Interest Exp. 267
CP8-2	2. Interest exp. $267
CP8-3	1. End. bal. $27,194
CP8-4	1. Warranty Exp. $25,000 2. Bal. $3,000
CP8-5	NCF
CP8-6	NCF
CP8-7	a. $97,500 b. $410,500
CP8-8	NCF
CP8-9	1/1/01 Interest Exp. $163
CP8-10	1. Bond carrying amt. 9/30/X2 $441,509
CP8-11	2. $17,500; 3. Interest exp. 9/30/X1 $19,575
CP8-12	3. $162.50 4. $178.75
CP8-13	b. Interest Exp. $178
CP8-14	EPS: Borrow $2.11; Issue stock $1.57
CP8-15	Total current liabilities $84,000

Exercises

E8-1	2. Warranty exp. $9,660 Est. warr. pay. $7,330
E8-2	12/31 Adjustment: Unearned Sub. Rev. 40 Subscrip. Rev. 40
E8-3	NCF
E8-4	12/31/X2 Interest Exp. $3,200
E8-5	Income tax pay. $141 mil.; Income tax exp. $365 mil.
E8-6	2. Debt ratio 0.53
E8-7	2. Est. Loss $1,100,000
E8-8	Pay $10,000
E8-9	Total current liab. $146,430
E8-10	2. Total cash received $993,333
E8-11	2. $555,200,000; 3. $351,200,000
E8-12	2. 12/31/X2 entry: Interest Exp. 14,943 Cash 14,000 Discount 943
E8-13	2. 12/31/01 entry: Interest Exp. 9,680 Premium 320 Interest Pay. 10,000
E8-14	Bond carrying amt. 12/31/X4 $593,836
E8-15	2. $396,400
E8-16	1. Extraordinary Loss $9,000
E8-17	EPS: Borrow $8.15; Issue stock $4.37
E8-18	NCF
E8-19	4. Interest exp. $27,050,000 5. Interest exp.: Year 1 $26,895,000 6. Pur. on 3/31/99: Pay $495,286

Problems

P8-1A	NCF
P8-2A	12/31/X4 Warranty Exp. $19,500; Interest Exp. $15,000
P8-3A	NCF
P8-4A	2. Interest pay. $40,000; Bonds pay. $2,000,000
P8-5A	4. Interest pay. $7,750; Notes pay., net $305,500
P8-6A	3. a. Interest exp. $43,000; b. Cash paid $40,000
P8-7A	2. Bond carrying amt. 9/30/yr.4 $124,423,000
P8-8A	1. Bond carrying amt. 12/31/X3 $314,688; 3. Convert. bonds pay., net $104,896
P8-9A	NCF
P8-10A	1. Total current liab. $66,200; Total LT liab. $767,000
P8-1B	NCF
P8-2B	12/31/X2 Warranty Exp. $2,900; Interest Exp. $6,000
P8-3B	NCF
P8-4B	2. Interest pay. $17,500; Bonds pay. $3,000,000
P8-5B	4. Interest pay. $14,167; Bonds pay., net $485,625
P8-6B	3. a. Interest exp. $83,000; b. Cash paid $80,000
P8-7B	2. Bond carrying amt. 9/30/yr.4 $123,639,000
P8-8B	1. Bond carrying amt. 12/31/X3 $474,920; 3. Convert. bonds pay., net $94,984
P8-9B	NCF
P8-10B	1. Total current liab. $141,000; Total LT liab. $868,000

Decision Cases

DC 1	EPS: A $4.72; B $4.45; C $4.53
DC 2	NCF

Financial Statement Cases

FS 1 3. $495,890,000
4. Pay off $29,721,500

Chapter 9

Check Points

CP9-1 NCF
CP9-2 NCF
CP9-3 NCF
CP9-4 1. $672 mil.
CP9-5 Balances in all accts. should be the same under both plans.
CP9-6 NCF
CP9-7 Total SE $192.8 mil.
CP9-8 a. $30.6 mil.;
b. $122.3 mil.;
c. $315.1 mil.
CP9-9 2. Total SE $32,100
CP9-10 2. Total SE $35,300
CP9-11 Total div. $31,000
CP9-12 1. $157,500;
4. Pfd. $472,500; com. $27,500
CP9-13 1. Debit RE for $65,000
CP9-14 2. Total SE $260,000
CP9-15 $62.65
CP9-16 NCF
CP9-17 ROA 24.2%; ROE 60.5%
CP9-18 Net cash outflow $54 mil.

Exercises

E9-1 NCF
E9-2 2. Total SE $12,000
E9-3 1. $83.74
E9-4 Total SE $245,500
E9-5 Total PIC $560,000
E9-6 Total SE $333,000
E9-7 Overall effect on SE $140,600
E9-8 NCF
E9-9 Total SE $13,061
E9-10 3. 378.3 mil. shares;
4. $48.85 per share;
5. Div. $751 mil.
E9-11 Total divs.: Pfd.-A $23,200; Pfd.-B $752,000; Com. $124,800
E9-12 3. Total SE $377,500
E9-13 2. Total SE $860,000
E9-14 a. Decrease SE by $6,375
E9-15 Total SE $1,584 mil.
E9-16 1. $16.17;
2. $16.10
E9-17 ROA .064; ROE .241
E9-18 NCF
E9-19 NCF
E9-20 NCF

Problems

P9-1A NCF
P9-2A 2. Total SE $330,900
P9-3A Total SE $767,000
P9-4A NCF
P9-5A Total SE $6,750,000
P9-6A 4. $22,500,000
P9-7A 2. Total SE $102,300
P9-8A NCF
P9-9A 1. Total assets $632,000;
Total SE $477,000
P9-10A 2. Total liabil.–net increase $593.9 mil.; Total SE–net decrease $565.5 mil.
P9-1B NCF
P9-2B 2. Total SE $250,300
P9-3B Total SE $452,000
P9-4B NCF
P9-5B Total SE $3,266,000
P9-6B 4. $212,080
P9-7B 2. Total SE $126,010
P9-8B NCF
P9-9B 1. Total assets $376,000; Total SE $238,000
P9-10B NCF

Decision Cases

DC 1 Total SE: Plan 1 $335,900; Plan 2 $350,900
DC 2 NCF

Financial Statement Cases

FS 1 3. Shares o/s: 1/30/99 571,973,354
5. Dividends $95,929,000

Chapter 10

Check Points

CP10-1 1. Dec. 31 Unrealized loss $262
CP10-2 1. Gain on sale $525
CP10-3 3. $101 mil.
CP10-4 Gain on sale $11.5 mil.
CP10-5 NCF
CP10-6 NCF
CP10-7 2. Cash interest $70,000;
4. Interest rev. $78,000
CP10-8 c. Amortization amt. $8,000
CP10-9 2. Investment carrying amt. $9,590
CP10-10 Apr. 19 FC Trans. Loss $100;
May 10 FC Trans. Gain $200
CP10-11 Aug. 28 FC Trans. Gain $30,000;
Sept. 29 FC Trans. Loss $462
CP10-12 NCF
CP10-13 NCF

Exercises

E10-1 d. Gain on Sale $2,400
E10-2 2. Unrealized Loss 8,750
Allowance 8,750
E10-3 End. bal. $855,000
E10-4 Gain on sale $545,000
E10-5 LT investment, at equity $175,200
E10-6 2. Total SE $670,000
E10-7 3. LT investment $19,250
E10-8 Dec. 16 FC Trans. Loss $40;
Dec. 30 FC Trans. Gain $1,200
E10-9 FC Trans. Adj. $40,000 credit
E10-10 Net cash used in investing $759 mil.
E10-11 NCF
E10-12 2. Cost $266,313 thou.;
3. Loss on sale $7,313 thou.

Problems

P10-1A 2. LT investment, at equity $796,300; Other comprehensive inc.- Unrealized gain $2,200
P10-2A 3. LT investments in affiliates $814,000
P10-3A 3. Consol. debt ratio .890
P10-4A 1. Consol. totals $846,000
P10-5A 2. LT investment in bonds $464,314;
Interest revenue $31,814
P10-6A June 21 FC Trans. Gain $3,000;
July 17 FC Trans. Loss $1,400
P10-7A 1. FC translation adj. $43,000 debit
P10-8A NCF
P10-1B 2. LT investment, at equity $868,300; Other comprehensive inc.- Unrealized loss $3,400
P10-2B 3. LT investments in affiliates $418,000
P10-3B 3. Consol. debt ratio .897
P10-4B 1. Consol. totals $1,233,000
P10-5B 2. LT investment in bonds $615,857;
Interest revenue $27,857
P10-6B June 18 FC Trans. Gain $1,500;
June 24 FC Trans. Loss $3,000
P10-7B 1. FC translation adj. $164,000 credit
P10-8B NCF

Decision Cases

DC 1 NCF
DC 2 NCF

Chapter 11

Check Points

CP11-1 NCF
CP11-2 NCF
CP11-3 Net inc. $21,000
CP11-4 Est. value of one share $37.50
CP11-5 EPS for net inc. $1.80
CP11-6 NCF
CP11-7 Comprehensive inc. $22,000
CP11-8 2. Net inc. $60,000

CP11-9 RE, 12/31/X5 $478,000

CP11-10 4. Par value $8,000
Market value $26,000

Exercises

E11-1 1. Net inc. $658 mil.;
2. Est. value $12,133.3 mil.

E11-2 Net inc. $10,200

E11-3 NCF

E11-4 5.8%

E11-5 EPS $1.20

E11-6 EPS for net inc. $3.42

E11-7 Def. Tax Liab. $16,000

E11-8 RE, 12/31/X9 $421.8 mil.

E11-9 a. Total SE $1,130,000

E11-10 Total RE, 12/31/X2 $6,432,000

E11-11 NCF

E11-12 NCF

Problems

P11-1A 1. Net inc. $35,000;
EPS for net inc. $1.04

P11-2A RE, 9/30/X3 $82,000

P11-3A Est. value of Delphi stock
$762,500

P11-4A 1. EPS for net inc. $0.92;
2. Est. value of Dexia stock at 8%
$13.75

P11-5A Comprehensive inc. $82,200;
EPS for net inc. $1.70

P11-6A 1. Taxable inc. $215,000;
3. Net inc. $149,500

P11-7A 1. $560 mil.
5. 5%

P11-1B 1. Net inc. $73,800;
EPS for net inc. $3.39

P11-2B RE, 11/30/X3 $114,800

P11-3B Est. value of Networking stock
$600,000

P11-4B 1. EPS for net inc. $3.07;
2. Est. value of TNT stock, at 8%
$36.375

P11-5B Comprehensive inc. $61,800;
EPS for net inc. $2.88

P11-6B 1. Taxable inc. $200,000;
3. Net inc. $136,500

P11-7B 1. $800 mil.
5. 10%

Decision Cases

DC 1 NCF

Financial Statement Cases

FS 1 3. Est. year-end price of stock
$52.06; $i = 2.7\%$

Chapter 12

Check Points

CP12-1 NCF

CP12-2 NCF

CP12-3 Cash bal. $(7) mil.

CP12-4 Net cash inflow–oper. $30,000

CP12-5 Net increase in cash $29,000

CP12-6 1. $180,000;
2. $94,000

CP12-7 a. $704,000;
b. $331,000

CP12-8 a. $48,000;
b. $154,000

CP12-9 a. $100,000;
b. $15,000

CP12-10 c. $84,000

CP12-11 1. $252,000

CP12-12 NCF

CP12-13 Net cash inflow–oper. $71,000

CP12-14 Net cash inflow–oper. $171 thou.;
Net cash outflow–finan. $83 thou.

CP12-15 NCF

Exercises

E12-1 NCF

E12-2 NCF

E12-3 NCF

E12-4 Net cash outflow–oper. $8,000

E12-5 NCF

E12-6 1. Net cash inflow–oper. $90,000;
Net cash inflow–finan. $4,000

E12-7 a. $85,000; b. $89,000

E12-8 a. $26,000; b. $6,000

E12-9 Net cash inflow–oper. $4,000

E12-10 NCF

E12-11 1. Net cash inflow–oper. $90,000;
Net cash inflow–finan. $4,000

E12-12 Net cash inflow–oper. $76,000

E12-13 NCF

E12-14 NCF

Problems

P12-1A NCF

P12-2A 1. Net inc. $120,000;
2. Total assets $303,000;
3. Net cash inflow–oper. $81,000

P12-3A 1. Net cash outflow–oper.
$30,000;
Cash bal., 7/31/X2 $68,300

P12-4A 1. Net cash inflow–oper. $70,600;
Net cash outflow–finan. $29,900

P12-5A 1. Net cash inflow–oper. $70,600;
Net cash outflow–finan. $29,900

P12-6A 1. Net inc. $120,000
2. Total assets $303,000
3. Net cash inflow–oper. 81,000

P12-7A Net cash inflow–oper. $94,000;
Net cash inflow–finan. $11,100

P12-8A 1. Net cash inflow–oper. $48,300;
Net cash inflow–finan. $120,600

P12-9A 1. Net cash inflow–oper. $77,200;
Net cash outflow–finan. $30,300

P12-10A 1. Net cash inflow–oper. $30,400;
Net cash outflow–finan. $37,100

P12-1B NCF

P12-2B 1. Net inc. $30,000;
2. Total assets $375,000;
3. Net cash outflow–oper.
$49,000

P12-3B 1. Net cash inflow–oper.
$115,700;
Cash bal., 4/30/X5 $56,600

P12-4B 1. Net cash inflow–oper. $72,900;
Net cash outflow–finan. $30,600

P12-5B 1. Net cash inflow–oper. $72,900;
Net cash outflow–finan. $30,600

P12-6B 1. Net inc. $30,000;
2. Total assets $375,000;
3. Net cash outflow–oper. $49,000

P12-7B Net cash inflow–oper. $75,200;
Net cash inflow–finan. $43,000

P12-8B 1. Net cash inflow–oper. $96,900;
Net cash inflow–finan. $31,000

P12-9B 1. Net cash inflow–oper. $67,800;
Net cash outflow–finan. $47,600

P12-10B 1. Net cash inflow–oper. $69,100;
Net cash outflow–finan. $95,200

Decision Cases

DC 1 1. Net cash inflow–oper.
$140 thou.;
Net cash outflow–finan.
$37 thou.

DC 2 NCF

Financial Statement Cases

FS 1 2. a. $9,054,462 thou.
b. $5,374,334 thou.

Chapter 13

Check Points

CP13-1 Revenue increase 19X6 35.9%

CP13-2 Revenues trend %: 19X6 215%

CP13-3 20X2: Cash 3.3%; PPE, net
52.7%

CP13-4 Net inc. %: Nike 8.5%; Home Depot 4.8%

CP13-5 Current ratio 19X8 3.20

CP13-6 1. 1998 acid-test ratio 0.99

CP13-7 a. 2.64 times
b. 62 days

CP13-8 1. 0.53
2. 34.3 times

CP13-9 b. 0.209
c. 0.425

CP13-10 1. EPS $1.92; P/E ratio 25

CP13-11 a. $4,264 mil.
d. $698 mil.

CP13-12 a. $631 mil.
e. $857 mil.

CP13-13 1. $2,184 mil.

Exercises

E13-1 W/C increase in 2001 21.8%

E13-2 Net inc. increased by 58.8%

E13-3 Trend % for net inc. year 5 173%

E13-4 PPE is 70.1% of total assets

E13-5 19X9 net inc. is 18.8% of total revenue

E13-6 NCF

E13-7 b. 0.61; c. 3.47 times; e. 55 days

E13-8 20X2 ratios; a. 2.09; b. 0.93 d. 4.34

E13-9 20X6 ratios: b. ROA .103; c. ROE .156; d. EPS $0.75

E13-10 20X4 ratios: P/E 19.2; Book value per share $7.25

E13-11 EVA® of IHOP $10.7 mil.

E13-12 Sales $6,639 mil.; Pretax inc. $1,183 mil.

E13-13 Total assets $19,565 mil.; Current liab. $6,752 mil.

Problems

P13-1A 1. Trend % for net rev. of 2003 123%; 2. ROE for 2003 14.2%

P13-2A 1. GP is 36.4% of net sales; Current assets are 77.8% of total assets

P13-3A NCF

P13-4A 2. a. Current ratio 1.38; Debt ratio 0.60; EPS No effect

P13-5A 1. b. 20X4 turnover 1.37 times; d. 20X4 ROE 0.357

P13-6A Jacobs-Cathey ratios: 1. 0.85; 2. 2.74 times 3. 35 days

P13-1B 1. Trend % for net rev. of 20X6 148%; 2. Return on sales for 20X6 0.081

P13-2B 1. GP is 31.8% of net sales; Current assets are 71.1% of total assets

P13-3B NCF

P13-4B 2. a. Current ratio 2.45; Debt ratio 0.51; EPS No effect

P13-5B 1. b. 20X6 turnover 1.18 times; e. 20X6 ROE 0.253

P13-6B Keyboards ratios: 1. 0.64; 2. 2.04 times; 3. 126 days

Decision Cases

DC 1 NCF

DC 2 NCF

Financial Statement Cases

FS 1 1. c. ROA for 1998 22.6%; d. ROE for 1998 52.2%
2. b. Turnover for 1998 5.94 times

Glossary

Accelerated depreciation method. A depreciation method that writes off a relatively larger amount of the asset's cost nearer the start of its useful life than the straight-line method does *(p. 321)*.

Account. The detailed record of the changes that have occurred in a particular asset, liability, or stockholders' equity during a period. The basic summary device of accounting *(p. 52)*.

Account format. A balance-sheet format that lists assets on the left and liabilities and stockholders' equity on the right *(p. 137)*.

Account payable. A liability backed by the general reputation and credit standing of the debtor *(p. 11)*.

Account receivable. An asset, a promise to receive cash from customers to whom the business has sold goods or for whom the business has performed services *(p. 18)*.

Accounting. The information system that measures business activities, processes that information into reports and financial statements, and communicates the results to decision makers *(p. 4)*.

Accounting cycle. The process by which accountants produce an entity's financial statements for a specific period *(p. 106)*.

Accounting equation. The most basic tool of accounting: Assets = Liabilities + Owners' Equity *(p. 4)*.

Accounts receivable turnover. Measures a company's ability to collect cash from credit customers. To compute accounts receivable turnover, divide net credit sales by average net accounts receivable *(p. 610)*.

Accrual. An expense or a revenue that occurs before the business pays or receives cash. An accrual is the opposite of a deferral. *(p. 112)*.

Accrual-basis accounting. Accounting that recognizes (records) the impact of a business event as it occurs, regardless of whether the transaction affected cash *(p. 106)*.

Accrued expense. An expense incurred but not yet paid in cash *(pp. 117, 362)*.

Accrued liability. A liability incurred but not yet paid by the company. Another name for *accrued expense (pp. 53, 362)*.

Accrued revenue. A revenue that has been earned but not yet received in cash *(p. 119)*.

Accumulated Depreciation. The cumulative sum of all depreciation expense from the date of acquiring a plant asset *(p. 116)*.

Acid-test ratio. Ratio (of the sum of cash plus short-term investments plus net current receivables) to (total current liabilities). Tells whether the entity can pay all its current liabilities if they come due immediately. Also called the *quick ratio (pp. 235, 608)*.

Adjusted trial balance. A list of all the ledger accounts with their adjusted balances *(p. 122)*.

Adjusting entry. Entry made at the end of the period to assign revenues to the period in which they are earned and expenses to the period in which they are incurred. Adjusting entries help measure the period's income and bring the related asset and liability accounts to correct balances for the financial statements *(p. 111)*.

Adverse opinion. An audit opinion stating that the financial statements are unreliable *(p. 516)*.

Aging-of-accounts-receivable. A way to estimate bad debts by analyzing individual accounts receivable according to the length of time they have been receivable from the customer *(p. 228)*.

Allowance for Doubtful Accounts. Also called *Allowance for Uncollectible Accounts (p. 226)*.

Allowance for Uncollectible Accounts. A contra account, related to accounts receivable, that holds the estimated amount of collection losses. Another name for *Allowance for Doubtful Accounts (p. 226)*.

Allowance method. A method of recording collection losses based on estimates of how much money the business will not collect from its customers *(p. 226)*.

Amortization. The systematic reduction of a lump-sum amount. Expense that applies to intangible assets in the same way depreciation applies to plant assets and depletion applies to natural resources *(p. 333)*.

Asset. An economic resource that is expected to be of benefit in the future *(p. 11)*.

Audit. A periodic examination of a company's financial statements and the accounting systems, controls, and records that produce them *(p. 173)*.

Authorization of stock. Provision in a corporate charter that gives the state's permission for the corporation to issue—that is, to sell—a certain number of shares of stock *(p. 413)*.

Available-for-sale investments. All investments not classified as held-to-maturity or trading securities *(pp. 220, 461)*.

Bad-debt expense. Another name for *uncollectible-account expense (p. 226)*.

Balance sheet. List of an entity's assets, liabilities, and owners' equity as of a specific date. Also called the *statement of financial position (p. 17)*.

Balance sheet approach. Another name for aging-of-accounts-receivable *(p. 228)*.

Bank collection. Collection of money by the bank on behalf of a depositor *(p. 178)*.

Bank reconciliation. A document explaining the reasons for the difference between a depositor's records and the bank's records about the depositor's bank account *(p. 177)*.

Bank statement. Document showing the beginning and ending balances of a particular bank account listing the month's transactions that affected the account *(p. 176)*.

Benchmarking. The practice of comparing a company to a standard set by other companies, with a view toward improvement *(p. 598)*.

Board of directors. Group elected by the stockholders to set policy for a corporation and to appoint its officers *(pp. 8, 410)*.

Bonds payable. Groups of notes payable (bonds) issued to multiple lenders called *bondholders (p. 367)*.

Book value (of a plant asset). The asset's cost minus accumulated depreciation *(p. 116)*.

Book value (of a stock). Amount of owners' equity on the company's books for each share of its stock *(p. 429)*.

Book value per share of common stock. Common stockholders' equity divided by the number of shares of common stock outstanding. The recorded amount for each share of common stock outstanding *(p. 617)*.

Brand name. See *trademark, trade name (p. 334)*.

Budget. A quantitative expression of a plan that helps managers coordinate the entity's activities *(p. 191)*.

Bylaws. Constitution for governing a corporation *(p. 410)*.

Callable bonds. Bonds that the issuer may call (pay off) at a specified price whenever the issuer wants *(p. 379)*.

Capital. Another name for the *owners' equity* of a business *(p. 11)*.

Capital charge. The amount that stockholders and lenders charge a company for the use of their money. Calculated as (notes payable + loans payable + long-term debt + stockholders' equity) times the cost of capital *(p. 618)*.

Capital expenditure. Expenditure that increases an asset's capacity or efficiency or extends its useful life. Capital expenditures are debited to an asset account *(p. 316)*.

Capital lease. Lease agreement that meets any one of four criteria: (1) The lease transfers title of the leased asset to the lessee. (2) The lease contains a bargain purchase option. (3) The lease term is 75% or more of the estimated useful life of the leased asset. (4) The present value of the lease payments is 90% or more of the market value of the leased asset *(p. 383)*.

Capitalize. To include a related cost as part of an asset's cost *(p. 315)*.

Cash. Money and any medium of exchange that a bank accepts at face value *(p. 11, 52)*.

Cash-basis accounting. Accounting that records only transactions in which cash is received or paid *(p. 107)*.

Cash equivalents. Highly liquid short-term investments that can be converted into cash with little delay *(p. 537)*.

Cash flows. Cash receipts and cash payments (disbursements) *(p. 536)*.

Chairperson. Elected by a corporation's board of directors, usually the most powerful person in the corporation *(p. 410)*.

Chart of accounts. List of all a company's accounts and their account numbers *(p. 76)*.

Charter. Document that gives a business the state's permission to form a corporation *(p. 408)*.

Check. Document instructing a bank to pay the designated person or business the specified amount of money *(p. 175)*.

Classified balance sheet. A balance sheet that shows current assets separate from long-term assets, and current liabilities separate from long-term liabilities *(p. 133)*.

Clean opinion. See *unqualified (p. 516)*.

Closing entries. Entries that transfer the revenue, expense, and dividends balances from these respective accounts to the Retained Earnings account *(p. 131)*.

Closing the accounts. The process of preparing the accounts to begin recording the next period's transactions. Closing the accounts consists of journalizing and posting the closing entries to set the balances of the revenue, expense, and dividends accounts to zero *(p. 131)*.

Closing the books. See *closing the accounts (p. 131)*.

Common-size statement. A financial statement that reports only percentages (no dollar amounts) *(p. 598)*.

Common stock. The most basic form of capital stock. Common stockholders own a corporation *(pp. 12, 412)*.

Comprehensive income. A company's change in total stockholders' equity from all sources other than from the owners of the business *(p. 507)*.

Conservatism. The accounting concept by which the least favorable figures are presented in the financial statements *(p. 271)*.

Consistency principle. A business must use the same accounting methods and procedures from period to period *(p. 270)*.

Consolidated statements. Financial statements of the parent company plus those of majority-owned subsidiaries as if the combination were a single legal entity *(p. 467)*.

Contra account. An account that always has a companion account and whose normal balance is opposite that of the companion account *(p. 116)*.

Contract interest rate. Interest rate that determines the amount of cash interest the borrower pays and the investor receives each year. Also called *stated interest rate (p. 370)*.

Contributed capital. See *paid-in capital (pp. 12, 411)*.

Controller. The chief accounting officer of a business *(p. 171)*.

Controlling (majority) interest. Ownership of more than 50% of an investee company's voting stock *(p. 466)*.

Convertible bonds (or notes). Bonds (or notes) that may be converted into the issuing company's common stock at the investor's option *(p. 380)*.

Copyright. Exclusive right to reproduce and sell a book, musical composition, film, other work of art, or computer program. Issued by the federal government, copyrights extend 50 years beyond the author's life *(p. 334)*.

Corporation. A business owned by stockholders. A corporation is a legal entity, an "artificial person" in the eyes of the law *(p. 8)*.

Cost of capital. A weighted average of the returns demanded by the company's stockholders and lenders *(p. 618)*.

Cost of goods sold. The cost of the inventory that the business has sold to customers. Also called *cost of sales* *(p. 260).*

Cost of goods sold model. Brings together all the inventory data for the entire accounting period: Beginning inventory + Purchases = Cost of goods available for sale. Then, cost of goods available − Ending inventory = Cost of goods sold *(p. 262).*

Cost of sales. Another name for *cost of goods sold (p. 260).*

Cost principle. Principle that states that acquired assets and services should be recorded at their actual cost *(p. 10).*

Credit. The right side of an account *(p. 64).*

Creditor. The party to whom money is owed *(p. 220).*

Cumulative preferred stock. Preferred stock whose owners must receive all dividends in arrears before the corporation can pay dividends to the common stockholders *(p. 425).*

Current asset. An asset that is expected to be converted to cash, sold, or consumed during the next 12 months, or within the business' normal operating cycle if longer than a year *(pp. 18, 133).*

Current installment of long term debt. The amount of the principal that is payable within one year *(p. 362).*

Current liability. A debt due to be paid within one year or within the entity's operating cycle if the cycle is longer than a year *(pp. 18, 133).*

Current ratio. Current assets divided by current liabilities. Measures a company's ability to pay current liabilities with current assets *(pp. 138, 606).*

Days' sales in receivables. Ratio of average net accounts receivable to one day's sale. Indicates how many days' sales remain in Accounts Receivable awaiting collection. Also called the *collection period (pp. 235, 611).*

Debentures. Unsecured bonds—bonds backed only by the good faith of the borrower *(p. 368).*

Debit. The left side of an account *(p. 64).*

Debt instrument. A payable, usually some form of note or bond payable *(p. 220).*

Debt ratio. Ratio of total liabilities to total assets. States the proportion of a company's assets that is financed with debt *(pp. 138, 612).*

Debtor. The party who has a debt *(p. 220).*

Default on a note. See dishonor of a note.

Deferral. See *prepaid expense (p. 112).*

Deficit. Debit balance in the Retained Earnings account *(p. 423).*

Depletion expense. That portion of a natural resource's cost that is used up in a particular period. Depletion expense is computed in the same way as units-of-production depreciation *(p. 332).*

Deposit in transit. A deposit recorded by the company but not yet by its bank *(p. 178).*

Depreciable cost. The cost of a plant asset minus its estimated residual value *(p. 318).*

Depreciation. Expense associated with spreading (allocating) the cost of a plant asset over its useful life *(p. 112).*

Direct method. Format of the operating activities section of the statement of cash flows; lists the major categories of operating cash receipts (collections from customers and receipts of interest and dividends) and cash disbursements (payments to suppliers, to employees, for interest and income taxes) *(p. 539).*

Direct write-off method. A method of accounting for bad debts in which the company waits until the credit department decides that a customer's account receivable is uncollectible and then debits Uncollectible-Account Expense and credits the customer's Account Receivable *(p. 230).*

Disclaimer. An audit opinion stating that the auditor was unable to reach a professional opinion regarding the quality of the financial statements *(p. 516).*

Disclosure principle. A business's financial statements must report enough information for outsiders to make knowledgeable decisions about the business. The company should report relevant, reliable, and comparable information about its economic affairs *(p. 271).*

Discount (on a bond). Excess of a bond's maturity (par value) over its issue price *(p. 369).*

Dividend yield. Ratio of dividends per share of stock to the stock's market price per share. Tells the percentage of a stock's market value that the company returns to stockholders as dividends *(p. 616).*

Dividends. Distributions (usually cash) by a corporation to its stockholders *(pp. 12, 413).*

Double-declining-balance (DDB) method. An accelerated depreciation method that computes annual depreciation by multiplying the asset's decreasing book value by a constant percentage, which is 2 times the straight-line rate *(p. 321).*

Double-entry system. An accounting system that uses debits and credits to record the dual effects of each business transaction *(p. 63).*

Double taxation. Corporations pay income taxes on corporate income. Then, the stockholders pay personal income tax on the cash dividends that they receive from corporations *(p. 409).*

Doubtful-account expense. Another name for *uncollectible-account expense (p. 226).*

Due date. See *maturity.*

Earnings per share (EPS). Amount of a company's net income per share of its outstanding common stock *(pp. 381, 505, 615).*

Economic value added (EVA). Used to evaluate a company's operating performance. EVA combines the concepts of accounting income and corporate finance to measure whether the company's operations have increased stockholder wealth. EVA = net income + interest expense − capital charge *(p. 618).*

Effective interest rate. Another name for *market interest rate (p. 370).*

Efficient capital market. A capital market in which market prices fully reflect all information available to the public *(p. 619).*

Q

R

S

T

U

V

W

X

Y

Z

Subject Index

C

D

E

F

G

H

I

J

L

M

N

S

T

U

V

W

Y